human resource management
Fifth edition - Raymond J Stone

WILEY

John Wiley & Sons Australia, Ltd

Fifth edition published 2005 by
John Wiley & Sons Australia, Ltd
33 Park Road, Milton, Qld 4064

Offices also in Sydney and Melbourne

Typeset in 9½ /11 pt Palatino

First edition 1991
Second edition 1995
Third edition 1998
Fourth edition 2002

© Raymond Stone 1991, 1995, 1998, 2002, 2005

National Library of Australia
Cataloguing-in-Publication data

Stone, Raymond J.
  Human resource management.

  5th ed.

  Includes index.
  ISBN 0 470 80403 3.

  1. Personnel management.
  I. Title.

658.3

Cover and internal design images:
© 2004 Digital Vision and Photodisc Inc.

Edited by Caroline Hunter, Burrumundi Partnership

Illustrated by Glenn Lumsden
and the John Wiley art department

Printed in Singapore by
Kyodo Printing Co (S'pore) Pte Ltd

10 9 8 7 6 5 4 3 2 1

To
Law King Han
To
Stella Currie,
whose dedicated assistance
made this book possible

brief contents

contents

The fifth edition of *Human Resource Management* emphasises a practical approach to the study of human resource management. Common themes running through the book include the linking of HRM to organisational strategic business objectives; HRM's potential to contribute to organisational success and employee wellbeing; the commonality of interests existing between employers and employees; the globalisation of business; and the need for organisations to become internationally competitive.

Every chapter from the fourth edition has been extensively revised. Each chapter has new case studies, questions and exercises (including online exercises). In addition, a 'Practitioner speaks' section, ethical dilemma sidebars and class debate topics have been included to promote individual thought and group discussion. The diagnostic model has been revised to provide a more comprehensive means for assessing environmental influences on HRM, demonstrating the link between strategic business objectives and HRM activities and measuring HRM performance in terms of organisational success and employee wellbeing.

The chapter material, diagnostic model, review questions, experiential exercises and cases are designed to highlight practical application. Australian and Asian source material, news items, examples and cases have been used extensively to reflect Australia's changing circumstances and to increase the relevance for students and practitioners alike. Learning objectives are given at the beginning of each chapter and mini ethical dilemmas are presented throughout. Each chapter ends with a summary, a list of key terms to know, review questions, a diagnostic model exercise, a practitioner speaks topic, a 'What's your view?' question, a Newsbreak exercise, a soapbox survey, an online exercise, an ethical dilemma, two case studies, online references, suggestions for further reading and end notes. The suggestions for further reading are specifically linked to standard Australian and Asian texts. There is also an extended case study at the end of each part.

The text has been divided into seven parts. Part 1 deals with the context of human resource management including strategic HRM, HR planning, HR information systems, and HRM and the law. Part 2 emphasises the importance of meeting the organisation's people requirements through job analysis, job design and the quality of work life, employee recruitment and selection. Part 3 deals with the development of human resources through human resource development, career planning and development, performance appraisal and performance management. Part 4 focuses on employee motivation, compensation, incentives and benefits. Part 5 is concerned with industrial relations, the management of change and workplace relations, negotiating in the workplace, employee health and safety, and managing diversity. Part 6 contains chapters on international human resource management and managing international assignments. The concluding section, part 7, deals with the assessment of human resource management.

Raymond J. Stone

Recognition must be given to the many people who assisted me in the preparation of this book: Samuel Aryee and Susanna Lo (Hong Kong Baptist University), Paula De Lisle (Watson Wyatt), Marianne Gloet (RMIT University), Caroline Rance (freelance journalist) and Robert Wright (Hong Kong Polytechnic University).

In particular, my gratitude goes to Ron Berenholtz, Joe Catanzariti (Clayton Utz), Maureen Fastenau (RMIT University), Graham O'Neil (Hay Group) and Lindsay Worledge (The Performance Consulting Group) for their text and chapter contributions; to David Poole (University of Western Sydney) for his provocative and thought provoking 'Letters to the Editor'; to Claudia Al-Bala'a (Starwood Hotels and Resorts), Peter Barrett (ODL), Mick Bennet (Hewitt Associates), Alfred Chown (EL Consultants), Roger Collins (AGSM), Paula De Lisle (Watson Wyatt), John Eddy (Citibank), Maura Fallon (Fallon International), Paul Gollan (London School of Economics), John Halfpenny (former Secretary, Trades Hall Council), Donald Hay (Hayco), Angela Horkings (TMP), Graham Hubbard (Mt Eliza Business School), Pamela Jackson (Q Concepts), David James (*BRW*), Suzanne Kallenbach (Lincoln Sentry Group), Sylvia Kidziak (St. Engineering), Maisie Lam (Citibank), Kristen Le Mesurier (*BRW*), Lesley Lewis (Consulting Psychologist), Sandra Li (Connections), Peter May (Deloitte Touche Tohmatsu), Graham O'Neill (Hay Group), Glenn Patmore (University of Melbourne), Robert Preston (Tabcorp), Cyndi Stow (John Wiley & Sons Australia, Ltd), Tatsuo Tanaka (Bank of Tokyo-Mitsubishi) and Mike Toten (CCH), and for their 'Practitioner speaks' contributions, and to Jenny Brinkies (Swinburne University), Erica French (Queensland University of Technology), Margaret Heffernan (RMIT University), Glenda Maconachie (Queensland University of Technology), John Shields (University of Sydney), Mohan Thite (Griffith University), Wendy Webber (Monash University) and the consultants HRM Consulting Pty Ltd for their challenging and comprehensive end-of-part case studies.

I am especially indebted to the reviewers Margaret Heffernan (RMIT University), Jenny Brinkies (Swinburne University), Sally Townsend (Swinburne University), Alison Sheridan (University of New England), Pamela Mathews (Charles Sturt University) and Maria Farrell (Charles Sturt University) for their insightful comments and suggestions.

The editorial and production team at John Wiley, including Dan Logovik, Rebecca Gollan, Jo Davis and Janine Burford, deserve my special thanks for their help and wise counsel. I particularly wish to express my appreciation to Caroline Hunter (Burrumundi Partnership) for her painstaking editing of the text.

Finally, I wish to say thank you to my sister-in-law, Stella Currie, and to my wife, Margaret, who with great patience and understanding undertook the monumental task of typing the manuscript.

Raymond J. Stone

The author and publisher would like to thank the following copyright holders, organisations and individuals for their permission to reproduce copyright material in this book.

figures

P. 200: Alfred Chown; fig. 9.3: © 1995 by the American Psychological Association. Adapted with permission; p. 237: © Ann Reinertsen Farrell; fig. 7.11: Reprinted from Personnel, January 1990, © 1990, American Management Association. Published by American Management Association International New York, NY. Used by permission of the publisher. All rights reserved. http://www.amanet.org; fig. 8.7: © K. Ludeman, Training and Development, vol. 49, no. 8, 1995; fig. 9.2: " January 1996 from T+D by

M. A. Gephart, V. J. Marsick, M. E. Buren and M. S. Spiro. Reprinted with permission of American Society for Training & Development; fig. 1.4: Butterworths; fig. 1.6, 2.9: BHP Billiton Annual Report 2003; pp. 153, 687: From The Wall Street Journal — Permission, Cartoon Features Syndicate; p. 342: Claudia Al-Bala'a; fig. 5.7: Australian Standard Classification of Occupations, © Commonwealth of Australia reproduced by permission; p. 205: " Woman & Work, issue 9/3, 1987, Department of Employment. © Commonwealth of Australia, reproduced by permission; fig. 7.3: © National Committee on Discrimination in Employment and Occupation. © Commonwealth of Australia reproduced by permission; fig. 3.4: HR Magazine by L.E. Adams. © 1992 by Society for Human Resource Management. Reproduced with permission of Society for Human Resource Management via Copyright Clearance Center; fig. 5.6: © 1983 by Academy of Management. Reproduced with permission of Academy of Management via Copyright Clearance Center; fig. 7.7, 7.12, 9.11: © 1998 by Society for Human Resource Management. Reproduced with permission of Society for Human Resource Management via Copyright Clearance Center; p. 720: © Cyndi Stow; fig. 9.13: © Fiona Sexton, HR Monthly, October 2002; fig. 1.1, 9.1: The permission of Foster's Group to reproduce this material is gratefully acknowledged; fig. 3.5: From Human Resource Information Systems, Development and Application 1st edn by Kavanagh, Guetal and Tannenbaum. © 1990. Reprinted with permission of South-Western, a division of Thomson Learning: www.thomsonrights.com. Fax 800 730-2215; fig. 9.7: Reprinted with permission of Global Sources Ltd. © 1992 Trade Media Holdings Ltd. and World Executives Digest. All Rights Reserved; p. 505: © Graham Hubbard; p. 464: Graham O'Neill; fig. 2.11: Harris Smith & Associates, Sydney, Australia; fig. 1.2: Reprinted by permission of Harvard Business School Press. From Human Resource Champions by D. Urlich. Boston, MA 1997, p.18. © 1997 by the Harvard Business School Publishing Corporation; all rights reserved; p. 14: Hayco Manufacturing/Donald Hay; fig. 12.8: © HayGroup Pty Ltd; fig. 5.11: Organizational Behaviour, 8th edn. Schermerhorn, J. R., Hunt, J. G and Osborn. © John Wiley & Sons, NY, 2003, this material is used by permission of John Wiley & Sons Inc; fig. 1.11: Courtesy of Johnson & Johnson; p. 516: FARCUS® is reprinted with permission from LaughingStock Licensing Inc., Ottawa, Canada. All Rights Reserved; p. 28: Leonie Ferguson, copyright holder for Gaynor Cardew; p. 62: Lesley Lewis; p. 301: Maisie Lam; fig. 1.3: Human Resources Masterfoods, Wyong; p. 606: Maura Fallon; fig. 6.4: Recruiting in Australia by W. Parkes, 1995, by Reed Books, Sydney; p. 781: Pamela Jackson; pp. 110, 754: © Paul Hartigan; p. 525: Paula DeLisle; p. 390: Peter Barrett; p. 280: © Robert Wright; p. 548: © Ron Tandberg; fig. 12.16: Reprinted by permission of Sage Publications/ K. M. Cofsky. Compensation & Benefits Review, vol. 25, no. 6, November–December, 1993, p. 49; p. 239: Suzanne Kallenbach; p. 679: © Sylvia Kidziak; p. 764: Tatsuo Tanaka; fig 6.7: The Office of Equal Employment Opportunity Western Australia (OEEO); fig 1.8: Westpac Banking Corporation.

text

p. 522: © Alison Kahler, *Australian Financial Review*, 22 May 2002; p. 202: © Annabel Day/*Australian Financial Review*, 19 September 2003; p. 427: Article reproduced, with permission, from Australian Connections — Asia's link with Australian business, August–September 2003; p. 8: *Australian Financial Review*, Catherine Fox; pp. 343, 563: *Australian Financial Review*, Cherelle Murphy; p. 727: *Australian Financial Review*, Fiona Buffini; pp. 782–3: *Australian Financial Review*, Catherine Fox, 23 September 2003; p. 423: Reprinted from *Management Review*, May 1996, © 1996 American Management Association. Published by American Management Association International New York, NY. Used by permission of the publisher. All rights reserved. http://www.amanet.org; p. 828: Reprinted from Personnel, June 1989, © 1989 American Management Association. Published by American Management Association International New York, NY. Used by permission of the publisher. All rights reserved. http://www.amanet.org; p. 441: *Remuneration Report*, BHP Billiton PLC *Annual Report 2002*; pp. 559, 679: Interviewed by Carolyn Rance for *HR Monthly*, May 2003; p. 571: © Commonwealth of Australia 2004 All legislation herein is reproduced by permission but does not purport to be the official or authorised version. It is subject to Commonwealth of Australia copyright; p. 669: Reproduced with the kind permission of CCH Aust Limited from 'Measuring management performance in occupational health and safety', *Journal of Occupational Health in Australia and New Zealand*, vol. 11, no. 6, 1995, p. 560. www.cch.com.au; p. 374: © Deirdre Macken, *Australian Financial Review*, 24–25 May, 2003; p. 789: © 1994, with permission from Elsevier/Reprinted from *Business Horizons*, vol. 37, no. 1, H. Tu and S. E. Sullivan, 'Preparing yourself for an international assignment', p. 68; p. 714: Equal Opportunity for Women in the Workplace Agency & Santa Sabina College; p. 648: © G. Kennedy et al, *Managing Negotiations* 3rd edn, Hutchison Business, 1987; p. 505: Graham Hubbard; p. 601: W. Cascio, 'Cutbacks threaten innovation', *HR Monthly*,

February 2003, p.14; p. 822: © Harry Onsman, *BRW*, 11 June 1999; p. 391: Reprinted by permission of *Harvard Business Review*. Excerpt from 'Is Management a Profession?' by P. Donham, vol. 40, issue.5, Sept.–Oct. 1962, p.64. © 1962 by the Harvard Business School Publishing Corporation; all rights reserved; p. 14: Hayco Manufacturing/Donald Hay; p. 449: HayGroup Pty Ltd; p. 105: Charles Power, Partner, Holding Redlich, Melbourne; p. 642: HREOC — Human Rights and Equal Opportunity Commission; p. 592: © Jan McCallum, Boss, June 2003; p. 844: © HRM Consulting/Jenny Brinkies; p. 603: © Joe Meissner, Personnel Journal, November, 1993; p. 86: John Eddy, *HR Monthly*; p. 49: © Peter Roberts, *BRW*, 3–9 July 2003; p. 419: © Jacqui Walker, *BRW*, 15–21 May 2003; p. 495: © David James, *BRW*, 19–25 June 2003; p. 632: © Kristen Le Mesurier, *BRW*, 16–22 October 2003; p. 662: Leighton Holdings Limited *Annual Report 2003*; p. 242: © Lisa Allen, *Australian Financial Review*, 16–17 August 2003; p. 755: © Lisa Allen, *Australian Financial Review*, 30 May 2003; p. 710: © Liz Porter, *Sunday Age*, 3 August 2003; p. 709: © Louise Bettison, *The Australian*, 23 May 2001; pp. 76, 150, 640: Marcus Priest, *Australian Financial Review*; p. 461:Martin Cox/ Bob Walker, *Australian Financial Review*; p. 552: Martin Foley, *HR Monthly*; p. 647: Matheson Publishing/Sally Matheson from the *Drake Business Review*; p. 661: J. M. Ivancevich, *Human Resource Management, 8th edn*, 2001, McGraw-Hill. Reproduced with permission of The McGraw-Hill Companies; p. 303: © Michael Cave, *Australian Financial Review*, 14 June 2002; p. 115: © Mike Toten, *HR Monthly*, July, 2003; p. 750: M. J. Marquardt, *Monash Mt Eliza Business Review*; pp. 666, 668: The National Occupational Health and Safety Commission (NOHSC) aims to improve public access to information about its activities and occupational health and safety information more generally. The vision of NOHSC is Australian workplaces free from injury and disease. Its mission is to lead and coordinate national efforts to prevent workplace death, injury and disease in Australia. This information can only assist you in the most general way. While NOHSC aims to keep the information accurate and up to date, NOHSC makes no warranties or representations regarding the quality, accuracy, completeness or reliability of information on the site. NOHSC accepts no liability arising from the use of or reliance on the material contained in this document, which is provided on the basis that NOHSC is not thereby engaged in rendering professional advice. Before relying on the material, users should carefully make their own assessment as to its accuracy, currency, completeness and relevance for their purposes, and should obtain any appropriate professional advice relevant to their particular circumstances. NOHSC also encourages you to contact the NOHSC Webmaster on info@nohsc.gov.au if you have any concerns about the information provided.; p. 663: OneSteel; p. 171: © Paul Gollan & Glenn Patmore, *HR Monthly*, June 2003; p. 315, 345, 363: Dr Philip Wright, Professor School of Business, Shue Yan College; p. 674: © Robin Robertson/*Australian Financial Review*, 6 November 2003, p. 15; p. 829: S. M. Kenney. *Compensation & Benefits Review*, vol. 27, 1, 1995, p. 26. Reprinted by permission of Sage Publications; p. 824: © Steve Van Emmerick/*HR Monthly*, April 2003, pp. 46–7; pp. 388, 452: Reprinted with permission from *2003 Compensation Report — Australia*. © 2003. Watson Wyatt Worldwide. For information visit www.watsonwyatt.com; p. 489, 490: Westpac Banking Corporation.

Every effort has been made to trace the ownership of copyright material. Information that will enable the publisher to rectify any error or omission in subsequent editions will be welcome. In such cases, please contact the Permissions Section of John Wiley & Sons Australia, Ltd, who will arrange for the payment of the usual fee.

Raymond J. Stone

BA, B.Com., Dip. Soc. Stud. (Melb); MA (Ottawa), PhD (HK), CMAHRI, FIHRM (Hong Kong), Registered Psychologist. Raymond J. Stone has over 30 years experience in international human resource management. He has held senior positions in Australia, Hong Kong, Japan and Korea. His work experience covers compensation and benefits, recruitment and selection, psychological appraisal, industrial relations, personnel research, training and development, human resource planning and policy development.

He has taught at universities in Australia, Japan and Hong Kong. He is the editor of *Readings in Human Resource Management*, Volumes 1, 2 and 3 (John Wiley & Sons) and is the co-author of two earlier books on human resource management.

His articles on negotiating and international human resource management have been published in leading academic and business journals in Australia, Hong Kong, Japan, Singapore, Britain and the United States.

Joe Catanzariti

Chapter 4 was written by Joe Catanzariti, BA, LLB (NSW). Catanzariti is a partner with the national law firm Clayton Utz. He is currently the Secretary of the Industrial Relations Society of Australia and is a counsellor of the New South Wales Law Society. He is a regular contributor to the *Law Society Journal* and other major industry journals.

Graham O'Neill

The original text for chapter 13 was prepared by Graham O'Neill, BA (Hons) (Tasmania), Dip. App. Psych. (Adelaide). O'Neill has edited several books on compensation and human resources and is a frequent commentator and contributor to professional journals on remuneration and HR issues.

Dr Maureen Fastenau

Chapter 19 was written by Dr Maureen Fastenau, Senior Lecturer in Management at RMIT University. Dr Fastenau practised for a number of years as a manager of EEO and AA programs, and continues to consult to private and public sector organisations in EEO, AA, diversity management, and sexual and racial harassment as well as to research in these areas. Dr Fastenau was until recently the EEO columnist for *HR Monthly*, the professional journal of the AHRI, and is the founding editor of the *International Employment Relations Review*.

how to use this book

Human Resource Management, 5th edition, has been designed with you, the student, in mind. The following features are included throughout the book to assist you in understanding the dynamic field of human resource management.

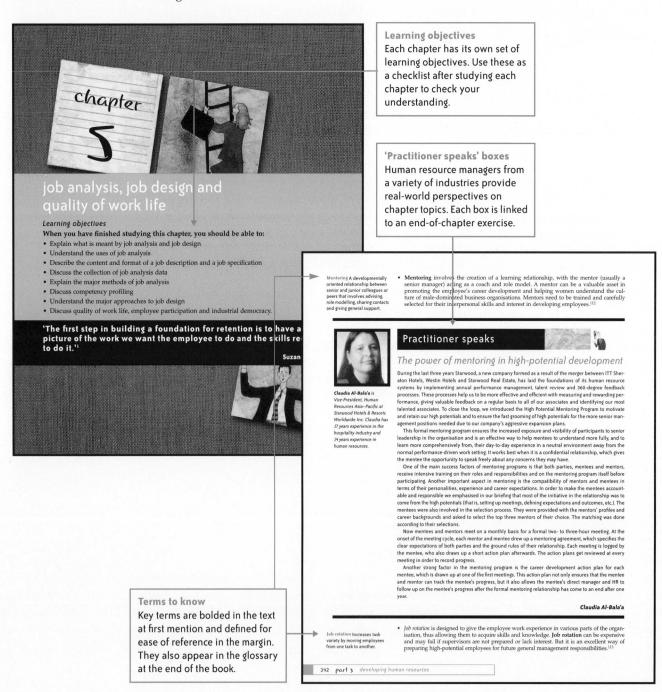

Learning objectives
Each chapter has its own set of learning objectives. Use these as a checklist after studying each chapter to check your understanding.

'Practitioner speaks' boxes
Human resource managers from a variety of industries provide real-world perspectives on chapter topics. Each box is linked to an end-of-chapter exercise.

Terms to know
Key terms are bolded in the text at first mention and defined for ease of reference in the margin. They also appear in the glossary at the end of the book.

---

chapter 5

job analysis, job design and quality of work life

Learning objectives
When you have finished studying this chapter, you should be able to:

• Explain what is meant by job analysis and job design
• Understand the uses of job analysis
• Describe the content and format of a job description and a job specification
• Discuss the collection of job analysis data
• Explain the major methods of job analysis
• Discuss competency profiling
• Understand the major approaches to job design
• Discuss quality of work life, employee participation and industrial democracy.

'The first step in building a foundation for retention is to have a [clear] picture of the work we want the employee to do and the skills re[quired] to do it.'[1]

Suzan[...]

Mentoring A developmentally oriented relationship between senior and junior colleagues or peers that involves advising, role modelling, sharing contacts and giving general support.

• **Mentoring** involves the creation of a learning relationship, with the mentor (usually a senior manager) acting as a coach and role model. A mentor can be a valuable asset in promoting the employee's career development and helping women understand the culture of male-dominated business organisations. Mentors need to be trained and carefully selected for their interpersonal skills and interest in developing employees.[112]

Practitioner speaks

The power of mentoring in high-potential development

Claudia Al-Bala'a is Vice-President, Human Resources Asia–Pacific at Starwood Hotels & Resorts Worldwide Inc. Claudia has 17 years experience in the hospitality industry and 14 years experience in human resources.

During the last three years Starwood, a new company formed as a result of the merger between ITT Sheraton Hotels, Westin Hotels and Starwood Real Estate, has laid the foundations of its human resource systems by implementing annual performance management, talent review and 360-degree feedback processes. These processes help us to be more effective and efficient with measuring and rewarding performance, giving valuable feedback on a regular basis to all of our associates and identifying our most talented associates. To close the loop, we introduced the High Potential Mentoring Program to motivate and retain our high potentials and to ensure the fast grooming of high potentials for the more senior management positions needed due to our company's aggressive expansion plans.

This formal mentoring program ensures the increased exposure and visibility of participants to senior leadership in the organisation and is an effective way to help mentees to understand more fully, and to learn more comprehensively from, their day-to-day experience in a neutral environment away from the normal performance-driven work setting. It works best when it is a confidential relationship, which gives the mentee the opportunity to speak freely about any concerns they may have.

One of the main success factors of mentoring programs is that both parties, mentees and mentors, receive intensive training on their roles and responsibilities and on the mentoring program itself before participating. Another important aspect in mentoring is the compatibility of mentors and mentees in terms of their personalities, experience and career expectations. In order to make the mentees accountable and responsible we emphasised that most of the initiative in the relationship was to come from the high potentials (that is, setting up meetings, defining expectations and outcomes, etc.). The mentees were also involved in the selection process. They were provided with the mentors' profiles and career backgrounds and asked to select the top three mentors of their choice. The matching was done according to their selections.

Now mentees and mentors meet on a monthly basis for a formal two- to three-hour meeting. At the onset of the meeting cycle, each mentor and mentee drew up a mentoring agreement, which specifies the clear expectations of both parties and the ground rules of their relationship. Each meeting is logged by the mentee, who also draws up a short action plan afterwards. The action plans get reviewed at every meeting in order to record progress.

Another strong factor in the mentoring program is the career development action plan for each mentee, which is drawn up at one of the first meetings. This action plan not only ensures that the mentee and mentor can track the mentee's progress, but it also allows the mentee's direct manager and HR to follow up on the mentee's progress after the formal mentoring relationship has come to an end after one year.

Claudia Al-Bala'a

Job rotation Increases task variety by moving employees from one task to another.

• *Job rotation* is designed to give the employee work experience in various parts of the organisation, thus allowing them to acquire skills and knowledge. **Job rotation** can be expensive and may fail if supervisors are not prepared or lack interest. But it is an excellent way of preparing high-potential employees for future general management responsibilities.[113]

342   **part 3**   *developing human resources*

Letters to the Editor

These letters provide a provocative viewpoint about chapter issues. What's your view? at the end of each chapter asks you to respond to the letters.

Letter to the Editor

While I'm happy for people to advance their careers as they see fit, I'm hamstrung by government regulations and bureaucratic red tape that inhibit me from supplying my organisation with the best people wherever I can find them. Whether it's politically imposed constraints such as immigration quotas, the petty-mindedness of government bureaucrats who fear that overseas workers may overstay their work visas or the high income taxes faced by employees in Australia, I cannot obtain the kinds of people I need at the time I need them.

Consider good IT staff, for example. Our universities produce a fixed number of IT graduates each year, yet supply is far short of demand for competent IT graduates. Why? Because the federal government cannot accurately predict the demand for IT graduates four and five years out from their graduation and so swings between overfunding and underfunding university courses from IT to teaching. Further, I find that the Australian university IT graduates I do interview often lack key verbal and written communication skills and fundamental IT competencies. I'm wondering whether some of these students should have been admitted to university in the first place.

So, the government and universities have a lot to answer for. In funding IT places, the government simply takes an educated guess about future economic and industrial conditions and funds universities accordingly. It is constrained by political realities from providing the IT graduates we need, and it knows that it will face a political backlash if it reduces funding for low-demand disciplines like the arts and some of the less-vocational sciences. At the same time, the universities accept marginally qualified entrants and are often years behind in teaching current IT competencies.

This makes very little sense to me. If our companies are to match the best in the world, we need the best people at the right time and at the right price. We are living in a globalised world where the move to free trade has helped to bring about times of great prosperity. People want freedom, whether it's freedom of religion or freedom to use their talents anywhere in the world. We need to deregulate the movement of people between one place and another, and also seek to abolish those industrial relations laws that make us pay a range of salaries and benefits out of kilter with the rest of the world.

I hope that other employers will join with me in getting government out of our pockets so that together we can become world competitive and join the global movement towards freer labour markets. We all stand to benefit, as do the countries in which we operate.

A concerned CEO

Source David Poole, University of Western Sydney.

Requirements for effective HR planning

Given that the success of an organisation ultimately depends on how well its human resources are managed, HR planning will continue to grow in importance. However, there is a danger that it may become a fad, failing because it cannot satisfy management's unrealistic expectations. Such expectations may be fuelled by planning theorists who advocate sophisticated analytical techniques. Mackay, for example, argues that 'planners, especially those trained in the quantitative approach, may be tempted to create esoteric systems that are incompatible with the practical needs of line managers'.[100]

Successful HR planning requires HR managers to ensure that:
- HR personnel understand the HR planning process
- top management is supportive
- the organisation does not start with an overly complex system
- the communications between HR personnel and line management are healthy

NEWSBREAK

Australia's reverse diaspora

By Peter Roberts

There is something very wrong here. A million Australians are working abroad — it has been called our very own diaspora. That is a cute idea, but a diaspora usually describes a dispersed group of desperate people who have fled oppression for a better life elsewhere. In Asia, there is a diaspora of Filipinos, many of whom flock to Singapore for menial and poorly paid jobs such as household maids. Their diaspora is incredibly valuable to the Philippine economy, with billions of dollars a year sent back to families at home.

But Australia's million-strong diaspora includes few maids or desperate people. They are often Australia's best and brightest — too often our elite business managers or managers from fast-growing small and medium-size companies.

In 2001–02, according to the Australian Bureau of Statistics, about 7300 more managers and professionals left the country than returned — a serious haemorrhage of talent. The previous year the number was closer to 13 000. The conditions they find in Asia are far better than Australia, where for business executives taxes are high and wages low on a world scale.

In Asia, executives occupy a respected position in society; in Australia, success and its rewards attract envy and even abuse. As the many poor Filipinos in menial jobs support their economy, so too does Australia's elite diaspora support its home economy, investing in cheap (by world standards) property in Sydney and on the Gold Coast.

Sitting at home in Australia, it is easy to think that 'they will be back'. But what will attract Australia's managerial and professional elite back home?

Australia's high taxes used to pay for quality public services such as free university education and free medical treatment. Today, those benefits are under attack, if not already gone.

In any case, no Australian university ranks among the world's top 100 in internationally recognised surveys, and the standard of medical care in places such as Kuala Lumpur and Bangkok is very good.

What Australia's policy makers seem to be pinning their hopes on is the country's environment and lifestyle, which are certainly invaluable assets in an increasingly crowded and polluted region. But we need look no further than Adelaide for the ultimate value of a great environment to draw successful expatriates back home.

For decades, Adelaide has endured the same exodus of talent, to the eastern states, that Australia now suffers internationally. Like a spring winding down, the South Australian economy has lost much of its vigor along with its talented and dynamic exports.

Certainly, some will return for the beaches and the Barossa, but most Adelaide people who have made it in Melbourne return only for family birthdays or to take the kids to Kangaroo Island.

Make no mistake: Australia is suffering a reverse diaspora. Our 'huddled masses' are staying at home while adventurous engineers and managers are finding a new future overseas. In an international economy, propelled by innovation and intellectual property, this can only impoverish us.

Source *BRW*, 3–9 July 2003, p. 50.

Newsbreaks

Media articles on HRM topics drawn from Australia and the Asia–Pacific region help demonstrate the chapter theory. Each Newsbreak is linked to an end-of-chapter exercise

Women in the work force

The growing role of women in the work force depends on improved childcare facilities, the availability of part-time work, job security after an absence for child-bearing, maternity leave, special parental leave and partners prepared to share home duties.

individual employee performance. Employee attitudes, behaviour and perceptions positively or negatively influence performance. High-performance HRM therefore cannot ignore HR outcomes from the employee's perspective.[107] This comprehensive strategic approach generates more informed and purposeful HR management. Articulating the organisation's mission or purpose (why it exists), its objectives (what it wants to achieve), its strategies (how the objectives are to be achieved) and plans (the action steps required) helps direct the setting of HRM objectives, strategies and plans. In turn, when applied to specific HRM activities such as recruitment and selection, the HR manager can better appreciate which specific action plans are required to support HRM and organisational strategic objectives. Organisations that adopt HRM strategies and high-performance HR policies and practices consistent with the demands of their internal and external environments outperform organisations that adopt less well-matched strategies and practices (see figure 1.10).[108]

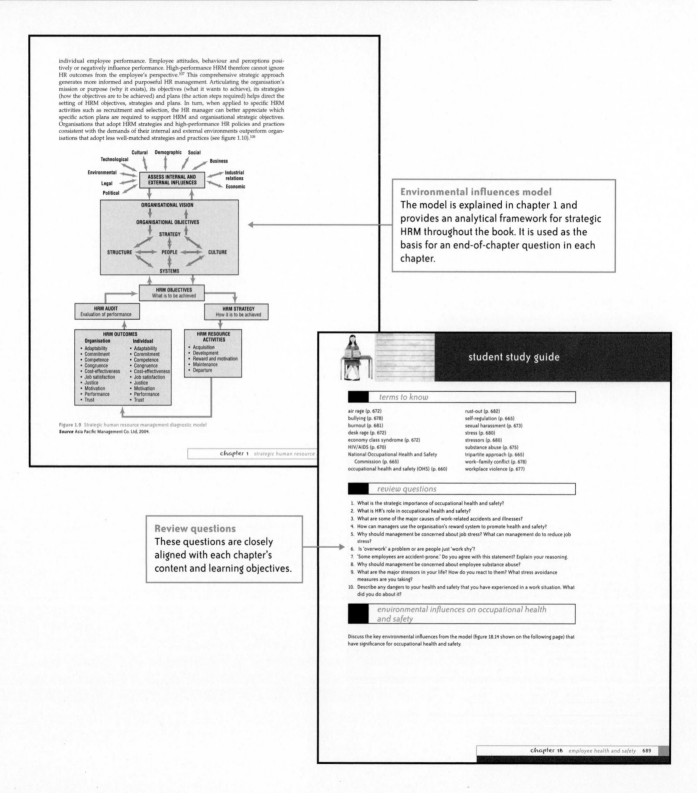

Figure 1.9 Strategic human resource management diagnostic model
Source Asia Pacific Management Co. Ltd, 2004.

Environmental influences model
The model is explained in chapter 1 and provides an analytical framework for strategic HRM throughout the book. It is used as the basis for an end-of-chapter question in each chapter.

student study guide

terms to know

air rage (p. 672)	rust-out (p. 682)
bullying (p. 678)	self-regulation (p. 665)
burnout (p. 681)	sexual harassment (p. 673)
desk rage (p. 672)	stress (p. 680)
economy class syndrome (p. 672)	stressors (p. 680)
HIV/AIDS (p. 670)	substance abuse (p. 675)
National Occupational Health and Safety Commission (p. 665)	tripartite approach (p. 665)
	work–family conflict (p. 678)
occupational health and safety (OHS) (p. 660)	workplace violence (p. 677)

review questions

1. What is the strategic importance of occupational health and safety?
2. What is HR's role in occupational health and safety?
3. What are some of the major causes of work-related accidents and illnesses?
4. How can managers use the organisation's reward system to promote health and safety?
5. Why should management be concerned about job stress? What can management do to reduce job stress?
6. Is 'overwork' a problem or are people just 'work shy'?
7. 'Some employees are accident-prone.' Do you agree with this statement? Explain your reasoning.
8. Why should management be concerned about employee substance abuse?
9. What are the major stressors in your life? How do you react to them? What stress avoidance measures are you taking?
10. Describe any dangers to your health and safety that you have experienced in a work situation. What did you do about it?

environmental influences on occupational health and safety

Discuss the key environmental influences from the model (figure 18.14 shown on the following page) that have significance for occupational health and safety.

Review questions
These questions are closely aligned with each chapter's content and learning objectives.

Class debates
A thought-provoking issue is provided on a topic in each chapter to encourage discussion of differing viewpoints.

Practical exercises
These individual or group-based activities are designed to facilitate experiential learning and your understanding of HRM theory.

Soapbox
This feature provides material for a class survey based on the content of each chapter.

class debate

Performance appraisal is simply a management technique operating under a scientific veneer to manipulate and control employees by reinforcing behavioural norms that the organisation considers desirable.
or
Australians are hard in their attitude towards non-performance on the sporting field but soft in their attitude towards non-performance in the workplace.

practical exercises

1. Break into groups of three: one member to play the role of the Sales Manager, one to be Judi Novak, the Sales Supervisor, and one to be an observer. The instructions for each role follow. After conducting an appraisal interview, each member should complete the performance appraisal feedback sheet provided above. Critically discuss your responses.
Sales Manager
You are the newly appointed Sales Manager of the Adelaide sales office and this is the first time that you have had to complete an appraisal of Judi Novak. The HR Manager has advised you that the annual performance appraisal for Judi is now due. You are somewhat anxious because Judi has a reputation for being aggressive and outspoken. She is technically very competent and has good relations with her subordinates and customers, but has upset several senior managers with her outspokenness. Consequently, you suspect that her personal advancement prospects are poor. You know, for example, that your superior dislikes her and you are worried that if you rate Judi too highly, you will have a problem with your boss. As a result, you plan to play it safe and give Judi the following ratings.

Name: Judi Novak					Position: Sales Supervisor	
Department: Office Equipment					Date: 23/03/04	
Factor	Rating					
	Poor			Average		Superior
Job knowledge	1 2 3			4 5 6		(7) 8 9
Human relations	1 2 3			(4) (5) 6		7 8 9
Organising ability	1 2 3			4 (5) 6		7 8 9
Planning ability	1 2 3			4 (5) 6		7 8 9
Creativity	1 2 3			4 (5) 6		7 8 9
Judgement	1 2 3			4 (5) 6		7 8 9
Initiative	1 2 3			4 (5) 6		7 8 9
Supervisory skills	1 2 3			4 5 (6)		7 8 9
Overall assessment: Average						

Judi Novak

You have been with the organisation for seven years and have generally been very highly rated. However, your ratings have dropped in the past two years. You feel this is because you challenged the

developing human resources

soapbox

What do you think? Conduct a mini survey of class members, using the questionnaire below. Critically discuss the findings.

1.	Management games are fun, but of little value in improving on-the-job performance.	YES	NO
2.	Only employees whose performance is unacceptable need training.	YES	NO
3.	The 'school of hard knocks' provides the best training.	YES	NO
4.	Companies should be required to spend a nominated amount each year on employee training and development.	YES	NO
5.	Training older workers is a waste of time and money.	YES	NO
6.	Trade unions should be involved in the design and implementation of all training and development programs.	YES	NO

online exercise

Visit one of the company web sites listed in appendix B on page 852. Find information relating to (a) the company's mission, objectives and culture and (b) the company's HRD activities and how they fit with its mission, objectives and culture. Prepare a three-minute presentation (to be given in class) summarising your findings.

ethical dilemma

A matter of discrimination at Jet Red

Jet Red, suffering from heavy losses, is undergoing major restructuring. Its new board of directors and top management are aggressive and results-oriented. They are under extreme pressure to turn the airline around before it collapses under the weight of excessive debt, passenger decline and savage competition. Jet Red's top management has a strong belief in HRD and has actively promoted employee development programs.

After completing a comprehensive training needs analysis, Linda Church, Jet Red's HR Manager, has introduced a customer service program. Jet Red's new management has made a policy change that requires training to be done in company and employee time. Consequently, the eight two-hour sessions are scheduled to start at 4 o'clock and finish at 6 o'clock. Linda is enthusiastic about the new program because it is job-related and has a demonstrable bottom-line impact.

Linda's thoughts are interrupted by the ringing of her phone. It is Annie O'Brien, the union representative. 'Linda, I'm shocked', Annie complained. 'I can't believe that you as a woman can allow this company to conduct a training program outside normal working hours. It's ridiculous. Apart from the question of overtime pay, the proposal is discriminatory and is an abusive intrusion on personal time. You as the HR Manager should be ashamed of yourself. You must be aware that women as partners and primary caregivers have limited time to attend such programs. Your thinking is so archaic, it's incredible.'
Linda shifted in her chair and said, 'Annie…'

Discussion questions
1. If you were Linda, what would you say to the union representative?
2. What do you think of Annie's arguments that out-of-hours training programs:
   (a) are discriminatory?
   (b) should attract overtime payments?
   (c) are an out-of-date concept?

362 **part 3** *developing human resources*

Online exercises
These exercises encourage further research and application of the chapter theory.

Ethical dilemmas
Case study-style ethical dilemmas are provided at the end of each chapter for analysis and discussion, and relevant ethical issues are highlighted in the chapter margins.

case studies

A friendly drink

You are enjoying your first Kaesing party in a Seoul restaurant. The food and entertainment have been lavish. Your Korean hosts have been very hospitable and everything seems to be progressing smoothly. Mr Park, the senior Korean, fills his glass with whisky and passes it to you to drink. You suddenly became concerned. You are worried about the health risks (especially AIDS and hepatitis) and about having to drink so much liquor in one hit. In fact, the whole idea of exchanging drinking glasses with others strikes you as repugnant.

Discussion question

What would you do? Why?

The noisy eater

Ken Shimada was happy. His interviews with the Executive Search Consultant, Michio Ishii, had gone extremely well and now he had been invited to dinner by Winston Eldridge III. Ken knew that if this meeting went well he would be certain to be offered the position of President for American Heritage Inc.'s Asian operations. As the Chairman and largest stockholder, Eldridge was the decision maker. A man in his early sixties, he was a Bostonian of conservative and aristocratic manner. All seemed to be progressing smoothly until the soup was served. Ken slurped the soup Japanese-style, making considerable noise. Eldridge was horrified. Suddenly, Ken sensed that he had lost the job.

Discussion questions

1. How could this situation have been avoided?
2. What would you do now assuming you were (a) Ken Shimada, (b) Michio Ishii and (c) Winston Eldridge?

The angry professor

Professor Harry Barbarian faced his Kowloon University class of year one business administration students. 'Okay', said Harry, 'let's see what you have learned from the case study.'

Harry noticed that suddenly all the students were staring intently at the floor. Willie Wong, in particular, seemed to be fascinated by the floor tiles.

'Mr Wong, you look like an intelligent fellow. Tell me, what do you think? How would you solve the problem?' Willie said nothing, and became even more absorbed in the floor tiles.

'Come on, man, you haven't lost your tongue, have you? Tell me, what would you do?' Willie muttered a desperate 'I'm not sure.'

Harry exploded 'What do you mean, you're not su[re?] Haven't you got a brain? Answer me, man, what do y[ou...]' Willie's face reddened. He continued staring at the [floor.]

Discussion questions

1. Why was Willie reluctant to answer the question?
2. Why did the professor behave the way he did?

> **End-of-chapter case studies and end-of-part case studies** A variety of real-world case studies are provided to illustrate the theory. Each case study includes questions for analysis. A running case study throughout the chapters helps to integrate the material.

part 6 case study

OUTSOURCING IT-ENABLED SERVICES TO INDIA: SOUND STRATEGY OR SOCIAL SUICIDE?
Mohan Thite, Griffith University

Robert Perry, the HR Director of Tel Alliance, a major telecommunications company in Australasia, had just come back to his office after addressing the annual meeting of HR professionals in the company. He had a smile on his face because the company had just posted handsome profits after many years of sluggish growth and declining revenue, and the board of directors had openly acknowledged the strategic contribution made by the HR Division in this remarkable turnaround.

With the smile still on his face, Robert turned his attention to the new email from his CEO, Jack Clinton, marked 'Urgent and confidential'. The email, addressed to all functional directors, said: 'I have called an urgent meeting of all directors on Monday morning to review our policy of outsourcing IT-enabled services (ITES) to strategic business partners in India.'

The message came as a surprise to Robert. He started wondering what could have prompted the CEO to call an urgent meeting on this issue, particularly as it was well known in the company that outsourcing ITES to India had had a very healthy impact on the company's bottom line. While walking to the coffee room, Robert recalled how Tel Alliance had come to rely more and more on Indian IT companies in IT services, including call centre operations.

It all started three years ago when Tel Alliance undertook a major review of its IT strategy. At that time, the IT Division was notorious for cost overruns, missing deadlines, a critical shortage of IT personnel with the latest skills and misreading technology trends affecting the business. Being a telecommunications company, Tel Alliance operated in an extremely volatile market characterised by hyper global competition, rapid technological obsolescence and heavy investment in technology with uncertain returns.

Robert recalled how the IT Director and the Finance Director had made an exciting presentation to management about the strategic benefits of outsourcing IT services to India. They pointed out that more than 50 per cent of Fortune 500 companies outsourced their IT-related operations overseas to countries like India, where labour costs offered dramatic savings — upwards of 70 per cent.[1] In fact, what was said at the meeting was open knowledge.

It was already being recognised worldwide that India, the world's largest democracy and home to one billion people, had surprisingly emerged as a software powerhouse in the global IT arena. From 1995 to 2000, exports of IT services by the Indian software industry grew at a staggering annual rate of 62.3 per cent.[2] At the time when the IT industry was experiencing an unprecedented boom period, due to a variety of factors such as the emergence of e-commerce, dot.coms and the Y2K scare, there was a worldwide shortage of IT personnel and India, with the world's second-largest pool of English-speaking scientific and technical professionals, offered high-quality and cost-effective IT services. What started with the outsourcing of low-level IT maintenance to Indian companies rapidly grew to include the development of critical IT projects. This IT outsourcing revolution was led by the United States, which issued more than 50 per cent of the work permits for foreign IT workers to Indian IT professionals.[3] This trend slowly picked up in other developed countries, such as Britain, Japan, Germany, Singapore and Italy.

Against this background, management did not need much convincing to follow the trend. In fact, many Indian IT professionals had already worked for Tel Alliance as subcontractors and provided excellent on-site services. Now the proposal was to use offshore IT services from Indian IT

introducing hrm

Part 1 deals with the context of human resource management and includes strategic HRM, HR planning, HR information systems, and HRM and the law. The case study at the end of the part incorporates these topics using the example of House Smart Furniture Company.

chapter

1

strategic human resource management

Learning objectives

When you have finished studying this chapter, you should be able to:

- Explain what is meant by human resource management
- Understand the relationship between human resource management and management
- Describe the HR manager's role
- Understand the human resource management activities performed in organisations
- Explain the meaning of strategy
- Explain the meaning of strategic human resource management
- Describe a strategic approach to human resource management
- Appreciate the strategic challenges facing human resource management.

'An HR manager's job requires that he or she confront issues of fairness and perceived injustice in the workplace.'[1]

D. P. Skarlicki and R. Folger

Human resource management (HRM) Involves the productive use of people in achieving the organisation's strategic objectives and the satisfaction of individual employee needs.

Objectives Measurable targets to be achieved within a certain time frame.

The focus of **human resource management (HRM)** is on managing people within the employer–employee relationship. Specifically, it involves the productive use of people in achieving the organisation's strategic business **objectives** and the satisfaction of individual employee needs.

Because HRM seeks to strategically integrate the interests of an organisation and its employees, it is much more than a set of activities relating to the coordination of an organisation's human resources. HRM is a major contributor to the success of an enterprise because it is in a key position 'to affect customers, business results and ultimately shareholder value'.[2] Says Gratton: 'The new sources of sustainable competitive advantage available to organizations have people at the centre — their creativity and talent, their inspirations and hopes, their dreams and excitement. The companies that flourish in this decade will do so because they are able to provide meaning and purpose, a context and frame that encourages individual potential to flourish and grow.'[3]

HRM is either part of the problem or part of the solution in gaining the productive contribution of people. Leading companies such as BHP Billiton, Foster's, General Electric, Coca-Cola, Johnson & Johnson, Macquarie Bank, Microsoft and Stockland recognise that human capital is their most important resource and take action to maximise it by focusing on selecting, developing and rewarding top talent, encouraging open communication, teamwork and collaboration, and refusing to tolerate poor performance or compromise their long-term objectives for short-term gains (see figure 1.1).[4] Lilian Clarke, Group General Manager, Human Resources at Stockland, says 'At Stockland, we have the right people with the right attitude and a dynamic inclusive structure that brings our vision, mission and values to life in everything we do'.[5]

For Foster's to consistently improve performance it is essential the group attracts, develops and retains the best people. Achieving this includes:
- Focusing on development and training opportunities that facilitate individual growth as well as meeting business needs.
- Ensuring Foster's and its businesses are challenging and rewarding places to work.
- Creating a work force of shareholders by encouraging employees to own shares in Foster's.

Figure 1.1 Creating an inspiring workplace at Foster's
Source Foster's Group, *Annual Report*, Melbourne, 2003, p. 26.

Pfeffer, after an exhaustive review of the research literature, identified seven dimensions of effective people management that produce substantially enhanced economic performance: employment security; rigorous selection; self-managed teams and decentralised decision making; comparatively high compensation linked to individual and organisational performance; extensive training; reduced status distinctions; and extensive sharing of financial and performance information throughout the organisation.[6] Guest similarly found that job design, employee participation and open communication, equal opportunities, family-friendly practices and anti-harassment practices are associated with higher work and life satisfaction.[7]

Other evidence indicates that such high-performance HR management policies and practices generate profitability gains, share price increases, higher company survival rates, increased sales, higher export growth and lower labour turnover.[8] Research by Chang and Chen found that HR activities such as training and development, human resource planning and performance appraisal had a significant impact on employee productivity.[9] Finally, a recent study by Bjorkman and Fan showed a positive relationship between organisational performance and the extent to which the organisation used 'high-performance' HRM policies and practices and integrated its HRM strategies with its business strategies.[10] The evidence is clear — high-performance HRM policies and practices generate superior organisational performance.[11] In addition, a Hay Group study showed that the most admired companies in the United States are more focused on strategic issues and more successful in creating a work force that is competent, loyal and committed.[12]

The HR manager, as with any other functional manager in marketing, production or finance, is responsible for performance. The position exists foremost to help achieve the strategic business objectives of the organisation. If it does not, the position will become redundant. According to Ulrich, HR people spend 60–80 per cent of their time in administrative activities and less than 20 per cent on the gutsy roles of strategic partner, employee advocate and consultant on important HR issues.[13] Consistent with this there is evidence indicating that line managers, rather than HR managers, are the organisation's change agents, and that HR managers are being marginalised.[14] Moreover, research indicates that HRM in many of the fastest-growing US firms is under-used, unrecognised and unnecessary as an in-house asset.[15] A study by Deloitte Touche also found that in most US companies HR activities are not seen as making an important contribution to the commitment of employees to either customers or the company.[16] More than 60 per cent of companies in another US survey reported that they had outsourced components of their HR activities.[17]

The HR function is recognised for contributing to the **'bottom line'**, not for being performed by nice people with good human relations skills.[18] Confusing people skills with people management is a common mistake made by many HRM practitioners. HR managers will never be accepted as strategic business partners until they fully understand the organisation's business and align high-performance human resource strategies, policies and practices with business strategies (such as customer satisfaction).[19] According to Walker, managers 'do not perceive people related issues and initiatives to be as important as financial, sales and other business concerns'.[20] This is despite studies showing that firms can benefit from having HR managers as part of their top management and that HR programs have a positive impact on organisational performance.[21] Australian research, for example, demonstrates that better-performing companies have HR representation at board level.[22] Consistent with this, Bartlett and Ghoshal argue that to develop a sustainable competitive advantage, HR activities must be viewed strategically with HR represented at top management level.[23] Clearly, there is a need for HR managers to create a better understanding among line managers of the valuable contribution to be made by HRM.[24]

Bottom line Refers to a final result, such as the net profit after taxes.

HRM and management

HRM is **management**, but management is more than HRM. HRM is that part of management dealing directly with people, whereas management includes marketing, management information systems, production, research and development, and accounting and finance. Because the purpose of HRM is to improve the productive contribution of people, it is intimately related to all other aspects of management. Managers manage people and the management of an organisation's human resources is primarily a line or operating management responsibility. However, the degree to which **HRM activities** are divided between line or operating managers and the HRM manager (and their department) varies from organisation to organisation (see the Letter to the Editor on page 11).

An HR specialist in one organisation may directly handle all negotiations with unions, for example, while in another organisation operating managers may take responsibility for union negotiations and the HR manager may have an advisory role or no involvement at all. Top management recognition of HRM's massive impact on organisational performance and an increasing belief that HR is too important to be left to HR managers has meant that some line managers now compete with HRM specialists for HR responsibilities.[25] For example, one survey found that line managers have increased their role and responsibility for HR matters (particularly in occupational health and safety, recruitment, selection and human resource development) and that HR managers have little or no influence over key decisions.[26] The precise balance between line and HR management is determined by an organisation's strategic business objectives, its culture and structure and the quality of its operating and HR managers[27] (see figures 1.2 and 1.3 overleaf). Some HR managers may also

Management The art of getting things done through people.

HRM activities HR activities such as job analysis, HR planning, recruitment, etc.

supervise another function: for example, ANZ has one executive responsible for both HRM and corporate affairs; St George's top HR executive's portfolio of responsibilities includes marketing, communications and group services; and Tandou's Human Resources Manager manages HR and community relations.[28]

Old myths	New realities
People go into HR because they like people.	HR departments are not designed to provide corporate therapy or as social or health-and-happiness retreats. HR professionals must create the practices that make employees more competitive, not more comfortable.
Anyone can do HR.	HR activities are based on theory and research. HR professionals must master both theory and practice.
HR deals with the soft side of a business and therefore is not accountable.	The impact of HR practices on business results can and must be measured. HR professionals must learn how to translate their work into financial performance.
HR focuses on costs, which must be controlled.	HR practices must create value by increasing the intellectual capital within the firm. HR professionals must add value, not reduce costs.
HR's job is to be the policy police and the health-and-happiness patrol.	The HR function does not own compliance — managers do. HR practices do not exist to make employees happy but to help them become committed. HR professionals must help managers commit employees and administer policies.
HR is full of fads.	HR practices have evolved over time. HR professionals must see their current work as part of an evolutionary chain and explain their work with less jargon and more authority.
HR is staffed by nice people.	At times, HR practices should force vigorous debates. HR professionals should be confrontative [sic] and challenging as well as supportive.
HR is HR's job.	HR work is as important to line managers as are finance, strategy, and other business domains. HR professionals should join with managers in championing HR issues.

Figure 1.2 Myths that keep HR from being a profession

Source Reprinted by permission of the Harvard Business School Press, from D. Ulrich, *Human Resource Champions*, 1997, p. 18. Copyright © 1997 by the Harvard Business School Publishing Corporation; all rights reserved.

When HRM is focused on records maintenance and employee recreation ('picnic and payroll') activities that typically no other function wants, it is regarded as a cost and largely irrelevant to the success of the business. With low status, HRM becomes a repository for the organisation's 'dead wood' and shunned by high-fliers. As a result, HR managers, whatever their individual competence, suffer the stereotypical image of being harmless people who spend their time worshipping policy manuals, arranging social activities and generally accomplishing little of fundamental importance.'[29]

Unfortunately, this depressing picture is all too accurate in many organisations. For example, research indicates that many companies have simply renamed their personnel function as 'HR' without any change in its administrative focus or the adoption of a strategic role.[30] Smith notes that the consequence is 'HRM functions are being disbanded, distributed and depleted as a result of takeovers, restructuring, company financial losses and funding cuts'.[31] HRM practitioners who do not add value have quickly proved to be dispensable. Organisations needing to trim overheads or reduce corporate flab cut HRM.[32] Job insecurity in times of economic downturn is a major source of stress for HR managers.[33] Says Mercer: 'Most human resource managers constantly feel the pressure that comes from being on a company's payroll without ever proving their worth in the company's actual bread and butter business. They do not thrive. For this reason, HRM managers never ensure for themselves secure positions or career progression' and they remain absent from the boardroom table.[34] 'Without being able to easily talk about finance, marketing, customers, technology, competitors and business strategies', says Ulrich, 'HR professionals will always be an afterthought.'[35]

The CEO of the company where you are HR Manager insists on a chauffeur-driven Mercedes and a luxury house in Mayfair for his personal use when visiting the London office.

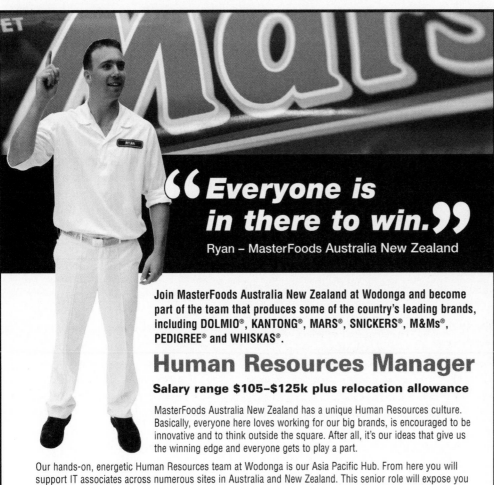

Figure 1.3 An advertisement for a Human Resources Manager
Source Masterfoods.

Best employers are real stars

By Catherine Fox

Australia's best employers are also among the strongest financial performers, according to an annual survey released last night.

Winning organisations in the 2003 study by researchers Hewitt Associates, are Flight Centre and Cisco Systems, followed by Diageo Australia, SEEK Communications and Virgin Blue.

But after a tough year, the study found even content employees were working harder and finding the work-life balance more difficult than ever.

The top companies have some core features in common. As well as being financially successful: they make an effort to recognise their employees and offer them a range of opportunities for progression.

As a result, they have much lower turnover rates and attract many more job applications than other comparable organisations.

Average revenue growth for best employers is 13 per cent, compared to 7 per cent for other companies.

This is the third, best employers survey. It involved 139 organisations in the public and private sectors and 28 000 Australian employees completed questionnaires.

According to Hewitt consultant Andrew Bell, the difficult conditions in 2002 did have an impact on the results but there was also evidence that some companies were sustaining their performance despite the downturn.

A number of the 2003 best employers were also in previous lists: Macquarie Bank, Lion Nathan, Cisco, Diageo, Nokia, Flight Centre, Nike, Johnson & Johnson, Merck Sharp and Dohme and Sales Force, Mr Bell said.

'The 2003 results show consistency in some key areas — the quality of senior leadership, a performance-driven culture which is aggressively managed by the leaders, passion for the organisation and the work employees do, and opportunities for employees to grow and develop.'

A survey of the CEOs from participating companies found best employers had leaders who spent far more time on people-related issues than other organisations.

Source *Australian Financial Review*, 14 March 2003, p. 11.

Approaches to HRM[36]

Instrumental HRM Stresses the rational, quantitative aspects of managing human resources. Performance improvement and improved competitive advantage are highlighted.

Humanistic HRM Recognises the need for the integration of HR policies and practices with the organisation's strategic objectives, but places emphasis on employee development, collaboration, participation, trust and informed choice.

Two extreme theoretical approaches to HRM can be distinguished: **instrumental HRM** and **humanistic HRM**. The *instrumental* (or *hard*) approach stresses the rational, quantitative and strategic aspects of managing human resources. Performance improvement and improved competitive advantage are highlighted. It is supremely important to the hard approach to HRM to integrate HR policies and practices with the organisation's business strategy, with the emphasis being on human resource management.

In contrast, the *humanistic* (or *soft*) approach, while still emphasising the integration of HR policies and practices with strategic business objectives, recognises that competitive advantage is achieved by employees with superior know-how, commitment, job satisfaction, adaptability and motivation. Employees are seen as proactive contributors to the organisation's strategic business objectives rather than as passive units to be allocated rationally along with any other factor of production. Consequently, the soft approach emphasises employee development, collaboration, participation, trust and informed choice. The aim is to generate resourceful employees through human resource management.

The hard approach clearly risks creating industrial conflict. Perhaps less obvious is that the soft approach can also create union problems. Trade unions, for example, may have serious objections on ideological and practical grounds to performance appraisal, pay-for-performance and incentive systems that reflect an individualistic rather than a collectivist approach to the management of the work force. Finally, HRM's stress on mutual interest, cooperation, communication and other soft aspects may be seen as nothing more than cynical manipulation and a means to weaken the power of the union. Consequently, HRM and trade unions may be regarded as incompatible, with HRM viewed as just 'old wine in a new bottle'.[37]

The role of the HR manager

As HRM becomes more business oriented and strategically focused, four key roles for the HR manager can be identified:
• strategic partner
• administrative expert
• employee champion
• change agent.

Strategic partner

'HR professionals', says Ulrich, 'play a strategic partner role when they have the ability to translate business strategy into action.'[38] This facilitating role allows the HR manager to become part of the business team. To achieve this, the HR manager must be able to ask appropriate questions and contribute to business decisions (see figure 1.4). Consequently, the HR manager must develop business acumen, a customer orientation and an awareness of the competition to be able to link business strategy to HR policies and practices. Alas, it seems that HR managers are not fulfilling their role of **strategic partner**. For example, research suggests that only a minority of CEOs involve their HR managers in formulating business strategy.[39] Australian firms similarly lag behind overseas firms in the adoption of sophisticated HRM policies and practices.[40] This is despite clear evidence that inappropriate HR policies and practices lead to alienation, reduced motivation and labour unrest.[41] More positively, there is evidence to indicate that there is a growing awareness of the need for HR managers to become actively involved at the strategic level and recognition that organisations that have a CEO who recognises the significance of HRM have a competitive advantage.[42]

> **Strategic partner** Refers to HR managers being an essential part of the management team running an organisation and contributing to the achievement of the organisation's objectives by translating business strategy into action.

1. Do the nuts and bolts of HR really well.
2. Get rid of HR efforts that don't add value.
3. Understand the business.
4. Develop relationships throughout the organisation.
5. Help line managers to become more confident in their HR role.
6. Develop an ability to articulate your point of view using 'line language'.
7. Become more flexible.
8. Become generalists who understand big-picture HR issues.
9. Focus on the same goals.
10. The three Cs: collaborate, cooperate and communicate.

Figure 1.4 Ten things HR professionals can do to improve their relationship with line managers
Source Ernst & Young Human Resources Consulting, 'All things considered', *Human Resources*, vol. 4, no.2, 2000, p. 18.

Administrative expert

According to Ulrich, to become **administrative experts** HR professionals must be able to: re-engineer HR activities through the use of technology, rethinking and redesigning work processes and the continuous improvement of all organisational processes; see HR as creating

> **Administrative experts** Refers to the efficiency of HR managers and the effective management of HR activities (such as selection, etc.) so that they create value.

value; and measure HR results in terms of efficiency (cost) and effectiveness (quality).[43] Research indicates that the competency levels of HR managers in high-performing firms are significantly higher than those of HR managers in low-performing firms.[44]

Employee champion

The HR professional must be able to relate to and meet the needs of employees. This can be achieved, says Ulrich, by being the employees' voice in management discussions, by being fair and principled, by assuring employees that their concerns are being heard and by helping employees to find new resources (for example, learn how to set priorities, eliminate non-value-added work, clarify goals, simplify complex processes, become involved in decision making, increase commitments, share in economic gains, and so on) that enable them to successfully perform their jobs.[45]

'These activities', says Ulrich, 'will help employees to contribute more fully because they will have the competence to do a good job and the commitment to do it right.'[46] The dual responsibility of strategic business partner and **employee champion**, however, can create tensions as the HR manager learns to balance the demands of both.[47] It is nevertheless incumbent on the HR manager to consider employee responses to any HR initiatives designed to enhance organisational performance (for example, not all employees desire participation in decision making, seeing it simply as extra work for the same pay).[48] Failure to do so will see HRM facing a loss of trust for losing sight of the 'needs, aspirations and interests of the workforce'.[49] Ignoring employee-related outcomes may result in lower job satisfaction, lower commitment and reduced performance, which, in turn, negatively affect organisational performance.[50]

> **Employee champion** Requires the HR manager to be the employee's voice in management decisions.

Change agent

> **Change agent** A person who acts as a catalyst for change.

The HR manager needs to act as a **change agent**, serving as a catalyst for change within the organisation. This can be achieved by leading change in the HR function and by developing problem-solving communication and influence skills. In short, the HR manager must know how to manage change.[51]

The HR function must change. 'It has to be transformed to deal creatively and pragmatically with emerging challenges. By accomplishing new roles and acquiring new competencies, the HR function will become more critical and strategic than ever before.'[52] Gloet, for example, argues that one way for HRM to reinvent itself is via the development and maintenance of learning environments, where knowledge creation, sharing and dissemination are valued.[53]

The Letter to the Editor opposite provides a provocative viewpoint. Do you agree? See 'What's your view' on page 33.

HRM activities

HRM involves the acquisition, development, reward and motivation, maintenance and departure of an organisation's human resources. Certain key HRM activities must be undertaken to satisfy these aims: each activity is interrelated and together they represent the core of HRM.

Job analysis defines a job in terms of specific tasks and responsibilities and identifies the abilities, skills and qualifications needed to perform it successfully. The products of job analysis are job descriptions (describes the job) and job specifications (describes the type of person needed for the job). Job analysis answers basic questions such as: Which tasks should be grouped together and considered a job? How should a job be designed so that employee performance is enhanced? Job analysis is significant because it represents a basic starting point for HR planning and other HR activities such as recruitment, selection, and training and development.

HR jobs are better done by line managers

Dear Editor,

There is one job for HR specialists and one job only. That is to advise line managers of the technical aspects of HR management. The real job of HR management can only ever be done well by line managers.

The HR 'industry' has not lived up to its claims and expectations. It has tried to make itself the equal of the 'applied' management functions and it has failed dismally. I mean, consider the strategic roles identified by Dave Ulrich as a case in point. Ulrich calls on HR managers to become 'strategic partners'. Partners with whom? If HR managers become partners with senior management, the workers see them both as enemies to be avoided or, at best, placated. If they partner the workers, senior managers won't take them or their ideas seriously. And in a world of specialists, can HR managers really become familiar with the detail of the worlds of finance, marketing, production and R&D? I doubt it.

Ulrich also expects HR managers to become 'administrative experts' with the ability to revolutionise HR activities. Maybe some change is possible; however, re-engineering is about a whole-of-business approach, and I cannot see the HR people leading such radical change processes in any organisation.

As for HR managers becoming 'employee champions', can there be a better way for HR managers to destroy their relationship with senior managers than to play the role of the 'workers' friend'? The role for senior managers is to minimise the costs of labour and to seek an amicable but not too close relationship with their employees. After all, we all know how wage and salary bills can spiral when employees and their unions obtain too much control over their work and the ways in which it is rewarded. Performing this role will therefore make HR managers the enemies of those with real organisational power, namely the senior managers.

This role also contradicts that espoused for HR managers as 'change agents'. Employees at every level hate change, and the agents of change are unanimously viewed as doing the dirty work of senior management. HR managers cannot simultaneously be both employee champions and change agents. The two roles are mutually inconsistent.

And, having said that, what does 'strategic' mean anyway? It's just another piece of management jargon designed to baffle everyone.

HR must be the responsibility of the managers and supervisors who operate close to the action, not those seeking some glorified role as experts in 'strategic HRM'. After all, we know our employees. We know what motivates them and how they like to be rewarded. We know how to handle their conflicts and to get the best out of them. With the development of new HR information systems we can perform most of the important HR roles ourselves. A little technical advice every so often is all we need, like providing updates on legislative and regulatory change, and assisting in the updating of HRM policies from time to time.

The theorists' idea of some 'strategic HRM utopia' is dying a rapid death. HRM should be put back where it belongs — in the hands of the real managers. And HR academics should get in touch with the real world of work.

A disgruntled line manager

Source David Poole, University of Western Sydney.

Human resource planning or *employment planning* is the process by which an organisation attempts to ensure that it has the right number of qualified people in the right jobs at the right time. It does this by comparing the present supply of people with the organisation's projected demand for human resources. This comparison produces decisions to add, reduce or reallocate employees internally. HR planning is used to achieve:

- more effective and efficient use of human resources
- more satisfied and better developed employees
- more effective equal opportunity planning.[54]

Recruitment is the process of seeking and attracting a pool of applicants from which qualified candidates for job vacancies within an organisation can be selected. A job vacancy may be filled from within or from outside the organisation. Some of the different methods used to recruit employees include job posting, advertising and executive search.

Selection involves choosing from the available candidates the individual predicted to be most likely to perform successfully in the job. Steps in the selection process include reviewing the application forms, psychological testing, employment interviewing, reference checking and completing a medical examination. Based on the information gathered, a selection decision is made.

Performance appraisal is concerned with determining how well employees are doing their job, communicating that information to the employees and establishing a **plan** for performance improvement. The information generated by the appraisal process is also used for linking rewards to performance, identifying training and development needs, and making placement decisions.

Plan Action step that shows how an objective or goal is to be achieved.

Human resource development activities focus on the acquisition of the attitudes, skills and knowledge required for employees to learn how to perform their jobs, improve their performance, prepare themselves for more senior positions and achieve their career goals. These activities substantially enhance employee (and organisational) knowledge, skills competitiveness and capacity to adapt and change. They are also a powerful communicator that the organisation is interested in the wellbeing of its employees.[55]

Career planning and development activities benefit both employees — by identifying employee career goals, possible future job opportunities and personal improvement requirements — and the organisation — by ensuring that qualified employees are available when needed.

Employee motivation is vital to the success of any organisation. Highly motivated employees tend to be more productive and have lower rates of absenteeism, turnover and lateness.[56] Employee motivation is concerned with why people do things and why one employee works harder than another.

Compensation refers to the cash rewards, such as the base salary, bonus, incentive payments and allowances, which employees receive for working in an organisation. Controversy exists over the precise motivational impact of cash rewards, but there is no doubt that they are an important mainspring in motivating employees and reinforcing employee behaviours demanded by the organisation's business strategies. Research indicates a positive relationship between pay systems and organisational performance.[57]

Benefits are sometimes referred to as indirect or non-cash compensation. They include superannuation, life insurance, disability insurance, medical and hospital insurance, long-term sickness and accident disability insurance, annual leave, sick leave, maternity leave and tuition refund programs. By improving the quality of work life, benefits reinforce the attractiveness of an organisation as a place to work and emphasise that it cares about its employees.[58]

Employee relations (ER) Deals primarily with employee attitudes and behaviour and the relationships between an organisation and its employees. Sometimes regarded as being the same as industrial relations (IR). However, ER focuses more on workplace relations than traditional IR, which emphasises industrial tribunals, trade unions, employer associations and government and their roles in the making of rules governing the employer–employee relationship.

Industrial relations (also called **employee relations (ER)** or employment relations) in this text deals primarily with employee attitudes and behaviour and the relationships between an organisation and its employees. If relationships are characterised by open communication, fair and equitable HR policies and practices, and high work and life satisfaction, there will be cooperation, trust, commitment and high performance. However, if they are characterised by poor communication, unfair and discriminatory HR policies and practices, and low work and life satisfaction, there will be conflict, mistrust, low commitment and poor performance.[59] Industrial relations also involves governments, industrial tribunals, employer associations, trade unions, industrial law, awards, terms and conditions of work, grievance procedures, dispute settlement, advocacy and collective bargaining.[60]

Effective *health and safety programs* help guarantee the physical and mental wellbeing of employees. Organisations are required to provide a safe work environment free from physical hazards and unhealthy conditions.

Learning to *manage diversity* and successfully integrate Australia's multicultural population into the work force to maximise the contribution of all employees represents a special challenge to HR managers. Australia is one of the most culturally diverse countries in the world, with almost 25 per cent of its population from non-English-speaking backgrounds. There is growing recognition that multicultural HR policies and practices provide significant benefits by lessening the time spent explaining instructions and directions, reducing mistakes caused by misunderstanding, and reducing industrial accidents and workplace tensions caused by poor communication. Some organisations, for example, have reported productivity increases of up to 20 per cent as a result of introducing English language classes.[61]

Ethical issues and HRM

HR managers today are increasingly faced with complex, ambiguous and conflicting issues involving questions of morality and standards of behaviour. What is good or bad or right and wrong? At times, there may be no clear-cut distinction between what is ethical or unethical. For example, is management's prime responsibility to shareholders (the owners of the business) or employees? Organisations must change to survive yet this may result in employee terminations, job insecurity and stress. Is it ethical for companies to require employees to use English at work? Should top managers receive performance bonuses while employees lose their jobs? Should companies monitor employee email? In developing economies, is the use of child labour acceptable?

Factors that influence 'ethical' behaviour include a person's personality and national culture, the situation and its importance to the individual, the corporate culture and the existence of clear, unambiguous organisational policies and codes of conduct. Failed insurer HIH had a culture of fear that led to cover-ups, tolerance of incompetence, misuse of company funds, misinformation, abrogation of responsibility and corruption.[62,63,64]

Throughout this text you will find ethical dilemmas highlighted in the margin where you see this icon and as case studies to challenge your thinking.

The CEO of the company where you are HR Manager publicly states that the company insists on the highest ethical standards. The company recently awarded study 'scholarships' in Australia to the children of its largest customer in China.

Strategy

What is strategy?

'Strategy defines the direction in which an organisation intends to move and establishes the framework for action through which it intends to get there.'[65] It involves a consistent approach over time and reflects the organisation's approach to achieving its objectives. The purpose of **strategy** is to maintain a position of advantage by capitalising on the strengths of an organisation and minimising its weaknesses. To do this, an organisation must identify and analyse the threats and opportunities present in its external and internal environments — for example, the change from a pro-union to a pro-business government (or vice versa), the elimination of tariffs, an increase in the rate of unemployment, an increase in interest rates and a decline in union membership all have significance for an organisation. Thus, organisations need to develop strategies to deal with these external influences if they are to avoid a **reactive**, short-term approach to management. Similarly, internal influences such as the quality of an organisation's human resources, its degree of management expertise and its structure and culture can each be a source of strength or weakness. Strengths in HRM, for example, will allow an organisation to better attract, retain and motivate quality employees. Consequently, HRM strategies need to be developed as an integral part of an organisation's overall strategy.[66]

Strategy Defines the direction in which an organisation intends to move and establishes the framework for action by which it intends to get there.

Reactive When managers wait until a problem occurs before taking action.

Practitioner speaks

The Hayco way

Donald Hay *is President/ CEO of Hayco Manufacturing Ltd, winner of the Hong Kong Business Award 2002. Hayco (www.hayco.com.hk) is a multimillion-dollar industrial and household brushware and cleaning products manufacturer employing 4500 people. Its customers include Procter & Gamble, Rubbermaid, 3M and Wal-Mart.*

Whichever way you look at it, the key to our success is our people. Although we are no longer a small company, we put a lot of effort into maintaining the 'Hayco family'. We emphasise empathy. If we can appreciate our people and utilise their skills, they will support us.

Our company has been very successful. We aim high and employ good people. A lot of top management effort goes into the recruiting and selection of Hayco people. We ask candidates what they think of us. What did they think of our hiring process? For senior appointments, we conduct at least three to four interviews and undertake a comprehensive psychological assessment using an independent consultant. We want to be the world's best at what we do. This means that we must have the right people. We demand performance but it is very seldom that we have to fire anyone.

Once a person joins us, we spend a lot of time and money on their development. We reward people well and link rewards to both individual and company performance. We use 360-degree performance appraisals. We make no bones about it — people have to perform. We tell candidates 'if you are not prepared to work hard, don't come here. We will develop you, reward you and give you opportunities, but you have to perform.' We treat our people with respect and use personal development as a key motivator. I tell our people 'Why would Hayco invest in you if we didn't think you are a valuable contributor to our success?'.

One of our strengths is that top management has never had a problem employing people who are smarter than we are. All the top managers are shareholders and their goal is a profitable business. We want our products to be in every home in the world. Unequivocally, we want to be the best in quality, price and distribution. That means we must have the best people. We foster teamwork and the sharing of knowledge by providing opportunities for people to get to know each other by attending training programs and social and recreational functions. Our plant in China has karaoke rooms, knitting classes, a football ground, badminton courts, a gym and a clubhouse. We give public recognition at our annual dinner to employees selected by their peers as making outstanding contributions to learning, innovation and customer service.

As we grow larger we have to fight bureaucracy to ensure that we are still emphasising freedom and giving people the right to make mistakes. We put a lot of effort into HR. Our philosophy is very simple — if we care about our people, they will care about Hayco. Many of our top people have been with us from the start and we have a number of long-serving employees. We have been very successful. The Hayco family ideal of cherishing people works.

Donald Hay

Strategic intent

Strategic intent Sustained obsession to achieve a challenging long-term objective.

Hamel and Prahalad claim that companies that have achieved global leadership 'invariably began with ambitions that were out of all proportion to their resources and capabilities. But they created an obsession with winning at all levels of the organisation and then sustained that obsession over the 10–20 year quest for global leadership.' Hamel and Prahalad call this obsession **'strategic intent'**.[67] Audacious goals can aid long-term vision. For example, in 1915 Citicorp had the goal 'to become the most powerful, the most serviceable, the most far reaching financial institution that has ever been'.[68] Southcorp's objective is 'to become the world's leading global branded wine company'.[69] Similarly, Collins and Porras found that companies that experience enduring success such as Hewlett-Packard, 3M, Johnson &

Johnson and Sony have core values and a core purpose that remain fixed 'while their business strategies and practices endlessly adapt to a changing world'.[70] Banners at South Korea's Samsung, for example, urge employees to beat Japan.[71] Honda proclaims 'We will destroy Yamaha!' The CEO at General Electric hammers, 'if you can't sell a top quality product at the world's lowest price, you are going to be out of the game'.[72] A core value at Philip Morris is 'winning — beating others in a good fight', and Merk aims for 'unequivocal excellence in all aspects of the company'.[73]

Many organisations desperately need HRM strategic intent: 'Improvements in the strategic management of people also requires a commitment to sustained long-term action.'[74] In addition, HRM needs leaders who can articulate direction and save their organisations from change via drift. Such managers, argues Kanter, 'create a vision of a possible future that allows themselves and others to see more clearly the steps to take'.[75]

Achieving this requires organisations to move from their traditional **conscript mindset** to a **volunteer mindset** where the discretionary effort of motivated and well-trained employees produces a competitive advantage.[76] It should be noted that this transition would be regarded as nothing more than a sophisticated form of exploitation by radical academics and trade unionists.[77]

What is strategic management?[78]

Thompson and Strickland define strategic management as 'the process whereby managers establish an organisation's long-term direction, set specific performance objectives, develop strategies to achieve these objectives in the light of all the relevant internal and external circumstances and undertake to execute the chosen action plans.'[79] The aims of strategic management are to help the organisation to achieve a competitive advantage — the special edge that permits an organisation to manage environmental influences better than its competitors do — and to ensure long-term success for the organisation. Strategic management does this by giving managers consistent guidelines for action and by allowing the anticipation of problems and opportunities. BHP Billiton, for example, defines itself as an international company headquartered in Australia and benchmarks itself against its global competitors. Just a few years ago, Mayne was a transport company; today, its primary business is pharmaceuticals. Companies are having to ask themselves: What is our core business? Are we in the right business? Can we pick the changes affecting our business?

Components of strategic management

Strategy formulation involves selecting an organisation's mission, or purpose, and key objectives (What is our business? What should it be?); analysing the organisation's internal and external environments (Who are our customers? Who should they be? Where are we heading? Is our market share growing or declining? Do we need to diversify? What major competitive advantages do we enjoy? Do we emphasise internal growth or growth through acquisition?); and selecting appropriate business strategies (Can we realistically expect to achieve an objective given our talents, resources and limitations? Which of the available alternatives is the best?). **Strategy implementation**, in turn, involves designing an organisation's structure and control systems and evaluating the selected strategy in achieving the organisation's key objectives (What remedial action is needed to make the strategy work? What changes need to be made to the original strategy?) (see figure 1.5).

Organisational mission and objectives

The first steps in strategic management are to define the mission (or purpose) and the prime objectives of the organisation. Jones and Kahaner claim that **mission statements** 'are the operational, ethical and financial guiding lights of companies. They are not simply mottoes or slogans; they articulate the goals, dreams, behaviour, culture and strategies of companies'[80] (see figure 1.6). The core purpose of 3M, for example, is 'to solve unsolved problems innovatively'; Hewlett-Packard exists 'to make technical contributions for the advancement and welfare of humanity'; Walt Disney 'to make people happy'; Nike 'to experience the emotion of competition, winning and crushing competitors'; and Mary Kay Cosmetics 'to give unlimited opportunity to women'.[81]

Conscript mindset Employees are externally motivated (that is, they are coerced by management) to perform.

Volunteer mindset Employees are internally motivated (that is, they are self-motivated) to perform.

Strategy formulation Involves selecting an organisation's mission, key objectives and business strategies.

Strategy implementation Involves designing an organisation's structure and control systems and evaluating the selected strategies in achieving the organisation's key objectives.

Mission statements The operational, ethical and financial reasons for an organisation's existence.

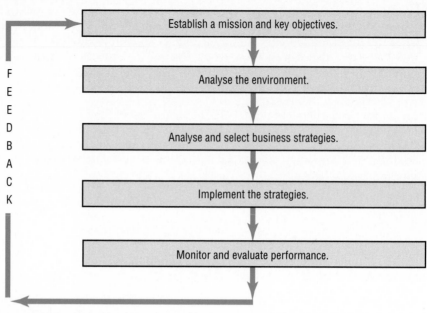

Figure 1.5 Strategic management model
Source Asia Pacific Management Co. Ltd, 2004.

The organisation's mission statement thus provides the context and direction for the formulation and evaluation of HRM objectives, strategies and action plans. The mission statement identifies why the organisation exists and what its focus is: What is the business of the organisation? What will it be? What should it be? The key objectives identify what the organisation plans to achieve. They are the concrete ends or goals that represent the ultimate purpose of the organisation. Strategies, in turn, represent the means through which these objectives are pursued at any given point of time.[82]

BHP BILLITON CHARTER

WE ARE BHP BILLITON, A LEADING GLOBAL RESOURCES COMPANY
Our purpose is to create value through the discovery, development and conversion of natural resources, and the provision of innovative customer and market-focused solutions.

To prosper and achieve real growth, we must:
- actively manage and build our portfolio of high-quality assets and services,
- continue the drive towards a high-performance organisation in which every individual accepts responsibility and is rewarded for results;
- earn the trust of employees, customers, suppliers, communities and shareholders by being forthright in our communications and consistently delivering on commitments.

We value:
- **Safety and the Environment** — An overriding commitment to health, safety, environmental responsibility and sustainable development.
- **Integrity** — Doing what we say we will do.

- **High Performance** — The excitement and fulfilment of achieving superior business results and stretching our capabilities.
- **Win–Win Relationships** — Having relationships which focus on the creation of value for all parties.
- **The Courage to Lead Change** — Accepting the responsibility to inspire and deliver positive change in the face of adversity.
- **Respect for Each Other** — The embracing of diversity, enriched by openness, sharing, trust, teamwork and involvement.

We are successful in creating value when:
- our shareholders are realising a superior return on their investment
- our customers and suppliers are benefiting from our business relationships
- the communities in which we operate value our citizenship
- every employee starts each day with a sense of purpose and ends each day with a sense of accomplishment.

Figure 1.6 BHP Billiton's charter
Source BHP Billiton, *Annual Report*, Melbourne, 2003, p. 63.

Environmental analysis

The objective of analysing the external environment is to identify any strategic opportunities and threats that may be present. Changes in government legislation may pose a threat by restricting business opportunities or by increasing competition. (A reduction in tariffs, for example, led Australia's biggest lingerie manufacturer to move its production to China and Indonesia.[83])

Similarly, analysis of the internal environment aims to identify the organisation's strengths and weaknesses. The organisation may possess special technological advantages, but lack the marketing expertise to successfully implement a strategy. To help determine what must be done to achieve the mission and objectives, it is critical that management analyses both the external environment and the organisation's internal capabilities and resources. Only then can the internal strengths and weaknesses be deployed to take advantage of external opportunities and to minimise external problems.[84]

Strategy selection

This step involves generating a series of strategic options based on the organisation's objectives and a comparison of its internal strengths and weaknesses and its external opportunities and threats (a **SWOT analysis**). Alternative strategies generated by a SWOT analysis are evaluated to identify which one will best achieve the organisation's objectives. The aim is to select the strategy that gives the best alignment or fit between the external and internal environments (see figure 1.7).

SWOT analysis Review of an organisation's strengths and weaknesses and the opportunities and threats in its environment.

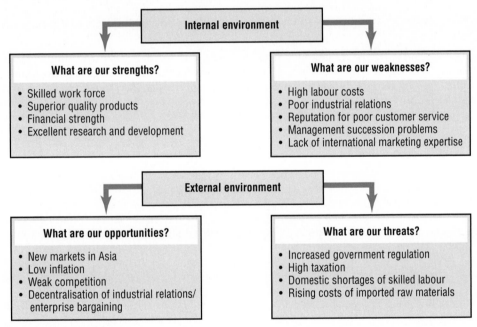

Figure 1.7 SWOT analysis
Source Asia Pacific Management Co. Ltd, 2004.

The selection of strategy thus involves managers being **proactive** (instead of reactive) to changes in their organisation's environment. The premise of **strategic choice** is that management can facilitate the organisation's successful adaptation to changing circumstances by shaping the organisation's objectives and policies. Thus, instead of permitting external influences to determine the future of the organisation, management anticipates change and actively develops long-term strategies to cope with environmental pressures. This also includes the development of an HR strategy to define 'the organisation's long-term objective with regard to human resource issues'.[85] Recognising the active role played by management in shaping HRM means rejecting the traditional view of management as being reactive and responding to trade union or other environmental influences. Finally, Debrah argues that the concept of strategic choice highlights the necessity of linking organisational strategies with HR strategies 'to achieve desirable outcomes in the workplace'.[86]

Proactive When managers anticipate problems and take corrective measures to minimise their effect.

Strategic choice Refers to managers being proactive (as opposed to reactive) in facilitating the organisation's successful adaptation to changes in its environment.

Strategy implementation

It is critical for successful strategy implementation that employees accept the changes demanded by the new or revised strategies. Similarly, an organisation's structure must be designed to enhance the implementation of a strategy. This involves arranging the organisation's physical and human resources to carry out the strategy. A strategy needs an appropriate structure if it is to work, and there are questions that must be answered — Should the structure be flat or tall? How are task responsibilities to be allocated (division of labour)? Is decision making to be centralised or decentralised (degree of delegation)? To what extent should the organisation be divided into sub-units such as divisions and departments (departmentation)? Other key issues include developing appropriate budgets, information systems, HR systems (control based or commitment based?) and policies and procedures to enhance strategy implementation. Wesfarmers, for example, rigorously applies target setting, performance measurement and reward systems with a strong **value-added** and accountability focus.[87]

Performance evaluation

Management must decide how to monitor and measure performance so the effectiveness of a strategy can be evaluated. One approach may involve setting performance objectives, measuring performance, comparing actual performance with targeted performance and taking any corrective action required. This **management by objectives (MBO)** approach has the advantage of integrating planning and control. Alternatively, management may decide to establish detailed bureaucratic controls involving impersonal rules and procedures and the standardisation of activities. For strategic planning to be successful, it is important to achieve a fit between the organisation's strategy, structure, culture and methods of control.

Feedback

Strategic management is an ongoing process. The implementation of a strategy must be monitored to determine the extent to which it is realising the organisation's major strategic objectives (see figure 1.7). In short, managers must ask whether the strategy is being implemented as planned, and whether it is achieving the desired results. Thus, feedback systems are necessary for management to determine whether its strategies are working as planned.

Conflict, politics and strategic change

Strategic management *appears* to be a process of rational decision making. This is not the case in reality. Conflict and politics arise with strategic change (see chapter 16). Individual functions and divisions have agendas that may not be identical, so conflict over resources and the need for change may produce power struggles within the organisation. Similarly, not all strategies are implemented in a logical way: they may be shaped, changed and developed by managers making small adjustments to existing strategies. That is, managers make *incremental* changes (as opposed to *revolutionary* changes) in strategy based on their experiences in managing the business.[88] Managers often have to make decisions and plan in rapidly changing environments (which frequently involve political and other pressures), so it is important that they remain 'focused on long-term objectives while still remaining flexible enough to master short-term problems and opportunities as they occur'.[89]

Types of strategies[90]

Growth

An organisation can expand either through internally generated growth (for example, McDonald's and Woolworths) or through acquisitions, mergers or joint venture (for example, National Australia Bank and Westpac). Growth may be concentrated on building existing strengths (for example, food for McDonald's and financial services for National Australia Bank) or on moving into new or unrelated areas of business (for example, the move from beer to wine for the brewers Foster's and Lion Nathan).

Retrenchment

The emphasis of retrenchment is on performance improvement by increasing productivity, cost cutting, downsizing, re-engineering and selling or shutting down business operations.

Commonwealth Bank of Australia, Nylex, Qantas and Telstra are examples of companies employing this strategy in an effort to become more competitive. Retrenchment strategies are common in today's cutthroat environment.

Stability

This is a neutral strategy that attempts to maintain the status quo by pursuing established business objectives. Stability strategy is often used when an organisation is performing well in a low-risk environment or when an organisation needs to consolidate after a period of rapid growth or restructuring.

Combination

An organisation can pursue more than one strategy at the same time. A large organisation, for example, may be expanding in some business or geographical areas and retrenching in others.

Choosing strategies

Different types of organisational strategies produce a need for particular HR strategies. Thus, it is important that HR strategies accurately reflect an organisation's master business strategy to ensure an appropriate fit. This enables HR action plans to support the master strategy and the direction of the organisation. Without this strategic alignment, confusion, frustration and inefficiencies result.[91]

The need for HRM strategies

Ever-increasing pressures have forced managers to critically rethink their approaches to HR management. People and their current and potential contributions were often overlooked in the past. A McKinsey survey, for example, revealed weaknesses in Australian firms relating to employee motivation, incentives and performance management.[92] According to Drucker, in the knowledge economy, employees are not labour, they are capital. Knowledge workers are the major wealth creators. It is now the productivity of capital (not its cost) that is decisive in determining organisational performance.[93] Merging business and HRM strategies is thus a critical source of competitiveness for organisations.[94]

Managers consequently must adopt a strategic mindset or way of looking at and thinking about the management of people (see figure 1.8). HR managers, in turn, have a responsibility to ensure that HRM is strategically aligned with the organisation's overall business objectives. If an organisation makes a strategic decision to expand, introduce new technology, reduce costs, improve quality or downsize, for example, HRM must support this choice. A differentiator between the corporate winners and losers in the twenty-first century clearly will be the quality of an organisation's human resources.[95]

The need for competitive advantage (and particularly sustained competitive advantage) has made the strategic management of HRM critical to long-term business success.[96]

The aims of HRM strategies

HRM strategies outline the organisation's people objectives and must be an integrated part of its overall business strategy. HRM strategies, like marketing or manufacturing strategies, are functional strategies — that is, they guide the actions to be taken within a specific function. HR activities such as recruitment and selection, training and development, for example, should be guided by an organisation's HRM strategies. The aim of a functional strategy is to support the organisation's business strategies. As a result, HRM strategies must focus on what line management sees as the main business issues. Only then can HRM activities be clearly related to the direction of the business. 'Asking the board to tack on HR's pet concerns to a business strategy', says Price, 'does not guarantee integration.'[97]

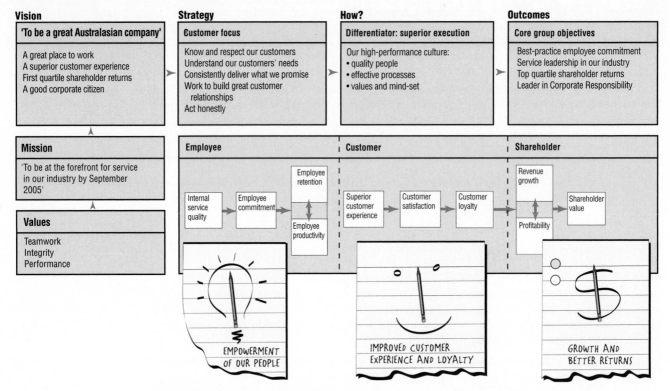

Figure 1.8 HRM strategy at Westpac
Source Westpac, *Annual Report*, Sydney, 2003, pp. 10–11.

HRM strategies aim to enable the organisation to achieve its strategic objectives by:

- ensuring that all business planning processes recognise from the outset that the ultimate source of value is people
- seeing that all concerned in strategic planning appreciate the HR implications of their proposals and understand the potential HR constraints if action is not taken
- achieving a close match between corporate business objectives and the objectives of the HR function
- designing and managing the culture, climate and organisational processes of the business to ensure that everyone can do their job better and that high-calibre people are found and kept
- identifying the firm's distinctive competencies and the types of people who will be needed to build and maintain those competencies
- ensuring that the resourcing activities of the organisation contribute to the development of competencies in the short and long term
- assessing the performance requirements needed to reach the organisation's strategic business objectives, and deciding how the requirements should be satisfied
- reviewing the levels of commitment throughout the organisation and planning ways to improve them where necessary.[98]

Overall, HRM strategic planning clarifies for employees and managers in an organisation and other stakeholders such as shareholders and unions how HRM intends to contribute, what methods it will use and what performance standards it is aiming for.

Strategic organisation and strategic HRM objectives

Strategic HRM Focuses on the linking of all HR activities with the organisation's strategic objectives.

Because they define the main issues to be worked on and determine policies and priorities, **strategic HRM** objectives must accurately reflect the strategic objectives and values of the organisation. Schuler, Galante and Jackson show that organisations can improve their environment for success by making choices about HR planning, staffing appraisal, compensation, training and development, and labour relations that are consistent with and support the corporate strategy.[99] This means that HR objectives, policies and plans must be integrated with the organisation's strategic business objectives.[100] When this happens, HRM becomes a true business partner in boosting the organisation's competitive advantage by helping achieve strategic objectives and employee growth.

HR objectives, policies and plans must be judged by how well they help achieve the organisation's strategic business objectives. The HR manager must ask: Do they work? Are they easy to understand and implement? Do they add value? Do they create a competitive advantage? Are they fair? Will they increase employee job satisfaction, commitment and motivation? Do they build the capacity for change? Do they promote a volunteer mindset? Do they reinforce the organisation's culture? Do they promote trust? Do they support the organisation's long-term business strategy? These questions are critical because research reveals that policies and practices are often inconsistent with strategy or are implemented in a piecemeal fashion.[101]

Without such a strategic view, HRM will remain a set of independent activities, lacking in central purpose and coherent structure. It will be reactive rather than proactive in shaping a relationship between the organisation and its employees. It will fail to optimise opportunities for the organisation's survival and growth. HRM must shed its non-strategic bureaucratic baggage or fade away unmourned. In a fast-changing, globally competitive world, it is human resources that provide the competitive edge. HR managers have a significant role to play in developing and implementing corporate strategy, especially when it is considered that the more effective HR becomes, the more competitive and differentiated the organisation becomes.[102]

Strategic HRM objectives and plans

Just as strategic HRM objectives must be in harmony with the organisation's overall aims, HRM activity plans must support the achievement of strategic HRM objectives. An organisation that has set profit improvement as a strategic business objective, for example, may need strategic HRM objectives that produce reduced labour costs (for example, improved employee performance, reduced headcount). These objectives, in turn, necessitate action plans for specific HR activities such as developing performance-linked reward systems to promote employee motivation and productivity, appropriate training programs to maintain and enhance employee competence, and an appraisal and exit program to accurately identify and remove poor performers.

Strategic HRM objectives and plans can be linked to strategic organisational objectives such as:
- *cost containment* — by focusing on cost reduction via reduced headcount, improved expense control, improved productivity, reduced absenteeism and lower labour turnover
- *customer service* — by focusing on achieving improved customer service through recruitment and selection, employee training and development, and rewards and motivation
- *organisational effectiveness* — by focusing on organisational structure, job design, employee motivation, employee innovation, adaptability to change, flexible reward systems and employee relations
- *social responsibility* — by focusing on legal compliance and improvements in areas such as equal opportunity, occupational health and safety, and minority opportunities and development
- *integrity* — by focusing on the enhancement of the organisation's reputation for ethical behaviour, fair treatment of employees, honesty in communications and honouring of agreements.

All strategic HRM objectives and activities must be evaluated in terms of how they contribute to the achievement of the organisation's strategic business objectives. This means that they must:
- be measurable

- include deadline dates for accomplishment
- identify and involve the key **stakeholders** and HR customers to ensure the necessary collaboration
- nominate the individual or parties responsible for implementation.

HRM policies and procedures

HRM **policies** are general statements that serve to guide decision making. As such, they direct the actions of the HRM function towards achieving its strategic objectives. HRM policies are generally put in writing and communicated to all employees. They typically serve three major purposes:

- to reassure employees that they will be treated fairly and objectively
- to help managers make quick and consistent decisions
- to give managers the confidence to resolve problems and to defend their decisions.[103]

Subjects covered by HRM policies include recruitment and selection, transfers, promotions, terminations and pay increases. The statement 'It is the policy of this organisation whenever feasible to promote from within', for example, gives a clear guideline to managers and employees about how promotional opportunities will be handled.

HRM **procedures** detail precisely what action is to be taken in a particular situation — for example, the specific steps to be followed when giving a pay increase, terminating an employee or handling a sexual harassment complaint. To promote trust in management and the organisation, it is extremely important that HR policies and procedures be perceived as fair and equitable.[104]

Strategic approach to HRM

Many factors affect HRM. Whether from the organisation's external or internal environment, the impact of a particular influence must be identified and considered by the HR manager. A diagnostic model thus provides the HR manager with an analytical framework to anticipate and prevent problems from arising (see figure 1.9). HRM does not operate in a vacuum. It is influenced by, and in turn influences, factors such as changes in technology, laws, social values and economic conditions that exist outside the organisation, as well as internal factors such as the organisation's culture, strategy, structure and systems.[105] All of these have a significant influence on the organisation's HRM objectives, strategies and action plans (see figure 1.9). Equal employment legislation, for example, has had a particular impact on the way organisations acquire, develop and reward human resources. Similarly, research shows that government intervention has had a significant impact on Australian industrial relations.[106] An integral part of strategic HRM therefore involves analysing **environmental influences** to identify those factors that inhibit the organisation and those that help achieve its objectives. An analysis of the strengths and weaknesses of the HRM function can also identify those positive and negative characteristics of HRM that promote or handicap the achievement of strategic objectives. Such analysis includes the quantity and quality of human resources available to the organisation.

If an organisation is to grow and remain competitive, its HR objectives and strategies must achieve the best alignment or fit between external opportunities and threats and the internal strengths and weaknesses of the organisation. The diagnostic model used in this book includes assessing internal and external influences, setting objectives and evaluating performance. Evaluation of outcomes provides feedback on HRM performance in the acquisition, development, reward and motivation, maintenance and departure of the organisation's human resources. It must be stressed that evaluation involves both employee and organisation-related outcomes. HRM is concerned with overall organisational performance and individual employee performance. Employee attitudes, behaviour and perceptions positively or negatively influence performance. High-performance HRM therefore cannot ignore HR outcomes from the employee's perspective.[107] This comprehensive strategic approach generates more informed and purposeful HR management. Articulating the organisation's mission or purpose (why it exists), its objectives (what it wants to achieve), its strategies (how the objectives are to be achieved) and plans (the action steps required) helps direct the setting of HRM objectives, strategies and plans. In turn, when applied to specific HRM activities such as recruitment and selection, the HR manager can better appreciate which specific action plans are required to support HRM and organisational strategic objectives. Organisations that adopt HRM strategies and high-performance HR policies and practices consistent with the demands of their internal and external environments outperform organisations that adopt less well-matched strategies and practices (see figure 1.10).[108]

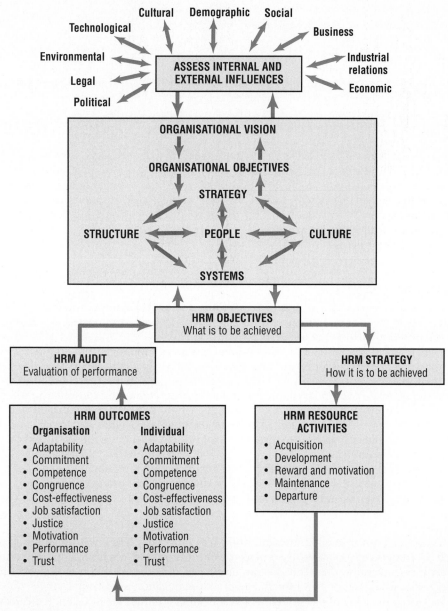

Figure 1.9 Strategic human resource management diagnostic model
Source Asia Pacific Management Co. Ltd, 2004.

Australian travel agency Flight Centre has exceptional performance in terms of its profitability and share price. It is recognized for its excellent HRM, marketing and operations strategies.

- *Recruitment and selection* — Flight Centre does not focus on industry experience or academic travel qualifications. It looks for people with a tertiary education who have travelled widely and appear to be highly motivated, likeable and achievement oriented.
- *HR development* — Flight Centre places a heavy emphasis on employee training and development with a focus on technical expertise in the company's systems and products and personal development.
- *Culture* — Flight Centre has a strong egalitarian culture with an emphasis on information sharing, minimization of status differences (all interpersonal communications are on a first name basis regardless of position and dress is smart casual).
- *HR outcomes* — Congruence between employee and company's interests.

Figure 1.10 HRM at Flight Centre

Source Adapted by the author from R. Dunford and I. Palmer, 'Managing for high performance? People management practices in Flight Centre', *Journal of Industrial Relations*, vol. 44, no. 3, 2002, pp. 376–96.

Assessment of influences

The diagnostic approach to HRM suggests that the HR manager must consider the nature of external and internal environmental influences before electing a particular course of action. This permits the HR manager to be *proactive*, rather than simply reacting to something after it occurs. It forces the HR manager to seek answers to such basic questions as:

- Where are we now?
- Where do we want to be in the future?
- What path is best for us?
- How and when can we implement it?

External influences

The HR manager must identify those external influences that will impact on the organisation and the management of its human resources. Some of the major influences existing outside of the organisation include the following:

- *Political:* political ideologies regarding human resources can range from an interventionist approach — where government regulation of HRM is comprehensive — to one of minimal involvement. Specifically, political attitudes towards business, unions, management rights, strikes, secondary boycotts and enterprise bargaining can differ markedly — federally, from state to state and internationally. Union relations with a federal Coalition government, for example, are less close than the business sector's relationship with the government, whereas union–government relations are distinctly closer in Labor states such as New South Wales.
- *Legal:* laws and regulations regarding hours of work, holidays, equal employment, affirmative action, sexual harassment, workers compensation, privacy, health and safety, fringe benefits and terminations clearly impact on HRM. EEO, for example, has seen the creation of new jobs such as sex equity expert, gender bias officer and harassment facilitator.[109]
- *Environmental:* government and community concerns regarding environmental issues — such as energy conservation, workplace beautification and environmental pollution — directly or indirectly affect job design, employee orientation and training, health and safety, industrial relations and the image of an organisation as an employer.[110]
- *Technological:* the level of technological advancement and the rate of technological change affect job design, recruitment, selection, training, motivation, compensation, health and safety, and industrial relations. The boom in portable PCs has changed the nature of some

jobs. Sales representatives using notebook computers now work from home and spend more time selling instead of wasting time commuting to the office. Similarly, computer networks have eroded traditional workplace hierarchies. Networks mean junior employees can join immediate online discussions with senior executives (where they are judged more on what they say than on where they sit on the corporate ladder). More and more the emphasis is on the application of knowledge and not physical exertion. Many agricultural and industrial jobs, for example, have become knowledge jobs. Factories and farms are operated using computer software instead of manual labour. The new economy is a knowledge economy calling for new skills, new ways of working and new organisational structures.

- *Cultural:* historical background, ideologies, values, norms and language all influence employee views on the role of HRM, EEO, job titles and specific aspects of HR such as job tasks and duties, education, rewards and motivation, and employee communication. Japanese, Australian and Filipino managers, for example, are most likely to support the right to strike, while the least likely managers to approve the right to strike are Singaporeans, Thais and Taiwanese.[111]
- *Demographic:* the nature of the human resources available to the organisation in terms of numbers, geographical distribution, age, sex, literacy, skill and the education levels of the population has an obvious impact on HRM. Labour shortages and the declining quality of local graduates in Hong Kong, for example, have spurred organisations to automate, dramatically increase compensation and benefits, and intensify their recruiting efforts overseas.[112]
- *Social:* changing values and attitudes towards issues such as dress, work, minorities, unions, management, social mobility, status, rewards, health and safety, job security, quality of life, employee privacy, sex roles and gay rights affect every aspect of HRM. Changing values and attitudes typically create new challenges for the HR manager — for example, how to handle dual career couples in an interstate or international transfer, whether benefits coverage should be extended to the partners of gay employees and how to deal with 'downshifters' (people who have decided on a lifestyle change involving less work, income and consumption).
- *Business:* In response to globalisation and increasing competition, organisations are merging, downsizing, restructuring, outsourcing and eliminating costs, all of which directly or indirectly affect HRM. A rising Australian dollar and increased import competition, for example, caused Paperlinx to cut staff.[113]
- *Economic:* factors such as the level of economic activity, the unemployment rate, public versus private ownership, the level of investment, the availability of credit, the degree of centralised economic planning, the amount of debt, and the level and type of taxes directly or indirectly influence recruitment, selection, compensation and benefits, industrial relations, retrenchments and labour turnover. Most of Australia's top export markets are now in Asia, generating demand for training in Asian languages, business cultures and cross-cultural negotiation, and the employment of expatriates.
- *Industrial relations (employee relations or employment relations):* factors relating to industrial relations — such as the industrial relations climate, the degree of unionisation, the existence of industrial tribunals, employee attitudes, employee commitment, employee input and the quality of work life — affect issues such as job design, absenteeism, labour turnover, industrial disputes, employee communication and pay rates. Unions, for example, often influence HR practices, particularly in the areas of compensation, job security arrangements and working conditions.

Internal influences

Internal environmental influences — organisational mission or purpose, objectives and strategies, culture, structure and systems — involve factors that are found within the organisation.

Organisational strategies

Strategies translate the organisation's strategic business objectives into action plans. They set the direction for the organisation and define how it plans to establish a sustainable competitive advantage. Strategies impact every part of the organisation. For example, if an organisation has an objective to become the fastest-growing, most profitable company in its industry, this influences the type of people it requires (highly competent, achievement-oriented), the HR system (high-performance), the culture (egalitarian, performance-oriented) and the structure (flat, non-hierarchical).

Organisational culture

An organisation's psychological and social climate forms its culture. The culture represents the values, beliefs, assumptions and symbols that define how the organisation conducts its business. **Organisational culture** tells employees how things are done, what is important and what kind of behaviour is rewarded. Kodak, for example, emphasises five principles: integrity, respect for the individual, trust, credibility and continuous improvement. Hewlett-Packard's core values include a deep respect for the individual, a dedication to affordable quality and reliability, a commitment to community responsibility and a view that the company exists to make technical contributions for the advancement and welfare of humanity. BHP Billiton is embedding a culture to promote vitality and a sense of urgency.[114] Culture thus impacts on employee expectations, behaviour and productivity. Organisational culture, for example, is one of the most critical determinants of safety performance.[115] Telstra's poor performance is in part attributed to a workplace culture drawn from a public sector mentality.[116]

Coles Myer CEO John Fletcher has identified cultural change as the number one issue given the company's past corrupt and sycophantic culture dominated by excess and personal fiefdoms.[117] The CEO of Johnson & Johnson says: 'The core values embodied in our credo [see figure 1.11] might be a competitive advantage but that is not why we have them. We have them because they define what we stand for, and we would hold them even if they become a competitive disadvantage in certain situations.'[118] Johnson & Johnson's unique decentralised culture, which fosters an entrepreneurial attitude, nevertheless has kept the company intensely competitive and very successful.[119] Another example is Nike, where employees who do not like the ferociously competitive culture do not last long.[120] Finally, culture distinguishes the organisation from other organisations. Although there is no one 'best' culture, there is a clear link between an organisation's culture and its effectiveness. Organisations with strong positive cultures have a much better chance of success than have those with weak or negative cultures.[121]

OUR CREDO

We believe our first responsibility is to the doctors, nurses and patients, to mothers and fathers and all others who use our products and services. In meeting their needs everything we do must be of high quality. We must constantly strive to reduce our costs in order to maintain reasonable prices. Customers' orders must be serviced promptly and accurately. Our suppliers and distributors must have an opportunity to make a fair profit.

We are responsible to our employees, the men and women who work with us throughout the world. Everyone must be considered as an individual. We must respect their dignity and recognize their merit. They must have a sense of security in their jobs. Compensation must be fair and adequate, and working conditions clean, orderly and safe. We must be mindful of ways to help our employees fulfill their family responsibilities. Employees must feel free to make suggestions and complaints. There must be equal opportunity for employment, development and

advancement for those qualified. We must provide competent management, and their actions must be just and ethical.

We are responsible to the communities in which we live and work and to the world community as well. We must be good citizens — support good works and charities and bear our fair share of taxes. We must encourage civic improvements and better health education. We must maintain in good order the property we are privileged to use, protecting the environment and natural resources.

Our final responsibility is to our stockholders. Business must make a sound profit. We must experiment with new ideas. Research must be carried on, innovative programs developed and mistakes paid for. New equipment must be purchased, new facilities provided and new products launched. Reserves must be created to provide for adverse times. When we operate according to these principles, the stockholders should realize a fair return.

Figure 1.11 Johnson & Johnson's organisational culture
Source Johnson & Johnson in *The Asian Manager*, vol. 6, no. 4, 1993, p. 35.

Thus, it is important for management to foster a culture that promotes the achievement of the organisation's strategic business objectives.[122] Campbell's Soup's strategic intent is to 'beat the competition . . . winning is what we are all about'.[123] This is articulated by Campbell's CEO: 'If you don't want to compete, if you don't like stretching, if you won't confront change and competition, I really don't think you are right for the company.'[124] By employing like-minded people, Campbell's is attempting to build its culture by strategic selection. Companies such as Harvey Norman, IBM, Microsoft, Proctor & Gamble and Westfield also assess job applicants more on how they fit the culture than on their job-related skills. For example, National Australia Bank values being conservative, liking hard work and being tough on cost control. Leading firms also spend a great deal of effort on selecting new employees (typically including both workers and managers in the screening process) and utilise well-established performance management systems to quickly identify selection errors.[125]

Similarly, an increasing number of firms are shaping their organisation's culture through employee orientation and training programs. McDonald's, for example, trains all of its new employees in the dominant values of 'quality, service, cleanliness and value'. Finally, organisations can use reward systems to shape their cultures. Employees who better fit the organisation's values can be rewarded more than others. A danger in such approaches, however, is that the inculcation of culture may become indoctrination, producing a lack of flexibility, a loss of individuality and unquestioning acquiescence.[126]

The link between organisational culture and HRM is important. HRM activities contribute to the development of an organisation's culture and provide it with a competitive edge by stimulating and reinforcing the specific behaviours needed to achieve the organisation's strategic objectives. This approach has been criticised by some academics as pseudoscientific, manipulative and anti-union.[127] Corporate culture programs in particular are seen as social engineering designed to create a servile uniformity in employee beliefs and behaviour.[128]

Hewlett-Packard's core values, by emphasising a belief in people, respect and dignity, recognition and performance, demonstrably influence the company's HRM objectives and strategies and make it one of the most successful companies in the United States.[129]

In contrast, the big four Australian banks (Westpac, National Australia Bank, ANZ and Commonwealth Bank of Australia), although seeking to change have cultures high on authority and low on warmth, teamwork, employee commitment and concern for performance.[130] Westpac's former culture, for example, has been described as old-style 'command and control'.[131] Don Argus, National Australia Bank's former CEO, was nicknamed 'Don't Argue' and former CEO Frank Cicutto reportedly oversaw an exodus of top talent replaced by 'yes men'.[132] Women too are notable for their absence in the senior executive ranks. Comments one female National Australia Bank employee: 'This is a bank from the 1960s or 1970s. They think you open doors for women, not take orders from them.'[133] Not surprisingly, the major banks (even after much hype regarding their concern for their customers) still cannot meet community expectations regarding service.[134]

Organisational structure

The effective implementation of an organisation's strategy requires management to ensure that the organisation's design helps achieve its strategic objectives. HRM is particularly concerned with **organisational structure** because it can directly affect employee productivity and behaviour.[135] Organisations with narrow spans of control that are hierarchical in structure, for example, tend to be authoritarian, rigid, formal, highly specialised and bureaucratic. In contrast, organisations with wide spans of control that are flat in structure tend to be more flexible, adaptable, informal, less specialised and more entrepreneurial. Thus, the structure of an organisation has a powerful influence over how jobs are designed, how decisions are made, how things get done and what type of employees are required for the organisation's success.

Organisational structure
Refers to the organisation's framework or design.

Organisational systems

The systems the organisation employs to achieve its objectives must be compatible. An efficient HR system that does not mesh with its functional counterparts will be ineffective. It is the HR manager's job to ensure that all HR systems are efficient and in harmony with accounting and financial, information and technology, purchasing and inventory, marketing, sales and distribution, and operations and service management systems. For example, if

HR's reward system (which includes the subsystems of compensation and benefits) does not promote marketing's goal of improving the sales performance of its sales representatives, then the overall performance of the organisation suffers. HR systems are influenced by (and will influence) the organisation's strategy, culture, structure and people. For example, an organisation seeking a risk-averse culture is unlikely to use a reward system emphasising at-risk compensation or to hire aggressive risk-takers.

Evaluating HRM objectives, policies and practices

HRM policies and practice should be evaluated in terms of their contribution to achieving the organisation's strategic business objectives and satisfying employee needs. Research has shown positive associations between HRM practices and perceptions of organisational performance and operational performance when matched with quality manufacturing strategies.[136] Similarly, there is evidence to indicate that an HR reputation for being employee-centred has a positive effect on labour turnover, sales, profitability and a company's share price.[137] Finally, an increasing number of studies highlight that it is people who limit or enhance the strengths and weaknesses of an organisation and that, when done well, HRM can improve organisational competitiveness, growth, adaptability and profitability.[138]

Adaptability Relates to the extent that HRM policies foster employee and organisational readiness for and acceptance of change.

Commitment Relates to the extent that HRM policies enhance employee identification with and attachment to their job and the organisation.

HRM outcomes and performance

HRM is concerned with both organisational performance and employee wellbeing. This means that any evaluation of HR's contribution must incorporate both perspectives — the organisation's and employees'. HRM's contribution to organisational performance involves aligning HR strategies with organisational strategies, managing the corporate culture to win employee commitment and being efficient in managing HR activities. HRM's contribution to individual wellbeing is demonstrated by employee attitudes and behaviour. High-performance HRM, which places the employee centre stage, has benefits for the organisation because the way employees respond to HRM initiatives is linked to their on-the-job performance — and ultimately to organisational performance.[139]

The following outcomes should be considered when evaluating HRM performance:

- **Adaptability:** To what extent do HRM strategies and policies foster organisational and employee flexibility? What is the readiness for change? Does the organisation exploit change or does it react? Are innovation and creativity encouraged or stifled? Is knowledge recognised as a critical asset? Does the organisation utilise people with different backgrounds and value systems?
- **Commitment:** To what extent do HRM strategies and policies enhance employee identification with and attachment to their job and the organisation? A high level of commitment can result in more loyalty, increased teamwork and reduced labour turnover, along with a

greater sense of employee self-worth, dignity, psychological involvement and feeling of being integral to the organisation. Macquarie Bank encourages commitment via profit sharing, share acquisition plans, flexible work arrangements, a flat management structure and promotion based on merit.[140]

- **Competence:** To what extent do HRM strategies and policies attract, retain, motivate and develop employees with the abilities, skills, knowledge and competencies required to achieve the organisation's business objectives?
- **Congruence:** To what extent do HRM strategies and policies generate (or sustain) congruence between management and employees, different employee groups, the organisation and the community, employees and their families, and within the individual? In other words, do HRM strategies promote the achievement of employee goals and, at the same time, satisfy the organisation's strategic business objectives? The lack of congruence can be costly to the organisation in terms of: time, money and energy; the resulting low levels of trust and lack of common purpose; and the stress and other psychological problems it can create.[141]
- **Cost-effectiveness:** To what extent do HRM strategies and policies reduce personnel-related costs, help correctly size the organisation, eliminate unnecessary work, optimise compensation and benefit expenditure, reduce labour turnover and absenteeism, improve employee health and safety, improve employee productivity and avoid costs from litigation and negative public relations?
- **Job satisfaction:** To what extent do HRM strategies and policies produce employees with positive attitudes and feelings about their work? Common job satisfaction facets include pay, promotion opportunities, fringe benefits, supervision, colleagues, job conditions, the nature of the work, communication and job security.[142] Employees frustrated and bored with repetitive and standardised work have low commitment.[143] A satisfied employee tends to be absent less often, make positive contributions, stay with the organisation and radiate positive feelings towards customers.[144]
- **Justice:** An organisation (and its management) may be trusted by its employees, but may not necessarily be seen as fair or just. This is because fairness is not an objective thing, but rather, like beauty, depends on the eye of the beholder. As a result, what is perceived as fair or just may vary from person to person. For example, employees may interpret what is fair in terms of *equality* (all people with the same qualifications performing the same work should receive the same rate of pay and the same pay increase — across-the-board pay increases, for example, are typically favoured by trade unions, but not by management) or *need* (low-income workers should receive more pay because they need the extra income to maintain a decent standard of living). Managers, on the other hand, may regard *competitive equity* (those that contribute the most are paid the most) and pay inequalities as being fair.

HR strategies, policies and practices are powerful communicators regarding management's trustworthiness, fairness and commitment to employees. If management is perceived favourably, employees reciprocate with increased commitment to the organisation.[145] However, downsizing, restructuring, job insecurity and increased work pressures have made many employees cynical. As a result, HR managers increasingly must face issues of trust and fairness, particularly in the areas of recruitment and selection, performance appraisals, compensation and benefits, promotions, demotions and terminations.

Three major perceptions of unfairness can be identified: distributive injustice, procedural injustice and interactional injustice.

- *Distributive justice* refers to whether scarce resources (such as the merit budget, superior performance ratings, promotional opportunities and expatriate assignments) are perceived as being allocated fairly.
- *Procedural justice* refers to how the HR process is administered. For example, is the company's selection process seen as fair or biased?
- *Interactional justice* refers to how managers interact with employees. Are they warm and friendly, open and respectful, or are they cold, arrogant, aloof and abusive?[146]

Given the diversity of fairness perceptions, it is unlikely that every employee (or manager) will be happy with every HR policy, practice or decision. HR managers must constantly ask: Is it fair? Why? Why not? Will it be seen as fair? Why? Why not? By ensuring that HR

Competence Relates to the extent that HRM policies attract, retain, motivate and develop employees with the abilities, skills, knowledge and competencies to achieve the organisation's strategic objectives.

Congruence Relates to the extent that HRM policies generate (or sustain) and promote the simultaneous achievement of employee goals and the organisation's strategic business objectives.

Cost-effectiveness Relates to the extent that HRM policies reduce personnel-related costs, help correctly size the organisation, eliminate unnecessary work, reduce compensation and benefit costs, reduce labour turnover, etc.

Job satisfaction The degree to which employees have positive attitudes about their jobs.

Justice Relates to perceptions of fairness.

policies and practices are perceived by employees as fair and equitable, HR managers can promote trust and a sense of fairness within the organisation. In particular, HR managers need to ensure that:

- communication exchanges are open, frequent and meaningful
- employees feel they are valued by the organisation (in other words, the organisation cares about their wellbeing)
- managers behave with integrity
- managers are competent
- employees are encouraged to express their feelings.

All of these factors clearly promote trust and perceptions of fairness and are within HR's ambit.[147]

- **Motivation:** To what extent do HRM strategies and policies stimulate employees to achieve a designated goal? Positive acts performed for the company (for example, creating customer satisfaction through personalised service) should be reinforced. Likewise, employees will be more motivated when they have clear goals to achieve.[148] Highly motivated employees work hard, come to work early and contribute more to the organisation's strategic objectives. A recent US study suggests that only 30 per cent of employees are truly loyal, committed and motivated; the rest are unhappy, prone to quit and less likely to provide satisfactory customer service.[149]

- **Performance:** To what extent do HRM strategies and policies contribute to employee on-the-job performance and productivity and the organisation's overall profitability, growth and success?
- **Trust:** To what extent do HR strategies, policies and practices promote trust between employees, management and the organisation? How willing are employees to share information, genuinely cooperate with one another and not take advantage of others? Is the corporate culture supportive of trusting behaviour and cooperative relations? Is the HR function seen as an independent voice that will offer an independent view on HR policies and practices? A trusting working environment has an economic pay-off via reduced transaction costs (for example, less time spent playing politics and checking up on others) and a more friendly, more predictable, more satisfying and less stressful work environment.[150] When trust is absent or broken, employees exhibit low job satisfaction, poor performance and high labour turnover.[151]

A recent survey depressingly indicates that most Australian workers have lost faith in their employer and almost half believe their company does not have their best interests at heart.[152] Other research in the United States similarly shows that less than half of all employees believe that management has a genuine interest in their wellbeing and barely half trust the information they receive from management.[153]

The HRM challenge

If HR managers are to be involved in strategic planning and decision making, they need to be — not just wish they were — strategic contributors. They need to tie dollar-and-cents implications to HR issues; they need to show management how to increase profitability through improved employee productivity by means of increased employee commitment, trust and perceptions of fairness; they need to be the employees' voice at the management table; and they need to demonstrate professional competence in HR activities such as compensation and benefits.

Management is developing high expectations of HRM. Productivity, improvement, restructuring and downsizing, industrial relations issues, the identification and development of talent, performance appraisal and reward systems, and change management increasingly occupy the attention of top management. Recognition of the important role that HRM plays in all aspects of a business requires HR professionals to lift their game. Organisations in today's competitive environment cannot risk giving HR managers unchallenged responsibility for HRM. It is up to HR managers to prove their worth by demonstrating the connection between what they do and organisational performance and employee wellbeing.

As Davidson states: 'Strategic HRM demands HR professionals who have competencies at a general management level and who are willing to accept responsibility for organisational performance outside HRM; who are skilful at selling HRM within their organisation so that they achieve the required level of influence and participation at executive and strategic management levels; and who thereby are able to bring their specialist HR functions more closely into alignment with corporate objectives and strategies.'[154]

Summary

The present climate of economic turbulence, savage competition and pressure for increased productivity has led to a need for HR managers to adopt a strategic approach, to be part of the top management team, to be involved in corporate planning, to develop business know-how, to become bottom-line oriented and to develop a vision for HRM. HRM activities such as job analysis, recruitment and selection, and human resource development must be part of a coordinated effort to improve the productive contribution of people in meeting the organisation's strategic business objectives. Inability to do so means that the organisation will ultimately stagnate and fail.

The shift from an industrial society to an information society also presents HRM with the major challenge of creating a fair and just workplace. Organisations today must manage people differently if they are to survive the erosion of trust caused by relentless restructuring, downsizing and work pressures.

In a world where human resources are the competitive advantage, a revolution in management and HRM thinking is needed if these challenges are to be met.

Thirty interactive Wiley Web Questions are available to test your understanding of this chapter at **www.johnwiley.com.au/ highered/hrm5e** *in the student resources area*

student study guide

terms to know

adaptability (p. 28)
administrative experts (p. 9)
bottom line (p. 5)
change agent (p. 10)
commitment (p. 28)
competence (p. 29)
congruence (p. 29)
conscript mindset (p. 15)
cost-effectiveness (p. 29)
employee champion (p. 10)
employee relations (ER) (p. 12)
environmental influences (p. 22)
HRM activities (p. 5)
human resource management
    (HRM) (p. 4)

humanistic HRM (p. 8)
instrumental HRM (p. 8)
job satisfaction (p. 29)
justice (p. 29)
management (p. 5)
management by objectives (MBO) (p. 18)
mission statements (p. 15)
motivation (p. 30)
objectives (p. 4)
organisational culture (p. 26)
organisational structure (p. 27)
performance (p. 30)
plan (p. 12)
policies (p. 22)
proactive (p. 17)

procedures (p. 22)
reactive (p. 13)
stakeholders (p. 22)
strategic choice (p. 17)
strategic HRM (p. 20)
strategic intent (p. 14)
strategic partner (p. 9)
strategy (p. 13)
strategy formulation (p. 16)
strategy implementation (p. 15)
SWOT analysis (p. 17)
trust (p. 30)
value-added (p. 18)
volunteer mindset (p. 15)

review questions

1. 'One of the aims of HRM is to give an organisation a competitive edge.' Do you agree or disagree with this statement? Explain your reasoning.
2. 'All managers are HR managers.' Do you agree or disagree with this statement? Explain your reasoning.
3. Why should top management be concerned about HRM?
4. The role of the HR manager involves being a strategic partner, an administrative expert, an employee champion and a change agent. Which role is the most important? Why?
5. What is HRM? What is its importance to an organisation? To employees?
6. Do you think liking people is the most important quality required for success as an HR manager? Explain your answer.
7. Describe the major types of HRM activities. Which do you think is the most important? Why?
8. What is organisational culture? What is its relationship to corporate strategy? What is its significance for HRM?
9. Identify and discuss three ways in which HRM can add value to an organisation. How would you measure the value added by HRM?
10. What do you think will be the two most significant challenges facing HR managers in the next five years? Explain your answer.

environmental influences on HRM

Describe the key environmental influences from the model (figure 1.12 shown opposite) that have significance for HRM.

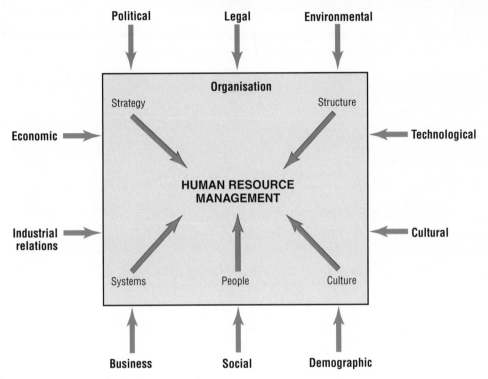

Figure 1.12 Environmental influences on human resource management

class debate

HR managers are not paid to be nice, they are paid to deliver results.
or
HR professional — employee champion or management stooge?

what's your view?

Write a 500-word response to the Letter to the Editor on page 11, agreeing or disagreeing with the writer's point of view.

practitioner speaks

What do you think is the most significant comment made by Donald Hay in the article on page 14. Why? As a class, discuss your viewpoints.

newsbreak exercise

Read the Newsbreak 'Best employers are real stars' on page 8. Do you agree or disagree with the writer's views? What are some possible implications for you and your career? How does the article relate to HRM?

What do you think? Conduct a mini survey of class members, using the questionnaire below. Critically discuss the findings.

1.	HR today is too concerned with profits.	YES	NO
2.	The prime purpose of HRM is to look after employee welfare.	YES	NO
3.	HR work is better done by line managers.	YES	NO
4.	HRM is increasing in importance.	YES	NO
5.	It is critical that HR managers be trusted by employees.	YES	NO
6.	HR managers who emphasise the 'bottom line' impact are unprofessional.	YES	NO

online exercise

Using the company web addresses provided in appendix B on page 852, summarise the mission, strategy and culture of two of the companies listed. Which company impressed you most? Why?

ethical dilemma

A new business for XYZ Ltd

John Kolikias, Managing Director of XYZ Ltd, fixed his gaze on the numbers on the screen. They were exciting. If correct, the innovation would be highly lucrative. The profits of their mobile phone subsidiary would literally explode. John sighed with relief. XYZ had been struggling for the last two years and its share price had plummeted by 40 per cent. If the business didn't turn around soon, a major restructuring would be necessary.

Keith Barnes, Financial Controller, switched off the PowerPoint presentation.

'Very impressive, Keith', said John. 'Well, what do the rest of you think?'

Vijay Mehta, Telco Divisional Manager, smiled. 'I think it's terrific. You know I have been arguing for this for months. This is exactly what we need — it is a licence to print money.'

'I agree', chipped in Robin Antoinetti, Manufacturing Manager.

John looked at the group of senior managers. 'All right, I take it the consensus is that we do it.'

Jo Santini, HR Director, leant forward to speak. 'Financially, the project is terrific. It's the moral issue that worries me.'

'What do you mean?' asked Vijay.

'Come on Vijay, providing soft porn for our mobile phone subscribers to download isn't something that I think our company should do.'

'Jo, you've seen Keith's projections. If they are even half correct, the move into soft porn could save our company from financial collapse.'

'I know, but I think it's morally wrong. It's not the sort of business I believe XYZ should be associated with.'

'I hope you feel just as moral, Jo, when you have to hand out the termination notices', interjected Keith.

'What we are proposing is perfectly legal. It's just that you haven't caught up with current community standards!' snapped Vijay.

'Look, just because something is legal doesn't mean that it's right', Jo fired back.

'Jo, I'm afraid Vijay is correct. Keith's figures are all too clear. We do this or we reduce headcount', said John.

'By at least 20 per cent. What is it to be Jo — porn, or people losing their jobs?' asked Keith.

Discussion questions

1. Who do you agree with? Why?
2. Should companies be concerned with moral issues or only profits?

Jet Red's new broom

Jet Red is a benevolent, paternalistic company. Many of its employees have more than 20 years of service. Highly bureaucratic, the company had until recently been protected from competition by government regulation. All blue-collar staff are unionised, as are all pilots and cabin crew. In addition, 60 per cent of the administrative and engineering staff are members of various unions. Altogether, Jet Red's employees are represented by a total of 16 unions. Seniority is recognised as the major determinant in promotions and pay increases. Although a performance appraisal program is in place for management staff, it is regarded as a formality and not something to be taken too seriously. Dismissals for poor performance at all levels are rare and, once employed, employees feel that they have a job for life.

The mood around the boardroom table was sombre. Jeff Davis, Jet Red's newly appointed Manager, Finance and Accounting, switched off the PowerPoint presentation. 'You can see the problems. We are losing more than $1 million a day. We must get our costs under control or we'll be out of business. Unrelenting competition, terrorism, the war in Iraq and SARS. We're in a do-or-die situation. Our passenger numbers on average are down by 40 per cent. On some routes, such as Hong Kong, we are down more than 60 per cent. We have 14 000 employees, which is at least 3000 more than we need. Our labour costs are excessive. Our wages and salaries are the highest in the industry, yet we have the most restrictive labour practices.

'You are all aware that Singapore Airlines' top managers have accepted pay cuts of up to 27.5 per cent and that they have fired almost 200 pilots and cabin crew.[155] We are facing our most difficult period in the company's 55-year history. We are the highest cost carrier in Australia. Virgin's cost base, in contrast, is one of its greatest strengths. In many areas, its costs are 30 per cent lower than Qantas's costs.[156] And we aren't even close to Qantas. To compete, we have to restructure. We must reduce our headcount, close unprofitable operations and reduce debt.' Jeff's words were met with silence.

Everyone in the room turned to face Alan Balkin, the new Managing Director. Alan, a highly respected and successful manager but without airline industry experience, looked slowly around and then spoke. 'As you know, I've been appointed to get results and I live or die by that. Nothing is going to deter me from ensuring that Jet Red survives. The fat and happy days are over. There has to be a sea change in attitude. If you haven't noticed, it's a dog-eat-dog world in international aviation. We have to deal with the reality of globalisation and overcapacity. No more sweetheart deals with the unions. No more jobs for life. No more pay increases based on seniority. No more five-star hotels for flight crews. Everything is up for scrutiny. Desperate times call for desperate measures. We can no longer be ambivalent about change. We have to cut $1 billion in costs just to survive. Our labour costs constitute the major difference between us and our competitors. Over 30 per cent of our total costs are labour costs. I want your thoughts on our immediate objective, which is how we can save Jet Red. I also want you to think longer term about how we can make Jet Red the most profitable and fastest-growing airline in the Asia–Pacific region. Next Friday, we will meet at our Gold Coast resort for a three-day retreat to finalise our objectives and action plans.'

Peter Wiley, Engineering Manager, tapped his pen, then interrupted. 'Excuse me, Alan, but that is rather short notice. I have a junior football league match to umpire next Saturday. Couldn't we postpone it until the end of the month? I know I would find it more convenient. I'm sure that there are others around the table who also have pressing commitments. Why can't we meet here in Melbourne during normal working hours?' A murmur of agreement echoed around the room.

Alan stiffened. 'We have 14 000 employees who are dependent on us for their jobs. We have shareholders who risk losing all their money. We are charged with saving an Australian icon and you talk about inconvenience? Alan, I have a simple message for you and everyone else sitting around this table. You are working for the new Jet Red. Performance and 100 per cent commitment are required. If you don't like it, find a job elsewhere. Can't you see that if we don't change and stop the financial haemorrhaging, there will be no Jet Red? We will be out of business. If Jet Red is to survive, we must position ourselves to compete against the other airlines. They are changing and they are reducing their cost structures. There is no alternative. I guarantee you two things. One, I will reward performance. And two, I will not tolerate non-performance. I expect you all to be at the retreat next Friday, prepared and ready to contribute!'

Peter's steely grey eyes pierced Alan. 'Alan, I must say that I find your attitude offensive. We all realise that the company is in difficulty, but that doesn't mean that we should be expected to drop everything. Jet Red doesn't own us.'

Alan, his face white with contained anger, paused then glared at Peter. 'Peter, I hear you. I'm demanding sacrifices because sacrifices are needed. This is a painful decision but one we have to make if we are going to survive. I'll work my guts out and I expect you to do the same. If any of you find this unacceptable, I'll accept your resignations now. It's your choice. Get on board, or leave. I cannot tolerate anything other than total commitment. Is that clear?' The room remained silent. Alan turned and, without saying another word, strode from the room.

Discussion questions

1. What HR challenges and issues are raised in this case?
2. What do you think of Alan's approach? What would you do?
3. Do you agree with Peter? Explain your answer.
4. If you were the HR Manager, what advice would you give to Alan? Why?

Exercise

Form into groups of four to six. Imagine you are part of Jet Red's senior management team. Prepare a set of corporate and HR objectives for Jet Red. Identify and discuss three major challenges you might face implementing your HR objectives.

practical exercises

1. Form into groups of four to six. Identify which external influences shown in figure 1.9 on page 23 affect the industry in which you work, the company for which you work and the job in which you work. What changes are these influences bringing about? Identify and discuss the implications for your organisation's HR management and for you personally.
2. Form into groups of four to six. Assume that you are the senior HR staff for an organisation that aims to be the fastest-growing, most profitable bank/manufacturer/retailer (select one industry) in the Asia–Pacific region. Identify and discuss the implications of this mission statement for the following HR activities:
   - recruitment and selection
   - training and development
   - compensation and benefits.
3. Form into groups of two or three. Research the stated 'core purpose' of three or four organisations with which you are familiar. You may gather the information from interviews and/or from published material such as company annual reports. Regroup as a class. Discuss what each stated core purpose tells you about the organisation and its culture. Is it credible? Is it reflected in the organisation's strategies, policies and practices? Identify which core purpose appeals to you the most and explain why.
4. Form into groups of four to six. Perform a SWOT analysis on your university (or business school) or an organisation you know well. Regroup and discuss your findings as a class.
5. Form into groups of four to six. Using the work sheet below, identify two or three trends for each category of external influence. Regroup as a class and discuss the impact each trend may have on employees, employers, trade unions and HRM.

IMPACT OF ENVIRONMENTAL TRENDS				
EXTERNAL INFLUENCES	**GROUP**			
	Employees	Employers	Trade unions	HRM
Political				
Legal				
Environmental				
Technological				
Cultural				
Demographic				
Social				
Business				
Economic				
Industrial relations				

6. Read BHP Billiton's mission statement on page 16 and Johnson & Johnson's organisational culture on page 26, then visit each company's web site (see appendix B on page 852). Briefly describe what you think each company would be like to work for and the type of person who would best 'fit' the culture.

suggested readings

Alexander, R. and Lewer, J., *Understanding Australian Industrial Relations*, 6th edn, Thomson, Melbourne, 2004, ch. 1

Bamgerger, P. and Meshoulam, I., *Human Resource Strategy*, Sage, Thousand Oaks, CA, 2000, chs 1, 2, 3.

Beardwell, I. and Holden, L., *Human Resource Management*, 3rd edn, Financial Times/Prentice Hall, London, 2001, chs 1, 2, 3.

Becker, B. E., Huselid, M. A. and Ulrich, D., *The HR Scorecard*, Harvard Business School Press, Boston, Mass., 2001, chs 1, 2.

Boxhall, P. and Purcell, J., *Strategy and Human Resource Management*, Palgrave Macmillan, Basingstoke, 2003, chs 1, 2, 3, 4.

CCH, *Australian Master Human Resources Guide*, CCH, Sydney, 2003, chs 1, 7, 8, 43.

De Cieri, H. and Kramar, R., *Human Resource Management in Australia*, McGraw-Hill, Sydney, 2003, chs 1, 2.

Fisher, C. D., Schoenfeldt, L. F. and Shaw, J. B., *Human Resource Management*, 5th edn, Houghton Mifflin, Boston, 2003, chs 1, 2, 10.

Gerrard, J. and Judge, G., *Employee Relations*, 3rd edn, CIPD, London, 2003, chs 1, 2, 6.

Gratton, L., *Living Strategy*, Financial Times/Prentice Hall, London, 2000.

Ivancevich, J. M., *Human Resource Management*, 8th edn, McGraw-Hill, Boston, 2001, chs 1, 2.

Ivancevich, J. M. and Lee, S. H., *Human Resource Management in Asia*, McGraw-Hill, Singapore, 2002, chs 1, 2.

Kamoche, K. N., *Understanding Human Resource Management*, Open University Press, Buckinghamshire, 2001, chs 1, 2, 3.

Mondy, R. W., Noe, R. M. and Premeaux, S., *Human Resource Management*, 8th edn, Prentice Hall, Upper Saddle River, NJ, 2002, chs 1, 2.

Nankervis, A. R., Compton, R. L. and Baird, M., *Strategic Human Resource Management*, 4th edn, Nelson, Melbourne, 2002, chs 1, 2, 18.

Ulrich, D., *Human Resource Champions*, Harvard University Press, Boston, 1997, ch. 1.

online references

Professional associations

www.ahri.com.au

www.aitd.com.au

www.apa.org

www.aps.psychsociety.com.au

www.bps.org.uk

www.hkihrm.org

www.ipd.co.uk

www.shri.org.sg

www.shrm.org

General information sources

aom.pace.edu/anjnew

aom.pace.edu/amr/

www.amazon.com

www.anzam.uts.edu.au

www.apa.org

www.atkearney.com

www.bizweb.com

www.blackboard.com

www.conference-board.org

www.econ.usyd.edu.au/acirrt

www.elibrary.com

www.haas.berkeley.edu/news/cmr/contents.html

www.hbr.org

www.hrisolutions.com/index2.html

www.hrps.org

www.mckinseyquarterly.com

www.mit-smr.com

www.nbs.ntu.ac.uk/staff/lyerj/hrm_link.htm

www.sagepub.co.uk/journals

www.shrm.org.hrmagazine

www.strategy-business.com

www.trainingsupersite.com

www.valberta.ca/~slis/guides/humares/homepage.htm

www.wfpma.com

www.workforceonline.com

www.yahoo.com/Business/Corporations/CorporateServices/HumanResources/

www1.sim.edu.sg

end notes

1. D. P. Skarlicki and R. Folger, 'Editorial fairness and human resource management', *Human Resource Management Review*, vol. 13, no. 1, 2003, p. 1.

2. E. L. Gubman, 'People are more valuable than ever', *Compensation and Benefits Review*, vol. 27, no. 1, 1995, p. 12; and P. M. Wright, G. C. McMahan and A. McWilliams, 'Human resources and sustained competitive advantage: a resource-based perspective', *International Journal of Human Resource Management*, vol. 5, no. 2, 1994, pp. 301–26.

3. L. Gratton, *Living Strategy*, Financial Times/Prentice Hall, London, 2000, p. 3.

4. C. P. McNamara, 'Making human capital productive', *Business and Economic Review*, vol. 46, no. 1, 1999, pp. 10–17; Macquarie Bank, *Annual Report*, Macquarie Bank, Sydney, 2003, pp. 12–15; and S. Spreier and S. Sherman, 'Staying ahead of the curve', *Fortune*, 3 March 2003, p. 42.

5. L. Clarke, 'Our people', *Stockland Annual Report*, Sydney, 2003, p. 14.

6. J. Pfeffer, *The Human Equation*, Harvard Business School Press, Boston, 1998, ch. 3.

7. D. Guest, 'Human resource management, corporate performance and employee well being: building the worker into HRM', *Journal of Industrial Relations*, vol. 44, no. 3, 2002, p. 335.

8. J. M. Ivancevich, *Human Resource Management*, 8th edn, McGraw-Hill, Boston, 2001, p. 10; A. K. Paul and R. N. Anantharaman, 'Business strategy, HRM practices and organizational performance: a study of the Indian software industry', *Journal of Transformational Management Development*, vol. 7, no. 3, 2002, pp. 27–51.

9. P. L. Chang and W. L. Chen, 'The effect of human resource management practices on firm performance: empirical evidence from hi-tech firms in Taiwan', *International Journal of Management*, vol. 19, no. 4, 2002, pp. 622–31.

10. I. Bjorkman and X. Fan, 'Human resource management and the performance of western firms in China', *International Journal of Human Resource Management*, vol. 13, no. 6, 2002, pp. 853–64; and J. Deng, B. Menguc and J. Benson, 'The impact of human resource management on export performance of Chinese manufacturing enterprises', *Thunderbird International Business Review*, vol. 45, no. 4, 2003, pp, 409–29.

11. J. Gould-Williams, 'The importance of human resource practices and workplace trust: a study of public sector organizations', *International Journal of Human Resource Management*, vol. 14, no. 1, 2003, p. 47; K. S. Law, D. K. Tse and N. Zhou, 'Does human resource matter in a transitional economy? China as an example', *Journal of International Business Studies*, vol. 34, no. 3, 2003,

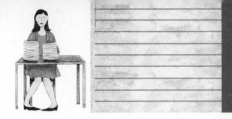

pp. 255–65; and M. A. Huselid, S. E. Jackson and R. S. Schuler, 'Technical and strategic human resource management effectiveness as determinants of firm performance', *Academy of Management Journal*, vol. 40, 1997, pp. 171–88.

12. Reported in S. Spreier and S. Sherman, op. cit., p. 41.

13. D. Ulrich, reported in Hewitt Associates, 'A reassessment of the true cost of HR could spur a transformation', *Hewitt Quarterly Asia Pacific*, vol. 2, no. 2, 2002, p. 3.

14. J. Purcell, 'The challenge of human resource management for industrial relations research and practice', *The International Journal of Human Resource Management*, vol. 4, no. 3, 1993, p. 518.

15. A. H. Church and G. C. McMahon, 'The practice of organisation and human resource development in the USA's fastest growing firms', *Leadership and Organisation Development Journal*, vol. 17, no. 2, 1996, pp. 31–2; and R. W. Mondy, R. M. Noe and S. R. Premeaux, *Human Resource Management*, 8th edn, Prentice Hall, Upper Saddle River, NJ, 2002, pp. 9–11.

16. Deloitte Touche, reported in 'The role of HR', *HR Focus*, 1999, p. 8; and J. Pfeffer, op. cit., p. 140.

17. Bureau of National Affairs and Society for Human Resource Management survey no. 62, reported in *Bulletin to Management*, 26 June 1997, p. 8.; J. Mace, 'Anyone home?', *HR Monthly*, February 2001, pp. 20–6; and A. Wai, 'Outsourcing helps firms focus on vital tasks', *South China Morning Post — Classifieds*, 18 October 2003, p. 23.

18. 'Bottom line: a term indicating the final result, such as the net profit after taxes', A. G. Giordano, *Concise Dictionary of Business Terminology*, Prentice Hall, NJ, 1981, p. 18.

19. E. L. Gubman, 'Aligning people strategies with customer value', *Compensation and Benefits Review*, vol. 27, no. 1, 1995, p. 22.

20. J. W. Walker, 'Are we business leaders?', *Human Resource Planning*, vol. 22, no. 4, 1999, p. 5.

21. T. M. Welbourne and L. A. Cyr, 'The human resource effect in initial public offering firms', *Academy of Management Journal*, vol. 42, no. 6, 1999, pp. 616–29; R. L. Simerly and J. M. Tomkiewicz, 'Management and economic performance: a strategic management approach', *International Journal of Management*, vol. 14, no. 2, 1997, pp. 282–91; T. C. Huang, 'The strategic level of human resource management and organizational performance: an empirical investigation', *Asia Pacific Journal of Human Resources*, vol. 36, no. 2, 1998, pp. 59–72; H. Vines, 'Body of evidence', *HR Monthly*, May 2002, pp. 18–23; and K. Singh, 'Strategic human resource orientation and firm performance in India', *International Journal of Human Resource Management*, vol. 14, no. 4, 2003, pp. 530–43.

22. CCH Australia and Australian Institute of Management study, reported in C. Fox, 'Powering up performance through HR', *Australian Financial Review*, 20 February 2001, p. 45.

23. C. A. Bartlett and S. Ghoshal, 'Building competitive advantage through people', *MIT Sloan Management Review*, vol. 43, no. 2, 2002, pp. 34–41.

24. J. W. Walker, W. E. Reif, L. Gratton and P. M. Swercz, 'Human resource leaders: capability, strengths and gaps', *Human Resource Planning*, vol. 22, no. 4, 1999, pp. 21–32; and C. Tebbel, 'Selling the concepts of strategic HR', *HR Monthly*, July 1999, pp. 16–19.

25. D. Guest, 'Personnel and HRM: can you tell the difference?', *Personnel Today*, June 1989, p. 10; and K. Truss, 'CEOs want a more strategic function', *People Management*, 8 August 1996, pp. 36–7.

26. Survey conducted by R. Kramar, Macquarie Graduate School of Business, in conjunction with the Centre for Australian Human Resource Management, Pricewaterhouse and the Australian Human Resources Institute. Reported in A. Moodie, 'Work programs cut office confrontation', *Australian Financial Review*, 30 May 1997, p. 65; R. Kramar, 'In with the new', *HR Monthly*, October 2000, pp. 48–52; and G. Michelson and R. Kramar, 'The state of HRM in Australia: progress and prospects', *Asia Pacific Journal of Human Resources*, vol. 41, no. 2, 2003, p. 133.

27. D. E. Guest, 'Personnel management: the end of orthodoxy?', *British Journal of Industrial Relations*, vol. 29, no. 2, 1992, p. 162.

28. ANZ, *Annual Report*, 2000, p. 24; St George Bank, *Annual Report*, 1999, p. 35; and Tandou, *Annual Report*, 2000, p. 51.

29. H. E. Meyer, 'Personnel directors are the new corporate heroes', in K. Perlman, F. L. Schmidt and W. C. Hammer (eds), *Contemporary Problems in Personnel*, 3rd edn, John Wiley & Sons, New York, 1983, p. 3; J. Pfeffer, 'When it comes to "Best Practices" why do smart organisations occasionally do dumb things?', *Organizational Dynamics*, vol. 25, no. 1, 1996, p. 39; and A. K. Paul and R. N. Anantharaman, op. cit., pp. 28–9.

30. M. Tayeb, 'Conducting research across cultures: overcoming drawbacks and obstacles', *International Journal of Cross Cultural Management*, vol. 1, no. 1, 2001, p. 100.

31. B. Smith, 'The future for human resources professionals — danger or opportunity', *HR Strategies*, Melbourne, 1998, p. 7.

32. M. W. Mercer, *Turning Your Human Resources Department into a Profit Center*, AMACOM, New York, 1989, p. 6; H. Meredith, 'Service provider can outsource HR functions', *Australian Financial Review*, 3 October 2000, pp. 6–9; and P. Wier, 'Anatomy of an HR outsource', *HR Monthly*, February 2000, pp. 6–9.

33. D. L. Nelson, J. C. Quick and M. A. Hitt, 'What stresses HR professionals?', *Personnel*, vol. 67, no. 8, 1990, p. 36.

34. M. W. Mercer, op. cit., p. 6.

35. D. Ulrich, quoted in L. Pickett, 'Turning strategy into results', *HR Monthly*, March 2000, p. 13.

36. This section is based on material drawn from D. Goss, *Principles of Human Resource Management*, Routledge, London, 1994, pp. 10–14; J. Storey, *Human Resource Management: A Critical Text*, Routledge, London, 1995, pp. 34–6; and J. Storey and K. Sisson, *Managing Human Resources and Industrial Relations*, Open University Press, Buckinghamshire, 1993, pp. 13–18.

37. For further discussion, see M. Gardner and G. Palmer, *Employment Relations*, 2nd edn, Macmillan, Melbourne, 1997, pp. 587–90; K. Legge, *Human Resource Management*, Macmillan, London, 1995, pp. 272–84; S. Deery, D. Plowman and J. Walsh, *Industrial Relations: A Contemporary Analysis*, McGraw-Hill, Sydney, 1997, ch. 2, especially pp. 2.5–2.6; and D. Grant and J. Shields, 'In search of the subject: researching employee reactions to human resource

management', *Journal of Industrial Relations*, vol. 44, no. 3, 2002, pp. 313–34.

38. D. Ulrich, *Human Resource Champions*, Harvard University Press, Boston, 1997, p. 79.

39. A. Nankervis, 'Small packages', *HR Monthly*, November 2000, pp. 42–3; and E. K. Johnson, 'The practice of human resource management in New Zealand: strategic and best practice?', *Asia Pacific Journal of Human Resources*, vol. 38, no. 2, 2000, pp. 69–83.

40. P. McGraw and B. Harley, 'Industrial relations and human resource management practices in Australian and overseas owned workplaces: global or local?', *Journal of Industrial Relations*, vol. 45, no. 1, 2003, pp. 1–22.

41. T. Jackson, 'The management of people across cultures: valuing people differently', *Human Resource Management*, vol. 41, no. 4, 2002, pp. 455–75.

42. C. Fisher and P. Dowling, 'Support for an HR approach in Australia: the perspective of senior HR managers', *Asia Pacific Journal of Human Resources*, vol. 37, no. 1, 1999, pp. 1–19; N. Way, 'A new world of people power', *Business Review Weekly*, 16 June 2000, pp. 62–6; and C. A. Bartlett and S. Ghoshal, op. cit., pp. 34–41.

43. D. Ulrich, 1997, op. cit., p. 121; and R. Blackburn and B. Rosen, 'Does HRM walk the TQM talk?', *HR Magazine*, July 1995, pp. 68–72.

44. A. Yeung, *Human Resource Competencies in Hong Kong: Research Findings and Applications Guide*, HKIHRM/University of Michigan Business School, Hong Kong, 1998, p. 4.

45. D. Ulrich, 1997, op. cit., pp. 123–49; and A. Yeung, W. Brockbank and D. Ulrich, 'Lower cost higher value: human resource function in transformation', *Human Resource Planning*, vol. 17, no. 3, 1994, p. 15.

46. D. Ulrich, 1997, op. cit., p. 149.

47. B. Ellig, 'HR must balance demands of dual roles', *HR News*, July 1996, p. 9.

48. C. Allan and K. Lovell, 'The effects of high performance work systems on employees in aged care', *Labour and Industry*, vol. 13, no. 3, 2003, p. 14.

49. T. Kochan, quoted in H. Trinca, 'HR needs to rebuild trust', *Australian Financial Review*, 11 November 2003, p. 59.

50. D. Guest, 2002, op. cit., p. 335.

51. A. Yeung, W. Brockbank and D. Ulrich, 1994, op. cit., p. 15; M. Foot and C. Hook, *Introducing Human Resource Management*, Longman, London, 1996, p. 11; and N. Tanner, 'I'm the HR consultant', *HR Monthly*, May 1997, pp. 19–20.

52. A. Yeung, W. Brockbank and D. Ulrich, 1994, op. cit., p. 16.

53. M. Gloet, 'The changing role of the HRM function in the knowledge economy: the links to quality knowledge management', paper presented at the 8th International Conference on ISO and TQM, Montreal, April 2003, pp. 1–7.

54. J. M. Ivancevich, *Human Resource Management*, 6th edn, Irwin, Chicago, 1995, p. 134.

55. K. E. Joyce, 'Lessons for employers from "Fortune's 100 best"', *Business Horizons*, vol. 46, no. 2, 2003, pp. 77–84.

56. L. L. Byars and L. W. Rue, *Human Resource Management*, 6th edn, McGraw-Hill, Boston, 2000, p. 303.

57. R. L. Heneman, *Merit Pay: Linking Pay Increases to Performance Ratings*, Addison-Wesley, Reading, Mass., 1992; and S. L. Rynes, A. E. Colbert and K. G. Brown, 'HR professionals' beliefs about effective human resource practices: correspondence between research and practice', *Human Resource Management*, vol. 41, no. 2, 2002, p. 157.

58. R. Levering and M. Moskowitz, '100 best companies to work for', *Fortune*, 20 January 2003, p. 87.

59. D. Guest, 2002, op. cit., pp. 335–58; and S. Albrecht and A. Travaglione, 'Trust in public sector senior management', *International Journal of Human Resource Management*, vol. 14, no. 1, 2003, pp. 76–92.

60. It should be noted that there is no one universally accepted definition of industrial relations. The definition used here reflects a unitarist perspective, which emphasises the mutual interests existing between employees and employers. In contrast, a pluralist definition emphasises the role of institutions and the making of rules to regulate conflict in the workplace. For further discussion, see chapter 15; S. Deery, D. Plowman and J. Walsh, *Industrial Relations: A Contemporary Analysis*, McGraw-Hill, Sydney, 2002, ch. 1; and R. Alexander and J. Lewer, *Understanding Australian Industrial Relations*, Thomson, Sydney, 2004, ch. 1.

61. See Office of Multicultural Affairs, *Multiculturalism at Work*, Canberra, undated, p. 4; and R. L. Tung, 'Strategic human resource challenge: managing diversity', *International Journal of Human Resource Management*, vol. 6, no. 3, 1995, pp. 482–93.

62. M. Westfield, *HIH: The Inside Story of Australia's Biggest Corporate Collapse*, John Wiley & Sons, Brisbane, 2003; A. Shand, 'The fatal weakness of Ray Williams', *Australian Financial Review*, 18–19 January 2003, pp. 21, 23; T. Sykes, 'They spoke of money that was never there', *Australian Financial Review*, 17–21 April 2003, p. 16; M. Priest, 'Judge urges directors to end the climate of fear', *Australian Financial Review*, 15 April 2003, pp. 1, 4; and A Main, 'HIH: Abbott to face charge', *Australian Financial Review*, 15 April 2003, pp. 1 and 4.

63. A. Shand, 'Going over the hill, or over the moon?', *Australian Financial Review*, 28 March–1 April 2002, p. 14; and S. Evans, 'Crossing the great divide', *Australian Financial Review*, 19 April 2002, p. 66.

64. Paul Coghlan, quoted in A. Cornell and S. Evans, 'Coles cracks up', *Australian Financial Review*, 14–15 September 2002, p. 23.

65. J. R. Schermerhorn Jr, *Management for Productivity*, John Wiley & Sons, New York, 1984, pp. 138–9.

66. Y. Debrah, 'Managerial strategic choice and the management of human resources', in A. R. Nankervis and R. L. Compton, *Readings in Strategic Human Resource Management*, Nelson, Melbourne, 1994, p. 50; S. Briggs and W. Keogh, 'Integrating human resource strategy and strategic planning to achieve business excellence', *Total Quality Management*, vol. 10, no. 4/5, 1999, pp. 447–53; and T. Grundy, 'How are corporate strategy and human resources strategy linked?', *Journal of General Management*, vol. 23, no. 33, 1998, pp. 49–72.

67. G. Hamel and C. K. Prahalad, 'Strategic intent', *Harvard Business Review*, May–June 1989, p. 64.

68. Cited in J. C. Collins and J. I. Porras, 'Building your company's vision', *Harvard Business Review*, September–October 1996, p. 72.

69. Southcorp, *Concise Annual Report*, 2000, p. 8.

70. J. C. Collins and J. I. Porras, op. cit., p. 65.

71. L. Kraar, 'How Samsung grows so fast', *Fortune*, 3 May 1993, p. 19.

72. Quoted in N. M. Tichy and S. Sherman, 'Jack Welch's lessons for success', *Fortune*, 25 January 1993, p. 64.

73. J. C. Collins and J. I. Porras, op. cit., p. 68.

74. R. R. Collins, 'The strategic contributions of the human resource function', *Human Resource Management Australia*, vol. 25, no. 3, 1987, p. 19.

75. R. Moss Kanter, *The Change Masters*, Counterpoint, London, 1983, pp. 294–5.

76. D. Guest, 2002, op. cit., p. 341.

77. F. M. Horwitz, 'HRM: an ideological perspective', *Personnel Review*, vol. 19, no. 2, 1990, pp. 10–15; and J. Purcell, 'The challenge of human resource management for industrial relations research and practice', *International Journal of Human Resource Management*, vol. 4, no. 3, 1993, pp. 515–17.

78. Much of this section is based on material drawn from C. W. L. Hill and G. R. Jones, *Strategic Management Theory*, 2nd edn, Houghton Mifflin, Boston, 1992, pp. 9–18; and G. D. Smith, D. R. Arnold and B. G. Bizzell, *Business Strategy and Policy*, Houghton Mifflin, Boston, 1991, pp. 2–16.

79. A. A. Thompson and A. J. Strickland, *Strategic Management: Concepts and Cases*, 4th edn, Business Publications, Plano, Texas, 1987, p. 4.

80. P. Jones and L. Kahaner, quoted in A. Farnham, 'Brushing up your vision thing', *Fortune*, 1 May 1995, p. 91. See also J. V. Quigley, G. E. Ledford, J. R. Wendenhof and J. T. Strahley, 'Realizing a corporate philosophy', *Organizational Dynamics*, vol. 23, no. 3, 1995, pp. 5–19; R. A. Stone, 'Mission statements revisited', *SAM Advanced Management Journal*, vol. 61, no. 1, 1996, pp. 31–7; D. Hoverden, 'Delivering inspiration', *HR Monthly*, March 2000, pp. 24–5; and H. Vines, 'Putting values to work', *HR Monthly*, April 2000, pp. 12–18.

81. Cited in J. C. Collins and J. I. Porras, op. cit., p. 69.

82. J. R. Schermerhorn Jr, *Management*, 5th edn, John Wiley & Sons, New York, 1996, pp. 161–2.

83. N. Bita, 'Lingerie workers lose jobs as Berlei admits local defeat', *Australian*, 14 August 1997, p. 3.

84. G. D. Smith, D. R. Arnold and B. G. Bizzell, op. cit., p. 3.

85. Y. Debrah, op. cit., p. 52.

86. Y. Debrah, op. cit., p. 54.

87. Wesfarmers, *Annual Report*, 1999, pp. 5–6.

88. J. R. Schermerhorn Jr, 1996, op. cit., pp. 172–4; C. W. L. Hill and G. R. Jones, *Strategic Management Theory*, 2nd edn, Houghton Mifflin, Boston, 1992, p. 17 and ch. 13; and J. C. Picken and G. G. Dess, 'Out of strategic control', *Organizational Dynamics*, vol. 26, no. 1, 1997, pp. 35–48.

89. J. R. Schermerhorn Jr, 1996, op. cit., p. 173.

90. Numerous other approaches to classifying strategies have been developed. See L. R. Gomez-Mejia, D. B. Balkin and R. L. Cardy, *Managing Human Resources*, 3rd edn, Prentice Hall, Englewood Cliffs, NJ, 2002, ch. 1; and B. Kane and A. Hermens, 'Strategic HRM and strategic management: should the link be tighter?', paper presented at the 1996 ANZAM Conference, 5 December 1996, Wollongong, pp. 1–22.

91. D. J. Cherrington, *The Management of Human Resources*, 4th edn, Prentice Hall, Englewood Cliffs, NJ, 1995, p. 47.

92. Reported in N. Field, 'People practices still a weak spot', *Australian Financial Review*, 11 June 1999, p. 25.

93. P. Drucker, 'They're not employees, they're people', *Harvard Business Review*, February 2002, p. 76.

94. D. Ulrich, 'Strategic and human resource planning: linking customers and employees', *Human Resource Planning*, vol. 15, no. 2, 1992, p. 47; and T. J. Galpin and P. Murray, 'Connect human resource management to the business plan', *HR Magazine*, March 1997, pp. 99–104.

95. S. Taylor, S. Beechler and N. Napier, 'Toward an integrative model of strategic international human resource management', *Academy of Management Review*, vol. 24, no. 4, 1996, p. 959; and M. Zigarelli, 'Human resources and the bottom line', *Academy of Management Executive*, vol. 10, no. 2, 1996, pp. 63–4.

96. M. Poole and G. Jenkins, 'Competitiveness and human resource management politics', *Journal of General Management*, vol. 22, no. 2, 1996, p. 18.

97. D. Price, 'How marketing can sell your personnel product', *People Management*, 13 June 1996, p. 21.

98. M. Armstrong, *Personnel and the Bottom Line*, IPM, London, 1989, pp. 91–2.

99. R. S. Schuler, S. P. Galante and S. Jackson, 'Matching effective HR practices with competitive strategy', *Personnel*, vol. 64, no. 9, 1987, p. 18.

100. CCH, 'Successful companies integrate HR practices with business goals and fully leverage employees', *Human Resources Management, Ideas and Trends*, 29 March 1995, pp. 56–7; and CCH, 'Bottom line reasons support HR's place at CEO's table', *Human Resources Management*, SHRM/CCH Survey, 21 June 1995, p. 1.

101. R. Kramar, 'Strategic human resource management: are the promises fulfilled', *Asia Pacific Journal of Human Resources*, vol. 30, no. 1, 1992, p. 3; and D. E. Guest, 1992, op. cit., p. 157.

102. R. W. Rowden, 'Potential roles of human resource management professionals in the strategic planning process', *SAM Advanced Management Journal*, vol. 64, no. 3, 1999, pp. 22–7; and J. Laabs, 'Strategic HR won't come easily', *Workforce*, vol. 79, no. 1, 2000, pp. 52–6.

103. D. J. Cherrington, *The Management of Human Resources*, Prentice Hall, Englewood Cliffs, NJ, 1995, p. 10.

104. S. Albrecht and A. Travaglione, 'Trust in public sector senior management', *International Journal of Human Resource Management*, vol. 14, no. 1, 2003, pp. 76–92; and B. Blunsden and K. Reed, 'The effects of technical and social conditions on

workplace trust', *International Journal of Human Resource Management*, vol. 14, no. 1, 2003, pp. 12–27.

105. T. Bramble, 'Strategy in context: the impact of changing regulatory regimes on industrial relations management in the Australian vehicle industry', *Asia Pacific Journal of Human Resources*, vol. 34, no. 3, 1996, pp. 48–62.

106. T. Bramble, op. cit., pp. 54–5.

107. D. Guest, 2002, op. cit., pp. 335–58.

108. G. A. Gelade and M. Ivery, 'The impact of human resource management and work climate on organizational performance', *Personnel Psychology*, vol. 56, no. 2, 2003, pp. 383–404; and C. A. Bartlett and S. Ghoshal, op. cit., pp. 34–41.

109. A. Lehn, 'Against all reason?', *Review*, vol. 49, no. 4, 1997, p. 31.

110. See M. Pitcher, 'Environmental integration can bring attractive returns', *HR Monthly*, September 1992, pp. 20–1; and P. Gilding and G. Mawer, 'Eco-competitiveness', *Management*, April 1996, pp. 8–10.

111. 'Managing in Asia', *Far Eastern Economic Review*, 16 September 1993, pp. 35–6.

112. R. Martin, 'New graduates face hard reality in competitive local job market', *Asian Wall Street Journal*, 'Hong Kong Week', 21 February 1994, p. 1; and C. Wan, 'Big headed graduates missing out', *Sunday Morning Post*, 25 June, 2000, p. 2.

113. B. Schneiders, 'Paperlinx feels weight of $A', *Australian Financial Review*, 28 November 2003, p. 62.

114. BHP, 'Coming out of a tight corner', *Report to Shareholders*, 2000, p. 21.

115. L. Ferraro, 'The culture of safety', *HR Monthly*, April 2003, p. 38.

116. N. Way, 'Call still waiting', *Shares*, May 2003, p. 37.

117. A. Shand, 2002, op. cit., p. 14; and S. Evans, 'Crossing the great divide', *Australian Financial Review*, 19 April 2002, p. 66.

118. R. S. Larsen, quoted in J. C. Collins and J. I. Porras, op. cit., p. 67.

119. A. Barrett, 'Staying on top', *Business Week*, 5 May 2003, pp. 42–7.

120. J. C. Collins and J. I. Porras, op. cit., p. 72.

121. J. P. Kotter and J. L. Heskett, 'How corporate culture affects performance', *World Executive's Digest*, July 1993, pp. 28–31; and J. C. Collins and J. I. Porras, op. cit., pp. 65–77.

122. R. J. Greene, 'Culturally compatible HR strategies', *HR Magazine*, June 1995, pp. 115–23.

123. Quoted in P. Sheehan, 'All souped up', *ABM*, January 1993, p. 86.

124. Quoted in P. Sheehan, op. cit., p. 86.

125. G. Hubbard, D. Samuel, S. Heap and G. Cocks, *The First XI: Winning Organisations in Australia*, John Wiley & Sons, Brisbane, 2002, pp. 209–19; and M. Priest, 'Trust and respect make work great', *Australian Financial Review*, 15 December 2003, p. 7.

126. K. N. Kamoche, *Understanding Human Resource Management*, Open University Press, Buckinghamshire, 2001, pp. 22–3.

127. B. Townley, 'Selection and appraisal: reconstituting "social relations"', in J. Storey (ed.), *New Perspectives on Human Resource Management*, Routledge, London, 1991, ch. 6; E. Ogbonna,

'Organization culture and human resource management: dilemmas and contradictions', in P. Blyton and P. Turnbull (eds), *Reassessing Human Resource Management*, Sage, London, 1992, ch. 5; and K. Kamoche, 'Human resource management: a multi-paradigmatic analysis', *Personnel Review*, vol. 20, no. 4, 1991, p. 11.

128. C. Fox, 'Workers by design', *Boss*, August 2003, p. 26.

129. L. Gratton, 2000, op. cit., pp. 6–8.

130. B. Kabanoff, 'An exploration of espoused culture in Australian organisations (with a closer look at the banking sector)', *Asia Pacific Journal of Human Resources*, vol. 31, no. 3, 1993, pp. 16–17.

131. J. Gray, 'Macho bank culture drives top women from Westpac', *Australian Financial Review*, 26 February 1997, p. 1; and K. Lyall, 'Bank women resigned to frustration', *Weekend Australian*, 8–9 March 1997, p. 6.

132. C. Ryan, 'The playmaker', *Australian Financial Review Magazine*, 2003, p. 53; A. Cornell, 'NAB: Who shrunk the bank?', *Australian Financial Review*, 11 April 2002, p. 42.

133. A. Cornell, 'Battered and bruised NAB under siege', *Australian Financial Review*, 4 February 2002, p. 53.

134. G. Lekakis and B. Pearson, 'Bank's standing at low point', *Australian Financial Review*, 25 October 2000, p. 7; Staff reporter, 'Brickbats for Westpac', *Australian Financial Review*, 5 November 2003, p. 46; J. Moullakis, 'CBA lags in customer survey', *Australian Financial Review*, 24 September 2003, p. 52; and J. Whyte, 'Bank customers vote with their feet on bad service', *Australian Financial Review*, 9 September 2003, p. 51.

135. W. F. Cascio, *Managing Human Resources*, 2nd edn, McGraw-Hill, Singapore, 1989, p. 46; J. Pfeffer, 1998, op. cit., pp. 74–9; and L. Gratton, 2000, op. cit., pp. 5–6.

136. J. T. Delaney and M. Huselid, 'The impact of human resource management practices on perceptions of organisational performance', *Academy of Management Journal*, vol. 39, no. 4, 1996, pp. 949–69; and M. A. Youndt, S. A. Snell, J. W. Dean and D. P. Lepak, 'Human resource management, manufacturing strategy and firm performance', *Academy of Management Journal*, vol. 39, no. 4, 1996, p. 858.

137. J. M. Hannon and G. T. Milkovich, 'The effect of human resource reputation signals on share prices: an event study', *Human Resource Management*, vol. 35, no. 3, 1996, pp. 405–24; J. M. Ivancevich, 2001, op. cit., pp. 9–10; and M. Ewing and A. Caruana, 'Strategic human resource effectiveness, internal marketing and performance in the public sector', *International Employment Relations Review*, vol. 5, no. 1, 1999, pp. 15–27.

138. J. M. Ivancevich, 2001, op. cit., p. 10; and R. S. Schuler, 'Human resource management', in M. Poole and M. Warner (eds), *The Handbook of Human Resource Management*, Thomson, London, 1998, p. 140.

139. D. Guest, 2002, op. cit., pp. 335–58.

140. Macquarie Bank, *Annual Report*, Macquarie Bank, Sydney, 2003, p. 15.

141. Adapted by the author from M. Beer, B. Spector, P. R. Lawrence, D. Q. Mills and R. E. Walton, *Managing Human Assets*, The Free Press, New York, 1984, p. 19.

142. P. E. Spector, *Industrial and Organizational Psychology*, 2nd edn, John Wiley & Sons, New York, 2000, p. 215.

143. E. Rose, 'The labour process and union commitment within a banking services call centre', *Journal of Industrial Relations*, vol. 44, no. 1, 2002, p. 40.

144. S. L. McShane and M. A. Von Glinow, *Organizational Behavior*, McGraw-Hill, Boston, 2000, p. 145; and G. A. Gelade and M. Ivery, op. cit., pp. 383–404.

145. E. M. Whitener, 'Do "high commitment" human resource practices affect employee commitment? A cross level analysis using hierarchical linear modeling', *Journal of Management*, vol. 27, no. 5, 2001, p. 515.

146. D. P. Skarlicki and R. Folger, op. cit., p. 1.

147. S. Albrecht and A. Travaglione, 'Trust in public sector senior management', *International Journal of Human Resource Management*, vol. 14, no. 1, 2002, pp. 76–92; and R. L. Holbrook Jr, 'Contact points and flash points: conceptualising the use of justice mechanisms in the performance appraisal interview', *Human Resource Management Review*, vol. 12, no. 1, 2002. p. 104.

148. S. P. Robbins, *Organizational Behavior*, 9th edn, Prentice Hall, Upper Saddle River, NJ, 2001, p. 166.

149. Study by Walker Information, reported in D. E. Lewis, 'Study of US workers finds that most feel "trapped" and lack loyalty', *International Herald Tribune*, 3 September 2003, p. 18.

150. J. Child and D. Faulkiner, *Strategies of Co-operation*, Oxford University Press, Oxford, 1998, pp. 46–7.

151. R. Zeffane and J. Connell, 'Trust and HRM in the new millennium', *International Journal of Human Resource Management*, vol. 14, no. 1, 2003, p. 5.

152. Survey by Kelly Services, reported in Australian Associated Press, 'Workers distrust bosses', *Australian Financial Review*, 24 September 2003, p. 6.

153. B. L. Katcher, 'Employees feel like slaves', *Human Resources*, May 2003, p. 6.

154. P. Davidson, 'Function struggles with potential of strategic HRM', *HR Monthly*, July 1996, p. 7.

155. 'SIA learns painful lessons amid virus woes', *South China Morning Post*, 26 May 2003, p. B6; and H. W. Tan and H. Amin, 'Singapore Air cuts jobs again amid weak demand', *International Herald Tribune*, 22 July 2003, p. B1.

156. J. Boyle, 'Virgin gives Qantas the blues', *Australian Financial Review*, 17–18 May 2003, p. 10.

chapter 2

human resource planning

Learning objectives

When you have finished studying this chapter, you should be able to:

- Explain the relationship between strategic HRM planning and HRM planning
- Appreciate the importance of HR planning
- Identify the key environmental influences on HR planning
- Understand the basic approaches to HR planning
- Describe the ways of forecasting HR requirements
- Understand the requirements for effective HR planning.

'For Foster's to consistently improve performance it is essential that the group attracts, develops and retains the best people.'[1]

Ted Kunkel, former President and CEO, Foster's Group Limited

Human resource planning and strategic HRM planning

Human resource planning and *strategic HRM planning* are often mixed up. To avoid such confusion, *human resource planning* (HRP) is better described as employment planning. This places HR planning at the operational level where it is concerned with detailed forecasts of employee supply (internal and external) and employee demand. Based on the HR forecasts, specific action can be taken to get the right numbers and types of employees doing the right work at the right time (that is, planning the flow of people into, through and out of the organisation). In contrast, *strategic HRM planning* is concerned with defining philosophy, objectives and strategy, and precedes HR planning.

To be of value, HR planning must be an integrated part of the organisation's overall strategic planning process (see figures 2.1 and 2.3).

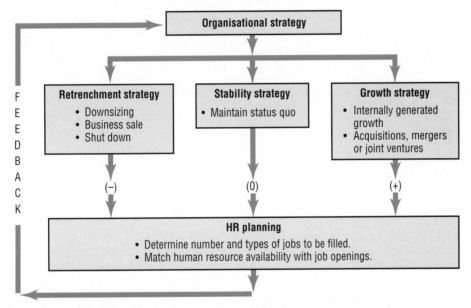

Figure 2.1 Organisational strategy and human resource planning
Source Asia Pacific Management Co. Ltd, 2004.

The importance of human resource planning

The focus of **human resource planning** or employee planning is on labour demand (the number of employees needed by the organisation) and labour supply (the number of qualified employees available to the organisation). HRP involves the entry of people into the organisation (acquisition), the development of employee skills (development) and the exit of employees from the organisation (departure). As a consequence, HRP is the responsibility of all managers — it is not just an HR department activity. Effective HRP is critical to the organisation's success because it matches the organisation and its HR objectives with its people requirements (see figure 2.2). Organisations with surplus employees will need to review their HR policies regarding permanent employment, outsourcing and retrenchments. Likewise, organisations with too many low-skilled and poorly qualified employees may face obstacles when introducing new technology, total quality management (TQM) and other

Human resource planning
The process of systematically reviewing human resource requirements to ensure that the required number of employees, with the required knowledge, skills and abilities, are available when needed.

change initiatives. Finally, organisations lacking a diverse employee mix may not meet their EEO objectives (see figure 2.2). Effective HRP ensures that the available talent is correctly allocated, labour costs are controlled, the employee headcount is appropriate, productivity is improved and talented employees are retained. Unfortunately, HRP receives scant attention from too many line managers.[2]

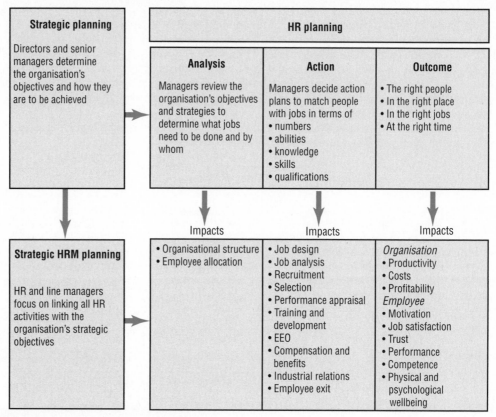

Figure 2.2 Strategic planning and HR planning
Source Asia Pacific Management Co. Ltd, 2004.

The purpose of HR planning

The purpose of HR planning is to ensure that a predetermined number of persons with the appropriate knowledge, skills and abilities are available at a specified time in the future. HR planning thus systematically identifies what must be done to guarantee the availability of the human resources required by an organisation to meet its strategic business objectives. Managers must ask: What mix of knowledge, skills and abilities do we require now? What mix will we require in the future? Do we have the right number of qualified employees today? How will employee numbers change in the future? How do our labour costs and productivity compare with our competitors?[3] Where will we find the people we need?

Scarcity of talent

Increasingly, what concerns managers is the scarcity of talent. Harold Clough, Chairman of Clough Ltd, says: 'We strongly believe that the future value and success of any company will depend on the quality of its people and their intellectual ability.'[4] Talent is now the prime source of competitive advantage, not raw materials, capital or technology.[5] One international survey of senior executives found that attracting talent and retaining talent are becoming the major drivers of corporate strategy.[6] A company's talent, moreover, is increasing in importance as a determinant of its share price.[7]

The major problems facing Sydney, Hong Kong, Kuala Lumpur, Shanghai and Singapore in their quest to be the business hub of the Asia–Pacific region are their lack of skilled people and a talent brain drain.[8] Australia, for example, has a persistent shortage of medical, nursing, teaching, accounting, engineering and technical employees and people with trade skills.[9] Overall, it is predicted that Australia will have 500 000 fewer workers than it needs by 2020.[10] China has a jobless rate exceeding 20 per cent, more than two million university students graduating per year and 150 million surplus rural labourers. Nevertheless, it faces severe skill shortages and an increasing brain drain.[11] (Australia is the number one destination for China's high-tech professionals.[12]) Less than 3.5 per cent of China's 70 million technical employees are skilled compared to 40 per cent in developed countries.[13] According to the Organisation for Economic Cooperation and Development (OECD), at least 15 per cent of adults in Australia, Britain, New Zealand and the United States have only rudimentary literacy skills, making it difficult for them to cope with the rising skill demands of industry.[14] It is similarly estimated that up to 500 000 Singaporeans lack the education to move into high-tech industries.[15]

Short-term versus long-term needs

A common mistake for HR managers is to concentrate on short-term replacement needs rather than on the organisation's long-range human resource requirements. Such a non-strategic approach causes management to be caught unawares by changes in employee availability and quality of labour, and creates a series of short-term dilemmas. Ad hoc HRP is inefficient because it is reactive and represents management-by-crisis. If the right numbers of qualified and skilled employees are not available, an organisation may not be able to meet its strategic business objectives. High-technology firms such as IBM and Motorola, for example, have strategies for developing new products or entering new markets that depend on the availability of appropriately qualified and skilled human resources.[16]

Cooperation between the HR function and line management is necessary for success. Such a partnership links HR planning with corporate strategic planning and ensures that HRM is proactive. It allows the HR manager to anticipate and influence the organisation's future HR requirements. Foster's move into China and its expansion into wine created demands for personnel with new skills and different experiences.[17] In contrast, Pacific Dunlop's strategic decision to exit the food and medical technology industries meant that it no longer required people with food and medical technology-related skills.[18] HR planning can thus be seen as a systematic process linking the management of human resources to the achievement of the organisation's strategic business objectives. It ensures a more effective and efficient use of human resources, more satisfied and better developed employees, more effective equal employment opportunity and affirmative action (AA) planning, and reduced financial and legal costs (see figures 2.1, 2.2 and 2.3).

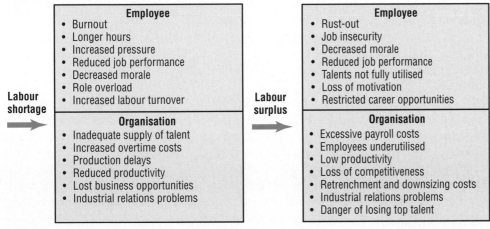

Figure 2.3 HR planning failure and labour imbalances
Source Asia Pacific Management Co. Ltd, 2004.

Environmental factors and human resource planning

As part of the strategic planning process, HR planning considers both the internal and external environmental influences on an organisation, its objectives, culture, structure, systems and HRM policies and practices (see figure 1.9 on page 23).

This is because HR planning must reflect the environmental trends and issues that affect an organisation's management of its human resources, including:

- economic factors (for example, Australia's high income tax rates make it difficult and expensive to attract international executives)
- social factors (for example, jobs shunned by Americans as being too hard, too dirty or too menial are done by some eight million illegal workers)
- demographic factors (for example, one in six Hong Kong residents will be 65 or older by 2015)
- and technological factors (for example, the Internet has made geographic location irrelevant, giving organisations the power to transfer jobs from rich countries with expensive labour to poor countries with cheap labour — Microsoft is shifting US-based jobs to India in an effort to reduce technical support and development costs[19]).

All these factors affect the type and availability of labour.[20]

Globalisation

'Globalisation is allowing skilled labour to move like capital across the world to locations that offer the best compensation and the best future.'[21] The United States attracts more educated immigrants than the rest of the world combined.[22] Australia is losing more than 80 000 residents per year — the majority being academics, managers and professionals — primarily to Britain, Hong Kong, Singapore and the United States (see the Newsbreak opposite). British schools are hiring teachers from Australia and Singapore.[23] Australian lawyers have gone global, creating a critical shortage of commercial lawyers, while the exodus of top academics risks a 'dumbing down' of Australian universities.[24]

In the United States, the shortage of business school faculty staff is reaching crisis point as fewer and fewer people with PhDs seek a career in academia, preferring more lucrative opportunities in consulting, think tanks and business. As a consequence, starting salaries for top talent now exceed US$130 000. To overcome the problem, existing staff are being asked to teach more classes, and people with non-business PhDs (for example, social sciences) are being hired along with practising managers.[25]

New Zealand too is experiencing a loss of talent as its managers and young professionals move abroad in increasing numbers.[26] As a consequence, New Zealand is seeking an extra 10 000 skilled and business immigrants per year (mainly from China, India, Japan and South Africa).[27]

China, India and Japan also are suffering brain drains.[28] Up to 50 per cent of India's top engineering and science graduates and 20 per cent of its medical graduates leave each year for jobs overseas.[29] It is estimated that more than 99 per cent of all Chinese graduates and two-thirds of all foreign PhD graduates in science and engineering remain in the United States.[30] Aggravating this situation are the concerted efforts of Japanese and European companies to capture Chinese and Indian talent. One consequence is that Hong Kong is experiencing unwanted competition for skilled mainland Chinese.[31] Japan similarly faces an alarming brain drain as its young and talented employees escape from its rigid, bureaucratic and seniority-ridden organisations in search of employers offering more flexibility, opportunity and rewards.[32]

NEWSBREAK

Australia's reverse diaspora

By Peter Roberts

There is something very wrong here. A million Australians are working abroad — it has been called our very own diaspora. That is a cute idea, but a diaspora usually describes a dispersed group of desperate people who have fled oppression for a better life elsewhere. In Asia, there is a diaspora of Filipinos, many of whom flock to Singapore for menial and poorly paid jobs such as household maids. Their diaspora is incredibly valuable to the Philippine economy, with billions of dollars a year sent back to families at home.

But Australia's million-strong diaspora includes few maids or desperate people. They are often Australia's best and brightest — too often our elite business managers or managers from fast-growing small and medium-size companies.

In 2001–02, according to the Australian Bureau of Statistics, about 7300 more managers and professionals left the country than returned — a serious haemorrhage of talent. The previous year the number was closer to 13 000. The conditions they find in Asia are far better than Australia, where for business executives taxes are high and wages low on a world scale.

In Asia, executives occupy a respected position in society; in Australia, success and its rewards attract envy and even abuse. As the many poor Filipinos in menial jobs support their economy, so too does Australia's elite diaspora support its home economy, investing in cheap (by world standards) property in Sydney and on the Gold Coast.

Sitting at home in Australia, it is easy to think that 'they will be back'. But what will attract Australia's managerial and professional elite back home?

Australia's high taxes used to pay for quality public services such as free university education and free medical treatment. Today, those benefits are under attack, if not already gone.

In any case, no Australian university ranks among the world's top 100 in internationally recognised surveys, and the standard of medical care in places such as Kuala Lumpur and Bangkok is very good.

What Australia's policy makers seem to be pinning their hopes on is the country's environment and lifestyle, which are certainly invaluable assets in an increasingly crowded and polluted region. But we need look no further than Adelaide for the ultimate value of a great environment to draw successful expatriates back home.

For decades, Adelaide has endured the same exodus of talent, to the eastern states, that Australia now suffers internationally. Like a spring winding down, the South Australian economy has lost much of its vigor along with its talented and dynamic exports.

Certainly, some will return for the beaches and the Barossa, but most Adelaide people who have made it in Melbourne return only for family birthdays or to take the kids to Kangaroo Island.

Make no mistake: Australia is suffering a reverse diaspora. Our 'huddled masses' are staying at home while adventurous engineers and managers are finding a new future overseas. In an international economy, propelled by innovation and intellectual property, this can only impoverish us.

Source BRW, 3–9 July 2003, p. 50.

Women in the work force

The growing role of women in the work force depends on improved childcare facilities, the availability of part-time work, job security after an absence for child-bearing, maternity leave, special parental leave and partners prepared to share home duties.

Working-class women are following the trend set by upwardly mobile career women and avoiding the 'mummy track' of staying at home and looking after children. It is estimated that 28 per cent of Australian women will never have children.[33] Singaporeans, despite government 'happy family' campaigns and child-relief incentives, also are having fewer children.[34] One in five Singaporean women with a higher degree now prefers to remain single, while in Japan, cultural traditions, lack of childcare facilities, long hours and after-work business entertainment force many women to make a stark choice between motherhood and career.[35]

Academic standards

The global proliferation of ever weaker and more diluted academic qualifications means that companies can no longer assume that because a person has graduated they are also qualified.[36] In the United Stares, 10 per cent of high school students cannot locate their home country on a blank map of the world.[37] In Australia, the increase in law degrees of varying quality has initiated discussion regarding the need for an independent bar exam.[38] According to some critics, grade inflation in Britain means that university degrees are now inferior to those of a decade ago. At one British university, for example, the proportion of electrical engineering graduates awarded first or upper second class honours degrees rose from 60 per cent to 74 per cent in five years.[39] In Hong Kong, employers are warned that it is up to them whether or not they recognise degrees obtained at overseas universities in Hong Kong. Furthermore, the perceived decline in English standards of Hong Kong graduates has forced employers to independently test graduate English skills and universities to introduce an internationally recognised English language test.[40]

Other environmental influences

Is it unethical for developed countries to recruit professionals such as doctors, nurses and teachers from developing countries?

Examples of other environmental influences that impact on HR planning include: demographic factors (for example, immigration, an ageing population, the number of women in the work force); the casualisation of the work force; employee literacy levels; skill shortages (the bursting of the Internet bubble has seen Australia go from a desperate shortage of computer science graduates to a surplus — an estimated 8000 computer professionals are now unemployed); acquisitions, mergers and divestures; deregulation; pay levels (low academic salaries in Australia have seen losses to the United States);[41] flexible work schedules; telecommuting; outsourcing; quality of life expectations; pollution (for example, Hong Kong is one of the world's most polluted and densely populated cities and so risks losing its attractiveness as a place to work);[42] government regulations (for example, the Australian government's ban on therapeutic cloning is reportedly causing the best stem cell scientists to seek work overseas); income tax levels (for example, the International Monetary Fund has warned that Australia's high marginal tax rates risk making the country uncompetitive and causing the loss of skilled workers);[43] and union attitudes (for example, unions in Australia, Hong Kong and the United States have opposed moves by companies to recruit overseas, seeing it as 'unpatriotic' and competition from cheap labour[44]).

Approaches to human resource planning

The human resource manager needs to be able to forecast the organisation's future HR requirements and determine from where they will be obtained. Three sets of forecasts are required:

- a forecast of the demand for human resources within the organisation
- a forecast of the supply of external human resources
- a forecast of the supply of human resources available within the organisation (see figure 2.4).

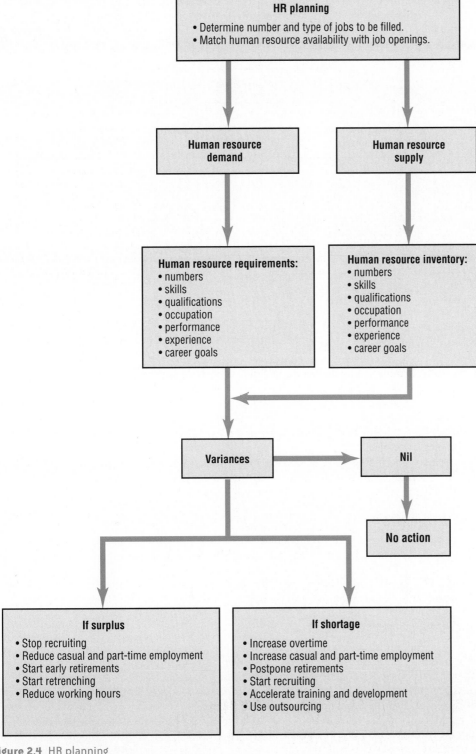

Figure 2.4 HR planning
Source Asia Pacific Management Co. Ltd, 2004.

These forecasts are an attempt to predict changes in the organisation's needs for human resources. They will be influenced by the organisation's strategic business objectives, the demand for its products and services, projected labour turnover, the quality and type of employees required and available, technological changes, financial resources and the general state of the economy. Although sophisticated techniques have been developed, HR forecasting is not an exact science and organisations continue to use elementary forecasting techniques such as the opinions of line managers and labour turnover statistics. Two approaches to HR forecasting planning can be identified — quantitative and qualitative (see figure 2.5).

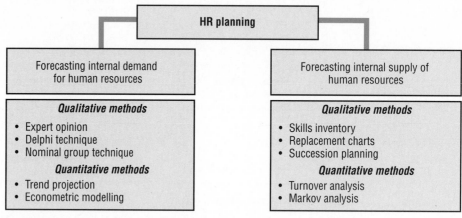

Figure 2.5 HR planning and HR forecasting

The quantitative approach

Quantitative HR forecasting uses statistical and mathematical techniques. It is primarily used by theoreticians and professional HR planners in large organisations.

The quantitative approach sees employees as numerical entities and groups them according to age, sex, experience, skills, qualifications, job level, pay, performance rating or some other means of classification. The focus is on forecasting HR shortages, surpluses and career blockages; its aim is to reconcile the supply and demand for human resources given the organisation's objectives.

Quantitative forecasting includes trend projection, econometric modelling and multiple predictive techniques. Such techniques often require specialised know-how, so the HR manager may have to rely on staff experts or outside consultants.

Trend projection

Trend projection, or time series analysis, makes predictions by projecting past and present trends into the future. Sales or production levels, for example, can be related to the organisation's demand for human resources. This technique is based on the assumption that the future will be a continuation of the past. Time series analysis is relatively simple and, provided historical data are available, can be performed quickly and inexpensively.[45]

Econometric modelling

Econometric modelling and multiple predictive techniques involve building complex computer models to simulate future events based on probabilities and multiple assumptions. Predictions are based on the statistical relationships discovered among the variables included in the models (for example, the relationship of sales, discretionary income and gross domestic product to employment). HR forecasts generally become more accurate when additional variables are considered. However, the cost of simultaneously considering numerous variables may be prohibitive. Furthermore, because they tend to rely heavily on past data, quantitative techniques may not be suitable in rapidly changing situations. Finally, no matter how sophisticated the technique, forecasts of HR needs are only estimates. Thus, the HR manager may be better advised to use simpler and more cost-effective approaches to HR forecasting, unless the time, effort and expense of a quantitative approach can be justified.

The qualitative approach

Qualitative HR forecasting uses expert opinion (usually a line manager) to predict the future (for example, the marketing manager will be asked to estimate the future personnel requirements for the marketing department). The focus is on evaluations of employee performance and promotability as well as management and career development. Estimates based on expert opinion, although not as sophisticated as the quantitative approach, are popular because they are simple, cheap and fast.

Qualitative HR forecasting The use of the opinions of experts to predict future HR requirements.

The Delphi technique

A refinement on this basic approach is the *Delphi technique*. A panel of experts, such as key line managers, make independent anonymous predictions in answer to questions relating to HR planning. The responses are analysed by the HR department and the confidential results are fed back to the experts along with another series of questions. The managers revise their original estimates in the light of this new information. This process is repeated until a consensus forecast is obtained.

The aim of the Delphi technique is to integrate the independent opinions of experts by eliminating personal influence and discussion. The technique is particularly useful when dealing with unknown or volatile situations where no precedents exist (for example, the 1997 return of Hong Kong to China) or where experts are physically dispersed or desire anonymity. There are two major disadvantages of the Delphi technique: it is time consuming and costly.

The nominal group technique

Another group-based forecasting method is the *nominal group technique*. After a problem has been presented, each team member, without discussion, independently generates as many solutions as possible and writes them down. Then, in turn, each member describes a solution to the group. No criticism or debate is undertaken, but team members can seek clarification. After all solutions have been presented, the group members silently and independently rank each proposed solution. The solution with the highest total ranking becomes the final decision.

The advantages of the nominal group technique are that it allows group members to meet without restricting the independence of their thinking, it produces more and better quality ideas than a traditional group, it is more effective than an individual in dealing with complex problems and it counterbalances any attempt by an individual to dominate the decision-making process.[46]

Forecasting human resource availability

Once the HR manager has estimated the HR needs of the organisation, the next challenge is to fill the projected vacancies. Present employees who can be promoted, transferred, demoted or developed make up the internal supply. The external supply consists of people who do not currently work for the organisation. Note that constraints may apply on the use of both internal and external labour supplies (for example, a 'promotion from within' policy, union restrictions, management preference and government regulations).

Forecasting the supply of internal human resources

Techniques for forecasting the internal supply of personnel include turnover analysis, skill inventories, replacement charts, Markov analysis and succession planning.

Turnover analysis

To accurately forecast the demand for labour, the HR manager must know how many people will leave the organisation. Labour turnover in an organisation may result from employee retirement, death, illness or disability, resignation, retrenchment or termination. The reasons why employees resign may be avoidable (for example, unfair treatment, poor supervision, lack of challenge) or unavoidable (for example, relocation to another state or overseas, return to university, serious illness). Employees may also quit because of dissatisfaction with their working conditions, pay and benefits, training and development, promotional opportunities, relationship with colleagues, and so on. Consequently, a detailed **turnover analysis** of why people leave the organisation is essential if meaningful information is to be obtained. Exit interviews giving information on employee reasons for leaving and labour turnover rates from past years are the best sources of information (see page 820 for more details on exit interviews). Turnover for each job classification and department should also be calculated because turnover can vary dramatically among various work functions and departments (see page 820 for more details on employee turnover and its calculation).

Skills inventories

The **skills inventory** is another method used to evaluate the internal supply of labour. This consolidates basic information on all employees within the organisation and permits the HR manager to:

- identify qualified employees for different jobs
- determine which skills are present or lacking in the organisation
- assess longer-term recruitment, selection and training and development requirements.

Information that can be listed in a skills inventory includes:

- personal data — age, sex, marital status, provided it is job-related (for example, young male actor)
- qualifications — education, job experience, training, licences (for example, driver's licence, electrician's licence)
- professional memberships — membership of professional associations (for example, Australian Human Resources Institute)
- skills — computer literacy
- languages — number and fluency
- employment history — jobs held, pay record
- test data — scores on psychological and employment tests (must be job-related)
- medical — health information (must be job-related)
- employee preferences — geographic location, management function (for example, marketing, production), type of job.

Skills inventories can be quite simple and manually kept, or detailed and maintained as part of an integrated HR information system (HRIS) (see figure 2.6). The method chosen depends on the HR objectives established for the skills inventory and the resources available. For example, Sims Group has a global database for its employees that enables management to identify employees with high potential and the required skills and experience for a position and to ensure that training and job exposure are tailored to meet individual needs.[47]

Employees also benefit from skills inventories. First, inventories provide a mechanism for filling positions by internal promotion, ensuring that existing employees are not overlooked. Second, selection for a more challenging position gives employees an opportunity to better fulfil their security, achievement, power and recognition needs (see figure 2.7).

SKILLS INVENTORY

Employee Name: John Pearson   Date: 4 November 2004

Number: HR 17923   Department: Human Resources

Division: Consumer Durables   Location: Sydney

Education

Degree	Major	Date
1. MBA	Marketing	2001
2. MA	Psychology	1997
3. BA	Japanese and Psychology	1996

Experience

From	To	Description
1. 2001	Present	HR Manager, Consumer Durables
2. 1999	2001	Sales Supervisor
3. 1998	1999	Sales Representative

Short courses

Course	Date
1. Leadership	2003
2. Job evaluation	2000
3. Sales training	1998
4. HRIS — vendor training	1998

Professional associations

1. Australian Human Resources Institute
2. Australian Psychological Society

Special licences

1. Registered Psychologist

Computer skills

1. Computer literate — spreadsheets, SPSS
2. PowerPoint

Other

- CEO's high-potential list
- Cash awards for outstanding performance, 1999, 2000, 2001, 2003, 2004

Languages

1. Japanese

Function preference

1. Marketing
2. HR
3. Business development

Location preference

1. Australia
   a. Sydney
   b. Melbourne
   c. Perth
2. Overseas
   a. Japan
   b. Hong Kong
   c. USA
   d. UK

Job preference

1. Product Manager, Consumer Durables
2. Sales Manager, Consumer Durables
3. HR Manager, Japan

Employee signature   HR Department

Date   Date

Figure 2.6 Skills inventory

Source Asia Pacific Management Co. Ltd, 2004.

SUCCESS REQUIREMENTS FOR A SKILLS INVENTORY SYSTEM

- **Clearly defined objectives.** If the skills inventory is not achieving the purposes for which it was designed, it should be revamped or scrapped, or it will degenerate into a wasteful and time-consuming activity.
- **Top management support.** If top management ignores the system, it will become a cosmetic activity that lacks credibility.
- **Employee acceptance.** Employees must perceive the system to benefit them through its ability to open up job opportunities within the organisation.
- **Current information.** Out-of-date information quickly makes a nonsense of any skills inventory system. Given the time and cost involved in updating, only essential data should be collected. Information overload can make a system unworkable because it can encourage managers to specify too many factors, with the result that many qualified employees are not considered because of out-of-date records.
- **Assured confidentiality.** Employees must be confident that all information in the system will be treated confidentially and accessed by authorised personnel only.
- **Accurate input.** All information must be checked for accuracy. Inaccurate information will quickly destroy the credibility of the system. Employees should be able to review their data files and have any wrong information corrected or deleted.
- **Use.** If managers do not use the system, it will quickly become a clerical exercise without benefit to the organisation or the individual employee. However, overuse by managers requesting information simply because it would be 'nice to know' can make the program uneconomical and increase the risk of loss of confidentiality.
- **Regular monitoring.** The performance of the system against its stated objectives must be regularly monitored to ensure that it remains efficient and effective.

Figure 2.7 Success requirements for a skills inventory system

Replacement charts

Replacement chart A visual representation of which employee will replace the existing incumbent in a designated position when it becomes vacant.

The **replacement chart** is less sophisticated than computerised skills inventories and is primarily used with technical, professional and managerial employees. Skills inventories are the source of data used in replacement charts. Typically, this information includes name, age, present position, performance rating, experience and an indication of promotion potential (see figure 2.8).

Replacement charts summarise this information in pictorial form for key managers so they can easily identify both the present incumbents and potential replacements (or lack of) for given positions. Appropriately designed and updated, replacement charts can give both the HR manager and line managers a visual overview of the organisation's human resources, helping identify potential problems in succession planning. A major criticism of replacement charts is that they focus attention on the skills and positions currently needed by the organisation and not those required for the future.[48]

Markov analysis

Markov analysis A mathematical technique used to forecast the availability of internal job candidates.

Markov analysis is a mathematical technique used to forecast the availability of internal job candidates. A matrix is developed to show the probability of an employee moving from one job to another or leaving the organisation. The Army, for example, needs to be able to calculate the likely replacement needs of its frontline infantry in battle conditions. The underlying assumption is that the departure or movement of personnel among various job classifications can be predicted from past movements. Unfortunately, any unexpected instability in the movements of employees or changes in job design reduce its usefulness. Furthermore, because quantitative techniques demand specialist expertise, and because Markov analysis requires at least 50 employees in any one job classification, its use is restricted to very large organisations.[49]

Succession planning

Succession planning A systematic, long-term career development activity that focuses on preparing high-potential employees to fill key professional and management positions so that the organisation can achieve its strategic objectives.

Succession planning is concerned with the filling of key professional and management vacancies. It stresses the development of high-potential employees and takes a long-term view of the organisation's HR needs. As such, it is a key driver for management commitment to human resource development and performance management. It makes use of replacement charts but generally expands on these to include additional information on current performance, promotability, developmental needs and long-term growth potential (see figures 2.9 and 2.10). More sophisticated plans may include job profiles that identify the essential competencies required for effective performance.[50] Westfield Holdings uses succession planning and executive development programs to ensure it has a cadre of world class managers competent in all aspects of the business and ready to assume major responsibilities.[51]

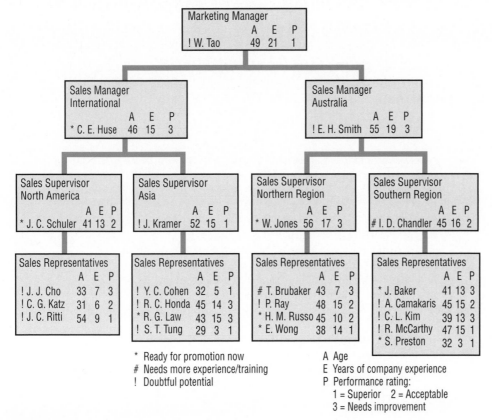

Figure 2.8 Determining human resource requirements
Source Asia Pacific Management Co. Ltd, 2004.

Board succession planning

The Board manages planning for its own succession with the assistance of the Nomination Committee. In doing so, the Board:

- considers the skill, knowledge and experience necessary to allow it to meet the strategic vision for the Group
- assesses the skill, knowledge and experience currently represented
- identifies any skill, knowledge and experience not adequately represented and agrees the process necessary to ensure a candidate is selected who brings those traits
- engages in a robust analysis of how Board performance might be enhanced both at an individual level and for the Board as a whole.

The Board engages the services of an independent recruitment organisation to undertake a search for suitable candidates.

Figure 2.9 Board succession planning at BHP Billiton
Source BHP Billiton Ltd, *Annual Report*, 2003, p. 38.

Performance pressures and the resultant massive downsizings, however, have led many organisations to deplete their managerial ranks and have made them less interested in formal succession planning and more willing to recruit talent from outside. Some experts furthermore argue that rapid changes in business and a mobile job market have made management development and succession superfluous. According to a McKinsey & Co. partner: 'Companies should think twice about spending a lot of time and money on someone who may walk out the door anyway. A healthier attitude today may be to consider the world as your bench.'[52] Consistent with this view, a survey found that almost half of all Australian companies do not have succession plans in place for their Chief Executive Officer and senior executives.[53]

SUCCESSION PLANNING CHART

Name: Rosanne F. Shapiro	Division: Australian Operation
	Location: Perth
Age: 34	Marital status: Not married
	Dependants: Nil
Date started	3 June 2000
Present position	Human Resource Manager Australia
	Promoted 2 August 2003
Current job size	Grade 8
Previous position	Compensation and Benefits Manager
	Appointed 3 June 2000
Other experience	2 years general HRM with Australian Heavy Industries Ltd
	2 years industrial relations experience with Widget Manufacturing Ltd
Qualifications	B. Com. (Qld) 1993, majors in accounting and economics
	MBA (Melb.) 1998, ranked 16th in class of 126 students
Professional associations	Chartered Member, Australian Human Resources Institute
Current performance rating	Superior
Previous performance rating	Superior
Promotability	At least 2 levels above present position
Experience required	Needs international exposure and head office experience in the United States
	Requires experience outside HR if to be considered for general management
Training and development	Company sales and marketing course, international management program at University of Michigan
Relocation	Free to locate interstate or internationally
Comments	Shapiro has general management potential. She has expressed interest in marketing and in working overseas. Awarded special performance bonus in 2000, 2001, 2002 and 2003 for outstanding achievement
Action	Transfer to the United States within 6 months. Arrange special 12-month project assignment in marketing in San Francisco head office and enrolment in international management program at University of Michigan. List as a candidate for product marketing manager in Pacific area head office (Hong Kong) on transfer of present incumbent. High-potential committee to review within 6 months of being transferred to the United States
Executive responsible for implementation	K. H. Law, Managing Director Australia

Figure 2.10 Succession planning chart, All Star Industries
Source Asia Pacific Management Co. Ltd, 2004.

Traditionally, managers have developed their own replacements, but this approach is often found wanting because of its ad hoc and subjective nature. Without a systematic approach, succession can be determined more by how skilful employees are at flattering their superiors than by the employees' objective qualifications.[54] Signs that there is a need for a strategic approach to succession planning include managers complaining that they have no suitable candidates when a vacancy occurs, high-potential employees deserting the organisation, a lack of women and minority candidates, a dependence on external searches to find suitable candidates, and ongoing complaints that promotion decisions are ad hoc, expedient and biased.[55] Effective development requires a systematic analysis of the manager's training and development needs, identifying appropriate learning experiences via job assignments, special projects and formal training programs. Some organisations now use assessment centres in conjunction with line management input to identify future senior managers and to assess their development needs.

The HR manager's role is to ensure that succession planning provides the organisation's future managers with the necessary preparation to successfully fill potential vacancies (see figure 2.11). This means having an effective performance appraisal system, needs-oriented training and development programs, and a corporate culture that fosters individual growth and promotion from within. Otherwise, succession planning becomes an academic exercise, producing only static charts and unwanted paperwork and causing line managers to complain that 'once they submit succession plans they never hear any more about them'.[56]

The traditional plan	The plan of the future

• Consider the key positions in today's organisation and the skills required in each.
• Take an inventory of the talent you have in the organisation right now.
• Decide whether you have a successor for each key position. Are they ready or not?
• Where is the development coaching required?
• Where is the recruitment of new talent the answer?
• *Warning*: Be careful you are not developing great executives for yesterday's business.
	• Use the traditional succession plan as a starting point.
	• Think about what your organisation will need to look like in three to five years. How is it different from today?
	• What new skills will you need in which position?
	• Who will be ready?
	• What does that view tell you about what actions to take today in:
	  – career management and retention of talent
	  – management development
	  – recruitment and release of talent
	  – performance management
	  – knowledge management.
	• Ask whether you have the systems in place to do this job.

Figure 2.11 Succession planning: changing face
Source N. Tabakoff, 'Replacing the boss in a wholistic way', *BRW*, 10 September 1999, p. 81.

Factors affecting the external supply of human resources

It is unrealistic to assume that every future vacancy can be filled from within an organisation. This is particularly true for disciplines where there is a global market for talent and the competition is fierce. Consequently, the organisation must tap into the external **labour market** (local, regional, interstate or international). The HR manager thus needs to be alert to demographic changes, such as an **ageing population**. The work forces of Australia, Hong Kong, Japan, Singapore, South Korea, Taiwan and the United States are all ageing. Already there are more than two million Australians aged 65 and over, and the number will double in the next 20 years.[57] In Hong Kong, 11 per cent of the population is 65 or older and this will

Labour market The geographical area from which employees are recruited for a particular job.

Ageing population Occurs when the number of older people increases relative to the number of young people in the population.

increase to 25 per cent in less than 30 years.[58] Japan, with more than 12 per cent of its population aged over 65 years, has become the world's most aged society, and this, combined with its extremely low birth rate, means its population is projected to shrink by 20 per cent over the next 50 years.[59] Europe too faces similar demographic problems. By 2020 more than one in three adults will be at least 60 years old.[60]

The average Singaporean worker aged over 40 years has no university education, is not proficient in English and is untrained. 'Older workers', says a former Executive Director of Singapore's National Productivity Board, 'will reduce potential output unless it is offset by productivity gain, industrial restructuring and technological progress.'[61] The ageing of the work force, combined with a global shortage of skilled personnel, will force employers to employ larger numbers of older workers. Fortunately, the use of technology will make work less physically demanding, permitting older people to work longer. 'An ageing work force', says one expert, 'will compel companies to rethink virtually every aspect of how they organise business in order to tap into the knowledge and experience of their older workers while keeping promotion opportunities open for younger employees.'[62] This has led to calls for the introduction of a government 'learning bonus' to encourage employee upskilling, more flexible working arrangements, the elimination of discriminatory workplace cultures that prevent older workers from participating in training, and an increase in the retirement age (especially given the predicted drain on government resources because of early retirement and longer life expectancies).[63]

Other changes occurring in the external labour market are increases in female **participation rates**, increases in school retention rates (less than half of all young Australians completed senior high school in 1985 compared with over 70 per cent today) and changes in the rate of immigration.[64] Foreigners, for example, make up 20 per cent of Singapore's work force.[65] Another trend is the rise in the use of child labour. The International Labour Organisation estimates that more than 127 million children in the Asia–Pacific region are forced to do work unsuitable for their age. Many are caught in the worst forms of child labour such as slavery, debt bondage, prostitution, pornography and forced recruitment for use in armed conflict.[66]

The casualisation of the work force

One dramatic trend is the casualisation of the work force in industrialised economies. Twenty-three million US workers, nearly 20 per cent of that country's total work force, now work part-time.[67] In Australia, 24 per cent of all employees are now casual workers.[68] Similarly, one in five workers in France is on a temporary or part-time contract, while in Britain, over 30 per cent of the work force is temporary or part-time.[69] Competitive pressures, changes in technology, the need for more flexible staffing, the increased use of outsourcing and unfavourable industrial relations legislation (which makes companies reluctant to hire permanent employees) have all contributed to this trend.[70] Critics argue that casualisation has disadvantaged workers (particularly young people and women) by marginalising them in terms of career paths, training and fringe benefits.[71] In addition, surveys indicate that most **contingent workers** would prefer to have full-time jobs.[72]

Outsourcing

Allied with the casualisation of the work force is the increasing use of strategic **outsourcing**. 'By strategically outsourcing and emphasising a company's core competencies', argue Quinn and Hilmer, 'managers can leverage their firm's skills and resources for increased competitiveness.'[73] According to Drucker, the restructuring of organisations has barely begun. Drucker claims that organisations will increasingly transfer work to the people, rather than moving people to the work. In addition, Drucker says, maintenance and clerical activities that do not offer opportunities for advancement into senior management or professional positions will be farmed out to external contractors.[74]

Outsourcing is becoming common in HRM, with some larger organisations actively outsourcing all but the most strategic HR activities. This has created a trend towards a greater use of contractors and a reduction in the number of permanent HR positions.[75] It is argued that this process is saving many HR professionals time and money, improving their

Your joint venture partner is an employer of child labour. The company argues that if it did not employ the children, their families would starve. They argue that you are imposing your moral values on them.

Participation rates Refers to the numbers of a particular group in the work force. For example, the increased participation rate of women in the work force is one of the most significant demographic changes to occur in recent times.

Contingent workers Temporary or part-time employees.

Outsourcing Subcontracting work to an outside company that specialises in and is more efficient at doing that kind of work. International outsourcing is called offshoring.

efficiency and enabling them to focus on competitive business issues.[76] Examples of outsourced functions include recruitment, benefits plan design, retirement services and HR record-keeping services. Faced with the continuing high cost of payroll, payroll taxes, fringe benefit taxes, Medicare levies and other expenses associated with full-time workers, organisations are under pressure to identify those activities that can be more productively performed externally (especially as labour cost savings of up to 80 per cent are possible).[77]

A survey of Australian employers showed that 90 per cent had outsourced some activities and more than half had outsourced cleaning, catering, transport and maintenance.[78] International law firm Baker & McKenzie has issued all its legal staff with digital dictaphones so that they can record documents and email them to a document service centre in the Philippines where the graduate operators transcribe, copy type, prepare PowerPoint presentations and edit documents, all at considerable cost savings.[79] Other Australian-based companies that reportedly have outsourced activities overseas include AXA, ANZ and GE Capital.[80]

Increasingly, many firms are reducing costs by utilising India's large pool of English-speaking, computer literate and relatively cheap university graduates. As a result, India is becoming the 'back office' to the world.[81] JP Morgan, Chase, Citigroup, Morgan Stanley, HSBC Holdings and AT Kearney all outsource much of their stock market research to India. Deloitte Consulting predicts that financial companies in the major industrialised nations will outsource some two million jobs worth more than US$100 billion to low-wage countries like India in the next five years.[82] Although regarded as necessary for competitive survival, outsourcing has faced union, public sector and political opposition (especially, when it involves the export of services).[83] Australia, however, because of its English-speaking work force, excellent telecommunications and low costs compared to Hong Kong, Japan and the United States, is favourably positioned to be a net importer of services.[84] Companies such as Hong Kong and Shanghai Bank, JP Morgan, UBS and Cathay Pacific have outsourced accounting and other back-room operations to Australia.[85]

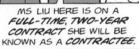

The reasons for organisations choosing to outsource include:

- *increased focus on core business* — organisations want to spend their discretionary management time and energy on the business of their business
- *cost and quality* — organisations assume that an external expert can do it better and more cheaply than they can do it internally
- *access to improved technology* — organisations with less sophisticated automation capabilities have greater tendencies to outsource than have organisations with better technology and automation capabilities
- *elimination of union problems* — outsourcing means that organisations may not have to worry about unions, restrictive work practices or demarcation problems.

Outsourcing by eliminating tasks that can be done more economically elsewhere, and by making organisations more cost-effective, appears to be the wave of the future. Nevertheless, outsourcing has generated criticism regarding reduced service, the poor quality of consultants, worsening industrial relations, production delays, the loss of essential personnel and excessive costs.[86]

Employees and unions often complain about outsourcing, especially to lower-cost, non-unionised suppliers or to foreign countries with lower wages and poorer working conditions, arguing that it destroys local jobs, reduces workers' pay and conditions and is anti-union. However, they welcome 'outsourced' jobs from high-cost locations such as Hong Kong, Japan and the United States.

International employees

Another recent change is that companies are increasingly seeking employees outside their domestic labour market. 'Chip' Goodyear (US) at BHP Billiton and John McFarlane (UK) at ANZ are examples of foreign executives heading major Australian corporations. Australian universities too are increasingly looking overseas to fill senior academic positions.[87] In contrast, Ansell International, the world's leading supplier of protective products to the health-care and industrial markets, employs only 60 people in its head office in Australia but over 5000 people in the Asia–Pacific region.[88] Labour exports earn China more than US$3 billion per year. It sends engineers, nurses, cooks, construction workers, garment makers, farmers and teachers to 150 countries including Singapore, South Korea, Japan and the United States. Likewise, JP Morgan, Lehman Brothers, Citigroup, Deutsche Bank, ABN Amro and HSBC are recruiting MBA graduates from India's top business schools to fill international vacancies.[89] Filling managerial and professional vacancies with Australians and Filipinos is also a convenient and relatively cheap solution for many companies in Asia.[90]

The Chairman of industrial giant ABB notes: 'We like to take Australians because their wages are half that of the Germans and they are quite well educated.'[91] Australian computer managers and financial analysts are also less expensive to hire than their counterparts in Hong Kong, Singapore and Japan. Indonesia, in turn, has some 2000 Filipinos working in managerial positions in its banks and financial institutions.[92] Taiwanese, Japanese and South Korean manufacturers are moving to the Philippines to escape exploding labour costs in their home markets and in previously favoured locations such as Singapore and Malaysia.[93] However, even the Philippines — with its abundant supply of low-cost, highly skilled, English-speaking workers — is experiencing competition from China and Vietnam where production costs can be as low as half as much.[94]

The union representing your Australian workers complains about the decision to outsource all manufacturing operations to a developing country. It says this is to avoid paying fair wages. The workers in the developing country argue that the union's complaints are an attempt to restrict competition and keep their living standards down.

***Lesley Lewis** is an education psychologist who studied in the United States and has been living in Hong Kong for over 19 years. She works in private practice as a personal, marital and family therapist and is a consultant and trainer to private business and government agencies.*

Practitioner speaks

Third-Cultured Kids

As cities and companies become increasingly international, a growing number of children are creating their own subculture. Often called TCKs (Third-Cultured Kids) or Global Nomads, these students can have a tremendously beneficial impact on the global community. They are 'raised in the margin of the mosaic' and learn to balance worlds from within.

Everyone who comes into contact with TCKs is affected. Parents must consider the impact of an international move on the family. But supporting TCKs during a transition is far more than just a family concern. Research shows the most common factor in overseas assignments that fail is family issues. Any company that relocates a family overseas must provide support — cross-cultural training, counselling and access to other support networks — if it is to ensure a successful transition to the new posting.

TCKs represent dozens of countries and a host of diverse cultures. Their numbers extend into the hundreds of thousands and are increasing each year on the back of easier travel and the globalisation of business and trade.

They tend to be highly mobile, culturally astute, educational achievers (the majority will attend university and receive an undergraduate degree), mature in their social skills, used to a privileged lifestyle, multilingual and able to adapt quickly to unfamiliar countries.

To an outsider a TCK's life may appear glamorous, but TCKs must overcome certain developmental challenges. Questions such as 'Who am I?', 'Where am I from?' and 'Where is home?' are constant. They often go unanswered, creating identity issues and a sense of rootlessness and restlessness. Commitment to decision making and 'feeling different from others' are other major factors.

Researching over 600 adolescents between the ages of 13 to 18 in eight different countries over the last two years, I have made some conclusions:

- Educational institutions must provide more programs and establish cross-cultural curriculums for TCKs. These students often enter school lonely, sad, angry and confused. And too often the TCKs enter or leave schools with little or no support.
- Just as importantly, companies must play a much larger role in the transition, adjustment and assimilation of their employees and families. Employers did not provide cross-cultural training to some 98 per cent of the families I worked with in my research. Spouses and children complained continuously over the lack of support from companies on pre- and post-arrival to assignments. Companies ignore this issue at their peril.

TCKs bring a deep knowledge from within and a special ability to compare international and local issues. They are the future cross-culturalists and, hopefully, future politicians, diplomats, executives and educators. TCKs have a deep understanding of human rights. They encounter a differing lifestyle compared to their monocultural peers. We can draw on their global experiences and incorporate this knowledge into our personal and professional lives. In doing so, we will reap unbelievable rewards and a true sense of satisfaction.

Lesley Lewis

Technological advances in communications and transportation and increased labour mobility have facilitated the internationalisation of business. A manufacturing company can now locate anywhere where there is an abundant supply of labour. Amcor now has 50 per cent of its total sales generated outside Australia, with acquisitions and greenfield developments in Europe, North America and Asia.[95] Companies clearly are no longer locked into using more expensive, less skilled and less productive domestic labour. Multinational electronics firms are starting to leave Malaysia for countries with cheaper labour such as China, Thailand and the Philippines.[96] US companies are shifting engineering and other technology-related jobs to China, Ireland, India and the Philippines.[97] Labour is now a global resource. The Singapore government is encouraging companies to relocate their labour-intensive operations to Malaysia and Indonesia.[98] Singaporean companies, however, face an acute shortage of managers who are prepared to relocate and who are capable of running an overseas operation.[99]

This Letter to the Editor provides a provocative viewpoint. Do you agree? See 'What's your view?' on page 67.

Letter to the Editor

Companies should be able to import labour without restrictions

Dear Editor,

In my view, governments place too many restrictions on the ability of organisations to attract the best people from around the world. As a CEO of a major Australian company, I have no choice but to watch as we continue to lose some of our best people to places like the United States and Asia. Many of these employees are attracted by better pay and the opportunity of rapid advancement in places like Silicon Valley. Others are attracted by the experience to be gained from foreign assignments in exotic and interesting locations.

(continued)

While I'm happy for people to advance their careers as they see fit, I'm hamstrung by government regulations and bureaucratic red tape that inhibit me from supplying my organisation with the best people wherever I can find them. Whether it's politically imposed constraints such as immigration quotas, the petty-mindedness of government bureaucrats who fear that overseas workers may overstay their work visas or the high income taxes faced by employees in Australia, I cannot obtain the kinds of people I need at the time I need them.

Consider good IT staff, for example. Our universities produce a fixed number of IT graduates each year, yet supply is far short of demand for competent IT graduates. Why? Because the federal government cannot accurately predict the demand for IT graduates four and five years out from their graduation and so swings between overfunding and underfunding university courses from IT to teaching. Further, I find that the Australian university IT graduates I do interview often lack key verbal and written communication skills and fundamental IT competencies. I'm wondering whether some of these students should have been admitted to university in the first place.

So, the government and universities have a lot to answer for. In funding IT places, the government simply takes an educated guess about future economic and industrial conditions and funds universities accordingly. It is constrained by political realities from providing the IT graduates we need, and it knows that it will face a political backlash if it reduces funding for low-demand disciplines like the arts and some of the less-vocational sciences. At the same time, the universities accept marginally qualified entrants and are often years behind in teaching current IT competencies.

This makes very little sense to me. If our companies are to match the best in the world, we need the best people at the right time and at the right price. We are living in a globalised world where the move to free trade has helped to bring about times of great prosperity. People want freedom, whether it's freedom of religion or freedom to use their talents anywhere in the world. We need to deregulate the movement of people between one place and another, and also seek to abolish those industrial relations laws that make us pay a range of salaries and benefits out of kilter with the rest of the world.

I hope that other employers will join with me in getting government out of our pockets so that together we can become world competitive and join the global movement towards freer labour markets. We all stand to benefit, as do the countries in which we operate.

A concerned CEO

Source David Poole, University of Western Sydney.

Requirements for effective HR planning

Should Australia allow the import and employment at lower rates of pay of domestic helpers from countries such as China, Indonesia, India and the Philippines to help overcome the problems of work–family conflict?

Given that the success of an organisation ultimately depends on how well its human resources are managed, HR planning will continue to grow in importance. However, there is a danger that it may become a fad, failing because it cannot satisfy management's unrealistic expectations. Such expectations may be fuelled by planning theorists who advocate sophisticated analytical techniques. Mackay, for example, argues that 'planners, especially those trained in the quantitative approach, may be tempted to create esoteric systems that are incompatible with the practical needs of line managers'.[100]

Successful HR planning requires HR managers to ensure that:
• HR personnel understand the HR planning process
• top management is supportive
• the organisation does not start with an overly complex system
• the communications between HR personnel and line management are healthy

- the HR plan is integrated with the organisation's strategic business plan
- there is a balance between the quantitative and qualitative approaches to HR planning.[101]

Summary

HR planning is an important part of an organisation's HR information system. This is because an HR plan affects all HR activities and acts as the strategic link between organisational and HRM objectives. An effective HR planning process is essential to optimising the utilisation of an organisation's human resources. The alternative is reactive decision making in a climate of increased risk and uncertainty, with the HR department contributing less to the achievement of the organisation's strategic business objectives.

An effective HR planning system is essential for an organisation to be proactive, because such information allows managers to make strategic decisions that ensure optimum performance. The HR manager should not forget, however, that an HR plan that is overly complex and generates masses of data is unproductive. A measure of the effectiveness of HR planning is whether or not the right people are available at the right time. This can only be achieved when HR planning is fully integrated into the organisation's strategic business plan. Charles Sturt University's Alan Fish comments: 'Given that human resource planning is the cornerstone of all HRM activity, it is astounding how many organisations still perceive the activity as little more than a headcount.'[102] This suggests that HR managers have yet to demonstrate that HR planning is relevant to both line managers and the successful achievement of the organisation's objectives.

Thirty interactive Wiley Web Questions are available to test your understanding of this chapter at **www.johnwiley.com.au/ highered/hrm5e** *in the student resources area*

review questions

1. What impact is globalisation having on labour demand and supply?
2. What is outsourcing? Why is it so controversial?
3. Describe the HR planning process.
4. What is the point of undertaking HR planning when there is so much change and uncertainty in the business world?
5. Which environmental factors will have the greatest impact on HR planning in the next five years?
6. How can HR planning help an organisation to achieve its strategic business objectives?
7. What is succession planning? Why is it important for an organisation to use succession planning?
8. What major demographic changes are likely to affect organisations in the near future? How can HR planning help organisations to successfully deal with these changes?
9. What can an organisation do when it is faced with (a) a surplus of human resources and (b) a shortage of human resources?
10. Do you agree that downsizing is the result of poor HR planning? Explain your answer.

environmental influences on HR planning

Identify and discuss the key influences from the model (figure 2.12 shown opposite) that have significance for HR planning.

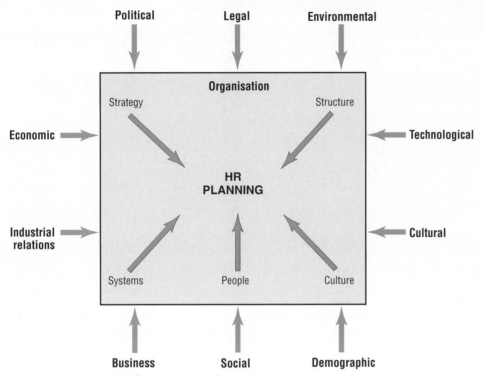

Figure 2.12 Environmental influences on HR planning

soapbox

What do you think? Conduct a mini survey of class members, using the questionnaire below. Critically discuss the findings.

1.	Downsizing allows companies to get rid of their 'dead wood'.	YES	NO
2.	International outsourcing destroys Australian jobs.	YES	NO
3.	The use of child labour is appropriate in developing economies.	YES	NO
4.	Older workers are inflexible.	YES	NO
5.	The casualisation of the labour force discriminates against women.	YES	NO
6.	High wages for low-skilled work is unfair.	YES	NO

online exercise

Conduct an online search for information on one of the following topics: child labour, older workers, outsourcing, casualisation of the work force, female workers or 'talent war'. Write a 300-word report on your findings. Include the web addresses that you found useful.

ethical dilemma

Jet Red's cabin crew problem[103]

'OK, we agree that the best way to get flexibility and reduce costs is to outsource all cabin crew, but how practical is this?', asked Alan Balkin, Jet Red's Managing Director.

'It makes sense', interrupted Bill Armstrong, Operations Manager. 'Our present cabin staff belong to a different era. They are used to tightly defined jobs, uniform pay rates and guaranteed job security. They are a bunch of prima donnas. We need more flexibility and more concern for the customer. If cabin crew would clean the planes, it would give us greater flexibility and save a bundle in wages and cleaning costs.'

Stan Vines, Marketing Manager, added, 'Our present crews don't meet with our marketing approach. Our in-flight service is terrible. It is a constant source of customer complaint. We want to use our crew as a strategic marketing tool — create a fresh young, dynamic image. The average age of our cabin crew is 34, which means we have some real geriatrics who don't meet our requirements.'

'I didn't hear that', snapped Linda Church, HR Manager.

'Like it or not, Linda, it's true. Our cabin crews are renowned for being old, fat and ugly. Everyone knows our "old boilers" can't compete with the "Singapore Girl". Survey after survey shows that our biggest-spending customers prefer young, attractive flight attendants. If we are going to get Jet Red more customers, we have to do something about the cabin crews', Stan retorted, his face flushed with anger.

'Well, we can't just sack them', growled Linda. 'Some of these people have given more than 20 years of loyal service.'

'Look Linda, times change. Loyalty is a great word but it doesn't exist anymore. We are going broke. We need to focus on what employees bring to the table now, not what they did in the past. How do you expect me to get customers if we don't offer them what they want?', countered Stan.

'There is one other consideration', said Bill.

'What's that?', sighed Alan.

'All cabin crew personnel are unionised. The Flight Attendants Union would never let us outsource. They are going broke. They need every member they can get.'

Alan slumped in his seat and sighed 'Terrific'.

Linda shifted nervously in her chair, then spoke. 'Alan, I suggest that until we can get our heads around this we freeze all recruitment. Let's investigate the possibility of a voluntary early retirement program to get the immediate numbers down. At the same time, we need to explore the use of part-time or casual staff and maybe even hiring overseas. We know we can get flight attendants in Thailand for about $9000 a year and New Zealand for $24 000.'

'What do our flight attendants earn?', asked Alan.

'Around $50 000 a year, which is about $5000 more than Qantas pays', answered Linda.

'Linda, anything that sheds jobs and makes us more competitive is worth looking at. What do the rest of you think of Linda's proposals?'

Discussion questions

1. What ethical issues are raised in this case?
2. If you were the HR Manager for Jet Red, how would you go about solving this dilemma?

case studies

Western University

Western University is the product of a merger between 115-year-old Sandstone University and 10-year-old Newtown Institute of Technology. Sandstone University has a traditional academic emphasis, which is reflected in its courses of study. In contrast, Newtown Institute of Technology offers applied programs of study oriented to the needs of business.

Part of the amalgamation is for the School of Economics at Sandstone University to combine with Newtown's School of Business. The School of Economics teaches economics, economic history, statistics, commercial law and accounting. Students major in either economics or accounting. Reflecting its different background and focus, the School of Business offers majors in accounting, marketing and HRM. Currently, the School of Economics employs 35 academics and has 700 students. Sandstone's student body is predominantly full-time and young (the average age is 21), while Newtown's is predominantly part-time, mature-age students (the average age is 33).

Sandstone University staff are highly qualified, with 90 per cent holding a PhD. All see themselves as research-oriented academics. Only a few have had any work experience outside of academia. Staff at the university are upset at being merged with a teaching university, and fear that their high academic standards and research will suffer.

Newtown staff are not so well qualified academically (only 20 per cent have a PhD). Most, however, have had extensive work experience. Institute staff take great pride in their reputation for teaching excellence. They aim to educate their students to go into the 'real world'. It is felt that Sandstone staff are too theoretical and divorced from the needs of business.

It is anticipated that the newly created School of Business will produce an increase in student enrolments of 20 per cent per year for the next three years.

Discussion questions

1. To formulate an HR plan, what further information would you need to gather about:
   (a) the existing academic staff and student body?
   (b) future students?
   What other information would you need to gather about Western University and its new School of Business?
2. How would you estimate the internal supply of academic staff in each department?
3. How would you predict the number of academic staff that will be needed in each department?
4. What HRM problems could be expected to arise in this merger? As HR consultant to Western University, what would you recommend (and do) to prevent or overcome such problems?

Keeping jobs at home[104]

Fiona Elliott, Manager for Information Technology, spoke: 'Look, the government's facing a budget deficit of $300 million. If we outsource our call centre work to India or the Philippines we can reduce our labour costs by at least one-third. We have a moral responsibility to the taxpayers of this state to operate as efficiently as possible.'

Simon Prystay, Director of Education, glared at Fiona. 'Yes Fiona, and we have to be realistic. Why should Australian jobs be shipped offshore to India or the Philippines? The government's concern is with the welfare of Australian workers. Why should Australian taxpayers' money end up in the pockets of foreign workers?'

Fiona snapped back, 'For the very good reasons that the work will be done at a much lower cost and with much higher quality results!'

Simon smiled. 'Fiona, wake up. How many politicians do you know who will be prepared to stand up and publicly declare that they are in favour of exporting Australian jobs? Outsourcing may be OK in the private sector, but in the public sector life is more complicated. Can you imagine the reaction of the unions when the Minister announces that the department is going to do away with 200 jobs?'

'OK, I take your point. But given the size of the government's deficit it really has to face up to the alternatives — cut services or increase taxes. The whole aim of outsourcing is to maximise value by saving money and improving services.'

Discussion questions

1. Who do you agree with? Why?
2. Should governments ban the outsourcing of jobs to foreign countries? Explain your answer.

suggested readings

Beardwell, I. and Holden, L., *Human Resource Management*, 3rd edn, Prentice Hall, London, 2001, ch. 4.

CCH, *Australian Master Human Resources Guide*, CCH, Sydney, 2003, ch. 3.

Clark, R. and Seward, J., *Australian Human Resources Management: Framework and Practice*, 3rd edn, McGraw-Hill, Sydney, 2000, ch. 3.

De Cieri, H. and Kramer, R., *Human Resource Management in Australia*, McGraw-Hill, Sydney, 2003, ch. 5.

Fisher, C. D., Schoenfeldt, L. F. and Shaw, J. B., *Human Resource Management*, 5th edn, Houghton Mifflin, Boston, 2003, ch. 3.

Ivancevich, J. M. and Lee, L. S., *Human Resource Management in Asia*, McGraw-Hill, Singapore, 2002, ch. 3.

Mondy, R. W., Noe, R. M. and Premeaux, S. R., *Human Resource Management*, 8th edn, Prentice Hall, Upper Saddle River, NJ, 2002, ch. 4.

Nankervis, A. R., Compton, R. L. and Baird, M., *Strategic Human Resource Management*, 4th edn, Thomas Nelson, Melbourne, 2002, ch. 3.

online references

www.hrps.org
www.nytimes.com/world
www.shrm.org
www.shrm.org.hrmagazine
www.stats.bls.gov/ocohome.htm
www.workforceonline.com

end notes

1. Foster's Brewing Group Ltd, *Annual Report*, 2002, Melbourne, p. 26.
2. M. Gardner and G. Palmer, *Employment Relations*, 2nd edn, Macmillan, Melbourne, 1997, pp. 269–72.
3. R. Maurer, 'Stop! Downsizing doesn't work', *Canadian Manager*, vol. 24, no. 1, 1999, p. 11.
4. W. H. Clough, *Clough Annual Report*, 2000, p. 6.
5. J. Byrne, 'The search for the young and gifted', *Business Week*, 4 October 1999, p. 64; and N. Way, 'Talent war', *Business Review Weekly*, 18 August 2000, pp. 64–70.
6. Survey conducted by Andersen Consulting and Economist Intelligence Unit cited in J. Byrne, op. cit., p. 67.
7. R. Gottliebsen, 'Star fever', *Shares*, January 2000, pp. 32–5.
8. Public Policy Institute of California study reported in *Asia Inc.*, October 1999, p. 7; M. A. Hamlin, 'Brain drain', *Far Eastern Economic Review*, 4 May 2000, p. 40; C. Prystay, 'Malaysia suffers tech brain drain', *Asian Wall Street Journal*, 30 November 2000, pp. 1, 6; and D. Narine, 'Asia faces shortage of skilled IT workers', *South China Morning Post — Technology*, 27 March 2001, p. 1.
9. P. Cleary, 'Business failing the skill test', *Australian Financial Review*, 19 August 2002, p. 1.
10. C. Murphy, 'Half a million workers short', *Australian Financial Review*, 21–22 June 2003, p. 8.
11. M. Dwyer, 'Alarming drop in graduate jobs', *Australian Financial Review*, 18 February 2003, p. 13.
12. R. Cheung, 'Talented workers stream overseas', *South China Morning Post*, 27 July 2002, p. 7.
13. 'Workforce lacking skills', *South China Morning Post*, 9 September 2002, p. 6.
14. Reported in Agence France-Presse, 'Workers lack skills for hi-tech economies', *South China Morning Post*, 15 June 2000, p. 14.
15. M. Shari, 'A brave new economy for Singapore', *Business Week*, 24 April 2000, p. 23.
16. D. Ulrich, 'Strategic and human resource planning: linking customers and employees', *Human Resource Planning*, vol. 15, no. 2, 1992, p. 47.
17. J. T. Ralph and E. T. Kunkel, 'Directors' report', *Annual Report 1996*, Foster's Brewing Group Ltd, Melbourne, pp. 7–8.
18. J. Gough, 'Chairman's report', *Annual Report 1996*, Pacific Dunlop Ltd, Melbourne, pp. 2–3.
19. Reuters, 'Microsoft's Indian recruitment puts US jobs under a cloud', *South China Morning Post*, 4 July 2003, p. B7.
20. M. Wong, 'Never too old to move on', *Sunday Morning Post*, 29 April 2001, p. 3; D. Kitney and N. Chenoweth, 'Global talent hard to lure when dollar keeps falling', *Australian Financial Review*, 12–16 April 2001, p. 3, The Guardian, 'Drugs, sex and sweat fuel US black market', *South China Morning Post*, 3 May 2003, p. A11; and A. Dhillon, 'India's outsourcing just a phone call away', *South China Morning Post*, 31 May 2003, p. B14.
21. D. Macken, 'A postcard from Australia's intellectual elite', *Australian Financial Review*, 28 September 1999, p. 16.
22. P. Johnson, 'The US, not the UN, speaks for humanity', *Forbes Global*, 9 June 2003, p. 14.
23. A. Lee, 'British schools want teachers from Singapore', *Straits Times*, 5 August 2000, p. 4; and C. Kennedy, 'UK looks abroad for skilled workers', *Sunday Morning Post*, 10 September 2000, p. 8.
24. B. Andrews, 'America calls', *Business Review Weekly*, 26 June–2 July 2003, p. 77; E. Wynhausen, 'Brain drain dumbs universities', *Weekend Australian*, 22–23 July 2000, p. 3; L. Cheung, 'Leadership crisis looms as senior academics leave', *South China Morning Post*, 9 September 2000, p. 5; and K. Towers, 'Who's gobbling up our legal talents?', *Australian Financial Review — Special Report*, 12 July 2000, p. 15.
25. J. Merritt, 'Brain drain at the B-schools', *Business Week*, 5 March 2001, p. 39.
26. L. Creffield, 'Brighter prospects lure many overseas for good', *South China Morning Post*, 2 March 2000, p. 15; and L. Creffield, 'Pursuit of big dollars speeds up brain drain', *South China Morning Post*, 4 December 2000, p. 12.
27. D. Barber, 'Immigration targets raised as brain drain takes its toll', *South China Morning Post*, 10 February 2001, p. 14.
28. H. Sender, 'India is combating brain drain with hefty pay, other perks', *Asian Wall Street Journal*, 18–20 August 2000, pp. 1, 4; M. Warner, 'The Indians of Silicon Valley', *Fortune*, 29 May 2000, pp. 57–65; and N. Chanda, 'The tug of war for Asia's brains', *Far Eastern Economic Review*, 9 November 2000, pp. 38–44.
29. S. N. M. Abdi, 'Indians weigh up the future, and leave', *South China Morning Post*, 17 January 2003, p. 10.
30. Knight Ridder, 'Luring back brainpower no easy task', *South China Morning Post*, 4 May 2000, p. 31; and C. Arrist, 'How the war on terror is damaging the brain pool', *Business Week*, 19 May 2003, p. 68.
31. Y. Sharma, 'Europe turns to China's IT staff', *South China Morning Post*, 11 April 2000, p. 19.
32. A. Cornell, 'Finance houses pay for being out of touch', *Australian Financial Review*, 26 March 2001, p. 9.
33. M. Gunn, 'The big baby bust', *Weekend Australian*, 20–21 November 1999, pp. 19, 22.
34. B. Porter, 'Lion city impotent over growth rate', *South China Morning Post*, 8 November 1999, p. 23; and M. H. Chua, 'Singapore is short of 200 000 babies', *Straits Times*, 20 October 1999, p. 3.
35. Agence France-Presse, 'Goh warns of decline in population', *South China Morning Post*, 14 October 1999, p. 13; and H. W. French, 'For women a struggle', *International Herald Tribune*, 25 July 2003, p. 4.
36. L. Yeung, 'City U sets lowest teacher hurdle', *South China Morning Post — Education*, 21 September 2002, p. 3.
37. J. Schmid, 'Low world education ranking leaves Germans stunned', *International Herald Tribune*, 7 February 2003, p. 5.
38. C. Merritt, 'Hearsay', *Australian Financial Review*, 9 May 2003, p. 58.

39. Research by the Higher Education Funding Council reported in Y. Sharma, 'Dumbing down a matter of degree', *South China Morning Post*, 26 July 2003, p. E2.

40. G. Cheung, 'HK English students two grades below peers', *South China Morning Post*, 7 October 2002, p. 1; Editorial, 'English test not enough', *South China Morning Post*, 30 July 2002, p. 15.

41. C. Martin, 'High debt a factor in brain drain', *Australian Financial Review*, 27 March 2003, p. 9.

42. B. Gilley and B. Dolven, 'Crunch time ahead', *Far Eastern Economic Review*, 9 March 2000, pp. 22–6; and S. Rabitaille, 'Hong Kong's competitiveness clouded by air pollution', *Asian Wall Street Journal*, 4 January 2000, p. 6.

43. Q. Hardy, 'Hello brain, goodbye rules', *Forbes Global*, 16 October 2000, pp. 110–11; B. Pleasant, 'Cloning ban driving top scientists overseas', *Australian Financial Review*, 8 April 2003, p. 9; M. Mellish, 'Cut taxes or lose skilled workers: IMF', *Australian Financial Review*, 20 September 2003, p. 1; and G. Maslen, 'Interest in Aussie tertiary IT courses falls dramatically', *South China Morning Post*, 29 March 2003, p. E6.

44. J. Boyle, 'Qantas hires abroad for long-term growth', *Australian Financial Review*, 28 August 2000, p. 7; K. C. Ng, 'Shortage of educated workers looms', *South China Morning Post*, 14 October 2000, p. 6; and A. Dhillon, op. cit., p. B14.

45. For a practical example in the hotel industry, see L. R. Gomez-Meija, D. B. Balkin and R. L. Cardy, *Managing Human Resources*, 3rd edn, Prentice Hall, Englewood Cliffs, NJ, 2001, pp. 161–2.

46. S. L. McShane and M. A. Von Glinow, *Organizational Behavior*, McGraw-Hill, Boston, 2000, pp. 358–9; S. P. Robbins, *Organizational Behavior*, 9th edn, Prentice Hall, Upper Saddle River, NJ, 2001, p. 245; and J. M. Ivancevich, *Human Resource Management*, 8th edn, McGraw-Hill, Boston, 2001, pp. 135–6.

47. Simsmetal Ltd, *Annual Report*, 2000, p. 23.

48. N. Gore, 'Managing talent replaces static charts in a new era of succession planning', *Canadian HR Reporter*, 11 September 2000, p. 17.

49. For further information, see D. M. Atwater, 'Workforce forecasting', *Human Resource Planning*, vol. 18, no. 4, 1995, pp. 50–3; and J. M. Ivancevich, op. cit., pp. 136–7.

50. K. M. Nowack, 'The secrets of succession', *Training and Development*, vol. 48, no. 11, 1994, p. 50.

51. Westfield Holdings Ltd, *Annual Report 2002*, p. 4.

52. R. Felton, quoted in J. A. Byrne, J. Reingold and R. A. Melcher, 'Wanted: a few good CEOs', *Business Week*, 11 August 1997, p. 41.

53. Korn Ferry International Survey of Boards of Directors reported in A. Main, 'Lack of chiefs in waiting', *Australian Financial Review*, 27 June 1997, p. 87.

54. T. A. Judge and G. R. Ferris, 'The elusive criterion of fit in human resource staffing decisions', *Human Resource Planning*, vol. 15, no. 4, 1992, pp. 47–67.

55. W. J. Rothwell, 'Putting success into your succession planning', *Journal of Business Strategy*, vol. 23, no. 3, 2002, p. 33.

56. C. Getty, 'Planning successfully for succession planning', *Training and Development*, November 1993, p. 32.

57. L. Russell, 'World order at the mercy of ageing populations', *Business Review Weekly*, 14 July 2000, p. 56.

58. P. Segal, 'Hong Kong Solutions', *Far Eastern Economic Review*, 20 March 2003, p. 14.

59. H. Nakame, 'Japan's aging population puts imperative on tax, pension reform', *Nikkei Weekly*, 7 March 1994, p. 1; and H. Restall, 'Japan and the Gaijin', *Asian Wall Street Journal*, 11 October 2000, p. 10.

60. G. Koretz, 'Europe faces a retiree crisis', *Business Week*, 15 May 2000, p. 18.

61. Koh Juan Kiat, quoted in Salil Tripathi, 'Singapore's cost crunch', *Asia Inc.*, June 1995, p. 53; and J. Lloyd-Smith, 'Singapore's quickly aging sector prompts calls for fast solutions', *South China Morning Post — Business*, 9 February 2001, p. 8.

62. C. Farrell, 'The economics of aging', *Business Week*, 19 September 1994, p. 50; and '90-year life span may be the norm by 2030', *South China Morning Post*, 10 February 2001, p. 16.

63. C. Murphy, 'Call to train older workers', *Australian Financial Review*, 9 May 2003, p. 11; C. Fox, 'Retirement poses risk of brain drain', *Australian Financial Review*, 6 May 2003, p. 59; and C. Murphy, 'OECD wants a stop to early retirement', *Australian Financial Review*, 7 February 2003, p. 23.

64. H. Van Leevwen, 'Asian born help change Australia', *Australian Financial Review*, 25 June 1996, p. 8.

65. Murray Hiebert, 'It's a jungle out there', *Far Eastern Economic Review*, 25 April 1996, p. 58.

66. Agence France-Presse, 'Child workers put at 246 billion', *International Herald Tribune*, 20 February 2003, p. 6.

67. E. McShulskis, 'Permanent part-timers', *HR Magazine*, September 1996, p. 19.

68. M. Wooden, 'The Australian labour market, March 1996: Main points', *Australian Bulletin of Labour*, vol. 22, no. 1, 1996, p. 2.

69. J. Templeman, 'A continent swimming with temps', *Business Week*, 8 April 1996, p. 22.

70. H. Van Leevwen, 'A trend to temporary employment', *Australian Financial Review*, 18 November 1996, p. 8; S. Long, 'More men finding part-time work', *Australian Financial Review*, 12 July 1996, p. 4; and M. Lawson, 'Temporaries take on a permanent look', *Australian Financial Review*, 13 August 1996, p. 3.

71. J. Burgess, 'Workforce casualisation in Australia', *International Employment Relations Review*, vol. 2, no. 1, July 1996, pp. 33–53.

72. J. Aley, 'The temp biz boom : why its good', *Fortune*, 16 October 1995, p. 40; and S. Bagwell, 'Employers are having the part time of their lives', *Australian Financial Review*, 10 July 1996, p. 17.

73. J. B. Quinn and F. G. Hilmer, 'Strategic outsourcing', *Sloan Management Review*, vol. 35, no. 4, 1994, p. 43.

74. P. Drucker, '1990s: The futures that have happened already', *Boardroom Reports*, 15 December 1989, p. 8.

75. J. Arnato, 'Contracting demand', *HR Monthly*, June 2002, p. 46.

76. J. C. Spee, 'Addition by subtraction', *HR Magazine*, March 1995, p. 38.

77. E. Conners, 'Protests fail to stem outsourcing', *Australian Financial Review*, 5 May 2003, p. 49.

78. S. Long, op. cit., p. 14.

79. J. Eyers, 'Long arm of the law spread word aboard', *Australian Financial Review*, 10 April 2003, p. 3.

80. M. Lawson, 'Making the switch from Dubbo to Delhi', *Australian Financial Review — Special Report*, 20 March 2003, p. 2.

81. Reuters, 'Back office boom spurs India's confidence as a global powerhouse', *South China Morning Post*, 1 May 2003, p. 86.

82. H. Bray, 'Outsourcing hits Wall Street', *International Herald Tribune*, 7 May 2003, p. 11; and Bloomberg, 'Multinationals call on India's low cost talent', *South China Morning Post*, 9 August 2003, p. B14.

83. S. Kitchens, 'Outsources? Out of the question!', *Forbes Global*, 12 May 2003, p. 16; and R. Stewart and S. Nagarajan, 'India graduates from the back office', *International Herald Tribune*, 8 August 2003 p. B2.

84. I. Thomas, 'Qantas offshore accounting upsets union', *Australian Financial Review*, 13 February 1998, p. 39; and E. Conners, op. cit., p. 49.

85. R. Stewart, 'JP Morgan moves staff to Asia to cut costs', *International Herald Tribune*, 9 April 2003, p. 81; and A. Grigg, 'Sydney to become help centre of UBS universe', *Australian Financial Review*, 25 July 2003, p. 54.

86. J. Mace, 'Anyone home?', *HR Monthly*, February 2001, pp. 20–6.

87. G. Maslen, 'Local hopefuls, crowded out of academic jobs', *Campus Review*, 22–28 February 1996, p. 5.

88. *Annual Report 1996*, Pacific Dunlop Ltd, Melbourne, p. 8.

89. M. O'Neill, 'SARS curbs threaten lucrative labour exports', *South China Morning Post*, 10 May 2003, p. B18; and Bloomberg, op. cit., p. B14.

90. P. Hartcher, 'Play the Asian way — patiently and viciously', *Australian Financial Review*, 29 October 1996, p. 15.

91. P. Barnevik, quoted in P. Seidlitz and D. Murphy, 'Don't go crying to embassy', *Sunday Morning Post*, 16 June 1996, p. 3.

92. T. Thomas, 'Asian brokers tap into Australia's talent bank', *Business Review Weekly*, 23 December 1996, pp. 84–5.

93. M. Clifford and S. V. Brull, 'The Philippines' new face', *Business Week*, 1 April 1996, pp. 38–41.

94. M. Clifford and S. V. Brull, op. cit., p. 41.

95. A. D. Lapthorne, 'Chairman's address', Amcor Ltd, Sydney, 25 October 1996, p. 3.

96. Reuters, 'Rising costs spark exodus', *Hong Kong Standard — Business*, 3 June 1997, p. 6.

97. J. Bjorhus, 'US engineering exodus raises white collar fears', *South China Morning Post*, 23 October 2002, p. B1.

98. Tan Chwee-Huat, 'Employee relations in Singapore — current issues and problems', *Employment Relations*, vol. 18, no. 3, 1996, p. 48.

99. C. P. Engardio, 'Coming home', *Business Week*, 31 August 1992, p. 25; and S. Tripathi, 'No can do, lah', *Asia Inc.*, October 1996, p. 20.

100. C. B. Mackay, 'Human resource planning: a four phased approach', *Management Review*, vol. 70, no. 5, 1981, p. 19.

101. J. Walker, 'Forecasting manpower needs', in E. H. Burack and J. W. Walker (eds), *Manpower Planning and Programming*, Allyn & Bacon, Boston, 1972, p. 94.

102. A. Fish, personal discussion with the author, January 2003.

103. Parts of this case study are based on A. Ferguson, 'Wounded kangaroo', *Business Review Weekly*, 10–16 July 2003, pp. 32–6; and S. Washington, 'The secret Qantas', *Business Review Weekly*, 10–16 July 2003, pp. 38–9.

104. Parts of this case study are based on S. Kitchens, op. cit., p. 16.

chapter 3

human resource information systems[1]

Learning objectives

When you have finished studying this chapter, you should be able to:

- Describe the relationship between strategic HRM and human resource information systems (HRIS)
- Explain the use of HRIS in contemporary HR functions
- Understand the decision-making process that needs to be followed when introducing HRIS
- Understand the key issues that will determine the success or failure of an HRIS
- Describe how an effective HRIS facilitates the achievement of HRM objectives.

'The e-revolution has finally freed HR to focus on strategies to support the company business — the acquisition, retention, and growth of the company's most important assets. Its people and their collective knowledge.'[2]

Watson Wyatt, HR consultants

Strategic HRM and HRIS

HR managers are under increasing pressure to become strategic business partners, to help the organisation better respond to the challenges of downsizing, restructuring and global competition by providing value-added contributions to the success of the business. HRM must work faster, be more accurate and be more productive. **Human resource information systems (HRIS)** have thus become a critical tool for integrating HR information into the organisation's business strategy and for demonstrating the positive contribution that HR can make to the bottom line through the more effective and efficient management of the organisation's human resources. Networks, PCs and automated telephone systems, for example, can give employees direct access to HR information and services, freeing HR personnel to focus on strategic value-added work and to make more informed decisions.[3]

An antiquated HRIS is a hindrance to both HRM and organisational performance. Slow, inflexible and retaining questionable data, such systems are no longer viable in a world of global competition where competitive advantage is built on distinctive human resources.[5] Unfortunately, according to one expert: 'Payroll is the only thing being used universally. The nexus between data and decisions has not been made.'[6] Boudreau, for example, argues that when HR managers think about HRIS, they tend to ask, 'How can we solve the most pressing administrative problems, cut our immediate costs, or deliver the report requested by our most vocal constituent?' The result is usually a system heavy on administrative efficiency and reports, but potentially light on strategic capability.[7] One way to make HRIS strategic is to ask 'What applications or systems will make people our most powerful organisational asset?'[8]

Clearly, HR managers need to reposition their role from that of an information source to that of a strategic resource.[9] However, one survey found that many Australian HR managers do not like being involved in strategy.[10] Evidence suggests that such people have no future.[11]

The critical priority for a successful HRIS is to ensure that it is aligned with the organisation's strategic business and HRM objectives. Thus, developing clear and precise corporate and HRM objectives is essential before any HRIS technology is introduced. 'The important issue to remember is not to automate for the sake of automating', says Blair, 'but to strategically analyse all HR business practices and develop a technology plan that truly integrates with the business.'[12] A major barrier to achieving maximum strategic benefit from HRIS is an unquestioning belief in the need for new systems and software: fascination with state-of-the-art technology can be fatal. The best approach is to settle for what can be completed.

HRIS, if used correctly, can provide a powerful competitive edge. As HR managers further assume the role of business partners with their line counterparts, the need to improve HRM productivity, planning and decision support services increases. The ability to analyse, estimate costs, savings or benefits, and determine and examine trends becomes vital if HRM is to become a value-adding function. 'There is no doubt', says Dr Peter Salmon of Salmon Cybernetics, 'that HR systems when viewed as information systems rather than administrative systems can contribute significantly to the corporate mission.'[13] The message is obvious: 'the focus of HR systems must be on the corporate business objectives, not simply the HR department's administrative problems.'[14]

Thus, HRIS is much more than a computerised record of employee information. It is an integrated approach to acquiring, storing, analysing and controlling the flow of HR information throughout an organisation.[15] It provides the necessary data for planning activities such as forecasting, succession planning, and career planning and development (see figure 3.1). The major benefit of HRIS is the accurate and timely access to diverse data that it provides to the HR manager and top management. In conducting HR planning, it is valuable (and simple) to examine various 'what if' scenarios or simulations to test out different strategic alternatives. 'This is particularly important', say Hall and Goodale, 'in large, decentralized organisations, where manual data collection would be almost impossible.'[16] Once again, it must be emphasised that if the HRIS is not related to the organisation's strategic business and HR objectives, there will be little or no return.[17] However, by applying HRIS technology appropriately, HRM can facilitate its transition from a reactive administrative role to that of a proactive strategic business partner.

Human resource information systems (HRIS) A computerised system used to gather, store, analyse and retrieve data, in order to provide timely and accurate reports on the management of people in organisations.[4]

Replacing HR people with technology may be more efficient but it depersonalises the HR function.

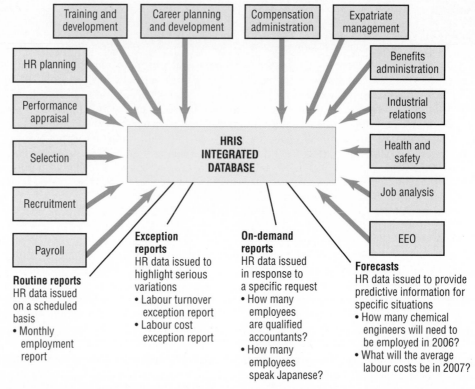

Figure 3.1 An HRIS model

NEWSBREAK

Beyond porn: cyberloafers in firing line

By Marcus Priest

Love is a priceless thing ... unless you and your beloved are sending and receiving affectionate messages 261 times over two days via your workplace email account. Then, the price of love could be your job.

In this case, the Sydney office worker caught cyber-smooching via Hotmail during a routine IT audit was lucky: she was counselled by her employer and told to do the job she was paid for.

In the past year local employers have begun to discipline and, if that fails, sack staff for unreasonable use of the internet and email.

Employers used to be more concerned about monitoring emails and internet usage for pornographic or inappropriate content, or leaking of confidential material. But now they are beginning to monitor productivity and crack down on internet and email usage that is not related to work.

'It is run on a pure productivity basis — it is a distraction from the work that you are paid for', says Clayton Utz workplace relations partner Joe Catanzariti.

This crackdown comes as something of a shock to some employees and unions. Also caught in the sweep at the

Sydney firm were 116 other workers, who had sent a total of 542 emails containing inappropriate images over the same period.

All the workers concerned managed to keep their jobs.

Many employees now routinely sign email policies when starting work and are aware that their emails can be monitored, but most do not realise the extent of the monitoring.

'Most people don't think privacy is an issue because they aren't looking at porn or committing fraud', Public Sector Association of NSW delegate Paul Petersen told Workers Online recently.

In the United States, a hardline approach to personal use of internet email is nothing new. Americans even have a word for it: cyberloafing.

Forty US employees at Xerox were fired for cyberloafing in 1999, and a survey of US workplaces in 2002 found the average employee spent about 220 hours a year surfing the web for non-business purposes.

In Britain, a study late last year estimated that medium-sized businesses lost 22 million work hours as staff sent e-cards and emails or organised Christmas parties. This resulted in a 15 per cent reduction in profits.

But in Australia — whether because employers have just been more relaxed or employees are only now turning en masse to the internet in work time for their shopping and banking needs — this kind of concern about productivity is new.

The Commonwealth Bank and Westpac say peak traffic time for net banking services is between 9.30 and 11 am — at the start of the business day. And the busiest day for net banking is Thursday — pay day. Online grocer Shopfast also reports a surge of users between 9.30 and 11am.

Banking and shopping sites are not the only sources of workplace distraction. Channel 10 reports that peak times for its *Big Brother* website are within hours of the nightly TV show and at 1 pm on week days, as workers eat a sandwich with one hand and click out their least favourite housemate with the other.

The spread of instant messaging software is another distraction for cyber-slackers.

It was screening for porn and fraud on the net that led employers to start cracking down on cyberloafing.

'First they want to stop viruses, then they become concerned about pornography, then spam, and eventually it comes to productivity',

says Chy Chuawiwat, the managing director of Clearswift Asia Pacific.

Chuawiwat, who runs the company that owns the local rights to the email and internet screening software Mimesweeper, says on average half the capacity of a workplace's internet and email system is taken up by non-work-related information and images.

Employers have a number of options to monitor employees' email and internet use. Chuawiwat says a number examine every email sent and received and every internet site visited by an employee. However, more common is a simple keyword search of all emails on the server, for words ranging from the sexually explicit to ones such as 'confidential' or 'CV'.

Another tack is to monitor employees who spend most time on the internet more closely.

Little research is done on the extent of email and internet monitoring in Australia, although anecdotal evidence indicates that monitoring is widespread. This recently prompted the State Chamber of Commerce of NSW to launch its own survey, which is yet to be finalised.

A recent survey in New Zealand found that about a quarter of workplaces monitored employees daily — almost equal to the number that did not monitor staff. What was most striking about the survey was that internet and email usage accounted for 59 per cent of all disciplinary matters in workplaces. Of these, 21 per cent related to inappropriate email or internet usage and 17 per cent to excessive use.

The trend by employers to use internet and email surveillance to monitor productivity has not gone unnoticed by unions, which have been pushing for tighter regulation of employer monitoring and protection for employee privacy.

The NSW Labour Council argue that email and internet monitoring has given employers something they have always wanted: constant monitoring of employees' work levels.

'The justification given for surveillance might be to monitor porn, but what in effect is happening is that employers are gathering a lot more information than they need to and employees are feeling that their every move is being watched when they are working', says NSW Labour Council assistant secretary Michael Gadiel.

There is no general constitutional or common law right to privacy in Australia, but laws were passed in 2000 preventing surveillance of employees being used as evidence or kept in employee records.

In NSW, the Law Reform Commission recommended that the general prohibition on covert video surveillance be extended to covert email and internet surveillance. The NSW Labour Council has since been lobbying the Carr government to implement the findings.

'In the past we had acceptance that monitoring of telephone calls was unacceptable, but with email and internet it has not yet reached a point where it has been recognised that there is a degree of privacy which is appropriate', Gadiel says.

The Carr government has resisted, citing constitutional concerns, but the Labour Council has renewed its push — and it is armed with a legal opinion from former state Labor attorney-general and now Supreme Court judge Jeff Shaw QC.

At the workplace level, unions are also seeking to restrict employer surveillance. Last month the Public Sector Union negotiated an agreement restricting the forms of surveillance that could be undertaken and introducing procedures to destroy email records after a certain period.

(continued)

'Surveillance is no substitute for good supervision and proper auditing. Our members are entitled to privacy', Petersen says. 'We've seen it all before in call centres. The employers use monitoring as a substitute for proper staffing to drive down their labour costs.'

Some employees are even greeted with a pop-up notice, which they must acknowledge, whenever they turn on their computer. But unions want these sorts of warnings to go further.

Gadiel says employers should at least tell employees when they are being monitored and should not merely issue general warnings. Further, employees should be told what employers look for — for example, the list of words they search for, what mechanisms are in place to protect the privacy of the information, how long it is kept, and who has access to it.

A study for the *Journal of Organisational Behaviour* last year also gave employers another option: provide a fairer workplace.

Organisational psychologist Vivien Lim, of the National University of Singapore, concluded that in many cases employees' motivation for wasting time on the internet and email was to even out perceived imbalances in the employment relationship.

Source *Australian Financial Review*, 6 June 2003, p. 22.

Computerisation through the payroll

The issue of HR versus payroll systems is an ongoing controversy.[18] One school of thought is that they should be integrated to create and maintain a 'complete' system and to prevent unnecessary duplication of effort (because much of the information kept in HRIS is replicated in payroll systems).[19] According to one expert, improvements in computer technology and the increased availability of PC-based HR and payroll packages 'means that human resource system integration is becoming not just a realistic possibility, but an absolute must'.[20] Given the commonality of information, argues Benson, there is much to be gained by streamlining data entry procedures.[21] The input of new hire details into an HRIS, for example, would automatically update both the superannuation scheme and the payroll, eliminating wasteful rekeying and potential discrepancies. Similarly, details of employee exits and the like can be communicated to payroll. This, says Benson, promotes 'increased operational efficiency and data consolidation'.[22] 'Furthermore, it is likely that the accuracy of shared information will be enhanced because payroll normally contains the most accurate and up to date information in any organization', for the simple reason that it is audited each pay period by every single employee.[23]

The second viewpoint is that payroll and HR are separate activities and should be treated as such. A payroll system is seen as essentially an accounting function that processes a large number of transactions, while an HRIS is used for HR planning and decision making. Payroll and HRIS also have other significant differences. For example: HRM transactions are variable and dynamic, whereas payroll transactions are run in batches and are mainly routine; HRM is event driven, whereas payroll is cyclical; HRM has historical records, whereas payroll usually maintains details only for the current year; online query capabilities are needed for HR personnel to do their work, whereas payroll updates records according to the pay cycle; HRM needs frequent ad hoc reports that range from simple to complex, whereas payroll reports are usually routine.[24] Finally, HRIS is specifically used for processing, manipulating and reporting HR information (see figure 3.2).

Database management
Involves the input, storage, manipulation and output of data.

Knowledge management
Deals with an organisation's ability to collect, store, share and apply knowledge in order to enhance its survival and success.

The driving mechanism of HRIS is **database management**. This involves the input, storage, manipulation and output of information. Generally, database management is to HRM what the spreadsheet has been to the accounting profession. Database management has opened up opportunities unavailable to the HR manager a decade ago, facilitating dramatic improvements in such things as the recruitment and tracking of job applicants, the processing of HR transactions (for example, pay increases), HR planning and **knowledge management** (see pages 334–5).

Address (work)	Grievance (outcome)	Phone number (mobile)
Address (home)	Grievance (type)	Phone number (work)
Annual leave (available)	Health plan coverage	Prior service (hire date)
Annual leave (used)	Health plan (# dependants)	Prior service (termination date)
Awards	Income tax number	Professional associations
Birth date	Injury (date)	Professional/technical licence (date)
Birth place	Injury (type)	Professional/technical licence (type)
Bonus	Job location	Schools attended
Child-support deductions	Job position number	Sex
Citizenship	Job preference	Share plan membership
Date on current job	Job title	Sick leave (used)
Department	Languages	Sick leave (available)
Disability status	Leave of absence (end date)	Skill function (type)
Discipline (appeal date)	Leave of absence (start date)	Skill subfunction (type)
Discipline (appeal outcome)	Leave of absence (type)	Skill (number of years)
Discipline (date of charge)	Medical exam (blood type)	Skill (proficiency level)
Discipline (hearing date)	Medical exam (date)	Skill (date last used)
Discipline (outcome)	Medical exam (restrictions)	Skill (location)
Discipline (type of charge)	Medical exam (outcome)	Skill (supervisory)
Division	Military service (branch)	Start date
Driver's licence (expiry date)	Military service (date)	Superannuation
Driver's licence (number)	Military service (discharge date)	Supervisor's title
Driver's licence (state)	Military service (discharge type)	Supervisor's work address
Driver's licence (type)	Military service (ending rank)	Supervisor's work phone
Education in progress (date)	Miscellaneous deductions	Termination (date)
Education in progress (type)	Name	Termination (reason)
Education degree (date)	Organisation property	Training (attended)
Education degree (type)	Pay	Training (date)
Education level attained	Pay compa ratio	Training (held)
Education major	Pay (previous)	Training (completed)
Education minor	Pay (change date)	Transfer date
Emergency contact (address)	Pay (change reason)	Transfer reason
Emergency contact (name)	Pay (change type)	Union deductions
Emergency contact (phone)	Pay (points)	Union membership
Employee code	Pay (range)	Union name
Employee number	Pay status (exempt/non exempt)	
Employee status	Performance increase ($)	
Full-time/part-time/casual	Performance increase (%)	
Garnishments	Performance rating	
Grievance (filing date)	Phone number (home)	

Figure 3.2 Example of HRIS data items

Uses of human resource information systems

An organisation's culture and HR philosophies and practices will influence the choice and design of its HRIS and its ease of introduction. For example, the Lend Lease culture of 'There must be a better way' allowed the immediate introduction of an HR **intranet**.[25] In high-tech companies, technology is seen as the key to a quantitative leap in the quality of HR

Intranet A network of computers that enables employees within an organisation to communicate with each other.

services.[26] Paperless HR, a computer on every employee's desk, a web page and an extensive intranet are standard.[27] Such an approach facilitates the decentralisation of time-consuming and expensive HR transactions. Managers and employees become empowered. Simon McCoy, National Human Resources Manager, Corporate Express, says, 'Rather than have all the information centralized where it is difficult to access, our plan is to have all our HR-related information at the fingertips of managers and employees alike to empower them to make decisions about payroll and HR-related issues.'[28] As a result, decision making is better informed and faster, and obsolete HR systems and programs can be quickly identified and dropped.[29]

In contrast, organisations with a more bureaucratic culture are likely to prefer an HRIS based on centralised data input and reporting via the accounting (payroll) and HR departments. However, competitive pressures and technological advances are promoting the increased use of decentralised systems. HR intranets, which are user-friendly, provide an efficient, cost-effective information hub for the organisation (see figure 3.3). Information on HR policies, recruitment, performance appraisal, training, compensation, benefits and so on, and news on company financials and performance is readily accessible. ANZ's intranet, for example, provides online leave forms, a global contact list, daily news, share price updates and business unit homepages (it receives over three million hits per month).[30]

In addition, an HR intranet facilitates more efficient management of low value-added HR and payroll activities (such as address changes and leave requests), because employees can access and update their personal information without going through the HR or accounting department. This means that low value-adding positions can be abolished.[31] The Insurance Commission of Western Australia estimates that three-quarters of the 4000 paper forms that its HR department receives annually will be eliminated in this way.[32] 'The result', says Grant Speight, the Commission's Manager, Human Resources, 'has been a decrease in the ratio of HR processing to HR management employees, and a move towards a more strategically oriented HR service.'[33] AXA Australia's HR department no longer handles basic and repetitive questions such as 'How much sick leave do I have?'[34] AXA claims that its HR department is now more proactive and focused, providing counsel on more complex and strategic issues.[35] Optus too has experienced similar benefits, including the removal of unnecessary layers of bureaucracy, improved data integrity and streamlined work flows.[36]

The challenge for HR managers is to embrace the new technology. Says HR expert John Sullivan: 'If you are going to change rapidly and continually improve, there is no industry where technology will not be a prime mover. If you are going to be faster, better, cheaper, it means you must use more and better technology, whether you are talking about a computer chip, a mobile phone or an HR department!'[37]

Flexibility of HRIS

Flexibility is an important feature in an HRIS. Whether buying or designing an HRIS, HR managers must remember that a key element to the system's success and future value is the ability to use data in ways that they might not originally think of when introducing the system.

Accountants talk about 'what ifs'. What if the profit margin could be increased by 10 per cent? How would this affect the bottom line? Depending on the size of the business, these questions may be applied to the actual figures or to a model of the business. It is for this reason that spreadsheet programs are the most prolific pieces of software ever sold.

HR professionals now have the same power. They can quickly estimate the cost of a 5 per cent pay rise across the organisation. They can also use multiple selection criteria, such as finding which employees speak Chinese, have engineering qualifications and are available to accept an international assignment.

Confidentiality of HRIS

HR data are typically confidential and sensitive. Consequently, a key concern with HRIS is the potential for the invasion (and abuse) of employee privacy by both authorised and unauthorised personnel.[38] To ensure employee and management confidence in an HRIS, it is important to thoroughly explore questions about user access, data accuracy, data disclosure, employee rights of inspection and **HRIS security**. Failure to do so may result in ethical, legal and employee relations problems of a magnitude that could destroy the credibility of the system.[39] Finally, HR managers of global organisations must ensure that their HRIS satisfies international data privacy laws. Non-compliance with the Hong Kong ordinance, for example, is a criminal offence.[40] An example of a PC security checklist is shown in figure 3.4. 'Establishing security and end user privileges', says O'Connell, 'calls for a balance of incorporating HR policy, system knowledge and day to day operations.'[41]

HRIS security Concerned with the protection of HRIS data from invasion and abuse by unauthorised parties.

Employment Manager
- How many applications have been received?
- How many have MBAs?
- How many are women?
- How many have been interviewed?

EEO Manager
- How many women are employed in management positions?
- What was the labour turnover rate for married women last year?
- What is the number of Aboriginal Australians employed?

HR Planning Manager
- How many chemical engineers are currently employed?
- How many chemical engineers will be required in 2006?
- What was the labour turnover of chemical engineers for 2004?

Compensation and Benefits Manager
- What is the year-to-date expenditure on health insurance?
- How much was spent on cash awards versus budget in 2004?

HRD Manager
- How many employees have enrolled in MBA programs?
- What is the year-to-date expenditure on apprenticeship training?
- What were the evaluations of the new graduate orientation program?

HRIS INTEGRATED DATABASE

Health and Safety Manager
- How many lost-time injuries were there in 2000, 2001, 2002, 2003 and 2004?

HR Manager
- What are the compensation and benefits expenses as a percentage of total operating expenses?
- What are the sales per employee?
- What is the net profit per employee?

Industrial Relations Manager
- How many working days were lost from strike action in 2004?
- What is the cost of granting an additional day's bereavement leave?

Line Manager
- What is the average age of employees in my department?
- When did Mary Brown receive her last pay increase?

Employee
- How much annual leave do I have?
- How much is my superannuation plan worth?
- Is my home address correct?

Figure 3.3 HRIS questions and answers
Source Asia Pacific Management Co. Ltd, 2004.

HR SECURITY CHECKLIST

- Review all PC-based HR applications.
- Verify that all users are properly trained in the secure use and handling of equipment, data and software.
- Ensure that all users sign-off (log-off) before they leave the PC unattended, regardless of how long they intend to be away.
- Caution users not to give or share their password with anyone. Each user should be accountable for everything done with their ID and password.
- Recommend a change of password on a monthly or quarterly basis.
- Caution users against duplicating not only copyrighted programs purchased from vendors but also programs and data that are proprietary to the company. Copies should be made only to provide necessary back-up.
- Ensure that all software acquired from sources other than vendors are run through a virus detection program prior to installing on your system.
- Consider the feasibility of separating the duties of the users (i.e. assigning the tasks of inputting data, balancing control totals, etc. to different people) to achieve and maintain confidentiality. Keep in mind the separation of some duties may cause users to lose the continuity of the entire task. Look at the whole function and how it relates to others in the department before separating duties.
- Review who will use the PCs and where their equipment will be located.
- Ensure that current and back-up copies, data files, software and printouts are properly controlled so that only authorised users can obtain them.
- Conduct reviews, scheduled and unscheduled, to ensure that an effective level of security is being maintained by PC users. Staff members who use PCs in their work must be responsible for ensuring that practices and administrative procedures adhere to security.

Figure 3.4 HR security checklist

Source Adapted by the author from L. E. Adams, 'Securing your HRIS in a microcomputer environment', *HR Magazine*, February 1992, p. 56.

Legal and management concerns

Internet A global network of electronic information sources. It enables people to send mail, access reference material, share documents electronically and send computer software directly from one computer to another.

Companies increasingly expect employees to stay late and work harder, yet they restrict web shopping and personal email.

Organisations today must be alert to the risk of litigation and abuse resulting from employee use of email and the **Internet**.[42] In Australia, for example, 35 per cent of employees use the Internet for personal reasons, 96 per cent use chat rooms and email, 37 per cent browse sexual sites and 32 per cent visit violence or crime sites.[43] Similarly, in the United States, it is estimated that up to 70 per cent of traffic on pornographic sites takes place during working hours. Web shopping in the United States is also on the increase because of its convenience and time saving (especially as job pressures mount), and it is estimated that more than half of all Internet purchases are made at work.[44] Employee abuse of the Internet and email is called *cyberloafing*. Other related problem areas include employees sending messages that disclose confidential information, breach intellectual property rights or attract defamation or harassment claims.[45] To combat such situations, nearly three-quarters of all major US companies now record and review employee communications (including telephone calls, email and Internet connections).[46] Others use special software to bar access to unwanted shopping, gambling and pornographic sites. Companies such as Merrill Lynch, Morgan Stanley and Goldman Sachs ban the use of personal email accounts.[47]

Carefully worded policies governing use of email and the Internet are essential.[48] One lawyer recommends that companies have a written policy advising their employees that their email messages are not private and can be read by their managers, that the technology they use at work belongs to the company and that the company reserves the right to monitor employee computer usage. All employees should sign the policy, acknowledging that they have read it and understand it.[49]

The challenge for HR managers is to find the right balance between permissiveness and surveillance. It should be noted that in some jurisdictions, privacy protection laws may prohibit the examination of employee emails. In Spain, for example, three Deutsche Bank executives are facing prison for reading employee emails (something that is routinely done elsewhere).[50] This makes employee training in the appropriate use of email essential.[51] Highlighting the problem, surveys have found ignorance, disagreement and confusion among Australian managers and employees in both the private and public sectors regarding the use of technology in the workplace.[52] Griffith University technology expert Tino Fenech claims that often company policies on Internet use are either inadequate or not properly communicated to employees. As a result, many employees remain unaware of the dangers of receiving unofficial communications such as joke emails that may contain viruses and illegal or obscene material.[53] The responsible use of technology is now a major HR and management issue.[54]

This Letter to the Editor provides a provocative viewpoint. Do you agree? See 'What's your view?' on page 93.

Letter to the Editor

Companies shouldn't be legally responsible for communications issued by their employees

Dear Editor,

I am deeply concerned about the rapid growth of employer surveillance of employee email and telephone use.

Not a week seems to pass by without stories in the media of employees sacked for inappropriate use of email systems. Similarly, one cannot ring an organisation these days without being informed by recorded message that the call may be monitored. It seems that the days of Big Brother watching us are finally here.

Of course, the immoral, illegal or illegitimate use of organisational communication systems cannot be condoned. Whether it is the sending of pornographic images over the Internet or the use of company telephones for long-distance personal calls, the exploitation of company resources for personal gain can never be justified.

On the other hand, perhaps we have gone too far in monitoring the work of our employees. Is it fair that senior managers can take long lunch hours and make personal calls while the same behaviour by other employees is punished? Surely there is a level of 'reasonableness' by which all can be similarly judged?

In this era of worker empowerment and the use of self-managing teams, surely our over-enthusiastic efforts to constrain all bad behaviour results in an understandable response from employees — a return to work to rule and the payment of lip service to managers' requests for creativity, loyalty and working beyond the call of duty when required. After all, monitoring is simply another form of managerial control over work.

A far healthier response from all concerned would be to return to that old value of trust, particularly because the monitoring and surveillance of work views workers as irresponsible and untrustworthy. Trust can be engendered through far less brutal approaches than those increasingly being used. In consultation with all employees, organisations can develop codes of ethics that signal how organisational resources should be expended and organisational systems administered and maintained. Such codes can serve as beacons for aspiring behaviour, as well as reminders of the sorts of behaviour that will not be tolerated by the organisation. They also indicate a willingness of people to work together in this age of the expendable employee.

New and existing staff can be requested to endorse the code to indicate their acceptance of the need to abide by its contents. Employees can be reminded of its relevance to their work through its public display and by the use of occasional reminder messages regarding its importance. Most importantly, managers can powerfully indicate the code's significance to the wider organisation by supporting it through their own work behaviours and actions.

In an era when senior managers seem to receive high salaries and perks whether or not they perform, and high payouts continue to be made to senior managers when they are given the sack for poor performance, it's about time that managers began to walk the talk of empowerment, participation and trust, and this is one clear way in which they can begin to do this.

At the end of the day, employees are not simply cogs in the great machinery of organisational life, bereft of emotions and other loyalties. People need breaks from time to time. Surely it is harmless in such cases to allow them to gain pleasure from surfing the Net and obtaining information of interest? We should also accept the need for employees to contact their friends and relatives from time to time for a range of reasons, whether to organise social events or to deal with sick parents or children. As long as these actions occur within boundaries specified by the agreed acceptance of what is 'reasonable', all will benefit. Employees will be more content with their wider lives and thus function more productively in their work lives, to the benefit of the organisations in which they work.

Let's back off this trend towards high-surveillance workplaces and remind each other that our shared humanity requires a little give and take from both sides.

A disinterested HR consultant

Source David Poole, University of Western Sydney.

Computerising the HR department: the decision-making process

The easiest way to justify the set-up costs of an HRIS is to highlight the dollar savings resulting from more effective management of HR records and compensation and benefits administration. Thus, it is natural that most systems commence with transferring these functions to the database.

Increasing legislative demands have added another batch of tasks to this 'grassroots' category. The requirements of affirmative action (AA), equal employment opportunity (EEO) and workers compensation legislation can be very effectively handled within the HRIS. Once it is known who is on the payroll, that they are being paid correctly and that all legal requirements are being met, more complex issues can be tackled.

Different HRIS users will have different requirements from the system (see figure 3.5). Operational users need to process routine transactions (for example, payroll) and to answer general enquiries relating to basic personnel records. Middle managers need to generate regular and ad hoc reports (for example, EEO compliance) for day-to-day planning, decision making and control. Finally, senior management needs an interactive capability to answer 'what if' questions dealing with strategic planning, policy formulation and decision making (for example, in developing HR projections).

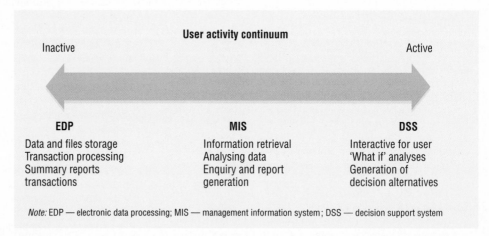

Figure 3.5 Types of computer-based HR systems

Source M. J. Kavanagh, H. G. Gueutal and S. O. Tannenbaum, *Human Resource Information Systems: Development and Application*, 1st edn. © 1990. Reprinted with permission of South-Western College Publishing, a division of Thomson Learning. Fax: 800 730 2215.

Three options exist when an organisation commits to introducing an HRIS.
- Design an in-house system using either internal or external resources, or a combination of both.
- Buy a system 'off-the-shelf' and commence operation.
- Buy a system as above but work with the vendor to modify it to better satisfy the organisation's requirements.

Each option has certain advantages and disadvantages. It is important to critically examine all of them to ensure that the organisation's choice best suits its needs and expectations.

The issues involved are related to some degree. Generally, the greatest concern relates to cost. Most management questions centre on purchase price and anticipated development costs, but these initial costs are the tip of the iceberg. Costs such as training, ongoing development and maintenance are typically underestimated or ignored.

Off-the-shelf Commercially available HRIS software.

Off-the-shelf systems offer users some comfort because set-up costs are known. In contrast, developing a customised system is not for organisations that are unwilling to provide significant upfront money. HR managers who have undertaken this task recount much frustration with cost overruns, programming errors and an inability to complete the project within a reasonable time frame.

An off-the-shelf product has the advantage of immediate availability. This approach clearly limits flexibility but there is no doubt that it is faster to get someone else to define the need, spend a lot of time developing a system and run tests to provide some certainty that it will work.

An off-the-shelf system often has a large user base, so the vendor is motivated to provide ongoing maintenance and, even more importantly, future development. Obviously, there is limited value in having a workable system now if it cannot cope with future changes in user requirements. Using a variety of off-the-shelf systems risks creating problems integrating and consolidating data sources into an effective strategic platform.[55] Guy Chapman, Information Services Manager for Optus, says: 'I think because Optus grew so fast, they went out and bought one of whatever was available, just to get the work done. This was fine at the time but it's ended up a bit of a shambles with lots of different systems'.[56]

Related to these issues is the question of the resources that are available in the HR department and the rest of the organisation. According to one expert, many systems fall down in their implementation because of the lack of resources to get them up and running.[57] The HR manager must ask questions such as: Are there sufficient computer-literate employees who understand operating systems and their minor difficulties? And to what extent will the HR department need to depend on the information systems department? (Any dependency can prove unsatisfactory.)

Documentation and user training also affect all systems. Who will write the documentation? Can it be understood? Who will be assigned to update it? Similarly, who will undertake user training? How can the HR manager ensure that there will be enough people in the organisation who can competently use the system?

Unfortunately, the perfect program has not yet been invented. There is no such software that works as it was intended and continues to do so even when minor modifications are made. In developing a system, the HR manager must be aware that another programming issue will arise just as the last one is resolved.

Legal advisers now oversee the development and consummation of contracts for the supply of an HRIS. Expert opinion is necessary because users and vendors can face a multitude of contractual problems and warranty issues. The HR manager must be prepared for this situation and the frustrations it involves.

Despite strong arguments in favour of off-the-shelf products, there is one issue that is quite critical. Such a product is generally one person's view of what an HRIS should look like. Thus, the HR manager is saddled with the vendor's preferences for managing data, designing the screens, constructing reports, and so on. Flexibility is rarely present in such generic systems. It is critical, therefore, that HR managers ensure that the product does what they want it to do and supports their HRIS strategy. For example, after the Commonwealth Bank of Australia abolished employee pay slips, the bank had employees access their pay information on the Internet and make a printout if required. However, the inability of the US-designed PeopleSoft software to cope with Australian taxes and payment cycles produced wrong pay amounts, and missed mortgage and debt repayments, resulting in employee and union anger and frustration.[58] The Commonwealth's CEO David Murray complained: 'I think you are entitled to expect that companies who represent that they can do things and deal with local complexities will do it.'[59] This is a reasonable comment, but as many HR managers involved with HRIS will attest, it is not necessarily realistic.

The buy-and-modify option is an attempt to get the best of both worlds. The vendor and/or specialist consultants take care of the painful and costly development work and modify the end product to suit the organisation's particular needs. However, once modifications commence, it is easy to reach a situation where the system is being rebuilt from the ground up (with the associated time and cost problems).

There is no best approach. Clearly the selection of a system reflects the organisation's specific needs and budget. The pragmatic option for the HR manager is to find a system that satisfies most of the organisation's needs. The proliferation of vendors means most organisations should be able to find something that satisfies their major needs. Finding an HRIS that satisfies 100 per cent is a task that shows a limited return for a large expenditure.[60]

John Eddy is HR Director at Citibank and has more than 30 years of HR experience with international organisations including Bristol-Myers Squibb, Philips and CIBA-Geigy.

Managing the impact

When HR information systems are introduced, it is typical that too much energy goes into enabling the technology and not enough into developing the HR operating model and preparing everyone for changes.

At Citibank, we have been going through an HR transformation for a number of years, including moving to a different operating platform. We are introducing PeopleSoft V8.3, with some customisation. We are also conscious of the impact the new technology will have on the roles and responsibilities of our HR people and the business users.

I got into HR by chance more than 30 years ago. I was working for BHP when I was asked to do some recruiting for the Whyalla Steel Works. Later I joined Hornibook, recruiting people to build bridges, roads and the Sydney Opera House. That was in the 1970s, when HR generally was very hands-on. There wasn't the proliferation of consultants or technology that there is today.

The emphasis now is on doing more with less — it's all about efficiency.

Citibank's new system will start with some basic self-service for employees and managers, and over time this will increase. Initially, people will make online changes to personal details, such as address and emergency contact. Managers will be able to make changes that used to require a third party.

We moved some years ago to a shared-services model in HR to handle transactional details and generalist services. People in specialist and generalist roles operate as internal consultants to the business. This offers opportunities and challenges for both groups. In the shared-services centre our people are being upskilled to become advisors to line managers and employees. They have less face-to-face contact with people, mainly utilising the telephone, e-mail and intranet, but the job is more interesting because they can work on a broader range of HR issues/projects.

Generalist HR practitioners often feel they need to be a business partner within the organisation. There's nothing wrong with that, but, if you want efficiencies, you may need to reorganise the way HR generalists work with the business. The people to look for are those who can build relationships with the business and then consult on the people issue before moving onto the next consulting challenge.

I believe there will always be some resistance to technological change in the HR community, but if people want to up-skill themselves and take advantage of new technology, there is plenty of opportunity. Don't get on board and there won't be a role for you in future; you have to adapt and manage the change.

HR strategy flows from an understanding of business strategy and direction, but you don't necessarily have to be part of the business to understand what the HR contribution should be. You also have to remember that HR works for the business and not the people. HR's prime focus should be on the requirements of the business rather than looking after the individual interests of every employee. HR is there to support that management responsibility, and advise managers and employees.

Some companies, such as Cisco, utilise HR technology more than most of us, but it will increasingly help us provide our businesses with more usable information about people. Our HRIS system is basic, focusing on records, turnover of staff, annual leave and workers compensation, etc. It would be nice to have systems that can provide more relevant data on areas such as talent management and succession planning.

Organisations have systems providing good information on their customers, but they have very little on their own people. At Citibank, climate surveys give us a guide on how we are tracking. They tell us if people are satisfied or dissatisfied. But they don't tell us if they are truly engaged.

There will always be limits to the use of technology in HR. Whether you are hiring people or they are leaving, voluntarily or involuntarily, people must be treated with courtesy and respect. Giving people notice by email will always be inappropriate.

John Eddy

Source *HR Monthly*, November 2003, p. 33.

Outsourcing

Outsourcing involves a company contracting out some (or all) of its HRIS activities to an information technology specialist.[61] Companies are attracted to outsourcing HRIS given the apparent lower costs, simplicity and convenience. Successful outsourcing also allows HR managers to concentrate on their core responsibilities rather than spending time struggling with complex (and peripheral) computing activities. However, some managers outsource HRIS because they do not understand HR information technology or because they have had problems with an HRIS in the past.

Outsourcing challenges HR managers to define their core business — that is, what do they want to do? Similarly, the HR manager must clearly define what the HRIS should be achieving, what it is costing and what parts the company is prepared to outsource. Outsourcing HRIS poses risks for the HR manager — for example, the outsourcing consultancy may lack the flexibility of an in-house HRIS, or it may prove to be more expensive and less time sensitive. In addition, a fine line exists between delegation of the HRIS and loss of control (and ownership) of data. An HRIS has an interface with the organisation's strategic planning process because it can influence or be influenced by the organisation's business strategy. (For example, does the organisation have sufficient qualified people to support a possible acquisition or entry into a new business area? If not, the organisation may have to alter or postpone the implementation of its strategy or recruit additional personnel.) Consequently, outsourcing poses a risk that the organisation may lose control over data, reducing the competitive advantage of a superior information system.

Resolution of key issues

A clear view of the HRM function

When embarking on the lengthy process of purchasing or developing an HRIS, the HR manager must have a clear picture of the HR function and its strategic objectives. This understanding will affect the time required to start up an effective system and the HR manager's ability to discriminate between software alternatives.

The 'bells and whistles' trap

The HR manager must also beware of the 'bells and whistles' trap (that is, buying a system that appears to have every known function regardless of whether it is useful). Some HRIS developers delight in creating systems that look good but are of little practical value. If the HR manager does not plan correctly, they risk buying a system designed by default using principles that the vendor's programmer thinks are important.

Payroll system or HRIS?

The HR manager must also decide whether a payroll system or an HRIS is wanted. The answer depends on whether the HR manager is seeking a transaction-based system for keeping wage and salary data, leave records and related information, or a more integrated system for collating a body of information that can be used for management planning.

Knowing the jargon

It is highly desirable that the HR manager be familiar with common HRIS jargon. The manager will not need to program a computer, but they should understand the fundamental issues as they relate to both **hardware** and **software**. This is necessary because there are new developments in the industry about which many hardware and software vendors will have inadequate knowledge. If the HR manager does not understand the basics, then they risk being given information that is inaccurate, misleading or unverifiable.

Hardware The physical parts of a computer; for example, the hard drive.

Software The program of instructions that makes computers perform.

Vapourware Software that purports to undertake certain tasks but in reality cannot accomplish them.

Using the 'show me' test

HR managers need to beware of **vapourware** (that is, software that purports to undertake certain tasks but in reality cannot accomplish them). Several systems displayed at one vendors' fair, for example, suggested an array of interesting menu items from which the HR manager could choose. However, when certain selections were made, it was obvious that about half the system had not yet been put in place. When questioned, the vendor replied that the missing modules would be available 'shortly'. The lesson is to learn to say 'show me'.

Ignore vendors who say that the processes are too technical and beyond the capacity of the HR manager to comprehend. All processes, whether related to software or hardware, can easily be explained. If the vendor is unable or unwilling to do so, the HR manager should be wary.

Extracting data and reports

Before purchasing and implementing an HRIS, the HR manager should work out how they want to extract **reports** and **data**. Report writing and data functionality should be determined against the organisation's requirements. Information must be reliable, readable, prompt and relevant to the needs of the user. If a manager requires a summary report, it is useless if all that can be generated is a 10-page detailed report.[62] Will the HRIS support decentralised **access**? Will the production of printed reports from HR suffice? Also, the matter of who will have access to HRIS-related data must be finalised — for example, does the organisation require fully decentralised access and data entry capability for all HRIS matters, or does it require limited access by managers to data relating to only their own subordinates?[63]

Knowing when to call for help

It is rare for an HR manager to have experienced as many HRIS implementations as a software vendor or HRIS consultant. Consequently, asking for help from someone with HRIS experience and expertise makes good sense and helps ensure a successful HRIS implementation.[64] However, the HR manager should exercise care in selecting an adviser because surveys indicate considerable client dissatisfaction with external software consultants.[65]

Seeking integration

A state-of-the-art computer supported by poor procedures and poorly trained users will produce an ineffective HRIS. It is the integration of the computer, people, policies/procedures and information flow that produces an effective HRIS.[66]

Relationship with the information technology department

The relationship between HR and the **IT (information technology) department** is also an area that requires some comment. The HR manager is fortunate if the IT department shares the same commitment to implementing a system, because IT specialists generally have considerable knowledge and expertise on computer systems, hardware and vendors.[67]

However, if the IT department is entirely committed to running the accounting system on the mainframe, the HR manager may receive little assistance (and possibly face considerable hindrance).

It is understandable that some business functions have to be undertaken on a regular basis and that these may take priority. Unfortunately, the IT department (as custodian of the organisation's data) is sometimes reluctant to release its responsibility for some business functions because it is more concerned with 'empire building'. In such cases, the HR manager may find that HRM efforts to access data are blocked. Even worse, the HR system may be used to help justify a significant cost injection into the organisation's mainframe; instead of a small, self-contained system, the HRIS becomes an integral part of the mainframe. This is an arrangement that may be difficult to justify later. But independence from the IT department can mean some difficulties for HR managers uninitiated in computer systems. However, with abundant and affordable new technology, user-friendly software and lower costs, microcomputers have given considerable independence to end users such as HR managers. Ideally, however, IT specialists and HR professionals should cooperate to achieve the organisation's strategic business objectives.

Relationship with other departments[68]

Implementing an effective HRIS requires a strong partnership not only with the IT department but also with other departments (for example, the HR department depends on the accounting department to record labour expenditure and leave liabilities in the organisation's general ledger). Consequently, the HR department must be outwardly (not just inwardly) focused if it is to receive the support it needs. This means that the HRIS should generate reports that help line managers to do their job. An HRIS must be aligned with the organisation's strategic business objectives. It must help increase sales and reduce costs — that is, help the organisation generate profit — instead of servicing only narrow HR interests. An HRIS can be a vehicle for the HR department to become a strategic business partner (with HRIS at the core of strategic planning).

Hardware issues

Technological advancements mean it is now increasingly difficult to distinguish the different characteristics of mainframes, minicomputers and microcomputers.

Mainframes are the biggest, fastest and most expensive class of computers. Originally, the term referred to the extensive array of large rack and panel cabinets that held thousands of vacuum tubes in early computers. Mainframes are large, possess huge data-handling capacities and typically serve as the information systems hub in large organisations.

Minicomputers are more powerful than microcomputers, but less powerful than mainframes. They can handle networks and other simultaneous arrangements at a relatively low cost. Local area networks (LANS) — where many computer stations share the same minicomputer software and peripherals (for example, printer, scanner and disk drives) — are common in many organisations. LANS can also be driven by mainframes or minicomputers and file servers or by PCs as 'peer-to-peer' systems, depending on the applications needed.[69]

Microcomputer is another name for a personal computer (PC). It is the smallest and least expensive class of computer. PCs are fully operational computers that use **microprocessors** as their **central processing unit (CPU)**. The introduction of PCs has decentralised control of information systems, moving them out from the IT department to departments throughout the organisation.

Technological advances have meant that differences are becoming increasingly blurred, particularly at the micro/mini end of the market. Falling costs and the increasing capacity of machines have lowered the barriers to entry to the computer market, encouraging HR managers to shift to microcomputers for running their HRIS. Furthermore, improved communication links to mainframes make it easier to use a mainframe computer for heavy

Mainframes The biggest, fastest and most expensive class of computer.

Minicomputers Computers that are more powerful than microcomputers but less powerful than mainframes.

Microcomputer The smallest and least expensive class of computer. Generally called a personal computer (PC).

Microprocessor The logic, mathematic and central functions contained in a computer chip.

Central processing unit (CPU) This is the computer's brain. It controls the interpretation and execution of instructions. It causes data to be read, stored, manipulated and printed.[70]

number crunching or networking. Finally, the growth of decentralised organisational structures has fostered the need for more client-oriented information services. Consequently, mainframes and traditional IT departments often reflect the organisational set-up of the past, while PCs and LANS are better suited to today's downsized, flat and empowered organisations.[71]

HRM and the Internet

Recruiting via the Internet is said to favour the affluent and the computer literate and disadvantage the economically less well off and the computer illiterate.

Increasingly, HR managers are going online with the Internet to recruit and select personnel, administer compensation and benefits, conduct research, access electronic databases, send email, network, advertise and undertake corporate promotion.[72] Some proactive HR managers use the Internet (and intranets) to post HR-oriented information such as company mission statements, company history, the company as an employer, HR policies (for example, EEO policies) and job openings, and to deliver online training and career assessment programs.

The Internet is an interconnection of millions of computers around the world, so files, documents, images and other forms of information can be exchanged quickly and relatively easily. By eliminating a lot of logistic activity, the Internet can free up the HR manager for strategic work and allow organisations to share valuable people resources.[73] In addition, the potential cost savings from the effective use of technology and the Internet in HR activities are compelling. IBM Corporation, for example, generated over US$100 million in cost savings through training online.[74]

Evaluating the HRIS

Data generated by the HRIS should help the HR manager and line managers to make better decisions. The HRIS should add value. Otherwise, its costs cannot be justified. Basic evaluation questions that the HR manager should ask include:

Employers are held responsible for the content of employee emails, yet employees and unions claim that monitoring emails is an invasion of privacy.

- Is the time spent on entering data justified by the accuracy, timeliness and value of the information generated?
- Is the HRIS response time appropriate?
- Is the HRIS integrated with the payroll system?
- Is the HRIS able to generate answers to specific HR questions?
- Is the HRIS able to generate ad hoc, on-request reports as well as regular detailed reports?
- Is the cost of the HRIS outweighed by its benefits?

Considering such questions should tell the HR manager whether or not the HRIS is value-adding, being used appropriately and helping managers to make better decisions.[75]

Summary

Thirty interactive Wiley Web Questions are available to test your understanding of this chapter at **www.johnwiley.com.au/ highered/hrm5e** *in the student resources area*

The primary purpose of an HRIS is to assist both the HR manager and line managers in decision making. Thus, an HRIS must generate information that is accurate, timely and related to the achievement of the organisation's strategic business objectives. Technology has created opportunities for HR to eliminate administrative overheads and become a strategic business partner.

The importance of analysing HRM needs must be stressed because each organisation will want to use its data in different ways. Some uses of HRIS include the management of personnel records, HR planning, recruitment and selection, performance appraisal, training and development, career planning and development, compensation and benefits, health and safety, and industrial relations.

The importance of flexibility in system design and use cannot be ignored. As the HRM function continues to change, so will the needs of the supporting systems. Because a computerised system must reflect these changes, the HR manager must ensure that it can adapt to the organisation's evolving needs. The process of introducing HRIS applications into an organisation is critical. A basic question is whether the organisation should design its own system, buy an off-the-shelf product or modify a bought system to suit its own needs. Further issues for the HR manager include ensuring the competence of vendors and their products and determining the role of the IT department in HRIS development.

student study guide

terms to know

access (p. 88)
central processing unit (CPU) (p. 89)
data (p. 88)
database management (p. 78)
hardware (p. 87)
HRIS security (p. 81)
human resource information systems
   (HRIS) (p. 75)
Internet (p. 82)
intranet (p. 79)

IT (information technology) department (p. 88)
knowledge management (p. 78)
mainframes (p. 89)
microcomputer (p. 89)
microprocessors (p. 89)
minicomputers (p. 89)
off-the-shelf (p. 84)
reports (p. 88)
software (p. 87)
vapourware (p. 87)

review questions

1. What are the benefits of HRIS to (a) the organisation, (b) the HR department and (c) the individual employee?
2. What should be the minimum capabilities of an HRIS?
3. Why have many HR managers faced serious problems when introducing or upgrading their HRIS?
4. What should be done to maintain the security of an organisation's HRIS?
5. How would you evaluate an organisation's HRIS?
6. How can an HRIS help line managers to better manage their HR responsibilities?
7. What is the difference between the Internet and an intranet?
8. How does an HRIS help HR managers to make better decisions?
9. What are the basic steps to consider in developing and implementing an HRIS?
10. What types of employee information should/should not be stored in an organisation's HRIS?

environmental influences on HRIS

Identify and discuss the key influences from the model (figure 3.6 shown opposite) that have significance for HRIS.

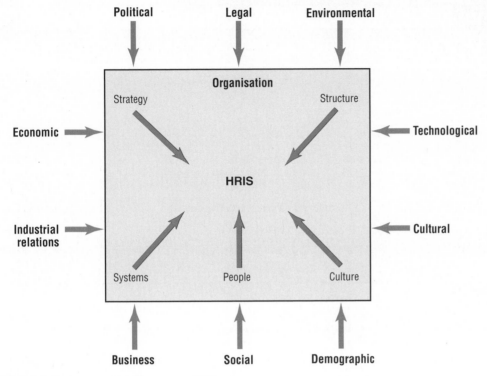

Figure 3.6 Environmental influences on HRIS

soapbox

What do you think? Conduct a mini survey of class members, using the questionnaire below. Critically discuss the findings.

1.	Managers must be able to monitor an employee's Internet usage.	YES	NO
2.	Employee emails should be private.	YES	NO
3.	Employees who visit pornographic sites during working hours should be fired.	YES	NO
4.	A company should be legally responsible for any sexist or racist emails sent by its employees.	YES	NO
5.	Personal web shopping during working hours is a necessary employee convenience.	YES	NO
6.	Any employee information entered into an HRIS should automatically become company property.	YES	NO

online exercise

Conduct an online search for information on commercially available HRIS programs. Prepare an executive briefing paper (750 words) describing one system, the vendor and purchasing details, provide examples of companies using the system and give your evaluation of the system. Include the web addresses you have accessed in your report.

ethical dilemmas

Email affection[76]

Peter Zimmerman, HR Manager for Allied International Ltd, snapped, 'Lucy, I am a reasonably tolerant person, but this is ridiculous! In the past two days you and your boyfriend have exchanged more than 250 messages. You are here to work, not advance your love life.'

Lucy Taylor's face flushed. 'You mean you have been reading our messages? That's an invasion of my privacy. What my boyfriend and I have to say to each other is none of your business.'

'Lucy, the company owns all email. I have an obligation to ensure that my people are not abusing the system and that their messages are not obscene, libellous or harassing. Your use is totally out of bounds. How can I possibly justify it? Spending so much time sending email messages to your boyfriend has got to affect your productivity. I should fire you,'

Lucy glared at Peter. 'Well, I think it is an abuse of my privacy and I am going to speak to my union about it.'

Discussion questions

1. Who do you think is right — Peter or Lucy? Why?

2. If you were Peter, would you fire Lucy?
3. If you were the union representative, what would be your response to Lucy's complaint?
4. What ethical issues are raised in this case?

A 'burning' problem

Brad Chatzky, financial analyst, pushed his chair away from his desk. 'All done.'

'What's that?' inquired Jessica Tong, HR specialist.

'I have downloaded all the music for Saturday night's party. It's really great. A couple of minutes work and I have the top 100 on CD. And it's free!'

'But that's theft, Brad. You know that downloading music online on company time is wrong', Jessica retorted.

'Oh, grow up Jessica. Everyone's doing it. What's so bad about burning a few CDs in company time?'

Discussion questions

1. Who do you agree with — Brad or Jessica? Why?
2. What ethical issues are involved in this case?

Party fun

The foreign exchange trading room was in uproar. Everyone was crowded around Jim McGraw's screen. Emily Mason, HR Vice-President for International Financial Services Ltd, asked curiously 'What's going on?'

'It's the year end bonus party — Jim's put it on the Net.'

'What?'

'It's a scream', commented Connie Finegold. 'I can't believe we did such things.'

Danny Maynard laughed. 'Boy, are there going to be some red faces in senior management. The boss better make sure his wife doesn't see his duet with Eva.'

Suddenly, Jim yelled 'Look, look, this is where Stacey throws up!' Everyone roared with laughter.

Emily was horrified. She screamed 'Stop it! Jim, do you realise what you have done?'

The people surrounding Jim's desk went quiet. 'What's up, Emily, can't you enjoy a bit of fun?'

Discussion questions

1. What ethical, legal and public relations issues are raised in this case?
2. If you were Emily, what would you do now?

No web shopping

John Boyd, HR Director for XYZ Ltd, fumed as he watched Joyce Lee surf various shopping sites. His face reddened as his anger increased. The whole department was flat out, yet for the past five minutes Joyce had done nothing but browse the Internet. 'Joyce, just what do you think you're doing? Everyone is flat out except you!' John barked.

Joyce turned and snapped, 'What's your problem? I have been working like a dog. I haven't taken a lunch break for the past two days and have worked back every night this week. Just when do you expect me to look after my personal affairs?'

Discussion questions

1. If you were John, how would you have handled this situation?
2. Should employees be allowed to shop online during working hours?
3. Should employers monitor employees' personal use of the Web?

1. Break into groups of four to six. Imagine you are a committee charged with introducing an HRIS to your organisation. Discuss the steps you would take, who you would involve, what information you would require and how you would access this information. Regroup as a class and discuss your recommendations.
2. Break into groups of four to six. Imagine you are a committee charged with developing company policies relating to HRIS security and employee privacy. List the major points that you think should be covered. Regroup as a class and discuss your findings.

3. Break into groups of four to six. Imagine you are a committee charged with developing a company's policy on employee use of the Internet. Specifically, you are asked to cover:
   (a) Internet shopping
   (b) playing computer games
   (c) accessing pornographic sites
   (d) personal email
   (e) downloading music.
   Prepare a short policy statement on each of these. Regroup as a class and discuss your policy statements.

4. Break into groups of six to eight, then break into two subgroups representing the HR and IT departments. Discuss the arguments for and against having the HRIS linked to the company's mainframe. Regroup as a class and discuss your recommendations.

5. Individually or as a group contact the HR manager of an organisation you are familiar with. Obtain information on the organisation's HRIS regarding its purpose, applications, security and effectiveness. Also ask how user-friendly the HRIS is, what major problems have been experienced and what recommendations the HR Manager would make to an organisation seeking to introduce an HRIS. Prepare a 750–1000 word report summarising your research. Regroup as a class and discuss your findings.

6. Individually or as a group contact an HRIS vendor and obtain details about its system. Write a 500-word report highlighting the advantages and disadvantages of the system. Regroup as a class and discuss your findings.

suggested readings

CCH, *Australian Master Human Resources Guide*, CCH, Sydney, 2003, ch. 5.

Clark, R and Seward, J., *Australian Human Resource Management: Framework and Practice*, 2nd edn, McGraw-Hill, Sydney, 2000, pp. 53–5.

De Cieri, H. and Kramar, R., *Human Resource Management in Australia*, McGraw-Hill, Sydney, 2003, ch. 5.

Fisher, C. D., Schoenfeldt, L. F. and Shaw, J. B., *Human Resource Management*, 5th edn, Houghton Mifflin, Boston, 2003, pp. 112–15.

Ivancevich, J. M., *Human Resource Management*, 8th edn, McGraw-Hill, Boston, 2001, pp. 142–5.

Mondy, R. W., Noe, R. M. and Premeaux, S. R., *Human Resource Management*, 8th edn, Prentice Hall, Upper Saddle River, NJ, 2002, ch. 6.

Nankervis, A. R., Compton, R. L. and Baird, M., *Strategic Human Resource Management*, 4th edn, Nelson, Melbourne, 2002, ch. 4.

online references

work.index.com
www.actnet.com
www.ahrm.org
www.anz.com/ols
www.employeeconnect.com.au
www.frontiersoftware.com.au
www.iplresearch.com
www.lir.msu.edu/hotlinks
www.mimesweeper.com.au./ads/freetrial.asp

www.mrchr.com
www.neller.com.au
www.payglobal.com
www.peoplesoft.com
www.PeopleWare.com/hk
www.rebussoftware.com
www.shrm.org.hrmagazine
www.teleport.com/~erwilson
www.workforceonline.com

end notes

1. This chapter is partly based on material prepared by Ron N. Berenholtz, B. Bus., Dip. Pers. Admin. (Deakin), CMAHRI (Australia).

2. Watson Wyatt, quoted in E. A. Ensher, T. R. Nielson and E. Grant-Vallone, 'Tales from the hiring line: effects of the Internet and technology on HR processes', *Organizational Dynamics*, vol. 31, no. 3, 2002, p. 224.

3. G. Wines and N. Lowenstein, 'Technology assumes HR's administrative role', *HR Monthly*, August 1996, p. 22; J. Boudreau, 'HRIS exploiting its real potential', *HR Monthly*, August 1995, pp. 8–13; and S. Greenard, 'Technology finally advances HR', *Workforce*, vol. 79, no. 1, 2000, pp. 38–41.

4. Definition provided by anonymous reviewer, November 2003.

5. J. Hannon, G. Jelf and D. Brandes, 'Human resource information systems: operational issues and strategic considerations in a global environment', *International Journal of Human Resource Management*, vol. 7, no.1, 1996, p. 245; and S. Liff, 'Constructing HR information systems', *Human Resource Management Journal*, vol. 7, no. 2, 1997, pp. 18–31.

6. D. Proud, 'Little quality data squeezed from HR systems, seminar told', *HR Monthly*, March 1997, p. 28.

7. J. Boudreau, op. cit., p. 13.

8. J. Boudreau, op. cit., p. 13.

9. G. Smith, 'Use systems to build high performance teams for knowledge age', *HR Monthly*, March 1999, pp. 30–1.

10. J. Macy, 'Survey asks HRIS to provide better strategic tools', *HR Monthly*, June 1996, p. 36.

11. P. Howes, 'Technological innovation driving demise of the HR department', *HR Monthly*, August 1998, pp. 52–3.

12. J. Blair, 'Leveraging technology in HR: the added edge', *HR News*, November 1992, p. A15; and W. A. Minneman, 'Strategic justification for an HRIS that adds value', *HRM Magazine*, December 1996, pp. 35–8.

13. P. Salmon, 'Focus on the business, not just HR administration', *HR Monthly*, June 1992, p. 24.

14. P. Salmon, op. cit., p. 24.

15. M. J. Kavanagh, H. G. Gueutal and S. O. Tannenbaum, *Human Resource Information Systems: Development and Application*, PWS-Kent, Boston, 1990, p. 29.

16. D. T. Hall, and J. G. Goodale, *Human Resource Management*, Scott Foresman, Glenview, Ill., 1986, p. 56.

17. S. Sherman, 'The new computer revolution', *Fortune*, 14 June 1992, p. 30.

18. For example, see S. Bernhardt, 'Integrated systems fail', *HR Monthly*, March 2000, pp. 40–1; S. Chapman, 'Realizing the tactical advantages of HRMS', *HR Monthly*, April 2000, p. 44; and 'Letters to the editor', *HR Monthly*, May 2000, pp. 8–9.

19. HRIS and payroll are linked because they share 10–20 per cent of the data on employees. S. O'Connell, 'Can you say "it's only payroll"?', *HR Magazine*, January 1995, p. 33.

20. J. Benson, 'Linking the 3Ps', *Multinational Employer*, March 1993, pp. 16–17.

21. J. Benson, op. cit., pp. 16–17.

22. J. Benson, op. cit., pp. 16–17.

23. J. Benson, op. cit., pp. 16–17.

24. S. O'Connell, op. cit., p. 34.

25. S. Casey, 'Benefits online', *HR Monthly*, April 2000, pp. 40–1.

26. C. T. Romm, N. Pliskin and Y. Weber, 'The relevance of organizational culture to the implementation of human resource information systems', *Asia Pacific Journal of Human Resources*, vol. 33, no. 2, 1995, pp. 63–80.

27. Adapted from J. Sullivan, 'Hi tech HR', *HR Monthly*, June 1998, pp. 14–16.

28. S. McCoy, quoted in 'The latest and greatest in employee self-service', *Human Resources*, July 2002, p. 18.

29. R. Sharp, 'New technology pushes HR information out into the business', *HR Monthly*, March 1999, p. 40.

30. *ANZ Annual Report*, 2000, p. 17.

31. P. Howes, 'Technological innovation driving demise of the HR departments', *HR Monthly*, August 1998, p. 52.

32. G. Speight, G. Edmunds and R. Lovell, 'Access all areas', *HR Monthly*, September 2000, p. 27.

33. G. Speight, quoted in G. Speight, G. Edmunds and R. Lovell, op. cit., p. 27.

34. J. Purcell and D. Perry, 'Merge right', *HR Monthly*, September 2000, pp. 28–9.

35. J. Purcell and D. Perry, op. cit., p. 29.

36. Reported in 'The latest and the greatest in employee self-service', *Human Resources*, July 2002, p. 19.

37. J. Sullivan, op. cit., p. 18.

38. W. Lenihan, 'Essentials of tight computer security', *Bottom Line Business*, vol. 24, no. 11, 1 June 1995, pp. 11–12; and J. M. Ivancevich, *Human Resource Management*, 8th edn, McGraw-Hill, Boston, 2001, pp. 144–5.

39. B. D. Weiss, 'Working in Cyberspace', *HR Focus*, September 1995, pp. 15–16; and V. Steggall, 'For whose eyes only?', *HR Monthly*, June 2000, pp. 16–20.

40. J. Macy, 'International data privacy laws place new strains on local HR systems', *HR Monthly*, February 1998, p. 48.

41. S. E. O'Connell, 'Security for HR records', *HR Magazine*, September 1994, p. 41.

42. V. Steggall, op. cit., pp. 16–20; and J. C. Hubbard, K. A. Forcht and D. S. Thomas, 'Human resource information systems: an overview of current ethical and legal issues', *Journal of Business Ethics*, vol. 17, no. 12, 1998, pp. 1319–23.

43. H. Zampetakis, 'Clean up wave could end surfers' paradise at work', *Australian Financial Review*, 26–27 February 2000, p. 19.

44. N. Wingfield, 'Bosses battle web shopping', *Asian Wall Street Journal*, 30 September 2002, p. A10.

45. A. Hepworth, 'Firms grappling with email anarchy', *Australian Financial Review*, 30 March 1999, p. 25. Also see R. Jackson and P. Wheelahan, 'The pop-porn culture', *HR Monthly*, April 2001, pp. 40–1; D. Neiger, 'Protection from "netnasties"', *HR Monthly*, April 2001, pp. 41–2; and E. Ross, 'The war against cyber-bludging', *Business Review Weekly*, 20 April 2001, pp. 68–9.

46. Adapted from M. Corvin, 'Workers, surf at your own risk', *Business Week*, 12 June 2000, pp. 78–9. See also M. J. McCarthy, 'Company's virtual voyeur keeps employees use of Internet in line', *Asian Wall Street Journal*, 11 January 2000, p. 8; and M. Bryan, 'NSW may ban e-mail monitoring', *Australian Financial Review*, 9 April 2001, p. 3.

47. M. Bryan and D. Crowe, 'Personal emails are wiped off screen', *Australian Financial Review*, 15 August 2003, p. 5.

48. D. Williams, 'Check your email policy', *HR Monthly*, May 2000, p. 35; E. Temperton, 'How to monitor e-communication', *People Today*, April 2001, pp. 24–7; and D. Henderson, 'See no evil', *HR Monthly*, September 2003, p. 28.

49. M. A. Nusbaum, 'Stepped up snooping arrives at the office', *International Herald Tribune*, 15 July 2003, p. 14.

50. N. Varchaver, 'The perils of e-mail', *Fortune*, 17 February 2003, p. 63.

51. N. Varchaver, op. cit., p. 58.

52. M. Bryan, 'Workers and managers are still worlds apart on email', *Australian Financial Review*, 24 March 2000, p. 3.

53. S. Strutt, 'Fun on the net . . . at the boss's expense', *Australian Financial Review*, 18 July 2003, p. 5.

54. N. Manktelow, 'Dark side of the net', *Weekend Australian*, 22–23 May 1999, p. 52.

55. 'The latest and the greatest in employee self-service', *Human Resources*, July 2002, p. 19.

56. G. Chapman, quoted in 'The latest and the greatest in employee self-service', *Human Resources*, July 2002, p. 19.

57. J. Ogier, 'Are you a tech wreck?', *HR Monthly*, September 2003, p. 23.

58. T. Boyed, 'Murray pays out on People Soft's failings', *Australian Financial Review*, 3 February 2003, p. 50; and J. Whyte, 'CBA promises end to payroll problems', *Australian Financial Review*, 16 July 2003, p. 48.

59. D. Murray, quoted in T. Boyed, op. cit., p. 50.

60. T. Shelds and J. Sale, 'How to avoid the system from hell!', *HR Monthly*, March 1994, pp. 17–19; and S. E. O'Connell, 'An alternative to the RFP', *HR Magazine*, September 1996, pp. 36–44.

61. This section is based on material drawn from M. Banaghan, 'Calling in the expert', *Business Review Weekly*, 16 September 1996, pp. 72–5; R. Langford, 'Can a business core be outside?', *Business Review Weekly*, 8 September 1997, pp. 92–3; and M. J. Kavanagh, H. G. Gueutal and S. O. Tannenbaum, op. cit., p. 32.

62. Based on anonymous reviewer comments, November 2003.

63. Based on anonymous reviewer comments, July 1997.

64. J. Schultz, 'Avoid the DDTs of HRIS implementation', *HR Magazine*, May 1997, p. 42.

65. Survey by Executive Connection (national network of chief executives) reported in D. James, 'Outsourcing fills the gaps created by recession', *Business Review Weekly*, 16 October 1995, p. 75.

66. M. J. Kavanagh, H. G. Gueutal and S. O. Tannenbaum, op. cit., p. 30.

67. M. R. Carrell, N. F. Elbert and R. D. Hatfield, *Human Resource Management*, 5th edn, Prentice Hall, Englewood Cliffs, NJ, 1995, p. 747; and B. Roberts, 'Who's in charge of HRIS?', *HR Magazine*, June 1999, pp. 130–40.

68. This section is based on anonymous reviewer comments (July 1997) and N. J. Beautell and A. J. Waler, 'HR information systems', in R. S. Schuler (ed), *Managing HR in the Information Age*, Bureau of National Affairs, Washington, 1991, pp. 6-197 to 6-198.

69. M. R. Carrell, N. F. Elbert and R. D. Hatfield, op. cit., p. 738.

70. Based on M. R. Carrell, N. F. Elbert and R. D. Hatfield, op. cit., p. 737.

71. M. R. Carrell, N. F. Elbert and R. D. Hatfield, op. cit., pp. 740–1.

72. This section is based on material drawn from C. Holden, 'Internet set to capture HR management', *HR Monthly*, August 1996, p. 28; S. Greenard, 'Catch the wave as HR goes online', *Personnel Journal*, July 1995, p. 59; S. Greenard, 'Home, home on the web', *Personnel Journal*, March 1996, pp. 26–33; Bureau of National Affairs, 'Special survey report: employers on the Internet', *Bulletin to Management*, 2 January 1997, pp. 1–20; and L. L. Byars and L. W. Rue, *Human Resource Management*, 6th edn, McGraw-Hill, Boston, 2000, ch. 2.

73. C. Holden, op. cit., p. 28.

74. E. A. Ensher, T. R. Nielson and E. Grant-Vallone, op. cit., pp. 224–5.

75. Based on material drawn from L. L. Byars and L. W. Rue, op. cit., p. 35; C. D. Diers, 'Personnel computing: make the HRIS more effective', *Personnel Journal*, May 1990, pp. 92–4; and M. Miller, 'Great expectations: is your HRIS meeting them?', *HR Focus*, April 1998, pp. 12–20.

76. Partly based on M. Priest, 'Beyond porn: cybernet loafers in firing line', *Australian Financial Review*, 6 June 2003, p. 22.

chapter 4

human resource management and the law[1]

This chapter was written by Joe Catanzariti, National Practice Group on Workplace Relations and Employment Law, Clayton Utz

Learning objectives

When you have finished studying this chapter, you should be able to:

- Understand the importance of the law as it relates to HRM
- Identify the sources of legal obligations in employment law
- Understand the importance of the contract of employment and its essential terms
- Identify the legal requirements at various stages of employee recruitment and selection
- Discuss the procedures for terminating employees
- Understand the employee's rights of review upon dismissal.

'**An employer who uses redundancy as a smoke screen for a performance-based termination will be exposing itself to several risks, including a claim for unfair dismissal.**'[2]

Michael Michalandos, Partner, Baker & McKenzie

HRM and the law

The relationship between an employer and their employees is governed by a myriad of legal issues with which successful HR managers must be familiar. At its broadest level, the HR profession needs to be familiar with what is termed 'labour law'. Labour law incorporates the law of employment, which governs the individual contract that all employees have with their employers, and industrial law, which regulates the manner in which employees, as a collective group, relate with employers, or indeed groups of employers. While it is beyond the scope of this chapter to provide an exhaustive analysis of labour law, what follows is an attempt to address the important legal issues that are faced daily by HR practitioners.[3]

Employee or contractor

An independent contractor is an independent, self-directed, self-sufficient worker. This person contracts their labour to another entity for a specified purpose but does not become an employee. As such, employers who enter into a relationship with independent contractors do not incur statutory obligations. Likewise, independent contractors do not have any statutory rights, such as the right to make an application for relief for unfair dismissal. Industries that rely heavily on such workers include the transport and construction industries.

Conversely, at common law, 'employees' are defined as workers employed under a contract of service, while independent contractors are defined as workers engaged under a contract *for* services. This seemingly simple distinction has been the subject of significant judicial consideration, with various legal tests being adopted over time, but with no 'golden formula' established pursuant to which practitioners can determine whether a person is an employee or an independent contractor.

Traditionally, the test used at common law was that of the nature and degree of control exerted by the 'master' over the 'servant'. As the employment relationship evolved in a modern context, a more flexible common law approach was required. To this end, the High Court held in *Stevens v. Brodribb Sawmilling Co. Pty Ltd* (1986) 63 ALR 513 that it is not just the level of control that should be considered, but the 'totality of the employment relationship'.

Sources of legal obligations

There are several sources of legal obligations that interact to form the law of employment: contracts (which may or may not incorporate workplace policies), statutes, statutory agreements, awards and the common law.

Contracts

Employment contract
An informal (oral) or formal (written) legally binding agreement between an employer and an employee specifying the legal rights and obligations of each party.

An **employment contract** will exist between the employer and the employee in all relationships of employment. It is a myth that contracts of employment need to be written. Contracts of employment can be either:
1. a written document signed by both parties
2. or a wholly or partly oral agreement (usually courts will infer the existence of a contract from when work commences).

In drafting contracts, employers often fail to consider terms other than remuneration and hours of work. This means that other important terms, such as probationary periods, termination notice periods, redundancy payments and non-competition clauses, are absent from the contract. In the interests of certainty, and in order to avoid the potential for costly and time-consuming litigation in the future, HR managers are advised to include all material terms of employment in the contract itself.

Types of employment contract

Broadly, contracts of employment may take one of two forms: **contracts of indefinite duration** and **contracts of a fixed term**. Contracts of indefinite duration are the most common type of employment contract and provide that the employee will remain employed until either the employer or the employee gives notice that they wish to terminate the employment. The requisite notice period is determined by statue, statutory agreements or the contract of employment itself.

A fixed-term contract is one that is determinable at an expressly defined date or upon the completion of a specific task. For example, an employee may be employed for a period of 12 months — the contract will come to an end after that period.

A contract will be for a fixed term only where the parties do not have the right to terminate the contract before the effluxion of time or the completion of the specific task. That is, a contract that provides for 12 month's service *and* provides that the employment may come to an end upon the giving of notice will not be construed to be a true fixed-term contract. A series of fixed-term contracts may indicate that a true construction of the relationship is one of continuing employment rather than one of a fixed term.

The importance of the distinction is that fixed-term employees may be excluded from state and federal unfair dismissal legislation.

Contracts of indefinite duration Continuing employment that ends only after one party gives the other party notice that they wish to terminate the contract.

Contracts of a fixed term Contracts of employment that provide that the employment will end on a specified date or upon the completion of a specific task.

The advantages of a written contract

There are many advantages to having a written contract of employment. In particular, it removes any doubts that the new employee may have about their rights and obligations. Surprisingly, parameters of the job are a major area of dispute between the parties in an employment relationship. Employees often comment, 'I did not think that that was part of my job description'. Drafting a written contract has the added benefit of forcing the parties to consider which terms they require in the contract. This means that the parties select the terms that govern their relationship rather than allowing the common law to imply terms that the parties may not desire.

Employment contracts need not be overly complex. They are inexpensive to draft and ultimately save a lot of time and money. However, conflict may arise if the terms of a contract are uncertain. Attention to detail at the outset of contractual formation is far less expensive than disgruntled ex-employees, both in terms of public relations and potential litigation. The more astute HR manager, ever concerned with the prospects of unnecessary litigation, should take the initiative by having all employees, and especially senior executives, enter into written contracts of employment. A well-planned, well-drafted contract of employment ensures that the employment relationship commences on the appropriate footing.

Figure 4.1 illustrates how a written contract provides for the essential aspects of the employment relationship.

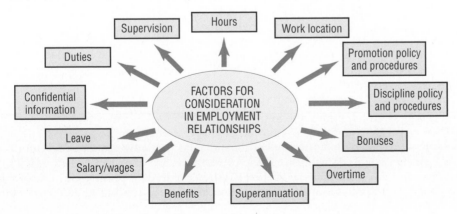

Figure 4.1 Essential terms of employment contracts

Workplace policy A document
of general application that is
prepared by the employer and
is designed to govern (either
with or without contractual
force) any and all aspects of the
conduct, rights and obligations
of the parties to a contract of
employment.

A further advantage of having a written contract of employment is that the parties can confidently know whether or not the contract, which provides for legally binding rights and obligations, incorporates a **workplace policy**. Workplace policies may take the form of a document that declares itself to be *The Workplace Policy* or it may take the form of guidelines or general directions to employees. What is important, however, is that they are of general application to employees, either as a whole or in defined groups.

A workplace policy can regulate virtually all aspects of employment, including recruitment, termination (including redundancy), disciplinary procedures, confidentiality, occupational health and safety, discrimination and equal employment opportunity. The following is a sample of an EEO policy:

[Company X] is an equal opportunity employer. This company is committed to equal employment opportunity and the prevention of discriminatory practices and behaviour.

Equal opportunity means that everyone's success is determined by their talents and abilities. Employees are judged on their ability to do the job based on their skills, qualification and experience. The company ensures that all employment policies and practices are based on this concept of equal opportunity. For example, all performance reviews only consider factors relating to an employee's performance of their duties and responsibilities.

Equal opportunity should be a common goal of all employees. It is everyone's responsibility to ensure that equal opportunity in the workplace is observed. The company recognises that all employees have a right to be treated equally. The company also expects all employees to treat their fellow employees with the same standard of treatment.

In the case of *Riverwood International Australia Pty Ltd v. McCormick*,[4] a case decided by the Full Bench of the Federal Court of Australia, a phrase in a contract that said 'you agree to abide by all company policies' was held to incorporate all the terms of the workplace policy in the legally binding contract. The incorporation of the policy in the contract permitted the employee to successfully sue the employer for the very favourable redundancy benefits that were contemplated by the policy. A workplace policy will, pursuant to the *Riverwood* decision, be incorporated into the contract of employment if:

1. the relevant policy is directly referred to in a document purporting to be the 'contract of employment'
2. or it appears to the court that it was the intention of the parties that the policy form part of the contract.

In the light of the *Riverwood* decision, best practice HR dictates a proactive approach in making the important decision of whether or not to incorporate the terms of a workplace policy into contracts with employees. The key benefit of incorporating policies into contracts is that it enables employers to enforce such things as disciplinary procedures against employees where those procedures are contemplated by the policy. On the other hand, the incorporation of policies into the contract may, as occurred in the *Riverwood* case, confer contractual rights on employees that are enforceable. Workplace policies are effective tools that employers can use to regulate the work environment. However, the prevailing implication of the *Riverwood* case is that employers must be mindful of 'locking themselves in' to the terms of a policy.

Restraint of trade

In the current climate of increasing competition and mobile employment, contracts of employment play an important role in minimising the losses incurred from employee turnover. They do so by attempting to limit an employee's ability to be engaged in a related business for a specific period after the termination and to divulge confidential information and/or customer connections. Historically, courts have not been inclined to uphold such clauses. The position at common law is that a restraint of trade is prima facie void as against public policy. In order to rebut the presumption, the person seeking to enforce a restraint must establish that the restriction is no wider than is *reasonably necessary to protect a legitimate interest*.

The employer will have to show that the former employee's knowledge of and relationship with customers, together with their acquaintance with the employer's trade secrets, would, if competition were allowed, enable the former employee to take advantage of the employer's connections or confidential information. The Courts have made it clear that even if the employer can prove that a restrictive covenant was intended to protect a legitimate interest, it will not be valid unless its scope is reasonable.

Reasonableness is assessed in terms of three factors that the covenant possesses, namely: (1) the *nature and extent of the activities* that the former employee is restricted from performing; (2) the *geographic area* in which those activities cannot occur; and (3) the *duration* of the restraint. The restraint must also be reasonable in the public interest. Reasonableness will be determined with reference to the actual or foreseeable circumstances at the time that it was entered into, rather than at the time when the employer sought to enforce it. Therefore, to be effective and act as a deterrent, trade restraint clauses need to be carefully drafted.

Confidentiality agreements

A related and equally important issue in employment contracts is making provisions for employee confidentiality during and after the course of employment. Although employer/employee common law duties are mentioned later in this chapter, a well-drafted confidentiality agreement will assist in clarifying the duties and obligations of an employee.

Confidentiality clauses in employment contracts have certain advantages over relying on the common law duties. The fact that the employment relationship has ceased will enliven the restrictive clauses. Rather than protecting specific information, restrictive clauses will prevent a former employee from misusing the information. Additionally, it is easier to frame legal action against a former employee around a breach of a contractual clause as opposed to an implied duty.

Workplace intellectual property

An invention created by an employee in the course of their employment will usually belong to the employer, not the employee. Having made a discovery or invention in the course of such work, the employee becomes a trustee for the employer of that invention or discovery, so that as a trustee the employee is bound to give the benefit of any such discovery or invention to the employer.

However, this depends on the consideration of all the circumstances in each case and an interpretation of the terms of employment. In the absence of a contractual obligation on the matter, the employer will have no legal claim to an invention. In such cases, it is open to a Court to take a restrictive approach to the employment relationship and hold that an invention was not made in the course of the employee's employment. The case review on the following page indicates that reliance upon generally accepted opinions may not prove sufficient to restrain employees.

Moral rights

Additionally, although an invention or discovery made by an employee in the course of their employment will generally belong to the employer, the employee may still have a number of moral rights. Since the enactment of the *Copyright Amendment (Moral Rights) Act 2000* (Cwlth), rights such as attribution of authorship, a right against false attribution of authorship and a right to maintain the integrity of a work may apply to an employee's creative endeavour.

These moral rights cannot be assigned, transferred or waived. This means that, irrespective of where the economic rights lie (that is, the copyright), the moral rights will remain with the author of the work. This may represent a serious impediment to the interests of the copyright owner in commercially exploiting the work. However, the Act does contain provisions whereby the author can consent to acts or omissions that would otherwise constitute an infringement of moral rights. However, such consent cannot be unconditional and limitations will apply.

Mr Collins worked as a Sales Manager for Spencer Industries, a company that is in the business of manufacturing equipment used in the tyre retreading business, particularly rasp blades, hubs and spacers and pins for hubs.

Mr Collins created an invention which was related to improvements in both the process and apparatus used for the retreading of tyres. In particular, the invention related to rasp blades and an improved assembly of such blades on tyre rasp hubs for buffing away the tread on worn tyres. The invention was later patented.

A dispute arose in relation to the entitlement to the patent when Spencer Industries applied for an extension of the term of the patent. In order to resolve this issue, the Delegate of the Commissioner of Patents had to determine whether the invention was created in the course of Mr Collins' employment.

Mr Collins was not employed pursuant to a written contract which clearly defined the scope of his employment. The job advertisement referred to 'sales and contracts and the authority to negotiate new agencies both in Australia and overseas'.

Decision of the delegate

The delegate concluded that the invention was not made by Mr Collins in carrying out his normal duties. The delegate held that even if the invention related to subject matter germane to, and useful for, his employer in their business, and even though the employee may have made use of his employer's time and servants and materials in bringing his invention to completion, and may have allowed his employer to use the invention while he was in their employment, this will not disqualify the employee from taking out a patent for an invention made by him during the term of his employment.

The employer, Spencer Industries, lodged a notice of appeal. It argued that Mr Collins made the invention with the consequence that the benefit of the invention vested in Spencer Industries.

Decision of the Federal Court

The Court accepted that relevant considerations in determining whether the invention was made during the course of Mr Collins's employment included the nature and seniority of Mr Collins's position with Spencer Industries, the nature of his duties as Sales Manager and whether he received a specific directive relating to the invention.

The Court found that Mr Collins was principally employed in a sales position, but due to the fact that the company was a small family owned one, he could be given reasonable directions by his employer to perform duties outside of the area of sales, as long as they were within the area of his technical skills and not incompatible with his principal responsibility for sales.

The Court rejected the submission by Spencer Industries that because Mr Collins had a duty as Sales Manager to advance the sales of Spencer Industries, any invention made by him which was capable of advancing the company's sales was an invention made by him within the course and scope of his employment.

The Court held that it was no part of Mr Collins's ongoing duties to invent products for Spencer Industries and neither was the invention the product of a direction by Spencer Industries (as Mr Collins informed Spencer Industries of the invention only after the inventive steps concerning it had been completed). The decision of the delegate was upheld.

Implications

An invention made during the term of a person's employment will not automatically belong to the employer, unless the invention was made in the course of employment as part of the employee's relevant duties.

For employers to have a legal claim over an employee's invention, it is advisable that they make it clear in the employee's contract of employment that all inventions made by them in the course of their employment will be the property of the employer.

See *Spencer v. Collins* (unreported, FCA No 97/2002, Branson J, 4 June 2003).

No winners under unfair dismissal law

By Charles Power

The Howard government undertook to reform unfair dismissal laws in 1996 to achieve a 'fair go all round' for employers and employees. It has arguably failed.

The federal unfair dismissal scheme is still clogged with unmeritorious claims. The remedies for proper claimants are paltry. Meanwhile, it is not clear that the laws are actually encouraging fairer approaches in handling employee issues.

Of the 150 or so federal unfair dismissal claims lodged each week in Australia, more than 75 per cent are settled before final hearing. There are few claims today that an employer would be better off defending rather than settling by a monetary payment.

The median monetary settlement at the conciliation phase is about eight weeks' pay, much less (assuming average weekly earnings) than the costs of defending a one-day hearing. The fact that the employer would win at final hearing usually offers little comfort, as costs are rarely awarded.

At the same time, the rewards for successful claimants are relatively meagre. Reinstatement is not available in most cases, and until recently, the average compensation award by the Australian Industrial Relations Commission was 13 weeks' pay.

The jurisdiction attracts a league of 'no win, no fee' organisations that take the lion's share of settlements or awards of compensation. The successful claimant is often exhausted, humiliated and distracted from the real task — getting another job.

The federal government clearly believes its 1996 reforms are not working, if its continuing campaign to change the legislation is any indication. The government recently presented its bill to exempt small business from unfair dismissal laws for the seventh time.

Senator Andrew Murray of the Australian Democrats has confirmed his party will again reject the bill and claims the government is looking for a double dissolution trigger.

In 2001 the Senate did pass laws restricting access to unfair dismissal laws and giving the AIRC power to dismiss claims that had no reasonable prospects of success. The commission has exercised its new powers in only a handful of cases, reflecting the primacy it gives to conciliating claims before any consideration of their merit. As the AIRC president, Justice Geoffrey Giudice, said in February: 'In one sense, and in an important one, the commission deals with individual disputes in relation to termination of employment in the same way as it has always dealt with collective industrial disputes. In both cases conciliation is the primary method of resolving the dispute, and arbitration is only available when it is clear that conciliation has failed.'

Yet parties to industrial disputes are still in employment and have a much greater degree of flexibility in devising remedies to solve disputes. The remedies in an unfair dismissal claim are, in the vast majority of cases, confined to monetary payments, which are rarely adequate compensation.

The government equates reform of unfair dismissal laws with micro-economic reform. Yet (as the OECD admitted in its March 2003 survey), it is not generally accepted that the scheme discourages employment.

The full Federal Court of Australia ruled in the Hamzy case (concerning casual exemption laws) in December 2001 that there was no evidence that the laws inhibited employment, remarking that, 'Employers are used to bearing many obligations in relation to employees (wage and superannuation payments, leave entitlements, the provision of appropriate working places, safe systems of work, even payroll tax).'

There is a better way for both employers and employees. Rather than restricting access to the jurisdiction, employers should be encouraged to ensure that dismissal disputes never find their way to the AIRC. Employers who have trained their managers in fair hiring and firing practices and have consistently applied that practice, should be able to mitigate their liability for unfair dismissal.

(continued)

Statutes

State and territory governments in Australia have legislated to prescribe minimum conditions of employment that apply despite any express provision in the contract. For example, equal opportunity **statutes** prohibit discrimination on the basis of such characteristics as race, colour, sex, transgender, sexual preference, age, physical or mental disability, marital status, family responsibility, pregnancy, religion, political opinion, national extraction or social origin, in areas such as hiring, remuneration, promotion and termination — for example, see *Human Rights and Equal Opportunity Commission Act 1986* (Cwlth), *Racial Discrimination Act 1975* (Cwlth), *Sex Discrimination Act 1984* (Cwlth) and *Disability Discrimination Act 1992* (Cwlth).

The scope of the employment relationship that statutes cover is broad and includes provisions to the effect that:

- Employers must not dismiss an employee without a 'valid reason' — *Workplace Relations Act 1996* (Cwlth).
- Employers must allow their employees to take annual leave and long service leave — for example, see *Annual Holidays Act 1944* (NSW), *Long Service Leave Act 1955* (NSW), *Long Service Leave Act 1992* (Vic.) and *Long Service Leave Act 1958* (WA).
- Employers must pay superannuation to their employees — see *Superannuation Guarantee (Administration) Act 1992* (Cwlth). (This is a complex area that usually requires professional advice.)
- Employers must obtain insurance against workers compensation claims — for example, see *Safety, Rehabilitation and Compensation Act 1988* (Cwlth), *Workers Compensation Act 1987* (NSW), *Accident Compensation Act 1985* (Vic.) and *Workers Compensation Act 1990* (Qld).
- An employer must ensure the health and safety of all employees and others in the working environment — for example, see *Occupational Health and Safety Act 2000* (NSW), *Occupational Health and Safety Act 1985* (Vic.), *Workplace Health and Safety Act 1995* (Qld), *Occupational Safety and Health Act 1984* (WA), *Occupational Health, Safety and Welfare Act 1986* (SA) and *Occupational Health and Safety Act 1989* (ACT).

Statutory agreements

In 1996, the *Workplace Relations Act* was enacted and introduced a sophisticated framework for individual and enterprise bargaining. The shift away from industry-wide bargaining has been facilitated by the introduction of Australian Workplace Agreements (AWAs) and provisions for non-unionised Certified Agreements.

Australian Workplace Agreements

AWAs are provided for by Part VID of the *Workplace Relations Act 1996*. AWAs are agreements made between an employer and an individual employee that govern the terms and conditions of that relationship. The Act provides that AWAs must incorporate certain minimum conditions, such as a discrimination clause and a dispute resolution clause. AWAs can continue to operate for a maximum of three years.

Statutes In the context of employment, statutes legislate the minimum conditions of employment that must apply in any employer–employee relationship.

Checking employee email is viewed as an invasion of privacy, yet employers may be liable for employee abuse of the system.

Certified Agreements

Part VIB of the *Workplace Relations Act 1996* regulates Certified Agreements, which facilitate collective enterprise bargaining. These agreements can be made between an employer and a group of employees. They can also be made between an employer and a union, or group of unions, if all unions involved have at least one member that will be subject to the agreement and that member has authorised the union to represent them. The terms of Certified Agreements prevail over the terms of an award. Having said that, however, the famous 'no-disadvantage' test must be met before the Australian Industrial Relations Commission will certify an agreement.

The 'no-disadvantage' test

As the terms of Certified Agreements prevail over awards (which prescribe the minimum employment conditions that provide a safety net for lower income employees), the *Workplace Relations Act* provides that an agreement will be certified only if it does not, on balance, effect a reduction in the overall terms and conditions of employment that are contained in an applicable award or statute (see Part VIE of the *Workplace Relations Act*). This provision raises difficult value judgements for the Commission as well as HR managers. The following case provides examples of the difficulties faced.

The company, Visy Paper Pty Ltd, made an application to the Australian Industrial Relations Commission for certification of an Agreement. The Commission refused to certify the Agreement given that it did not pass the 'no-disadvantage' test. There were a number of clauses in the Agreement that the Commission had concerns with, including the following:

Wage rates

The company submitted that the rates stipulated in the Agreement would provide a net benefit. However, in calculating those rates, it included bonus payments that were contingent on employees achieving *all* Key Performance Indicators (KPIs). In order to achieve 100 per cent of the payment, the targets of attendance, nil sick days, 85 per cent uptime, 71 per cent yield, productivity over 85 tonnes per person per month, and nil time lost to injury, must be achieved. If these are not achieved, or are only partly achieved, it would result in a reduction in earnings vis-a-vis the award.

The KPI bonus is a benefit that is not provided for in the Award. However, the Commission noted: *'It is not appropriate to include the maximum benefit payable under that scheme in a costing comparison document as it has the capacity to distort the figures.'* If the KPI payments were removed from the calculation, the employees would suffer a net detriment when compared to the Award. Further, it was difficult to assess the benefit of this provision given that the scheme was subject to variation.

Casual rates of pay

The casual rates set out in the Agreement were less than those provided in the Award. The company made an undertaking to pay casuals at a rate that was at least as beneficial as the payments they would receive under the Award, or time off in lieu of such payments. In calculating those payments, any KPI payments may be taken into account.

The Commission had a number of difficulties with this provision and the associated undertaking. First of all, the rate specified in the Agreement was less than that provided for in the Award. Further, the performance payment, which was contingent on the achievement of all KPIs, would be offset against the award entitlement. This would diminish the possible benefit of the KPI payment. Finally, the Commission was unclear as to how the time off work, as opposed to current payment for the work performed, would counteract the disadvantage inherent in the clause.

Annual and long service leave

The Agreement provided that on agreement between the parties, annual and long service leave could be cashed out if the employee had accrued at least 4 weeks leave. (Note: the relevant legislation prohibits employers from cashing out leave; however, where the amount accrued is in excess of 4 weeks, that extra amount can be cashed out.) On the assumption that the (4 weeks) accrued leave is to be taken (as opposed to cashed out), the Commission held that this clause does not disadvantage employees as compared with the legislative entitlement.

Sick leave

The Agreement provided for 38 hours sick leave in the first year and 60.8 hours in the years thereafter. The Award also made provision for 38 hours in the first year, but this increased to 76 hours each year thereafter. The Agreement entitlement was held to be less beneficial to employees.

Redundancy

The company submitted that the redundancy provision contained in the Agreement was an advantage to the employees. However, the Commission rejected this contention. It adopted the statement made by Senior Deputy President Lacy in *Re Genesis Holdings WA Pty Ltd Collective Agreement 2003* (PR936265 13 August 2003): '... *it is not appropriate to take into account contingent benefits under a benchmark instrument*'. In this case, the contingency is that an employee/s would be made redundant.

Conclusion

The Commission concluded that the Agreement did not pass the no-disadvantage test and refused to certify the Agreement. However, it did give the company the opportunity to take steps to make the Agreement certifiable.

See *Visy Paper Pty Ltd; Visy Recycling — Rydalmere MRF Enterprise Bargaining Agreement 2003* (unreported, AIRC No. AG2003/6464, Commissioner Larkin, 29 September 2003).

Other requirements for agreement certification

The Commission will also refuse to certify an Agreement for other reasons, including:

- the Agreement has not been approved by a valid majority of employees who will be subject to the terms and conditions of the Agreement
- the terms and conditions of the Agreement have not been appropriately explained to those who will be subject to the Agreement having regard to any particular needs of the employees
- there is no dispute resolution clause in the Agreement
- an employee has been coerced by the employer to not request that they be represented by an employee organisation such as a union or to remove such a request.

The duration of Certified Agreements

Certified Agreements will remain in force until a new agreement is made by the parties and is certified by the Commission. Having said that, however, it is a legislative requirement that Certified Agreements must contain a 'nominal expiry date', which is to be no more than three years from the date of certification. The importance of the 'nominal expiry date' is that industrial action by either party (such as strikes in the case of employees/unions and lock-outs in the case of employers) is prohibited before the nominal expiry date has passed.

Awards

In the past, awards were the primary source of employment obligations for most Australian employees and employers. However, the *Workplace Relations Act* has lessened the importance of awards through its award simplification provisions and its encouragement of individual bargaining under AWAs.

With the enactment of the *Workplace Relations Act* in 1996, federal awards are now limited to dealing with 20 allowable matters that relate to minimum conditions only. These matters are outlined in s. 89A(2) of the Act.

By limiting the scope of awards, additional terms and conditions can be made only at the industrial level (as opposed to the contractual level) through Certified Agreements and AWAs. Therefore, legislative reform has encouraged a shift in the way the employment relationship is governed, with awards increasingly being supplanted by enterprise and individual bargaining.

Despite this, it is still necessary for HR managers to understand what an award is, and be aware of all awards relevant to their organisation. Awards specify minimum terms and conditions of employment. They are created by state and federal industrial tribunals and are legally binding on the parties to them. They can cover conditions such as minimum pay, hours of work, types of leave and the regulation of employment termination. An employer may provide more favourable terms than those provided by the relevant award.

Copies of awards and information on them can be obtained from state and federal departments of industrial relations. Employees should be informed which award applies to their work and where they can inspect a copy.

Common law

The **common law** is 'case law' that has developed in the court system. On one level, the body of previous judgements that comprise the common law guides how we should interpret the other sources of law such as statutes. Further, the common law is itself a source of legal rights and obligations. The doctrine of precedent holds that the Courts must decide like cases alike. On this basis we can predict how courts will decide cases before them and define the law on that basis. The general duties of the parties to an employment relationship are prescribed by the common law.

Employers' and employees' common law duties

At common law employers have clear obligations to their employees. These include the **employers' duties** to:
- pay employees' wages, as well as reasonable expenses incurred in the course of the employment
- give employees reasonable notice of termination of employment
- take reasonable care for the health and safety of the employees
- indemnify an employee for losses incurred by the employee during the course of employment
- cooperate with their employees — that is, not conduct themselves in a manner likely to seriously damage the necessary relationship of trust and confidence that must exist between the employee and employer
- provide work for employees who are paid on commission or on a piece rate, or who need to maintain their public profile (such as actors).

However, employers are under no common law duty to:
- provide work for employees other than those described above; however, the employer will remain bound by the implied duty to pay wages notwithstanding that no work is required
- provide a reference for former or current employees
- provide medical care to employees while they are at work (although an employer must obtain medical care if there is an accident)
- provide accommodation to employees.

It must be noted that the employer may have duties such as those above if such duties are expressly provided for in the contract.

Similarly, employees' owe common law duties to their employers. These include the **employees' duties** of:
- obedience — employer's directions/orders that are lawful and reasonable must be followed
- good conduct — employees owe their employers a duty to not misconduct themselves in the course of their employment; misconduct includes theft, being under the influence of intoxicating substances and violence in the workplace
- working in a skilful manner, where the employee made a representation that they possessed such skills
- indemnifying their employer for losses incurred by the employer while performing duties under the contract of employment (this duty has been overturned by statute in New South Wales, South Australia and the Northern Territory — see, for example, s. 3 of the *Employees Liability Act 1991* (NSW)).
- cooperating with their employer — that is, not conducting themselves in a manner likely to seriously damage the necessary relationship of trust and confidence that must exist between the employee and employer
- fidelity and good faith — the employee owes their employer a duty to:
  - not accept bribes or secret commissions/profits for work that is done in the course of employment
  - hold on trust for the employer the benefit of any inventions that they make during the course of employment

The more legal restrictions are imposed on employers, the less likely they are to employ local workers and the more likely they are to outsource overseas.

– not disclose or otherwise use the employer's confidential information in a manner inconsistent with the wishes of the employer.

Employees are under no common law duty to:

- volunteer information about their past or present misconduct
- conduct work that is demonstrably different from that which they contracted to perform.

A myriad of laws govern arrangements for selecting and engaging employees. These laws are well established and need to be considered by HR managers. The following areas require particular consideration in the pre-employment phase:

- the job advertisement
- the job description
- the application form
- the interview.

Before discussing these areas, it is necessary to provide an overview of the anti-discrimination laws.

Discrimination

Discrimination Any practice that makes distinctions between different groups based on characteristics such as sex, race, age, religion and so on, which results in particular individuals or groups being advantaged and others disadvantaged.

Unfair **discrimination** is a central concern for HR managers as it pervades all stages of the pre-employment process. As noted earlier, employers must not unfairly discriminate against employees on the basis of race, colour, sex, transgender, sexual preference, age, physical or mental disability, marital status, family responsibility, pregnancy, religion, political opinion, national extraction or social origin, in areas such as hiring, remuneration, promotion and termination — for example, see *Human Rights and Equal Opportunity Commission Act 1986* (Cwlth), *Racial Discrimination Act 1975* (Cwlth), *Sex Discrimination Act 1984* (Cwlth) and *Disability Discrimination Act 1992* (Cwlth).[5]

It should be noted, however, discrimination on some grounds such as age will not be unlawful if there is a genuine occupational requirement and/or inherent requirement of the job that would render certain individuals unsuitable for the position. Indeed, some discrimination is specifically required by legislation. For example, because each Australian state provides that liquor may be sold only by persons above the age of 18 years, it is lawful for a seller of alcoholic beverages to refuse to employ a person under the age of 18 years.

In other cases, differing treatment of classes of persons on the basis of gender, for example, is permitted, if not encouraged, under statute. For example, at the federal level, the *Equal Opportunity for Women in the Workplace Act 1999* (Cwlth) requires private companies with

I agree entirely, Samantha — may I call you Samantha — these days, far too much weight is put on intellectual capital.

more than 100 employees to develop an equal opportunity in the workplace program. These employers must lodge an annual report on the assessment of the program with the Equal Opportunity in the Workplace Agency. An equal opportunity program need not be limited to gender equality. The introduction of special measures such as flexibility in uniforms to cater for differing cultural/religious requirements is a simple provision that may assist in demonstrating that a previously disadvantaged group is better represented in the work force.

Unfair discrimination involves making a distinction between individuals or groups so as to disadvantage some and advantage others in an unreasonable or unjust manner. It can be direct or indirect (see table 4.1). Direct discrimination is the most easily identifiable form, and occurs where a person or group is treated less favourably than another person or group would be treated in similar circumstances. Indirect discrimination involves practices that appear to be inoffensive but that result in a person or group being disadvantaged.

Table 4.1	Direct discrimination versus indirect discrimination	
	DIRECT DISCRIMINATION	**INDIRECT DISCRIMINATION**
Definition	Treating a person or group less favourably than another person or group in similar circumstances.	A practice that appears inoffensive but that results in a person or group being disadvantaged.
Example	An employer dismisses a woman purely on the basis of her gender.	A company makes promotion dependent upon five years continuous service. This disadvantages women who may be more likely to take time off to have children.
Remedy	Damages — pecuniary loss, hurt, loss of career prospects, stress, humiliation.	Damages — pecuniary loss, hurt, loss of career prospects, stress, humiliation.

The following is an example of a decision concerning discrimination in the pre-employment phase.

In this interesting case the Equal Opportunity Division of the Administrative Decisions Tribunal of NSW awarded a man $40 000 in damages arising from unlawful discrimination in pre-employment on the basis of disability. The applicant, Mr Peck, was offered the position of 'Overseer Catering' at a minimum security gaol on the condition that he pass a criminal background check and a medical examination to confirm that he was physically capable of being a prison officer. Mr Peck was examined by a doctor who stated that he was unfit to meet the physical demands of the position because of a knee injury he sustained 10 years previously. This injury prevented him only from bending his left knee beyond a 90 per cent angle.

The Commissioner for Corrective Services argued in response to the claim of discrimination that the inherent requirements of the job demanded prison officers be physically capable of chasing and physically restraining prisoners who may be acting in a violent manner. Although this argument was recognised as valid by the Tribunal, evidence that Mr Peck was a particularly fit and strong candidate was not given sufficient weight by the employer. The Tribunal found that even if his knee was a hindrance, that hindrance would not be any greater than that suffered by other prison officers who might not be as physically fit as Mr Peck or as young as Mr Peck (Mr Peck was 30 years of age at the date of the discrimination). The Tribunal concluded that Mr Peck was the victim of unfair discrimination in pre-employment.

See *Peck v. Commissioner of Corrective Services* [2002] NSWADT 122.

Senior politicians make equal employment opportunity laws but surround themselves with people they regard as loyal and trustworthy.

This case serves as a practical example to HR professionals that unlawful discrimination is taken very seriously by the law and can result in expensive litigation when things go wrong. More specifically, this case indicates that employers will be able to rely on the defence that their discrimination was lawful because of the inherent requirements of the job only if all the relevant circumstances of the case are adequately considered.

The job advertisement and legal requirements

HR managers must be careful when publicising a job vacancy that the advertisement does not indicate, or could not reasonably be understood to indicate, an intention to act in a manner that is discriminatory under any of the legislation. The Acts make it clear that an employer need not actually do anything discriminatory. The legislation is specifically concerned with an indication, or terminology within an advertisement that could reasonably be understood as an indication, of an intention to contravene the provisions. An advertisement that includes such phrases as 'housewife preferred' or 'seeking an office boy', for example, would offend the provisions. Single gender references such as 'waiter required' or 'cameraman needed' should also be avoided in favour of gender-neutral references such as 'waiter/waitress required' or 'camera operator needed'.

Two groups of people are caught — the employer who causes the advertisement to be published, and the publisher. The fine imposed may not be great, but HR specialists should be careful to operate within the legislative requirements. Aside from the bad public relations, any hint of discrimination at the recruitment stage may be used later by a disgruntled employee alleging discrimination in an unfair dismissal action.

The following case concerned discriminatory language in a job advertisement.

In this New Zealand case, the employer owned a service station and advertised for a 'keen Christian person aged 16–18 who is not afraid of work' to apply for the position of service station attendant. The test for discrimination was the same as the test under the New South Wales act and the federal act: namely, whether the advertisement could reasonably be understood as indicating an intention to breach the act — that is, indicating an intention to either employ or give preference to Christians. The Equal Opportunity Tribunal rejected an argument that the term 'Christian' was intended to denote qualities such as honesty and trustworthiness that any employer would seek in a prospective employee. The Tribunal found that decisions to refuse employment would, as evidenced by the advertisement, be made on the basis of an applicant's religious beliefs.

See *Human Rights Commission v. Eric Sides Motor Company Limited*.[6]

The job description and the law

To ameliorate the danger of later accusations of discrimination, or complaints that an employee's duties are not part of their role, it is important to prepare a concise and accurate description of the position to be filled. The preparation of an unambiguous job description is also a prudent manner in which HR managers can ensure that a prospective employee is not misled in any way about the nature of the job. Misleading or deceptive information given to applicants in the pre-employment process may breach s. 53B of the *Trade Practices Act 1974* (Cwlth), which specifically prohibits conduct liable to mislead persons seeking employment. The job description should generally be made available at the interview, if not before.

An HR manager preparing a job description should not reuse old versions (which may be out of date) or reproduce samples from other organisations (which may be inappropriate). Instead, the HR manager should consider the employer's present and future expectations of the employee performing the particular job being described. In doing this, the HR manager should leave sufficient capacity in the job description for the job to evolve. Having said that, in order for the job description to be meaningful, it should contain the following information:

- the title of the position
- the qualifications required
- the level of experience required
- the level of responsibility that the position holds
- the person to whom the employee must report.

Application forms

While there are no direct legal requirements in Australia regarding application forms, there are certain enquiries that are prohibited by relevant equal opportunity and anti-discrimination legislation.

The application form should be concise and include enquiries that are relevant only to deciding whether an applicant should be interviewed for the particular position. Other relevant but non-essential areas should be covered at the interview.

It may be appropriate for a company to utilise more than one type of application form. The information required may vary depending on the position to be filled. For example, the information required from a person applying for a wage-based position may be different from that sought from a person applying for a salaried position.

An application form should contain no discriminatory language and must not mislead or deceive prospective applicants with respect to any facet of the job.

Enquiries as to the applicant's age, religion, gender, country of birth, nationality and marital status (unless it is specifically relevant to a genuine occupational requirement) should not be included. Enquiries should focus on the inherent requirements that are relevant to the applicant's capacity to perform the requisite functions of the job.

Freedom of (and from) association

Part XA of the *Workplace Relations Act 1996* (Cwlth) seeks to ensure that, in accordance with the Australian democratic tradition of freedom of association, employees are free to join or not to join organisations such as trade unions. A prospective employer must not refuse to employ a person on the basis that they are, or are not, a member of an employee organisation such as a trade union. In the case of *Jones v. Britax Rainsford Pty Ltd*,[7] Commissioner Larkin was critical of an application form that asked the question: 'Are you a member of a union or staff association? If yes, name the organisation.' The Commissioner commented that this question was not relevant to the job and that an employee found to have answered the question dishonestly could not be terminated on this ground. At appeal, the Full Bench of the Commission did not vary this conclusion.[8]

Age

Application forms often ask job applicants to disclose their age. However, as discrimination on the grounds of age is unlawful, employers should avoid questions pertaining to age wherever possible.

An exception to the general prohibition against pre-employment enquiries concerning age relates to the employment of juniors. Employers are permitted to advertise for and employ juniors under the age of 21 and pay them junior rates. Questions aimed at identifying an applicant's age for this purpose are not discriminatory. Employers may also need to question juniors as to their age in order to determine whether they are legally permitted to work. Generally, it is an offence for employers to employ a child unless the child has attained the age of 15.

Sex

Commonwealth, state and territory anti-discrimination legislation makes it clear that discrimination on the basis of sex, marital status, pregnancy or family responsibilities in employment is prohibited. At the Commonwealth level the *Sex Discrimination Act 1984* (Cwlth) provides that only where there is a genuine occupational qualification to be of a certain sex is such discrimination permitted. For example, s. 30 of the Act provides that where the employment is for a dramatic performance and for the purposes of 'authenticity, aesthetics or tradition' the role is required to be performed by a member of a particular sex, discrimination on that basis is not unlawful. Questions on application forms should therefore not enquire about a person's sex, marital status, state of pregnancy or otherwise, or family responsibilities. Having said that, however, if the position requires a great deal of travel or time away from home, it is entirely lawful to ask applicants whether or not they are willing to meet such requirements of the position.

Physical and mental capacity

Questions regarding physical and mental capacity are proscribed by most state legislation. Generally, such questions are unnecessary unless it can be demonstrated that a particular physical or mental attribute is required. In this case, questions should be carefully worded so as to avoid contravening the legislation (and offending the person applying for the job!). The wording should tie the question to the applicant's ability to perform the required duties — for example, 'Can you work under certain conditions, such as wet or humid environments?' or 'Can you distinguish between different colours and accurately identify, for instance, whether a particular electric wire is red or green?'

If the selection criteria include the ability to perform tasks that clearly require certain physical attributes, the applicant may be required to undergo a medical examination or produce a recent medical certificate. Such physical requirements should be described in the job advertisement.

Criminal convictions

It is quite common for application forms to contain questions regarding criminal convictions. Although it is generally permissible to ask questions relating to past criminal convictions (although not to previous arrests), it is necessary to be aware of the 'spent convictions' legislation that exists in many states and is being considered in others. Nuances of this area of the law will depend entirely upon the relevant jurisdiction. In New South Wales, the relevant legislation is the *Criminal Records Act 1991* (NSW). Part II of this Act provides that a conviction, except one in which a prison sentence of six months or more was imposed or a conviction for a sexual offence, becomes 'spent' after a 10-year crime-free period. A person with a spent conviction is not required to disclose that spent conviction to any other person, unless that disclosure relates to certain proscribed appointments or employment, such as a judge, magistrate, justice of the peace, police officer, prison officer, teacher, teachers aide or a provider of childcare services. Further exclusions are provided for in the *Criminal Records Regulation 1999* (NSW).

A decision of the Anti-Discrimination Commission of the Northern Territory indicates that a requirement that applicants submit to a criminal background check may be inappropriate in certain cases. In the case of *Hosking v. Fraser t/a Central Recruiting*,[9] an application form produced by a company that required applicants for the position of nurse in a isolated Aboriginal community to submit to a criminal background check without any reference to the relevance of the check, the relevance of any criminal record and to such matters as 'spent convictions' was found to be unreasonable.

References and previous employment

The application form will usually provide for the applicant to nominate referees. The HR manager, in contacting any person not nominated as a referee, should seek the applicant's permission. The HR manager should also consult the applicant before contacting previous employers or checking academic qualifications. Later in the interview the applicant may be asked why they left a previous position of employment.

In making an application for employment, a prospective employee has no obligation or duty to reveal information such as past faults or misconduct if it is not asked of them. In the famous English case of *Bell v. Lever Bros*,[10] Lord Atkin stated the position of the common law regarding the rejection of any imposition on employees to voluntarily disclose past acts:

> the [employee] owes a duty not to steal, but, having stolen, is there superadded a duty to confess that he has stolen? I am satisfied that to imply such a duty ... would be to create obligations entirely outside the normal contemplation of the parties.

In the case of *Concut Pty Ltd v. Worrell and Another*,[11] the High Court of Australia considered this position of the law. However, it is lamented that the Court missed an opportunity to make a clear authoritative statement regarding disclosure of past acts in employment. As such, the law remains that unless an applicant is directly asked to disclose relevant past misconduct, there is no obligation to volunteer such information.

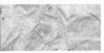

Mike Toten is HR analyst and writer, CCH Australia (www.cch.com.au).

Practitioner speaks

HR policies and procedures: the legal impact

Many cases have been contested in industrial relations tribunals over whether employers were entitled to dismiss employees for alleged breaches of HR policies and procedures. Frequent topics of contention have included alleged misuse of the employer's email or internet facilities, damage/misuse of company vehicles, breaches of occupational health and safety procedures and rules, and non-compliance with employers' dress codes.

While employers are entitled to issue workplace policies and procedures and give directions to employees in relation to them, dismissal of employees for non-compliance with them may, depending on the circumstances of the case, be ruled unfair. It is unlikely to be sufficient merely to issue a policy or procedure and demand that employees comply with it. The following steps should also be taken:

- The policy itself must be in compliance with all relevant law and its contents must be 'reasonable' in all the circumstances. For example, the policy must not breach equal opportunity legislation by treating certain groups of people less favourably (for example, on the basis of gender). Nor should it be targeted to disadvantage particular individuals.
- The policy should be issued to all employees affected by it and clearly explained to them. There have been cases where employees have successfully argued that, even though they were issued with a copy of an HR policy, they were not aware of its contents, and that the implications and requirements of it had not been personally explained to them. That defence has succeeded even in cases where the employee was required to acknowledge that they had received a copy of the policy and understood that they were bound by it. Merely requiring the employee to sign such an undertaking may be insufficient if the employer does not back it up with direct action to ensure that the employee has access to the policy and understands the contents.
- Employers must be able to demonstrate that the employee clearly understands the policy/procedure. If necessary, the employer should provide training (including refresher training).
- The employer must be consistent in its application, not applying it rigidly to some employees and overlooking breaches by others.
- The employer must not substantively alter a policy or procedure without telling employees. The changes must be announced in advance and widely publicised. Again the changes should be clearly explained to employees and the employer should ensure they understand what the changes mean.

Mike Toten

Source *HR Monthly*, July 2003, p. 30.

An example of the absence of any duty to voluntarily disclose past conduct is found in the case of *Hollingsworth v. Commissioner of Police (No. 2)*.[12] The case involved a student police officer who did not volunteer in her application for the NSW Police Force that she had been a stripper and prostitute in the past. When this information was revealed, her contract of employment was terminated on the basis of her non-disclosure. The Full Bench of the Industrial Relations Commission of NSW held that a prospective employee has a duty to disclose all 'relevant' information only if asked by the employer in the pre-employment process, and not afterwards. The Full Bench commented that a prospective employee does not have to be frank about matters that may disqualify them from appointment except to honestly answer the questions asked. Additionally, a prospective employee is not obliged to answer incriminating questions. However, there is no restriction on the inferences an employer may draw from a refusal to answer on that ground.

Testing employees

A growing issue for HR managers in Australia is the use of pre-employment testing of applicants. Traditionally, the use of medical testing has been used in industries that require employees to have a certain level of physical fitness in order to carry out the inherent requirements of the position. In order to avoid indirect discrimination, HR managers considering medical tests should ensure that the tests are carried out by a qualified medical practitioner, are relevant to the inherent requirements of the position and that the results of the tests are not disclosed to third parties without the consent of the applicant.

More recently, HR practitioners are beginning to rely on psychological and psychometric testing to assess the suitability of applicants for a position. There is no doubt that such testing can assist in reducing the costs associated with making poor recruitment decisions. However, such testing must, for legal as well as practical reasons, be relevant to the requirements of the position.

Another cutting-edge issue for HR managers and the law in Australia is the use of genetic testing in the pre-employment process. In May 2003, the Australian Law Reform Commission's report entitled *Essentially Yours: The Protection of Human Genetic Information in Australia* was tabled in the Commonwealth Parliament. The report found that although there are few examples of the use of genetic testing of applicants in Australia, more numerous examples exist in other countries. There is currently no prohibition on employers using an applicant's genetic information in pre-employment where that applicant has consented to the process.

Having said that, however, the report noted that discriminatory treatment on the basis that a person's genetic information indicates that they have some form of disability will be lawful only if the genetic information indicates that the applicant will not be capable of fulfilling the 'inherent requirements' of the position. Among the report's 144 recommendations are the recommendations that anti-discrimination legislation should be amended to prohibit discrimination based on a person's real or perceived genetic status and that employers should not be permitted to collect or use genetic information except in rare circumstances where such testing is required to maintain occupational health and safety standards. There is no doubt that this issue will become increasingly important for Australia's legislatures and HR managers in the future.

The interview

An interviewer should not conduct an employment interview without careful planning and forethought. Failure to be aware of discrimination legislation in particular could lead to court and tribunal intervention.

Where possible, interviews should be held in an accessible venue. Reasonable alternative arrangements should be made to accommodate a candidate who is unable to access a venue because of a disability. In *W v. P Pty Ltd*,[13] the Human Rights and Equal Opportunity Commission held that the arrangement of an interview in an inaccessible building that had 16 steps, despite the applicant informing the prospective employer that she had a mobility problem, was unlawfully discriminatory.

It is also necessary to consider whether the interview should be conducted on a one-to-one basis. Apart from affording the organisation the benefit of an additional contributor to the selection process, a second interviewer may represent an important back-up if an applicant later accuses the employer of discrimination or of making false statements that misled or deceived the applicant. Section 53B of the *Trade Practices Act 1974* (Cwlth) prohibits the making of statements that are liable to mislead an applicant as to the availability of employment or the terms and conditions of that employment. A prudent HR manager should therefore conduct the interview with another person from the organisation. In all cases, comprehensive notes should be made of the interview so there is an up-to-date record available in the event of any legal challenge. A useful approach is to comment on a printed sheet containing space for each selection criterion.

This Letter to the Editor provides a provocative viewpoint. Do you agree? See 'What's your view?' on page 129.

Employers should be able to test potential employees for substance abuse

Dear Editor,

I am sick and tired of hearing from all those objectionable civil libertarians who oppose the use of employee testing for evidence of substance abuse.

Who are they kidding? Do they seriously believe their own argument that such testing is only relevant for those in specific occupations such as bus and truck driving and the operation of machinery? On any grounds, such arguments cannot be justified.

For instance, as a taxpayer, you can bet that it matters to me whether or not my child's schoolteachers and university lecturers walk into class free of drugs, whether we are talking about alcohol or cocaine. Not only will their teaching suffer, but my child will receive a second-rate education from those affected by such substances. In addition, who is to know what weird and wild philosophical arguments will emanate from teachers under the influence?

Similarly, as the manager of a finance company, I am deeply concerned that my staff offer only the best financial information to our clients. This can be assured only if they are sober both in their work and personal habits. I have long believed that our public character is a direct reflection of our private character, and I constantly stress this view both to my employees and to potential new clients of my company.

In addition, as the use of various illegitimate substances could affect the judgement of my employees, I can ill afford to be sued by clients for the poor financial advice potentially given by drug-affected staff.

Employers have a right to know whether employees are affected by drugs while undertaking their employment obligations, since employers are directly responsible for employees and their decisions. By accepting an employment contract, employees are making a commitment to their employer that they will work to the best of their ability. How can this occur under the influence of any illegal or unacceptable drugs or other substances of abuse?

In closing, I would also note my belief that this argument should be extended to those with contagious diseases and disabilities. Employers have a responsibility of care to all employees in their workplaces, and it is to everyone's advantage that senior managers are fully aware of the health of their staff so that steps can be taken to ensure that everyone works in a harmonious and healthy environment.

Managing Director, Financial Planning Company

Source David Poole, University of Western Sydney.

Legal issues for HR professionals during employment

The legal issues that HR professionals face are by no means limited to hiring and firing. During the life of the contract of employment between an employer and their employees, HR professionals must manage a myriad of legal issues ranging from compliance with relevant occupational health and safety legislation to managing the statutory entitlements of employees.

Occupational health and safety requirements

Governments at the state and federal level have introduced legislation obliging employers to be responsible for occupational health and safety.[14] The purpose of the legislation is to balance the inevitable health and safety risks associated with industry against social justice issues. Employees should not be exposed to unacceptable levels of hazard at work, and those who are injured at work should be fairly and sufficiently compensated.[15] Basically, an employer must provide and maintain, so far as is practical, a working environment that is safe and without risks to the employee's health. Safety standards set out in the regulations to the Occupational Health and Safety Acts aim at preventing injuries. The legislation also deals with compensation schemes for injured workers.

Importantly, case law suggests that labour hire agencies may be deemed to be the employer of staff they hire out and may therefore attract occupational health and safety obligations, which they cannot simply delegate to clients.[16] There is thus an obligation on employers that hire out their employees to ensure that the working conditions of their employees are safe, notwithstanding that another organisation is directing their actual work.

When hiring employees, HR managers must provide all the necessary information, instruction, training and supervision for the employees to perform their work. The duty of the employer also extends to:
- providing and maintaining plant and systems of work that are safe and without risks to health
- making arrangements for safety in connection with the use, handling, storage and transport of plant equipment and substances
- maintaining the workplace in a condition that is safe and without risks to health
- providing adequate facilities for the welfare of employees at the workplace.

In New South Wales, the legislation also creates a general duty of employers: 'Every employer shall ensure the health and safety and welfare at work of all employees.'[17] The duty is an absolute obligation. It is not even qualified by the usual words, 'so far as is reasonably practicable'! However, employees should be aware that where, during normal hours, they deviate from their duties and engage in a 'frolic' outside the scope of their employment, their employer is not required to compensate them for any injury suffered.

The NSW legislation also contains extensive provision on an employer's duty to consult with employees on occupational health and safety matters.[18]

Discriminatory treatment of employees

It is often the responsibility of the HR manager to ensure that individual employees, or groups of employees, are not unfairly discriminated against in employment. Where an employee is unfairly discriminated against and subsequently resigns, the law may find that the action of discrimination, perpetrated by the employer, constitutes a 'constructive dismissal', which means that the dismissal is at the initiative of the employer, not the employee. The significance of this is that the 'constructively dismissed' employee will be able to seek a remedy such as reinstatement, re-employment or compensation in lieu of reinstatement in the relevant state or federal industrial tribunal.

An example of unfair discrimination in the workplace is found in the case of *Daghlian v. Australia Postal Corporation*.[19] In this case, the Federal Court of Australia held that a middle-aged woman who had a physical disability was unfairly discriminated against in contravention of the *Disability Discrimination Act 1992* (Cwlth). The woman in question had served the employer for over 11 years in a customer service capacity. The woman suffered from osteoarthritis of the lower back, spondylitis, bilateral varicose veins and bilateral spurs of the heels, which rendered her, according to medical evidence heard at trial, unable to stand for extended periods. This condition made it impossible for her to comply with a new company policy that forbade sitting while serving customers. Justice Conti held that the application of this policy unfairly discriminated against the woman who, but for the discrimination, was capable of performing the inherent requirements of her job.

Statutory benefits

Employee entitlements are primarily governed by the terms and conditions of the contract of employment. However, the states and territories have enacted legislation setting standard minimum employee entitlements that HR professionals need to be familiar with:

- The payment of wages — because the most fundamental benefit employees receive from their work is the payment of wages, the states have legislated to provide that wages must be paid in money (rather than by way of the provision of goods or services) and at reasonable intervals.[20]
- The provision of leave — the various states and territories have also enacted legislation to provide employees with minimum leave entitlements. Relevant legislation is too numerous to list, but New South Wales is a typical example, providing for four weeks annual leave per annum.[21]

Terminating employees

Types of dismissal

Dismissals invariably fall into one of four broad categories:

1. Dismissal based on an employee's serious ('repudiatory') breach of the contract demonstrating an intention that the employee no longer wishes to be bound by its terms — this is known as **summary dismissal**. Summary dismissal has been described as the 'ultimate sanction' for employee misconduct. An example of conduct displaying an intention to no longer be bound by the contract is an employee stealing from the employer. Summary dismissal effectively means dismissal without giving notice of dismissal.

2. Dismissal pursuant to the express or implied terms of the employment contract whereby either the employer or the employee terminates the contract by giving the other party **notice** of the termination or **payment in lieu of notice** — this is known as dismissal 'on notice'. The requisite notice period that must be given will be determined by relevant legislation, an industrial instrument such as an award, the contract of employment or the Court. Where such instruments are silent with respect to notice, the common law implies that **reasonable notice** must be given. What is 'reasonable' will depend on the circumstances of the case. However, factors such as the seniority of the position, the employee's age and the prospect of obtaining alternative employment will be relevant considerations. According to common law principles, a dismissal on notice can be for any reason, not limited to performance or conduct. More stringent requirements are placed on employers by the various state's unfair dismissal legislation.

3. Dismissal based on the employer's commercial or economic decisions regarding the management of the business — this is called **redundancy**.

4. Where an employer acts in a manner that indicates they no longer wish to be bound by the terms and conditions of the contract of employment, the affected employee will, if they resign, be considered to have been dismissed by the employer. This is known as **constructive dismissal**. Constructive dismissal occurs when an employee is effectively forced to resign. If, for example, the employer says to an employee 'resign or you will be fired', the law will determine that the employee, if they resign, will have been dismissed by the employer and not at their own initiative. The importance of this is that an employee cannot bring an action for unfair dismissal unless they have been dismissed by their employer. Other examples of constructive dismissal exist where an employee resigns because they do not accept the employer's unilateral variation of the terms of the contract of employment (for example, changes to the work location, duties or remuneration).

Summary dismissal

The right of an employer to terminate summarily (that is, without notice) is only enlivened when the employee acts in a manner inconsistent with the continuation of the contract of employment. It is a powerful tool that may have a drastic effect on the livelihoods of those who are dismissed. Therefore, the common law restricts the employer's right to summarily dismiss an employee to occasions where the employee's conduct is in direct and serious breach of the employee's obligations. As stated in the much-quoted speech of Lord Evershed MR in *Laws v. London Chronicle (Indicator Newspapers) Ltd*:[22]

Summary dismissal Dismissal based on an employee's serious ('repudiatory') breach of the employment contract. Effectively, dismissal occurs without giving any notice.

Notice Notice of termination is required if one party to a contract of employment wishes to bring the contract to an end.

Payment in lieu of notice Payment of all wages that would have been receivable if the employee was required to work during the notice period.

Reasonable notice The amount of notice to be given in individual circumstances where no period is contemplated in the contract.

Redundancy Termination of the employment contract by the employer due to the permanent elimination of the position.

Constructive dismissal Dismissal by the employer where the employer acts in a manner suggesting that they no longer wish to be bound by the terms of the contract.

if summary dismissal is claimed to be justifiable, the question must be whether the conduct complained of is such as to show the [employee] to have disregarded the essential conditions of the contract [of employment].

And then at 288:

… I … think … that one act of disobedience or misconduct can justify dismissal only if it is of a nature which goes to show (in effect) that the [employee] is repudiating the contract.

The following are substantive grounds upon which summary dismissal is often based:

- serious misconduct
- physical/verbal abuse
- disobedience of a lawful and reasonable direction
- drunkenness
- incompetence in cases where the employee has presented themselves as competent to perform the job
- neglect of duties
- dishonesty/bribery
- criminal behaviour in connection with employment
- absenteeism.

Notice of dismissal

Except for a valid summary dismissal (where no notice is required), employers may not terminate employment unless they have given the employee sufficient notice of impending termination. Otherwise, compensation (payment in lieu of notice) must be paid. The worker should be notified in writing of the decision to terminate employment and is entitled to receive a statement of reasons for the termination. This is to ensure clarity and avoid confusion. If employers do not abide by these regulations, the termination may be deemed unfair.

Table 4.2	Period of notice required

EMPLOYEE'S PERIOD OF CONTINUOUS SERVICE	MINIMUM PERIOD OF NOTICE
Not more than 1 year	1 week
More than 1 year but not more than 3 years	2 weeks
More than 3 years but not more than 5 years	3 weeks
More than 5 years	4 weeks

The period of notice is increased by 1 week if the employee is over 45 years old and has completed at least 2 years continuous service.

How much notice is given depends on the contract of employment. The *Workplace Relations Act 1996* (Cwlth) sets a statutory minimum notice period, as shown in table 4.2 above. This legislative minimum notwithstanding, the contract of employment may stipulate a longer, but not a shorter, period of notice. Where the contract of employment is silent with respect to the length of notice, the common law implies that the employer must give the employer reasonable notice. What is 'reasonable' will depend entirely on the circumstances of the individual case. At the highest end of the scale, the NSW Industrial Relations Commission in Court Session held that a reasonable period of notice for a 57-year-old senior executive with 35 years service to the employer was 18 months.[23] At the lowest end of the scale, statutory provisions have been deemed reasonable.

Under current unfair dismissal laws it is generally easier and cheaper for employers to 'pay up' rather than defend an unwarranted claim.

Redundancy

Redundancies are dismissals that are based on commercial and economic considerations. The dismissals may arise for a number of reasons, including technological change, a downturn or seasonality in business, and restructuring of the enterprise. Because the employer no longer needs the job to be filled, the dismissal is through no fault of the employee.

The respective rights of employers and employees in relation to redundancy are now almost exclusively governed by awards and legislation. The *Termination, Change and Redundancy Case 1984*[24] (which concerned an application by the Australian Council of Trade Unions to amend the Metal Industry Award) is of major importance to the law on redundancy. This was a test case. In its decision, the former Australian Conciliation and Arbitration Commission discussed the general principles to be included in a redundancy provision in an award. The Commission laid down recommendations in relation to consultation, information, notice, transmission of business, time off during the redundancy period, an employee leaving during the notice period, the transfer to other duties of an employee, employee entitlements such as severance pay, ordinary and customary turnover of labour, superannuation, incapacity to pay, and provision of alternative employment where possible.

The descision in the *Redundancy Test Case 2004*[25] was handed down recently, which most importantly increased the levels of severance pay entitlements for federal award employees and partially removed the exemptions for small businesses (with fewer than 15 employees) in relation to making severance payments to employees. The appropriate levels of severance payments are determined by the contract of employment, statutory agreements, awards and legislation. By way of example, the *Redundancy Test Case 2004* provides for a scale of minimum severance payments for employees covered under federal awards (see table 4.3).

Table 4.3 Redundancy requirements	
EMPLOYEE'S PERIOD OF CONTINUOUS SERVICE	**SEVERANCE PAY**
Less than 1 year	Nil
1–2 years	4 weeks pay
2–3 years	6 weeks pay
3–4 years	7 weeks pay
4–5 years	8 weeks pay
5–6 years	10 weeks pay
6–7 years	11 weeks pay
7–8 years	13 weeks pay
8–9 years	14 weeks pay
9–10 years	16 weeks pay
More than 10 years	10 weeks pay*

* The amount is decreased to account for the fact that employees with this length of service are entitled to long service leave payments and thus will not suffer the same extent of losses from non-transferable credits.

The rationale behind redundancy pay (severance) is not the same as that for notice of termination. While notice of termination is required to give the employee a reasonable opportunity to adjust to the end of the employment relationship, severance pay is compensatory. Severance pay attempts to compensate employees whose positions have been made redundant for the loss of non-transferable entitlements such as sick leave.

It is the duty of employers to hold discussions with employees and unions once a definite decision has been made that may lead to redundancies. Furthermore, alternative positions in the company must be considered by those affected by the redundancy.

For instance, in *Shop Distributive and Allied Employees' Association of NSW v. WD & HO Wills Holdings Ltd*,[26] WD & HO Wills merged with Rothmans and offered its employees either continued employment with the merged entity or with another employer, Imperial. The employees were assured that both the merged entity and Imperial would honour and continue their current leave and other entitlements. Two of WD & HO Wills's former employees refused the offer of employment with Imperial and sought a redundancy package instead. The NSWIRC held that the offer of employment with Imperial constituted 'reasonable alternative employment', so that WD & HO Wills was under no obligation to make redundancy payments to its two former employees.

Constructive dismissal

In a recent decision of the Industrial Relations Commission of NSW, *Colosimo and Banana Traders of Australia Pty Ltd t/a PW Chew & Co.*,[27] an employee was found to have been constructively dismissed by the employer. Mr Colosimo was employed as a banana trader when, due to an alleged downturn in business, the employer asked him to take his accrued annual leave entitlements before saying words to the effect that he should work for wages provided for by the relevant award until the financial difficulties affecting the industry improved. Mr Colosimo was being paid around $58 800 per annum, so working under award wages would constitute a reduction in remuneration of 65 per cent. Mr Colosimo submitted to the Commission that such a reduction in wages by the employer was a unilateral imposition of less favourable terms, constituting a constructive dismissal. The Commission found that a 65 per cent reduction in wages 'could not be viewed as acceptable'. As a result, the Commission found the dismissal to be 'harsh and unjust'. Mr Colosimo was awarded $13 575.70 (the equivalent of 12 weeks pay) by way of compensation in lieu of reinstatement.

This case is an important reminder to employers and HR managers that, notwithstanding an industry downturn, attempting to unilaterally reduce the terms or conditions of employees may be likely to result in a finding of unfair dismissal. In such circumstances, employers may choose to make a position redundant. However, in doing so employers must be mindful that they have obligations to:

- give reasonable notice to employees and/or their unions of the expected redundancy
- adequately consult with employees and/or their unions on the impact of the proposed changes
- explore genuine alternative options for redundancy, such as redeployment or relocation
- ensure such options are fairly offered to the affected employees
- provide reasonable standards of redundancy benefits
- provide appropriate ancillary services, such as time off to seek alternative work, retraining opportunities, outplacement services or financial planning
- ensure employees nominated for redundancy are fairly selected on an objective and unbiased basis.[28]

Recent cases have also found that demotion may be construed as constructive dismissal in certain circumstances. A demotion may represent a repudiation of the employment contract where the contract does not include express provisions allowing the employer to reclassify a position at will. In the case of constructive dismissal, the employee has the same rights as if they had been dismissed.

The following is an example of a decision in which a demotion has been found to constitute constructive dismissal.

Advertiser Newspaper v. Grivell[29] was the first decision to recognise demotion as a form of constructive dismissal. However, it was relevant only in so far as it applied to South Australian legislation. In this case the plaintiff, some period after promotion, was advised that he would be required to work in the promoted position only on an irregular basis. The reasons given for the demotion were based on cost-efficiency, not performance. The plaintiff protested his demotion but continued to work for the defendant in the position to which he was demoted.

The Commission interpreted the word 'dismissal' broadly and decided that an employee who was demoted and had not left the employment of his employer could nevertheless bring an unfair dismissal claim if the employee's contract had not allowed for the employer to reclassify his position at will.

Under s. 170CD(1B) of the *Workplace Relations Act 1996* (Cwlth), a demotion will not be considered a termination of employment if the demotion does not result in a significant reduction in remuneration and the employee remains employed with the employer.

Procedures for dismissal

Under the *Workplace Relations Act 1996* (Cwlth) a regime of substantive and procedural fairness is imposed on employers (who are subject to the legislation) with respect to dismissing an employee. The concept of substantive fairness requires that there is a 'valid reason' for the dismissal (for example, drunkenness), while the concept of procedural fairness requires that the employee accused of drunkenness is afforded an opportunity to respond to the allegation and have that response considered before any final decision to dismiss is made. Therefore, when an employer wishes to dismiss an employee, both substantive and procedural fairness must be considered. The Act further provides that in considering a dismissal the Commission must bear in mind the principle of a 'fair go all round' — that is, a 'fair go' for both employer and employee.

Valid reason — substantive fairness

As noted above, under the *Workplace Relations Act 1996* (Cwlth), as well as various state acts, it is wrongful to dismiss an employee without a 'valid reason'. This is the case regardless of which of the abovementioned four forms of dismissal it takes. Section 170CG of the Act states (to paraphrase) that in determining whether a dismissal is unfair, the Commission is to have regard to, among other things, whether there is a valid reason for the termination relating to the capacity or conduct of the employee or to the employer's operational requirements. Therefore, the dismissal cannot be for an arbitrary reason. Rather, there must be a substantive reason for the dismissal.

Unlawful termination for proscribed reasons

The *Workplace Relations Act 1996* (Cwlth) provides that certain reasons cannot be 'valid reasons' under the Act. Pursuant to s. 170CK(2), employers are prohibited from terminating an employee's employment for reasons of:

- temporary absence from work because of illness or injury within the meaning of the regulations
- trade union membership or participation in trade union activities outside working hours or, with the employer's consent, during working hours
- non-membership of a trade union
- seeking office as, or acting or having acted in the capacity of, a representative of employees
- the filing of a complaint, or the participation in proceedings, against an employer involving alleged violation of laws or regulations or recourse to competent administrative authorities
- race, colour, sex, sexual preference, age, physical or mental disability, marital status, family responsibilities, pregnancy, religion, political opinion, national extraction or social origin
- refusing to negotiate in connection with, make, sign, extend, vary or terminate an AWA
- absence from work during maternity leave or other parental leave
- temporary absence from work because of carrying out a voluntary emergency management activity, where the absence is reasonable having regard to all the circumstances. This clause was added into the *Workplace Relations Act 1996* (Cwlth) in 2003. The purpose of this amendment was to give effect to International Labour Organisation Recommendation 166 concerning Termination of Employment. (Article 5 of the Recommendation refers, inter alia, to absence from work due to civic obligation as not constituting a valid reason for termination.)

Where an employee is absent from work because they are ill or injured, it will be regarded as temporary absence if:

- the employee has complied with the requirements set out in *Workplace Relations Regulation 30C* and obtained a medical certificate of absence stating the illness and the duration of absence from work as temporary
- the employee has complied with the terms of an award or agreement to notify the employer of any absence and to give a reason.

Employers can raise a defence to an otherwise unlawful termination if the termination was based upon the inherent requirements of a particular position. Under s. 170CK(3) of the *Workplace Relations Act 1996* (Cwlth), the 'inherent requirements' defence to unlawful termination claims can apply to terminations based upon race, colour, sex, sexual preference, age, disability, family responsibilities, pregnancy, religion, political opinion, national extraction or social origin.

The defence was applied by the High Court of Australia in the case *Qantas Airways Ltd v. Christie*.[30] Christie, a pilot with Qantas, was terminated when he reached the age of 60. Under the *Convention on International Civil Aviation*, parties (of which Australia is one) may exclude from their airspace any aircraft flown by a pilot who is over 60 years of age. Although the rules do not apply in Australia, as Qantas is an international airline its retirement policy states that pilots should not continue in employment beyond the age of 60. On his termination, Mr Christie commenced proceedings based on the grounds of age discrimination. The High Court adopted a broad interpretation of s. 170CK(3) and found that age was an inherent requirement of Mr Christie's position. Consequently, the termination was not unlawful.

The employer's right to 'hire and fire'

Prohibited reasons for dismissal aside, it is the basic right of management (often called a 'managerial prerogative') to choose which employees it wishes to have working for the company. In determining whether or not an employer had a 'valid reason' to dismiss an employee, the Courts and industrial tribunals, such as the Australian Industrial Relations Commission, do not assume to be expert business managers. The focus of termination of employment proceedings is to ensure that the parties receive 'a fair go all round'. In considering a reinstatement order, the Commission and/or Court will look to factors such as the effect of the order on the viability of the employer's business, the length of the employee's service with the employer and the efforts of the employee to mitigate their loss.

An example where the New South Wales Industrial Relations Commission refused to intervene concerned the termination and suspension of a man's employment with Blayney Abattoir.[31] The man was employed as a labourer on the mutton slaughter floor. The employer argued before the Commission that the labourer had left the abattoir without permission even after several warnings. The Australasian Meat Industry Employees' Union, New South Wales branch, contended that the labourer had not been given a 'fair go' and that he had been treated in a cruel, harsh and unjust manner by the company. After finishing work, the employee had looked for his supervisor but, unable to find him, had gone home without permission. The Commission found that the company had been very easy on the employee, especially considering his record of walking off the job, fighting, being lazy, abusing fellow employees and incurring 'a string of reprimands a mile long', including a previous suspension. Considering all the circumstances, it was determined that the labourer had been treated fairly and was dismissed for a valid reason.

Procedures for termination

However, having a valid reason for dismissing an employee is not of itself sufficient to effect that dismissal fairly, in compliance with the statutory regime. Although an employee may have acted in an entirely reprehensible manner (such as stealing from the employer), the employee remains entitled to be dealt with in a procedurally fair manner. That is, the employee is entitled to:

1. be furnished with *reasons* for the impending dismissal (for example, the employer has reason to believe that the employee stole from the employer)
2. a *fair hearing*, so that the employee is afforded a *right to respond* to those reasons (for instance, to explain that they honestly believed they were permitted to take the item)
3. an *unbiased* decision-making process that takes the employee's response into account before any final decision is made. Furthermore, alternatives to dismissal such as a mere warning should be considered.

The importance of procedural fairness is displayed in the case of *Morgan v. Bindaree Beef*.[32] The employee in this case was employed as a boner/trainee foreman at Bindaree Beef. The employee brought an action for unfair dismissal under s. 170CE of the *Workplace Relations Act* for being summarily dismissed for what the employer described as a 'breach of contract' and 'gross misconduct' arising out of two separate incidents.

First, the employee was accused of directing fellow employees to defraud the employer by entering a 'sign-off' time on their time sheets that was at least one hour later than the time at which they actually finished work. Second, the employer alleged that the employee fraudulently reported that the weight of meat processed by himself and other employees was greater that it actually was. The purpose of this fraudulent activity was to mitigate a financial loss sustained by the employees during a three-hour stoppage in work that occurred earlier in the day. Upon the discovery by the employer of the above activity, the employer conducted an investigation that consisted of a series of interviews with employees including the applicant.

During the applicant's first interview he denied any involvement and was 'stood down' without pay. The following day the applicant was interviewed for a second time. The employer's HR Manager gave evidence that the company had decided prior to this second interview that the applicant would be dismissed regardless of what transpired at the interview. The only question remaining for the employer was whether to contact the police in relation to the alleged fraudulent conduct. During the interview the applicant was informed that he was dismissed. After determining that the applicant's dismissal was substantially unfair because the Commission could not determine on the test of the balance of probabilities that the applicant was actually guilty of the alleged misconduct, Commissioner Cargill held that the dismissal was also procedurally unfair. The applicant was not afforded procedural fairness because:

1. the applicant was not told of the reasons for the dismissal prior to the decision being made
2. the reasons given by the employer after dismissal ('breach of contract' and 'gross misconduct') were neither put in sufficiently plain and comprehensible language nor were they sufficiently detailed
3. the applicant was not afforded the opportunity to respond to the allegations.

Due to substantive as well as procedural unfairness, the Commission awarded the employee compensation to be determined between the parties in lieu of reinstatement.

The rights of the employee

A dismissed employee has various means of appeal. The most important ones are:
* a statutory action including that for unfair or unlawful dismissal
* a common law action for wrongful dismissal in breach of contract
* a statutory action for unfair contract for those in New South Wales and Queensland (s. 106 of the *Industrial Relations Act 1996* (NSW) and s. 276 of the *Industrial Relations Act 1999* (Qld)).[33]

Unfair dismissal

At both the state and federal level, legislation provides that an employee can challenge the fairness of their dismissal in an industrial tribunal. The availability, jurisdiction and remedies for an action for **unfair dismissal** vary from state to state. Thus, the factors considered by tribunals in determining a claim also differ from state to state. By way of a typical example, the *Workplace Relations Act 1996* (Cwlth) provides that the Commission has jurisdiction to remedy unfairly dismissed employees where the dismissal is *harsh, unjust or unreasonable*.

Unfair dismissal Occurs where a dismissal is harsh, unjust or unreasonable, but need not involve a fundamental breach of the employment relationship.

Eligibility under the federal regime
Eligibility to bring an unfair termination proceeding is limited, for Constitutional reasons, to the following categories of employees:
* Commonwealth public sector employees
* territory employees
* federal award employees who are employed by constitutional corporations
* federal award employees who are waterside workers, maritime employees or flight crew officers and who are employed in the course of, or in relation to, trade and commerce between Australia and a place outside Australia, between the states, within a territory, between a state and a territory, or between two territories

- Victorian employees (in 1996, Victoria referred its employment powers to the Commonwealth).

The following categories of employees are exempted from the termination of employment provisions:
- employees engaged under contract of employment for a specific period of time
- employees engaged under contract for a specified task
- employees serving a bona fide period of probation or a qualifying period of employment
- casual employees hired for a short period of time
- trainee employees
- employees not employed under award conditions whose remuneration exceeds $85 400 (or such other amount that is set by the Regulations).

To comply with Australia's international treaty obligations, the unlawful termination jurisdiction is broader than that which applies to unfair dismissals. As well as the above-mentioned categories, it applies to 'employees' in general.

Remedies for unfair dismissal

Under new changes to the federal Act, employees will be able to seek redress for unfair dismissal in the Australian Industrial Relations Commission. If an employer unfairly or unlawfully terminates someone's employment, the employer may face a claim for compensation and/or reinstatement.

The Commission has outlined detailed criteria for termination of employment that are required in applications. It requires the employer to submit a detailed statement as a response. Failure to do this could irrecoverably damage the employer's defence. Advice should be sought immediately.

If amicable settlement cannot be achieved between the parties, the Commission may make orders for the employee to be returned to the same position as if the employment had not been terminated. Commission orders may include:
- declaring the termination to have contravened the provisions of the Act
- requiring the employer to reinstate the employee
- ordering compensation.

If a compensation order is made, the maximum amount that can be awarded for an employee who is employed under award conditions is the equivalent of six months remuneration. For an employee not covered by an award, the maximum amount that can be awarded is the lesser of six months remuneration or $42 700 (indexed from time to time in accordance with the formula in Regulation 30BF of the *Workplace Relations Regulations 1996* (Cwlth)).

Wrongful dismissal

Wrongful dismissal Occurs when an employee's employment is terminated by an employer for reasons that are in breach of the employment contract.

An employee may make a **wrongful dismissal** claim when an employer breaches the terms of the contract of employment. Termination on insufficient notice, for example, constitutes a wrongful dismissal. Usually, the dismissed employee can claim damages for wages lost as a result of the short dismissal period. An employee has a duty to mitigate the loss by making reasonable steps to find alternative employment. Wrongful dismissal actions are heard in common law courts, and are expensive to run and defend. Thus, actions for wrongful dismissal in the common law courts are rare and tend to be reserved for those ineligible to bring an action under the relevant unfair dismissal jurisdiction of industrial tribunals.

Table 4.4 compares wrongful and unfair dismissals.

Table 4.4	Comparison of wrongful dismissal and unfair dismissal		
	TRIGGER	ACTION	REMEDY
Wrongful dismissal	Fundamental breach of employment contract by employer	Common law	Damages
Unfair dismissal	Dismissal is harsh, unjust or unreasonable	Statute	Reinstatement, re-employment or compensation

Unfair contracts in New South Wales and Queensland

In New South Wales and Queensland, employees and non-employees who provide work (such as independent contractors) may bring an action before their relevant state industrial commission arguing that their contract for the provision of work was an **unfair contract**. In New South Wales this right is provided for by s. 106 of the *Industrial Relations Act 1996* (NSW) and in Queensland it is provided for by s. 276 of the *Industrial Relations Act 1999* (Qld).

At the federal level, s. 127A of the *Workplace Relations Act 1996* (Cwlth) empowers the Australian Industrial Relations Commission to vary unfair contracts for independent contractors, but not for employees.

The unfair contracts jurisdiction of the relevant state industrial tribunals is exercisable by all workers, not merely those who have been dismissed. Having said that, unfair contract actions are often used by dismissed employees who do not have access to the unfair dismissal provisions under the relevant statute because they are an excluded class of employee. Furthermore, the jurisdiction is a convenient alternative to the long waiting lists and costs associated with a common law action for wrongful dismissal.

Under both New South Wales and Queensland provisions the relevant commission has the power to vary any contractual term that is deemed to be unfair, harsh or unconscionable.

In 2002, the New South Wales unfair contracts jurisdiction was amended by the *Industrial Relations (Unfair Contracts) Amendment Act 2002* (NSW). The amendment imposed a remuneration cap of $200 000 per annum on workers seeking to have the Commission deem their contracts unfair. The effect of the remuneration cap is that those earning above $200 000 per annum cannot bring an unfair contracts action. Queensland has a far smaller remuneration cap, which is presently $85 400.

In *Sheffield v. Brambles Australia Limited (2002)*,[34] decided by the Industrial Relations Commission of NSW in Court Session, a contract of employment was varied under the unfair contracts jurisdiction of the Commission under s. 106 of the *Industrial Relations Act 1996* (NSW). The employee was a senor executive with over 12 years service to the employer. The employee sought to vary the terms in his contract that governed notice of termination and the vesting rights of share options.

With respect to notice of termination, the contract provided for six month's notice. The Commission found that given the seniority of the position and the length of service rendered, that contractual term was unfair. The Commission varied the contract to extend the notice of termination period to 12 months. With respect to the contractual term that governed the vesting of share options, the contract provided that outstanding share options would lapse 60 days after the senior executive ceased to hold office, making allowance for employer discretion. The Commission held that because the contract did not contemplate different circumstances of termination of employment and because discretion was applied inconsistently, the contract should be varied to provide for the automatic vesting of options in the senior executive.

Unfair contract A contract that a relevant industrial tribunal can vary if the contract is unfair, harsh or unconscionable.

Summary

The law governs the parameters of all employment relationships. These legal obligations arise from employment contracts, legislation, statutory agreements, awards and the common law. Careful drafting, strict observance of legislation and an awareness of legal obligations generally will help to minimise an organisation's exposure to dispute and litigation. From hiring an employee to terminating the employment relationship, the same level of care should be shown. Good HR managers balance all these skills and add value to their organisations by minimising workplace disruptions caused by bad employment practices.

Thirty interactive Wiley Web Questions are available to test your understanding of this chapter at **www.johnwiley.com.au/ highered/hrm5e** *in the student resources area*

common law (p. 109)

constructive dismissal (p. 119)

contracts of indefinite duration (p. 101)

contracts of a fixed term (p. 101)

discrimination (p. 110)

employers' duties (p. 109)

employees' duties (p. 109)

employment contract (p. 100)

notice (p. 119)

payment in lieu of notice (p. 119)

reasonable notice (p. 119)

redundancy (p. 119)

statutes (p. 106)

summary dismissal (p. 119)

unfair contract (p. 127)

unfair dismissal (p. 125)

workplace policy (p. 102)

wrongful dismissal (p. 126)

review questions

1. What are the five sources of legal obligations in employment law?
2. What are the two broad types of employment contracts? How do they differ?
3. What is a workplace policy? When will an employer be contractually bound by its terms?
4. What are three statutes that affect working relationships?
5. What is the difference between an Australian Workplace Agreement and a Certified Agreement?
6. What are five common law duties of employers and employees?
7. What is the difference between direct discrimination and indirect discrimination?
8. What should HR managers avoid asking in interviews and on application forms?
9. What is the difference between summary dismissal and dismissal on notice?

What is the difference between unfair dismissal and wrongful dismissal?

environmental influences on legal aspects of HRM

Describe the key environmental influences from the model (figure 4.2 shown opposite) that have significance for the legal aspects of HRM.

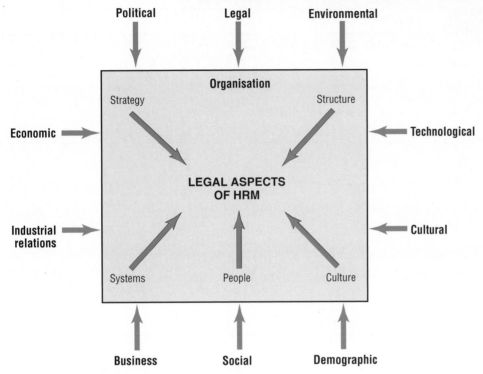

Figure 4.2 Environmental influences on legal aspects of HRM

class debate

The increasing involvement of the law in HRM has a destructive effect on the employer–employee relationship.

what's your view?

Write a 500-word response to the Letter to the Editor on page 117, agreeing or disagreeing with the writer's point of view.

practitioner speaks

Read the article on page 115. Prepare a policy statement on employee termination.

newsbreak exercise

Read the Newsbreak 'No winners under unfair dismissal law' on pages 105–06. As a class, review the policies. Do you agree or disagree with the author that regulation to protect the rights of sacked workers is failing? Explain your reasons.

The corporate senior executive

Dr Gluttonous is the Chief Executive Officer of a global financial institution called Colossus. After the retirement of the Director of the Futures Trading Branch, Dr Gluttonous became aware of the high-flying young executive called Ms Corruptus who might be a suitable candidate for the vacant directorship. The only problem is that Ms Corruptus currently works for a competing bank called Diminutive. Dr Gluttonous is not perturbed by this, as he wants the best person for the job.

Dr Gluttonous arranges to meet Ms Corruptus at a new restaurant called *La pretentious yuppia* to discuss the opportunity. At the meeting, Ms Corruptus informs Dr Gluttonous that she is loath to leave her secure current job. Dr Gluttonous tells her not to worry: the new job at Colossus will be just as secure as her old job. What he does not tell her is that Colossus will be amalgamating the Futures Trading Branch with another

branch in 12 months, which could potentially put the job of Director of the Futures Trading Branch in jeopardy. Upon being reassured that the position is secure, Ms Corruptus accepts the offer, not telling Dr Gluttonous that she is currently being investigated by the Australian Securities and Investments Commission for insider trading.

Discussion questions

1. Is it lawful of Dr Gluttonous to tell Ms Corruptus that the job will be as secure as her old job, even though he knows that to be wrong? What if he had said nothing?

2. Is the fact that Ms Corruptus is under investigation relevant or irrelevant? Should she volunteer that information at the meeting? Can she be fired later for not doing so?

3. What action can Ms Corruptus take if she is made redundant in 12 months?

case studies

The Jet Red contract

Peter Smart is a senior sales executive with Jet Red. His title is Sales Manager, New South Wales. Peter has been employed by Jet Red for eight years and is currently earning $150 000 per year. He is also provided with a fully maintained company car. No written contract of employment exists. The only written record is a letter dated 1 April 1996, which says: 'Welcome on board. We look forward to having you on our team. Your commencing salary will be $50 000 per year.'

There has been no serious misconduct by Peter, whose performance is consistently rated acceptable (but with no potential for further advancement). A serious downturn in business has caused Stan Vines, Jet Red's Marketing Manager, to raise a number of questions with Linda Church, HR Manager, regarding Peter's continued employment. Specifically, Stan wants to know:

- How can the company successfully terminate Peter's employment?
- What restrictions apply to Peter if he leaves and joins a competitor?
- What happens if Peter provides confidential marketing information to a new employer?
- What happens if Peter lures away and hires other staff currently employed by Jet Red?

Discussion questions

1. If you were Linda Church, how would you respond to Stan Vine's questions?
2. Draft a suggested restraint of trade clause (which ought to have been included in Peter's original written contract). *Hint:* Make sure it is reasonable in relation to duration, extent and geography.

Eastern University's changed contract

Harry Young was dumbfounded. He had just been informed by Raymond Wong, Assistant HR Manager for Eastern University, that the offer of employment that he had accepted by telephone in Australia was to be changed.

'This is unbelievable', gasped Harry. 'I accepted an offer made by phone by Dr Mark De Chillo, the Head of the Management Department, and now that I am in Hong Kong, you sit there and calmly tell me that the university is not going to pay for my airfares?'

'Yes', replied Raymond, 'It is quite simple. You told Dr De Chillo that you were planning to relocate to Hong Kong for family reasons, so why should the university pay for your airfares? You were coming to Hong Kong anyway.'

'But I was told that they would be paid', Harry said pointedly.

Poker-faced, Raymond replied, 'That was a mistake made by Dr De Chillo. He has no authority to make an offer of employment. What he did was to explain possible terms of employment. The exact terms are here in the formal contract — this is what applies, not something Dr De Chillo may or may not have said. You are being offered the position of Visiting Scholar, which is not a regular position. This means that your salary will be fixed for the duration of the two-year contract. You also will receive a gratuity and medical insurance for your wife and yourself, but not for your children.'

Flabbergasted, Harry asked, 'What about the relocation allowance of one month's salary, does that still apply?'

Raymond sighed. 'No, of course not. As a Visiting Scholar, you are not entitled to this benefit.'

'In other words', said an angry Harry, 'now that I am in Hong Kong you are changing all the conditions just like that?'

'I am sorry', replied Raymond, 'but there is nothing more I can do. Will you accept the position?'

Discussion questions

1. Why has this problem come about? How could it have been avoided?
2. If you were Harry, what would you do now?
3. What advice would you give to Harry?
4. How could a trade union help Harry?
5. What are the ethical questions involved in this case?

Is it a private matter?

Star Selection is a leading executive recruitment firm. Long established, it has built a network of blue-chip clients. Although not a major part of its business, it has developed a niche as a successful recruiter for the private school sector. Helen Moskowitz, a senior consultant with Star Selection, is currently handling an assignment to recruit a live-in housemistress and senior History teacher for the Blue Mountain Catholic Girls College. An old school, the college has produced many leading figures in the arts, education and medicine. Highly regarded for its academic standards and traditional Christian values, the college is a very popular choice among Catholic professionals and businesspeople for educating their daughters.

After interviewing nine candidates, Helen has short-listed three: Patricia O'Malley, Susanna Mann and Angela Napoli. All are highly qualified and well capable of doing the job.

After completing the standard Star Selection background check, however, Helen is somewhat concerned. Her investigations have revealed that Patricia is a lesbian, Susanna is not Catholic and is divorced, and Angela is a convert to Islam.

Discussion questions

1. Is any of this personal information relevant? Is it any business of the college?
2. In cases such as this, should employers be allowed to discriminate?

suggested readings

Alexander, R. and Lewer, J., *Understanding Australian Industrial Relations*, 6th edn, Thomson, Melbourne, 2004, ch. 5.

Beardwell, I. and Holden, L., *Human Resource Management*, 3rd edn, Financial Times/Prentice Hall, London, 2001, chs 10, 11.

Catanzariti, J., *Essential Facts: Recruitment and Termination*, Thompson CPD, Victoria, 2003.

Catanzariti, J. and Baragwanath, M., *The Workplace Relations Act — A User Friendly Guide*, Newsletter Information Services, Manly, New South Wales, 1997.

CCH, *Australian Master Human Resource Guide*, CCH, Sydney, 2003, chs 11, 18, 19, 20, 24, 25, 26, 30, 35, 36, 37, 38, 39.

Creighton, B. and Stewart, A., *Labour Law: An Introduction*, 3rd edn, The Federation Press, Sydney, 2000.

De Cieri, H. and Kramar, R., *Human Resource Management in Australia*, McGraw-Hill, Sydney, 2003, chs 3, 6, 8.

Fisher, C. D., Schoenfeldt, L. F. and Shaw, J. B., *Human Resource Management*, 5th edn, Houghton Mifflin, Boston, 2003, chs 5, 14, 15.

Macken, J. J., O'Grady, P., Sappideen, C. and Warburton, G., *The Law of Employment*, 5th edn, Law Book Company, Sydney, 2002.

Nankervis, A. R., Compton, R. L. and Baird, M., *Strategic Human Resource Management*, 4th edn, Nelson, Melbourne, 2002, chs 5, 13, 14.

online references

www.actu.asn.au
www.ahir.com.au
www.airc.gov.au
www.dewrsb.gov.au
www.eeo.gov.au

www.ilo.org (the International Labour Organisation is a specialised agency of the UN)
www.shrm.org/hrnews
www.workforceonline.com
www.workplace.gov.au

end notes

1. This chapter was written by Joe Catanzariti, BA, LLB (UNSW). Joe leads the Clayton Utz National Practice Group on Workplace Relations and Employment Law and is one of Australia's foremost experts in the field. Joe is Secretary/Treasurer of the Industrial Relations Society of Australia and Chair of the Industrial Law Committee of the Law Society of New South Wales. Joe is a member of the editorial board of the *Journal of Industrial Relations*. He is also a regular contributor to the *Law Society Journal*. The author advises that this area of the law changes rapidly, which may affect some of the issues discussed in the chapter.

2. M. Michalandos, 'Don't play with fire', *HR Monthly*, November 2002, p. 26.

3. The following abbreviations are used in this chapter: Commonwealth (Cwlth), section (s.), sections (ss.) and trading as (t/a).

4. (2000) 177 ALR 193.

5. See also *Anti-Discrimination Act 1977* (NSW), *Equal Opportunity Act 1984* (Vic.), *Anti-Discrimination Act 1991* (Qld), *Equal Opportunity Act 1984* (SA), *Equal Opportunity Act 1984* (WA), *Discrimination Act 1991* (ACT) and *Anti-Discrimination Act 1992* (NT). The grounds of discrimination that are prohibited vary from state to state.

6. (1984) EOC para 92–006.

7. Unreported, AIRC, PR903204, 12 April 2001.

8. See *Britax Rainsford Pty Ltd v. Jones* (2001) 109 IR 381.

9. (1996) EOC 92–859.

10. [1932] AC 161.

11. (2000) 176 ALR 693; (2000) 75 ALJR 312.

12. (1999) 47 NSWLR 151; 88 IR 252.

13. [1997] HREOCA 24 (26 May 1997).

14. *Occupational Health and Safety (Commonwealth Employment) Act 1991* (Cwlth), *Occupational Health and Safety Act 2000* (NSW), *Workplace Health and Safety Act 1995* (Qld), *Occupational Health, Safety and Welfare Act 1986* (SA), *Occupational Safety and Health Act 1984* (WA), *Workplace Health and Safety Act 1995* (Tas), *Work Health Act 1986* (NT) and *Occupational Health and Safety Act 1989* (ACT).

15. Each state, as well as the federal government, has legislated to provide for minimum workers compensation rights. See s. 170VR(2)(b) *Workplace Relations Act 1996* (Cwlth), *Seafarers Rehabilitation and Compensation Act 1992* (Cwlth), *Safety Rehabilitation and Compensation Act 1988* (Cwlth), *Workers' Compensation Act 1987* (NSW), *Accident Compensation Act 1985* (Vic.), *Workcover Queensland Act 1996* (Qld), *Workers'*

Rehabilitation and Compensation Act 1986 (SA), *Workcover Corporation Act 1994* (SA), *Workers' Rehabilitation and Compensation Act 1988* (Tas), *Workers' Compensation and Rehabilitation Act 1981* (WA), *Work Health Act 1986* (NT), *Workers' Compensation Act 1951* (ACT) and *Workers' Compensation Supplementation Fund Act 1980* (ACT).

16. *Swift Placements Pty Ltd v. WorkCover Authority of NSW (Inspector May)* (2000) 96 IR 69; and *Inspector Guillarte v. Integrated Group Ltd* [2003] NSWIRComm 98.

17. Section 8(1) of the *Occupational Health and Safety Act 2000* (NSW).

18. Sections 13–19 of the *Occupational Health and Safety Act 2000* (NSW).

19. [2003] FCA 759 (29 July 2003).

20. See *Industrial Relations Act 1996* (NSW), ss. 117–121; *Industrial Relations Act 1999* (Qld), ss. 370, 391–394; *Industrial and Employment Relations Act 1994* (SA), s. 68; *Minimum Conditions of Employment Act 1993* (WA), Part 3A; and *Industrial Relations Act 1984* (Tas), ss. 47, 51.

21. (*Annual Holidays Act 1944* (NSW), s. 3(1)), long service leave (*Long Service Leave Act 1955* (NSW)), parental leave (*Industrial Relations Act 1996* (NSW), s. 55) and sick leave (*Industrial Relations Act 1996* (NSW), s. 26)

22. [1959] 2 A11 ER 285 at 287.

23. See *David Jones Ltd v. Cukeric* (1997) 78 IR 430.

24. (1983–84) 8 IR 34.

25. AIRC PR032004, 26 March 2004.

26. [2000] NSWIRComm 98.

27. [2003] NSWIRComm 72.

28. *Colosimo and Banana Traders of Australia Pty Ltd t/as PW Chew & Co.* [2003] NSWIRComm 72 at [125].

29. (1998) SAIRComm 65 (27 July 1998) and at appeal (2000) SAIRComm 36.

30. (1998) 152 ALR 365.

31. *Dorsett v. Blayney Abattoir Pty Ltd* (unreported, IRC, NSW, 2237/92, 9 November 1992).

32. (Unreported, AIRC, PR 913415, 18 January 2002.)

33. Pursuant to s. 106 of the *Industrial Relations Act 1996*, the Industrial Commission in Court Session can make an order varying, or even declaring void, any part or the whole of a contract or arrangement that it determines is unfair, harsh, unconscionable or against the public interest.

34. 112 IR 369.

HOUSE SMART FURNITURE COMPANY
Margaret Heffernan, RMIT University

Colin Moreland could not believe that his company, which had once had the reputation as an industry leader with an exciting future, could be facing bankruptcy. He wondered how the company's financial position could have deteriorated in such a short time. His intuition told him that the situation was the direct result of 'people problems' in the Australian manufacturing plant and the Hong Kong office.

As he waited to meet with his finance manager, Colin reflected on the events of the last six months.

Background

House Smart Furniture Company, founded in Sydney in 1986, had long been the industry leader in the design and manufacture of self-assembled, compact, low-cost furniture. The company was successful because of both its ability to react quickly to market trends and the reliability of its hardworking employees. In addition, House Smart had an established distribution network in Singapore, which was a money-maker despite experiencing intense competition from European imports.

Colin had been in the furniture business all his life and knew what it took to run a factory. Demand for House Smart's products was constant. Employees felt secure and had a harmonious working relationship with management. Colin saw no need to develop a strategic business plan or to introduce formal HR policies, believing that they would make the company inflexible and unable to seize business opportunities as they arose. House Smart had no HR Department. HR activities were undertaken by line managers, with all key decisions being made by Colin. Although this sometimes resulted in unfair and contradictory decisions, Colin believed it gave the company speed and flexibility. Colin micro-managed all operational activities including relationships with key customers. He provided constant guidance to employees and stressed his expectation that all his employees work hard. He treated his employees like family and placed great emphasis on loyalty and obedience. Company-sponsored social gatherings were frequent and all employees were expected to attend.

In 2001, in order to take advantage of the company's strong market position and to increase growth opportunities, Colin decided to open a sales office in Hong Kong. This required borrowing A$550000.

Despite lacking an HR skills inventory and any real awareness of the Hong Kong labour market, Colin decided that the manager of the Hong Kong office should be selected from existing staff. He believed that someone who had an understanding of Chinese culture, and who was enthusiastic and hardworking, would be ideal.

Jane Fleming, a sales representative in Sydney, was delighted when she was offered the job. In her late twenties, Jane had lived in Hong Kong with her parents during her high school years. Jane was ambitious, loyal and had no dependants. She saw this as a golden opportunity. Jane and Colin both believed that she could comfortably manage sales and marketing, HR and accounting because she had studied these subjects in her BBA degree.

Jane's first task was the recruitment and selection of staff for the Hong Kong office. House Smart had no written job descriptions or person specifications because Colin regarded such things as bureaucratic nonsense. Jane and Colin agreed that in order to penetrate the competitive Hong Kong market, 11 employees were needed — seven sales representatives, a secretary, a receptionist, an accounts clerk and a sales clerk. Jane sought applicants who were enthusiastic and ambitious, had a sales and marketing background, and were fluent in English and Cantonese. Because of the weak labour market, Jane found that she was able to hire university graduates for all positions. Although this meant paying slightly higher salaries, Jane felt it was worth it. Jane was somewhat disappointed (and frustrated) when Colin queried the costs and insisted that payroll be administered by head office in Sydney.

Jane felt confident that the Hong Kong office could maintain effective communication with head office via the company's intranet. However, problems soon began to surface because of the poor written English skills of some of the Hong Kong employees. This resulted in more and more telephone calls to clear up communication misunderstandings.

For the first six months the Hong Kong office seemed to be performing well. A major mail order company with a large distribution network had asked Jane to expand the business into Taiwan and Japan via a joint venture. Jane saw this as a great opportunity to show off her managerial abilities to Colin.

However, the furniture styles that appealed to House Smart's traditional customers failed to gain continuing market acceptance in Hong Kong. The competitive situation worsened with the arrival of an aggressive European company that had more appealing designs and lower prices. The joint venture proposal was dropped. Tensions rose among the Hong Kong employees due to Jane's unrealistic sales targets, the refusal by head office to change designs or reduce prices, and ongoing payroll problems (due to the inability of head office's HRIS to cope with Hong Kong's taxation system, pension fund contributions and payment cycles). As the pressures to improve performance increased, Jane became more aggressive and demanding (and her employees more passive and sullen).

Costs in the Hong Kong office were increasing, and Colin was angrily expressing his concern to Jane and others. In addition, a downturn in the economies of Hong Kong and Singapore due to the SARS epidemic had severely reduced consumer spending. Disappointed with the results, Jane lost confidence in her employees and insisted that they constantly check with her. Jobs that had given people responsibility, freedom to make decisions and use their initiative became routine as Jane increasingly assumed all decision making, with even minor matters having to be referred to her. Jane's heavy workload along with head office pressure caused her to become extremely quick-tempered. Staff morale plummeted as Jane's outbursts became more frequent. Her secretary and two sales representatives quit after Jane's anger exploded when she caught the sales clerk shopping on the Internet and fired her on the spot. When challenged by the employee, Jane screamed that an Internet policy was not needed as anyone with commonsense would know that personal shopping during work hours was not allowed. Shortly afterwards, the company received a letter from a legal firm acting on behalf of the sales clerk demanding compensation for wrongful dismissal. Jane was further horrified when the incident was negatively reported in the local press.

By the end of the year, House Smart had lost most of its market share. Morale was at an all-time low, with employees openly discussing the future of the company and their likely termination benefits.

In addition to the problems the company was experiencing in Hong Kong and Singapore, the Australian operation had been affected by its first ever strike. Environmentalists had discovered that the timber used to make the furniture was taken from protected rainforests. They immediately joined with the trade union movement to make an example of House Smart. The slowdown in production meant that orders were being delivered late, causing several key customers to cancel their orders. Colin felt betrayed by his workers and began to marginalise those who had been active in the strike.

Although House Smart had been able to meet its first loan repayment, the second repayment was now overdue. Credit for advanced purchase of materials was withdrawn and the company's bank was applying pressure for all loans to be repaid.

Colin became frantic. He now realised that the Hong Kong office was a mistake and that Jane lacked the management experience and know-how to successfully manage the Hong Kong sales operation. He reluctantly decided that for the parent company to survive he had to close the Hong Kong office. Colin worried that this could result in House Smart being faced with large claims for breach of contract regarding employment and leasehold arrangements. In particular, he worried about what he should do with Jane. Although no written employment contract existed, Colin had verbally promised Jane that she could stay in Hong Kong for at least two years.

Questions

1. Describe the HRM practices that were conducted at House Smart. What evidence is there that the four key roles of an HR manager were applied? What impact did this have on organisational growth and survival?
2. Analyse the life cycle of the organisation and compare it with the HR planning and forecasting needs to encourage growth and sustainability. What influence would effective HR planning have had on House Smart's latest expansion strategy?
3. Was the purpose of Colin's plans evident? How did they fit with his 'strategic intent'? What must House Smart do to implement more effective strategic management?
4. Applying a SWOT analysis, consider what aspects of the internal and external environment were considered when House Smart planned for its human resources. What techniques would have assisted Colin and Jane when forecasting human resource needs?
5. What assumptions did Jane make about House Smart's recently established HRIS? What processes did she ignore?
6. What are some issues that House Smart should have considered when applying Australian employment law to offshore locations? What consequences should Colin have foreseen?
7. Develop an HRM recovery plan for House Smart.

part

2

determining, attracting and selecting human resources

Part 2 emphasises the importance of meeting the organisation's people requirements through job analysis, job design, the quality of work life, employee recruitment and selection. The case study at the end of the part looks at the issue of discrimination in the selection process.

chapter 5

job analysis, job design and quality of work life

Learning objectives

When you have finished studying this chapter, you should be able to:

- Explain what is meant by job analysis and job design
- Understand the uses of job analysis
- Describe the content and format of a job description and a job specification
- Discuss the collection of job analysis data
- Explain the major methods of job analysis
- Discuss competency profiling
- Understand the major approaches to job design
- Discuss quality of work life, employee participation and industrial democracy.

'The first step in building a foundation for retention is to have a clear picture of the work we want the employee to do and the skills required to do it.'[1]

Suzanne Dibble

Introduction

Organisations today are depending more on their human resources. Revolutionary change, complex technologies and global competition mean increasing vulnerability. Organisations that fail to have the right people in the right place at the right time are at risk. A proper match between work and employee capabilities is now an economic necessity. Moreover, work itself is in a state of constant flux as organisations downsize, outsource, restructure and re-engineer their work processes and introduce self-directed work teams to gain a competitive advantage. Such workplace changes dramatically affect the work lives of employees.

Organisations that change their existing strategies, or develop new business strategies, for example, need to reassess their structures. If there is a poor fit between the chosen strategy and the organisation's structure, the structure will need to be redesigned. This means that the arrangement of the organisation's parts and the allocation of work will change. The move from a tall, hierarchical structure to a flat structure involves eliminating layers of management. This will produce wider spans of control, more delegation of responsibilities, increased empowerment and decentralised decision making.

Thus, changes in strategy affect not only how work is performed, but also the skills, knowledge and attitudes required by workers. Job restructuring, for example, may highlight gaps in the current skill levels of employees, calling for new recruitment, training and development, coaching, redeployment and outsourcing programs. This means that HR managers need a good understanding of work and how it is organised to ensure that the organisation's strategic business objectives are being supported and employee needs are being met. Job analysis and job design provide the foundations for this knowledge.

It is said that change is necessary for organisational survival, but change also creates job loss, insecurity and stress.

Job analysis

Job analysis A systematic investigation of the tasks, duties and responsibilities of a job and the necessary knowledge, skills and abilities a person needs to perform the job adequately.

Job analysts People who collect information about job content, how the job is done and the personal requirements needed to do the job successfully.

Job analysis is a basic HR activity because it focuses attention on the job content, the job requirements and the job context. It identifies what employees are expected to do. Knowledge about jobs and their requirements is collected through job analysis, which may be defined as the process by which jobs are divided to determine what tasks, duties and responsibilities they include, their relationships to other jobs, the conditions under which work is performed, and the personal capabilities required for satisfactory performance.[2]

Larger organisations usually have HR specialists called **job analysts** who undertake this systematic collection, evaluation and organisation of job information. Smaller organisations usually make the task part of the HR manager's job portfolio.

The purpose of job analysis

The purpose of job analysis is to obtain answers to the following questions:
1. Why does the job exist?
2. What physical and mental activities does the worker undertake?
3. When is the job to be performed?
4. Where is the job to be performed?
5. How does the worker do the job?
6. What qualifications are needed to perform the job?
7. What are the working conditions (such as the levels of temperature, light, offensive fumes and noise) of the job?
8. What machinery or equipment is used in the job?
9. What constitutes successful performance?

The components of job analysis

Job analysis provides information about three basic aspects of a job:

1. Job *content* describes the duties and responsibilities of the job in a manner that can range from global statements to very detailed descriptions of tasks and procedural steps.
2. Job *requirements* identify the formal qualifications, knowledge, skills, abilities and personal characteristics that employees need to perform the content of the job in a particular situation or context.
3. Job *context* refers to situational and supporting information regarding the particular job: its purpose; where it fits within the organisation; scope data (such as the magnitude of financial, human or material resources managed); the availability of guidelines; the potential consequences of error; the amount and closeness of supervision received or provided; and the work setting, cultural context, physical demands and working conditions.[3]

Figure 5.1 shows the type of information typically provided in a job analysis.

INFORMATION TYPE	DETAILS
General information	Details of position, including job number, title, branch/department/section, classification, job title of immediate supervisor, educational level, special licences (e.g. crane, forklift, money dealers, valuers) Main objectives of position: usually four to six short statements on key result areas
Job context	Reporting relationships (how many people report directly and indirectly to the position), degree of autonomy, problem-solving and decision-making responsibilities Contacts with other departments in an average week, external contacts (customers, suppliers, other organisations) Budgetary responsibilities Physical requirements (travelling, shift work, after-hours work, work from home, hot, dirty, high or confined-space work) Psychological aspects (workload, tight deadlines, time pressures, repetitious activities, dealing with routine or serious complaints, listening to personal problems, counselling) Monetary and non-financial incentives
Machines	Machines, tools, equipment, work aids and vehicles used
Job-related operations	Materials processed, products made Special knowledge required (e.g. chemical testing, occupational health and safety requirements) Services provided (e.g. handling customer enquiries, vehicle maintenance) Supervisory and controlling activities Other activities (communication, safety regulations, etc.)
Work performance	Work measurement (time taken, frequency of performing particular task) Work standards Error analysis Reworking procedures Other aspects
Personnel requirements	Job-related knowledge, skills and abilities (education, training, work experience) Personal attributes (aptitudes, physical characteristics, personal qualities, interests, ability to work unsupervised/work in a crowded area for lengthy periods) Special requirements

Figure 5.1 Types of information typically provided in a job analysis

Source Adapted from E. J. McCormick, 'Job and task analysis', in Marvin D. Dunnette (ed.), *Handbook of Industrial and Organizational Psychology*, John Wiley & Sons, New York, 1983, pp. 652–3.

Approaches to job analysis

There are two basic approaches to job analysis: a job-oriented (or task) approach and an employee-oriented (or behaviour) approach. A job-oriented approach is concerned with what gets done — that is, the tasks, duties and responsibilities of the job (job content). The employee-oriented approach focuses on how the job is done — that is, the human behaviour required to perform the job (job requirements). Job requirements (knowledge, skills and abilities) can be determined from a description of the job content, but not the other way around.

Job analysis and job design

Job information is gathered, analysed and recorded as the job exists, not as the job should exist. Industrial engineers, methods analysts or technical specialists initially structure work to achieve the organisation's strategic business objectives. Job analysis is normally conducted after the job has been designed, the worker has been trained and the work has been performed.[4] The organisation can then use the information generated via the written job descriptions (what the job entails) and job specifications (what kind of people to hire for the job) in the design or redesign of jobs (see figure 5.2).

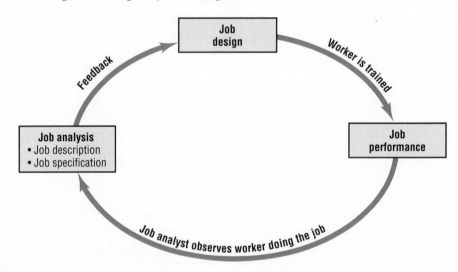

Figure 5.2 The relationship between job analysis and job design
Source Asia Pacific Management Co. Ltd, 2004.

When to analyse a job

Job analysis must keep up with job changes, but it is not possible to identify precisely how often a job should be reviewed. Cherrington identifies three occasions when job analysis is generally undertaken:[5]

1. when the organisation commences and the job analysis program is started
2. when a new job is created
3. when a job is changed significantly as a result of new methods, new procedures or new technology — for example, flight attendants with new low-cost US airline Song are expected, in addition to their standard duties, to be able to crack jokes, sing, dance and generally entertain passengers.[6]

Indicators that a job analysis may be needed include:

*   no evidence of any job analysis having ever been done
*   a considerable period having passed since the last job analysis was undertaken
*   increasing employee grievances regarding job content and/or working conditions
*   disagreement between a supervisor and a job holder on the work to be performed

- reorganisation, restructuring or downsizing that involves job changes or the creation of new jobs
- changes in technology whereby new processes, machinery or equipment are introduced — for example, hotel concierges, bellhops and housekeepers are now required to understand the basics of broadband and wireless Internet access, while hotel managers are expected to have additional IT troubleshooting skills[7]
- the replacement of long-serving employees who may have modified a job to meet their personal needs and abilities
- the use of new sources of recruitment, leading to new employees who may have different expectations from those of people hired in the past.[8]

Figure 5.3 outlines the job analysis process.

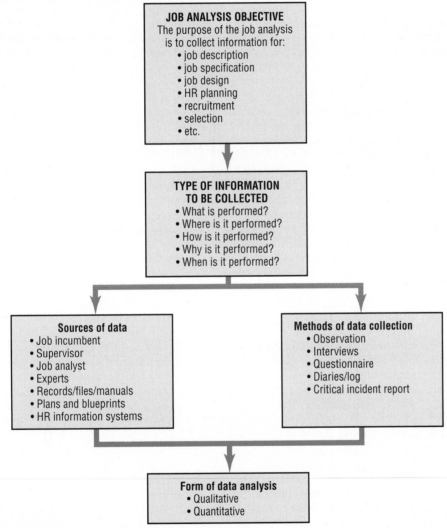

Figure 5.3 The job analysis process
Source Asia Pacific Management Co. Ltd, 2004.

The uses of job analysis

The information produced by job analysis is used extensively in HRM. 'It is in fact', says Ivancevich, 'difficult to imagine how an organisation could effectively hire, train, appraise, compensate or use its human resources without the kinds of information derived from job analysis.'[9]

Job descriptions define what a job is by identifying its content, requirements and context. Providing a written summary of the duties and responsibilities of the job, job descriptions help managers and current and prospective employees to understand what the job is and how it is to be performed.

Job specifications focus on the personal characteristics and qualifications that an employee must possess to perform the job successfully.

Job design identifies what work must be performed, how it will be performed, where it is to be performed and who will perform it. Job analysis information is invaluable in determining which tasks should be grouped together to form a job, and for structuring jobs so that employee satisfaction and performance can be enhanced.

Job analysis information can help identify and clarify the organisational structure and design. By clarifying job requirements and the interrelationships among jobs, job content, tasks, duties and responsibilities can be specified at all levels, thus promoting efficiency by minimising overlap or duplication.[10]

HR planning involves 'getting the right number of qualified people into the right job at the right time'.[11] Job analysis information is essential for HR planning because it helps to accurately determine the number and types of employees to be recruited or exited from the organisation.

Job analysis information aids the recruitment process by establishing the job requirements to be met and thus identifying who to recruit (and how and where to recruit them), helping the HR manager to attract better qualified candidates. In addition, job analysis identifies irrelevant and/or distorted job information, thus permitting the HR manager to provide realistic job previews.

Job analysis information assists the selection process by identifying what the job is by defining its duties and responsibilities. This facilitates the development of job-related selection techniques, helps ensure that EEO requirements are met and increases the likelihood of a proper matching of an applicant with the job.

Effective job orientation requires a clear understanding of the work to be performed, which is exactly what job analysis provides. A new employee cannot be properly taught how to do a job if job duties and responsibilities are not clearly defined.

Job analysis information is essential to the establishment of performance standards and performance appraisal. It provides a thorough understanding of what the employee is supposed to do. Without this information, acceptable levels of performance cannot be determined and an accurate measure of actual performance cannot be obtained.

Job analysis information is used to design and implement training and development programs. The job specification defines the knowledge, skills and abilities required for successful job performance. This allows the HR manager to establish training and development objectives, design programs and determine whether a current or potential employee requires training.

HR managers are better placed to offer career planning and development guidance when they have a good understanding of the types of jobs existing in an organisation. Similarly, by identifying jobs and job requirements, employees become aware of their career options and what constitutes a realistic career objective for them in the organisation.

The job description is the foundation of job evaluation. It summarises the nature and requirements of the job and permits its evaluation relative to other jobs. Once the relative worth of a job has been determined, an equitable level of compensation and benefits can be assigned.

Job analysis information helps create a healthy and safe working environment. Jobs with hazardous conditions, methods or procedures can be identified, and the work can be redesigned to eliminate or reduce exposure to health and safety hazards.

Misunderstandings and disagreement among managers, employees and unions over job content is a major source of grievance and demarcation disputes. Job analysis information promotes good industrial relations by helping to avoid such disputes, by providing a clear description of tasks and responsibilities and by identifying the formal qualifications, skills, abilities, knowledge and experience required to perform the work successfully.

Increasingly, HR managers face legal requirements prohibiting discriminatory HR practices, particularly in employment. Given that systematic job analysis can identify the critical elements of a job (that is, the duties and responsibilities that must be performed) and the necessary knowledge, skills, abilities and other personal characteristics required for successful job performance, it provides insurance that an organisation's HR policies and practices are legally defensible.

Job descriptions

A **job description** or position description is a written statement explaining why a job exists, what the job holder actually does, how they do it and under what conditions the job is performed (see the example in figure 5.4).[12] There is no standard format used for writing a job description; the format, in fact, depends on management preference and how the job description will be used. However, most job descriptions contain information on:

- job identification
- job objectives
- duties and responsibilities
- relationships
- know-how
- problem solving
- accountability
- authority
- special circumstances
- performance standards
- trade union or professional memberships
- licences
- other requirements.[13]

Job description A written statement explaining what a job holder does, how the work is performed and where and when it is performed.

Components of job descriptions

1. Job identification
The job identification section locates the job in the organisational structure. It includes information on the employee's job title, department and reporting relationships. The job title should be descriptive, meaningful and consistent with comparable positions in the organisation. A title that accurately identifies a job is valuable for:
- providing employee information and fostering self-esteem
- identifying job relationships
- comparing the position with similar jobs in other organisations.[14]

Additional information can include the job code, the job status (exempt/non-exempt, full-time/part-time/casual), the job grade or points, the pay range, the date written, the name of whoever wrote the job description, and the name and position of the person approving the description.

2. Job objective
The job objective describes in a nutshell why the job exists — that is, the primary purpose or objective of the position. Ideally, it should describe the essence of the job in 25 words or less.

3. Duties and responsibilities
This section includes a listing of the major job duties and responsibilities. It is the heart of the job description and should indicate clearly and specifically what the employee must do. Given rapid change, the need for improved performance, flexibility and multiskilling, duties and responsibilities are increasingly being expressed as performance standards derived from the organisation's strategic business objectives. Nevertheless, many job description formats still list performance standards separately (or not at all).

Five to eight statements of key duties and responsibilities are sufficient to describe most jobs. A common mistake in this section is to list every task, duty and responsibility regardless of importance. A task or duty that is performed frequently is not necessarily significant in achieving the job's objectives. A major duty and responsibility is one of such importance that non-performance or substandard performance will significantly affect the required results and demand remedial action by management.[15] Job holders, in particular, are especially prone to padding job descriptions when they know they are being used for job evaluation purposes. Thus, it is essential that these statements be clear and concise and give an accurate word picture of the major duties and responsibilities encompassed by the job. They are best expressed as a list of results that the job is designed to achieve so that job performance can be measured objectively.

4. Relationships
This section identifies the relationships with other positions (within and external to the organisation) that are necessary for satisfactory job performance. For example, what positions report directly to this job? What are the job's most frequent contacts within the organisation? What are the job's most frequent and important contacts outside the organisation?

JOB DESCRIPTION

Position: Vice-President, Human Resources, Asia–Pacific
Location: Hong Kong
Division: Asia–Pacific
Incumbent: Y. Tanaka
Department: Human Resources
Job status: Exempt
Job code: CAP-HRM-001
Reports to: President Asia–Pacific (administrative), Vice-President, Human Resources — Corporate (functional)
Written by: Monica Lim, Job Analyst
Date: 2 April 2003
Approved by: J. A. Wong, President, Asia–Pacific (administrative superior)
W. J. Smith, Vice-President, Human Resources — Corporate (functional superior)

Job objective

Under the administrative direction of the President, Asia–Pacific, and the functional guidance of the Vice-President, Human Resources — Corporate, develop, recommend and implement approved HRM strategies, policies and practices that will facilitate the achievement of the company's stated business and HRM objectives.

Duties and responsibilities

- Develop and recommend HRM strategies, policies and practices that promote employee commitment, competence, motivation and performance, and that facilitate the achievement of the Asia–Pacific region's business objectives.
- Provide policy guidance to senior management regarding the acquisition, development, reward, maintenance and exit of the division's human resources so as to promote the status of the company as an ethical and preferred employer of choice.
- Identify, analyse and interpret for Asia–Pacific regional senior management and corporate HR management those influences and changes in the division's internal and external environment and their impact on HRM and divisional business objectives, strategies, policies and practices.
- Actively contribute as a member of the Asia–Pacific Board of Directors to the development, implementation and achievement of the Asia–Pacific region's overall business objectives, strategies and plans.

Relationships

Internally, relate with senior line and functional managers within the Asia–Pacific region and corporate headquarters in New York. Externally, successfully relate with senior academic, business, government and trade union personnel. Directly supervise the following positions: Manager, Compensation and Benefits, Asia–Pacific and Manager, Training and Development, Asia–Pacific. Functionally supervise the HR managers in 13 geographic locations within the Asia–Pacific region.

Know-how

University degree is required, along with seven to 10 years broad-based HRM experience in a competitive and international (preferably Asian) business environment. A proven track record in managing change is essential. Fluency in English is essential and fluency in Chinese or Japanese is desirable. Excellent human relations and communication skills are essential. Previous experience in marketing, finance or manufacturing is desirable. Computer literacy in spreadsheets and HRIS is essential. The ability to positively represent the company at the most senior levels and to actively contribute as a Director of the Asia–Pacific Regional Board is essential.

Problem solving

Diverse cultures and varying stages of economic development within the Asia–Pacific region create a unique and tough business environment. The incumbent will often face complex HR and business problems demanding solutions that need to be creative and, at the same time, sensitive to local and company requirements.

Accountability

Employees: 3000. Sales: US$4 billion. Direct budget responsibility: US$2.7 million. Assets controlled: US$780 000. Locations: Australia, China, Hong Kong, India, Indonesia, Japan, South Korea, Malaysia, New Zealand, the Philippines, Singapore, Taiwan, Thailand.

Authority

This position has the authority to:

- approve expenditures on budgeted capital items up to a total value of US$100 000 in any one financial year
- hire and fire subordinate personnel in accord with company policies and procedures
- approve expense accounts for subordinate personnel in accord with company policies and procedures
- authorise all non-capital item expenditures within approved budgetary limit
- exercise line authority over all direct reporting positions.

Special circumstances

Successful performance requires the incumbent to work long hours, to travel extensively (50–60 per cent of the time), to quickly adapt to different cultures and business conditions, to successfully handle high-stress situations and to constantly work under pressure in a complex and very competitive business environment.

Performance indicators

Performance indicators will include both quantitative and qualitative measures as agreed by the President, Asia–Pacific Division, the Vice-President, Human Resources — Corporate and the incumbent. Indicators may be market based (e.g. share price improvement), business based (e.g. division profitability, budget control, days lost through industrial unrest, positive changes in employee commitment, job satisfaction and motivation) and individual based (e.g. performance as a leader and manager as assessed by superiors, peers and subordinates). Performance expectations and performance indicators generally will be defined on an annual basis. A formal performance appraisal will be conducted at least once a year.

Figure 5.4 Global Chemicals Inc. job description for Vice-President, Human Resources, Asia–Pacific
Source Asia Pacific Management Co. Ltd, 2004.

5. Know-how

The know-how section is concerned with the minimum levels of knowledge, skills, abilities, experience and formal qualifications required to do the job. For example, what are the minimum academic qualifications required? What IT capabilities are required? How much and what type of experience is needed to perform the job successfully?

6. Problem solving

The problem-solving section identifies the amount of original thinking required in decision making and the environment in which problem solving takes place. For example, does the job require simple, routine and repetitive solutions or complex, varied and creative solutions? Is the business environment stable or dynamic? (for example, is competition non-existent or cutthroat?).

7. Accountability

Accountability details the financial impact of the job by identifying the dollar value of assets, sales volume, payroll, and so on for which the job is accountable. It measures the answerability for actions taken on the job.

8. Authority

This identifies the specific rights and limitations that apply to the position's decision-making authority — in other words, the freedom to act. For example, what decisions can be made without reference to a superior? What decisions must be referred to a superior? Does the job involve the right to hire and fire? What specific dollar limits exist on decision-making authority?

9. Special circumstances

The special circumstances section is concerned with what is special, unusual or hazardous about the position and/or the environment in which the job is performed (for example, dirty, dusty, dangerous, high pressure, long hours, etc.).

10. Performance standards

This section identifies (a) the standards required for effective performance and (b) the measures for evaluating performance.

11. Trade union/professional associations

This section identifies any professional association or trade union membership required.

12. Licences

This section highlights any special licences or registrations required (for example, a licence to practise psychology or medicine).

Job description guidelines

Although the style and format of job descriptions are largely determined by their use and organisational preference, there are some standard guidelines for writing effective job descriptions:

- List duties and responsibilities in logical sequence.
- State separate duties and responsibilities clearly, simply and concisely.
- Begin each sentence with an action verb.
- Use quantitative terms where possible to achieve greater objectivity and clarity.
- Use specific rather than vague terms.
- Use standardised terminology.
- Answer the questions of how, what, when and why. This will help produce a complete job description.
- Clearly identify the end results or standards on which performance will be evaluated.

Clarity and simplicity of expression are prerequisites for job descriptions and specifications. If job descriptions are to be read, understood and accepted by all levels of employees, they must be written in plain and simple English.

Job specifications

The **job specification** or person specification is derived from the job description. It identifies the experience, education, skills, abilities and knowledge, personal characteristics and special requirements needed to perform the job successfully. The job specification is an essential part of the selection process because it identifies in job-related terms what kind of candidates need to be recruited and how they should be assessed. It should be noted that some job specifications identify not only the essential criteria required to perform a job successfully, but also those criteria deemed to be desirable. In this case, care must be exercised to ensure that preconceived attitudes or prejudices do not lead to the inclusion of criteria that are not job related. The job specification may be incorporated into the job description form or documented separately. A sample job specification is shown in figure 5.5.

JOB SPECIFICATION

Position: Department/section:
Location: Division/unit:
Job status: Date:
Job code:

Key selection criteria

Experience
What type of and how much experience is required to perform this job successfully?

Qualifications
What are the minimum formal educational qualifications required to perform this job successfully? Are any special qualifications legally required to perform this job?

Skills, abilities and knowledge
What skills, abilities and knowledge are required to perform this job successfully?

Personal qualities
What personal qualities (physical characteristics/ personality) are required to perform this job successfully? (For example, 20/20 vision, outgoing personality, etc.)

Special requirements
What special requirements must be satisfied to perform this job successfully? (For example, ability to work shift work, travel interstate/overseas, be away from home for extended periods, work long/irregular hours)

Ideal industry background
What industries/organisations would provide an ideal background for doing this job?

Ideal current organisation
What would be the ideal organisation for the candidate to be employed in at this moment?

Ideal current position
What would be the ideal position for the candidate to be employed in at this moment?

Route up
What would be the ideal career path for the candidate to have followed as preparation for this position?

Remuneration
What salary and benefits should the candidate currently be receiving to make this position financially attractive?

Figure 5.5 Global Chemicals Inc. job specification
Source Asia Pacific Management Co. Ltd, 2004.

Job descriptions, job specifications and unions

The language used in writing job descriptions and job specifications is extremely important. It is particularly important when a job description is to become part of an award or negotiated agreement involving a union. Badly written job descriptions and job specifications restrict management's freedom to change job tasks, duties and responsibilities and to assign work to employees. To avoid disputes, it is critical that job descriptions and job specifications be clear, concise and understandable. This is particularly so with jobs that have hierarchical skill and responsibility classifications (for example, machinist grade A or grade 1, highest level; machinist grade B or grade 2, next level down; and so on). Such jobs must be carefully distinguished by job title and clearly involve different job content and job requirements.

If ABC-type classifications have developed because of 'historical' reasons, it is essential to check that more than one level of the job actually exists. Otherwise, claims for 'higher duties' payments or for an upgrade to a higher classification are likely to be an ongoing source of grievances. Precise job descriptions cannot overcome incompetent management or inadequate wage and salary administration, but they do help.

Job analysts or HR managers preparing job descriptions that are subject to award or contract negotiation can minimise the risk of disputes by attending to the following matters:

- Job descriptions and job specifications for higher level positions should include only job content and job requirements that reflect the highest level of difficulty encountered by the job holder on a regular and consistent basis. Tasks, duties and responsibilities performed occasionally should not be included if they already appear in lower level job descriptions.
- Job descriptions and job specifications for jobs at each level should use only terms and definitions that have the complete agreement and common understanding of employees, union representatives, supervisors and managers.
- The job content or job requirements should not be identical for jobs covered by rival unions present on the same site.
- Job content and job requirements should be examined for possible union demarcation disputes.
- Job description language should be kept clear and simple to avoid the union argument that the job sounds 'difficult to do'.
- Job specifications should identify the minimum requirements needed to satisfactorily perform the job, thus avoiding the union argument that the job is 'highly skilled'.
- Job descriptions should be concise. Long job descriptions allow the union to argue, 'If the employee has to do ALL this . . .'
- Job descriptions for jobs at different levels should use clearly different titles and clearly different language.[16]

Criticisms of job descriptions

The traditional job description has been criticised for being a straitjacket suitable only for repetitive work.[17] Being a static written description, it ignores the dynamics of the job. Cascio describes job descriptions as being behaviourally sterile![18] This is especially true for problem-solving and managerial work 'where incumbents have a great deal of influence over their work activities, the percentage of time they allot to different work activities, and the way in which the activities are carried out'.[19]

Furthermore, Peters argues that 'it is imperative today that managers and non-managers be induced to cross 'uncrossable' boundaries as a matter of course day after day'.[20] Japanese companies, for example, avoid specialisation and generalise training programs to promote flexibility in the assignment of personnel.[21] Thus, their job descriptions are merely a general guide, with everyone crossing job boundaries.[22] Job fluidity such as this undermines the effectiveness of traditional job descriptions and means that they risk being out of date and counterproductive as guides for selection, job evaluation, and so on.[23] Today's good job description may be irrelevant tomorrow.

'At best', says Townsend, 'a job description freezes the job as the writer understands it at a particular instant in the past. At worst, they are prepared by personnel people who can't write and don't understand the jobs.'[24] Thus, job descriptions are seen as being appropriate only for stable, predictable and bureaucratic organisations.[25] According to Brass, 'there is considerable evidence that "jobs" are created by organizations and bureaucracies merely because this makes organizational life more ordered and more easily controlled from the top'.[26] Townley, for example, argues that the job description is the first stage in controlling work by making employee behaviour and performance predictable and calculable.[27] On the other hand, if trade unions control skill definition and allocation of job duties, management's power and labour flexibility is reduced.[28] Ironically, research suggests that union opposition to output-based pay fosters jobs that are more repetitive, have more measurable criteria and involve less judgemental criteria and data analysis.[29]

Finally, job descriptions are seen as archaic because the traditional job comprising set tasks is disappearing. Automation of routine office and factory work means that employees

Organisations want increased flexibility to reduce costs via outsourcing, the use of casual and temporary labour and multiskilling to remain competitive. Employees and unions complain that this leads to overwork, lower wages and poorer conditions.

increasingly work on projects that are 'conceived, staffed up, completed and shut down'.[30] The conventional concept of a job thus 'has reached its use by date'.[31] Kiechel argues that, 'If a job is defined "as a regular set of duties with regular pay, and regular hours and a fixed place in an organization's structure", then it increasingly seems an obsolescent social artefact of the Industrial Revolution'.[32] In the chemical industry, for example, some companies 'specify only output quantities, quality specifications, and plant utilization rates, leaving how the work will be done to the team of employees who contract with them to operate the plant for a particular period'.[33]

Project-based work instead of position-based work signals the demise of the traditional job and the traditional job description. As a result, employees psychologically tied to a job title and a job description are vulnerable because they lack flexibility.[34] Today, says Peters, 'the job description is a loser'.[35] The conventional view, in contrast, argues that job descriptions should be prepared for all jobs.[36] This debate indicates to the HR manager that traditional 'tools of the trade' should not be used unthinkingly. Competition, technical innovation and changing workplace values have created the need for a work environment where jobs are reinvented totally. 'To be satisfying', says Townsend, 'a job should have variety, autonomy, wholeness and feedback. In other words, no job descriptions.'[37] Nevertheless, legal and equal employment opportunity requirements, industrial relations realities, management needs and organisational inertia suggest that job descriptions still have their place.

NEWSBREAK

Long hours part of the job

By Marcus Priest

Next time people in your office complain about working long hours, don't bother telling them to do something about it. They wouldn't even if they could.

Research from Griffith University shows that many people who do have a large say over work-times work long hours.

It's not because they want to, mind, but because they have 'internalised' their employer's business objectives.

The study also finds that the behaviour of other workers also creates a workplace culture of long working hours.

Last year, the Australian Industrial Relations Commission ruled that workers should have the right to refuse unreasonable overtime.

But instead of giving staff greater say over their working hours, the research supports a push from sections of the union movement to impose a cap on working hours as a more effective way of controlling the hours.

'For an agreed ceiling on working hours to be effective, there must be enforcement mechanisms in place; otherwise a minority of employees and unsympathetic supervisors can subvert its operation.'

The critical aspect of controlling working hours is not the ability to have a say over hours but rather the ability to have a say over workload, says the report.

The study looked at 17 workplaces in Queensland between 2001 and 2002 over a number of industries, including manufacturing, mining, construction, banking, law, retail, government, education and law enforcement, and found support for an external cap across all workplaces.

The research by David Peetz, Keith Townsend, Bob Russell, Chris Houghton, Andrea Fox and Cameron Allan was funded by the Queensland Department of Industrial Relations and the Australian Research Council, and appears in the latest edition of the *Australian Bulletin of Labour*.

'The culture of long hours is something that is more complex than simply the employers telling workers they have to work long hours against their will, it's a culture that has been bought into by working people', ACTU assistant secretary Richard Marles said.

'Hours caps are a really important tool in changing the whole working hours' culture because they are an external intervention into an existing culture which has been bought into by both parties.'

Author Dr Peetz said the research highlighted how the provision of

Collection of job analysis information

There are numerous ways of collecting job analysis information (varying in complexity, cost and effectiveness). The most appropriate data collection method depends on the purpose of the job analysis, the types of information to be collected, the sources of information, the means of information collection and the way in which the data are to be analysed and reported. The five most common data collection methods are *observation*, *interview*, *questionnaire*, *diary/log* and *critical incident reports*. Other approaches include film and video, a computerised system and job analyst participation. Each can be used alone or in conjunction with one or more of the other data collection methods. Using job observation and employee interviews together, for example, is a practical and common way of obtaining job information. Employees (and union officials where appropriate) should be fully informed about the collection of job analysis data to ensure their cooperation and to avoid the risk of industrial disputation.

Common data collection methods

To understand what an employee does, along with how, why and where they do it, the job analyst observes an employee working and records a description of the tasks and duties performed. Direct **observation** is primarily used for standardised, repetitive short job cycle or manual jobs. Jobs that are predominantly made up of observable actions, therefore, are best suited for analysis by observation. In contrast, jobs that involve thinking yield almost no information to the observer. For example, there is often no way in which an observer can obtain an accurate description of the mental energy, personal pressures, contemplative and planning activities, and subtleties of interpersonal relationships that make up a significant part of a manager's job. Similarly, if a job cycle is irregular or extends over a long period of time, job observation will be difficult. Thus, job analysts often combine observation with an interview when analysing managerial jobs.[38]

However, the process of observation can create an unrealistic situation and cause the employee to behave differently. This problem can be particularly serious when an employee knows that a job description will be used to determine their job grade and compensation.[39] Consequently, it is important that the job analyst observe a representative sample of employees to avoid biased or inaccurate descriptions. This can be extremely time consuming, requiring many hours of direct observation. Much writing and analysis of narrative is also usually involved.[40] Such problems have led to the use of videotapes or films of employee job performance.

Observation The job analyst observes an employee working and records the duties performed.

Interviews The job analyst interviews the job holder about the duties performed.

Job analysis data can be obtained by interviewing the job holder and their supervisor. Interview information is especially valuable for managerial and professional jobs that involve difficult-to-observe behaviour. **Interviews**, in fact, are probably the most widely used method of collecting job analysis information. The interview method generally requires that the job analyst visit the job location and meet with the employee performing the job. The job place is the most desirable location at which to conduct the interview, but whether this is realistic depends on such conditions as noise, weather, safety, accessibility, secrecy, privacy or management preference. Interviews can be conducted with a single employee, a group of employees or a manager who is knowledgeable about the job. Usually a structured questionnaire is used to obtain the job information and to facilitate comparisons. Interviews are valuable in verifying and augmenting information collected by observation.

Limitations of the interview method include the following:

- Developing a questionnaire, establishing rapport between the job analyst and the employee and interviewing multiple job holders (especially those in managerial and professional positions) can be expensive and time consuming.
- The job analyst needs considerable skill to ensure that only accurate and unbiased information is recorded. Given the risk of information distortion, Cascio recommends against using an interview as the sole method of job analysis.[41]

Job analysis questionnaire Questionnaire specially designed to collect information about job content, how the job is done and the personal requirements needed to do the job successfully.

The major advantage of the **job analysis questionnaire** method is that information on a large number of jobs can be collected within a relatively short time. Consequently, the use of questionnaires is usually the most economical of job analysis methods. Another advantage of the questionnaire technique is that it permits the job analyst to put standard questions to all participants.

However, there is a danger (especially with open-ended or narrative questionnaires) that employees may not complete the questionnaire, may misinterpret it or may take an excessively long time to return it.[42] Furthermore, some questions — such as: What type of formal education do you consider to be the minimum requirement for satisfactory performance of your job? What do you think is the most complex or difficult part of your job? What contacts inside and outside the organisation are necessary in performing your job? — allow the employee to fully describe the job as it is being performed, but may be perceived as threatening, invasive, complicated, time consuming and annoying. Moreover, the quality of the job analysis depends on the employees' writing skills. The checklist questionnaire attempts to overcome some of these problems by reducing the employees' time and effort in completing the form. It also facilitates statistical analysis by computer. However, the problems of employee understanding, accuracy and motivation remain. Thus, precautions must be taken to ensure that employees have interpreted the questions correctly and that they have supplied all the required information in the proper form. This explains why the questionnaire and interview methods are often combined.

Job analysts disagree about the exact format and degree of structure that a job analysis questionnaire should exhibit. Nevertheless, there are some established guidelines to make the questionnaire easier to use.

- Keep it as short as possible. Employees do not generally like to complete forms.
- Explain how the questionnaire results are being used. Employees want to know why they must answer the questions.
- Keep it simple. Do not try to impress employees with jargon or technical language to make a point or ask a question.
- Test the questionnaire before using it. To improve the questionnaire, ask some employees to complete it and to comment on its features. This means that the format can be adjusted before the questionnaire is used in its final form.[43]

Diary/log A written record of the duties performed by an employee.

Job information can be obtained by getting employees to maintain written records of what they do in performing their jobs. These records may take the form of a time log or daily diary. The **diary/log** is useful when analysing professional and management jobs that are difficult to observe. If a diary/log is accurately recorded and kept up to date, it is a valuable source of job information. If maintained for an extended period of time, it is especially useful in identifying irregular or infrequent duties and tasks. Time logs are a valuable means of helping employees identify how their time is spent and what they actually do each day.

However, the diary/log method requires considerable effort to complete. Unfortunately, employees often lack the necessary self-discipline and they may see the diary/log as an unwelcome chore. Finally, employees may lack the writing skills to clearly and concisely record their activities. The portable tape-recorder can overcome this latter problem by allowing the employee to verbally describe job activities as they are performed.

Critical incident reports are snapshot accounts of effective or ineffective job performance. If a large amount of incident information is collected, describing what led up to the incident, what the employee actually did and why the performance was effective or ineffective, then the job requirement can be defined. However, the critical incident technique does not identify the routine activities performed by the employee, so it is best suited for use in performance appraisal and training and development. Critical incident reports require the employee's supervisor to keep written records of the employee's activities that have contributed to success or failure on the job. Like the diary/log method, this can be viewed as an onerous task. Furthermore, without proper training, the supervisor may find it difficult to distinguish between critical and typical job behaviour.

Critical incident An example of employee behaviour that illustrates effective or ineffective job performance.

'Sure I can handle multitasking. Can you handle multipaying?'

Combining data collection methods

Used alone, the observation, interview, questionnaire, diary/log or critical incident methods are unlikely to be a comprehensive source of job information. A combination of methods increases the probability of better results, so multiple methods are frequently used. The job analyst ultimately must decide which method or combination of methods is required to produce a thorough job analysis (see figure 5.6). This decision should not be made on the basis of immediate need. It is critical that the purposes of the job analysis (for example, recruitment and selection, performance appraisal or job evaluation) be clearly stated before the data collection method is determined (see figure 5.3).[44]

CRITERIA	DEFINITION
1. Purposes served	Can the data collected be used for a variety of purposes?
2. Versatility	Can the method be used to analyse many different jobs?
3. Standardisation	Does the method provide data that can be easily compared to data collected by other methods?
4. User acceptability	Do users of the method accept it as a reasonable way to collect job data?
5. Training required	How much training is needed before individuals can use it to collect data in the organisation?
6. Sample size	How large a sampling of information sources is needed before an adequate picture of the job can be obtained?
7. Off-the-shelf	Can the method be used directly off-the-shelf, or must considerable development work be done to tailor it for use in a particular organisation?
8. Reliability	Does the method produce reliable data?
9. Time to complete	How long does it take to analyse a job using the method?
10. Cost	How much does the method cost to implement and use?

Figure 5.6 Criteria for assessing job analysis methods
Source E. L. Levine, R. A. Ash, M. Hall and F. Sistrunk, 'Evaluation of job analysis methods by experienced job analysts', *Academy of Management Journal*, vol. 26, 1983, pp. 339–48.

Job analysis techniques

The above data collection methods, although presented in general terms, underpin the composition of many popular job analysis techniques, such as Functional Job Analysis and the Management Position Description Questionnaire outlined below.

Functional Job Analysis (FJA) was developed by the US Training and Employment Service. FJA uses standardised statements and terminology to describe the nature of jobs and to prepare job descriptions and job specifications. It produces a description of a job in terms of data, people and things. FJA is based on the following key assumptions:

- Jobs are concerned with data, people and things.
- A distinction must be made between what gets done and what employees do to get things done.
- Mental resources are used to describe data; interpersonal resources are used with people; and physical resources are applied to people.
- Each duty performed on a job draws on a range of employee talents and skills. FJA has the advantages of being intuitively appealing, relatively easy to learn and based on a standardised format, but it has been criticised for being labour-intensive, subjective and difficult to use.[45]

The Australian Standard Classification of Occupations (ASCO) 'is a skill-based classification of occupations developed in Australia as a national standard for the production and analysis of labour force statistics, human resources management, education planning, the listing of job applicants and vacancies, the provision of occupational information and for vocational guidance'.[46] It comprises more than 1000 distinct occupations distributed

Functional Job Analysis
Job analysis technique that uses standardised statements and terminology to describe the nature of jobs and to prepare job descriptions and job specifications.

among eight major job classifications: managers and administrators, professionals, para-professionals, tradespersons, clerks, salespersons and personal service workers, plant and machinery operators, and drivers and labourers and related workers. Job information is given on skill levels, tasks and duties performed and related occupations or occupation titles. ASCO is useful to job analysts as a source of background job information and generic job descriptions (see figure 5.7).

The **Position Analysis Questionnaire** (PAQ) is a job analysis instrument and scoring/reporting service that is marketed commercially.[47] Developed by Purdue University, the PAQ is a structured questionnaire for quantitatively assessing jobs. It contains 194 questions divided into six major categories:

- *Information input* — where and how does the employee get the information needed to perform the job?
- *Mental processes* — what reasoning, decision making, planning and information-processing activities are involved in performing the job?
- *Physical activities* — what physical activities does the employee perform and what tools or devices are used?
- *Relationships with other people* — what relationships with other people are required in the job?
- *Job context* — in what physical or social contexts is the work performed?
- *Other job characteristics* — what activities, conditions or characteristics, other than those described above, are relevant to the job?

The big advantage of the PAQ is that it can be used to analyse almost any type of job. In addition, it has been widely used and researched and appears to be both valid and reliable.[48]

Position Analysis Questionnaire Job analysis method that uses a structured questionnaire for quantitatively assessing jobs.

HUMAN RESOURCES OFFICER

Provides staffing and administration services in support of an organisation's human resource policies and programs.

Skill level

The entry requirement for this occupation is a Bachelor's degree or higher qualification or at least five years relevant experience. In some instances, relevant experience is required in addition to the formal qualification.

Tasks include:

- conducts analyses to determine staffing needs
- arranges for advertising of vacancies, interviewing and testing of applicants and selection of staff
- provides advice and information to management on personnel policies and procedures, staff performance and disciplinary matters
- assists in the planning and provision of staff services such as canteens, recreational facilities and amenities

- maintains personnel records and associated human resource information systems
- analyses and prepares job descriptions
- arranges the induction of staff and provides information on conditions of service, salaries and promotional opportunities
- may counsel employees or discuss their individual grievances, problems and difficulties
- may assist in the development and implementation of equal opportunity, anti-discrimination and similar programs
- may assist in the organisation of safety programs and procedures
- may supervise personnel clerks.

Specialisation

Work force planning analyst

Figure 5.7 Generic job description for human resources officer
Source Australian Bureau of Statistics, *Australian Standard Classification of Occupations*, AGPS, Canberra, 1997, p. 143.

The **Management Position Description Questionnaire** (MPDQ) is a 197-item, behaviourally oriented, structured questionnaire for describing, comparing, classifying and evaluating management positions.[49] The latest version of the MPDQ is divided into 10 sections: general information; decision making; planning and organising; supervising and controlling; consulting and involving; contacts; monitoring business indicators; overall ratings; know-how; and an organisational chart.[50] The MPDQ has been found useful for selecting managerial employees, planning careers, diagnosing training needs and evaluating jobs.[51]

Management Position Description Questionnaire Job analysis method that uses a behaviourally oriented, structured questionnaire to describe, compare, classify and evaluate management positions.

**Position Classification
Inventory** Job analysis
questionnaire that can be used
to classify occupations and
assess person–job fit.

The **Position Classification Inventory** (PCI) is a job analysis inventory based on Holland's RIASEC theory that can be used to classify occupations and to assess person–job fit.[52] It can help the HR manager to:

- describe skills required within specialised occupations
- compare employee views and supervisor views of the position
- enhance person–job fit
- understand sources of satisfaction and dissatisfaction with a position or occupation.

The 84-item inventory can be completed in less than 10 minutes.[53]

Widely used in job evaluation, the Hay Guide Chart Profile Method is commercially available through the Hay Group.[54] Job content is analysed in terms of three major factors that are present to some degree in every job. These are know-how (the knowledge and skills needed for satisfactory job performance, expressed in terms of specialised knowledge, managerial skills and human relations), problem solving (the amount of original, self-starting thinking required by the job, expressed in terms of the environment in which thinking takes place and the challenge presented by the thinking to be done) and accountability (the answerability for actions and for the consequences of those actions, expressed in terms of freedom to act, job impact on end results and magnitude). A fourth factor, working conditions, is used for those jobs for which hazards, an unpleasant environment and/or particular physical demands are significant elements. The Hay Guide Chart Profile Method allows the organisation to define job requirements and to accurately measure and compare job content. It facilitates organisational analysis and planning, HR appraisal, planning and development and EEO compliance.

New multi-method approaches to job analysis based on computer technology and sophisticated quantitative techniques are now coming into use. There are some common characteristics of such job analysis methods:

- They use multidimensional perspectives on the source of job information, the type of data analysed and the response scale formats.
- They are designed to concurrently support multiple HR applications.
- They are structured questionnaires to be completed by employees, supervisors and/or subject-matter experts.
- They use computer-friendly computer systems that may perform complex multivariate statistical procedures but that also provide graphical, quality reports for ease of data interpretation.[55]

Multi-method approaches can efficiently analyse a geographically dispersed work force, track and document rapidly changing job content and, for large organisations, produce results that are very cost-effective. In addition, these methods have the advantage of supporting the development of an integrated HR information system (such as Job Scope, Career Directions, HR Focus and Hay Value).[56]

Evaluation of traditional job analysis techniques

Job analysis suffers from research neglect, although the studies that have been undertaken to evaluate its reliability and validity suggest that job analysis ratings are reasonably reliable.[57] However, the results from task-oriented approaches are less conclusive. Similarly, research on the validity of job analysis ratings suggests that they are a source of useful information but certainly are not perfect.[58]

Competency profiling

The usefulness of task-oriented approaches to job analysis has been reduced by changes in the workplace: widespread corporate downsizing; improvements in information technology; the introduction to the workplace of flexible job design, teamwork, multiskilling and project assignments; and the demise of authoritarian hierarchies and the replacement of specialisation with a new style of generalism.[59] Lawler, for example, says: 'Despite its historic utility, there is growing evidence that it may be time for many organizations to move away from a focus on jobs and towards a focus on individuals and their competencies ... Instead of thinking of people as having a job with a particular set of activities that can be captivated in a relatively permanent and fixed job description, it may be more appropriate and more effective to think of them as human resources that work for an organization.'[60]

As a result, HR managers have increasingly focused on person-oriented approaches such as critical incident reporting and behaviour–event interviews to identify the skills and behaviours needed to perform a job, which is known as **competency profiling**.[61] These occupational requirements are referred to as competencies (see figure 5.8). Specifically, a competency is 'an underlying characteristic of a person that leads to or causes superior or effective performance'.[62] This attributes model of competencies has three key elements:

- *Underlying characteristics:* the competency is an integral part of a person's personality.
- *Causality:* the competency causes or predicts behaviour and performance.
- *Performance:* the competency actually predicts effective (that is, minimally acceptable) or superior performance as measured on a specific criterion or standard.[63]

Competency profiling Job analysis method that focuses on the skills and behaviours needed to perform a job successfully.

COMPETENCIES FOR HR PROFESSIONALS

1. Goal and action management abilities cluster
   - Efficiency orientation
   - Planning
   - Initiative or efficacy
   - Attention to details
   - Self-control
   - Flexibility
2. Interpersonal/people management cluster
   - Empathy
   - Persuasiveness
   - Networking
   - Negotiating
   - Self-confidence
   - Group management or team leadership
   - Developing others
   - Oral communications
3. Analytic reasoning or cognitive cluster
   - Systems thinking
   - Pattern recognition
   - Social objectivity
   - Written communication

Figure 5.8 Competencies for HR professionals
Source A. K. Yeung, 'Competencies for HR professionals: an interview with Richard Boyatzis', *Human Resource Management*, vol. 35, no. 1, 1996, pp. 120–1.

Competency characteristics[64]

- *Motives:* what drives, directs and selects behaviour towards certain actions or goals and away from others. Example: achievement-motivated people consistently set challenging goals, take responsibility for accomplishing them and use feedback to do better.
- *Traits:* physical characteristics and consistent responses to situations or information. Example: reaction time and good eyesight are physical trait competencies of fighter pilots.
- *Self-concept:* a person's attitudes, values or self-image. Example: self-confidence, a person's belief that they can be effective in almost any situation, is part of that person's concept of self.
- *Knowledge:* information a person has in specific content areas. Example: a surgeon has knowledge of the nerves and muscles in the human body.
- *Skill:* the ability to perform a certain physical or mental task. Example: a computer programmer should be able to organise 50 000 lines of code in logical sequential order.

It should be noted that knowledge and skill competencies tend to be visible, while self-concept, trait and motive competencies tend to be hidden and more central to personality.[65] Consequently, the surface competencies are easier to develop than the deeper competencies (see figure 5.9). According to Spencer and Spencer, it is therefore more cost-effective for HR managers to use training for focusing on the visible competencies and to use selection for focusing on the hidden competencies.[66] Partly because of the difficulties associated with assessing and developing the hidden competencies, some HR managers and theorists prefer to concentrate on developing universal standards of performance expressed in terms of outputs rather than inputs. This approach is called the standards model and it emphasises minimal standards of performance.[67] Competencies are more restrictively defined as 'the ability to perform activities within an occupation to the standards expected in employment' or 'the observable behaviours that are required of job incumbents to perform their jobs effectively'.[68]

In developing a competency standard, HR managers typically ask three questions:
1. What action must the employee demonstrate? (the element)
2. What performance standards must be met? (performance criteria)
3. What are the conditions under which the action must be carried out? (range of variables)
   For example:

- *Element:* Must record and store information.
  Performance criteria: Must record information accurately and in sufficient detail for its significance and use.
  Range of variables: Must use manual and electronic methods of information recording, storage and retrieval.
- *Element:* Must type at 50 words per minute.
  Performance criteria: Must have a maximum 10 per cent error rate.
  Range of variables: Must use computer, copy of typing test.[69]

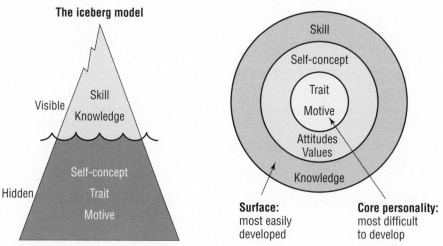

Figure 5.9 Central and surface competencies
Source L. M. Spencer and S. M. Spencer, *Competence at Work*, John Wiley & Sons, New York, 1993, p. 11.

The standards model has found favour in Australia and Britain with consultants, academics, bureaucrats, managers and trade union officials (who frequently see it as an indirect avenue to win pay increases).[70]

In contrast, Spencer and Spencer's attributes model distinguishes between competencies that are 'threshold' and those that are 'differentiating'. *Threshold competencies* are the essential characteristics (for example, the ability to read and write) that everyone in a job needs to be minimally effective. *Differentiating competencies* are the characteristics that distinguish superior from average performers (for example, achievement orientation, which causes superior sales representatives to set higher goals than those required by the company).[71]

Thus, to improve performance, organisations 'should use the characteristics of superior performers as their "template" or "blueprint" for employee selection and development. Failure to do so', argue Spencer and Spencer, 'is essentially to select and train to mediocrity.'[72]

The behavioural event interview

The Behavioural Event Interview (BEI) is a development of critical incident reporting. It generates information not only about the job but also about what the job holder thinks, feels and hopes to achieve in the job. This helps the HR manager to identify and measure competencies such as achievement motivation and logical problem solving. Spencer and Spencer argue that BEI is an advancement over the critical incident approach because it identifies the competencies required to do the job well rather than just identifying aspects of the job.[73]

It is claimed that specific advantages of the BEI method are: empirical identification of competencies; precise expression of a competency; identification of how superior performers handle specific tasks or problems; freedom from racial, gender and cultural bias; and the generation of data for assessment, training and career pathing.[74] However, the time, expense and interviewer expertise needed mean that BEI is inappropriate for analysing a large number of jobs. The focus on critical incidents also means that some important job tasks may be missed.[75]

Criticisms of competency profiling

There are a number of criticisms levelled at competency profiling:

- *The ambiguous meaning of competency:* there is no universal agreement as to what competency means. For example, competency is sometimes used to refer 'to behaviours or actions, sometimes to the abilities or characteristics underlying behaviour and sometimes to the outcomes or results of actions'.[76]
- *Its generic 'off-the-shelf' nature:* it is argued that particular companies/industries and organisational and national cultures require competencies tailored to their specific situation.[77] Raelin and Sims, for example, found that the use of off-the-shelf instruments may be unreliable and invalid without situational customisation.[78]
- *Its focus on the past:* many competency models are based on 'what has made for successful performance in the past, rather than what will make for successful performance in the future'.[79]
- *Its emphasis on 'technical' competencies:* competencies such as creativity and sensitivity, which are difficult to measure, are often ignored.[80]
- *Its assumption of rationality:* Townley sees competency profiling as being based on the false assumption that managers behave rationally and truly understand their jobs. In addition, Townley argues that the political dimensions of the job along with the gender and racial imbalances present in most organisations are ignored, thus raising serious questions about 'what gets identified as requisite behaviour'.[81]

Despite these criticisms, proponents argue that competency profiling, by identifying specific occupational requirements that facilitate the achievement of the organisation's strategic objectives, fosters competitiveness and a more strategically focused approach to HRM.[82]

Spencer and Spencer, for example, claim that 'competencies provide a common language and method that can integrate all human resource functions and services — selection, performance appraisal, career and succession planning, training and development and compensation — to help people, firms and even societies to be more productive in the challenging years ahead'.[83]

Job analysis and EEO

Job analysis is a systematic process for understanding jobs. To guarantee compliance with EEO requirements, managers must 'know the job'.[84] Job analysis can provide the hard evidence of job relatedness and thus help the HR manager to establish organisational adherence to EEO requirements. The HR manager must be careful when writing job specifications and descriptions to ensure that the final documentation is consistent with the job analysis and that the level of detail does not exceed that generated by the job analysis.[85]

Specifically, it is necessary to avoid the following pitfalls:

- There should be no obvious or disguised violations of EEO requirements (for example, stating that normal colour vision is required when the job analysis shows that colour-related tasks could be identified and performed using factors other than colour).
- Avoid listing lengthy experience requirements (for example, 10–15 years) unless no one with less experience could satisfactorily perform the job.

- Job specifications and job descriptions should not be based on opinion without a proper job analysis being undertaken.[86]

Finally, to ensure the legality of the job analysis itself, job analysts should be able to demonstrate the following:
- the accuracy of the job analysis information
- the extent to which individuals who provide job information agree with one another about job content and job requirements
- the extent to which the different methods of job analysis yield similar results (if different methods are used)
- whether the selected job analysis method is appropriate to the particular purpose for which it is being used.[87]

Practical problems with job analysis

Some problems that arise in job analysis are the product of human behaviour, while others stem from the nature of the job analysis method. The following are some of the more common problems:
- lack of top management support
- the use of only one method of job analysis
- the use of only a single source for collecting job information
- lack of participation by supervisors and job holders in the design of the job analysis exercise
- the fact that the job analyst, the supervisor or the job holder have not been trained in job analysis
- employees' lack of awareness of the importance of job analysis
- employees seeing job analysis as a threat to their job status, pay level, job security or workload
- lack of reward for employees for providing quality job information
- insufficient time allowed to complete the job analysis
- intentional or unintentional distortion of job content and job requirements
- the absence of a review of the job to determine whether it is being done correctly or whether improvements can be made.[88]

Theoretical criticisms of job analysis

Traditional approaches to job analysis are mostly criticised for their basic assumption that jobs are static, when 'jobs are unlikely to remain static for any period of time'.[89] Furthermore, as discussed earlier, the validity of the job concept itself is questionable. The following are other criticisms concerning job analysis:
- Some methods rely on what people say they do rather than on what they actually do.
- There may be no agreement regarding whether a task is actually performed as part of the job or on the skill level required.
- Workers generate different information about jobs according to their sex, age and level of education. For example, older and less educated workers typically describe their work as less important and less complex.[90]
- 'Issues of hierarchy, power, imbalance and socio-political determination of what constitutes activity and work are neglected.'[91] According to Townley, the nature of skill, for example, is bound up with the sexual division of labour, with 'natural' female skills such as dealing with the sick and disabled and being responsive to the needs of others being either devalued or ignored.[92]

Job design

Are employees committed? Do they demonstrate pride in their work? Do they feel free to make decisions? Will they accept responsibility? Are they frequently absent? Are they productive? **Job design** is frequently the key to the answers to these questions.[93] But when such problems arise, managers often blame employees rather than the design of the job.[94] People today expect more from their jobs. However, the gap between what employees want from their jobs and what they actually get appears to be widening. Significant numbers of Australians are dissatisfied with the quality of their working lives. HR managers must promote employee productivity by finding ways to unlock the potential that exists in the overwhelming majority of employees.[95]

Better job design is one way of doing this, because productivity, job stress and quality of work life are tied to job design.[96] But there is no one best way to design a job. The different approaches to job design can emphasise either efficiency or employee satisfaction. Trade-offs inevitably occur because job design is influenced by numerous factors such as management philosophy, corporate culture, government regulations, union requirements, economic conditions and employee numbers and availability.[97] This means that some jobs will be more or less efficient or satisfying than others. Regardless, poorly designed jobs result in lower productivity, employee turnover, absenteeism, sabotage, resignations and unionisation.[98] In contrast, a well-designed job promotes the achievement of the organisation's strategic business objectives by structuring work so it integrates management requirements for efficiency and employee needs for satisfaction. Thus, effective job design presents a major challenge for the HR manager.

Job design Specification of the content of a job, the material and equipment required to do the job, and the relation of the job to other jobs.

Methods of job design

The various methods of job design are illustrated in figure 5.10 and discussed below.

	JOB SPECIALISATION	JOB ENLARGEMENT	JOB ROTATION	JOB ENRICHMENT
Job • definition • nature • complexity • variety	Narrow Repetitive Limited Limited	Narrow Repetitive Limited Some	Narrow Repetitive Limited Some	Broad Changing Considerable Considerable
Decision making	Limited	Limited	Limited	Considerable
Responsibility	Limited	Limited	Limited	Considerable
Loading	None	Horizontal	Horizontal	Horizontal and vertical

Figure 5.10 Job design methods
Source Asia Pacific Management Co. Ltd, 2004.

Job specialisation or simplification

Job specialisation or simplification involves using standardised work procedures and having employees perform repetitive, precisely defined and simplified tasks. This job design method is used by industrial engineers and time and motion analysts. Specifically, time and

Job specialisation or simplification Involves employees performing standardised, repetitive and routine tasks.

motion studies require the careful observation of a good or standard worker. The job analyst records the various movements made in performing the job, clocks the time taken for each movement and undertakes rational or 'scientific' job analysis to:

- redesign the job to make movements simpler and quicker to perform
- develop more efficient patterns of movement so employees can do the job faster and with less fatigue
- set standards for designated jobs, which can be used to determine pay rates and performance measures
- develop thorough job descriptions and job specifications to facilitate employee recruitment, selection, orientation and training.[99]

Job specialisation is exemplified by Frederick Taylor's scientific management, which basically saw job design as a three-step process:

1. Management determined the one best way of doing the job.
2. Management hired workers according to their qualities that best matched the job requirements.
3. Management trained workers in the one best way to do the job.[100]

Advantages of job specialisation

Scientific management meant that all planning, organising and controlling of work was done solely by management.

The potential advantages of job specialisation include: improved operating efficiencies through the use of low-skill and low-cost labour; the need for minimum on-the-job training; the easy control of production quantities; and the fewer errors made when workers perform simple routine jobs.[101] The resulting potential for reduced labour costs has been a prime motivator among industrial engineers in their promotion of job specialisation.

Problems of job specialisation

- *Repetition:* employees perform only a few tasks that have to be repeated many times. Boredom and lack of challenge to learn anything new or to improve the job quickly surface as problems and cause low organisational commitment. As a result, high levels of managerial control and surveillance become necessary.[102]
- *Mechanical pacing:* employees are restricted by the speed of the assembly line, which requires them to maintain a regular work pace. Thus, employees cannot take a break when needed or transfer their attention to some other aspect of the job. Instead, their constant attention and effort have to be maintained at a set speed — often too fast for some and too slow for others.
- *No end product:* employees find that they are not producing any identifiable end product, so develop little pride or enthusiasm in the job.
- *Limited social interaction:* employees complain that because the assembly line requires their constant attention, there are few opportunities to socialise with other employees. This inhibits the development of informal groups and reduces job satisfaction.
- *No employee involvement:* employees complain that they have no decision-making authority over how the job is done. Lack of autonomy decreases job satisfaction and worker interest in introducing job improvements. Workers become powerless and dependent.
- *Higher costs:* employees frequently dislike highly specialised jobs, so they tend to quit or absent themselves. Absenteeism and high labour turnover increase the costs of recruitment, selection and training, and pressure employers to pay higher rates to try to keep employees on the job. Finally, problems associated with poor quality, poor customer service, sabotage, employee stress and grievances appear, adding to costs.[103]
- *Lack of flexibility:* employees cannot cover for each other, which creates problems when employees are absent or have to leave the workplace.

These problems, along with union pressures and the changing nature of the work force, have led to considerable attention been devoted to improving the quality of work life by finding ways to make meaningless, repetitive jobs more rewarding.[104] It should be noted, however, that research indicates that the negative relationship between job specialisation and job satisfaction is not universal. It is true that highly specialised jobs cause job dissatisfaction for many workers, but there are some workers who prefer narrower, restricted jobs.

Employees with low growth needs, for example, will be less satisfied in expanded and challenging jobs than will individuals with high growth needs.[105]

Job enlargement

Job enlargement seeks to expand a job by **horizontal loading** — that is, adding to the variety of tasks to be performed. As organisations downsize and become flatter, multiskilling and increasing work interest are becoming increasingly important. Task variety is assumed to offset some of the disadvantages of job specialisation, thereby increasing employee performance and satisfaction. However, although sometimes effective, job enlargement is often resisted because:

- the enlargement is seen as just adding more routine, boring tasks to the job
- the advantages of job specialisation are reduced
- unions oppose job enlargement on the grounds that it means more work and encourages reductions in the number of employees
- some workers like repetitive tasks or, at worst, express no real preference for changing things — repetitive work allows workers to daydream and socialise without improving their productivity.[106]

Job enlargement The horizontal expansion of a job by adding similar level responsibilities.

Horizontal loading Job enrichment through the addition of tasks of a similar nature.

Job rotation

Job rotation increases task variety by periodically shifting employees between jobs involving different tasks. It is closely related to job enlargement but, rather than having more tasks to do, the employee rotates between different jobs with similar skill requirements. Job rotation aims to reduce boredom by diversifying the employee's tasks. However, if all the tasks are boring and routine, there will be similar employee problems to those found with job enlargement. For the organisation, job rotation may increase training costs, disrupt work groups and lower productivity (for example, where an inefficient worker replaces an efficient worker).

In contrast, if job rotation is used to place employees in more challenging jobs, it can be effective for improving job satisfaction, helping an employee develop a generalist perspective, increasing skills and increasing work force flexibility.[107] Japanese companies, for example, move their managers between functions, offices and geographic locations so they get to know the organisation's people, problems and procedures.[108] Other benefits of job rotation include control of repetitive stress injuries, reduced work stress, reduced absenteeism, lower turnover rates and increased motivation.[109]

A major potential restriction on the use of job rotation exists in highly unionised workplaces where inter-union rivalry can lead to ongoing demarcation issues and union antagonism. Job rotation also has several other drawbacks:

- increased training costs
- lower productivity when an employee is moved into a new job where they are less efficient
- disruption when members of a work group may not accept the rotated employees
- increased supervisory time spent answering questions and monitoring the work of rotated employees
- demotivation of intelligent and ambitious trainees who seek specific responsibilities in their chosen specialty.[110]

Job rotation Increases task variety by moving employees from one task to another.

Job enrichment

Job enrichment involves making basic changes in job content and level of responsibility. The **vertical loading** gives the employee the opportunity to experience greater achievement, recognition, responsibility and personal growth, and the horizontal loading increases the complexity of work to promote interest. Thus, job enrichment builds motivating factors into the job content by:

- *combining tasks* — fractionalised tasks are combined to increase skill variety and task identity

Job enrichment The vertical expansion of a job by adding planning and decision-making responsibilities.

Vertical loading Job enrichment through increased opportunities for responsibility, decision making, recognition, personal growth and achievement.

- *creating natural work units* — the job is changed so the employee is responsible for, or 'owns', an identifiable body of work, leading them to view the work as important and meaningful rather than irrelevant and boring
- *establishing client relationships* — a direct relationship is established between the employee and their client (that is, the user of the product or service that the employee produces) wherever possible
- *expanding jobs vertically* — vertical loading gives employees responsibilities and control formerly reserved for higher-level positions; it seeks to close the gap between the 'doing' and the 'controlling' aspects of the job, thus increasing employee autonomy
- *opening feedback channels* — more and better ways for giving employees feedback on their performance are identified. Increased feedback means the employees not only learn how they are going, but also whether their performance is improving, deteriorating or remaining at a constant level. Ideally, this feedback should be received as the employee does the job, rather than occasionally from a supervisor.[111]

Whirlpool (Australia), for example, restructured the work of its sales representatives and renamed them 'account managers'. Says Whirlpool's Managing Director: 'In the past, our salespeople, like most whitegoods companies' salespeople, were order takers. They'd go to a retailer, take an order, and move on to the next retailer. Now they act as business development managers, focused on the quality of the sale. They talk to retailers about our products and marketing strategies, the retailers' marketing strategies and put together business plans that will help both parties.'[112]

Introducing job enrichment

Job enrichment means many workers work harder and are more productive because they become internally motivated. It is argued that this is a subtle form of management manipulation.

Job enrichment has received wide publicity but has not always produced favourable results in the workplace. A great deal of debate exists over the benefits and limitations of job enrichment: it clearly is not for everyone. Thus, HR managers thinking of introducing a job enrichment program should consider the following matters:
- Is there widespread discontentment among employees?
- Is it economically and technically feasible to enrich jobs?
- Are there natural units of work?
- Can employees be given control over their jobs?
- Do employees perceive their jobs as meaningful to society?
- Is there a reward for assuming increased responsibility?
- Can performance feedback be given?
- Is there some form of consumer identification?
- If enriched jobs require the interaction of several employees, can compatible employees be grouped together?
- Is management style compatible with job enrichment?
- Do employees want enriched jobs?
- Is there union opposition to job enrichment?
- Are some managers opposed to job enrichment?
- Are the jobs easy to enrich?
- Is motivation central to the problem?
- Is there an easier way?
- Are compensation benefits and working conditions satisfactory?
- Are the jobs deficient in intrinsic rewards?[113]

Benefits of job enrichment

Job enrichment can lead to improvements in both job performance and job satisfaction. A survey of almost 100 research studies found job enrichment resulted in greater productivity, improved product quality, fewer employee grievances, improved worker attitudes, reduced absenteeism and labour turnover, and lower costs.[114] Thus, improved quality of working life brought about by job enrichment has not only social benefits but also bottom-line benefits to the organisation.[115]

This Letter to the Editor provides a provocative viewpoint. Do you agree? See 'What's your view?' on page 176.

Job enrichment is just an exploitative management technique

Dear Editor,

Everybody seems to speak of the benefits of job enrichment. Unfortunately, no one seems to mention the costs. Is this the way with all of the allegedly 'empowering' methods of management, or do managers and management writers gloss over the 'dark side' in the hope that no one will notice?

A couple of years ago, my job was 'enriched'. My senior manager will tell you that I freely consented to the changes to the content and responsibilities of my job. I'm here to tell you otherwise. I had no choice. If I wanted to keep my job, there was no alternative but to agree to the changes. Of course, I sought to appear enthusiastic in response to my manager's 'suggestions'. But really, did I have a choice? Of course not, for to reject the changes would have been to place my position in jeopardy.

You see, that's what job enrichment is all about. It's merely an enforced change to jobs in order for the company to obtain higher productivity from its workers. I call it a betrayal, and here's why. When I joined the company, I agreed to the job description provided to me. It clearly stated what I needed to do to perform my job satisfactorily. I also joined the organisation on the assumption that if my job changed significantly in any way, particularly in terms of more work, then I would be given a higher salary and other benefits to compensate for the changes. When my job was 'enriched', however, I received nothing. To the contrary, my boss could not be more enthusiastic about how much I would enjoy the extra responsibility and autonomy being given to me!

Frankly, I couldn't care less about more responsibility and autonomy. I have three kids at home and drive a 10-year-old car that has seen better days. What I want is more money to make life a little easier, not some gratuitous job enrichment program that only makes things harder.

To me, job enrichment has meant more work for no more reward. I have been given new administrative responsibilities that only get in the way of the real work I am employed to do. My phone never stops ringing, the boss seems to want me to write more memos and reports than ever, and I have to answer hundreds of unnecessary email messages every week.

If this is what job enrichment is all about, then I hope it is just another passing management fad that will go the way of other fads like strategic planning, business process re-engineering and management by objectives. 'Job enrichment' is a misnomer. It should be called 'job imprisonment'.

A weary, but 'enriched' supervisor

Source David Poole, University of Western Sydney.

Socio-technical enrichment

Socio-technical enrichment focuses on the relationship between technology and groups of workers. The aim is to integrate people with technology. It is of interest to the HR manager confronted with situations where specialised group tasks exist and where technological change disrupts the social group to such an extent that the new technology becomes inefficient. Socio-technical enrichment often means creating self-managing or autonomous work groups to perform a job that was previously done on an assembly line. It is usually difficult and expensive to change the technology of an existing operation, so socio-technical enrichment works best when an entirely new operation is being designed.[116]

Socio-technical enrichment
Focuses on the relationship between technology and groups of workers. The aim is to integrate people with technology.

Autonomous work teams

Autonomous work teams represent job enrichment at the group level. The employer sets up self-managed work teams who are responsible for accomplishing defined performance objectives. Planning and decision making are done within the group. Typically, the team sets its own output and quality standards. Team members may elect their own leader or decide to

Autonomous work teams
Represents job enrichment at the group level. This is achieved by creating self-managed work teams responsible for accomplishing defined performance objectives.

make decisions jointly. They may even establish pay levels and train and certify team members as being qualified in required job skills. As a result, supervisory positions are reduced in importance and may even be eliminated.[117]

Team members typically are able to:

- rotate their tasks to enhance skill variety
- work together on a product that is a whole identifiable piece of work
- relate to other members of the team
- decide as a group who will belong to the team and what tasks various members will perform
- obtain feedback from other team members about their performance
- count on the assistance and support of other team members if and when needed.[118]

Consequently, having the 'right mix' in the work group is essential for success.[119]

Volvo in Sweden is the most famous example of a company applying autonomous work teams. But several other firms have also used this approach, including Saab–Scania, IBM, General Electric and Xerox.[120] The outcomes are similar to those obtained from job enrichment. The benefits claimed by Volvo, for example, included:

- improved worker attitudes
- improved quality of output
- lower absenteeism and labour turnover
- ease in covering absent workers
- reduced numbers of supervisory personnel.[121]

It should be noted that, because of changes in technology and cost pressures, Volvo has now closed its plants using autonomous work teams.[122] Again, as with job enrichment, a small but significant number of workers are likely to resist autonomous work teams.[123] Supervisors may resist because it changes their role and threatens job security, and skilled workers may resist because they fear it reduces their power and status. Unions, in turn, complain that 'job enrichment programs are management ploys to get more out of workers for less money'.[124] There is also evidence to suggest that the impact in some situations may be only minimal, or that it may lower job satisfaction, organisational commitment and trust in management.[125] Finally, research suggests that enriching a job beyond a certain level can have a detrimental effect on workers, increase error rates, increase training costs and create industrial relations problems.[126]

Comprehensive job enrichment: the Hackman–Oldham Job Characteristics Model

Job Characteristics Model
An example of comprehensive job enrichment. It combines both horizontal and vertical loading to stimulate employee motivation and satisfaction.

The **Job Characteristics Model** (JCM) is an example of comprehensive job enrichment. It is a type of job design that combines both horizontal and vertical improvements to stimulate employee motivation and satisfaction.[127] The idea is that employees perform better when they perceive their work as being meaningful, have responsibility for outcomes and receive feedback on the results of their activities.[128] According to Hackman and Oldham, five core job characteristics are especially important to job design, as detailed below. A job that is high in these core characteristics is said to be enriched.[129]

Skills variety The degree to which a job holder requires a variety of activities, skills and talents to perform the job.

1. **Skills variety** refers to the degree to which a job holder must carry out a variety of different activities and use a number of different personal skills in performing the job (that is, the extent to which the job requires a variety of activities, skills and talents to carry out the work).

Task identity Means doing an identifiable piece of work, thus enabling the worker to have a sense of responsibility and pride.

2. **Task identity** refers to the degree to which performing a job results in the completion of a whole and identifiable piece of work and produces a visible outcome that can be recognised as the result of personal performance (that is, the extent to which the job allows the employee to complete whole tasks rather than just parts of tasks).

Task significance Means knowing that the work one does is important to others in the organisation and outside it.

3. **Task significance** refers to the degree to which a job has a significant impact on the lives of other people, whether those people are colleagues in the same organisation or individuals outside the organisation (that is, the extent to which the job is regarded as important to people inside and outside the organisation).

4. **Autonomy** refers to the degree to which the job holder has the freedom, independence and discretion necessary to schedule work and to decide which procedures to use in carrying it out (that is, the extent to which the job provides the employee with freedom to plan, schedule and decide work procedures).

5. **Feedback** is the degree to which performing the activities required by the job provides the employee with direct and clear information about the effectiveness of their performance (that is, the extent to which the job permits the employee to obtain clear and direct knowledge about how well they are doing).[130]

These five core job characteristics, in turn, influence the extent to which employees experience three critical psychological states. Skills variety, task identity and task significance influence experienced meaningfulness of work, autonomy affects experienced responsibility for work outcomes, and feedback affects knowledge of results (see figure 5.11).[131]

1. *Experienced meaningfulness of the work* — the degree to which employees experience their jobs as having an outcome that is useful and valuable to them, the company and the community.

2. *Experienced responsibility for outcomes of the work* — the degree to which employees feel personally accountable and responsible for the results of their work.

3. *Knowledge of actual results of the work* — the degree to which employees maintain an awareness of the effectiveness of their work.[132]

Collectively, these three critical psychological states determine the level of employee motivation, job satisfaction and performance. Hackman and Oldham claim, for example, that if employees feel their jobs are interesting, challenging and important, they will be motivated (that is, the job itself will 'turn them on'). Similarly, it is argued that high levels of the critical psychological states, in addition to high internal motivation, lead to improved work performance and job satisfaction and reduced absenteeism and labour turnover.[133]

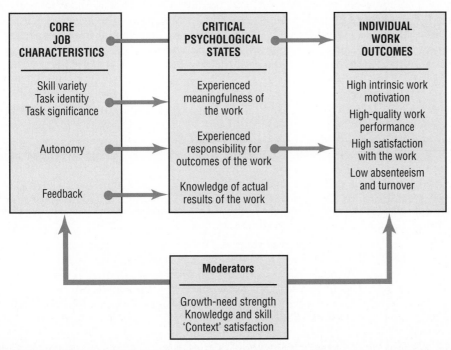

Figure 5.11 Job design implications of job characteristics theory
Source J. R. Schermerhorn, J. G. Hunt and R. N. Osborn, *Organizational Behavior*, 8th edn, John Wiley & Sons, New York, 2003, p. 156.

However, these outcomes are expected only for employees who have the necessary knowledge and skills to do the job successfully: other employees are likely to feel frustrated by their inability to do the job. Similarly, employees who do not desire challenge and responsibility are likely to feel overburdened by the opportunities presented to them. Finally, employees who feel exploited and dissatisfied — because they are poorly paid, lack job security, have abusive colleagues or suffer unfair treatment from management — are likely to view any attempt at job enrichment as just one more type of exploitation.[134]

Consequently, before the HR manager or line manager attempts to change the job characteristics, it is important to assess the personality and the situation of employees to ensure that the desired outcomes will be achieved. Nevertheless, the JCM remains a viable and popular approach to job design.[135]

Quality of work life

Quality of work life Involves the implementation of HRM policies and practices designed to promote organisational performance and employee wellbeing (including management style, freedom to make decisions, pay and benefits, working conditions, safety, and meaningful work).

Quality of work life (QWL) programs incorporate principles of job enrichment and socio-technical enrichment in a comprehensive effort to improve the quality of the work environment. QWL programs especially seek to integrate employee needs and wellbeing with the organisation's desire for higher productivity.[136] They bring management, the union (if present) and employees together to determine what needs to be done to improve the work environment, job satisfaction and employee productivity. The establishment of such channels of communication gives employees a much greater say in decision making. Consequently, QWL programs emphasise cooperative relationships among employees, unions and management. Thus, QWL can significantly change the way in which employee relations are conducted in an organisation — conflict being replaced with cooperation.[137]

The major criteria for improving QWL include:

- *Adequate remuneration:* How adequate are pay and benefits in terms of helping employees maintain an acceptable standard of living?
- *Safe and healthy environment:* Are physical conditions hazardous? What job conditions affect the employee's physical and psychological wellbeing?
- *Development of human capabilities:* To what extent does a job enable employees to use and develop their skills, knowledge and abilities and undertake tasks that are satisfying?
- *Growth and security:* What career potential exists in the job?
- *Social integration:* Is there an opportunity to relate to others? Is advancement based on merit? Does equal opportunity exist?
- *Constitutionalism:* How much dignity and respect exists for employees? Can employees give honest opinions and be treated like adults? What are employees' rights and how are they protected?
- *Total life space:* Is there a balance between work and life away from work? Is there an absence of high levels of job stress?
- *Social relevance:* Do employees view the organisation as socially responsible? Does the organisation account for society's values when developing and implementing its policies and practices concerning employees, customers, competitors and the community?[138]

Organisations that have adopted QWL programs include General Foods, General Motors, Xerox, IBM and Proctor & Gamble. Substantial evidence supports the effectiveness of QWL programs, although their introduction has not always been without problems.[139] Mandell offers the following cautionary measures for HR managers considering a QWL program:

- HR managers need to recognise QWL for what it is — an experiment. No matter how excited any member of the organisation may be about introducing a QWL program, there is no guarantee it will be successful.
- HR managers who are prepared to take the risk should ensure that QWL has total commitment. The program is certain to fail without organisation-wide understanding and support.
- The HR manager must determine whether all employees are capable of (and interested in) participating in a QWL program. Training in group problem solving and decision making may be necessary before the program is introduced.
- If the introduction of a QWL program results in increased productivity and financial gains, the organisation should be prepared to share these gains with employees (especially if the program requires additional responsibility and participation for employees).

- The HR manager must determine whether a QWL program is culturally compatible. Westwood, for example, argues that the acceptance of authority, status differences and use of power in many Asian cultures may create barriers to the implementation of QWL programs involving egalitarian and participative behaviour.[140]
- The success or failure of a QWL program may be difficult to prove. The HR manager must be prepared to accept possible criticism.[141]

Quality circles

Quality circles were developed and refined in Japan in the post–World War II years. But their concept is based on the work of US quality experts Edward Deming and J. M. Juran.[142] Consequently, the exact meaning of quality circles can vary from organisation to organisation and country to country.[143]

Quality circles usually consist of small groups of five to 10 workers who meet on a regular basis. Meetings generally involve the group's supervisor (although the supervisor may not be the quality circle leader).[144] The objective is to identify problems as a group, process suggestions and examine alternatives for improving (at relatively low cost) productivity, raising product and service quality, and increasing worker satisfaction. Some groups may also discuss how to improve working conditions. Quality circles have been used to develop job descriptions, inspect products, design workplace layouts, determine equipment needs and suggest procedures and process improvements.[145] They are based on the premise that employees often know best. The recommendations of the quality circle are presented to management for final approval. There is no reward for the group's members other than the recognition and satisfaction they receive. Quality circles act independently and are not part of the formal organisation. Members volunteer to participate and they choose which problems to discuss and analyse.

Quality circles are credited with producing impressive results when correctly implemented. However, evidence of success is mostly anecdotal and there is little hard data to support their effectiveness.[146] Existing research evidence suggests that quality circles have little effect on productivity but can enhance employee feelings of satisfaction and involvement.[147] But the impact of these groups is less than that of job enrichment because quality circle members must still perform boring, routine jobs.[148] Also, given the continuing adversarial relationship between employers and employees, it is argued that quality circles are unlikely to be more than a passing fad; the indications are that such groups have a life span of only about two years.[149] Research indicates that only a minority of Australian workplaces use quality circles.[150] Finally, there is evidence to suggest that cultural differences may act as a major barrier to management and workers' acceptance of quality circles and, hence, the groups' effectiveness.[151] Many companies in the United States are now dropping quality circles for this reason.[152]

Eunson also points out that educational and cultural differences between Australian and Japanese employees may inhibit the success of quality circles in Australia when compared with their success in Japan. Specifically, Eunson cites Australia's emphasis on individualistic behaviour (versus group behaviour in Japan); lack of job flexibility and concerns over demarcation; poor training and low education of workers; and the perception of quality circles by employees as a management 'rip-off' if productivity gains are not shared.[153]

Why quality circles fail

Orpen says that, despite their potential for improvement and adoption by many organisations, quality circles frequently fail because:
- managers often feel threatened
- managers often pressure employees into starting quality circles instead of leaving employees to initiate them (research suggests that if management consults with employees about establishing and operating quality circles, they are much more likely to lead to perceived increases in productivity or efficiency)[154]
- in many organisations, high labour turnover and frequent job changes among quality circle members make it difficult, if not impossible, to maintain any continuity of membership

> **Quality circles** Small groups of employees who meet regularly to identify and solve work-related problems.

- many groups focus on problems that they have no control over or that are beyond their level of expertise to solve
- some organisations restrict the number of meetings and the time spent in meetings because quality circle gatherings require members to be absent from their jobs
- quality circles are often beset with problems that derive from union–management relations. When management and unions see each other as adversaries, for example, there is a tendency for quality circles to focus on employee grievances about pay and conditions and the union's role. There is also a strong chance that union representatives may use quality circles as a bargaining weapon in any negotiations with management. For example, the union will support the establishment of quality circles if management agrees to union claims. If the claims are ignored or rejected, the union will oppose the introduction of quality circles.

Requirements for successful quality circles

To overcome these problems, it is recommended that HR managers ensure:

- *Use of a pilot study:* given the high failure rate of quality circles, it is advisable to run trials before committing the organisation to an extensive quality circle program. A pilot study allows evaluation and finetuning and ensures realistic expectations.
- *Provision of adequate training:* employees frequently need training in how to behave in groups and quality circle leaders especially must be able to lead in an atmosphere of equity and to promote contributions from other members.
- *Middle management involvement:* quality circles stand a much better chance of success if managers are involved in their establishment and are committed to the concept.
- *An organisational culture consistent with the quality circle philosophy:* the prevailing culture should emphasise participation and individual responsibility for solving problems.
- *Delegated decision making:* unless decision making is pushed to the lowest level possible, quality circles will not be effective.
- *Top management commitment:* quality circles work best with top management support.
- *Recognition of quality circle achievements:* if the recognition of achievements is not clearly articulated, understood and agreed to by all involved, the entire quality circle program may be sabotaged.
- *Union support:* to gain union support, managers should meet with union representatives and reach agreement on the charter of quality circles, their authority and safeguards for the legitimate interests of the unions (and management).
- *Monitoring of results:* quality circles need to keep notes of their meetings, suggestions, implementation and feelings, while management should audit quality circles for their effectiveness and members' feelings.
- *Emphasis on employee development:* quality circles will suffer if the emphasis is on organisational interests only and employee development is ignored.
- *Voluntary membership:* employees forced to join a quality circle are likely to be negative in their attitudes and contributions.
- *Relevance to the members' actual tasks, duties and responsibilities:* if quality circle projects are not relevant to the members' actual jobs, interest is unlikely to be high.
- *Use of quality circle suggestions:* some quality circle recommendations need to be adopted, or team members will lose interest, their participation will quickly decline and the groups will fade away.[155]

Employee participation and industrial democracy

Industrial democracy Type of employee participation that involves a redistribution of decision-making power from management to employees (often via a trade union).

Industrial democracy is often confused with the less emotive terms *employee participation* and *employee involvement*. It has even been used by both unions and management to mean similar (if not identical) things.[156] In fact, industrial democracy and employee participation have been described as different aspects of the same concept. A former federal Labor government discussion paper on industrial democracy and employee participation, for example, claims that industrial democracy is the ideal, while employee participation is the process leading to employee influence in corporate decision making.[157] But the reality, as Teicher indicates, 'is that employee participation and industrial democracy have quite distinct meanings and implications'.[158] Industrial democracy implies at least the 'redistribution of decision making power'.[159] 'To democratise', says Ramsay, 'is to redistribute power from those in management, who for the most wield it, to their subordinates in work organisations.'[160]

Practitioner speaks

New option for worker participation

Employee democracy has had a short and colourful history in Australia. Its continual, phoenix-like re-emergence over the last 30 years testifies to the power of the idea and its capacity to capture the collective imagination. Equally, its fading from the political agenda is evidence of the tenacity of the powerful forces that stand against it. Employee democracy is the great unfulfilled promise in Australian industrial relations.

With little expected out of current enterprise bargaining — in terms of new consultation mechanisms — many are now looking to Europe's 'social partnership' model as one that may be workable and functional in Australia. In Europe, the term 'social partner' refers to government, employers, employees and union representatives and 'social partnership' means the role that social dialogue plays in both developing and maintaining forms of employee participation. According to the social partnership model, participants in a business enterprise have both an economic and a social function.

An example of the social partnership model is seen in the European Works Council Directive that mandates the establishment of a European Works Council in all large, multinational enterprises. Some key purposes of this directive are to foster and improve workers' fundamental social rights to information, consultation and participation and to promote dialogue between management and labour to harmonise cross-border mergers, takeovers and joint ventures.

Features of social partnership can also be found in a new information and consultation directive aimed at employees in small and medium-sized enterprises. Its principal purpose is to improve information and consultation on pertinent workplace and company matters and its objectives include promoting social trust and extending economic benefits to all citizens. Unlike the European Works Council Directive it does not mandate the establishment of a works council, but leaves open the kinds of arrangements that might be implemented.

The overall aim of the social partnership agenda is to modernise the way work is organised. It moves organisations into new thinking based on high skill, high trust, high quality, and the involvement of employees. Examples of this new thinking include lifelong learning, the adaptation of social legislation and reshaped tax systems, new means of remuneration, working time and equal opportunities. It raises new policy challenges for managers, unions and governments.

Three main arguments arise when considering how such a model might be received or applied in Australia.

Critics say that European information and consultation arrangements are incompatible with Australia's free market economy, which is based on conflictive negotiations over wages and conditions. It is also suggested that the current culture and attitudes of government and employers in Australia would be a major barrier and that it would be premature to devote time and resources to establishing information and consultation structures along the lines of works councils.

However, these European initiatives have been successfully applied to a range of national industrial relations systems throughout Europe with highly diverse cultures.

Paul J. Gollan is a lecturer in the department of industrial relations at the London School of Economics.

Glenn Patmore is a senior lecturer in law at the University of Melbourne. They are editors of a forthcoming book Partnership at Work: The Challenge of Employee Democracy *(Pluto Press, Australia).*

(continued)

The second criticism of the 'partnership' idea is that it creates a false impression that employers and employees have equal bargaining power. The argument goes that, even though it may be possible for the idea of 'partnership' to be given more substantive meaning, without equal bargaining it will not be possible to actually achieve a non-adversarial model of workplace democracy. Some have suggested that the law of employment reinforces this inequality by making workers legally subordinate to employers. This creates a fundamental conflict between employees and employers such that the employment relationship is not treated as a partnership by law and cannot be a partnership in fact — no matter how cooperative employers and employees become, within existing structures.

However, these European initiatives usher in new legal arrangements, creating new legal rights and entitlements for employees. As such, they serve a power-balancing function and redress some of the inequalities in the employment relationship.

The third criticism of partnership is that it offers little in the way of direction and is 'all things to all people'. This argument, however, overlooks the fact that specific laws and obligations govern the European model of social partnership.

These new cooperative mechanisms do not fully eliminate the adversarial element in organisations — but they do channel it. In this way, the pattern of tensions shifts due to the changing expectations of employees, and the interpretation of these expectations by their representatives. Employees and employers have the means and opportunity to understand each other's points of view more fully, and this, in turn, enables a richer, more productive form of consultation.

Paul Gollan and Glenn Patmore

Source HR Monthly, June 2003, pp. 42–3.

Furthermore, such increased employee power is to be achieved primarily through union action. (Ironically, while unions are at the forefront of pushing industrial democracy in the workplace, they frequently do not encourage participation in union decision making and can remain ignorant and unresponsive to their members' needs.[161]) Employer associations, not surprisingly, are opposed to the more radical concept of industrial democracy, seeing it as a vehicle to destroy management prerogatives and increase union power. When industrial democracy is equated with employee participation, however, managers tend to view it more favourably, believing that it can increase productivity, reduce turnover and improve industrial relations.[162] Unions are similarly divided in their reactions. Some union officials favour industrial democracy because they believe that it increases worker involvement, produces greater job satisfaction and improves industrial relations. In contrast, other unionists believe that it involves 'hopping into bed with the boss' and is improper and detrimental to the class war.[163]

It is obvious that such differing perceptions spring from different understandings of industrial democracy. The former federal Labor government's discussion paper included joint consultation, changing work roles, self-management, financial participation and worker representation on corporate boards as being under the industrial democracy umbrella.[164] Management, in turn, sees its real purpose as being to develop trust, enthusiasm, innovative behaviour and commitment towards a common goal.[165] It is evident that this view does not allow for any significant sharing of power but rather 'emphasises personal development, attitude change, healthy work relationships, increased productivity and economic revitalisation. The role of trade unions moreover is downplayed.'[166] This is consistent with the job enrichment approach of Herzberg and others and with socio-technical job enrichment, which do not allow for any significant involvement of employees (or unions) in job design or the allocation of work. For these reasons, many unions genuinely fear that employee participation schemes will undermine their authority and reduce their power in the workplace.[167] Cooperation, as a result, is seen as benefiting the employer, with political and industrial action still being necessary to change traditional power structures.

Radical unionists believe that industrial democracy involves a major restructuring of society and the workplace. According to this view, unions exist to impose limits on the power of management and the state. The primary union commitment is to the welfare of its members and not to a firm, an industry or a country.[168] This approach makes the acceptance of common objectives between unionised employees and management difficult, if not impossible. Employee participation (as distinct from industrial democracy) is seen as manipulative and little more than corporate propaganda designed to destroy the links between unions and their members.[169] The National Research Centre of the Australian Metal Workers Union, for example, criticised Orica's Botany plant program when it introduced semi-autonomous work groups.[170] Finally, many Australian unions are as conservative as management in their attitudes and approaches to innovation.[171] Australian workers, as a result, often remain suspicious and unmoved by the declaration, 'We're all in this together'.[172]

Management is also often opposed to employee participation (and industrial democracy), given its entrenched attitudes and the perceived threats to its power and position. Recent research, for example, shows that foreign-owned organisations in Australia have more consultation and devote more resources towards relationship maintenance with employees.[173]

Finally, Australian governments have adopted different approaches to employee participation depending on their political persuasion. Labor governments, while being more vocal in their support for industrial democracy, in practice have taken little action.[174] The result is that Australia has not seen much legislative intervention or actual reform.[175] The Australian Workplace Industrial Relations Survey, for example, found that the majority of workplaces did not regularly provide information to employees or inform (let alone consult!) the relevant unions about organisational changes that would affect employees.[176]

Trade unions resist change to protect their members. As a consequence, organisations relocate overseas or go out of business.

It seems inevitable, however, that Australian organisations and unions, given the ever-increasing competitive pressures and the rise of HRM, will increasingly embrace some form of employee participation.[177] In fact, the evidence indicates that employee participation has become more widely practised, but that it is managerially driven and employees continue to lack empowerment and discretion at work.[178] This confirms some experts' fears that the decline in union power means that participative practices will be more likely the result of unilateral management decision making.[179] In the present industrial relations climate, industrial democracy appears to have little future, although the Labor party is considering introducing laws requiring employee representation in management decision making.[180] Vaughn, for example, comments that worker participation and industrial democracy seem like terms from an old and outmoded vocabulary of work force management.[181] What is certain is that, when raised, the issue of industrial democracy will continue to divide management and union opinion.

Summary

Job analysis is a fundamental HRM activity. It is the process whereby jobs are studied to determine their tasks, duties and responsibilities, their relationships to other jobs, the conditions under which work is performed and the personal qualities required for satisfactory performance. The major job analysis data collection methods include observation, interviews, questionnaires, employee diary/logs, critical incident reporting and competency profiling. The products of job analysis are job descriptions and job specifications. Job descriptions provide a written summary of the duties and responsibilities of the position, and job specifications focus on the personal characteristics and qualifications that are required to successfully perform the job. Job design identifies what work must be performed, how it will be performed, where it is to be performed and who will perform it.

Job specialisation involves using standardised work procedures and having employees perform repetitive, precisely defined and simplified tasks. Job enlargement, in contrast, seeks to increase the breadth of a job by adding to the variety of tasks to be performed. Job rotation increases task variety by periodically shifting employees between jobs involving different tasks. Job enrichment builds motivating factors such as achievement, recognition, responsibility and opportunities for personal growth by vertical and horizontal loading. Autonomous work teams represent job enrichment at the group level. QWL programs represent a comprehensive effort to improve the quality of the work environment by integrating

Thirty interactive Wiley Web Questions are available to test your understanding of this chapter at www.johnwiley.com.au/ highered/hrm5e in the student resources area

employee needs and wellbeing with the organisation's need for higher productivity. Quality circles attempt to overcome job specialisation by giving employees the opportunity to participate in the management of their jobs instead of modifying the job content.

Industrial democracy is often equated with employee participation. Industrial democracy involves a redistribution of power in an organisation, whereas employee participation schemes (such as quality circles) do not. Industrial democracy is subject to controversy and management resistance, whereas employee participation schemes, while also controversial, appear to have a greater chance of acceptance.

student study guide

review questions

1. What are the major steps involved in job analysis? What environmental issues influence the design of jobs in organisations? In what way do they have an influence?
2. What is job enrichment? Should all jobs be enriched? Justify your answer.
3. Who should conduct a job analysis? Why?
4. Job analysis is described as a basic HRM activity. Why?
5. What is the relationship between job analysis and job design?
6. What is the difference between a job description and a job specification?
7. What is competency profiling? What are the arguments for and against its use?
8. Explain the differences between job specialisation, job rotation, job enlargement and job enrichment.
9. What is meant by the terms employee participation and industrial democracy?
10. Why is industrial democracy such a controversial issue?

environmental influences on job design

Discuss the key environmental influences from the model (figure 5.12 shown on the next page) that have significance for job design.

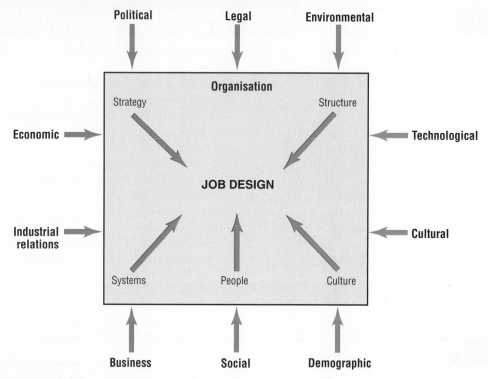

Figure 5.12 Environmental influences on job design

class debate

The problem today is that people are either 'dollar rich' and 'time poor' or 'time rich' and 'dollar poor'.

what's your view?

Write a 500-word response to the Letter to the Editor on page 165, agreeing or disagreeing with the writer's point of view.

practitioner speaks

Read the article on pages 171–2. As a class, discuss the views expressed by Paul Gollan and Glenn Patmore about how a social partnership model might be applied in Australia. Which comments do you agree with or disagree with? Explain your answer.

newsbreak exercise

Read the Newsbreak 'Long hours part of the job' on pages 150–1. Do you agree or disagree that a ceiling should be placed on working hours? Explain your reasoning. Critically discuss the impact of any restriction on working hours and individual rights.

soapbox

What do you think? Conduct a mini survey of class members, using the questionnaire below. Critically discuss the findings.

1.	Job descriptions are a waste of time.	YES	NO
2.	Job enrichment is an exploitative technique to get people to work harder.	YES	NO
3.	Employees are interested in money, not job enrichment.	YES	NO
4.	Employee participation is a myth in most organisations.	YES	NO
5.	Industrial democracy means an increase in union power.	YES	NO
6.	These days there is no quality of work life.	YES	NO

online exercise

Conduct an online search on (a) how globalisation is changing the workplace and (b) the impact of technology on the workplace. As a class, discuss your findings and prepare a list of the most useful web sites you found.

ethical dilemma

HR's new responsibility at Jet Red

Stan Vines, the Marketing Manager, said, 'Well, that's it, except for the visit next month of our biggest customer Ichiban Tours. I want to review the arrangements just to make sure that everything goes off without a hitch. These Ichiban guys work hard and play hard and it's up to us to make sure that we do everything to keep their business. Our present travel products, unfortunately, are 'me-too' products given the cutthroat competition. The only competitive advantages we have are on price and service. We have to do everything to keep a major customer like Ichiban happy. I've asked Sam Selznick, our Marketing Manager for Asia–Pacific, to review the schedule for the visit.'

Sam spoke up. 'Well, as Stan has mentioned, Ichiban is our bread and butter. They make up 50 per cent of our Asia–Pacific region sales. It's critical that everything goes off like clockwork or we will all be out of a job. I have finalised the arrangements regarding the resort visits and product presentations with Robin

Antoinetti in Marketing Services so the formal side of the visit is taken care of. All that's left are the "three Gs".'

Everyone laughed except for Linda Church, the newly appointed HR Manager.

'As in the past', continued Sam, 'I'll take responsibility for the golf arrangements and Robin will look after things with the casino. That leaves 'G' number three. Because girls come under Human Resources, I think that should be Linda's responsibility.'

Everyone laughed and looked at Linda Church, who was shocked. 'I bet they didn't tell you that was part of your job description', smiled Robin.

Discussion questions

1. If you were Linda Church, what would you do? Why?
2. Do the activities described above constitute 'legitimate' business entertainment? Explain your answer.
3. What ethical issues are raised in this case?

New job description at Jet Red

'Let's get started. As you all know, I announced at the press conference yesterday our attack on Jet Red's cost structure. We have to better the competition or we are history. Our overall personnel numbers and expenses are way out of line with the competition. We have to reduce costs. There is no alternative.' As he spoke, Alan Balkin, Jet Red's Managing Director, showed the mounting pressure.

'Alan, I think we should tackle the cabin crew situation first. Our people numbers and labour expenses are way above those of the competition and our productivity is terrible. Jet Red's cabin crew expenses exceed our worst performing competitor by more than 30 per cent', said Jeff Davis, Manager, Finance and Accounting.

Bill Armstrong, Jet Red's Operations Manager, shifted uneasily in his seat as Alan's gaze focused on him.

'Is that correct, Bill?', questioned Alan.

'Yes, Alan, I'm afraid it is.'

'How in the hell did we get into such a situation?', barked Alan.

Bill leant forward, his face flushed. 'Very easily Alan. We have given the unions everything they asked for over the years because we could pass on the extra costs. It was a nice sweetheart arrangement. We paid and they gave us no trouble. It worked well when there was no competition. Now it is dog eat dog and we are hurting.'

'OK, I appreciate the history, but what do you suggest we do now?', asked Alan.

'I recommend we reduce flight crew numbers to bring them into line with competitive practice. This will result in an immediate 20 per cent reduction in people numbers. Next, I suggest we expand the job duties to be performed, which will also save us money by allowing more rapid turnarounds, further people reductions in cleaning staff and lower costs.'

'I'm not sure what you mean Bill', asked Linda Church, HR Manager.

'It's simple. The cabin crew become multi-tasked. Instead of just the standard duties of serving and looking after passengers, they can also clean the plane at the end of each flight and take on check-in duties if required.'

'Bill, this is crazy. The unions will never accept it.'

'Linda, I don't see what the problem is. Our competition is already doing this. At Virgin Blue flight attendants clean the planes, including the toilets.[182] If our unions can't see the need for change, then we might as well pack up and go home now.'

'Why don't we fire the lot and simply outsource from New Zealand and the Philippines?', questioned Jeff Davis. 'We need more flexibility and lower costs, and outsourcing gives us that.'

'I agree with Jeff', chipped in Stan Vines, the Marketing Manager. 'Our flight attendants have developed very bad work habits over the years. They know that they can't be fired and that their pay increases are guaranteed. It's no wonder we have a reputation for surly service. Our flight attendants are a major marketing problem.'

Linda snapped, 'You realise that there will be a major union backlash!'

'So what, Linda?', retorted Stan. 'This company has been playing "Father Christmas" for too long. It's about time people realised that we are a global company competing against airlines with lower costs. Lack of competition, government ownership and union power have given this company an unsustainably high cost base.'

'You forgot lousy management. This airline's problem is that its management is too bureaucratic and too resistant to change. It's the quality of our management that stinks, not our people!', Linda flared.

Alan Balkin interrupted the sharp exchange. 'Can we get back to business please? Picking up on Bill's suggestion that we introduce a new job description for the flight attendants. If the savings are as great as Bill indicates, we could pay the flight attendants more. We really need to look at how we can convince the unions to help us reduce costs. We must have the flexibility to manage our human resources properly. In case you haven't all noticed, time is running out for Jet Red.'

Discussion questions

1. Critically examine the various arguments proposed in this case. Who do you agree with? Explain your reasons.
2. As a class, discuss the viability of the various proposals made.

Exercises

1. Form into groups of four to six. Imagine you are a member of a task force assigned to reduce flight attendant numbers, expand job responsibilities and increase flexibility. Develop an action plan and highlight how you propose to overcome any predicted obstacles.
2. Form into groups of four to six. Half the groups will represent Jet Red's management and the other half will represent Jet Red's unions. Negotiate management's demands that (i) flight crew numbers be reduced by 20 per cent and (ii) flight crews assume additional responsibilities for cleaning the plane cabins.

Job enrichment at Jet Red

Sitting in Singapore's Changi Airport, Ashley Wood was surprised to see the familiar faces of John Wong and Teresa Hayman. All three had studied economics at University. After some small talk, John asked Ashley what she had been doing.

'Well, as you know, I went to Melbourne and took a job as a marketing trainee with Jet Red. It was a disaster. Every year, six trainees joined the Marketing Department whether they were really needed or not. The result was that there wasn't much to do, and some of the more experienced people weren't interested in helping us because the turnover of new graduates was so high. Also, with the downturn in business, the graduate training program was cancelled and some of the new trainees were fired. I was given the job of understudying one of the sales representatives, which simply meant following him around and observing what he did. I was never allowed to say anything or try to make a sale myself. If you ever did anything, you had to do it by the book and constantly check with the boss.

'Another thing that really frustrated me was all the commotion that took place after I completed an assignment on customer relations for one of the product marketing managers. It was a great assignment and I really got involved — the only problem was that the previous Marketing Manager, Tom Medley, thought the results were too controversial and reflected badly on the department. So it was simply filed and nothing was done.

'After that, I was put in charge of expense reports, which meant calculating the expenses of all sales representatives and checking that they had filled in their expense claim forms correctly. When I asked Tom for something else to do, he told me not to be so impatient, that it had taken him 25 years to get where he was and I had better realise that my degree didn't make me anyone special. If he had his way, he said, he would do away with hiring university graduates and get some

practical people who didn't expect to be made general manager in a week.

'One thing I did to fill in time was start reading everything I could on marketing — unfortunately, Tom seemed to think I was "goofing off" if he ever saw me reading, so I stopped. Then I developed a new expenses claim procedure that was a lot simpler and meant I could do my job in less than two days if I really worked hard.

'Instead of being happy, Tom was upset because I wanted to change the system. His exact words were, "I don't care if you say it is better. The present system is serving us well and I don't want it changed! If there are any changes to be made around here, I'm the one who will make them!"'

'It seems strange, but although I had virtually nothing to do, I was starting to feel tired and suffer from insomnia. Worse, my boyfriend said my temper had become unbearable and ended our relationship. I can tell you, I was really at rock bottom. I only stayed because one of the sales representatives quit after an argument with Tom. Although they advertised the job, they couldn't get anyone to accept it because the money was so bad. So they offered it to me with the promise of a pay review in six months if I did okay.

'I really worked. I picked up several new accounts and increased the business with the existing clients by almost 20 per cent. In fact, I had the top sales performance in the group. So you can imagine how I felt when Tom told me that I was going to get a cost-of-living increase plus 2 per cent. When I asked why my pay wasn't going to be increased in line with my performance, I was told I was already earning a lot for a woman and not to be greedy.

'That's when I asked myself, what sort of job is this?'

'Did you quit?', asked John.

'No', replied Ashley. 'There was a revolution. The old board of directors got thrown out and most of the senior managers including Tom were fired.'

(continued)

'What's your new boss like?', asked Teresa.

'Stan Vines? Well, he's completely different from Tom, that's for sure.'

'How do you mean?', questioned John.

Ashley smiled. 'He is totally results oriented. Perform and Stan gives you all the freedom in the world. I love it.'

'What happens if you don't perform?', asked Teresa.

'Three strikes and you're out. Stan allows you to make mistakes, but not the same ones. If you are a slacker or not 100 per cent committed, you're dead. Some of the old timers can't stand the pressure and have either quit or been fired. But me, I love it! Every day is exciting. In fact, it sounds crazy, but I can't wait to go to work. I really get a buzz. No one questions what I do or when I work. I am my own boss. I have all the responsibility I can handle. No one says you can't do it because you're too young or female.'

'Sounds good', smiled John, 'But what about the money?'

'Since Stan took over, I have had three pay increases and a performance bonus. I actually feel that I'm making something of my life now. It makes such a big difference if you enjoy your work. I work like a dog, but I love it!'

Discussion questions

1. What changes in job design have contributed to Ashley's new perception of her job at Jet Red?
2. Identify and discuss the demotivators and motivators present in Ashley's various jobs at Jet Red.
3. Would you prefer to work at the 'old' or the 'new' Jet Red? Justify your answer.
4. Do you think Ashley's new 'love of work' is the product of cunning management manipulation? Explain your reasoning.

practical exercises

1. Break into groups of three or four. Using the information in this chapter, select one student to be interviewed about a job with which they are familiar. After completing the job analysis interview, write a job description and a job specification for the position. Critically review the process and the end products.
2. Break into groups of three or four. Using the example shown on page 148, write a job specification for the position of (a) Vice-President, Human Resources, Asia–Pacific region (using the job description shown on page 146 as a guide) or (b) your present job or a job you are aiming to get.
3. Prepare a competency profile using the standards model illustrated on page 157 for one of the following positions:
   (a) police officer
   (b) lecturer in HRM
   (c) football coach
   (d) exotic dancer
   (e) your present job or a job you are aiming at.
4. Select a job you are familiar with and analyse it for its motivation potential in terms of skills variety, task identity, task significance, autonomy and feedback. How would you redesign the job to improve its motivation potential?

suggested readings

Alexander, R. and Lever, J., *Understanding Australian Industrial Relations*, 6th edn, Thomson, Melbourne, 2004, pp. 263–71.

Beardwell, I. and Holden, L., *Human Resource Management*, 3rd edn, Financial Times/Prentice Hall, London, 2001, ch. 5, pp. 236–8, 329–31.

CCH, *Australian Master Human Resources Guide*, CCH, Sydney, 2003, chs 9, 13.

De Cieri, H. and Kramar, R., *Human Resource Management in Australia*, McGraw-Hill, Sydney, 2003, ch. 4.

Deery, S., Plowman, D., Walsh, J. and Brown, M., *Industrial Relations: A Contemporary Analysis*, 2nd edn, McGraw-Hill, Sydney, 2001, ch. 10.

Fisher, C. D., Schoenfeldt, L. F. and Shaw, J. B., *Human Resource Management*, 5th edn, Houghton Mifflin, Boston, 2003, ch. 4.

Ivancevich, J. M., *Human Resource Management*, 8th edn, McGraw-Hill, Boston, 2001, ch. 6.

Ivancevich, J. M. and Lee, S. H., *Human Resource Management in Asia*, McGraw-Hill, Singapore, 2002, ch. 4.

Mondy, R. W., Noe, R. M. and Premeaux, S. R., *Human Resource Management*, 8th edn, Prentice Hall, Upper Saddle River, NJ, 2002, ch. 4.

Nankervis, A. R., Compton, R. L. and Baird, M., *Strategic Human Resource Management*, 4th edn, Nelson, Melbourne, 2002, ch. 6.

Robbins, S. P., *Organizational Behavior*, 9th edn, Prentice Hall, Upper Saddle River, NJ, 2001, chs 14, 15.

Schermerhorn, J. H., Hunt, J. G. and Osborn, R. N., *Organizational Behavior*, 8th edn, John Wiley & Sons, New York, 2003, ch. 8.

online references

www.econ.usyd.edu.au/acirrt
www.shrm.org.hrmagazine
www.workforceonline.com

end notes

1. S. Dibble, *Keeping Your Valuable Employees*, John Wiley & Sons, New York, 1999, p. 35.

2. Every job is composed of tasks, duties and responsibilities. A job differs from a position, which is a collection of tasks, duties and responsibilities performed by one person. A job may include more than one position. For example, if an HR department has two training officers, there are two positions (one for each person), but just the one job of training officer. A job is an organisational unit of work. Responsibilities are obligations to perform accepted tasks and duties. A task is a distinct, identifiable work activity — for example, asking questions of a job candidate. A duty is composed of a number of tasks and constitutes a larger segment of work — for example, interviewing a job candidate. It should be noted that because tasks and duties both describe activities it is not always easy (or necessary) to make a distinction between them. For a list of definitions, see C. D. Fisher, L. F. Schoenfeldt and J. B. Shaw, *Human Resource Management*, 5th edn, Houghton Mifflin, Boston, 2003, pp. 143–4.

3. Adapted by the author from R. C. Page and D. M. Van De Voort, 'Job analysis and HR planning', in W. F. Cascio (ed.), *Human Resource Planning, Employment and Placement*, BNA, Washington, DC, 1989, pp. 2.35–2.36.

4. R. W. Mondy, R. M. Noe and S. R. Premeaux, *Human Resource Management*, 8th edn, Prentice Hall, Upper Saddle River, NJ, 2002, p. 88.

5. D. Cherrington, *The Management of Human Resources*, 4th edn, Prentice Hall, Englewood Cliffs, NJ, 1995, p. 183.

6. M. Burke, 'Funny business', *Forbes Global*, 9 June 2003, p. 35.

7. R. Lebihan, 'Hotel staff turn techno geeks', *Australian Financial Review*, 23–24 August 2003, p. 7.

8. D. Yoder, H. G. Heneman, J. G. Turnbull and C. H. Stone, *Handbook of Personnel Management and Labor Relations*, McGraw-Hill, New York, 1958, p. 5.23.

9. J. M. Ivancevich, *Human Resource Management: Foundations of Personnel*, 8th edn, Irwin, Homewood, Ill., 2001, p. 156.

10. W. F. Cascio, *Managing Human Resources*, 4th edn, McGraw-Hill, New York, 1995, p. 129.

11. C. F. Russ, 'Manpower planning systems: part 1', *Personnel Journal*, January 1982, p. 41.

12. G. Dessler, *Human Resource Management*, 7th edn, Prentice Hall, Englewood Cliffs, NJ, 1997, p. 96; and S. Robbins, *Organizational Behavior*, 9th edn, Prentice Hall, Upper Saddle River, NJ, 2000, pp. 475–6.

13. Some organisations use 'elastic' or 'safety' clauses such as 'performs other duties and responsibilities as assigned'. These (in

theory) permit managers to assign duties and responsibilities different from those the employees normally perform. Such clauses, while having an intuitive appeal of flexibility, actually reflect sloppy job analysis and poor management and, when invoked, become a source of employee grievance.

14. R. I. Henderson, *Compensation Management*, 3rd edn, Reston, Virginia, 1979, p. 159.

15. R. I. Henderson, op. cit., p. 160.

16. Much of this section is based on D. W. Belcher, *Wage and Salary Administration*, 2nd edn, Prentice Hall, Englewood Cliffs, NJ, 1962, pp. 223–4.

17. C. D. Fisher, L. F. Schoenfeldt and J. B. Shaw, op. cit., pp. 143–6.

18. W. Cascio, *Applied Psychology in Personnel Management*, 4th edn, Prentice Hall, Englewood Cliffs, NJ, 1991, p. 192.

19. W. Cascio, 1991, op. cit., p. 192.

20. T. Peters, *Thriving on Chaos*, Pan, London, 1989, pp. 500–1.

21. R. J. Ballon, *Foreign Competition in Japan: Human Resource Strategies*, Routledge, London, 1992, p. 34.

22. W. H. Whitely, *Business Systems in Asia*, Sage, London, 1992, p. 39.

23. A. Downs, 'Job descriptions are outdated', *Bottom Line/Business*, vol. 24, no. 13, 1995, p. 8.

24. R. Townsend, *Further up the Organization*, Coronet, London, 1985, p. 115.

25. T. Peters, op. cit., pp. 500–1.

26. C. Brass, 'Life without jobs', *HR Monthly*, April 1995, p. 11.

27. B. Townley, *Reframing Human Resource Management — Power, Ethics and the Subject of Work*, Sage, London, 1994, pp. 52–3.

28. W. H. Whitely, op. cit., p. 236

29. J. Garen, 'Unions, incentive systems and job design', *Journal of Labor Research*, vol. 20, no. 4, 1999, pp. 589–603.

30. T. A. Stewart, 'Planning a career in a world without managers', *Fortune*, 20 March 1995, p. 46.

31. C. Brass, op. cit., p. 11.

32. W. Kiechel II, 'A manager's career in the new economy', *Fortune*, 4 April 1994, p. 54.

33. C. Brass, op. cit., p. 13.

34. T. A. Stewart, op. cit., p. 49.

35. T. Peters, op. cit., pp. 500–1.

36. G. Nosworthy, 'Generic or non generic job descriptions?', *Personnel Journal*, February 1996, p. 102; and D. A. Grigson and G. W. Stoeffel, 'Job analysis and job documentation', in L. A. Berger and D. R. Berger (eds), *The Compensation Handbook*, 4th edn, McGraw-Hill, New York, 1999, ch. 5.

37. R. Townsend, op. cit., p. 115; and S. Robbins, op. cit., pp. 475–6.

38. S. Tyson and A. York, *Personnel Management*, Heinemann, London, 1982, p. 91.

39. D. J. Cherrington, op. cit., p. 188.

40. R. C. Page and D. M. Van De Voort, op. cit., p. 2.43.

41. W. F. Cascio, *Managing Human Resources*, 3rd edn, McGraw-Hill, New York, 1992, p. 14.

42. R. I. Henderson, op. cit., p. 138.

43. Adapted by the author from J. M. Ivancevich, op. cit., pp. 161–2.

44. N. R. Lange, 'Job analysis and documentation', in M. L. Rock and L. A. Berger (eds), *The Compensation Handbook*, 3rd edn, McGraw-Hill, New York, 1991, p. 50.

45. L. L. Byars and L. W. Rue, *Human Resource Management*, 6th edn, Irwin, Ill., 2000, pp. 103–4.

46. Australian Bureau of Statistics, *Australian Standard Classification of Occupations*, AGPS, Canberra, 1997, p. 143.

47. Further information can be obtained from the Occupational Research Center, Department of Psychological Sciences, Purdue University, West Lafayette, Indiana, 47907, USA.

48. E. J. McCormick, A. S. De Nisi and J. B. Shaw, 'Use of Position Analysis Questionnaire for establishing the job component validity of tests', *Journal of Applied Psychology*, vol. 64, no. 1, 1979, pp. 51–6; and W. F. Cascio, 1991, op. cit., p. 206.

49. W. W. Tornow and P. R. Pinto, 'The development of a managerial job taxonomy: a system for describing, classifying and evaluating executive positions', *Journal of Applied Psychology*, vol. 61, 1976, pp. 410–18.

50. W. F. Cascio, 1991, op. cit., pp. 136–8.

51. W. W. Tornow and P. R. Pinto, op. cit., pp. 410–18; and L. R. Gomez-Meijia, R. C. Page and W. W. Tornow, 'Development and implementation of a computerized job evaluation system', *Personnel Administrator*, February 1979, pp. 46–52.

52. Based on Positive Classification Inventory (PCI) information given in the *ACER Personnel Selection and Human Resource Development Catalogue of Tests and Materials 1995–96*, Australian Council for Educational Research, Camberwell, 1995, p. 33.

53. For further information contact the Australian Council for Educational Research, 19 Prospect Hill Road, Camberwell 3124. Tel: (03) 9277 5656; fax: (03) 9277 5678.

54. This section is based on A. O. Bellak, *The Hay Guide Chart — Profile Method of Job Evaluation*, Hay Group, Melbourne, 1991, pp. 1–10; and C. W. G. Van Horn, 'The Hay Guide Chart — Profile Method', in M. L. Rock (ed.), *Handbook of Wage and Salary Administration*, McGraw-Hill, New York, 1972, pp. 2.86–2.97.

55. R. C. Page and D. M. Van De Voort, op. cit., p. 2.49.

56. R. C. Page and D. M. Van De Voort, op. cit., pp. 2.49–2.58.

57. O. Lundy and A. Cowling, *Strategic Human Resource Management*, Routledge, London, 1996, p. 231.

58. P. E. Spector, *Industrial and Organizational Psychology*, John Wiley & Sons, New York, 1996, pp. 68–70.

59. R. Lles and G. Salaman, 'Recruitment, selection and assessment', in J. Storey (ed.), *Human Resource Management*, Routledge, London, 1995, p. 214; and S. Sherman, 'A brave new Darwinian workplace', *Fortune*, 25 January 1993, pp. 30–3.

60. E. E. Lawler III, 'From job based to competency based organizations', *Journal of Organizational Behavior*, vol. 15, 1994, p. 4.

61. R. Lles and G. Salaman, op. cit., p. 214 and D. Blancero, J. Boroski and L. Dyer, 'Key competencies for a transformed human resource organization: results of a field study', *Human Resource Management*, vol. 35, no. 3, 1996, pp. 383–403.

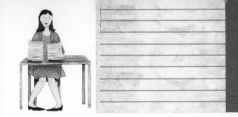

62. A. K. Yeung, 'Competencies for HR professionals: an interview with Richard E. Boyatzis', *Human Resource Management*, vol. 35, no. 1, 1996, p. 119.

63. Based on A. K. Yeung, op. cit., pp. 119–31; and L. M. Spencer and S. M. Spencer, *Competence at Work*, John Wiley & Sons, New York, 1993, p. 9.

64. Based on L. M. Spencer and S. M. Spencer, op. cit., pp. 9–12.

65. L. M. Spencer and S. M. Spencer, op. cit., p. 11.

66. L. M. Spencer and S. M. Spencer, op. cit., p. 11.

67. P. D. Rutherford, *Competency Based Assessment*, Pitman, Melbourne, 1995, pp. 1–19.

68. R. Iles and G. Salaman, op. cit., p. 216; C. Foley, 'Development of competencies', *Training and Development in Australia*, vol. 22, no. 4, 1995, p. 19; and P. D. Rutherford, op. cit., p. 257.

69. Adapted by the author from P. D. Rutherford, op. cit., pp. 67–9.

70. T. Keighley, 'Incompetence marks competency debate', *Business Review Weekly*, 11 July 1994, p. 101; and P. Horrocks, 'A case for developing generic management standards in Australia', *The Practising Manager*, vol. 14, no. 1, 1993, pp. 18–23.

71. L. M. Spencer and S. M. Spencer, op. cit., p. 15.

72. L. M. Spencer and S. M. Spencer, op. cit., p. 15.

73. L. M. Spencer and S. M. Spencer, op. cit., p. 98.

74. L. M. Spencer and S. M. Spencer, op. cit., pp. 98–9.

75. L. M. Spencer and S. M. Spencer, op. cit., p. 99.

76. P. Iles and G. Salaman, op. cit., p. 216 and J. A. Raelin and A. Sims, 'From generic to organic competencies', *Human Resource Planning*, vol. 18, no. 3, 1995, pp. 25–6.

77. P. Iles and G. Salaman, op. cit., p. 216.

78. J. A. Raelin and A. Sims, op. cit., pp. 24–33.

79. P. Iles and G. Salaman, op. cit., p. 216.

80. B. Townley, *Reframing Human Resource Management*, Sage, London, 1994, p. 62.

81. B. Townley, op. cit., pp. 62–3.

82. P. Iles and G. Salaman, op. cit., p. 218 and D. Ulrich, 'Profiling organizational competitiveness: cultivating capabilities', *Human Resource Planning*, vol. 16, no. 3, 1993, pp. 1–7.

83. L. M. Spencer and S. M. Spencer, op. cit., p. 347; and C. Foley, op. cit., pp. 19–20.

84. K. H. Pritchard, 'Job analysis is the key to ADA compliance', *HR News*, June 1992, p. A8.

85. K. H. Pritchard, op. cit., p. A8.

86. Based on K. H. Pritchard, op. cit., p. A8.

87. C. D. Fisher, L. F. Schoenfeldt and J. B. Shaw, *Human Resource Management*, 4th edn, Houghton Mifflin, Boston, 1999, pp. 157–9.

88. L. L. Byars and L. W. Rue, pp. 94–7.

89. O. Lundy and A. Cowling, op. cit., p. 231.

90. B. Townley, op. cit., p. 58.

91. B. Townley, op. cit., p. 59.

92. B. Townley, op. cit., p. 59

93. G. T. Milkovitch and J. W. Boudreau, *Human Resource Management*, 8th edn, Irwin, Ill., 1997, p. 69.

94. R. W. Mondy and R. M. Noe III, *Human Resource Management*, 6th edn, Prentice Hall, Upper Saddle River, NJ, 1996, p. 110.

95. M. A. Campion, 'How do you design a job?', *Personnel Journal*, January 1989, p. 43.

96. W. H. Glick, C. D. Jenkins and N. Gupta, 'Method versus substance: how strong are underlying relationships between job characteristics and attitudinal outcomes?', *Academy of Management Journal*, vol. 29, no. 3, 1985, pp. 441–64; D. A. Ondrack and M. Evans, 'Job enrichment and job satisfaction in quality of working life and non quality of working life work sites', *Human Relations*, vol. 39, no. 9, 1986, pp. 871–89; and S. Caudron, 'Job stress is in job design', *Workforce*, vol. 77, no. 9, 1998, pp. 21–3.

97. F. Luthans, *Organizational Behavior*, 7th edn, McGraw-Hill, New York, 1995, pp. 175–6.

98. W. B. Werther and K. Davis, *Human Resources and Personnel Management*, 5th edn, McGraw-Hill, New York, 1996, pp. 136–8.

99. J. R. Schermerhorn, J. G. Hunt and R. N. Osborn, *Organizational Behavior*, 8th edn, John Wiley & Sons, New York, 2003, p. 153.

100. F. W. Taylor, *The Principles of Scientific Management*, Harper & Row, New York, 1947.

101. J. Schermerhorn, J. Hunt and R. Osborn, op. cit., 2003, p. 153.

102. E. Rose, 'The labour process and union commitment within a banking services call centre', *Journal of Industrial Relations*, vol. 44, no. 1, 2002, p. 40.

103. M. R. Carrell, N. E. Elbert and R. D. Hatfield, *Human Resource Management*, 5th edn, Prentice Hall, Englewood Cliffs, NJ, 1995, pp. 213–14.

104. J. Halfpenny, 'Benefits of higher skills come with job redesign', *HR Monthly*, July 1992, p. 14; and S. L. Perlman, 'Employees redesign their jobs', *Personnel Journal*, November 1990, pp. 37–40.

105. C. L. Hulin and M. R. Blood, 'Job enlargement, industrial differences, and worker responses', *Psychological Bulletin*, vol. 69, no. 1, 1968, pp. 41–53; and J. L. Pierce and R. B. Dunham, 'Task design: a literature review', *Academy of Management Review*, vol. 1, no. 4, 1976, pp. 83–97.

106. D. C. Feldman and H. J. Arnold, *Managing Industrial and Group Behavior in Organizations*, McGraw-Hill, Tokyo, 1983, pp. 231–4; and S. Altman, E. Valenzi and R. M. Hodgetts, *Organizational Behavior: Theory and Practice*, Academic Press, Orlando, Florida, 1985, p. 392.

107. T. R. Mitchell, P. J. Dowling, B. V. Kabanoff and J. R. Larson, *People in Organisations*, McGraw-Hill, Sydney, 1988, p. 512.

108. A. M. Whitehall, *Japanese Management*, Routledge, London, 1992, pp. 164–5.

109. T. Ellis, 'Implementing job rotation', *Occupational Health and Safety*, vol. 68, no. 1, 1999, pp. 82–4; and D. D. Triggs and P. M. King, 'Job rotation', *Professional Safety*, vol. 45, no. 2, 2000, pp. 32–4.

110. S. P. Robbins, op. cit., p. 459.

111. S. P. Robbins, op. cit., p. 460; and G. Dessler, op. cit., p. 328.

112. M. O'Neill, quoted in N. Shoebridge, 'Whirlpool's smaller ripples are turning the tide', *Business Review Weekly*, 9 June 1997, p. 76.

113. The material in this section is based on P. Mears, 'Guidelines for the job enrichment practitioner', *Personnel Journal*, May 1976,

pp. 210–11; G. Dessler, op. cit., p. 328; R. Aldag and A. Brief, *Task Design and Employee Motivation*, Scott Foresman, Glenview, Ill., 1979, pp. 83–101; and S. Altman, E. Valenzi and R. M. Hodgetts, op. cit., pp. 393–7.

114. See R. E. Kapelman, 'Job redesign and productivity: a review of the evidence', *National Productivity Review*, vol. 4, 1985, pp. 237–55.

115. D. Hellriegel and J. W. Slocum, *Management*, 6th edn, Addison Wesley, Reading, Mass., 1992, p. 438.

116. D. Hellriegel and J. W. Slocum, op. cit., pp. 438–42.

117. J. R. Schermerhorn, *Management for Productivity*, 5th edn, John Wiley & Sons, New York, 1996, pp. 274–5.

118. J. A. Wagner and J. R. Hollenbeck, *Management of Organizational Behavior*, Prentice Hall, Englewood Cliffs, NJ, 1992, p. 659.

119. S. Robbins, op. cit., p. 461.

120. J. A. Wagner and J. R. Hollenbeck, op. cit., p. 662.

121. J. R. Schermerhorn, op. cit., p. 275.

122. E. M. Davis and R. D. Lansbury, *Managing Together*, Longman, Melbourne, 1996, pp. 201–2.

123. J. A. Wagner and J. R. Hollenbeck, op. cit., p. 662.

124. S. L. McShane and M. A. Von Glinow, *Organizational Behavior*, McGraw-Hill, Boston, 2000, p. 118; and R. Hodson 'Dignity in the workplace under participative management: alienation and freedom revisited', *American Sociological Review*, vol. 61, 1996, pp. 719–38.

125. J. R. Gordon, *Organizational Behavior*, 4th edn, Allyn & Bacon, Boston, 1993, pp. 628–9. See also J. L. Cordery, W. S. Mueller and L. M. Smith, 'Attitudinal and behavioural effects of autonomous group working: a longitudinal field study', *Academy of Management Journal*, vol. 34, no. 2, 1991, pp. 464–76.

126. J. M. Ivancevich, op. cit., p. 176; and S. L. McShane and M. A. Von Glinow, op. cit., pp. 118–19.

127. J. A. Wagner and J. R. Hollenbeck, op. cit., p. 653.

128. V. G. Scarpello, J. Ledvinka and T. J. Bergmann, *Human Resource Management*, 2nd edn, South-Western, Cincinnati, Ohio, 1995, p. 181.

129. J. R. Schermerhorn, J. G. Hunt and R. N. Osborn, op. cit., p. 156.

130. J. A. Wagner and J. R. Hollenbeck, op. cit., 1992, pp. 654–5; and V. G. Scarpello, J. Ledvinka and T. J. Bergmann, op. cit., p. 181.

131. S. P. Robbins, op. cit., pp. 447–9.

132. J. A. Wagner and J. R. Hollenbeck, op. cit., p. 655.

133. P. E. Muchinsky, *Psychology Applied to Work*, 4th edn, Brooks/Cole, Pacific Grove, CA, 1993, p. 434.

134. J. A. Wagner and J. R. Hollenbeck, op. cit., p. 656.

135. G. Moorhead and R. W. Griffin, *Organizational Behavior*, 4th edn, Houghton Mifflin, Boston, 1995, p. 168.

136. H. R. Berkman and L. L. Neider, *The Human Relations of Organizations*, Kent, Belmont, CA, 1987, p. 337.

137. L. M. Oyley and J. S. Ball, 'Quality of work life: initiating sources in labor-management organizations', *Personnel Administrator*,

May 1982, pp. 27–9; and 'The new industrial relations', *Business Week*, 11 May 1981, pp. 85–98.

138. H. R. Berkman and L. L. Neider, op. cit., p. 340, B. Mandell, 'Does a better work life boost productivity?', *Personnel*, vol. 66, no. 10, 1989, pp. 48–9.

139. J. P. Gordon, J. A. Pearce and E. C. Ravlin, 'The design and activation of self regulating work groups', *Human Relations*, vol. 40, 1987, pp. 751–82.

140. R. I. Westwood, *Organizational Behaviour, Southeast Asian Perspectives*, Longman, Hong Kong, 1992, pp. 228–9.

141. Adapted from B. Mandell, op. cit., p. 52.

142. W. L. Mohr and H. Mohr, *Quality Circles: Changing Images of People at Work*, Addison Wesley, Reading, Mass., 1983, p. 13.

143. B. Eunson, *Behaving: Managing Yourself and Others*, McGraw-Hill, Sydney, 1987, p. 388.

144. B. Eunson, op. cit., p. 388.

145. U. Thomas, 'Productivity improvement through people: some new approaches', *Management Decision*, vol. 27, no. 4, 1989, p. 59.

146. J. R. Gordon, op. cit., p. 634; and P. E. Spector, op. cit., p. 317.

147. J. A. Wagner and J. R. Hollenbeck, op. cit., p. 664. See also R. P. Steel and R. Lloyd, 'Cognitive, affective and behavioral outcomes of participation in quality circles: conceptual and empirical findings', *Journal of Applied Behavioral Science*, vol. 24, 1988, pp. 1–17.

148. J. A. Wagner and J. R. Hollenbeck, op. cit., p. 664.

149. R. H. Hall, *Sociology of Work*, Pine Forge, Thousand Oaks, CA, 1994, pp. 296–7.

150. R. Callus, A. Morehead, M. Cully and J. Buchanan, *Industrial Relations at Work*, Commonwealth Department of Industrial Relations, Canberra, 1991, p. 304.

151. P. S. Kirkbride and S. F. Y. Tang, 'From Kyoto to Kowloon: cultural barriers to the transference of quality circles from Japan to Hong Kong', *Asia Pacific Journal of Human Resources*, vol. 32, no. 2, 1994, pp. 100–11.

152. M. R. Carrell, N. E. Elbert and R. D. Hatfield, op. cit., p. 70.

153. B. Eunson, op. cit., pp. 389–90.

154. E. M. Davis and R. D. Lansbury, op. cit., p. 76.

155. Based on C. Orpen, 'Quality circles, what is needed to make them work?', *Professional Administrator*, vol. 40, no. 2, March–April 1988, pp. 30–2. See also E. R. Ruffner and L. P. Ettkin, 'When a circle is not a circle', *Advanced Management Journal*, vol. 52, 1987, pp. 9–15; M. O'Donnell and R. J. O'Donnell, 'Quality circles — the latest fad or real winner', *Business Horizons*, vol. 26, 1984, pp. 48–52; and R. Mitchell, 'Quality circles in the US: rediscovering our roots', *The Journal for Quality and Participation*, vol. 22, no. 6, 1999, pp. 24–8.

156. J. Teicher, 'Theories of employee participation and industrial democracy: towards an analytical framework', in B. Dabscheck, G. Griffin and J. Teicher (eds), *Contemporary Australian Industrial Relations*, Longman Cheshire, Melbourne, 1992, p. 476. See also S. Deery, D. Plowman and J. Walsh, *Industrial Relations: A Contemporary Analysis*, McGraw-Hill, Sydney, 1997, pp. 11.3–11.5.

157. R. Willis, 'Industrial democracy and employee participation: summary of key points', *Human Resource Development in Action*, January 1987, p. 1.

158. J. Teicher, op. cit., p. 476.

159. J. Teicher, op. cit., p. 476; and M. Marchington, 'Involvement and participation', in J. Storey (ed.), *Human Resource Management: A Critical Text*, Routledge, London, 1995, p. 282.

160. H. Ramsay, 'Industrial democracy and the question of control', in E. Davis and R. Lansbury (eds), *Democracy and Control in the Workplace*, Longman Cheshire, Melbourne, 1986, p. 53.

161. See S. J. Deery and D. H. Plowman, *Australian Industrial Relations*, 3rd edn, McGraw-Hill, Sydney, 1991, p. 230; and P. Berry and G. Kitchener, 'Can unions survive?', *BWIU*, ACT Branch, 1989, pp. 6–7.

162. S. J. Deery and D. H. Plowman, op. cit., p. 460; and R. Callus, 'Technological change and employee participation in a public instrumentality', in R. D. Lansbury and E. M. Davis (eds), *Technology, Work and Industrial Relations*, Longman Cheshire, Melbourne, 1984, pp. 103–4.

163. M. Derber, 'Reflections on aspects of the Australian and American systems of industrial relations', in W. A. Howard (ed.), *Perspectives on Australian Industrial Relations*, Longman Cheshire, Melbourne, 1984, p. 32.

164. R. Willis, op. cit., p. 1.

165. F. G. Hilmer, P. A. McLaughlin, D. K. Macfarlane and J. Rose, *Avoiding Industrial Action: A Better Way of Working*, Business Council of Australia, Allen & Unwin, Sydney, 1991, p. 71.

166. R. Clark, *Australian Human Resources Management: Framework and Practice*, 2nd edn, McGraw-Hill, Sydney, 1992, p. 231.

167. S. J. Deery and D. H. Plowman, op. cit., p. 463.

168. B. Brooks, *Why Unions?*, CCH Australia, Sydney, 1980, p. 81.

169. N. Hooper, 'The growing trend to worker participation', *Business Review Weekly*, 15 April 1988, p. 62; and N. Ruskin, 'Union policy on industrial democracy: the case of the AMWU', in E. Davis and R. Lansbury (eds), *Democracy and Control in the Workplace*, Longman Cheshire, Melbourne, 1986, pp. 179–80.

170. N. Ruskin, op. cit., pp. 179–80.

171. G. W. Ford and L. Tilley, 'Industrial democracy in Australia: the forces of change and tradition', in G. W. Ford, J. M. Hearn and R. D. Lansbury, *Australian Labour Relations: Readings*, 4th edn, Macmillan, Melbourne, 1987, p. 414.

172. J. Smith, 'Making worker participation work', *Australian Business*, 13 September 1989, p. 98; and S. V. Volard, 'Developments in industrial democracy in Australia', *The Practising Manager*, vol. 4, no. 1, 1984, p. 33.

173. P. McGraw and B. Harley, 'Industrial relations and human resource management practices in Australian and overseas owned workplaces: global or local?', *Journal of Industrial Relations*, vol. 45, no. 1, 2003, p. 11.

174. S. J. Deery and D. H. Plowman, op. cit., pp. 467–8.

175. S. Deery, D. Plowman and J. Walsh, op. cit., pp. 11.19–11.20.

176. E. M. Davis and R. D. Lansbury, op. cit., p. 11.

177. See E. Vaughn, 'The romance and theatre of managing together', in E. M. Davis and R. Lansbury (eds), op. cit., pp. 25–40; S. Deery, D. Plowman and J. Walsh, op. cit., p. 11.20; and D. P. Gollan and G. Patmore, 'New option for worker participation', *HR Monthly*, June 2003, pp. 42–3.

178. B. Harley, H. Ramsay and D. Scholarios, 'Employee direct participation in Britain and Australia: Evidence from AWIRS 95 and WERS 98', *Asia Pacific Journal of Human Resources*, vol. 38, no. 2, 2000, pp. 42–54.

179. S. Deery, D. Plowman and J. Walsh, op. cit., p. 11.20.

180. M. Priest, 'ALP looks at workplace democracy', *Australian Financial Review*, 23 June 2003, p. 5.

181. E. Vaughn, op. cit., p. 25. See also T. Wallace, 'Industrial democracy struggles to survive', *Australian Financial Review*, 9 January 2001, p. 33.

182. A. Ferguson, 'Wounded Kangaroo', *Business Review Weekly*, 10–16 July 2003, p. 35.

chapter
6

recruiting human resources

Learning objectives

When you have finished studying this chapter, you should be able to:

• Describe strategic recruitment
• Discuss the major internal and external sources of human resources
• Explain the major recruitment methods and their advantages and disadvantages
• Discuss the recruitment of women, people with disabilities, older workers and minorities
• Evaluate the recruitment activity.

'Recruiting is the HR process arguably most influenced by the Internet.'[1]

E. A. Ensler, T. R. Nielson and E. Grant-Vallone

Strategic recruitment

The pressures of competition, cost saving, downsizing and global skill shortages have made recruitment a top priority.[2] The competition for talent means that skilled workers are today's prized trophies. For many companies, talented people are the prime source of competitive advantage.[3] **Recruitment** (the process of *seeking and attracting* a pool of qualified candidates for a job vacancy) and **selection** (the process of *choosing* the candidate who best meets the selection criteria) are used today as major levers to bring about strategic and cultural change.[4] An organisation must attract qualified candidates if it is to survive and grow.

Leading US companies such as Microsoft have created an 'employment brand' to convey their personality and image to potential employees and to attract top talent.[5] Marketing techniques are being applied to persuade candidates to join an organisation and stay.[6] Says Ann Sherry, Westpac's Group Executive, People and Performance, 'Employment branding can create a unique proposition for potential employees, separate one company from another and attract key talent'.[7]

Management must anticipate changes in the organisation's environment to ensure that people who are recruited have the unique skills, know-how and values required by the organisation's strategic business objectives. **Strategic recruitment** does this by linking recruiting activities to the organisation's business objectives and culture (see figure 6.1).[8]

Recruitment The process of seeking and attracting a pool of qualified applicants from which candidates for job vacancies can be selected.

Selection The process of choosing from a group of applicants the best qualified candidate.

Strategic recruitment The linking of recruiting activities to the organisation's strategic objectives and culture.

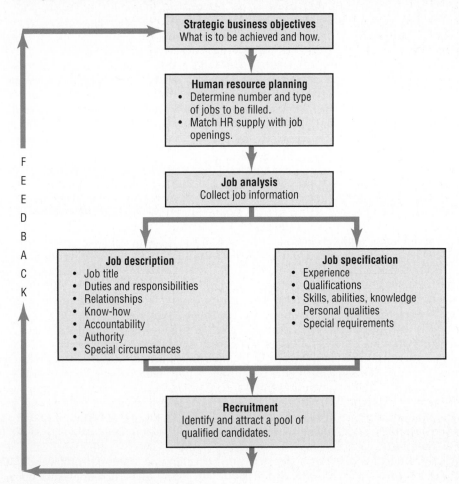

Figure 6.1 Strategic recruitment
Source Asia Pacific Management Co. Ltd, 2004.

The increasing use of teams and ongoing demands for greater flexibility and multiskilling have seen a change in emphasis from the traditional approach to recruitment (attracting candidates whose academic qualifications and past employment history match the formal job requirements) to one highlighting individual attitudes, behaviour and potential.[9] This, in turn, has led to candidate profiling accentuating person-oriented (rather than job-oriented) characteristics. Boxhall and Purcell argue that if an organisation seeks high performance and agility, it is important to recruit for long-run trainability and adaptability rather than specific job know-how (which can be acquired over time — assuming the individual has both the intelligence and motivation to learn).[10]

The core purpose of Nike, for example, is 'To experience the emotion of competition, winning and crushing competitors'.[11] Consequently, this creates a need to recruit people who are stimulated by the competitive spirit and the urge to be ferocious.[12] Other organisations have other objectives and values: Nordstrom stresses hard work and productivity, service to the customer and a sense of never being satisfied; and Philip Morris highlights competition, individual initiative, hard work and continuous self-improvement.[13] Investment bank UBS seeks highly intelligent, hard-working, entrepreneurial team players.[14] In contrast, the President of Boyden International (Japan) declares: 'I don't look for nice guys — they tend to be weak managers. Also great men have great appetites. I'm not so keen to place goody-goodies who don't smoke or drink and never play around.'[15]

Recruitment is thus a means of delivering behaviours seen as necessary to support the organisation's culture and strategies.[16] The current emphasis on employee competencies illustrates this role. Organisational strategies and culture determine whether the focus is on technical skills and formal qualifications or on personality, the ability to 'fit in' and the potential for development.[17] Toyota, for example, seeks people who can work as a team, have ideas for improvement and can demonstrate an ability to learn.[18] Similarly, Nissan favours attention to quality, pride in the job, a spirit of teamwork and cooperation, and a desire for continual improvement.[19] Leading UK food retailer Pret A Manger emphasises personality rather than experience. Alison McLaughlin, Pret A Manger's HR Manager says, 'We want people who are enthusiastic, energetic and have a natural empathy for servicing'.[20] A Qantas manager similarly says, 'Now we are looking a lot more to hiring people for their attitude'.[21] In Hong Kong, 'having the right attitude' is now the most important selection criterion to become a teacher.[22] A critic acidly comments 'this sort of inanity reinforces poor selection decisions'.[23]

A consequence of this emphasis on employee characteristics has been an increasing use of psychological testing to assess candidate behavioural and attitudinal characteristics (also see pages 234–6). In addition to being a valuable tool in employee recruitment and selection, testing has proven helpful in training and development and in reducing the chances of litigation arising from the hiring of incompetent, dishonest or potentially violent employees.[24] This has aroused some criticism because it results in the recruitment of 'a young "green" labour force, without years of acculturalisation in traditional manufacturing methods in heavily unionised plants' and marginalises unions.[25] Storey and Townley, for example, condemn such strategies because they dehumanise applicants, result in cloning and promote management control by producing a compliant, non-unionised work force.[26] Trade unions not surprisingly are also opposed to the use of psychological testing.[27]

Recruiting is also affected when organisations make fundamental strategic changes as a result of asking questions such as: What is our core business? What business should we be in? What is it we want to achieve? Mayne was a land transport company, but today its core business is pharmaceuticals. Clearly, the organisation now requires people with different know-how, skills and abilities. Consequently, an organisation can destroy its unique competitive advantage if it ignores its strategic mission, objectives and culture in recruiting personnel. In addition, it places at risk the careers of those applicants who do not match the organisation's strategic requirements. Attracting such candidates is simply a costly waste of time for all involved.

Strategic recruitment avoids this by locating and attracting the 'right' potential candidates to the 'right' job openings within an organisation (see figure 6.1). Such applicants form a pool from which those who most closely match the job specifications can be offered employment. Recruitment begins with identifying HR requirements and ends with receiving

A friend asks you to act as a referee for a job that involves a significant promotion. You regard your friend as unsuitable for the position.

applications. It involves determining where qualified applicants can be found (**recruitment sources**) and choosing a specific means of attracting potential employees to the organisation (**recruitment methods**). It immediately precedes the selection process and involves attracting qualified and interested candidates (from either inside or outside) who have the capacity to generate a sustainable competitive advantage for the organisation. Recruitment is a two-way process: information is given and received by both the applicants and the organisation. It is concerned both with satisfying the organisation's strategic HR requirements and with helping potential candidates decide whether they meet the job requirements, are interested in the position and want to join the organisation. Unfortunately, many HR managers forget this. Organisations that are the most satisfying to work for are also those that have the least trouble getting good candidates.[28]

Successful recruiting means clearly outlining each job, which involves job analysis (see chapter 5). Products of the job analysis process are the job description (which highlights duties and responsibilities, relationships, required know-how, accountability, authority and special circumstances) and the job or person specification (which identifies the job's human requirements in terms of qualifications, experience, skills, abilities and knowledge, and personal and special requirements).

> **Recruitment sources** Where qualified individuals are located.
>
> **Recruitment methods** The specific means by which potential employees are attracted to an organisation.

Recruitment policy

An organisation's recruitment policy provides the framework for recruiting action and reflects the organisation's recruitment objectives and culture. It details the overriding principles to be followed by management in general and by the HR manager in particular. Some items to be considered in the development of a recruitment policy include:

- EEO — will EEO (equal employment opportunity) policies be applied only where legally required or universally (for example, even in countries which have no, or only limited, EEO requirements)?
- promotion from within — will internal or external candidates be preferred?
- recruiting personnel from local, interstate or international sources
- permanent part-time and casual employment
- hiring people with disabilities
- hiring women and members of minority groups
- employees taking early or normal retirement
- employing gay and lesbian personnel
- employing relatives and friends of existing employees
- employing children domestically and internationally
- employing union/non-union members
- the balance of the emphasis on technical skills and formal qualifications and the emphasis on the values held by the applicant
- the selection of methods and media to recruit personnel — which positions will be advertised? Which will be placed with executive search firms?
- the decision about to what extent to inform applicants about the position, career opportunities, the company, its products, and so on — will the information be realistic (that is, a **realistic job preview**)? Will some subjects be glossed over?
- the decision about how and when to inform applicants about the job, the company, and so on.

These fundamental decisions must be articulated and checked to ensure that they are consistent with the organisation's strategic and HR objectives, culture and all legal requirements.

> **Realistic job preview** A method of conveying job information to an applicant in an unbiased manner, including both positive and negative factors.

Recruitment activities

Effective recruitment requires the HR manager to undertake the following actions:

- determine and categorise the organisation's long-range and short-range HR needs
- keep alert to changing conditions in the **labour market**
- develop appropriate recruitment advertisements and literature

> **Labour market** The geographical area from which employees are recruited for a particular job.

- record the number and quality of applicants from each recruiting source
- follow up on applicants to evaluate the effectiveness of the recruiting effort (see figure 6.2).[29]

Recruitment is a form of economic competition. Organisations compete with each other to identify, attract and employ qualified human resources. The proposition that 'people make the difference' means that recruitment is a key marketing tool for organisations seeking a competitive edge. The way in which the recruitment process is handled affects the organisation's image as an employer and, in turn, its ability to attract qualified people.

Given that there is often pressure to promote both the job and the organisation in the most favourable light, the HR manager must ensure that applicants do not receive misleading or inaccurate information. Failure in this task can create unrealistic expectations among candidates. In turn, this may produce job dissatisfaction, lower commitment and higher turnover.[30]

EMPLOYMENT CHECKLIST

Before beginning the hiring process, the HR manager should review and receive agreement from all involved managers on the following issues:

1. Is there a genuine need for this job to be filled? Could the work be reallocated? Is the work really necessary? Would the work be better outsourced?
2. Should the job be filled internally or externally?
3. What is the budget for filling the position? Which departments will be charged the recruitment costs?
4. What are the duties, responsibilities, reporting relationships, qualifications, experience, skills and personal qualities required? (An agreed job description and job specification are essential.)
5. What is the job size? What is the job title?
6. What salary and fringe benefits will the position attract? What are the conditions of employment? Which department/s will the payroll costs be charged to?
7. How will candidates be recruited: job posting? newspaper advertisement? executive search consultant? personnel agency?
8. What advertisement copy/layout/style will be used? Will the advertisement be prepared in-house or by an advertising agency? Who will approve the final version? Who will be responsible for placing the advertisement? Which newspapers, magazines and other communication media will be used to relay the advertisement to potential applicants?
9. Who will be involved in the recruitment and selection process? Who will conduct the interviews? Who will make the hire/reject decisions? Will psychological tests be used? Will a medical examination be required?
10. Who will handle the induction? Who will be responsible for placing the new hire on the payroll?
11. Who will give the job instructions? Who will arrange for any special training required?
12. Who will review the new hire's performance during the probation period? Who will be involved in the decision to confirm or terminate employment? Who will make the decision?

Figure 6.2 Employment checklist
Source Asia Pacific Management Co. Ltd, 2004.

Unfortunately, although research indicates that truthfulness is a key characteristic preferred by many applicants, recruiters still give general, glowing descriptions of the company rather than a balanced or honest presentation.[31] But to be effective, recruitment must satisfy the needs of the candidate as well as the needs of the organisation. 'You have to tell candidates what you have to offer as well as finding out what they can offer you', advises consultant David Reddin.[32] This is best done honestly, or the HR manager risks both the integrity of the organisation and their own status as an HR professional. Numerous research studies show that realistic job previews bring about success in improving retention, job satisfaction and performance.[33]

Recruitment methods

Internal or external recruitment?

When a job vacancy exists, the first replacement source to consider is within the organisation. Organisations such as BHP Billiton, Cathay Pacific, IBM, Lend Lease, Dow Chemical and Shell have a policy of filling vacancies through internal transfer and promotion. One early study found that almost 80 per cent of organisations filled more than half of their supervisory and managerial vacancies via internal promotion.[34] But such results are no longer so common. Downsizings, financial costs and the increased legal requirements associated with maintaining a full-time work force have motivated employers to make greater use of independent contractors, temporary workers and executive leasing.[35] As a result, despite the claimed advantages of internal promotion — improved morale, reduced orientation and training requirements, and so on — many organisations now prefer to recruit from outside their existing pool of employees.[36]

Promotion from within is not without its disadvantages. Employees who apply for jobs and are rejected can become discontented; the pool of candidates may be restricted; creativity can be stifled as a result of inbreeding; and management's time involvement and expense may be excessive (see figure 6.3). Levi Strauss management recognised that it had a major problem because of inbreeding and now mandates that one-third of all vacancies be filled by outsiders.[37]

Promotion from within Policy that gives preference to existing employees when filling a job vacancy.

Nevertheless, the advantage of internal recruitment is that management's perceptions of an employee are likely to be more accurate, thus providing a better prediction of success than information gained about external candidates. Human resources constitute an enormous investment for most organisations, and it makes economic sense to try to improve the return on this investment by making full use of the abilities of existing employees.

Internal recruitment methods

Different organisations use various methods to locate qualified internal candidates and to inform their existing employees about job vacancies. These methods include computerised record systems and job posting.

Computerised record systems

Computers have enabled the creation of databanks that contain the personal details, qualifications and work history of each employee. Such information can also be specially presented in the form of skills inventories and replacement charts. These permit the HR manager to quickly locate potential candidates within the organisation's work force. However, because it can be difficult for an HR manager to know if an employee is genuinely interested in the vacancy, job posting is often used.

Job posting

The purpose of **job posting** is to inform employees about job vacancies. The organisation may do this via bulletin boards, newsletters, personal letters or, increasingly, by computerised posting programs, which allow employees to match a job vacancy with their skills, qualifications and experience. Some multinationals, such as BP Amoco, operate global electronic job posting systems that bring a vacancy to the notice of all employees irrespective of location. Successful job posting programs have the following characteristics:

Job posting Advertising of job openings to current employees via bulletin boards, newsletters, personal letters or computerised posting programs.

1. Jobs are posted in prominent places or advertised so interested employees are likely to see them.
2. All permanent promotions and transfer opportunities are posted.
3. Job openings are posted before external recruiting is begun.
4. A job specification is included with the listing so employees can judge whether they possess the necessary knowledge, skills and abilities, formal qualifications and personal requirements.

5. The position's eligibility rules and the criteria for selection are clear. An applicant should know, for example, whether the decision will be based on seniority (that is, length of service with the employer), performance or a combination of both, and if they must fulfil minimum length-of-service requirements in the present job before applying for a promotion/transfer.

6. Once the decision is made, all applicants are informed about the decision and unsuccessful candidates are counselled as appropriate.[38]

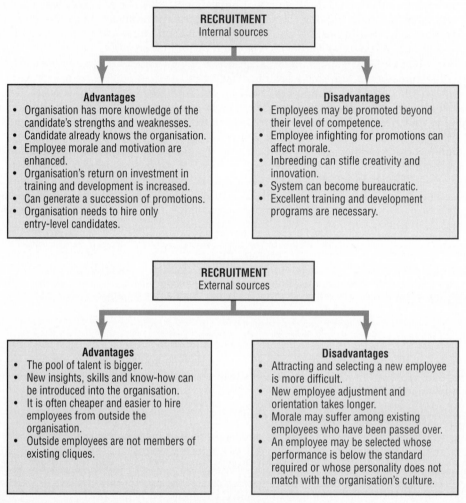

Figure 6.3 Recruitment (internal versus external sources)
Source Asia Pacific Management Co. Ltd, 2004.

External recruitment

HR departments can use various approaches to locate and attract external candidates, often looking to more than one source. Government employment agencies, private employment agencies, recruiting consultants, executive search firms, educational institutions and professional organisations are popular sources, as are advertisements, employee referrals and unsolicited applications.

To choose an approach, the HR manager must know which recruitment channel is likely to be most successful in targeting a particular labour group. An electrician, a computer specialist and a general manager will each have their own preferred recruitment channels (for example, employment agency and newspaper advertisement, the Internet, and an executive search firm, respectively).

Research on recruiting channels is mixed. Decker and Cornelius suggest that employee referrals are the best source, while newspaper advertisements and employment agencies are among the worst. Similarly, Kirnan, Farley and Geisinger found in favour of informal recruiting channels. In contrast, a study by Swaroff, Barclay and Bass found no relationship between recruitment channel and job tenure or employee productivity. The message is that each organisation should conduct its own audit of recruitment channels in terms of cost, candidate quality and ultimate performance.[39]

The state of the economy can also influence the value of a particular recruiting method. High unemployment usually means that unsolicited applications are more frequent and of better quality than they are when the labour market is tight. A situation of full employment is likely to force the HR manager to use several recruiting channels simultaneously to generate even a few qualified candidates.

Advertising

Although online recruiting is changing the way HR managers approach recruiting, advertising in local, state and national newspapers is still used by many organisations.

To be effective, an employment advertisement must have attention-grabbing headlines and applicant-friendly copy, and must specify the personal qualities, formal qualifications and knowledge, skills and abilities necessary for success. Moreover, the advertisement must enhance the image of the organisation as a good place to work (see figure 6.4).[40]

THE AIDA TECHNIQUE

AIDA stands for Attention, Interest, Desire, Action. It gives information, creates interest and stimulates replies.

Attention

An eye-catching, descriptive title is the key to getting attention. The title of the advertisement need not be the actual job title (which may not have a particularly appealing sound) but it should highlight the attractive features of the job. If needed, subtitles or the first sentence of the copy immediately following the heading can be used to expand on this theme. Attention is also gained in the first paragraph, which should be stimulating and contain much of the information about the job.

Interest

This will include some but not all of the critical points of interest such as job detail, reporting relationships and qualifications. The details should be contained in one or two paragraphs in an easy-to-read, logical style.

Desire

Having caught the attention of a reader and created interest, you want to make a special, individual and direct appeal to this prospective candidate. You do this by offering such incentives as higher status, better remuneration, more security, realistic promotional prospects, greater professionalism and more progressive employee policies. Apart from the salary, your appeal will be an emotive one.

Action

Finally, you call for action. This must be more than just giving your address or telephone number. Ask the candidate to write, *invite* him or her to telephone, *ensure* him or her of complete confidentiality. Give your name so the candidate may contact you direct.

Figure 6.4 How to create advertisements that enhance the image of the organisation as a good place to work

Source W. Parkes, *Recruiting in Australia*, Reed, Frenchs Forest, 1995, pp. 34–5.

Your company has had no success in filling a vacant position. You decide to alter the job advertisement to make the job sound more attractive than it really is.

Unfortunately, much recruitment advertising is organisation-centred, unattractive and boring to read. A survey by the Newspaper Advertising Bureau of Australia found a marked discrepancy, particularly with 'professional' recruitment, between what job applicants want to know and what organisations want to include in the advertisement.[41]

Contrary to popular opinion, studies show that prospective applicants are less concerned with the compensation package than with what they would be doing, what type of industry they would be working in, and the experience, personal characteristics and qualifications required.[42]

Research has also shown that when employers limit job-related content to promote their corporate image, the employment advertisement is less effective.[43] Mathews and Redman, as a result, recommend that less money be spent on creative visuals and more on research to identify the critical personal attributes required for success in the company.[44]

Other discrepancies exist regarding the placement of advertisements. The Newspaper Advertising Bureau of Australia survey revealed that professional applicants were less influenced by advertisements placed in the news section. In contrast, an earlier study found that advertisements placed in the news section attracted more applicants.[45]

The size of an advertisement has also been shown to have an influence on applicants' responses, particularly with professional and managerial staff. More than 75 per cent of respondents to a survey regarded larger advertisements as being positively influential.[46]

Managers, however, can be put off by the use of some words such as 'dynamic' and 'proactive'.[47] Job hunters, it seems, want hard facts not hype.[48]

Finally, there is evidence to suggest that cultural factors may help determine an advertisement's effectiveness. UK advertisements, for example, stress personal attributes such as communication skills, enthusiasm, interpersonal skills and initiative, while German advertisements emphasise technical qualifications.[49] Similarly, terms such as 'hard hitting', 'strong' and 'aggressive' may dissuade women from applying.

HR managers can write more attractive and response-evoking recruitment advertisements by following some basic guidelines:

- Critically examine the company's current advertisements. Do they stand out? Do they create the right image? How do they compare with the competition? Do they target the potential employees sought by the company?
- Specifically examine the format, design and copy of the advertisements. Are they eye-catching? Do they make creative use of borders, colour, graphics, photographs, typefaces, margins and space? Do they accurately communicate the company's culture? Do they portray the company as a preferred employer? Is the copy reader-friendly? Does it speak to the reader directly? Does it give sufficient (and accurate) information for the reader to properly evaluate the job and the company? Does it explain why employment with the company is different from and better than employment with other companies? Does it describe what the company offers in terms of compensation and benefits, career development, and so on? Does it emphasise what is unique and interesting about the job, and the company? Does it tell the reader the qualifications, skills, abilities, knowledge and personal characteristics required for success in the job? (For example, communication skills, initiative, enthusiasm, interpersonal skills, motivation, flexibility.)
- Do the advertisements make it easy for potential candidates to take action? Are a contact name, telephone number, fax number, email address and postal address included? Is confidentiality assured? Can candidates make quick enquiries?
- Critically examine employee advertisements for their consistency with the company's overall advertising and public relations programs. Are they in harmony? Does the recruitment copy reinforce existing corporate advertising and public relations programs? Prepare a style manual for HR staff and line managers to ensure consistency in format and quality.
- Monitor and evaluate the success of the advertisements. Are they attracting a sufficient number of suitable applicants? Are the advertisements cost-effective? Does the company obtain discounts for multiple advertisements?

Advantages and disadvantages of the major types of advertising media are shown in figure 6.5.

Government employment agencies

Government employment agencies Typically specialise in assisting blue-collar clerical and secretarial personnel to find employment.

Although they cover a range of job vacancies, **government employment agencies** or government-sponsored employment services such as Job Network are mostly used for clerical, sales, technical, industrial and manual positions. Eligibility for unemployment benefits typically requires people to be available for 'suitable employment', so government employment agencies can be a good source of potential candidates. However, there is evidence to suggest that many employers are frustrated with government employment agencies because they will not tolerate discrimination on the basis of age, race or sex. Private employment agencies are apparently more willing to accede to employer requests to use subjective criteria such as physical appearance.[50]

TYPE OF MEDIUM	ADVANTAGES	DISADVANTAGES	WHEN TO USE
Newspapers	• Short deadlines • Ad size flexibility • Circulation concentrated in specific geographic areas • Classified sections well organised for easy access by active job seekers • Corporate branding opportunity	• Easy for prospects to ignore • Considerable competitive clutter • Circulation not specialised — you must pay for great amount of unwanted readers • Poor printing quality	• When you want to limit recruiting to a specific area • When sufficient numbers of prospects are clustered in a specific area • When enough prospects are reading help-wanted ads to fill hiring needs
Magazines	• Specialised magazines reach pinpointed occupation categories • Ad size flexibility • High-quality printing • Prestigious editorial environment • Long life — prospects keep magazines and reread them	• Wide geographic circulation — usually cannot be used to limit recruiting to specific area • Long lead time for ad placement	• When job is specialised • When time and geographic limitations are not of utmost importance • When involved in ongoing recruiting programs
Directories	• Specialised audiences • Long life	• Not timely • Often have competitive clutter	• Only appropriate for ongoing recruiting programs
Direct mail	• Most personal form of advertising • Unlimited number of formats and amount of space • Names can be selected by geographical area, professional skills and other demographics, permitting precise targeting	• Difficult to find mailing list of prospects by occupation at home addresses • Cost for reaching each prospect is high	• If the right mailing list can be found, this is potentially the most effective medium — no other medium gives the prospect as much a feeling of being specially selected • Particularly valuable in competitive situations
Radio and television	• Difficult to ignore • Can reach prospects who are not actively looking for a job better than newspapers and magazines • Can be limited to specific geographic areas • Creatively flexible • Can dramatise employment story more effectively than printed ads • Little competitive recruitment clutter	• Only brief, uncomplicated messages are possible • Lack of permanence; prospect cannot refer back to it (repeated airings are necessary to make an impression) • Creation and production of commercials — particularly TV — can be time consuming and costly • Lack of special interest selectivity; paying for waste circulation	• In competitive situations when not enough prospects are reading your printed ads • When there are multiple job openings and there are enough prospects in a specific geographic area • When a large impact is needed quickly; a 'blitz' campaign can saturate an area in two weeks or less • Useful to call attention to printed ads
Outdoor (roadside billboards) and transit (posters on buses and subways)	• Difficult to ignore • Can reach prospects as they are literally travelling to their current jobs • Precise geographic selectivity • Reaches large numbers of people many times at a low cost	• Only very brief message is possible • Requires long lead time for preparation and must be in place for long period of time (usually one to three months)	• When there is a steady hiring need for large numbers of people that is expected to remain constant over a long period of time

(continued)

Figure 6.5 Advantages and disadvantages of the major types of advertising media

TYPE OF MEDIUM	ADVANTAGES	DISADVANTAGES	WHEN TO USE
'Point-of-purchase' (promotional materials at recruiting location)	• Calls attention to employment story at time when prospects can take some type of immediate action • Creative flexibility	• Limited usefulness; prospects must visit a recruitment location before it can be effective	• Posters, banners, brochures, audiovisual presentations at special events such as job fairs, open houses and conventions • As part of an employee referral program • At outfitting placement offices, or whenever prospects visit at organisation facilities
Internet	• Can target a global or local pool of labour • Increasingly not limited to high-tech positions • Short lead times and comparatively low cost • Job postings can target active job seekers • Banners, newsletters and email can target passive job seekers • Niche sites can target prospects with unique skills • An employment homepage can provide detailed employment information to prospects and serve as the centre of recruitment activities	• Prospects must be computer literate and/or have access to the Internet • Increasing competitive clutter • May discriminate against economically deprived social or ethnic groups and/or those who are computer illiterate	• When there is a need to attract high-tech computer literate personnel or run high-volume recruitment campaigns • When a quick response is needed • When there is a need to target a global labour pool

Figure 6.5 Advantages and disadvantages of the major types of advertising media
Source Adapted by the author from Bernard S. Hodes of Bernard Hodes Group (www.hodes.com).

Recruitment consultancies

Recruitment consultancies
Privately owned employment agencies.

Recruitment consultancies are privately owned employment agencies. Traditionally, they specialise in clerical and secretarial positions, but some have expanded their activities to include the recruitment of junior accounting, information technology, sales and technical personnel. Recruitment consultancies also differ in the range of services they offer, the professionalism of their consultants and their fees. One survey found that more than 60 per cent of client companies felt that recruitment consultants did not possess the necessary qualifications and experience.[51] A critic claims that this is not surprising because recruitment firms hire consultants for their selling skills rather than their HR expertise and use reward systems similar to those used by real estate agencies and car yards.[52]

Most reputable recruitment consultants are members of the Recruitment and Consulting Services Association. The association acts as a governing body, setting examinations and policing professional ethics. Given that membership is not compulsory and the association's powers are limited, there are still unethical and incompetent recruitment consultants in the industry.

According to one survey, employers' biggest complaint is that many consultants are 'body shops' where candidates are not screened properly.[53] Another survey showed that many companies believe that they get much less service than expected from recruitment companies.[54] A Monash University survey found that owners of small- and medium-sized businesses felt that the use of consultants was an ineffective way of recruiting.[55]

Consequently, the HR manager should exercise considerable care in selecting the services of a recruitment consultant. The importance of this is reinforced by a University of Western

Australia survey, which found that the use of agencies is not cost-effective, and a study by Harris, Toulson and Livingston, which found that recruitment consultants regularly use selection methods that are of little or no value.[56]

Fees charged by recruitment consultancies vary widely (with substantial discounts being available to large customers). A range equivalent to 2 to 12 per cent of the recruited employee's gross annual compensation (that is, base pay, allowances, superannuation and benefits) is common. It should be noted, however, that some of the more aggressive consultancies have very flexible fee structures that are open to negotiation.

Management recruitment consultants

Management recruitment consultants concentrate on advertised recruiting for professional and managerial positions. There is a myriad of firms, producing great diversity in professionalism, ethics and fee structures. This, in turn, has contributed to considerable criticism and scepticism about the use of management recruitment consultants. Unfortunately, this is often the case because anyone can work as a recruitment consultant. Consequently, some recruitment consultancies operate in a haphazard manner and have poor success rates.

> **Management recruitment consultants** Concentrate on advertised recruiting for professional and managerial positions.

Reputable management recruitment consultants have a strict code of ethics, employ qualified staff and use a systematic approach to recruitment and selection. Services that the HR manager can expect from a professional consultant include: a detailed client background study; preparation of a job description and ideal candidate profile; development of the recruitment strategy; creation of the job advertisement; candidate screening and evaluation; reference checking; and post-appointment counselling.

The advantages of using a professional recruitment consultant are:
- *Time:* management time is at a premium. Using a consultant reduces the involvement of the organisation's management in screening, interviewing, and so on.
- *Confidentiality:* business sensitivities mean that it may not be practical to advertise under the organisation's own name. The use of a consultant can ensure confidentiality. Similarly, applicants may prefer to remain unidentified to the client while they explore the details of the position and before they decide to submit a formal application.
- *Expertise:* professional management recruitment consultants possess considerable expertise in recruiting and selecting professional and managerial personnel. This can save an organisation's time and money, and reduce the chances of a failed recruiting campaign or a bad appointment.
- *Reputation:* first-class management recruitment consultants have a reputation that motivates high-calibre personnel to apply. This is of special advantage to small or unknown organisations that lack attraction on their own.

Fees range from 10 per cent to 20 per cent of the candidate's total remuneration package and are usually paid in two instalments — 50 per cent on acceptance of the assignment (or on the presentation of a short list of candidates) and 50 per cent on the successful completion of the assignment. Advertising, travel and other related expenses are added to this. Such items may be charged at cost or with a service premium added.

Executive search firms

Executive search is a technique for recruiting senior managers and professionals. Commonly called 'head-hunting', it is favoured when:
- the personnel with the required skills and experience are not known to be seeking a job change
- the number of people with the necessary qualifications and experience is limited
- maximum confidentiality is desired.

> **Executive search** Sometimes called 'head-hunting'. Executive search firms specialise in identifying top-level executives for key positions and approaching them directly.

Although surrounded in considerable mystique, the executive search process is quite straightforward. The Egon Zhender executive search process involves the following steps:
- Hold the initial client meeting to define the client problem or need.
- Confirm the proposed method, targets, timing, consultants responsible and fees.
- Conduct a systematic search through research, approaching sources in a position to comment and finding targets.
- Interview potential candidates and prepare confidential reports.

- Present candidates and check references.
- Assist with offer negotiations and follow-up.

Other leading executive search firms adopt similar approaches.[57] These firms do not often advertise, mainly because it is felt that successful managers do not read advertisements or apply for jobs.[58]

Executive search is expensive. Fees of 25–40 per cent of total remuneration are paid in three instalments: one-third in advance, followed by two scheduled payments. The fee is paid whether or not a candidate is hired. Expenses are billed separately and often are not itemised.

The high cost, along with questionable performance and conflicts of interest over the raiding of existing clients, has raised questions about the value of executive search. It is claimed that only 50–60 per cent of all searches result in the hiring of the individual who was initially specified. In effect, 40–50 per cent of the money, time and effort expended on an executive search may be wasted.[59] An *Economist* study of 300 European-based companies, for example, found more than half felt executive searches were less than 60 per cent effective. Criticisms centred on the search method itself, the poor quality of the candidates, the time taken to complete an assignment and the 'off-limits' problem (where the consultant cannot look for potential candidates inside companies that are existing clients).[60]

In spite of these criticisms, executive search is well entrenched as a means of recruiting senior personnel. The use of executive search is also booming as multinationals expand into Asia.[61] However, HR practices such as lifetime employment in Japan and the dominance of Chinese family companies and their use of *guanxi* (relationships) can create barriers that make searches in Asia both time consuming and costly.

When choosing an executive search firm, the HR manager should review the following points to ensure that the search firm is compatible with the organisation's requirements and that their conduct will be professional.

1. *Fee structure* — How is the fee charged? Will payment be in cash or equity (or a combination)? What is included and excluded? How are expenses charged? Will an itemised account be presented?[62]
2. *Parameters of the search* — What will the organisation get for its money — for example, which countries/geographic areas and which industrial sectors and companies will be covered? The details can be worked out at a subsequent meeting with the chosen firm, but it is important to be clear about this from the start to avoid later misunderstandings.
3. *Time scale* — When can the organisation expect to see candidates, and how many? When will reference checks be conducted? Reference checks ideally should be completed before short-listed candidates are presented to the client organisation. However, most search firms check references only after the candidate has been selected by the client. According to one search consultant, 'These late running reference checks are unlikely to turn up anything short of a felony, because the search consultant is already booking the search as complete'.[63]
4. *Client status* — What happens if the organisation would like some companies included in the search process that are existing clients of the search firm? Are there any conflicts of interest?
5. *Responsibility* — Who will be working on the organisation's assignment? Will there be one consultant or two? Who will do the research work, the contacting of potential candidates and the interviewing?
6. *Problems* — What happens if no candidates can be found or if the organisation considers that none is suitable? This is critical because the most common cause of client dissatisfaction is the executive search firm's failure to find a suitable candidate.[64]
7. *Off-limits rule'* — Does the search firm have an 'off-limits rule'? What is it? Will the firm recruit its own placements? Note that some search firms recruit their own placements again and again while some have 'off-limits rules' that apply for only one year, and others regard any company that is merged or sold as 'fair game'.[65]

Outplacement firms

Outplacement Special assistance given to terminated employees to help them to find jobs with other organisations.

The ongoing restructuring and downsizing of organisations have meant that **outplacement** firms such as Right Management Consultants and Thomson DBM have become valuable sources of highly qualified candidates. Outplacement firms, moreover, are cost-effective because no recruiting fee is normally charged.

Executive leasing

Executive leasing is similar to temporary help except that the focus is on supplying management and/or professional personnel. Executive Leasing and TMP eResourcing are examples of Australian international consulting firms that provide executive leasing services. Typically, such firms charge an agreed fee to the client organisation for providing the executive and for performing all the associated HR activities of recruitment, compensation, and so on. Executive leasing is flexible and cost-effective but it can present problems relating to employee loyalty and commitment.

University recruiting

To attract young professionals and management trainees, many public and private organisations recruit directly from universities and colleges. Generally, this is done via a university appointments board or careers advisory service.

Vacancies are advertised via email or on noticeboards and campus interviews are arranged. The time, expense and high labour turnover involved are major problems associated with campus recruiting: these may be partly a result of the ineffectiveness of the recruiting program. HR managers, for example, have been criticised for their poor recruiting techniques. There is also evidence that campus recruiters frequently lack sufficient knowledge of their organisation and do not use effective interview techniques.[66] Other weaknesses of the university recruiting program include an inability to use the appointments board properly, mismanagement of candidate company visits, failure to follow up, attempts to visit too many campuses, and management indecision. Correcting such deficiencies should be of primary concern for the HR manager.

Employee referrals

Recommendations made by current employees can be a useful source of applicants. Notices of vacancies with requests for referrals can be posted on the organisation's bulletin boards and internal email system. Prizes and cash bonuses may be given to employees who recommend a candidate who is subsequently hired. Deloitte Touche Tohmatsu, Pricewaterhouse-Coopers and McKinsey all give cash or other rewards for a successful referral.[67] One US software company offers a new Ferrari for the first employee who refers 10 new hires.[68]

However, the success of such an approach largely depends on the morale of existing employees, the accuracy of the job information and the closeness of the friend.[69] Major drawbacks in the use of employee referrals are that cliques may develop and referring employees may become upset if their candidate is rejected. Finally, reliance on employee referrals may be regarded as discriminatory or disruptive of EEO goals if it tends to maintain the present employee mix by nationality, race, religion and sex.[70]

Unsolicited applications

Unsolicited applications, often called 'walk ins' and 'write ins', can also be a source of qualified personnel. 'Walk ins' are people who approach the HR department seeking a job. 'Write ins' are those who submit a written enquiry about job opportunities. Neither should be ignored. Good public relations demands that all applicants be treated in a professional manner. Interestingly, the performance of 'walk ins' and 'write ins' when employed has been found to be superior to candidates recruited from placement services or newspaper advertisements.[71]

You desperately need a job. You decide to include a few 'white lies' on the application form to enhance your résumé.

Professional associations

Professional associations such as those representing accountants, engineers and HR practitioners can be good recruitment sources. Most journals of professional associations accept advertisements and some even list mini résumés of members. The big advantage of using professional associations is that the HR manager can easily target a specialised labour market. However, time lags can be a problem.

Alfred Chown *is Principal of E.L. Consult, a regional executive search and interim management provider founded in Australia in 1974. Alfred has contributed numerous articles on human resource management and is a regular writer on the subject for the* South China Morning Post.

Practitioner speaks

Leased Executives

A vast amount of commercial activity is project-oriented, yet most projects are not staffed with experts or even people highly experienced in the particular field called for by the project. Rather, most projects are undertaken by the human resources that a company has available at that given point in time. No wonder corporates experience so many cost overruns and delays in trying to achieve their objectives.

Surely the sensible thing to do when undertaking a project would be to bring on a person or people who have a track record in delivering on the type of task to be performed — not as a permanent hire but on a temporary basis — for the duration of the project.

Enter the Leased Executive or the more commonly termed Interim Manager. Leased Executives are typically experienced senior level managers with a specialist skill. On appointment, in conjunction with the company, they will establish a list of deliverables and their success will be gauged against achieving those deliverables in the designated time. As such, these individuals are highly focused and immune to the office 'politicking' that so often accompanies any new initiative or goal. From their first day on the job, they are driven to meet time scales and stated objectives. Being experienced and generally 'over' qualified for the role they undertake, they need no training period or learning curve. They simply 'roll up their sleeves' and begin work, adding value immediately.

Of great benefit too is the fact that Leased Executives attract no complex remuneration structure. Their services are supplied on a cash-only basis — no annual leave calculations, no training budget, no sick leave — they are paid only for the work they do, and once it is done, they leave — no redundancy, no long service.

Mercenary? Well yes, but as independent contractors, that is what the Leased Executive expects and wants. They do not desire a traditional employer–employee relationship; Leased Executives want the freedom to move from one company to another undertaking assignments of interest that have a definite beginning and a definite end. They aim to escape the drudgery of a permanent position with its year in, year out grind and incremental advances.

Critics point out that it is this 'footloose' feature of Executive Leasing that is its greatest disadvantage. Because the executive is employed for a short time, that same executive may not be available to return at some later point for follow-up work. Thus, the critics say, the corporation will be disadvantaged because there is no guarantee of continuity. While this point is valid, what guarantee of continuity is there with a permanent employee? They are free to resign at any time and often do. Further, what is wrong with having a new person and new input? Isn't this one way to foster innovation and change, both highly sought in the modern corporation?

Another oft-cited criticism of Executive Leasing is that by allowing a Leased Executive into your company, you run the risk of confidential information leaving the company and falling into the hands of competitors. While anything is possible, who is more likely to leak information — a Leased Executive whose next assignment, and thus way of life, is dependent on honouring all commitments including confidentiality on each and every assignment they undertake, or a permanent employee recently head-hunted by the competition?

In short, Executive Leasing offers a very viable alternative to traditional employment modes and allows corporates yet another way to better manage human capital.

Alfred Chown

Trade unions

Trade unions can be a recruiting service for certain types of labour. In industries such as coal-mining and stevedoring, unions traditionally were involved in supplying workers to employers. The union covering mineworkers in Australia, for example, previously compiled an industry list of retrenched employees from which companies had to hire.[72]

Electronic recruiting

Electronic recruiting, cybercruiting or recruiting on the Internet (and intranet for internal recruiting) present a major change to the way in which companies traditionally recruit personnel. IBM now accepts applications for its annual graduate intake online only through its own **web site**.[73] Companies can now post their vacancies by location and occupation via their own web site or online job centres. Similarly, job seekers can post their résumés and job interests (see figure 6.6).[74] Companies increasingly are accepting job applications via email and using email alert matching services to gain a direct and personalised advertising channel to targeted candidates. Web sites can avoid the problems of print deadlines, space limitations, time delays, limited exposure and high advertising costs. Companies can immediately advertise a job vacancy, 24 hours a day, seven days a week, include detailed and comprehensive information about the job and the company, reach large numbers of potential applicants and expect an almost immediate response. Candidates, in turn, enjoy the speed, accuracy and convenience of instantly seeing only those vacancies that match their requirements.[75]

Electronic recruiting Recruiting via the Internet (external) and intranet (internal). Sometimes called cybercruiting.

Web site The web address or location of an organisation; for example, the web site for BHP Billiton is www.bhpbilliton.com.

When you are job seeking online:
- Research carefully to find the right sites.
- Check whether a site belongs to a head-hunter or is a general recruitment site.
- Check that job adverts are updated regularly.
- Don't expect too much.

Before posting your résumé online:
- Check how confidentiality issues are handled at each site.
- Don't post personal details such as your address (although you may need to leave your phone number).
- Think carefully about sending your résumé, as having your résumé on too many sites can make you look desperate and probably isn't necessary.
- Re-post your résumé regularly so that it appears near the top of any search.

Figure 6.6 Checklist for job seekers looking online

Source Based on H. Johnstone, 'Job seekers turn to cyberspace', *Sunday Morning Post — Money*, 27 September 1998, p. 10.

Most criticisms of Internet recruitment centre on the need for better screening of candidates (by the recruiting web site) to avoid being swamped with irrelevant and/or poor quality applications, the need for better quality information about the candidates and the need to streamline the management response process.[76] Adrian Bell, Recruitment Manager for Mount Isa Mines (MIM), says: 'We receive applications from people all around the world and, in many cases, they are not relevant to the position. It takes time to sort through the applications for the suitable candidates.'[77]

For applicants, US data show that the odds of finding a job online are about 40 per cent for technical positions but only 5 per cent for non-technical jobs.[78] Finally, US experience suggests that most web applicants are young, white males, which may pose potential EEO problems (especially in technical fields where women and minorities tend to be underrepresented).[79]

In deciding which recruiting web site to use, Sunderland recommends the HR manager consider quantity (traffic and job volume), the quality of candidates and their online applications (as delivered by the site), and HR and back-end technical interface support.[80]

'The ability to display graphics, dynamic linking between files, and audio and video capabilities make a web site an incredibly rich source of information about an employer, its products or services, culture, sites and accompanying lifestyles, and — naturally — current openings', says Gibbon.[81] Regardless, newspapers still remain a significant recruiting source, generating 10 responses to every one from the Internet.[82] Apart from niche areas such as graduate recruitment, education and technology, older, middle and senior managers still prefer to use newspaper advertisements or recruitment consultants in their job searches.[83] This perhaps explains why many organisations remain undecided about advertising job vacancies online, preferring to stress the importance of the human element in their recruitment activity. Comments one expert: 'Recruiting requires more touch and less tech. Evaluating candidates and persuading them to accept a job offer remain interpersonal issues.'[84]

Nevertheless, recent research shows that managers are likely to job hunt via the Internet when:
- the geographical scope of the job hunt is wide
- a major pay increase is sought
- both small and large companies are being canvassed
- a facility with Internet navigation exists.[85]

NEWSBREAK

Fruit loophole puts lawyers to the test

By Annabel Day

Amanda dipped out when asked what fruit she was. 'I said I wanted to be a mango because I like mangoes, but apparently they were looking for grapes — because you worked well both in a bunch or individually.'

For Susan, it was when she was asked: 'If you had a plane ticket to anywhere in the world, where would you go and who would you have sitting next to you?' When she said Baghdad, they didn't bother asking who her travel partner was.

Yes, it's recruitment time for summer clerks in the legal profession. Thousands of elite, penultimate-year law students around the country are sweating through group interviews, cocktail parties and questions on fruity personalities — competing for a few prized positions that could set them up for life.

And all this just for 12 weeks, or in some cases three weeks, work.

For many big law firms, the recruitment of seasonal or summer clerks is the only graduate recruitment they carry out, which is why they take it so seriously.

It's why the students do as well, because those who fail to win a clerkship the first time around are often locked out of the big firms.

The director of executive search firm Russell Reynolds Associates, Graham Willis, says some of the recruitment techniques used by the firms are a way of getting around the fact that most candidates didn't yet have a track record against which they could be judged.

In addition to questions about fruit and travel, students have been asked about the last book they read or, in the case of Phillips Fox, groups of students

have to choose from a list of professionals like doctors and solicitors who they would vote off a desert island. And it goes a lot further than that.

Cocktail parties are a famous part of the clerk recruitment process. The Baker & McKenzie party in NSW is not a continuation of the interview but a chance for students to mingle with partners and lawyers and to ask questions they didn't want to ask earlier, human resources consultant Claire Storey says.

'These are the people you'll be working with, you'll spend more time with these people than with your friends and family', Storey says, so candidates had to know if they would get on with them.

But Susan says she felt she had to be 'on good behaviour' during the party.

Storey confirmed that photos taken of the candidates before the party were shown afterwards to partners and lawyers, who were asked if they had met the students and what their impressions were. But the impact of that on who was recruited was minimal, she says.

Many firms put their candidates through at least two interviews, which at Baker & McKenzie come before and after the cocktail party. The first takes place in groups of three or four with a partner and senior associate who work in the student's area of interest. There are no set questions; partners are encouraged to ask about books, travel and what candidates would do with an hour's free time. The point, Storey says, is to test 'interpersonal skills, listening skills and cultural fit'.

Only some students will proceed to the next interview.

The fruit, book and travel type of questions were part of a new trend in interviewing to ask, 'the killer question, the knock out, the one that throws them a bit', says Patrizia Anzellotti, a specialist in legal and graduate recruitment with recruitment company Robert Walters. And the answers show 'how the person thinks, how lateral they are. The fruit question is really to get to another layer of the person — how do you really see yourself?'

Gilbert + Tobin hopefuls have to give up half their weekend to attend the 'Super Saturday' recruitment extravaganza during which they are put through formal interviews, informal chats with the managing partner over a coffee, tours of the practice with graduate lawyers and either a buffet lunch or evening drinks — or both if they're really keen.

All candidates have two interviews, both with a partner and senior lawyer, which come before and after coffee with managing partner Danny Gilbert and human resources director Carmel Harrington. Over coffee the students, in groups of 14, are encouraged to ask questions following a short talk given by Gilbert. During the meeting, an 'impressionistic assessment' is made of the candidates, Harrington says.

Group interviews like this are 'a pitched battle', Willis says. 'At the end of the day it's quite unreasonable to put people competing for a role in the same situation. What are you going to do? Be collegial or try and trip up your competitors?'

But Anzellotti says the group interview identifies leaders.

Following the interviews, Gilbert + Tobin candidates attend a lunch, tour of the office and drinks, all designed to make students 'as relaxed as possible' and to give them a sense of the Gilbert + Tobin culture, Harrington says.

At lunch, partners often sit with groups of students and while there is no formal assessment going on, partners or lawyers do comment if someone they spoke to was outstanding, human resources coordinator Melissa Leslie says.

'The candidate had the opportunity to take it as far as they wanted in that setting. If they wanted to network they could', she says.

Mallesons Stephen Jaques' Melbourne practice also includes coffee with junior lawyers as part of the interview process, staff partner Jo Cameron says.

Some students suspect the informal coffees and office tours are just another chance for the firms to distinguish among candidates. During one of his interviews, Ben from Melbourne was taken on an office tour by an articled clerk who he suspects 'then reported back and gave their opinion. So if you've got like a bad attitude or something like that, then they report back.'

Willis says techniques like socialising over coffees and cocktails tend to favour 'confident, outgoing people with a stronger ego than quiet achievers', even though quiet achievers could be equally as good as lawyers.

That is the point of such settings, Anzellotti says. They relax candidates so they can 'be more themselves' and are a way of getting past students' marks 'to see who the natural allrounders are'.

'You can hire someone who's got great results ... but [the firms are] also looking for potential partners — for the future leaders of the organisation', she says.

The pressure is so high on candidates because clerkships are the single entry point into many of the top-tier — and even second-tier — firms. Gilbert + Tobin, as well as the NSW practices of Baker & McKenzie and Clayton Utz are among the firms that do not have graduate recruitment programs this year, depending solely on intake from the clerkships — 70 per cent of article clerks taken on by Mallesons Stephen Jaques' Melbourne office have been seasonal clerks, Cameron says.

Firms such as Clayton Utz are highly unlikely to hire a graduate 'just on instinct' when they've had the benefit of getting to know a clerk over 12 weeks as is the case in NSW, graduate HR consultant Jill Steele says.

So, not surprisingly, competition for a place is fierce.

Baker & McKenzie's NSW office receives some 1100 applications each year, Clayton Utz's about 1000 and this year Gilbert + Tobin received about 965. Of those firms, Baker & McKenzie take on 12 summer clerks, Clayton Utz take 20 and Gilbert + Tobin take about 14.

(continued)

In Melbourne, Mallesons Stephen Jaques have three different three-to-four-week intakes of 20 seasonal clerks for which they receive 700 to 900 applications.

Freehills' Queensland office has two four-week intakes a year, choosing eight clerks from 250 applicants.

Some of the clerkships offer students the chance to travel — clerks at Baker & McKenzie for instance go to Asia for five weeks — or to work on non-law projects such as a website for future summer clerks like the one set up by clerks at Gadens Lawyers.

The pay is not bad, usually between $500 and $700 net a week. But according to Ben, the wage has nothing to do with the clerkships' popularity.

'I'd do it for free, a lot of people would, I think, if they could. It's not really about the money, for most people it's really about the opportunity to get your foot in the door.'

So what are the firms looking for?

The first thing is marks. Without those, a CV will never get past the rubbish heap. But beyond that they want personality.

At Clayton Utz they want 'interesting' candidates.

'They've made use of their vacations, they've had really varied work experience, also during the time that they're not studying they really show motivation, they're involved in clubs and societies and they might be good at sport, good at music', Steele says.

Source *Australian Financial Review*, 19 September 2003, pp. 1, 54.

Equal employment opportunity and recruitment

Australian organisations have clear legal obligations to provide for equal employment opportunity (EEO) in the workplace. EEO legislation requires fair treatment for all members of the community and the elimination of discrimination. EEO is about merit. It means selecting the best person for the job in terms of their job-related skills. Thus, candidates should be treated fairly irrespective of differences in race, sex, religion, nationality or other non-job-related factors.

Good HRM demands that organisations have well-defined EEO objectives and policies. In turn, these must be communicated to all employees and must be clearly seen to have top management support (see chapters 4 and 19 for further discussion).

An employment agency says it is prepared to filter applicants so that your company does not appear to be using discriminatory hiring practices.

Recruitment of women

Women make up the largest group among the disadvantaged members of the work force. Although women's participation rate in the work force continues to increase, they are still predominant in the low-paid occupations. While more women are in the active work force, they face considerable time pressures if in full-time work, thus often preferring casual or part-time employment (women do four times as much housework as men, three times as much food preparation and cleaning up, and eight times as much laundry).[86]

Women, moreover, still encounter barriers to gaining highly paid positions and the numbers of women in managerial positions remain low.[87] According to federal government statistics, women make up only 24 per cent of Australia's managers and administrators. Of the more than 2000 board directorships in Australia's top 300 companies, only a little over 10 per cent are held by women.[88] Women make up only 550 of the 5500 professors, associate professors and readers in Australia. Women are also overrepresented among junior academics and those on short-term contracts or limited tenures.[89] Not surprisingly, one survey found 62 per cent of women believe it is still a man's world in the workplace.[90]

In Europe, the progress of women has been negligible, while only 61 of the 500 largest companies in the United States have (a) a woman among their top five income earners or (b) one-quarter or more of their officers who are women.[91] Seventeen of the 33 biggest companies in Hong Kong have no women directors and none has a woman chief executive. (Those women who are directors are the sister, wife or mother of the male founder.[92]) A recent Hong Kong government survey also found that men outnumber women three to one in senior management positions.[93] Says legislator, Tse Wing-ling: 'It boils down to Chinese culture. Women are indoctrinated to have low expectations of themselves.'[94] A recent Census and Statistics Department survey shows that Hong Kong men enjoy more leisure and do less housework than Hong Kong women and continue to hold traditional gender stereotypes.[95]

Working women in Japan are limited to six hours of overtime per week, are almost universally prohibited from working between 10 pm and 5 am, and are pressured to quit after they marry, have children or (if still single) reach their forties.[96] 'Whether hailing from an elite university or a finishing school', claims Craft, 'Japanese women invariably are relegated to the numbing and servile routine of tea serving, fax sending, ashtray wiping, phone answering and staple refilling. They are expected to scurry when a male co-worker demands an eraser, needs a button sewn back on or asks to have a torn sheet of paper glued back together.'[97]

Barriers encountered by women

A major barrier faced by women is stereotyped thinking.[98] Yet a study by US Army researchers revealed that women, with appropriate strength training, can load trucks, fix heavy equipment and march under the weight of a loaded backpack as well as many men.[99] Recent UK military trials have also shown that women can stand up to the rigours of combat just as well as men, which could see women being allowed into frontline infantry positions.[100] In New Zealand, female apprentice jockeys now outnumber their male counterparts.[101] Furthermore, recent US research indicates that female managers are outshining their male counterparts.[102] Women, it is claimed, think through decisions better than men, are more collaborative and seek less personal glory. Former Affirmative Action Agency Director Valerie Pratt says, 'We need to get rid of myths such as women don't make good managers'.[103]

In a US Gallup poll of both male and female workers, more female than male workers indicated that they would prefer to have a male boss. Another international survey also found an overwhelming preference among men and women for a male boss. US research indicates that capable women who are on the rise are more likely to be 'shot down' by female superiors who see them as threatening.[104] In fact, women 'do best in industries rocked by change — computers, telecommunications, financial services — because competition puts a premium on sheer talent'.[105] There are still irritations such as being called 'girls' and being referred to as 'dragons' while their equally efficient male colleagues are regarded as 'good operators'.[106]

'The issue of our time', says one feminist, 'is that women have gone through an extraordinary metamorphosis over the past three decades and what is staggering is the degree to which men haven't changed.'[107] The Chairman of Hainan Airlines, for example, explains that there are no women on the board of directors because 'If ladies too beautiful are too close to me — I will forget my work'.[108] Male government officials in China's Sichuan province likewise have been prohibited from hiring women as personal assistants or drivers in an effort to stamp out corruption. No restriction has been imposed on women cadres because there are so few in positions of authority.[109]

Glass ceiling

One invisible barrier to women rising to the top is the **glass ceiling**. This phenomenon is typically experienced when a woman attempts to move from middle management into general management. Australian women remain poorly represented in management. Less than half of Australia's top 200 companies have a woman in an executive management

Glass ceiling Occurs when people can see higher level positions but are blocked by an unseen barrier, such as discrimination.

position.[110] Research also suggests that women academics are constrained by the same glass ceiling.[111] It is argued that this is a product of male sexism, ingrained corporate thinking and women's self-doubt.[112] Recent evidence suggests that for women to climb the corporate ladder, it is necessary to have a partner who will set aside their own career so that the prime breadwinner's career can flourish.[113]

Other barriers to the advancement of women include inadequate education, poor self-image, child-rearing responsibilities and lack of childcare facilities.[114] Educators, for example, claim the preference for 'softer subjects' channels women into lower-status, lower-paid service industries.[115] According to one study, less than 12 per cent of postgraduate engineering students are women.[116] Similarly, almost 70 per cent of US adults who have access to the Internet are men.[117] A study by the University of Technology, Sydney, found that computing science is viewed as a masculine career and associated with 'geeks', high levels of mathematical competence and poor social skills. Male dominance of the computer world begins young, with research indicating that even at kindergarten, boys use aggressive behaviour to keep the computers for their own use.[118]

Glass walls

According to Alison Watkins, Group General Manager of Strategy for ANZ, 'one of the biggest issues is getting women into line roles; it is about **glass walls** as opposed to glass ceilings'.[119] These walls, it is claimed, have created 'women's ghettos' such as HR, public relations and community affairs. In Australia, 70 per cent of the most senior women are in either HR or PR, while in the United States women hold less than 7 per cent of line management positions — the profit and loss jobs that are the most common route to top management.[120] This has led to the comment that some 'businesses view women only as workhorses, well suited for demanding careers in middle management but not for prime jobs'.[121] Black, Hispanic and Asian women in the United States are even less well represented in line management than their white counterparts.[122]

Women in trades and non-traditional occupations

Women have a long history of employment in manufacturing industries. During World War II, women worked as welders, assemblers and machine operators. Despite this and recent EEO drives, only a small percentage of women enter apprenticeships and other non-traditional occupations. This is because they often face a hostile environment and a lack of support.[123]

One early study, for example, found that girls in technical schools shunned subjects taught in workshops because they 'suffer in the rigidly and aggressively masculine ethos of this environment, often experiencing paternalism, verbal and physical harassment and a sense of being unwelcome intruders'.[124] Girls have also been discouraged from seeking engineering careers by their parents and peers because there is a perception that it lacks status.[125] Similarly, girls have been advised against pursuing science and mathematics in high school because careers in these areas are regarded as a male domain.[126] Recent research highlights the importance of mentoring and summer internships in the selection of science careers by adolescent girls.[127]

Women in sales

Selling success is directly related to performance, so sales is a field in which women can demonstrate their abilities. Yet few women occupy professional sales positions. Most are found in low-status, poorly paid retailing jobs. Some are earning six-figure incomes in real estate, computers, financial services and insurance. Even so, barriers exist and few have found their sales success a springboard into senior management.[128]

Recruitment of minorities

Migrants make up one-quarter of Australia's work force. They face problems such as:
- language and cultural barriers
- lack of recognition of their qualifications

- concentration in unskilled jobs with a lack of opportunity for advancement
- high rates of unemployment.[129]

A survey of the hiring practices of Victorian employers found significant discrimination against Vietnamese and Greeks. One reason suggested was that male Greeks suffered from the concept of 'Mediterranean back', involving the perception that they make excessive workers compensation claims.[130] Another study by McAllister and Moore of the University of New South Wales found that Asians were the most disliked racial group, followed by 'blacks' and Aborigines. Islam was the most disliked religion.[131] Research by Watson found that the cultural biases of Australian managers form a barrier to people from non-English-speaking backgrounds wanting to enter management positions. However, migrants from former British colonies such as Hong Kong, India and Sri Lanka faced fewer obstacles. Managers appear to generally prefer to employ clones of themselves.[132] Asian males, in addition, suffer from the stereotyped image in Australia and the United States of being good team players but not good team leaders.[133] In Hong Kong, there is considerable prejudice against Filipinos, Indians, Nepalis, Pakistanis and mainland Chinese.[134] In one study, Hong Kong people described themselves as smart, materialistic, fashionable, diligent and efficient, and mainlanders as poor, corrupt, out of style, conservative and backward.[135] Having a dark skin in Hong Kong has caused domestic helpers to be fired, tenants to be rejected and students to be denied entrance to schools.[136]

The Letter to the Editor overleaf provides a provocative viewpoint. Do you agree? See 'What's your view?' on page 213.

Recruitment of people with disabilities

According to the Australian Bureau of Statistics, there are approximately two million Australians with a disability. It is claimed that nine out of 10 people with disabilities experience difficulty in finding work and are subjected to considerable discrimination.[137] Unemployment among vision-impaired people, for example, is at least three times higher than that of the rest of the community.[138] Some universities in Hong Kong have expressed a fear that admitting a greater number of disabled students may undermine their academic standards, while Hong Kong employers have sacked employees because of physical deformities and are reluctant to hire ex-mental patients. In mainland China, two Chinese universities refused to enrol an award-winning student on the grounds that his ugly face would scare away other students,[139] and a Shenzhen woman was rejected for a civil service position because she was too short.[140] People with a disability in Japan also face blatant discrimination.[141]

However, a US study found that employees with disabilities were more dependable, had better attendance, were more loyal and were better employees than were their counterparts without disabilities.[142] In addition, Australian and Hong Kong case studies show that people with disabilities, if matched to the right job, can bring benefits to the workplace.[143]

Recruitment of older workers

'Although older people are a major human resource', states Lansbury, 'age discrimination remains one of the most insidious forms of prejudice in Australian society.'[144] A **grey ceiling** exists with negative stereotypes prevalent. One leading management consultant remarked: 'There is a broad community view that we are all old farts at 55.'[145] Research by Snape and Redman shows that older workers experience longer periods of unemployment, get fewer job interviews and are more likely to be selected for redundancy.[146] To be aged 55 years or older and thrown out of employment can be disastrous because many companies believe that the ideal age for employees is 25–35 years.[147] In a study of the Australian labour market, Vanden Heuvel concluded that mature age workers are a clearly disadvantaged group. In Singapore, Debra found that private sector employers often retired employees when they became 55 years old, hiring younger workers in their place.[148] Age discrimination in Hong Kong, especially against women, is also rampant.[149] A recent government survey found that one in five people over 50 years of age reported being discriminated against by Hong Kong employers because of their age.[150]

Grey ceiling Occurs when people can see higher level positions but are blocked by age discrimination.

Recruiting for ethnic diversity is government social engineering

Dear Editor,

Like any manager, I appreciate the potential benefits of a diverse work force. What I dislike, however, are the subtle and not-so-subtle efforts of governments of all persuasions to pressure managers to hire people just for the sake of diversity. In my view, diversity for the sake of diversity is not just politically correct — it can potentially reduce organisational effectiveness rather than improve it. In any event, why don't political parties practise what they preach by applying EEO to their own candidate selection processes?

Certainly, recruiting a diverse work force can assist some organisations in some contexts. I have seen at first-hand how organisations like the Hotel Nikko in Sydney benefit from having a work force in which the staff can speak a total of 34 languages. Customer service levels are certainly enhanced when the staff can communicate appropriately with the diverse range of customers who stay at the Nikko. Similarly, I'm aware that Qantas Catering Services has secured over $10 million in catering contracts from other airlines by using its multicultural staff to develop menus and food preparation to meet the culinary requirements of different cultural groups.

There are problems, however, with recruiting simply for diversity's sake. For one thing, organisations that are not already diverse will have to meet the costs of adapting to a diverse work force. The costs of developing more appropriate communication systems for a plethora of English literacy levels and the costs of meeting the religious needs of some ethnic groups can be significant, particularly for small- and medium-sized businesses.

There are also philosophical problems with the push for work force diversity. On one level, governments continue to exhort organisations to employ on merit and ensure that they get the best person for the job no matter who the person is or where they're from. That's a philosophy with which I'm comfortable. On another level, however, governments virtually plead that we somehow 'weight' the applications of job applicants from non-Anglo backgrounds to ensure that they have a better chance of obtaining jobs. These philosophies are completely contradictory, and together they send mixed messages to managers everywhere. The concept of 'merit' is becoming completely twisted by government to mean anything that they want it to mean, from favouring Indigenous Australians who apply for employment to weighting the applications of returned soldiers.

There is nothing wrong with having a diverse work force. As I've said, diversity can bring benefits for many organisations, particularly those operating in a global environment seeking to meet the needs of international customers. For many small- and medium-sized enterprises, and for those organisations providing generic products and services in relatively undifferentiated markets, these benefits may be illusory at best. Any consideration of recruiting for diversity must take these differences into account, and must be tempered by the overriding consideration of employing the best person for the job, whether they're from Sydney, Singapore or Senegal.

A concerned middle manager

Source David Poole, University of Western Sydney.

Yet research by Bennington and Tharenou indicates that negative stereotypes of older workers — relating to absence, performance, memory, intelligence, ability to fit in and job satisfaction — are not true.[151] Older workers, for example, have been found to be a better recruitment investment for the call centre industry because they are more likely to remain as long-term employees with the one organisation.[152] Research also indicates that older workers are more reliable than younger workers and have a greater ability to handle complex issues.[153] Shanghai Airlines introduced a 'mature woman policy' for cabin crew, with female staff under 30 grounded. Management believes older women are more reliable and homely.[154] Other companies promoting the greater use of older workers include Alcoa, IBM and Westpac. Westpac, for example, is using mature employees to better match with its older customers.[155]

Unfortunately, older people have not received as much attention as some other disadvantaged groups. But there is a growing realisation that Australia cannot afford to have productive people leaving the work force at the present rate.[156] Regardless, the prejudiced belief, 'If you are over 45, you are over the hill', persists.[157] Disappointingly, research indicates that HR managers hold the most negative attitudes towards the employment of older workers.[158] One survey of senior executives and HR managers found that none would employ managers or executives in their fifties.[159] Worse, the over-sixties are perceived as having passed their economic use by date and as being a burden on others.[160] Not surprisingly, age discrimination in employment remains a major concern among older workers.[161]

Recruitment of Aboriginal Australians and Torres Strait Islanders

Although Aboriginal Australians and Torres Strait Islanders comprise just 1.5 per cent of the Australian population, their depressed social conditions are of national concern.[162] Aboriginal Australians are the most disadvantaged group in the Australian labour market.[163] Indigenous people have an unemployment rate four times the national average (in the Northern Territory, only one in six Aboriginal Australians has a full-time job and only one in 50 earns the average wage), their income barely exceeds two-thirds that of other workers and most are employed in less-skilled industries. Sixty per cent of male Aboriginal workers are found in production, process work, labouring, farming and fishing.[164] Aboriginal Australians also have a life expectancy that is 10 to 20 years less than that of other Australians (death rates among Aboriginals aged between 25 and 54 are up to five times higher than the rest of the population); only a one-in-four chance of completing secondary school; a twenty times greater likelihood of living in poverty; a fifteen to twenty times greater chance of being jailed (almost one-third of Aboriginal males over the age of 13 have been arrested in the past five years) and, for Aboriginal women, a thirty-three times greater chance of dying from domestic violence.[165]

Coupled with negative community images of them as 'drunken, lazy layabouts', all these issues have undermined Aboriginal Australians' confidence and dignity.[166] Research by the Australian Bureau of Statistics shows that Aboriginal Australians see their lives as being dominated by suffering, poverty, unemployment and ill health.[167] Only a small minority of Australian organisations have a formal Aboriginal employment policy.[168]

Figure 6.7 suggests some guidelines for employers in helping Aboriginal Australians starting in a new job and avoiding discrimination and prejudice.

Recruitment of gay and lesbian workers

Discrimination based on sexual orientation is a growing issue in Australia and elsewhere.[169] Although employers and employees are more willing to discuss sexual orientation and a number of organisations have non-discriminatory policies, the employment of gay and lesbian workers remains controversial.[170] The National Council of Churches, for example, requested that the Singapore government withdraw its policy of hiring gays for the civil service, arguing that gay lifestyles were 'sinful and unacceptable'.[171] The US Army recently dismissed nine linguists because they were gay.[172] However, according to one recruitment consultant, some companies are targeting gay and lesbian personnel because they tend to be highly educated, mobile and have a reputation for honesty and loyalty, as well as being conscientious, organised and well presented.[173] 'Like all forms of discrimination', says Segal, 'discrimination on account of sexual orientation usually is grounded in fear. Through training, education, clear policies and strong leadership from the top, the fear can be channeled into acceptance and understanding, the result being greater productivity and workplace fulfilment.'[174]

Transition to work

The transition from Aboriginal to non-Aboriginal society is not an easy one. The dilemma for many Aboriginal people is to determine which aspects of Aboriginal culture may be helpful in the new environment, and more importantly, which valued aspects of Aboriginal culture may be lost or threatened through the change.

The dilemma is heightened when joining the work force, where people from more traditional cultures may experience forms of culture shock.

The adjustment to a new workplace is made more difficult for Aboriginal people where little managerial support or communication is offered. Many Aboriginal employees report being left on their own in a new job, with little attempt to involve them in the work or the work group.

A problem that may impact on work time if the new employee has had to relocate to gain employment is the difficulty of finding accommodation. Aboriginal employees may find it hard to rent because of discrimination in the general community.

Discrimination and prejudice

As with all staff, supervisors need to appreciate the adjustment required when joining a new workplace. For Aboriginal employees, supervisors must also be aware of the reactions of colleagues and make an effort to eradicate any discrimination or prejudice.

Attempts at humour involving racial stereotypes may offend those who are the brunt of the joke. Supervisors should ensure that there are no instances of humorous 'put downs' and take positive action where negative insinuations are disguised as humour. While some people may be able to brush off humour, others find it offensive and demoralising.

Aboriginal employees frequently report the patronising attitudes of supervisors and other employees. Subtle inference of difference such as:

'You are OK' (implies that other Aboriginals are not)

'You can't help being Aboriginal'

'You are not really like other Aboriginal people'

are all examples of an ethnocentric attitude — 'Aboriginal people are generally less than acceptable.'

Reactions to a new workplace vary. Supervisors should be alert to reactions such as withdrawal and absenteeism, and avoid simplistic stereotypes in seeking to understand the issues. Supervisors should also be aware that Aboriginal employees may experience some difficulty contributing to discussions if they are the only Aboriginal person present.

When feeling isolated in the workplace, Aboriginal employees may seek contact with other Aboriginal employees. Unfortunately, many supervisors have restricted this contact during working hours, often resulting in further demoralisation and isolation.

Figure 6.7 Assisting Aboriginal staff
Source *Are You Employing Aboriginal Staff?*, Director of Equal Opportunity in Public Employment, Perth, Western Australia, 1996, p. 5.

Evaluation of recruitment

According to Lles and Salaman: 'Organizations tend to evaluate success of their recruitment initiatives in immediate short term ways, such as whether vacancies are filled with minimally qualified people at acceptable cost, or whether recruitment efforts produce a rise in the number of applicants.'[175] Measures of effectiveness, such as the quality of applicants and those who accept a job offer, are often ignored. Similarly, measures of efficiency, such as the acceptance-to-offer ratio and the cost per applicant are also rarely evaluated.[176] Research suggests that less than one-quarter of companies calculate the costs of executive recruitment, with even fewer bothering to calculate the cost of executive turnover.[177]

Philips recommends that assessment of recruitment activity focus on:

• *Productivity:* this measures the number of applicants generated by a particular recruitment source or method. Specific measures include:
  – applications per recruiting source/method
  – applicants interviewed per recruiting source/method
  – applicants selected per recruiting source/method.
• *Quality:* this measures the on-the-job performance and tenure of employees recruited using a particular source or method. Specific measures include:

- employee performance ratings by recruiting source/method
- early turnover (for example, first three months) by recruiting source/method
- tenure by recruiting source/method
- applications per candidate hired for a recruiting source/method.

- *Costs:* costs include advertising expenditure, employment agency and executive search firm fees, applicant and staff travel, and interviewer/s' remuneration. A specific measure is cost per applicant per recruiting source/method.
- *Time:* time is important in recruitment, especially for critical positions that must be filled quickly or in highly competitive labour markets. A specific measure is response time — that is, the time from when the recruiting action is initiated until an application is received.
- *Soft data:* soft data focus on the applicants' and management's satisfaction with the recruiting method/s employed. Specific measures include:
  - applicants' satisfaction with a particular recruiting method
  - applicants' reasons for applying to the organisation
  - line managers' satisfaction with a particular recruiting method.[178]

Evaluation of the recruitment activity is important for meeting strategic business objectives, controlling costs, satisfying EEO objectives and improving recruitment performance.

A recruitment consultancy that you have selected for a large assignment invites you to an all-expenses-paid HR conference in Hawaii.

Summary

Recruitment is the process of locating and attracting qualified candidates for job vacancies within an organisation. It is a form of business competition. To achieve their strategic business objectives, organisations require candidates with the appropriate knowledge, skills, abilities and personal qualities. Thus, the job to be filled must be identified and precisely defined.

Next, the type of candidate required must be specified. Potential candidates have to be made aware of job vacancies. This can involve a number of methods such as advertising or using consultants, educational institutions and professional associations.

EEO legislation requires organisations to eliminate discriminatory recruiting practices and to take specific action to ensure that disadvantaged groups are given fair access to job opportunities. Organisations that are regarded as good employers have the least trouble attracting high-quality candidates.

Evaluation of the recruitment activity is necessary to ensure that the organisation is meeting its strategic business objectives, containing costs, satisfying EEO objectives and improving recruitment efficiency and effectiveness.

Thirty interactive Wiley Web Questions are available to test your understanding of this chapter at
www.johnwiley.com.au/ highered/hrm5e
in the student resources area

terms to know

electronic recruiting (p. 201)

executive search (p. 197)

glass ceiling (p. 205)

glass walls (p. 206)

government employment agencies (p. 194)

grey ceiling (p. 207)

job posting (p. 191)

labour market (p. 189)

management recruitment consultants (p. 197)

outplacement (p. 198)

promotion from within (p. 191)

realistic job preview (p. 189)

recruitment (p. 187)

recruitment consultancies (p. 196)

recruitment methods (p. 189)

recruitment sources (p. 189)

selection (p.187)

strategic recruitment (p. 187)

web site (p. 201)

review questions

1. What are the advantages and disadvantages of internal and external recruitment?
2. How appropriate is Internet recruitment for (a) graduate trainees, (b) plant operators and (c) senior managers?
3. How can an organisation change its recruitment activities to improve employee diversity?
4. What role do line managers play in the recruitment process? Describe the advantages and disadvantages of utilising line managers in the recruitment process and provide examples.
5. What are the arguments for and against stating the compensation and benefits in a job advertisement for (a) a graduate trainee, (b) an electrician and (c) a general manager?
6. How would you evaluate a firm's recruitment activity? Why is evaluation important?
7. Explain what is meant by 'strategic recruitment'. Give practical examples to illustrate your answer.
8. What is the role of (a) a job description and (b) a person specification in recruitment?
9. What role should the HR department play in recruitment?
10. What arguments would you use to persuade top management that an executive search firm (head-hunter) should or should not be retained to recruit a new divisional general manager?

environmental influences on recruitment

Discuss the key environmental influences from the model (figure 6.8 shown opposite) that have significance for employee recruitment.

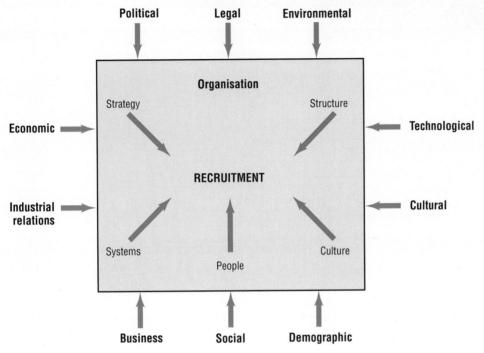

Figure 6.8 Environmental influences on recruitment

class debate

Women should be allowed to serve in active combat roles in the military.

what's your view?

Write a 500-word response to the Letter to the Editor on page 208, agreeing or disagreeing with the writer's point of view.

practitioner speaks

Read the article 'Leased Executives' on page 200. As a class, critically discuss the advantages and disadvantages of executive leasing from the point of view of (a) the organisation and (b) the individual.

newsbreak exercise

Read the Newsbreak 'Fruit loophole puts lawyers to the test' on pages 202–4. As a class, critically review the approaches to recruitment and selection described. If you were an applicant, how would you feel?

What do you think? Conduct a mini survey of class members, using the questionnaire below. Critically discuss the findings.

1.	EEO policies should be applied only when legally necessary.	YES	NO
2.	Recruiting activities should be outsourced.	YES	NO
3.	Promotion from within is best.	YES	NO
4.	The Internet is the best way to recruit.	YES	NO
5.	It is socially acceptable to lie on an application form.	YES	NO
6.	It is critical that compensation details be shown in an employment advertisement.	YES	NO

online exercise

Select a company web site from the list shown in appendix B on page 852. Evaluate the site as a recruiting tool. Identify its strengths and weakness. Write a 300-word report on how you would make the site more effective (and attractive).

ethical dilemma

A matter of restricted recruitment

Sachin Meta looked at the President of Asia Industries. Sitting across the highly polished mahogany table of the boardroom, Justin Whiterow was an imposing figure. Tall, hard and about 60 years old, Whiterow had commenced his career working for an international construction company. While still in his 20s he had established a property development company. From this small beginning, he had built a company with interests in property, tourism and hotels and with an annual turnover in excess of $2 billion.

Sachin tried to focus as Justin Whiterow spoke. 'Mr Meta, I have heard some excellent things about you. I look forward to having you work with us.' Sachin nodded and smiled.

Obviously, things had progressed even further than he had been led to believe by Amy Tran, HR Director and Whiterow's personal assistant. She had simply asked him to meet with Whiterow to discuss the possibility of undertaking an executive search assignment. But Whiterow was speaking as if he already had the job. Sachin hoped it was the case. Business had been depressed for almost a year and his firm was on the verge of bankruptcy.

'Mr Meta, Amy may not have mentioned this, but we are looking to fill eight senior positions. The first is President of a new construction company we are establishing in Indonesia. If you can handle this assignment to my satisfaction, Amy will give you the details of the rest.'

Amy Tran smiled. 'Mr Meta, the minimum package we are offering for each of these positions is $300 000 — so you can see this is a major assignment.'

'Yes, I can see that', replied Sachin. A quick calculation indicated fees well in excess of $700 000. Sachin was overwhelmed. He was saved.

'There is one thing, Mr Meta.' Whiterow looked directly at him. 'Yes, Mr Whiterow, what is that?' asked Sachin. Whiterow waited a few seconds then said, 'The President of our Indonesian operations cannot be an ethnic Chinese or a woman.' Sachin was stunned. 'But you must be aware that such restrictions are discriminatory?'

'Mr Meta, Indonesia is Indonesia. It's not my country. I'm going there to do business, not to teach Indonesians about equal opportunity. The success of this business depends a great deal on our relationships with local officials and I am not going to have it jeopardised. We are guests in their country. What right do we have to impose our values on them? Moreover, Mr Meta, this is my company. I built it from nothing. I own every share. I will not have you or some bureaucrat in Canberra telling me who I can and cannot employ. It is not the government's money, it is mine and I will spend it as I please. Do I tell you which doctor to consult or what products to buy when you go to the supermarket? No, I do not. So please don't tell me how to spend my money. Now Mr Meta, do you want the assignment or not?'

Sachin was silent for a moment then replied, 'Mr Whiterow . . .'

Discussion questions

1. If you were Sachin, how would you respond?
2. Do you regard Justin Whiterow's demands as reasonable? Explain your reasoning?
3. What are the possible legal consequences of Justin Whiterow's approach?
4. Should one country's attitudes to equal opportunity be 'exported' to another country where differing cultural, social, religious or political values apply?
5. If Sachin accepted the assignment, would you regard his decision as ethical? Explain your answer.

case study

Cabin crew for Jet Red

'So, we're all agreed', said Alan Balkin, Managing Director of Jet Red. 'We need to change.'

Stan Vines, Marketing Manager, leant forward. 'Alan, it's imperative. We're losing market share. The competition is killing us. We're seen as a safe but boring way to fly. Our in-flight service at best is average, and our crew are seen as surly and not service-oriented. We're just not competitive.'

'I agree with Stan', growled Operations Manager, Bill Armstrong. 'Our present crew are not with it — they're too old. They don't present a modern image. We need people who are young, attractive, cheerful and dynamic. If we're going to turn around this airline, we need to do something. Some of the male crew look like absolute slobs with their beer guts and some of the women have backsides the size of a barn! It's no wonder we can't compete with Virgin and Singapore. Their crews are attractive, cheerful and service-oriented. As a passenger, you get greeted with a smile, not a snarl.'

'It seems to me', snapped Linda Church, HR Manager, 'that this sorry state of affairs is a reflection of our bad management!'

'For heaven's sake, Linda. We're trying to run a business, not a social welfare organisation. Face reality, customers prefer to be served by young, attractive crew. Our competition realises that. Listen to what Malaysia Airlines corporate services senior general manager, Mohammadon Abdulla, was reported as saying: "Customers prefer to be served by young, demure and pretty stewardesses, especially Asian ladies."[179] Who wants to be served by a bunch of ageing couch potatoes and old boilers?'

'I can't believe you said that!' snapped Linda. 'What you are saying is so blatantly discriminatory that it's not funny.'

'It's not just me Linda. Look at this newspaper clipping. The writer makes it clear what passengers want.'

'What does it say?' questioned Alan.

'To quote', smiled Bill, 'a charming face with a captivating smile has a more positive impact than a wrinkled face with a forced smile.'[180]

'Really Bill, you're being ridiculous', sighed Linda.

'Please, let's remain focused', Alan interrupted. 'We have a problem and we have to do something. We're losing market share and money. We can't continue with the old ways or we'll be out of business. Now, what do you suggest?'

'Hire all new cabin crew', enthused Stan.

'I'm prepared to explore the option, Stan, but it seems to me that Linda has raised some valid objections', responded Alan. 'Linda?' questioned Alan.

'Alright, I'll go along with the exercise. But first we need to clearly define the type of people we need.'

'Well, if our aim is to be the fastest-growing, most profitable airline in the Asia–Pacific region, that means we need people who are motivated and have a strong service orientation. They must fit with our image as a young, dynamic, "with it" Australian airline that has an international outlook and is going places', said Stan.

'So, we are the young, confident, progressive airline that proclaims its "Australianness" but at the same time communicates its cultural diversity', said Alan. 'Mmm, sounds interesting. You three get together and articulate the specific qualities we should look for and identify where we are going to find such people', requested Alan.

Discussion questions

1. As a class, critically review the points raised. Which do you agree with? Which do you disagree with? Why?
2. Form into groups of four to six. Imagine you are Jet Red's executive team.
   (a) Define the experience, qualifications, know-how, personal qualities and any special requirements for the new cabin crew to be recruited.
   (b) Outline the recruiting action you plan to take to attract a pool of suitably qualified applicants. Use the recruitment grid shown below to illustrate your action plans.

   Regroup as a class and discuss your recommendations.

VACANT POSITIONS				
Recruiting medium and source of employees	Blue collar	Office/clerical	Professional/technical	Executive/managerial
High schools				
Colleges, TAFEs				
Universities				
Professional associations				
Competitors				
Other firms				
Overseas				
Private employment agencies				
Government employment agencies				
Executive search firms				
Unsolicited applications				
Employee referrals				
Applications on file				
Temporary help				
Summer interns				
Former employees				
Existing employees				
Employee leasing				
Newspaper advertisements				
Magazines				
Direct mail				
Radio/TV				
Job fairs				
Internet				
Trade unions				
Military				
Personal contacts				

practical exercises

1. Form into groups of three to four.
   (a) Review the employment section of a major daily newspaper and identify two advertisements that you regard as effective and two that are ineffective. Explain your selections.
   (b) Select a job in an industry that you are familiar with and prepare the copy and layout of an advertisement for the job for publication. Pass your group's completed advertisement to another group for critical review. Use the advertisement rating grid below to help you (1 means NO, 3 means MAYBE, 5 means YES).

ADVERTISEMENT RATING GRID					
	1	2	3	4	5
Attention getting					
Eye-catching title					
Creates interest					
Gives sufficient information about:					
Job duties and responsibilities					
Prospects					
Rewards					
Qualifications required					
The company					
Location					
Makes it easy for the candidate to take action					
Uses space effectively					
Makes attractive use of colour					
Uses attractive typeface					
Has attractive graphics					
Has an attractive border					
Is an appropriate size					
Creates a strong positive image of the company					
Satisfies EEO requirements					
Presents a distinctive corporate image likely to persuade good candidates to apply					

2. Form into groups of four to six. Imagine that you are part of a management group given the task of writing a recruitment policy for your organisation. Identify the items you plan to include and prepare a policy statement. Regroup as a class and review your policy statements.

suggested readings

Beardwell, I. and Holden, L., *Human Resource Management*, Financial Times/Prentice Hall, London, 2001, ch. 6.

CCH, *Australian Master Human Resource Guide*, CCH, Sydney, 2003, ch. 10.

Compton, R. L., Morrissey, W. J. and Nankervis, A. R., *Effective Recruitment and Selection Practices*, CCH, Sydney, 2002, chs 2, 4, 5, 10, 13.

De Cieri, H. and Kramar, R., *Human Resource Management in Australia*, McGraw-Hill, Sydney, 2003, ch. 6.

Fisher, C. D., Schoenfeldt, L. F. and Shaw, J. B., *Human Resource Management*, 5th edn, Houghton Mifflin, Boston, 2003, chs 5, 6.

Ivancevich, J. M., *Human Resource Management*, 8th edn, McGraw-Hill, Boston, 2001, ch. 7.

Ivancevich, J. M. and Lee, S. H., *Human Resource Management in Asia*, McGraw-Hill, Singapore, 2002, ch. 5.

Mondy, R. W., Noe, R. M. and Premeaux, S. R., *Human Resource Management,* 8th edn, Prentice Hall, Upper Saddle River, NJ, 2002, ch. 5.

Nankervis, A. R., Compton, R. L. and Baird, M., *Strategic Human Resource Management*, 4th edn, Nelson, Melbourne, 2002, chs 5, 7.

online references

jobsearch.dewrsb.gov.au
www.adcorp.au
www.airsdirectory.com
www.ambition.com.au
www.asia.jobpilot.net
www.asiaxpat.com
www.careerbuilder.com
www.careermosaic.com
www.careerpath.com
www.careertimes.com.hk
www.deetya.gov.au
www.employment.com.au
www.erecruiting.com.au
www.execunet.com
www.headhunter.net
www.HotJobs.com.au
www.jobsbank.com.sg
www.jobsdb.com

www.kfselection.com
www.monster.com.au
www.monster.com.hk
www.monster.com.sg
www.newsemployment.com.au
www.positionsvacant.com.au
www.recruitasia.com
www.recruitersonline.com.au
www.researchmatters.net
www.resumenetwork.com.au
www.seek.com.au
www.shrm.org.hrmagazine
www.staffsure.com.au
www.vault.com
www.versantsolutions.com
www.work.asn.au
www.workforceonline.com

end notes

1. E. A. Ensler, T. R. Nielson and E. Grant-Vallone, 'Tales from the hiring line: effects of the Internet and technology on HR processes', *Organizational Dynamics*, vol. 31, no. 3, 2002, p. 226.

2. 'The top HR issues of 2000', *HR Focus*, April 2000, p. 1.

3. N. Way, 'Talent war', *Business Review Weekly*, 18 August 2000, pp. 64–70; and T. Thomas, 'The battle for talent', *Business Review Weekly*, 12 April 2001, pp. 72–3.

4. P. Lles and G. Salaman, 'Recruitment, selection and assessment', in J. Storey (ed.), *Human Resource Management. A Critical Text*, Routledge, London, 1995, p. 206.

5. A. Sherry, 'Put some branding iron into your image', *Business Review Weekly*, 21 July 2000, p. 66; R. Lawrence, 'Employers R. us', *HR Monthly*, February 2001, pp. 48–51; and P. Lyons, 'Employers with a "brand name" got the better staff', *South China Morning Post — Classifieds*, 21 June 2003, p. 1.

6. J. McClurg and A. Hall, 'Strong branding boosts organization image', *HR Monthly*, May 1998, p. 36.

7. A. Sherry, op. cit., p. 66.

8. D. Allen, 'Recruitment management: finding the right fit', *HR Focus*, April 1995, p. 15.

9. I. Beardwell and L. Holden, *Human Resource Management*, 3rd edn. Financial Times/Prentice Hall, London, 2001, p. 225.

10. P. Boxhall and J. Purcell, *Strategy and Human Resource Management*, Palgrave Macmillan, Basingstoke, Hants, 2003, p. 142.

11. Reported in J. C. Collins and J. I. Porras, 'Building your own company's vision', *Harvard Business Review*, September–October 1996, p. 69.

12. J. C. Collins and J. I. Porras, op. cit., p. 72.

13. J. C. Collins and J. I. Porras, op. cit., p. 68.

14. A. Campbell, 'Letter to the Editor', *Australian Financial Review*, 8 January 2004, p. 44.

15. A. Tsukada, 'Outlook', *Asian Business*, April 1996, p. 68.

16. P. Lles and G. Salaman, op. cit., p. 207.

17. M. Gardner and G. Palmer, *Employment Relations*, 2nd edn, Macmillan, Melbourne, 1997, p. 272.

18. Reported in J. Storey and K. Sisson, *Managing Human Resources and Industrial Relations*, Open University Press, Buckingham, 1993, p. 111.

19. Reported in K. Legge, *Human Resource Management*, Macmillan, London, 1995, pp. 232–3.

20. A. McLaughlin, quoted in Staff Writer, 'Pret's hunger for quality starts with staff recruitment', *South China Morning Post — Classifieds*, 31 May 2003, p. 24.

21. Quoted in J. Eastway, 'Quantum leaps in service for the flying Kangaroo', *Business Review Weekly*, 22 October 1999, p. 12.

22. Hong Kong Baptist University survey reported in P. Hui, 'Attitude, not background, gives teachers top marks', *South China Morning Post*, 14 October 2003, p. C4.

23. Anonymous reviewer, November 2003.

24. J. Storey, *Developments in the Management of Human Resources*, Blackwell, Oxford, 1992, pp. 98–100; J. A. Byrne 'The search for the young and gifted', *Business Week*, 4 October 1999, pp. 64–8; and E. Hoffman, *Psychological Testing at Work*, McGraw-Hill, New York, 2002, p. 6.

25. K. Legge, op. cit., p. 233.

26. B. Townley, *Reframing Human Resource Management*, Sage, London, 1994, p. 98; B. Townley, 'Selection and appraisal: reconstituting social relations?', in J. Storey (ed.), *New Perspectives on Human Resource Management*, Routledge, London, 1992, p. 96; and J. Storey, *Developments in the Management of Human Resources*, Blackwell, Oxford, 1992, p. 100.

27. A. Day, 'Job applicants go psycho when put to the test', *Australian Financial Review*, 31 December 2003–1 January 2004, p. 5.

28. B. Schneider and N. Schmitt, *Staffing Organizations*, 2nd edn, Waveland Press, Ill., 1992, p. 170.

29. R. L. Mathis and J. H. Jackson, *Personnel/Human Resource Management: Contemporary Perspectives and Applications*, 6th edn, West Publishing, St Paul, 1991, p. 189.

30. S. L. Premack and J. P. Wanous, 'A meta analysis of realistic job review experiments', *Journal of Applied Psychology*, vol. 70, 1985, pp. 706–19; and J. M. Ivancevich, *Human Resource Management*, 8th edn, McGraw-Hill, Boston, 2001, pp. 199–200.

31. J. M. Ivancevich, op. cit., pp. 199–200.

32. D. Reddin, quoted in C. Rance, 'Sell to get the best staff', *Age Employment Section*, 7 May 1988, p. 1.

33. B. Schneider and N. Schmitt, op. cit., pp. 162–4.

34. J. H. Sweeney and K. S. Teel, 'A new look at promotion from within', *Personnel Journal*, August 1979, pp. 531–5.

35. R. L. Mathis and J. H. Jackson, *Human Resource Management*, 8th edn, West Publishing, St Paul, 1997, p. 220; and J. Burgess, 'Workforce casualisation in Australia', *Journal of International Employment Relations Review*, vol. 2, no. 1, 1996, pp. 33–54.

36. J. A. Byrne, J. Reingold and R. A. Melcher, 'Wanted: a few good CEOs', *Business Week*, 11 August 1997, pp. 38–42.

37. N. Mink, 'How Levi's trashed a great American brand', *Fortune*, 12 April 2000. p. 42.

38. D. J. Cherrington, *The Management of Human Resources*, 4th edn, Prentice Hall, Englewood Cliffs, NJ, 1995, p. 203.

39. P. J. Decker and E. T. Cornelius, 'A note on recruiting sources and job survival rates', *Journal of Applied Psychology*, vol. 64, 1979, pp. 463–4; J. P. Kirnan, J. A. Farley and K. F. Geisinger, 'The relationship between recruiting source, applicant quality, and hire performance: an analysis by sex, ethnicity, and age', *Personnel Psychology*, vol. 42, no. 2, 1989, pp. 293–308; and P. G. Swaroff, L. A. Barclay and A. R. Bass, 'Recruiting sources: another look', *Journal of Applied Psychology*, vol. 70, no. 4, 1985, pp. 720–8.

40. K. Smith, 'Colour and creativity feature in world's best ads', *HR Monthly*, May 1998, p. 39.

41. Reported in 'Recruitment advertising in Australia', *Armstrong's Recruitment Review*, March 1990, p. 1.

42. 'Content of recruitment advertisements', *Armstrong's Recruitment Review*, March 1990, p. 1; and B. P. Mathews and T. Redman, 'Getting personal in personnel recruitment', *Employee Relations*, vol. 18, no. 1, 1996, p. 68.

43. 'Content of recruitment advertisements', *Armstrong's Recruitment Review*, March 1990, p. 1.

44. B. P. Mathews and T. Redman, op. cit., p. 76.

45. C. D. Fyock, 'New ways to say "help wanted"', *Personnel Administrator*, March 1988, p. 100.

46. Reported in 'Recruitment advertising in Australia', *Armstrong's Recruitment Review*, March 1990, p. 1.

47. B. P. Mathews and T. Redman, op. cit., p. 76.

48. 'Job hunters want facts not hype, survey finds', *HR Monthly*, May 1991, p. 25.

49. B. P. Mathews and T. Redman, op. cit., p. 69.

50. J. Foreshew, 'Bosses prefer breasts to skill', *Australian*, 14 July 1994, p. 3. For further details, see P. Boresham, A. Roan and G. Whitehouse, *Privatisation of Labour Market Policy: The Role of Employment Agencies*, Department of Government, University of Queensland, Brisbane, 1994.

51. G. Penna, 'Recruitment firms, are they delivering?', *HR Monthly*, December 2002, p. 34.

52. G. Penna, op. cit., pp. 34–5.

53. Reported in J. McBeth, 'Body Shop approach discredits recruiters', *Business Review Weekly*, 14 July 1989, p. 89.

54. G. Penna, op. cit., p. 34.

55. 'The best and worst ways to get good staff', *Business Review Weekly*, 11 July 1994, pp. 54–5; and M. Darke, 'The recruitment industry — buyer beware', *HR Monthly*, April 2000, p. 53.

56. Study by C. Mulvey and C. Short reported in M. Abbott, 'Professional headhunting costs health industry', *Australian Financial Review*, 10 November 1989, pp. 46–7; and N. J. Harris, P. K. Toulson and E. M. Livingston, 'New Zealand personnel consultants and the selection process', *Asia Pacific Journal of Human Resources*, vol. 34, no. 2, 1996, pp. 71–87.

57. G. Hines, 'Search process now fills most executive jobs', *HR Monthly*, September 1996, p. 22.

58. J. Gagliardi, 'Thrill of the hunt', *South China Morning Post — Features*, 20 April 2001, pp. 1–2.

59. T. J. Hutton, 'Increasing the odds for successful searches', *Personnel Journal*, September 1987, p. 140.

60. *Financial Times*, 'Headhunters in Europe fail to deliver, poll finds', *Australian Financial Review*, 2 February 1990, p. 42.

61. J. Dobrzynski, 'Executive 'head hunters' busier in US', *South China Morning Post — Business*, 10 March 1997, p. 6.

62. For a detailed discussion of fees, see N. Tabakoff, 'Headhunters become the hunted', *Business Review Weekly*, 10 March 2000, pp. 80–4.

63. W. G. Hetzel, 'Negotiate up front when using search firms', *HR Magazine*, October 1996, p. 64.

64. D. James, 'What firms want from headhunters', *Business Review Weekly*, 7 February 1994, p. 57.

65. W. G. Hetzel, op. cit., pp. 62–6; and B. Pavlik, 'Recruiting a recruiter: seven steps to success', *HR Focus*, September 1998, pp. 513–14.

66. J. M. Ivancevich, op. cit., pp. 198–9.

67. A. Fabro, 'In-house staff good bait for the big fish', *Australian Financial Review*, 17 November 2000, p. 48.

68. D. Leonard, 'They're coming to take you away', *Fortune*, 29 May 2000, pp. 41–54.

69. J. P. Kirnan, J. A. Farley and K. F. Geisinger, op. cit., pp. 293–308.

70. J. P. Kirnan, J. A. Farley and K. F. Geisinger, op. cit., p. 306; and K. Tyler, 'Employees can help recruit new talent', *HR Magazine*, September 1996, pp. 57–60.

71. J. A. Breaugh, 'Relationship between recruiting sources and employee performance, absenteeism and work attitudes', *Academy of Management Journal*, vol. 24, no. 1, 1981, p. 145.

72. P. Maher, 'Coal strike sparks reform tussle', *Bulletin*, 28 September 1993, p. 69.

73. T. Roussety, 'How have online recruitment technologies affected your recruitment activities?', *HR Monthly*, December 2000, p. 9.

74. More than 200 000 Australians posted their CVs online in 2000. K. Sunderland, 'The rise and rise of e-recruitment', *HR Monthly*, December 2000, pp. 34–41.

75. P. Bassat, 'Logged on', *HR Monthly*, December 2000, pp. 42–4; and K. Sunderland, op. cit., p. 35.

76. K. McCormick, 'On line recruitment: how connected are you?', *Human Resources*, October 1999, p. 18; and S. D. Wildstrom, 'Wanted: better job listings', *Business Week*, 20 September 1999, p. 10.

77. A. Bell, quoted in G. Bryant, 'Now for a real jobs network', *Business Review Weekly*, 25 June 1999, p. 118.

78. H. G. Heneman III, T. A. Judge and R. L. Heneman, *Staffing Organizations*, 3rd edn, McGraw-Hill, Boston, 2000, p. 287.

79. H. G. Heneman III, T. A. Judge and R. L. Heneman, op. cit., p. 288.

80. K. Sunderland, op. cit., p. 36.

81. T. Gibbon, 'Superhighway going through!', *HR Monthly*, May 1995, p. 18.

82. N. Jones, 'People look where the jobs are — in the newspaper (still)', *HR Monthly*, May 1996, p. 19.

83. P. Allen and J. Pillinger, 'From evolution to brewing internet revolution', *HR Monthly*, May 1996, p. 23; N. Jones, op. cit., pp. 18–19; S. Jones, 'Hands on', *HR Monthly*, December 2000, pp. 43–5; and M. Wooden and D. Harding, 'Recruitment practices in the private sector: results from a national survey of employers', *Asia Pacific Journal of Human Resources*, vol. 36, no. 2, 1998, pp. 73–87.

84. R. Fein, 'Traditional or electronic tools: how do people get hired?', *Journal of Career Planning and Employment*, vol. 58, no. 4, 1998, p. 43.

85. D. C. Feldman and B. S. Klass, 'Internet job hunting: A field study of applicant experiences with on line recruiting', *Human Resource Management*, vol. 41, no. 2, 2002, p. 175.

86. Reported in 'The Bulletin snapshot', *Bulletin*, June 1993, p. 38.

87. T. Vilkinas, 'Poor educational access slows women's climb into senior jobs', *HR Monthly*, October 1995, pp. 20–1.

88. S. Long, 'Still no cracks in glass ceiling', *Australian Financial Review*, 29 March 2000, p. 3.

89. I. Moses, 'Where are the women?', *Campus Review*, 26 October–1 November 1995, p. 11.

90. Morgan and Banks Ltd, 'It's still a man's world', *Recruitment Journal*, June 2000, p. 26.

91. P. Dwyer, M. Johnston and K. Lowry Miller, 'Europe's corporate women', *Business Week*, 15 April 1996, pp. 40–2; and L. Bernier, 'Out of the typing pool into career limbo', *Business Week*, 15 April 1996, pp. 43–6.

92. *South China Morning Post* survey reported in G. Manuel, 'Women at the top prove thin on the ground', *Sunday Morning Post*, 27 December 1996, p. 3.

93. Women's Commission Survey reported in S. Schwartz, 'Top jobs still prove elusive to women', *South China Morning Post*, 19 November 2002, p. 6.

94. Quoted in G. Manuel, op. cit., p. 3.

95. Reported in P. Moy, 'Housework — it's a woman's job say HK males', *South China Morning Post*, 30 August 2003, p. C1.

96. Workplace equality still coming in Japan', *International HR Update*, November 1996, p. 3; and N. Wasson, 'Equality elusive in Japan's offices', *Hong Kong Standard*, 19 December 1995, p. 13.

97. L. Craft, 'Honour thy office lady', *Asian Wall Street Journal*, 27 May 1996, p. 8.

98. E. P. Kelly, A. O. Young and L. S. Clark, 'Sex stereotyping in the workplace: a management's guide', *Business Horizons*, vol. 36, no. 2, 1993, pp. 24–9; and V. E. Schein, R. Mueller, T. Lituchy and J. Liu, 'Think manager — think male: a global phenomenon?', *Journal of Organizational Behavior*, vol. 17, no. 1, 1996, pp. 33–41.

99. Reported in Associated Press, 'Women able to compete in military', *Eastern Express*, 31 January 1996, p. 8. See T. J. Robertson, 'Gender cooperation, an organizational advantage', *Asia Pacific Journal of Human Resources*, vol. 33, no. 1, 1995, pp. 1–21.

100. Reported in 'Tests show women ready for combat', *South China Morning Post*, 26 December 2000, p. 7.

101. 'Changing scene in NZ', *Straits Times*, 25 July 1996, p. 46.

102. R. Sharpe, 'As leaders, women rule', *Business Week*, 27 November 2000, pp. 104, A2–A11; and R. Sharpe, 'Women bosses: greatness is still not good enough', *Australian Financial Review*, 20 November 2000, pp. 28–9.

103. Quoted in S. Plunkett, 'Women managers most under-used source', *Office News and Automation*, March 1987, p. 43.

104. S. Bagwell, 'Power plays in workplace', *Australian Financial Review*, 25 September 1996, p. 21; and L. Rudman, *Bottom Line Business*, vol. 25, no. 1, 1996, p. 15.

105. A. B. Fisher, 'Where women are succeeding', *Fortune*, 3 August 1987, p. 68.

106. G. Koretz, 'Women in the boardroom', *Business Week*, 25 September 2001, p. 13.

107. B. Campbell, quoted in A. Ramsey, 'Men will be men, feminists learn', *Australian*, 24 April 1996, p. 4; and G. Maslen, 'Why women log off when it comes to computing degrees', *Campus Review*, 13–19 November 1996, p. 32.

108. Chen Feng, quoted in Reuter, 'Air hostesses find little cause to smile', *Hong Kong Standard — Business*, 15 February 1997, p. 3.

109. A. J. Cai, 'Sichuan puts male officials out of temptation's way', *South China Morning Post*, 15 July 2003, p. 1.

110. J. Walker, 'Boys' clubs under siege', *BRW*, 14–20 August 2003, p. 22.

111. N. Subramaniam and C. Lambert, 'Status of women academic accountants in Australia', reported in Accountancy Hotline, *Business Review Weekly*, 4 June 1993, p. 108; and M. Byrne, 'Equality doesn't quite add up', *Australian Financial Review*, 8 March 2001, p. 4.

112. L. Still, 'Where to from here? Women in management, the cultural dilemma', *Sydney Papers*, vol. 6, no. 3, 1994, pp. 1–12.

113. B. Morris, 'Trophy husbands', *Fortune*, 14 October 2002, p. 72.

114. G. Kovetz, 'Superwoman? Good luck', *Business Week*, 30 October 1995, p. 12; S. Barr, 'Up against the glass', *Management Review*, vol. 85, no. 9, 1996, pp. 12–17; and C. Arnst, 'Being a mother doesn't pay', *Business Week*, 12 March 2001, p. 8.

115. A. Messina, 'VCE: girls lead the way', *Age*, 9 July 1996, p. 1.

116. Study by Monash University PhD student, Wendy Smith, reported in J. Veale, '"Maleness" engineers women out', *Australian*, 2 October 1996, p. 36.

117. Survey by O'Reilly and Associates reported in 'Who's on the Internet?', *Bottom Line Business*, vol. 25, no. 5, 1996, p. 6.

118. Reported in A. Hepworth, 'Girls and IT: hard drive on', *Australian Financial Review*, 15–16 May 1999, p. 18; and S. Green, 'Battle of sexes moves to cyberspace', *South China Morning Post*, 2 October 1995, p. 25.

119. A. Watkins, quoted in C. Fox, 'Secret women's business', *Australian Financial Review*, 21 August 2000, p. 38.

120. M. Cave, 'It's a guy thing', *Boss*, May 2000, p. 46; and Knight Ridder, 'Uphill battle into corporate ranks', *South China Morning Post — Business*, 15 November 1999, p. 4.

121. R. Sharpe, 'As leaders, women rule', *Business Week*, 27 November 2000, pp. 104, A4.

122. Knight Ridder, op. cit., p. 4; and S. Holmes, 'Coke sued over colour filtering', *Business Review Weekly*, 30 April 1999, p. 22.

123. M. Fasteneau, 'Young woman's dream shattered through lack of HRM preparation', *HR Monthly*, April 1997, pp. 40–1.

124. K. Kizilos, 'Why girls don't get technical', *Age*, 3 January 1986, p. 8.

125. C. Collins, 'Engineering seen as unsuitable for women', *Australian*, 3 April 1990, p. 3.

126. C. Collins, op. cit., p. 3.

127. B. W. L. Packard and D. Nguyen, 'Science career related possible selves of adolescent girls: a longitudinal study', *Journal of Career Development*, vol. 29, no. 4, 2003, p. 261.

128. F. Carruthers, 'Women lose battle of the boardrooms', *Weekend Australian*, 8–9 February 1997, pp. 1, 6; and F. Carruthers, 'Women struggle to break $80 000 barrier', *Australian*, 14 March 1997, p. 5.

129. National Committee on Discrimination in Employment and Occupation, *Equal Opportunity*, AGPS, Canberra, 1984, p. 14; and A. Sinclair, 'Race around the office', *Boss*, April 2001, pp. 49–53.

130. Study by P. Riach and J. Rich, cited in J. Masanauskas, 'Study shows ethnic bias by employers', *Age*, 24 October 1991, p. 6.

131. Study by I. McAllister and R. Moore, 'Ethnic prejudice in Australian society: patterns, intensity and explanations', cited in K. Middleton, 'Vietnamese, Muslims, least liked', *Herald*, 19 July 1989, p. 5.

132. I. Watson, 'Opening the glass door: overseas born managers in Australia', reported in C. Jones, '"Glass door" blocks migrant managers', *Australian*, 22 November 1995, p. 7.

133. Associated Press, 'Educated Asians lose out on wages', *South China Morning Post*, 10 December 1995, p. 8.

134. R. Shamdasani, '40 pc of South Asians without work' and 'Pakistanis complain of job discrimination', *South China Morning Post*, 9 June 2003, p. A2.

135. Reported in K. Forestier, 'School projects bridge the gap', *Sunday Morning Post*, 6 October 1996, p. 12; and A. Nadel and A. Woo, 'Fear

and loathing', *Far Eastern Economic Review*, 31 October 1996, pp. 44–6.

136. Editorial, 'At long last, a chance to outlaw racism', *South China Morning Post*, 12 June 2003, p. A12; and V. Rajwani, 'Time's up for racial discrimination', *South China Morning Post*, 28 August 2003, p. 14.

137. ACTU, 'A new deal for the disabled', *Workplace*, no. 7, 1992, pp. 34–8; L. Yeung, 'Disabled by an air of discrimination', *Sunday Morning Post*, 15 September 1996, p. 2; and G. Brooks and T. Horwitz, 'Aboriginal issues stir diverseness as Olympics loom', *Asian Wall Street Journal*, 22 August 2000, pp. 1, 7.

138. Cited in 'Focus of jobs for blind people', *AHRI Victoria News*, September 1992, p. 6.

139. E. Lee, 'Special study fund proposed for disabled', *Eastern Express*, 2 January 1995, p. 3; 'New face of discrimination', *Campus Review*, 12–18 October 1995, p. 28; A. Lau, '$150 000 award for sacked maid', *South China Morning Post*, 15 August 2002, p. 2; and E. Wu, 'Ex-mental patients beset by job woes', *South China Morning Post*, 11 October 2003, p. C4.

140. C. Y. Chow, 'Too small woman gets short shrift', *South China Morning Post*, 11 February 2004, p. 1.

141. N. Kristof, 'Shameful attitude towards the disabled', *South China Morning Post,* 12 April 1996, p. 24.

142. D. J. Petersen, 'Paving the way for hiring the handicapped', *Personnel*, March–April 1981, p. 51.

143. R. Langford, 'Disabled workers prove their worth', *Business Review Weekly*, 11 November 1996, p. 50; M. Fasteneau, 'Able or disabled: does it affect competence, or your comfort level?', *HR Monthly*, September 1996, pp. 39–40; and C. Saltau, 'Staff commitment adds an extra dimension', *Business Review Weekly*, 12 August 1996, p. 64.

144. Quoted in J. Smith, 'Retired and back on the payroll', *Golden Wing*, March 1990, p. 22.

145. J. Egan, quoted in M. Cave, 'Old problems: CEOs hit the grey ceiling', *Australian Financial Review*, 26–27 July 2003, p. 6.

146. E. Snape and T. Redman, 'Too old or too young? The impact of perceived age discrimination', *Human Resource Management Journal*, vol. 13, no. 1, 2003, p. 79.

147. M. Lawson, 'Age may not weary, but can mean no job', *Australian Financial Review*, 12 February 1997, p. 6.

148. A. Vanden Heuvel, 'Mature age workers: are they a disadvantaged group in the labour market?', *Australian Bulletin of Labour*, vol. 25, no. 1, 1999, pp. 11–22; and Y. A. Debra, 'Tackling age discrimination in employment in Singapore', *International Journal of Human Resource Management*, vol. 7, no. 4, 1996, pp. 813–31.

149. C. Wong, 'Survey reveals age bias in jobs', *South China Morning Post*, 8 June 1996, p. 6; and R. J. Stone, 'Human resources as a competitive advantage: a Hong Kong overview', *International Employment Relations Review*, vol. 1, no. 1, 1995, p. 58.

150. P. Moy, 'Over 50s suffer discrimination at work', *South China Morning Post*, 15 July 2003, p. C4.

151. L. Bennington and P. Tharenou, 'Older workers: myths, evidence and implications for Australian managers', *Asia Pacific Journal of Human Resources*, vol. 34, no. 3, 1986, pp. 63–76.

152. S. Long, 'High staff turnover plagues call onlines', *Australian Financial Review*, 21 November 2000, p. 34.

153. N. Tabakoff and R. Skeffington, 'The wise old heads are back', *Business Review Weekly*, 3 November 2000, pp. 60–4.

154. 'Homely flights', *Asia Inc.*, June 1999, p. 7.

155. M. McLachlan, 'Older workers must stay on', *Australian Financial Review*, 24–27 April 2003, p. 6.

156. Agence France-Presse, 'Firms are urged to hire older workers', *South China Morning Post*, 27 August 2003, p. B10.

157. C. Fox, 'Time for action on ageing workforce', *Australian Financial Review*, 19 August 2003, p. 59.

158. S. Wilson, 'Encouraging an age-neutral culture', *Management*, April 1996, pp. 13–16.

159. S. Long, 'The death of loyalty', *Australian Financial Review*, 7 June 2000, p. 61.

160. B. Jones, 'Not yet over the hill', *BRW*, 24–30 July 2003, p. 53.

161. C. D. Fyock, 'Finding the gold in the graying of America', *HR Magazine*, February 1994, pp. 74–6; and C. M. Solomon, 'Unlock the potential of older workers', *Personnel Journal*, October 1995, pp. 56–66.

162. Associated Press, 'Scuffles greet guilt free speech of past Aboriginal injustices', *South China Morning Post*, 16 November 1996, p. 12.

163. M. Davis, 'Indigenous and invisible', *Australian Financial Review*, 29 March 1999, p. 20.

164. Associated Press, 'Aborigines lose battle', *South China Morning Post*, 22 February 1995, p. 14; and L. McLean, 'Aborigines bear brunt of unemployment', *Australian*, 6 June 1995, p. 6.

165. D. Schulz and S. Milson, 'Trapped in the money-go-round', *Bulletin*, 28 February 1995, pp. 31–3; R. Maynard, 'Aborigines dying younger: study', *South China Morning Post*, 27 December 2000, p. 10; and R. Maynard, 'Shocking state of Aboriginal health revealed', *South China Morning Post*, 1 September 2003, p. A13.

166. S. Green, 'Locked into a world of despair', *South China Morning Post*, 13 January 1996, p. 19; and N. Pearson, 'Welfare state hurts Aborigines', *Australian Financial Review*, 17 August 2000, p. 41.

167. Reported in S. Green, 1996, op. cit., p. 19.

168. J. O'Flynn, K. Lau, A. Sammartino and S. Nicholas, 'Indigenous employment — a jobs treaty', *HR Monthly*, June 2002, p. 28.

169. S. Macklin, 'Battle over British ban on gays in armed forces', *South China Morning Post*, 20 May 1999, p. 4; M. Chulov, 'Gays should not be in the army, RSL', *Weekend Australian*, 4–5 March 2000, p. 9; and M. Davey, 'Church panel accepts gay bishop', *International Herald Tribune*, 5 August 2003, p. 4.

170. G. K. Kronenberger, 'Out of the closet', *Personnel Journal*, June 1991, pp. 40–4; and 'Sexual orientations policies common', *HR News*, April 1993, p. A3.

171. Associated Press, 'Policy on gays opposed', *International Herald Tribune*, 31 July 2003, p. 4.

172. Associated Press, 'US army sacks nine linguists for being gay', *South China Morning Post*, 16 November 2002, p. 9.

173. G. Kelly, reported in 'Gay and lesbian staff in demand for special skills', *Australian Financial Review*, 21 January 1997, p. 19.

174. J. A. Segal, 'The unprotected minority?', *HR Magazine*, February 1995, pp. 27–33. See also S. Caudron, 'Opening the corporate closet to sexual orientation issues', *Personnel Journal,* August 1995, pp. 42–55.

175. P. Lles and G. Salaman, op. cit., p. 213.

176. P. Lles and G. Salaman, op. cit., pp. 213–14; and W. Cascio, *Managing Human Resources*, 4th edn, McGraw-Hill, New York, 1995, p. 183.

177. M. Excell, 'People a neglected asset', *Business Review Weekly*, 3 November 2000, p. 12.

178. This section is based on J. J. Philips, *Accountability in Human Resource Management*, Gulf Publishing, Houston, 1996, pp. 203–5.

179. A. L. Nanik, 'Beauty and the air traveller', *South China Morning Post*, 12 October 2003, p. 10.

180. M. Abdullah, quoted in P. Walbrook, 'Travellers' checks', *Post Magazine*, 12 October 2003, p. 48.

chapter

7

employee selection

Learning objectives

When you have finished studying this chapter, you should be able to:

- Explain strategic selection
- Understand the need for validation of employee selection procedures
- Describe some of the major research findings on selection
- Evaluate the use of psychological tests in selection
- Appreciate the factors that make for successful selection interviewing
- Discuss the compensatory and successive hurdles approaches to selection decision making.

'... if an HR person is trying to choose people for an organization, knowing their values is very important — if they are not consistent with the organization's values, they are not likely to stay very long.'[1]

Professor Roger Collins, Australian Graduate School of Management

Strategic selection

The hiring and retention of key human resources is a critical issue for organisations. Increased international competition, pressures for improved performance, corporate mergers and rationalisations, and industry restructuring mean that organisations cannot afford the luxury of poor employee selection. Because an organisation's success depends on it having the right people in the right jobs at the right time, the organisation's strategic business objectives and culture should determine the people selected. In other words, the choice of **selection criteria** should be consistent with the organisation's strategic direction and culture. **Strategic selection** aligns employment activities with the organisation's business strategies to produce a positive contribution to organisational performance.[2]

Microsoft's Director of Recruiting says:

> The best thing we can do for our competitors is to hire poorly. If I hire a bunch of bozos, it will hurt us, because it takes time to get rid of them. They start infiltrating the organization and then they themselves start hiring people of lower quality. At Microsoft, we are always looking to hire people who are better than we are . . . we look for smarts and experience, but we also want to know . . . are they flexible? Can they learn new concepts? In this industry, things are changing on a daily basis, and if you're not capable of learning new things, you won't be successful.[3]

The Microsoft case illustrates the increasing emphasis that organisations are giving to the behavioural and attitudinal characteristics of employees. The emergence of such changes requires the precise definition of job objectives and the utmost care in the selection of employees.[4] As a result, attention is increasingly being focused on psychological testing to assess applicant behavioural and attitudinal characteristics.

Jaguar UK, for example, uses psychometric tests to measure independence of thought, team working and cooperativeness.[5] For its senior management appointments, Dell Computer Corporation has a consultant conduct a lengthy behavioural interview and extensive pencil and paper testing.[6] Because the 'Singapore Girl' is such a critical symbol of Singapore Airlines' marketing strategy, senior management is involved in the selection of stewardesses. At Microsoft, hiring a strong work force that contributes to achieving its strategic objectives is also taken so seriously that senior executives are as actively involved as everyone else.[7] For Japanese companies, a personal philosophy compatible with the organisation's culture is considered essential.[8] Mazda (USA) uses an application form, written aptitude tests, personal interviews, a group problem-solving assessment and simulated work exercises to weed out 'druggies, rowdies and unionists'.[9] The HR Director of Komatsu (UK) says, 'we haven't necessarily taken on the most skilled people, but the ones who have the right attitude to team working and flexibility'.[10] Similarly, Malay, Thai and Chinese family companies emphasise personnel relationships in selection to ensure loyalty and compatibility.[11] In Korea and Japan, a good quality education at a prestigious university and harmonious personality traits are also favoured by major organisations.[12]

'By employing like minded people', says Ogbonna, 'organizations are able to increase the strength of their culture and reduce the possibility and consequences of undesired behaviors.'[13] This trend, not surprisingly, has its critics. Screening for cultural fit and attitude is viewed not as a matter of efficiency but one of power. Townley, for example, claims the use of systematic selection techniques (particularly the use of personality inventories and bio data questionnaires) is a way for an organisation to acquire a compliant, non-unionised work force. Selection based on applicant attitudes, motivation and behavioural criteria, Townley argues, is aimed at eliminating 'cultural differences' between the employee and management, thus promoting management control. The role of the HR manager is to give a veneer of professional legitimacy to what in reality is a sophisticated exercise in management power. Unions, not surprisingly, are often fiercely opposed to the use of psychometric testing.[14]

Regardless of such controversies, the reality is that the process through which organisations assess people applying for jobs has undergone little change. The application form,

Selection criteria Key factors in making a decision to hire or not to hire a person. May include qualifications, experience, special skills, abilities or aptitudes. Selection criteria must be job-related.

Strategic selection The linking of selection activities to the organisation's strategic business objectives and culture.

personal interview and reference check remain the most commonly used selection methods.[15] The interview, despite its recognised unreliability and poor predictive validity (see below), continues to be the dominant method of employee selection.[16] As a consequence, selection decisions in many organisations are idiosyncratic and jeopardise organisational effectiveness.[17] However, the desire to match applicant personality characteristics with the organisation's culture and strategic business requirements suggests that the use of personality inventories in selection will increase (particularly as research shows that cultural fit and value congruence between employees and their organisations are significant predictors of labour turnover and job performance).[18]

Consistent with this, Pfeffer found that high-performance organisations employ rigorous selection procedures that have been refined and developed over time to identify people with the attitudes and skills they require.[19]

It is obvious that ad hoc selection equals increased cost. Poor selection decisions result in increased training time, labour turnover, absenteeism, accidents, industrial unrest, job dissatisfaction and poor performance. Selection decisions must be based on accurate and objective information if managers are to make an informed choice. A systematic selection process is essential to ensure that the person and the job match.[20]

Selection policy

For an organisation to achieve its human resource objectives, selection decisions must conform with corporate policy. A good policy is essential as it communicates clearly what a company's selection goals are. Factors that management needs to consider in the development of its selection policy are:

- **Equal employment opportunity (EEO)**. What are the company's attitudes and approaches towards hiring women? Minorities? Older employees? People with disabilities? What will be the selection criteria?
- *Quality of people.* Does the company want to hire the top MBA graduates from the best universities? High school graduates? How will the 'suitability' of candidates be measured? Will the emphasis be on cultural fit and attitude? Technical skills? Qualifications?
- *Source of people.* Does the company want to promote from within? Have a mix of internal and external people? Rely solely on external sources? Generate applicants domestically? Internationally?
- *Management roles.* Who in the company will make the final decision to hire? What is the role of the HR department? What is the role of the line manager? To what extent will senior executives be involved? Hewlett-Packard, for example, has shifted much of its hiring responsibilities from HR to line management.[21]
- *Selection techniques.* Will multiple interviews be employed? Will psychological tests be used? Will assessment centres be used for executive selection? How will specific skills be tested? Will all applicants be required to undertake a medical examination? Will **genetic screening** or **HIV/AIDS testing** be undertaken?
- *Employment consultants.* Will external employment agencies, management recruitment consultants or executive search consultants be used? If so, for what positions? In what situations? Who will choose the consultant?
- *Industrial relations.* Are there any trade union restrictions or membership requirements regarding employment?
- *Legal issues.* Are there any legal restrictions or requirements regarding employment (for example, only a licensed person can be employed as an electrician or nurse)? Or the use of certain selection techniques (for example, the polygraph)?
- *Organisational strategic business objectives.* Are the company's selection policies and practices in harmony with the organisation's strategic business objectives? Do the candidates selected have the qualities and qualifications required by the organisation's strategic business objectives?

Equal employment opportunity (EEO) Giving people a fair chance to succeed without discrimination based on unrelated job factors such as age, race, sex or nationality.

Genetic screening Biological testing that can determine whether a job applicant is genetically susceptible to certain diseases, such as cancer and heart disease or to specific chemical substances.

HIV/AIDS testing Medical tests designed to determine the presence of AIDS in job applicants or existing employees.

- *Costs.* What is the budget? Who will pay the costs? HR or the line department? Who will authorise payments?

It is important that the selection process be recognised by managers as a systematic gathering of information. Its aim is to generate as much job-related data as possible to enable the manager to choose the right individual to fill a job. The selection process can also be viewed as a series of hurdles that the candidate must successfully pass before being offered a job.

Validation of selection procedures

A decision to hire (or not to hire) requires that line managers and the HR manager clearly identify the criteria that distinguish successful from unsuccessful job performance and use only predictive measures of job success that are reliable and valid. Without a systematic approach that examines reliability and validity, no relationships can be demonstrated between selection criteria and selection predictors. Decisions thus remain subjective, of dubious value and open to legal challenge. In contrast, the stronger the relationship between predictors and criteria, the more accurate the employment decision and the easier it is to satisfy EEO requirements that selection procedures be objective, non-discriminatory and result in the best candidate being selected. Finally, as Cascio points out, 'more accurate predictions result in greater cost savings (monetary as well as social)'.[22]

Validity

In selection, **validity** refers to the extent to which a **predictor** (that is, a selection criterion such as level of education or scores on an aptitude test) correlates with criteria identified as measuring job performance (such as measures of productivity — for example, sales, absenteeism and performance ratings) (see figure 7.1). The stronger the relationship between a predictor and the criterion of job success, the higher the **correlation coefficient**. While correlation coefficients range from +1.0 to –1.0 in the real world of the HR manager, it is rare to find such perfect relationships. Typically, predictor validities range from 0.20 to 0.50.[23]

Validity refers to the ability of a predictor to measure what it is supposed to measure. Two basic approaches are used by HR managers to determine the validity of criteria — concurrent and predictive.

Concurrent validity

This involves identifying a criterion predictor (for example, an aptitude test such as mechanical reasoning) and giving it to a group of existing employees and correlating their scores with their job performance. If an acceptable correlation exists, the criterion predictor can be used in the selection of new employees. While this method is generally regarded by HR managers as being both convenient and efficient, it risks challenge from EEO authorities because the population of existing employees may not be representative.

Predictive validity

To determine if a criterion predictor actually predicts acceptable job performance, the criterion predictor is administered to all applicants but the test scores are ignored when making the selection decision. After a specified period of time (for example, six months) the results are reviewed and correlated with a criterion such as job performance. If the validity coefficient is satisfactory, the predictor can be used in the selection process in the future. Unfortunately, while often regarded as the more 'scientific' of the two approaches, predictive validity tends to be time consuming and expensive. In addition, because the original predictive results are ignored, it means that there is an increased risk that incompetent personnel may be hired.[24]

Validity The ability of a test or other selection technique to measure what it sets out to measure.

Predictor A selection criterion, such as the level of education or scores on an intelligence test.

Correlation coefficient A statistical procedure showing the strength of the relationship between two variables; for example, between an employee's test score and on-the-job performance.

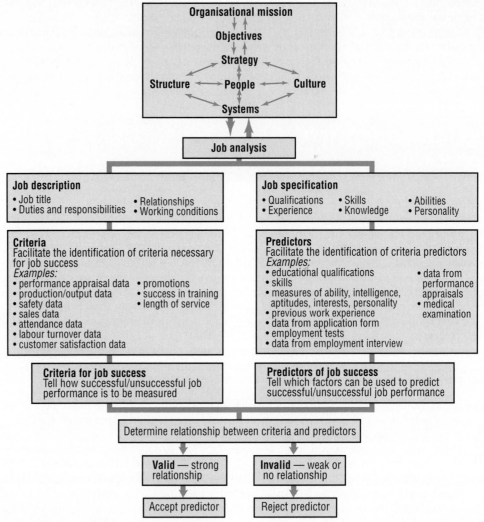

```
                        Organisational mission
                               ↕
                            Objectives
                               ↕
                            Strategy
                               ↕
        Structure  ←→      People     ←→    Culture
                               ↕
                            Systems
                               ↕↑
                          Job analysis
```

Job description
- Job title   • Relationships
- Duties and responsibilities • Working conditions

Job specification
- Qualifications   • Skills   • Abilities
- Experience   • Knowledge   • Personality

Criteria
Facilitate the identification of criteria necessary for job success
Examples:
- performance appraisal data   • promotions
- production/output data   • success in training
- safety data   • length of service
- sales data
- attendance data
- labour turnover data
- customer satisfaction data

Predictors
Facilitate the identification of criteria predictors
Examples:
- educational qualifications
- skills   • data from performance appraisals
- measures of ability, intelligence, aptitudes, interests, personality
- previous work experience   • medical examination
- data from application form
- employment tests
- data from employment interview

Criteria for job success
Tell how successful/unsuccessful job performance is to be measured

Predictors of job success
Tell which factors can be used to predict successful/unsuccessful job performance

Determine relationship between criteria and predictors

Valid — strong relationship

Invalid — weak or no relationship

Accept predictor

Reject predictor

Figure 7.1 Strategic selection
Source Asia Pacific Management Co. Ltd, 2004.

Reliability

Reliability The ability of a test or other selection technique to produce similar results or scores for an individual on separate occasions.

In selection, **reliability** refers to the consistency of measurement of a predictor. A predictor is reliable if individuals obtain essentially the same scores, ratings or rankings each time they are tested or assessed. A predictor is thus reliable if it consistently produces similar results. A predictor will be regarded as unreliable if the same individual obtains very different scores, ratings or rankings on separate occasions. For example, a general intelligence test would be regarded as reliable if an individual initially obtained a score of 120 and then a similar score when retested at a later date. If, however, the two scores differed significantly (for example, 120 compared with 90) the reliability of the test would be suspect.

When a predictor lacks reliability, little confidence can be placed in the results it generates because the same candidate can do well one time and poorly the next. The predictor will thus be regarded as undependable and not trustworthy. Typically, subjective measures such as the employment interview do not give very consistent results and thus have low reliability (and low validity). This is because the interaction between the interviewer and the interviewee may differ from interview to interview, interviewer skills may vary and different interviewer personalities may affect the candidates' responses.[25] Interviewers also may have great difficulty achieving agreement on their evaluation of a candidate's personality or potential.[26] Finally, only interviewer ratings of intelligence appear to be consistent and ratings of sociability to be both reliable and valid.[27] This is because of differences in interviewer standards used to evaluate candidates and because interviewers typically do not base their decisions on the same factors. For example, some interviewers may rely on a single factor, such as work experience, while others may emphasise interpersonal skills and communication skills.[28]

Predictor reliability is measured using one of three methods — test/retest, split halves and parallel forms. The test/retest method involves the applicant being subjected to the same predictor on two separate occasions. The scores, ratings or rankings are then correlated. If the correlation is high, the predictor is considered reliable. The split halves method involves the predictor being divided into two parts. For example, a test may be split into two parts — the even number items being considered as one test (test A) and the odd number items as the second test (test B). Again, the correlation between the two results is calculated. The final method, parallel forms, involves the development of two identical versions of the same predictor. For example, an intelligence test may have a Form A and a Form B, both of which ask similar questions in a similar way. The results on both predictors are correlated to estimate their reliability.[29]

Steps in the selection process

Selection procedures vary from organisation to organisation. Company objectives, culture, size, type of industry, geographic location, the state of the labour market, and the type and level of the position all impact on the type, order and number of steps an organisation uses in its selection process. The selection steps shown in figure 7.2 are representative of a full-scale selection process. Note that selection steps may vary in sequence; some steps may be ignored or additional steps introduced, depending on the organisation's HR selection policy and available resources.

SELECTION STEPS

1.	Reception of applicant
2.	Preliminary interview
3.	Application form
4.	Tests
5.	Interview
6.	Background investigations
7.	Preliminary screening by the human resource department
8.	Final selection by line managers
9.	Medical examination
10.	Placement on the job

Figure 7.2 Selection steps

Reception of applicants

The importance of giving the applicants a favourable impression at this stage cannot be overemphasised. Rudeness, disinterest or discrimination at reception may cost the organisation a good applicant and foster negative attitudes about the company and its products or services.

Telephone screening

In situations where large numbers of applicants are anticipated, initial screening may be done over the telephone to avoid sifting through hundreds of written applications. Applicants can be asked a few simple questions relating to critical job requirements (for example, 'Are you a licensed electrician?', 'Are you a qualified accountant?', 'Are you able to work weekends?'). Questions to be asked should be prepared beforehand and asked in the same way for each applicant. If candidates satisfy the minimum requirements, they then can be asked to submit a written application or attend an interview. Others can be informed immediately that they do not have the required qualifications. All telephone applicants should be treated politely and with efficiency. Under no circumstances should applicants be kept on hold or told to ring back.

Electronic applications

Increasingly, for high-tech, graduate and large, high-volume appointments, companies are using Internet technology to receive and process job applications. Cisco Systems, for example, uses 'résumé-less' candidate screening via the use of 'profiler' systems on its web page.[30] The main advantage is the very quick turnaround. The use of commercial/third-party electronic databases (electronic head-hunters) to select candidates, however, so far appears to have had only marginal acceptance.[31] According to Sunderland, the basic online application process requires candidates to reply by email and attach a CV. More sophisticated approaches include the use of customised forms that allow a database of candidate information to be compiled, searched (by the use of key words or various criteria such as job skills, years of work experience, education, study major, grade point average, etc.) and compared.[32] A common complaint is that biographical data are not well matched with the job requirements, resulting in too many inappropriate résumés, which clog up the whole system.[33] International HR consultancy SHL claims that this is because most online recruitment sites have time-intensive, unstructured and inadequate screening processes.[34] Nevertheless, it is apparent that in the near future better pre-screening via online psychometric and skills-based assessment will be integrated into the online application and selection process.[35]

The preliminary interview

The preliminary or initial screening interview may be used to check quickly on language skills, qualifications, willingness to do shift work, union membership, and the like. The preliminary interview is typically brief and centred on very specific job requirements. However, it should be carried out in a courteous, non-discriminatory and efficient way (as should all stages of the selection process). The negative public relations impact of discriminatory, rude or inefficient treatment cannot be overemphasised.

The application form

Application form Basic source of employment information covering qualifications, experience and other job-related data.

The **application form** is the basic source of all employment information for use in later steps of the selection process. It is also a valuable tool in screening out unqualified applicants. For example, if the job requires a trade qualification and the applicant indicates that they do not have one, there is no need to process the application further. Biographical data are considered by many researchers to be the best predictor available; however, they are often used in a subjective and haphazard way.[36]

Weighted application forms

Although designed to overcome interviewer subjectivity caused by an implicit weighting of factors that the interviewer thinks are important, very few organisations use weighted application forms.

Developing a weighted application form basically involves identifying the relationship between an application form item and job performance measures, such as productivity, absenteeism, tenure and theft. An explicit weight is then assigned to the points for level of education, number of previous jobs, specific work experience, military service or other nominated application form items to produce a weighted score. Applicants with the highest weighted point scores are deemed to be the best candidates.

While weighted application form scores are often highly predictive, it should be stressed that an application form item that has good predictive power for one job may not necessarily have the same predictive power for other jobs.[37] Finally, although weighted application forms are developed using a statistically proven relationship between the application form item and performance, they may be seen to be against the spirit of EEO. Items such as age, national origin, race, religion or sex, for example, may act as a red flag to the EEO authorities. Consequently, such items are probably best avoided by the HR manager when developing a weighted application form.

Application forms and EEO requirements

Equal employment opportunity bodies claim that many application forms and interview questions discriminate against women and minorities because they are not job-related. As a result, some traditional questions are best avoided. Examples of questions that should *not* be asked include the following (refer to chapter 4 for a discussion of their legal implications):

- *Marital status:* enquiries into family circumstances, relationships, spouse's situation, family planning or any related circumstances are not acceptable. The applicant may be asked if they are willing and able to be transferred, to travel and/or to work weekends, shifts or overtime, and under what conditions.
- *Residency status:* applicants may be asked their residency status if Australian residency is a job requirement.
- *National or ethnic origin:* no enquiries seeking information about national or ethnic origin may be made. This includes references to birthplace, first language, nationality or foreign residence. Applicants may, however, be asked to provide evidence of their eligibility to work legally in the country.
- *Organisations:* applicants may not be asked to list all the clubs and organisations to which they belong.
- *Photographs:* these may not be requested prior to interview except where job-related (for example, acting and modelling). Photographs may be required for identification purposes after appointment.
- *Race or colour:* information about a person's race, colour, complexion, or colour of eyes, hair or skin may not be sought.
- *Relatives:* no information about relatives, including names, addresses and relationships, may be required of the applicant. The names and addresses of a person or persons to be notified in the case of an emergency may be required after the selection decision has been made.[38]

Furthermore, job-related information involving the applicant's criminal record and/or traffic convictions and accidents should not be requested on the application form but should be asked for during the interview.

Additional information that may be job-related in some circumstances includes the following:

- *Age:* applicants may be asked only to indicate if they have reached minimum age or are below any maximum age that may apply by law to employment. Verification of age may be obtained during the interview.
- *Sex:* information as to a person's gender should not be requested unless it is an inherent job requirement. However, some organisations seek the applicant's preferred form of address at the interview stage.
- *National or ethnic origin:* the employer may ask if the applicant is legally entitled to work in Australia. Documentary proof of this eligibility may be asked for at the short-listing stage.
- *Name:* if the applicant was previously employed under a different name, it is relevant to employment history and may be requested.

A convicted sex offender applies for a job as a taxi driver. The employer wishes to be fair but worries about the potential danger to female passengers.

- *Languages:* questions on which languages the applicant speaks, reads or writes should be made only if language skills are job-related.
- *Religion:* no details of religious affiliation or practices may be sought unless an inherent job requirement exists. The employer may enquire if the applicant is willing to work a specified work schedule.
- *Military service:* questions on military service should be asked only if they are job-related.
- *Physical disability:* the application form may enquire about the existence of a physical disability only if it is relevant to the job, if it would preclude the applicant from performing the duties of the job satisfactorily, or would be hazardous to the safety of the applicant or colleagues, clients or the public.
- *Medical information:* application forms may indicate that a job offer is conditional on the passing of a medical examination if there is a bona fide occupational requirement for it. A medical examination should be conducted only after the selection decision has been made, and only where required.
- *Height and weight:* questions on height and weight may be asked only if they are relevant to the job.

Consequently, considerable care and attention must now be given to the design of the employment application form if charges of discrimination are to be avoided. An example of the type of form recommended by EEO authorities is shown in figure 7.3.

APPLICATION FORM

Position applied for Permanent ☐ Temporary ☐ Part-time ☐

Surname **Given names**
Address **Telephone no.**
  Postcode

Educational qualifications Please list any technical, secondary, tertiary qualifications and/or special skills, training undertaken, etc.

Previous employment Please list previous employers, positions held and length of time positions held and name under which you were employed.

Referees Please list names and telephone numbers of at least three people who can be contacted or attach written references.

Any further information you may wish to provide in support of this application.

Appointment to this position may require a medical examination. If this is so, you will be advised of this condition by the interviewing officer.

Figure 7.3 Example of an application form recommended by EEO authorities
Source Reproduced with the permission of the National Committee on Discrimination in Employment and Occupation.

Despite comprehensive anti-discrimination legislation, recent research suggests that many employers still regard EEO requirements as irrelevant or something to be worked around, and that discrimination in selection is still commonplace.[39] For example, Hewson claims that pre-selection processes and interviews for aspiring Australian politicians appear to have little to do with objective criteria but everything to do with gossip, innuendo, personal lifestyle and preferences.[40] According to Dwyer, the only prerequisite for Tung Chee-hwa's appointment as Chief Executive of the Special Administrative Region of Hong Kong 'was unswerving loyalty to the masters in Beijing'.[41] Similarly, former Japanese Prime Minister Mori's cabinet was selected not on merit but to repay favours, reward time serving and balance factional demands.[42]

Tests

If the applicant shows no obvious job-related deficiencies that would cause disqualification, then tests or an in-depth interview can be given. The choice between tests or an interview will depend on company policy, the type of job applied for, the cost of the test and the qualifications of the candidate. Applicant reactions to interviews (especially where the interviewer asks questions with **face validity**) are more favourable than they are to other selection techniques.[43] Face validity has also been shown to be important in applicant perceptions of the fairness of a selection technique. Research indicates that general intelligence and conscientiousness relate strongly to performance across a wide range of jobs and situations.[44] It has also been found that tests which are perceived by applicants as being job-related are positively correlated with organisational attractiveness.[45] This suggests that HR managers need to demonstrate to job applicants the face validity and job-relatedness of the selection technique employed.[46] Finally, evidence suggests that the use of psychological testing (especially for managerial and professional positions) is increasing. Australian corporate users include ANZ, Citibank, Corrs Chambers Westgarth, Lion Nathan, Macquarie Bank and Qantas.[47]

Figure 7.4 outlines some guidelines for the use of tests.

Face validity Refers to where a test item or question appears to make sense or to be logical.

- Analyse the job thoroughly to determine the precise requirements needed to perform the job successfully.

- Review the types of tests available that measure the 'critical factors' for successful job performance identified by the job analysis.

- Check that the 'climate' in your organisation is right for testing. Will there be employee opposition? Will the trade unions react negatively? Will testing deter good candidates?

- Ensure that your company has an objective performance appraisal system. Unless you can clearly discriminate between high- and low-performing employees, it is difficult to demonstrate that a test is an effective predictor. Consequently, any EEO challenge concerning the validity of the test will be virtually impossible to refute.

- Ensure that the conditions under which tests are administered are appropriate and the same for all candidates.

- Ensure that tests are administered by qualified personnel and that the results are treated as strictly confidential.

- Ensure that all applicants are advised of the results and are properly counselled.

Figure 7.4 Guidelines for the use of tests
Source Asia Pacific Management Co. Ltd, 2004.

This Letter to the Editor provides a provocative viewpoint. Do you agree? See 'What's your view?' on page 257.

Letter to the Editor

Psychological tests dehumanise applicants and promote management control

Dear Editor,

We appear to be returning to the days of the 'man in the grey flannel suit', with organisations increasingly hiring only those people who reflect and espouse the company's culture and value system. Given the inherent problems with personality tests, I'm not sure that this is such a good thing.

There are two problems here. One is with the tests themselves. It should be hoped that psychological testing would improve with time; however, this does not appear to be the case. During the mid-1980s, I took a psychological test administered by the Australian Army for the purposes of identifying future officers. One of the questions that has stuck in my mind is 'I am ashamed of . .', with candidates required to complete the sentence. I was honest enough to write something occurring in my past about which I wasn't particularly proud. Other candidates told me that they wrote 'nothing' in order to appear courageous. Who wrote the best answer? Something could be said for both. Whatever the merits of the answer, I wondered what right the Army had to ask such a private question, a question that appeared to have no relationship to the job being considered, and a question whose answer could be faked easily by those completing the test.

More recently, I completed a test providing scores on each of Hofstede's cultural dimensions, including individualism-collectivism, power distance and long/short-term time orientation. After undertaking the test, I discovered that my scores were in the 'moderate' range for every dimension. What does this tell me? Absolutely nothing, for 'moderate' is a label devoid of meaning, and the absence of significant differences between my scores for each dimension similarly generates a result deficient of any practical significance.

Psychological tests are generally characterised by ambiguously worded questions and a level of simplicity far removed from the complexities of human behaviour. Furthermore, environmental characteristics and situational constraints may be just as important in influencing organisational decision making as psychological influences. Psychological characteristics and personality may be of little assistance in predicting behaviour in these settings.

A second significant problem concerns the nature of contemporary organisations. Cultural conformity is not a particularly helpful defining characteristic for organisations seeking to survive in increasingly globalised and turbulent markets. The new environment demands creativity rather than conformity, and it demands deliberate efforts to create internal organisational conflict instead of operating under old frameworks of consensus. Attempts to culturally homogenise the work force may thus fly in the face of contemporary organisational realities.

While selecting people to ensure cultural conformity can bring benefits, it can also create the spectre of 'organisational man' operating in lemming-like fashion to endanger organisational health in today's complex and rapidly changing environment.

A management consultant on organisational change

Source David Poole, University of Western Sydney.

Employment tests

Employment tests Attempt to assess the match between the applicant and the job requirements. Examples include typing, welding and driving tests.

Employment tests attempt to assess the match between the applicant and the job requirements. Classic examples are driving, welding, typing and shorthand tests.

Employment tests, because they are job-related, tend to be accurate and objective predictors of particular skills that are needed on the job. Many problems involving unsatisfactory job performance and dismissal (because of poor technical skills) could be avoided by the use of employment tests. Less valid, and certainly more controversial, are psychological questionnaires that attempt to measure the applicant's interests, aptitudes, intelligence and personality.[48] Irrespective of such controversy, 'psychological assessment', according to consulting psychologist Alison Brady, 'provides an objective and cost-effective method of determining an individual's strengths, behavioural style, motivation and values'.[49] Consistent with this view, a recent survey indicates that almost 70 per cent of Australian HR directors believe that psychometric assessment is extremely valuable in the selection process.[50]

Interest tests

Interest tests aim to measure how an applicant's interest patterns compare with the interest patterns of successful people in a particular job. The underlying assumption in the use of interest tests is that applicants are more likely to succeed in a job they like. Unfortunately, in the employment situation, applicants may be motivated to fake their answers, with the result that interest tests often have limited value as a selection tool.[51] They are, however, useful for helping individuals choosing a career or contemplating a career change. Popular tests currently in use include Holland's Vocational Preference Inventory, the Strong Interest Inventory and the Rothwell-Miller Interest Blank.

Aptitude tests

Aptitude tests are tests of special abilities that are required in specific jobs. Examples are tests of mechanical, clerical, linguistic, musical and artistic abilities; manual dexterity; reaction time; and hand/eye coordination.

Such tests are often used to predict aptitude for a particular job or type of training. Thus, the use of aptitude tests can be of value in situations where an applicant has had little or no experience related to the job requirements — for example, in the selection of apprentices. Research suggests aptitude tests are valid for virtually all jobs. According to Schneider and Schmidt, an identification of the job family to which a particular job belongs should adequately identify the appropriate aptitude tests suitable for predictors of job performance.[52]

Some of the more common tests of aptitude are the Stromberg Dexterity Test (physical coordination), the Minnesota Paper and Form Board (spatial visualisation) and the Australian Council for Educational Research (ACER) Mechanical Reasoning Test (understanding of mechanical ideas).

Intelligence tests

Intelligence tests are designed to measure an applicant's intelligence or 'IQ' (intelligence quotient). Specific tests measuring ability to reason with numbers, words and abstract items are given. Such tests are good indicators of a candidate's ability to learn quickly and are the best established predictor of job performance (especially for jobs that involve conceptual thinking and problem solving).[53] Not surprisingly, managerial success is forecast most accurately by tests of general intellectual ability.[54] However, care must be taken to ensure that such tests are not culturally biased. Some psychologists do not see this as a problem and believe that any cultural bias is more often the result of test misuse.

Of course, a high intelligence is not a requirement for all jobs (for example, routine jobs with limited opportunities to exercise discretion). Intelligence scores rise with managerial level, but executives with unusually high scores are less likely to be successful in managerial positions than are those who score at intermediate levels.[55] The ACER ML-MQ, AL-AQ and B40 tests, the Wechsler Adult Intelligence Scale and Raven's Standard Progressive Matrices are examples of widely used intelligence tests. The latter, because it is a measure of non-verbal intelligence, is regarded as non-discriminatory and 'culture fair'.[56]

A fast-food chain employs people with mental and physical disabilities. Customers complain that they find it upsetting.

Personality tests

Personality tests or temperament tests are designed to measure basic aspects of an applicant's personality, such as level of introversion/extroversion, emotional stability and motivation. Personality tests are the most difficult tests to evaluate and use in employee selection. This is because the concept of personality itself is hazy and the relationship between performance on the job and personality is often vague or nonexistent. In addition, the applicant can fabricate answers easily. Some personality tests, as a consequence, tend to have limited value in employee selection and their use may be extremely difficult to justify if challenged by EEO authorities. Finally, some tests may include questions that could be regarded by applicants as an invasion of privacy. In the United States, questions about religious beliefs and sexual orientation, for example, have been construed as both invasive and discriminatory and have resulted in heavy financial penalties.[57]

In contrast, Hogan, Hogan and Roberts, after an exhaustive review of the literature, concluded that '(a) well constructed measures of normal personality are valid predictors of performance in virtually all occupations; (b) they do not result in adverse impact for job applicants from minority groups; and (c) using well developed personality measures for pre-employment screening is a way to promote social justice and increase organisational productivity'.[58] Fisher and Boyle similarly argue that conceptual and methodological advances have enhanced the credibility of personality as a predictor in employee selection. Even so, they advise managers to proceed cautiously because of the many poor tests on the market.[59]

Overall, the validity of personality tests as a predictor of performance appears to depend greatly on the degree to which they are able to measure the 'Big Five' personality dimensions of adjustment, agreeableness, conscientiousness, extroversion and inquisitiveness. Conscientiousness (being dependable, organised, persevering, thorough and achievement-oriented) especially appears to be a good predictor of performance.[60]

The disparity of opinion regarding the use of personality tests in selection, however, virtually guarantees controversy and a polarisation of attitudes between HR managers.[61]

Personality tests in common use include the IPAT Sixteen Personality Factor Questionnaire (16PF), the Guilford-Zimmerman Temperament Survey, Edwards Personal Preference Schedule, FIRO-B, the California Psychological Inventory (CPI), DISC, the Humm-Wadsworth Temperament Scale, Kostick's Perception and Preference Inventory, Gordon's Personal Profile Inventory, the Myers-Briggs Type Indicator (MBTI) and the Occupational Personality Questionnaire.

An organisation aims to be an equal opportunity employer. Its major customer refuses to deal with sales representatives who are not of the same religious and ethnic background.

Testing and EEO

EEO requires that, if tests are to be used in making employment decisions, they must:
- be proven as being able to predict job performance
- not discriminate
- be job-related.

EEO authorities consequently caution that any selection tests used by an organisation be checked to ensure that they do not include any discriminatory elements.[62]

HR managers, however, should not become over fearful of testing because of concerns about language or cultural bias. If done properly, testing can be a valuable selection tool for promoting work force diversity.[63] For example, tests using the 'Big Five' personality dimensions have been shown to be valid across racial, ethnic and linguistic lines and to provide useful information on career choice and performance.[64]

Questions for the HR manager to ask

- *Current and past users.* Which companies use the test now? Which companies used it in the past? Why did they stop using the test? What is the present user's experience with the test?
- *Test literature.* What literature is available on the test and its application in employee selection? Is there a manual available? What research exists on its reliability and validity?
- *Reviewer comments.* Who has reviewed the test? What did they say about the test? Is the test listed in the standard reference sources? If not, why not? What do independent professional bodies such as the Australian Council for Educational Research have to say about the test?[65]
- *Country studies.* What country studies have been undertaken? What were the results? Were they conducted by people with a vested interest or by independent researchers?
- *Equal opportunity.* What do state and federal EEO bodies have to say about the use of the test in employee selection? Do they regard it as discriminatory and not job-related, or a good predictor of on-the-job performance?
- *Legal liability.* What is the situation if the test is found to be discriminatory? Who is liable? What is the position of the company's consultant?
- *Job-relatedness studies.* If required, who will conduct, interpret and pay for them — the company or the consultant?[66]

Interviews

The **employment interview** is the most widely used selection technique. It is a conversation with a purpose between an interviewer and a job applicant. The interview can be relatively unstructured and non-directive or highly structured and patterned. The **structured interview** makes use of a predetermined outline. By following this outline, the interviewer ensures that all relevant information on the candidate is systematically covered. As would be expected, research indicates that the use of a structured interview yields more accurate results than an **unstructured interview**.[67] On the other hand, some interviewers do not like the patterned interview approach, believing that it is too restrictive. Australian managers, for example, appear to have a strong preference for unstructured or minimally structured interviews.[68] In the United States, about 70 per cent of organisations use unstructured interviews (where they often consist of 'superficial, shoot from the hip questions').[69] In Europe, interview styles vary from country to country. Structured interviews are favoured in Britain, Scandinavia, Germany, Austria and Spain, while non-structured interviews are preferred in Italy, Luxembourg, Portugal and Switzerland.[70]

Regardless of which interview method is adopted, questions asked must be job-related. Under EEO legislation, irrelevant and unnecessary questions may lead to charges of discrimination. As a consequence, many HRM experts feel that the safest and fairest types of interviews are the structured or patterned interviews as they ensure that the same standardised questions are asked of all job applicants. For a brief look at some of the major research findings on the employment interview see figure 7.5.

'I see … so, the gaps in your employment correspond to each of your alien abductions?'

Behavioural interviews

A special type of structured interview is the behavioural or situational interview. This is based on a detailed analysis of the skills required to perform the job to be filled. Behavioural specifications aim to depict the job in terms of how the individual must function in order to perform successfully. Questions are developed from the definitions of the desired skills. The skill specifications are listed so that they can be systematically explored during the interview.[71]

Questions in a behavioural interview should be aimed at specific life history events that give the interviewer insight into how the candidate will perform in the job. 'Behaviour descriptions', says Janz, 'reveal specific choices applicants have made in the past, and the circumstances surrounding those choices. The interviewer probes the details of the situation and what the applicant did in that situation, or what the applicant did the next time that same situation arose.'[72] This allows the interviewer to judge how well the applicant performed in that situation and to develop an idea of the applicant's typical behaviour patterns. Behavioural interviews are thus based on the assumption that the best predictor of future performance is past performance in similar circumstances. Psychologist Dr Paul Green recommends questions such as 'Give me an example of a time when you had to deal with a difficult person at work'. He is not in favour of questions that begin 'How do you feel about … ?' or 'What would you do if … ?' Green believes that by focusing on skills rather than personality traits the interview is less likely to prejudice the candidate.[73] While research suggests that behavioural interviews have much greater validity than unstructured interviews, the expense and time required for development means that they are not widely used.[74]

Many women in senior executive positions lie in interviews about having children for fear of risking their careers. Is this unethical?

- When the number of women candidates is 25 per cent or less of the total number of applicants, they will be evaluated less favourably.[75] The same is also true for older applicants.[76]
- Interviewers develop their own stereotypes of a good applicant and select those who match that stereotype.[77]
- Experienced interviewers who have not learned how to conduct effective interviews simply are experienced bad interviewers.[78]
- Being disabled has a positive impact on qualified candidates but a negative impact on unqualified candidates.[79]
- Interviewers are more lenient in evaluating men who are interviewed after a woman than in evaluating a woman who follows a man.[80]
- Unfavourable information outweighs favourable information.[81]
- Interviewers are more likely to change their initial opinion of an applicant from positive to negative than from negative to positive.[82]
- Interviewers' post-interview ratings are highly related to their pre-interview impressions.[83]
- Interviewers' reactions to applicants are strongly influenced by appearance (dress, physical attractiveness and use of grooming aids). Candidates judged to be attractive and/or appropriately groomed are more highly evaluated than unattractive or inappropriately dressed candidates.[84] Major Japanese companies, for example, are opposed to hiring applicants with dyed hair, while Chinese parents pay for plastic surgery for their daughters to help them find a good job after graduation. According to a recent University of Hong Kong survey, most Hong Kong women want to look young for their age, believing it will boost their self-confidence, create a good impression and help their employment prospects.[85]
- Candidates who are above average in attractiveness enjoy a distinct advantage over others. Less attractive female applicants are especially at a disadvantage, regardless of their experience.[86]
- Obesity (especially for women) has a negative influence on interviewer perceptions of the applicant's personality.[87]
- Women wearing more masculine clothing (for example, a dark blue suit) are judged to be more forceful, self-reliant, dynamic, aggressive and decisive than those wearing more feminine clothing (for example, a soft beige dress).[88]
- Candidates being interviewed before or after a very good or very bad candidate can have their evaluation seriously distorted.[89]
- Interviewees who play hard to get are rated more highly.[90]
- Applicants who demonstrate greater eye contact, head moving, smiling and other similar positive, non-verbal behaviour receive higher evaluations.[91]
- When interviewers exhibit cold, non-verbal behaviour (for example, no eye contact or smiling), applicants' verbal and non-verbal behaviours are rated less favourably.[92]

Figure 7.5 Research and the employment interview

How to interview successfully

1. Know the job

To select the right person, the HR manager and line managers must know the job to be filled, otherwise how can an accurate match be obtained? The job description should list the key responsibilities, determine reporting relationships, identify where the position fits into the organisation, analyse the organisational climate and its impact on the job, and determine aspects about the job that make it unique, such as regular international travel (see pages 145–50). Research indicates that when job information is used to develop interview questions as well as to evaluate the applicant's answers, the validity of the interview is enhanced. Moreover, interviewers who are given more complete job information make selection decisions with higher inter rater reliability.[93]

2. Know the personal attributes, experience, skills and qualifications

It must be stressed that the qualifications, experience and special skills required must be job-related — that is, they must be present if the applicant is to satisfactorily perform the job. To establish unnecessary requirements may eliminate many good candidates and lead to charges of discrimination. Requirements should be reduced to four or five critical elements that are absolutely essential and can be clearly shown to be job-related. If candidates are to

Practitioner speaks

Employee selection

Suzanne Kallenbach is National Human Resource Manager for the Lincoln Sentry Group, a privately owned supplier and distributor of componentry to the glazing, window, security, hardware and cabinet-making industries. The company has 23 sites throughout Australia and New Zealand. Suzanne is a Council Member of AHRI for Queensland and undertook a scholarship to the United States in 2001 to explore international best practice in recruitment and selection. Suzanne has experience in both public sector and private sector management and has presented at a number of national conferences on HR matters.

Employee selection is a time-consuming and labour-intensive task. Far too often the process is compromised in order to 'save time', only to find that a poor selection choice results in considerably more time being spent doing the job again. The value of 'doing it right the first time' cannot be overemphasised.

Frequently, new HR practitioners are designated to the 'recruitment' section because it is considered to be 'good for beginners'. This really could not be further from the truth unless they are guided by an experienced and competent mentor. Applicants are becoming quite savvy with the recruitment and selection process and the legal requirements are possibly the most complex in the world. There are any number of traps for an unsuspecting beginner.

Where do beginners go wrong? First and foremost they become too emotionally involved in the recruitment process. Selection criteria must be applied to each position (whether in the public or private sector). This should cover the educational standards required, previous role and industry experience as well as attitude, personality, geographic and demographic factors if relevant to the role in question.

Consistency is the key! All applicants whether internal, external or your best friend should be treated exactly the same. This is particularly relevant with regards to interview questions, pre-employment assessments and reference checks where it is tempting to cut corners if you 'know the person'. It is consistently amazing what you 'don't' know about someone you think you know well! It is not uncommon to dislike the people we 'need'. Keep your 'wants' and your 'needs' distinct and impartial.

Keep your applicants informed. Too often the emphasis is on those who are in the running and those who miss out at each stage get neglected. These could be your future people — don't waste a public relations opportunity. 'Rejection' calls are the most unpleasant feature of the job, but in fact require the greatest skill and ability on the part of the recruiter.

Don't overstate the job you are offering! Tell it like it is. Be sure to give all the details of the role, including those unspoken norms such as company culture, social culture, meal breaks and areas, perks, and so on. These are often the most important details to your candidate after salary, hours and location! The phrase 'underpromise and overdeliver' is particularly relevant to the selection role. Applicants will tend to have a rosy view of what you are presenting and many times hear only part of what you say. It is your job to be very, very clear so there are no disappointments in those first few weeks on the job.

In times of tighter labour markets you need to think in terms of relative skills. Judge how applicants can apply their skills base to a number of tasks and duties. We no longer have the luxury of finding the 'perfect fit'. This can call for creativity and innovation on your part.

Selection can be the most rewarding aspect of the HR role. It can also be the most challenging. Take your time, pay attention to detail and be consistently impartial and you are well on your way to becoming a professional recruiter.

Suzanne Kallenbach

be measured on common standards, it is vital for the HR manager to discuss critical selection factors with line managers involved in the selection process. According to Rowe: 'Before human resource managers start interviewing, they need to know what they want. For example, is the job really necessary in the first place? How does it contribute to the business? What are the results wanted from the job? This leads to detailing the characteristics of the person wanted. This generally is not done well and so cannot be overemphasised.'[94]

3. Set specific objectives

HR managers must establish what information they wish to get (and give) and what topics they wish to cover. It is important to note that the interview should not be a rehash of questions on the application form. The purpose of the employment interview is to give and get information that will help the interviewer to make a decision about the applicant's suitability. 'One needs to keep in mind that the interview is being used to predict future performance on the job and that performance is a function of both motivation and ability and not of ability alone', argues McCarthy. 'Accordingly, preparation for the interview is critical. Time should be taken beforehand to develop a range of questions pertinent to the job and the applicant's background to enable the development of sustained themes of questioning. The lines of questioning followed in the interview will determine the success or otherwise of judgements about the motivation and ability of potential employees.'[95] Moreover, if interviewers know what they are looking for, they are more likely to detect its presence or absence in applicants.

4. Provide the proper setting for the interview

The interview is important to the applicant and to the image of the company. Consequently, the interview should be conducted in private and in a setting free from interruptions. Lighting, temperature, seating arrangements and accessibility for disabled applicants must also be considered. Not to do so creates a negative image to applicants by communicating that the interviewer does not really think that they are important enough to justify the courtesy of a professionally conducted interview. Research by Harn and Thornton, for example, has found that the behaviour of interviewers towards applicants can influence their decision to accept or reject a job offer. This is particularly so when interviewing job applicants with a disability (see figure 7.6). Similarly, applicants react very negatively to interviewers who are uncertain and hesitant.[96] According to Goldrick, 'Interviewers who have the interviewing skills and confidence to make a good impression and facilitate open communication will create a positive experience for candidates, enhance organisational image, be perceived as fair and increase the number of job offers accepted'.[97]

When interviewing any applicant with a disability:
- Always offer to shake hands. Do not avoid eye contact, but don't stare either.
- If you feel it appropriate, offer the applicant assistance (for example, if an individual with poor grasping ability has trouble opening a door), but don't assume it will necessarily be accepted. Don't automatically give assistance without asking first.
- If you know in advance that an applicant has a particular disability, try to get some information before the interview on how the limitations of the disability may affect the performance of the essential functions of the job.

When interviewing an applicant who uses a wheelchair:
- Don't lean on the wheelchair.
- Make sure you get on the same eye level with the applicant during the interview.
- Don't push the wheelchair unless asked.
- Keep accessibility in mind. (Is that chair in the middle of your office a barrier to a wheelchair user? If so, move it aside.)
- Don't be embarrassed to use natural phrases such as 'Let's walk over to the plant'.

When interviewing an applicant who is blind:
- Identify yourself and others present immediately, cue a handshake verbally or physically.

- Be descriptive in giving directions. ('The table is about five steps to your left.')
- Don't shout.
- Don't be embarrassed to use natural phrases like 'Do you see what I mean?'
- Keep doors either open or closed, not half opened, as this is a serious hazard.
- Don't touch an applicant's cane. Do not touch or pet a guide dog.
- Offer assistance in travel by letting the applicant grasp your left arm, just above the elbow.

When interviewing an applicant who is deaf:
- You may need to use a physical signal to get the applicant's attention.
- If the applicant is lip reading, enunciate clearly, and place yourself where there is ample lighting.
- Communicate by using a combination of gestures, facial expressions and note passing.
- If you don't understand what the applicant is telling you, ask them to repeat the sentence(s). Don't pretend that you understand if that is not the case.
- If necessary, use a sign language interpreter, but be sure to always speak directly to the applicant. Don't say to the interpreter, 'Tell her that ...'

Figure 7.6 Etiquette for interviewing candidates with disabilities
Source *Managing Diversity*, February 1992.

5. Review the application form or résumé

The interviewer should review the written application to determine whether additional information is needed. Examples of items that may need clarification or expansion include: unexplained gaps in employment history, such as dates left out and employers not named; questions not answered or only partly answered; vague wording; inconsistencies such as a 'promotion' without a pay increase; inflated job titles; danger signs such as frequent job changes; vague reasons for leaving previous jobs; unusual number of previous employers who are now out of business; health problems; inability to work overtime; and place of residence a long distance from work.

One technique that enables the interviewer to do this is the matching sheet. This lists the most important job dimensions on the left-hand side of a page. When sorting through the résumés, the interviewer jots down each person's relevant qualifications in the right-hand column. This makes matches and mismatches obvious and can save time in reaching an objective decision on who to interview.

6. Beware of prejudices

Most people have prejudices of some sort. If applicants are to be appraised objectively, it is important that these prejudices do not impinge on the selection decision, otherwise the interviewer runs the risk of losing good candidates and leaving the way open to charges of discrimination. Interviewers must 'know their prejudices and recognise when they exist', advises Pontifex. 'Whilst we believe that they have a basis in the reality of our own experiences, most of them do not stand up to scrutiny. It is also worth trying to identify the line manager's prejudices before starting to recruit so that the interviewer has the opportunity to counter them before the event.'[98]

7. Don't make snap decisions

Research indicates that interviewers make a judgement about an applicant in the first three to five minutes of the interview.[99] From that point on, the interviewer hears and sees only information that confirms initial impressions. In fact, research shows that employers still follow male and female stereotypes when considering applicants for jobs. A study by Arvey, Miller, Gould and Burch, for example, found that women are given higher evaluations than similarly qualified men for jobs that are stereotypically female.[100] As more information becomes available to the interviewer, however, reliance on stereotypes diminishes.[101]

Interviewers must be alert to this tendency to make instant judgements about the suitability of a candidate. Judgement must be reserved until all relevant information about the applicant has been gathered. If this is done, the danger of making a snap judgement and the introducing of bias is minimised.

8. Put the applicant at ease

Rapport must be established with applicants by putting them at ease so that the interview will flow freely. Talking about neutral topics of mutual interest until the ice has been broken permits the interviewer to move comfortably into the interview. Any interviewer who acts in a superior way and is overly formal will fail to get all the facts. An executive search consultant says, 'The good interviewer needs to establish rapport quickly and have the ability to delve with sensitivity and the ability to evaluate objectively'.[102]

9. Watch the body language

The interviewer should look for non-verbal signals, such as facial expressions, fidgeting, arm movements and the like, which can give important clues as to what the applicant is really thinking or feeling. According to Braysich, **body language** is 'the art of seeing what others are thinking', and because it stems from the subconscious, it is 'a more accurate indicator of feeling than the carefully chosen word'.[103] A single body movement, however, may be unclear and by itself may not have a precise or universally accepted meaning. Interviewers especially must be alert to cultural differences. For example, in high-context cultures such as Japan and China (see pages 753–5), subtlety is valued. Reading non-verbal behaviour is crucial for understanding a communication. In contrast, in low-context cultures such as Australia and the United States, much greater emphasis is given to the spoken word.[104] Similarly, different cultures may attach different meanings to specific aspects of non-verbal behaviour. For example, Thais can use the smile to indicate amusement, to express thanks, to excuse themselves, to show embarrassment or to sidestep a difficult issue.[105]

Body language Non-verbal signals (such as facial expressions) that can indicate what a person is really thinking or feeling.

NEWSBREAK

For some men talent is not enough

By Lisa Allen

It's hard to believe, but some men actually think that plastic surgery can enhance their job prospects. But believe it. The figures show that men are increasingly vulnerable to the lure of surgical self-improvement. Apparently, in some industries men reaching their early forties are viewed as too old for the corporate life where youth is perceived as smarter and edgier.

Male IT and advertising executives, management consultants, and even financial sector employees are queuing for plastic surgery as they hit middle age and desperately cling to their careers. The rate of Australian men seeking out the surgeon's scalpel has doubled since 1998.

Eyelid lifts correcting droopy, saggy eyes and eyebrows which make executives look tired have become increasingly popular. But the eyelid lift is often just the start of elective procedures with executives progressing to full face lifts and hair transplants as they hit their late forties and fifties.

Australian plastic surgeon Norm Olbourne, who brought 1200 of the world's leading plastic surgeons to Sydney for a cosmetic and plastic surgery conference this week, says 'older people are perceived to have lost it which is common in the IT industry where the younger people are perceived as smarter.

'There is pressure on the older man who might be in his early to late forties who may feel the need to do something about it', says Olbourne.

'In these industries there is terrific turnover — as the economy goes up and down the jobs go up and down.'

Olbourne says in 'consulting firms like McKinseys executives work very hard, long hours and often the young turks give the impression of being more energetic. So men in their forties may come to have surgery.'

Olbourne says male patients seeking eye lifts and full face lifts have doubled in the past five years.

Human rights lawyer Geoffrey Robertson QC, lecturing on plastic surgery and the law at the World Congress of Plastic Surgery in Sydney this week, says there is an endemic discrimination against those perceived as ugly. 'In most walks of life, particularly those involving personal contact with the public, physical attractiveness is a career asset. It is well established that it enhances confidence and in turn the prospects of success.

'A recent comprehensive study in the United Kingdom of men in their mid-thirties showed that those who were attractive earned 15 per cent more than those with otherwise equivalent qualifications. We have had European studies of careers in advertising and sales finding very pronounced discrimination in favour of those with good looks.

'[In a] Society where survival of the fittest is coming to mean survival of the prettiest, there is obviously an increased demand for surgery which boosts career prospects, confidence and self-esteem.'

Brazilian plastic surgeon Ivo Pitanguy who has performed 8000 plastic surgery operations, for 'kings, actresses, and presidents', says the main complaint from men is they look tired.

'The most important thing for men is to fix the eyelids … they make them look tired, they think in the office this guy is tired when in fact he was at home all night', Dr Pitanguy told *The Weekend Australian Financial Review*.

The world renowned plastic surgeon and medical professor says men made up just 6 per cent of patients during 1980 to 1990. Today male plastic surgery cases account for 18 to 20 per cent.

But Dr Pitanguy says he does not like doing male patients whose only reason for surgery is to get a better career path. 'They won't get a better job and they will just be frustrated with the surgery.'

Dr Pitanguy, who is well into his seventies and says he has not had surgery — although he has performed plastic surgery for many of his medical colleagues — says after he has fixed the eyelids, men want more. They want facelifts and pockets of fat removed from the thighs, he says.

Weak chins are also augmented to make males appear more virile. Some men think this will help them appear more dominant and in control in aggressive workplaces or tough management situations.

'Many men have chin [augmentation] because they think a weak chin doesn't give the sign of virility', says Dr Pitanguy.

They also want their acne scars removed. Most executives with ugly noses have already had them fixed well before they get the top job. 'People are more fit these days but the law of gravity is still the same. If you are having a motivation that is healthy you should do it.'

Alfred Lewis president of the Australian Society of Plastic Surgeons says there are about 50 000 plastic surgery procedures carried out in Australia each year.

In the United States rates of cosmetic surgery are soaring, and men now make up almost 15 per cent of the market.

Certified surgeons performed more than 7 million cosmetic procedures last year on 2 million patients, five times as many as in 1992, according to the American Society of Plastic Surgeons.

Overall last year Americans handed over $14 billion to their surgeons in return for cosmetic procedures.

The most popular operations are liposuction, eyelid surgery and nose re-shaping.

Older women remain the bulk of those who go under the knife, but the numbers of men are rapidly increasing.

Of the 370 000 nose jobs in the US last year, 136 000 were done on men.

The most popular procedures, that don't involve surgery, include chemical peels, botox injections and lasers to remove hair or 'rejuvenate' skin.

Of the 1 million faces injected with Botox to remove frown lines last year, 100 000 of them were male. Of the 1.4 million chemical peels, 168 000 were for men.

At an average surgeon's fee of $1000 for a chemical peel or a botox injection, $6000 for a nose job, and $4400 for 'laser skin resurfacing' the total size of these markets is clearly enormous.

In September a journal called *Medical Laser Insight* estimated that globally in 2001 $6 billion was paid in fees to doctors for laser treatments, $3.6 billion for botox injections, and $4.8 billion for chemical peels. The journal suggested 20 per cent of those seeking 'skin rejuvenation' were men.

Olbourne says there are more reasons why men are being enticed to have plastic surgery. 'More and more men are considering face lifts because the techniques of face lifts are developing so there are less invasive

operations, scars are hidden and there is less down time', he says.

Some men with deteriorating eyelids and sagging eyebrows are advised to go the next step and have a mini face lift, lifting their forehead to make them appear more youthful, says Olbourne.

'But almost everybody who has cosmetic surgery doesn't want to advertise it', he says. 'Often it's hard to keep from your family, but the patient will often go on a holiday.'

There are very few people — men or women — who want a neon sign saying 'I've had cosmetic surgery', says Olbourne, whose conference in Sydney was sponsored by the Australian Plastic Surgery Society, which is part of the Royal Australasian College of Surgeons. 'But over the last five years the number of men seeking cosmetic surgery in my practice would have doubled. More and more men are considering face lifts. You can't stereotype people but these are trends', says Olbourne.

The surgeon says an eyelid lift will cost about $5000 and a facelift will set a male executive back about $10 000.

Source Australian Financial Review, 16–17 August 2003, p. 29.

10. Encourage the applicant to do most of the talking

While the interviewer is talking, they are not learning about the applicant. The more the applicant talks (on the subjects the interviewer wants to hear about), the more the interviewer is going to learn about them. 'The interviewer can never probe enough', stresses Bongazoni.[106]

Rather than asking questions that simply require a 'yes' or 'no' answer, the interviewer should encourage the applicant to talk by asking open-ended questions such as: 'Tell me what you did in your last job', 'What are the most important contributions you've made in your current job?' and 'What is your best guess as to what your boss would say about your strengths, weaknesses and overall performance?' Negative questions can also be useful in job interviews, for example, 'That's an impressive achievement — can you tell me about a time when things didn't go as well?' Follow-up questions such as 'How did the situation arise?' and 'What did you do?' are vital if specific information is to be obtained. This approach is reinforced if the interviewer makes sure of being an attentive and sympathetic listener. According to Dwyer, 'Many managers feel uncomfortable with silence and do not know which questions to ask and therefore tend to talk too much during an interview'.[107] An occasional 'Uh-huh!', 'Really', 'Is that so' or 'I see' by the interviewer is very effective in keeping the applicant talking.

The interview can be ruined if the interviewer monopolises the conversation with a string of favourite stories. The employment interview is not a social occasion. It is a business meeting with a specific purpose. Figure 7.7 provides a list of sample questions to ask at interviews.

Questions to reveal integrity/honesty/trustworthiness
- Discuss a time when your integrity was challenged. How did you handle it?
- What would you do if someone asked you to do something unethical?
- Have you ever experienced a loss for doing what is right?
- Have you ever asked for forgiveness for doing something wrong?
- In what business situations do you feel honesty would be inappropriate?
- If you saw a colleague doing something dishonest, would you tell your boss? What would you do about it?

Questions to reveal personality/temperament/ability to work with others
- What brings you joy?
- If you took out a full-page ad in the *New York Times* and had to describe yourself in only three words, what would those words be?
- How would you describe your personality?
- What motivates you the most?
- If I call your references, what will they say about you?
- Do you consider yourself a risk-taker? Describe a situation in which you had to take a risk.
- What kind of environment would you like to work in?
- What kinds of people would you rather not work with?
- What kinds of responsibilities would you like to avoid in your next job?
- What are two or three examples of tasks that you do not particularly enjoy doing? Indicate how you remain motivated to complete those tasks.
- What kinds of people bug you?
- Tell me about a work situation that irritated you.
- Have you ever had to resolve a conflict with a colleague or client? How did you resolve it?
- Describe the appropriate relationship between a supervisor and subordinates.
- What sort of relationships do you have with your associates, both at the same level and above and below you?
- How have you worked as a member of teams in the past?
- Tell me about some of the groups you've had to get cooperation from. What did you do?

- What is your management style? How do you think your subordinates perceive you?
- As a manager, have you ever had to fire anyone? If so, what were the circumstances, and how did you handle it?
- Have you ever been in a situation where a project was returned for errors? What effect did this have on you?
- What previous job was the most satisfying and why?
- What job was the most frustrating and why?
- Tell me about the best boss you ever had. Now tell me about the worst boss. What made it tough to work for him or her?
- What do you think you owe to your employer?
- What does your employer owe to you?

Questions to reveal past mistakes
- Tell me about an objective in your last job that you failed to meet and why.
- When is the last time you were criticised? How did you deal with it?
- What have you learned from your mistakes?
- Tell me about a situation where you 'blew it'. How did you resolve or correct it to save face?
- Tell me about a situation where you abruptly had to change what you were doing.
- If you could change one (managerial) decision you made during the past two years, what would that be?
- Tell me of a time when you had to work on a project that didn't work out the way it should have. What did you do?
- If you had the opportunity to change anything in your career, what would you have done differently?

Questions to reveal creativity/creative thinking/ problem solving
- When was the last time you 'broke the rules' (thought outside the box) and how did you do it?
- What have you done that was innovative?
- What was the wildest idea you had in the past year? What did you do about it?
- Give me an example of when someone brought you a new idea, particularly one that was odd or unusual. What did you do?
- If you could do anything in the world, what would you do?

Figure 7.7 Know what to ask

- Describe a situation in which you had a difficult (management) problem. How did you solve it?
- What is the most difficult decision you've had to make? How did you arrive at your decision?
- Describe some situations in which you worked under pressure or met deadlines.
- Were you ever in a situation in which you had to meet two different deadlines given to you by two different people and you couldn't do both? What did you do?
- What type of approach to solving work problems seems to work best for you? Give me an example of when you solved a tough problem.
- When taking on a new task, do you like to have a great deal of feedback and responsibility at the outset, or do you like to try your own approach?
- You're on the phone with another department resolving a problem. The intercom pages you for a customer on hold. Your manager returns your monthly report with red pen markings and demands corrections within the hour. What do you do?
- Describe a sales presentation when you had the right product/service, and the customer wanted it but wouldn't buy it. What did you do next?

Miscellaneous good questions

- How do you measure your own success?
- What is the most interesting thing you've done in the past three years?
- What are your short-term or long-term career goals?
- Why should we hire you?
- What responsibilities do you want, and what kinds of results do you expect to achieve in your next job?
- What do you think it takes to be successful in a company like ours?
- How did the best manager you ever had motivate you to perform well? Why did that method work?
- What is the best thing a previous employer did that you wish everyone did?
- What are you most proud of?
- What is important to you in a job?
- What do you expect to find in our company that you don't have now?
- Is there anything you wanted me to know about you that we haven't discussed?
- Do you have any questions for me?

Figure 7.7 Know what to ask

Source C. Hirschman, 'Playing the high-stakes hiring game', *HR Magazine*, March 1998, pp. 86, 88.

11. Keep control of the interview

The specific objectives that the interviewer has set for the meeting must be constantly kept in mind. This ensures that the applicant talks about relevant subjects. The interviewer must make certain to get all the facts needed to make a decision. 'Don't ignore information that needs to be explored', cautions Grigg.[108] To do so means that employment decisions will be made on incomplete and/or inaccurate information, thus increasing the probability of selection failure.

Already in the United States negligence in hiring is grounds for a lawsuit. Where an employee assaults, robs or injures a third party and the injured party demonstrates that the employer knew or should have known of the unfit or dangerous character of the employee, the employer can be found liable.[109]

12. Explain the job

The interviewer must explain the key aspects of the job and where it fits in. This should be done without overselling the job, the employment conditions or the company as this only leads to later dissatisfaction. To make a decision, the candidate needs accurate information about the job, the organisation and the terms and conditions of employment. The interviewer should always ask candidates if they have any questions or need any more information.

Selection is a two-way process. In fact, some writers recommend that the term 'employment decision' should be used instead of 'selection decision', because the latter implies a one-way decision-making process in which organisations evaluate candidates and make decisions about who will be accepted or rejected. In reality, a two-way decision-making process exists in which candidates are involved in decision making. A candidate, if offered a job, has the right to accept or reject it.[110]

13. Close the interview

Closing the interview should be done in a friendly way. If the applicant is clearly not the person the interviewer is seeking, they should be told tactfully. If the applicant appears suitable and is to proceed to the next step in the selection process, the interviewer should say so. If not in a position to give an answer on the spot, the interviewer should say when the applicant might expect to hear from the company.

The public relations aspects of employment interviewing can never be ignored. Berenholtz says: 'Those responsible for recruiting need to be aware that they represent a window into the organisation. As a consequence of this, they are in a position to either greatly enhance or diminish the company's public image.'[111]

14. Write up the interview

One of the biggest deficiencies in interviewing is the failure by interviewers to write up the results of the interview while it is still fresh in their minds. Accuracy is increased if facts and impressions are recorded as soon as possible (this can also be done during the interview). Checklists and/or rating forms can help make this a less onerous job (see figure 7.8). Finally, accurate records are vital in proving that the selection decision was not discriminatory.

Comments regarding key selection criteria, in particular, are invaluable in this respect. For example, if excellent communication skills are an essential job requirement, recorded examples of the applicant's poor English, lack of fluency, and so on, are invaluable. Likewise are examples of the applicant's good English, fluency, articulation, and so on. Assessments supported by objective, accurately recorded evidence give credibility to the selection interview process and ensure that any questions regarding a selection decision can be justified when subjected to external scrutiny. Post-interview write-ups are a mark of the professional interviewer and should be done automatically at the end of each interview.

15. Check references

This is critical. The interviewer should wait until the interview is over before making a decision and should never make a job offer until a thorough reference check has been completed. One of the biggest mistakes in reference checking is to talk to only one referee. The interviewer should talk to a cross-section of people — peers, superiors, former bosses, customers — and compare the responses. Research indicates that validity is best when the referee is well acquainted with the applicant's work and/or is the applicant's supervisor.[112]

The most serious validity problem remains the unwillingness of referees to give frank opinions and evaluations for fear of defamation claims.[113] The growth in Britain and the United States of negligent hiring lawsuits, however, means that companies must also be concerned about giving a reference that is favourably false. A company may now be held liable for an economic loss suffered by another company if it fails to disclose negative information about a former employee related to the job in question.[114] Personal references from family friends and the like should obviously be avoided. Catanzariti warns: 'a few kind words today could see you in court tomorrow — and a few bad words could too!'[115] Companies can minimise the chances of experiencing defamation or negligent referral claims by making sure the information provided is factual and can be substantiated.[116] It is a foolish HR manager who assumes that the recruitment consultant will thoroughly check a candidate's references.[117] Responsibility for checking references should be clearly detailed in the recruitment contract. Questions regarding applicant identity and résumé accuracy must be covered.[118]

Academic and professional qualifications in particular must be checked. In the United States, it is estimated that up to one-third of all higher education claims are false.[119] Studies conducted by Western embassies in Beijing show that up to one-third of applications to study in overseas universities are fraudulent.[120] A recent survey by Pricewaterhouse Coopers found that more than 60 per cent of applicants for positions in the Australian financial sector lied about their qualifications and experience.[121] Such fraudulent practices have seen the introduction of special reference-checking consultancies that verify information on employment, convictions, finances, identity, drug abuse, education and professional licences. Reference checking, says Dunn 'should be seen as an aggressive, proactive way to reduce turnover and maintain a higher quality workforce'.[122]

Failure to conduct an adequate background check can be expensive and embarrassing. The facts must be known before a decision to hire is made. As Rowe points out, the interviewer must think about the strategic nature of what they are about to do.[123]

Figure 7.9 outlines some guidelines for giving references.

APPLICANT EVALUATION FORM

CONFIDENTIAL

Position applied for: _____

Date: _____/_____/_____ Interview location: _____

PERSONAL INFORMATION

Full name of applicant: _____

Address: _____

City: _____ State: _____ Post code: _____

Contact details: _____ (private) _____ (business)

_____ (mobile) _____ (email)

Education/qualifications: _____

_____

FIRST IMPRESSION

What type of first impression does the applicant make?

[ ] Very poor early impression

[ ] Rather poor early impression

[ ] Good impression in some ways, poor in others

[ ] Good early impression

[ ] Very good early impression

COMMENT: _____

APPEARANCE

How does the applicant's appearance impress you?

[ ] Untidy, unkempt, sloppy

[ ] Overdressed, flashy

[ ] Professional appearance

COMMENT: _____

SELF-EXPRESSION

How well does the applicant use correct English, and articulate their views?

[ ] Very poor — indistinct, confused

[ ] Poor — difficult to understand, monotonous, boring

[ ] Average — fairly easy to understand, but does not have great fluency

[ ] Good — clear speech, easy to understand

[ ] Very good — fluent, logical, persuasive

COMMENT: _____

BEHAVIOUR

What was the applicant's behaviour during the interview? (please circle)

Timid, overbearing, rude, arrogant, immature, ingratiating, nervous, irritating, indifferent, aggressive, confident, self-assured, tactful, relaxed, enthusiastic, friendly, pleasant, passive.

COMMENT: _____

RESPONSIVENESS

How alert was the applicant?

[ ] Withdrawn, dull, uninvolved in the interview, slow to catch on

[ ] Responded only to direct questions, did not volunteer information, evasive

[ ] Good listener, responded well, grasped ideas quickly

[ ] Alert, attentive, asked intelligent questions; spontaneous, quick to grasp concepts

COMMENT: _____

(continued)

Figure 7.8 Applicant evaluation form

BACKGROUND

How well do the applicant's experience, education and training fit the job?

[ ] Little or no relationship between background and the job; insufficient experience

[ ] Background and education partly related to job; has adequate education for the job

[ ] Background well-suited to job; appropriate experience; good education match

[ ] Background and education fit the job exceptionally well; ideally fitted for the job; unusually well qualified

COMMENT: _____

TRACK RECORD

[ ] Little evidence of past success; background questionable

[ ] Good record of accomplishment and potential for growth

[ ] Outstanding past record; exceptional potential for growth

COMMENT: _____

TEAMWORK

Ability to work with others

[ ] Evidence of friction with supervisors, peers, subordinates

[ ] Appears to be a 'loner', but able to work with others if required

[ ] Appears to be an excellent team player

COMMENT: _____

PLANS FOR FUTURE

[ ] Poorly defined goals; appears to act without purpose

[ ] Wants the job, but is not thinking beyond it

[ ] Ambitious, industrious, and has plans for getting ahead

COMMENT: _____

APPLICANT'S MOTIVATION

What factors appear to be influencing the applicant's consideration of a position with our company at this time? Why is the applicant leaving their present position?

_____

POSSIBLE RESERVATIONS

What reservations or concerns (if any) does the applicant have about the position? (Consider factors such as work location, travel, compensation, advancement, opportunities, etc.)

_____

OTHER POSITIONS

Does the applicant seem to be more suitable for another position or location?

_____

APPARENT ASSETS AND LIMITATIONS

What are the applicant's apparent assets and limitations? What training and development (if any) is recommended?

_____

ADDITIONAL COMMENTS: _____

_____

DATE AVAILABLE: _____

OVERALL EVALUATION

[ ] Good   [ ] Fair   [ ] Unfavourable

Would you recommend the applicant be given a

Further interview   [ ] Yes   [ ] No

Job offer   [ ] Yes   [ ] No

INTERVIEWER'S NAME: _____ SIGNATURE: _____

INTERVIEWER'S POSITION: _____

Figure 7.8 Applicant evaluation form
Source Asia Pacific Management Co. Ltd, 2004.

GIVING REFERENCES

- Don't respond to telephone requests — get all requests in writing. You cannot assume that people on the telephone are who they say they are.
- Have all reference enquiries directed to the HR department. Educate employees not to make personal comments about former employees over the telephone.
- Ask the enquiring organisation to have the applicant verify that a reference is to be given (especially important where additional information, apart from dates of employment, position held etc., is being sought).
- Obtain releases from existing employees granting the company the right to supply references.
- Stick to the facts. Provide only information that can be substantiated — dates of employment, salary, attendance, awards, job responsibilities, etc.

Figure 7.9 Guidelines for giving references
Source Adapted from E. Bahnsen and A. Loftin, 'Handle reference requests consistently; stick to the facts', *HR News*, December 1995, p. 16; P. M. Perry, 'Cut your risk when giving references', *HR Focus*, May 1995, pp. 15–16; and M. Magee, 'Reference traps', *Boardroom Reports*, 1 April 1994, p. 10.

16. Evaluate the interview

The HR practitioner must ensure that all the information required has been gleaned, that the interview objectives were achieved, that the interview and the interviewing technique are evaluated, and the 'batting average' reviewed — are winners or losers being selected? This can be done by looking at labour turnover figures and by comparing performance appraisal assessments against the assessments made during the employment interview.

The medical examination

The **medical examination** is usually given by a company doctor or by a doctor approved and paid for by the organisation. The aim of the pre-employment medical is to obtain information on the medical condition of the applicant.

Medical examination Examination to determine whether an applicant is physically fit to perform a job.

Such information is useful in:

- ensuring that people are not assigned to jobs for which they are physically unsuited
- safeguarding the health of present employees through the detection of contagious diseases
- identifying applicants who have symptoms of alcohol and drug abuse
- ensuring that applicants are not placed in positions that will aggravate an existing medical condition
- protecting the organisation from workers compensation claims by identifying injuries and illnesses present at the time the employee was hired
- determining the applicant's eligibility for group life, health and disability insurance.

Because of the cost, some organisations give applicants a medical questionnaire to complete. If no serious medical problems are indicated by the questionnaire, the applicant is not required to have a physical examination. It should be noted that EEO authorities sanction the use of a medical examination only if a legitimate job requirement exists. If medical examinations systematically screen out those with disabilities or diseases that are not directly related to the person's ability to perform the job and/or do not adversely affect the health or safety of others, they will likely be regarded as discriminatory.

Screening for AIDS

Other controversial issues involve AIDS, drug and genetic screening.[124] A Federal Court decision that addiction or drug dependency is a disability has thrown into question the legality of such screening practices.[125] Although private employers' associations and trade unions recommend that employers should not test for AIDS, all Australian Defence Force recruits are. The Army bans HIV-positive recruits because soldiers are expected to fight and bleed. The Army has similar bans on recruits with diabetes and gout.[126] Australians wanting to work in China, South Korea and Singapore likewise have to prove that they do not have AIDS before a work permit is granted. How organisations satisfy such requirements while not being able to demand an AIDS test is unclear.

Screening for substance abuse

The screening of personnel for alcohol and drug abuse is also a sensitive issue. Australian companies such as Hanson, Qantas and WMC Resources use random drug tests, arguing that they are necessary to guarantee a safe working environment. Unions, on the other hand, feel that such testing is an invasion of employee privacy and ignores other factors (such as stress and fatigue) that affect employee performance.[127] Yossi Berger, National Occupational Health and Safety Officer for the Australian Workers Union, complains: 'When I say to employers that if you take a sample of drugs of this worker at 3 am to check for your favourite drugs and alcohol, then I want 50 per cent of the sample so I can test for what the workplace is putting into their system — for things like fumes and diesel as well as what the roster may be doing to his hormones — they get very shy about that equity.'[128] However, research consistently shows significant differences in absenteeism, involuntary turnover rates, disciplinary actions, vehicular accidents and medical costs between employees who test positive and those who do not.[129] The National Health and Safety Commission, for example, claims that in almost 40 per cent of all workplace deaths the cause is alcohol.[130] Organisations that administer compulsory drug tests should exercise caution because of the considerable risk of litigation, expense, union opposition and negative impact on employee morale.[131]

Genetic screening

Advances in technology have now made genetic screening available to organisations. This permits the company to identify applicants who may be hypersensitive to pollutants in the workplace, thus facilitating their placement to a 'safe' work area. Genetic screening, however, can also be used to identify applicants who are susceptible to various diseases and physical or mental conditions. As a consequence, genetic screening practices are seen as intrusive, highly controversial and subject to increasing legislative control.[132] The Australian Law Reform Commission nevertheless recently recommended genetic testing be allowed for occupational health and safety reasons or because of job requirements. This has met with strong union opposition because of fears of privacy concerns and abuse by unscrupulous employers.[133] The challenge for HR managers is to ensure that the individual's right to privacy is balanced with the organisation's right to information about the person.[134]

Figure 7.10 lists some symptoms that may indicate employee drug use.

How do you know if an employee is abusing alcohol, illegal drugs or prescription drugs? You seldom can tell for sure, says Gary Topchik, director of Silver Star Enterprises. But possible indicators include the following:
- deteriorating productivity
- inappropriate or angry interactions with colleagues or customers
- frequent absences or lateness
- continuous rapid or wandering speech
- drowsiness or frequent breaks
- changes in productivity after lunch
- occasional, unpredictable flashes of outstanding performance

- accidents, errors, carelessness or sloppy work
- regularly borrowing money from colleagues
- drunken behaviour, with or without the odour of alcohol
- possession of drug paraphernalia
- drug mottos on clothing or at workstation; drug-inspired jewellery
- possession of a variety of medicines
- association with known drug users.

Topchik reminds managers that the same symptoms can also result from other causes. Managers who observe them should report them to a trained professional who knows how to diagnose drug-related problems and make referrals.

Figure 7.10 Symptoms of employee drug use
Source Silver Star Enterprises, Newsletter, Los Angeles, March–April 1993, quoted in *Training & Development*, vol. 49, no. 10, 1995, p. 13.

Other selection techniques

Biographical information blanks

Biographical information blanks (BIBs) are one of the oldest methods for predicting job success and are closely related to the weighted application form. The BIB typically includes more items than a standard application form and has various types of questions relating to attitudes, hobbies, sports, club membership, years of education, health, early life experiences, investments, sales experiences and the like that have been identified as success criteria. A multiple-choice questionnaire is used to collect the responses of job applicants. For example, the applicant might be asked:

How did you do at school?	*How old were you when you started work?*
1. Always among the top students	1. Younger than 16
2. Below the top group, but better than average	2. 16–17
3. About average	3. 18–19
4. Below average but not in the bottom group	4. 20–21
5. Always among the bottom students	5. 22–23

The responses given are then compared with the responses of high-performing employees. Thus, using seemingly irrelevant questions, characteristics associated with high performance are identified and measured. Research suggests high validity for the BIB as a predictor of job success.[135] While basically a simple and inexpensive technique, the costs of introducing a BIB can be very high if external consultants are used. There is also the risk that unless great care is taken with the design of the questionnaire, it may appear discriminatory and not job-related.

Panel interviews

Panel interviews or board interviews are conducted by two or more interviewers. This allows all interviewers to evaluate the applicant on the same questions and answers at the one time. It also overcomes any idiosyncratic biases that individual interviewers might have. However, research shows that in racially mixed panels where there is a lone white or black interviewer, the interviewer identifies more with other panel members than their own racial group. This suggests that it is important that the membership of racially mixed panels be balanced.[136] Provided thorough preparation is undertaken by panel members before the interview, the same panel members ask the same questions of each candidate and there is discussion of the candidates between interviews, the interview process can be improved.[137] Although a thorough questioning of the applicant is likely, the experience can be quite stressful for the interviewee. Another disadvantage can be the time and cost of involving senior managers as panel members. The panel interview is widely used in the military, universities and the public sector.

Group interviews

Group interviews often take the form of a problem-solving exercise or a leaderless group discussion, with the interviewers acting as observers. According to Anderson, organisations using such methods are likely to place emphasis on a candidate's personality, attitudes, and social, influencing, communication and intellectual skills.[138] Group interviews are probably best used when dealing with young applicants, such as new university graduates, or as part of an assessment centre process.

Computer screening

A recent interviewing innovation is the use of computers to screen applications via résumé scanning and to conduct preliminary screening interviews and online testing. The typical computer-aided interview has about 100 questions and can be completed in less than 20 minutes (see figure 7.11). However, some are highly sophisticated and include online testing and assessment procedures designed to generate information on the candidate's intelligence, leadership, verbal assertiveness, drive, emotional control and other personal qualities.[139] A big advantage is that a lot of information can be obtained quickly and economically from a large number of candidates. The well-designed computer system avoids the common weaknesses of face-to-face interviews because 'it conducts the interview with perfect memory, patience, accuracy and consistency that enhance the cognitive power and decision-making capability of the subsequent human interviewer'.[140] Hard or embarrassing questions, for example, are asked without fear or favour.

Interestingly, in a study by Martin and Nagao, candidates answered more accurately to the computer than to human interviewers.[141] While computerised screening and interviewing are user-friendly and provide instant feedback, research indicates that there is disenchantment with 'personality test' type questions and that applicants for higher-level positions desire more personal attention. This last point suggests that computerised screening and interviewing are probably best suited to lower-level positions.[142] Finally, concerns have been raised regarding faking, privacy, security of information, equity and union opposition.[143]

Computers present job applicants with questions that, though they are multiple choice, require reflection, and can spot inconsistent or problematic answers. Here's a brief sample:

1. Steve, if you were given a supervisory job, how would you evaluate your chances for success?
   A. Very poor, this would not be a good job for me.
   B. Poor, I don't think I would perform well.
   C. Fair, I think I could do an adequate job.
   D. Good, I think I would perform above average.
   E. Excellent, I think I would be highly successful.
   F. I am not sure how I would perform.

2. Steve, how would your supervisor rate your performance at your former job?
   A Very poor.
   B. Poor.
   C. Fair.
   D. Good.
   E. Excellent.
   F. I'm not sure how it would be rated.

3. Steve, could we have your permission to contact Bill Winters [Steve's previous supervisor] to see how he would rate your performance at ABC Brick Company?
   A. Yes.
   B. No.

Figure 7.11 A computer interview

Source B. Mitchell, 'Interviewing face to interface', *Personnel*, vol. 67, no. 1, 1990, p. 24. Reproduced by permission of publisher. © 1990 American Management Association, New York (www.amanet.org). All rights reserved.

Video interviewing[144]

Another recent approach to employment interviewing involves the use of video. This is particularly advantageous for organisations when conducting interviews with applicants who are resident interstate or overseas. Management at the hiring organisation, for example, can evaluate the video candidates and then nominate a short list for further interviews at their office. Cost savings in management time, transportation and accommodation charges obviously can be considerable. A disadvantage is where a candidate expresses reluctance to being video interviewed. Similarly, some candidates complain about the lack of feedback and the lack of the human element[145] (see figure 7.12). According to one expert, however, for most candidates, initial reluctance is quickly overcome.[146] A final problem centres on visual quality, which may not always be consistent and can be a source of annoyance to both the applicant and the interviewer.

According to Dr Karl Magnusen of the College of Business Administration at Florida International University, the main problem with videoconferencing as a means of employment interviewing is the inexperience of the participants. Employers who conduct interviews through videoconference technology have expressed a need for more training materials for the technique. While those materials are being developed, Dr Magnusen offers the following advice:

Do

- Wear solid colours, keeping in mind that light blue shirts or blouses look better than white.
- Begin the interview with a smile, since you won't be able to shake hands.
- Keep in mind there will be a half-second delay in transmission. Participants need to listen more carefully as a result.
- Behave as though talking to a television with ears — and remember, the other party can hear everything unless the mute feature is turned on.
- Always check time zone differences when scheduling.

Don't

- Be late — besides being obviously rude, it's costly.
- Wear clothes, scarves or ties with busy patterns — they're distracting. Similarly, avoid jewellery or cuff links that clink next to the microphone.
- Make too many movements. While normal movement is fine, excessive gesturing will wash out on the screen, since data transmission is not as complex as on television.
- Forget that you are talking to a real person like yourself. Concentrate on the interview, not the technology.
- Neglect to thank the other person when the interview is over.

Figure 7.12 Tips for videoconferencing
Source Extract by Elizabeth Shelley in *HR Magazine*, August 1995, p. 72.

Assessment centres

Assessment centres are a 'state-of-the art' selection technique that involves a series of tests, exercises and feedback sessions conducted over a one- to five-day period. In addition, assessment centres can be used to help organisations to identify and assess individual and organisational strengths and limitations after a merger or downsizing and 'to recognize where the talent pool lies for succession planning'.[147] While there is no one best procedure, the following activities are indicative of what is generally involved:

- **In-basket exercises:** applicants are required to deal with a series of memos, letters and so on, relating to a number of business activities or problems.
- *Group discussions:* applicants take part in at least one group discussion. Typically, these deal with a business problem such as how to cut staff, increase sales or improve productivity.
- *Psychological tests:* applicants undergo a variety of psychological tests. A typical test battery would include intelligence, aptitude and personality tests and tests measuring leadership style and attitudes towards conflict resolution.
- *Interviews:* applicants are interviewed by a number of people including line managers, HRM specialists and industrial psychologists.
- **Business games:** assessment centres generally include some type of business game that requires the applicants to engage in role-playing and group decision making.

After each activity, applicants are evaluated by a group of assessors. At the end of the assessment centre program, the assessors combine their evaluations in an effort to reach a consensus regarding the suitability of each applicant. Assessment centres, because of their focus on group activities and problem solving, are especially suitable for assessing team leaders.[148]

Although common in Britain and the United States (especially for graduate recruitment), assessment centres have had limited use in the Asia–Pacific region. Organisations that utilise assessment centres for internal selection (promotion) and employee development include BHP Billiton, Cathay Pacific, Coles Myer, Hong Kong and Shanghai Bank, National Australia Bank and the State Government of NSW.[149] While research studies indicate that assessment centres have a higher validity than other selection techniques, the cost associated with their use is a major disadvantage and tends to restrict their use to large companies.[150] Nevertheless, if researched and implemented appropriately, assessment centres can be shown to be economically worthwhile.[151]

Assessment centres Use interviews, tests, simulations, games and observations to evaluate an individual's potential.

In-basket exercises A simulation in which the participant is asked to establish priorities for handling a number of business papers, such as memoranda, reports and telephone messages, that would typically cross a manager's desk.

Business games Simulations that represent actual business situations.

The polygraph

The **polygraph** ('lie detector') is an instrument used to record bodily changes that take place when an applicant is subjected to pressure. Stressful questions such as 'Do you take drugs?' and 'Have you ever stolen anything?' are interposed with neutral questions such as 'Is your name Smith?'. As a test of honesty, the polygraph is used in the United States, Israel, Japan and Canada and reportedly is becoming popular in Europe.[152] However, with the introduction of the *Employee Polygraph Protection Act 1988* in the United States, the use of pre-employment 'lie detector' tests by private employers has been severely restricted. The polygraph has never been a popular screening device in Australia because of its questionable reliability and validity, perceived threat to civil liberties, and employee and trade union opposition.[153]

Given the potential legal and public relations costs involved, organisations tempted to use the polygraph should exercise the utmost caution. Any attempt to use the polygraph in employee selection should be made only after legal advice has been obtained and employer associations, government authorities and trade unions consulted.

Honesty tests

The curtailment of the polygraph in the United States has seen the widespread adoption of written honesty or integrity tests (especially in the retail industry).[154] **Honesty tests** are designed to ask applicants about their attitudes towards theft and dishonesty or about admissions of theft or illegal behaviour. Most tests have satisfactory reliability and, according to Milkovich and Boudreau, have shown validities in the 'range of 0.50 with self-reported dishonest activity, though their relationship to objectively or observed theft or dismissal due to illegal activity is usually lower'.[155]

A two-year study by the American Psychological Association, in fact, concluded that professionally developed honesty tests are valid predictors of dishonest and counterproductive behaviour in the workplace.[156] Even so, honesty tests are not without their critics. Charges that some tests are deceptive, ask questions that are intrusive, have questionable validity and present a real danger that applicants who fail will be labelled as dishonest have all been made. Consequently, honesty tests should be used with great caution, always in conjunction with a detailed reference check, and should be restricted to those jobs where an actual opportunity for serious theft exists.[157] Similarly, an applicant should never be rejected solely on the basis of an honesty test result. Although it is estimated that Australian businesses lose some $2.5 billion per year because of security problems, it is very debatable whether honesty tests will gain acceptance because of union and employee resistance.[158] Nevertheless, integrity tests have been recommended as an essential part of the selection process for entry into the NSW Police Force.[159]

Graphology

Graphology is based on the premise that a person's personality is revealed through their handwriting. Despite its lack of validity, it is still used as a selection technique in Europe (especially France).[160] Reputable companies such as Renault and Helena Rubenstein, for example, have employed consulting graphologists.

The selection decision

The final step in the selection process requires the line manager (often in conjunction with the HR manager) to make a decision to hire or reject an applicant. The selection decision can be made using either a compensatory approach or a successive hurdles approach.

The compensatory approach

In the **compensatory approach**, the manager considers all the selection data (favourable and unfavourable) for candidates who have successfully passed the initial screening. This allows the manager to form an overall impression of the applicants. Because it employs more information and does not rely on just one selection technique, the compensatory approach should lead to more accurate hiring decisions. In jobs where a minimum amount of some ability, skill or knowledge is critical, however, a successive hurdles approach is recommended. Finally, because each candidate must complete all the steps in the selection process before the selection decision is made, the compensatory approach can be time consuming and expensive.

The successive hurdles approach

In the **successive hurdles approach** or multiple hurdle approach, the selection predictors are ranked according to their effectiveness (that is, from most valid and reliable to least valid and reliable). For example, if an intelligence test has the highest correlation with job success, it will be used as the first hurdle or step in the selection process. Candidates who pass move on to the next hurdle, such as the interview, reference check and so on, until the selection process is completed. Candidates who fail any hurdle are automatically rejected. The successive hurdles approach can be very economical (especially when selecting a few candidates from a large pool of applicants) by using predictors such as an intelligence test to screen out the best candidates early in the selection process, thus saving the more expensive predictors, such as panel interviews, for use with a small group (see figure 7.13).

Successive hurdles approach
Involves the screening out of candidates at each stage of the selection process.

COMPENSATORY APPROACH

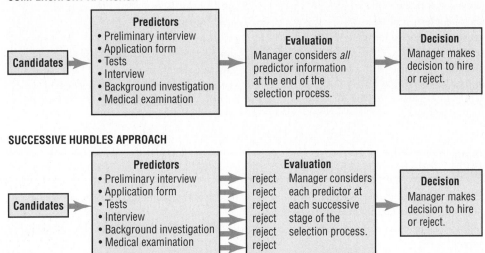

SUCCESSIVE HURDLES APPROACH

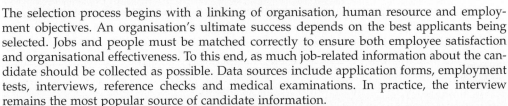

Figure 7.13 Selection decision approaches
Source Asia Pacific Management Co. Ltd, 2004.

Summary

The selection process begins with a linking of organisation, human resource and employment objectives. An organisation's ultimate success depends on the best applicants being selected. Jobs and people must be matched correctly to ensure both employee satisfaction and organisational effectiveness. To this end, as much job-related information about the candidate should be collected as possible. Data sources include application forms, employment tests, interviews, reference checks and medical examinations. In practice, the interview remains the most popular source of candidate information.

HR specialists and line managers who conduct employment interviews should be trained in interview planning and in assessing applicants in job-related terms. EEO requirements can be satisfied only if objective measures are employed. Consequently, the value of employment tests, biographical information blanks and assessment centres should not be overlooked. As much selection activity is unsophisticated and ad hoc, HR managers have a key role to play in educating management on the importance of a systematic selection process to the successful realisation of the organisation's strategic business objectives.

Thirty interactive Wiley Web Questions are available to test your understanding of this chapter at
www.johnwiley.com.au/ highered/hrm5e
in the student resources area

chapter 7 *employee selection* 255

application form (p. 230)	HIV/AIDS testing (p. 226)
aptitude tests (p. 235)	honesty tests (p. 254)
assessment centres (p. 253)	in-basket exercises (p. 253)
biographical information blanks (BIBs) (p. 251)	intelligence tests (p. 235)
	interest tests (p. 235)
body language (p. 241)	medical examination (p. 249)
business games (p. 253)	panel interviews (p. 251)
compensatory approach (p. 254)	personality tests (p. 235)
correlation coefficient (p. 227)	polygraph (p. 254)
employment interview (p. 237)	predictor (p. 227)
employment tests (p. 234)	reliability (p. 228)
equal employment opportunity (EEO) (p. 226)	selection criteria (p. 225)
	strategic selection (p. 225)
face validity (p. 233)	structured interview (p. 237)
genetic screening (p. 226)	successive hurdles approach (p. 255)
graphology (p. 254)	unstructured interview (p. 237)
group interviews (p. 251)	validity (p. 227)

review questions

1. Why is it important to check references? What are some of the problems involved in checking references? How would you overcome them?
2. What are the major types of employment interview? What are the advantages and disadvantages of each?
3. Describe the typical selection steps you would use when hiring a taxi driver, a graduate trainee and a university lecturer in HRM.
4. Which do you think are the most critical steps in the selection process? Why?
5. What are the arguments for and against screening for substance abuse?
6. What are the pros and cons of using personality tests in employee selection?
7. Explain what is meant by the terms reliability and validity. What is their significance in employee selection?
8. What are the most common mistakes made by interviewers? How would you overcome them?
9. Why is it important to evaluate the selection process? Describe how you would go about it.
10. Why should an organisation's strategic business objectives define the type of people to be hired?

environmental influences on selection

Discuss the key environmental influences from the model (figure 7.14 shown opposite) that have significance for employee selection.

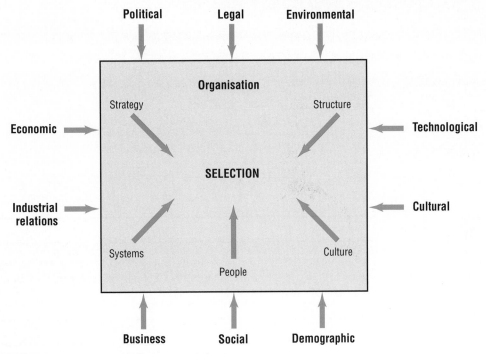

Figure 7.14 Environmental influences on selection

██ *class debate*

Employers should be free to hire whomever they like.

██ *what's your view?*

Write a 500-word response to the Letter to the Editor on page 234, agreeing or disagreeing with the writer's point of view.

██ *practitioner speaks*

As a class, critically discuss the article on page 239. What was the most valuable piece of advice given by the author? Explain your reasoning.

██ *newsbreak exercise*

Read the Newsbreak 'For some men talent is not enough' on pages 242–3. Do you agree or disagree with the author's view? Why? As a class, critically examine the situation described.

██ *soapbox*

What do you think? Conduct a mini survey of class members, using the following questionnaire. Critically discuss the findings.

1. The selection of candidates with attitudes and values the company desires is anti-union.	YES	NO
2. Employees should be fired if it is discovered that they have lied on their application form.	YES	NO
3. People with criminal records should not be hired as schoolteachers.	YES	NO
4. Drug testing should be compulsory for all employees.	YES	NO
5. People with red hair are hot-tempered.	YES	NO
6. Reference checking is a waste of time.	YES	NO

online exercise

Conduct an online search for information on one of the following: personality tests, polygraph and honesty tests, intelligence tests or online psychological tests. Summarise your findings in a report of 500–750 words. Include the web addresses that you found useful.

ethical dilemmas

Jet Red's medical exam

'Look, as Managing Director of this company I have both a legal and moral obligation to protect the interests of our employees, customers and shareholders. I say we should test for anything that could possibly have an adverse impact on our medical and health insurance costs or workers compensation costs or that is a potential health and safety risk. Testing for drug use, AIDS or potential heart attack victims is fine with me. What are we running here — a business or a welfare organisation?' Alan Balkin thumped the table, his face red with anger.

'I'm afraid it's not that simple Alan', replied Linda Church, HR Manager. 'There are matters regarding the employee's right to privacy, the need for a medical exam to be job-related and not to be in any way discriminatory. We cannot refuse to hire drug addicts just because they are drug dependent. If we do, we could be in breach of the federal Disability Discrimination Act. There are legal and ethical issues to be considered.'

'You're telling me!' snapped Alan. 'It's obvious that the people who thought this up don't have to run an airline. Do they realise that one in eight applicants for flight attendant jobs have been found to be using drugs? What do we tell our passengers? How can we in all honesty claim that we are a "safe" airline if we employ drug addicts or people who are about to drop dead?'

Discussion questions

1. Do you think it is ethical for companies to demand comprehensive medical examinations for the following positions?
   - Check-in clerk
   - Flight attendant
   - Pilot
   - HR manager
   - Maintenance engineer
2. Is conducting a urinalysis to check for drug use an invasion of privacy? Is it unethical?
3. Should employees be tested for AIDS? Pregnancy? Allergies? Disabilities?
4. How would you reconcile Alan's health and safety concerns with the employee's right to privacy?

Western University's selection committee

'Well, Harry, I see you have been nominated to the selection panel for the Associate Professor's job in Engineering.'

'Yes, Heaven knows why they picked me', replied Professor Harry Young as he sipped his red wine. 'Mmm, not a bad choice. Not bad at all. You certainly can pick wine.'

Professor James Wong smiled. 'Harry, I trust you know how to pick Associate Professors.'

'What do you mean?' asked Harry.

'Well, for starters, the reason you were nominated for the panel is that you are an outsider. You are from the business school.'

'So?' queried Harry.

'The rest of the panel are the Dean of Engineering's stooges — you give the panel an air of legitimacy, perhaps even respectability.'

'I don't understand James.'

'Surely you don't think David Ong in Engineering is going to let a panel choose his new Professor? David will have already selected his man and, believe me, it will be a man. The rest of you are there to make up the numbers.'

'James, as far as I am concerned it will be the candidate that I believe is best for the job who will get my vote.'

'Harry, whenever will you learn? You have been appointed to legitimise David's choice, not select the best candidate.'

'James, you can't be serious?'

'Of course I'm serious. When does your contract come up for renewal Harry?'

'Next month. Why?'

'Really Harry, you continue to amaze me. Organisational politics isn't your game, is it?'

'What are you getting at James?'

James smiled. 'You mean you don't know who is chairing the panel to review your renewal application?'

Harry's face whitened. 'You mean it's David Ong?'

'Naturally. Another glass of red, Harry?'

Discussion questions

1. What ethical issues are raised in this case?
2. If you were Harry, what would you do?

case study

Selection at Western University

Professor Harry Young sipped his red wine and savoured the flavour.

'Not bad, is it?' The questioning voice belonged to James Wong, Professor of Economics. James seated himself next to Harry. 'What's on your mind Harry? You look like you were deep in thought.'

'Actually, I was thinking about a telephone call I received earlier from Anna Tan at All Star University. She is interested in applying for the Vice-Chancellor's job.'

James smiled. 'Anna would be an ideal candidate. She is highly qualified and has an outstanding reputation as an administrator. But tell her not to waste her time.'

'What do you mean, James?'

'The new Vice-Chancellor has already been selected.'

'How can that be? The advertisements appeared in the press only last Saturday.'

'Really, Harry, for someone who has worked at Western University for as long as you have, you really are wet behind the ears.'

Harry stiffened. 'What you do mean?'

'Come on, Harry, you mean you really don't know?'

'Know what?' snapped Harry.

'The new Vice-Chancellor is going to be the Dean of Arts, Anthony Grimes.'

'James, you're kidding me? Grimes hasn't published anything for years. And his reputation as an administrator is nothing to write home about.'

'Aha, you don't understand, do you?'

'What do you mean?' Harry asked.

'You may be correct in your assessment of Grimes, but you have ignored three important factors. First, he is more than acceptable to the present government. Second, he has all the necessary connections with the university power brokers. And third, he will maintain the status quo. No one will be threatened.'

'I don't believe you James. That's just rumour.'

'Well, Harry, my friend, you forget who is heading the selection committee. David Ong, the Dean of Engineering. And who is the Dean of Engineering's best friend? The Dean of Arts. I suggest you read the job description more carefully Harry. You will see it fits Anthony Grimes to a tee. Scholarship is downplayed and things like knowledge of the university, an understanding of its educational values and so on are all highlighted. Grimes has been with this university for over 20 years. Who's going to outscore him? No one.'

(continued)

'James, if what you say is true, it is most disappointing. Particularly as this university needs to undergo major change if it is to become anything but second rate.'

'Ah!' smiled James.

'What are you smiling at, James? I think what you have told me, if it is true, is most depressing.'

'Harry, the best is yet to come.'

'What do you mean?

'As a "reward" for doing his job so well, our good friend David Ong will be promoted to the exalted position of Assistant Vice-Chancellor when Carmel Sklovsky retires next year.'

'James, now I know you're kidding me. That guy's reputation is terrible. He's lazy and an obstacle to change. Everyone knows that to survive in his department you have to be a "yes man".'

'All true, Harry, but such is life at Western University. Another glass of red, Harry?'

Discussion questions

1. What issues are raised in this case?
2. If you were the HR Manager at Western University, what would you do (given that HRM is a profession)?
3. Do you think the situation described in this case represents common or uncommon organisational behaviour?

practical exercises

1. Airline Jet Red is undergoing a turbulent period in its corporate history. Plagued by heavy financial losses it is trying to reinvent itself to become the fastest-growing, most profitable airline in the Asia–Pacific region. As part of the change process it has been decided to use the cabin crew as a key marketing tool in communicating Jet Red's new image — young, motivated, service-oriented, confident and fun to travel with. The company wants to emphasise its 'Australianness' but at the same time communicate its cultural diversity.

   The company currently has two vacancies for cabin crew. The following eight applications have been received:

Name:	**Edward Ma**		
Address:	1/28 Pearl Street, Ashwood, 2000	Marital status:	Single
Age:	23 years	Qualifications:	BBA Eastern University (Major in Marketing)
Height:	168 centimetres	Languages:	English, Cantonese and Mandarin
Weight:	65 kilograms	Experience:	Part-time waiter, Tino's Pizza Parlour
Place of birth:	Hong Kong	Interests:	Mah-jong, poker, karaoke
Nationality:	Australian	Awards:	Australian Amateur Poker Champion, 2004

Name: Mary Papadopoulos

Address:	23 Weir Street, Burwood, 2011
Age:	26 years
Height:	162 centimetres
Weight:	63 kilograms
Place of birth:	Greece
Nationality:	Australian
Marital status:	Single parent with one child (4 years, Robert)
Qualifications:	Studying part-time for BA at All Star University (majoring in English Literature). Expects to complete her final two subjects within the next 12 months.
Languages:	English, Greek
Experience:	Currently works full-time as a teaching assistant in an exclusive girl's school. Only other job since leaving school was as a receptionist in a small private medical practice.
Interests:	Playing the piano and listening to classical music
Other:	Computer literate, typing skills
Awards:	University Scholarship for the best overall results in Year One

Name: Carmelita Conti

Address:	85 Brunswick Road, Fernwood, 2006
Age:	27 years
Height:	180 centimetres
Weight:	54 kilograms
Place of birth:	The Philippines
Nationality:	Australian
Marital status:	Divorced
Qualifications:	Completed year one of BA degree, Manila University
Languages:	English, Tagalog
Experience:	Two years with Allwell Pharmaceutical company in HR (the Philippines). One year as a sales representative for Oriental Foods Co. Ltd (Singapore). Two years as a marketing specialist with Kiwi Manufacturing Ltd (New Zealand). One year doing part-time modelling and working as an Assistant Manager of the Copacabana Night Club (Hawaii). Lives in Sydney. Seeks a permanent position with career prospects.
Interests:	Aerobics, modelling, reading and cooking
Awards:	Finalist — Miss University; Second prize — Miss Gold Coast; Winner — Miss Photogenic, *Star Magazine*
Other:	Short-sighted

Name: David Misa

Address:	1/46 Jackson Road, Springhill, 2003
Age:	28 years
Height:	182 centimetres
Weight:	76 kilograms
Place of birth:	Kenya
Nationality:	Australian
Marital status:	Single
Qualifications:	BA degree from the University of East London (Majors in Economics and History). Currently studying part-time for an MBA at Western University.
Languages:	English, Swahili
Experience:	Worked for Ajax Pharmaceutical Company as a senior sales representative. Retrenched two months ago because of company closure. Currently unemployed.
Awards:	Sales representative of the year, 2003
Interests:	Travel, classical music, ballet, and fine food and wines
Other:	Secretary, Gays in Business

Name:	**Wayne Peters**		
Address:	6/2 Bentleigh Avenue, Westland, 2009	Experience:	US Army, infantry (weapons specialist) for three years. Currently working as an insurance sales representative.
Age:	26		
Height:	198 centimetres		
Weight:	100 kilograms		
Place of birth:	USA	Interests:	Unarmed combat and pistol shooting
Nationality:	Australian	Awards:	Honourable discharge from the Army; black belt in Karate; university heavyweight boxing champion
Marital status:	Married (wife is Australian)		
Qualifications:	BA (major in Religious Studies) from American Christian University		
		Other:	Facial scars and two fingers missing from left hand
Languages:	English, Spanish		

Name:	**Sarah Menon**		
Address:	115 Alison Avenue, Rosewood, 2004	Qualifications:	BSc from Oz Institute of Technology
Age:	33 years	Languages:	English, Hindi
Height:	166 centimetres	Experience:	Worked for All State Airlines Ltd in sales and marketing. Current position is Marketing Representative, South Australia.
Weight:	58 kilograms		
Place of birth:	India		
Nationality:	Australian	Other:	Former mental patient
Marital status:	Married, no children	Interests:	Knitting, embroidery, reading, gardening

Name:	**Jimmy Cockatoo-Wallace**		
Address:	3/11 Warrigal Street, Eastwood, 2006	Qualifications:	PhD in Sociology from Southern University
Age:	27 years	Languages:	English
Height:	178 centimetres	Experience:	Casual work as a bartender and rock musician (bass guitar).
Weight:	76 kilograms		
Place of birth:	Australia	Interests:	Music, rugby
Nationality:	Australian	Other:	Professional footballer with the Mirrabooka Magpies
Marital status:	Single		

Name:	**Ibrahim Azizi**		
Address:	7/28 Best Road, Blue Waters, 2015	Languages:	English, Arabic, Turkish
Age:	24	Experience:	Employed as a maintenance engineer with Wonderful Hotels
Height:	180 centimetres		
Weight:	80 kilograms	Interests:	Travel, surfing and soccer
Place of birth:	Iraq	Awards:	Apprentice of the Year, 2002
Nationality:	Australian	Other:	Vice-President, Association for the Liberation of Oppressed Peoples
Marital status:	Single		
Qualifications:	Qualified electrician		

Questions

(a) Develop a list of the key selection criteria in terms of experience, qualifications, know-how, personal qualities and special requirements (see the form below).

(b) Outline how you would evaluate the candidates on each criterion.

(c) On reviewing the list of candidates, would you anticipate any bias (favourable or unfavourable)? List any instances and discuss as a class.

(d) Who would you choose for the positions? Why?

(e) If the unsuccessful candidates were to challenge your selection because of perceived bias, how would you defend your choice of candidates?

KEY SELECTION CRITERIA

Experience What type of and how much experience is required to perform this job successfully?

Qualifications What are the minimum formal educational qualifications required to perform this job successfully?

Know-how What special skills, abilities and knowledge are required to perform this job successfully?

Personal qualities What special personal qualities (physical characteristics and personality characteristics) are required to perform this job successfully?

Special requirements What special requirements are required to perform this job successfully?

Role-play

Select two or three class members to interview the candidates and eight others to play the roles of the candidates and conduct the interview process for the eight candidates. Remaining class members should do the following:

(a) Evaluate the interviews, paying particular attention to EEO concerns.

(b) Select two applicants based on their observations.

(c) Use the interview rating sheet that follows to evaluate the interviews.

(d) As a class, critically review the findings.

INTERVIEW RATING SHEET

Interviewer's name: _____

Directions Rate the interviewer by using the five-point rating scale below. Avoid making ratings in the middle of the scale.

1. Did the interviewer pay attention to the applicant?
   Attentive   1 2 3 4 5   Inattentive
2. Did the interviewer allow the candidate full opportunity to speak?
   Interruption   1 2 3 4 5   Full opportunity to speak
3. Did the interviewer seem interested?
   Interested   1 2 3 4 5   Bored
4. Did the interviewer vary the tone of voice?
   Monotonous   1 2 3 4 5   Varied
5. Did the interviewer let the interview drag?
   Rushed   1 2 3 4 5   Dragged
6. Did the interviewer probe for more information?
   Probed   1 2 3 4 5   Ignored leads
7. Were the questions clear?
   Not clear   1 2 3 4 5   Clear
8. Did the interviewer get all the necessary information to make a decision to hire?
   No   1 2 3 4 5   Yes
9. How was the interviewer's explanation of the job duties and responsibilities?
   Poor   1 2 3 4 5   Good
10. How was the interviewer's description of the company?
    Poor   1 2 3 4 5   Good
11. Did the interviewer's questions satisfy EEO requirements?
    Hardly ever   1 2 3 4 5   Always
12. How was the manner in which the interviewer put the candidate at ease?
    Good   1 2 3 4 5   Poor
13. Was the interview concluded smoothly?
    Smooth   1 2 3 4 5   Abrupt
14. Did the interviewer thank the candidate?
    Yes   No
15. Overall, the interviewer was:
    Very good   _____
    Good   _____
    OK   _____
    Poor   _____
    Very poor   _____
16. Comments: _____
    _____
    _____

2. Assume you are interviewing an applicant for the position of HR management trainee. Indicate which of the following questions you feel are appropriate or inappropriate to ask the applicant. As a class, review your responses and discuss any areas of disagreement.

	Appropriate	Not appropriate
Why did you study HRM?		
Do you belong to a political party?		
How old are you?		
Are you a member of a union?		
Do you have any children?		
Why did you leave your last job?		
What is your nationality?		
Are you a hard worker?		
What is your career goal?		
How long do you plan to stay with our company?		
Do you have a criminal record?		
Are you married?		
Why do you want to work for our company?		
What are your hobbies?		
Are you healthy?		
Which languages do you speak?		
How much do you weigh?		
How tall are you?		
Do you hold a driver's licence?		
Are you renting or buying a home?		
Do you own a car?		
What clubs do you belong to?		
Why should we hire you?		
What are your greatest strengths/weaknesses?		
Are your parents Australian?		
How do you plan to continue developing yourself?		
Are you religious?		
Do you smoke?		
Do you drink?		
Do you take drugs?		
What is your father's occupation?		
What does your mother do?		
Are you assertive?		
How would you describe yourself?		
What do you think of the government?		
Do you like to travel?		
Are you a gambler?		
Where were you born?		
Do you play golf?		

3. Critically examine the applicant evaluation form in figure 7.8 on pages 247–8 and design a new, improved form for candidate evaluation. Explain the reasons for the changes made.

suggested readings

Beardwell, I. and Holden, L., *Human Resource Management*, Financial Times/Prentice Hall, London, 2001, ch. 6.

CCH, *Master Human Resources Guide*, CCH, Sydney, 2003, ch. 10.

Compton, R. L., Morrissey, W. J. and Nankervis, A., *Effective Recruitment and Selection Practices*, CCH, Sydney, 2002, chs 6, 7, 8, 10.

De Cieri, H. and Kramer, R., *Human Resource Management in Australia*, McGraw-Hill, Sydney, 2003, ch. 6.

Fisher, C. D., Schoenfeldt, L. F. and Shaw, J. B., *Human Resource Management*, 5th edn, Houghton Mifflin, Boston, 2003, chs 7, 8.

Ivancevich, J. M., *Human Resource Management*, 8th edn, McGraw-Hill, Boston, 2001, ch. 8.

Ivancevich, J. M. and Lee, S. H., *Human Resource Management in Asia*, McGraw-Hill, Singapore, 2002, ch. 6.

Mondy, R. W., Noe, R. M. and Premeaux, S. R., *Human Resource Management*, 8th edn, Prentice Hall, Upper Saddle River, NJ, 2002, chs 6, 7.

Nankervis, A. R., Compton, R. L. and Baird, M., *Strategic Human Resource Management*, 4th edn, Nelson, South Melbourne, 2002, ch. 8.

online references

www.apa.org
www.aps.pyschsociety.com.au
www.bps.org.uk
www.drugfreeworkplace.org
www.integrolearning.com
www.oeeo.wa.gov.au
www.onetest.com.au
www.polycomasia.com/bw
www.polygraph.org
www.proveit.com

www.psch.com.au
www.psychassessments.com.au
www.psychologicalscience.org/links.htm
www.queendom.com/tests/index.html
www.shl.com.au
www.shrm.org.hrmagazine
www.telelabor.com/eduverify/tesper.htm
www.test-and-train.com
www.workforceonline.com

end notes

1. Quoted in C. Rance, 'Mindful selection', *HR Monthly*, April 2003, p. 34.

2. A. P. O. Williams and P. Dobson, 'Personnel selection and corporate strategy', in N. Anderson and P. Herriot (eds), *International Handbook of Selection and Assessment*, John Wiley & Sons, Chichester, 1997, p. 242.

3. D. Pritchard, quoted in R. Lieber, 'Wired for hiring: Microsoft's slick recruiting machine', *Fortune*, 5 February 1996, pp. 67–8.

4. G. Anderson, 'Selection', in B. Towers, *The Handbook of Human Resource Management*, Blackwell, Oxford, 1992, p. 168.

5. J. Storey, *Developments in the Management of Human Resources*, Blackwell, Oxford, 1992, pp. 98–9.

6. J. Byrne, 'The search for the young and gifted', *Business Week*, 4 October 1999, p. 67.

7. R. Smith, *The Unofficial Guide to Getting a Job at Microsoft*, McGraw-Hill, New York, 2000, pp. 72–3.

8. A. M. Whitehill, *Japanese Management*, Routledge, London, 1993, p. 136; and D. Torrington, *International Human Resource Management*, Prentice Hall, Hemel Hempstead, 1994, p. 152.

9. R. Delbridge and P. Turnbull, 'Human resource maximisation: the management of labour under just-in-time manufacturing systems', in P. Blyton and P. Turnbull (eds), *Reassessing Human Resource Management*, Sage, London, 1992, p. 57.

10. Quoted in R. Delbridge and P. Turnbull, op. cit., p. 61; and C. H. Tan and D. Torrington, *Human Resource Management for Southeast Asia and Hong Kong*, 2nd edn, Prentice Hall, Singapore, 1998, pp. 212–22.

11. C. H. Tan and D. Torrington, op. cit., pp. 219–22.

12. H. C. Lee, 'Transformation of employment practices in Korea Business', *International Studies of Management and Organization*, vol. 28, no. 4, 1998–1999, pp. 26–9.

13. E. Ogbonna, 'Organization culture and human resource management: dilemmas and contradictions', in P. Blyton and P. Turnbull (eds), op. cit., p. 81.

14. B. Townley, 'Selection and appraisal: reconstituting "social relations"?', in J. Storey (ed.), *New Perspectives on Human Resource Management*, Routledge, London, 1992, ch. 6; P. Lles and G. Salaman, 'Recruitment, selection and assessment', in J. Storey, *Human Resource Management: A Critical Text*, Routledge, London,

1995, p. 204; K. Legge, *Human Resource Management*, Macmillan, 1995, London, pp. 232–3 and M. Priest, 'ATO to psych test staff', *Australian Financial Review*, 15 August 2003, p. 3.

15. L. M. Graves and R. J. Karren, 'The employee selection interview: a fresh look at an old problem', *Human Resource Management*, vol. 5, no. 2, 1996, pp. 163–80; and S. P. Robbins, *Organizational Behavior*, 9th edn, Prentice Hall, Upper Saddle River, NJ, 2001, pp. 476–7.

16. R. L. Dipboye, *Selection Interviews: Process, Perspectives*, Southwestern, Cincinnati, 1992; and S. R. Fuller and V. L. Huber, 'Recruitment and selection', in M. Poole and M. Warner (eds), *The Handbook of Human Resource Management*, Thomson, London, 1998, p. 626.

17. L. M. Graves and R. J. Karren, op. cit., pp. 163–80. Also see M. Tenopyr, F. Erwin and C. Russell, 'Rigorous evaluation needed to cut staff selection risks', *Mt Eliza Business Review*, vol. 3., no. 1, 2000, pp. 47–56.

18. D. E. Bowen, G. E. Ledford and B. R. Nathan, 'Hiring for the organization, not the job', *Academy of Management Executive*, vol. 5, no. 4, 1991, pp. 35–51; C. A. O'Reilly, J. A. Chatman and D. F. Caldwell, 'People and organizational culture: a profile comparison to assessing person organization fit', *Academy of Management Journal*, vol. 34, 1991, p. 487; and J. Pfeffer, *The Human Equation*, Harvard Business School Press, Boston, 1998, p. 73.

19. J. Pfeffer, op. cit., pp. 74–9.

20. J. Pfeffer, op. cit., pp. 73–4.

21. J. Sullivan, 'Recruitment in the next millennium', *RCSA Journal*, November 1998, p. 10.

22. W. Cascio, *Applied Psychology in Personnel Management*, 4th edn, Prentice Hall, Englewood Cliffs, NJ, 1991, p. 281.

23. L. L. Byars and L. W. Rue, *Human Resource Management*, 6th edn, Irwin, Homewood, Ill., 2000, pp. 186–9.

24. V. G. Scarpello, J. Ledvinka and T. Bergmann, *Human Resource Management*, 2nd edn, Southwestern, Cincinnati, Ohio, 1995, pp. 269–71; and W. F. Cascio, *Applied Psychology in Human Resource Management*, 5th edn, Prentice Hall, Upper Saddle River, NJ, 1998, pp. 103–4.

25. P. E. Spector, *Industrial and Organizational Psychology*, 2nd edn, John Wiley & Sons, 2000, pp. 109–12.

26. C. D. Fisher, L. F. Schoenfeldt and J. B. Shaw, *Human Resource Management*, 5th edn, Houghton Mifflin, Boston, 2003, pp. 340–3.

27. B. Schneider and N. Schmidt, *Staffing Organizations*, 2nd edn, Waveland Press, Prospect Heights, Ill., 1992, pp. 385–6.

28. L. M. Graves and R. J. Karren, op. cit., pp. 164–6.

29. D. R. Cooper and P. S. Schindler, *Business Research Methods*, 6th edn, McGraw-Hill, Singapore, 1998, pp. 171–4.

30. J. Sullivan, op. cit., p. 8.

31. R. Fein, 'Traditional or electronic tools: how do people get hired?', *Journal of Career Planning & Employment*, vol. 58, no. 4, 1998, pp. 40–3.

32. K. Sunderland, 'The rise and rise of a recruitment', *HR Monthly*, December 2000, p. 37.

33. R. Turner, 'Previous applicants will be deleted', *Boss*, November 2000, p. 12.

34. K. Sunderland, op. cit., p. 37.

35. P. Bassat, 'Logged on', *HR Monthly*, December 2000, p. 44; and D. Crowe, 'E-recruitment the latest frontier', *Australian Financial Review*, 26 April 2000, p. 39.

36. P. E. Spector, op. cit., pp. 108–9; and H. G. Heneman, T. A. Judge and R. L. Heneman, *Staffing Organizations*, 3rd edn, McGraw-Hill, Boston, 2000, pp. 383–93.

37. W. F. Cascio, *Managing Human Resources*, 4th edn, McGraw-Hill, New York, 1995, pp. 198–9.

38. National Committee on Discrimination in Employment and Occupation, *Equal Employment Opportunity*, AGPS, Canberra, 1984, pp. 22–6.

39. L. Bennington and R. Wein, 'Discrimination the real story', *HR Monthly*, July 2000, pp. 26–7.

40. J. Hewson, 'Public deserves far better', *Australian Financial Review*, 24 November 2000, p. 74.

41. M. Dwyer, 'Opinion polls don't spell end for Beijing's man', *Australian Financial Review*, 1 August 2000, p. 14.

42. A. Cornell, 'Outrage over Mori's "old boy" cabinet', *Australian Financial Review*, 6 July 2000, p. 10.

43. R. A. Posthuma, F. P. Morgeson and M. A. Campion, 'Beyond employment interview validity: a comprehensive narrative review of recent research and trends over time', *Personnel Psychology*, vol. 55, no. 1, 2002, p. 80.

44. O. Behling, 'Employee selection: will intelligence and conscientiousness do the job?', *Academy of Management Executive*, vol. 12, no. 1, 1998, pp. 77–86.

45. T. Bauer, E. D. Maetz, M. Dolen and M. Champion, 'Longitudinal assessment of applicant reactions to employment testing and test outcome feedback', *Journal of Applied Psychology*, vol. 83, 1998, pp. 892–903.

46. J. M. Phillips and S. M. Gully, 'Fairness reactions to personnel selection techniques in Singapore and the United States', *International Journal of Human Resource Management*, vol. 13, no. 8, 2002, pp. 1186–1205.

47. C. Fox, 'Psychometric tests used in 25 pc of job placements', *Australian Financial Review*, 9–10 September 2000, p. 4.

48. R. Hogan, J. Hogan and B. R. Roberts, 'Personality measurement and employment decisions', *American Psychologist*, vol. 5, 1996, pp. 469–77; H. G. Heneman, T. A. Judge and R. L. Heneman, op. cit., pp. 427–32; and P. Taylor, 'Personnel selection: what the researchers tell us', *Human Resources*, vol. 2, no. 6, 1998, pp. 7–15.

49. A. Brady, 'Testing positive', *HR Monthly*, February 2003, p. 44.

50. S. Dahl and A. Moore, 'The technology trap', *HR Monthly*, February 2003, p. 42.

51. D. Schultz and S. E. Shultz, *Psychology and Work Today*, 7th edn, Prentice Hall, Upper Saddle River, NJ, 1998, p. 115.

52. B. Schneider and N. Schmidt, 1992, op. cit., pp. 306–37.

53. F. L. Schmidt and J. E. Hunter, 'The validity and utility of selection methods in personnel psychology: practical and theoretical

implications of 85 years of research findings', *Psychological Bulletin*, vol. 124, 1998, pp. 262–74.

54. W. F. Cascio, 1998, op. cit., pp. 226–7.

55. C. Bahn, 'Can intelligence tests predict executive competence?', *Personnel*, vol. 56, no. 4, 1979, p. 53; and S. P. Robbins, 2001, op. cit., p. 37.

56. R. M. Kaplan and D. P. Saccuzzo, *Psychological Testing*, 3rd edn, Brooks/Cole, Pacific Grove, CA, 1993, p. 378.

57. J. A. Mello, 'Personality tests and privacy rights', *HR Focus*, March 1996, pp. 22–3.

58. R. Hogan, J. Hogan and B. W. Roberts, op. cit., p. 469. See also C. M. Solomon, 'Testing at odds with diversity efforts?', *Personnel Journal*, vol. 75, no. 4, April 1996, pp. 131–40.

59. C. D. Fisher and G. J. Boyle, 'Personality and employee selection: credibility regained', *Asia Pacific Journal of Human Resources*, vol. 35, no. 2, 1997, pp. 26–40.

60. M. R. Barrick and M. K. Mount, 'The big five personality dimensions and job performance — a meta analysis', *Personnel Psychology*, vol. 44, 1991, pp. 1–26; and S. L. Rynes, A. E. Colbert and K. G. Brown, 'HR professionals' beliefs about effective human resource practices: correspondence between research and practice', *Human Resource Management*, vol. 41, no. 2, 2002, p. 156.

61. For example, see A. Ferguson, 'Science, cynicism and the cult of personality testing', *Business Review Weekly*, 23 September 1996, pp. 82–4; and J. Packard, 'The wrong turns to avoid with tests', *People Management*, 8 August 1996, pp. 20–5.

62. E. Hoffman, *Ace the Corporate Personality Test*, McGraw-Hill, New York, 2000, p. 16.

63. C. M. Solomon, 'Testing is not at odds with diversity efforts', *Personnel Journal*, March 1993, pp. 100–4.

64. M. S. Hammond, 'The use of the Five Factor Model of Personality as a therapeutic tool in career counselling', *Journal of Career Development*, vol. 27, no. 3, 2001, p. 163.

65. The Australian Council for Educational Research (ACER) is a highly reputable national independent organisation. It is the largest marketer of psychological tests in Australia. ACER is located at 19 Prospect Hill Road, Camberwell 3124. Tel: (03) 9277 5656; fax: (03) 9277 5678.

66. M. Dray and G. Lawrence, 'Appropriate choice and usage will give the best results', *HR Monthly*, November 1995, pp. 21–2; and R. M. Yandrick, 'Employers turn to psychological tests to predict applicants' work behaviour', *HR News*, November 1995, pp. 2, 13.

67. M. A. Campion, E. D. Pursell and B. K. Brown, 'Structured interviewing: raising the psychometric properties of the employment interview', *Personnel Psychology*, vol. 41, no. 1, 1988, pp. 25–41; and J. H. Philbrick, 'Pre-employment screening: a decade of change', *American Business Review*, vol. 17, no. 2, 1999, pp. 75–85.

68. E. Vaughn and J. McLean, 'A survey and critique of management selection practices in Australian business firms', *Asia Pacific Human Resource Management*, vol. 27, no. 4, 1989, p. 26.

69. L. M. Graves and R. J. Karren, op. cit., p. 164.

70. M. Tixier, 'Employers' recruitment tools across Europe', *Employee Relations*, vol. 18, no. 6, 1996, p. 70.

71. D. Schultz and S. E. Schultz, op. cit., pp. 85–6.

72. T. Janz, 'The patterned behavior description interview: the best prophet of the future is the past', in R. W. Eder and G. R. Ferris (eds), *The Employment Interview: Theory, Research and Practice*, Sage, Newbury Park, CA, 1989, p. 159.

73. Reported in 'How to conduct a behavioral interview', *IMPACT*, 9 August 1989, p. 4.

74. A. M. Starcke, 'Tailor interviews to predict performance', *HR Magazine*, July 1996, pp. 49–54.

75. M. E. Heilman, 'The impact of situational factors on personnel decisions concerning women: varying the sex composition of the applicant pool', *Organizational Behavior and Human Performance*, vol. 26, 1980, pp. 386–96.

76. J. N. Cleveland, R. M. Festa and L. Montgomery, 'Applicant pool composition and job perceptions: impact on decisions regarding the older applicant', *Journal of Vocational Behaviour*, vol. 32, 1988, pp. 112–25.

77. P. M. Rowe, 'Individual differences in selection decisions', *Journal of Applied Psychology*, vol. 47, 1963, pp. 304–7.

78. R. Jacobs and J. E. Baratta, 'Tools for staffing decisions: what can they do? What do they cost?', in W. F. Cascio (ed.), *Human Resource Planning, Employment and Placement*, Bureau of National Affairs, Washington, DC, 1989, pp. 2.159–2.199.

79. R. A. Posthuma, F. P. Morgeson and M. A. Campion, op. cit., p. 26.

80. W. E. Seigfried and C. E. Pohlman, 'Order and task effects in the evaluation of female and male applicants', *Academic Psychology Bulletin*, vol. 3, 1981, pp. 89–96.

81. T. D. Hollman, 'Employment interview errors in processing positive and negative information', *Journal of Applied Psychology*, vol. 56, 1972, pp. 130–4.

82. Study by M. M. Okanes and H. Tschirgi, 'Impact of the face to face interview on prior judgments of a candidate', cited in C. D. Fisher, T. L. F. Schoenfeldt and J. B. Shaw, *Human Resource Management*, Houghton Mifflin, Boston, 1990, p. 269.

83. T. M. Macan and R. L. Dipboye, 'The relationship of interviewers' pre-interview impressions to selection and recruitment outcomes', *Personnel Psychology*, vol. 43, no. 4, 1990, pp. 745–8.

84. R. A. Baron, 'Impression management by applicants during employment interviews: the "too much of a good thing" effect', in R. W. Eder and G. R. Ferris (eds), *The Employment Interview: Theory Research and Practice*, Sage, Newbury Park, CA, 1989, p. 205.

85. P. Murphy, 'A job to dye for: it's back to black', *International Herald Tribune*, 3 February 2003, p. 6; J. Ma and A. Yan, 'Cosmetic solutions growing in popularity', *South China Morning Post*, 1 September 2003, p. A6; and H. Lee, '80 pc of women prize youthful looks', *South China Morning Post*, 10 September 2003, p. C4.

86. C. M. Marlowe, S. L. Schneider and C. E. Nelson, 'Gender and attractiveness biases in hiring decisions: are more experienced managers less biased?', *Journal of Applied Psychology*, vol. 81, no. 1, 1996, pp. 11–21.

87. R. Pingitore, B. L. Dugoni, R. S. Tindale and B. Spring, 'Bias against overweight job applicants in a simulated employment interview', *Journal of Applied Psychology*, vol. 79, 1994, pp. 909–17.

88. S. M. Forsythe, 'Effect of applicants clothing on interview decisions to hire', *Journal of Applied Social Psychology*, vol. 20, 1990, pp. 1579–95.

89. R. E. Carlson, 'Effects of applicant sample on ratings of valid information in an employment setting', *Journal of Applied Psychology*, vol. 54, 1970, pp. 217–22.

90. R. A. Posthuma, F. P. Morgeson and M. A. Campion, op. cit., p. 13.

91. R. Arvey and J. Campion, 'The employment interview: a summary and review of recent research', *Journal of Applied Psychology*, vol. 35, 1982, p. 305.

92. R. A. Posthuma, F. P. Morgeson and M. A. Campion, op. cit., p. 9.

93. P. E. Spector, op. cit., p. 112.

94. B. Rowe, personal correspondence with the author, 1989.

95. T. McCarthy, personal correspondence with the author, 1989.

96. T. J. Harn and G. C. Thornton, 'Recruiter counseling behaviours and application impressions', *Journal of Occupational Psychology*, vol. 54, 1988, pp. 165–73; and D. P. Rogers and M. A. Sincoff, 'Favourable impression characteristics of the recruitment interviewer', *Personnel Psychology*, vol. 31, 1978, pp. 495–504.

97. P. Goldrick, 'What makes a selection system best practice?', *HR Monthly*, June 1997, p. 27.

98. M. Pontifex, personal correspondence with the author, 1989.

99. W. F. Cascio, 1998, op. cit., pp. 195–6.

100. R. D. Arvey, H. E. Miller, R. Gould and P. Burch, 'Interview validity for selecting sales clerks', *Personnel Psychology*, vol. 40, 1987, pp. 1–2.

101. R. D. Arvey and J. E. Campion, 'Unfair discrimination in the employment interview', in R. W. Eder and G. R. Ferris (eds), op. cit., p. 67.

102. P. Royce, personal correspondence with the author, 1989.

103. J. Braysich, *Body Language*, Joseph Braysich, Sydney, 1979, p. 125; and S. P. Robbins, 2001, op. cit., pp. 293–4.

104. N. A. Boyacigiller and N. J. Adler, 'Methodological considerations in studying cross-cultural management behaviour', in T. Jackson (ed.), *Cross-Cultural Management*, Butterworth-Heinemann, Oxford, 1995, p. 23.

105. R. Cooper and N. Cooper, *Culture Shock: Thailand*, Times Books International, Singapore, 1986, pp. 8–12.

106. C. Bongazoni, personal correspondence with the author, 1989.

107. M. Dwyer, personal correspondence with the author, 1989.

108. P. Grigg, personal correspondence with the author, 1989.

109. G. Munchus, 'Check references for safer selection', *HR Magazine*, June 1992, pp. 75–7; and C. D. Fisher, L. F. Schoenfeldt and J. B. Shaw, op. cit., pp. 349–51.

110. See G. Anderson, 'Selection', in B. Towers (ed.), op. cit., p. 169.

111. R. Berenholtz, personal correspondence with the author, 1989.

112. B. Schneider and N. Schmidt, 1992, op. cit., p. 383.

113. E. Bahnsen and A. Loftin, 'Handle reference requests consistently; stick to facts', *HR News*, December 1995, p. 16; and P. Barada, 'Reference checking is more important than ever', *HR Magazine*, November 1996, pp. 49–51.

114. S. Long, 'References come back to haunt', *Australian Financial Review*, 28 June 1996, pp. 1, 12; J. Catanzariti, 'To whom it may concern — beware', *Weekend Australian*, 20–21 July 1996, p. 44; and P. W. Barada, 'Reference checking is more important than ever', *HR Magazine*, November 1996, pp. 49–51

115. J. Catanzariti, op. cit., p. 44.

116. P. M. Perry, 'Cut your risk when giving references', *HR Focus*, May 1995, pp. 15–16; and G. Beacher, 'Safe pathway possible through reference minefield', *HR Monthly*, March 1999, pp. 44–5.

117. See 'Stockford caught by hiring blue', *Business Review Weekly*, 10 November 2000, p. 115.

118. S. Lawrence, 'Recruitment agencies must be vigilant', *Australian Financial Review*, 11 April 2003, p. 67.

119. C. D. Fisher, L. F. Schoenfeldt and J. B. Shaw, op. cit., p. 349.

120. R. Tillay, 'A degree of deceit', *Asia Inc.*, vol. 9, no. 4, July 2000, pp. 10–11.

121. Reported in G. Maslen, 'Fake degrees commonplace in CVs', *South China Morning Post*, 6 September 2003, p. E2.

122. P. A. Dunn, 'Pre-employment referencing aids your bottom line', *Personnel Journal*, February 1995, p. 68.

123. B. Rowe, personal correspondence with the author, 1989.

124. J. M. Walsh and L. L. Maltby, 'Is workplace drug testing effective?', *HR News*, April 1996, p. 5; and G. Dessler, J. Griffiths, B. Lloyd-Walker and A. Williams, *Human Resource Management*, Prentice Hall, Sydney, 1999, pp. 292–4.

125. S. Long, 'Court rules drug addiction is a disability', *Australian Financial Review*, 23 November 2000, p. 3.

126. Y. Preston, 'Very public politician's business', *Bulletin*, 19 December 1995, p. 98.

127. A. Hepworth, M. Priest and A. Day, 'Drug tests in the office: You may be next', *Australian Financial Review*, 3 October 2003, pp. 1, 72.

128. Quoted in A. Hepworth, M. Priest and A. Day, op. cit., p. 72.

129. J. Norman, S. D. Salyards and J. J. Mahoney, 'An evaluation of pre-employment drug testing', *Journal of Applied Psychology*, vol. 75, 1990, pp. 629–39; and D. C. Parish, 'Relation of pre-employment drug testing to employment status: a one year follow-up', *Journal of Internal Medicine*, vol. 4, 1999, pp. 44–7.

130. A. Hepworth, M. Priest and A. Day, op. cit., p. 72.

131. J. E. Bahls, 'Dealing with drugs', *HRM Magazine*, March 1998, pp. 104–16; R. W. Mondy, R. M. Noe and S. R. Premeaux, *Human Resource Management*, 8th edn, Prentice Hall, Upper Saddle River, NJ, 2002, pp. 188–9; and R. Thompson, 'Passing the screen test', *HR Monthly*, December 2003, p. 35.

132. Based on S. R. Fuller and V. L. Huber, 'Recruitment and selection', in M. Poole and M. Warner (eds), *The Handbook of Human Resource Management*, Thomson, London, 1998, p. 626; and H. G. Heneman, T. A. Judge and R. L. Heneman, op. cit., p. 399. See also 'Genetic testing needs scrutiny', *HR Monthly*, June 2001, p. 7.

133. M. Priest, 'Unions: genetic testing a threat', *Australian Financial Review*, 2 June 2003, p. 6.

134. R. Robertson, 'The law should protect our genes', *Australian Financial Review — Special Report*, 17 July 2003, p. 5.

135. R. R. Reilly and G. T. Chao, 'Validity and fairness of some alternative employee selection procedures', *Personnel Psychology*, vol. 35, no. 1, 1982, pp. 1–62; and K. R. Murphy and N. Luther, 'Assessing honesty, integrity and deception', in N. Anderson and P. Herriot, *International Handbook of Selection and Assessment*, John Wiley & Sons, Chichester, 1997, pp. 374–5.

136. A. J. Prewett-Livingston, H. S. Field, J. G. Veres and P. M. Lewis, 'Effects of race on interview ratings in a situational panel interview', *Journal of Applied Psychology*, vol. 81, 1996, pp. 178–86.

137. W. F. Cascio, 1991, op. cit., p. 276; and G. Dessler, J. Griffiths, B. Lloyd-Walker and A. Williams, op. cit., pp. 311–12.

138. G. Anderson, 'Selection', in B. Towers (ed.), op. cit., pp. 179–80.

139. M. Abernethy, 'The selector weeds out corporate pretenders', *Australian Financial Review*, 14 March 1997, p. 54.

140. B. Mitchell, 'Interviewing face to interface', *Personnel*, vol. 67, no. 1, 1990, p. 24.

141. C. L. Martin and D. H. Nagao, 'Some effects of computerized interviewing on job applicant responses', *Journal of Applied Psychology*, vol. 74, 1989, pp. 72–80.

142. C. L. Martin and D. H. Nagao, op. cit., 1989; and E. A. Ensher, T. R. Nielson and E. Grant Vallone, 'Tales from the hiring line: effects of the Internet and technology in HR processes', *Organizational Dynamics*, vol. 31, no. 3, 2002, p. 229.

143. V. Porzsolt, 'Leaping the digital divide', *HR Monthly*, October, 2002, p. 35; HR Gateway, 'Online applicant tests encourage ambitious fakers', *Human Resources*, January 2003, p. 2; 'Workplace testing offensive, says Australian union', *Human Resources*, February–March 2003, p. 4.

144. This section is based on M. Johnson, 'Lights, camera, interview', *HR Magazine*, April 1991, pp. 66–8; and HRM Update, 'A wave of the future', *HR Magazine*, April 1993, p. 28.

145. R. Rimmer Hurst, 'Video interviewing — take one', *HR Magazine*, November 1996, pp. 100–4.

146. M. Johnson, op. cit., p. 68; and K. O. Magnusen and K. Galen Kroeck, 'Video conferencing maximizes recruiting', *HR Magazine*, August 1995, pp. 70–2.

147. A. McGibbon and A. Ball, 'Assessment centres or "assassination centres"?', *HR Monthly*, June 1997, p. 32; and H. G. Heneman, T. A. Judge and R. L. Heneman, op. cit., p. 523.

148. A. Armstrong, 'Using assessment centres to select team leaders', *Asia Pacific Journal of Human Resources*, vol. 35, no. 2, 1997, p. 67.

149. M. Lawson, 'Assessing "real" candidates', *Australian Financial Review*, 2 August 1996, p. 15.

150. P. A. Iles and I. T. Robertson, 'The impact of personnel selection procedures on candidates', in N. Anderson and P. Herriot (eds), *International Handbook of Selection and Assessment*, John Wiley & Sons, Chichester, 1997, pp. 551–2; and M. Tixier, op. cit., p. 77.

151. S. B. Keel, D. S. Cochran, K. Arnett and D. R. Arnold, 'ACs are not just for the Big Guys', *Personnel Administrator*, May 1989, pp. 98–101.

152. H. Bior, 'Yes, (just strap this on) the boss trusts you', *International Herald Tribune*, 24 February 2003, p. 7.

153. D. A. De Cenzo and S. P. Robbins, *Human Resource Management*, 6th edn, John Wiley & Sons, New York, 1999, pp. 199–200; and K. R. Murphy and N. Luther, 1997, op. cit., p. 380.

154. S. P. Robbins, 2001, op. cit., p. 479.

155. G. T. Milkovich and J. W. Boudreau, *Human Resource Management*, 7th edn, Irwin, Homewood, Ill., 1994. pp. 367–70; and H. G. Heneman, T. A. Judge and R. L. Heneman, op. cit., pp. 448–50.

156. 'Study validates integrity testing', *Personnel Journal*, May 1991, p. 17; and K. R. Murphy and N. Luther, 1997, op. cit., pp. 371–4.

157. J. W. Townsend, 'Is integrity testing useful?', *HR Magazine*, July 1992, p. 96.

158. R. Brown, 'Employees are allies in the battle against loss', *IPA Review*, vol. 46, no. 1, 1993, p. 39; and M. Fenton-Jones, 'Shoplifters: retail feels the pinch', *Australian Financial Review*, 30 September 2003, p. 47.

159. K. Glasscott, 'Wood attacks culture of greed', *Australian*, 16 May 1997, p. 1.

160. M. Tixier, op. cit., p. 77; V. Shackleton and S. Newell, 'International assessment and selection', in N. Anderson and P. Herriot, *International Handbook of Selection and Assessment*, John Wiley & Sons, Chichester, 1997, p. 89; and R. W. Mondy, R. M. Noe and S. R. Premeaux, 2002, op. cit., p. 191.

LAURA LEARNS A LESSON
Wendy Webber, Monash University

Laura was newly promoted to section head when Molly, the section receptionist, handed in her resignation pending the birth of her first child. Upon receiving the resignation, Laura rang a colleague, Amy, to say that she wanted her to replace Molly as soon as Molly left. Laura then contacted the HR Department to advise them that she wanted to appoint Amy to replace Molly.

The HR Department advised that all job vacancies must be advertised externally and that as the supervisor, Laura's role was to form a panel of four people to short-list, assess and interview prospective candidates. The panel should then give a final recommendation to the HR Department as to which candidate should be selected.

Laura felt that as she was the supervisor she should not be forced to advertise, but because it was company policy, she had better make it look good. Laura then rang Amy and told her that although she thought she was the best one for the job, Amy would have to apply for the position once it was advertised.

The HR Department clarified with Laura and Molly that the job description was still accurate and then advertised the vacancy in the local paper. Laura asked Molly and two other women from her section to be on the selection panel. The panel met to discuss all applications and determine which tests they would use to check the applicants' skills and suitability for the team. Six applications were received and all met the essential selection criteria stated in the position description. The panel decided they would interview the best four applicants and agreed to give them a typing test, a numeracy test and a personality test, which Laura had downloaded from the Internet. After the candidates had completed the tests, they would be interviewed by the panel. The panel prepared their interview questions based on the selection criteria and agreed that they would ask the same questions to all candidates.

Molly rang all four candidates to arrange for the tests and the interview. When she contacted a candidate called Ben, he asked what had caused the vacancy. Molly was very helpful and explained that she was pregnant and was leaving to have her baby. Ben asked why she had not taken maternity leave. Molly answered that no one in the company had ever taken maternity leave and she thought the company would not like it if she did.

The next week all the candidates were interviewed. All four seemed to do very well in at least one of the tests but no one was the best at all the tests. The committee started to get itself confused as to who was the best candidate and agreed that all candidates were appointable. Laura took the lead in the discussion. She commented that although Ben was best at the numeracy test, she was not too sure about having a man as her assistant, especially as his personality test showed he was high on 'judging' and she did not like people who were judgemental. Carla was best at typing and scored high in the interview. She was friendly, professional and very experienced in reception work. Don was hard to interview, he was very nervous and laughed too much. Although his personality test showed him as a friendly kind of person, the panel found him irritating and a know-all who really should lose some weight. Amy was the last one interviewed.

In the panel discussion after the interviews, Laura said she thought Amy was the best candidate, especially as she was already employed with the company and was known to everyone. Molly said she had heard that Amy was sometimes a troublemaker. Laura said it was better to 'hire the devil you know' than risk the 'unknown'. The panel agreed that as Laura was the supervisor, she should have the final say, and so Amy should be hired.

The next week, the HR Manager rang Laura to advise that, due to a formal complaint, he was contacting all members of the selection panel to investigate whether the selection process had been satisfactory. He was very concerned, because there had been a written complaint from the legal representative of one of the applicants, Ben. The complaint alleged that the all-female selection panel had discriminated against Ben, who thought he was the best candidate for the job and felt that he had been unsuccessful because he was a man. Ben's lawyer also said that he had heard that discrimination was systemic in the organisation because eligible female staff were too scared to apply for maternity leave, which is their legal entitlement under Australian law.

The HR Manager also asked Laura to explain why he had heard office gossip that Amy had been promised the job even before it had been advertised.

Questions

1. What evidence is there that employment discrimination has taken place in this selection process?
2. Who would you have put on the selection panel to ensure the best selection result? Why?
3. How could the panel have been more objective in distinguishing the strengths and weaknesses of each candidate?
4. Discuss the validity and reliability of the selection tests used in this selection process.
5. Identify the formal and informal events relating to the selection process in this case.
6. What impressions does this selection process give to future internal and external job applicants?
7. What should the HR Department do to improve the selection process in the organisation?
8. How can the HR Department assess and address the claim that discrimination is systemic in the organisation?
9. What lessons about the selection process do you think Laura can gain from this experience?

developing human resources

Part 3 deals with the development of human resources through performance appraisal and performance management, human resource development, and career planning and development. The case study at the end of the part incorporates these topics using the example of ABC Manufacturing.

appraising and managing performance

Learning objectives

When you have finished studying this chapter, you should be able to:

- Discuss the relationship between strategy, performance management and performance appraisal
- Understand the objectives of performance appraisal
- Identify the sources of error in performance appraisal
- Discuss the major types of performance appraisal systems
- Understand the importance of goal setting in performance improvement
- Appreciate the impact of EEO on performance appraisal.

'The problem we must wrestle with is that good intentions in the performance appraisal area have often been associated with disappointing outcomes.'[1]

Peter Boxhall and John Purcell

Organisations need ever-improving performance to survive and prosper in today's competitive world: individual and organisational performance improvements are the keys to competitive advantage. Rapid change, tighter budgets, downsizing and restructuring, and pressures for greater employee accountability are placing greater emphasis on **performance management** by translating the organisation's objectives and strategies into individual job objectives and performance standards. A US study shows that top global organisations use performance measures 'that focus on all the drivers of their business — financial performance, shareholder value, employees and customers'.[2] Research by Nankervis and Leece indicates that organisations are trying to relate individual outcomes more directly to their strategic business objectives.[3] In addition, performance-related rewards that target those who meet the performance requirements signal the types of employee behaviour and organisational culture demanded by the organisation's strategic business objectives.[4] Critics argue that this produces a market-oriented, entrepreneurial, individualistic culture that weakens the influence of trade unions, undermines collective bargaining, strengthens the role of the line manager and enhances employee commitment to the organisation rather than the union.

The evaluation of organisational and employee performance permits managers to check that strategic business objectives are valid, are being successfully communicated throughout the organisation and are being achieved. In short, performance management ensures that jobs are properly designed and that qualified personnel are hired, trained, rewarded and motivated to achieve the organisation's strategic business objectives. Performance management promotes the organisational and employee behaviour and performance required to improve bottom line results. Research demonstrates that companies that manage performance outperform companies that do not, with higher profits, better cash flows, stronger stock market performance, productivity gains, higher sales growth per employee and overall better financial performance.[5]

Performance management, in turn, provides a strategic link by auditing the organisation's employees in terms of their skills, abilities, knowledge and behaviours. It generates information about how well the organisation's human resources satisfy the needs of the organisation's present and future business strategies. It gives feedback to management on the strategic alignment of employee behaviours. Are people doing what is required to achieve organisational objectives? Are people feeling satisfied about being effective contributors? Is the organisation recognising and rewarding the behaviours needed to achieve strategic goal achievement and reinforce the desired organisational culture?

Performance appraisal, by providing a dynamic link to employee recruitment, selection, training and development, career planning, compensation and benefits, safety and health, and industrial relations, is a vital tool for strategy execution. It signals to managers and employees what is really important; it provides ways to measure what is important; it fixes accountability for behaviour and results; and it helps to improve performance.[6] Finally, it's necessary to defend the organisation against individuals who legally challenge the validity of management decisions relating to promotions, transfers, salary changes and termination.[7]

Appraising and managing performance are critical management responsibilities and a vital part of the organisation's strategic management process. In practice, however, performance appraisal systems are often ad hoc and divorced from the organisation's strategic business objectives.[8] A recent survey, for example, found that many companies do not link their strategic objectives with individual employee performance criteria.[9] Moreover, highly unionised, university and public sector organisations often have cultures that promote strong opposition to any form of performance evaluation (despite ineffective control and performance monitoring systems being an important factor in the poor performance of the public sector).[10]

Unions, for example, see performance appraisal and pay for performance as focusing on the individual, thus creating a competitive culture, coercing higher output and promoting management by control.[11] In the public sector, the cultural preference for collaboration rather

Performance management
Aims to improve organisational, functional, unit and individual performance by linking the objectives of each. Incorporates job design, recruitment and selection, training and development, career planning, and compensation and benefits, in addition to performance appraisal.

Performance appraisal
Concerned with determining how well employees are doing their jobs, communicating that information to employees, agreeing on new objectives and establishing a plan for performance improvement.

than competition means that peer competitiveness can be seen as a strong negative factor in employee job satisfaction.[12] One academic claims, 'As professionals, as colleagues, as scholars, and as members of national and international discipline and research communities, performance management is not appropriate for us'.[13] Similarly, an academic from the University of Western Australia argues that performance appraisal is an attack on academic freedom because it could be used to monitor and control staff and prevent the pursuit of unpopular research or public discussion of questions not supported by the university.[14] Disagreeing, one pro-vice-chancellor states: 'Unions have carefully confused egalitarian principles, a feature of university philosophy, to obfuscate accountability and productivity ... academics are required to teach four to 12 hours a week for 30 weeks a year, prepare study materials and undertake research, often in excess of 60 hours a week all year. Other academics teach four to 12 hours for only 30 weeks and have the same salary privileges and rights as their active scholarly colleagues.'[15]

Nevertheless, sufficient research exists to suggest that the introduction of appraisal-based merit pay into the public sector needs to be considered very carefully, as it requires major conceptual shifts in individual thinking and behaviour and organisational culture.[16]

Performance management

It is argued that performance appraisal is a management technique designed to reward those employees whom management favours and punish those employees whom management dislikes.

Organisational interest in performance management has increased as a result of competitive pressures, the influence of HRM and the individualisation of the employment relationship.[17] Storey and Sisson define performance management as 'an interlocking set of policies and practices which have as their focus the enhanced achievement of organisational objectives through a concentration on individual performance'.[18]

The key elements of performance management are:
- the creation of a shared vision of the organisation's strategic business objectives
- the establishment of performance objectives (derived from the organisation's strategic business objectives) for each function, group and individual to ensure that their performance is aligned with the needs of the business
- the use of a formal review process to evaluate functional, group and individual progress towards goal achievement
- the linking of performance evaluation and employee development and rewards to motivate and reinforce desired behaviour.[19] Thus, performance management involves goal establishment, performance evaluation, employee development and reward. It provides the link between the organisation's strategic business objectives, employee performance, development and rewards, and organisational results (see figures 8.1, 8.2 and 8.3).

Performance management thus can have a significant impact on the success of an organisation through promoting cooperative effort towards common goals; encouraging teamwork and more open communications; increasing individual and group performance; and facilitating change. Firms with an effective performance management program should outperform those without such a system.

Performance appraisal

Performance appraisal may be viewed as an overall measure of organisational effectiveness: organisational objectives are met through the effort of individual employees. If employee performance is improved, the organisation will lift its performance. However, it should be noted that some experts do not accept these assumptions. Deming, for example, argues that:
- individual employees do not differ significantly in their work performance and that any observed differences are simply the result of sampling error
- any variation in employee performance is predominantly a result of factors outside the individual's control
- management appraisers are incapable of distinguishing between employee-caused and system-caused variations in performance.[20]

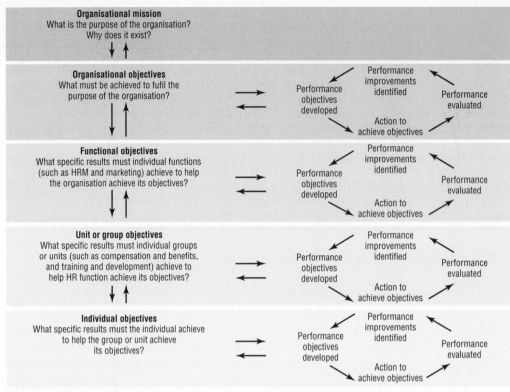

Figure 8.1 Performance management
Source Asia Pacific Management Co. Ltd, 2004.

Performance management

There is no universal agreement as to what constitutes performance management, but the following characteristics are generally present:

- Performance management is a much broader concept than performance appraisal. It aims to improve organisational, functional, unit and individual employee performances.
- Performance management has a focus on strategic planning and development. It aims to link the organisation's key objectives and strategies with organisational, functional, unit and individual objectives and strategies.
- Performance management measures the progress being made towards the achievement of an organisation's strategic business objectives. It does so by evaluating organisational, functional, unit and individual performance; identifying needed performance improvements; developing new performance objectives; and activating mechanisms for converting improved performance into rewards.
- Performance management, given the above, may incorporate job design, recruitment and selection, training

and development, career planning, and compensation and benefits, in addition to performance appraisal. Production workers, for example, whose jobs have been redesigned to include feedback concerning their own performance quality, are more likely to demonstrate improvement than those who receive feedback from external sources such as quality control officers.[21]

Performance appraisal

Performance appraisal typically involves measuring how well an individual employee is doing their job against a set of criteria (for example, personal competencies, behavioural characteristics or achievements), providing feedback and creating a development plan. The performance process generates information that may be used for administrative purposes (such as rewards, promotions, transfers and terminations) and/or developmental purposes (such as training and development, coaching and career planning) and/or research purposes (such as validating selection procedures and evaluating the effectiveness of training). Performance appraisal is a key part of an organisation's performance management system.

Figure 8.2 Performance management and performance appraisal
Source Asia Pacific Management Co. Ltd, 2004.

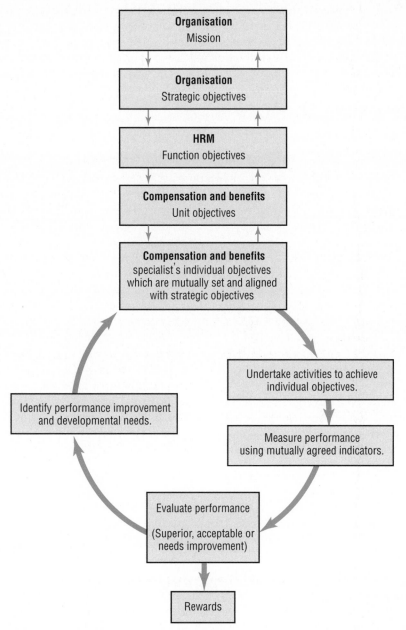

Figure 8.3 The strategic link between organisational objectives and performance and individual objectives and performance

Source Asia Pacific Management Co. Ltd, 2004.

Deming's position is in stark contrast with the generally accepted view that there are meaningful differences in employee performance that should and can be measured. Interestingly, Carson, Cardy and Dobbins claim that both Deming's assumptions and the conventional HRM assumptions regarding performance appraisal remain largely untested. Their exploratory studies do suggest, however, that separating person and system factors is difficult. Appraisal of employee performance nevertheless remains a critical and ongoing management activity. This is because managers are continually observing and judging their employees. This evaluation process may be formal or informal. Either way, it has a direct impact on the employees' pay increases, promotions, demotions, terminations, training and career development.

Despite the importance of performance management, many organisations do not have any systematic method of appraisal or use a system that lacks congruence with the organisation's culture and strategic business objectives (see figure 8.4). In one survey, more than half the responding companies reported that their performance appraisal system offered little or no value to the organisation.[22] After a review of the literature, Newton and Findlay similarly concluded that appraisal schemes rarely work as their formal procedures suggest because in practice they are predominantly concerned with surveillance, accountability and control.[23]

PERCEPTIONS OF PERFORMANCE APPRAISAL

A study based on 100 interviews looked at how Hong Kong Chinese HR managers and line managers perceived performance appraisal in their organisation.[24] The study found that both groups held very different views as to what made performance appraisal systems effective. On the one hand, HR managers were most concerned with issues dealing with performance appraisal guidelines and HR's role as custodian of the system. On the other hand, line managers were concerned with the need for performance appraisals to be better linked to strategy, to be more objective and to have a clearer system of measurement. They also expressed considerable frustration at not being sufficiently involved in the design, implementation and evaluation of the performance appraisal system in their organisation. Alarmingly, line managers felt that performance appraisals did not add value or help to achieve business objectives.

Other findings from the study showed that performance appraisal training, performance appraisal forms, performance appraisal guidelines and the standards used to evaluate performance were inadequate. In particular, appraisal training was seen as having no impact. Even worse, both HR managers and line managers perceived the performance criteria and standards used to appraise performance as not being linked to their organisation's business strategies. All managers desired more 'control' over the appraisal system, and line managers in particular wanted greater involvement in any performance appraisal initiatives coming out of the HR department.

Figure 8.4 A study of Chinese line managers' and HR managers' perceptions of performance appraisal
Source Robert Wright, School of Business, Hong Kong Polytechnic University, 2003.

Thus, HR managers have a critical and challenging role in educating their organisation's management and staff on the significance and use of performance appraisal in employee development, performance improvement and achievement of the organisation's strategic business objectives.[25]

It should be noted that not all HR writers would accept this viewpoint. Barbara Townley, for example, expresses some serious concerns about the real intent of performance appraisal. For Townley, performance appraisal is little more than a pseudo-scientific management technique for handling labour relations. The real purpose of performance appraisal, she argues, is to monitor and control employees. This is done by emphasising the assessment of current performance (as opposed to future development) and using trait rating rather than job-based criteria. Townley says that because of the increased discretion being given to employees, it has become critical for organisations to ensure that they can continue to control employee behaviour. Internal controls rather than external controls, she says, have now become of paramount importance. Consequently, a key function of performance appraisal is to communicate organisational norms or culture so that employees internalise the organisation's values. Townley thus perceives performance appraisal as nothing more than a personalised application of power in the workplace, with the ultimate aim being to control employee behaviour.

A checklist for introducing a performance appraisal program is shown in figure 8.5.

STEPS FOR INTRODUCING A PERFORMANCE APPRAISAL PROGRAM

1. Clearly define the purposes of the performance appraisal program — that is, what it is you want to achieve.
2. Ensure that the type of program you plan to introduce is consistent with the organisation's objectives and culture and is perceived by managers and employees as fair in its design and application.
3. Ensure there is full understanding of and support for the program by top management, employees and the unions (if applicable).
4. Involve employees, managers and the unions (if applicable) in the development of the program.
5. Ensure that performance standards and the method of evaluation are clear, job-related, fair and as objective as possible.
6. Establish training sessions for managers and employees on the objectives of the program and the skills and responsibilities required.
7. Provide a formal procedure to allow employees to challenge performance appraisal evaluations that they consider inaccurate or unfair.
8. Constantly monitor the program to check that it is meeting its objectives (and particularly that it is perceived by managers and employers as having fair procedures and generating fair outcomes).

Figure 8.5 Introducing a performance appraisal program
Source Asia Pacific Management Co. Ltd, 2004.

Performance appraisal objectives

Discrimination

A manager must be able to objectively discriminate between those who are contributing to the achievement of the organisation's strategic business objectives and those who are not. A performance-oriented organisation has no room for egalitarianism: inadequate performance cannot be tolerated. Those who are underperforming should be given the opportunity and assistance to improve. If an employee still cannot make the grade, corrective action such as transfer, demotion or termination should be taken. One senior executive says: 'You don't do anybody any favours by tolerating failure or incompetence. All you really do is put a lot of other people's jobs at risk.'[26] Research shows that the best companies and the best CEOs never hesitate to fire when they must (and yet are more people-oriented).[27] Microsoft annually weeds out about 5 per cent of its employees through its performance appraisal system. Intel also employs a tough 'up or out' program.[28] The costs of keeping non-performers are significant and send the wrong signals to other employees who are performing well.[29] Lost sales, high rejection rates, customer dissatisfaction and damaged public image are just some of the obvious costs. Hidden costs include loss of motivation among good performers and the diversion of management resources.[30]

Leniency leading to inaccurate performance appraisals is a long-standing problem.[31] Interestingly, poor performers tend to have unrealistic (and inflated) perceptions regarding their performance relative to good performers.[32] According to one survey, more than 60 per cent of Australian employees felt their companies were too lenient with poorly performing employees.[33] Another survey indicates that 20 per cent of academics have not published anything in five years, despite having the same research time and sabbaticals as their more productive colleagues.[34]

The Commander of the New South Wales Police Service's Professional Responsibility Branch states, 'One of the problems that the Police Service has always had is that we have never been able to get rid of those officers who are simply lazy, have poor attitudes or are simply incompetent'.[35] Private sector organisations similarly can show reluctance to deal with non-performance.[36]

Apart from weak management and poor corporate governance, incompetence and unprofessional behaviour are often tolerated because union power makes it difficult to remove poor performers.[37] In Hong Kong, less than one in 7500 teachers is dismissed for non-performance. Principals say they are reluctant to fire substandard teachers because of the bureaucratic procedures involved and union opposition.[38] Dismissal too is almost impossible in the rest of the civil service — it takes at least two years to fire a civil servant whose performance is unsatisfactory.[39] A recent Watson Wyatt survey, moreover, found that Hong Kong civil servants' average total remuneration was 229 per cent more than their private sector counterparts.[40] Critics are demanding changes in the civil service culture and for the Hong Kong government to strengthen its reward and punishment system.[41] Hong Kong's civil service, not surprisingly, has been criticised for being slack, overstaffed, pampered, overpaid, wasteful and resistant to change.[42] Civil service unions, however, continue to oppose staff reductions and pay rises based on merit (preferring automatic pay increases regardless of performance).[43]

According to the National Commission of Audit, the extraordinary complexity of the Australian Public Service personnel system similarly protects inefficiency because the delays in proceedings, the manipulation of rights of appeal and the frequent recourse to generous redundancy payouts make it difficult to dismiss inefficient public servants.[44] The rigidities and the lack of accountability in dealing with underperforming employees are among the toughest issues facing public sector managers.[45]

According to one expert, 'The only way to make a business live up to its potential is to get tough'.[46] Gail Kelly, CEO of St George Bank, says one of management's most important tasks is to get the wrong people off the bus.[47] Former legendary Port Adelaide Football Club coach Foster Williams illustrates this when he says: 'Any club worth its salt will clear out its no-hopers from the doorman to the head trainer to the captain. Keeping no-hopers in these positions is a mark of a non-successful club. You have to weed out the people who breed an atmosphere of non-professionalism. They are there for the bloody joke, the social life, the prestige. They are not there to win.'[48]

Employees who achieve want to be recognised and rewarded for their efforts while poor performers prefer egalitarian pay plans.[49] To motivate performance, outstanding performers therefore must be identified and rewarded. Merit increases must be significantly different in size to reward those who deserve it. The effectiveness of pay as a motivator, however, 'depends on the extent to which performance can be measured and the extent to which it is possible to discriminate between individual employees'.[50] A study by the Australian Institute of Management in Western Australia found that a major disincentive to productivity was attributable to everyone getting the same pay rise regardless of how hard they work.[51] Ninety per cent of employees in a survey by the American Productivity and Quality Center said recognition for good performance is a top priority in job satisfaction, yet only 55 per cent said they actually get such recognition. And while 85 per cent of respondents said fair performance reviews are critical, only 38 per cent said they receive fair ones.[52]

Unfortunately, research indicates that ingratiating subordinates are better liked and receive more pay increases, more favourable performance appraisals and more promotions than do equally qualified, non-ingratiating workers.[53] Managers admit that political considerations are nearly always part of the evaluation process.[54] Research, nevertheless, shows a positive relationship between merit pay systems and organisational performance.[55]

Discrimination on the basis of performance is an organisational necessity. It is part of the managerial role that cannot be avoided. If an organisation is to survive and grow, and retain and motivate its top performers, effective performance management is a must.

Reward

To encourage performance, it is obvious that it must be rewarded. Consequently, most organisations claim that they do just that. Employees who have contributed the most to the achievement of the organisation's strategic business objectives should receive the greatest rewards. If not, how are employees to be motivated to perform?

The big question is: if no objective measure of performance exists within the organisation, how does management know what is being rewarded? Embarrassingly, organisations often reward membership, seniority, a servile demeanour or some other factor that has little or nothing to do with the achievement of strategic objectives. Research shows that employees who flatter and fawn on their supervisors receive higher ratings, better pay increases and more promotions than do their counterparts.[56] The result 'is the over-rewarding of incompetence and the under-rewarding of superior performance'.[57]

There is now evidence, however, to suggest that organisations are increasingly rewarding performance even though the key factor in determining rewards in the past has been membership.[58] For example, the difference in pay increases between excellent and poor performers in the Hong Kong civil service equates to about A\$3 per month.[59] A civil service union official says in response, 'Pay rises should not be used as a reward as this would complicate human resources management'.[60]

Private sector senior management also is not averse to rewarding non-performance. Former AMP CEO George Trumbull's penalty for 'almost ruining the unruinable company' was to walk away with \$23 million.[61]

Membership-based rewards include 'across-the-board' pay increases, cost-of-living increases, seniority payments, and so on. Performance-based rewards include piecework payments, commissions, incentives, bonuses or other forms of merit pay plans.[62] Performance-based rewards are 'at risk' rewards. They are based on the continual achievement of job goals.[63]

Employees are not stupid. They quickly learn to exhibit the behaviour that they know will be recognised and rewarded by management. A study on police ethics, for example, found that being ethical leads to punishment for many police officers, with the result that most police officers believe being dishonest is the only way of being promoted.[64] Immigration officers in Hong Kong similarly found that being polite to travellers was punished because it was too time consuming.[65]

An objective performance appraisal system in which high performers receive higher rewards and low performers receive lower rewards is essential for encouraging performance-oriented behaviour and a performance-oriented culture. Linking employee contributions and rewards also ensures that the organisation gets maximum value for its compensation dollar.

Development

Employee development is the third aim of performance appraisal (and one that is often overlooked). Performance improvement comes about by building on strengths and overcoming weaknesses. It is the manager's job to remove blocks to employee performance and to help each employee to grow and develop. Performance appraisal must be a positive and dynamic process for this to occur. 'Developmental schemes enhance the appraisal process by encouraging communication and employee participation', says Lansbury.[66] For example, performance ratings are of significantly better quality when made for developmental purposes than for administrative purposes.[67] The research evidence is clear: the higher the level of employee participation, the greater the employee's satisfaction (and sense of fairness) with the appraiser and the appraisal process.[68] If perceived as having unfair procedures or outcomes, however, performance appraisal can generate emotional stress among employees.[69] One major US company calls its performance appraisal program 'the employee development system' to emphasise the importance of coaching and development.[70]

Unfortunately, performance appraisals are negative and static in too many organisations. They are concerned with past performance rather than with improving future performance.[71] The emphasis is on looking back at and judging where an employee has been. No attempt is made to explore how the individual can grow and develop, even though research indicates that most employees want performance appraisal to be used primarily for employee development.[72] Similarly, any organisation seeking to pursue quality over an extended period of time must make development a primary concern.[73] Without this emphasis, performance appraisal becomes a negative experience, leading employees to see performance appraisals as an unfair 'report card' to be given on the annual day of judgement.[74] Furthermore, employees who constantly receive negative feedback risk emotional burnout.[75]

Negative experiences also explain why there is often considerable management, employee and union opposition to performance appraisal. Particularly for top executives whose behaviour is a primary contributor to an organisation's culture and whose strategic leadership fosters a common vision and sense of organisational direction, feedback that can lead to top management awareness, insight and development is critical. Unfortunately, top executives often do not perceive the need for feedback and change.[76] But if appraisals are not done at the top, the message sent to the rest of the organisation is that appraisals are unimportant and should not be taken seriously. Moreover, research suggests that such attitudes result in managers deliberately distorting and manipulating appraisals for political purposes.[77]

Feedback

Managers are responsible for evaluating the performance of their employees and for accurately communicating that assessment. This requires the manager to identify the employees' deficiencies and determine how they can be overcome, to know what specialised training and development are needed, and to ensure that opportunities are created for any new job experiences required.

Communicating clear, specific expectations and giving both positive and negative feedback are essential parts of the performance appraisal process.[78] Unfortunately, discussing such matters with a subordinate can be very stressful. Managers may prefer to avoid the unsettling experience of making decisions that affect the lives of employees.

A survey of US managers found that 'evaluating staff members' performance' and 'having to make decisions that affect the lives of individual people that I know' were major managerial stressors.[79] Says Kiechel: 'Most managers hate conducting performance appraisals ... If they think they can get away with it, they will skip such "potential" unpleasantness entirely.'[80] Stress is aggravated when the organisation's performance appraisal scheme is subjective, is unfair in its procedures and outcomes, has managers who are untrained or who are inadequately prepared, causes employees to lose face or results in constant negative feedback.[81] Many Chinese managers in Hong Kong and the People's Republic of China, for example, feel it is impolite to even say something negative about another person.[82] Singaporean managers similarly dislike performance appraisals because the cultural influence of face is so powerful.[83] Consequently, managers are reluctant to give open and honest feedback to their subordinates. Companies, in turn, use 'closed' systems where no feedback is given to the subordinate.[84] Less than one-third of Japanese managers compared with 70 per cent of US managers, for example, feel the best management policy is to evaluate and inform each employee of their strengths and weaknesses. Most Japanese managers prefer to mention only positive things to their better employees or say nothing at all.[85]

Managers are also often confused about what they should accomplish with the appraisal, or are unaware that the appraisal is more than a recital of employee shortcomings. The performance review, says Schotes, 'is the most stilted, anxiety ridden, posing conversation ever devised by human beings'.[86] As a result, many managers in face-to-face interviews make the appraisal a general get-together and avoid conflict by inflating poor ratings.[87]

Not surprisingly, performance appraisals are often ambiguous, incomplete and peppered with generalities such as 'Try harder!' and 'Keep on doing what you are doing, but do it better!'. One international study of more than 8000 respondents found that nearly half felt that their superior 'was not clear, frank or complete in telling them what they thought of their work performance',[88] while a Canadian study found that less than two-thirds of employees understood the measures used to evaluate their performance.[89] Such vagueness may cause Australian and North American employees stress because they feel anxious and uncertain about how their manager sees their performance.

Although subordinates generally prefer to have a clear understanding of 'How am I doing?' and prefer to be able to answer 'What does my manager really think? How can I improve? Why didn't I get a promotion? What is my likely future in this company?', this is not universal. Japanese employees, for example, typically prefer a far greater degree of ambiguity, do not want their weaknesses discussed and, in many cases, want appraisal results kept secret and not discussed at all.[90] Hofstede recommends giving feedback indirectly in such situations — for example, withdrawing a favour or passing on information through a third party trusted by both the manager and the employee.[91] Finally, when employees are allowed to express their feelings and managers give thorough explanations and use objective standards, employee perceptions of fairness increase.[92]

Rater of employee performance

The evaluation of employee performance is done by the immediate supervisor in most organisations.[93] However, performance appraisal can be done by anyone who:

- is familiar with the job's responsibilities and performance objectives
- has sufficient opportunity to observe the employee's job performance
- has the know-how to distinguish between behaviours that produce effective or ineffective job performance.[94]

Consequently, immediate supervisors, peers, customers and employees themselves (individually or in combination) can all provide information on employee performance. In fact, the demand for greater objectivity, the increased use of teams and the emphasis on customer service and quality has created interest in using multiple sources to generate performance evaluation data.

Supervisor evaluation

Overwhelmingly, performance appraisals are the responsibility of the immediate supervisor. This is because it is assumed that the supervisor best knows the job, the performance standards to be met and the actual performance of the individual employee. Research indicates that supervisory ratings have a higher inter-rater reliability than do peer ratings.[95] Moreover, performance appraisals are a powerful vehicle for supervisors to monitor and direct employee behaviour and to reinforce their formal authority and control. Disadvantages of this approach include the subjectivity of the supervisor (particularly if there is a personality conflict or the supervisor perceives the employee as a threat), manipulation of ratings to justify pay increases or promotions, discrimination and supervisor incompetence and lack of expertise.[96] To check such problems, organisations usually subject the supervisor's evaluation to management review and/or provide a mechanism for employee appeal and train supervisors to become more accurate raters.[97]

Peer evaluation

Organisations employing total quality management (TQM) concepts and teams are increasingly using **peer evaluations**. This is because peer ratings:

- are often more accurate because team members usually know each other's performance better than does the supervisor

Peer evaluation Employees at the same level in the organisation rate one another's performance. Sometimes called peer review.

- mean that employees are subject to peer pressure, which is a powerful motivator to improve performance
- increase team members' commitment and productivity
- involve several opinions, not just the supervisor's
- tend to yield more valid predictors of leadership performance than do immediate supervisor ratings
- show good reliability and validity
- are a valuable supplement to the immediate supervisor's ratings
- lead to a greater acceptance of performance appraisal.

However, research indicates that effective peer appraisals require a high level of trust among team members, a non-competitive reward system and frequent opportunities for colleagues to observe each other's performance.[98] This perhaps explains a trend evidenced in some companies to use appraisal systems that incorporate both individual and team evaluations.[99]

Self-evaluation

Self-evaluation Occurs where employees evaluate their own performance.

Some organisations use **self-evaluation** as a supplement to supervisor and/or peer evaluations. This is particularly so in organisations that aim to promote a less authoritarian culture and encourage employee participation and self-development. Research indicates that self-evaluation produces:
- more satisfying and constructive performance review discussions[100]
- less defensiveness among employees regarding the appraisal process
- improved job performance through greater commitment to organisational goals.[101]

Problems associated with self-evaluation include leniency, the employee's preference for being rated by the supervisor, lack of agreement between supervisor ratings and self-ratings, and bias when the ratings are being used for pay and promotion purposes. Consequently, self-evaluations are probably best used for self-development and the identification of training needs.[102] Finally, it is essential that employees receive proper training in self-evaluation and that both the supervisor and the subordinate have good interpersonal skills.[103]

Subordinate evaluation

Subordinate evaluations Sometimes called upward appraisals. Involve the subordinate evaluating the performance of their superior.

Although upward appraisals are a seldom-used management tool, organisations using total quality management and seeking continuous improvement increasingly employ this technique to evaluate manager performance.[104] The justification is that subordinates are in an excellent position to appraise a manager's leadership skills and ongoing performance. Consequently, **subordinate evaluations** are seen as a powerful indicator of how well the organisation's managers are managing others.[105] A common example of this approach is found in universities with student evaluations of lecturer performance. Examples of questions include: 'My manager does not "shoot the messenger"' and 'My manager encourages people to learn from one another'.[106]

The claimed benefits of upward appraisals are that they:
- generate unique information about the manager
- improve communication and worker satisfaction
- create an incentive for the manager to change
- enhance employee job satisfaction
- reduce power and status differences and make the workplace more democratic
- identify competent managers with leadership skills
- improve managerial performance (especially of poorly performing managers).

Disadvantages of upward appraisals include:
- information may be limited to situations involving personal interaction with the employee
- pressure may result in the manager making popular rather than right decisions
- the authority and status of some managers may be undermined, reducing their effectiveness
- employees may resist evaluating their manager because they fear reprisal or because they feel it is not part of their job
- some managers may be unable to cope emotionally with negative feedback.[107]

To implement upward appraisal effectively, it is important to:
- guarantee anonymity to participants
- use the upward performance appraisal for development not evaluation
- not conduct it at the same time as the formal performance appraisal
- make known the results of the appraisal as soon as possible
- ensure that everyone clearly understands who will see the results and what will be done with the information
- provide support for the employee being appraised
- train all participants (a critical factor for success)
- have top management commitment
- get people involved and keep them informed
- use only raters who volunteer to participate
- focus only on the observable aspects of the job
- include both average and range information in results provided to the employee being appraised
- control for bias.[108]

Multisource evaluations

Multisource evaluations (or **360-degree appraisals**) are gaining increasing popularity with some companies as they strive to improve organisation and individual performance. One survey, for example, reveals that 360-degree programs are now nearly universal among Fortune 500 companies.[109] In contrast, Nankervis and Leece found that the use of 360-degree feedback is minimal among Australian companies.[110]

Multi-rater feedback can: help achieve strategic business objectives and facilitate change by identifying the knowledge, skills and competencies needed; create the required training and development programs; and track employee progress in applying new learning on the job. It also fits well with organisations that have introduced teams, employee involvement and TQM programs.[111]

The objectives of the 360-degree evaluation are to identify areas of organisational and individual performance that need improvement. The first step in designing 360-degree evaluations is to identify observable managerial and leadership behaviours that are critical to the organisation's business success and culture enforcement. Next, superiors, peers, subordinates and others are asked to rate the manager using a comprehensive questionnaire (see figure 8.6).[112] The manager similarly rates their own performance. Finally, results are compiled by an independent consultant or the HR department and fed back to the manager. The manager then uses the information to identify those areas where differences exist and explore possible reasons for different perceptions. This type of feedback has been found to be a powerful performance diagnostic tool by enhancing information quality, providing specific performance feedback, targeting developmental areas and improving employee performance.[113]

360-degree feedback can also be used to communicate and reinforce for employees the organisation's mission, values and strategic business objectives (see figure 8.7).[114] AT&T, for example, requires any manager supervising three or more people to go through an annual evaluation based on the company's value statement. An essential factor in determining the overall value of 360-degree feedback is the follow-up on the required training and development activities identified by the feedback. Such evaluations should be seen as a part of the overall management development process and not a one-time event. If feedback does not encourage development, managers 'will likely be sceptical about participating in such an "opportunity" again'.[115]

There is some evidence to suggest that using 360-degree systems to make pay decisions that are not linked to accomplishment or results, and not maintaining confidentiality by limiting the amount of information the boss gets to see, undermines trust in the appraisal process.[116] Also, because the questionnaires are often lengthy and time consuming to complete, respondents can suffer from survey fatigue and the costs to the organisation can be high (see figure 8.8).[117] Finally, autocratic hierarchical organisations will probably find 360-degree evaluations a major source of stress and managerial resistance to results being shared with colleagues both up and down.[118]

Multisource evaluations (360-degree appraisals) Seek performance feedback on employees from their colleagues, superiors, customers and subordinates. Popular in companies with teams, TQM and employee involvement programs.

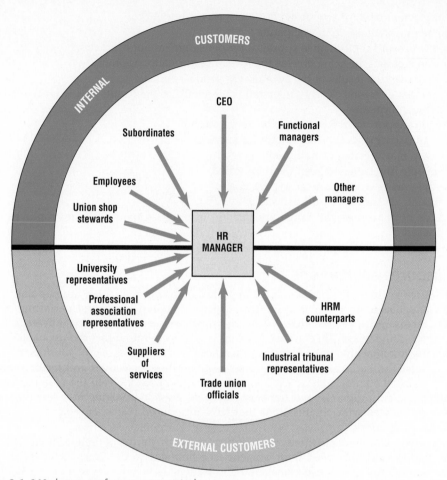

Figure 8.6 360-degree performance appraisal

Team appraisals

Economic, social and technological changes have seen organisations become less hierarchical in structure, adopt more participative management styles and introduce self-managed work teams. Conventional employee appraisal schemes, with their focus on the individual, now require modification. In addition to recognising and rewarding individual performance, appraisal schemes must measure the performance of the group and reward its achievements in a way that promotes team effort and commitment. Unfortunately, **team appraisals** pose a number of challenges for the HR manager because:

- it is not always clear *what* results should be measured
- it is not clear *how* performance should be measured
- performance measurement has to be done at both the team and individual level. Individual performance, however, may be difficult to measure in some team activities. As a result, this can produce dissatisfaction and feelings of inequity among more individualistic and/or hardworking members (especially if some team members make less of an effort than when they are working alone). Such **'social loafing'** is a major disadvantage of the team approach. It is most evident in groups (particularly large ones) where individual contributions are difficult to identify (for example, how does a lecturer accurately measure the contribution of an individual student to a group assignment?)
- teams vary in personality, diversity, size and the type of work performed, so it is not easy to design a program that has universal application
- team and individual measures of performance are in conflict (for example, a football team receives a bonus for each game it wins, but individual players are awarded a bonus for each goal they score).

Team appraisals Appraisals that are specially designed to evaluate how well a team has performed.

Social loafing Occurs when an employee expends less effort and performs at a lower level when working in a group than when working alone.

EXECUTIVE APPRAISAL

Here are some items included on a 360-degree feedback instrument. Respondents are to indicate whether the person exhibits them.

Vision and strategy

- Creates an inspired mission and a sense of core purpose, based on a clear vision for the future.
- Makes the vision real to managers and other employees. Communicates a view of the future so compelling that others are drawn to follow.
- Develops breakthrough strategies and tactical plans to take advantage of future trends and market changes.

Innovation and change

- Leads the way in creating new approaches. Stimulates new thinking in goals, technologies, business conditions, organisational structures and people.
- Goes beyond current thinking to seek new perspectives and different ways of doing things. Challenges old techniques and strategies. Explores different options before making a decision.
- Manages successfully in an ambiguous and changing environment. Initiates effective action in unstructured situations.

Collaboration

- Helps businesses work together to meet goals and solve problems.
- Actively works with the executive team to create a positive, optimistic and cooperative work environment.
- Uses appropriate interpersonal and management styles to work with others. Varies approach with different people and situations.

Coaching

- Accurately identifies strengths and development needs in others. Coaches others in the development of their skills and stimulates them to make changes and improvements.
- Deals promptly and directly with performance that is below expectations. Confronts issues before they worsen.

Personal leadership

- Knows own personal strengths, weaknesses and limits. Seeks feedback to improve performance and to make any necessary changes.
- Takes responsibility for problems rather than making excuses or blaming others.
- Can be counted on to hold things together during tough times.

Figure 8.7 Executive 360-degree assessment
Source K. Ludeman, 'To fill the feedback void', *Training and Development*, vol. 49, no. 8, 1995, p. 40.

Advantages

- Develops desired corporate skills, abilities, knowledge and behaviours.
- Increases employees' accountability to their customers.
- Supports team initiatives.
- Creates a high-involvement work force.
- Decreases hierarchies, promotes streamlining.
- Detects barriers to success.
- Assesses developmental needs.
- Avoids discrimination and bias by providing a more comprehensive view of employee performance.
- Enhances employee self-development.[119]
- Increases the credibility of the performance appraisal process.

Disadvantages

- May intimidate people.
- May raise conflicting opinions — questions of who is right.
- May not be perceived by employees as accurate or reliable feedback.
- May not result in truthful feedback.
- May not result in anonymous and confidential feedback.
- May use an unreliable or invalid feedback instrument.
- May need a feedback expert to interpret the results.
- Does not ensure follow-up on development plans.
- Links feedback to pay and promotions.[120]
- Can be time consuming and administratively complex.
- Requires training and significant change effort to be effective.

Figure 8.8 Multisource evaluations: advantages and disadvantages

To reduce the negative impact of such problems, the HR manager should try to ensure that a team-based appraisal scheme:
- has clearly defined group goals that are accepted by all team members
- has group rewards that are linked to the achievement of group goals
- is applied where the personality of the team members and the nature of the work to be performed are compatible with a team approach

- involves team members in the design of the appraisal program, the setting of goals and the defining of performance measures
- has measures of individual and team performance that are transparent, accepted and not in conflict with each other.[121]

Sources of error in performance appraisal

Research evidence indicates that managers can clearly discriminate between performing and non-performing employees.[122] However, their ratings will not necessarily reflect their actual judgements. This is because managers often distort their evaluations when completing performance appraisal forms.[123] Managers need to recognise this when considering the validity and accuracy of their organisation's performance appraisal system (see figure 8.9).

Validity

To be valid, a performance appraisal must measure actual employee performance. Consequently, only factors related to successful job performance should be measured. Extraneous factors and factors that the employee cannot control (such as economic conditions) must be excluded from the evaluation process. Thus, a thorough job analysis is essential to ensure that performance-related and not irrelevant factors are being assessed.

Reliability

To be reliable, a performance appraisal must generate consistent results. If an employee, for example, is evaluated quite differently for achieving the same standard of performance at different times or by different managers at the same time, then the appraisal is unreliable.

Figure 8.9 Validity and reliability

Management attitude

If management is committed to performance appraisal, it will work. However, if managers see performance appraisal as something imposed on them by the HR department, the process will lack the genuine support of senior management and will simply become a cosmetic process to be treated with indifference. 'Management commitment', according to Regel and Hollman, 'is vital to an effective performance appraisal program. All members of the management team need to understand appraisal's purpose(s) and should agree that it is critical for management to participate in and support the system.'[124]

Performance appraisal is valued when it is seen as facilitating the accomplishment of the organisation's strategic business objectives by motivating employees to improve their performance and reach their potential. Performance appraisal systems are thus a key element in using and developing an organisation's human resources.[125] A survey by KMPG, however, found that while 80 per cent of Australian company directors recognise that there is a link between their company's performance and that of its directors, only less than 40 per cent actually evaluate board performance.[126]

Rater errors

Rater errors Errors in the evaluation of an employee's performance resulting from leniency, strictness, bias, central tendency, prejudice, recency effect and the like.

Most managers and employees are aware of the **rater errors** that arise in performance appraisal. 'Easy' and 'tough' managers and managers who play favourites create situations that result in unfair and inaccurate ratings. Such managers teach employees that performance does not count. Moreover, because there are inequities, the performance appraisal system becomes a nonsense and fosters employee frustration and animosity. Seventy per cent of civil servants in Hong Kong are rated as 'outstanding' or 'very good', forcing the Public Service Commission Chairman to comment, 'It's a bit ludicrous'.[127]

The halo effect

If a manager gives an employee the same rating on all factors by generalising from one specific factor, this causes a 'halo effect' error. Research shows that people with good attendance records are viewed as intelligent and responsible. Similarly, workers with poor attendance records are considered poor performers, even though the tardy person may produce work of far greater quantity and quality than the punctual employee.[128]

Central tendency

Central tendency is a problem caused by a manager giving everyone an average or acceptable rating, regardless of actual performance. Obviously, such ratings are useless for the purposes of rewards and training and development. A study by Pearce and Porter found that employees actually perceive a performance rating of 'satisfactory' as negative, and that the rating significantly reduces the employee's commitment.[129] Central tendency errors arise from 'playing safe', having few opportunities to observe the employee's performance and being unwilling to justify high or low ratings to the employee or the organisation. Murphy and Cleveland point out that these explanations are essentially hypotheses (although widely accepted) that have not been adequately tested.[130]

Leniency/strictness bias

A leniency or **strictness bias** occurs when managers rate their employees either consistently high or low. Examples include managers who give their subordinates the highest possible ratings indiscriminately, or who require their subordinates to 'walk on water' before they can receive an above-average rating. Research by Jawahar and Williams found that managers who know they are rating an employee for administrative purposes (for example, a merit increase or promotion) are likely to be more lenient and less accurate than when evaluating performance for research, feedback or employee development purposes.[131] Other reasons given by managers for inflating or deflating appraisals are shown in figures 8.10 and 8.11.

Prejudice

If a manager has a negative or positive **prejudice** towards an individual or group, this causes a rater-generated error. One study, for example, found rater bias against the 'performance capacity' and 'potential for development' of employees aged 60 years or more.[132] Other research shows that older workers receive lower performance ratings than younger employees.[133] Cook reviewed 40 separate studies and found substantial bias against older employees.[134] There is also evidence to suggest a race bias exists in performance appraisal (that is, whites favour whites, blacks favour blacks).[135] In another study, a sex bias was found, with high-performing females rated significantly higher than high-performing males.[136] Other biases may also exist. One Hong Kong publicly listed company, for example, has a long-standing policy banning male employees from taking mainland mistresses. Says the Managing Director: 'We want our managers to be faithful to their wives. It's good for the company and good for business … If they take a mistress and I find out about it, they're fired.'[137] Clearly, all managers need to have an understanding of EEO and legal issues and how they affect the performance appraisal process.[138]

The recency effect

If a manager overemphasises the employee's most recent behaviour, this results in a 'recency effect' error. The cunning employee uses this bias by ensuring, just before appraisal time, that they submit some outstanding piece of work, come to work early, leave late and appear highly motivated. The manager is overimpressed by the dramatic improvement in the employee's performance, evaluating only this segment of work rather than the employee's performance over the full review period.

MAKING IT SOUND BETTER

- Executives inflated the appraisal to provide ratings that would effectively maintain or increase the subordinate's level of performance (the primary concern was not the accuracy of the ratings).
- Inflated ratings occur primarily on the overall performance rating, as opposed to the individual appraisal items.
- Executives sometimes inflated the appraisal:
  - to maximise the merit increases a subordinate would be eligible to receive, especially when the merit ceiling was considered low
  - to protect or encourage a subordinate whose performance was suffering because of personal problems (feeling sorry for a subordinate also resulted in an inflated appraisal)
  - to avoid hanging dirty laundry out in public if the performance appraisal would be reviewed by people outside the organisation
  - to avoid creating a written record of poor performance that would become a permanent part of a subordinate's personnel file
  - to avoid a confrontation with a subordinate with whom the manager had recently had difficulties
  - to give a break to a subordinate who had improved during the latter part of the performance period
  - to promote a subordinate 'up and out' when the subordinate was performing poorly or did not fit in the department.

Figure 8.10 Inflating the appraisal

Source C. O. Longenecker, H. P. Sims and D. A. Gioia, 'Behind the mask: the politics of employee appraisal', *Academy of Management Executive*, vol. 1, no. 3, 1987, p. 189.

MAKING IT SOUND WORSE

- Executives indicated that they were very hesitant to consciously deflate a subordinate's ratings because there were potential problems associated with such a tactic.
- Nevertheless, they sometimes deflated appraisals:
  - to shock a subordinate back onto a higher performance track
  - to teach a rebellious subordinate a lesson about who is in charge
  - to send a message to a subordinate that they should consider leaving the organisation
  - to build a strongly documented record of poor performance that could speed up the termination process.

Figure 8.11 Deflating the appraisal

Source C. O. Longenecker, H. P. Sims and D. A. Gioia, 'Behind the mask: the politics of employee appraisal', *Academy of Management Executive*, vol. 1, no. 3, 1987, p. 190.

The relationship effect

A recent US study found that employees in high-quality, trusting relationships with managers receive higher ratings regardless of how long they have worked for the manager, whereas employees in more distant, low-quality relationships receive higher than expected ratings only when the relationship is long term. Similarly, the research showed that ratings on subjective criteria, such as dependability and trustworthiness, were more heavily influenced by the quality and duration of the relationship.[139] This is called a **relationship effect.**

Other rater-related errors are produced when the manager varies the ratings for political reasons or for a specific purpose, such as helping a subordinate to obtain a pay increase or promotion.

It should be remembered that if performance appraisal is to remain an effective management tool, the system must be consistently monitored to ensure that its results are fair, accurate and related to performance.

This Letter to the Editor provides a provocative viewpoint. Do you agree? See 'What's your view?' on page 313.

Relationship effect Occurs where the nature of the superior/ subordinate relationship influences a performance rating.

Performance appraisal is like smoking pot: the harder you suck, the higher you get

Dear Editor,

I have been reading reports that many organisations have been improving their performance appraisal (PA) systems, and I am writing to argue that the newer PA systems have a long way to go if they are to be effective. Personally, I have yet to see a PA system that can outsmart those employees who make a genuine effort to outsmart the PA system.

Here's how my colleagues and I ensure that we 'smell like roses' at every appraisal.

First, we seek to have the PA session conducted within a day or two following an important work 'victory'. The victory may be a major sale, the development of a new product or service or the receipt of excellent customer feedback, some of which we may deliberately solicit ourselves! This ensures that the boss is in a positive frame of mind regarding our performance.

Second, we know that managers at all levels are time-starved. Mintzberg's seminal research attests to that, and little has changed in the three decades since that research was conducted. Time-starved managers are likely to undertake appraisals superficially and seek to emphasise the positives, as identifying negatives requires subsequent employee counselling and development. To assist our senior managers to avoid these time-consuming tasks, we emphasise that our busy schedules only allow 20 or 30 minutes for appraisals,

and that even this amount of time is tough for us to find, since it takes us away from our customers and our 'real work'.

Third, we remind ourselves that performance appraisals are a flawed process. For example, the targets against which we are evaluated often have no basis in reality, but are simply last year's objectives plus 10 or 15 per cent. This can make for an unrealistic appraisal, since much of what we do is affected by economic, market and industry conditions over which we have no control. For this reason, we emphasise during our appraisals that the positive aspects of our performance were the result of our individual brilliance, while those objectives not achieved were due to circumstances beyond our control, and we request that our managers appraise us accordingly. That also provides our managers with an excuse for their own failure to meet the department's objectives! Of course, we also indicate that our successes have much to do with their great management skills!

Finally, we avoid any type of conflict with our managers and appraisers in the period leading up to the appraisal. Performance appraisals are primarily a 'feel good' exercise, and we try hard to make sure everyone is feeling really good for the appraisal process. We do this by tidying our desks, getting to work on time and staying late, and writing long-overdue reports and memos full of creative ideas for improving our organisation. Bringing fresh flowers into the office and buying cakes for the tearoom also works a treat!

Yes, performance appraisals are nothing to be feared. And they are like smoking pot: the harder you suck, the higher you get!

A contented sales rep (with a new company car)

Source David Poole, University of Western Sydney.

An emphasis on subjective performance criteria

An examination of many traditional performance appraisal systems reveals an emphasis on subjective criteria such as personality, loyalty and initiative, as opposed to objective criteria such as number of units produced, days absent per year, dollar value of sales and number of late arrivals at work. Nankervis and Leece found that subjectivity was one of the most commonly reported difficulties with performance appraisals.[140] Galin similarly found that a large number of the appraisal methods studied were heavily based on opinion with little regard to the facts (see figure 8.12).[141] Nearly 60 per cent of NSW government CEOs received bonus payments regardless of whether performance agreements and performance appraisal systems were in place.[142] Furthermore, the most important criteria for performance appraisal in some cultures, such as the People's Republic of China, include subjective factors such as ideological and political purity.[143]

Personal-based	Performance-based*
Initiative	Work quantity
Dependability	Sales volume
Leadership ability	Earnings or profit generated
Attitude towards safety	Costs incurred
Willingness to cooperate	Number of clients
Verbal communication skills	Number of rejects
Enthusiasm for job	Amount of scrap produced
Ability to work under stress	Attendance record

*This distinction often rests on the observability of the performance-based criteria.

Figure 8.12 Examples of personal-based and performance-based criteria
Source S. J. Carroll and G. E. Schneider, *Performance Appraisal and Review Systems*, Scott Foresman, Glenview, Ill., 1982, p. 36.

Appraisal systems such as the one illustrated by figure 8.13 are vague, subjective and open to charges of discrimination; they create a culture of 'yes' men and women and generally should be avoided. But ultimately, the nature of the job and the purposes of the assessment determine the type of criteria to be used.[144] Thus, it is not uncommon for organisations to use a combination of objective and subjective criteria. Singapore Airlines, for example, uses performance criteria relating to quality and quantity, job attitudes and behaviour (for example, dependability, teamwork, cooperation) and management skills (supervision and communication).[145] Nevertheless, as Gardner and Palmer point out, the litigious potential of performance appraisal under EEO legislation suggests that criteria should be carefully examined for their reliability and validity.[146]

Employee's name:

Position:

Department:

Circle the appropriate score for each factor that best describes the work performance of the employee.

1 — unsatisfactory 2 — needs improvement 3 — satisfactory 4 — above average 5 — outstanding

Write a short statement in the space provided, supporting your rating.

(a) **Output:** ability to meet required standards of quality and quantity	1 2 3 4 5
(b) **Job knowledge:** clear understanding of the job	1 2 3 4 5
(c) **Organisation and planning:** ability to devise work methods, anticipate needs and meet deadlines	1 2 3 4 5
(d) **Judgement:** ability to make effective decisions without undue delay	1 2 3 4 5
(e) **Work relations:** human relations and leadership skills	1 2 3 4 5
(f) **Delegation of authority:** frees self of routine work	1 2 3 4 5
(g) **Initiative:** seeks increased responsibilities, self-starting, unafraid to proceed alone	1 2 3 4 5
(h) **Capacity for advancement:** potential to assume additional responsibility	1 2 3 4 5
(i) **Personal qualities:** personality, appearance, sociability, integrity	1 2 3 4 5
(j) **Overall performance:** all factors in consideration	1 2 3 4 5

Reasons: ....
....
....

Figure 8.13 Employee appraisal record
Source Asia Pacific Management Co. Ltd, 2004.

Finally, research shows that employees assessed by an appraisal system emphasising objective performance criteria are significantly more satisfied with the way in which they were evaluated.[147]

Major types of performance appraisal systems

When choosing an employee performance appraisal system to introduce, managers must consider the strategic business objectives of the organisation as well as specific performance evaluation purposes (such as training and development, rewards linked to performance). The system selected should also be compatible with the organisation's culture.[148]

Ranking

Ranking is the oldest and simplest form of rating. It compares each person's performance, with the manager ranking all subordinates from 'best' to 'worst' using a single overall rating or ranking each employee using various criteria (for example, job knowledge, quality of work, quantity of work, attendance, punctuality, and so on). It is assumed that the manager thoroughly understands the job of every subordinate and is able to simultaneously compare them overall on selected criteria. The technique's apparent simplicity is thus misleading.

In practice, it is suitable for dealing with only a small number of employees whose jobs have a high degree of commonality and are familiar to the manager. Even then, ranking can be highly subjective, very cumbersome, inaccurate and misleading. For example, in figure 8.14, Caplan is ranked 1, Monicelli 2 and Uzan 3, yet Caplan is only just better than Monicelli, while Monicelli is twice as good as Uzan. In addition to ignoring relative differences, ranking gives no indication of actual performance. For example, all employees may be superior or unsatisfactory. In other words, the person ranked last in one group may be a superior performer, while the person ranked first in another group may simply be the best of a bad lot. Finally, ranking involves considerable difficulty in discriminating between employees in the middle and does not give any indication as to why one employee is superior to another.

Ranking The manager compares their subordinates' performance then ranks each in order from 'best' to 'worst'.

| Name | RANKING CRITERIA | | | | OVERALL | |
	Job knowledge	Quality of work	Quantity of work	Attendance	Total	Rank
Caplan, J.	1	1	2	2	6	1
Monicelli, P.	2	2	1	2	7	2
Uzan, K.	4	4	3	3	14	3
Koshiyama, T.	5	6	4	4	19	5
Singh, S.	3	2	5	6	16	4
Ricco, I.	7	5	7	5	24	6
Smith, J.	6	7	6	7	26	7
Bennett, A.	9	8	10	8	35	8
Page, D.	8	9	8	10	35	9
Da Silva, L.	10	10	9	9	38	10

Figure 8.14 Ranking method
Source Asia Pacific Management Co. Ltd, 2004.

Grading

The **grading** system describes specific performance levels, such as superior, good, acceptable, marginal, unsatisfactory. Employees' performance is compared with the grade definitions, and then the employees are placed in the grade that best describes their performance.

A refinement of the grading system is forced distribution, whereby a fixed percentage of employees are allocated to each grade — for example, 5 per cent are superior, 15 per cent are good, 60 per cent are satisfactory, 15 per cent are marginal and 5 per cent are unsatisfactory (see figure 8.15). There are some strong arguments in favour of using the forced distribution technique because it overcomes the problems of managers overrating, underrating or rating everyone as average. Moreover, it forces managers to think seriously about their employees, so there is a much greater likelihood of identifying performers and non-performers. Texas Instruments, for example, requires that its managers clearly identify the top 10 per cent and bottom 10 per cent of their subordinates.[149]

| Unsatisfactory | Marginal | Satisfactory | Good | Superior |

Figure 8.15 Illustration of a forced distribution

However, forced grades generally meet with considerable resistance. As one critic says: 'the bell shaped curve is a misguided attempt to overcome the lack of precise performance standards for each unique job. It is intended to upgrade organisational performance and control pay increase budgets. Instead, it erodes trust. Rather than fair performance appraisals, the organisation ends up with guerrilla warfare.'[150] Absolute standards, on the other hand, provide definite goals for employees without the worry of competing with peers.[151]

Graphic scales

Graphic scales are one of the most popular methods of performance appraisal.[152] Typically, the manager can choose one of five degrees for each specific criteria (for example, see figure 8.13). The selection of criteria to be measured can be centred on subjective factors (such as initiative and dependability) and/or on objective factors (such as quality and quantity of work). Graphic scales, while appearing to be scientific, are notoriously unreliable. Another problem is that criteria may be important in one job but not in another. For example, creativity may be critical for success as an advertising director but of little importance to good performance as a data entry operator. Research also suggests that many criteria commonly chosen on graphic rating scales are intercorrelated. One study on the performance evaluation of a group of engineers, for example, found that successful performance was the function of only two of the 10 rating criteria used — technical ability and interpersonal relations.[153]

Critical incidents

This method requires the manager to record those occurrences or **critical incidents** of employee job behaviour that highlight good or bad job performance. Incidents typically take the form of a story or anecdote and are recorded as soon as possible after they occur. The manager then uses the record of critical incidents to assess the employee's performance when it is time for performance appraisal. By focusing on specific examples when discussing the evaluation with the employee, the rater can emphasise that performance, not personality, is being judged.[154] In addition, the critical incident technique increases the probability that a manager's evaluation will cover the entire period subject to appraisal, not just recent happenings.

Research by Peters and De Nisi, for example, found a statistically significant improvement in the quality of performance ratings when managers kept a diary on employee performance rather than simply relying on memory during appraisals. Similarly, diary-keeping managers were shown to be less lenient, not given to making inflated appraisals and more critical in their reviews than were other managers.[155] However, it should be noted that the critical incidents technique can be prone to recency error, makes it difficult to compare individual employees and can be very time consuming for managers.

> **Critical incidents** Examples of employee behaviour that illustrate effective or ineffective job performance.

Behaviourally anchored rating scales

Behaviourally anchored rating scales (BARS) are designed to evaluate behaviour demonstrated in performing a job. Profiles of good and bad performance in a particular job are collected from supervisors and/or people familiar with the work. These examples are then grouped into various job dimensions such as job knowledge, customer relations and safety. Next, specific examples of job behaviour are placed on a scale, which is usually graded from one to seven (see figure 8.16). It is argued that BARS reduce bias and subjectivity because the positions along the scale are defined in terms of job behaviour. In addition, there is some evidence to suggest that subordinates are more committed, less tense and more satisfied than those subject to other types of appraisal systems. However, in terms of rating errors and problems, research fails to demonstrate any superiority of BARS over other techniques.[156]

A major drawback with BARS is that they take a great deal of management time and effort to develop. In addition, because separate rating forms must be developed for different jobs, their use is restricted to a minority of big organisations with generic jobs performed by large numbers of incumbents.[157] One recent US survey, in fact, reported that there was not one organisation using BARS.[158]

> **Behaviourally anchored rating scales (BARS)** A performance appraisal method that combines elements of the traditional rating scale and critical incidents method.

EMPLOYMENT OFFICER

Superior performance	7	Could be expected at all times to be developing, implementing and refining selection procedures and their own interviewing techniques to the highest professional standard.
Very good performance	6	Could be expected to have an excellent knowledge of the company, its products and job vacancies, and to be accurate and thorough in matching applicants with jobs.
Good performance	5	Could be expected to interview in-depth and treat applicants with courtesy and respect and inform them fully about the job, the company and its products.
Acceptable performance	4	Could be expected to talk with an applicant about the job, their interests, etc. and to cover key questions regarding suitability.
Marginal performance	3	Could be expected to show little personal interest in the candidate and possess only basic knowledge about the job, the company and its products.
Poor performance	2	Could be expected to keep applicants waiting, interview haphazardly and have little or no knowledge about the job, the company and its products.
Unsatisfactory performance	1	Could be expected to disclose confidential information about applicants, be rude, ask questions that are not job-related and keep applicants waiting.

Figure 8.16 Behaviourally anchored rating scale for an employment officer
Source Asia Pacific Management Co. Ltd, 2004.

Behaviour observation scales

Behaviour observation scales (BOS) Performance appraisal system that uses critical incidents to develop a list of desired behaviours needed to perform a specific job successfully.

Behaviour observation scales (BOS) use critical incidents to develop a list of the desired behaviours needed to perform a specific job successfully. The employee is then evaluated by the manager on the frequency with which they demonstrate such behaviour on the job, using a five-point scale ranging from 'almost never' (1) to 'almost always' (5). The manager calculates an overall rating by adding up the scores on each behavioural item. There is evidence that both managers and employees prefer appraisals based on behaviour observation scales to those based on BARS and graphic rating scales. Legal opinion suggests that behaviour observation scales may be more defensible than the other two in EEO challenges.[159] Nevertheless, as with BARS, the job-specific nature of the technique makes it costly and time consuming to develop (see figure 8.17).

EMPLOYMENT OFFICER

1. Gives the applicant a clear description of the job
   (almost never)   1   2   3   4   5   (almost always)
2. Gives the applicant a clear description of the pay and benefits offered
   (almost never)   1   2   3   4   5   (almost always)
3. Conducts in-depth interviews with applicants
   (almost never)   1   2   3   4   5   (almost always)
4. Treats all applicants in a non-discriminatory and courteous manner
   (almost never)   1   2   3   4   5   (almost always)
5. Undertakes thorough reference checks
   (almost never)   1   2   3   4   5   (almost always)

Total score
   5–9: Needs improvement   10–14: Acceptable   15–19: Good   20+: Superior

---

Figure 8.17 Behaviour observation scale for an employment officer
Source Asia Pacific Management Co. Ltd, 2004.

Essay description

Essay description A written statement describing an employee's strengths, weaknesses, past performance and future development prepared by the rater.

Some organisations use an **essay description** to try to determine performance levels (see figure 8.18). A manager may be asked to describe, in their own words, the employee's performance (covering the quantity and quality of work performed, job know-how, human relations skills, strengths and weaknesses, promotability, and so on). The major problems associated with this approach are subjectivity, the impact of the manager's writing skills on the impression conveyed in the report, and the difficulty in comparing reports written by different supervisors. Finally, managers can find essay reports a time-consuming bureaucratic annoyance (especially if they have a large number of subordinates). For these reasons, few private organisations employ this approach. However, essay descriptions are still used in the public sector — for example, the Hong Kong Police uses essay appraisals.

Management by objectives

Management by objectives (MBO) Involves setting specific measurable goals with each employee and then periodically reviewing the progress made.

Management by objectives (MBO) is a technique whereby the manager and the subordinate mutually identify common goals, define the subordinate's major areas of responsibility in terms of expected results, and use these as measures in assessing the subordinate's performance. It should be stressed that goals without measurement remain a statement of good intentions that the manager and the employee can agree to, but for which no one can be held accountable. Measurement creates discipline. 'Numbers always tell the story', says Campbell's Soups former Chief Executive Officer David Johnson.[160] Management by objectives is popular with both managers and subordinates.[161] This is because it is easy to understand, is objective and involves the subordinate in the appraisal process. Research shows that user acceptance is critical to the success of a performance appraisal system, and this is a major plus for the MBO approach.[162]

```
Name:

Position:

Department:

Date started on job:

Date of last rating:

Date of this rating:

Appraisal of performance: ...............................................................................................

............................................................................................................................................

............................................................................................................................................

............................................................................................................................................

............................................................................................................................................

Suggestions for development: .........................................................................................

............................................................................................................................................

............................................................................................................................................

............................................................................................................................................

............................................................................................................................................

Prepared by:                                    Position:

Manager's signature:                       Employee's signature:
```

Figure 8.18 Example of an essay description performance appraisal format

It should be noted, however, that research by Hofstede suggests that the effectiveness of an MBO program may depend on national culture. Furthermore, MBO programs can require considerable expense, time and effort to develop.[163]

To make MBO easier to understand and implement, some companies employ the acronym SMART:

Specific/Stretching
Measurable
Agreed/Achievable
Realistic
Time-bounded.

Is it fair that failed executives who have destroyed shareholder wealth and cost employees their jobs are rewarded with lucrative exit payouts?

- *Specific:* objectives must be clear and precise (for example, 'increase sales by 10 per cent' and not vague (for example, 'try harder') or generalised (for example, 'to provide high quality service').
- *Stretching:* objectives must have 'stretch' built in. In other words, they must be challenging (but not impossible) to achieve. Objectives that are too easy to achieve result in undera-chievement and the demotivation of those with high achievement needs.
- *Measurable:* objectives should be measurable and quantifiable.
- *Agreed:* objectives must be jointly agreed upon by the supervisor and the subordinate. Objectives that are imposed on the subordinate by the superior risk being rejected. For subordinates to be motivated, they must have a sense of ownership of the objectives.
- *Achievable:* objectives must be achievable. Impossible objectives will lead to employees giving up, becoming demoralised and feeling antagonistic towards the process.
- *Realistic:* objectives must take into account current circumstances (for example, the state of the economy, market conditions, political instability, and so on).
- *Time-bounded:* objectives must have a specific deadline or time frame by which they are to be achieved (for example, 15 November 2006).

The balanced scorecard

Balanced scorecard (BS) A performance management technique that evaluates organisational performance in four key areas: people, internal operations, customer satisfaction and financial.

The **balanced scorecard (BS)** is a performance management technique that evaluates organisational performance in four key areas: people, internal operations, customer satisfaction and financial. Objectives and performance measures are set for each key area. The BS emphasises that all areas are important to organisational performance and that balance should exist between them. According to Dolmat-Connell, the BS 'is a tool for translating vision to action. It translates vision and strategy into a tool that effectively communicates strategic intent and motivates and tracks performance against the established goals'.[164]

The balanced scorecard highlights an organisation's focus on future success by setting and measuring performance against people, internal operations, customer and financial factors:

1. *People* — the BS directs attention to learning and innovation (see the learning organisation on page 332–3). Performance measures include:
   - employee satisfaction
   - employee retention
   - employee productivity
   - employee abilities, knowledge and skill.
2. *Internal operations* — the BS directs attention to the development of a learning organisation. Performance measures include:
   - innovation (for example, percentage of sales from new products)
   - operational efficiency
   - service (for example, time from order to delivery).
3. *Customer satisfaction* — the BS directs attention to the needs of the customer. Performance measures include:
   - market share
   - customer acquisition
   - customer retention
   - customer satisfaction
   - customer profitability
   - service/product quality
   - image/reputation.
4. *Financial* — the BS directs attention to the financial results that drive the business. Performance measures include:
   - revenue growth and mix
   - cost reduction
   - productivity improvement
   - return on investment
   - return on sales
   - asset utilisation.[165]

Grouped together, these generate a balanced view of the organisation's overall performance and specific employee performance.

The advantages of the BS approach include:
- It creates an alignment between organisational, departmental and individual objectives.
- It balances short-term and long-term objectives.
- It focuses attention on four key performance areas.
- It provides guidance for change.
- It provides performance feedback.

The disadvantages of the BS approach include:
- It can become overly complex and incomprehensible to employees.
- The four factors may not be equally important drivers of performance.
- The selection and classification of the four factors is arbitrary.
- It requires extensive training.
- It requires extensive communication.
- It requires the setting of objectives throughout the organisation.[166]
- Managers overemphasise areas that they believe are key drivers or key performance criteria.[167]

The effectiveness of the balanced scorecard in the real world is debatable and it risks being labelled as yet another management fad.

Maisie Lam *is Vice-President of a major multinational bank and has over 15 years experience in human resources. She has held responsibilities for various HR activities, including staffing and leadership development, compensation and benefits, and training and development.*

Practitioner speaks

The balanced scorecard

The balanced scorecard is the foundation of the performance management process. Establishing a balanced scorecard facilitates:

- setting key objectives for the year
- aligning individual and team objectives with business objectives
- planning individual development
- providing/receiving performance feedback
- reviewing and evaluating performance
- linking rewards to the performance of the individual and the business.
  An effective balanced scorecard should have the following features:
- key categories or performance drivers that are critical to the success of the company, both in terms of short-term financial results and long-term franchise growth — some key categories often include customers, operation processes, controls, risks, people, community and financial performance
- performance objectives and expected results
- action plans
- measurements and results.

The balanced scorecard is gaining increasing popularity as it benefits all parties — the company, the manager and the employee (see chart below). When everyone in the company uses the same scorecard categories, cascaded down through successive management levels, it supports the scorecards of peers, managers and the business. This ensures that everyone is working towards common goals and speaking the same language around performance and results.

While achieving financial results is important, it is not the only critical measure if the company wants to grow. The company needs to perform well in other performance drivers, giving rise to the 'balanced' concept, which financial results are dependent upon. Although some performance drivers may or may not be more relevant or important to employees assuming different roles in the organisation, adopting the balanced scorecard will deter employees from focusing only on their area of relevance, upholding their own agenda and being unwilling to cooperate, and will work in the best interests of the organisation.

The benefits of the balanced scorecard

COMPANY	MANAGER	EMPLOYEE
Consistency of alignment • Supports the company vision • Ensures all levels of the organisation understand the strategy, and that both departmental and individual objectives are aligned Objectivity • Promotes a more motivated and less sceptical work force Productivity • Increases efficiency as all work towards common goals	• Understands the priorities • Makes communication to subordinates easier • Focuses on measurable results, facilitates evaluation and communication • Promotes greater teamwork and coordination	• Understands how their actions contribute to overall departmental objectives • Knows what needs to be done and the results expected; reduces subjectivity • Increases job satisfaction and appreciation of work environment

(continued)

Although the balanced scorecard may have many benefits, there may also be deficiencies if it is not applied appropriately:

- Too many key categories will diminish the area of focus and lose sight of the priorities.
- If the measurements and results are too high level, junior employees may not feel that it is within their own sphere of influence.
- Some employees may find difficulties in developing actions to contribute to those performance drivers that are not so relevant to their job role.
- Like any other objective-setting program, goals that are too vague, too easy or lack specific measurement will undermine the effectiveness of the scorecard.
- Not even the balanced scorecard can completely eliminate subjectivity.

Maisie Lam

Assessment centres

Assessment centre Uses interviews, tests, simulations, games and observations to evaluate an individual's potential.

The primary purpose of an **assessment centre** is typically to identify promotable or high-potential employees. Assessment centres are rarely used for performance appraisal purposes because they are costly and time consuming.[168] Evaluations are not made on the job but are the product of observations of behaviour and test results generated from simulated activities such as interviews, in-basket exercises, group discussions and business games. Consequently, exhaustive job analysis is necessary to attain a close relationship between the assessment centre activity and the actual job. Finally, the reliability and validity of the assessment centre approach can be markedly influenced by the use (or non-use) of trained assessors and psychologists.[169] It should be noted that an assessment centre is a process of assessment and not a physical place.

Workplace surveillance

The introduction of workplace surveillance equipment to monitor employee performance and behaviour is rapidly becoming a matter of considerable controversy. A survey conducted by PricewaterhouseCoopers found that more than half of Australia's leading companies use video surveillance to monitor their employees.[170] In Hong Kong, more than 60 per cent of 500 companies surveyed reported installing some type of workplace surveillance.[171] Scrutiny of employee use of email, the Internet and the telephone is commonplace in some industries (often without employees being told that their activities are being monitored). In Hong Kong, domestic helpers are increasingly being secretly monitored by employers via hidden video cameras. Introduced as a result of a series of high-profile child abuse cases, such surveillance has created heated debate between employers (concerned about their children's welfare) and domestic helpers (concerned about their right to privacy).[172]

Likewise, companies concerned about the huge financial and public relations risks associated with inappropriate email and Internet use by employees feel compelled to increase surveillance. Employers cite three main threats: *diminished productivity* (it is estimated that cyberloafing accounts for 30 to 40 per cent of lost worker productivity); *potential legal liability* (a British company was forced to pay more than US$700 000 because of a defamatory email, while US investment bank Morgan Stanley faces a US$60 million damages claim from two Afro-American employees after a white colleague distributed a racist joke); and *information theft*.[173] In an effort to counteract fears that white supremacists are infiltrating their ranks, British police plan to monitor the attitude and conduct of all new recruits via the use of informers.[174]

Electronic performance monitoring is objective; however, it can also be viewed as an invasion of employee privacy and as a marker of management's lack of trust of its employees.

Employee surveillance and electronic monitoring have been subjected to considerable criticism from unions and others who claim that they are symptomatic of a low-trust approach to people management, produce anxiety and stress, cause alienation and loss of morale, are invasive and constitute yet another mechanism for controlling employees.[175]

Smile, the boss has you on 'dunny cam'

By Michael Cave

How would you feel about your employer setting up video cameras in each toilet cubicle?

An Australian mining company — concerned about secret drinking or drug-taking by heavy equipment operators — was seriously considering this just three or four months ago.

It is one of the more bizarre workplace surveillance scenarios that has crossed the desk of Federal Privacy Commissioner Michael Crompton over the past year.

But while the dunny-cam did not go ahead, Australian workers should come to terms with the fact that the boss is listening in to almost everything they do.

There is virtually nothing workers can do in the workplace today that can't be monitored by an employer. Talking on the phone, surfing the internet, walking down the corridor, riding in the elevator or just sitting in the office — the boss might be listening, monitoring or watching.

Surveillance has become so all-encompassing in the workplace that it's not even noticed.

And that could be a dangerous thing, according to Graham Sewell, a work surveillance expert at Melbourne University's Department of Management.

'Every organisation with a PABX phone system or an email system — and that means effectively every business in the country — is monitoring their employees', said Dr Sewell, who has studied the issue for 13 years.

'But what is interesting is how companies use that information and how we police the policers.'

Workplace surveillance has existed since the industrial revolution, but where it was once obvious and bureaucratic, today it is embedded in technology and virtually invisible.

Companies can count the number of keystrokes per day on a worker's computer to monitor how hard they are working, or monitor the mobile phone to track movements during the day.

'Surveillance seems to have snuck in under the radar because it is embedded in the technology we use every day', Dr Sewell said.

He is calling on business to be more open about the use of surveillance, and for the community to debate the issue. He believes it is time for people to be made aware just how much of their lives is under scrutiny.

Mr Crompton said privacy complaints and enquiries to his office are on track to rise 300 per cent over last year.

'There is no doubt that all forms of surveillance — in the workplace and elsewhere — is on the increase, and there is a genuine need for people to be more aware of the fact they are being watched and about their rights in relation to the information being gathered about them', he said.

A PricewaterhouseCoopers survey last year found almost half of all Australian companies monitor staff email and internet traffic, while 40 per cent use cameras to snoop on staff.

'The paradox is that at a time when human resource departments are celebrating buzzwords like reciprocal commitment, teamwork and trust, we have never been more closely scrutinised', Dr Sewell said.

Source *Australian Financial Review*, 14 June 2002, p. 4

Static and dynamic performance appraisals

For effective performance management, performance appraisal should be dynamic. It should emphasise employee growth and development and the setting of new goals, not just judgemental decisions about performance.[176] The evidence suggests that this kind of performance appraisal is 'more likely to be effective, credible and sustainable'.[177] A recent survey by the Hay Group for *Fortune* magazine's Global Most Admired list found that the most admired companies set more challenging goals, link compensation to achievement of those goals and are more oriented towards long-term performance.[178] Says Hay Group Managing Director Vicky Wright: 'It's not about keeping score. It's about learning how to motivate people — how to link those performance measures with real rewards.'[179] Yet, in practice, the evaluation of past employee performance remains the dominant purpose of performance appraisal.[180]

The characteristic feature of static appraisal programs is that they look back. They focus on the past, not the future. In contrast, a dynamic performance appraisal program helps employees to know where they are going, how they are going to get there and when they will get there. Judgemental decisions in performance appraisal require information on 'what happened'; developmental decisions require information on 'how it happened'. One emphasises punishment, the other learning and growth. Performance appraisals are most effective and preferred by employees when managers guard against overemphasising the negative aspects of performance.[181]

Characteristics of a dynamic performance appraisal program

Goal A specified desired result. Goals are the qualitative or quantitative values set for an indicator.

Dynamic performance appraisal programs are characterised by three key qualities:
- **goal** establishment
- performance feedback
- performance improvement (see figure 8.19).

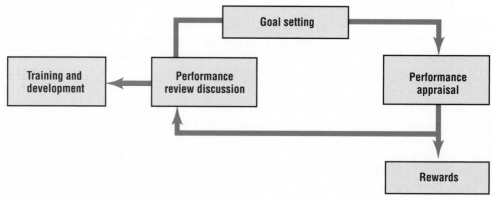

Figure 8.19 Dynamic performance appraisal program

Good performance measurement is an absolute necessity for effective feedback. Feedback in turn is also necessary for a quality goal-setting program because it allows employees to see how well they are performing and helps them to set new goals. Setting goals without establishing a way of measuring achievement is useless. Nevertheless, it is critical that there is not an overemphasis on quantity at the expense of quality.[182] If they are well designed, goal-setting programs can be powerful tools for increasing employee motivation and performance.[183] An example of the **responsibilities**, **indicators**, goals (RIGs) approach to **goal setting** is shown in figure 8.20.

Responsibilities Major areas in which the employee is accountable for achieving results.

Indicators A means for measuring progress towards meeting a responsibility.

Goal setting The process of defining an objective or target to achieve. Gives a sense of purpose or direction to an action.

Importance of goal setting in performance improvement

Employee motivation and performance are improved if the employee clearly understands and is challenged by what is to be achieved. In general, research findings indicate that:
- the setting of specific goals is more likely to lead to higher performance than simply telling an employee to 'do your best'

Responsibilities	Indicators	Goals
1. Order service	(a) percentage error (b) customer feedback (c) field sales representative feedback (d) sales manager	(a) less than 1 per cent (b) favourable (c) favourable (d) favourable
2. Customer service	(a) answer all enquiries (b) communications (c) price change notice (d) self-originated new 'ideas'	(a) within seven days (b) effective (c) 24 hours (d) one per month
3. Credit	(a) major complaints from Credit Department (b) customer opinion	(a) none (b) favourable
4. Customer relations	Feedback from (a) sales manager (b) field sales representatives (c) customer complaints	(a) favourable (b) favourable (c) minimum
5. Other relationships (a) boss (b) other office sales representatives (c) field sales representatives (d) secretary	(a) opinion (b) opinion (c) opinion (d) working relationship	(a) favourable and reviewed each six months (b) favourable (c) favourable (d) effective
6. Self-development	(a) industry-related journals (b) other magazines and books (c) course X completed (d) professional meetings	(a) three per month (b) six per month (c) by X date (d) one per year
7. Prepare self for field sales assignment	(a) knowledge of selling techniques (b) knowledge of other product groups (c) field sales experiences during office assignment	(a) successful completion of company selling skills course (b) successful completion of company product knowledge test (c) minimum of four

Figure 8.20 RIGs for an office sales representative
Source Asia Pacific Management Co. Ltd, 2004.

- goals that are perceived to be difficult to achieve or require stretch tend to result in better performance than goals that are perceived as easy (providing that the employee accepts the goals)[184]
- employee participation in goal setting tends to lead to higher goals being set than when the manager unilaterally sets the goals
- frequent performance feedback results in higher performance
- employees will set higher goals if they are evaluated on performance rather than simply on goal attainment.[185]

When using goal setting in performance appraisal, it is important not to:
- evaluate employees on factors over which they have no influence or control — for example, general economic downturn and changes in exchange rates
- subject employees to 'punishment' because they improve their performance — for example, being transferred from Melbourne to Sydney or being ostracised by work mates.

'If performance appraisal is to have a developmental purpose', says Kearney, 'it must concentrate on the process of getting results. That process must be examined in terms of the job-related behaviours over which the individual has control.'[186]

Performance appraisal record

Performance appraisal record
Document used to record the performance ratings and supervisor comments on an employee's performance.

The **performance appraisal record** is the document that is used to record the ratings and comments for an employee (see figure 8.21). A well-designed performance appraisal form is essential because it ensures that the appraisal process focuses on those aspects of job performance identified as important to the achievement of the organisation's strategic business objectives.[187] Properly designed, it is a valuable tool for:
- goal setting
- defining performance levels
- facilitating job performance review discussion
- identifying training and development needs
- identifying low- and high-potential employees
- rewarding performance.

It must be stressed that the completion of an evaluation sheet is a part of the performance appraisal process. Completion of the sheet is not the complete process.

Performance review discussion

Research shows that three factors are important in producing effective performance appraisal interviews:
1. the manager's knowledge of the employee's job and performance
2. the manager's support of the employee
3. the manager's involvement of the employee in the discussion.[188]

Performance review discussion Where the manager and subordinate mutually review the employee's job responsibilities, performance improvement and career goals.

The absence of any of these factors will have a negative impact on the quality of the performance appraisal interview and on its ultimate value. Obviously, the **performance review discussion** is critical to any effective performance appraisal program because this is when the manager sits down with their subordinate to:
- mutually review the employee's responsibilities
- mutually examine the employee's performance
- mutually explore what each can do to ensure performance improvement
- mutually review the employee's short-term and long-term goals.

The performance appraisal interview should be a positive experience for the manager and the employee. Yet, all too frequently, it becomes stressful and unpleasant. This is because managers have not received any training in conducting a job performance review, do not undertake sufficient preparation and fail to give objective feedback or give it in a mechanical way. Consequently, the appraisal interview is often the weakest part of the whole appraisal process. Instead of generating an improvement in performance, it produces a demotivated and angry employee and results in performance decline.[189]

PERFORMANCE APPRAISAL RECORD

Name	Department	Company
Job title	Date employee joined company	Review period from to
How long employee has worked in this position		Date of discussion with employee
Supervisor	Department manager	Date of discussion with supervisor

KEY PERFORMANCE STRENGTHS AND AREAS OF IMPROVEMENT

	Outstanding	Good	Acceptable	Marginal	Unsatisfactory	Comments
Technical skills/ knowledge						
Problem solving/ creativity						
Accountability for results						
Planning and organising						
Interpersonal skills						
Communication skills						
Development of others						
Decision making						
Leadership						
Motivation						
Representative of the company						
Quality commitment						
Safety commitment						
Achievement of results						

OBJECTIVES AND RESULTS

Established objectives What did you specifically agree with the employee that he/she would achieve during the review period? (List in terms of importance/priority.)	Achieved objectives To what extent were these objectives met (not met)?	Rating Base your rating on the degree to which expected results were achieved.

DESIRED PERFORMANCE OBJECTIVES FOR NEXT APPRAISAL PERIOD (Be sure goals and performance standards are clearly established.)

Figure 8.21 Performance appraisal record

CAREER PLANNING. What are this employee's career interests and goals? Recommend possible future positions. Describe any major requirements needed to achieve career goals.

RECOMMENDED TRAINING AND WORK EXPERIENCE

EVALUATION OF OVERALL PERFORMANCE. Circle the classification which most closely describes the employee's overall performance. (Select only one rating.)

Outstanding	Good	Acceptable	Marginal	Unsatisfactory

SUPERVISOR'S SUMMARY

Signature _____   Date _____

EMPLOYEE'S COMMENTS	**SUPERVISOR'S COMMENTS**
This is an opportunity for the employee to read the review and to make any comments.	

Supervisor's signature _____

Date _____

Employee's signature _____

HR manager's signature _____

Date _____

Date _____

Figure 8.21 Performance appraisal record
Source Asia Pacific Management Co. Ltd, 2004.

Preparation required for the performance review discussion

Good, solid preparation leads to a successful performance review discussion. Before meeting an employee, the manager should undertake the following tasks.

- Review the employee's job description to ensure that it is still accurate and that nothing has been overlooked. Check that there is a proper match between the job and the employee's skills, knowledge, abilities and interests. Research indicates that a manager's lack of knowledge about an employee's job can significantly undermine the credibility of the performance review.[190]
- Read the employee's last performance appraisal report to be refreshed on key points and to identify areas of improvement and areas still requiring emphasis.
- Check the employee's actual performance against the mutually agreed goals. Check that the employee's entire performance (not just positive or negative factors) has been considered.
- Consult with other managers who have contact with the employee in the performance of the job.
- Alert the employee well in advance about the forthcoming performance review discussion so they can undertake the necessary preparation (such as completing a self-appraisal, reviewing the job description, examining goal achievement, thinking about career steps, and so on).
- List all key points to be discussed in the interview. It is also desirable to ask the employee to do the same. This ensures that the discussion is perceived as being of mutual benefit and not just the manager passing judgement.
- Ensure that there is sufficient time available for the appraisal discussion and that there are no interruptions. Failure to do so simply communicates to the employee that the manager regards the appraisal discussion as unimportant.

Conduct of the performance review discussion

Listed below are some research-based guidelines that HR managers need to consider if they are to help their organisations to conduct effective performance review discussions.[191]

- Problems should be discussed as problems and not as criticisms. In other words, the manager should be constructive, not destructive. The supportive mutual review of problems and their solutions leads to improved performance. Criticism has a negative effect on goal achievement. Similarly, dwelling on isolated incidents should be avoided.
- The performance appraisal review should not be used as a vehicle to attack the employee's personality. This simply makes the employee defensive and increases their dissatisfaction with the performance appraisal process.
- The employee should be encouraged to talk. The manager should not monopolise the discussion. The more employees are allowed to participate, the more satisfied they feel with the appraisal discussion. However, strong social inhibitions in some cultures may prevent such openness. Shaikh, for example, found that Indian subordinates are reluctant to ask questions or express an opinion for fear of being thought arrogant.[192] Below are some examples of questions that can be used to bring an employee into the discussion:
  - What can I do to help you to do your job better?
  - How can I give you better feedback on your performance?
  - How involved do you see yourself in the work of the department?
  - How do you feel about the amount of responsibility I am delegating to you?
  - What training/development do you feel you need?
  - What do you see as your next move?
  - What are your future career interests?

- Specific performance improvement objectives should be set. General criticism is not effective in achieving performance improvement. 'Increase the number of sales calls per week by 5 per cent' is quite specific, for example; 'try harder' is not.
- Discuss only those things that can be changed. Feedback is most effective when it is confined to behaviour that employees can change. Drucker, for example, recommends that managers tolerate weaknesses in employees if those weaknesses do not hinder performance.[193]
- The manager should avoid using positional authority. The meeting should be held on neutral ground and in an atmosphere that indicates that the discussion is one of joint problem solving, not one where the manager sits in judgement. Mutual goal setting, not criticism, improves performance.

It should be stressed that there is nothing magical about these factors. They can be taught to and learned by managers responsible for conducting performance appraisal interviews.

Are the following situations fair?

(a) An employee who has been trying hard but cannot perform to standard is terminated.

(b) A student who has been studying hard but cannot perform to standard is failed.

(c) A professional footballer who is trying hard but who is not performing is dropped from the team.

Performance appraisal and EEO

Performance appraisals must satisfy EEO requirements. For example: 'Transfer or promotion must be based on a fair assessment of an employee's potential, ability and work record. Ideally the work record should reflect an objective assessment of the employee's performance.'[194] In addition, it is desirable for employees to include progress in EEO as part of the performance assessment of managers.[195]

Although the Asia–Pacific region lags behind the United States in EEO, local managers ultimately will have their performance evaluations subjected to public scrutiny. US managers, for example, have been involved in several court cases focusing on performance appraisal and there seems little doubt that many EEO authorities will refer to US legislation and court decisions for guidance.

The US Equal Employment Opportunity Commission's guidelines make it clear that performance appraisals must be job-related and non-discriminatory. A review of US legal cases indicates that the following practices should be used if an organisation is to successfully defend its appraisal system as being non-discriminatory:
- Job analysis must be used to develop the system.
- The performance appraisal scheme must be behaviour-oriented rather than trait-oriented.
- Managers must be given definite instructions and training on how to make appraisals.
- Results must be communicated to employees.
- There must be a provision for appeal in the case of disagreement.[196]

According to some experts: 'Without a valid system of performance management, organisations risk an eventuality where even unintentional discrimination may consume large amounts of time and money on employee complaints, grievances and suits. The impact on public relations, managerial confidence in personnel decisions, and employee morale may be even more devastating.'[197] Thus, like it or not, managers increasingly will find their performance appraisals subject to challenge and external review. HR managers must not only stress this to their management but also provide the know-how within the organisation that ensures performance appraisals are objective and non-discriminatory.

Summary

Appraising and managing performance involves evaluating performance, communicating that evaluation to the employee and establishing a plan for improvement. Performance appraisal is a dynamic process with the emphasis on self-development, the establishment of performance standards and the giving and receiving of feedback. Performance appraisal is a management program; it is not just an HR department responsibility. It is also an important motivator and employee development tool. Finally, the HR manager, in searching for performance improvement, has a responsibility to ensure that management understands that an organisation's strategic business objectives are better achieved through satisfying individual goals, and that the fairness of the performance appraisal program strongly affects how employees feel about the organisation.

Thirty interactive Wiley Web Questions are available to test your understanding of this chapter at **www.johnwiley.com.au/ highered/hrm5e** in the student resources area

terms to know

assessment centre (p. 302)

balanced scorecard (BS) (p. 300)

behaviour observation scales (BOS) (p. 298)

behaviourally anchored rating scales (BARS) (p. 297)

central tendency (p. 291)

critical incidents (p. 297)

essay description (p. 298)

goal (p. 304)

goal setting (p. 304)

grading (p. 296)

graphic scales (p. 296)

halo effect (p. 291)

indicators (p. 304)

management by objectives (MBO) (p. 298)

multisource evaluations (p. 287)

peer evaluations (p. 285)

performance appraisal (p. 276)

performance appraisal record (p. 306)

performance management (p. 276)

performance review discussion (p. 306)

prejudice (p. 291)

ranking (p. 295)

rater errors (p. 290)

recency effect (p. 291)

relationship effect (p. 292)

responsibilities (p. 304)

self-evaluation (p. 286)

social loafing (p. 288)

strictness bias (p. 291)

subordinate evaluations (p. 286)

team appraisals (p. 288)

360-degree appraisals (p. 287)

review questions

1. What is performance management? Describe how it relates to the organisation's strategic business objectives.
2. What are some of the common sources of bias in performance appraisals? How might these sources of bias be overcome?
3. What are the advantages and disadvantages of using 360-degree appraisals?
4. How can supervisors make their performance appraisal feedback sessions more effective?
5. Describe the preparation required of (a) the manager and (b) the employee before a performance appraisal meeting.
6. What is MBO? What are its advantages and disadvantages?
7. What is performance? What factors might influence employee performance?
8. Describe some factors that might make an organisation's performance appraisal system illegal. What can an organisation do to avoid such issues?
9. What factors could cause employees to perceive that an organisation's performance appraisal system is (a) fair or (b) unfair?
10. Explain the difference between performance appraisal and performance management.

environmental influences on performance appraisal

Describe the key environmental influences from the model (figure 8.22 shown below) that have significance for performance appraisal.

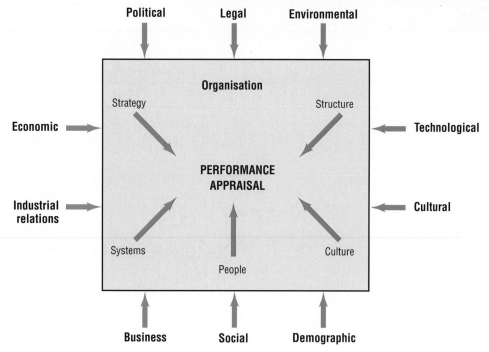

Figure 8.22 Environmental influences on performance appraisal

class debate

Performance appraisal is simply a management technique operating under a scientific veneer to manipulate and control employees by reinforcing behavioural norms that the organisation considers desirable.

or

Australians are hard in their attitude towards non-performance on the sporting field but soft in their attitude towards non-performance in the workplace.

what's your view?

Write a 500-word response to the Letter to the Editor on page 293, agreeing or disagreeing with the writer's point of view.

practitioner speaks

Read the article on pages 301–2. (a) Write a 200-word summary report highlighting the key points made by Maisie Lam. (b) Write a 200-word executive summary recommending/not recommending the introduction of the balanced scorecard to an organisation.

newsbreak exercise

Read the Newsbreak 'Smile, the boss has you on "dunny cam"' on page 303. As a class, critically discuss how you feel about surveillance in the workplace and the use of technology to observe and measure performance.

soapbox

What do you think? Conduct a mini survey of class members, using the questionnaire below. Critically discuss the findings.

1. For group assignments, every student in the group should receive the same mark.	YES	NO
2. Pay increases should not be discussed during the performance appraisal interview.	YES	NO
3. Performance appraisal is for management's benefit and not the employee's benefit.	YES	NO
4. Getting a good performance rating depends on ingratiation and not actual performance.	YES	NO
5. Performance appraisal is just an opportunity for managers to play god.	YES	NO
6. Pay increases should be linked to individual performance.	YES	NO

online exercise

Conduct an online search for information on (a) team-based appraisals, (b) trade union attitudes towards performance appraisal, (c) electronic monitoring of performance or (d) alternative performance appraisal approaches. Summarise your findings in 500–750 words. List the web addresses you found useful.

ethical dilemma

Jet Red's sick employee

Jet Red has had a financially disastrous year. Sales have plummeted by more than 30 per cent. Cutthroat competition, SARS and the global terrorism threat have savaged the company's business. Every department is under enormous pressure to cut costs and reduce its headcount. Employees have extremely heavy workloads and are being pushed to their limits.

Jet Red's Marketing Department, in particular, is under pressure to improve its performance. A key member of the marketing team is the Customer Service Manager, James Wheatley. James is regarded as competent and hardworking. However, over the past few months, James has been taking more and more days off work because of illness. Initially, other members of the department were sympathetic, but James's absences have become a source of discontent as his colleagues have had to do his work as well as their own.

Stan Vines, the Marketing Manager, is becoming increasingly frustrated with James. Under considerable pressure from management, he is stretched to the limit. Stan's subordinates have started asking: Why is James always sick? Why does James have to go to the doctor's all the time? Why do I have to do James's work? James has become evasive when approached, simply stating that he is suffering from a particularly severe form of shingles. Resentment has continued to increase and rumours have begun that James has AIDS. Maureen Bylinsky, the senior customer service representative and one of the department's top performers, has heatedly told Stan that she and several others are going to quit if something isn't done about James.

At breaking point, Stan has decided to talk the problem through with Linda Church, the HR Manager.

Discussion questions

1. If you were Linda, how would you handle this situation? What advice would you give to Stan? What would you do about James?
2. What ethical issues, if any, are raised in this case?

Jet Red's training problem

Mike Burdell cracked his tenth crude joke of the session and the class of maintenance supervisors laughed loudly. Mike glanced at his watch. 'Five o'clock. I guess that's it for today, guys — see you next week!' As they filed out someone shouted, 'Hey, Mike . . . come and have a beer with us!' Someone else said, 'Great course, Mike!'

Observing this was Linda Church, Jet Red's new HR Manager. Linda shook her head. She had seen this type of trainer before. Every session was a slick hour of entertainment. People loved it, but they seldom took the trainer or their training seriously. 'People like Mike', she decided, 'give training a bad name.'

Having refused the offer to go for a drink, Mike walked back to his office. 'Oh, hi Linda. I didn't know you were still around.'

'Yes Mike. I want to speak to you for a moment.'

'Hey, those guys think this course I'm giving is great! Did you notice that 15 have signed up for the next one already?'

'That's what I want to talk to you about, Mike — the next course.'

'What about it, Linda? Everything's going great!'

'Is that so? Mike, top management wants us to prove that what we are doing gets results. Training has to add value. We are in the business of improving performance, not providing entertainment.'

'What are you worrying about Linda? The guys love my stuff. Look at the evaluations!'

'You mean the "happy sheets"? The participants might be happy, but I'm not. There are no tangible results. The money spent on training in this company is being wasted.'

Mike looked shocked. 'What's got into you, sweetheart? Everyone knows I do a terrific job.'

'Why do you think I've been hired, Mike?', Linda retorted.

'Linda . . . I know you're my boss, but take a word of advice from an old pro. I've been in this game for over 20 years. Every now and then this value-added thing comes up. I play the game for a while and then the top brass forget all about it. Let me tell you, keeping participants happy will keep you in your job much longer than tough courses and lots of fancy statistical evaluations.'

Linda paused then said, 'Unfortunately Mike, it's not going to keep you in yours.'

'What the hell do you mean by that Linda?' snapped Mike.

Discussion questions

1. Should management expect all training courses to add value?
2. What measures can be used to evaluate Mike's training program?
3. How much 'entertainment' and how much 'learning' should there be in a training program?
4. If you were Linda, how would you evaluate Mike's performance?
5. What are the differences between Linda's and Mike's performance expectations? How could these differences be avoided?

Source Dr Philip Wright, Professor, School of Business, Shu Yan College, Hong Kong, and co-author of *Managing Performance Through Training and Development*, 2nd edn, Nelson, Scarborough, Ontario, 2000.

XYZ'S performance problem

Following the retirement of Fred Marshall as the Director of Human Resources for XYZ Ltd, Jo Santini, Manager, Compensation and Benefits, has been promoted to the position. The Managing Director, John Kolikias, has a very high opinion of Jo.

Since Jo was promoted, the next most senior position in the HR Department, Jo's previous role, Manager, Compensation

and Benefits, has remained vacant. John has left the responsibility of filling the position to Jo. It is company policy to promote from within, so the choice has come down to Justin Toppel, Manager, Industrial Relations, or Anna Kepitis, Manager, Training and Development.

Anna Kepitis has been with the company for three years and has shown herself to be dedicated, results-oriented and enthusiastic. She has also received above-average

(continued)

performance ratings during her employment with XYZ Ltd. In Jo's opinion, Anna is her natural successor.

Justin Toppel has been with the company for 15 years and is regarded as a reliable and competent manager. He has shown unusual ability in handling industrial relations problems. However, Jo feels that Justin is too quiet and serious to hold the secondmost senior HR position in the company. Jo feels that Justin is not a leader and lacks Anna's charisma. She therefore decides to promote Anna.

Jo communicates her decision to Anna, but does not discuss the matter with Justin or give him any advance notice of her decision. When Justin sees the announcement on the noticeboard, he immediately goes to Jo's office to express his disappointment. He also takes the matter to the Managing Director. During his meeting with John, Justin makes it clear that he had counted on getting the promotion because of his good performance and his long service. Moreover, in response to Jo's criticism that he lacks leadership ability, Justin reveals

that he has recently been elected as President of the Institute of Human Resource Management. But John tells Justin that the decision is final and that he expects him to cooperate with Jo and Anna.

After this, Justin seems less than enthusiastic. He continues to perform satisfactorily, but becomes increasingly withdrawn. His attitude towards Jo and Anna is polite but cool.

Two months later, when recommendations for performance increases are being considered, Jo and Anna decide that Justin should be passed over. Completing the appraisal form, Jo shows it to Anna: judgement — average; initiative — average; communication — below average; quality of work — above average; quantity of work — average; cooperation — below average. She then takes it to Justin, who signs it without comment.

Justin also makes no comment when he does not receive a merit increase. But Jo and Anna feel that he has become even more distant and business-like in his dealings with them.

Discussion questions

1. What has brought about this situation? How could it have been avoided?
2. If you were Jo, how would you have handled the situation? If you were Justin, what would you have done?
3. What key elements in the appraisal process are missing in this case? What is the impact of their absence on employee perceptions of fairness?

Role-play

Select two class members to play the roles of Jo and Justin in a performance review discussion. The remaining class members should complete the performance appraisal feedback sheet shown below. As a class, critically discuss your responses and highlight the three major lessons learned from this exercise.

PERFORMANCE APPRAISAL FEEDBACK SHEET

(a) How would you describe the general tone of the session? (Circle your answers and give examples in the space provided.)

- stiff and formal ....
- authoritarian ....
- participative ....
- one-sided ....
- casual ....
- candid ....
- friendly ....
- planned ....
- results-oriented ....
- wishy-washy ....
- disorganised ....
- emotional ....
- confrontational ....
- honest ....
- evasive ....

(b) List three ways in which the session could have been improved.

(i) ....

(ii) ....

(iii) ....

practical exercises

1. Break into groups of three: one member to play the role of the Sales Manager, one to be Judi Novak, the Sales Supervisor, and one to be an observer. The instructions for each role follow. After conducting an appraisal interview, each member should complete the performance appraisal feedback sheet provided above. Critically discuss your responses.

Sales Manager

You are the newly appointed Sales Manager of the Adelaide sales office and this is the first time that you have had to complete an appraisal of Judi Novak. The HR Manager has advised you that the annual performance appraisal for Judi is now due. You are somewhat anxious because Judi has a reputation for being aggressive and outspoken. She is technically very competent and has good relations with her subordinates and customers, but has upset several senior managers with her outspokenness. Consequently, you suspect that her personal advancement prospects are poor. You know, for example, that your superior dislikes her and you are worried that if you rate Judi too highly, you will have a problem with your boss. As a result, you plan to play it safe and give Judi the following ratings.

Name: Judi Novak Department: Office Equipment		Position: Sales Supervisor Date: 23/03/04	
Factor	**Rating**		
	Poor	**Average**	**Superior**
Job knowledge	1 2 3	4 5 6	⑦ 8 9
Human relations	1 2 3	④ 5 6	7 8 9
Organising ability	1 2 3	4 ⑤ 6	7 8 9
Planning ability	1 2 3	4 ⑤ 6	7 8 9
Creativity	1 2 3	4 ⑤ 6	7 8 9
Judgement	1 2 3	4 ⑤ 6	7 8 9
Initiative	1 2 3	4 ⑤ 6	7 8 9
Supervisory skills	1 2 3	4 5 ⑥	7 8 9
Overall assessment: Average			

Judi Novak

You have been with the organisation for seven years and have generally been very highly rated. However, your ratings have dropped in the past two years. You feel this is because you challenged the ratings given by your previous manager (who is now your supervisor's boss). You believe that the ratings were very subjective and not based on your actual job performance. You are very concerned about how your new manager is going to rate you. You have had no feedback at all on your performance since his arrival six months ago. You suspect he is very keen to make a good impression on his boss. You have documented all your achievements and want to know what the organisation thinks of you personally, your performance and your prospects, and why.

2. **Performance appraisal design**

    Break into groups of three or four. Select one of the major types of performance appraisal systems discussed in this chapter and design a performance appraisal form to measure and document an employee's performance for one of the following positions:

    (a) HRM lecturer

    (b) HRM student

    (c) HR manager

    (d) professional basketball player

    (e) pop singer

    (f) taxi driver.

    Critically discuss your choice of system, the factors you selected to measure, the objectivity of the system and the advantages and disadvantages you can identify in using such a system.

3. **Performance appraisal survey**

    (a) Use the questionnaire below to survey friends and classmates. Critically discuss the individual findings.

    (b) Group the individual findings as though they represent employees from one company and prepare a brief report for management discussing the results and your recommendations.

APPRAISAL SURVEY

1. In my company, if you get a good performance rating, you will get a good pay increase.
   (Strongly disagree)   1   2   3   4   5   (Strongly agree)

2. My company's performance appraisal system emphasises development.
   (Strongly disagree)   1   2   3   4   5   (Strongly agree)

3. My company's performance appraisal system uses mainly objective factors to measure performance.
   (Strongly disagree)   1   2   3   4   5   (Strongly agree)

4. People in my company regard performance appraisal as a positive experience.
   (Strongly disagree)   1   2   3   4   5   (Strongly agree)

5. Performance appraisals in my company are top down.
   (Strongly disagree)   1   2   3   4   5   (Strongly agree)

6. Performance appraisals in my company are seen as an HR Department program.
   (Strongly disagree)   1   2   3   4   5   (Strongly agree)

7. Managers in my company are trained in performance appraisal management.
   (Strongly disagree)   1   2   3   4   5   (Strongly agree)

8. Performance appraisals in my company are a source of good feedback on employee performance.
   (Strongly disagree)   1   2   3   4   5   (Strongly agree)

9. The performance appraisal system in my company is easy to understand.
   (Strongly disagree)   1   2   3   4   5   (Strongly agree)

10. Employees in my company regard the performance appraisal system as fair.
    (Strongly disagree)   1   2   3   4   5   (Strongly agree)

suggested readings

Beardwell, I. and Holden, L., *Human Resource Management*, 3rd edn, Financial Times/Prentice Hall, London, 2001, ch. 12.

CCH, *Australian Master Human Resource Guide*, CCH, Sydney, 2003, ch. 14.

De Cieri, H. and Kramar, R., *Human Resource Management in Australia*, McGraw-Hill, Sydney, 2003, ch. 9.

Fisher, C. D., Schoenfeldt, L. F. and Shaw, J. B., *Human Resource Management*, 5th edn, Houghton Mifflin, Boston, 2003, ch. 11.

Ivancevich, J. M., *Human Resource Management*, 8th edn, McGraw-Hill, Boston, 2001, ch. 9.

Ivancevich, J. M. and Lee, S. H., *Human Resource Management in Asia*, McGraw-Hill, Singapore, 2002, ch. 9.

Mondy, R. W., Noe, R. M. and Premeaux, S. R., *Human Resource Management*, 8th edn, Prentice Hall, Upper Saddle River, NJ, 2002, ch. 10.

Nankervis, R. L., Compton, R. L. and Baird, M., *Strategic Human Resource Management*, 4th edn, Nelson, Melbourne, 2002, ch. 11.

Robbins, S., *Organizational Behavior*, 9th edn, Prentice Hall, Upper Saddle River, NJ, 2001, pp. 485–94.

Schermerhorn, J. R., Hunt, J. G. and Osborn, R. N., *Organizational Behavior*, 8th edn, John Wiley & Sons, New York, 2003, ch. 7.

online references

www.actu.asn.au
www.aeufederal.org.au
www.austin-hayne.com
www.cam.org/~steinbg/trends.htm

www.cpsu.org/psu/index.htm
www.members.xoom.com/perform
www.npr.gov
www.performance-appraisal.com/into.htm

www.performanceimpact.com.au
www.schoonover.com
www.shrm.org.hrmagazine
www.shrm.org/performance-review

www.sicore.com.au
www.ssc.com.au
www.vitascope.com
www.workforceonline.com

end notes

1. P. Boxhall and J. Purcell, *Strategy and Human Resource Management*, Palgrave Macmillan, Basingstoke, 2003, p. 145.
2. M. Stark and W. Alper, quoted in N. Stein, 'Measuring people power', *Fortune*, 2 October 2000, p. 62.
3. A. R. Nankervis and P. Leece, 'Performance appraisal: two steps forward, one step back?', *Asia Pacific Journal of Human Resources*, vol. 35, no. 2, 1997, p. 91.
4. K. Legge, *Human Resource Management*, Macmillan, London, 1995, p. 167.
5. D. McDonald and A. Smith, 'A proven connection: performance management and business results', *Compensation and Benefits Review*, vol. 27, no. 1, 1995, p. 59.
6. C. E. Schneider, D. G. Shaw and R. W. Beatty, 'Performance measurement and management: a tool for strategy execution,' *Human Resource Management*, vol. 30, no. 3, 1991, p. 279.
7. J. Ghorpade and M. M. Chen, 'Creating quality driven performance appraisal systems', *Academy of Management Executive*, vol. 9, no. 1, 1995, p. 32; and J. S. Lublin, 'Firms are re-evaluating their performance reviews', *Asian Wall Street Journal*, 7–8 October 1994, p. 5.
8. A. R. Nankervis and P. Leece, op. cit., p. 80; and V. L. Huber and S. R. Fuller, 'Performance appraisal', in M. Poole and M. Warner (eds), *Handbook of Human Resource Management*, Thomson, London, 1998, pp. 596–7.
9. Hay Group survey, reported in C. Fox, 'Business leaders urged to support staff', *Australian Financial Review*, 31 July 2001, p. 51.
10. K. Russ, 'Public service HR lags behind best practice', *HR Monthly*, 1997, pp. 8–9; and L. Yeung, 'Poly U staff condemn performance review', *South China Morning Post — Education*, 9 November 2002, p. 3.
11. M. Ferguson and M. Ogden, 'Union approach to performance measurement', *Work and People*, vol. 14, no. 3, 1993, p. 2; and T. Harris, 'Teachers and the learning curve', *Australian Financial Review*, 18 April 2000, p. 20.
12. C. Fletcher and R. Williams, 'Performance management, job satisfaction and organisational commitment', *British Journal of Management*, vol. 7, no. 2, 1996, p. 177.
13. L. Hort, 'Performance management skills neither new nor relevant', *Campus Review*, 16–22 October 1996, p. 8.
14. M. de la Harpe, 'UWA lecturer fails to block appraisals', *Campus Review*, 28 March–3 April 1996, p. 4.
15. M. Irving, 'Expenditure review must take account of academic career paths', *Campus Review*, 11–17 September 1996, p. 8.
16. P. J. Taylor and J. L. Pierce, 'Effects of introducing a performance management system on employees' subsequent attitudes and effort', *Public Personnel Management*, vol. 28, no. 3, 1999, pp. 423–52.
17. A. R. Nankervis and P. Leece, op. cit., pp. 80–92.
18. J. Storey and K. Sisson, *Managing Human Resources and Industrial Relations*, Open University Press, Buckingham, 1993, p. 132.
19. J. Storey and K. Sisson, 1993, op. cit., p. 132; and P. Stiles, L. Gratton, C. Truss, V. Hope-Hailey and P. McGovern, 'Performance management and the psychological contract', *Human Resource Management Journal*, vol. 7, no. 1, 1997, p. 57.
20. For further details see W. E. Deming, *Out of Crisis*, Cambridge University Press, Cambridge, 1982; K. P. Carson, R. L. Cardy and G. H. Dobbins, 'Performance appraisal as effective management or deadly management disease', *Group and Organization Studies*, vol. 16, no. 2, 1991, pp. 143–59; R. Rudman, 'One more time: just what's wrong with performance appraisal', *Human Resources*, vol. 1, no. 2, 1996, pp. 11–13; and F. Nickols, 'Don't redesign your company's performance appraisal system — scrap it', *People Today*, October 2000, pp. 30–5.
21. B. N. Smith, J. S. Hornsby and R. Shirmeyer, 'Current trends in performance appraisal: an examination of managerial practice', *SAM Advanced Management Journal*, vol. 61, no. 3, 1996, p. 15.
22. Survey by William M. Mercer, reported in D. McNerney, 'Improved performance appraisals: process of elimination', *HR Focus*, July 1995, p. 1; and M. M. Markowich, 'We can make performance appraisals work', *Compensation and Benefits Review*, vol. 26, no. 43, 1994, pp. 25–6.
23. T. Newton and P. Findlay, 'Playing God? The performance of appraisal', *Human Resource Management Journal*, vol. 6, no. 3, 1996, pp. 42–58; and V. Marshall and R. E. Wood, 'The dynamics of effective performance appraisal: an integrated model', *Asia Pacific Journal of Human Resources*, vol. 38, no. 3, 2000, pp. 62–90.
24. R. P. Wright, 'Perceptual dimensions of performance management systems in the eyes of different sample categories', *International Journal of Management*, vol. 19, no. 2, 2002, pp. 184–93.
25. See B. Townley, 'Selection and appraisal: reconstituting "social relations"?', in J. Storey (ed.), *New Perspectives on Human Resource Management*, Routledge, London, 1992, ch. 6. See also G. Coates, 'Performance appraisal as icon: Oscar winning performance or dressing to impress?', *Journal of International Human Resource Management*, vol. 5, no. 1, 1994, pp. 167–91; and T. Newton and P. Findlay, op. cit., pp. 42–58.
26. I. Gow, quoted in *Business Review Weekly*, 15 January 1988, p. 57.

27. R. Chamran and G. Colvin, 'Why CEOs fail', *Fortune*, 21 June 1999, pp. 47–53; P. Hjelt, 'The world's most admired companies', *Fortune*, 3 March 2003, pp. 30–5; and G. Hubbard, D. Samuel, S. Heap and G. Cocks, *The First XI: Winning Organisations in Australia*, Wrightbooks, Melbourne, 2002, pp. 228–30.

28. D. Grote, 'The secrets of performance appraisal best practices from the masters', *Across the Board*, vol. 37, no. 5, 2000, pp. 14–20.

29. B. H. Holmes, 'The lenient evaluator is hurting your organization', *HR Magazine*, June 1993, p. 76; and C. A. Bartlett and S. Ghoshal, 'Building competitive advantage through people', *MIT Sloan Management Review*, vol. 43, no. 2, 2002, p. 38.

30. J. Johnson, 'Work relationships', *Human Resources*, April 2003, p. 37.

31. J. T. Austin, P. Villanova, J. S. Kane and H. J. Bernardin, 'Construct validation of performance measures: issues, development and evaluation of indicators', in G. R. Ferris and K. M. Rowlands (eds), *Research in Personnel and Human Resource Management*, vol. 9, JA1 Press, Greenwich, 1991, pp. 159–234.

32. J. Kruger and D. Dunning, 'Unskilled and unaware of it: how difficulties in recognizing one's own incompetence lead to inflated self-assessments', *Journal of Personality and Social Psychology*, vol. 77, 1999, pp. 1121–34.

33. M. Lawson, '"Soft" bosses ignoring problem workers, survey finds', *Australian Financial Review*, 7 August 1996, p. 4.

34. Reported in R. Storey, 'UWA tests waters', *Australian*, 16 October 1996, p. 46.

35. R. Bridge, '100 police to lose jobs after corruption probe', *South China Morning Post*, 10 August 1996, p. 10.

36. R. Harby, 'Higgins out with $6.7m', *Australian Financial Review*, 21 February 2003, p. 75; and A. Kohler, 'Sour grapes and Southcorp's fate', *Australian Financial Review*, 8–9 March 2003, p. 10.

37. S. Neales, 'University challenge', *Australian Financial Review Magazine*, August 2003, pp. 12–16; A. Cornell and J. Macken, 'Australian universities pay the price', *Australian Financial Review*, 1–2 March 2003, p. 26; P. Lawnham, 'Steele trap', *Australian*, 1 May 2002, p. 23; and New York Times, 'New York schools system perpetuates incompetency', *South China Morning Post*, 7 June 2003, p. E2.

38. P. Hui, 'Heads call for help to sack failing leaders', *South China Morning Post*, 15 February 2003, p. E1.

39. K. Sinclair, 'Running a tighter ship in the civil service', *South China Morning Post*, 31 May 1999, p. 17.

40. J. Van der Kamp, 'Soft pedal on survey fails to hide civil servant secret', *South China Morning Post*, 14 February 2003, p. B18; and K. Chan and M. S. Hon, 'Civil servants under attack in pay survey', *South China Morning Post*, 13 February 2003, p. 2.

41. C. Yeung, 'Culture change in civil service a must', *South China Morning Post*, 26 November 2001, p. 4. J. Tien, 'Stop indulging civil service', *South China Morning Post*, 29 February 2000, p. 17; and G. Cheung, '1000 civil servants promoted despite drive to cut costs', *South China Morning Post*, 22 October 2003, p. C3.

42. S. M. H. May and A. Li, 'Slack departments ordered to report', *South China Morning Post*, 11 February 1999, p. 6; C. Yeung, 2001, op. cit., p. 4; and P. Yeung, 'Why civil servants are sitting pretty', *South China Morning Post*, 4 December 2003, p. A17.

43. J. Cheung, 'Automatic pay rise queried', *Sunday Morning Post*, 6 June 1999, p. 2; and M. S. M. Hon, 'Unions oppose pay rises on merit', *South China Morning Post*, 19 January 2000, p. 6.

44. A. Mitchell, 'Clear directions for Costello', *Australian Financial Review*, 26 June 1996, p. 20.

45. N. Hooper, 'Time running out for fat cat ways', *Business Review Weekly*, 9 July 1993, p. 30.

46. A. Pearson, 'Muscle builds the organisation', *Harvard Business Review*, April 1987, p. 49.

47. Reported in L. Murray, 'Kelly gang takes over the bus', *Australian Financial Review*, 23 September 2002, p. 49.

48. F. Williams, quoted in A. Ramsey, 'Port live by Williams' creed on no hopers', *Australian*, 24 February 1997, p. 28.

49. A. E. Barber and M. J. Simmering, 'Understanding pay plan acceptance: the role of distributive justice theory', *Human Resource Management Review*, vol. 12, no. 1, 2002, p. 37.

50. R. Wood, quoted in J. Mundy, 'How to be a better manager', *Australian Business*, 21 September 1988, p. 85. Also see L. Gratton, *Living Strategy*, Financial Times/Prentice Hall, London, 2000, pp. 105–6.

51. Reported in 'Factors for performance', *Flight Deck*, no. 28, 1989, p. 61.

52. Reported in 'On personnel', *Boardroom Reports*, 15 February 1989, p. 15. See also C. E. Labig Jr and Y. C. Tan, 'Problems with performance appraisal? Remedies for HR executives', *Research and Practice in Human Resource Management*, vol. 4, no. 1, 1996, pp. 107–13.

53. W. L. Gardiner, 'Lessons in organizational dramaturgy: the art of impression management', *Organizational Dynamics*, vol. 21, no. 1, 1992, pp. 33–46.

54. C. O. Longenecker, H. P. Sims and D. A. Gioia, 'Behind the mask: the politics of employee appraisal', *Academy of Management Executive*, vol. 1, no. 3, 1987, p. 184; and D. A. Gioia and C. O. Longenecker, 'Delving into the dark side: the politics of executive appraisal', *Organizational Dynamics*, vol. 22, no. 3, 1994, pp. 47–57.

55. S. L. Rynes, A. E. Colbert and K. G. Brown, 'HR professionals' beliefs about effective human resource practices: correspondence between research and practice', *Human Resource Management*, vol. 41, no. 2, 2002, p. 157.

56. G. R. Ferris and T. A. Judge, 'Personnel/human resources management: a political influence perspective', *Journal of Management*, vol. 17, 1991, pp. 1–42; and G. R. Ferris, T. A. Judge, K. M. Rowland and D. E. Fitzgibbons, 'Subordinate influence and the performance evaluation process: test of a model', *Organizational Behavior and Decision Processes*, vol. 58, 1993, pp. 101–35.

57. S. P. Robbins, *The Administrative Process*, Prentice Hall, Englewood Cliffs, NJ, 1976, p. 314.

58. M. Bennett, 'Future directions in remuneration management', in A. R. Nankervis and R. L. Compton, *Readings in Strategic Human Resource Management*, Nelson, Melbourne, 1994, p. 294.

59. M. S. M. Hon, '"Failure not an option" in reform package', *South China Morning Post*, 23 April 1999, p. 6.

60. C. C. Leung, quoted in M. S. M. Hon, 'Unions oppose pay rises on merit', *South China Morning Post*, 19 January 2000, p. 6.

61. A. Burrell, 'Execs pocket millions in year of excess', *Australian Financial Review*, 21 June 2000, p. MW16.

62. 'BHP charters a new world', *Australian Financial Review*, 27–28 March 1999, p. 64; and J. Hurst, 'BHP has some explaining to do', *Australian Financial Review*, 21 December 1999, pp. 46, 48.

63. W. B. Bruce, 'Deciding what's important in pay for performance', *HR Monthly*, 1997, p. 6.

64. Practical ethics in the police service survey conducted by the National Police Research Unit in Adelaide and the University of New South Wales, reported in K. Towers and S. Lunn, 'Police regard honesty as a career barrier', *Australian*, 26 June 1996, p. 5. See also E. Davis, 'Overcoming obstacles to good performance management', *HR Monthly*, February 1999, pp. 14–18.

65. C. Parsons, 'Thankless task for travellers under pressure', *South China Morning Post — Markets*, 11 February 2000, p. 20.

66. R. Lansbury, 'Performance management: a process approach', *Human Resource Management Australia*, vol. 26, no. 2, 1988, p. 47. See also P. E. Spector, *Industrial and Organizational Psychology*, John Wiley & Sons, New York, 2000, pp. 73–4.

67. G. J. Greguras, C. Robie, D. J. Schleicher and M. Goff, 'A field study of the effects of rating purpose on the quality of multi source ratings', *Personnel Psychology*, vol. 56, no. 1, 2003, p. 1.

68. G. Latham and K. Wexley, *Increasing Productivity Through Performance Appraisal*, Addison Wesley, Reading, Mass., 1982; and R. L. Holbrook, 'Contact points and flash points: conceptualizing the use of justice mechanisms in the performance appraisal interview', *Human Resource Management Review*, vol. 12, no. 1, 2002, p. 104.

69. M. Brown and J. Benson, 'Rated to exhaustion? Reactions to performance appraisal processes', *Industrial Relations Journal*, vol. 34, no. 1, 2003, p. 77.

70. R. Soines, S. Quisenberry and G. W. Sawyer, 'Business strategy drives three pronged assessment system', *Compensation and Benefits Review*, vol. 26, no. 5, 1994, p. 74.

71. A. M. Mohrman Jr and S. A. Mohrman, 'Performance management is running the business', *Compensation and Benefits Review*, vol. 27, no. 4, 1995, p. 74.

72. I. H. S. Chow, 'An opinion survey of performance appraisal practices in Hong Kong and the People's Republic of China', *Asia Pacific Journal of Human Resources*, vol. 32, no. 3, 1994, p. 72.

73. J. Ghorpade and M. M. Chen, 'Creating quality driven performance appraisal systems', *Academy of Management Executive*, vol. 9, no. 1, 1995, p. 35.

74. R. J. Sahl, 'Involve employees in performance appraisals', *HR Magazine*, April 1997, p. 24.

75. M. Brown and J. Benson, 2003, op. cit., p. 78.

76. K. A. Guinn, 'Assessment techniques for top executives', *Career Development International*, vol. 1, no. 3, 1996, p. 9; and K. Ludeman, 'To fill the feedback void', *Training and Development*, vol. 49, no. 8, 1995, pp. 38–41.

77. C. O. Longenecker, H. P. Sims and D. A. Gioia, 1987, op. cit., pp. 183–91.

78. K. Tyler, 'Careful criticism brings better performance', *HR Magazine*, April 1997, p. 57; and M. Thornber and A. Kelly, 'Performance anxiety', *HR Monthly*, July 2000, p. 29.

79. W. H. Gmelch, *Beyond Stress To Effective Management*, John Wiley & Sons, New York, 1982, p. 76; and A. Nankervis, R. Compton and M. Baird, *Strategic Human Resource Management*, 4th edn, Thomson, Melbourne, 2002, pp. 406–7.

80. W. Kiechel III, 'How to appraise performance', *Fortune*, 12 October 1987, p. 74.

81. M. Brown and J. Benson, 2003, op. cit., pp. 67–81, D. P. Skarlicki and R. Folger, 'Editorial fairness and human resource management', *Human Resource Management*, vol. 13, no. 1, 2003, pp. 1–5; J. R. Schermerhorn, J. G. Hunt and R. N. Osborn, *Organizational Behavior*, 8th edn, John Wiley & Sons, New York, 2003, p. 409; and J. M. Ivancevich and S. H. Lee, *Human Resource Management in Asia*, McGraw-Hill, Singapore, 2002, pp. 250–6.

82. I. H. S. Chow, op. cit., p. 77.

83. B. Lawrence, 'Performance appraisal', in G. Thong, *Human Resource Issues in Singapore*, Addison Wesley, Singapore, 1996, p. 121.

84. B. Lawrence, op. cit., p. 122; and Y. Paik, C. M. Vance and H. D. Stage, 'The extent of divergence in human resource practice across three Chinese national cultures: Hong Kong, Taiwan and Singapore', *Human Resource Management Journal*, vol. 6, no. 2, 1996, pp. 20–31.

85. A. M. Whitehall, *Japanese Management*, Routledge, London, 1992, p. 203.

86. P. Schotes, quoted in R. Rudman, 1996, op. cit., p. 13.

87. R. L. Holbrook, 2002, op. cit., p. 116.

88. L. Pickett, 'People make the difference', *HR Monthly*, May 2000, pp. 28–9.

89. T. Davis and M. Landa, 'A contrary look at performance appraisal', *The Canadian Manager*, vol. 24, no. 3, 1999, pp. 18–19.

90. A. M. Whitehall, 1992, op. cit., p. 203.

91. G. Hofstede, 'Managerial values', in T. Jackson (ed.), *Cross-Cultural Management*, Butterworth-Heinemann, Oxford, 1995, p. 157.

92. R. L. Holbrook, 2002, op. cit., pp. 103–4.

93. A. R. Nankervis and P. Leece, op. cit., p. 88 and E. Soltani, R. Van der Meer, J. Gerrard and T. Williams, 'A TQM approach to HR performance evaluation criteria', *European Management Journal*, vol. 21, no. 3, 2003, p. 331.

94. V. G. Scarpello, J. Ledvinka and T. J. Bergman, *Human Resource Management*, 2nd edn, Southwestern, Cincinnati, Ohio, 1995, p. 608.

95. C. Viswesvaran, D. S. Ones and F. L. Schmidt, 'Comparative analysis of the reliability of job performance ratings', *Journal of Applied Psychology*, vol. 81, no. 5, 1996, pp. 557–74.

96. S. P. Robbins, *Organizational Behavior*, 9th edn, Prentice Hall, Upper Saddle River, NJ, 2001, p. 492.

97. D. McGee-Wanguri, 'A review, an integration and a critique of cross-disciplinary research on performance appraisals, evaluations and feedback, 1980–1990', *Journal of Business Communication*, vol. 32, no. 3, 1995, p. 273; and Robbins, 2001, op. cit., p. 492.

98. D. J. Cherrington, *The Management of Human Resources*, 4th edn, Prentice Hall, Englewood Cliffs, NJ, 1995, p. 296; M. G. Aamodt, *Applied Industrial/Organizational Psychology*, 2nd edn, Brooks/Cole, Pacific Grove, CA, 1996, pp. 260–1; M. L. Ramsay and H. Lehto, 'The power of peer review', *Training and Development*, vol. 48, no. 7, 1994, pp. 38–41; and D. McGee-Wanguri, op. cit., pp. 273–4.

99. A. R. Nankervis and P. Leece, op. cit., p. 82.

100. B. N. Smith, J. S. Hornsby and R. Shirmeyer, 1996, op. cit., p. 14.

101. D. J. Cherrington, op. cit., p. 296; and Y. Baruch, 'Self performance appraisal vs direct manager appraisal', *Journal of Managerial Psychology*, vol. 11, no. 6, 1996, pp. 50–65.

102. D. J. Cherrington, op. cit., p. 297; M. G. Aamodt, 1996, op. cit., pp. 261–2; and J. Ghorpade and M. M. Chen, 'Creating quality driven performance appraisal systems', *Academy of Management Executive*, vol. 9, no. 1, 1995, p. 38.

103. V. G. Scarpello, J. Ledvinka and T. J. Bergman, op. cit., p. 607; P. M. Muchinsky, *Psychology Applied to Work*, 4th edn, Brooks/Cole, Pacific Grove, CA, pp. 243–4; and F. J. Yammarino and L. E. Atwater, 'Implications of self–other rating agreement for human resources management', *Organizational Dynamics*, vol. 25, no. 4, 1997, pp. 35–44.

104. J. L. Hall, J. K. Leidecker and C. Di Marco, 'What we know about upward appraisals of management: facilitating the future use of UPAs', *Human Resource Development Quarterly*, vol. 7, no. 3, 1996, p. 209.

105. A. Gome, 'How staff can give their boss a rating', *Business Review Weekly*, 15 January 1996, p. 38.

106. J. S. Lublin, 'Workers are being asked to size up bosses in US', *Asian Wall Street Journal*, 10 October 1994, p. 9.

107. D. J. Cherrington, op. cit., pp. 295–6; M. G. Aamodt, 1996, op. cit., p. 261; D. McGee-Wanguri, op. cit., p. 274; J. L. Hall, J. K. Leidecker and C. Di Marco, op. cit., pp. 210–11; J. S. Lublin, op. cit., p. 10; and M. Thatcher, 'Allowing everyone to have their say', *People Management*, 21 March 1996, p. 30.

108. Taken from J. L. Hall, J. K. Leidecker and C. Di Marco, 1996, op. cit., pp. 211–17.

109. F. J. Yammarino and L. E. Atwater, op. cit., p. 35. See also D. W. Bracken, 'Straight talk about multi-rater feedback', *Training and Development*, vol. 48, no. 9, 1994, pp. 44–51.

110. A. R. Nankervis and P. Leece, op. cit., p. 90.

111. S. H. Gebelein, 'Multi rater feedback goes strategic', *HR Focus*, January 1996, pp. 1, 4; and S. P. Robbins, 2001, op. cit., p. 489.

112. W. J. Heisler, '360 degree feedback: an integrated perspective', *Career Development International*, vol. 1, no. 3, 1996, p. 20; and R. Noe, *Employee Training and Development*, McGraw-Hill, Singapore, 2000, p. 229–32.

113. D. Coates, 'Multisource feedback: seven recommendations', *Career Development International*, vol. 1, no. 3, 1996, p. 32; M. R. Edwards, 'Improving performance with 360 degree feedback', *Career Development International*, vol. 1, no. 3, 1996, p. 5; and S. L. McShane and M. A. Von Glinow, *Organizational Behavior*, McGraw-Hill, Boston, 2000, p. 48.

114. B. O'Reilly, '360 degree feedback can change your life', *Fortune*, 17 October 1994, p. 78; and P. Brotherton, 'Candid feedback spurs changes in culture', *HR Magazine*, May 1996, p. 52.

115. C. D. McCauley and R. S. Moxley Jr, 'Development 360: how feedback can make managers more effective', *Career Development International*, vol. 1, no. 3, 1996, p. 19.

116. D. E. Coates, 'Don't tie 360 feedback to pay', *Training*, vol. 35, no. 9, 1998, pp. 68–78.

117. K. A. Guinn, 'Assessment techniques for top executives', *Career Development International*, vol. 1, no. 3, 1996, p. 10; and C. Hymowitz, 'New job: review fad is dubious tool', *Asian Wall Street Journal*, 19 December 2000, p. 6.

118. M. R. Edwards and A. J. Ewen, '360 degree feedback: a royal folly or holy grail?', *Career Development International*, vol. 1, no. 3, 1996, p. 29; and B. O'Reilly, op. cit., p. 78.

119. R. Hoffman, 'Ten reasons you should be using 360 degree feedback', *HR Magazine*, April 1995, pp. 82–5; and J. F. Milliman, R. A. Zawacki, C. Norman, L. Powell and J. Kirksey, 'Companies evaluate employees from all perspectives', *Personnel Journal*, vol. 73, no. 11, 1994, p. 103.

120. M. Vinson, 'The pros and cons of 360 degree feedback: making it work', *Training and Development*, vol. 50, no. 4, 1996, pp. 11–12; and J. F. Milliman et al., 1994, op. cit., p. 103.

121. This section is based on T. Welbourne and L. R. Gomez-Mejia, 'Optimizing team based incentives' and J. Zigon, 'Measuring the hard stuff: teams and other hard-to-measure work', in L. A. Berger and D. R. Berger (eds), *The Compensation Handbook*, 4th edn, McGraw-Hill, New York, 1999, chs 22, 34; S. P. Robbins, 2001, op. cit., pp. 267, 461; and S. L. McShane and M. A. Von Glinow, 2000, op. cit., pp. 288–9.

122. K. R. Murphy and J. N. Cleveland, *Performance Appraisal: An Organizational Perspective*, Allyn & Bacon, Boston, 1991, p. 236.

123. K. R. Murphy and J. N. Cleveland, op. cit., p. 236; and C. O. Longenecker, H. P. Sims and D. A. Gioia, op. cit., p. 190.

124. R. W. Regel and R. W. Hollman, 'Gauging performance objectively', *Personnel Administrator*, vol. 32, no. 6, 1987, p. 78.

125. R. W. Regel and R. W. Hollman, op. cit., p. 75.

126. Bloomberg, 'Directors focus on their role', *South China Morning Post — Business*, 12 October 1998, p. 4.

127. A. J. Cheung, 'Ludicrous praise for bureaucrats', *South China Morning Post*, 20 February 1999, p. 1; and P. E. Spector, op. cit., p. 87.

128. J. R. Schermerhorn, J. G. Hunt and R. N. Osborn, *Managing Organizational Behavior*, 5th edn, John Wiley & Sons, New York, 1994, p. 155; and P. E. Spector, op. cit., pp. 87–8.

129. J. Pearce and L. Porter, reported in 'On personnel', *Boardroom Reports*, vol. 16, no. 7, 1987, p. 15; and P. E. Spector, op. cit., p. 89.

130. K. R. Murphy and J. N. Cleveland, op. cit., p. 219.

131. Research by I. H. Jawahar and C. R. Williams, reported in 'Research on performance appraisal wins award', *HR News*, July 1997, p. 13; and P. E. Spector, op. cit., p. 89.

132. B. Rosen and T. H. Jerdee, 'The nature of job related age stereotypes', *Journal of Applied Psychology*, vol. 61, 1976, pp. 180–3.

133. E. Snape and T. Redman, 'Too old or too young? The impact of perceived age discrimination', *Human Resource Management Journal*, vol. 13, no. 1, 2003, p. 79.

134. M. Cook, 'Performance appraisal and true performance', *Journal of Managerial Psychology*, vol. 10, no. 7, 1995, p. 3.

135. M. Cook, op. cit., p. 3.

136. W. J. Bigoness, 'Effect of applicant's sex, race and performance on employer's performance ratings: some additional findings', *Journal of Applied Psychology*, vol. 61, 1976, pp. 80–4.

137. P. Ngan quoted in A. T. Cheng, 'The iron butterfly', *Asia Inc.*, June 2002, pp. 12–13.

138. W. S. Hubbart, 'Bring performance appraisal training to life', *HR Magazine*, May 1995, p. 166.

139. J. M. Forray, 'A good relationship with the boss pays off', *Academy of Management Executive*, vol. 9, no. 1, 1995, p. 79; and N. T. Duarte, J. R. Goodson and N. R. Klich, 'Effects of dyadic quality and duration on performance appraisal', *Academy of Management Journal*, vol. 37, no. 3, 1994, pp. 499–521.

140. A. R. Nankervis and P. Leece, op. cit., p. 83.

141. A. Galin, 'The criteria method of performance appraisal', *Human Resource Management Australia*, vol. 17, no. 2, 1979, p. 21.

142. L. Allan, 'Top pay deals under the gun', *Australian Financial Review*, 31 August 2000, p. 3.

143. I. H. S. Chow, op. cit., p. 75.

144. P. E. Spector, op. cit., pp. 74–9.

145. D. Torrington, *International Human Resource Management*, Prentice Hall, Hemel Hempstead, 1994, p. 154.

146. M. Gardner and G. Palmer, *Employment Relations*, 2nd edn, Macmillan, Melbourne, 1997, p. 334.

147. S. Murray, 'A comparison of results oriented and trait based performance appraisals', *Personnel Administrator*, June 1983, pp. 100–35; and S. L. McShane and M. A. Von Glinow, 2000, op. cit., pp. 84–5.

148. B. N. Smith, J. S. Hornsby and R. Shirmeyer, op. cit., p. 15.

149. D. Grote, op. cit., p. 15; and 'Performance management as culture change', *HR Focus*, March, 1998, p. 4.

150. 'The bell shaped curve that inspires guerrilla warfare', *Personnel Administrator*, May 1987, p. 41; and D. Grote, op. cit., pp. 14–20.

151. J. Ghorpade and M. M. Chen, 'Creating quality driven performance appraisal systems', *Academy of Management Executive*, vol. 9, no. 1, 1995, p. 37.

152. A. R. Nankervis and P. Leece, op. cit., p. 85; and B. N. Smith, J. S. Hornsby and R. Shirmeyer, op. cit., p. 12.

153. P. M. Muchinsky, op. cit., p. 227; and V. L. Huber and S. R. Fuller, 'Performance appraisal' in M. Poole and M. Warner (eds), *The Handbook of Human Resource Management*, Thomson, London, 1998, p. 599.

154. W. F. Cascio, *Managing Human Resources*, 4th edn, McGraw-Hill, New York, 1995, p. 286; and J. M. Ivancevich, *Human Resource Management*, 5th edn, McGraw-Hill, Boston, 2001, pp. 255–6.

155. Research by A. S. Denis and L. H. Peters cited in 'Studies note ways to improve appraisals', *HR Focus*, February 1992, p. 14.

156. J. M. Ivancevich, op. cit., pp. 256–7.

157. A. R. Nankervis and P. Leece, op. cit., p. 85.

158. B. N. Smith, J. S. Hornsby and R. Shirmeyer, op. cit., p. 12.

159. U. Wiersman and G. P. Latham, 'The practicality of behavioral observation scales, behavioral expectation scales and trait scales', *Personnel Psychology*, vol. 39, 1989, pp. 619–28; and J. M. Ivancevich, op. cit., pp. 257–8.

160. D. Johnson, quoted in L. Grant, 'Stirring it up at Campbell', *Fortune*, 13 May 1996, p. 52.

161. A. R. Nankervis and P. Leece, op. cit., p. 85; and B. N. Smith, J. S. Hornsby and R. Shirmeyer, op. cit., p. 12.

162. J. W. Hedge and M. S. Teachout, 'Exploring the concept of acceptability as a criterion for evaluating performance', *Group and Organization Management*, vol. 25, no. 1, 2000, pp. 22–44.

163. G. Hofstede, *Culture's Consequences*, Sage, Beverly Hills, CA, 1984, pp. 261–3; and V. L. Huber and S. R. Fuller, op. cit., p. 602.

164. J. Dolmat-Connell, 'Changing measures for changing times', in L. A. Berger and D. R. Berger, *The Compensation Handbook*, 4th edn, McGraw-Hill, New York, 2000, p. 473.

165. J. Dolmet-Connell, 2000, op. cit., pp. 473–4; and E. M. Olsen and S. F. Slater, 'The balanced scorecard competitive strategy and performance', *Business Horizons*, vol. 45, no. 3, 2003, pp. 11–16.

166. J. Dolmet-Connell, 2000, op. cit., p. 476; G. Kenny, 'A new perspective', *HR Monthly*, March 2003, pp. 34–6; and A. C. Maltz, A. J. Shenhar and R. R. Reilly, 'Beyond the balanced scorecard: refining the search for organizational success measures', *Long Range Planning*, vol. 36, no. 2, 2003, pp. 187–204.

167. T. Leahy, 'Tailoring the balanced scorecard', *Business Finance*, August 2000, pp. 53–6.

168. S. P. Robbins, 2001, op. cit., p. 479.

169. W. F. Cascio, *Applied Psychology in Personnel Management*, 4th edn, Prentice Hall, Englewood Cliffs, NJ, 1991, p. 331; and P. E. Spector, op. cit., pp. 113–17.

170. S. Long and S. Beer, 'Big brother is watching at a workplace near you', *Australian Financial Review*, 10 September 1998, p. 3.

171. M. Carlson, 'Fears increase over snooping bosses', *South China Morning Post*, 17 August 2000, p. 3.

172. V. Kwong and A. Lau, 'Camera catches maid assaulting toddler', *South China Morning Post*, 19 September 2000, p. 3; and H. Phillips and A. Lo, 'Maids advised "never, never" to admit to guilt', *South China Morning Post*, 20 November 2000, p. 3.

173. M. Bryan, 'Every step you take, every move you make...', *Australian Financial Review*, 4–5 March 2000, p. 27; M. Conlin, 'Workers, surf at your own risk', *Business Week*, 12 June 2000, p. 78; S. Long, 'Think before you click and forward', *Australian Financial Review*, 15 November 2000, p. 51; and M. Fenton-Jones, 'Intellectual theft a growing problem for business', *Australian Financial Review*, 21 October 2003, p. 49.

174. L. O'Donnell, 'UK police to act after TV report uncovers racism', *South China Morning Post*, 26 October 2003, p. 8.

175. S. Long and S. Beer, op. cit., p. 3.

176. C. O. Longenecker, H. P. Sims and D. A. Gioia, op. cit., p. 190.

177. G. Anderson, 'Performance appraisal', in B. Towers (ed.), *The Handbook of Human Resource Management*, Blackwell, Oxford, 1992, p. 188.

178. N. Stein, op. cit., p. 62; and L. Gratton, op. cit., pp. 104–5.

179. V. Wright, quoted in N. Stein, op. cit., p. 62.

180. A. R. Nankervis and P. Leece, 1997, op. cit., p. 83.

181. B. N. Smith, J. S. Hornsby and R. Shirmeyer, op. cit., p. 10.

182. P. P. Carson and K. D. Carson, 'Deming versus traditional management theorists on goal setting: can both be right?', *Business Horizons*, vol. 36, no. 5, 1993, p. 80; and S. Sherman, 'Stretch goals: the dark side of asking for miracles', *Fortune*, 13 November 1995, pp. 165–6.

183. R. D. Pritchard, P. L. Roth, S. D. Jones, P. J. Galgay and M. D. Watson, 'Designing a goal setting system to enhance performance: a practical guide', *Organizational Dynamics*, vol. 17, no. 1, 1988, p. 71; and S. L. McShane and M. A. Von Glinow, op. cit., pp. 84–6.

184. S. Tully, 'Why go for stretch targets?', *Fortune*, 14 November 1994, pp. 95–100; and S. L. McShane and M. A. Von Glinow, op. cit., p. 85.

185. M. G. Aamodt, 1996, op. cit., pp. 466–7.

186. W. J. Kearney, 'Performance appraisal: which way to go?', *MSU Business Topics*, vol. 25, no. 1, 1977, p. 60.

187. R. W. Regel and R. W. Hollman, op. cit., p. 76.

188. D. Cederblom, 'The performance appraisal interview: a review, implications, and suggestions', *Academy of Management Review*, vol. 7, no. 2, 1982, p. 219.

189. H. H. Meyer, E. Kay and J. R. P. French, 'Split roles in performance appraisal', *Harvard Business Review*, January 1965, pp. 123–9.

190. J. S. Y. Lee and S. Akhtar, 'Determinants of employee willingness to use feedback for performance improvement: cultural and organizational interpretations', *International Journal of Human Resource Management*, vol. 7, no. 4, 1996, p. 87.

191. See R. J. Burke, W. Weitzel and T. Weir, 'Characteristics of effective employee performance review and development interviews: replication and extension', *Personnel Psychology*, vol. 31, 1978, pp. 903–19; D. Cederblom, op. cit., pp. 219–27; and S. H. Applebaum and A. Hare, 'Self efficacy as a mediator of goal setting and performance', *Journal of Managerial Psychology*, vol. 11, no. 3, 1996, pp. 33–47.

192. T. S. Shaikh, 'Appraising job performance — to be or not to be? An Asian dilemma', *International Journal of Career Management*, vol. 7, no. 5, 1995, pp. 13–18.

193. P. Drucker, quoted in 'On personnel', *Boardroom Reports*, 1 December 1987, p. 15.

194. National Committee on Discrimination in Employment and Occupation, *Equal Employment Opportunity*, AGPS, Canberra, 1984, p. 29; and P. E. Spector, op. cit., pp. 92–3.

195. *Equal Employment Opportunity*, op. cit., p. 37.

196. W. H. Holley and H. S. Field, 'Will your performance appraisal system hold up in court?', *Personnel*, vol. 5, no. 1, 1982, pp. 61–3; J. M. Ivancevich, op. cit., pp. 246–8; and G. A. Nofsinger, 'Performance measures: an overview', in L. A. Berger and D. R. Berger (eds), *The Compensation Handbook*, 4th edn, McGraw-Hill, New York, 2000, pp. 425–7.

197. P. Hersey and M. Goldsmith, 'The changing role of performance management', *Training and Development Journal*, vol. 34, no. 10, 1980, p. 22; and J. R. Schermerhorn, *Management*, 7th edn, John Wiley & Sons, New York, 2002, p. 320.

chapter 9

human resource development[1]

Learning objectives

When you have finished studying this chapter, you should be able to:

- Understand the importance of human resource development to organisational success
- Explain the meanings of strategic human resource development, learning organisations and knowledge management
- Explain the need for a systematic approach to training and development
- Distinguish between training and development
- Outline the major human resource development methods and techniques
- Describe the key characteristics of an effective orientation program
- Understand the main principles of learning psychology.

'Training represents an investment in performance.'[2]

Mindtheme Consulting

Human resource development (HRD) has come to prominence because organisations have to improve their productivity and international competitiveness. A well-trained, multiskilled work force is essential to economic survival. Moreover, many employees now look to the company they work for to provide them with growth and learning opportunities to improve their employability.[3] Research shows that investments in human resources are a potential source of competitive advantage and have a positive relationship with stock market performance and profits.[4] In fact, virtually all descriptions of high-performance management, according to Pfeffer, emphasise training.[5] Ford Australia, for example, claims that worker training in its manufacturing plant halved absenteeism and dramatically reduced labour turnover.[6] Similarly, it is claimed that Toyota's Technical Skills Academy is the cornerstone of its success.[7]

Unfortunately, many organisations spend little on HRD and Australian governments are among the most parsimonious when it comes to expenditure on education. According to an Australian Bureau of Statistics training practices survey, only a minority of employers provide training for their employees. In Hong Kong, it is less than 10 per cent (even though only slightly more than half the work force has an education beyond form three).[8] A recent survey shows that almost 80 per cent of Australian workers do not think their employer is providing sufficient training for them to do their job properly.[9] It is also claimed that Australian universities are increasingly employing academics on a flexible part-time basis and give little (or no) training in teaching, marking or course design.[10] According to the Australian Centre for Industrial Relations Research and Training: 'There is little evidence of a strong training culture within Australian workplaces. Much of employer provided training in Australia is aimed at the barest minimum and does little to contribute to a knowledge based economy.'[11]

Motorola, which has one of the finest reputations for quality in the United States, gives all employees at least 40 hours training per year (a figure it plans to quadruple), while other leading US companies such as General Electric and Intel spend around 6–8 per cent of their payroll on training and development.[12] Says Motorola's CEO: 'If knowledge is becoming antiquated at a faster rate, we have no choice but to spend on education. How can that not be a competitive weapon?'[13] HRD expenditure, moreover, sends a powerful signal to employees of the organisation's commitment to its people.[14]

To be competitive in the global marketplace, many organisations need to rethink their approach to HRD. In the new information-based economy, the most important intellectual property is what is inside employees' heads. People, not physical assets, are now critical. But people, unlike coalmines and factories, cannot be owned. Organisations therefore must create an environment that makes the best people want to stay.[15] Having employees with the 'right' training and education is essential.

Australia's education system, however, is failing to produce people with the skills, attitudes or abilities needed by business. One in three Year 9 students lack literacy skills, 2.6 million adults are at the lowest level of literacy and Australian students rate poorly on maths and science skills compared with their Asian counterparts.[16] Australian schools and universities are being subjected to change and criticism. Controversy rages over classroom hours, inadequate education facilities, the impact of political ideology, mediocrity versus meritocracy, academic pay systems, low teaching standards, performance assessment, language and Asian studies, hard versus soft subjects, private versus state education, academic shortages and declining academic standards.[17]

Such ferment in training and development and **education** is symptomatic of the fact that change is necessary if Australia is to have a work force that possesses the creativity, flexibility and skills necessary for economic survival. A study by the University of South Australia, for example, found that 40 per cent of CEOs are intimidated by technology.[18] According to some experts, Asian countries have an advantage because their Confucian belief in the educated person, the self-advancing person, produces a highly skilled and motivated work force.[19] Hitachi's management-developing efforts are based on the corporate

Human resource development (HRD) Includes training and development, career planning and performance appraisal. Its focus is on the acquisition of the required attitudes, knowledge and skills to facilitate the achievement of employee career goals and organisational strategic objectives.

Who owns the knowledge an employee acquires by attending training and development programs paid for by the organisation?

Education Activities designed to improve the knowledge, understanding and abilities of an individual.

Should companies be responsible for teaching employees basic literacy skills because of failures in the education system?

Competency-based training (CBT) Training that develops the skills, knowledge and attitudes required to achieve competency standards.

belief that the most important responsibility of a manager is to educate and develop their subordinates.[20] Similarly, leading US companies recognise that human resource development can be a powerful tool for generating change and creating a competitive advantage. A survey by the American Management Association shows a strong correlation between profit growth and productivity improvements and increased expenditure on human resource development.[21] Research also shows that higher levels of skills training are positively associated with higher levels of quality management.[22]

Accepting such attitudes will require a fundamental change in workplace culture for many organisations. The former Labor government's Training Guarantee Scheme was a recognition of the seriousness of the situation and of Australian companies' general failure to invest in people. The scheme, however, proved ineffective in dealing with Australia's skill shortage and unemployment problems and was ultimately abandoned.[23]

Additional controversy involved the Carmichael and Mayer reports and their advocacy of **competency-based training (CBT)**.[24] Although embraced by the former Labor government and the trade union movement, employers and some academics have been less than enthusiastic.[25] CBT seeks to improve the relevance of education and training to industry, as well as to maximise the use of individual skills. According to Whittingham, CBT 'focuses on competencies gained by an individual, rather than on the training process' and this characteristic has inflamed the debate.[26] Andrewartha and others, for example, argue that this emphasis on outcomes inhibits intellectual development.[27] Pennington claims it downgrades knowledge, while other critics claim that its real intention is to spread qualifications as widely as possible and to foster expectation of a higher wage level on reaching agreed competency levels, whether or not the skills are relevant for the job for which trainees are employed.[28] Other criticisms of CBT centre on its administrative requirements, centralised control, facilitation of union power and claims of social engineering.[29] Needless to say, the value of CBT has produced heated division among training experts.[30]

Advocates of CBT claim it promotes 'greater quality assurance, industry relevant training, portability of credentials, recognition of prior learning and articulated pathings between education, training and industry'.[31]

A further controversial initiative of the former Labor government was the creation of a special task force, headed by David Karpin, to examine the performance of Australian managers, identify the managerial skills needed to improve Australia's competitiveness and determine the role of educational institutions in developing Australia's future business leaders.[32] The assumption was that good managers are the key to improved economic performance. According to the Karpin Report, the majority of Australia's managers do not have the equivalent education or skill levels of managers from Australia's major trading partners. Critics claim that too many Australian companies are run by managers who are obsessed with control, and who lack strategic perspective, flexibility and leadership skills.[33]

In contrast, Karpin believes that Australian managers' strengths include being hardworking, innovative, technically competent and egalitarian. Karpin also argues that most Australian educational and training institutions are not world class, are out of touch, and focus on producing graduates with technical operational skills rather than graduates who understand how to lead and communicate.[34] To develop greater entrepreneurial spirit and better quality managers, the report recommended:
- creating a positive enterprise culture
- upgrading vocational education and training and business support
- capitalising on the talents of diversity
- achieving best-practice management development
- reforming management education.[35]

Specifically, the task force identified eight critical areas in which Australian managers need to improve their skills: 'soft' or people skills, leadership skills, strategic skills, international orientation, entrepreneurship, broadening beyond technical specialisation, relationship-building skills across organisations and the use of diverse human resources.[36] According to Karpin, the profile of the future senior manager will be quite different from the profile of many of today's managers. There will be more women, more people from different ethnic backgrounds and more MBAs. Careers will be varied and international. Managers will be more prepared to share information and to delegate. Their environment will be constantly changing and their tenure will be short. Not surprisingly, such managers will be subject to high pressure and will be driven by results.[37]

The Karpin Report has clear implications for HR managers and their organisations and can be used, says Moore, 'to demonstrate the benefits of directly linking management development and corporate strategy'.[38] However, the Coalition government has shown little enthusiasm for its contents. Moreover, the report has been the subject of much criticism. Emery, for example, argues that Karpin ignores the major changes that have occurred in the workplace, such as enterprise bargaining, self-managing teams, union amalgamation, decentralised industrial relations, and so on. Emery also claims that the report is based on false assumptions and suffers from poor analysis.[39] Other critics have branded its recommendations as narrow, 'motherhood and apple pie', elitist, abstract, outdated and having negligible impact.[40]

The need for human resource management

HRD is an important activity. Today, it is employee know-how that represents a key source of sustainable competitive advantage.[41] Newly hired employees need to be trained to perform their jobs. Existing employees need to acquire new skills and knowledge. Changes, particularly in technology and organisational restructuring, mean that people and organisations are continually faced with situations that require learning and the exploitation of knowledge.

Business and economic changes

Deregulation, international competition, tariff reductions, global outsourcing and restructuring are just a few of the dislocating factors affecting organisations today. Philips Electronics, for example, faced bankruptcy several years ago. Poor strategic decision making and staggering debt combined with a competitive onslaught from new and more agile competitors meant only a dramatic intervention could save the company.[42] 'It was important', says a senior Philips executive, 'first to realize that the company needed restructuring in order to improve operational performance. We had to improve quality, costs and cycle time, and it was also necessary to reduce our head count. But it was important to do more than just restructure the company — we needed to revitalize it. We wanted to seek out new opportunities for growth and provide stretch goals for the entire organization. Central to achieving these goals was our capacity to develop the organizational and individual capabilities required for future competitiveness. It was also critical to communicate the key changes in strategic direction in an efficient and effective manner. This is where education served to support our strategic processes. Executive education at Philips was used as a vehicle for communicating vital messages and making informed decisions about our future, for building core capabilities and for leading continuous change.'[43]

Viewed strategically, HRD can be 'a platform for organizational transformation, a mechanism for continuous organizational and individual renewal and a vehicle for global knowledge transfer'.[44]

Specifically, HRD can be a powerful tool in:
- implementing a new policy
- implementing a strategy
- effecting organisational change
- changing an organisation's culture
- meeting a major change in the external environment
- solving particular problems.[45]

It is clear that the increasingly competitive and ever-changing business and economic environment requires HRD to support the organisation's business strategies and play a pivotal role in shaping its culture.[46]

Technological change

The rate of technological change is now greater than it has ever been. No employee or organisation can escape its whirlwind impact. The majority of US workers are now knowledge workers and 80 per cent of new jobs are in information-intensive sectors of the economy. Added value is being created by brain power and not physical effort.[47] The application of computer technology and microprocessors in the retail industry over the past decade, for example, has had considerable impact on functions such as accounting, inventory control, storage, stock control and warehouse operations. The introduction of point-of-sale electronic cash registers, optical scanning and electronic funds transfer are technological developments that are even more obvious.

Similarly, technology is revolutionising much of manufacturing. The advent of microprocessors, computer-controlled machinery and data advances in telecommunications require employees to possess new skills and know-how. Technology creates redundancies and employee obsolescence, making continuing work force skilling and re-skilling essential. Today, employees (and organisations) can compete only if they learn faster than their competitors. Marketable skills are the key to worker employability and organisational survival. A US study, for example, found that companies that increased their long-term training budget after job cuts were 75 per cent more likely to show increased earnings and nearly twice as likely to improve employee productivity, compared with those companies that reduced their training expenditure.[48]

Organisational change

Organisational change also creates HRD needs. Organisations are becoming more flexible, participative and simultaneously tougher and more humane. They increasingly value both accountability and creativity and seek competitive advantage through people strategies. McLagen has identified six key areas of organisational change that are impacting HRD:

1. Pressures for work force productivity have intensified, with organisations and industries looking beyond obvious efficiency gains to more systemic and 'breakthrough' ways of being low-cost producers of high-quality products and services.
2. The pace of change continues to accelerate. Cycle times are being reduced, the useful life of information is shrinking, work is changing as a result of advances in technology and time is becoming a more valuable resource. The bottom line is that organisations that work in less time have a competitive advantage.
3. Organisations continue to shift their focus to the customer and quality. That shift is more than a fad or a fleeting tactic. It is pervasive because it is a key competitive characteristic. A customer and quality focus permeates the superior organisation, with every employee clear about the value they add in both areas for internal and external customers.
4. The arena for an organisation's planning and action is becoming global. Markets, resource pool competition and partnerships are crossing national lines. Some competitors are now also suppliers, customers or partners. Relationships, in short, are becoming complex and the boundaries between the organisation and its environment blurred.
5. Business strategies now depend even more on the quality and versatility of the human resources. Whether they rely on improved productivity, quality or innovation, strategies cannot be delivered if an organisation's people are not capable and committed. Organisations that apply only money and technology to problems, without involving people, will not survive. This is especially the case in industries where people's knowledge, attitudes, skills and willingness to change are critical to the organisation's competitive advantage.
6. Work structure and design are changing dramatically, building on changes that have already begun. Hierarchies are melting into, or being displaced by, flatter and more flexible organisational designs. The boundaries between individual jobs are blurring, with more team accountability and flexible, multiskilled job designs. Autocratic decision structures are giving way to more participative modes.[49]

McLagen cautions, however, that the changes that organisations must make to survive will be successful only if employees adapt, develop and grow, and if organisations can mobilise themselves as social systems to work in different ways.[50]

Social, legal and other changes

Finally, changes in social attitudes, legal requirements, industrial relations, and so on generate training and development needs. Occupational health and safety, enterprise bargaining, smoking in the workplace, substance abuse, sexual harassment, the management of diversity and EEO requirements, for example, demand new skills, attitudes and knowledge on the part of employees and organisations. An ageing population (the average age of trained aircraft mechanics is 55 years), the negative attitudes held by young people towards trade-related apprenticeships (which are not seen as 'cool') and the promotion of university and TAFE qualifications have contributed to skills shortages in the building, food, electrical and engineering industries.[51] Some experts also argue for women-only management courses to provide a positive and supportive environment for the development of women managers.[52]

Should it be compulsory for employees to attend certain types of training programs (for example, on sexual harassment or equal employment opportunity) if they find them embarrassing or if they are in conflict with their personal values or national culture?

Strategic HRD

HRD has an important role to play in generating improved organisational performance and individual growth, but it must be aligned with corporate objectives if an organisation is to gain any real benefit from expenditure. If a company's strategic business objective is to provide the best customer service in the industry, for example, then training must specifically address this aim.[53] HRD activities emphasising key behaviours and competencies must be similarly highlighted in the organisation's performance appraisal and reward systems.[54]

Failure to link HRD to business objectives means that the organisation's competitive strategy will not be supported. Training and development will take place for their own sake. Popularity and fashion will be paramount. A strategic approach to HRD, in contrast, aims to meet an organisation's specific business objectives. The ultimate purpose of HRD is to help the organisation and individuals to compete more effectively, now and in the future. It involves a strategic, long-term and systematic way of thinking about people. Yet the research evidence suggests that many organisations do not understand the value of using HRD for strategic ends.[55] A study by Curtain found that most Australian companies believe technology and innovation are important but they do not include HRD as a key element in their business strategy.[56] To add value, HRD activities 'must be derived from an explicit strategy that is consciously linked to the business strategy'.[57] The closer the alignment between HRD and the organisation's strategy, the greater the likelihood that learning will be transferred to the job.[58]

The HR manager should ask questions such as: What are the strategic business objectives of the organisation? What needs to be done to build the employee attitudes, skills and knowledge needed to achieve those objectives? What is the business need we are addressing? Well-designed HRD programs can help realise objectives such as improving customer service, increasing the quality of the company's product or service and boosting productivity. Cuts to training budgets and lack of top management support for HR managers can occur because much training and development has little positive impact on an organisation's ability to compete. For example, the BBC Staff Training Department spent UK£1400 on leaflets telling employees how to negotiate revolving doors, while another BBC training leaflet instructed employees on how to use the office kettle.[59] Some companies similarly are sending their managers to cooking classes to learn 'teambuilding'.[60] In contrast, Siemens' university management education program not only pays for itself but saves the company millions of dollars annually.[61] Thus, HR managers must be obsessive about linking individual and organisational development to the bottom line, ensuring that HRD programs deliver exactly what the business needs.[62] The HR manager can also contribute to employee development by reminding management of the strategic importance of training and development and by ensuring that the organisation is attractive to talented employees.[63]

Strategic HRD is virtually non-existent in many organisations. One Australian survey suggested that 70 per cent of training was a waste.[64] Below are some reasons for the absence of strategic HRD:

- Organisations lack or have ill-defined strategic objectives.
- Top management views training and development as a necessary evil, something nice to do or an employee benefit.
- Organisations neglect long-term considerations and concentrate on the short term.
- Organisations do not analyse training and development needs.
- Evaluation of training is ignored or emphasises employee satisfaction rather than performance improvement.

How much longer organisations can hide from the strategic imperatives of inadequate and inferior HRD is a moot point. The increasing pressures of international competition are making it harder for unskilled managers and workers to compete. 'Competitive organizations today', says Jones, 'require knowledge workers who are empowered decision makers capable of carrying out their jobs in alignment with carefully defined corporate goals.'[65] Recognising this need, Singapore has established a Skills Development Fund, which offers training subsidies of up to 80 per cent to organisations that ensure that their training programs promote the achievement of their strategic business objectives.[66] The global economy will not spare Australia. 'The productivity of modern economies depends heavily on investments in the acquisition of knowledge and skills ... no nation can thrive in the modern world without investing in its people', says Nobel Laureate G. S. Becker.[67] Hong Kong, likewise, is in danger of losing its competitive edge because of declining academic standards and poor English and Chinese language skills.[68] According to the American Chamber of Commerce in Hong Kong, the education system is not equipping students to meet the demands of a knowledge-based economy, to think creatively and to communicate effectively in both Chinese and English.[69]

Learning organisations[70]

Learning organisations
Organisations where the focus is on the acquisition, sharing and utilisation of knowledge to survive and prosper.

Learning organisations focus on the acquisition, sharing and utilisation of knowledge to survive and prosper. The development and empowerment of every employee is supported and encouraged. A learning organisation represents a strategic orientation that promotes a critical capability to compete. Managers are explicit in their strategic commitment to change, innovation and continuous improvement (see figures 9.1 and 9.2).[71] They constantly strive to create organisations that gather, organise, share and analyse knowledge to achieve strategic business objectives. The culture of such organisations is characterised by risk-taking, open communication, and employee empowerment and development. Team-oriented structures, systems and policies promote the learning and development of all employees. Compensation systems, for example, reward employees for seeking, sharing and creating knowledge. HRD is given top priority for developing quality, creativity, leadership and problem solving (see figure 9.3).

PEOPLE DEVELOPMENT AT FOSTER'S

Foster's is absolutely committed to the development of its people across all levels of the business around the world.

In an effort to ensure the best possible skill set for our business leaders, all Foster's businesses conducted global talent reviews during the year. This process helped identify key actions to ensure our people are well equipped to continue their strong leadership now and into the future.

Individual development is encouraged at Foster's. Employees are offered opportunities to participate in on the job training, special projects, secondments and mentoring projects. In addition, a number of tailored courses are offered to employees year round and higher education sponsorship is offered.

Foster's is a global company, so we believe that it is important to provide our people with the opportunity to gain international work experience. Almost 40 employees are now in key expatriate roles in Australia, the US, Europe and Asia.

Figure 9.1 People development at Foster's
Source T. Kunkel, former President and CEO, Foster's Group Limited, Concise Annual Report, Melbourne, 2003 p. 8.

Feature	Description
Continuous learning	Employees share learning with each other and use their jobs as a means for applying and creating knowledge.
Knowledge generation and sharing	Systems are developed for creating, capturing and sharing knowledge.
Critical systematic thinking	Employees are encouraged to think in new ways, see relationships and test assumptions.
Learning culture	Learning is rewarded, promoted and supported by management.
Encouragement of flexibility and experimentation	Employees are encouraged to take risks, innovate, explore new ideas, try new processes, and develop new products and services.
Valuing employees	The focus is on the development and wellbeing of employees.
Strategic focus	Learning and the management of knowledge are tied to the achievement of the organisation's strategic business objectives.
Organisational renewal	Emphasis is given to the constant renewal and revitalisation of the organisation.

Figure 9.2 Features of a learning organisation

Source Adapted by the author from M. A. Gephart, V. J. Marsick, M. E. Van Buren and M. S. Spiro, 'Learning organizations come alive', *Training and Development*, vol. 50, no. 1, 1996, pp. 34–45; and M. Gloet, 'The changing role of the HRM function in the knowledge economy: the links to quality knowledge management', paper presented at the 8th International Conference on ISO and TQM, Montreal, April 2003, pp. 1–7.

Conduct a cultural audit to determine whether there is an organisational value for learning. For each statement below, indicate whether you:

1 strongly disagree   2 disagree   3 neither agree nor disagree   4 agree   5 strongly agree

1. Job assignments are challenges that stretch employees' knowledge to the limit. 1 2 3 4 5
2. Supervisors give recognition and credit to those who apply new knowledge and skills to their work. 1 2 3 4 5
3. Employees are able to provide reliable information about ways to improve job performance. 1 2 3 4 5
4. There is a performance appraisal system that ties financial rewards to technical competence. 1 2 3 4 5
5. Job assignments consistently expose employees to new technical information. 1 2 3 4 5
6. Supervisors can match an employee's need for personal and professional development with opportunities to attend training. 1 2 3 4 5
7. Employees tell each other about new information that can be used to increase job performance. 1 2 3 4 5
8. There is excellent on-the-job training. 1 2 3 4 5
9. Job assignments are created in an employee's area of interest and are designed to promote personal development. 1 2 3 4 5
10. Supervisors encourage independent and innovative thinking. 1 2 3 4 5
11. My organisation is highly innovative. 1 2 3 4 5
12. My organisation expects continuing technical excellence and competence. 1 2 3 4 5
13. My organisation has a progressive atmosphere. 1 2 3 4 5
14. My organisation attempts to be better than its competitors. 1 2 3 4 5
15. My organisation expects high levels of work performance. 1 2 3 4 5

Figure 9.3 Checklist for a learning culture

Source Adapted from J. B. Tracey, I. T. Scott, S. I. Tannenbaum and M. J. Kavanagh, 'Applying training on the job: the importance of the work environment', *Journal of Applied Psychology*, vol. 80, no. 2, 1995, pp. 239–52.

In the information economy, knowledge is the critical factor driving organisational success. Globalisation, Internet technologies and the push for higher value-added products and services have placed a premium on innovation and value creation. Economic success now centres on data, know-how, and idea generation and manipulation. **Knowledge management** aims to exploit the **intellectual capital** residing in an organisation. Intellectual capital includes:

- **Human capital:** the knowledge, skills and abilities of employees.
- **Renewal capital:** the intellectual property (patents, trademarks, copyright, licences) that has marketable value.
- **Structural capital:** the knowledge captured and retained in an organisation's systems and structures.
- **Relationship capital:** the value of an organisation's relationships with its suppliers, customers and competitors.

An organisation's knowledge — its intellectual capital — is its major source of competitive advantage. Intellectual capital, for example, is clearly recognised as having an impact on the company's share price and economic success.[73] Companies such as Microsoft have few assets other than the knowledge of their employees. The central theme of knowledge management is to leverage and reuse the organisation's intellectual capital to maximum effect. Learning organisations do this by:

- capturing, storing, retrieving and distributing tangible knowledge assets, such as copyright, patents and licences
- gathering, organising and disseminating intangible knowledge, such as professional know-how and expertise, individual insight and experience, creative solutions, and the like — for example, to effectively leverage its human capital, Lend Lease employs a knowledgeable management system called 'i know', which facilitates the identification, storage and access of valuable knowledge and expertise present in the organisation
- creating an interactive learning environment where people readily transfer and share what they know, internalise it and apply it to create new knowledge — Grace Chopard from IBM Consulting Services says: 'Technology obviously facilitates knowledge harvesting and knowledge transfer but I think it is really important to recognize that, ultimately, organizations have to create the environment that encourages knowledge management'[74]
- creating the kind of culture and reward systems that attract, retain and motivate top talent (see figures 9.1 and 9.2).

These practices encourage employees to share information and make it easy for them to identify sources of information and best practices and eliminate wasted time and effort on 'reinventing the wheel'. The reuse of existing knowledge thus becomes a routine way of working and the creation of new knowledge encouraged. The strategic management of knowledge (and HRD) is recognised as key to increasing individual and corporate competitive advantage.

Choosing a knowledge management approach will have a direct impact on several processes and strategies within an organisation, including TQM and HRM. Knowledge management is a long-term strategy, so serious consideration must be given to choosing approaches that are compatible with the organisation's goals, strategies, products and services. If the approaches are well considered and aligned with organisational strategy, then knowledge management can act as a strong enabling mechanism for quality HRM practices within the organisation. On the other hand, a poorly aligned approach can affect quality HRM practices through conflict arising from fundamental differences in values and assumptions.

HRM practitioners need to be aware of knowledge management processes and their effects, as these have a bearing on HRM functions, including the following:

Knowledge management Deals with an organisation's ability to collect, store, share and apply knowledge in order to enhance its survival and success.

Intellectual capital The knowledge that exists within an organisation.

Human capital The knowledge, skills and abilities of an organisation's employees.

Renewal capital The intellectual property (patents, trademarks, copyrights, licences) of an organisation that have marketable value.

Structural capital The knowledge that is captured and retained in an organisation's systems and structures.

Relationship capital The value of an organisation's relationships with its suppliers, customers and competitors.

- *HRM strategy:* knowledge management is a long-term strategy, and demonstrates a proactive rather than a reactive approach to business planning and execution. HRM practitioners can play an important role in this regard by building linkages between overall business strategy, knowledge management strategy and HRM strategy. Building and securing management support for HRM and knowledge management strategy throughout the organisation, and communicating the strategy up, down and across the organisation, are also important aspects of a strategic HRM approach.
- *Staffing:* the organisation needs to ensure that people with appropriate knowledge, skills and attitudes are brought into the organisation through recruitment and selection procedures. This means having a clear understanding of the nature and substance of the jobs the people will undertake.
- *Human resource development:* the success of a knowledge management approach is dependent on the participation of all employees at all levels of the organisation. This is because every employee is both a teacher and a learner, continuously learning and transferring knowledge to others in the organisation.[75] HRM practitioners thus need to encourage the full development and utilisation of the skills and abilities of all employees. This includes developing future managers who possess appropriate skills for managing in the new knowledge economy.
- *Nurturing an appropriate organisational culture:* HR practitioners can contribute significantly through managing change and building an egalitarian culture that sees knowledge and learning as fundamental to the organisation's existence. Continuous learning, sharing, teamwork and a recognition that benefits cannot always be measured simply in economic terms are attributes of good quality HRM practice, and these can complement, support and strengthen knowledge management practices within an organisation.
- *Motivation, reward and recognition:* the organisation must understand the needs of knowledge workers and provide appropriate incentives to acquire, share and disseminate knowledge. Employees must be empowered to make decisions, to experiment, to take calculated risks and to continuously improve organisational performance.[76]

HRD methods and techniques

HRD involves 'the acquisition of knowledge and attitudes to facilitate the achievement of career goals and corporate objectives'.[77] It is interconnected with performance management and knowledge management and encompasses both training and development. The focus is on improving corporate effectiveness by enhancing the performance of the organisation's human resources. High-performance organisations integrate HRD with strategy to ensure that employees are competent and motivated to work towards organisational objectives.[78] As key parts of HRD, training and development are concerned with changing employee behaviour and improving job performance.[79] **Training** typically emphasises immediate improvements in job performance via the procurement of specific skills (for example, computer skills). **Development**, on the other hand, aims to prepare the employee for future job responsibilities through the acquisition of new experiences, knowledge, skills and attitudes (for example, management development via an MBA). Although training emphasises the improvement of present job performance, its benefits may continue throughout an employee's entire career and help prepare them for future promotions. The reality is that 'the distinction between training (now) and development (future) is often blurred and primarily one of intent'.[80]

Training Represents activities that teach employees how to better perform their present jobs.

Development Involves those activities that prepare an employee for future responsibilities.

The scope of training programs

The aim of entry training for new employees is to provide them with the skills necessary to meet the performance standards of the job. Once base-level competence has been achieved, further training and development provides additional skills and know-how to enable the employee to advance to positions of higher responsibility. This leads to personal growth and enhanced self-esteem. Another important aim of training is to remedy substandard job performance. Performance appraisal is an important source of information on training needs; it highlights specific weaknesses and deficiencies in the employee's range of job skills and know-how (see figure 9.4). Yet research suggests that few organisations explicitly link performance appraisal information with training.[81]

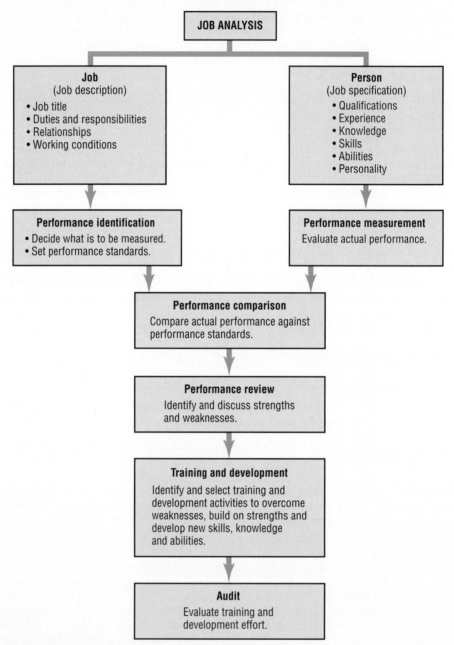

Figure 9.4 Performance appraisal and training needs
Source Asia Pacific Management Co. Ltd, 2004.

As mentioned earlier, changing technology generates training and development needs. The benefits of new technology depend on employees being equipped with the necessary skills, so work force re-training becomes necessary. Moreover, existing competencies may become redundant. In Australia, technical training is increasingly seen as the responsibility of the Technical and Further Education Colleges (TAFE) and the tertiary education sector.

This is not without its problems, because universities and colleges have been slow in adapting to changing business conditions, lack high-quality staff and often operate with obsolete equipment.[82] Moreover, there is increasing criticism that universities are 'dumbing down' and that poor-quality fee-paying students are being passed regardless. For example, one student graduated despite being caught more than once plagiarising essays,[83, 84] while a Hong Kong student who paid his tutor to sit his exam was allowed to continue his studies. MBA programs, in particular, are an area of concern.[85] Besides being devalued by their sheer numbers, the academic standards are often questionable, the program content out of date and the competence of graduates questionable.[86] Comments one critic '... the product that universities sell is qualifications, not education'.[87] Advertisements for overseas university programs marketed in Hong Kong now carry the rider: 'It is a matter of discretion for individual employers to recognize any qualifications to which these courses may lead.'[88]

Training beyond immediate job requirements

HR planning examines the organisation in terms of its capacity to achieve its objectives by having qualified people in the right place at the right time. To do this the organisation must provide training and development to ensure that employee skills and knowledge match future HR requirements. If top management does not insist that employees continually improve their skills and knowledge, the organisation's competency and overall competitiveness will decline.

There is also an increasing belief among some experts that non-job-related training (such as personal skills training in time management, assertiveness, stress management and liberal arts subjects) produces on-the-job benefits. Training and development is an obligation organisations have to employees. In times of decreasing job security, training and development makes employees more valuable and enhances their marketability. Leading companies seek to upgrade their employees' skills because they can no longer promise lifetime employment. Instead, by investing in employee development, they hope to guarantee their employees lifelong employability. Finally, from the employee's viewpoint, expenditure on training and development reinforces the belief that the organisation is interested in their welfare (also see chapter 10).

In an era of high job mobility, why should employers spend money on employee training and development?

A systematic approach to training and development

The effectiveness of training and development is enhanced when training activities are preceded by comprehensive analysis. This permits the HR manager to demonstrate how training and development contribute to the organisation's strategic business objectives. According to Michaud, 'Without information about what and how critical the needs are, training and development efforts are likely to continue the "spray and pray" strategies which have too often characterised them.'[89]

Training and development should be as cost-effective as any other functional activity. Training and development are investments in the human 'capital' of the organisation. Accordingly, it is essential to measure the adequacy of the 'return on investment' for training and development activities. The return is likely to be higher if a **systematic approach to training** and development is taken rather than an ad hoc one. An example of a systematic approach is shown in figure 9.5.

Logical sequence is the essence of this particular system:

1. *Assessment:* establish what is needed, by whom, when and where, so that training objectives can be determined.
2. *Training activity:* select the training methods and learning principles to be employed.
3. *Evaluation:* measure how well the activity met the training and development objectives.

These three steps are discussed in more detail below.

Systematic approach to training A three-step approach to training that involves: (a) assessment of training needs; (b) conduct of the training activity; and (c) evaluation of the training activity.

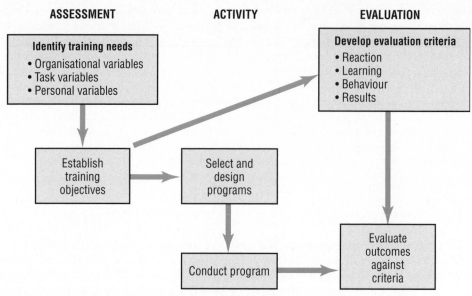

Figure 9.5 A systematic training and development model

Assessment phase

The determination of training needs, and the translation of those needs into training objectives, provides direction and purpose for the training effort (see figure 9.6). If the **assessment phase** is inadequate, training may not be consistent with actual needs. Unfortunately, the evidence suggests that organisations usually either do a poor job of assessing training needs or do not do it at all.[90] According to Wexley and Latham, 'too often training and development programs get their start in organisations simply because the program was well advertised and marketed, or because "other organisations are using it"'.[91]

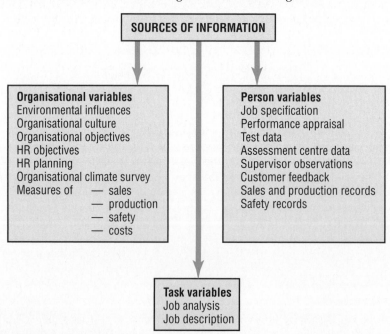

Figure 9.6 Training needs analysis

Organisation, task and person model

- *Organisational variables*. Organisational objectives determine the quality and quantity of resources allocated to the training effort. The climate and culture of the organisation also limit what can be achieved by training. Promoting employee participation in an autocratic organisation, for example, will only create problems. Similarly, employees whose training-learned skills are ignored in the workplace typically become alienated from the job and from the organisation. Finally, the organisation's external environment should be analysed, because legal, social, technological and other changes can generate training needs. Thus, organisational analysis looks at the organisation as a whole. Its primary purpose is to determine in which parts of the organisation training activities should be conducted (that is, where are they needed?) and could be conducted (that is, where will they be successful?).[92]

- *Task variables*. Nominating job tasks is essential for identifying the employee competencies necessary to perform the job. This analysis helps to identify job performance standards and the knowledge, skills and abilities needed to perform these tasks.
- *Person variables*. Person analysis is concerned with how an employee performs their tasks. Thus, the emphasis is on how well the employee actually demonstrates the knowledge, skills and abilities required by the job. Person analysis answers the question: Who needs training and what kind?[93]

The end product of **training needs analysis** should be a comprehensive set of behavioural objectives that provide direction for the training effort and benchmark the evaluation of training.

Activity phase

Once objectives are set, the next question is how to best achieve these objectives. The **activity phase** involves considering both content and process. Particular issues in designing training and development activities include:

- location — on-the-job versus off-the-job, in-house versus out-of-house
- timing — in-hours versus out-of-hours, session length (that is, spaced versus massed learning)
- presenters — in-house versus external (for example, consultants or academics).

Operational realities will determine what is possible, because organisations are generally reluctant to operate without employees for extended periods of time. Unfortunately, this can prevent optimal training and development decisions.

Process methods

Some major ways of delivering off-the-job training and development are listed below.

Classroom activities

If formal teaching is required, the classroom represents an economically viable way of reaching a mass audience. The classroom may also provide a forum for exchanges of views and experiences among trainees, thus promoting a shared learning environment. A big disadvantage is the loss of individuality in instruction and learning. Figure 9.7 outlines the best room arrangements for training groups of people.

Simulation

In some situations, the costs and risks involved in training on real equipment are unacceptably high. The use of simulators and simulated experience to approximate the real thing provide relevant learning in risk-controlled learning environments.

Forms of **simulation** include the following.

- *Machine simulators*. Facilities designed to replicate the operating environment have been developed to instruct airline pilots, car drivers and money-market dealers. Trainees using these facilities are able to acquire skills in an environment where the consequences of 'getting it wrong' are carefully controlled.
- *Interactive simulation*. Developed from the technology used for flight simulators to train pilots, interactive simulation is a leading-edge technology. The training can be subject-specific (for example, credit management) or general (for example, supervisory skills). Using interactive CD-ROMs, simulations can train both large and small numbers of employees.[94]
- *Part simulations*. These replicate a critical or different portion of the task without providing a complete replication of the operating environment — for example, using pig's feet to teach suturing techniques to medical students.[95]

Training needs analysis Identifies training needs and translates them into training objectives.

Activity phase Concerned with selecting the training methods and learning principles to be employed in a training program.

Simulation A training device designed to reproduce a real-world situation in a risk-controlled learning environment.

Choose the arrangement that best suits the atmosphere you want to create.

	Type	Advantage	Disadvantage
(circle arrangement)	Circle	Allows participants to see each other. Is conducive to expressing ideas and opinions. Allows leader to join circle as an equal.	Creates a 'touchy-feel' tone if there are no tables. Is unwieldy with a large group. May make participants sitting next to the leader feel uncomfortable.
(classroom arrangement)	Classic classroom (participants in rows, with you in front)	Is conducive to imparting information. Is convenient for use of visual aids. Enhances leader's authority. Is more comfortable for taking notes.	Can be associated with school set-up. Feels artificial with a small group. Discourages spontaneity and interaction. May make people at the back feel left out.
(squared-off U arrangement)	Squared-off U (tables like three sides of a square, with you in front)	Allows interaction; squareness sets a more businesslike tone than the circle or semi-circle. Leaves lots of room for you to move around in the middle of the 'U'. Is convenient for use of visual aids.	Can make the room feel empty. Will not work well with more than 20 people.
(semi-circle arrangement)	Semi-circle (with you in front)	Accommodates more people than circle or squared-off 'U'. Lets leader be both authoritative and open to group participation.	Can feel more crowded than a circle or classic classroom.
(square arrangement)	Square (one large table or small ones forming a large one)	Is better than circle for taking notes. Fosters more team spirit than the other options.	May not leave enough elbow room. Can get cluttered with distracting items.

Figure 9.7 Picking the best room arrangement
Source *World Executive's Digest*, November 1992, p. 78.

- *Vestibule training.* Often used in training plant operatives, the vestibule is a separate part of the factory where trainees can develop skills on actual equipment, without the pressures of having to meet production schedules. Once competency has been achieved, trainees are transferred back to the main operation. The rationale of **vestibule training** is that practice and learning will be more effective in an environment created specifically for training.
- *Management training.* Management training and development often require trainees to undergo the demands and pressures of management work by experiencing 'real-life' situations. Techniques include:
  - *Case studies:* these require trainees to use analytical and problem-solving skills to produce workable solutions to real or hypothetical situations. The case method requires participants to listen to and consider others' opinions. As such, according to Niemyer, it is a powerful tool for dealing with discrimination and sexual harassment.[96] Case

Vestibule training Training that takes place away from the production area on equipment that closely resembles the actual equipment used on the job.

studies that are job-related are the most effective in bringing about a transfer of learning.[97] The success of the case study method is heavily reliant on the skills of the trainer in asking probing questions and keeping everyone involved.[98]

– *Incidents:* these are mini case studies requiring the development of a specific response. Unless well written, they can appear superficial and of limited relevance to the actual job. This technique is popular but there is no evidence that the use of incidents actually improves management decision making in the work situation.[99]

– *Role-plays:* **role-plays** are an interactive technique whereby trainees act out a particular role to develop their behavioural skills in interviewing, counselling and negotiating. A disadvantage of role-playing is that it depends on the willingness of the trainees to play the roles and to take the situation seriously.[100]

– *In-basket exercises:* **in-basket exercises** call for the trainee to make decisions (often in writing within a specified time) on the letters, memos and notes typically found in a manager's in-basket or in-tray. These exercises are relatively economical and easy to administer and can be effective if well written and job-related.[101]

– *Gaming:* business games force trainees to make decisions under time and competitive pressures. Thus, they can mirror real life. Computerised formats permit rapid feedback on the consequences of the decisions made. Business games tend to be motivating because they have intrinsic interest and high trainee involvement. Some research suggests that if the games are well designed, there can be considerable **transfer of training** to the job. However, most of the appeal of gaming stems from its face validity and the persuasiveness of its advocates.[102]

– *Adventure training:* **adventure training** or wilderness training presents managers with physical and mental challenges in the hope of teaching them something about themselves and about working with other people.[103] One participant has commented: 'It teaches you to be very confident, to rely on yourself, because you come to know your own limitations. As a team you learn you have an enormous amount of strength — provided everyone's going in the same direction the same thing applies at work.'[104] Nevertheless, there is little hard evidence to suggest that challenges such as abseiling a rock face, crossing rope bridges and bushwalking with colleagues yield any long-term benefits.[105] Apart from being controversial, adventure training can present potential legal and safety pitfalls.[106] A KFC training program, for example, saw 20 employees treated for burns after walking over hot coals.[107] Organisations using adventure training include AMP, ANZ, Kellogg's Australia, Manulife, Westpac and Woolworths.[108]

– *Cookery training:* a recent innovation, cookery training aims to promote communication, cooperation and teamwork. It is claimed that the training involves mentoring, articulating a common goal (and working towards it) and opportunities for conflict resolution.[109] However, there is no research evidence to support these claims.

On-the-job experience

Experience as a basis for learning is central to the concept of employee development. The use of 'real work' in 'real time' as a basis for learning is very attractive because there are no problems with transferring from the learning situation to the job. Much operator and apprenticeship training is done in this way. This approach also has value in non-trade settings, including the development of managers. There are a number of possible methods of on-the-job experience:

• **Coaching** is planned one-to-one instruction. The coach sets a good example of what is to be done, answers questions, provides insight into the manager's interpersonal relations and generally offers counsel and strategic business advice. Coaching takes a work situation and turns it into a learning opportunity. When combined with job rotation, coaching can be a very effective technique of learning by doing.[110]

• **Understudy assignment** is an appointment to gain exposure to some specific knowledge and/or skills. Understudy assignments are frequently used to prepare an employee to fill a particular job. Jobs such as assistant HR officer, assistant to the HR manager and HR trainee often involve an understudy role. The benefits from this type of training depend on the manager's ability to teach effectively via oral communication and behaviour modelling.[111]

Role-plays Training activities in which participants assume the roles of specific people in situations (such as the roles of interviewer and job applicant), act out the event and then review the implications of their behaviour.

In-basket exercises A simulation in which the participant is asked to establish priorities for handling a number of business papers, such as memoranda, reports and telephone messages, that would typically cross a manager's desk.

Transfer of training Relates to the transfer of training to the work situation. The greater the transfer, the more effective the training.

Adventure training Adventure or wilderness training presents managers with physical and mental challenges such as abseiling, canoeing and bushwalking. The aim is to promote self-awareness, confidence and teamwork.

Coaching An on-the-job approach to management development in which the manager is given an opportunity to teach on a one-to-one basis.

Understudy assignment An appointment to gain exposure to some specific knowledge and/or skill.

Mentoring A developmentally oriented relationship between senior and junior colleagues or peers that involves advising, role modelling, sharing contacts and giving general support.

- **Mentoring** involves the creation of a learning relationship, with the mentor (usually a senior manager) acting as a coach and role model. A mentor can be a valuable asset in promoting the employee's career development and helping women understand the culture of male-dominated business organisations. Mentors need to be trained and carefully selected for their interpersonal skills and interest in developing employees.[112]

Practitioner speaks

Claudia Al-Bala'a is Vice-President, Human Resources Asia–Pacific at Starwood Hotels & Resorts Worldwide Inc. Claudia has 17 years experience in the hospitality industry and 14 years experience in human resources.

The power of mentoring in high-potential development

During the last three years Starwood, a new company formed as a result of the merger between ITT Sheraton Hotels, Westin Hotels and Starwood Real Estate, has laid the foundations of its human resource systems by implementing annual performance management, talent review and 360-degree feedback processes. These processes help us to be more effective and efficient with measuring and rewarding performance, giving valuable feedback on a regular basis to all of our associates and identifying our most talented associates. To close the loop, we introduced the High Potential Mentoring Program to motivate and retain our high potentials and to ensure the fast grooming of high potentials for the more senior management positions needed due to our company's aggressive expansion plans.

This formal mentoring program ensures the increased exposure and visibility of participants to senior leadership in the organisation and is an effective way to help mentees to understand more fully, and to learn more comprehensively from, their day-to-day experience in a neutral environment away from the normal performance-driven work setting. It works best when it is a confidential relationship, which gives the mentee the opportunity to speak freely about any concerns they may have.

One of the main success factors of mentoring programs is that both parties, mentees and mentors, receive intensive training on their roles and responsibilities and on the mentoring program itself before participating. Another important aspect in mentoring is the compatibility of mentors and mentees in terms of their personalities, experience and career expectations. In order to make the mentees accountable and responsible we emphasised in our briefing that most of the initiative in the relationship was to come from the high potentials (that is, setting up meetings, defining expectations and outcomes, etc.). The mentees were also involved in the selection process. They were provided with the mentors' profiles and career backgrounds and asked to select the top three mentors of their choice. The matching was done according to their selections.

Now mentees and mentors meet on a monthly basis for a formal two- to three-hour meeting. At the onset of the meeting cycle, each mentor and mentee drew up a mentoring agreement, which specifies the clear expectations of both parties and the ground rules of their relationship. Each meeting is logged by the mentee, who also draws up a short action plan afterwards. The action plans get reviewed at every meeting in order to record progress.

Another strong factor in the mentoring program is the career development action plan for each mentee, which is drawn up at one of the first meetings. This action plan not only ensures that the mentee and mentor can track the mentee's progress, but it also allows the mentee's direct manager and HR to follow up on the mentee's progress after the formal mentoring relationship has come to an end after one year.

Claudia Al-Bala'a

Job rotation Increases task variety by moving employees from one task to another.

- *Job rotation* is designed to give the employee work experience in various parts of the organisation, thus allowing them to acquire skills and knowledge. **Job rotation** can be expensive and may fail if supervisors are not prepared or lack interest. But it is an excellent way of preparing high-potential employees for future general management responsibilities.[113]

- *Project assignments* can provide the trainee with exposure to a range of specialist skills and knowledge. The employee can also develop skills in working with others in a team environment.
- *Small site management* exposes the trainee to a range of management problems in a small operation, independent of headquarters, and can provide valuable general management experience and decision-making responsibility.
- *Secondments*, temporary assignments within the organisation or with an outside organisation, can provide the employee with the opportunity to gain specific skills or differing viewpoints.

NEWSBREAK

Call to train older workers

By Cherelle Murphy

Two leading business lobbies have urged the federal government to do more to boost the skills of older workers to counteract the effect of Australia's ageing population.

The Financial Planning Association said in a submission to a Senate committee that older workers should be able to use parts of their superannuation contributions to fund retraining.

'We believe there is scope to give older Australians access to part of their voluntary contributions in a lump sum to specifically fund up-skilling', the submission said.

The association said that when older workers were made redundant, they often had no government or corporate assistance to help them get back in the workforce.

The Australian Chamber of Commerce and Industry also called on the federal government to introduce a 'learning bonus' to encourage up-skilling of the workforce as the population ages.

The bonus would be paid to employers whose existing employees undertake formal retraining in a similar way that payments are made to employers who take on young apprentices.

'When the government came in, they made some sensible decisions about the budget and cut a lot of training programs, but we think they need to revisit something like the learning bonus', ACCI chief executive Peter Hendy said.

Older workers are often discriminated against when it comes to training, and Australia's workplace culture often prevents older workers from showing an interest in re-training.

But this is a practice that Australia cannot afford as the workforce ages, according to Mr Hendy. 'We need to encourage mature age workers to take the training', he said.

The average age of the Australian worker is increasing. That's a problem because as older people leave the workforce, fewer young people are left to pay taxes.

Economic forecaster Access Economics predicts the working age population, which grows by around 170 000 people a year, will grow by just 125 000 for the entire decade of the 2020s.

The Prime Minister, John Howard, told *The Australian Financial Review*, participation among older workers was a major issue for the government's third term.

Source *Australian Financial Review*, 9 May 2003, p. 11.

- **Behaviour modelling**, or observational learning, is how people learn from others' experience. It takes place in two steps: acquisition and performance. First, the employee observes the actions of others and acquires a mental picture of the act and its consequences. Second, the employee performs the observed act. If the consequences of imitating the model are rewarding, the trainee is likely to act that way again.[114] Thus, by the relatively simple approach of imitation, interpersonal skills can be developed and retained. Trainers at IBM and General Electric have found that supervisory, sales and customer relations skills are learned faster and more effectively when taught from a modelling base.[115] Following are the basic steps in behaviour modelling:

Behaviour modelling The process of learning from other people's experience by simulating (copying) their behaviour.

– Provide trainees with suitable models by videotape or film. The models should demonstrate effective approaches in handling 'real-world' problems.
– Allow trainees to rehearse and practise the behaviours they have seen demonstrated by models. Use repetition until high levels of skill are evidenced.
– Systematically reinforce trainees by allowing them to see whether their behaviour approximates that of the model. Use videotaping to provide feedback to trainees; this provides reinforcement by demonstrating progress towards skills acquisition.
– Develop mechanisms to encourage transfer of skills to the job. This involves practice and reinforcement until the desired behaviour emerges as reflex. Overall, behaviour modelling that uses the power of imitation has been shown to be an important process by which people learn new behaviours and/or modify the probabilities of using known behaviours.[116]

Action learning

Action learning is based on learning by experience. It differs from traditional management training in several respects. The material of action learning is not books or written cases but actual organisational problems (which are less easily predicted or solved than classroom problems). The technique 'is based on the straightforward pedagogical notion that people learn most effectively when working on real time problems occurring in their own work setting'.[117] Trainees are formed into a small group and asked to work on a defined project taken from their own organisation. Each trainee, with the help of a group adviser, undertakes research and develops a solution that can be implemented in the workplace. Group members share experiences and support each other. Action learning tries to create the conditions in which managers learn from their own experience in solving a real-life problem. Thus, problem solving and personal development become equal parts of the same learning process. 'Action learning', says Brearley, 'is based on the principles that adults learn but when they want to learn, when they have to face up to problems and when learning is a co-operative and social process and that a lot of learning involves the restructuring of what is already known rather than the acquisition of new knowledge.'[118] Organisations employing action learning include IBM, Lend Lease and National Australia Bank.[119]

Competency-based training

Competencies are the demonstrable and assessable skills that distinguish effective from ineffective job performance. In other words, they are things that employees need to do to be productive. CBT is a skills approach to employee development. Its focus is on performing specific tasks to a predetermined standard. Advocates argue that CBT 'has the potential to enhance managerial performance, and ultimately lift international competitiveness in Australia'.[120] CBT involves the following steps:

1. Capability profiling:
   • Identify the competencies needed in the job.
   • Rank the importance of the competencies.
   • Evaluate the job holder against the competencies standards.
   • Identify strengths and areas needing remedial attention.
2. Select training programs or other learning events (either on or off the job) that can develop the desired skills.
3. Produce a personal training plan for each employee.
4. Assess the competency.[121]

Some writers have expanded the concept to include knowledge and attitudes in an effort to define managerial effectiveness and to use competence assessment in recruitment, selection, performance appraisal and succession planning.[122] Objections to this trend are numerous. Concerns include: the possibility that competencies will become a list of traits; the inability to define a universal list of management competencies; the lack of validity in equating competence with performance; restriction on innovative thinking; the fostering of dependence on prescribed procedures; and the fact that it has not been shown to be more objective than other methods of assessment.[123] Regardless, the former Labor government had competency standards as a key element in its training reform agenda and some organisations are trying to develop relevant competency profiles to identify and train managers.[124]

This Letter to the Editor provides a provocative viewpoint. Do you agree? See 'What's your view?' on page 361.

Letter to the Editor

It's time to explode training myths

Dear Editor,

I have often thought that managers place too much blind trust in training. This attitude has spawned a worldwide, multibillion-dollar industry. In fact, training has become a corporate religion, complete with a liturgy, high priests and rituals. Yet, if one asks the average manager what return on investment is expected from the corporate training budget, all you'll get is a blank stare.

There is a myth, then, that training somehow is 'good' and need not be subject to the same financial controls as other expenditures. As this mythology permeates most corporate cultures, some of my colleagues are suggesting that up to 70 per cent of all training expenditures are wasted! In any other area, that sort of wastage would cause heads to roll, but trainers just keep going on and on and on!

One problem is the myth that training has a direct effect on productivity — except for basic (and necessary!) on-the-job training, this rarely is the case. Productivity improvement stems from a far more complex process, the application of the social sciences and the physical sciences to a business problem. Training is only one factor in this multidisciplinary combination.

For training to be effective, we must first separate symptoms from 'trainable' problems. Stress management training, for example, rarely works, because stress is a symptom of some characteristic in the work environment. Unless the stressor is addressed first, then employees go back into the same culture, with the same stress load and soon forget everything they learned on the course. Similarly, training needs to 'fit' into the culture. Try applying the latest management technique you learned on that last course and you will be greeted with amused stares and told 'that won't work here'. Of course not! You are trying to change a culture without all the lengthy preparation required to transform an organisation.

In my view, organisations should rarely have a training budget. They should have a productivity improvement budget of which training is a part. Trainers should work closely with line managers, solving their problems and improving their operations. Of course, then there wouldn't be any need for trainers, only for 'productivity improvement specialists', so an entire profession could be obsolete. So be it! It's time to move on. Let's stop wasting money in support of the training myth and concentrate on what really counts — increasing productivity in some measurable way.

A frustrated trainer

Source Dr Philip Wright, Professor, School of Business, Shu Yan College, Hong Kong.

Training within industry

Developed in the United States during World War II, training-within-industry (TWI) programs aim to improve productivity by developing the skills of first-line supervisors. The programs have wide adoption in many countries but particularly Japan. In fact, a number of Japanese management practices such as *Kaizen* (continuous improvement) trace their roots to the training-within-industry technique. The programs are distinctive, according to Robinson and Schroeder, not because they cover accepted principles of good management, but because they are successful in getting them used.[125]

Training-within-industry programs create a multiplier effect by using a standard method in which employees are trained; these employees, in turn, train others to use the method. To guarantee a program's effectiveness, each course is rigorously field tested before it is released. In addition, stringent quality control is demanded through instructor training, ongoing practice and strict adherence to set lesson outlines. The aim is to improve supervisory skills via three core programs — job instruction training, job methods training and job relations training. *Job instruction training* teaches supervisors the importance of training and how to be an effective instructor. *Job methods training* focuses on how to generate and implement ideas for methods improvement. Finally, *job relations training* promotes better supervisor–worker relations.

All programs are structured in the same way: five two-hour sessions made up of 10 to 12 employees who are expected to learn by doing. Although developed 50 years ago, the skills in instruction, method improvement and leadership needed by supervisors have changed relatively little.[126] Japan's success with TWI suggests that Australian industry could also benefit.

Corporate universities

Organisations that are serious about employee training and development are increasingly partnering with academic institutions to gain a competitive edge.[127] Intercontinental Hotels and Southern Cross University, for example, have joined together to form The Hotel School at Intercontinental Sydney to provide certificate, diploma and degree study in hotel management.[128] Other major organisations with corporate universities include BHP Billiton, Coles Myer, Ford and Qantas.[129] Corporate universities enable companies to ensure that the teachers are first class and that all employees receive the same message and learn a common vocabulary.[130] As one academic points out: 'It's just common sense that when you have a specialized degree program, which focuses on improving those specific skills that people use at work, you're going to end up with higher skilled workers who are well trained to do that particular job much more efficiently and to the best of their ability.'[131] Furthermore, corporate universities recognise that training and development are not just a nice thing for employees to do but are 'a strategic resource that corporations must use to specifically move forward into the next century'.[132] Corporate universities in the United States are at the forefront of learning innovations and are rapidly increasing in number (there were more than 1600 in 1999).[133] According to the President of Motorola University, 'We figure if we can out-learn our competitors we can beat them every time'.[134]

Training technologies

Programmed instruction

Programmed instruction employs the principles of reinforcement theory. Material to be learned (generally factual information) is broken down into a series of developmental steps. Initially the content is easy, but gradually it becomes more difficult. A correct answer allows the trainee to advance to new and/or more complex material. If a trainee's answer is incorrect, the step is repeated. Programmed instruction material may be presented in a written format or via a computerised program. However, the advantages of self-teaching, portability and sound application of learning principles (active participation, immediate and continuous feedback, and positive reinforcement) are offset by the high cost of program development.[135]

Computer-based training

Developments in personal and microcomputing have enabled the widespread use of computers as a learning vehicle. The memory and storage capabilities of computers, along with extensive software developments, make it possible to provide interactive drills, problem solving, simulations and gaming. Instructional staff are used only as reference points with the emphasis being on self-managed learning. Both programmed instruction and **computer-based training** generate high levels of activity from the learner, and allow trainees to work through the material at their own pace. Examples of computer-based training include the teaching of computer literacy skills, typing skills and the training of flight crews.[136]

Audiovisual

Closed-circuit television and videotape-recording equipment have become popular as training resources (especially in skills training). Videotape permits comprehensive and objective feedback, which is important in behavioural training. The portability of videocassettes allows their use in remote locations and ensures standardisation of presentation. Videotape has made large inroads into the market of training films because it is easy to use. McDonald's, for example, regards videotape explanation and instruction as its most effective training tool. Federal Express uses interactive video to help employees to study their jobs, company policies and procedures, and customer service issues.[137]

Multimedia training[138]

Multimedia training combines computer-based and audiovisual training technologies to activate all the learning senses. Text, graphics, animation, audio and video become integrated. Programs are delivered via the Internet or intranet, allowing 24-hour-a-day unlimited accessibility from anywhere. Because computers can simulate situations where skills, knowledge or behaviours can be practised (and tested), training is given a 'real-life' feel. This means that learning time is reduced and learner retention, motivation and interaction are improved.[139] Other advantages of multimedia training include immediate feedback and guidance, and consistency of content and delivery, which enables trainees to track their progress, test themselves and certify their mastery. Major disadvantages of multimedia training are high development costs (limiting it to large companies), the expense and time needed to update programs and the dislike of technology by some learners. Finally, although holding much promise, there is still debate regarding the superiority of multimedia training compared with the more traditional training methods.

Multimedia training Training that combines audiovisual training methods with computer-based training.

Web-based training

Web-based training refers to training that is delivered on public or private computer networks and is displayed by a web browser. Intranet-based training refers to training delivered by a company's own computer network. Internet- and intranet-based training use similar technologies. The major difference is that intranet training is restricted to a company's employees. Internet and intranet training cover simple communication, online referencing and actual delivery of training and storage of the organisation's intellectual capital or knowledge. Internet and intranet training have similar advantages to multimedia training.[140] The disadvantages of web-based training include bandwidth and virus problems, the need to control and bill users, and the difficulties (and costs) of writing (and revising) training programs. A recent US study found that while online teaching can be highly effective, the costs in developing and supporting web-based training programs may be higher than those involved with face-to-face learning.[141] Finally, while viewed as being good for technical training and transferring information, web-based training is seen as inappropriate for 'soft' skills such as interpersonal relations and teaching people to think strategically.[142] Companies using web-based learning include Cathay Pacific, Cisco, Motorola, PricewaterhouseCoopers and Sun Microsystems. At Home Depot, one of the largest retailers in the United States, a cashier can fix a jammed cash register tape by watching a 20-second training video downloaded directly to a screen on the cash register.[143]

Web-based training Refers to training that is delivered via the Internet.

Online university courses have given rise to concerns regarding educational quality, academic standards, high drop-out rates, boring programs and copyright. In the United States, there are already 13 web sites that post lecture notes taken by students.[144] Nevertheless, in the United States there are now three million students studying for cyber degrees (US colleges and universities offer more than 6000 accredited courses on the Web), and the online University of Phoenix, Arizona is now the largest university in the world.[145] ANZ provides its managers with university-accredited online degrees via its intranet.[146] In Asia, it is estimated that the accredited postgraduate education market amenable to online delivery is worth between US$5 and $10 billion per year.[147] For example, in China fewer than 5 per cent of people have college degrees (compared with 26 per cent in the United States). To reach US levels, it is estimated that China would have to build at least 400 000 new universities.[148]

Evaluation phase

Training and development, if they are to be justified, must contribute to the achievement of the organisation's objectives. Unfortunately, many HR managers do not include an **evaluation phase** as part of the training and development activities within their organisation.[149] Those who do undertake evaluation tend to measure program popularity (which is often a measure of entertainment, not of the transfer of learning).[150] The problem, according to Ramlall, is that HR practitioners are not trained in assessment and research methodologies and are thus inclined to use 'happy sheet' evaluations[151] (see figure 9.8).

Evaluation phase Concerned with measuring how well a training activity met its objectives.

Management will believe that the money spent on training and development is worthwhile only if the programs help improve employee performance and have profit impact. If training and development add measurable value, management will regard them as being as essential to the organisation's success as are finance, marketing or production; if not, they will be viewed as an overhead expense waiting to be cut.[152] To date, the evidence suggests that there is minimal organisational value derived from much management training and development, despite training practices being shown to have a significant effect on organisational performance.[153] As a consequence, management often views training and development initiatives as ineffective.[154] It is therefore critical that HR managers be able to assess and communicate the benefits of all HRD interventions.[155]

Measures of training effectiveness

To evaluate training, it is necessary to compare the intended outcome with measurements of actual achievement and to analyse and explain any variances. Kirkpatrick suggests four ways to measure the effectiveness of training:[156]

- *Reactions:* these can be measured during or at the end of the training activity. Reactions can be based on impressions, opinions and attitudes, and they identify how much the participants liked the program, including its content, the trainer, the methods used and the surroundings in which the training took place.[157] As a result, such questionnaires are referred to as 'happy sheets'. Reactions, it must be stressed, are not hard evidence of learning or performance improvement.

TRAINING PROGRAM EVALUATION

The following form is designed to help you to evaluate the content of the training program. On this evaluation, we're concerned with getting your feedback on how well the program was prepared and presented.

Directions: Rate each of the following program elements on a scale of 1 to 5.

1. PROGRAM OBJECTIVES
How clear were the program's learning objectives?

1	2	3	4	5
Unclear		Fairly clear		Very clear

2. PROGRAM RELEVANCE
How relevant to your job was the material taught?

1	2	3	4	5
Totally irrelevant		Somewhat relevant		Highly relevant

3. INSTRUCTIONAL DESIGN
Were the learning activities designed to lead from the simple to the more complex?

1	2	3	4	5
Never		Usually		Always

4. TRAINING TECHNIQUES
How appropriate were the training techniques employed?

1	2	3	4	5
Inappropriate		Generally appropriate		Very appropriate

5. PROGRAM LEADER'S KNOWLEDGE
How well did the seminar leader know the material?

1	2	3	4	5
Minimally		Satisfactorily		Expertly

Figure 9.8 A sample program evaluation or 'happy sheet'

6. PROGRAM LEADER'S INSTRUCTIONAL ABILITY

Apart from the leader's knowledge of the subject, how about their ability to impart understanding?

1	2	3	4	5
Poor		Satisfactory		Excellent

7. PARTICIPANT INTEREST

How much interest did the program generate?

1	2	3	4	5
None		Some		A great deal

8. TRAINING VALUE

What value will this program be to you in your job?

1	2	3	4	5
Useless		Somewhat helpful		Highly valuable

9. FACILITIES

How would you rate the facilities?

1	2	3	4	5
Unsatisfactory		Satisfactory		Excellent

10. CATERING

How would you rate the catering arrangements?

1	2	3	4	5
Unsatisfactory		Satisfactory		Excellent

11. OVERALL

How would you rate the program?

1	2	3	4	5
Unsatisfactory		Satisfactory		Excellent

GENERAL COMMENTS

1. What I liked most about this program _____

_____

2. What I liked least about this program _____

_____

3. Other comments _____

_____

Figure 9.8 A sample program evaluation or 'happy sheet'

Source Asia Pacific Management Co. Ltd, 2004

- *Learning:* this can also be measured during or at the end of the training activity. Special or standardised tests (for example, typing tests) are used to measure how well the trainees have learned a particular skill or piece of know-how — that is, did the participants actually learn what the instructor taught them?

- *Behaviour:* this measurement involves identifying changes in job behaviours, interpersonal relationships, and so on that can be attributed to the training activity. It is actually about examining transfer of training — have participants improved their on-the-job performance as a result of the training? Evidence can be obtained from direct observation, from the comments of supervisors and colleagues and from performance appraisals.
- *Results:* this measures the effects of training on the achievement of the organisation's objectives. It provides the HR manager with a cost–benefit analysis of the training effort. 'Hard data' reports, giving information on productivity, sales, quality, absenteeism costs, and so on before and after training are used to determine the bottom-line impact of the training activity.

A recent innovation has been the use of return on investment (ROI) in training. This adds a fifth level to the four-level model developed by Kirkpatrick. Basically, the ROI question is whether the monetary value of the results exceeds the cost of the program.[158]

Figures 9.9 and 9.10 illustrate various techniques used to evaluate training and development.

A number of firms now use **benchmarking**, identifying the training policies, practices and programs of organisations recognised as excelling in the training and development area (for example, costs, training staff/employee ratios, types of delivery systems, and so on).

Benchmarking The identification of best practices among competitors and non-competitors that make them superior performers.

MEASURES	INDICATORS	HOW MEASURED
Reactions	• Satisfaction • Enjoyment	• Questionnaire • Interviews • Focus groups
Learning	• Knowledge (e.g. OH&S regulations, EEO requirements) • Skill (e.g. computer program or machine operation)	• Pencil and paper test • Oral examination • Work sample • Observation of performance • Performance ratings
Behaviour	• Changes in attitudes, behaviour, motivation	• Observation of performance • Performance ratings • Third-party feedback (e.g. customer feedback)
Results	• Productivity • Sales • Quality • Absenteeism • Labour turnover • Accident frequency	• Production statistics • Sales statistics • HR statistics • OH&S statistics
Return on investment	• Dollar value	• Cost–benefit analysis

Figure 9.9 Measures of training effectiveness
Source Asia Pacific Management Co. Ltd, 2004.

GROUP		EVALUATION	
Number	**Type**	**Timing**	**Comparison**
One	Trained	After training	None
One	Trained	Before training After training	Before and after training scores
Two	Trained Untrained	After training	Scores of trained and untrained groups
Two	Trained Untrained	Before training After training	Scores of trained and untrained groups before and after training

Figure 9.10 Methods of training evaluation

Source Adapted by the author from A. R. Montebella and M. Haga, 'To justify training, test again', *Personnel Journal*, January 1994, p. 85.

Orientation

Employee **orientation** or induction, although often forgotten, is a key part of the training and development process.[159] It is the systematic introduction of new employees to their job, colleagues and the organisation. New employees have particular training and development needs: they need to learn about the organisation and its culture, learn how to do their jobs and be introduced to workmates. The focus on specific job skills permits new employees to improve their performance and thus feel a sense of achievement. The organisation, in turn, has a need to accelerate the employees' integration and make them operationally competent.[160]

Orientation The introduction of new employees to their job, their colleagues and the organisation.

The benefits of employee orientation

Researchers have found that formal orientation can achieve significant cost savings by reducing the anxieties of new employees and by fostering positive attitudes, job satisfaction and a sense of commitment at the start of the employment relationship.[161] Thus, orientation reduces the likelihood of new employees quitting before they feel bonded to the organisation. Most labour turnover (particularly at operator levels) occurs in the first six months of employment, so helping new employees to feel part of the organisation can reduce labour turnover costs and improve organisational profitability and competitiveness.[162]

However, orientation per se is not necessarily beneficial. The programs must be well planned, conducted and evaluated. The HR manager should remember that orientation is likely to be more successful if it is done over a period of time so the new employee is not overloaded with information, it involves a combination of learning styles and it begins immediately.[163]

Orientation program content

The content of the orientation program should be clearly laid out and comprehensive in its coverage. A checklist is often used to ensure coverage of all important points about the organisation (history, philosophies, HR policies, products and services, and so on) and about the job (duties and responsibilities, safety requirements, and so on) (see figures 9.11 and 9.12). The content must provide essential information on the employment relationship, build identification with the organisation and establish high performance expectations.[164]

WHAT NEW EMPLOYEES WANT TO KNOW

- What is really expected of me?
- How do I gain acceptance around here?
- How do I get ahead in this company?
- How do I get rewarded for a good job?
- What is the boss really like?
- I know the policies and procedures, but what are the real rules of the game?
- How do I fit into the total picture here?
- Just how much security do I have?
- What in the devil does this company really do?

Figure 9.11 What new employees want to know

Source A. M. Starcke, 'Building a better orientation program', *HR Magazine*, November 1996, p. 113.

The timing of orientation

Ideally, planned orientation activities should commence as soon as the new employee joins the organisation. One early study found that the impressions formed by new employees within their first 60 to 90 days are lasting, with the first day being particularly crucial.[165] If not planned, there is a risk that new employees will learn about the organisation and their job from someone who may be untrained, ill informed or dissatisfied. Such erroneous information can quickly lead to frustration, poor performance and the development of a negative attitude towards the organisation.

Formal orientation programs

If the numbers permit, it is worthwhile having a formal orientation program in which new employees can participate. Such programs can include presentations from senior management (ideally giving a clear picture of the CEO's vision for the organisation), public relations materials such as corporate videos, and presentations from recent entrants about their experiences working in the organisation. Major benefits of this approach are the sharing of experiences, the reduction of individual anxiety, the opportunity to raise matters of concern and the representation of the organisation's 'human face' by personal contact with senior managers.

Informal orientation

Some organisations prefer a less formal approach to employee orientation, believing it makes for a more relaxed and personalised introduction to colleagues, the job and the organisation. This approach often uses mentors or sponsors who act as advisers and role models for the new employee. Such mentors are extremely important because they impart organisational culture through dress, associations and actions, as well as by what they say.

Orientation packages

It can be expensive and difficult to conduct orientations in large organisations with many operating locations. To overcome these problems and to provide a standard induction program, self-administered induction materials are often used. These include CD's, videotapes and audiocassettes, workbooks, booklets and brochures.

ORIENTATION CHECKLIST

Name:
Position:
Supervisor:

Starting date:
Department:
Mentor:
Reviewed:
By: Date:

Company overview
History
Products and services
Key personnel
Values, mission and strategic business objectives

Health and safety
Medical examination
First aid
Safety and accident prevention
Safety equipment and clothing
Sexual harassment
Smoking
Substance abuse
Workplace violence

Employee relations
Terms and conditions of employment
Probationary period
Mentor
Performance appraisal
Absenteeism
Lateness
Sickness
Grievance procedures
Union membership

Discipline
Email, Internet and telephone use
Termination of employment
Dress code
Equal employment
Employee privacy
Employee survey
Gambling
Theft
Electronic surveillance
Security
Training and development

Job description
Responsibilities
Performance expectations
Performance evaluation
Reporting relationships
Assistance available

Compensation
Pay
Overtime
Shift pay
Holiday pay
Pay reviews
Facilities

Benefits
Medical insurance
Life insurance
Disability insurance
Workers compensation
Holidays
Special leave
Superannuation
Share purchase scheme
Social club
Cafeteria
Car park
Tuition refund scheme
Counselling service

Location tour
Rest rooms
Cafeteria
Car parking
First aid
Supplies and equipment
Workplace

Introductions
Mentor
Union representative
Human resource representative
Social club secretary
Fellow employees
Key managers

I have received the information and participated in the activities checked above. I understand my employment duties and the conditions of my employment.

Employee: _____   Date: _____

Supervisor: _____   Date: _____

Figure 9.12 Subjects to cover at orientation

Follow-up

Follow-up interviews with new employees are an essential part of a well-planned orientation program. Interviews with the employee's supervisor and a representative of the HR department ensure that any unanswered questions and misunderstandings are clarified. Such interviews also provide a good basis on which to evaluate the effectiveness of the orientation program.

Supervisory and management training

Employees do not automatically have the competencies necessary for the effective performance of supervisory and management roles. The competencies that lead to success as an operator may have little relevance when an employee is promoted from a 'doing' role to a 'delegating to get things done' role. Supervisory appointments are seen as the first step on the management hierarchy. As a first-line manager, the supervisor requires basic skills in planning, leading, organising and controlling. The skills and competencies required by middle managers also include an understanding of organisational behaviour and functional know-how in areas such as finance, marketing or production. It is increasingly important for senior managers to have a focus on strategy, the management of change and global competitiveness. Figure 9.13 outlines how Siemens develops its managers.

SIEMENS

Telecommunications multinational Siemens employs 450 000 people in more than 190 countries. Siemens Management Learning is run as a global program aligned to regional demands. The main objective of the program, says regional learning manager Robyn Williamson, is to develop transformational leaders who can function at both operational and strategic levels, to better service a global market. SML covers a suite of programs for target groups ranging from employees with high potential (usually recent graduates) to senior executives. Content ranges from self-management and teamwork at entry level, up through soft skills in management capabilities, entrepreneurial thinking and turnaround management, to structuring of implementation of corporate issues at the most senior level. Entry-level courses are taught locally, while more senior programs are run regionally/globally. Potential candidates are identified through staff dialogues with HR and line managers, and each course runs for around 12 months. Programs are structured around face-to-face workshops, business-driven action learning and e-learning/e-collaboration.

Figure 9.13 How Siemens develops its managers
Source F. Cameron, 'Pick of the bunch', *HR Monthly*, October 2002, p. 18.

In practice, many employees move up the management hierarchy without the benefit of a systematic preparation. 'While Australian managers are practical', says Milton-Smith, 'they are poorly educated with only 30 per cent having degrees compared with 80 per cent in the USA and Japan.'[166] This low level of formal education may help explain the poor training and development record of Australian organisations and the fact that our major customers rate Australian managers as inferior to managers from Japan, the United States, Germany and Britain.[167] Similarly, a study conducted by the Department of Foreign Affairs and Trade concluded that Asians see Australian businesspeople as naive and lacking in both self-esteem and international experience.[168] McKinsey and Co. also concluded that low aspirations by Australian managers produce a lack of innovation and failure to develop long-term skills.[169] Moreover, some employees appear to resist undertaking further training and development because they are costly and inconvenient and infringe on personal time.[170] Unlike Asia, Australia seems to be a country where it is 'cool to be a fool'.[171] According to some experts, Australia has 'not provided an education in the talents, toils and street wisdom necessary to prosper in a global labour market where there are now hundreds of millions of minds bustling to seize all available opportunities'.[172]

It is also questionable whether the Australian emphasis on self-training is appropriate for today's managers. An emerging development route favoured by CEOs is to pursue formal qualifications alongside challenging job experiences, together with short courses throughout the manager's career. SmithKline Beecham Corporation, for example, requires its best people to gain experience in two business units, two functional areas (for example, finance and marketing) and two countries.[173]

Psychological principles of learning

The psychology of learning provides some important principles for HR managers concerned with delivering effective training.

Pre-conditions for learning

The trainability of employees is an important preliminary consideration. A function of ability and motivation, it affects the selection of process methods and training technologies. Group processes, for example, reduce the effectiveness of individual training but promote the sharing of experiences. The desire to learn involves motivation. If a training program helps an employee to satisfy their needs, then learning will take place. Showing trainees 'what is in it for them' is critical.

The best situation is one where people learn because they want to learn. Curiosity, achievement and enhanced self-esteem all create internal motivation. The HR manager must also consider trainee attitudes and expectations because these can support or inhibit learning and influence the overall reaction to the training program.[174]

Core concepts in learning

- *Relevance:* learning is enhanced when trainees can see that training is relevant and capable of implementation. Thus, the presentation of material should be made as meaningful as possible. This can be done by relating training material directly to the trainee's work environment.
- *Reinforcement:* strengthening of behaviour is called **reinforcement**. It occurs in learning when a reward follows the behaviour. To increase the probability that the behaviour will be repeated the reward must be seen as a consequence of the behaviour. Rewards can be tangible or psychological. A trainer's approval or congratulations, for example, may have reinforcing value. Similarly, if an employee can solve a problem by using a particular process, there is increased probability that they will use the process again. The timing of the reinforcement is important. Generally, the reward is most effective if it immediately follows the behaviour. The effectiveness of the reinforcement also depends on the trainee's personality. What is a powerful reinforcer to one trainee may have no impact on another. Behaviour modelling and behaviour modification both depend on the reinforcement of desired behaviour to change behaviour.
- *Transfer of training:* if employees cannot transfer their training to the work situation, the training effort may have been wasted. Obviously, the greater the gap between the training situation and the job, the greater the possibility of transfer loss. Given its relevance, **on-the-job training** has the advantage of avoiding transfer problems. Factors that reduce transfer include the employee not being able to remember all the training information and not having an opportunity to use the new skills and knowledge. Action planning is used to facilitate transfer. It acts as a link by requiring trainees to develop a detailed strategy

Reinforcement The strengthening of a behaviour through the use of rewards and punishments.

On-the-job training Employment training that takes place at the job site and tends to be directly related to the job.

for applying their training on return to the workplace. Typically, the plan includes checkpoints for evaluating their progress.

- *Knowledge of results:* improved performance depends on trainees being made aware of their present performance standard. This feedback enables them to establish the size of the learning task. For example, a trainee who knows his current production is five widgets, against 10 for a fully competent operator, can clearly understand the skill development yet to be achieved. Obviously, it is easier to comprehend training needs when the size of the learning task can be quantified. Some skills such as customer relations are not easily quantifiable and thus are more difficult to assess. The feedback element is also important. This shows the trainee where their performance is satisfactory or requires improvement. Without feedback there is no basis for a change in behaviour. But a trainee is likely to improve performance if told of their deficiencies and shown how to overcome them.

- *Distribution of learning:* **distribution of learning** relates to the scheduling of training activities. Trainee concentration and ability to 'digest' material are important variables in determining the most appropriate training format. When selecting training formats, the HR manager needs to consider trainee time off the job, content divisibility, practice needs and material complexity. Spacing out training usually produces more rapid learning and better retention. However, spacing can mean extra time costs because it is necessary to link sessions, recapitulate, and provide a warm-up and icebreaker in each session.[175]

- *Whole versus part learning:* sometimes, the learning of a task will require the mastery of the parts to comprehend the whole. Given this need to focus on the relevant 'building blocks' or competencies at each stage, the capacity to break things into component parts is important. One popular approach is to give the trainee a brief overview of the job as a whole, then break it into building blocks for detailed instruction.[176]

- *Practice and learning:* there is a direct relationship between skills acquisition and practice, in the same way that lack of practice leads to skill diminution. The 'hands-on' aspect is vital to the acquisition of skills and is a central concept in adult learning. Repetition (or practice) helps the trainee reach a level of performance where the skill is instinctive or reflexive in practice. Unfortunately, one consequence of practice is boredom, which can reduce the trainee's enthusiasm for learning. Thus, the use of variety in practice obviously makes for more effective training.[177]

- *Activity versus passivity:* a feature of adult learning is the emphasis it places on 'learning by doing'. Thus, it is important to design training activities that are trainee-centred in terms of activity, simulation and variety. People learn better when more senses are involved, so training material should require the use of as many senses as possible. Experiential exercises and action learning recognise the value of structured activity as a learning tool. Also, in tertiary education, the small group tutorial with its significant opportunity for activity can compensate for the passive, one-way communication style of lectures.[178]

- *Learning styles:* everyone has a unique learning style that emphasises some learning abilities over others. Wolfe and Kolb have said that 'some people develop minds that excel at assimilating disparate facts into coherent theories, yet these same people are incapable of, or uninterested in, deducting hypotheses from the theory. Others are logical geniuses but find it impossible to involve and surrender themselves to an experience'.[179] One instrument that measures differences in learning style is the Learning Style Inventory. It measures an individual's relative emphasis on the four learning abilities — concrete experience, reflective observation, abstract conceptualisation and active experimentation.[180] The concept of learning styles can also be applied to groups. This permits the trainer to identify the best way of addressing learning situations in terms of group composition.

Learner-centred learning

Adults learn differently from children. They bring with them a wealth of untapped resources via their life experiences. Thus, they require a less-controlled, trainer-directed approach to learning. Malcolm Knowles, the father of andragogy (the art and science of helping adults learn), has defined the most important assumptions about adults as learners:

1. *The need to know.* According to Knowles, adults learn more effectively if they understand why they need to know or be able to do something. Trainers should demonstrate how a program will help adult participants in their job or career development. The more directly adults can experience or see the benefits, the more motivated they will be to learn.[181]

2. *The need to be self-directing.* Adults have a psychological need to take responsibility for their own lives. Adults need to be self-directing rather than dependent learners. Knowles says that when adult trainees 'take some responsibility in the learning process they learn more, retain what they learn longer and learn more efficiently'.[182] Trainers are advised to involve employees in planning and directing their learning activities.[183]

3. *Greater volume and quality of experience.* 'Adults, by virtue of having lived longer, accumulate a greater volume and different quality of experience than children.'[184] Says Knowles, adults have done more things, have worked, been married, had children and had the responsibilities of being an adult citizen. This means that adults as a group will have very varied backgrounds. Consequently, training needs to be tailored to account for individual differences. Because adults have more experience, they provide the trainer with a rich source of learning on which to draw. This is why an emphasis on experiential techniques such as group discussions, problem-solving exercises, and so on — techniques that tap into the experiences of the trainee — are recommended.[185]

4. *Readiness to learn.* Training opportunities that are timed to coincide with the trainees' readiness to learn are more likely to be effective. Trainers should not force employees to attend training programs for which they are not ready.[186]

5. *Orientation to learning.* Compared with children who have been conditioned to have a subject-centred orientation to learning, adults have a life-centred, task-centred or problem-centred orientation. This has a major implication for the trainer in designing a training program. A trainer in a computer skills course, for example, should not

emphasise technical details but, instead, should organise the learning around life tasks such as how to write a letter or a report.[187]

The learning curve

Learning curve A graphical representation of the rate at which a person learns something over time.

The rate of learning does not necessarily proceed at a constant pace. One method for demonstrating the cumulative change in a measurable behaviour is the use of a **learning curve**, which reflects performance over time (see figure 9.14). Many learning situations have periods in which progress does not occur. These periods, represented horizontally on the learning curve, are called plateaus. The plateau may be caused by fatigue, diminished motivation, ineffective learning methods or a mindset of having reached the optimum performance level. Advancement from the performance plateau requires an understanding of the cause so that it can be eliminated. The form and length of learning curves vary considerably. Learning curves are frequently used in operator training because the easy quantification of performance outcomes makes it relatively simple to measure skills acquisition.[188]

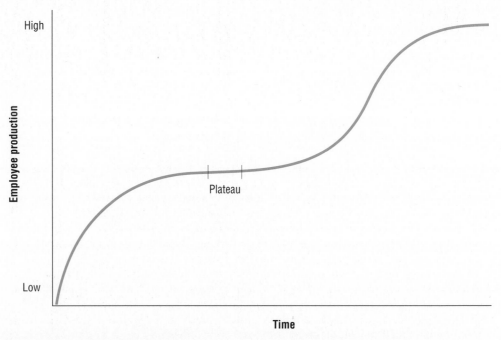

Figure 9.14 A typical learning curve

Summary

Thirty interactive Wiley Web Questions are available to test your understanding of this chapter at **www.johnwiley.com.au/ highered/hrm5e** *in the student resources area*

Accelerating rates of change and global competition have meant that HRD has become an important organisational and national issue. HRD is now recognised as critical to competitive success. It is not simply a desirable HRM activity but a powerful contributor to the achievement of the organisation's strategic business objectives. It involves employee training and development and the exploitation of knowledge. Learning organisations that focus on the acquisition, sharing and utilisation of knowledge give HRD top priority.

Training starts when an employee enters the organisation. The need to orientate employees and generate a feeling of belonging is critical to avoiding problems of incorrect job instruction, labour turnover and reduced morale. To improve performance and avoid employee obsolescence, the employee should undergo further training and development. Training and development activities reflect the capacity for people to grow and change.

A systematic approach to training and development involves assessing needs, selecting training methods and evaluating their effectiveness. Evaluation is necessary to ensure that training is contributing to the success of the business. Funds should be allocated to training and development activities only when the HR manager has assessed the expected returns. It is useful for the HR manager to understand and implement the principles of learning when planning, conducting and evaluating training and development programs and ensuring their success.

student study guide

review questions

1. Describe a training course that you have undertaken. Have you been able to apply what you learned? Why or why not?
2. In your own words, describe the term knowledge management. Why is it so important for organisations to manage knowledge?
3. What are the key features of a learning organisation? Which feature do you regard as the most important? Why?
4. What are the advantages and disadvantages of computer-based training?
5. Explain how training and development can motivate employees.
6. Define the term orientation. What are the purposes of an orientation program?
7. What is a strategic approach to HRD and why is it so important?
8. What is the difference between training and development? Give examples to illustrate your answer.
9. Explain how you would evaluate a training and development program.
10. What is action learning? What are its advantages and disadvantages?

environmental influences on HRD

Discuss the key environmental influences from the model (figure 9.15 shown opposite) that have significance for HRD.

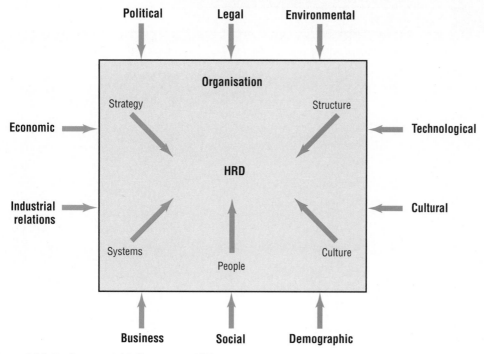

Figure 9.15 Environmental influences on HRD

class debate

The 'learning organisation' is a theoretical ideal that cannot be achieved in the workplace.

what's your view?

Write a 500-word response to the Letter to the Editor on page 345, agreeing or disagreeing with the writer's point of view.

practitioner speaks

Read the article on page 342. Critically examine the role of mentoring in the development of high-potential personnel. Explain the roles of (a) the mentor and (b) the mentee.

newsbreak exercise

Read the Newsbreak 'Call to train older workers' on page 343. Outline in one page how you would tackle the problem. As a class, discuss your individual viewpoints.

soapbox

What do you think? Conduct a mini survey of class members, using the questionnaire below. Critically discuss the findings.

1.	Management games are fun, but of little value in improving on-the-job performance.	YES	NO
2.	Only employees whose performance is unacceptable need training.	YES	NO
3.	The 'school of hard knocks' provides the best training.	YES	NO
4.	Companies should be required to spend a nominated amount each year on employee training and development.	YES	NO
5.	Training older workers is a waste of time and money.	YES	NO
6.	Trade unions should be involved in the design and implementation of all training and development programs.	YES	NO

online exercise

Visit one of the company web sites listed in appendix B on page 852. Find information relating to (a) the company's mission, objectives and culture and (b) the company's HRD activities and how they fit with its mission, objectives and culture. Prepare a three-minute presentation (to be given in class) summarising your findings.

ethical dilemma

A matter of discrimination at Jet Red

Jet Red, suffering from heavy losses, is undergoing major restructuring. Its new board of directors and top management are aggressive and results-oriented. They are under extreme pressure to turn the airline around before it collapses under the weight of excessive debt, passenger decline and savage competition. Jet Red's top management has a strong belief in HRD and has actively promoted employee development programs.

After completing a comprehensive training needs analysis, Linda Church, Jet Red's HR Manager, has introduced a customer service program. Jet Red's new management has made a policy change that requires training to be done in company and employee time. Consequently, the eight two-hour sessions are scheduled to start at 4 o'clock and finish at 6 o'clock. Linda is enthusiastic about the new program because it is job-related and has a demonstrable bottom-line impact.

Linda's thoughts are interrupted by the ringing of her phone. It is Annie O'Brien, the union representative. 'Linda, I'm shocked', Annie complained. 'I can't believe that you as a woman can allow this company to conduct a training program outside normal working hours. It's ridiculous. Apart from the question of overtime pay, the proposal is discriminatory and is an abusive intrusion on personal time. You as the HR Manager should be ashamed of yourself. You must be aware that women as partners and primary caregivers have limited time to attend such programs. Your thinking is so archaic, it's incredible.'

Linda shifted in her chair and said, 'Annie…'

Discussion questions

1. If you were Linda, what would you say to the union representative?
2. What do you think of Annie's arguments that out-of-hours training programs:
   (a) are discriminatory?
   (b) should attract overtime payments?
   (c) are an out-of-date concept?

case study

Jet Red's attention trained on Janice

Janice Almira, Training Manager for Jet Red, has a PhD in the social sciences and a firm belief that every manager and employee should be 'people'-oriented. Accordingly, she 'sold' the idea to Jet Red's former senior management that human relations, communication, team building and similar courses are a prerequisite for improved organisational performance. Given a free hand, Janice hired expensive training consultants and saw to it that all managers and most employees were exposed to 'people training'.

After the dismissal of the former senior management team, Janice was called into the office of Jet Red's new HR Manager, Linda Church. 'Well Janice', Linda began, 'I have

some disturbing news. It would appear from the consultant's market research report that all our competitors are leading us in terms of customer satisfaction, innovation and level of management sophistication. We have lost our position in the marketplace and Alan Balkin wants corrective action now. All this wonderful "people" training you've been pushing has been a disaster. I regret I'm going to have to let you go. There is no place in the new Jet Red for activities or people who do not add value. I'm sorry, Janice, but there is no alternative.'

With that, Linda pressed a button and a tall, grey-haired figure entered the room. It was the outplacement consultant. Janice's career with Jet Red was over! Janice suddenly realised that she was wet with perspiration.

Discussion questions

1. Critique Janice's approach to training and development.
2. What approach to training and development should Janice have taken?
3. What would you do now if you were Janice?
4. What responsibility should management take in this situation?
5. If you were Linda, how would you have handled this situation?

Source Dr Philip Wright, Professor, School of Business, Shu Yan College, Hong Kong, and co-author of *Managing Performance Through Training and Development*, 2nd edn, Nelson, Scarborough, Ontario, 2000.

suggested readings

Beardwell, I. and Holden, L., *Human Resource Management*, Financial Times/Prentice Hall, London, 2001, chs 7, 8, 9.

Belcourt, M., Wright, P. C. and Saks, A. M., *Managing Performance Through Training and Development*, 2nd edn, Nelson, Scarborough, Ontario, 2000.

CCH, *Australian Master Human Resources Guide*, CCH, Sydney, 2003, chs 4, 15, 45.

De Cieri, H. and Kramar, R., *Human Resource Management in Australia*, McGraw-Hill, Sydney, 2003, chs 10, 11.

Fisher, C. D, Schoenfeldt, L. F. and Shaw, J. B., *Human Resource Management*, 5th edn, Houghton Mifflin, Boston, 2003, chs 9, 10.

Ivancevich, J. M., *Human Resource Management*, 8th edn, McGraw-Hill, Boston, 2001, ch. 13.

Ivancevich, J. M. and Lee, S. H., *Human Resource Management in Asia*, McGraw-Hill, Singapore, 2002, ch. 7.

Mondy, R. W., Noe, R. M. and Premeaux, S. R., *Human Resource Management*, 8th edn, Prentice Hall, Upper Saddle River, NJ, 2002, ch. 8.

Nankervis, A. R., Compton, R. L. and Baird, M., *Strategic Human Resource Management*, 4th edn, Nelson, Melbourne, 2002, ch. 9.

Noe, R. A., *Employee Training and Development*, 2nd edn, McGraw-Hill, New York, 2002.

online references

hotelschool.scu.edu.au
trainingpays.anta.gov.au
www.ahrd.org
www.aitd.com.au
www.anta.gov.au
www.anta.gov.au/currissu/marshman.html
www.apscommunications.com.au
www.astd.org
www.buseco.monash.edu.au/courses.MBA
www.careermosiac.com
www.fuqua.duke.edu/admin/gemba
www.hightechcampus.com
www.mindresources.net

www.shrm.org.hrmagazine
www.skillsoft.com
www.stada.org.sg
www.tcm.com/trdev
www.thetraininglink.com.au
www.train.gov.au/trai1853.htm
www.training.com.au
www.traininghouse.com
www.trainlink.com
www.umva.edu/distance
www.unext.com
www.workforceonline.com

end notes

1. This chapter draws partly on material originally prepared by L. A. Worledge, BA, B.Com. (Melbourne), M.Admin. (Monash), MAITD, registered psychologist, Director of The Performance Consulting Group. Much of the material in the section on knowledge management on pages 344–5 was prepared by Marianne Gloet, School of Management, RMIT University.

2. Quoted in Mindtheme Consulting, 'Value of training outweighs cost', *South China Morning Post — Classifieds*, 14 June 2003, p. 24.

3. E. M. Garger, 'Holding on to high performers. A strategic approach to retention', *Compensation and Benefits Management*, vol. 15, no. 4, 1999, pp. 10–17.

4. M. Huselid, S. E. Jackson and R. S. Schuler, 'Technical and strategic human resource management effectiveness as determinants of firm performance', *Academy of Management Journal*, vol. 40, no. 1, 1997, p. 186.

5. J. Pfeffer, *The Human Equation*, Harvard Business School Press, Boston, Mass., 1998, p. 85.

6. M. Corben, 'Why corporate unis don't have all the answers', *Australian Financial Review — Special Report*, 5 September 2002, p. 13.

7. Reuters, 'Prosperity begins at Toyota talent school for staff', *South China Morning Post*, 16 August 2003, pp. 13, 14.

8. Reported in P. Roberts, 'Failing grades in new tests of excellence', *Australian Financial Review*, 14 February 1997, p. 61; K. Y. No, 'Give staff time off to be trained, says Tung', *South China Morning Post*, 23 November 2000, p. 2; and J. Cheung, 'Highbrow future may leave behind the low-skilled', *South China Morning Post*, 4 October 2003, p. A3.

9. Research by the Spherion Group, reported in Research Bites, *HR Monthly*, November 2002, p. 7.

10. B. Toohey, 'Degree of irony in rich list's top three', *Australian Financial Review*, 24–25 May 2003, p. 49.

11. Quoted in C. Murphy, 'Employers take training too lightly', *Australian Financial Review*, 14 June 2002, p. 21. Also see M. Priest, 'Call for more training', *Australian Financial Review*, 7 November 2003, p. 8.

12. 'The six sigma dogma', *Bulletin*, 16 July 1996, p. 41; and K. Kelly and P. Burrows, 'Motorola: training for the millennium', *Business Week*, 28 March 1994, p. 58.

13. G. L. Tooker, quoted in K. Kelly and P. Burrows, op. cit., p. 58.

14. J. Pfeffer, op. cit., p. 295.

15. P. Coy, 'The creative economy', *Business Week*, 21–28 August 2000, p. 41.

16. C. Jones, 'One in three year nine students lack literacy skills', *Australian*, 22 October 1996, pp. 1, 6; and P. O'Brien, 'School must teach job skills', *Weekend Australian — Recruitment*, 21–22 August 1999, p. 1.

17. B. Toohey, 'A degree of value', *Australian Financial Review*, 3–4 February 2001, pp. 22–3; C. Martin, 'The business of higher learning', *Australian Financial Review*, 18 August 2003, p. 60; C. Golis, 'Dumbing down of the MBA is starting to add up', *Australian Financial Review*, 17 November 2003, p. 42; and A. Norton, 'Time to restore teaching as universities' "cardinal role"', *Australian Financial Review*, 24 November 2003, p. 38.

18. Reported in H. Zampetakis, 'CEOs can become mouse-trained', *Australian Financial Review*, 3 March 1997, p. S.3.

19. *The Economist*, 'Trained to succeed', reported in *South China Morning Post*, 24 September 1996, p. 23.

20. Reported in 'The bookshelf', *HR Magazine*, December 1990, p. 16.

21. P. Gollan, 'Training reveals its value', *HR Monthly*, May 1997, p. 11.

22. M. V. Gee, 'Strategic fit between skills training and levels of quality management: an empirical study of American manufacturing plants', *Human Resource Planning*, vol. 22, no. 2, 1999, pp. 12–23.

23. From July 1992, until the scheme's suspension in 1994, organisations with annual payrolls of more than $214 000 were required to spend 1.5 per cent of their payroll on eligible training schemes. Any employer not spending the required amount on training had to make up the difference as a tax penalty. For further details, see A. Smith, 'Australian training and development in 1992', *Asia Pacific Journal of Human Resources*, vol. 31, no. 2, 1993, pp. 71–2; K. Beresford and J. Gaife, 'Training Guarantee Act: suspended or ended?', *HR Monthly*, October 1994, pp. 17–18; and C. Nobel, 'International comparisons of training policies', *Human Resource Management Journal*, vol. 7, no. 1, 1997, pp. 10–12.

24. The Mayer Reports, *Employment Related Competencies*, AGPS, Canberra, May 1992, and *Putting General Education to Work: The Key Competencies Report*, AGPS, Canberra, November 1992; The Carmichael Report of the Employment and Skills Formation Council, *The Australian Vocational Certificate Training System*, AGPS, Canberra, March 1992. Also see A. Smith, *Training and Development in Australia*, Butterworths, Sydney, 1996, pp. 204–5.

25. A. Smith, 1993, op. cit., pp. 68–9.

26. T. Whittingham, 'Vocational training: a competency management system', *Management*, no. 3, April 1993, p. 11.

27. G. Andrewartha, 'New wave training is just another set of labels', *HR Monthly*, March 1993, p. 27; A. Henderson, 'No brownie points for the Mayer Report', *Commercial Issues*, no. 13, 1993, pp. 6–7; and D. Pennington, 'Excellence, not competence', *IPA Review*, vol. 46, no. 1, 1993, pp. 26–30.

28. D. Pennington, op. cit., p. 29; A. Henderson, 'Laurie Carmichael's yellow brick (training) road', *Commercial Issues*, no. 11, 1992, p. 5; and H. M. Boot, 'Training, wages, and human capital: the economic costs of Keating and Carmichael', *Policy*, vol. 8, no. 3, 1992, pp. 13–17.

29. 'Skills education fails the business test', *ABM*, June 1993, pp. 136–7; D. Pennington, op. cit., p. 27; and H. M. Boot, op. cit., p. 16.

30. For example, see G. Andrewartha, 'Competency based training is doomed to failure', *HR Monthly*, April 1993, pp. 23–4; T. Hampstead, 'CBT offers pathway to real changes', *HR Monthly*, June 1993, p. 26; G. Andrewartha, 'New wave training is just another set of labels', *HR Monthly*, March 1993, p. 27; and D. J. Lange, 'Competency based training: beware the dangers', *HR Monthly*, March 1993, pp. 22–3.

31. T. Whittingham, op. cit., p. 11.

32. *Enterprising Nation*, Report of the Industry Task Force on Leadership and Management Skills, AGPS, Canberra, 1995.

33. A. Harris, 'Management or leadership? Australia ticks the wrong box', *Australian Financial Review*, 15–16 April 2000, p. 32; B. Clegg, 'The very model of the millennium manager', *Australian Financial Review*, 25 August 1999, p. 16; and N. Chinoweth, 'It's alibi time for the poor CEO', *Australian Financial Review*, 7–8 July 2001, p. 25.

34. D. Nettle, 'The Karpin enquiry and the role of management education in Australia, history revisited?', *Labour and Industry*, vol. 7, no. 2, 1996, p. 103. Also see M. Priest and S. Moran, 'Report card: 2003 MBA rankings', *Boss*, September 2003, pp. 63–71; K. Marshall, 'Management training goes in house', *Australian Financial Review — Special Report*, 2 October 2003, p. 2; and T. Dodd, 'Storm in lucrative export', *Australian Financial Review*, 10 November 2003, pp. 31–2.

35. See D. James, 'Karpin prompts business schools to take stock', *Business Review Weekly*, 3 July 1995, pp. 74–7.

36. M. Davis, 'The not so clever country is urged back to school', *Business Review Weekly*, 1 May 1995, p. 63.

37. D. Karpin, 'In search of leaders', *HR Monthly*, June 1995, p. 11.

38. F. Moore, 'Huge opportunities flow from Karpin Report', *HR Monthly*, June 1995, p. 27.

39. F. Emery, 'Karpin task force manages to get confused', *Business Review Weekly*, 24 July 1995, p. 72.

40. E. Moody, 'Karpin report branded "motherhood and apple pie"', *Australian*, 6 June 1995, p. 63; N. Way, 'Karpin critics', *Business Review Weekly*, 15 April 1996, pp. 12–13; 'Barely managing', *Workplace*, Spring 1995, p. 26; and A. Moddie, 'Australians reject US model', *Australian Financial Review*, 27 June 1997, p. 55.

41. R. Elsdon and S. Iyer, 'Creating value and enhancing retention through employee development: the Sun Microsystems experience', *Human Resource Planning*, vol. 22, no. 2, 1999, pp. 39–47.

42. D. A. Ready, 'Educating the survivors', *Journal of Business Strategy*, vol. 16, no. 2, 1995, p. 28.

43. N. Freedman, quoted in D. A. Ready, op. cit., pp. 28–9.

44. D. A. Ready, op. cit., p. 29.

45. D. E. Hussey, 'Management training: a key tool for strategy implementation', *Strategic Change*, vol. 5, no. 5, 1996, p. 264.

46. R. J. Torraco and R. A. Swanson, 'The strategic roles of human resource development', *Human Resource Planning*, vol. 18, no. 4, 1995, p. 11.

47. D. Tapscott, *The Digital Economy*, McGraw-Hill, New York, 1996, p. 7.

48. American Management Association study, reported in G. Koretz, 'Economic trends', *Business Week*, 25 November 1996, p. 14.

49. P. A. McLagen, 'Models for HRD practice', *Training and Development Journal*, vol. 43, no. 9, 1989, p. 50.

50. P. A. McLagen, op. cit., p. 50.

51. S. Goss, 'All the right ingredients for a positive outcome', *Age*, 13 September 2003, p. 21; J. Moullakis, 'Industry's apprentice woes', *Australian Financial Review*, 26 August 2003, p. 48; and Editorial, 'Time to act on skills shortage', *Australian Financial Review*, 20 August 2002, p. 62.

52. T. Vilkinas, 'Poor educational access slows women's climb in to senior jobs', *HR Monthly*, October 1995, pp. 20–1.

53. C. Harp, 'Link training to corporate mission', *HR Magazine*, August 1995, p. 65.

54. J. Pfeffer, op. cit., pp. 111–12.

55. D. E. Hussey, op. cit., p. 263.

56. Study by R. Curtain, reported in P. Roberts, 'Failing grades in new tests of excellence', *Australian Financial Review*, 14 February 1997, p. 61.

57. D. T. Hall, 'Executive careers and learning: aligning selection, strategy and development', *Human Resource Planning*, vol. 18, no. 2, 1995, p. 15.

58. S. Ramlall, 'A critical review of the role of training and development in increasing performance', *Journal of Compensation and Benefits*, vol. 18, no. 15, 2002, p. 17.

59. 'BBC instructs staff on how to boil water', *Sunday Morning Post*, 24 December 2000, p. 7.

60. S. Long, 'Cooking up careers', *Australian Financial Review*, 26 April 2000, p. 23.

61. J. Ewing, 'Siemens building a "B School" in its own backyard', *Business Week*, 15 November 1999, pp. 109–10.

62. D. Plunkett, G. Greenstein and N. Street, 'A strategy for success: performance based human resource development', *Human Resource Planning*, vol. 17, no. 1, 1994, p. 59.

63. B. Barry, 'The development of management education in Australia', *Asia Pacific Journal of Human Resources*, vol. 34, no. 2, 1996, p. 54.

64. J. Pfeffer, op. cit., pp. 111–12; and K. Marshall, '70 pc of training a waste: survey', *Australian Financial Review*, 31 October 2000, p. 28.

65. B. Jones, 'Developing human capital', *Management Review*, vol. 85, no. 2, 1996, p. 10.

66. Reported in *SIHRM Monthly Digest*, November 1996, p. 13.

67. G. S. Becker, 'Human capital: one investment where America is way ahead', *Business Week*, 11 March 1996, p. 8.

68. P. Wonacott, 'Hong Kong survey reveals concerns', *Asian Wall Street Journal*, 13 December 2000, p. 3; R. Stone, 'English in Hong Kong: ACER Word Knowledge Test Skills — a case of declining standards?', *Hong Kong Linguist*, nos. 19, 20, 1999, pp. 23–8; and R. Stone, 'English in Hong Kong: word knowledge skills of science undergraduates', *Hong Kong Journal of Applied Linguistics*, vol. 4, no. 1, 1999, pp. 93–100.

69. M. Brooker, 'Amcham stresses reforms', *South China Morning Post*, 21 January 2000, p. 1; and G. Cheung 'Students flock overseas to pursue education', *South China Morning Post*, 16 October 2000, p. 5.

70. This section is based on M. Belcourt, P. C. Wright and A. M. Saks, *Managing Performance Through Training and Development*, Nelson, Scarborough, Ontario, 2000, pp. 343–5; and M. Gloet, 'The changing role of the HRM function in the knowledge economy: the links to quality knowledge management', paper presented at the 8th International Conference on ISO and TQM, Montreal, April 2003, pp. 1–7.

71. S. P. Robbins, *Organizational Behavior*, 9th edn, Prentice Hall, Upper Saddle River, NJ, 2001, p. 560; and M. Gloet, P. Lovett and E. Nunez, 'Knowledge management and the HRM function: a best practice case study', paper presented at the 8th International Conference on ISO and TQM, Montreal, April 2003, p. 3.

72. This section is based on L. Wah, 'Behind the buzz', *Management Review*, vol. 88, no. 4, 1999, pp. 16–19; S. L. McShane and M. A. Von Glinow, *Organizational Behavior*, McGraw-Hill, Boston, 2000, pp. 19–24; M. Belcourt, P. C. Wright and A. M. Saks, op. cit., pp. 343–51; and V. Lee, 'Creating value in the knowledge economy', *HR Monthly*, April, 1998, pp. 12–17.

73. S. L. McShane and M. A. Von Glinow, op. cit., p. 20; and Lend Lease, *Report to Shareholders*, Sydney, 2000, p. 40.

74. Quoted in S. Moran, 'Keeping up on the knowledge highway', *Australian Financial Review*, 16 September 2003, p. 59.

75. C. James, 'Designing learning organizations', *Organizational Dynamics*, vol. 32, no. 1, 2003, pp. 53–4.

76. C. James, op. cit., p. 55.

77. M. Belcourt, P. C. Wright and A. M. Saks, op. cit., p. 3.

78. M. Belcourt, P. C. Wright and A. M. Saks, op. cit., p. 4.

79. J. Lawrie, 'Differentiate between training, education and development', *Personnel Journal*, vol. 69, no. 10, October 1990, p. 44.

80. W. B. Werther Jr and K. Davis, *Human Resources and Personnel Management*, 5th edn, McGraw-Hill, New York, 1996, p. 282.

81. M. P. O'Driscoll and P. J. Taylor, 'Congruence between theory and practice in management training needs analysis', *International Journal of Human Resource Management*, vol. 3, no. 3, 1992, pp. 593–603.

82. F. Emery, 'Universities could lose business education', *Business Review Weekly*, 1 July 1996, p. 68; and T. Coady (ed.), *Why Universities Matter*, Allen & Unwin, Sydney, 2000.

83. B. Adams, 'Degrees of concern', *South China Morning Post*, 17 August 2003, p. 12.

84. G. Maslen, 'HK exam cheat beats conviction', *South China Morning Post*, 18 January 2003, p. E1.

85. N. Way, 'Degrees for sale', *Business Review Weekly*, 28 July 2000, pp. 72–8; J. Molony, 'Australian universities today', in T. Coady (ed.), op. cit., p. 73; and B. Adams, op. cit., p. 12.

86. D. Brown, 'MBA programs strive to catch up with real world', *Canadian HR Reporter*, 11 September 2000, pp. 3, 15; N. Way, op. cit., pp. 72–8; D. Spender, 'Up to universities to upgrade their products', *Boss*, February 2001, p. 21; K. Marshall, 'Many MBAs lack day to day skills', *Australian Financial Review*, 1 August 2003, p. 19; and K. Marshall, 'Aspiring MBAs spoilt for choice', *Australian Financial Review*, 25 July 2003, p. 23.

87. J. Davidson, 'Radical reform needed in tertiary education', *Business Review Weekly*, 18 August 2000, p. 12.

88. See advertisements in the *South China Morning Post*, 6 May 2000, pp. 6, 15, 16, 21, 22.

89. R. E. Michaud, 'The self development function — assessing training needs', *Training and Development Journal*, vol. 32, no. 8, 1978, p. 78.

90. A. R. Nankervis, R. L. Compton and M. Baird, *Strategic Human Resource Management*, 4th edn, Nelson, Melbourne, 2002, p. 331.

91. K. N. Wexley and G. P. Latham, *Developing and Training Human Resources in Organizations*, Harper Collins, New York, 1991, p. 36.

92. K. N. Wexley and G. P. Latham, op. cit., p. 37; and P. Taylor, 'Training', in M. Poole and M. Warner (eds), *The Handbook of Human Resource Management*, Thomson, London, 1998, pp. 643–6.

93. I. L. Goldstein, *Training in Organizations*, Brooks/Cole, Pacific Grove, CA, 1993, p. 22.

94. Taken from K. Cole, 'Learning by experience', *HR Monthly*, June 1999, pp. 48–9.

95. I. L. Goldstein, op. cit., pp. 260–5; and K. N. Wexley and G. P. Latham, op. cit., pp. 191–4.

96. E. S. Niemyer, 'The case for case studies', *Training and Development*, vol. 49, no. 1, 1995, p. 50; and A. A. Einsiedel Jr, 'Case studies: indispensable tools for trainers', *Training and Development*, vol. 49, no. 8, 1995, pp. 50–3.

97. K. N. Wexley and G. P. Latham, op. cit., pp. 261–3; and I. L. Goldstein, op. cit., pp. 281–3.

98. L. L. Byars and L. Rue, *Human Resource Management*, 6th edn, McGraw-Hill, Boston, 2000, p. 235.

99. K. N. Wexley and G. P. Latham, op. cit., pp. 263–4.

100. K. N. Wexley and G. P. Latham, op. cit., pp. 271–3; and I. L. Goldstein, op. cit., pp. 283–5.

101. J. M. Ivancevich, *Human Resource Management*, 8th edn, McGraw-Hill, Boston, 2001, pp. 395–6.

102. K. N. Wexley and G. P. Latham, op. cit., pp. 273–6.

103. P. Harrell, 'Make an adventure of the learning experience', *HR Monthly*, October 1994, pp. 18–19; and R. Morarjee, 'Off the wall', *Post Magazine*, 20 July 1997, pp. 12–15.

104. Quoted in S. Macmillan, 'Corporate punishment', *Australian Magazine*, 1–2 December 1990, p. 75. See also H. Campbell, 'Adventures in teamland', *Personnel Journal*, May 1996, pp. 56–62.

105. M. Mason, 'About those team building retreats', *Asian Wall Street Journal*, 29 April 1993, p. 6; and R. J. Wagner and C. C. Roland, 'How effective is outdoor training?', *Training and Development*, vol. 46, no. 7, 1992, pp. 61–6.

106. See S. W. Kezman and E. K. Connors, 'Avoid legal pitfalls in non traditional training', *HRM Magazine*, May 1993, pp. 71–4; and C. Clements, R. J. Wagner and C. C. Roland, 'The ins and outs of experiential training', *Training and Development*, vol. 49, no. 2, 1995, pp. 52–6.

107. Reported in 'Getting a warm feeling?', *HR Monthly*, April 2002, p. 12.

108. A. McKenzie, 'The weird world of management training', *Asian Business*, March 1995, pp. 46–8.

109. S. Williams, 'Executive recipe for success in business', *Australian Financial Review*, 12 September 2003, p. 73.

110. K. N. Wexley and G. P. Latham, op. cit., pp. 156–9.

111. See K. N. Wexley and G. P. Latham, op. cit., pp. 277–8; and J. M. Ivancevich, op. cit., pp. 398–9.

112. K. N. Wexley and G. P. Latham, op. cit., pp. 161–2; and C. Bell, 'Mentoring: a powerful form of professional development', *Management*, July 1995, pp. 24–6.

113. K. N. Wexley and G. P. Latham, op. cit., pp. 163–5.

114. J. M. Ivancevich, op. cit., p. 397.

115. J. M. Ivancevich, op. cit., p. 397.

116. P. Goldrick, 'Behaviour modelling still a versatile skill building', *HR Monthly*, February 1997, pp. 36–8; and J. M. Ivancevich, op. cit., p. 397.

117. J. A. Raelin, 'Action learning and action science: are they different?', *Organizational Dynamics*, vol. 26, no. 1, 1997, p. 21.

118. L. Brearley, quoted in C. Rance, 'Adding an extra dimension to learning skills at work', *Age — Employment Section*, 17 February 1996, p. 2.

119. P. Roberts, 'Action learning shifts focus to the workplace', *Australian Financial Review*, 18 July 1997, p. 30.

120. J. B. Hunt and J. Wallace, 'A competency-based approach to assessing managerial performance in the Australian context', *Asia Pacific Journal of Human Resources*, vol. 35, no. 2, 1997, p. 52; and R. Bishop, 'The future of competency based training', *HR Monthly*, June 1999, pp. 36–7.

121. For further discussion, see A. Smith, 1996, op. cit., pp. 47–53, 60, 79–81, 103–5, 136–8.

122. G. Hearn, A. Close, B. Smith and G. Southey, 'Defining generic professional competencies in Australia: towards a framework for professional development', *Asia Pacific Journal of Human Resources*, vol. 34, no. 1, 1996, p. 45.

123. E. P. Antonacopoulous and L. Fitzgerald, 'Reframing competency in management development', *Human Resource Management Journal*, vol. 6, no. 1, 1996, pp. 27–48.

124. M. Belcourt, P. C. Wright and A. M. Saks, op. cit., pp. 53–4.

125. A. G. Robinson and D. M. Schroeder, 'Training, continuous improvement, and human relations: the US TWI programs and the Japanese management style', *California Management Review*, vol. 35, no. 2, 1993, pp. 35, 51.

126. A. G. Robinson and D. M. Schroeder, op. cit., p. 55.

127. M. H. Peak, 'Go corporate U!', *Management Review*, vol. 86, no. 2, 1997, p. 33; and D. Ashenden and S. Milligan, 'Universities are open for business', *HR Monthly*, September 1999, p. 34.

128. See advertisement for The Hotel School, Intercontinental Sydney, *Australian Financial Review*, 4–5 October 2003, p. 5.

129. M. Corben, 'Why corporate universities don't have all the answers', *Australian Financial Review — Special Report*, 5 September 2002, p. 13.

130. M. H. Peak, op. cit., p. 34.

131. J. Van Dyke, quoted in P. R. Theibert, 'Train and degree them — anywhere', *Personnel Journal*, February 1996, p. 37.

132. M. H. Peak, op. cit., p. 37.

133. D. Spender, 'Corporate universities', *Boss*, November 2000, p. 19; and M. Schrage, 'Sorry, no keg parties here. This university is on the desktop', *Fortune*, 7 June 1999, p. 93.

134. W. Wiggethorn, quoted in D. A. Ready, op. cit., p. 35.

135. D. Schultz and S. E. Schultz, *Psychology and Work Today*, Prentice Hall, Upper Saddle River, NJ, 1998, pp. 181–2.

136. D. Schultz and S. E. Schultz, op. cit., pp. 183–4.

137. W. Wilson, 'Video training and testing supports customer service goals', *Personnel Journal*, June 1994, p. 47.

138. Much of this section is based on M. Belcourt, P. C. Wright and A. M. Saks, op. cit., pp. 138–40; and R. A. Noe, *Employee Training and Development*, McGraw-Hill, Boston, 2000, pp. 194–5.

139. J. Salopek, 'Quotient', *Training and Development*, vol. 52, no. 11, 1998, pp. 21–34.

140. Based on R. A. Noe, op. cit., pp. 199–202.

141. A Griffiths, 'e-learning slow to take off', *HR Monthly*, June 2000, pp. 26–8; and Mindtheme Consulting, 'The pros and cons of e-learning in the business world', *South China Morning Post — Classifieds*, 18 October 2003, p. 24.

142. P. Gibbins, 'The virtual professor', *Business Review Weekly*, 20 October 2000, p. 104.

143. B. Upbin, 'Profit in a big orange box', *Forbes Global*, 24 January 2000, p. 31.

144. K. Morris, 'Wiring the ivory tower', *Business Week*, 9 August 1999, pp. 58–60; A Sanders, 'Urlazy.com', *Forbes Global*, 15 May 2000, p. 137; D. Svetcov, 'The virtual classroom versus the real one', *Forbes Global*, 18 September 2000, pp. 114–16; and S. Hamm, 'The wired campus', *Business Week — E. Biz*, 11 December 2000, pp. EB69–EB77.

145. J. Macken, 'University on the line', *Australian Financial Review*, 14 January 1999, p. 17; and G. S. Becker, 'How the web is revolutionizing learning', *Business Week*, 27 December 1999, p. 11.

146. K. Marshall, 'Degrees online for ANZ staff', *Australian Financial Review*, 6 October 2000, p. 17.

147. V. Kwong, 'Online distance learning on course for growth amid steady demand', *South China Morning Post — Business*, 13 October 2000, p. 5.

148. B. Johnstone, 'Ivory servers', *Forbes Global*, 11 December 2000, p. 139.

149. V. K. Kumar, 'Training instruments for human resource development', *Personnel Psychology*, vol. 52, no. 4, 1999, pp. 1101–4.

150. K. N. Wexley and G. P. Latham, op. cit., pp. 109, 113. See also L. F. Gingerella, 'Seven ways to sell management on training', *Training and Development*, vol. 49, no. 3, 1995, pp. 11–14; and P. Taylor, op. cit., pp. 650–3.

151. S. Ramlall, op. cit., p. 15.

152. E. A. Davidore and P. A. Schroeder, 'Demonstrating ROI of training', *Training and Development*, vol. 46, no. 8, 1992, pp. 70–1.

153. M. Clarke, 'Management development as a game of meaningless outcomes', *Human Resource Management Journal*, vol. 9, no. 2, 1999, pp. 38–49; and G. H. Harel and S. S. Tzafrir, 'The effect of human resource management practices on the perceptions of organizational and market performance of the firm', *Human Resource Management*, vol. 38, no. 3, 1999, pp. 185–99.

154. D. V. McCain, 'Aligning training with business objectives', *HR Focus*, February 1999, pp. 51–3.

155. S. Ramlall, op. cit., p. 16.

156. D. L. Kirkpatrick, 'Four steps to measuring training effectiveness', *Personnel Administrator*, November 1983, pp. 19–25; and P. E. Spector, *Industrial and Organizational Psychology*, 2nd edn, John Wiley & Sons, New York, 2000, pp. 163–9.

157. K. N. Wexley and G. P. Latham, op. cit., p. 109.

158. J. J. Phillips, 'ROI: the search for best practices', *Training and Development*, vol. 50, no. 2, 1996, pp. 42–7; J. J. Phillips, 'Was it the training?', *Training and Development*, vol. 50, no. 3, 1996, pp. 28–32; J. J. Phillips, 'How much is the training worth?', *Training and Development*, vol. 50, no. 4, 1996, pp. 20–4; and J. Brown, 'Getting started', *HR Monthly*, September 2003, p. 46.

159. L. Norman, 'Induction becomes first stage of ongoing training', *HR Monthly*, June 1997, p. 4; and J. Brown, 2003, op. cit., p. 46.

160. M. I. Finney, 'Employee orientation programs can help introduce success', *HR News*, October 1995, p. 2.

161. E. F. Halton III, 'New employee development: a review and reconceptualization', *Human Resource Development Quarterly*, vol. 7, no. 3, 1996, pp. 234–6.

162. J. M. Ivancevich, op. cit., pp. 381–2.

163. A. M. Starcke, 'Building a better orientation program', *HRM Magazine*, November 1996, p. 108.

164. F. X. Mahoney, 'Human resource management', in L. Nadler and Z. Nadler, *The Handbook of Human Resource Development*, 2nd edn, John Wiley & Sons, New York, 1990, p. 28.

165. E. J. McGarrell, 'An orientation system that builds productivity', *Personnel Administrator*, October 1983, pp. 75–85.

166. J. Milton-Smith, quoted in D. Kitney, 'Education gap puts us behind', *Australian Financial Review*, 5 August 1996, p. 6.

167. D. MacLean, 'Education and small business', *Corporate Management*, vol. 45, no. 5, 1993, p. 122; D. Kitney, op. cit., p. 6.

168. Reported in I. Jarrett, 'Old images stick fast', *Asian Business*, June 1995, p. 70.

169. McKinsey & Co. study, reported in P. Roberts, op. cit., p. 61.

170. Business Services Industry Training Board, 'Marketing, education and training report', cited in B. Hutchings, 'Workers snub call for extra training', *Weekend Australian*, 11–12 September 1993, p. 53.

171. J. Wilson, 'Students stifled by language change', *Australian*, 5 June 1995, p. 12.

172. R. Little and W. Reed, authors of *The Tyranny of Fortune*, quoted in P. Roberts, 'Australia, a victim of "the tyranny of fortune"', *Australian Financial Review*, 26 September 1997, p. 21.

173. J. A. Byrne, J. Reingold and R. A. Melcher, 'Wanted: a few good CEOs', *Business Week*, 11 August 1997, p. 42.

174. J. M. Ivancevich, op. cit., pp. 384–5.

175. I. L. Goldstein, op. cit., pp. 104–5; and K. N. Wexley and G. P. Latham, op. cit., pp. 75–6.

176. I. L. Goldstein, op. cit., p. 109; K. N. Wexley and G. P. Latham, op. cit., pp. 76–7.

177. I. L. Goldstein, op. cit., pp. 110–11 and K. N. Wexley and G. P. Latham, op. cit., pp. 73–5.

178. I. L. Goldstein, op. cit., p. 114.

179. D. M. Wolfe and D. A. Kolb, 'Career development, personal growth and experiential learning', in D. A. Kolb, I. M. Rubin and

J. M. McIntyre, *Organizational Psychology — Readings on Human Behavior in Organizations*, 4th edn, Prentice Hall, Englewood Cliffs, NJ, 1984, p. 130.

180. The learning style inventory is contained in D. A. Kolb, I. M. Rubin and J. M. McIntyre, op. cit., p. 23.

181. M. S. Knowles, 'Adult learning: theory and practice', in L. Nadler and Z. Nadler (eds), *The Handbook of Human Resource Development*, 2nd edn, John Wiley & Sons, New York, 1990, pp. 6–8.

182. M. S. Knowles, op. cit., pp. 6–10.

183. J. Reed in 'Learner centred learning', *Training and Development*, vol. 47, no. 6, 1993, p. 20.

184. M. S. Knowles, op. cit., pp. 6–10.

185. M. S. Knowles, op. cit., pp. 6–10; and J. Reed, op. cit., pp. 20–2.

186. M. S. Knowles, op. cit., pp. 6–11.

187. M. S. Knowles, op. cit., pp. 6–12.

188. K. N. Wexley and G. P. Latham, op. cit., pp. 83–4.

chapter 10

career planning and development

Learning objectives

When you have finished studying this chapter, you should be able to:

- Understand the importance of career planning and development
- Identify the responsibility for career planning and development
- Explain the HR department's role in career planning and development
- Discuss some of the major factors contributing to successful career development
- Understand the preparation desirable for a career in HRM.

> **'Young people who don't finish 12 years of education are the future underclass in Australia.'**[1]
>
> **Katie Lahey, CEO, Business Council of Australia**

The importance of career planning and development

Until recently, employees could join an organisation fully expecting to stay with it for their entire career.[2] Now, lifelong careers are a thing of the past. Executive Vice-Chairman Thomas Patrick Sr was terminated from Merrill Lynch after 25 years of service. His two secretaries and chauffeur were escorted from the building by security guards, his computers were unplugged and his email account was shut down. Patrick, regarded as a shrewd investment banker with a strong track record, had lost in a political power play.[3] Tom Fraser, head of AMP's UK operations, thought his own performance was good. The Chairman of AMP had told the Financial Services Authority that Fraser, along with Andrew Mohl, was one of two candidates being considered for the position of CEO. Fraser was fired shortly after by the new CEO, Mohl. According to one commentator, Fraser had paid the price for being on the wrong side.[4]

Some naive employees still feel that they are immune to the ongoing reductions because they are doing good work and adding value to the organisation. However, globalisation, increasing competition, rapid technological change, relentless restructuring and downsizing mean that high performance no longer protects employees from dismissal. According to one survey, only 55 per cent of employees believe that their organisation provides security for good performers.[5] Employees are now on their own. 'The paternalistic model of long term employment', says Henkoff, 'is dead and buried.'[6]

Max Ogden, the ACTU's coordinator for workplace change, says 'in the pursuit of world best practice, the work force must be highly skilled, motivated and prepared to undertake retraining, and change jobs'.[7] People increasingly will move from opportunity to opportunity without regard for traditional job boundaries. These **boundaryless careers**, claim Jones and De Fillippi, will 'unfold as people move among firms for projects, develop market niches rooted in competencies and strategies, and create opportunities based on prior performance and networks of professional contacts'.[8] Part-time work will become more important.[9] Some experts predict that soon full-time careers will no longer be the norm.[10] Job insecurity is already one of the most common sources of social anxiety.[11] An added insecurity is the risk of choosing an occupation or profession that will be rendered obsolete by technological change.[12]

Management guru Charles Handy argues that employees must 'begin to think of their careers as a sequence of jobs that may or may not be in the same organization'.[13] Handy stresses that employees today must look out for themselves because the future is no longer guaranteed. He notes that in these circumstances education becomes an investment and varied experience becomes an asset.[14] 'But for those who end up with merely their time to sell', warns Handy, 'a bleak future lurks ever closer.'[15] Those most likely to suffer include young adults with limited education, semi-skilled manufacturing workers, people over 40 years of age in large organisations and 'anyone still expecting a 30 year career with the same company'.[16]

In Singapore, those without qualifications are three times more likely to be unemployed. In Australia, the chances of getting a job are twice as great for those with post-secondary qualifications and there is evidence to suggest that graduates are increasingly competing with school leavers for lower-level jobs.[17] As a result, it is likely that the 80 000 young Australians who do not complete 12 years of education in the next decade will face long-term unemployment. Welfare recipients, in particular, will have especially limited prospects (given their negative attitudes, lack of workplace skills and poor work ethic).[18] In addition, graduates have significantly more earning power and better promotion prospects than non-graduates.[19] A degree, however, is no guarantee of getting a good job. The number of graduates in China exceeds two million each year, with only about 70 per cent expected to find suitable employment. As in Australia and elsewhere, graduates are taking jobs from the lesser skilled. The Vice-President of China's Institute of Personnel and Human Resources states, 'When it comes to the Chinese labour market, there are now three radishes for every hole'.[20]

Boundaryless careers Careers that involve switching jobs, specialisations, companies, industries and locations. They may involve upwards, downwards and sideways moves.

The ever-changing work environment means employees are vulnerable to career disruption or stagnation, so career planning is critical.[21] Managers today are younger and their tenures are shorter.[22] According to a survey conducted by management consultants Booz Allen Hamilton, Australian CEOs have an average shelf life of just 4.4 years.[23] Government officials in Singapore have warned workers that their complacency and inertia concerning the acquisition of new skills mean that they are in danger of becoming jobless.[24] This is because job security now centres not on having a job but on being employable. 'In the New Economy', says Cisco Systems CEO John Chambers, 'you expect life long learning, not necessarily life long employment.'[25] Thus, employees must continue to develop their skills to ensure they possess the competencies that the market needs.

Realistic career planning forces employees to be proactive and to anticipate problems and opportunities. It does this by making them establish and examine their career objectives. Furthermore, employees' careers are subject to dual influences: individual employees choose occupations, organisations and positions, while organisations recruit and select individual employees.

Thus, **career planning and development** involve two processes — *career planning* (employee-centred) and *career management* (organisation-centred). Employee benefits include better self-understanding and better identification of desired career goals. Organisational benefits include communication of career opportunities to employees, a better match between employee career aspirations and organisational opportunities, and achievement of EEO goals. Career management is integral to HR planning, but HR planning and/or career management do not exist or are not integrated in some organisations. It makes little sense, however, to train and develop employees without having suitable positions available, or to forecast employee requirements without having a program to satisfy them (see figure 10.1).

Ideally, career planning and development should be seen as a process that aligns the interests and skills of employees with the needs of the organisation. This means that careers must be managed strategically so the skills demanded by the organisation's strategic business objectives are understood and a work force with a matching profile of skills is developed. Employees must be informed of the organisation's business direction and be encouraged to build their career goals around the organisation's future. Career planning and development play a major part in ensuring that the organisation has a competitive and knowledgeable work force. Thus, organisations need to make this process a key business strategy if they want to survive in an increasingly competitive business environment where employee know-how is a critical source of competitive advantage.

Career planning and development Giving employees assistance to develop realistic career goals and the opportunities to realise them.

HR planning and career planning and development

Employees and organisations are paying more attention to career planning and development because:
- employees are increasingly concerned about their quality of life
- there are EEO legislation and requirements
- educational levels and employee aspirations are rising
- workers are making the transition from **vertical careers** to **lateral careers**
- organisations have an increasing sense of obligation to employees — 'The most valuable thing that a business can give its members', says Handy, 'is no longer employment but employability, the security of a saleable skill'[26]
- shortages of skilled workers are producing a global talent war[27]
- older employees are experiencing longer periods of unemployment, longer job searches and fewer job interviews.[28]

Finally, career planning and development should be important to every employee because the consequences of career success or failure are so closely linked with each person's self-concept, identity and satisfaction with life.[29] Career experts claim that employees 'who take time to invest in their own development find increased job satisfaction and a new feeling of control over their lives'.[30]

Vertical careers Traditional career path where an employee enters the organisation at a junior level and progresses upward to more senior positions over a period of time.

Lateral careers Career path where an employee undertakes a series of lateral moves (often in different functions) instead of moving upward within the organisation.

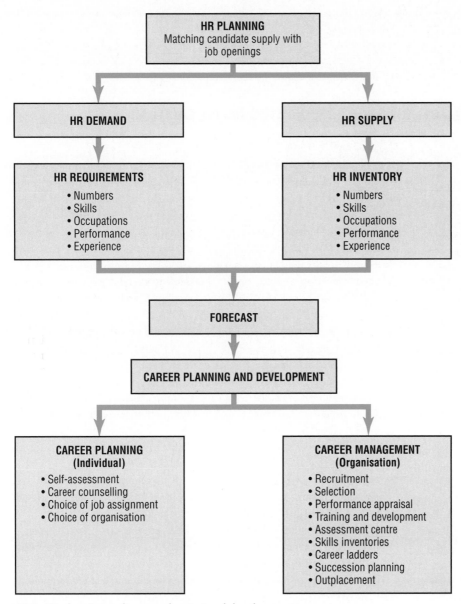

Figure 10.1 HR planning and career planning and development
Source Asia Pacific Management Co. Ltd, 2004.

The employee's responsibility

All employees should be concerned about their own career planning and development. They need to analyse their situation, identify their career objectives and develop action steps to achieve their objectives. Today, with no job guaranteed, employees are responsible for keeping themselves marketable. Organisations, in turn, should provide opportunities for self-evaluation and training. Says one writer: 'Forget old notions of advancement and loyalty. In a more flexible, more chaotic world of work, you're responsible for your career.'[31] Employees need to think of themselves as self-employed, working for 'Me Inc.'.[32] Unfortunately, many employees ignore this responsibility, preferring to leave it to the organisation. By adopting such a passive stance, employees give up control of their career, limit their future **employability** and reduce their chances of achieving their career goals.

Employability Having marketable skills (skills that are attractive to employers).

When a career becomes hard labour

By D. Macken

Maybe it's the sight of all those obstetricians handing baby back to mum so they can head off to the golf course, but there's a lot of chatter about dropping out at the moment. Much of it is coming from early boomers who are clicking over into that black hole of the working life, the 55–59-year old period — an age when last drinks are called at the bar of opportunities.

The fact that the average age of obstetricians is 55 years doesn't augur well for the profession even though the politicians have made a late dash to rescue the whitecoats from liability in perpetuity.

While sceptics don't believe that too many midwives will be left holding the baby, there are many social and historic reasons why some of the leaders of the original hippie generation are being tempted to drop out.

At the end of another working week, it's probably redundant to say that pressures in the workforce are making the full-time commitment less attractive than ever.

You don't have to be delivering babies to be working at 2 am these days; there are lawyers in the office at 10 pm, builders on the job at 7 pm, traders online throughout the night.

Moreover, the pleasures of working one's butt off have paled in the past few years because of the fees that many professionals pay for the right to overwork. The series of insurance crises and the opportunistic shenanigans in the industry have forced all sorts of service providers to pay a ransom for their work ticket.

It begs the question: why would anyone pay tens of thousands of dollars to go to university for a decade, so they can begin paying insurance premiums of $120 000 a year for the pleasure of being called out at 2 am to deliver a baby?

For the money, of course.

Most of these beleaguered professions are not starving. But the prosperity of the past decade — the increases in property values, professional fees, salaries and retail sales — is making it easier for history's hippies to drop out rather than tethering them to the earn/spend cycle.

This is especially the case for those in their 50s who have benefited most from property booms, are freed from the bulk of child-rearing costs, and are the first generation to have had two full-time wages coming into the house for most of the past three decades.

They are now post-economic (or at least one of them is).

Dinner party talk, chats across the tax accountant's table and quiet conversations with redundancy lawyers may reflect more of a dreaming than a mass exodus, but the statistics show a continual bleed from commitment to the nine-to-nine grind.

Staff are both turning over faster and ditching their suits earlier. A survey by the Australian Institute of Management this week shows there was a 20 per cent rise in staff turnover last year — a disgruntlement rate that was sheeted home to overworked, underpaid and undervalued staff.

But it's the permanent downshifters who reflect most poorly on the state of work today.

In the year to March, the proportion of employed men aged 55 to 59 years who were working full-time fell half a percentage point; the proportion of employed women of the same age who were working full-time dropped one and a half percentage points.

While the historic shift to early retirement that began in the 1980s was largely structural (most were redundancies in blue-collar jobs which disappeared forever), the second wave seems a reaction to the changing nature of the workforce and is more of a voluntary movement.

What's more, most aren't disappearing to the backyard shed but are maintaining links with the workforce through affiliated career, small business or more creative work.

The drift is not so much into retirement but into less commitment as more men stay in the workforce after 55 but not as many stay in full-time work.

The more leisured worker is not a drain on society, and therefore not a great worry to the Treasurer, but the voluntary outworker still represents a withdrawal from mainstream society.

We used to chide people for taking the bat home: now we champion the idea.

Of course, the hard-line jobs will still get done but they'll be done by other sorts of people.

Obstetrics, stripped of white male rugger-buggers, might be done by midwives, GPs or immigrants.

A study published in *People and Place* magazine a few months ago found that the exodus of psychiatrists from the public health system had forced government departments to look further afield for specialists, especially for rural placements. Now, in fact, 41 per cent of public psychiatrists are overseas-born.

Migrant labour has traditionally been associated with cleaning toilets, picking fruit or working 24/7 in ethnic restaurants.

Migrants are still doing jobs Australians don't want, but they're now in those professions that have been penalised by the uncivil society.

Source *Australian Financial Review*, 24–25 May 2003, p. 28.

In contrast, proactive employees continually ask questions:
- What do I really want to do?
- What do I know how to do?
- What career opportunities can I expect to be available?
- Where do I want to go?
- What do I need to get there?
- How can I tell how well I am doing?
- How marketable will my skills be in five years time? Am I in an occupational growth area?
- What opportunities do I have to learn and grow?
- Who is there who will help and encourage my development?
- How can I get out of the box I am in?[33]
- Is my organisation successful? Will it continue to grow?
- Do I want to remain in this industry?
- What can I do now?

Although some organisations provide in-house career planning and development, this is often geared to the organisation's needs and not those of the individual employee. Unless employees are motivated to seek ongoing personal development, they increase the risk of declining performance and job loss by becoming professionally obsolete.

Individual career planning means that the employee must critically examine their personal and vocational interests, personal and career goals, and current skill and ability levels. The HR department and the employee's superior can both help with this process.

The employee has the ultimate responsibility for developing an action plan to achieve a particular career objective, because only the employee can answer some key questions:
- How hard am I prepared to work?
- What is important to me?
- What kind of trade-offs between work, family and leisure am I prepared to make?
- Am I prepared to undertake further study?
- Am I prepared to make the necessary sacrifices such as relocation overseas to achieve my career goals?
- What are my financial resources?

Career planning and development require a conscious effort on the part of the employee — the process does not happen automatically. Effective career planning depends on the joint efforts of the employee, their manager and the HR department.

The HR department's responsibility

Proactive HR managers recognise the importance of career planning and development in satisfying individual and organisational needs. If the HR department is fully aware of the organisation's future HR needs, career openings and training and development opportunities, then it is well placed to promote career planning among employees. The HR department can do this by providing career education information, vocational guidance, **career counselling** information on job opportunities and career options, and by publicising training

Career counselling Involves the giving of information and advice to employees to facilitate their career planning and development.

and development programs. By supporting career planning and development, HR managers can realise a number of benefits for their organisations (see figure 10.2).

WHY USE CAREER PLANNING?

- *It aligns strategy and internal staffing requirements.* By assisting employees with career planning, the HR department can better prepare them for anticipated job openings identified in the HR plan, resulting in a better mix of the talents needed to support company strategies.
- *It develops promotable employees.* Career planning helps develop internal supplies of promotable talent to meet openings caused by retirement, resignations and growth.
- *It facilitates international placement.* Global organisations use career planning to help identify and prepare for placement across international borders.
- *It assists with work force diversity.* When they are given career planning assistance, workers with diverse backgrounds can learn about the organisation's expectations for self-growth and development.
- *It lowers turnover.* Increased attention and concern for individual careers may generate more organisational loyalty and lower employee turnover.
- *It taps employee potential.* Career planning encourages employees to tap more of their potential abilities

because they have specific career goals. Not only does this prepare employees for future openings, it can lead to better performance among incumbents in their current jobs.
- *It furthers potential growth.* Career plans and goals motivate employees to grow and develop.
- *It reduces hoarding.* Career planning causes employees, managers and the HR department to become aware of employee qualifications, preventing selfish managers from hoarding key subordinates.
- *It satisfies employee needs.* With less hoarding and improved growth opportunities, an individual's esteem needs, such as recognition and accomplishment, are more readily satisfied.
- *It assists affirmative action plans.* Career planning can help members of protected groups to prepare for more important jobs. This preparation can contribute to meeting affirmative action timetables.

To realise these benefits, companies are supporting career planning through career education, information and counselling.

Figure 10.2 Career planning benefits
Source W. B. Werther and K. Davis, *Human Resources and Personnel Management*, 5th edn, McGraw-Hill, New York, 1996, p. 317.

Factors in career development

Individual employees must accept the responsibility for their own career development. Failure to do so will prevent smooth and optimal career progression. Following are some factors that are important to successful career development and growth.

Performance

This is the foundation to career success. Employees who perform badly are rarely considered for training and development opportunities, international assignments or promotion.

It is critical that employees fully understand their managers' performance expectations and what they regard as good performance. Misunderstandings regarding performance expectations are an all too common cause of **career meltdown** (see figure 10.5). Moreover, a key criterion for success is the willingness to stay and do whatever needs to be done (irrespective of anything else in your life). The reality is that in many companies, to make it to the top you have to be available 24 hours a day, seven days a week, 52 weeks a year.[34]

Exposure

If an employee is to succeed, they must become known to senior management. Even good performers can miss out on important career opportunities if they lack **exposure** (see figure 10.3). Many employees think self-promotion is unnecessary or demeaning and that the quality of their work should speak for itself. It won't. To be successful, employees need to learn to play the game of self-promotion.[35] Employees can become known to the

Career meltdown Occurs when an employee's career commences a downward spiral. Typically characterised by termination, demotion, being bypassed for promotion and being politically marginalised.

Exposure Employee behaviour designed to make management aware of the employee's abilities and achievements.

organisation's decision makers through superior performance, leading a high-profile project, report writing, presentations (the ability to deliver a first-class presentation is now an indispensable corporate survival skill) and involvement in company training and development programs and social activities.

CAREER MYTHS

- A university degree is a guarantee for getting a good job.
- Big, profitable companies offer job security.
- If you perform well, your job will be secure.
- Ability and hard work will get you to the top.
- If you are good at your job, you don't have to promote yourself.
- Top performers get the promotions and the big pay increases.

- You can have a balanced work/family life and get to the top.
- If your performance is outstanding, you will be rewarded.
- Networking and mentoring are not necessary for success if you are a top performer.
- If you keep yourself up to date, you will always be guaranteed a good job.

Figure 10.3 Some career myths
Source Asia Pacific Management Co. Ltd, 2004.

A recent trend in the United States is for high-flying executives to use executive talent agencies (similar to those used by sports stars and celebrities) to promote their careers by identifying jobs, providing career coaching, negotiating compensation packages and arranging speaking engagements and other activities to build visibility.[36]

Qualifications

US research indicates that a strong correlation exists between graduate earnings and the quality of the university they attended. Graduates from universities in the top quintile, for example, earn about 20 per cent more than comparable graduates from universities in the bottom quintile.[37] A survey of major companies in Japan overwhelmingly showed that company presidents came from the country's most prestigious universities such as Tokyo, Kyoto and Waseda.[38] Similarly, graduates from traditional or 'sandstone' universities in Australia win jobs at a rate above the average.[39] The big four accounting firms, for example, tend to choose their recruits from a small number of sandstone universities such as the University of Melbourne, the University of NSW and the University of Queensland.[40] Leading companies such as The Boston Consulting Group likewise specify that applicants should have an outstanding academic record from a top tier university.[41]

Universities also are trumpeting the importance of prestige. One university bluntly states, 'It's not the letters after your name, it's the name after your letters' while another proclaims 'Academic excellence counts'.[42] Macquarie Graduate School of Management claims it has the number one MBA program in Asia and Australia 'where successful people go to go further'.[43] The proliferation of MBA degrees means that graduates from elite schools such as the Australian Graduate School of Management, Melbourne Business School, Hong Kong University of Science and Technology and the National University of Singapore have a competitive advantage. Interestingly, the cost of an MBA program appears to be related to its prestige.[44] A recent trend is for many top US business schools to promote combined courses of study to further differentiate their students in the marketplace. It is estimated that around 30 per cent of students at top US business schools now pursue two masters degrees. Popular additions include law, engineering, science and public policy.[45]

Should companies be able to employ talented people from anywhere in the world, irrespective of the need to provide job opportunities for local graduates?

Leading US universities such as Chicago, Columbia, Dartmouth, Duke, Harvard, Michigan, MIT, Northwestern and Pennsylvania produce graduates who consistently get the best job offers and highest salaries. Anecdotal evidence suggests that holding a US degree carries more weight than an Australian or Hong Kong qualification. Undoubtedly, the 'brand' of a business school carries enormous weight and can have a direct impact on employee marketability.[46]

The global reputation of a business school, for example, is critical for graduates seeking a career with leading multinational companies.[47] Graduates from less well known institutions or distance learning programs risk having their qualifications discounted.[48] Careers expert Professor Samuel Aryee calls this **negative educational equity**.[49] This arises with 'Mickey Mouse' degrees where quality control is poor or nonexistent. The result is that employers regard both the qualification and the applicant negatively. The degree, instead of enhancing job opportunities, reduces them. One critic publicly claimed that academic standards at one of Hong Kong's newer universities were so low that its campus would better serve the community as a car park.[50] Such concerns have led some employers to restrict job applications to nominated 'premier' universities.[51]

Employer reputation

Some organisations have a 'star' reputation as breeding grounds for high-potential employees. Consequently, getting a job with the right company can be an important factor in career success and long-term employability. Macquarie Bank, known as the 'millionaire factory' (it takes about five years for a recruit to become a millionaire) selects only 100 graduates from the more than 6000 who apply. Recognised for their intelligence, ambition, aggressiveness and team culture, Macquarie Bank alumni are highly marketable.[52] Other leading companies such as Citigroup, Rio Tinto, General Electric, McKinsey & Co., IBM and Unilever are also renowned for their managerial excellence.[53]

Says Hilton Sack, Visa Executive Vice-President, Australia and New Zealand: 'Citibank has always been known as the university bank. It puts training as a higher priority than any other bank I know. We were always told to challenge the status quo and to find a point of difference in winning over a customer base. One excellent principle at Citibank is that you were given a lot of responsibility but you were allowed to make mistakes. As long as you had done your homework, there was no question of being punished.'[54] Similarly, Helen Nugent says, 'At McKinsey, there was superb training and desire to get in deep on all subjects. At its best, it was a school for life; they really believe their main asset is people.'[55] Companies such as these are fertile hunting grounds for executive talent and give employees a competitive edge in the marketplace.

Finally, people who have worked in industries that are exposed to major change (such as services and technology) and that have a strong marketing emphasis will be in demand.[56]

Nepotism

Is it ethical for publicly listed companies to promote family members into senior management positions?

Thirty per cent of publicly listed companies in Hong Kong have boards of directors on which half or more of the executive directors are related as family members.[57] The Bank of East Asia Board of Directors, for example, includes Chief Executive David Li Kwok Po, Chairman Li Fook Wo (David's uncle), Director Li Fook-shu (David's father), Director Alan Li Fook Sum (David's cousin), Director Arthur Li Kwok Cheung (David's brother), Director Sean Li Fook Simm (David's uncle) and Director Aubrey Li Kwok Sing (David's son). Interestingly, the Li family is not a major shareholder.[58] Most big companies in Asia are still characterised by nepotism and a lack of professional management.[59] The children of senior communist party officials in China are called 'princelings' and are noted for their overwhelming presence in key positions in business and government.[60] In Australia, family dynasties are evident in major companies such as News Corporation, Visy Industries and Consolidated Press Holdings Ltd.[61] Says James Packer, heir to the Consolidated Press empire: 'University is fantastic for people who don't have the opportunity to get a job without it.'[62]

Mentors

Successful managers usually have a **mentor** or sponsor who helps advance their career by offering advice, giving instruction and opening up career opportunities.[63] The mentor is usually an older, experienced senior manager. Organisations may formally establish sponsorships as part of an employee's orientation or such arrangements may develop informally. Research suggests that for the mentoring experience to be perceived positively, the values, personality and interests of the mentor and mentee should be similar.[64]

Mentoring activities

- The mentor may advance the career of the protégé by nominating them for promotion or membership of a high-profile project team.

- The mentor may provide the protégé with visibility in the organisation or profession by personal introduction and recommendation.
- The mentor may protect the protégé from controversial situations and provide coaching by suggesting appropriate coping strategies.
- The mentor may provide counselling about work and personal problems and generally act as a role model.[65]

Benefits of mentoring
- The protégé, by developing more skills and self-confidence, performs better and provides longer service to the organisation.
- Mentoring, by identifying talent, helps companies encourage and capitalise on diversity.
- Mentoring provides a structure for the growth and development of all employees.[66]
- Mentoring helps inculcate corporate values.
- Mentoring improves employee job and career satisfaction, motivation, and career success.[67]
- Mentors can buffer women from discrimination and help them to overcome gender-related barriers to advancement.[68]

Unfortunately, women and minorities often find themselves excluded from mentoring relationships. This is because mentoring is frequently based on personal relationships built up outside working hours. In addition, some men dislike taking on female protégés because of the sexual innuendoes or fear of sexual harassment claims that often accompany such relationships.[69] Also, many organisations have few female senior managers available to become mentors and these women are often reluctant to take on mentoring roles.[70] Finally, mentoring may play a less important role in authoritarian cultures (except for a lucky few) and in family companies (except for those with family connections).[71]

Ingratiation

Ingratiation may be an effective career strategy, especially when associated with competence. Research suggests that ingratiators receive higher pay rises and more promises of pay increases than do equally competent non-ingratiators. Ingratiating behaviour includes doing favours for the target person (usually a superior), agreeing with their opinions, using praise and flattery, and persuading the target of one's positive qualities and good intentions. Using ingratiation as a career strategy to establish a good image with superiors appears to be more common among managers than among employees with a professional or scientific orientation.[72] There is also evidence to suggest that certain types of ingratiatory behaviour may be more appropriate in some cultures than others.[73] Finally, research indicates that a task-oriented leadership style discourages ingratiation, while a participative leadership style facilitates ingratiation.[74]

Is it ethical to use ingratiation to promote your career?

Development

Ongoing expansion of skills and knowledge makes an employee more valuable and therefore more attractive to the organisation. Employees with business and economics postgraduate degrees such as MBAs and Masters of Commerce, for example, are among the most highly compensated.[75] According to one expert, 'the conscious acquisition of skills and experience improves the options available and the desirability of the person to a prospective employer'.[76] Self-development also overcomes the problems of career plateauing and professional obsolescence.

But it is critical that technological, managerial and other acquired skills relate to the demands of the job market. People with academic qualifications not needed by today's market now constitute a relatively greater proportion of the long-term unemployed in the United States than do high school drop-outs.[77] In Taiwan, hundreds of college graduates have applied for jobs as garbage collectors, and in Hong Kong, graduates have taken jobs as security guards.[78] In Malaysia, almost one-quarter of fresh graduates cannot find a suitable job because they studied courses not wanted by employers.[79] Australian humanities and social science graduates are twice as likely to be unemployed and are unlikely ever to earn high salaries (see figure 10.4).[80]

Employees who do not upgrade their skills and know-how in the light of economic, social and technological change will become the victims in company takeovers and company reorganisations.

- A graduate with a science degree asks: why does it work?
- A graduate with an engineering degree asks: how does it work?
- A graduate with a business administration degree asks: how much does it cost?
- A graduate with an education degree asks: do you want fries with that?

Figure 10.4 A matter of degree

This Letter to the Editor provides a provocative viewpoint. Do you agree? See 'What's your view?' on page 394.

Letter to the Editor

Employers don't regard MBAs to be of much value

Dear Editor,

I am writing to see whether any of your readers can assist me with some career advice.

Several years ago, I completed a double degree in science and business at a major metropolitan university. Since then, I have become a supervisor at a medium-sized manufacturing company in the suburbs of Melbourne. While the position is a good one, I would like to advance my career by undertaking postgraduate study; however, I am beset by conflicting views about the value of completing an MBA.

Some of my colleagues believe that enrolling in an MBA is nothing but an exercise in futility. They argue that MBAs vary so much in quality that employers cannot pick the good ones from the bad. They also state that it is doubtful whether I would recoup the costs of undertaking an MBA. My research indicates that the cost of MBAs in Australia varies from around $10 000 to more than $40 000. Another argument put by these colleagues is that MBAs are the outcome of 'credentialism' in our society, whereby MBAs are merely the contemporary equivalent of a good first degree in days gone by. They state that the academic standard of many

MBAs is barely undergraduate level, and that only an idiot or a snob would pay $40 000 or more for a questionable academic qualification. I am also a little concerned that the subjects in an MBA would merely be a rehash of those completed in my undergraduate business degree.

Other colleagues, particularly those who have an MBA, put a different position. Their view is that it doesn't matter that there may be overlap between my undergraduate degree and an MBA, since the fact is that people like me need an MBA to at least match the CVs of competitors for senior positions at this company and at other organisations. In any event, they say that I will be exposed to a range of new management theories and concepts that have been developed since my undergraduate days. They also argue that the opportunities for networking with faculty and fellow students at the more prestigious business schools may prove invaluable in building my career over the longer term.

One day, I find the arguments of the anti-MBA colleagues convincing. The next, I find that I'm motivated by my MBA-holding colleagues to phone the leading MBA schools for information and application forms. Who is right? What should I do?

An anxious junior manager

Source David Poole, University of Western Sydney.

International experience

International experience is increasingly a key to career success (particularly for those aspiring to top management).[81] Companies' growing realisation that business does not have geographic boundaries has created a demand for global managers who understand how business is done in other countries and who feel comfortable working at home or abroad. Leading companies continue to expand their international business operations, so an expatriate assignment is becoming a dominant factor in career progression. An overseas assignment, furthermore, can offer much greater responsibility, freedom and broader experience than can an equivalent position in Australia.[82] Finally, because Australia faces marginalisation in the global economy with increasing numbers of major companies moving (or contemplating moving) their headquarters offshore, non-mobile employees risk having their careers capped at 'branch office' level.[83]

Language skills

The internationalisation of business and the development of global business centres such as Hong Kong and Singapore demand that fast-track managers possess not only good English skills but competency in a second (or third) language. For example, Hong Kong graduates who want to land top jobs are expected to have fluency in English, Cantonese and Mandarin. Similarly, Westerners wishing to work in Asia now require good language skills.[84] According to Srivastava, in the information age non-English speakers increasingly risk being left behind and marginalised.[85] In recognition of this, Malaysia has restored English as a teaching language in its schools and universities.[86]

Computer and keyboard skills

To have a competitive advantage, computer literacy is a must. High-skilled employees must be 'technology capable'. The use of email has transformed work practices — gone are the typing pools and the support staff. 'Keyboarding' (typing) is a must-have skill (even workers in jobs once considered 'low tech' now need keyboard skills). Productivity is the driving force. According to one expert, once employees learn to touch-type they can save at least one hour per day. In addition, occupational health and safety requirements mean that bad typing habits that produce posture and muscle strain problems cannot be tolerated. Finally, research shows that poor typing skills are linked to technology-related stress, making employees reluctant to use email and computers. Sun Microsystems CEO Scott McNealy says, 'If your boss can't type, doesn't do email and doesn't surf the Web, get out'.[87] To be employable means embracing technology. Companies such as Fortis Australia now make it compulsory for their employees to learn to type.[88]

Networking

It is extremely important for an employee to build a network of contacts who are likely to be useful to career development. Two-thirds of retrenched executives, for example, find their new jobs through networking.[89] Employees who are not part of a network are at a career disadvantage because members typically favour each other in all manner of business situations. **Networking** is really about maintaining friendships and keeping visible. It is a process for letting people know who you are and what you are doing.[90] Experts recommend that networking be regarded as an ongoing lifetime project, requiring consistent effort and commitment. It is important to find comfortable ways of keeping in touch. Personal notes, thankyou letters and recognition of special occasions are all examples. 'Successful people', says Lloyd, 'know that the way to opportunities and advancement often comes from a network that is carefully maintained.'[91] Potential sources of contacts include business, governments, trade unions, professional bodies, universities and trade and commercial associations. However, the richest source for networking is an employee's circle of informal contacts such as friends, relatives and business associates.

Networking Using informal contacts inside and outside an organisation.

Goal setting

Career education expert Dr Betty Levy says: 'successful career planners are self motivated, self starters who are hard working, and most important of all, goal directed. They have established what goals they want to achieve and how to go about it. Young people may find their final career goals change along the way and they will inevitably develop new goals to strive after. This is an important aspect of life and an outcome of the changing environment and personal development and achievement.'[92] Without **goal setting**, employees will find it difficult to realise their maximum potential. Their careers will be without focus and subject to aimless drift. Successful career development requires a goal-oriented approach if it is to have purpose and give the employee a sense of direction and achievement.

Goal setting The process of defining an objective or target to achieve. Gives a sense of purpose or direction to an action.

Financial planning skills

Today, savvy employees know that there are no lifelong employment guarantees. The loyalty contract has disappeared. Companies make employment decisions based on financial considerations. Life at work is harder and less certain.[93] In an era of portable careers and short-term work assignments interspersed with periods of unemployment, financial planning skills are essential. Employees must think of themselves as a business, 'Me Inc'.[94] This involves developing marketing (especially networking), career planning and financial know-how. Employees need expertise in insurance, investments and superannuation. Unfortunately, schools and universities rarely teach these skills, preferring to prepare people for an industrial age that no longer exists. In the information age people must be concerned with wealth creation and financial independence. Financial guru Robert Kiyosaki argues: 'Your boss's job is not to make you rich. Your boss's job is to make sure that you get your pay cheque. It is your job to become rich.'[95] To ignore such advice is likely to prove financially and psychologically painful; the company will not take care of you.

Golf

Golf is at the centre of business, especially in Asia where most major business deals are concluded on the golf course.[96] The golf course is now called the boardroom of the new millennium, because business discussions that start on the golf course often end up in the boardroom. Recognition of this has led leading companies, such as IBM, to pay for their employees to attend golf seminars.[97] Comments one senior executive: 'They say that business and pleasure should never mix, but golf is the exception to that rule. I have been able to develop a network of wonderful clients, many of whom I now call my friends.'[98] Liz King, Senior Manager Corporate Sponsorship with Ernst & Young, similarly says, 'Being able to play a round of golf has proved advantageous at work'.[99] Golf is a universal language, it fosters relationships, develops networks and provides access to senior managers.[100] Poor golf skills, moreover, have been identified as a blocking factor to the advancement of women in business.[101] 'What you see in a person on the golf course', says Mark Woodward, General Manager, Panasonic, 'is a good indication of how they are in life, including business.'[102]

Appearance

There is ample evidence to indicate that appearance plays an important role in compensation and career success. Likewise, some companies believe that if employees look old, they are less dynamic and have only old ideas. This has promoted increased interest in cosmetic surgery (especially among middle-aged male managers). In certain professions, such as sales, retail, hospitality, entertainment and consulting, good looks appear to be an unspoken requirement. Cosmetics, fashion and being figure-conscious are now becoming as important for modern males or metrosexuals (à la David Beckham) as for women.[103] One research company, for example, predicts that the global men's skin-care market will grow by 50 per cent within the next few years.[104] Comments one writer, 'Whatever a man's cosmetic shortcoming, it's apt to be a career liability'.

Research shows, for example, that job applicants who are highly attractive are evaluated as being better qualified than unattractive candidates. For women, however, the type of position for which they apply also has an impact. Attractive females tend to get higher ratings for non-managerial jobs, while less attractive females get higher ratings for managerial jobs. Looking good is a potent consideration in hiring and promotion decisions.[105] In China, universities that specialise in training future government employees reject short students (those less than 1.6 metres tall) irrespective of their examination results because of their bleak employment prospects.[106]

Career plateauing

Career plateau Point in an individual's career where the probability of further advancement is negligible..

A **career plateau** refers to that point in an employee's career at which the probability of an additional promotion is minimal. This may stem from the employee's decision to make a trade-off between career progression and a more balanced lifestyle. The progression of most employees up the organisational hierarchy must stop at some time. When this happens, employees find themselves blocked and unable to achieve further advancement (see figure 10.5). (Women appear to top out at the same ages and rates as men.[107]) If an employee is to avoid plateauing, it is critical that they have the ability to adapt and develop in the face of change or **career transition**.[108] Employee plateauing creates problems for both the individual and the organisation. According to Professor Judith Barwick, this is especially the case for those employees who have been successful because it can destroy their motivation, allegiance, commitment and productivity.[109]

Employees are now 'reaching plateaus earlier in their careers than did their predecessors — and far earlier than their own expectations — [so] it is important for organisations and individuals to prepare to cope with the phenomenon successfully, particularly when the signs of an impending plateau are observed'.[110] Aryee, for example, found that the risk of obsolescence is less if organisations accept responsibility for employee development and if employees are prepared to invest time in their development.[111] Similarly, if organisations do not neglect plateaued employees, but instead provide feedback and challenging jobs, those employees remain productive even when they do not receive any opportunities for promotion.[112]

Career transition Involves a significant change in an employee's career via transfer, demotion, promotion, overseas assignment or switch from one occupation to another.

Dual careers

As more women enter the work force, HR managers must develop specific policies and programs designed to accommodate the **dual career** aspirations of employees and their partners (see figure 10.6). HR managers must be particularly alert to the implications of an employed partner when providing career counselling to an employee.[113] Problems may arise because each partner works different shifts, because both strongly identify with their chosen professions or because a relocation is incompatible with a partner's career plans. One survey, for example, found that almost 60 per cent of companies reported difficulty in moving dual career couples.[114] This is not surprising because many organisations are unresponsive and provide little support.[115] Organisations and employees can both suffer loss of flexibility as a result of dual career demands. Tensions can arise over basic issues such as who stays late at the office, whose turn it is to travel or whose turn it is to pick up the children. As a result, dual careers have been described as a high wire act.[116]

Dual career Situation where both spouses or partners have career responsibilities and aspirations.

SIGNS OF CAREER MELTDOWN

Watch out if your career exhibits the following danger signs. It could be a signal to start looking elsewhere before you reach career meltdown.

- You are over 45, highly paid and work in a cost centre.
- Your company is outsourcing.
- You have been passed over for promotion or demoted.
- Your relationships with your colleagues and superiors are deteriorating. You are no longer invited for drinks after work or to other social activities.
- You are being marginalised. Slowly, but surely, you are being eased out of the communication loop. You no longer get selected for interesting jobs or projects.
- Your company's strategic direction has changed. Your abilities, skills and experience are no longer relevant.
- The corporate culture has changed. You don't fit with the new values.
- New technology is being introduced. You are not viewed as being technically savvy, flexible or as ready to embrace change.

- You are perceived as a 'quality of life' type and not a 'work' person.
- Your mentor or your boss has been fired.
- Your company has been taken over.
- Your department is being reorganised.
- You haven't had a pay increase (but everyone else has).
- You are perceived as a 'moaner and groaner'.
- Your performance is unsatisfactory, but you won't admit it.
- You are 'invisible'. No one in senior management knows who you are or what you do.
- You are perceived as a threat by your boss or other powerful managers.

However, not all these signs mean you have reached career meltdown. You may have been blocked, bypassed or terminated because you are the wrong sex, race, religion, nationality, colour, height, weight or whatever — you are just wrong. But that doesn't mean that you should be a passive patsy. Learn the rules of the game — it's your insurance for a bright and independent future.

Figure 10.5 How to avoid career meltdown
Source Asia Pacific Management Co. Ltd, 2004.

- Women are more likely to choose a career in science if they undergo summer internship programs and have a mentor.[117]
- Career satisfaction for women is most adversely affected by work–family conflict.[118]
- The major barriers to career advancement reported by women in their mid-20s to mid-30s were personal and family responsibilities, lack of mentoring, lack of experience and stereotypical views of women's roles and responsibilities.[119]
- Prevailing attitudes and unrelenting job pressures undermine supportive family-friendly HR policies.[120]
- Non-managerial women
  - do not have a clear career strategy but adjust career goals to accommodate others and circumstances in their lives
  - are more hesitant to explore other career options than managerial women.
- For non-managerial women
  - career choices are greatly influenced by other life choices such as parental responsibilities
  - career planning assistance, mentoring, training and tuition refund programs are absolutely critical to career development.[121]
- Senior executive women are recognising the importance of having partners who will set aside their own careers and support them in their advancement. One-third of *Fortune* magazine's most powerful women in business have husbands at home either full-time or part-time.[122]
- The most influential person in determining career choice for both male and female youth is the mother.[123]

Figure 10.6 Women and careers

Dual career couples need to be flexible, to be mutually committed to both careers, to adopt coping mechanisms (such as clearly separating work and non-work roles) and to develop the skills of career planning. Organisations, in turn, can provide flexible work schedules, counselling, effective career management, childcare and support with transfers and relocations.

Work–family conflict

Increasing education, the liberation of women, the rising cost of living and increasing career opportunities for women have led more and more women to enter the work force. This has eroded the traditional support given by the wife to the husband and his career. Consequently, the demands of work have increasingly intruded into family life (and vice versa). One managing director, for example, says he expects his employees to be thinking about customers even when they are taking a shower.[124] An employee states: 'Working at Cisco is like being strapped to a rocket. It never stops.'[125]

Work–family conflict The conflicting demands made on an individual by home and work.

Work–family conflict is evidenced by the dual-income family and the single-parent family. People today are faced with problems of redefining what is meant by success and how to balance work and family. Particularly for women, the integration of work and family responsibilities can be difficult because job demands compete with the traditional family demands of being mother, wife and housekeeper.[126] One UK case, for example, involved a 'high-flying' career woman who was sacked after she refused to have an abortion.[127] The harsh reality is that if women (like men) are not prepared to work the long hours, their career suffers. They do not get the good projects, the challenging assignments or the financial recognition.[128]

Some companies, in turn, are favouring young, unmarried people. Says the CEO of Sun Microsystems, 'It's really hard to do a start up with two kids at home'.[129] This has led one writer to argue that women have to stop believing that they can 'have it all'. It is unrealistic, says McKenna, to expect to achieve success as it is traditionally defined while serving as a family's primary caregiver and housekeeper and in a myriad other domestic roles. 'Pursuit of this ideal', according to McKenna, 'creates stress, depression, and ultimately burnout.'[130]

Men who place family first also face a problem with companies and colleagues. Devoted dads irritate colleagues (especially childless colleagues) who expect them to put the job first.[131] Comments one critic: 'Parents are getting more than non-parents. Every time someone takes time off for that sick child, someone else has to do the work.'[132] This has led some HR experts to question whether it is fair to pay employees who are not prepared to make sacrifices the same rate of pay as those who are.[133] In addition, employees without family responsibilities increasingly claim they are being discriminated against.[134] The more senior a person's position and the older they are, the more likely they are to feel the competing pressures of work and family.[135] Recent research shows that the career satisfaction of women and older males is most adversely affected by work–family conflict — women are affected throughout their working lives and men are affected once they reach 40 years of age or older. It appears that as employees age, they are less willing to endure work–family conflict for the sake of their career.[136]

Family-responsive policies such as the provision of childcare or assistance with childcare expenses, the introduction of flexible work schedules, part-time work, home work, job sharing and flexible leave provisions not only help, but also result in increased employee commitment.[137] Recent research, however, shows that family-friendly policies are often contradicted by prevailing attitudes, long working hours, high levels of unpaid overtime and work intensification.[138] According to ANU's Professor Peter McDonald: 'Firms tend to value and reward those who put in a 60-hour week, not those only wanting to work nine-to-five.'[139] The reality is that families are a problem for companies.[140] Says one writer: 'More and more the business world seems to regard children not as the future generation of workers but as luxuries you are entitled to after you've won your stripes. It's fine to have the kids' pictures on your desk — just don't let them cut into your billable hours.'[141]

In addition, downsizing and the internationalisation of business have created demands for accomplishing more in less time with fewer people, for 24-hour service and for frequent overseas travel. The result is increased conflict between work and family, with the demands of the job becoming all consuming.[142] 'In a world that's a village', says Morris, 'the corporate hero is the one free to fly to Singapore on a moment's notice, not the poor chump who has to get home to relieve the nanny.'[143] Philip Greenspun, Chairman of US software company ArsDigita says: 'Your business success will depend on the extent to which programmers essentially live at your office. Long hours for programmers are a key to profitability.'[144] To get employees to work longer, Greenspun advocates making the office a nicer place to be than home — a big screen TV, rockclimbing wall, indoor garden, aquarium, gym and pinball machines — the all-providing, all-consuming workplace.[145]

Is it unfair for people who are not prepared to work long hours to be paid the same rate of pay as those who are?

CEOs, too, are under unprecedented pressure to perform or be pushed out. Two-thirds of all major companies worldwide replaced their CEO at least once during the past five years.[146] And the evolution of law from a profession to a business with increased pressures for more billable hours has created long hours and dissatisfaction (even though large law firms in Australia provide a range of benefits such as casual Fridays, in-house yoga, after-hours meal services, gym membership and in-house massage, aromatherapy and reflexology).

In such situations, it is not surprising that more and more employees are reporting dissatisfaction with their work–family balance.[147] This has produced **downshifters** — employees who make a conscious decision to cut back on the time they spend at work in order to rebalance their lives — and the **flame-out track** — where employees work to excess, make (and save) lots of money, acquire lots of share options and then quit after five

Downshifters Employees who make a voluntary long-term lifestyle change involving less work, less income and less consumption.

Flame-out track A situation where employees work to excess, make lots of money, acquire lots of assets and then quit to take an open-ended sabbatical.

to 10 years to take an open-ended sabbatical.[148] A recent Newspoll survey found that almost 25 per cent of the Australian population under the age of 60 has downshifted.[149]

How to deal with the competing demands of work and family is a major challenge facing employees, employers and HR managers.

Outplacement

Outplacement is a special type of counselling designed to help a terminated employee to locate a new career. Services provided by outplacement consultants vary but generally include: advice on termination procedures; career evaluation; psychological appraisal; interview training; résumé preparation; job-search techniques; and the provision of office and secretarial services. Its use by industry has grown rapidly as a result of economic conditions, business rationalisations and organisations' recognition of their obligation to help displaced employees to establish new careers. It is claimed that organisations are now 'very conscious of public image and the damage that can be done if they are seen as unjust employers'.[150] Employees who are outplaced include top as well as poor performers, although recent research shows that an executive about to be retrenched is likely to have suffered a marked career plateau within the past five years.[151] Downsizing especially has increased the likelihood that good people will be let go.

An outplacement consultant provides emotional support and identifies new career opportunities, benefiting the employee and the organisation. Outplacement is a balance, sustaining the corporate image while furthering the wellbeing of the exiting employee. Outplacement is an alternative within the career planning process because it creates better prospects for terminated employees. It can also be seen as a contribution to society, as well as remuneration to the individual for past service.

Careers in human resource management

The choice of career for most people plays an important part in their lives. Those contemplating a career in HRM need to think carefully about their career objectives and how they plan to achieve them. HRM offers many exciting opportunities but also has its limitations. Few HRM practitioners, for example, become managing directors or achieve the same status and income as their counterparts in line management.[152] Opportunities in growth sectors such as financial services, high-tech businesses and management consulting, however, are increasing and successful practitioners can expect high incomes, high status and challenging, responsible work. To enhance personal satisfaction and professional success, individuals should thoroughly assess their own needs and expectations, and gather as much information as they can about HR work, career paths, opportunities, rewards, and so on.

Figure 10.7 provides some guidelines on evaluating a particular job offer once you have decided on a career move.

Job variety

Job opportunities exist for both generalists and specialists in HRM. Generalists are involved in a range of HR activities. Typically, such positions at junior levels are found in smaller organisations where the resources do not exist to employ specialists in recruitment and selection, training and development, industrial relations and other HR activities.

Management positions in HR are also generalist in nature, with a focus on planning, leading, organising and controlling the HR function rather than direct involvement in HR operating activities. Executive or top management HR positions emphasise strategic planning, change management and policy development responsibilities.

Specialists, on the other hand, focus on a particular HR activity. Some larger organisations (or management consultancies) may have a whole department or unit to focus on one HR activity and this can provide management opportunities for the employee who wishes to remain a specialist in compensation, change management, industrial relations, training or another HR activity.

A recent trend in some large companies such as IBM and JP Morgan is for HR professionals to be employed in service centres where they wear headsets, sit at screens, answer telephone calls and give advice. These HR specialists spend about 20 per cent of their time on project assignments away from the telephone. It is predicted that more and more people pursuing HR careers in large companies will commence work in a service centre.[153]

HOW TO EVALUATE A JOB OFFER

Changing jobs is an important career step. Don't rush in. Investigate the situation thoroughly before you decide. Some things you should consider include the following:

- Does your personality fit with the culture of the new company? Does the company hold values that are important to you?
- What is the company's reputation? Is the company admired? Is it regarded as ethical? Does it treat its employees well?
- Is the company financially sound? Is it a growth industry? Is it well managed? What do financial analysts say about the company? Is the company likely to be downsized or taken over?
- Does the job excite you? Will it give you the challenges, personal development opportunities and advancemnet you desire?

- Are the rewards competitive? Will you be satisfied with your pay and benefits?
- What does your family think?
- Are they supportive? Will the demands of the job lead to work–family conflict?
- Is the company prepared to spend money on your development? Will you enhance your marketable skills by taking the job?
- What is your boss like? What are the key people you will have to work with like? Will you be comfortable working with them?

Say 'yes' when you feel confident that the indicators are positive. Say 'no' or do some more homework if you are not sure. Changing jobs involves risk. Be thorough and move carefully to minimise this risk.

Figure 10.7 How to evaluate a job offer
Source Asia Pacific Management Co. Ltd, 2004.

Remuneration

Remuneration for HRM employees has lagged behind that paid to employees in functions such as finance and marketing. Australian and US data suggest that the median earnings of full-time HR professionals are in decline and that male HR professionals, on average, still earn more than their female counterparts.[154] However, as HRM moves away from its traditional status of a cost centre to that of a profit contributor and strategic business partner, the magnitude of the monetary differential is reducing (particularly in banking and financial services and high-tech companies). Anne Sherry, Group Executive, People & Performance at Westpac, has total compensation in excess of $970 000, while P. S. Wilson, Amcor's Executive General Manager, Human Resources and Operating Risk, has total remuneration above $900 000.[155] Recent income figures are shown in table 10.1.

Working conditions

HR departments are frequented by applicants, employees, union representatives, government officials and visitors, so they need to present a favourable image of the organisation as a place of employment. Consequently, most HR offices tend to be clean and pleasant places in which to work. HR people work a standard 35- to 40-hour week, but increasingly longer hours are being demanded. This is especially the case for more senior managers and during activities such as union negotiations and graduate recruiting. Most HR practitioners spend their time in the office, but some may travel extensively — for example, executive recruiters and industrial relations specialists.

Position 53
Head of Human Resources and Administration II (Regional)
Number of incumbents: 29
Number of companies: 17

Position description
The position reports to the Chief Executive Officer (Regional). Responsible for the overall direction and control of all human resources services such as recruitment and selection, training and development, compensation and benefits, employee services and industrial relations. Serves as part of the management team and has significant involvement in planning for broad administration and office management. Supervises one or more human resources teams. Operates in a large or diversified organisation in several countries in the Asia–Pacific region, possibly directing personnel specialist managers. Minimum 12 to 15 years relevant experience.

ANNUAL COMPENSATION DATA AS OF 1 JANUARY 2001

	Minimum	Lower decile	Lower quartile	Median	Upper quartile	Upper decile	Maximum	Weighted average
Company characteristics								
2000 annual sales volume (HK$m)	–	282	389	460	728	1396	—	686
Number of employees	29	40	56	109	322	411	546	271
Incumbent characteristics								
Years of service with the co.	—	1	2	5	7	8	—	5
Years of relevant experience	5	6	8	10	12	15	15	11
Cash compensation (HK$'000)								
Basic salary	726	872	1126	1240	1560	1642	2072	1298
Basic guaranteed	787	389	1159	1297	1661	1704	2244	1380
Basic guaranteed + bonuses	810	954	1246	1456	1690	2032	2767	1507
Total cash	884	996	1246	1456	2033	2117	2767	1579
Cash components (HK$'000)	**% receiving**							
Allowances	35	—	24	71	185	305	352	—	173
Fixed bonus	59	—	67	92	118	129	135	—	109
Variable bonuses	76	24	60	91	185	291	372	523	161
Cash components analysis								
Allowances as % of basic salary	—	1.7	4.5	16.6	23.3	24.3	—	13.5
Fixed bonus in no. of months of basic salary	—	1.0	1.0	1.0	1.0	1.0	—	1.0
Variable bonuses in no. of months of basic salary	0.4	0.7	0.9	1.8	2.6	3.0	3.0	1.4

Note: A$1 = HK$5.50 (approximately).
Source Watson Wyatt, *Compensation Report — Hong Kong*, Hong Kong, 2003.

Career preparation

Education

Some people work in HRM without academic qualifications, but it is evident that the increasing demands by employers for professional competence and know-how make tertiary education essential.[156] Accredited qualifications are now mandatory for practitioners seeking professional membership of the Australian Human Resources Institute (AHRI).

But what tertiary qualifications are best for a career in HRM? There is no evidence to suggest that specialist undergraduate courses in HRM better prepare aspiring HR practitioners for their career than do other courses of study. In fact, behavioural science backgrounds have been criticised for teaching HR professionals to be reactive and producing a glaring ignorance of other aspects of the business.[157]

Such deficiencies partly explain why HR managers are least likely to become CEOs. According to a survey by a leading executive search firm, most CEOs come from sales and marketing, finance, and manufacturing and operations. HRM as a source does not rate a mention.[158] Finally, given the devolution of many HR activities to line managers, the widespread adoption of shared services, and the outsourcing of HR activities such as compensation, recruitment and training, job prospects in HRM risk lagging behind those in finance, marketing and general management.[159]

Competencies

Ulrich argues that the HR manager of the future should be a strategic business partner, an administrative expert, a champion for employees and a change agent. This, says Ulrich, demands competence in knowledge of the business (financial, strategic and technological), knowledge of HR practices (staffing, development appraisal, rewards, organisational planning and communication), change management (ability to create meaning, problem solving, innovation, relationship influence and role influence) and credibility (accuracy, consistency, meeting of commitments, personal chemistry, appropriate confronting of issues, integrity, thinking outside the box, confidentiality and ability to listen to and focus on executive problems).[160]

Other research suggests the following professional skills and abilities are required: anticipates the effect of internal and external changes; exhibits leadership for the HR function and corporation; demonstrates the financial impact of all HR activities; defines and communicates the HR vision for the future; educates and influences line managers on HR issues; takes appropriate risks to accomplish objectives; has broad knowledge of many HR functions; knows about competitors' HR practices; focuses on the quality of HR services; has international experience; influences peers in other companies; has experience in other key business areas; and has line management experience and a business orientation.[161]

Experience

Probably the most beneficial entry to HRM is from a line management function such as marketing. This enables the individual to better understand the problems faced by line managers and to appreciate the importance of bottom-line impact. It also promotes flexibility and provides increased career opportunities outside HRM (a major advantage in an era of boundaryless careers).

The significance of this is emphasised by Andrews, who claims that 'young professionals working upward in the human resources field are systematically trained, by a frequent and continuous series of experiences, to be reactive and rule oriented'.[162] Consequently, too many HR practitioners prefer to be active in HR reporting in lieu of making profitable contributions to the business.[163] Obviously, such people are not seen as potential senior managers or given much status by their colleagues. To be successful, HR professionals must make the effort to become businesspeople who happen to work in HR, rather than HR people who happen to find themselves in a business.[164] Apart from technical proficiency in HR, organisations are now seeking competency in goal setting, functional and organisational leadership, influence management and business knowledge.[165] Increasingly, HR people will have to consider themselves as managers who can work in functions such as finance and marketing and not just as HR specialists. Failure to do so creates the risk of career stagnation, the loss of market attractiveness and job loss.

Peter Barrett *is the Managing Director of Organisation Development Limited, a multipurpose regional consultancy engaged in management consultancy and providing advice to family firms on professionalisation, strategy, corporate governance and succession. He is a Council Member of the Hong Kong Institute of Directors, the Management Consultancies Association of HK and the Employers' Federation of Hong Kong.*

Practitioner speaks

Preparing HR managers for board representation

HR managers are disadvantaged in that being highly specialised in a continuously changing legal and theoretical environment, they have to work hard to keep up to date. In Hong Kong and the Asia–Pacific, since the Asian financial crisis and the impact of SARS, many HR managers have become more like board members and are often consulted by their CEOs.

Some HR managers will be invited to join the board. But do they know how boards work? Do they know what their responsibilities will be? HR managers should begin to think strategically. They should seek to influence the corporate plan and to be involved in its creation. They certainly should be asked to comment on the organisational structure, which may change as a consequence of the plan, and give technical advice on compensation policy changes and strategic changes related to succession plans and organisational development.

How should HR managers prepare themselves to become board members?

1. First, they must understand the elements of corporate governance. How do boards function? What are directors responsible for? What are their fiduciary duties? They should join their local Institute of Directors to help them to comprehend the world of directors, which is different to the world of management.

2. As specialists, HR managers focus on human resources, but they also need to broaden their background and understand marketing (perhaps by joining the local Institute of Marketing) and become more familiar with the operational details of their company. HR managers will never succeed at board level unless they have a complete understanding of finance.

3. The competencies required of a director are quite extensive and HR managers in the main do have several of these, particularly in the areas of communication and interpersonal relationship skills. They need to develop their helicopter thinking quality, rising above the detail to understand overall trends. They also need to understand strategic planning.

4. To be a director, HR managers need to think like a director. One way to do this is to read some of the best literature. I can recommend the following:
   Thin on Top (Professor Bob Garratt, Nicholas Brealey Publishing Ltd, 2003)
   The Fish Rots from the Head (Professor Bob Garratt, Profile Business, 2003)
   Chairing the Board (John Harper, Kogan Page, 2000)
   Corporate Governance and Chairmanship (Adrian Cadbury, Oxford University Press, 2002)
   The Power of Strategic Thinking (Michel Robert, McGraw-Hill, 2000)
   The Board Game (Peter Waine, John Wiley & Sons, 2002).

All directors are responsible at law for the company's actions. The code of conduct in each country makes it imperative that directors' behaviour in managing the board is strictly circumscribed. In addition, directors are legally responsible for the actions of the board. Ignorance is no excuse.

Peter Barrett

Accreditation

Admission to the AHRI is open to graduates and non-graduates. However, grading as a chartered member requires the possession of a recognised academic qualification and approved HR experience. AHRI professional grades are Fellow and Chartered Member, and subprofessionals are classified as Member (which includes Student). Canadian experience suggests that professional membership is valuable for those early in their careers, but is not relevant for senior managers (where work history and expertise count).[166]

HRM as a profession

Whether or not HRM is a profession has long been debated.[167] What is not questioned is whether HR managers should be 'professional' in terms of their qualifications and performance. Comparing HRM against the characteristics of a profession (see figure 10.8) suggests that it is still a long way from meeting the criteria. Getting a job in HRM does not require the candidate to be licensed or registered, to have passed any particular examination or to be a member of the AHRI or any other professional association. 'It should be understood', says Clark, 'that one can be professional without being engaged in a profession. A professional is a person who is skilled in the theoretical, scientific and practical aspects of an occupation, and who performs with a high degree of competence.'[168] Unfortunately, it seems that too many HR academics and practitioners are concerned with professional status rather than professional contribution.[169] **Accreditation** is desirable, if the aim is to improve practitioner expertise and not to make entry into HRM more exclusive and restrictive.

Accreditation The process of certifying the professional competence of HR specialists.

CHARACTERISTICS OF A PROFESSION

1. A profession is characterised by a systematic body of specialised knowledge of substantial intellectual content.
2. A profession is characterised by a motive of service, by standards of conduct, which govern all professional relationships and which take precedent over personal gain and by acceptance of the social responsibility inherent in the profession.
3. A profession is characterised by a recognised educational process and standards of qualification for admission.
4. A profession is an organisation devoted to the advancement of the profession's social obligation and the enforcement of standards of admission and membership.

Figure 10.8 What makes a profession?
Source P. Donham, 'Is management a profession?', *Harvard Business Review*, September–October, 1962, p. 64.

Professional associations

The **professional association** with the largest membership is the AHRI. It conducts conferences, seminars and workshops, provides online learning, publishes *Asia Pacific Journal of Human Resources* and *HR Monthly*, and offers valuable opportunities for networking. Apart from the AHRI, the HR professional will find it beneficial to join other leading associations in the field, such as the Australian Institute of Training and Development, the Industrial Relations Society and the Australian Institute of Management. Major professional associations in Asia include the Hong Kong Institute of Human Resource Management and the Singapore Institute of Human Resource Management.

Professional association Group of specialists who join together to advance their profession and enhance their own personal development.

Professional literature

Ongoing personal development requires awareness of the **professional literature**. Some important publications with which students and practitioners should be familiar are:

Professional literature Literature relating to a particular academic discipline or professional occupation.

- *Asia Pacific Journal of Human Resources* (Australia)
- *British Journal of Industrial Relations* (UK)
- *Compensation and Benefits Review* (USA)
- *Human Resource Management* (USA)
- *Human Resource Planning* (USA)
- *HR Monthly* (Australia)
- *Human Resources* (New Zealand)
- *International Employment Relations Review* (Australia)

- *International Journal of Employment Studies* (Australia)
- *International Journal of Human Resource Management* (UK)
- *Journal of Industrial Relations* (Australia)
- *Labour and Industry* (Australia)
- *Organizational Dynamics* (USA)
- *Personnel Psychology* (USA)
- *Research and Practice in Human Resource Management* (Singapore)

Newspapers and periodicals covering the general field of business and management also contain articles pertaining to human resource management. Among these are *The Asian Wall Street Journal, The Financial Times, Forbes Global, Harvard Business Review, Business Week, Fortune, BRW* and the *Australian Financial Review.*

Thirty interactive Wiley Web Questions are available to test your understanding of this chapter at www.johnwiley.com.au/ highered/hrm5e *in the student resources area*

Summary

Increasing competition, accelerating change and relentless restructuring have made career planning and development critical for both organisations and employees. Effective career planning is essential for employees if they are to fully achieve their career objectives. Organisations, in turn, must realise a better match between employee career aspirations and job opportunities to obtain the supply of qualified human resources needed to achieve strategic organisational objectives.

Although some HR departments provide assistance via information and counselling, the prime responsibility for career planning is with the employee. Important factors contributing to successful career development include performance, exposure, mentoring, personal development, international experience, networking and goal setting. A career plateau is reached at some stage in an employee's career when further promotions or opportunities are unavailable. At this stage, the employee may require outplacement counselling. Conducted by specialists, this counselling is designed to help a terminated employee to locate a new career.

A career in HRM provides opportunities for both generalists and specialists. Remuneration for HRM personnel is improving but has generally lagged behind that for other functions. Working conditions are generally good. Increasingly employers are demanding tertiary qualifications for positions in HRM. It is also desirable to have some experience in line management before entering a position in HRM. Membership with the AHRI provides accreditation and access to professional conferences, seminars, workshops and publications.

student study guide

review questions

1. What is a boundaryless career? Does it appeal to you? Explain your answer.
2. What is career meltdown? What are common signs of career meltdown?
3. What are some of the key factors influencing career progression? Which do you think is the most important? Why?
4. What can an employee do to avoid the problem of career plateauing?
5. Why is job flexibility becoming so important to an employee's career progression?
6. What are the advantages and disadvantages of a career in HRM?
7. What is outplacement? Describe the benefits of outplacement from the employer's and the employee's viewpoint.
8. What are some of the challenges faced by dual career couples? How might these challenges be overcome?
9. How are careers changing? Why do you believe this is so? What further changes do you believe will occur over the next 20 years?
10. What special career problems do older employees face? How do you feel organisations and employees can best manage these challenges?

environmental influences on career planning and development

Describe the key environmental influences from the model (figure 10.9 shown on the next page) that have significance for career planning and development.

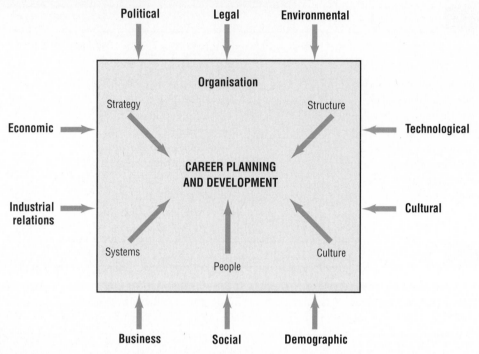

Figure 10.9 Environmental influences on career planning and development

class debate

HRM is a profession.

or

If you want to get to the top, you must be 100 per cent committed to your career — everything else is secondary.

what's your view?

Write a 500-word response to the Letter to the Editor on page 380, agreeing or disagreeing with the writer's point of view.

practitioner speaks

Read the article on page 390. As a class, critically discuss the author's viewpoints, explaining why you agree or disagree with them.

newsbreak exercise

Read the Newsbreak 'When a career becomes hard labour' on pages 374–5. Break into small groups and critically discuss the author's comments. Regroup as a class and discuss your findings.

soapbox

What do you think? Conduct a mini survey of class members, using the questionnaire below. Critically discuss the findings.

1. Having a mentor is critical to career success.	YES	NO
2. Employees are responsible for keeping themselves up to date.	YES	NO
3. 'Liking people' is critical for success in HR.	YES	NO
4. A major in HRM is necessary to be an HR professional.	YES	NO
5. If you want to get to the top, you have to be totally committed to work.	YES	NO
6. All HR specialists should be members of a professional association.	YES	NO

online exercise

Visit three of the web sites listed in the online references on page 400. Write a brief 100-word critique on their usefulness for career planning and development. As a class, discuss your findings.

ethical dilemma

Overqualified, undereducated and unemployed[170]

'Look, Harry. It's ridiculous. I'm getting sick and tired of interviewing graduates who barely know which day of the week it is.' Harry Young, Associate Professor in Management at Western University, nodded his head in acknowledgement.

'Applicants arrive at my office proudly flaunting their collection of certificates and are devastated when I tell them I can't employ them because they don't have the skills I need. Don't the universities understand that companies like mine desperately need people with good communication skills and at least a basic knowledge of the subjects they studied? I hate to tell you this, but I interviewed one of your HRM graduates last week and when I asked him what he knew about cafeteria benefits, he told me it was when a company provided a cafeteria so that employees could get cheap meals. Really Harry, what do you teach people at your place?'

Harry examined the flushed face of Ken Duckett, General Manager of Oz Industries Ltd. The fury and frustration were obvious.

'I know the problem, Ken, but that's the name of the game these days. Everyone graduates. It's becoming a joke. Students know that once they're in the system, they will pass. Students today are customers. They pay their fees and genuinely feel they are entitled to a qualification. It's a business — get as many customers as you can and then spew them out as quickly as possible. Certification is the end prize, not an education.'

'Well, I tell you Harry, I don't intend to waste any more of my time. If I receive another application from one of your graduates, it will go straight into the rubbish bin.'

Discussion questions

1. What ethical issues are raised in this case?
2. Critically discuss the opinions expressed in this case. What are your views?

case studies

Bye-bye Joe and Mary

Joe and Mary were hot contenders to replace Jet Red's CEO Fred Jackson on his retirement. Both actively sought the backing of individual board members. In addition, several key managers aggressively lobbied colleagues on their behalf. After an acrimonious meeting, the board was split on their selection. Senior management also became divided. Personal attacks increased and the work climate became bitter.

In response to major shareholder criticism, the Chairman, Stan Smith, resigned. His replacement, John Mehta, was a tough, no-nonsense executive and immediately took action. Fred's retirement was brought forward, and Alan Balkin, a close associate of John's, was appointed as Jet Red's new Managing Director. John simultaneously requested the resignations of Joe and Mary. A list of directors and senior managers involved in lobbying activities or seen as being closely linked with Joe and Mary was drawn up. A press conference was called at which John announced several board changes and a major management reorganisation. Within three months, all those associated with the succession campaign were gone.

Discussion questions
1. What career issues does this case highlight?
2. Do you think that Joe and Mary were treated appropriately?

'Quality of life' Peter

Peter Wiley, Jet Red's Engineering Manager, was a new age man. He was concerned with equity and quality of life. Always punctual, he arrived at his desk at 8.55 am and left on the dot at 5.00 pm. Peter took tea and lunch breaks at the allocated time. He worked hard (but not too hard) and never took work home. On those occasions that it was necessary for Peter to work overtime (unpaid), he complained bitterly about the company's unfair intrusion into his private life. When assigned to a project team, others quickly got into arguments with Peter about his approach to work. Some colleagues protested when placed on a team with Peter, as they felt he was too 'public service', and more concerned with his entitlements than getting the job done. When the new management took over, Peter was the first one to be let go.

Peter was devastated.

Discussion questions
1. What career mistake did Peter make?
2. Is quality of life incompatible with career success?

Marginalising Mary

The first hint Mary got was when she was not given share options. 'This year, the options are being channelled to junior employees', Stan Vines, Jet Red's Marketing Manager, explained. Later, Mary heard on the grapevine that a number of her colleagues had received share options. She dismissed the disappointment.

Mary's concerns again rose when she was not listed to meet with Alan Balkin, the new Managing Director. Mary was told that because of Alan's tight schedule, a meeting was not possible. On a subsequent business trip to Melbourne head office, Mary found that she was left on her own, or entertained by junior personnel. The senior people were polite, but protested heavy commitments at this time. On her return to Sydney, Mary was informed that as part of a cost-cutting exercise, she was to be relocated to a smaller office. Her old office was to be occupied by a newly appointed marketing specialist — an appointment that Mary had heard nothing about. Somewhat shocked, Mary again hid her feelings.

Shortly afterwards, Mary applied to attend a one-day seminar. Linda Church, the HR Manager, emailed Mary explaining that because of budgetary constraints, attendance was not possible. Mary would have to wait until the next financial year.

A few weeks later, Mary's position was declared redundant. She was given 30 minutes to clear her desk.

Discussion questions

1. What career mistakes did Mary make?
2. What advice would you give to Mary?

Changing Marion

Marion had worked with Jet Red for 22 years as Administration Manager. Because of the company's poor performance and heavy financial losses, it had seen major changes in its board and senior management. Many of Marion's colleagues had 'resigned' and been replaced by outsiders.

Three weeks after the appointment of Linda Church as HR Manager, Marion was called to her new boss's office. Linda told Marion that her position was secure, and that she was being given the new title of Human Resources Manager, Operations. Marion was also told that she would no longer be responsible for payroll, as Jet Red's new accounting policy required that payroll and HR be separated. Marion would now report administratively to Bill Armstrong, Operations Manager, and functionally to Linda.

Marion accepted the rationale for the change but soon became frustrated with Head Office reporting requirements and policy changes. In particular, Marion felt upset when some programs that she had personally introduced were replaced by Head Office initiatives. Although consulted by Linda and Bill, Marion increasingly sensed that she wasn't fitting in. Everyone was under pressure to lower costs and to match Jet Red's new performance goals. More and more emphasis was being given to achievement, academic qualifications and potential.

Younger employees began to be promoted over those with more seniority. Long-time employees began complaining that the company was not the same. The close family culture was dying. Marion increasingly found herself resenting the changes and the relentless focus on the bottom line. She furiously argued that the new performance appraisal program with its emphasis on goal setting and individual accountability was not suitable for Jet Red. Linda replied bluntly that to survive Jet Red had to change and that the new performance program was part of the change process. Marion reluctantly accepted the decision. She began to share her frustrations with other long-serving employees. Two months later a reorganisation was announced. Marion's position (together with those of several other old timers) was declared redundant.

Discussion questions

1. What career mistakes did Marion make?
2. What advice would you give to Marion?

Unknown Angela

Aged 41, Angela joined Jet Red 10 years ago as a human resources specialist. Her colleague Paula, 36, with two years less service, had just been promoted (her second in the last four years). Angela was perplexed. She had worked as hard, if not harder, than Paula. The quality of her work was good. But the breaks never seemed to go her way. Paula appeared to have been sprinkled by magic dust by their boss Linda Church.

Angela is quiet, doesn't believe in blowing her own trumpet, and feels that the quality of her work should speak for itself. However, senior managers like Managing Director Alan Balkin and Jeff Davis, Manager, Finance and Accounting, don't really know her, what she does or the quality of her work.

In contrast, everyone knows Paula. She is always active in company events, communicating with everyone, offering support, letting others know what she is doing and what she has achieved.

When Alan Balkin required the HR Department to reduce its headcount, no one questioned why it was Angela's and not Paula's name on the separation list.

Discussion questions

1. What career mistakes did Angela make?
2. As a career counsellor, what advice would you give to Angela?

practical exercises

1. Interview someone who is currently employed about their views of the career myths listed in figure 10.3 on page 377. As a class, discuss your findings.

2. Interview a friend or family member who is currently employed regarding their views on their company's approach to:
   (a) employee selection
   (b) career planning and development
   (c) employee communication
   (d) employee motivation
   (e) reward management.

   Prepare a report identifying any problems that could arise in these areas and your recommended solutions.

3. Break into small groups and discuss how you would respond to the following questions:
   (a) Why do you want to work for our company?
   (b) Why should we hire you?
   (c) When you were studying, which courses did you like best? Why?
   (d) Why did you choose to study HRM?
   (e) What do you know about our company?
   (f) What do you think produces success in a career in HRM?
   (g) What are your greatest strengths? Weaknesses?
   (h) What are your career objectives? How do you plan to achieve them?

4. This exercise is designed to get you thinking about your career development.
   (a) Individually, complete the following self-assessment questionnaire.
   (b) Break into groups of three or four and review the results of the self-assessments.
   (c) Still in groups of three or four, review the career action plan that each person developed in part 8 of the questionnaire.

SELF-ASSESSMENT QUESTIONNAIRE

1. List your three ideal jobs. These may relate to your present work or be daydreams.

2. List three of your strengths and three things you need to improve.

Strength	Need to improve
1.	1.
2.	2.
3.	3.

3. List your major skills/areas of know-how/special abilities/interests.

4. List all your qualifications, certificates, diplomas, degrees.

5. Indicate what you want from a job by rating the factors listed below
(from 1 = unimportant to 5 = very important):

(a)	High pay	1	2	3	4	5
(b)	Job security	1	2	3	4	5
(c)	Opportunities for travel	1	2	3	4	5
(d)	Opportunities for advancement	1	2	3	4	5
(e)	High status/prestige	1	2	3	4	5
(f)	Interesting work	1	2	3	4	5
(g)	Lots of variety	1	2	3	4	5
(h)	Lots of freedom	1	2	3	4	5
(i)	Lots of power	1	2	3	4	5
(j)	Opportunities to work with people	1	2	3	4	5
(k)	Time to spend with my family	1	2	3	4	5
(l)	Opportunities to develop myself	1	2	3	4	5

6. List three things you would 'hate' in a job.

7. Consider your responses to questions 2, 3, 4, 5 and 6. How well does your present job match with the requirements of your 'dream' job? Are there any mismatches or deficiencies? How can these be overcome?

8. Develop a career action plan using the format shown below.
(a) Self-assessment — Who am I? (abilities, knowledge, skills, interests, personality)
(b) Goal setting — What do I want? (career, lifestyle, financial, educational, family, spiritual, and so on)
(c) Career goal — What do I need to achieve?
—People resources: Who do I know? Who knows about me? Who can help me achieve my goal? How can they help me? What do I have to do to get them to help me?
—Financial resources: How much do I earn? How much do I own (cash, shares, fixed interest, property or other assets)?
—Obstacles: What obstacles exist? How can these be overcome?
—Action plan: How am I going to achieve it? (state how you will achieve your goals)
—Timing: When am I going to achieve it? (set a specific date)

suggested readings

CCH, *Australian Master Human Resources Guide*, CCH, Sydney, 2003, ch. 16.

De Cieri, H. and Kramar, R., *Human Resource Management in Australia*, McGraw-Hill, Sydney, 2003, ch. 11.

Fisher, C. D., Schoenfeldt, L. F. and Shaw, J. B., *Human Resource Management*, 5th edn, Houghton Mifflin, Boston, 2003, pp. 36–44, 742–54.

Gomez-Mejia, L. R., Balkin, D. and Cardy, R., *Managing Human Resources*, 3rd edn, Prentice Hall, Upper Saddle River, NJ, 2001, ch. 9.

Ivancevich, J. M. and Lee, S. H., *Human Resource Management in Asia*, McGraw-Hill, Singapore, 2002, ch. 8.

Nankervis, A. R., Compton, R. L. and Baird, M., *Strategic Human Resource Management*, 4th edn, Nelson, Melbourne, 2002, ch. 10.

online references

executive.seek.com.au
jobsguide.com.au
www.afrboss.com.au/downloads/mbasurvey2002.pdf
www.agsm.edu.au
www.ahri.com.au
www.apesma.asn.au/education/mba
www.asx.com.au
www.bm.ust.hk/execprog/etec
www.business-week.com/bschools/index/html
www.careeremag.com
www.careerone.com.au
www.careers.com
www.careertrainer.com

www.companydirectors.com.au
www.cweb.com
www.deakin.edu.au/home/courses/2001occg
www.futurestep.com.au
www.hbs.harvard.edu
www.mycareer.com.au
www.ncda.org
www.nyuonline.com
www.seek.com.au
www.shrm.org.hrmagazine
www.uniasia.edu
www.workforceonline.com

end notes

1. Quoted in M. Cave, 'Unskilled, unloved and underemployed', *Australian Financial Review*, 15 April 2003, p. 69.

2. A career may be defined as 'a sequence of positions occupied by a person during the course of a lifetime'. See E. Super and D. T. Hall, 'Career development and planning', *Annual Review of Psychology*, vol. 29, 1978, p. 334.

3. L. Thomas, 'Merrill chief breaks with firm's past', *International Herald Tribune*, 5 August 2003, pp. 11, 14.

4. C. Ryan, 'AMP the bloody coup', *Australian Financial Review*, 23–24 August 2003, pp. 19–22.

5. R. Henkoff, 'Companies that train best', *Fortune*, 22 March 1993, p. 58.

6. R. Henkoff, op. cit., p. 58.

7. Quoted in J. Rowbotham, 'Where the new jobs will come from', *Business Review Weekly*, 17 April 1992, p. 39.

8. C. Jones and R. J. De Fillippi, 'Back to the future in film: combining industry and self knowledge to meet the career challenges of the 21st century', *Academy of Management Executive*, vol. 10, no. 4, 1996, p. 89.

9. P. Herriot, 'Careers', in M. Poole and M. Warner (eds), *The Handbook of Human Resource Management*, Thomson, London, 1998, pp. 469–71.

10. J. Pfeffer, *The Human Equation*, Harvard Business School Press, Boston, 1998, ch. 6.

11. ACIRRT, *Australia at Work*, Prentice Hall, Sydney, 1999, p. 126.

12. P. Coy, 'Limiting the risk — and pain — of capitalism', *Business Week*, 14 April 2003, p. 9.

13. Quoted in 'The new professionals', *World Executive's Digest*, May 1993, p. 14.

14. Quoted in 'The new professionals', op. cit., p. 14.

15. C. Handy, 'Intelligence — capitalism's most potent asset', *HR Monthly*, December 1996, p. 8.

16. W. Kiechel, 'A manager's career in the new economy', *Fortune*, 4 April 1994, p. 52; B. Juddery, 'Statistics confirm the value of a degree', *Campus Review*, 15–21 January 1997, p. 8; and K. Murphy, 'Men more likely to be retrenched', *Australian Financial Review*, 10 October 2000, p. 7.

17. C. Martin, 'ALP: Teach our children early about tertiary level', *Australian Financial Review*, 17 July 2003, p. 8.

18. R. Wolf, 'Welfare to work not an easy road', *USA Today*, 13 March 1997, p. 3A; R. Hawes and B. Hutchings, 'A chance to learn and earn', *Australian*, 12 March 1997, pp. 1–2; K. Marshall, 'Flood of graduates squeezes out school leavers', *Australian Financial Review*, 9 July 2003, p. 6; and M. Cave, 'Unskilled, unloved and underemployed', *Australian Financial Review*, 15 April 2003, p. 69.

19. Graduate Careers Council Survey, reported in K. Marshall, 2003, op. cit., p. 6.

20. Quoted in M. Dwyer, 'Alarming drop in graduate jobs', *Australian Financial Review*, 18 February 2003, p. 13.

21. A. Yeung, 'Human asset management', *People Today*, December 2000, pp. 22–6.

22. P. McGeehan, 'Even at top seniors struggle to keep jobs', *International Herald Tribune*, 4 February 2003, p. 12.

23. Reported in H. Trinca, 'CEOs crash and churn', *Australian Financial Review*, 18 September 2003, p. 1.

24. Workers "too complacent" about skills', *Straits Times*, 28 August 2000, p. 1.

25. Quoted in J. Byrne, 'The search for the young and gifted', *Business Week*, 4 October 1999, pp. 65–6.

26. C. Handy, op. cit., p. 11.

27. J. Byrne, op. cit., pp. 64–8; and D. Leonard, 'They're coming to take you away', *Fortune*, 29 May 2000, pp. 41, 54.

28. E. Snape and T. Redman, 'Too old or too young? The impact of perceived age discrimination', *Human Resource Management Journal*, vol. 13, no. 1, 2003, p. 79.

29. W. F. Cascio, *Managing Human Resources*, 4th edn, McGraw-Hill, New York, 1995, p. 309.

30. R. Henkoff, op. cit., p. 49; and A. Bradfield and A. Rubins, 'Six key steps to career management', *HR Monthly*, April 1999, p. 50.

31. S. Sherman, 'A brave new Darwinian workplace', *Fortune*, 25 January 1993, p. 30.

32. T. A. Stewart, 'Planning and career in a world without managers', *Fortune*, 20 March 1995, p. 46.

33. R. L. Mathis and J. H. Jackson, *Personnel — Contemporary Perspectives and Applications*, 3rd edn, West Publishing, St Paul, 1982, p. 271; and R. Ream, 'Changing jobs? It's a changing market', *Information Today*, February 2000, pp. 18–20.

34. B. Morris, 'Trophy husbands', *Fortune*, 14 October 2002, p. 81.

35. L. Taylor, 'She didn't brag, she missed the bonus', *Australian Financial Review*, 24–27 April 2003, pp. 28–9.

36. N. Stein, 'You have a career: now you need an agent', *Fortune*, 12 May 2003, p. 68.

37. Study by K. Daniel, D. Black and J. Smith, cited in G. Koretz, 'Sheepskins to show off', *Business Week*, 29 April 1996, p. 12.

38. Top companies conservative in picking the boss', *Nikkei Weekly*, 24 July 1995, p. 9.

39. J. Richardson, 'Traditional unis best for jobs', *Australian*, 29 November 1995, p. 3.

40. B. Andrews, 'The graduate edge', *BRW*, 31 July–6 August 2003, pp. 70–1.

41. The Boston Consulting Group advertisement for careers in strategic consulting, *South China Morning Post — Classifieds*, 26 July 2003, p. 2.

42. See classified advertisements for ANU, *Australian Financial Review*, 4 July 2003, p. 41 and *Australian Financial Review*, 27 September 2002, p. 10; and Warwick Business School, *South China Morning Post*, 29 June 2002, p. 11.

43. Macquarie Graduate School of Management advertisement, *South China Morning Post*, 28 August 2003, P. A10.

44. R. Turner, 'MBA price hikes only add to the prestige', *Australian Financial Review*, 22 November 2002, p. 16.

45. R. Weber, 'When an MBA isn't enough', *Business Week*, 17 March 2003, p. 76.

46. N. Way, 'Degrees for sale', *Business Review Weekly*, 28 July 2000, pp. 72–8; C. Fox, 'Rival business schools compete for MBA students', *Australian Financial Review*, 29 December 2000, p. 4; B. Bennett, 'The new masters of the universe', *Australian Financial Review — Special Report*, 1 November 2000, pp. 14–20; and P. Hui, 'Local MBA graduates spurned by global firms', *South China Morning Post*, 27 January 2002, p. 2.

47. C. Fox, 'Why MBA?', *Boss*, January 2001, pp. 16–20; and 'The best schools', *Business Week*, 2 October 2000, pp. 79–98.

48. N. Quacquarelli, 'Corporates seek Chinese MBAs', *South China Morning Post — Special Supplement*, 8 July 2000, p. 8; and 'The best B schools', *Business Week*, 2 October 2000, pp. 79–98.

49. S. Aryee, personal discussion with the author, 5 September 2003.

50. J. Van der Kamp, 'Professor's spend thrift advice ignores home truths', *South China Morning Post*, 4 March 2003, p. B26.

51. For example, see Flytech advertisement, *South China Morning Post*, 31 August 2002, p. 12.

52. A. Shand, 'Macquarie: the bank that makes millionaires', *Australian Financial Review*, 3 January 2001, pp. 1, 14.

53. D. Orr, 'Shell game', *Forbes Global*, 26 May 2003, pp. 12–13.

54. H. Sack, quoted in J. Kirby, 'Companies that teach you to be a star', *Business Review Weekly*, 29 September 1997, pp. 58, 60.

55. H. Nugent, quoted in J. Kirby, op. cit., p. 60.

56. J. Kirby, op. cit., pp. 54–60.

57. R. Callick, 'Accountants deplore strong family ties on HK boards', *Australian Financial Review*, 30 January 1997, p. 10; and L. Kraar, 'Inside Li Ka-Shing's empire', *Fortune*, 29 May 1999, p. 35.

58. F. G. Manuel, 'All in the family', *South China Morning Post — Business*, 7 January 1995, p. 14.

59. M. Mackey, 'Asian crisis was more a crisis of management', *Correspondent*, April–May 2000, p. 19.

60. Staff reporter, 'Princelings march into the corridors of power', *South China Morning Post*, 3 March 2002, p. 10; and M. Dwyer, 'Rise of red princelings', *Australian Financial Review*, 24 October 2002, p. 18.

61. K. Legge, 'In the name of the father', *Australian Magazine*, 14–15 December 1996, pp. 10–19; L. Chang and R. Frank, 'The rise and rise of Wandi Dang', *Australian Financial Review*, 3 November 2000, pp. 80–1; M. McLachlan, 'Pratt the younger in no hurry to see father abdicate', *Australian Financial Review*, 2 January 2003; and

N. Chenoweth, 'A mortal Murdoch accesses his world', *Australian Financial Review*, 12 June 2002, p. 18.

62. J. Packer, quoted in K. Legge, op. cit., p. 13. See also H. Bosch, 'Inherent risks', *Shares*, May 2001, pp. 120–1.

63. M. Chipperfield, 'Someone to watch over you', *Boss*, 8 October 2000, pp. 22–5.

64. T. D. Allen and L. T. Eby, 'Relationship effectiveness for mentors: factors associated with learning and quality', *Journal of Management*, vol. 29, no. 4, 2003, pp. 469–86.

65. K. Tyler, 'Prepare managers to become career coaches', *HR Magazine*, June 1997, p. 101.

66. B. A. Reid, 'Mentorships ensure equal opportunity', *Personnel Journal*, November 1994, pp. 122–3.

67. T. A. Scandura, M. J. Tejeda, W. B. Werther and M. J. Lankau, 'Perspectives on mentoring', *Leadership and Organization Development Journal*, vol. 17, no. 3, 1996, pp. 50–6; and S. E. Murphy and E. A. Ensher, 'The role of mentoring support and self management strategies on reported career outcomes', *Journal of Career Development*, vol. 27, no. 4, 2001, p. 240.

68. B. R. Ragins and J. L. Cotton, 'Wanted: mentors for women', *Personnel Journal*, April 1993, p. 20.

69. S. Feinstein, 'Women and minority workers in business find a mentor can be a rare commodity', *Wall Street Journal*, 10 November 1987, p. 39; W. F. Cascio, A. E. Harley and E. A. Farenson-Eland, 'Challenges in cross gender mentoring relationships: psychological intimacy, myths, rumours, innuendoes and sexual harassment', *Leadership and Organization Development Journal*, vol. 17, no. 3, 1996, pp. 42–9; and B. R. Ragins and J. L. Cotton, 'Jumping the hurdles: barriers to mentoring for women in organizations', *Leadership and Organization Development Journal*, vol. 17, no. 3, 1996, pp. 37–41.

70. B. R. Ragins and J. L. Cotton, op. cit., p. 20; and A. Vincent and J. Seymour, 'Profile of women mentors: a national survey', *SAM Advanced Management Journal*, vol. 60, no. 2, 1995, pp. 4–5.

71. E. C. Yuen, 'Does having a mentor make a difference? An empirical study of mentoring and career outcomes, in Singapore', *International Journal of Employment Studies*, vol. 3, no. 1, 1995, p. 13.

72. S. Aryee, A. D. Yaw and W. C. Yue, 'An investigation of ingratiation as a career management strategy: evidence from Singapore', *International Journal of Human Resource Management*, vol. 4, no. 1, 1993, pp. 191–212.

73. S. Aryee, T. Wyatt and R. Stone, 'Early outcomes of graduate employees: the effect of mentoring and ingratiation', *Journal of Management Studies*, vol. 33, no. 1, 1996, p. 113.

74. S. Aryee, T. Wyatt and R. Stone, op. cit., p. 113.

75. Graduate Careers Council of Australia survey, reported in K. Marshall, 2003, op. cit., p. 6.

76. Lionel Parrott, quoted in R. Allen, 'Managing a career requires a strategy', *Business Review Weekly*, 14 October 1988, p. 114.

77. Egghead blues', *Fortune*, 13 January 1997, p. 85.

78. '5000 Taiwanese apply for 300 garbage-collector jobs', *Straits Times*, 28 August 2000, p. 20.

79. 'Malaysia's "misfit" graduates', *Human Resources*, June 2000, p. 5.

80. Centre for Independent Studies report, cited in J. Richardson, 'Arts students in jobs strife', *Australian*, 19 July 2000, p. 33.

81. A. G. Perkins, 'The multinational CEO', *Harvard Business Review*, November–December 1994, pp. 12–13; and M. Loeb, 'The real fast track is overseas', *Fortune*, 21 August 1995, p. 95.

82. M. Dixon, 'Lucre lures young Turks to Singapore', *Australian Financial Review*, 9 September 1997, pp. 1, 14; and M. Ketchell, 'People are going overseas', *Sunday Age*, 16 July 2000, p. 13.

83. L. Colquhoon, 'ASX battles backwater status', *South China Morning Post — Markets*, 12 December 2000, p. 12; A. Ferguson, 'Left behind', *Business Review Weekly*, 14 July 2000, pp. 60–5; and M. Gibson, 'It's bye bye, big Australians', *Australian Financial Review*, 18 April 2001, p. 54.

84. T. Boyd, 'The essential skills needed to land a job in Japan', *Australian Financial Review — Japan Special Report*, 17 October 1996, p. 53; and E. McShulskis, 'Bilingual employees more valuable', *HRM Magazine*, April 1996, p. 16.

85. S. Srivastava, 'English as a ticket to the good life', *International Herald Tribune*, 3 September 2003, p. 9.

86. B. Kuppusamy, 'English is back as Malaysia's language of learning', *Sunday Morning Post*, 5 January 2002, p. 6.

87. Quoted in B. Schendler, 'The odd couple', *Fortune*, 1 May 2000, p. 69.

88. Based on D. Meagher, 'Corporate Australia searches for keyboard competency', *Australian Financial Review*, 7–8 October 2000, p. 4; and D. Meagher, 'Keys to success', *Boss*, October 2000, pp. 45–7.

89. 'Retrenched executives find better paying jobs', *HR Monthly*, July 1997, p. 9; and D. Townsend, 'Moving forward', *HR Monthly*, November 2002, pp. 52–3.

90. K. S. Wolfer and R. G. Wong, *The Outplacement Solution*, John Wiley & Sons, New York, 1988, p. 124.

91. J. Lloyd, *The Career Decision Planner*, John Wiley & Sons, New York, 1992, p. 218.

92. Quoted in C. Rance, 'Set goals for success', *Age — Employment*, 7 January 1988, p. 1.

93. ACIRRT, 1999, op. cit., p. 176.

94. P. O'Brien, 'Mark me, management reminded', *Weekend Australian — Recruitment*, 25–26 September 1999, p. 1; and H. Trinca, 'The board called you', *Boss*, January 2001, pp. 14–15.

95. Quoted in K. Suter, 'Fatherly financial advice', *Australian Financial Review*, 22 September 2000, p. 11.

96. B. Cheesman, 'Tiger finds intrigue is par for the course', *Australian Financial Review*, 15 November 2000, p. 17.

97. A. Quamby, 'Around the traps with ...', *Australian Financial Review*, 9–10 September 2000, p. 55.

98. K. Pfahl, 'Around the traps with ...', *Australian Financial Review*, 28–29 August 1999, p. 63.

99. Quoted in L. King, 'Around the traps with ...', *Australian Financial Review*, 24–28 December 1999, p. 63.

100. Wall Street executives learning the art of fairway business', *Australian Financial Review*, 29–30 January 2000, p. 55.

101. A. Gome, 'Women against odds too great to be ignored', *Business Review Weekly*, 8 December 2000, p. 56; M. Byrne, 'Equality doesn't quite add up', *Australian Financial Review*, 8 March 2001, p. 4; and L. Taylor, 2003, op. cit., p. 29.

102. Quoted in N. Wall, 'New business links are par for the golf course', *Business Review Weekly*, 3 December 1999, p. 62.

103. R. Meredith and M. Wells, 'Today's man', *Forbes Global*, 15 September 2003, p. 73.

104. R. Burbury, 'Metrosexual: this year's must-have male', *Australian Financial Review*, 30–31 August 2003, p. 12.

105. G. G. Critser, 'Let them eat fat', *Australian Financial Review*, 24 March 2000, p. 5; A. C. Copetas, 'Some executives look at plastic surgery for an edge', *Asian Wall Street Journal*, 1 May 2001, p. N7; and S. Robbins, *Organizational Behavior*, 9th edn, Prentice Hall, Upper Saddle River, NJ, 2000, p. 480.

106. H. Doran, 'Tall order sees those with ambition cut down to size', *South China Morning Post*, 4 September 2003, p. 1.

107. J. Connelly, 'Have you gone as far as you can go?', *Fortune*, 26 December 1994, p. 163.

108. E. Van Velso and J. B. Leslie, 'Why executives derail: perspectives across time and cultures', *Academy of Management Executive*, vol. 9, no. 4, 1995, pp. 68–9.

109. J. M. Bardwick, *The Plateauing Trap*, AMACOM, New York, 1986, p. 3.

110. J. W. Slocum Jr, W. L. Cron and L. C. Yows, 'Whose career is likely to plateau?', *Management Review*, vol. 13, no. 4, 1988, p. 3; and D. Rotondo, 'Individual difference variables and career related coping', *Journal of Social Psychology*, vol. 139, no. 4, 1999, pp. 458–71.

111. S. Aryee, 'Combating obsolescence: predictors of technical updating among engineers', *Journal of Engineering and Technology Management*, vol. 8, 1991, pp. 103–19.

112. Y. W. Chay, S. Aryee and I. Chew, 'Career plateauing: reactions and moderators among managerial and professional employees', *International Journal of Human Resource Management*, vol. 6, no. 1, 1995, p. 76.

113. M. K. Quaintance, 'Internal placement and career management', in W. F. Cascio (ed.), *Human Resource Planning, Employment and Placement*, BNA, Washington, 1989, p. 2.211.

114. Study by Wendy Coyle and Associates, reported in N. Way, 'Moving on', *Business Review Weekly*, 4 December 1995, p. 13. See also W. Coyle, 'Dual career couples become main inhibitor to relocation', *HR Monthly*, April 1995, pp. 4–5.

115. J. Pierce and B. L. Delahaye, 'Human resource management implications of dual career couples', *International Journal of Human Resource Management*, vol. 7, no. 4, 1996, p. 921.

116. B. Morris, 2002, op. cit., p. 74.

117. B. W. L. Packard and D. Nguyen, 'Science career-related possible selves of adolescent girls: a longitudinal study', *Journal of Career Development*, vol. 29, no. 4, 2003, pp. 251–63.

118. L. L. Martins, K. A. Eddleston and J. F. Veiga, 'Moderators of the relationship between work/family conflict and career satisfaction', *Academy of Management Journal*, vol. 25, no. 2, 2002, pp. 399–409.

119. 2001 survey by Catalyst, reported in B. Morris, 2002, op. cit., p. 74.

120. S. A. Hewlett, 'Executive women and the myth of having it all', *Harvard Business Review*, April 2002, pp. 66–73.

121. L. M. Hite and K. S. McDonald, 'Career aspirations of non-managerial women: adjustment and adaptation', *Journal of Career Development*, vol. 29, no. 4, 2003, pp. 221–35.

122. B. Morris, 2002, op. cit., pp. 71–81.

123. L. B. Otto, 'Youth perspectives on parental career influence', *Journal of Career Development*, vol. 27, no. 2, 2000, pp. 111–18.

124. John Taylor, Managing Director of Australia Pacific Projects (APP), reported in L. Nicklin, 'Distress breeds success', *Bulletin*, 7 October 1997, p. 37.

125. Quoted in A. Serwer, 'There's something about Cisco', *Fortune*, 15 May 2000, p. 36.

126. N. D. Marlow, E. K. Marlow and V. A. Arnold, 'Career development and women managers: does "one size fit all"?', *Human Resource Planning*, vol. 18, no. 2, 1995, p. 46; and S. Aryee and V. Luk, 'Balancing two major parts of adult life experience: work and family identity among dual career couples', *Human Relations*, vol. 49, no. 4, 1996, pp. 465–87.

127. J. Macartney, 'Employers with attitude; time for a change, baby', *Australian Financial Review*, 26 September 1997, p. 16.

128. S. A. Hewlett, 2002, op. cit., p. 73.

129. S. G. McNealy, quoted in 'Too much of a good thing?', *Business Week*, 25 August 1997, p. 81.

130. Reported in N. Freundlich, 'Maybe working women can't have it all', *Business Week*, 15 September 1997, p. 10. Also see E. P. McKenna, *When Work Doesn't Work Anymore — Women, Work and Identity*, Delacorte, New York, 1997.

131. '"New Age" dads irritate colleagues as kids come first, work second', *Asian Wall Street Journal*, 14 June 1995, pp. 1, 6; and L. Porter, 'Don't call me Mr Man', *Sunday Life (The Sunday Age)*, 16 July 2000, pp. 12–14.

132. Quoted in B. Summerskill, 'You must be kidding', *South China Morning Post — Features*, 21 August 2000, pp. 1, 3.

133. H. Trinca, 'Workers who want life in the slow lane still pay price', *Australian Financial Review*, 24–27 January 2003, p. 5.

134. S. Long, 'Singles "hijacking" work for life polices', *Australian Financial Review*, 11 October 1999, p. 100.

135. J. Brouard, 'Corporate dads', *Australian Financial Review Magazine*, September 1997, p. 38.

136. L. L. Martins, K. A. Eddleston and J. F. Veiga, 2002, op. cit., p. 406.

137. T. Moore, 'Work and family — a balancing act', *Asia Pacific Journal of Human Resources*, vol. 34, no. 2, 1996, pp. 119–25; and S. Aryee, V. Luk and R. Stone, 'Family response variables and retention-relevant outcomes among employed parents', *Human Relations*, vol. 50, no. 20, 1997, pp. 1–15.

138. Research studies by the Centre for Applied Social Research at the Royal Melbourne Institute of Technology, reported in S. Long, 'Unpaid hours leave deposit of ill will', *Australian Financial Review*, 7 July 2000, p. 21; and Juliet Boorke of the University of New South Wales, reported in N. Field, 'Work still not flexible study finds', *Australian Financial Review*, 15–16 July 2000, p. 4. Also see S. A. Hewlett, 2002, op. cit., pp. 66–73.

139. P. McDonald, quoted in C. Murphy, 'Gap grows between low, high earners', *Australian Financial Review*, 6 August 2003, p. 6.

140. W. Coyle, 'Most companies find dual careers a problem, survey finds', *HR Monthly*, October 1995, pp. 6–7.

141. M. Gunn, 'Bosses don't care for working parents' needs', *Australian*, 14 February 1997, p. 3; and M. Gunn, 'Family friendly jobs hard to find', *Australian*, 4 September 1996, p. 2.

142. B. Morris, 1997, op. cit., p. 53. See also G. B. Knecht, 'American Express loses president to fatherhood', *Asian Wall Street Journal*, 23 November 1995, pp. 1–9; and J. Ferman, 'It's 2 a.m., let's go to work', *Fortune*, 21 August 1995, pp. 64–9.

143. B. Morris, 1997, op. cit., p. 48.

144. Quoted in S. Long, 'Don't even think about going home', *Australian Financial Review*, 20 December 2000, p. 31.

145. S. Long, 2000, op. cit., p. 31.

146. A. Bianco and L. Lavelle, 'The CEO trap', *Business Week*, 11 December 2000, p. 48, J. S. Lublin and M. Murray, 'CEOs leave their posts faster than ever before', *Asian Wall Street Journal*, 21 October 2000, p. 8; and L. Schmidt, 'Law is hell', *Business Review Weekly*, 29 September 2000, pp. 66–70.

147. R. Callus, 'Fairness and flexibility', *HR Monthly*, March 1999, pp. 10–13.

148. S. Long, 'Taking time for the soul', *Australian Financial Review*, 17 May 2000, p. 23; and C. Hymowitz, 'Burnt out tech managers increasingly opt for a life', *Asian Wall Street Journal*, 29 February 2000, p. 8.

149. Reported in C. Flanders, 'The word: downshifters', *Boss*, 10 July 2003, p. 10.

150. Quoted in R. Gill, 'Big business embraces the gentle art of "outplacing"', *Sunday Age — Money Section*, 30 September 1990, p. 4.

151. Research by DBM Australia and the University of Southern Queensland, reported in M. Lawson, 'Sackings force managers to move', *Australian Financial Review*, 29 August 1997, p. 15; and D. Watkins, 'Why top performers get outplaced', *Management*, April 1995, pp. 19–20.

152. G. Flynn, 'HR is not necessarily the quickest route to the top', *Personnel Journal*, April 1995, p. 24.

153. J. Pickard, 'Centre of attention', *People Today*, November 2000, pp. 41–3.

154. 'Demographic profile of the HR profession', *Workplace Visions*, September–October 1997, p. 5; and A. Hepworth, 'Women still behind the pay ball', *Australian Financial Review*, 12 May 2000, p. 12.

155. Westpac, *Concise Annual Report*, 2002, p. 52; and AMCOR, *Concise Annual Report*, 2002, p. 30.

156. M. Finney, 'Degrees that make differences', *HR Magazine*, November 1996, pp. 75–82.

157. J. R. Andrews, 'Where doubts about the personnel role begin', *Personnel Journal*, June 1987, pp. 86–7; and G. G. Gordon, 'Getting in step', *Personnel Administrator*, April 1987, p. 48.

158. Reported in *Success*, vol. 35, no. 2, 1988, p. 28.

159. C. Le Coic, 'Oversupply of graduates', *HR Monthly*, June 2002, p. 46; and J. Amato, 'Contracting demand', *HR Monthly*, June 2002, p. 46.

160. D. Ulrich, *Human Resource Champions*, Harvard Business School Press, Boston, 1997, pp. 251–4.

161. M. A. Huselid, S. E. Jackson and R. S. Schuler, 'Technical and strategic human resource management effectiveness as determinants of firm performance', *Academy of Management Journal*, vol. 40, no. 1, 1997, pp. 171–88.

162. J. R. Andrews, 1987, op. cit., p. 87.

163. M. J. Thompson, 'Defining the dilemma', *Personnel Administrator*, May 1987, p. 6.

164. R. Korn, 'Managing line resistance', *Personnel Administrator*, May 1987, p. 6.

165. T. E. Lawson and V. Limbrick, 'Critical competencies and developmental experiences for top HR executives', *Human Resource Management*, vol. 35, no. 1, 1996, pp. 67–85.

166. J. Hampton, 'CHRP more of an asset to climbers than execs', *Canadian HR Reporter*, 11 September 2000, p. 1.

167. J. M. Jenks, 'Let's stop professionalising', *Personnel Journal*, July–August 1958, pp. 96–7; T. R. Lawson, 'In defense of professionalising', *Personnel Journal*, November 1958, pp. 221–2; F. B. Miller, 'The personnel dilemma: profession or not?', *Personnel Journal*, June 1959, pp. 53–5, 79; and R. P. Cunningham, 'The personnel manager — a professional', *Personnel Journal*, December 1960, pp. 263–5, 271.

168. R. Clark, *Australian Human Resources Management — Framework and Practice*, 2nd edn, McGraw-Hill, Sydney, 1992, p. 18.

169. B. A. Rowe, 'Are your employees an investment or a cost?', *Management Review*, July 1990, pp. 5–6.

170. Partly based on A. Qiu, 'Overqualified, undereducated and unemployed', *South China Morning Post*, 9 April 2003, p. A14.

DEVELOPING HUMAN RESOURCES AT ABC MANUFACTURING

Jenny Brinkies, Swinburne University

'We'll worry about induction later!' fumed Fred, the Customer Service Manager at ABC Manufacturing. 'It's taken HR long enough to find a replacement for Sandra, and now we finally have someone starting, we'd better get her onto the job right away.'

'Fred, all new employees should participate in an induction training program', replied Helen, the Team Supervisor.

'Yes', continued Fred, 'but the program that HR developed is only delivered on a six-monthly basis. All new employees, regardless of their position within the organisation, must attend this new program. They're putting all new employees in the same training session! Yes, you heard right! It doesn't matter whether the new employee is a process worker or a manager! The program is totally useless.'

'Shall we see what the induction procedure states?' suggested Helen.

'What procedure? Do we have an induction procedure? I haven't seen one! Unless it's in my in-basket, with all the other urgent matters from the past three months. We just don't get enough time around here … and that's just why Sue should get right into it. No need for useless induction programs.'

'Fred, we do have an induction procedure. It clearly states that all employees should participate in a departmental induction program on their first day, and later they attend the generic six-monthly program.'

Fred was getting angry. 'Helen, please understand. We have too much work to worry about induction, and I would like Sue to get started on the filing. That's pretty easy stuff, and nothing can really go wrong! As supervisor, you should be glad the work will get done. You can introduce Sue to the team and then get her started. She should be in a position to take customer calls within a few days.'

Helen sighed, and realised she would not get anywhere.

Sue, the new Customer Service Administrator, was welcomed by the receptionist. Unfortunately, Helen had rung in sick, so Fred spent the first half hour with Sue, explaining the job content in much the same way as he had already done during her interview. He then advised Sue of the enormous filing backlog, and commented that it was best she get straight on with the job. As people came into the department, Sue was introduced. By lunchtime, Fred felt quite good about his new employee, and he was confident in leaving her alone for the rest of the day. At home that same evening, Sue advised her family that she might have made a mistake in accepting the job.

Despite Sue's concerns, she stuck it through to the end of her probationary period, at which time a performance appraisal meeting with Fred was scheduled. Again Fred was too busy, so he delegated the task to Helen. Fred was aware that Helen had never conducted a performance appraisal meeting before, so he filled her in with some basic how-to instructions.

Sue came to the meeting equipped with questions and suggestions, and was prepared to give it her best. Five minutes into the meeting there was a knock on the door. It was Fred.

'I'm really sorry to interrupt', he said, 'but I urgently require the XYZ customer file. Could you please bring it into my office as soon as possible?'

Helen sighed. She did not want the meeting interrupted, but realised the matter was urgent. She picked up the phone, and delegated the task to Peter.

As the meeting continued, Helen referred to Sandra, who held the same job for many years and knew every customer inside out. 'You know', said Helen 'you are very much like Sandra. Sandra was excellent in her job, and I'm hoping you will turn out just like her. In fact, you two even look alike!'

After a while the two women got quite chatty, and Helen spoke about Fred, telling Sue how little direction he gives, that he never praises his staff and generally is not very good at people management.

'I've worked that out myself', said Sue 'but quite frankly, I can handle him. I thought this meeting was about my performance, not Fred's.' The meeting ended on a sour note.

'How did the meeting with Sue go?', asked Fred.

'Oh, not too good', Helen replied.

'I know. She has already come to see me and complained. She wants me to conduct the meeting again, but I simply haven't got the time just yet. I told her I will do it in a week or two.'

'I really could do with some training so I can do it better next time.'

'Well, you better organise some training before I let you loose again', commented Fred. 'In fact, I've just received notification that we have $10 000 in the training budget that must be spent before the end of the financial year.'

'In that case', responded Helen 'could I also attend a course to upgrade my computer skills?'

'Maybe', replied Fred 'but first let's see whether anyone else has any interest in attending a training program. We should distribute the money equally among the department.'

The next month, Sue attended a full-day induction training program with all the other new employees. The program commenced with a general description of the US headquarters, continued with an overview of customers and competitors, an outline of the most important policies and procedures, and concluded with a hands-on session on the new telephone system, installed some five months ago. There were 12 'new' employees in the session: two process workers, three stores people, five general office staff and two managers. When Sue spoke to her family about the training session, she emphasised the social lunch they provided and the opportunity she had to spend some time with two senior employees. She had also finally learned more about the product the organisation manufactured, because they were taken for a tour through the manufacturing department, which was normally out of bounds for office workers.

Later in the year Helen attended her performance management training program, and returned highly motivated and enthusiastic to apply what she had learned. The annual appraisals were due in a few months, and she intended to work hard to maintain the skills she had learned during the training. Fred had confirmed that she could conduct the appraisals for her five team members.

Time for appraisals! Helen prepared herself well, and also gave her team members plenty of time to prepare. She organised an appropriate meeting room, advised the receptionist not to put calls through, and requested Fred not to interrupt the meeting. Helen remembered what she learned at her training session. She listened carefully to what her staff had to say and provided constructive feedback where appropriate. She also remembered to discuss objectives for the coming year and how these could be achieved. The final topic was career aspirations. She felt pleased with the outcome.

When it came to her own appraisal, Fred suggested that she was now so experienced in conducting performance appraisal meetings, there really was no need for the two of them to sit down together. 'You're doing an excellent job. I'm really happy with your performance, and I'm sure you will let me know if you have any problems', advised Fred.

Helen looked at Fred and frowned. 'Fred, everyone deserves to have their performance appraised by their manager and I'm no different. You should have participated in the training program! You know, they even said in the program that career planning should be part of the performance appraisal meeting, and I would like the opportunity to discuss my career with you.'

'Career!' fumed Fred 'What career? Everyone is responsible for their own career, and that includes you! Why should I spend time discussing your career aspirations with you? You wouldn't be after my job, would you?'

Questions

1. Why did Sue feel unhappy on her first day? What could have been done to improve the situation?
2. Do you think a six-monthly induction program such as that conducted by ABC Manufacturing is effective? Provide a detailed justification, including recommended changes/additions to the program, if any.
3. Comment on the two different types of appraisal meeting Helen had with her staff. Is there room for improvement? Justify your answer.
4. What training would be of benefit to Fred? Provide an outline of a relevant program for Fred and describe the training methods you would apply. How would you measure the success of the program?
5. Using Kirkpatrick's model of training evaluation, how could the effectiveness of Helen's performance management training be measured?
6. Consider the $10 000 training budget. What would be your approach to utilising this budget?
7. What advice would you give to Helen about managing her own career?
8. What HR strategies could ABC Manufacturing apply to ensure effective career planning?

rewarding human resources

Part 4 focuses on employee motivation, compensation, incentives and benefits. The case study at the end of the part incorporates these topics using the example of strategic reward management at Winton Wynne Moore and Associates, Commercial Law Partners.

chapter

11

employee motivation

Learning objectives

When you have finished studying this chapter, you should be able to:

- Understand the importance of strategic motivation
- Discuss the features of the major theories of motivation
- Describe the relationship between motivation and performance
- Understand the implications of motivation theory for HRM
- Explain the effectiveness of money as a motivator.

'It's fantastic to have the feeling of achievement — to see the opportunity where no one else sees it; to figure it out and then pull it off'.[1]

Frank Lowy, Chairman, Westfield Holdings Ltd

Strategy and motivation

Increasing cost pressures, work force diversity, downsizing and the advent of contingent workers and the lean organisation have focused management attention on the strategic importance of employee motivation. Strategic business objectives seeking competitive advantage through higher productivity and improved customer service can be achieved only if employees are strongly motivated to perform. Job design, the system of rewards, management style, corporate culture, organisation structure and change management all impinge on employee motivation. Consequently, management places the achievement of its strategic business objectives at risk if it downgrades employee motivation in relation to financial and other strategic objectives. Finally, management decisions based on valid models of employee motivation are much more likely to achieve success than those based on wrong or inappropriate assumptions.[2]

The importance of motivation

Employee motivation is one of the most challenging aspects of HRM. It manifests itself through employee morale, output, absenteeism, effort, labour turnover, loyalty and achievement. Generally, managers do not understand motivation and its essence remains enigmatic. Just what is it that makes the 'high flyers' fly? Why is it that some employees demonstrate a burning desire to achieve and seek increased responsibility, while others remain passive or openly hostile? These and similar questions are frequently asked by managers and HR specialists.

Motivation That which energises, directs and sustains human behaviour.

Unfortunately, there are no clear-cut answers. **Motivation** is generally defined as an internal state that induces an employee to engage in particular behaviours, or as a set of factors that cause employees to behave in certain ways, but it is extremely complex. This is because employee motivation is the product of many interacting factors such as the culture of the organisation, management's leadership style, the structure of the organisation, job design, and HR policies and practices. The employee's personality, skills, knowledge, abilities and attitudes also play a part.

Not surprisingly, there is no one generally accepted explanation of what motivates employees at work.[3] One perception is that motivation is concerned with behavioural direction (that is, the choice of specific behaviours from a large number of possible behaviours — for example, choosing to call in sick and stay at home watching television instead of going to work), persistence (that is, continuing engagement in a behaviour over time — for example, continuing to work even after finishing time to complete something the employee feels motivated about) and intensity (that is, the amount of effort an employee puts into performing a task — for example, giving '110 per cent' effort to work or taking it easy and working at half pace).

Conversely, another view is that motivation is concerned with the employee's desire to achieve some goal (that is, motivation by wants, needs or desires — for example, being highly motivated to achieve a promotion, a salary increase or a bigger job title).[4] Because employees differ in what motivates them to work, it is impossible to find a universal answer. What motivates a 45-year-old executive with three teenage children and a mortgage, a 29-year-old highly paid single studying an MBA part-time, a part-time worker in a low-skilled job, a single parent with two children in nursery school and a newly arrived migrant with few possessions and limited English skills may be quite different. Management thus needs to consider its employees as individuals and recognise that they have different needs. Employee diversity also means managers must be flexible in designing jobs, work schedules, rewards, and training and development programs.

Finally, cultural differences also play a part. Asian and Latin American employees, for example, may feel uncomfortable with a manager who delegates authority and asks them to express their opinions. North Americans and Scandinavians, in contrast, expect their managers to employ a participative approach and involve them in decision making.[5] Managers therefore need to exercise flexibility and adapt their management style to recognise individual differences.

Motivation remains a subject 'that pervades all of management' and is one that line managers and HR managers cannot ignore.[6] HR policies and practices, for example, have both a direct and indirect impact on employee motivation. Rigorously enforced health and safety policies and practices can create a sense of wellbeing; and well-designed incentive plans can increase employee effort and goal achievement. On the other hand, poorly designed jobs, subjective performance appraisals and discriminatory hiring and promotion can harm employee motivation and satisfaction.[7]

What is the employer's responsibility towards an individual who lacks the motivation to work? Should companies in today's competitive environment have to spend time and money on such people?

Management and motivation

What really motivates employees? What force drives employees to perform well? Ability and skill determine whether an employee can do the job, but motivation determines whether the employee will do the job properly.[8] Is it money? Status? Power? Self-fulfilment? Managers have been struggling with such questions for decades. However, it is a mistake for managers to simply regard motivation as a problem of 'how to get employees to work harder'. Motivation (or lack of it) can be seen in absenteeism, labour turnover, punctuality, quality and safety.

Taking a 'sickie' because you have a boring job is okay.

Similarly, it is wrong for managers to assume that motivation is the singular key to increased performance. Many other factors influence individual performance in an organisation. No amount of employee effort can compensate for factors such as lack of ability or skill, outdated equipment, inefficient systems, poor organisational structure or financial constraints.

Finally, it is important that managers distinguish between motivation and **job satisfaction**. Motivation is the 'why' of behaviour. Job satisfaction reflects an employee's feelings about various aspects of work. Managers have to get their employees to act in a specific, goal-directed way so as to meet the organisation's strategic business objectives. If this is done so employees receive what they want from the job, then job satisfaction is achieved. Thus, satisfaction is an end state resulting from the attainment of some goal.

Job satifaction The degree to which employees have positive attitudes about their jobs.

The employee's attitude towards work and life in general, and their age, health, level of aspiration, social status and political and social activities, all influence the level of job satisfaction.[9] Managers have traditionally believed that a satisfied employee is a motivated employee. However, happy employees are not necessarily productive. Job satisfaction does not automatically cause employees to work harder.[10] In fact, the weight of evidence suggests that job performance leads to job satisfaction rather than the other way round. However, satisfaction is related to tenure, turnover, absenteeism and tardiness.[11] Encouraging an employee to feel positively about work can have a direct impact on HR costs and the organisation's effectiveness in achieving strategic business objectives. Employees are more likely to behave honestly on the job, for example, when they believe a company is committed to their wellbeing and career advancement.[12]

Early theories of motivation

Scientific management Explanation of employee motivation based on the work of Frederick Taylor. Emphasises the division of labour, task specialisation, time measurement and the use of monetary rewards.

Scientific management

Traditional explanations of employee motivation are based on the work of Frederick Taylor and others in the **scientific management** school. Division of labour, task specialisation, time measurement and the use of monetary rewards are at the heart of this management approach to motivation. The key assumption is that money is the primary employee motivator, that human beings have the rational characteristics of a robot. Employees are not robots and they have needs and feelings, so the economies of specialisation are frequently more than offset by the diseconomies of employee dissatisfaction. The boredom and dissatisfaction created by some forms of specialisation result in increases in absenteeism, labour turnover and industrial unrest — negatives that are costly to organisations.[13] Money also has proved to be ineffective as a universal panacea to overcome low employee motivation.

The human relations movement

The **human relations movement** discarded the mechanistic view of employees in favour of a more humanistic approach. It recognised that employees seek more than financial rewards from their jobs. Money was regarded as an effective motivator only when it was used to facilitate and not oppose the satisfaction of employee needs. This dramatic shift in management thinking resulted primarily from a series of studies conducted from the early 1920s through to the mid-1930s at the Hawthorne Works of Western Electric. Involving Australian sociologist Elton Mayo, the Harvard University research team studied how productivity was affected by rest pauses, financial incentives, friendly supervision and informal group norms.[14]

It should be noted that the human relations movement did not challenge the scientific management school's emphasis on division of labour, task specialisation or management control. Rather, it added a social dimension to management's orientation. The human relations movement (especially Mayo) has been severely criticised and dismissed as little more than 'the twentieth century's most seductive managerial ideology'.[15] But, despite criticisms of the Hawthorne studies as being publicity seeking, oversimplified and scientifically weak, the studies' historical significance cannot be denied. They stimulated management interest and research in:

- the impact of the work group on employee attitudes and productivity
- the employee's need for recognition, security, status and a sense of belonging
- the effect of management style on employee morale and productivity
- the need for managers to possess good interpersonal skills
- the 'grapevine' as a means of communication.

The Hawthorne studies were the first attempt to systematically analyse human behaviour at work. As such, they set an important precedent.

Theory X and Theory Y

All managers have their favourite theories about what motivates employees. In reality, these are not always stated or even recognised. They often operate as hidden policies. McGregor argued that some of these are remarkably pervasive and influence every managerial decision or action.[16] He concluded that managers develop their views on employee motivation based on one of two propositions — what he called **Theory X** and **Theory Y**.

Managers guided by Theory X assumptions are directive, narrow and control-oriented in their treatment of employees. Passive, dependent and reluctant subordinates are the result. Managers following a Theory Y orientation, in contrast, will delegate authority, encourage employee participation in decision making, and grant greater job autonomy and task variety. Highly productive employees with initiative and commitment to the organisational goals are created when these higher order needs are satisfied. McGregor saw Theory Y as a 'process primarily of creating opportunities, releasing potential, removing obstacles, encouraging growth and providing guidance'.[17] Essentially, Theory X emphasises management control and Theory Y emphasises employee self-control.

The appeal of Theory Y to many managers is obvious. Unfortunately, there is little evidence to confirm that either set of assumptions is valid, or that a Theory Y approach results in more motivated employees.[18] In fact, Theory Y is more of a program than scientific theory.[19] Nevertheless, McGregor's approach to employee motivation has had great significance. It has encouraged managers to:

- delegate authority
- enlarge and enrich jobs
- increase the variety and responsibilities of employees
- improve the free flow of communication within organisations
- use participative management-by-objectives performance appraisal
- promote employee empowerment and self-management.[20]

Content theories of motivation

Content theories attempt to explain motivation in terms of factors that initiate employee behaviour. They are called content theories because they define what is motivating the person. Thus, content theories give the manager an insight into employee needs and how these affect employee behaviour and attitudes at work.

Content theories Attempt to explain motivation in terms of factors that initiate employee behaviour.

Maslow's needs hierarchy theory

Maslow's **needs hierarchy** theory is one of the most popular motivation theories among practising managers. It argues that employees are motivated to satisfy five basic types of needs (physiological, safety, social, esteem and **self-actualisation**). According to Maslow, these are arranged in a hierarchy of importance, with lower order needs requiring adequate satisfaction before the next higher order need can motivate behaviour (see figure 11.1).

Needs hierarchy Sequence of five human needs, as proposed by Maslow — physiological, safety, social, esteem and self-actualisation needs.

Self-actualisation Becoming what one is capable of becoming.

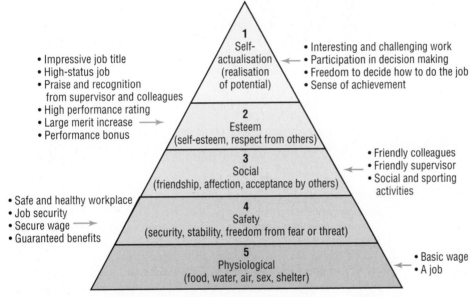

Figure 11.1 Maslow's hierarchy of needs and employee work needs
Source Adapted from J. R. Schermerhorn, *Management*, 7th edn, John Wiley & Sons, New York, 2002, p. 99.

Maslow's theory alerts managers to the danger of unsatisfied needs dominating employee attention and influencing their attitudes and behaviour at work. Also, once a need is satisfied, it may no longer act as an effective motivator of employee behaviour.

Many organisations apply Maslow's approach to employee motivation through their job design, award, and compensation and benefit programs. IBM's compensation strategy, for example, aims to provide employees with:
- a sense of security by paying very competitive salaries that permit employees to feed, clothe and house their families

- significant financial incentives that encourage excellent performance and high levels of productivity
- awards and rewards such as cash, gifts or trips that demonstrate appreciation of superior performance or a specific accomplishment.[21]

The intuitive logic and ease of understanding of Maslow's theory appeals to managers, but a number of criticisms can be made:[22]

- There is little evidence to support the claim that there are five distinct levels of needs.
- There is no obvious proof that the motivational power of a need diminishes once the need has been satisfied.
- Variables such as age, race, personality, cultural background and the size of the firm influence the relative strength of a need in individual employees. It is important for Japanese employees, for example, to be recognised for their achievements and to belong to a social group.[23] Low-income Indian employees place most importance on satisfying basic physiological needs, and Hong Kong private-sector managers favour opportunities for advancement and high pay.[24] Finally, Hofstede argues that 'self-actualisation' is a product of an individualistic society and thus does not apply to collectivist societies.[25] This argument is supported by studies of Asian employees, which suggest that concerns for garnering social approval, conforming to social expectations, maintaining harmonious relations and avoiding social embarrassment are powerful motivators.[26]

Despite such drawbacks, the needs hierarchy remains popular with managers (if not with academics) as a motivation theory because recognition, enrichment and a safe workplace do increase employee satisfaction. Pizza Hut (USA) uses 'The Big Cheese Award' to recognise loyalty and performance. Chief People Officer, Joe Bosch, says such recognition is crucial to staff retention. 'It's a stupid piece of foam', says Bosch. 'But you see these hardcore, 20-year veterans get tears in their eyes when they get one.'[27] Research shows that Australian managers similarly rate recognition very highly as a motivator.[28] A US study of 400 companies found that the ability to form friendships at work was a key indicator of highly productive workplaces, while a Watson Wyatt survey found a positive link between workplace friendliness and stock price performance.[29]

Below are some managerial implications of Maslow's theory:
- Managers should identify the most important needs of their employees and make their satisfaction contingent on performance.
- Managers should create an environment that encourages employees to reach their maximum potential.
- Managers who do not address these matters are likely to suffer employee frustration, labour turnover and decreased performance.[30]

Herzberg's two-factor theory

(see figure 11.2)

Motivators Job-centred factors such as achievement and responsibility which, when present in a job, motivate employees.

Hygiene factors Lower order employee needs that are met by pay, working conditions, interpersonal relations, supervision, company policy and administration.

Job dissatisfaction Employee dissatisfaction caused by poor pay, working conditions, supervision and/or company policy and administration.

Sometimes called the motivation–hygiene theory, the two-factor theory has gained wide acceptance in management circles and has had a major impact on job design (see figure 11.2). It defines a two-tier hierarchy of needs:
- **Motivators** are higher order needs for achievement (recognition, intrinsic interest in the work, responsibility and advancement). These determine job satisfaction and performance.
- **Hygiene factors** are lower order needs that are met by pay, working conditions, interpersonal relations, supervision, company policy and administration. Herzberg argued that these factors do not motivate by themselves but can prevent motivation from occurring.

Traditionally, managers regarded job satisfaction and **job dissatisfaction** as opposite ends of the same continuum. Herzberg's two-factor theory challenged this notion.

Factors that produce job satisfaction are true motivators and are directly related to job content. Factors leading to dissatisfaction, according to the theory, are hygiene or maintenance factors. Herzberg primarily associated these with the work environment (see figure 11.2). Herzberg concluded from this dichotomy that only the presence of motivators can produce employee satisfaction and performance; the presence of hygiene factors merely prevents employee dissatisfaction. In other words, hygiene factors do not motivate but their absence can result in job dissatisfaction. This theory is supported by an Australian study that concluded that 'bad working conditions can be a potent source of dissatisfaction but very good conditions do not do much to create work motivation'.[31]

Focusing management attention on the job as a key factor in employee motivation, two-factor theory highlighted the need for job design that stimulates employees to work harder and be more satisfied.

Herzberg's theory, however, has been subject to considerable academic attack. Because it is related to the needs hierarchy theory of motivation, it has experienced many similar criticisms. Moreover, controlled studies have produced mixed results and led to suspicions about Herzberg's methodology.[32] As a result, the theory remains controversial.

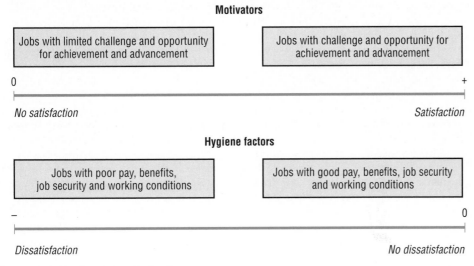

Figure 11.2 Herzberg's two-factor theory

Job characteristics theory

Job characteristics theory is a more sophisticated development in relating the nature of the job to performance. The argument, as with Herzberg's theory, is that employees are motivated by the intrinsic nature of the job. According to job characteristics theory, five core characteristics of a job (skill variety, task identity, task significance, autonomy and feedback) significantly affect the levels of employee motivation and satisfaction. Studies on the job characteristics model have produced mixed results. Although not a universal panacea for employee motivation and satisfaction problems, it is generally regarded as useful. Leading companies such as Citicorp, IBM, Motorola and Texas Instruments have applied it to job design (see pages 161–8 for further discussion).

Job characteristics theory
An example of comprehensive job enrichment. It combines both horizontal and vertical loading to stimulate employee motivation and satisfaction.

McClelland's achievement motivation theory

McClelland's theory argues that certain personality variables explain why some employees achieve and others do not. **Achievement motivation** is seen as the desire to perform in terms of a standard of excellence, or a desire to be successful in competitive situations. The achievement motivation of each employee depends on childhood, personal and work experiences, and on the type of organisation in which they work. Using projective techniques, McClelland identified four characteristics that describe high achievers:

1. a liking of situations in which they take personal responsibility for finding solutions to problems
2. a tendency to take moderate risks rather than low or high risks

Achievement motivation
The desire to be successful in competitive situations or to perform in terms of a standard of excellence.

3. a desire for concrete feedback on their performance
4. a tendency, once having selected a goal, to be totally preoccupied with that goal until it is achieved.[33]

McClelland indicated that the effect of monetary incentives on high achievers is complex. High achievers have a high sense of their own worth, so they expect to be well paid. Consequently, they are unlikely to stay with an organisation that does not sufficiently reward them. Conversely, because high achievers are naturally motivated, it is doubtful whether an incentive plan will actually improve performance. Money is a symbol of achievement. Moreover, achievement motivation does not operate when employees with high achievement needs are undertaking jobs that are routine, boring and lacking in competition. McClelland suggests four ways to enhance employee achievement motivation:

1. arrange for accomplishment feedback so employee success is reinforced
2. identify achievement models within the organisation and encourage the employee to emulate them
3. help employees to modify their self-image so they desire personal challenge, responsibility and feedback or success
4. encourage employees to repeat words of self-encouragement and to eliminate negative thoughts.

Similarly, McClelland favoured the building of achievement factors into jobs — responsibility, participation, moderate goal setting and fast, clear feedback on performance. If the job does not offer implicit feedback, it is critical for the manager to provide high achievers with frank, detailed appraisals of their performance.

McClelland also recognised power and affiliation needs. He saw power needs as the desire to manipulate others or to be superior to them, and affiliation needs as the desire for friendly and close interpersonal relationships. According to McClelland, both needs tend to be closely related to managerial success. His research suggested that the best managers are high in their need for power and low in their need for affiliation.

Interestingly, while high achievers get things done at an individual level, they are often ineffective as managers. Nevertheless, the need for achievement is an important factor in career success.[34]

Limitations of content theories

The theories of Maslow, Herzberg and McClelland seek to identify what motivates employee behaviour. They concentrate on particular employee needs and their satisfaction. Thus, content theories give managers an understanding of work-related factors that initiate motivation. However, managers should not accept them as the only explanations of employee motivation. Content theories serve a useful purpose in focusing a manager's attention on employee needs and their satisfaction, but they are limited by their inability to explain the underlying dynamics of motivation. They give only a restricted understanding of why employees choose certain behaviours to satisfy their needs. In contrast, this choice factor is the central focus of **process theories** of how motivation works.

> **Process theories** Attempt to explain motivation in terms of the thought processes that employees go through in choosing their behaviour.

Process theories of motivation

Vroom's expectancy theory

Expectancy theory relates to choice behaviour and is based on the logic that employees will do what they can, when they want to. It assumes that employees are thinking, reasoning people who have beliefs and anticipations about future events. Expectancy theory argues that an employee's choice of behaviour depends on the likelihood that their action will bring about a specific result that is attractive to them. To better understand this process, Vroom suggests that managers know the following three factors:

1. **Expectancy** (effort–performance link): the employee's perceived probability that exerting a given amount of effort will lead to performance. Expectancy equals zero if the employee believes it is impossible to reach a given performance level and one if the employee is certain that the performance level can be achieved.
2. **Instrumentality** (performance–reward link): the degree to which the employee believes that performing at a specific level will bring about a desired result. Instrumentality also varies from zero to one.
3. **Valence** (attractiveness): the value or importance that the employee places on the potential result or reward that can be achieved. Valences can be either positive or negative and range on a scale from minus one (very undesirable) to plus one (very desirable). Obviously, the more positive an employee feels about an outcome, the more attractive it will be.

Expectancy The employee's perceived probability that exerting a given amount of effort will lead to performance.

Instrumentality The degree to which an employee believes that performing at a specific level will bring about a desired result.

Valence The value or importance that an employee places on a potential result or reward that can be achieved.

NEWSBREAK

Secrets of profitability

By Jacqui Walker

Richard Ramsay, founder of the wholesaler Juice Clothing, watched sales fall last year after three years of meteoric business growth. With a new focus on the bottom line, Ramsay has turned to employees to improve their productivity. Unproductive staff have left and difficult suppliers that required excessive management by his staff have been dropped. He has also redefined many of his employees' jobs to increase the amount of work they get done.

Ramsay is not alone in searching for ways to increase productivity this year. Enterprise bargaining within workplaces, the pressure of globalisation and a squeeze on margins has made businesses more aware of the importance of employee productivity, says Heather Ridout, deputy chief executive of Australian Industry Group.

Studies show that the biggest worry for many businesses is maintaining a skilled workforce. Paul Orton, the policy manager at Australian Business, an advice and networking organisation, says the need for increased employee productivity is at the heart of this concern.

The chief economist for Yellow Pages, Steven Shepherd, says there is a trend toward improving productivity. 'In the January quarter, overall sales for small businesses went up significantly but the workforce only increased marginally. The difference is being met through increased labour productivity.'

About 60 per cent of the entrepreneurs running the fastest-growing small and medium-size companies in Australia, who took part in the *BRW Fast 100* survey in 2002, said they were adopting new measures to improve productivity. These ambitious firms are doing what might be expected to increase worker productivity — improving recruiting techniques, benchmarking performance against key performance indicators and offering bonuses and financial incentives. Only 28 per cent of the *Fast 100* companies surveyed said financial rewards were the key to motivating staff. Instead, they are focusing on new ideas, technology and psychology.

The managing director of the recruiting and training company Ingeus, Therese Rein, says: 'Work is about more than take-home pay. I believe that work is about being part of a community,

being part of a team, about developing and learning, and having the opportunity to do that.'

Productive employees are motivated employees who have clear definable goals, know the value of their work, and have goals they believe are achievable. If a goal does not seem achievable, it's hard to get motivated because you feel as if you are failing', Rein says. Employers must help employees understand how their particular role contributes to the organisational values, which Rein defines for her company as 'improving the quality of people's lives'. When employees can see how their work contributes to this, they are motivated and contribute what Rein terms 'huge amounts of discretionary effort'.

Although some may criticise Rein's approach as offering nothing tangible, it has proved successful. In 1989, her occupational therapist consultancy, Work Directions Australia, had one employee: Rein. Now it is called Ingeus and is a multi-disciplinary organisation with 650 employees, 48 offices in Australia and two in London.

(continued)

Rein says that productivity improvements come from recruiting people into roles that fit their personal values; then they will find the work inherently rewarding. 'The sort of work we do is not good for rampant individualism.' Her company tries to hire people who will be happy to work in teams of people with different and complementary skills.

The acting chief executive of the business consultancy Shirlaws, Chris Dionne, believes his staff are productive because the culture of the business allows them to meet their personal goals. Shirlaws provides business advice to small and medium-size businesses. Many of the staff have joined the company — which was set up four years ago and turned over $4.4 million in 2001–02 — from senior executive roles in much larger companies. They have been frustrated by working in large organisations, are already financially secure, and join Shirlaws because they want to use their skills to help small and medium-size businesses. Dionne says their altruistic goals mean they are very productive for Shirlaws.

Origin Healthcare, which appeared on the *BRW Fast 100* at number 64 in 2002, has gone to extraordinary lengths and used high-tech equipment to motivate its workers and ensure greater productivity. It has created a workplace for staff in which they can see the effect of their efforts on the business.

The office resembles NASA's space million control room at Houston. It has six plasma screens that display every aspect of the company's business in colorful graphics. The information, such as measurements of client demand and capacity-to-supply, is coded so that when certain performance goals are reached, lights flash and the colors change, not unlike the way falling stock prices are represented in red on stock exchange boards. In full view of the screens in the middle of the office, the company has a cafe bar. Origin Healthcare's chief executive, Russell Bateman, says: 'If you are doing a lot of repetitive work, it can become very dull.'

Most of the company's staff are tertiary qualified but spend much of their time on the telephone to health-care facilities trying to solve problems. 'They are doing work that can be isolating and therefore stimuli and involvement is very important. 'The company has designed its office to keep people interested and Bateman says this has improved profitability by about 20 per cent. 'It allows people to benchmark themselves against others in a non-threatening way. People know whether they fit in and they know what is going on. Most employee stress comes from a lack of understanding. When expectations are clear, it's a very positive experience.'

Ramsay of Juice Clothing says that staff work more efficiently when they understand their employer's expectations. 'What I've definitely learnt is that if I employ staff, I have to invest enough time in training them and making it clear what their role is.'

He found that his previous laissez-faire approach to management, whereby staff were given broad goals but had to work out how to reach them, left them confused. 'They tended to get a little bit lost and to become a little unproductive.' Ramsay is trying to fix the problem by giving them more guidance. 'I'm trying to create a less stressful environment through more effective time management of employees. I don't want them working harder, just more effectively.'

Net Options, a Brisbane-based technology consultancy that employs 70 staff, is also using technology to improve worker productivity. Its chief executive, Richard McAlary, says allowing people to work from home more often, improving the integration of off-site work practices and having modern communications and data storage capabilities, has enabled the company to increase its number of service staff and reduce the number in administration. New communications technology has helped cut staff meetings from every month to each quarter. He says focusing on productivity has improved operating profit.

McAlary says that to keep employees motivated, the company has created an attractive, safe and clean work office. The building has a swimming pool, a tennis court, everyone has a view outside, and the walls are decorated with plants and paintings.

Training is becoming a popular way to improve worker productivity. Data releases by the Australian Bureau of Statistics show the proportion of employers providing structured and unstructured training increased from 61 per cent to 81 per cent between 1997 and 2002.

Tony Talevski, the owner of STM Group, a rapidly growing accounting and financial services provider that specialises in franchisees, believes that training improves productivity even when it is not directly related to the employee's job. The company, which he started in 1997 and which will turn over almost $4 million in 2002–03, is paying for six staff to attend personal motivation seminars. Talevski says bonuses have a limited effect on morale. 'If staff are not happy, they leave no matter what you pay them.'

Source BRW, 15–21 May 2003, pp. 68–9.

Vroom claims that the relationship between motivation (M), expectancy (E), instrumentality (I) and valence (V) can be expressed as follows: $M = E \times I \times V$. This multiplicative relationship means that the motivational impact of a particular employee decision is dramatically reduced whenever expectancy, instrumentality or valence approach zero. Likewise, for a reward to have a positive motivational impact, the employee must feel favourably about the expectancy, instrumentality and valence associated with the reward (see figure 11.3).

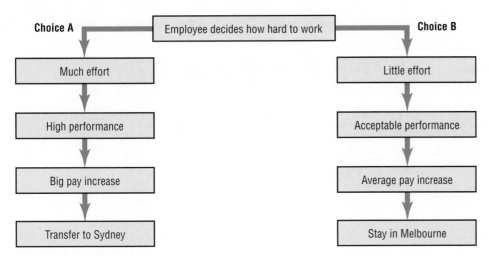

Figure 11.3 The employee thought process
Source Asia Pacific Management Co. Ltd, 2004.

This multiplier effect has important implications for managers trying to create high levels of employee motivation by allocating rewards. It clearly points out that managers must take action to maximise all three motivational components, because a low value for expectancy, instrumentality or valence will result in low or zero motivation.

Expectancy theory also recognises that more than one result can occur. In the example in figure 11.3, the employee believes that increased effort may improve their performance and lead to both a large pay increase (positive) and a transfer to Sydney (negative). Consequently, the attractive result (money) may be countered by a negative result (transfer). The informed manager, suggests Schermerhorn, will always try to identify and understand multiple outcomes from the employee's standpoint and adjust the use of rewards accordingly.[35]

Major problems exist in the practice of expectancy theory because few organisations actually reward performance, and even fewer managers have the authority to tailor rewards to meet particular employee needs.[36] Rather than invalidating the theory, this provides a rational explanation of why so many employees are unmotivated to perform.

In making choices, employees constantly ask themselves: What's in it for me? If employees are to be motivated to perform, they must see a clear pay-off that is attractive to them. It is the manager's difficult job to see that this happens.

Equity theory

Employees want to be treated fairly. Equity theory states that if an employee sees a discrepancy between the outcomes they receive and their input, compared with those of other employees, that employee will be motivated to do more (or less) work. The employee may question working harder than others, for example, if given a merit increase or recognition that is lower than that given to other employees.

In essence, employees ask: How well am I doing compared to others? See figure 11.4.

An employee's view of fair monetary and non-monetary compensation is obviously subjective, yet it is critical in determining their behaviour. Perceived inequity produces tension within the individual and this motivates them to eliminate or reduce the tension by striving to make the balance equal.

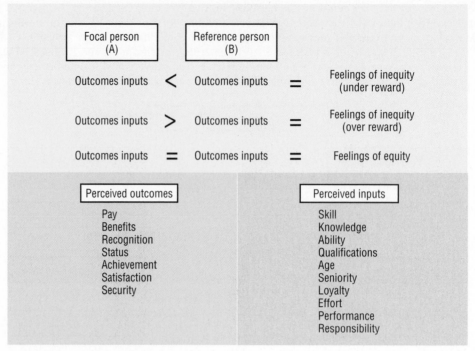

Figure 11.4 Major components of equity theory

In an effort to restore equity, employees may:
- change inputs — employees can put more or less effort into the job
- change outcomes — employees can push for wage increases and other benefits without any corresponding increases in inputs
- psychologically rationalise inputs or outcomes — rather than actually changing inputs or outcomes, employees change their perception of what they are putting in or getting out (for example, by artificially increasing the status of the job or by convincing themselves that their effort is less than it is)
- leave — employees can transfer to another job or simply quit the organisation
- psychologically distort the inputs or outcomes of others — employees may come to believe that others work harder than they do and thus deserve greater rewards
- change the comparison — an employee may decide that a particular person (or group) is no longer appropriate for comparison and may select another that yields a more favourable outcome.

Through such actions, employees attempt to cope with situations that they perceive as unfair. Perceptions of inequity are most typically seen in organisations when employees performing the same job receive different scales of pay. In Australia, this is evidenced by the considerable pressures exerted by unions to maintain one wage rate for all employees in the same award classification. Equity theory is important in that it forces HR managers to ensure that organisational rewards are equitably allocated both in absolute and relative terms.

Equity theory intuitively makes sense, but the research evidence is mixed. Personal factors such as sex, IQ and social values also appear to affect the individual's perception of inequity.[37]

Goal-setting theory

When an employee does not perform as a manager expects, it is often because the employee does not really know what is expected. Employees may think that they are performing well, then be shocked to discover that the performance is not what the manager wants.

This is unfortunate because the evidence indicates that intentions articulated as goals are a potent motivating force.[38] Research suggests the following conditions are needed for goal setting to be an effective motivator:

- Managers must set clear and specific goals. Vague or generalised goals such as 'Do your best' lack motivational impact.
- Employees must accept the goals as their own. Employee participation in the goal-setting process is essential if commitment to the goal and employee job satisfaction are to be achieved.
- Goals must be difficult but not impossible to achieve. Impossible or easy goals do not lead to high performance. (They may even bring about a reduction in performance.) Daniels recommends that, instead of setting over-ambitious goals, managers should set goals that employees can reach 80–90 per cent of the time because this promotes frequent positive reinforcement and makes employees eager to set new goals.[39]
- Managers must give employees frequent feedback on performance (preferably developmental not evaluative feedback).

In summary, goal setting is a strong employee motivator if goals are specific, difficult but attainable, and acceptable to employees, and if managers provide feedback on progress.[40]

Reinforcement theory

Learning by **reinforcement** (sometimes called operant conditioning or behaviour modification) is not strictly a theory of motivation. Unlike the theories discussed above, reinforcement theory is not concerned with individual thought processes. It does not try to explain employees' behaviour in terms of need satisfaction or expectations. Rather, it focuses on rewards and punishments and the effect they have on behaviour (see figure 11.5). Reinforcement theory is based on a fundamental principle of learning — the law of effect — whereby 'behaviour that results in a pleasant outcome is likely to be repeated; behaviour that results in an unpleasant outcome is not likely to be repeated'.[41] If organisations require certain behaviour from employees (for example, high productivity), they should reward such behaviour. Conversely, unwanted behaviour should be ignored or punished. Nevertheless, says Kerr, 'numerous examples exist of reward systems that are fouled up in that the types of behaviour rewarded are those which the rewarder is trying to discourage, while the behaviour desired is not being rewarded at all'.[42] Companies may seek teamwork, for example, but reward individuals, or they may desire innovative thinking and risk-taking but reward the use of proven methods and the absence of mistakes.[43]

Reinforcement The strengthening or weakening of a behaviour through the use of rewards or punishment.

MOTIVATION CHECKLIST

- Do employees feel that meritorious performance is consistently rewarded?
- Does your organisation's reward system send clear and unambiguous messages to employees about what is really important?
- Is 'getting the right results' rewarded much more frequently than 'getting to work'?
- Do employees get excited about the rewards your organisation offers?
- Do your employees feel adequately recognised for their efforts?
- Does your organisation reward employee contributions promptly and creatively?
- Do employees have input into the rewards they receive?
- Do employees perceive the reward system in your organisation as being fair and objective?

Figure 11.5 How motivating are your rewards?

Source D. E. Spitzer, 'Power rewards: rewards that really motivate', *Management Review*, vol. 85, no. 5, 1996, p. 47.

Organisational behaviour modification

Organisational behaviour modification (OBM) is a means of applying **operant conditioning** techniques in the workplace. It aims for the systematic reinforcement of behaviour desired by the organisation and the non-reinforcement or punishment of unwanted behaviour. As a result, its use has generated considerable debate. This controversy is heightened by claims that individuals can be controlled and shaped by organisational behaviour modification yet still feel free. Westwood, for example, expresses concern that the technique infringes human rights, violates the dignity of the individual and reduces the employee to the level of a laboratory rat subject to the manipulations of a manager playing 'God'.[44] Others regard the technique as a cynical attempt by management to destroy workers' sense of collective solidarity along with the influence and power of unions in the workplace. These critics believe that using rewards to create employee commitment is a type of 'manufactured consent', which ensures employees work for management's interests and not their own.[45]

Such criticisms should not be dismissed but they overestimate the effectiveness of organisational behaviour modification.[46] Despite reinforcement being a useful management tool, human behaviour is not so easy to understand and modify.

Using motivation theories in the workplace to improve performance is an exercise in employee manipulation. It is unethical and exploitative.

Employees (and unions) are not so gullible as to be deceived by such cynical manipulation. In any organisation (public, private or trade union), much employee behaviour is already subject to reinforcement. For example, employees have their pay docked for being late or for an unauthorised absence, they receive a pay increase or promotion for good performance, and so on. It is inevitable that managers influence the behaviour of their employees. By definition, management is the art of getting things done through people. To do the job well, managers must be successful in influencing their employees. In short, behaviour control is an unavoidable part of every manager's job.

However, it should not be forgotten that employees also 'manage' their managers. They reward managers by offering praise, being on time, and so on, and punish them by not finishing tasks, complaining to the boss's boss, and so on. The real question, according to Schermerhorn, 'may not be whether it is ethical to control behavior, but whether it is ethical NOT to control behavior well enough that the goals of both the organization and the individual are served'.[47] Nevertheless, HR managers should not ignore the ethical questions involved in organisational behaviour modification.

Approaches to organisational behaviour modification

There are four basic approaches to OBM: positive reinforcement, negative reinforcement, punishment and extinction.

1. **Positive reinforcement:** the manager actively encourages a desired behaviour by repeatedly pairing the desired behaviour or outcomes with rewards or feedback — for example, a manager thanks a subordinate for a helpful suggestion. According to Levinson, young workers particularly need positive reinforcement about what they are doing right because they are under intense pressure from parents and superiors.[48]
2. **Negative reinforcement:** also called avoidance learning, the manager withdraws or withholds punishment when the desired behaviour occurs — for example, a supervisor ceases to reprimand an employee who is often late for work when that employee is punctual.
3. **Punishment:** the manager provides negative consequences after an undesired behaviour, with the intent of decreasing the frequency of the behaviour — for example, a supervisor docks the pay of an employee who is always late for work.[49]
4. **Extinction:** the manager withdraws a positive reinforcer so the undesired behaviour becomes weaker and eventually disappears — for example, a manager fails to reward (with money, praise and so on) an employee who consistently comes to work late, causing the behaviour to cease.

Punishment

Behaviourists generally do not recommend the use of punishment. First, unless handled correctly, the technique may suppress (and not eliminate) the behaviour. Second, the employee may become bitter and feel anger towards the manager and the organisation. Third, the punishment may be offset by positive reinforcement from another source, such as another manager or fellow workers. Fourth, the employee may experience severe stress, causing unpredictable behaviour. And finally, the unwanted behaviour may not change because the employee does not identify the desired behaviour.[50]

To avoid such problems, Schermerhorn suggests the following guidelines for managers:

1. Discuss with the employee what is wrong about their performance. Clearly identify the undesirable behaviour that is the reason for punishment.
2. Explain to the employee what is right. Desirable behaviour (that is, the preferred alternative to the behaviour that is being punished) should be clearly established.
3. Punish in private. Avoid publicly embarrassing people by punishing them in front of others.
4. Follow the laws of contingent and immediate reinforcement. Make sure the punishment is contingent on the undesirable behaviour and follows its occurrence as soon as possible.
5. Make the punishment match the behaviour. Be fair in equating the magnitude of punishment with the degree to which the behaviour is truly undesirable.[51]

Reinforcement schedules

A reinforcement schedule charts how reinforcements are being administered. **Continuous reinforcement** means that rewards are given after each desired behaviour — that is, the desired behaviour is rewarded each and every time. While quickly establishing a connection between behaviour and reward, the learned behaviour is subject to rapid extinction once it is no longer rewarded. Furthermore, continuous reinforcement is not practical in the work situation. Few managers (and especially those with many subordinates) have the time or resources to reward employees every time they perform properly.[52]

Partial reinforcement occurs when rewards are occasionally given after a desired behaviour; the desired behaviour is not rewarded every time. Less efficient in establishing a connection between behaviour and reward, partial reinforcement nevertheless produces higher levels of performance and is more resistant to extinction. Partial reinforcement also has the advantage of being less expensive and awkward to administer.

There are four basic types of partial reinforcement (see also table 11.1):

1. **Fixed interval schedule:** the frequency of reinforcement is determined by an interval of time (for example, hour, day, week, month, year). A monthly pay cheque or a Christmas bonus are examples of rewards administered according to a fixed schedule. The employee knows the reward is coming and expects it. Given that the reward is contingent on employee behaviour meeting some minimal standard (for example, attendance at work), fixed interval schedules generally do not promote high or sustained levels of performance and their use of pay as a reward has never been associated with increases in performance, whereas fixed ratio schedules (see below) have.[53,54]
2. **Fixed ratio schedule:** an employee is rewarded after producing a fixed number of items or performing an activity a fixed number of times. A typical example is a piece-rate system whereby employees are paid for each unit they produce. Rewards are tied to performance by a ratio of rewards to results (for example, five dollars for each item produced). Fixed ratio schedules can produce high levels of performance, but performance rapidly decreases when the reward is not given. Managers should note that continuous and fixed schedules encourage employees to expect that they will be rewarded. If these expectations are not met, an employee may perceive that they have been punished. This not only leads to extinction of the desired behaviour, but also to employee hostility and resentment.[55]
3. **Variable interval schedule:** rewards are administered at varied intervals, so employees never know precisely when the rewards are going to be received. An example is when merit dates vary because the period between increases is contracted or expanded based on employee performance. This is opposed to fixed date reviews such as 1 January each year. Variable interval schedules can achieve high levels of consistent performance and tend to be resistant to extinction.[56]
4. **Variable ratio schedule:** rewards are administered only after an employee has performed the desired behaviour a number of times. A sales representative may receive a bonus, for example, after selling five units, then 12 units, then 18 units, and so on. The average level of sales required to be rewarded is fixed (for example, 10 units), but the sales

Continuous reinforcement Occurs when rewards are given after each desired behaviour.

Partial reinforcement Occurs when rewards are given occasionally after each desired behaviour; that is, the desired behaviour is not rewarded each and every time.

Fixed interval schedule The frequency of reinforcement is determined by an interval of time (for example, hour, day, week, month, year).

Fixed ratio schedule Occurs when an employee is rewarded after producing a fixed number of items or performing an activity a fixed number of times.

Variable interval schedule Rewards are administered at varied intervals.

Variable ratio schedule Rewards are administered only after an employee has performed the desired behaviour a number of times.

representative never knows exactly when they will receive the next bonus. Variable ratio schedules generate consistently high levels of performance and extinction of the desired behaviour is slow.

Table 11.1	Schedules of partial reinforcement			
SCHEDULE OF REINFORCEMENT	**NATURE OF REINFORCEMENT**	**EFFECTS ON BEHAVIOUR WHEN APPLIED**	**EFFECTS ON BEHAVIOUR WHEN PERCEIVED**	**EXAMPLE**
Fixed interval	Reward on fixed time basis	Leads to average and irregular performance	Quick extinction of behaviour	Weekly pay cheque
Fixed ratio	Reward consistently tied to output	Leads quickly to very high and stable performance	Quick extinction of behaviour	Piece-rate pay system
Variable interval	Reward given at variable intervals around some average time	Leads to moderately high and stable performance	Slow extinction of behaviour	Monthly performance appraisal and reward at random times each month
Variable ratio	Reward given at variable output levels around some average output	Leads to very high performance	Slow extinction of behaviour	Sales bonus tied to selling X accounts, but X constantly changes around some mean

Source R. M. Steers and J. S. Black, *Organizational Behavior*, 5th edn, Harper Collins, New York, 1994, p. 114.

Implementing organisational behaviour modification
To effectively introduce this technique, Miner recommends the following steps.
1. Select rewards that are reinforcing for an individual employee.
2. Wherever possible, identify and use new types of rewards.
3. Look for rewards that are naturally occurring, such as praise and profit sharing.
4. Give out enough of the reward so that it is worthwhile for the employee to respond.
5. Provide rewards contingent on the performance of appropriate work behaviour.
6. Set up reinforcers so they follow desired behaviours as quickly as is practical.
7. Make sure that rewards follow rather than precede the desired behaviour.
8. Make sure that rewards are contingent on specific behaviours such as an increase in an individual's sales figures, rather than on broad outcomes such as an overall increase in sales.
9. Start out by rewarding behaviour that is close to the employee's current behaviour.
10. Reward small steps of improvement towards a final goal.
11. Establish a system that rewards too much rather than too little for desired behaviours.
12. State objectives in positive terms — that is, emphasise rewards and de-emphasise punishment.[57]

It is obvious that management must reward the behaviour it wishes to encourage. Reinforcement theory is one way of doing this. But managers should remember that if the organisation claims to value one thing but rewards something else, employees will become cynical and will not trust management in the future.

Finally, rewards must be important to employees before they can motivate individuals to behave in particular ways. Employees choose behaviours that they perceive as leading to the rewards they value. According to Lawler, an organisation 'that is able to tie valued rewards to the behaviors it needs to succeed is likely to find that the reward system is a positive contributor to its effectiveness'.[58]

Practitioner speaks

A private preference

TOP AUSTRALIAN TEACHERS CHOOSE TOP SCHOOLS

Australian teachers have an ability to relate to students and make them feel comfortable which makes them valuable assets attracting overseas parents to send their children for secondary education in Australia, a highly-regarded private school principal said.

'Australian teachers have a fine reputation to the extent that international schools often target Australia as a source for quality teachers', The King's School principal Tim Hawkes said.

'They have an energy, a "can-do" quality and a wonderful capacity to relate to students which I have not seen in other countries', Hawkes said.

Over the past 20 years, there has been a growth in quality teachers at independent schools that has dramatically eclipsed the public sector as non-government schools continue to attract more students.

Australian Bureau of Statistics figures, which reflect a rising preference for private schooling, revealed an 84 per cent increase in the number of full-time equivalent teachers in non-government schools compared with just eight per cent in the public sector.

Cranbourne Christian College teacher Mark Fancett made the move two years ago from a government to a private school. He said the rise in teachers going to private schools is linked to the number of students also making the change.

'I've noticed that it's not only the students that are "opting out". As the numbers of students leaving the government sector increase, it necessitates a move in teachers from the government to private sectors', Fancett told Melbourne newspaper, *The Age*.

Brisbane Grammar School deputy headmaster Brian Short said it is also the advantages of teaching in a private school that affects the migration of quality teachers to private schools.

Short said teaching in a private school offers staff the four main advantages of stability, high interest and involvement from the parents, being part of a real mission and purpose, and extended professional development.

Schools like Brisbane Grammar School have large professional development budgets used to improve staff during school time and in holidays.

'The benefits of private schools in the professional development sense is that they are able to investigate and source tailored professional development programs and then evaluate them', Short said.

'Many staff members are able to attend national and international conferences. We encourage professional development for the purpose of developing teachers and bring the information back to share and teach others', he said.

The King's School Tim Hawkes said private schools search out gifted educators that can make strong contributions of educational debate. Most of the general staff at King's have co-authored mathematics and science textbooks. He himself speaks at least four times a year at teaching conferences and has written a best-selling book on boys education.

'There is a level of accountability in non-government schools that makes it more imperative to offer quality education. Also, it's important because parents pay a lot more in school fees to get this difference', he said.

Communications director of The Scots College, Amanda Hovell said that because stakeholders are now expecting even more from their schools, it is essential the independent sector attract and retain the best possible teachers.

Out of the 90 full time teaching staff at the College, 30 per cent hold Masters degrees, 30 per cent hold Honours degrees and three hold a PhD. Acknowledged experts are also invited to the school to lead seminars on different fields of education.

(continued)

Sandra Li is a freelance features writer and education journalist for Australian Connections magazine. She has a Bachelor of Arts in Mass Communications and Journalism from Murdoch University and lives in Perth.

In addition to higher school fees, private schools receive better funding from the Australian government. According to this year's new Federal budget, funding of non-government schools is estimated to hit A$5.3 billion by 2006.

These funds are used to improve school facilities and environment, as well as provide an added incentive through teachers wages.

The Adelaide Advertiser reported most private school teachers are now renegotiating enterprise agreements, seeking pay rises of up to 13 per cent to take most to about A$62 500 by mid-2005. This is substantially more than the annual salary for teachers in government schools.

Since 2001, annual federal funding to The King's School went from A$1.44 million to A$3.23 million. 'We pay 20 per cent above award wage per month. The school can afford the pay rise and attract more quality teachers', Hawkes said.

Besides better pay, there are other reasons why teachers might prefer to work for independent schools. Most non-government schools are on larger grounds and surrounded by lush scenery, making it a pleasant environment to work in.

Hawkes even believes the students are better balanced.

'I guess to a certain extent we can control them because of the minimum standards met and the students are already more disciplined', he said.

At Brisbane Grammar School, Short ensures staffing is taken very seriously.

'We see teaching as a tripartite role, in the classroom, pastoral care and extra-curricular', Short said. 'Not only must a teacher be an excellent teacher but also must contribute to the quality of extra-curricular activities and also provide a role in the pastoral care and development of students.'

Due to these duties, teachers become part of a culture which supports its staff as well as its students. The extended role they play in the students' lives may also rouse a better quality of job satisfaction. However, this requires most private school teachers to be expected to work after hours and on weekends.

'We pay more but demand more. A normal working day is probably longer than in some state schools. This is because there is a great level of accountability in carefully monitoring on staff performances and educational development', Hawkes said.

'This is the best way to ensure quality education.'

Sandra Li

Source Connections, August–September 2003, pp. 18–19.

Money and motivation

Money plays a complex role in employee motivation. It is not the sole motivator but it does motivate, and some researchers argue that it is the most important single motivator used in organisations.[59] Equity, expectancy and reinforcement theories all show the value of money as a motivator. It is instrumental in satisfying employee needs because it facilitates the purchase of food, shelter and clothing and provides the means to pursue leisure activities. Money can also serve as a symbol of achievement, recognition and status. It acts as a message from the organisation to employees about how much it values their contribution.[60]

Employees compare money earned to determine how they rank. The result of such ranking can affect employee satisfaction and performance.[61] American whiz-kid billionaire Mark Cuban says, 'Money is a scoreboard where you can rank how you are doing against other people'.[62] Industrial disputes, for example, have frequently arisen in Australia when traditional wage relativities have been threatened. The issue is so sensitive with employees that unions generally strongly resist any proposed change to existing relativities.[63] In Hong Kong, money is consistently rated most important by employees.[64] One explanation for this is that it is society's yardstick of success and a key determinant of community respect.[65] In Hong Kong, Japan and Singapore, women rate income level as an overriding concern in their choice of a partner.[66] Finally, a recent European study found money to be the main cause of divorces, separations and rows between couples.[67]

This Letter to the Editor provides a provocative viewpoint. Do you agree? See 'What's your view?' on page 433.

Letter to the Editor

Money is what motivates people

Dear Editor,

I'm sick of hearing all this stuff about money not being important to people. As far as I can tell, money is at the centre of our society and remains the single most important motivator for the great majority of people.

Consider this. I attended the most academically successful high school in Australia. After completing Year 12, I was interested to see the academic choices of my school friends and colleagues. What amazed me was that many who chose the most prestigious and best-paying careers appeared to make choices far removed from their preferences until that time. For instance, a whole group of students who had never studied economics, business studies or legal studies enrolled in combined arts/law and economics/law degrees at the most prestigious universities. Clearly, they were chasing the dollars, even though they had shown little interest in the law or business while at school.

Similarly, I often discuss career issues with friends in occupations like stock broking, futures trading and investment management. Do you think they would be in these occupations if they weren't going to become rich in the process? Of course not! They convince themselves that they like their careers since they need some rationalisation for being paid so much. They work horrendous hours, step over their colleagues in the pursuit of advancement and are under so much stress that it's unbelievable. Do they do it for the money? You'd better believe it! Yet they convince themselves otherwise so that they can tell their friends that they really do enjoy their work and they are making a real contribution to the community.

We even have state governments in Australia creating new incentives in an effort to attract men into primary school teaching. This is a noble profession, probably more valuable to our community than investment banking will ever be, yet there are few men who want to do it. It appears that teaching is viewed as an unattractive profession for the primary reason that it doesn't pay enough. I am seriously concerned what this says about the state of our society's values.

Please convince me that our doctors and medical specialists, lawyers, management consultants and property developers do their work for the sheer joy of it, or for some other altruistic reason. I bet you can't!

A motivational realist (not a 'pop psychology' motivational theorist)

Source David Poole, University of Western Sydney.

Pay and motivation

Pay will motivate employees only if certain conditions are met:
- Employees must attach a high positive valence to pay.
- Employees must believe that good performance leads to high pay. (Superior performers resent automatic and indiscriminate pay increases for all employees.)
- Employees must believe that the quality of their job performance primarily reflects how hard they are trying.
- Employees must see the positive outcomes tied to good performance as being greater than the negative ones (such as moving into a higher tax bracket or being ostracised by workmates).
- Employees must see good performance as the most desirable of all possible behaviours.

Being underpaid by a company means that it is okay to 'steal' the difference.

- Employees must perceive a performance-related pay increase as being significant. US research indicates that merit increases must be at least 7 per cent of base pay if they are to be perceived as motivating.[68]

There are some circumstances under which pay will not motivate employees:

1. There is little trust between management and employees.

2. Employee performance is difficult to measure. If pay is tied to performance, the performance standards must be clearly identified and employee performance must be accurately measured. Otherwise, employees will not perceive any connection between pay and performance. In addition, if pay is tied to only those aspects of performance that are measurable, employees may give all their attention to these aspects while neglecting other tasks.

3. Employee performance is too often measured subjectively and performance ratings are seen as biased. Appraisal in the Australian public service, for example, tended 'to be on the basis of whether a particular officer was liked or not, whether they worked in a high profile area, whether their boss was ranked highly and whether they were based in a state office or Canberra'.[69] According to one survey of Australian companies, barely half had an appraisal system yet almost all claimed to be rewarding outstanding performance.[70] The Australian public service experience shows that a performance appraisal system will be ineffective if it is poorly designed and implemented and if it conflicts with the corporate culture. Some Australian government departments, for example, give all their senior staff the same performance ratings and the same performance-based pay increase.[71]

4. Large pay increases cannot be given to the top performers. Australian companies seem more reluctant than US firms to relate pay and performance or to build in significant pay differences between various jobs.[72] Furthermore, where unions are present, management may have no discretion to reward performance.

5. Employees do not feel that their pay is related to performance. One survey, for example, showed that the majority of Australian organisations rewarded employees on an 'across the board' basis rather than on individual performance.[73] Other research has shown that pay levels and pay increases are affected by such things as physical attractiveness, 'face time' (that is, employees who spend longer time at work are perceived more favourably) and ingratiation.[74]

6. The absolute amount of the pay increase does not clearly discriminate between good and poor performers. This situation is worsened by high marginal income tax rates that make the after-tax difference minuscule. This has led to claims that 'It is about time Australia started to reward performers rather than trying to bring everyone down to the lowest common denominator'.[75]

7. Money is viewed as the sole motivator. Ultimately, motivation comes from within the individual employee. Organisations must create an environment in which employees feel they can make a contribution and advance as far as talent and ambition will take them. Money is a major element in that environment, but it is just that — one element.[76] Says Virgin's Richard Branson: 'It's not about making $2 billion or $3 billion. It's about not wasting one's life.'[77]

Summary

Motivation theories give the HR manager an insight into the importance of:
- identifying and understanding employee needs
- examining the range of employee behavioural choices and their respective attractiveness
- clarifying goals and performance expectations
- ensuring that rewards are closely tied to performance
- ensuring that rewards satisfy needs that are important to employees
- ensuring that employees perceive rewards as equitable.

The theories offer the HR manager a framework for systematically analysing a whole range of HRM activities such as job design, performance appraisal, training and development, career planning and development, compensation and benefits, industrial relations, and occupational health and safety. They also provide considerable insight into why employees behave and perform the way they do. Such insights increase the effectiveness of the HR manager in helping managers to successfully motivate their employees to achieve the organisation's strategic business objectives.

Thirty interactive Wiley Web Questions are available to test your understanding of this chapter at **www.johnwiley.com.au/ highered/hrm5e** *in the student resources area*

student study guide

review questions

1. What is the relationship between pay and motivation?
2. Have you experienced inequity in a job or in a class? What was the inequity? How did it affect your performance?
3. What are the key motivators that your lecturer uses to motivate you? Are they effective? Explain your answer.
4. What factors can influence employee motivation?
5. What is the difference between content and process theories of motivation? Which approach do you think has the greater relevance for HR managers? Explain your answer.
6. A manager is confronted with an employee motivation problem. As an HRM practitioner, which questions would you ask in attempting to find a solution?
7. Identify a job in which you were highly motivated or demotivated. What characteristics of the work, the people and/or the organisation made you feel this way?
8. Think of a really bad boss. Describe what made the boss so awful. Which employee needs were not satisfied by the boss's behaviour?
9. Define motivation. What is its relationship to employee performance?
10. Think of a job you have done. How could it have been enriched?

environmental influences on employee motivation

Describe the key environmental influences from the model (figure 11.6 shown opposite) that have significance for employee motivation.

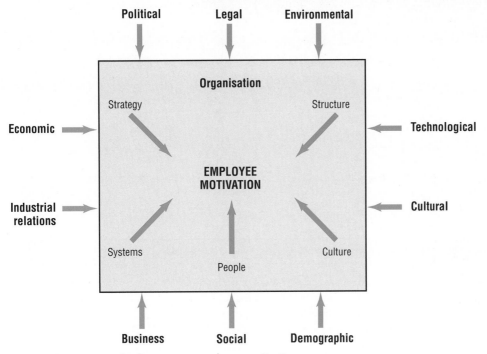

Figure 11.6 Environmental influences on employee motivation

class debate

Motivation is simply a sophisticated management technique to intensify worker effort without increasing costs.

what's your view?

Write a 500-word response to the Letter to the Editor on page 429, agreeing or disagreeing with the writer's point of view.

practitioner speaks

Read the article on page 427–8. Using one of the motivation theories studied in this chapter, explain why private schools appear to be more attractive to quality teachers. As a class, critically discuss Sandra Li's viewpoints.

newsbreak exercise

Read the Newsbreak 'Secrets of profitability' on page 419–20. Write a 500-word critical review of the article based on your personal feelings and experience.

soapbox

What do you think? Conduct a mini survey of class members, using the questionnaire below. Critically discuss the findings.

1. Money motivates people.	YES	NO
2. Men and women are motivated by the same things.	YES	NO
3. Income tax 'kills' employee motivation.	YES	NO
4. Most companies reward 'belonging' and not performance.	YES	NO
5. Australian society 'punishes' high achievers.	YES	NO
6. What gets employees motivated is fear of losing their job.	YES	NO

online exercise

1. Conduct an online search on the compensation of professional athletes, senior executives and senior academics (making specific reference to equity theory). As a class, review your findings.
2. Conduct an online search on motivation. Identify other viewpoints and examples relating to the theories described in this chapter. As a class, review your findings.

ethical dilemma

'Good people deserve to be rewarded'

George Brown, CEO of ABC International, believed that people were the company's greatest asset. He spent millions of dollars on gifts and bonuses to employees he favoured, arguing that it was important for employee motivation. Even as ABC International's financial position deteriorated, Brown's largesse continued. He spent over $100 000 on gifts for long-serving employees. At Christmas, every one of ABC International's employees was given either an expensive box of chocolates or a bottle of wine, accompanied by a 'thank you' note personally signed by Brown. Although this took an enormous amount of time, Brown believed it personalised the company's culture and gave it a family feel. Some senior managers privately disapproved of the time taken and questioned the value of the practice. None, however, was prepared to challenge Brown, fearing that to do so would put their own emoluments at risk.

Brown fuelled the hidden criticism when he allowed his secretary to take a holiday at the company's expense and awarded another long-serving employee a $60 000 round-the-world trip with his wife to farewell old friends and colleagues.

Brown described the payments as rewards for outstanding achievement and loyalty.

People who challenged Brown quickly found themselves marginalised. Invitations to company functions were withheld, scheduled bonus payments withdrawn and membership of key committees denied. In contrast, those employees perceived as loyal and willing to follow Brown's directions were lavished with praise, gifts, promotions and financial rewards.

Despite the company's dire financial position, Brown continued to spend money on motivating employees. Extravagant functions at five-star hotels were held for top-performing salespeople and others whom Brown favoured. To enhance the company's image, Brown initiated a major donation program to several leading charities and universities. A sizeable donation to one university resulted in Brown being awarded an honorary doctorate. As a result, he ordered all employees to now refer to him as Dr Brown. On business trips, he travelled first class and booked two seats so that he would not be disturbed as he worked. All frequent flyer points were subsequently credited to his personal account.

Brown dismissed all criticisms of his generous treatment of ABC International employees, arguing that 'good people deserve to be rewarded', especially during tough business times. In private, senior managers described the situation as 'human resource management gone mad'. Many other employees, however, adored Brown and saw him as a strong and caring leader.

Discussion questions

1. Critically analyse ABC International's approach to employee motivation.
2. Which theory of motivation best describes George Brown's behaviour?
3. What ethical issues are raised in this case?

case studies

Bricks beat brains[78]

'I don't believe it!' shouted Steve Plovnick, Associate Professor in Organisational Behaviour at Western University. 'I have a PhD and over 15 years working experience and I don't earn anything like this! Who said Australia was the clever country? This place rewards brawn not brains. Damn it, it makes me angry!' Plovnick threw the newspaper down and looked at his colleagues. 'It says here that brickies are earning $100 000 a year. Tell me how smart do you have to be to lay bricks? How long do you have to study to become a bricklayer?'

'I know', said Cindy Castelli, Lecturer in Sociology. 'I work very hard and spent years studying to get my PhD — and for what? A salary not even half of that earned by someone who didn't even complete high school. How do you expect to motivate people to sacrifice and study if there are no rewards? It's very unfair.'

'Why don't you guys stop complaining and face reality?' snapped Professor Angela Simons. 'There is a building boom, which means there is an acute shortage of bricklayers. The community demand for brickies is simply greater than it is for academics who teach Sociology and OB.'

'I don't care', retorted Plovnick, 'it's neither right nor fair.'

Discussion questions

1. Do you agree with the views expressed above? Explain your answer.
2. Why are Steve and Cindy complaining about their pay? Which motivation theory do you think best explains their feelings?

Why burst a boiler?

Valerie Firestone, Vice-President, Sales, for ABC Ltd, scanned the sales report. Every representative had exceeded quota by at least 20 per cent. The one exception was Jack Murphy. Jack had made quota, but only just. Until six months ago, Jack, aged fifty-five, was the company's top sales representative. Recently, however, he seemed to have lost his edge. The company's incentive program allowed representatives to earn unlimited cash bonuses and was regarded as the best in the industry. Valerie wondered why

Jack's performance was down as he had always been extremely 'hungry'.

When Valerie raised the matter with Jack, he smiled. 'Valerie, you know I have been a top sales rep for many years.' Valerie nodded. 'Well, my wife Mary and I saved pretty hard and put all our money into Sydney real estate. Given the property boom we have made a killing. Mary and I are property millionaires. I just don't need the dough. All the effort to exceed quota and the extra tax just don't make it worthwhile. I'm sorry, Valerie, I'll do my job, but don't expect me to push myself like I have in the past.'

Discussion questions

1. What motivational factors are at work here?
2. Which motivational theory best explains Jack's behaviour?
3. If you were Valerie, what would you do to get Jack to improve his performance?

practical exercises

1. Form into groups of four to six. Discuss how you would motivate employees in the following jobs using one of the theories studied in this chapter:
   (a) taxi driver
   (b) domestic helper
   (c) nurse
   (d) supermarket checkout operator
   (e) graduate trainee
   (f) university lecturer
   (g) HR manager
   (h) exotic dancer.
2. Form into groups of four to six. Brainstorm a list of innovative ways to motivate employees to achieve outstanding performance — and be creative! After 10 minutes, compare your suggestions. Pick the top 10 for originality and likely effectiveness. Identify and discuss the employee needs they satisfy. Select a reward for the group with the best suggestions.
3. (a) Complete the employee survey questionnaire shown below.

EMPLOYEE SURVEY QUESTIONNAIRE

	Very dissatisfied			Very satisfied	
My opportunities for advancement	1	2	3	4	5
My recognition from my boss	1	2	3	4	5
My pay	1	2	3	4	5
My benefits	1	2	3	4	5
My relationship with my colleagues	1	2	3	4	5
My status	1	2	3	4	5
My relationship with my boss	1	2	3	4	5
My working conditions	1	2	3	4	5
My job's health and safety	1	2	3	4	5
My training and development	1	2	3	4	5
My job security	1	2	3	4	5
My job	1	2	3	4	5
My work–life balance	1	2	3	4	5
My performance appraisal ratings	1	2	3	4	5
My company's HR policies and practices	1	2	3	4	5

(b) Score the class results.

(c) Break into discussion groups of four to six members. Analyse and critically discuss the survey results using one of the theories of motivation studied in this chapter.

(d) If you were an HR manager, what would you point out to an organisation that obtained similar results? What corrective actions would you recommend?

4. Interview someone you know who has working experience. Ask them to give an actual example of (a) when they felt highly motivated and (b) when they felt highly demotivated. Use one of the theories studied in this chapter to explain their motivation or lack of it.

5. Form into groups of four to six. Imagine that you are the board of directors of a newly formed fast-food company. Discuss how you plan to motivate your employees to:

(a) work hard

(b) be punctual

(c) give excellent customer service

(d) be flexible regarding work assignments

(e) work safely

(f) cooperate with each other and work as a team

(g) be committed to the company

(h) work long hours.

suggested readings

Boxhall, P. and Purcell, J., *Strategy and Human Resource Management*, Palgrave Macmillan, Basingstoke, 2003, pp. 146–61.

CCH, *Australian Master Human Resources Guide*, CCH, Sydney, 2003, ch. 13.

De Cieri, H. and Kramar, R., *Human Resource Management in Australia*, McGraw-Hill, Sydney, 2003, ch. 13.

Fisher, C. D., Schoenfeldt, L. F. and Shaw, J. B., *Human Resource Management*, 5th edn, Houghton Mifflin, Boston, 2003, pp. 600–2.

Ivancevich, J. M., *Human Resource Management*, 8th edn, McGraw-Hill, Boston, 2001, pp. 298–301.

Ivancevich, J. M. and Lee, S. H., *Human Resource Management in Asia*, McGraw-Hill, Singapore, 2002, pp. 36–7, 82–4, 295–9.

McShane, S. L. and Von Glinow, M. A., *Organizational Behavior*, McGraw-Hill, Boston, 2000, chs 3, 4.

Robbins, S., *Organizational Behavior*, 9th edn, Prentice Hall, Upper Saddle River, NJ, 2001, chs 6, 7.

Schermerhorn, J. R., Hunt, J. G. and Osborn, R. N., *Organizational Behavior*, 8th edn, John Wiley & Sons, New York, 2003, ch. 6.

online references

www.aps.psychsociety.com.au
www.econ.usyd.edu.au/acirrt
www.shrm.org.hrmagazine

www.workforceonline.com
www.workplaceinfo.com.au

end notes

1. F. Lowy, quoted in R. Harley, 'Lowy wraps up his biggest shopping expedition', *Australian Financial Review*, 27 March 2002, p. 55.

2. O. Lundy and A. Cowling, *Strategic Human Resource Management*, Routledge, London, 1996, pp. 296–302.

3. P. E. Spector, *Industrial and Organizational Psychology*, John Wiley & Sons, New York, 1996, p. 192.

4. Based on P. E. Spector, op. cit., p. 192.

5. J. R. Schermerhorn, *Management*, 7th edn, John Wiley & Sons, New York, 2002, pp. 131–7.

6. D. Hellriegel and J. W. Slocum, *Management*, 6th edn, Addison-Wesley, New York, 1993, pp. 429–30.

7. W. B. Werther Jr and K. Davis, *Human Resources and Personnel Management*, 5th edn, McGraw-Hill, New York, 1996, p. 500.

8. M. G. Aamodt, *Applied Industrial/Organizational Psychology*, 2nd edn, Brooks/Cole, Pacific Grove, CA, 1996, p. 439.

9. G. Moorhead and R. W. Griffin, *Organizational Behavior*, 4th edn, Houghton Mifflin, Boston, 1995, p. 584.

10. G. Bassett, 'The case against job satisfaction', *Business Horizons*, vol. 37, no. 3, May–June 1994, pp. 61–8.

11. D. J. Cherrington, *Organizational Behavior*, 2nd edn, Allyn & Bacon, Boston, 1994, pp. 280–1.

12. Research conducted by London House and Food Marketing Institute, cited in 'Employees respond well to company commitment', *Personnel Journal*, vol. 74, no. 7, 1995, p. 23.

13. S. P. Robbins, *Organizational Behavior*, 9th edn, Prentice Hall, NJ, 2001, pp. 21–2.

14. F. J. Roethlisberger and W. J. Dixon, *Management and the Worker*, Harvard University Press, Cambridge, Mass., 1939.

15. A. Carey, 'The Hawthorne studies: a radical criticism', *American Sociological Review*, vol. 32, 1967, pp. 403–16; and R. H. Franke and J. D. Kaul, 'The Hawthorne experiments: first statistical interpretations', *American Sociological Review*, vol. 43, 1978, pp. 623–43.

16. D. McGregor, *The Human Side of Enterprise*, McGraw-Hill, New York, 1960, p. 33.

17. D. McGregor, cited in E. L. Deci (ed.), *Management and Motivation*, Penguin, Middlesex, 1970, p. 315.

18. S. P. Robbins, op. cit., p. 158.

19. M. Rose, *Industrial Behaviour*, Penguin, Middlesex, 1985, p. 189.

20. A. D. Szilagyi and M. J. Wallace, *Organizational Behavior and Performance*, 5th edn, Scott Foresman, Glenview, Ill., 1990, p. 94; and J. R. Schermerhorn, op. cit., p. 101.

21. B. Rodgers, *The IBM Way*, Harper & Row, New York, 1986, pp. 184–5.

22. M. A. Wahba and L. G. Bridwell, 'Maslow reconsidered: a review of the research on the need hierarchy theory', *Organizational Behavior and Human Performance*, vol. 15, 1976, pp. 212–40; and V. F. Mitchell and P. Moudgill, 'Measurement of Maslow's need hierarchy', *Organizational Behavior and Human Performance*, vol. 16, 1976, pp. 334–49.

23. G. G. Alpanda and K. D. Carter, 'Strategic multinational intra-company differences in employee motivation', *Journal of Managerial Psychology*, vol. 6, no. 2, 1991, pp. 25–32.

24. R. Mead, *International Management: Cross Cultural Dimensions*, Blackwell, Oxford, 1995, p. 205.

25. G. Hofstede, 'Cultural dimensions in management and planning', *Asia Pacific Journal of Management*, vol. 1, no. 2, 1984, pp. 81–99.

26. R. I. Westwood, 'On motivation and work', in R. I. Westwood (ed.), *Organizational Behavior, Southeast Asian Perspectives*, Longman, Hong Kong, 1992, pp. 299–391.

27. *The Dallas Morning News*, 'Pizza Hut chief ignites the passion to win', *South China Morning Post — Business*, 6 September 1999, p. 4.

28. Research by SHL, reported in C. Fox, 'Never fear, Aussies are here', *Australian Financial Review*, 29 June 2000, p. 38.

29. Gallup study, reported in S. Shellenbarger, 'Friendly workers work better', *Australian Financial Review*, 20 January 2000, p. 50.

30. D. R. Spitzer, 'Power rewards: rewards that really motivate', *Management Review*, vol. 85, no. 5, 1996, pp. 45–50.

31. F. E. Emery and M. Phillips, *Living At Work*, AGPS, Canberra, 1976, p. 33.

32. G. Gardner, 'Is there a valid test of Herzberg's two-factor theory?', *Journal of Occupational Psychology*, vol. 50, 1977, pp. 197–204; and J. Schneider and E. A. Locke, 'Critique of Herzberg's classification system and a suggested revision', *Organizational Behavior and Human Performance*, vol. 6, 1971, pp. 441–58.

33. F. Luthans, *Organizational Behavior*, 7th edn, McGraw-Hill, New York, 1995, pp. 145–6.

34. S. L. McShane and M. A. Von Glinow, *Organizational Behavior*, McGraw-Hill, New York, 2000, p. 71.

35. J. R. Schermerhorn, op. cit., pp. 371–2.

36. R. I. Henderson, *Compensation Management*, 7th edn, Prentice Hall, Upper Saddle River, NJ, 1997, pp. 412–14.

37. J. R. Schermerhorn, op. cit., pp. 369–70.

38. G. P. Latham and E. A. Locke, 'Goal setting: a motivation technique that works', *Organizational Dynamics*, Autumn 1979, pp. 72–6.

39. E. A. Locke, K. N. Shaw, L. M. Saari and G. P. Latham, 'Goal setting and task performance', *Psychological Bulletin*, vol. 90, 1981, pp. 125–52; T. Matsui, A. Okada and R. Mizuguchi, 'Expectancy theory prediction of the goal theory postulate', *Journal of Applied Psychology*, vol. 66, 1981, pp. 54–8; and M. Erez, 'Feedback, a necessary condition for the goal setting performance relation', *Journal of Applied Psychology*, vol. 62, 1977, pp. 624–7.

40. L. A. Wilk and W. K. Redmon, 'The effects of feedback and goal setting on the productivity and satisfaction of university admission staff', *Journal of Organizational Behavior*, vol. 18, 1998, pp. 45–68.

41. E. L. Thorndike, *Animal Intelligence*, Macmillan, New York, 1911, p. 244.

42. S. Kerr, 'On the folly of rewarding A, while hoping for B', *Academy of Management Executive*, vol. 9, no. 1, 1995, p. 7.

43. S. Kerr, op. cit., p. 15.

44. R. I. Westwood (ed.), op. cit., p. 311.

45. K. Legge, cited in J. Storey (ed.), *New Perspectives on Human Resource Management*, Routledge, London, 1992, ch. 2 (especially p. 37); T. Keenoy, 'HRM: a case of the wolf in sheep's clothing', *Personnel Review*, vol. 19, no. 2, 1990, pp. 3–9; and F. M. Horwitz, 'HRM: an ideological perspective', *Personnel Review*, vol. 19, no. 2, 1990, pp. 10–15.

46. A. D. Szilagyi and M. J. Wallace, op. cit., p. 139; P. E. Spector, op. cit., pp. 199–200.

47. J. R. Schermerhorn, op. cit., p. 376.

48. H. Levinson, 'Positive reinforcement — the powerful under used management tool', *Boardroom Reports*, 1 December 1993, pp. 5–6.

49. J. B. Miner, *Industrial-Organizational Psychology*, McGraw-Hill, Singapore, 1992, p. 97.

50. R. D. Arvey and J. M. Ivancevich, 'Punishment in organizations: a review, propositions and research suggestions', *Academy of Management Review*, vol. 5, 1980, pp. 123–32.

51. J. R. Schermerhorn, op. cit., pp. 374–6.

52. R. L. Daft and R. M. Steers, *Organizations: A Micro/Macro Approach*, Scott Foresman, Glenview, Ill., 1986, p. 110.

53. R. L. Daft and R. M. Steers, op. cit., p. 110.

54. S. M. Klein and R. R. Ritti, *Understanding Organizational Behavior*, 2nd edn, Kent, Boston, Mass., 1984, p. 218.

55. S. M. Klein and R. R. Ritti, op. cit., pp. 217–18.

56. P. E. Spector, op. cit., pp. 198–200.

57. J. B. Miner, op. cit., pp. 99–100.

58. E. E. Lawler III, cited in M. L. Rock and L. A. Berger (eds), *The Compensation Handbook*, 3rd edn, McGraw-Hill, New York, 1991, p. 594.

59. J. M. Ivancevich, *Human Resource Management*, 8th edn, McGraw-Hill, Boston, 2001, pp. 298–9.

60. S. Robbins, *Organizational Behavior*, 9th edn, Prentice Hall, Upper Saddle River, NJ, 2001, p. 179.

61. G. Milbourn, 'The relationship of money and motivation', *Compensation Review*, vol. 12, no. 2, 1980, pp. 33–44.

62. M. Cuban, quoted in R. Patterson, 'Man in a billion', *South China Morning Post — Review*, 17 June 2000, p. 8.

63. J. D. Hill, W. A. Howard and R. D. Lansbury, *Industrial Relations: An Australian Introduction*, Longman Cheshire, Melbourne, 1982, p. 154; S. J. Deery and D. H. Plowman, *Australian Industrial Relations*, 3rd edn, McGraw-Hill, Sydney, 1991, pp. 388–91.

64. Survey reported in *China Staff*, vol. 6, no. 1, November 1999, p. 34.

65. S. G. Redding, *The Spirit of Chinese Capitalism*, de Gruyter, Berlin, 1990, pp. 194–5.

66. Survey conducted by the Social Development Service, reported in J. Hee and T. Tan, 'Eight out of 10 don't regret saying I do', *The Sunday Times*, 6 August 2000, p. 27; J. James and S. Yap, 'Marriage not top priority for singles', *The Strait Times*, 18 April 2001, p. H6; and

'Mr Right must be rich, say Japanese singles', *Sunday Morning Post*, 8 April 2001, p. 9.

67. Study by the Department of Psychology, University of Vienna, reported in M. Leidig, 'It's money, honey, if you want to get on with me', *South China Morning Post*, 30 November 2000, p. 18.

68. S. Robbins, op. cit., pp. 170, 179; and A. Mitra, N. Gupta and G. D. Jenkins Jr, 'The case of the invisible merit raise: how people see their pay raises', *Compensation and Benefits Review*, May–June, 1995, pp. 71–6.

69. P. Roberts, 'Work appraisal is good, but skip the bonus pay', *Australian Financial Review*, 3 October 1997, p. 46.

70. Ibis, Deloitte Haskins and Sells-Rydges, 'Stimulate productivity, stem mediocrity, reward performance', *Rydges*, November 1984, p. 129.

71. P. Roberts, op. cit., p. 46.

72. M. Pascoe, 'Million dollar failures', *Bulletin*, 7 October 1997, pp. 52–3.

73. Recruitment Solutions report into remuneration and recruitment, reported in 'Succession still being left to chance, survey reveals', *HR Monthly*, September 1997, p. 9.

74. Society for Human Resource Management, 'Reasonable accommodation necessary in 'Appearance' policy', *Issues in HR*, January–February 1994, p. 1; G. Koretz, 'When layers are lookers', *Business Week*, 8 January 1996, p. 10; and L. Harper, 'Even among bricklayers, beauty works the hunks for higher pay', *Asian Wall Street Journal*, 26–27 November 1993, pp. 1, 5.

75. Executive Director of the Association of Professional Engineers, quoted in N. Hooper, 'Executives raise the ante on Hawke's call', *Business Review Weekly*, 26 February 1988, p. 28.

76. D. J. McLaughlin, 'Does compensation motivate executives?', in F. F. Foulkes (ed.), *Executive Compensation*, Harvard, Boston, 1991, pp. 78–9; and M. M. Markowich, 'Does money motivate?', *Compensation and Benefits Review*, vol. 26, no. 1, 1994, pp. 69–72.

77. R. Branson, quoted in B. O'Reilly, 'What it takes to start a startup', *Fortune*, 7 June 1999, p. 68.

78. Partly based on B. Schneiders, 'Elusive brickies earn $100k as trade skill shortage bites', *Australian Financial Review*, 6 June 2003, p. 17.

employee compensation

Learning objectives

When you have finished studying this chapter, you should be able to:

- Understand the need to link compensation policies and practices with an organisation's strategic business objectives
- Identify the key objectives of employee compensation
- Explain the components of a systematic compensation program
- Understand the mechanics of common job evaluation systems
- Explain the steps in compensation planning
- Understand current issues in executive compensation
- Explain how to link pay to performance.

> **'Sanity should be restored to the sheltered workshop of executive remuneration.'**[1]
>
> **Robert Samuelson, Member, Washington Post Writers Group**

Strategic compensation

Compensation is one of the most important HRM activities. It can help to reinforce the organisation's culture and key values and facilitate the achievement of its strategic business objectives. By rewarding desired results, an organisation's compensation policies and practices can reinforce employee behaviour that realises its strategic business objectives. Research shows that organisations seeking a competitive advantage employ remuneration practices that encourage, facilitate and reward desired employee behaviours.[2] Leading companies such as ANZ, BHP Billiton (see figure 12.1), Foster's and Westpac have aligned their executive remuneration to shareholder-based measures. Foster's, for example, aligns management rewards with shareholder interests, the achievement of business objectives and the profitability of the company.[3] 'Compensation thus can be an important tool for motivating higher levels of job performance and enhancing organizational effectiveness.'[4]

> **Compensation** What employees receive in exchange for their work. Includes pay and benefits (total compensation) or just pay (cash compensation).

Remuneration policy

The Committee recognises that the Group operates in a global environment and that its performance depends on the quality of its people. To prosper, the Group must be able to attract, motivate and retain highly skilled executives willing to work around the world.

The key principles that underpin Group remuneration policy are:

- competitive rewards are provided to attract and retain executive talent on a global basis
- demanding key performance indicators apply to delivering results across the Group and are applied to a significant portion of the total reward
- rewards to executives are linked to the creation of value to shareholders
- the criteria used to assess and reward executives include financial and non-financial measures of performance
- remuneration arrangements should ensure equity between executives and should facilitate the deployment of human resources around the Group
- severance payments due to executives on termination are limited to pre-established contractual arrangements which do not commit the Group to making any unjustified payments in the event of non-performance.

The remuneration policy assists the Group to achieve its business strategy and objectives. The Committee recognises that, while remuneration is a key factor in recruiting the right people, it is not the only factor. The Group's values, and its ability to provide interesting and challenging career opportunities, also play an important part.

Figure 12.1 BHP Billiton's remuneration policy
Source *BHP Billiton Annual Report*, 2003, p. 47.

Moreover, **strategic compensation** is a formidable communicator and can be a powerful instrument for change and a major determinant of the culture of an organisation. For example, pay-for-performance programs communicate to employees the organisation's expectations regarding flexibility, dynamism and contribution. They also symbolise that continued employment is contingent upon performance.[5] It should be noted that reward systems by themselves will not change a culture, but they can help reinforce a desired culture.[6]

Critics argue that **pay for performance**, with its emphasis on individual performance, recognition and reward, undermines collective employment relations, discourages union membership, marginalises unions and increases management control, which, in turn, explains trade union hostility.[7] Furthermore, if there is a significant mismatch between compensation and organisational strategy, it is likely to result in major barriers to the achievement of strategic business objectives.[8] This is critical because organisations must control costs and reward performance if they are to compete successfully in a global economy.[9]

> **Strategic compensation** Involves compensation practices being aligned with the achievement of the organisation's strategic business objectives.

> **Pay for performance** A pay system that rewards employees on the basis of their performance.

However, few companies have any idea of what they want to achieve through their compensation programs.[10] One survey, for example, found that while companies call for team players, only 7 per cent of those surveyed had linked team performance to performance pay plans.[11] Similarly, a Towers Perrin survey showed that only 37 per cent of companies with executive option schemes applied some form of performance criteria.[12] Such findings are consistent with overseas research, which indicates that there is a significant gap in many organisations between management pronouncements linking pay and performance and actual practice.[13]

Finally, for many organisations, employee compensation is the biggest single cost of doing business. 'Pay and benefit costs', according to O'Neill, 'are the largest single operating expense for most service companies, and typically the second or third highest expense category in manufacturing.'[14] Compensation, in turn, is a necessity of life for employees: pay is the means by which they provide for their own and their family's needs.[15] As such, it is the only reason to go to work. This does not mean that non-financial or intrinsic rewards are unimportant and can be ignored; it simply recognises that money is a powerful source of motivation (see figure 12.2).

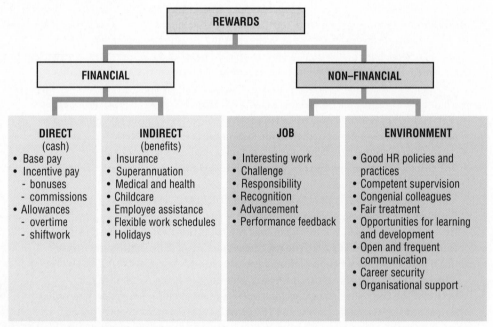

Figure 12.2 Types of employee rewards
Source Asia Pacific Management Co. Ltd, 2004.

Compensation philosophy

An organisation's general approach to compensation must be consistent with its overall strategic business objectives (see figure 12.3). Compensation policies and practices should emanate from the organisation's strategic business objectives because these determine the performance and behaviours to be motivated, the kind of people to be attracted and retained, and the structure of the organisation.[16] Unfortunately, too many organisations have not clearly articulated the rationale underlying their compensation program and therefore react in an ad hoc way to compensation issues instead of viewing each issue as part of a comprehensive whole.[17] As a result, organisations do not achieve optimum value from the compensation dollars they spend.

Compensation cannot be looked at in isolation if a high-performance environment is to be created. The HR manager must change the emphasis from immediate questions — How much do we need to pay? How should it be packaged? — to more strategic questions — What does the organisation want in return for its pay? How can compensation policies and practices achieve these objectives?[18] If an organisation's stated objective is to attract, retain and motivate the 'best' people in its industry, then it is pointless to compensate employees at below-market rates.[19] Likewise, if an organisation wants to be an ethical employer and a good 'corporate citizen', then questionable tax avoidance and shadowy tax minimisation schemes should not be used. Similarly, if improved customer service is sought, the compensation system must stimulate and reward the employee behaviours that produce superior service performance.

A formal compensation policy should:
- reflect the organisation's strategic business objectives and culture
- articulate the objectives that an organisation wants to achieve via its compensation programs
- be communicated to all employees
- be perceived as fair and equitable
- provide the foundation for designing and implementing compensation and benefits programs (see figure 12.1).

Australian taxpayers have to work 132 days for the federal government before they start working for themselves.

Objective and policy setting phases
Stage 1 Develop strategic business objectives.
Stage 2 Develop HRM objectives.
Stage 3 Develop employee compensation objectives.

Compensation administration phases
Stage 4 Job analysis
Identify, describe and place jobs to create the desired organisation structure, considering:
- job analysis
- job description
- job specification
- job titles
- performance standards.

Stage 5 Job evaluation
Establish the internal equity and importance of jobs to the organisation, considering:
- job ranking
- job grading

- point system
- factor comparison.

Stage 6 Pay survey
Establish the external equity, considering:
- own surveys
- professional association surveys
- consultants' surveys
- employer association surveys
- government surveys.

Stage 7 Job pricing
Match the job's internal and external worth, considering:
- job evaluation worth (worth within the company)
- labour market worth (what other employers are paying).

Determine competitive market posture.
Establish pay ranges.

Stage 8 Implementation
Administer, communicate, monitor and review the compensation program.

Figure 12.3 Strategic compensation
Source Asia Pacific Management Co. Ltd, 2004.

Compensation program objectives

Following are some common compensation program objectives.
For the organisation
- Attract and keep the desired quality and mix of employees.
- Ensure fair and equitable treatment.
- Motivate employees to improve their performance continually and to strive to achieve the organisation's strategic business objectives.
- Reinforce the organisation's key values and the desired organisational culture.
- Drive and reinforce desired employee behaviour.
- Ensure compensation is maintained at the desired competitive level.
- Control compensation costs.
- Ensure optimum value for each compensation dollar spent.
- Comply with legal requirements.

For the employee
- Ensure fair and equitable treatment.
- Accurately measure and appropriately reward performance and contribution to the achievement of the organisation's strategic business objectives.
- Provide appropriate compensation changes based on performance, promotion, transfer or changing conditions.
- Provide regular compensation and performance reviews.

Compensation program components

To achieve these objectives, it is essential that organisations have a systematic approach to compensation. Inadequate compensation planning is characterised by:
- failure to link compensation strategies to the organisation's strategic business objectives
- a haphazard approach in the reward of performance (if there is no measure of performance, what is being rewarded?)
- lack of control over compensation costs (if a company does not know its total compensation costs — base pay, bonus, cash incentives, and so on — how can it effectively budget and control costs?)
- no defined market posture (if a company does not know its position in the marketplace and likely future pay movements, how can management forecast and budget accurately?)
- gross overpayment or underpayment of employees, giving rise to employee dissatisfaction because of the lack of 'fairness'
- disjointed internal relationships, with junior positions being paid more than senior positions (typically where seniority rather than responsibility and performance is rewarded)
- the granting of pay increases on the 'squeaky wheel' principle, leading to further anomalies, dissatisfaction and de-motivation among employees
- lack of compliance with applicable state and federal laws and industrial awards.

Components of a systematic compensation program include:
- job analysis — accurately identifies job duties and responsibilities (**job description**) and the employee characteristics needed to perform the job successfully (**job specification**)
- job evaluation — accounts for each job's relative value to the organisation
- pay survey — establishes the competitiveness of pay levels compared with other organisations
- performance evaluation — determines the level of performance of each employee
- pay for performance — relates pay increases to performance and desired employee behaviours.

Job description A written statement explaining what a job holder does, how the work is performed, where and when it is performed and the performance standards to be met.

Job specification A written statement of the qualifications, skills and know-how a person needs to perform a given job successfully.

Job evaluation The systematic determination of the relative worth of jobs within an organisation.

Job evaluation

Job evaluation is a systematic method of determining the worth to the organisation of a job in relation to the worth of other jobs. It is concerned with 'how big' or 'how small' a job is. The aim is to ensure that jobs of different sizes or relative worth attract the appropriate pay differentials.

An accounting manager's job, for example, would require greater know-how and responsibility than would the work of an accounting trainee, so the management job would be worth more to the organisation in helping it achieve its objectives. Thus, the pay range for the job of accounting manager should be higher than that for the job of trainee.

Job evaluation forms the basis for establishing the organisation's job hierarchy and associated pay structure. Australian senior HR managers, for example, firmly believe that a formal job evaluation system is essential to effective pay administration.[20]

Job evaluation systems

There are many methods used to evaluate jobs and each is subjective to some degree. All are based on the assumption that jobs can be differentiated by evaluating the information in a job description. The most common job-based systems include job ranking and job grading or classification, which are qualitative, and the points and factor comparison methods, which are quantitative (see figure 12.4). These traditional systems evaluate jobs and require up-to-date, well-written job descriptions. In contrast, new person-centred or skill-based evaluation systems focus on the employee role or skills, competencies or knowledge as the basis for pay. Typically, these require tests or measures to determine whether an employee possesses the designated skills, competencies or knowledge.

| | SCOPE OF COMPARISON | |
Basis for comparison	Whole job (qualitative)	Job factors (quantitative)
Job versus job	Job ranking	Factor comparison
Job versus scale	Job grade	Point system

Figure 12.4 Job evaluation systems
Source Asia Pacific Management Co. Ltd, 2004.

Job ranking

Job ranking is the quickest, simplest, easiest to understand and oldest job evaluation method. The evaluator ranks the jobs from 'biggest' to 'smallest'. Obviously, accuracy depends on the evaluator's knowledge of the jobs and degree of objectivity. Ranking, while measuring relative worth, does not measure the magnitude of difference between jobs: we know that an a general manager's job is 'bigger' than that of the accounting manager, but not how much 'bigger'. Thus, the job ranking method is too subject to bias and too clumsy to be used in any but the smallest of organisations (see figure 12.5).

Job ranking A job evaluation method that sizes jobs by placing them in rank order.

Figure 12.5 Example of job ranking
Source Asia Pacific Management Co. Ltd, 2004.

Job grading or job classification

A refinement on job ranking is the system of **job grading** or job classification. The first step is to use a number of job-related factors, such as education, experience and responsibilities, to determine classes or grades of job. The next step is to create generic or 'benchmark' job descriptions for each grade or class. To establish the relative worth of an individual job, the job is compared with the benchmark description for each of the grades or classes, then assigned to the appropriate one.

A major problem with this method is that satisfactory descriptions have to be written for each of the grades or classes. This can become extremely complex in large organisations and is often unworkable. One way of attempting to overcome such problems is to use functional (or job family) gradings or classifications such as engineering, finance or sales and marketing. These can simplify gradings or classifications within a function, but comparing jobs cross-functionally remains a problem (see figure 12.6).

Job grading does not provide a precise classification. It is best suited to organisations with

Job grading A job evaluation method that sizes jobs using a series of written classifications.

benchmark jobs that have well-known and understood standardised characteristics and thus are a valid and reliable guide to grading or classification. Job grading or classification does have the advantage of being relatively inexpensive. It is often used in the public sector in industrial awards, and for engineering and scientific jobs.

SALES REPRESENTATIVE GRADES: TECHNICAL SALES

Grade 1 Entry-level sales position. Requires a university degree in chemistry or chemical engineering. One or two years of related work experience desirable. Sells company products to assigned accounts.

Grade 2 Requires a university degree in chemistry or chemical engineering plus a good working knowledge of company products and a minimum of two to three years of successful sales experience. Sells company products to assigned and potential accounts. Prepares monthly report and monthly sales forecast.

Grade 3 Requires a university degree in chemistry or chemical engineering, associated with considerable knowledge of the company's products. A minimum of five years of sales experience (with at least two to three years in the company) is required. Sells company products to larger existing and potential accounts. Prepares monthly report and monthly sales forecast.

Grade 4 Requires a university degree in chemistry or chemical engineering associated with in-depth knowledge of the company's products. A minimum of seven to eight years of sales experience is required with at least two years experience of working with major accounts. Must be capable of working with a minimum of supervision and dealing with personnel at the most senior levels. Sells company products to major accounts only. Prepares monthly report and monthly sales forecast.

Figure 12.6 Example of job grading
Source Asia Pacific Management Co. Ltd, 2004.

The point system

Point system An approach to job evaluation in which numerical values are assigned to specific job factors and the sum of those values provides a quantitative assessment of a job's relative worth.

The **point system** involves quantifying a set of job factors — such as education, experience, responsibility and working conditions — by allocating points to each factor. Typically, each factor is divided into a number of levels, each with a specific definition. The education level required by the job, for example, could be graded as in figure 12.7. This process is followed for each job factor. The points allocated for individual factors are totalled to determine the job's relative worth to the organisation.

This system appears to be precise, but quite subjective decisions are involved in choosing the relative weights for each factor, the gradations within each factor, the factors themselves and the number of factors. For example, should the number of points be the same for each of the factors? How does responsibility equate with education, experience and working conditions? Should the points allotted increase by jumps of 50, as in the example in figure 12.7? Why not by 20 or 30 or 100? Should they increase by equal steps of 50 points? Why not by steps of 50, 75, 100, and so on?

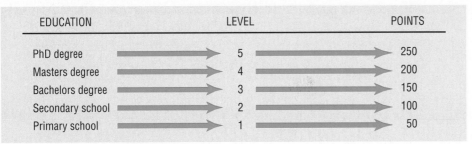

EDUCATION	LEVEL	POINTS
PhD degree	5	250
Masters degree	4	200
Bachelors degree	3	150
Secondary school	2	100
Primary school	1	50

Figure 12.7 Example of a point system

These are questions that each HR manager must be able to resolve, and more importantly justify, when explaining the system to employees. Point plans require the use of a manual that contains a description of the factors, the number of levels within a factor and the number of points allotted to each factor and to each level.

All of this can be time consuming, expensive and difficult. As a result, many organisations prefer to use a system developed by a specialist consultant to obtain a credible job evaluation program at reasonable cost.

The factor comparison system

The **factor comparison system** is a refinement of the ranking and point systems. Like the point system, it uses job factors such as education, experience, responsibility and working conditions, and allocates points to quantify these factors. The basic principle is that all jobs should be compared and evaluated independently against each of the job factors. This is a refinement of the ranking system, where jobs are ranked as whole jobs.

Jobs are ranked by one factor at a time under this system, so all jobs are compared independently a number of different times (once for each factor). The separate rankings are assigned point values and the points for each factor are totalled to give the overall point value of the job. To maintain consistency in the development of the company's job hierarchy, key or benchmark jobs (for example, sales representative) are used as standards of comparison.

A major problem with the factor comparison system is that it is complex and not easily understood by employees. It can also be expensive to introduce and maintain, thus limiting its application to larger organisations.

> **Factor comparison system** A job evaluation technique that involves comparing (ranking) jobs on a range of factors such as know-how, responsibility, etc. Each factor ranking for each job is converted to points. The total number of points for the factors equals the job size.

'Pre-packaged' or proprietary job evaluation systems

A number of job evaluation systems are commercially available. These vary considerably in complexity, cost and usefulness. Some of the better-known systems are discussed in the following text.

Hay Group
1. *The Hay Group guide chart profile* This method of job evaluation uses three factors deemed to be required for all jobs — know-how, problem solving and accountability. These three factors are each broken down into subfactors. Know-how consists of specialised knowledge, management breadth and human relations skill. Problem solving looks at the thinking environment and thinking challenge. Accountability consists of freedom to act, nature and level of impact. A matrix chart is used for each factor and associated subfactors to identify, define and score the worth of each factor (see figure 12.8). The sum of the points allocated for each factor represents the worth of the job. Hay Group offers PC software to process evaluation judgements and to assist with salary administration.

   Given that know-how, problem solving and accountability are present to some degree in all jobs, it is possible to use the Hay job evaluation method to compare jobs within a function, jobs in different functions and jobs in different locations. Comparisons can be made on the basis of overall job size as well as on specific factors. Such comparisons can provide insight into the structure of reporting relationships. If a supervisor's job, for example, requires only minimally higher know-how from that of a subordinate, the HR manager may ask whether the supervisory job will add significant value to the work of the subordinate job.

HayGroup

HAY GUIDE CHART FOR EVALUATING
KNOW-HOW

··· HUMAN RELATIONS SKILLS

1. **BASIC:** Ordinary courtesy and effectiveness in dealing with others is required.
2. **IMPORTANT:** Understanding, influencing and communicating with people are important but not overriding considerations.
3. **CRITICAL:** Skills in influencing, developing and/or motivating people are critical to the achievement of job objectives.

·· PLANNING, ORGANISING, CONTROLLING — BREADTH OF MANAGEMENT KNOW-HOW

· DEPTH AND RANGE OF TECHNICAL KNOW-HOW

Column definitions:

T. TASK — Performance of a task (or tasks) highly specific as to objective and content and not involving the supervision of others.

I. ACTIVITY — Performance or supervision of work which is specific as to objective and content with appropriate awareness of related activities.

II. RELATED — Internal integration of operations which are relatively homogeneous in nature and objective, and which involve external integration with associated functions.

III. DIVERSE — Operational or conceptual integration of activities which are diverse in nature and in objective in an important management area, or central co-ordination or a strategic function.

Depth & Range		T. TASK 1	2	3	I. ACTIVITY 1	2	3	II. RELATED 1	2	3	III. DIVERSE 1	2	3
A PRIMARY: Jobs requiring elementary plus some secondary (or equivalent) education, plus work indoctrination.		38	43	50	50	57	66	66	76	87	87	100	115
		43	50	57	57	66	76	76	87	100	100	115	132
		50	57	66	66	76	87	87	100	115	115	132	152
B ELEMENTARY VOCATIONAL: Jobs requiring familiarisation in uninvolved, standardised work routines and/or use of simple equipment and machines.		50	57	66	66	76	87	87	100	115	115	132	152
		57	66	76	76	87	100	100	115	132	132	152	175
		66	76	87	87	100	115	115	132	152	152	175	200
C VOCATIONAL: Jobs requiring procedural or systematic proficiency, which may involve facility in the use of specialised equipment.		66	76	87	87	100	115	115	132	152	152	175	200
		76	87	100	100	115	132	132	152	175	175	200	230
		87	100	115	115	132	152	152	175	200	200	230	264
D ADVANCED VOCATIONAL: Jobs requiring some specialised (generally non theoretical) skills gained by on the job experience or through part professional qualification.		87	100	115	115	132	152	152	175	200	200	230	264
		100	115	132	132	152	175	175	200	230	230	264	304
		115	132	152	152	175	200	200	230	264	264	304	350
E BASIC PROFESSIONAL: Jobs requiring sufficiency in a technical, scientific or specialised field based on an understanding of concepts and principles normally associated with a professional qualification or gained through a detailed grasp of involved practices and procedures.		115	132	152	152	175	200	200	230	264	264	304	350
		132	152	175	175	200	230	230	264	304	304	350	400
		152	175	200	200	230	264	264	304	350	350	400	460
F SEASONED PROFESSIONAL: Jobs requiring proficiency in a technical, scientific or specialised field gained through broad and deep experience built on concepts and principles or through wide exposure to complex practices and precedents.		152	175	200	200	230	264	264	304	350	350	400	460
		175	200	230	230	264	304	304	350	400	400	460	528
		200	230	264	264	304	350	350	400	460	460	528	608
G PROFESSIONAL MASTERY: Jobs requiring determinative mastery of concepts, principles and practices gained through deep development in a highly specialised field or through comprehensive business experience.		200	230	264	264	304	350	350	400	460	460	528	608
		230	264	304	304	350	400	400	460	528	528	608	700
		264	304	350	350	400	460	460	528	608	608	700	800

Side labels: PRACTICAL PROCEDURES · SPECIALISED TECHNIQUES · PROFESSIONAL DISCIPLINES

Figure 12.8 Hay Group guide chart
Source Hay Group Pty Ltd.

Users of Hay Group's method of job evaluation include 'blue-chip' Australian companies and leading foreign multinationals who apply it at management level and, in many cases, award level (that is, to non-exempt employees). Users include ANZ Banking Group, BHP Billiton, Dow Chemical, Hoechst, Hong Kong and Shanghai Bank, Shell and Telstra. This wide use gives the Hay method a distinct advantage by making it easier for client companies to compare jobs and salaries for external equity and competitiveness. Proprietary methods of job evaluation, such as the Hay system, are sometimes criticised for their cost, inflexibility and their 'one size fits all' approach.[21] But recent innovations in the application of the Hay method have attempted to meet these criticisms. Hay Group has developed alternative guide charts, for example, for organisations with differing work cultures and value systems.

2. *Role-based evaluation* A recent innovation, role-based salary administration combines elements of job evaluation with a 'person-centred' approach. This effectively redefines work as something other than the traditional static view of a job. Rather, it views work in terms of evolving roles that reflect the growing ability of incumbents to add value to an organisation. This 'added value' may not be captured by traditional job-centred evaluation methods, so role-based evaluation methods have been developed. Hay Group, for example, has combined elements of its job evaluation method with its competency modelling approach. The integration of these two approaches is based on the premises that job evaluation captures the value of 'full proficiency' in a role and that competency modelling defines the added value of an exemplary performer. It is made relevant by the use of 'just perceptible difference' scales to judge both types of factors. In addition to traditional job evaluation factors, these role-based factors may include mental and social behaviours (see figure 12.9).

CUSTOMER SERVICE ORIENTATION

Customer service orientation implies a desire to help or serve others, to know more about their problems or issues, to meet their needs. 'Customers' include external customers and internal colleagues, or anyone that the person is trying to help.

1. *Clarifies needs, follows up:* asks direct questions of customer to clarify needs. Follows through on customer enquiries, requests and complaints.
2. *Maintains clear communication:* maintains clear communication with customer regarding mutual expectations. Checks out customer satisfaction. Distributes helpful information. Keeps customer up-to-date.
3. *Takes personal responsibility:* personally good to investigate customer service problems. Questions and involves those closest to the problem. Takes personal responsibility for correcting problems promptly and undefensively.
4. *Acts to make things better:* calls on others who are not personally involved to get their views, background information, experience, etc. Makes concrete attempts to make things better for the customer in some way.
5. *Identifies areas for organisational improvement:* identifies similarities between a current customer problem and things that have happened before. Challenges the way things are done in the organisation by suggesting specific improvements to a function, structure or process.

Figure 12.9 Being concerned with customer service
Source Hay Group Pty Ltd.

Mercer

The Mercer method measures three key factors — cognition, education and decision accountability. As with the Hay Group guide chart profile method, each of these three factors is broken down into a further eight subfactors. These consider the knowledge, experience and skill requirements of jobs, their breadth of influence, the environmental complexities and challenges surrounding them, the jobs' reasoning requirements and the overall impact of each position. Factor ratings are converted to point scores using matrix charts. Mercer software is available to perform evaluations and to administer compensation.

The Mercer system is used for management and non-management positions in both large and small organisations. Users of Mercer's services include Coles Myer, Coca-Cola Amatil, Commonwealth Bank of Australia, Qantas and Woolworths.

Watson Wyatt

Watson Wyatt has two job evaluation systems — FACTORCOMP™ and MULTICOMP™.

FACTORCOMP™ involves the selection of a set of compensable factors and the development of a point scale for each factor, representing increasing levels of worth. The content of each job is rated separately on each of the selected factors, and is assigned a corresponding number of points, which are totalled to produce the total relative worth of jobs.

Interdisciplinary in approach, Watson Wyatt's MULTICOMP™ draws on recent advances in computer technology, psychometrics and statistics. MULTICOMP™ employs a specially designed questionnaire that is filled out by incumbents or their supervisors to create a comprehensive company database. The database measures how each job reflects the specific compensable factors that the organisation values most.

Using multiple regression analysis, MULTICOMP™ then evaluates questionnaire responses and competitive data to develop a statistical model for the organisation's benchmark positions. Once the mathematical relationships between benchmark data and salary grades are established, the model assigns preliminary pay scales for management review and approval, greatly reducing the time ordinarily required to evaluate each job.[22]

Major users of Watson Wyatt's job evaluation systems include AMP, New South Wales local government, Colgate Palmolive, Electricity Trust of South Australia and National Foods.

Which system should be used?

No one system is perfect. There are advantages and disadvantages associated with each type and between internally developed and commercially available systems. The HR manager should consider the factors listed below before selecting a system:

- *Objectives:* what are the organisation's strategic business objectives in introducing job evaluation? Will the selected plan satisfy these objectives?
- *The size of the organisation:* the smaller the organisation, the easier it is to use a simple system such as job grading. Larger organisations may find more sophisticated (and more expensive) point or factor comparison plans appropriate.
- *Organisational resources:* are the personnel and expertise available to develop an internal plan? How much can the organisation afford to spend on introducing and maintaining a particular plan? Will the expected benefits exceed the cost? Job evaluation is an ongoing exercise and plan maintenance can prove expensive, particularly with the more complex point and factor comparison plans.
- *Plan users:* which organisations use which type of plans? What do similar organisations in the same industry use? What is the experience of other organisations with their particular plans? It is especially important when assessing commercially available plans to talk to organisations that use them. Ask about costs, employee acceptance and satisfaction with the plan's consistency and accuracy. Ask about the 'after-sales' service provided by the consultant.
- *Corporate culture:* the job evaluation plan selected must reflect the organisation's culture. It is pointless to introduce a highly structured plan designed for large bureaucratic organisations if the organisation is small, fast moving and entrepreneurial.
- *Employee attitudes:* no matter how good a job evaluation system is, it will fail if not understood and accepted by employees as being fair and equitable. Particularly with the more complex systems, it is essential that employees be given a thorough explanation of how the system works. This can prevent many later disruptive arguments and disputes.

Job description

A necessary requirement of any job evaluation scheme is an appropriate job description (see pages 145–50). A job description is the vehicle used by most job evaluation systems to translate words into numbers. Job description formats vary from brief summaries to essay-type descriptions and may follow a rigid format or be relatively unstructured. The job description is a product of job analysis, so the method of job analysis chosen should be consistent with the organisation's strategic business objectives and culture. In designing the format of and writing the job description, the HR manager must always keep in mind its purpose.

The job description is a blueprint that profiles the design of the job, making its potential usefulness to management almost limitless. Nevertheless, much criticism of job descriptions stems from misuse, incompatibility with the organisation's strategic business objectives and culture, difficulty in comprehension, inflexibility, rapid obsolescence, time spent on writing the description, and cost.[23] Using an inaccurate, incomplete or incompatible job description as a guide in HR decision making can seriously damage an organisation by clouding employee roles and organisational objectives.[24]

'Ninety per cent of job descriptions', says Reddin, 'are created to justify the change in salary differentials. They are used as pseudo scientific means of saying that this job is worth relatively more than that job.'[25]

Moreover, special problems such as gender stereotyping can affect the wording of job descriptions.[26] An Australian study found major differences in the language used to describe jobs for men and women.[27] Similarly, a UK study by McNally and Shimmin found firmly held views concerning gender characteristics and the relative value of men's and women's work. Managers (mostly men), lay and official trade union representatives (mostly men) and members of job evaluation committees (mostly men) showed a tendency to positively evaluate the work of men and to hold relatively negative assumptions about the inherent worth of women's jobs.[28]

Pay surveys

The **pay survey** is the vehicle for relating an organisation's pay rates to those for similar jobs in other organisations. Thus, pay surveys are a key plank in the design of an organisation's compensation program. Pay survey data provide the raw material for job pricing by translating job sizes into dollars. There are two main types of pay survey. One is based on matching similar jobs according to their content; the other is based on matching jobs according to their job size using a common job evaluation method (for example, the Hay Group guide chart profile method). The job match approach can be less expensive to implement, but proponents of the job size approach argue that it is also less precise.

Figure 12.10 illustrates a typical format for a job match pay survey. The survey gives information on base pay and benefits. This can be used by the HR manager to calculate the organisation's competitive position and to plan any corrective action required. To begin this process, the HR manager must identify the appropriate labour market and those organisations that it competes with for labour. In other words, does the organisation want to compare itself with:
- organisations in the same or related industries?
- organisations in the same geographic area?
- 'best-practice' companies?
- domestic companies?
- multinationals?
- organisations of a similar size in terms of sales, number of employees and assets?
- the general community?
- private sector companies only?
- a mix of private and public sector organisations?

Pay survey The vehicle for relating an organisation's pay rates to those for similar jobs in other organisations.

POSITION 48: Head of Human Resources
Number of incumbents: 182
Number of companies: 170
Position description
Reports to Chief Executive/Managing Director. Supervises Human Resources Manager(s). Responsible for ensuring the most effective utilisation of the organisation's staff resources. Develops the HR contribution to the company's strategic planning so that its long-term people needs are identified and accommodated within its business plans and management decisions. Develops, submits for approval and manages the implementation of HR policies throughout the organisation that comply with legal requirements and minimise disruption, penalties and adverse publicity. Ensures that all skills requirements within the organisation are met through ongoing work force planning, staff development programs and external recruitment. Ensures all staff administration records are effectively maintained on the HRIS. Conducts negotiations with industrial unions as required and ensures compliance with appropriate awards and determinations. Tertiary level qualifications with at least 12 years or more experience in all aspects of human resources management.

ANNUAL COMPENSATION DATA AS OF 1 JANUARY 2003							
		Lower decile	Lower quartile	Median	Upper quartile	Upper decile	Average
Company characteristics							
FY2000 annual turnover (A$'000)		25 000	65 000	175 000	750 000	1 625 000	871 358
Number of employees		102	207	460	1 444	5 000	2 271
Cash compensation (A$)							
Basic salary		100 000	114 216	142 963	187 710	251 142	158 220
Nominal base salary		100 000	116 577	154 541	189 988	254 500	161 277
Guaranteed cash		100 000	116 577	147 390	192 588	254 755	162 121
Total cash		103 832	126 864	162 773	221 809	304 620	191 643
Total remuneration		111 523	141 641	182 523	244 792	321 881	209 846
Total employer cost (TEC)		120 491	155 057	194 638	268 029	349 539	226 748
Compensation elements (A$)							
	% receiving						
Salary sacrifice superannuation	28	2 500	5 456	7 000	10 204	18 000	10 909
Fixed allowances	27	798	1 365	1 716	2 724	4 118	3 073
Variable payments	73	7 641	16 466	27 250	47 944	65 488	40 704
Company superannuation	100	9 123	11 205	13 816	20 615	29 369	16 091
Company car benefit	58	10 867	15 080	18 663	23 792	30 321	19 688
Other FBT items	44	500	1 776	2 608	4 700	9 555	4 541
Fringe benefits tax (FBT)	62	1 706	2 825	8 870	14 187	18 626	9 635
Compensation element analysis							
Salary sacrifice superannuation as a % of basic salary		1.1	3.8	5.0	5.4	17.5	7.3
Fixed allowances as a % of basic salary		0.5	1.3	1.3	1.4	3.3	1.9
Variable payments as a % of basic salary		7.0	10.9	19.9	30.0	35.0	21.8
Company superannuation as a % of basic salary		9.0	9.0	9.0	11.2	15.0	10.7
Company car benefit as a % of basic salary		7.0	10.3	12.8	16.6	20.3	13.4
Other FBT items as a % of basic salary		0.3	1.1	1.9	3.3	5.8	3.2
FBT as a % of basic salary		1.2	2.2	6.0	9.0	11.0	6.4

Figure 12.10 Pay survey for Head of Human Resources
Source Watson Wyatt, *2003 Compensation Report — Australia*, 2003.

Answering such questions helps the HR manager to clarify the type of data needed, to ensure comparisons are from the appropriate labour marketplace and to determine the type of pay survey required.

An organisation needs to ask the following questions if a pay survey is to be worthwhile:

- Does the survey provide participants with clear, concise job descriptions and adequate written instructions?
- Are the data screened for consistency and accuracy? Are part-time, temporary or contract employees excluded?
- Who are the participants? Are they best-practice companies, or unsophisticated, unknown entities?
- Who has access to the published information? Some organisations may be reluctant to disclose information if the survey is commercially available and not restricted to participants.
- How was job matching completed? By personal interview? By computer input? By comparing job titles? By looking at pay levels? By matching job descriptions? By comparing job points?
- Who did the matching? An experienced compensation and benefits administrator or a junior clerk? If the survey is to have value, it is critical that 'apples be compared with apples'. The saying 'garbage in, garbage out' is especially applicable to pay surveys.
- Who is conducting the survey? Are they professional? Are they ethical? Are they specialists in compensation and benefits survey methods?
- How is the survey information to be presented? Is it in a format that is meaningful, easy to understand and statistically correct?
- Is professional assistance available to help with interpretation if required?
- Does the survey cover an appropriate range of relevant jobs for the organisation's requirements? Are there sufficient good job matches to make participation worthwhile? In practice, organisations do not survey every job. Instead, key or **benchmark jobs** are selected. Benchmark positions must be stable in job content and widely occurring within the organisation to be surveyed, precisely defined and performed in a similar way.
- How old is the information? When was the survey conducted?
- What does the survey cost? Is the price appropriate?

Benchmark jobs Jobs that are similar or comparable in content across firms.

Getting valid data from a survey requires considerable preparation and hard work. There is a direct relationship between the quality of results and the effort made by the participants to ensure that jobs are matched properly and that pay data are reported correctly. The most common shortcoming of pay surveys is the lack of job compatibility.[29] Other problems relate to the inclusion of mainly high-paying (or low-paying) organisations, poor definition of benchmark jobs and misinterpretation of the data.

Exchange of information between HR managers is also facilitated if organisations use the same job evaluation method. Most compensation and benefits specialists are prepared to exchange information and to spend time ensuring that guesswork is eliminated from job matching.

Job evaluation and the pay survey

Job evaluation determines the relative worth of each job to the organisation — that is, job evaluation is concerned with internal equity. The pay survey makes it possible to assign appropriate pay ranges to each job — that is, the pay survey helps to ensure that external equity is achieved and maintained.

Pay structure

Individual pay rates within an organisation are normally determined by job size and employee performance. Job size is established by job evaluation and performance is measured by performance appraisal. Once job sizes have been established, each job level is given a pay range showing the minimum and maximum pay to be paid. The **pay structure** presents all pay ranges over the whole spectrum of job sizes and is an essential tool in compensation administration.

Pay structure Presents all pay ranges over the whole spectrum of job sizes.

The pay line or curve

Pay line Graphically depicts the compensation currently being paid for jobs related to job size.

The **pay line** or curve graphically depicts the compensation being paid for jobs related to job size. The purpose of the pay line is to show the relationship between the size of a job and the average compensation paid for it. The pay line permits companies to 'price' jobs by providing the basis for establishing pay ranges (see figure 12.11).

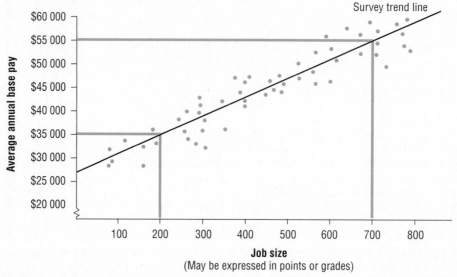

Figure 12.11 Pay trend line

Pay ranges

The standard range

Pay range Sets the minimum and maximum scheduled amounts paid for a job at a particular job size.

The most generally accepted **pay range** for professional and managerial positions is plus or minus 20 per cent from the midpoint. The minimum may be $40 000, the midpoint may be $50 000 and the maximum may be $60 000. The pay range in this example is $20 000 (maximum rate of $60 000 minus minimum rate of $40 000 equals $20 000). The maximum rate is 150 per cent of the minimum rate (150 per cent of $40 000 equals $60 000). A range of this magnitude gives ample room for discrimination on the basis of experience and performance. It also permits pay growth without the need for constant reclassification because the employee has hit a pay ceiling (see figure 12.12).

Broadbanding

Broadbanding Collapses numerous job grades with narrow pay bands in a pay structure into a few broad job grades with wide pay bands.

Broadbanding involves the clustering of numerous individual pay grades into a few broad pay grades. Organisations using hierarchical pay grades with small midpoint-to-midpoint progression (10 per cent) between grades and narrow spreads in the pay ranges (plus or minus 5 to 10 per cent from the midpoint) can find that job flexibility and multiskilling are restricted (for example, a higher grade 10 employee may be reluctant to do a lower grade 8 job), customer service is hindered and career growth opportunities are limited. In addition, restructuring and downsizing have changed the concept of promotion from one of pay grade progression to one of undertaking more varied job duties and responsibilities. According to one survey, organisations favour broadbanding because it reflects their flatter structures, facilitates internal transfers and job mobility, emphasises promotion, gives employees greater pay potential and supports their new organisational culture.[30]

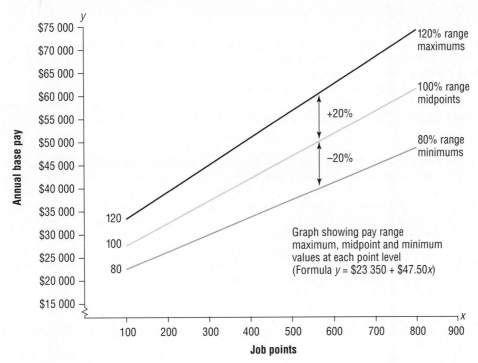

Figure 12.12 Pay ranges

The collapsing of multiple pay grades into fewer pay grades creates much broader pay ranges. A study by Hewitt Associates found that although broadbanding pay ranges vary, the range maximum is typically 100 per cent of the range minimum. Consequently, the range midpoint loses its value as a control point. Four control points within the band are used under a system of expanded pay ranges — the minimum, the maximum and two control points. These control points guide managers making pay decisions and are a barometer of market competitiveness. It should be noted that broadbanding still requires jobs to be analysed, described and evaluated. Finally, broadbanding involves considerable cultural change and should not be attempted without appropriate employee communication and training. Thus, a critical role for the HR manager is to train line managers to properly manage employee compensation.[31]

Broadbanding may be an attractive pay system for organisations wanting to restructure and flatten, redefine career paths and encourage personal growth through lateral job movement — it can support both the new strategy and culture.[32] 'To be successful', stresses Abosch, 'broadbanding must be compatible with an organization's culture, vision and business strategy.'[33]

Market posture

An organisation can adopt one of the three basic **market postures** outlined below:
- *Pay above market average.* Organisations that select this market posture pay better-than-average compensation. These organisations believe that paying higher rates of pay enables them to attract, retain and motivate superior employees.
- *Pay market average.* This is a common market posture. The aim is to compensate employees at a level equal to the prevailing market rate in the geographic area or industry in which they operate.
- *Pay below market average.* This posture is taken by organisations that want to pay the minimum level needed to hire sufficient employees to stay in business. The long-term implications for attracting, retaining and motivating a qualified work force are obvious. However, it may be the only option available in the short run, especially if the business is in financial difficulty.

Market postures Determine where an organisation seeks to be in the pay market — above market, market average or below market.

Selecting a pay policy line

Pay survey data are historical information. The compensation specialist uses these data to determine the organisation's current competitive position and to develop the organisation's new pay policy line.

Pay policy line A graphical representation of the organisation's predicted pay midpoints.

The **pay policy line** is a graphical representation of the organisation's predicted pay midpoints for the 12-month period ahead. Its purpose is to ensure that the organisation's stated market position is achieved and maintained.

For example, many organisations review pay rates on 1 January each year. If the pay survey were based on December data, the compensation and benefits specialist would need to predict the general pay movement for the next 12 months. Then they could quite accurately establish what the market trend line would be at 1 January. If pay rates were expected to move by an average 10 per cent in this period, and if the organisation did not need to make any other adjustments to achieve its stated market position, then the pay line would be simply moved up by 10 per cent.

The situation is not quite so simple in practice. The organisation may find that its position is satisfactory at the lower job levels but has fallen behind by about 5 per cent of the market at 800 points. In this case, the pay line will need to be tilted upwards at the higher job levels to regain the organisation's desired market position (see figure 12.13).

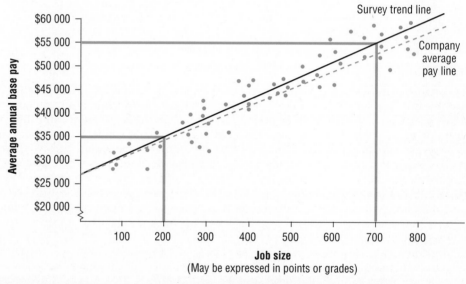

Figure 12.13 Pay trend lines (survey trend compared to company average pay rates)

Equitable compensation

Pay secrecy

Equity in compensation is a major concern of employees. Where inequities are perceived to exist, the impact on morale and motivation can be devastating. Management can try to avoid this problem by maintaining **pay secrecy**, especially in organisations that do not have an objective and defensible compensation program.

Pay secrecy Occurs where pay rates are kept confidential between the employer and the employee.

However, research by Lawler suggests that secrecy over pay can generate mistrust of the compensation program, reduce employee motivation and inhibit the organisation's effectiveness.[34] Nevertheless, pay secrecy remains the norm in most private sector organisations with some organisations requiring employees to sign confidentiality agreements. (In contrast, information on public sector pay is readily available.) Private sector pay rates are being subjected to increasing publicity via consultants' surveys, business magazine articles and changing legal requirements (for all publicly listed companies, details of the compensation for directors and the five most highly paid managers are now given in company annual reports), which facilitate comparisons.

Pay compression

Pay compression occurs when employees feel that the difference is too small between their pay and that of other employees in jobs above or below them. Pay compression can occur when pay rates for new hires increase at a faster rate than those of employees already on the payroll, or when pay increases are given for low-level jobs without commensurate adjustments for high-level positions. First-line supervisors often experience compression when the pay rates for unionised employees are increased. Similarly, compression can occur between skilled and unskilled employees when flat sum increases are given instead of percentage-based increases. Finally, unions sometimes have the industrial power to win large pay increases for unskilled or semi-skilled employees, producing pay rates that are better than those of supervisors or employees performing jobs requiring far more knowledge, skill and responsibility. It should be noted that reactive managements — ones that always adjust non-union employees' pay rates after the union wins increases — just promote pro-union sentiment among their union-free employees. Whatever its cause, pay compression generates dissatisfaction and makes employees reluctant to acquire new skills, competencies or knowledge or to strive for promotion.[35]

Senior executive pay rates

Globalisation, talent shortages, the increased practice of granting stock options, the star status given to executives and executive pay disclosures have seen a dramatic upsurge in executive remuneration.[36] Shareholders, trade unions and politicians increasingly are expressing concern about the levels of senior executive compensation.[37] In the United States, the average CEO earns 475 times the average wage. In Australia, the ratio is 23:1, in Britain it is 24:1 and in Japan it is 11:1.[38] Comments ACTU Secretary, Greg Combet: 'In almost every industry when unions go to negotiate wage increases for workers they are confronted with the argument that companies need to reduce costs due to international pressure and yet the very same arguments are being used to justify massive increases in executive salaries.'[39] Billionaire Chairman of Berkshire Hathaway, Warren Buffet, claims executive pay has become the benchmark against which CEOs measure each other: 'It's ego, and it can only rocket upwards.'[40] Another US board member has likened some corporate compensation to 'putting a rat in the granary'.[41]

Furthermore, a Stanford Business School study suggests that broad managerial powers and discretion under corporate law may enable senior managers to distort the goals and indicators of performance-based pay.[42] Similar concerns have also been expressed about CEO motives in negotiating a company merger or sale because of non-performance-related executive 'golden parachutes'.[43] According to the Australian Institute of Directors, common defects in many pay-for-performance packages include inadequate hurdles, lack of downside risk for poor performance and salvation for executives via option repricing.[44] Some experts also argue that in Australia's case many industries do not require the payment of globally competitive salaries. Comments one consultant: 'They are simply coming along for the ride and using globalization as an excuse to ramp up salaries.'[45] Commonwealth Bank CEO David Murray's compensation jumped from $450 000 to $7 million in less than 10 years.[46] Another concern is that the income divide in Australia (and Hong Kong and the United States) is widening, producing a cultural shift in power and privilege and increasing tensions between the haves and have-nots.[47] An ACTU spokesman, for example, claims that skyrocketing executive compensation is an issue that infuriates Australian workers.[48]

Finally, all too often senior executive pay levels appear to have little to do with responsibility or performance. According to Warren Buffett, 'Not only does executive pay seem more decoupled from performance than ever, but boards are conveniently changing their

Details of the total remuneration for federal government ministers and top Commonwealth public servants remain a tightly guarded secret. In contrast, the remuneration of private sector senior executives is subject to intense public scrutiny.

definition of "performance"'.[49] Hong Kong's Pioneer Industries International (Holdings), for example, gave its directors a 200 per cent rise in performance-related pay despite experiencing a sixfold increase in its net loss.[50] One Australian survey found no discernible relationship between CEO pay and anything at all (except company size) — profit growth, share price gain and return on equity counted for little. Furthermore, a recent study of Australia's 100 biggest companies by Sydney University's School of Business showed that the higher the CEO's pay, the lower the company's profit, and vice versa.[51]

Keith Lambert, held responsible for almost destroying Southcorp Ltd, was paid $6.19 million for seven month's work in 2002–2003, the same year that the company suffered a record loss of $923 million.[52] Frank Cicutto, former National Australia Bank CEO, received almost $14 million following his resignation and a foreign exchange scandal (NAB was one of the worst performing major banks in Australia during Cicutto's term).[53] The huge sums paid to executives has led to a public outcry and increasing concern about the growing divide between executives and other employees.[54]

One survey of Australia's largest companies disappointingly found that most non-executive directors did not think that their compensation should be linked to performance.[55] 'In today's market', claim Reingold and Grover, 'the only true conclusion is that if greed is good, it's best for the CEO.'[56] Comments another critic: 'CEOs have to commit a crime of "moral turpitude" — like rape or murder — to become ineligible for severance. As a result, some CEOs walk away with a lot more than they would have gotten if they had completed their terms.'[57] Australian and US studies show that good corporate governance enhances the efficiency of executive pay arrangements and that poor corporate governance is linked to excessive remuneration.[58]

The Letter to the Editor opposite provides a provocative viewpoint. Do you agree? See 'What's your view?' on page 473'.

Setting pay rates

Seniority-based pay

Pay increases based on seniority are determined not by performance but by the employee's length of time on the job. Organisational membership, not individual achievement, is the prime criterion for the allocation of pay increases. **Seniority-based pay** is most effective in keeping employees within the organisation. However, this may reduce labour turnover too heavily, resulting in many poorly motivated (and poor performing) employees staying on until retirement. Seniority-based pay does not lead to improved employee productivity; rather, employees do the minimum necessary to stay in the organisation.[59] Consequently, management prefers to use merit or pay-for-performance systems to motivate employees.

However, unions favour seniority as the basis for pay increases. Unions believe that performance appraisal and merit pay are subjective, open to bias and permit management to play favourites; but they see seniority as providing objective criteria to measure the employee's loyalty, skill improvement and the increased competency that comes with experience. Finally, unions look on seniority as the most important measure of job security for employees.

Thus, while seniority is an anathema to most managers because it rewards length of service and not performance, it does:
- avoid the problems of biased managers
- provide a quick, easy and painless way of making pay increase decisions
- recognise the correlation between experience and performance
- reward the loyal employee who has worked for the organisation for many years.

Nevertheless, the incidence of performance-related pay is increasing in Australian workplaces. For example, more than 30 per cent of union-certified agreements now include some element of performance pay. There are, however, major differences between union and non-union agreements. Union agreements tend to use objective criteria, while non-union agreements often rely on subjective and arbitrary appraisals.[60]

Is it right for CEOs to have multimillion-dollar packages while some of their employees are earning only minimum wages?

Seniority-based pay Occurs where pay levels and increases are determined by length of time on the job and not performance.

Senior executive salaries are outrageous and promote inequality

Dear Editor,

The levels of remuneration paid to senior executives in this country are simply outrageous! The growing disparity between top-level management and workers cannot be long tolerated.

How can anyone justify the salaries of these glorified administrators? One only has to eyeball the figures to see that they cannot be defended. For instance, after years of lack-lustre performance David Higgins of Lend Lease received a payout of more than $5 million. Similarly, Frank Cicutto, former NAB CEO, was paid almost $8 million in 2002–2003, even though NAB was the worst-performing major bank in Australia! These executives are being paid world-class salaries but where is the world-class performance?

In many cases, the salaries are paid for simply achieving cutbacks in staff numbers, product lines and customer service outlets. This was certainly the case with the leaders of the banks, and is also true for people like 'Chainsaw Al' Dunlap, who received millions for implementing massive cost reduction programs at places like Sunbeam and Australian Consolidated Press.

One Australian salary survey has found that senior management received pay increases averaging almost 115 per cent in a decade, while the average rise for middle managers was less than 60 per cent. Clearly, the gap between those at the top and those in the middle continues to widen.

The gap between senior managers and lower-level workers is even wider. Australia appears to be following the US trend where people at the bottom get peanuts and those at the top get millions.

At a time when senior managers continue to lament the weakening of the psychological contract, their own compensation (which they often set themselves in cahoots with their cronies) continues to rise to ridiculous and unjustifiable levels. This only serves to deepen the divisions between workers and managers, or 'us and them', and it makes a mockery of management calls for restrained wage demands and industrial peace.

The level of greed that we are witnessing in executive salaries can only mean one thing, namely a return to the industrial relations chaos of previous eras in the name of fairness and equity.

A senior union official

Source David Poole, University of Western Sydney.

Pay for performance

The objective of **merit pay** or performance-based compensation 'is to develop a productive, efficient, effective organization that enhances employee motivation and performance'.[61] Alas, many organisations have not been aggressive in relating pay to performance. The use of merit increases has been influenced by tax considerations, award changes, the cost of living, seniority, the number of employees supervised, internal relativities, the desirability of the job and factors such as ingratiation, greed, personal attractiveness and time spent at the desk (see figure 12.14).[62]

For example, US researchers found that people who are perceived as 'good looking' — education, experience and other characteristics being equal — earn an average 10 per cent more than do those viewed as 'homely'. A National Bureau of Economic Research study found that smokers working full-time earned 4–8 per cent less on average than did comparable non-smokers. Similarly, another US study found that young adults who are overweight and men who are shorter than average earn less than do their slimmer and taller counterparts, respectively. Recent US research shows that the individual net worth of obese women is on average 40 per cent lower than for women of normal weight.[63]

Merit pay Any pay increase awarded to an employee based on their individual performance.

Another problem is that merit increases for outstanding performers often have not been much greater than increases paid to average or poor performers, and therefore have offered little incentive. Finally, it has not always been clear why an employee is given a higher or lower merit increase.[64] Many employees thus distrust merit or pay-for-performance plans.[65]

In practice, merit plans do not reward performance when:
• employees fail to make the connection between pay and performance
• other employees perceive the secrecy of the reward as inequity
• the size of the merit increase has little effect on performance
• the performance evaluation system is inadequate.[66]

However, competitive pressures and the demand for higher employee productivity mean that organisations are being forced to better ensure that merit increases reflect performance. Performance pay plans based on the achievement of job goals and performance criteria mutually agreed to by managers and employees are therefore becoming popular. Similarly, shareholders are demanding that top executive pay be more performance-based as criticism of executive overcompensation increases.

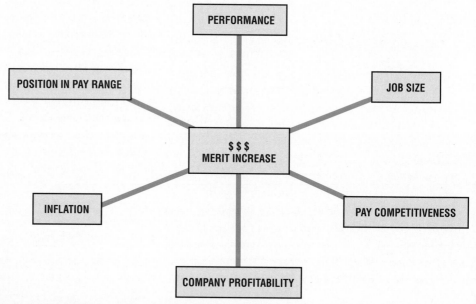

Figure 12.14 Major factors affecting merit pay increases
Source Asia Pacific Management Co. Ltd, 2004.

Merit increases incur a 'fixed cost' for the organisation by increasing the base salary component that must be paid irrespective of future employee performance; thus, it is becoming more common that organisations give employees a one-time reward (such as a performance bonus) instead of an increase to base salary.[67] Unfortunately, there is no single right answer or objective solution to what or how an employee should be rewarded.[68] Some research findings, for example, 'suggest that using pay as a motivator of performance is uncertain as to consistency of outcome'.[69] Similarly, it is argued that it is not really known at what point a merit increase becomes large enough to be motivational.[70] What is acceptable, motivating and fair to employees is highly subjective. Nevertheless, research does suggest that:
• a merit increase must be at least 6–7 per cent of base pay to produce the desired effects on employee attitudes and behaviour
• increasing the size of a merit raise beyond a certain point is unlikely to improve motivation and performance
• merit increases that are too small will negatively affect motivation and morale
• cost-of-living adjustments, seniority and other non-merit parts of an increase should be clearly identified.[71]

The HR manager should be aware — given that communication, participation and trust significantly influence an employee's perception of pay — that the process of introducing a pay system can be as important as the system itself.[72]

NEWSBREAK

An executive's worth is the multimillion-dollar question

There was indignation this week at the enormous salaries paid to executives. The Australian chief executive of the International Chamber of Commerce, Martin Cox, argues that these result from a properly functioning market. But Bob Walker, professor of accounting at the University of NSW, says inflated salaries are unfair to shareholders and wage earners.

Martin Cox

What's happening in the executive salary market? How does David Murray get an extra $4.7 million for staying at the Commonwealth Bank and John Fletcher get $7.7 million from Brambles for not staying? Does this sort of thing give market capitalism a bad name, as Tony Abbott has said? Or is it even, as others say, an example of market failure?

Here are two places *not* to go for the answers:

1. Community sentiment. With due respect, the community knows as much about efficiently setting executive wages as it does about quantum mechanics.

Wittingly or not, the press often simplifies issues, lumping the One.Tel, Enron and HIH scoundrels in with the genuine wealth-creating executives such as Microsoft's Bill Gates and Westfield's Frank Lowy.

It's fair enough for the crowd to bay for the blood of One.Tel directors and the like. If the allegations are proved, what we had there is simply old-fashioned fraud. Hardly market failure.

But it's altogether another thing to assume — as many do — that every highly paid executive must be somehow swindling the shareholders and workers.

2. Comparing executive wages with average wages. This ignores one of the basic principles of economics: namely, that companies base their investment decisions (such as whom to hire as the next CEO) on whether the investment (the salary package) is likely to be profitable.

Put simply: if a company believes that hiring Mavis Jones on a salary package of $15 million will boost profits (net of her package) more than hiring Fred Brown for $3 million, then it makes sense to hire Mavis over Fred. That's regardless of how much more Mavis is getting than Tom the fitter and turner.

The notion that one can extrapolate the worth of Mavis the CEO from that of Tom the fitter and turner is just pure fantasy.

And there are other productivity-related reasons why CEOs are paid so much.

In contrast to shareholders who have diversified portfolios, newly hired top executives have all their (human) capital tied up in one firm. That tends to make them more risk averse, when they're hired precisely to undertake bold, risky, but hopefully high-yielding ventures. Golden parachutes help overcome risk aversion.

Meanwhile, top executives are vulnerable to raiders from other firms who wish to avoid their own search costs, so often there's a retainer component.

Firms today deliberately employ more mid-level managers than they can promote, and then create a tournament for the top job. The best way to encourage contestants in this low-probability bout is to top up the value of the prize.

Of course, in the delicate art of executive appointment, mistakes will be made. But face it: who among the finger-pointers has come up with an infallible method for netting the best candidate at the lowest possible price, and keeping her there?

When allowed to operate freely, the market is the best means of discovering and eliminating faulty strategies. Companies that persist in overpaying executives for keeping duds in the chair make themselves candidates for hostile takeovers.

Instead of moralising about greedy executives, politicians should sharpen the competitive edge by deregulating takeovers and mergers, and opening the economy to foreign investment.

More fundamental, they should move away from politics of envy. Huge as they sometimes seem, the amounts earned by the handful of top executives are a tiny fraction of a shareholder's dividend.

Rather than mulling over how to make the rich poorer, consider how the market economy has lifted the living standard of the masses beyond those dreamed of by kings of old.

Bob Walker

Let's face it, some corporate executives are overpaid. Even if CEOs were the most intelligent, insightful, diligent, committed, hard working, proactive, inspirational and visionary people on the planet — which is doubtful — it's hard to see that any would be worth a million dollars a year.

(continued)

Nor, for that matter, are failed CEOs worth massive termination bonuses. Top executives get paid top salaries partly in anticipation of good performance, and partly in compensation for the risk of being sacked if they fail. Their packages already include humiliation money. When boards and CEOs part company, payouts of more than a year's salary reflect either board weakness or poorly designed contracts.

Remuneration arrangements should reward good performance. But to work well, those arrangements must be fair, independent and linked to real achievement (not simply sector-wide movements in share prices, or paper profits).

It's not fair to bestow generous benefits on just one person — the CEO — who happens to lead the management team. If a board wishes to reward managers for their successful implementation of its strategy, then those rewards should be based on fair assessments of achievement, and should cascade down within the organisation. Anything less just damages morale.

The same corporations which have given multimillion-dollar bonuses or retention allowances to CEOs have been silent about how remuneration arrangements have been linked to the achievement of the board's strategy. That suggests that many board remuneration committees are simply doing deals with managers rather than focusing on the achievement of short- and long-term targets.

Many boards rely on reports from remuneration consultants. Typically, a CEO commissions a report on revised pay rates in terms of market conditions. The consultant, therefore, is not independent. Would any remuneration consultant report that the CEO is already overpaid? Consultants have to provide the right advice to get repeat work.

The methodology used by remuneration consultants involves a mix of assessing the responsibilities associated with specific positions, and presenting data about what comparable jobs are paying. If the latter places reliance on published data, then the benchmark figures may already include bonuses paid by other firms.

Consultants commonly present a salary range, suggesting that bonuses be linked to performance. But how should performance be assessed? Most consultants leave the hard part to directors, who (they say) would have a better understanding of the industry.

Yet experience suggests that many boards use very crude tools to measure or reward performance. Many have chosen to reward CEOs with options — sometimes issued at a token amount, and funded with interest-free loans. This might seem a way of aligning the interests of CEOs and shareholders. Yet CEOs can get rewarded just for being there in a bull market.

Some boards link bonuses to short-run improvements in profits. This can be a source of amusement to readers of financial reports — the game is to spot the accounting changes that will boost reported profits in the short term. Changes in depreciation rates? Newly capitalised expenditure? Provisions for restructuring? Boards that lack financial skills are probably unaware of such subtle manipulation.

Overall, recent surprise announcements of big payouts to surviving or departing CEOs point to poor corporate governance — to a failure to link rewards to individual contributions and to overall performance in meeting strategic targets and adding to long-term shareholder value.

Source *Australian Financial Review*, 5–6 October 2002, p. 50.

Failed CEOs who have destroyed shareholder wealth and cost employees their jobs should not receive million-dollar severance packages.

Pay-for-performance requirements

To establish an effective pay-for-performance or merit plan, HR managers need to ensure that:

- The plan creates a link between reward and performance.
- The plan provides fair and equitable compensation.
- The plan reflects the organisation's strategic business objectives and culture.
- The plan involves a high level of communication and employee participation.
- The cost of the plan is consistent with the financial state of the business.
- The plan is based on universally accepted criteria that motivate employees to contribute to the achievement of the organisation's objectives.
- The plan uses accurate performance appraisals that have the confidence of employees and management.
- There is a minimum time lapse between performance appraisal and the pay increase.
- There is effective feedback during the performance appraisal so employees are aware of expected performance.

- Managers are trained in performance appraisal and the administration of the merit plan.
- The plan has top management and employee support.
- Employee reward needs are compatible with the plan and the organisation's compensation philosophy.[73]

Most compensation systems are flawed, but this does not mean that they cannot be powerful tools in motivating employees, facilitating change, reinforcing the organisation's culture and achieving its strategic objectives.[74]

Skill-based pay

Skill-based pay, or pay for competencies or knowledge, compensates employees on the basis of the job-related skills, competencies and knowledge they possess. The purpose of this system is to motivate employees to gain additional skills, competencies and knowledge that will increase their personal satisfaction and value to the organisation.

It should be noted that some writers see skill-based pay systems as being designed to reduce the sense of collective action among employees and to increase the organisation's control over the employee. Treating employees on an individual basis, it is argued, results in a reduction of the collectivist culture and a weakening of the trade unions. Finally, pay for performance is seen as underpinning a unitarist (as opposed to a pluralist or a Marxist) view of employee relations.[75] Some organisations apply the terms 'competency-based pay' or 'person-based pay' to the skill-based pay plans they design for knowledge workers because (a) they are more appealing terms and avoid the connotation of subprofessional or submanagerial work, (b) they clearly identify the plan as applying to professional and managerial employees and (c) they allow compensation consultants to differentiate their products in the marketplace.[76]

Under skill-based pay systems, employees are paid for the skills, competencies and knowledge they are capable of using, not for the job they are performing, their job title or their seniority. This is radically different from traditional job-based pay plans, which pay employees for the jobs they hold (see figure 12.15).[77] Skill-based pay is also called competency-based pay, pay for knowledge, pay for skills, multiskilled compensation and role-based or person-centred compensation.[78] It is often used for autonomous work groups or other job enrichment programs. Consequently, organisations that adopt skill-based pay tend to have a participative organisational culture and a high commitment to employee training and development.[79] Research suggests that skill-based pay is more likely to be adopted by organisations that encourage employee involvement, use total quality management and face strong market challenges from foreign competition.[80] Skill-based pay also depends on the employees wanting to increase their knowledge and skills. Employees earn pay increases by learning and demonstrating competency. They can then be rotated to jobs that require the new skill, competency or knowledge.[81]

Supporters of a skill-based pay system claim that it:
- recognises that the discrete job is becoming obsolete, given technological change, downsizing, re-engineering and increasing teamwork — rather than paying for the job, companies must now pay people for their skills
- fits the strategic business focus on core competencies[82]
- gives management greater flexibility in rostering, allocating work and covering for absenteeism and labour turnover
- gives employees additional job security, job mobility and the chance to increase earnings without being moved permanently to a higher level job (which can be important where promotional opportunities are limited)
- leads, under some conditions, to higher performance, lower staffing levels, greater productivity, improved quality, faster response to customer orders, more effective problem solving, lower absenteeism and reduced labour turnover[83]
- allows for multiskilling, which reinforces a high-involvement management style whereby employees are given responsibility
- results in a better trained work force
- motivates employees through the growth and development associated with continued learning and job progression.[84]

Graham O'Neill *is Director of Reward and Recognition for the Hay Group. Apart from some 20 years in consulting, Graham has held corporate positions in remuneration and HR line management. He is also an adjunct professor at RMIT University's School of Management.*

Rewarding strategies

When I first joined the Hay Group in 1980 remuneration planning was concerned with using job evaluation to establish relativities between different jobs and with providing reliable pay benchmarks from the external market.

Performance-related pay, where it existed, was largely based on determining how the annual review percentage would be allocated among salaried employees. For example, how do we carve up the six per cent budget to ensure our top performers get more than the budgeted amount and the poor performers receive less?

The HR practitioner's focus was on developing a remuneration management structure based on internal consistency, with some attempt to factor in performance, and also on determining the appropriate external positioning of pay — very much about building a sound administrative framework.

Spiralling inflation in the 1980s led to an accelerated 'bracket creep' as employees quickly drifted into the top marginal tax rate. As a direct result there was an almost exponential growth in the provision of benefits such as vehicles, travel, entertainment and the like as tax-effective components of remuneration.

Introduction of Fringe Benefits Tax (FBT) legislation in 1986 aimed to ensure better collection of taxation liabilities accruing from the provision of non-cash benefits. As such, it legitimised salary packaging, thus providing a new emphasis for HR managers in planning and administering a 'total employment cost' — the total cost the organisation was prepared to pay, whether in cash salary or benefits, plus the applicable FBT.

While the administrative implications added to the complexity of overall salary management, some HR managers recognised that the freedom to package (or cash-out) benefits could provide a modest medium-term competitive advantage for some firms, particularly where remuneration packaging was used as an inducement to get people out of the award system.

The early 90s saw a very significant shift from discretionary bonuses to target-based incentive plans based on the 'do this-get that' principle of plan design. This was accompanied by a rapid spread of performance pay plans to cover almost all supervisory and management positions. This in turn prompted the HR function to re-engineer performance planning to ensure the integrity of performance plans and their link with pay.

The other change was the widespread introduction of equity-based, long-term incentives. Only the three executive directors participated in the ANZ Bank's option plan when I joined the bank in 1994. By 1996 the number had grown to some 100 participating executives and managers.

Many HR managers found themselves grappling with significant governance issues following amendments to the Corporations Law in 1998. There was greater disclosure of executive remuneration and a requirement that annual reports state the policy or philosophy by which executive and management remuneration is determined, and an explanation of the link between remuneration and performance.

What does all this tell us as we look back over the past 20 years? In summary, the HR profession has always known the essence of remuneration is to attract, retain and motivate people. Now there is recognition that it must also demonstrate a sound business focus that effectively balances the capacity to pay with the need to pay — a balance that requires a clear medium to longer term reward strategy.

Looking forward there is a looming challenge for HR practitioners. Notwithstanding changes to Corporations Law and the newly released ASX guidelines, recent spectacular corporate collapses have prompted cries from both sides of politics that if business will not regulate its own house then government will. This has the potential to create significant issues in the planning and determination of executive remuneration.

Graham O'Neill

Source *HR Monthly*, September 2003, p. 33.

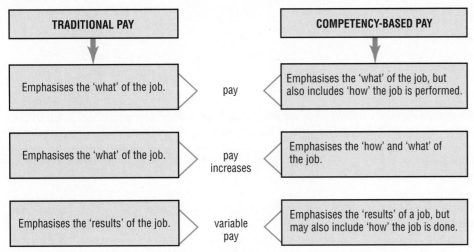

Figure 12.15 Traditional versus competency-based pay

Source K. M. Cofsky, 'Critical keys to competency based pay', *Compensation and Benefits Review*, vol. 25, no. 6, 1993, p. 49.

However, skill-based pay has some potential disadvantages:
- It can lead to increased pay and training costs, which may not be offset by cost savings.
- Employees with newly acquired skills may become restless and want to move prematurely from job to job.
- If too many skills are permitted, the plan may become too complex and thus difficult to administer and difficult for employees to understand.
- Employees trained in several different jobs may be unable to perform all of them better than a group of workers trained in only one job. In other words, specialised employees may improve efficiency.
- Pricing jobs in the marketplace may be more difficult if few (or no other) organisations use a skill-based pay plan.
- Some employees may not have the ability or the desire to acquire new skills or knowledge, so may resist skill-based pay.
- Some companies may not be willing to examine, question and possibly discard their traditional objectives, strategy and culture.[85]

Nevertheless, it appears that skill-based pay programs are increasing in popularity and that employees with multiple skills are in high demand as organisations restructure and eliminate layers of management and specialists.[86] Employers that have successfully used skill-based systems include Johnson & Johnson, General Electric and Procter & Gamble.[87]

Relating pay to performance

The compa ratio or pay index

The **compa ratio** is the ratio or pay index between the average pay for a particular job point or grade and the midpoint of the pay range for that point or grade. It assumes that the pay midpoint (sometimes referred to as the target or control pay) is the desired level of payment for acceptable performance.

For example:
1. *Group*

$$\text{Compa ratio} = \frac{\text{average of all pay rates in the grade}}{\text{midpoint of the standard pay range}} \times 100$$

> **Compa ratio** The ratio between the average pay rates for a particular job point or grade and the midpoint of the pay range for that point or grade.

$$\text{Compa ratio} = \frac{\text{average of all pay rates at a job point}}{\text{midpoint of the standard pay range}} \times 100$$

2. *Individual*

$$\text{Compa ratio} = \frac{\text{actual pay rate}}{\text{midpoint of the standard pay range}} \times 100$$

The compa ratio is a control index that is useful in auditing pay practices. Assuming a plus or minus 20 per cent pay range, an index of 100 equates with the midpoint pay; an index of 80 equates with the pay range minimum; and an index of 120 equates with the pay range maximum.

A low index can reflect:
- underpayment
- a large number of young or new employees in the job grade
- hard performance ratings.

An index of around 100 typically indicates that there is an acceptable distribution of employees throughout the pay range.

A high index may suggest:
- a large number of senior, experienced employees in the job grade
- soft performance ratings
- pay midpoints that are not competitive.

It should be noted that a compa ratio or pay index can be calculated for an individual as well as for groups of employees at a particular job level. Consequently, it is a useful management tool for aligning merit increases with performance ratings.

The performance index

Performance range A pay administration technique used to better align performance with rewards.

The compa ratio or pay index indicates where an employee is being paid in their pay range. Using the same concept, it is possible to develop a corresponding **performance range** and index. Then it is a simple matter of matching the performance index with the pay index (compa ratio) to determine the appropriate increase that best equates with performance (see figure 12.16).

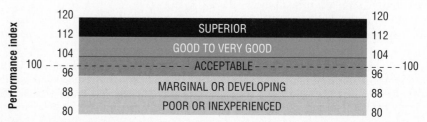

Figure 12.16 Performance ranges

The performance range (like the standard pay range) has a spread of plus or minus 20 per cent from the midpoint (100) and is divided into five bands. By using this technique, the manager can broadly identify where the employee should be located in the range — for example, superior, acceptable — then make a more precise decision as to where the employee lies within the band. This means that the manager is able to distinguish between several employees rated as 'acceptable'. If one employee just makes the grade of 'acceptable' and the other is on the verge of being rated 'good', for example, then the manager may allocate performance indexes of 96 and 104, respectively. These numbers are directly comparable with each employee's pay index, so they can be used to link pay to performance.

An example in figure 12.17 shows the performance–pay differential. Brown is being underpaid relative to his performance, Smith is being paid fairly and Jones is being paid too much relative to her performance level. Thus, in terms of their claim to a share of the merit budget, Brown has the strongest claim, while Jones has the least claim. Using this technique, the manager can allocate the funds available for pay increases in a way that links compensation to performance and is justifiable to the employees.

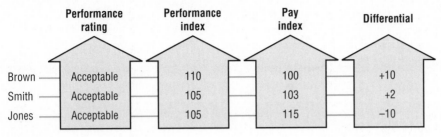

Figure 12.17 Linking pay to performance

The merit grid

Another way to link pay to performance is to use a **merit grid**. As can be seen from figure 12.18, the amount of pay increase depends on employee performance and on the employee's position in the pay range (compa ratio). The better the performance rating and the lower the position in the pay range, the larger the percentage increase.

Merit grid A technique used to allocate rewards linked to performance.

Performance rating	POSITION IN PAY RANGE			
	First quartile (80–89) % increase	Second quartile (90–99) % increase	Third quartile (100–109) % increase	Fourth quartile (100–120) % increase
Superior	13–14	11–12	9–10	6–8
Good	11–12	9–10	7–8	5–6
Acceptable	9–10	7–8	5–6	3–4
Marginal	5–6	3–4	Delay increase	Delay increase
Poor	Nil	Nil	Nil	Nil

Figure 12.18 Sample merit grid

Pay increases

Pay increases recognise the employee's contributions to the achievement of the organisation's objectives. Most organisations review pay rates annually. This should not mean that everyone is guaranteed an increase every 12 months. A poor performer (say, performance index 83) with a high pay rate (say, salary index 108), for example, is already being well compensated relative to their contribution and a further increase would be difficult to justify.

The systematic review of pay rates is facilitated by having all the necessary information presented in a logical format. A typical compensation review sheet is shown in figure 12.19. Linking pay to performance is even simpler if PC spreadsheet programs are used. Performance ratings and other related data can be quickly transformed into a scheduled merit increase. Moreover, these increases can be quickly and accurately costed.

Name	Hire date	Age	Job points	Pay range			Current pay	PI	PR	Proposed increase				
				Minimum	Midpoint	Maximum				Amount	%	Date	New pay	New PI
Anderson, R. P.	92	28	180	31 200	39 000	46 800	39 000	100	A					
Andrews, S. A.	87	37	230	33 200	41 500	49 800	33 200	80	A					
Davies, H.	94	26	130	29 200	36 500	43 800	43 800	120	S					
Dunlop, K. G.	82	47	330	37 200	46 500	55 800	36 000	77	S					
Kuzmits, W. L.	96	39	230	33 200	41 500	49 800	48 000	116	G					
Li, W. W.	89	41	330	37 200	46 500	55 800	44 000	95	A					
Milkovich, J. J.	90	37	230	33 200	41 500	49 800	41 500	100	U					
Ng, C. H.	93	51	390`	39 600	49 500	59 000	61 000	123	G					
Pagonis, G. W.	89	63	230	33 200	41 500	49 800	45 000	108	M					
Rosenberg, D.	87	59	180	31 200	39 000	46 800	53 000	136	S					
Saad, K. K.	88	49	270	34 800	43 500	52 200	35 000	80	M					
Sadhwani, M. L.	91	33	330	37 200	46 500	55 800	39 000	84	U					
Tse, D. K.	93	31	180	31 200	39 000	46 800	28 000	71	A					
Ziegenmeyer, S.	95	27	180	31 200	39 000	46 800	30 000	77	G					

Note: PI = pay index (compa ratio) (80 = range minimum, 100 = range midpoint, 120 = range maximum);
PR = performance rating (S = superior, A = acceptable, G = good, M = marginal, U = unsatisfactory)

Figure 12.19 Compensation review planning sheet

Merit increases

In most organisations, merit increases are a composite of payments for merit, cost of living and inflation. Few organisations grant a pure merit increase because there is no set answer regarding how much of a pay increase should reflect merit. Ultimately, the answer depends on factors such as the organisation's strategic objectives, culture, compensation philosophy, business results, competitiveness in the pay market and the age and growth rate of the organisation. Whatever the figure, the merit increase must be seen as significant by employees or its motivational impact will be negated.

Although most senior HR managers believe that rewards must be linked to performance, one survey found that:
- the best employees are not usually rewarded with extra dollars
- the merit increase program is insufficient to provide an incentive to excel and change behaviour
- inadequate funds are available to pay for performance
- performance review programs in use are ineffective.[88]

Promotional increases

A **promotion** involves a change to a bigger job with a higher pay range. This is a significant milestone in an employee's career and should be appropriately recognised. It should be noted that the promotional increase, unlike the merit increase which typically contains an economic component, represents a significant increase in purchasing power. However, situations do arise where an employee is being overpaid, and a further pay increase is not warranted in such cases (see figure 12.20).

Promotion The movement of a person to a higher level position in the company.

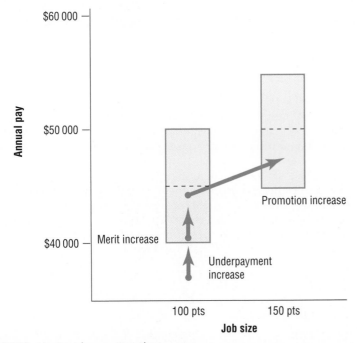

Figure 12.20 Merit and promotional increases

There is no fixed formula to determine the amount of a promotional increase. Factors that need to be considered are:
- the employee's position in the pay range (compa ratio) before and after the promotion
- the size of the promotion
- the probability of future promotions
- the pay rates of other employees at the new job level

- the size of previous pay increases (which generally should not be larger than the proposed pay increase)
- the employee's age and length of service
- the timing of the increase (whether it should be paid at the commencement of the promotion, or after the completion of a probationary period).

General adjustments

If pay for performance is a compensation objective, then **across-the-board increases** should be avoided. Such increases have little or no motivational impact and can engender the feeling that employees are entitled to the increase regardless of individual performance or the organisation's competitive position. 'Organisations that fail to pay for performance will receive less in terms of effort and contribution from their employees' and 'are more likely to discourage and even lose their best performers'.[89] Nevertheless, one US survey found that only a minority of participants rated their compensation programs as successful in relating pay to performance.[90] Organisations that follow an entitlement philosophy often refer to employee pay increases as cost-of-living increases even though the link between the size of the increase and the movement in the cost of living indicators may be weak.[91]

Automatic progression

Automatic progression or incremental pay scales are not concerned with relating pay increases to performance and should be avoided. Typically, such pay programs reward membership of the organisation and longevity in the job; they do not encourage employees to improve their performance. There is no motivation, for example, for an employee who knows that they will automatically progress to the next predetermined pay level along with everyone else, regardless of performance. Such programs, common in the public sector, are ineffectual, demoralising to top performers and a waste of compensation dollars.

Blue and red circle pay rates

Blue circle pay rates are individual anomalies that are adjusted because the pay rates are below the minimum of the pay range, or within the pay range but considered too low in relation to the employee's performance and experience. Increases to fix underpayment should not be given to marginal or unsatisfactory employees unless the organisation wishes to retain them for some special reason.

Red circle pay rates are those above the range maximum for the job. Generally, organisations do not cut such pay rates but rather freeze them until the pay range moves up and can accommodate them. Unless handled with great care, this approach can lead to high turnover among long-term employees. To avoid 'red circle' situations, it is important to slow the rate of pay increases as the pay moves into the upper ends of the pay range, and to start an aggressive career development program for affected employees.

Pay reviews

There are three main types of **pay reviews**:
1. *Fixed-date reviews:* the standard fixed-date review applies from 1 January each year. The big advantage is that it considerably simplifies compensation administration by getting everything over 'all at once'. It also has the advantage that everyone is reviewed under the same business conditions. Fixed-date reviews, however, tend to produce widespread employee comparison of pay rates, pressure management to give everyone an increase (especially if the increases are announced just before Christmas or Chinese New Year), create problems with employees who have just joined (for example, does an employee who joined late in the year qualify for a January increase?) and dilute pay for performance.

2. *Anniversary reviews:* pay rates are reviewed at 12-month intervals from the employee's date of hire. The advantages of this approach are that employee comparisons are more difficult and that each employee can be handled individually. Furthermore, managers are better able to reward performance because they do not have to deal with groups of disappointed and emotional employees at the same time.

3. *Flexible-date reviews:* these reviews generally operate within a time span of nine to 18 months, based on the employee's anniversary date of hire. Using variable timing increases flexibility. In addition, superior-performing employees who are low in their pay ranges can be rewarded more frequently. Conversely, those high in their pay ranges or with poor performance ratings can be placed on a 'stretch out' program to slow down the timing of their pay increase.

Summary

Compensation is a critical part of strategic HRM. Compensation policies and practices should reinforce employee behaviours that help achieve the organisation's strategic business objectives and reinforce its desired culture. In short, money must match the message.

No system for compensating employees is perfect. Details of administration always involve the element of human judgement. However, a systematic approach to compensation reduces the level of subjectivity and increases the likelihood of an organisation attracting, retaining and motivating suitable employees and gaining a competitive advantage. Without a systematic approach to compensation, an organisation will have difficulty monitoring cost-effectiveness, legal compliance, pay equity, the relationship between pay and performance, and whether its compensation program supports its business strategy.

Thirty interactive Wiley Web Questions are available to test your understanding of this chapter at
www.johnwiley.com.au/ highered/hrm5e
in the student resources area

student study guide

terms to know

across-the-board increases (p. 470)
automatic progression (p. 470)
benchmark jobs (p. 453)
blue circle pay rates (p. 470)
broadbanding (p. 454)
compa ratio (p. 465)
compensation (p. 441)
factor comparison system (p. 447)
job description (p. 444)
job evaluation (p. 444)
job grading (p. 445)
job ranking (p. 445)
job specification (p. 444)
market postures (p. 455)
merit grid (p. 467)
merit pay (p. 459)

pay compression (p. 457)
pay for performance (p. 441)
pay line (p. 454)
pay policy line (p. 456)
pay range (p. 454)
pay reviews (p. 470)
pay secrecy (p. 456)
pay structure (p. 453)
pay survey (p. 451)
performance range (p. 466)
point system (p. 446)
promotion (p. 469)
red circle pay rates (p. 470)
seniority-based pay (p. 458)
skill-based pay (p. 463)
strategic compensation (p. 441)

review questions

1. How can an organisation ensure that its employee compensation program supports its strategic business objectives?
2. How can an organisation's culture affect employee compensation? How can employee compensation affect an organisation's culture?
3. Describe the advantages and disadvantages of the major types of job evaluation systems.
4. Is performance-based pay appropriate for university lecturers? Explain your answer.
5. What is a pay survey? What is the best way to conduct a pay survey?
6. What are the advantages and disadvantages of linking pay to performance?
7. Why should an organisation have a pay policy? Describe the key elements that should be present in a pay policy.
8. What are the advantages and disadvantages of (a) pay openness and (b) pay secrecy?
9. What are the arguments for and against across-the-board pay increases?
10. What is the difference between 'guaranteed' pay and 'at-risk' pay? Which would you prefer to be compensated by? Why?

environmental influences on employee compensation

Describe the key environmental influences from the model (figure 12.21 shown opposite) that have significance for employee compensation.

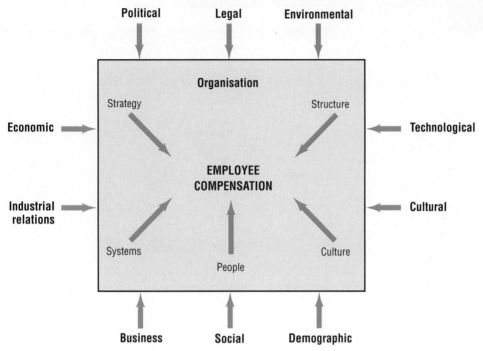

Figure 12.21 Environmental influences on employee compensation

Class debate

Australian tax rates punish high income earners.
or
The government should pass legislation to limit the maximum amount that CEOs can be paid.

what's your view?

Write a 500-word response to the Letter to the Editor on page 459, agreeing or disagreeing with the writer's point of view.

newsbreak exercise

Read the Newsbreak 'An executive's worth is the multimillion-dollar question' on pages 461–2. Which of the writers do you agree with? Why?

practitioner speaks

Read the article on page 464. As a class, critically discuss the author's views.

What do you think? Conduct a mini survey of class members, using the questionnaire below. Critically discuss the findings.

1.	Pay for performance is an attack on the Australian spirit of egalitarianism.	YES	NO
2.	Complaints regarding CEO salary levels are just 'sour grapes'.	YES	NO
3.	Pay for performance aims to weaken union power.	YES	NO
4.	There should be a cap on executive pay.	YES	NO
5.	Across-the-board increases promote mediocrity.	YES	NO
6.	Every worker is entitled to an annual pay increase.	YES	NO

online exercise

1. Conduct an online search for information on (a) levels of CEO pay, (b) CEO pay and performance and (c) attitudes towards CEO pay. As a class, discuss your findings.
2. Conduct an online search for information on competency-based pay and performance-based pay. Write a 500-word report on your findings. Include the web addresses that you found useful.

ethical dilemmas

Executive pay 'rip-off'

Jerry Barnes barked, 'You blokes are nothing but a bunch of thieves. You collude with the directors of this company to ramp up your own pay, but won't give the poor bloody workers a cent!'

The three senior executives of XYZ Ltd glared at the union representative sitting opposite them. 'What do you mean?' thundered George Slattery, the HR Director.

'You know as well as I do George. It's a case of you scratch my back and I'll scratch yours. The performance of this company stinks, but you lot are all on multimillion-dollar packages. You couldn't organise a chook raffle in a pub, but in a week you earn over 20 times what my members do.'

'That's because we are better qualified and have more responsible jobs. You know that Jerry.'

'Look, what irks my members and the union is that you and the board are talking garbage and you won't admit it. Everyone knows that the board and senior management of this company are involved in one great shareholder rip-off.'

'Watch it, Jerry, you are going too far!' snapped George.

'Too far? You blokes are unbelievable. You gave John Andrews a $10 million goodbye present after that hopeless idiot almost destroyed the company and cost 1500 of my members their jobs. And what about your executive share option program? The company's profits dropped $60 million this year, yet the directors voted themselves an increase and gave you blokes performance bonuses and more options. It's a farce. It's a straight-out transfer of shareholder funds into your own pockets.'

'Issuing options aligns management's interests with the shareholders. Surely you can see that.'

'What I see', snarled Jerry, 'is a bunch of no-hopers with their hands in the till. It's no wonder my members are hopping mad.'

Discussion questions

1. What ethical issues are raised in this case?
2. Who do you agree with? Why?
3. If you were George, how would you respond to the union's criticisms

The credit card

Clara Ng smiled as she sat down and took in the luxury of the CEO's office. Jim Brodzinski quickly dealt with the details of Clara's remuneration package. All was straightforward. Clara felt very satisfied. Her appointment as Vice-President of Human Resources for Pacific Investment Bank was a major career move.

'Oh, I almost forgot your credit card.'

'My credit card?' asked Clara, somewhat confused.

'Yes, sorry about that. It's not in your contract. It's just a little extra something we give our senior staff to help compensate for the long hours and missed weekends. Sixty hours is an easy week

here', smiled Jim. 'You will see that the card is in the name of our Hong Kong affiliate. You can charge your personal travel and entertainment expenses on this. It keeps the Australian tax people out of our hair.'

'My personal entertainment expenses?' questioned Clara.

'You got it. You can spend up to $50 000 per year, no questions asked. It's strictly for your personal use. Entertain whoever you like and charge it. Enjoy!' laughed Jim.

Discussion questions

1. What ethical issues are raised in this case?
2. If you were Clara, what would you do? Why?

---

case studies

Market rates

Leon Poon, Dean of Business Administration at Western University, stood to speak before the university's Remuneration Committee. 'I propose that we do away with the present system of standard pay rates for staff irrespective of discipline. The Business School is suffering because we cannot offer competitive compensation packages. We are constantly losing our best people. This year we have lost two senior lecturers in Accounting and one Associate Professor in Marketing.

'We have to have more flexibility. The Business School generates more money for this university than any other school, yet we cannot reward our people because of the rigid system we are forced to follow. I cannot see the logic in paying a senior lecturer in Accounting the same rate as a senior lecturer in Social Work. They do not bear any relationship to each other. Yet I am forced to pay my people at below market rates so that other schools can pay their people rates above what their jobs are worth. It is extremely unfair and is preventing our school from attracting and keeping the best talent.

'We also need to have more flexibility in how we reward performance. At the moment everyone, regardless of their performance, gets an automatic step increase until they hit the top of their pay range. This is crazy. We should be able to discriminate and give more to those who are performing and less (or maybe nothing) to those who are not contributing. It's

time for the university to change. We should no longer be locked into such an antiquated remuneration system.'

Professor Millie Orman, Dean of Social Work, rose to address the committee. 'I am very disheartened to hear my colleague's comments. What he proposes strikes at the heart of the university's collegial system. What Professor Poon wants is to create the dog-eat-dog world of the free market. What will it do to the university if a senior lecturer in Accounting is paid more than a senior lecturer in Social Work? I note that only one senior lecturer in Accounting has a PhD, yet all my senior lecturers have terminal degrees. Where is the justice in paying them less?

'As for pay for performance, this is just a managerial ploy to turn colleague against colleague. How is performance to be measured? I doubt that Professor Poon can offer us an objective measure of academic performance. I do not believe it is possible to accurately assess the work of academics. So much of what we do is intangible. Trying to link pay to performance is a manipulative technique. All it will do is breed discontent and increase disputes over pay. Under the present system, the good people get promoted. The others do not.

'I strongly recommend to the committee that it ignores Professor Poon's recommendations. I suggest instead that we develop a program to educate the community about our plight and press the government for more money.'

Discussion question

Who do you agree with? Explain your reasoning.

Conduct a mini survey of your lecturers regarding their views on the advantages and disadvantages of introducing 'pay for performance' for academics. As a class, discuss your findings.

Big bucks upset at Western University[92]

'You guys make me laugh', interjected Stella Chatzky.

'Why is that, Stella?', asked Eric Martin, Associate Professor in Management.

'Well, you're always complaining about how much this CEO or that CEO earns, but I never hear you complain how much sporting stars or entertainers earn. You seem to only get annoyed when businesspeople get compensated in the millions.'

'Stella's right', smiled Percy Samuels, senior lecturer in Organisational Behaviour. 'You two have this crazy sense of inequity. Why shouldn't CEOs be paid like movie stars? Surely, you aren't going to tell me that someone who can kick a ball or strum a guitar contributes more to society than a CEO?'

'That's not the point', barked John Smith, Head of the Management Department. 'Senior management pay in this country is obscene. Why should a CEO earn 20 or 30 times what an average worker earns? Surely, you are not going to argue that that is morally right?'

'Yeah! And especially when you take into account their pay is determined more by the size of the company they work for and not their contribution', shouted Steve Plovnick, Associate Professor in Organisational Behaviour, his face flushed with anger. 'Everyone knows it's some big sweetheart deal between compliant boards and greedy executives.'

'I agree', snapped Cindy Castelli, lecturer in Sociology. 'It's an outrageous conflict of interest. No wonder the workers and the unions are screaming. At least when footballers don't perform they get dropped from the team.'

'So do CEOs!', Stella shouted back.

'But at what price?', questioned Cindy. 'Look at the multimillion payouts to CEOs after they almost destroy a company.'

'Yeah', interrupted Steve. 'You can bet the poor idiots at the bottom of the corporate ladder who lost their jobs because of the CEO's incompetence got diddle. It really stinks. How are such huge payouts justified? It's not by performance. If we get fired for non-performance, we won't get anything like that.'

'That's irrelevant, Steve. When did anyone get fired for incompetence at this university? Contracts not renewed, yes, but can you tell me one person with tenure who has been fired?' said Stella.

Steve grimaced. 'Stella, you know as well as I do that academia is quite different from the corporate world. Besides, we are grossly underpaid compared with private sector managers.'

'That's true, Stella, you can't deny that', added Cindy.

'Hey, you lot should stop arguing and read this', interrupted Ron Mazzochis. 'It says here in the *Financial News* that at the top 181 Australian companies the ratio between CEO pay and the average wage is 74 to 1.'

'You're kidding!' cried Steve.

'No, read it for yourself.'

'So much for Australia being an egalitarian society', sighed Cindy. 'We are getting more like the United States every day.'

'It's disgraceful', muttered Steve.

Discussion questions

1. Who do you agree with? Why?
2. As a class, discuss your views on the issues highlighted.

practical exercises

1. (a) You are the Marketing Manager for XYZ Ltd. Using the compensation review planning sheet data in figure 12.19 on page 468, calculate the planned salary increases and new salary indices for your staff for the next calendar year. The HR Department has informed you that the anticipated rate of inflation is 3 per cent and that the proposed overall rate of increase for the company is 7 per cent. Your present salary payments total $576 500 and your allowable merit budget is 7 per

cent of this amount (that is, $40 355). Apart from the restriction of not exceeding the merit budget, you are free to allocate the money as you choose.

(b) When you have completed the exercise, form into groups of three or four. Discuss your recommendations.

2. Break into small groups of four to six. Individually rank the following jobs from 'biggest' to 'smallest' and place them on an organisation chart. Then compare and review your results as a group. Discuss the basis on which you made your evaluations. What difficulties (if any) did you experience in 'sizing' the jobs?

Rank	Job title
_____	Accounting Manager
_____	Compensation and Benefits Manager
_____	Cost Accountant
_____	Cost Clerk
_____	Electrician
_____	Electrical Engineer
_____	Executive Secretary
_____	General Manager
_____	Graduate Trainee (Marketing)
_____	HR Manager
_____	Manufacturing Manager
_____	Marketing Manager
_____	Market Research Officer
_____	Mechanical Engineer
_____	Paymaster
_____	Receptionist
_____	Safety Officer
_____	Sales Representative
_____	Sales Supervisor
_____	Senior Sales Representative
_____	Training Manager
_____	Treasurer

3. Break into small groups of four to six. Individually, use the following job grade descriptions to evaluate the jobs of Stella Chow, Theo Camakaris, Joe Epstein, Deborah Kleiner, Stephen Overman and Kate Petrini from 'biggest' to 'smallest'. Then compare and review your results as a group. Discuss the basis on which you made your evaluations. What difficulties (if any) did you experience in 'sizing' the jobs?

Job grade	Description
1	Carries out simple, routine clerical tasks such as photocopying, filing and sorting mail. Works under close supervision. Junior high school education required. No previous experience necessary.
2	Carries out routine clerical work requiring basic arithmetic skills. Works under close supervision. Senior high school education desirable. Some previous job-related experience desirable.
3	Carries out routine clerical tasks but occasionally works on more complex tasks. Works under moderately close supervision. Makes decisions on simple, routine matters. Senior high school education required. Six to twelve months related work experience required.

4	Carries out more complex clerical tasks. Works under minimum supervision. Senior high school education required with additional training in basic accounting. At least one to two years related work experience.
5	Supervises the work of five to six clerks. Undertakes complex clerical tasks. Makes minor decisions involving non-routine matters. Senior high school education required with additional training in accounting and the use of spreadsheets. Two years related work experience. Some previous supervisory experience necessary.

Stella Chow
- able to write correspondence in English
- up to six months work experience
- makes decisions on routine matters
- junior high school education
- dealings limited to own work unit
- used to normal office conditions

Theo Camakaris
- able to use basic accounting and computer skills
- one to two years related work experience
- able to analyse complex non-technical matters
- subprofessional accounting qualification
- dealings limited to own work unit
- used to normal office conditions

Joe Epstein
- able to read English memos and fill in forms
- two to three years work experience
- makes decisions on simple facts
- senior high school education
- dealings with junior-level persons within and outside the organisation
- used to normal office conditions

Deborah Kleiner
- able to prepare technical reports in English
- five to seven years work experience
- able to analyse complex non-technical matters
- senior high school education
- dealings with senior management inside and outside the organisation
- used to normal office conditions

Stephen Overman
- able to deal with abstract and concrete ideas
- two to three years work experience
- exercises high degree of judgement on complex issues
- university degree in business administration
- involvement in negotiations with senior management inside and outside the organisation
- used to normal office conditions

Kate Petrini
- able to read and write simple English
- up to six months work experience
- no decision-making responsibility

- junior high school education
- able to give and receive routine information
- regularly exposed to noise and dirt

4. Break into small groups of four to six. Individually, use the point plan below to size the jobs of the six employees from exercise 3. Compare and review your results. What difficulties did you experience in 'sizing' the jobs?

Point plan — non-managerial salaried positions

Factors		Degree of points							
		1	2	3	4	5	6	7	8
I	Education	20	40	60	80	100	120		
II	Experience	10	30	50	70	90	110	130	150
III	Decision making	10	30	50	75	100			
IV	Relationships	10	30	50	70	90			
V	Working conditions	5	15	25	50				

I Education

This factor measures the general level of education required to perform the job

Degree	Definition	Points
1	Follow simple instructions; add, subtract, multiply, divide and count whole numbers; read and write simple sentences.	20
2	Carry out detailed but simple instructions; add, subtract, multiply and divide, including use of decimals and fractions; read simple drawings and memoranda; fill out standardised routine forms.	40
3	Compute such items as discount, interest, percentage, ratio and volume; draw simple graphs or charts; read mechanical drawings, instructions and specifications; write routine reports.	60
4	Prepare correspondence of a non-routine or elementary technical nature; prepare reports requiring explanations; apply know-how involving basic principles of accounting, electronics, etc.	80
5	Apply at a professional level knowledge of accounting, engineering, etc.; read complex drawings and specifications; prepare correspondence and reports of an involved or technical nature.	100
6	Apply specialised and advanced knowledge in the physical sciences or behavioural sciences; prepare reports concerning technically involved subjects; deal with a variety of abstract and concrete concepts.	120

(continued)

II Experience

This factor evaluates the number of months/years work experience needed to perform the job.

Degree	Months or years	Points
1	Less than 1 month.	10
2	1 month but less than 3 months.	30
3	3 months but less than 6 months.	60
4	6 months but less than 1 year.	70
5	1 year but less than 2 years.	90
6	2 years but less than 4 years.	110
7	4 years but less than 6 years.	130
8	6 years and over.	150

III Decision making

This factor evaluates the complexity of decision making required to do the job

Degree	Definition	Points
1	Follow established routine with no decision-making responsibilities.	10
2	Work from detailed or written instructions; make minor decisions.	30
3	Analyse varied or complex non-technical information; make decisions in accordance with established procedures.	50
4	Analyse complex technical information; make decisions using general guidelines.	75
5	Analyse complex technical and non-technical information; exercise high degree of originality and independent judgement in areas where there are few guidelines for precedents.	100

IV Relationships

This factor evaluates the nature of relationships required to perform the job.

Degree	Definition	Points
1	Deal only with employees and supervisor within own work unit.	10
2	Deal with staff both within own department and in other departments or other organisations; give and receive routine information.	30
3	Deal with staff in other departments and in other organisations; give and receive various oral and written information.	50
4	Deal with staff both within and outside the organisation; discuss, explain and agree on matters of importance to the functioning of the job or department.	70
5	Deal with staff both within and outside the organisation; often negotiate, persuade and make agreements.	90

V Working conditions

This factor evaluates both general working conditions and safety and health hazards.

Degree	Definition	Points
1	Normal office conditions.	5
2	Infrequent exposure to disagreeable conditions such as heat, cold or dirt; little or no exposure to any health and safety hazards.	15
3	Occasional exposure to disagreeable conditions such as noise, heat, cold, dirt and fumes; some exposure to health and safety hazards.	25
4	Frequent exposure to objectionable conditions such as noise, heat, cold, fumes, vibration, etc.; frequent exposure to serious health and safety hazards.	30

5. Break into groups of four to six. Individually, using the factor comparison chart shown on the following page, size the jobs of Stella Chow, Theo Camakaris, Joe Epstein, Deborah Kleiner, Stephen Overman and Kate Petrini. (Remember to select one job as the benchmark job and compare the others with it, factor by factor.) Next compare and review your results. Discuss the basis on which you made your decisions. What difficulties did you experience in making your evaluations? What additional information would have been helpful?

6. Compare the four methods used in exercises 2–5. Describe how you feel about their ease of use, understandability and accuracy. Which method do you prefer? Why?

FACTOR COMPARISON CHART

Points	Education	Experience	Decision making	Relationships	Working conditions
330					
305					
290					
275					
260					
245					
230					
205					
190					
175					
160					
145					
130					
115					
100					

7. You are the HR Manager for Oz Manufacturing Ltd. You have been requested by the Managing Director to design a job evaluation system for the company. The company is a small, one-plant company employing approximately 160 people. The organisation is shown in the figure opposite. Annual sales are $20 million. The products manufactured are technically simple but unique in design. The company sells only domestically and has no intention of developing an export market.

(a) What type of job evaluation system would you recommend? Why?

(b) Would you recommend that those executives reporting to the Managing Director all be given the same job size and be paid alike? Explain your reasoning.

(c) Suppose you decide to design a point job evaluation plan. Identify the factors to which you would assign points and the number of points you would allocate to each factor. Calculate the total points you would give for the positions of Managing Director, Accounting Manager, HR Manager, Production Manager and Sales Manager.

(d) Would you recommend the same job evaluation system for all employees or different systems for employees doing different work or located at different levels in the organisational hierarchy? Why?

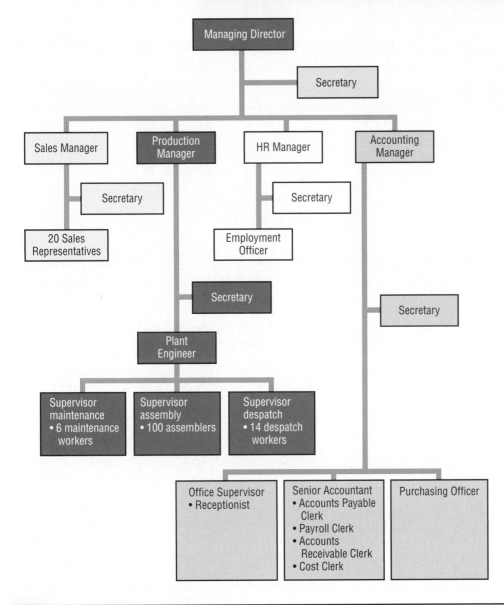

suggested readings

Beardwell, I. and Holden, L., *Human Resource Management*, 3rd edn, Prentice Hall, London, 2001, ch. 12.

CCH, *Australian Master Human Resources Guide*, CCH, Sydney, 2003, ch. 12.

Clark, R. and Seward, D., *Australian Human Resources Management: Framework and Practice*, 3rd edn, McGraw-Hill, Sydney, 2000, ch. 11.

De Cieri, H. and Kramar, R., *Human Resource Management in Australia*, McGraw-Hill, Sydney, 2003, chs 12, 13.

Fisher, C. O., Schoenfeldt, L. F. and Shaw, J. B., *Human Resource Management*, 5th edn, Houghton Mifflin, Boston, 2003, chs 12, 13.

Henderson, R. I., *Compensation Management in a Knowledge-Based World*, 9th edn, Pearson Education, Upper Saddle River, NJ, 2003.

Ivancevich, J. M. and Lee, S. H., *Human Resource Management*, McGraw-Hill, Singapore, 2002, chs 10, 11.

Mondy, R. W., Noe, R. M. and Premeaux, S. R., *Human Resource Management*, 8th edn, Prentice Hall, Upper Saddle River, NJ, 2002, ch. 11.

Nankervis, A. R., Compton, R. L. and McCarthy, T. E., *Strategic Human Resource Management*, 4th edn, Nelson, Melbourne, 2002, ch. 12.

online references

www.acaonline.org
www.afr.com
www.haygroup.com
www.imercer.com
www.jobsmart.org

www.mercerhr.com
www.shrm.org.hrmagazine
www.watsonwyatt.com
www.workforceonline.com
wwwtowersperrin.com

end notes

1. R. Samuelson, 'Fortunes are fit for kings, not CEOs', *Australian Financial Review*, 1 May 2003, p. 71.
2. G. L. O'Neill, 'Framework for developing a total reward strategy', *Asia Pacific Journal of Human Resources*, vol. 35, no. 2, 1995, pp. 103–17; and J. E. Nelson, 'Linking compensation to business strategy', *The Journal of Business Strategy*, vol. 19, no. 2, 1998, pp. 25–7.
3. Foster's Group, *Concise Annual Report*, Melbourne, 2002, p. 38.
4. J. Franklin, 'For technical professionals: pay for skills and pay for performance', *Personnel*, vol. 65, no. 5, 1988, p. 20.
5. I. Beardwell and L. Holden, *Human Resource Management*, Prentice Hall/Financial Times, London, 2001, p. 524.
6. D. J. McLaughlin, 'The rise of a strategic approach to executive compensation', in F. K. Foulkes (ed.), *Executive Compensation*, Harvard Business School Press, Boston, 1991, pp. 11, 22; T. Turnasella, 'Aligning pay with business strategies and cultural values', *Compensation and Benefits Review*, vol. 26, no. 5, 1994, p. 65; and J. Hale, 'Strategic rewards: keeping your best talent from walking out the door', *Compensation and Benefits Management*, vol. 14, no. 3, 1998, pp. 39–50.
7. I. Kessler, 'Reward systems', in J. Storey (ed.), *Human Resource Management: A Critical Text*, Routledge, London, 1995, p. 262, and I. Beardwell and L. Holden, op. cit., pp. 524–5.
8. D. Brown, 'A guide for matching compensation with company strategy and structure', *Compensation and Benefits Review*, vol. 25, no. 5, 1993, pp. 47–52.
9. T. R. Tudor, R. R. Trumble and L. Flowers, 'Strategic compensation management, the changing pattern of pay and benefits', *Journal of Compensation and Benefits*, vol. 12, no. 2, 1996, p. 34.
10. G. O'Neill and A. Berry, 'Remuneration of Australian executives: a practitioner review', *Asia Pacific Journal of Human Resources*, vol. 40, no. 2, 2002, p. 243.
11. Reported in 'Succession still being left to chance, survey reveals', *HR Monthly*, September 1997, p. 9.
12. Reported in M. Lawson, 'Australian options schemes hit competitiveness: survey', *Australian Financial Review*, 3 October 1997, p. 20.
13. P. Taylor, 'When pay for performance fails to perform', *Human Resources*, vol. 2, no. 4, October 1997, pp. 17–19; and J. Storey and K. Sisson, *Managing Human Resources and Industrial Relations*, Open University Press, Buckinghamshire, 1993, pp. 138–44.
14. G. O'Neill, 'Cost, entitlement or investment?', *HR Monthly*, December 1994, p. 11.
15. J. M. Ivancevich, *Human Resource Management*, 8th edn, Irwin, Chicago, 2001, p. 287.
16. O. Lundy and A. Cowling, *Strategic Human Resource Management*, Routledge, London, 1996, p. 304.
17. G. O'Neill and A. Berry, op. cit., p. 243.
18. G. O'Neill and R. R. Clark, 'Executive remuneration in the 1990s: major issues and trends', in G. O'Neill (ed.), *Corporate Remuneration in the 1990s*, Longman Cheshire, Melbourne, 1990, p. 17.
19. L. R. Gomez-Mejia, D. B. Balkin and R. L. Cardy, *Managing Human Resources*, 3rd edn, Prentice Hall, Englewood Cliffs, NJ, 2001, pp. 331–2.
20. Survey of senior HR managers' attitudes. See R. J. Stone, *Human Resource Management*, 2nd edn, John Wiley & Sons, Brisbane, 1995, Appendix I, p. 581.
21. J. G. Berg, *Managing Compensation*, AMACOM, New York, 1976, pp. 113–15.
22. Based on material supplied by Paula DeLisle, Director, Watson Wyatt (Hong Kong), 2003.
23. R. E. Sibson, *Wages and Salaries*, rev. edn, AMA, New York, 1967, p. 207; and CCH, *Australian Master Human Resources Guide*, CCH, Sydney, 2003, pp. 170–1.
24. P. C. Grant, 'What use is a job description?', *Personnel Journal*, February 1988, pp. 45–6.

25. W. Reddin, quoted in S. Y. Tsang, 'Another look at managerial effectiveness', *World Executive's Digest*, November 1989, p. 68.

26. H. Fisher, 'Job evaluation: problems and prospects', *Personnel*, vol. 61, no. 1, 1984, p. 55.

27. C. Burton, R. Hag and G. Thompson, *Women's Worth: Pay Equity and Job Evaluation in Australia*, AGPS, Canberra, 1987, pp. 45–63.

28. J. McNally and S. Shimmin, 'Job evaluation: equal work — equal pay?', *Management Decision*, vol. 26, no. 5, 1988, pp. 22–7.

29. M. A. Conway, 'Salary surveys: avoid the pitfalls', *Personnel Journal*, June 1984, p. 64.

30. See 'Broadbanding gains favour slowly', *HR Focus*, October 1992, p. 6.

31. S. Arasu, 'Broadbanding adds flexibility and speed to pay structure', *HR Monthly*, December 1995, p. 21.

32. Much of this section is adapted from S. L. O'Neill, 'Aligning pay with business strategy', *HR Magazine*, August 1993, pp. 76–9.

33. K. S. Abosch, 'The promise of broadbanding', *Compensation and Benefits Review*, vol. 27, no. 1, 1995, p. 58.

34. E. Lawler III, *Pay and Organizational Development*, Addison Wesley, Reading, Mass., 1981, pp. 43–8.

35. C. D. Fisher, L. F. Schoenfeldt and J. B. Shaw, *Human Resource Management*, 5th edn, Houghton Mifflin, Boston, 2003, p. 578.

36. J. A. Knight, 'Performance and greed', *Journal of Business Strategy*, vol. 23, no. 4, 2002, p. 24.

37. M. Hovy, 'Executive pays go to market', *HR Monthly*, May 2003, p. 36.

38. M. Cave, 'I'm worth it, baby', *Australian Financial Review*, 2–3 December 2000, pp. 21–3.

39. Quoted in M. Cave, op. cit., p. 23.

40. Quoted in Agencies, 'Buffet turns back on "boring" equities', *South China Morning Post — Business*, 2 May 2000, p. 1.

41. Quoted in D. Gibson, 'Buffet compares frenzy to chain letter', *Asian Wall Street Journal*, 1 May 2000, p. 9.

42. Cited in J. Hill and C. Yablon, 'What's in our pay checks?', *Australian Financial Review*, 29 November 2000, p. 42. Also see G. Morgenson, 'Stock options are not a free lunch', *Forbes Global*, 18 May 1998, pp. 50–4.

43. J. Reingold and B. Wolverton, 'Why bosses get rich from selling the company', *Business Week*, 30 March 1998, pp. 33–4.

44. Reported in J. Hill and C. Yablon, op. cit., p. 42.

45. Quoted in M. Cave, op. cit., p. 23.

46. T. Boyd, 'World class', *Boss*, November 2002, p. 34.

47. S. Long. 'Professionals' pay takes off,' *Australian Financial Review*, 22 March 2000, p. 5; M. Conlin, P. Coy, A. T. Palmer and G. Saveri, 'The wild new workforce', *Business Week*, 6 December 1999, pp. 53–7; A. Cornell, 'Up, up and away', *Boss*, November 2002, p. 42; and M. Priest, 'Workers rail at executive pay', *Australian Financial Review*, 31 January 2003, p. 3.

48. Reported in Agence France-Presse, 'Top executive takes heavy pay cut as public anger grows', *South China Morning Post — Business*, 26 October 2002, p. 4.

49. W. Buffett, quoted in J. Useem, 'Have they no shame?', *Fortune*, 28 April 2003, p. 40.

50. Y. M. Hui, 'Directors face call to reveal salaries', *South China Morning Post — Business*, 3 December 1999, p. 4.

51. A. Kohler, 'CEOs do soft shoe shuffle', *Australian Financial Review*, 2 November 1999, p. 18; A. Ferguson and T. Watts, 'CEOs tack into stormy waters', *Business Review Weekly*, 23 November 1998; NZPA, 'Chief's pay rise fuels debate', *Australian Financial Review*, 6 January 2004, p. 13; R. Turner, 'The new rules', *Boss*, November 2002, p. 46; and research by the Australian Council of Superannuation Investors, reported in G. Weaven, 'The tide of excess', *BRW*, 28 August–3 September 2003, p. 66.

52. S. Evans, '$6.2m for Southcorp woes', *Australian Financial Review*, 10 September 2003, p. 14; A. Kohler, 'Sour grapes and Southcorp's fate', *Australian Financial Review*, 8–9 March 2003, p. 11; and A. Grigg, 'Homing in on Lambert's folly', *Australian Financial Review*, 7 April 2004, p. 48.

53. A. Choudhury and K. Foley, 'Australian bank's new CEO gets high marks', *International Herald Tribune*, 4 February 2004, p. B4; Bloomberg, 'Police to investigate dealers at hapless NAB', *South China Morning Post*, 16 January 2004, p. 4; S. Oldfield, 'Queries in capital strength dog NAB', *Australian Financial Review*, 8 January 2004, p. 38; S. Oldfield, 'Cicutto's still standing after all the tears', *Australian Financial Review*, 15–16 November 2003, p. 13; A. Cornell, 'Can Frank Cicutto survive?', *Australian Financial Review*, 17–18 January 2004, pp. 18–19; and S. Oldfield, 'Great Scot: NAB pays $21m', *Australian Financial Review*, 28 May 2004, p. 3.

54. T. Harris, 'Executive pay out of step', *Australian Financial Review*, 1 October 2002, p. 70; C. Fox, 'The new pay track', *Boss*, November 2003, p. 42; and G. O'Neill and A. Berry, 'Remuneration of Australian executives: a practitioner review', *Asia Pacific Journal of Human Resources*, vol. 40, no. 2, 2002, p. 229.

55. Cullen Egan Dell survey, reported in M. Carr, 'Directors reject performance link to salaries', *Australian Financial Review*, 29 July 1998, p. 19.

56. J. Reingold and R. Grover, 'The bosses are rolling in it', *Australian Financial Review*, 10–11 April 1999, p. 11; and Agence France-Presse, 'Labor cries foul on Cicutto's payout', *South China Morning Post*, 4 February 2004, p. B6.

57. S. Koudsi, 'Why CEOs are paid so much to beat it', *Fortune*, 29 May 2000, p. 18.

58. G. Koretz, 'Did the CEO deserve the raise?', *Business Week*, 24 April 2000, p. 12; and research by G. Fleming of Australian National University's School of Finance, reported in A. Cornell, 'Salary survey 2002', *Boss*, November 2002, p. 46.

59. D. Katz and R. L. Kahn, *The Social Psychology of Organizations*, John Wiley & Sons, New York, 1966, pp. 355–6.

60. Study by J. Shields, School of Business, University of Sydney, reported in S. Long, 'Ordinary workers moving to performance related pay', *Australian Financial Review*, 24 March 2000, p. 23.

61. V. A. Hoevemeyer, 'Performance based compensation: miracle or warfare', *Personnel Journal*, July 1989, p. 64.

62. G. O'Neill and R. Payne, 'Performance based pay — is it appropriate for Australia?', *Personnel Today*, February 1989, p. 12; D. Torrington, 'Sweets to the sweet: performance related pay in Britain', *International Journal of Employment Studies*, vol. 1, no. 2, 1993, pp. 149–64; and D. Foust, 'CEO pay: nothing succeeds like failure', *Business Week*, 11 September 2000, p. 44.

63. Harper, 'Even among bricklayers, beauty marks the hunks for higher pay', *Asian Wall Street Journal*, 26–27 November 1993, pp. 1, 5; G. Koretz, 'When lawyers are lookers', *Business Week*, 8 January 1996, p. 10; Society for Human Resource Management, 'Reasonable accommodation necessary in "Appearance" policy', *Issues in HR*, January–February 1994, p. 1; G. Koretz, 'Wages that go up in smoke', *Business Week*, 25 March 1996, p. 11; B. Johnson, 'Work overdose produces little for British executives', *Eastern Express*, 1 November 1995, p. 11; N. Gupta and G. D. Jenkins, 'The politics of pay', *Compensation and Benefits Review*, vol. 28, no. 2, 1996, pp. 23–30; and S. Long, 'Fat not just a feminist issue — but a financial one', *Australian Financial Review*, 6 December 2000, p. 35.

64. D. Brookes, 'Merit pay, the hoax', *HR Magazine*, February 1993, p. 117; and D. Brookes, 'Merit pay: does it help or hinder productivity', *HR Focus*, January 1993, p. 13.

65. C. D. Fisher, L. F. Schoenfeldt and J. B. Shaw, op. cit., pp. 612–14.

66. J. M. Ivancevich, *Human Resource Management*, 8th edn, Irwin, Chicago, 2001, p. 325.

67. S. Kerr, 'Risky business: the new pay game', *Fortune*, 22 July 1996, pp. 77–80; and B. Hoffman, 'Strategy remix emphasises "at risk" pay components', *HR Monthly*, December 1996, pp. 14–15.

68. W. Bruce, 'Deciding what's important in pay for performance', *HR Monthly*, March 1997, p. 6.

69. G. Bassett, 'Merit pay increases are a mistake', *Compensation and Benefits Review*, vol. 26, no. 2, 1994, p. 21.

70. A. Mitra, N. Gupta and G. D. Jenkins, 'The case of the invisible merit raise: how people see their pay raises', *Compensation and Benefits Review*, vol. 27, no. 3, 1995, p. 71.

71. A. Mitra, N. Gupta and G. D. Jenkins, op. cit., pp. 75–6.

72. M. Beer, B. Spector, P. R. Lawrence, D. Q. Mills and R. E. Walton, *Human Resource Management: A General Manager's Perspective*, The Free Press, New York, 1985, pp. 424–5.

73. Adapted by the author from J. P. Guthrie and E. P. Cunningham, 'Pay for performance for hourly workers: the Quaker Oats alternative', *Compensation and Benefits Review*, vol. 24, no. 2, 1992, p. 20; and 'ACA: performance based plans get high grades', *Compensation and Benefits Review*, vol. 24, no. 5, 1992, p. 10.

74. 'ACA: performance based plans get high grades', op. cit., pp. 9–10; L. Thornburg, 'Study shows pay for performance plans work', *HR News*, July 1992, p. A15; and R. L. Heneman, *Merit Pay*, Addison Wesley, Reading, Mass., 1992, p. 12.

75. C. Lockyer, 'Pay, performance and reward', in B. Towers (ed.), *The Handbook of Human Resource Management*, Blackwell, Oxford, 1992, ch. 12.

76. G. E. Ledford, 'Paying for the skills, knowledge and competencies of knowledge workers', *Compensation and Benefits Review*, vol. 27, no. 4, 1995, p. 56; and E. E. Lawler III, 'Competencies: a poor foundation for the new pay', *Compensation and Benefits Review*, vol. 28, no. 6, 1996, p. 20.

77. G. E. Ledford Jr, 'The design of skill-based pay plans', in M. L. Rock and L. A. Berger (eds), *The Compensation Handbook*, McGraw-Hill, New York, 1990, p. 199; and R. McPaul, 'Fine tuning competency pay', *HR Monthly*, October 2000, pp. 28–9.

78. G. E. Ledford Jr, 1990, op. cit., p. 200.

79. G. E. Ledford Jr, 1990, op. cit., p. 205.

80. E. E. Lawler III, G. E. Ledford Jr and L. Chang, 'Who uses skill based pay and why', *Compensation and Benefits Review*, vol. 25, no. 2, 1993, pp. 22–6.

81. G. T. Milkovich and J. W. Boudreau, *Human Resource Management*, 8th edn, Irwin, Chicago, 1997, p. 481.

82. G. E. Ledford, 1995, op. cit., p. 57.

83. S. Caudron, 'Master the compensation maze', *Personnel Journal*, June 1993, p. 64J.

84. Based on G. E. Ledford Jr, 1990, op. cit., p. 203; G. T. Milkovich and J. W. Boudreau, op. cit., p. 479–85; and C. D. Fisher, L. F. Schoenfeldt and J. B. Shaw, op. cit., p. 568.

85. Based on G. E. Ledford Jr, 1990, op. cit., p. 203; G. T. Milkovich and J. W. Boudreau, op. cit., pp. 479–85; J. L. Morris, 'Lessons learned in skill based pay', *HR Magazine*, June 1996, pp. 136–42; and K. M. Cofsky, 'Critical keys to competency based pay', *Compensation and Benefits Review*, vol. 25, no. 6, 1993, pp. 46–52.

86. E. E. Lawler III, G. E. Ledford Jr and L. Chang, op. cit., p. 26; G. E. Ledford Jr, 1990, op. cit., p. 217; and R. G. Layman, 'Building a business focus through competency based pay', *Journal of Compensation and Benefits*, vol. 12, no. 1, 1996, pp. 34–9.

87. B. Leonard, 'New ways to pay employees', *HR Magazine*, February 1994, p. 62.

88. R. Stone, 1995, op. cit., p. 582.

89. J. F. Sullivan, 'The future of merit pay programs', *Compensation and Benefits Review*, vol. 20, no. 3, 1988, p. 24.

90. Cited in 'Compensation trends', *Compensation and Benefits Review*, vol. 20, no. 3, 1988, p. 13.

91. R. L. Mathis and J. H. Jackson, *Human Resource Management*, 8th edn, West Publishing, St Paul, 1997, pp. 377–8.

92. Partly based on J. Durie, 'Vivid reminder of BHP value lost', *Australian Financial Review*, 23 May 2003, pp. 66, 84; A. Cornell, 'The great shareholder rip-off', *Australian Financial Review*, 8 March 2002, p. 12; M. Priest, 31 January 2003, op. cit., p. 3; M. Priest, 'CEO pay study: more means less', *Australian Financial Review*, 23 May 2003, p. 8; G. Hughes, 'Top executives can no longer be trusted', *Australian Financial Review*, 27 February 2003, p. 67; S. Evans, 'Anger at $4.4m Lambert payout', *Australian Financial Review*, 26 February 2003, p. 48; and S. Evans, 10 September 2003, op. cit., p. 14.

chapter 13

incentive compensation[1]

Learning objectives

When you have finished studying this chapter, you should be able to:

- Understand the importance of linking incentives to strategic business objectives
- Explain the concept of incentive compensation and why its use is spreading
- Identify the key objectives of incentive compensation plans
- Describe the major types of incentive pay systems and their advantages and disadvantages
- Understand the role of incentive pay in the overall context of employee rewards.

'Of all the big lies out there, the one that corporate executives' pay is linked to the performance of their companies takes the prize.'[2]

Gretchen Morgenson, *International Herald Tribune*

Globalisation, increased competition, and cost and performance pressures have promoted the growing use of flexible compensation programs linked to individual, group or company performance. For example, a basic idea underlying share option plans is that because employees see themselves as owners of the business, they are motivated to work harder. Such incentive compensation is called **at-risk compensation** because, unlike base pay which is 'guaranteed' irrespective of performance, flexible rewards such as bonuses and stock options are contingent upon the successful achievement of specific performance targets.

Relating pay to individual performance has never been as important in Australian compensation practice as it has in the United States. According to one expert, more than two-thirds of US workers are compensated by a mix of **base pay** and performance bonus.[3] Top performers in Microsoft have stock or share **options** valued in the millions. (It is estimated that about one-third of Microsoft employees are millionaires.[4])

Although many Australian companies require some form of performance criteria to be applied before granting options, the evidence indicates that performance standards are subjective and that rewards have balloned for non-performance.[5] This has led them to being referred to as 'soft options' and the personification of easy money.[6] As a result, share options increasingly are regarded as an unsound way to align the interests of employees and shareholders. Primarily, this is because they carry no cost and no actual downside risk. Executives thus share the gains with the shareholders but do not share the losses when things go wrong.[7] One critic caustically comments that when share prices drop, directors start handing out 'effort' bonuses.[8]

Executive bonus schemes are often treated as 'add-ons' to base pay, irrespective of performance.[9] Jodee Rich and Brad Keeling received $15 million prior to the collapse of One.Tel. Likewise, just before Ansett's demise, performance bonuses were paid to 16 senior executives — justified by CEO Gerry Twomey on the grounds that performance goals had been achieved.[10] Such cases and the growing divide between senior executive and ordinary employee compensation have made incentive compensation a controversial social issue subject to increasing public scrutiny.[11]

Many Australians, furthermore, see individual-based performance (or incentive) pay striking at the heart of egalitarian values that stress 'mateship' and worker solidarity.[12] Many public servants, for example, find performance pay divisive and alien to the collective nature of public service work. Consequently, in some departments, all senior staff are given the same performance rating and the same performance pay increase.[13] The NSW Auditor-General found that nearly 60 government CEOs had received bonus payments regardless of whether performance agreements and performance appraisals were in place.[14]

The Australian focus has been on issues such as comparative wage justice, establishing and maintaining award relativities, and ensuring pay equity through equal pay for equal work. The United States has legislation to provide for pay equity, but that country has always had much greater emphasis on rewarding individual effort and contribution. Stanley and Danko also point out that 'it takes considerable courage to work in an environment in which one is compensated according to one's performance'.[15] This has prompted one writer to highlight 'the US notion of equality of opportunity compared with the Australian concern with equality of outcome'.[16] Nevertheless, Australian corporate practice is changing. A study by the Hay Group shows a continuing growth in both the size and incidence of incentive compensation.[17] Hills Industries, for example, has introduced remuneration schemes enabling all employees to participate in the growth and profit of individual business units. Westpac's senior executive remuneration program has three main components: base salary, annual performance bonus and long-term incentives (see figure 13.1 and table 13.1).[18] At Harvey Norman, only 20 per cent of an executive's remuneration is fixed — the rest is based on performance. Says CEO Harvey Norman: 'If you don't perform, you don't deserve to get paid.'[19]

Three factors have prompted both public and private sector organisations to take an active interest in incentive pay. First, Australians are coming to appreciate — and increasingly

Executive share options are an expense to shareholders — they create a transfer of wealth from the owners of the business to the managers without any associated risk.

Should non-performing executives receive multimillion-dollar payouts for destroying jobs and shareholder wealth?

demand — the opportunity to be rewarded for their individual contribution to an organisation's success (see figure 13.2).[20]

Second, since the introduction of enterprise bargaining, the onus is increasingly on individual enterprises to achieve workplace productivity gains. This has led organisations to review their work practices and to include job redesign and variable pay systems in their award restructuring agenda. Says Dr John Shields from Sydney University's Work and Organisational Study Group, 'There is a definite movement from time-based payment to individualized pay-at-risk for ordinary workers'.[21] The issue now is not so much whether the concept is acceptable, but how to design variable and incentive pay systems so that they meet the needs of each organisation.

HOW WESTPAC REWARDS EXECUTIVE PERFORMANCE

Independent remuneration consultants are used to support both the Board Remuneration Committee and the CEO in ensuring that our pay and reward policies reflect market practice.

The structure of our executive pay and reward system

Executive pay and reward is made up of four parts:
- base pay
- short-term performance incentives
- long-term equity-linked performance incentives
- other compensation, such as superannuation.

The combination of these comprises the executive's total compensation.

Base pay

Executives are offered a competitive base pay that reflects the fixed component of pay and rewards. Base pay is set to reflect the marketplace for each position. It is generally not revised annually unless an executive has been promoted or there has been a marked structural shift in marketplace rates.

Short-term performance incentives

If individual performance objectives are met — always designed around key and specific business goals — a short-term incentive may be provided.

Long-term equity-linked performance incentives

Our long-term incentives for the CEO and senior executives are designed to align their financial interests with those of our shareholders by making use of carefully designed share-based incentives. We believe that this will provide an extra incentive to ensure Westpac has a healthy and growing share price, and delivers sustained growth in value for all shareholders.

Other benefits — superannuation

All executives and staff are required to be members of one of Westpac's staff superannuation funds.

Figure 13.1 How Westpac rewards executive performance

Source Westpac, *Concise Annual Report*, Sydney, 2003, p. 53.

Third, there is an increasing demand for pay structures to provide a more direct link between employee rewards and organisational objectives. Terms such as new pay, strategic pay, **contribution-based pay** and alternative reward strategies are prominent in the literature promoting greater use of incentive pay for employees.[22] Traditional merit pay plans are criticised because the true merit component is only a small proportion. Also, because each annual merit increase is incorporated into base salary and becomes the basis of the next year's pay increase calculation, traditional merit pay plans contribute to increased fixed remuneration overheads.

Incentive pay plans are not new. Despite varying degrees of success, if properly designed they can play an important role in motivating employees and recognising performance.[23] Incentive pay plans can effectively focus employee attention on those objectives that the organisation wishes to reinforce through its pay practices. It is critical that the design of a variable or incentive pay plan considers the results being measured and ensures that the incentives provided are appropriate.[24]

HR managers should remember that incentive-based pay is not the prime means for getting employees to work to their fullest capacity. If it is the only motivator, then there are other, different issues at stake — for example, a poor work climate, unsuitable management style, faulty job design and a lack of clarity about job duties and responsibilities. Incentive

Contribution-based pay A pay plan designed to directly link rewards to the contributions made by an individual employee.

compensation is not a panacea for all the ills of the organisation. Second, HR managers must remember that performance-based pay systems need to be straightforward in design and simple to communicate. Incentive pay plans most often fail because they are too complex.

| Table 13.1 | Westpac's senior executive compensation |

	BASE PAY[1] ($)	SHORT-TERM INCENTIVES[1, 2] ($)	OTHER[3] ($)	TOTAL CASH REMUNERATION ($)	TOTAL EQUITY-BASED REMUNERATION[4] ($)
David Morgan Managing Director and Chief Executive Officer	1 575 000	1 700 000	645 681	3 920 681	3 447 277
Ilana Atlas Group Executive People and Performance	512 100	325 000	45 695	882 795	423 270
Philip Chronican Chief Financial Officer	525 000	550 000	117 824	1 192 824	1 040 382
David Clarke Chief Executive Officer BT Financial Group	750 000	650 000	0	1 400 000	2 237 192
Philip Coffey Group Executive Westpac Institutional Bank	550 000	705 000	49 310	1 304 310	579 438
Michael Coomer Group Executive Business and Technology Solutions and Services	625 000	550 000	56 034	1 231 034	561 671
Michael Pratt Group Executive Business and Consumer Banking	674 875	865 000	0	1 539 875	378 148
Ann Sherry Group Executive New Zealand and Pacific Banking	533 375	560 000	406 083	1 499 458	663 718

1. Base Pay is the total cost to Westpac of salary and packaged benefits (including motor vehicles and parking) received in the year to 30 September 2003 and includes fringe benefits tax. Short-term incentive figures reflect annual performance awards accrued but not yet paid in respect of the year ended 30 September 2003.
2. The amount above is the entire short-term incentive (STI) relating to performance for this year. Where actual STI for senior executives exceeds their target STI, a portion of the STI is deferred. The deferred portion is the amount over the executive's target STI and the deferral period is up to three years from the first payment date. A portion of the deferred STI payment becomes due each year. Interest is applied to the balance outstanding each year and paid annually. Amounts paid in each year in respect of deferred STI are not included as part of the executives remuneration. In certain circumstances, any unpaid deferred payment (including interest) may be forfeited.
3. Other remuneration is determined on the basis of the cost to Westpac and includes notional surchargeable superannuation contributions (as determined by the Plan's actuary) for those executives who are members of the Westpac Staff Superannuation Plan, housing and other benefits (such as commencement incentives, relocation costs, staff discount on Westpac products and separation payments) and all fringe benefits tax.
4. The amount included in equity-based remuneration relates to the current year amortisation of the fair value of all share options, performance options and performance share rights granted (in the current and previous years) that have either vested during the financial year or remain unvested at 30 September 2003 and the increase in value of vested cash settled equity-based remuneration arrangements. The calculation of fair value for the purpose of the above table follows Australian Securities and Investments Commission (ASIC) guidelines issued in June 2003 on the value of options that should be included in the disclosure of the emoluments of each director and each senior executive. Included in David Morgan's equity-based remuneration is an amount related to the increase in value in the year ended 30 September 2003 of stock appreciation rights granted in 1997 in lieu of share options.

Source Westpac, *Concise Annual Report*, Sydney, 2003, p. 51.

GUARANTEED	
BASE PAY	Weekly wage Monthly salary + Step increases Cost-of-living increases
AT-RISK	
Individual incentives	Merit pay increases Sales commissions Piece-rate incentives Individual bonuses Share options
Group incentives	Group incentives Group bonuses
Company-wide incentives	Gainsharing plans (Rucker, Scanlon) Profit-sharing plans Employee share options

Figure 13.2 Pay components
Source Asia Pacific Management Co. Ltd, 2004.

Why introduce incentive compensation?

Organisations introduce **incentive compensation** for essentially four reasons:
1. *To promote employee identification with the organisation's objectives.*
   Many organisations attempt to focus employee attention on their strategic business objectives by linking the achievement of objectives to employee rewards. This builds employee commitment and gives employees a 'stake' in the overall success of the organisation (as well as helping the organisation to achieve its strategic business objectives). Incentive plans designed to build employee commitment in this way include annual bonuses and employee **profit sharing**.
2. *To encourage individual, team or business unit performance.*
   The aim here is to make the incentive reward dependent on specific work outcomes that the employee, or the work group, directly affects. (This is often referred to as maintaining a direct 'line of sight' between employee performance and pay.) Examples of this type of variable pay include sales **commission**, production **piece-rates** and other such incentives linked to agreed targets.
3. *To control fixed compensation costs.*
   One way of controlling compensation costs is to designate a portion of pay as **'at-risk' compensation** if predetermined business unit, team or individual objectives are not achieved. Thus, the organisation gears its total compensation costs to meeting its objectives. If the objectives are met, employees receive their full pay; if the objectives are exceeded, they receive more; and if the organisation does not meet its objectives, some or all of the 'at-risk' component is not paid.
4. *To increase remuneration competitiveness.*
   Another reason for adopting incentive pay is to make the organisation's compensation practices more competitive than other organisations' practices. This provides a visible

Incentive compensation Compensation that is linked to performance by rewarding employees for actual results achieved instead of seniority or hours worked.

Profit sharing A plan whereby employees share in the company's profits.

Commission An individual incentive system whereby an employee is paid either a percentage or flat sum amount on the revenue of sales volume they generate.

Piece-rates Incentive system in which compensation is based on the number of units produced or sold.

'At-risk' compensation Variable rewards that are payable only when a performance target is met.

signal to employees that the organisation is willing to reward good performance at a significantly higher level than do other organisations. The aim is to use variable pay to provide employees with the opportunity of earning well above their regular salary levels.

Regardless of its reasons for adopting an incentive-based pay system, an organisation will expect to see improvements in performance. Key performance indicators may be expressed as quantitative measures related to an organisation's financial or operating performance. Examples include a return on assets managed, revenue growth, a share price increase, a reduction in the unit cost of production, higher stock turnover and reduced lost time from accidents. Alternatively, many performance-based pay systems reward employees for their performance using qualitative measures. Examples include teamwork, employee attitudes and customer satisfaction ratings.

As a general rule, senior managers have their performance measured against indicators of the overall financial performance of the business unit or function under their control (for example, net operating profit after tax, return on equity, gain in share price and economic value added).[25] This is consistent with the fact that the impact of these jobs is much broader and is likely to affect the overall wellbeing of the organisation. Further down the hierarchy, performance indicators tend to focus more on work group indicators (for example, team productivity, branch sales) or highly specific personal goals (for example, number of units produced per shift).

Types of plan

There are a variety of ways of categorising incentive compensation plans. A useful introduction to the range of variable performance pay systems is to consider them under the headings of individual, small group (for example, work team), large group (for example, business unit or organisation wide) and recognition programs. There is considerable scope and latitude for plan design under each of these headings. Ultimately, the choice of plan — who it rewards, for what and how — depends on the objectives to be achieved, the management processes to be supported and reinforced, and what is likely to be successful within the existing structure and culture of the organisation.

Bonus versus incentive

Bonus A discretionary reward provided after the achievement of a goal.

A **bonus** is a discretionary reward provided after the event. It may be awarded for a well-defined accomplishment or it may simply be given to recognise 'extra effort' or 'a job well done'. A bonus is determined and given after the job is done and it makes no guarantee that future work or effort will be rewarded similarly.

Incentive A reward to be given if a specified goal is achieved.

Whereas a bonus is reactive, an **incentive** is proactive. The aim of an incentive is to focus an employee's behaviour by establishing performance objectives and rewarding the achievement of these objectives. Thus, an incentive provides a very direct message to an employee: 'If you achieve this level of performance, you will receive this amount of reward.'

Because a bonus is determined after the fact and is discretionary, it does not require clear performance measurement systems. An incentive system, by its very definition, depends on some formal means of measuring performance. Consequently, an incentive system is more likely to result in improved performance because it clarifies job expectations and directly links pay to performance.

Pay-for-performance link

Attitude surveys suggest that employees perceive only a weak link between performance and pay.[26] Rather, pay is seen as dependent on non-performance factors such as position and length of service. Variable pay systems and particularly incentive-type plans aim to strengthen the perceived link between pay and performance.

The relationship between pay and performance is especially effective when it is based on those aspects of the work that are under the individual employee's direct control and influence — if you sell or produce more, you earn more! This establishes an immediate relationship between results and rewards. The relationship between employee control and influence over the end result is referred to as the **line of sight**. The more immediate the employee's line of sight, the more likely it is that the incentive plan will generate improved performance. An incentive that rewards a manager for the performance of their department has a stronger line of sight (or pay-for-performance link) than one that rewards the manager for the overall performance of the organisation.

Line of sight The relationship between employee control and influence over the end result. The more direct the relationship, the stronger the line of sight.

Variable and 'at-risk' pay

Any pay system that provides a bonus or incentive is a variable pay system. The bonus or incentive paid for a particular period may or may not be paid the next time period. The amount of the bonus or incentive varies and cannot be predetermined. Clearly, if the amount of bonus or incentive does not vary or if it can be determined beforehand, regardless of the results to be achieved, the link between pay and performance is nonexistent.

Some variable pay systems allow the bonus or incentive to be an 'add-on' to normal pay. If an employee's normal pay is $60 000, for example, then the bonus or incentive is paid on top of this amount. However, other systems are based on the notion of some portion of pay being 'at-risk' against specified levels of performance. A production superintendent's regular salary is $60 000, for example, but her monthly pay is based on $50 000 with the remaining $10 000 to be paid out when she achieves predetermined objectives. In this case, the variable and 'at-risk' component is the $10 000 incentive to reach the required performance objectives.

Some employees find the idea of 'at-risk' pay and pay for performance stressful. Should this be of any concern to a company?

A clear principle in the design of an 'at-risk' incentive system is that the employee must have the opportunity to earn more than the target amount (more than $60 000 in the production superintendent's example). A good rule of thumb is to allow twice the amount at-risk for above-target achievement (that is, the production superintendent should be able to earn up to $80 000).

Individual incentive plans

Individual incentive plans are those that reward the employee for reaching or exceeding specific performance criteria. They can be used only where there are accurate and reliable measures of individual performance. The prime objectives of **individual incentives** are to increase individual performance and to permit the pay system to actively discriminate in favour of top performers.

Individual incentives Incentives directly linked to individual (as opposed to group or team) performance.

Two conditions need to exist for individual incentive plans to succeed. First, the organisation must emphasise individual contribution as distinct from team or work group effort. Second, the job must be designed to allow each employee to work independently and with autonomy and discretion.

A basic individual incentive plan is designed so an employee's pay depends solely on their output. In Australia, the agricultural industry has traditionally made extensive use of this form of pay. Sheep shearers and fruit and vegetable pickers, for example, have always been paid on their individual output. Similarly, a door-to-door sales representative, whose pay consists only of a commission on sales revenue or volume, is another example of an employee working under an individual incentive pay system.

Today, it is more usual to use a combination of a minimum base salary and a **variable pay component**. Many sales representatives, for example, receive a retainer with commission. A major consideration in the design of sales compensation plans is the relative amounts (the 'mix') of fixed and variable pay. If the base salary is high, the incentive is not likely to commence until the person comes close to achieving their predetermined targets for sales revenue or volume. If the fixed component is low, the variable component will cut in much earlier, possibly with the first dollar or unit sold.

Variable pay component That part of pay that is not guaranteed and is at-risk; that is, it is paid only if the performance target is met.

Individual incentive plans can be categorised according to the way in which the employee's performance objectives are set. Generally, there are three criteria for setting performance objectives:

1. *Internal benchmark:* performance must meet or exceed some past performance level established within the organisation. The process of setting performance on the basis of internal benchmarks can be applied from shop floor to management employees. Variable pay plans based on this type of performance measure are typically found in direct operational areas where there is production, processing or sale of some clearly defined output. It is critical for incentive systems based on improvement over past performance that accurate baseline data are available to establish the benchmark standard.
2. *External benchmark:* performance must meet or exceed some performance level established outside the organisation. These performance measures are usually more global and tend to be used for technical, professional and managerial employees. The aim is to increase performance relative to a general industry standard or compared with a selected group of organisations.
3. *Strategic business objectives:* performance is measured against the strategic business objectives set for the organisation. Middle- and senior-level managers typically have their performance objectives based on the strategic objectives of the organisation. The performance requirements vary according to the specific accountability of each manager and may range from successful divestment of low-performing business units or high return on assets managed to specific profit or share price targets.

Individual incentive plans are the most common form of variable pay currently used in Australian and overseas firms.[27] They can have a dramatic impact on individual and organisational performance. However, they must be designed with care if they are to realise their potential in the workplace. Their advantages and disadvantages are outlined in figure 13.3.

INDIVIDUAL INCENTIVE PLANS

Advantages
- Provide a clear link between individual pay and work contribution.
- Discriminate in favour of high performers.
- Can have a significant impact on key performance indicators such as productivity, quality and sales.
- Link total compensation costs to organisational objectives.

Disadvantages
- May encourage individualism and non-productive competition.
- Require comprehensive and credible systems of individual performance measurement. If these are not already in place, they may be expensive to design and introduce.
- Can sometimes end up paying for performance that would have been achieved without an incentive plan.
- May leave the organisation no better off if improvements from one employee are offset by another's poor performance.
- May become an administrative burden.

Figure 13.3 The advantages and disadvantages of individual incentive plans

The following key principles need to be considered in the design and implementation of an individual incentive plan:
- *Simple design and clear goals.* The plan should be simple to understand and to communicate and should be based on measurable performance objectives. The objective of an individual incentive plan is to focus employee behaviour on highly specific targets, so simplicity and clarity are essential.
- *Identified source of funding.* How are the incentives to be funded? A well-designed plan will fund incentive payments from increases in productivity (or decreases in costs). Incentive plans that do not have clearly defined funding sources become an additional cost overhead and are unlikely to succeed in the medium or longer term.

- *Performance tracking and management systems.* Effective incentive plans are supported by good data tracking systems that enable employees to monitor their progress. Supervisors and managers should reinforce this with constructive feedback and assistance so employees can maximise their performance and earning opportunities.
- *Frequent reward.* The best plans pay employees frequently. The closer the link between performance and reward, the more effective the system will be in improving and maintaining individual focus and direction.
- *Pay for performance.* The most successful plans continually emphasise the link between individual performance and reward. Similarly, successful plans pay strictly on the basis of results achieved. All employees quickly learn that the rewards are there if they meet or exceed performance targets. Conversely, there are no consolation prizes if employees do not perform at the required levels.
- *Periodic review.* It is necessary to ensure that the plan continues to meet the organisation's objectives and employee needs. A periodic review of the plan from a business perspective is a chance to evaluate its cost and balance that against increased productivity or decreased costs. It is also important for the organisation to know whether employees support the plan and whether it provides them with appropriate rewards for their efforts.
- *No shifting of the goal posts.* Constant changing of the targets to be achieved can lead to employee frustration and disillusionment (especially if targets are moved upwards because employees are perceived by management to be earning 'too much').

NEWSBREAK

The pay puzzle

By David James

Public outrage over excessive executive pay, severance payouts and stock options has created much political heat, but it is doing little to protect the needs of shareholders. The reason? Many boards are no closer to understanding how to structure incentives to ensure high-quality senior executive performance.

Much attention is given to well-known examples of board 'weakness' in permitting big salary increases for chief executives, and to the widening gap between the rewards of employees and senior executives. But the deeper problem is not what executives are being paid; it is how they are being paid. Boards are failing to create sound financial incentives. It is even questionable that monetary rewards should be the focus in any case: most senior executives rise to the top of their industry for a wide variety of reasons, of which remuneration is only one.

A central puzzle in the governance of public companies is 'agency theory': finding the right way to align the interests of shareholders with the interests of senior management. It is assumed that some form of share ownership, or performance target, is, in addition to the base salary, necessary to create the right kind of incentives. High executive rewards are considered acceptable, or at least defensible, as long as shareholders also get rich. There is an alignment between the interests of the owners and the managers.

A recent survey by the Labor Council of New South Wales, *The Bucks Stop Here: Private-Sector Remuneration in Australia*, caused a stir by offering evidence that incentives seem to work poorly in Australia's larger corporations. Assessed as the 'human resource managers' of senior executives, boards are underperforming. It may even be that in paying high executive salaries, boards are inevitably attracting chief executives who are more interested in personal financial rewards than the building of healthy businesses.

The survey examines the relationship between pay and performance using three measures: the return on equity, changes in the share price, and changes to earnings per share. It concludes that the increases in executive remuneration — which grew from 22 times average weekly earnings in 1992, to 74 times in 2002 — represented 'systematic rent extraction' rather than 'optimal principal-agent bargains'. That is, senior executives are being paid more regardless of their performance, rather than as a way of aligning the interests of shareholders and senior managers.

(continued)

However, high executive pay is largely beside the point. Harvard Business School's Professor Michael Jensen, in his book *Foundations of Organisational Strategy*, writes that the crucial point is not what executives are paid, it is how they are paid. 'The critics have it wrong. There are serious problems with chief executive compensation, but "excessive" pay is not the biggest issue … in most publicly held companies; the compensation of top executives is virtually independent of performance. Is it any wonder that so many chief executives act like bureaucrats rather than the value-maximising entrepreneurs companies need to enhance their standing in world markets?'

There is a focus now on 'shareholder activism': financial institutions acting more aggressively to curtail greedy or incompetent senior executives. The problem is, this is not strictly shareholder activism; it is funds manager activism, conducted supposedly on behalf of shareholders. The stockmarket tends to be controlled by two groups of managers, neither of which owns substantial portions of what they control: senior executives and the managers of the larger funds. Adam Lewis, senior partner at consultants McKinsey & Company, says: 'Chief executives should pay a lot less attention to analysts, who are looking myopically at short-term, Australian domestic operations.'

That intermediaries (institutions and funds managers) mostly represent shareholders' interests has profound, and rarely explored, implications for the proper incentive structures for senior executives. Agency theory is typically seen as the problem of finding the best interaction between senior executives and shareholders. Attend any annual general meeting, and there is no lack of shareholders ready to criticise management. But

usually these individuals control very little stock.

The dominant shareholdings are typically in the hands of the large institutions and even if they decide to be more active, they are acting only on what they think are the real shareholders' interests. In this sense, they differ little from the chief executives. The financial structure is designed in such a way that direct shareholder influence is rarely available, despite the rise in direct share ownership in Australia in the past decade.

Worse, there is another interpreter of shareholder interest: boards. Boards mediate between the large stockholders (institutions of fund managers) and senior executives. Little surprise that they start to mirror the mostly short-term interests of the funds and that their decisions start to reflect the priorities of performance tables rather than the long-term interests of the company.

One problem is the shortening of senior management tenure, which makes it less likely that the (mostly long-term) savings interests of shareholders will match the more short-term interests of chief executives. It certainly makes it less likely that the interests of the corporation will be well served. The corporation may not be 'permanent' (in contrast with its 'transitory' shareholders), as management guru Peter Drucker once claimed. But it is supposed to be around longer than three years.

Bernard Cronin, the chief executive of the Australian Institute of Management, says shortening tenures have changed the dynamics of selecting chief executives. 'The board appoints the chief executive, and the board knows that, on average, chief executives don't last more than three years. And the board is under pressure to maximise the return to shareholders.

So, in three years, the chief executive has to provide good dividends and increase shareholder value.

'To get a person to do that — which, let's face it, is not a natural thing — you have to pay over the odds. I do think some of the payouts are obscene, but if you don't provide an extraordinary package you won't get them [quality chief executives].'

Three main methods are used to supposedly align the interests of shareholders and chief executives: share ownership, performance bonuses and stock options. Jensen argues that the most powerful link between shareholder wealth and executive wealth is direct stock ownership. Bonuses, he says, do not cause big fluctuations in chief executive compensation (because they are not sufficiently sensitive to differences in a company's performance to meaningfully affect the behavior of a senior executive).

'Compensation for chief executives is no more variable than compensation for hourly and salaried employees', Jensen writes. 'Most commentators look at chief executive stock ownership from one of two perspectives — the dollar value of the chief executive's holdings or the value of his shares as a percentage of his annual cash compensation. But when trying to understand the incentive consequences of stock ownership, neither of these measures counts for much. What really matters is the percentage of the company's outstanding shares the chief executive owns. By controlling a meaningful percentage of the total corporate equity, senior managers experience a direct and powerful 'feedback effect' from changes in market value.'

By Jensen's best measure, share ownership, only three of the 20 highest-paid executives in Australia in 2001–02 have the best kind of incentive for reflecting shareholder interests: Rupert Murdoch of News Corporation, and Frank Lowy and Peter Lowy of Westfield Holdings. All three have large shareholdings in the companies they manage. Six of the 20 top executives, at June 30, 2002, owned no shares in the companies they led.

Among the 20 highest-paid chief executives in 2001–02, the balance between bonuses and base salary was about equal: on average, $3.67 million and $3.73 million respectively. This supports Jensen's argument that bonuses do not vary sufficiently to create genuine incentive for senior executives.

However, stock options were worth much more. Among the top 20 executives, the average value of stock options was almost 10 times that of their base salary. Options are a questionable form of incentive because they reward executives only on the upside (if the shares reach the strike price for the options). The only penalty for poor performance is missing out on a windfall. Options are also less sensitive than share ownership to changes in company performance. Jensen says options, on average, change by less than $1 when the share price changes by $1: he estimates 60c as the average figure.

The Labor Council of NSW report lists five other problems with stock options. The link between rewards and performance is remote because there are so many uncontrolled variables affecting the share price. They often represent only a temporary form of ownership because once the options are exercised, the shares can be sold, misaligning the generally long-term interests of investors and the shorter-term interests of executives.

Options dilute the shareholder equity by creating more shares (although this is not of itself unusual: it happens whenever there is a share bonus issue). They are a cost to the company (although exactly what the cost is remains problematic because they are not strictly an expense but a derivative). And options can encourage market manipulation. The Labor Council report says: 'Options invite market manipulation. Simply by releasing overly optimistic forward profit figures or by raising the possibility of a takeover, the executive can make a windfall gain.'

The greatest misalignment of shareholder and senior executive interests is also that which attracts the most controversy: large redundancy payouts. Almost by definition, this severs the link between shareholder and executive interests by mitigating the pain of failure (a pain no doubt deeply felt by shareholders). If boards consider large redundancy payouts necessary to get good-quality executives, then they should probably spend a lot of time examining their selection methods.

Agency theory has shortcomings; it tends to concentrate on chief executives or senior executives. Although the quality of leadership is vital to a company's performance, success equally depends on how the whole staff performs. A survey by the consulting firm William Mercer suggests that average chief executive remuneration in Australia is a quarter that of British chief executives and a fifth of the level in the US. By world standards, Australian executive remuneration is not excessive.

The widening gap

But the appearance of greater inequality has implications for the management of companies that should be of great interest to shareholders. The Labor Council report says the average pay of the 50 highest-paid chief executives rose from 22 times average annual full-time adult earnings in 1992 to 74 times in 2002. 'The decade of the 1990s witnessed a transfer of wealth from ordinary workers to executives via corporate cost cutting via downsizing'.

The irony was that much of this downsizing happened to middle-class savers who indirectly hold shares through the institutions. Those same institutions were putting pressure on senior executives to cut costs. Although this may have encouraged greater efficiency, the short-term gain has created long-term difficulties. The Labor Council report says: 'The implication is that if senior management truly want employee commitment and involvement, then the trend to wider pay inequality between senior management and ordinary employees will have to be reversed.'

The challenges of corporate governance extend beyond shareholders. There is an increasing pressure on companies to reflect the interests of the wider community as well as shareholders. Even if the 'agency problem' — the aligning of shareholder and executive incentives — is resolved, it may still not be enough.

Cronin says large companies are now walking a tightrope between being a good corporate citizen and the demands of an increasingly aggressive financial community and shareholders. 'So if you could get the perfect package where everyone's interests are looked after, and where the community of shareholders is catered for, would you attract the right people? You just have to use common sense to work it out so the stakeholders benefit.'

Source BRW, 19–25 June 2003, pp. 64–6.

Small-group incentive plans

Small-group incentives
Incentives designed to reward work teams, project groups or departments.

The key principles outlined earlier also apply to the reward of small groups (for example, work teams, project groups and departments). The focus on **small-group incentives** has increased markedly in the past decade or so. This reflects several important changes in the design and management of work. First, complex technologies and highly competitive business environments have led to greater reliance on specific-purpose project teams in some industries (for example, information technology and defence). Second, there has been a worldwide trend of downsizing in private and public sector organisations, thus reducing the levels of management and creating flatter organisational structures that focus on the work team and self-management. Third, research and experience have shown that work group effectiveness is strongly correlated with employee involvement, communication and a supportive management style.[28]

In this environment, small-group incentives can provide a highly effective link between pay and performance. An important aspect of small-group incentives is their ability to increase flexibility in job assignment by focusing on team accomplishments rather than individual ones. This promotes a strong group perspective rather than individual focus. The performance objectives of work groups are similar to those of individual incentive plans and relate to financial, productivity and other specific targets. The key difference is the deliberate encouragement of a group or team ethos.

Gainsharing

Gainsharing An incentive system that shares the gains from productivity improvements with the employees who made the improvements.

Gainsharing is a small-group incentive system that shares the productivity improvements with the employees who make the improvements. It is one of the fastest-growing pay-for-performance reward systems.[29] The plan involves measuring improvements in performance over some agreed baseline data, calculating the financial impact of any improvements (typically measured in reduced costs) and sharing the financial gain with employees. Gainsharing plans operate in addition to the normal wage structure. The aim is to create a work climate in which employees benefit financially from increased productivity. Thus, increased productivity and employee rewards are clearly linked.

The Letter to the Editor provides a provocative viewpoint. Do you agree? See 'What's your view?' on page 509.

Letter to the Editor

Incentive plans discriminate against those who value quality of life

Dear Editor,

I believe that the trend towards incentive plans is a worrying feature of contemporary organisational reward systems. As with all management fads and fashions, incentives may be worthwhile for some employees, but I find them dissatisfying in a number of ways.

Unlike many of the 'hyper' Type A individuals who populate our companies, I am a more relaxed person who values quality of life over level of income. Don't get me wrong — I am happy to work as hard as the next person, but long experience in the work force has led me to place less value on the symbols and 'trinkets' associated with many incentive programs. I would rather put in a reasonable but not excessive number of hours and aim to live a balanced and harmonious home and work life.

One problem with incentive plans is that they seem to create a workplace that reminds me of one of those *Survivor* television programs. It's all about the survival of the fittest, and the single-minded pursuit of goals appears to be the order of the day. I would much prefer the older way of working, where people looked after each other and helped their colleagues during periods of high workload and on occasions where family problems required a little time out of the office. This type of cooperation is now a distant memory in my workplace.

Another problem is that incentive plans push people into working excessive hours. Most evenings, I seem to be the first to leave the office, and when I drive past our office building at night and even on weekends I often see colleagues working themselves to the bone in an effort to meet their incentive targets. This can't be good for anyone. It can't be good for the physical and mental health of my overworked colleagues, it can't be good for their families and friends, and it can't be good for our organisation, since it will surely lose out in the longer term as staff reduce the quality of their work in exchange for higher quantities of work.

With the pressures of new technologies, the opening of global markets and the constant rush to release new products and services more quickly than in the past, organisations are far more stressful and intense places to work than ever before. The trend towards incentive plans only serves to make things worse, and does nothing for anyone's quality of life. As the saying goes, no one on their deathbed regrets not having spent more time in the office!

A reflective, older middle manager

Source David Poole, University of Western Sydney.

The earliest gainsharing plan — the **Scanlon plan** — was named after Joe Scanlon, a union official in a US steel mill.[30] The mill was losing money and on the verge of closing. Scanlon proposed a system of joint union–management involvement aimed at improving the operating processes and productivity of the plant to make it profitable. Interestingly, the original plan focused on joint involvement and employee communication only; sharing financial benefits was a second step added when the mill became profitable again (see figure 13.4).

Scanlon's emphasis on participative management and employee involvement is a critical aspect of gainsharing plans. Research conducted on existing pay plans shows that the correlation between productivity and pay is strongest where there is a commitment to employee involvement and an open management style that supports participative management.[31]

The Scanlon plan defines productivity as 'payroll costs per dollar of net sales'. The financial gain (productivity increase) comes from achieving the same or better production levels for the period with lower payroll costs than in the agreed baseline data. Whatever financial gain is made is shared between the employees and the organisation. A typical Scanlon plan split is 75 per cent to employees and 25 per cent to the organisation. Payments to employees are made on a regular basis (such as monthly or quarterly). But usually not all the employee share is paid out at the end of the payment period: a portion of the employee share is held in

Scanlon plan A gainsharing plan designed to link employee rewards to the firm's performance.

a reserve to offset periods when there is no gain. The aim is to even out employee payments over the year. The residual amount in reserve is paid out to participating employees at the end of the plan year.

Gross sales for period	5 000 000
Less returns	112 500
Net sales	4 887 500
Plus stock on hand	437 500
Value of production for period	5 325 000
Baseline payroll costs (25 per cent of value of production)	1 331 250
Actual payroll costs for period	1 064 100
Bonus pool	267 150
Organisation's share of bonus pool (30 per cent)	80 145
Employee share of bonus pool (70 per cent)	187 005
Payment to reserve fund (25 per cent of 70 per cent)	46 751
Payment available for distribution to employees	140 254
Actual payroll costs for period	1 064 100
Gainsharing percentage (140 254/1 064 100)	13.18%

Figure 13.4 An example of a Scanlon plan

Rucker plans Gainsharing plans that calculate employee gains using a value-added formula.

Scanlon plans are only one example of gainsharing plans. **Rucker plans**, named after US economist Allan Rucker, calculate their gains on a value-added formula.[32] Similarly, Improshare[TM] plans measure gains on the basis of standard hours for production (based on industrial engineering calculations) against actual hours taken.[33] Overall, there is a general move away from predefined formulae to custom-designed approaches that reinforce the link between pay and performance within the particular work group.[34] This trend recognises that each work situation is different and that the overriding objective is to encourage all employees to use their combined skills and talents to solve the particular problems and challenges present in their own work environment.

Paying for quality and customer service

Small-group incentives are increasingly being used as a means of rewarding work teams for achievements in quality and customer service. Typically, manufacturing companies focus on product quality while service organisations such as banks and hotels focus on customer service. Each team member shares equally in the incentive pool as predetermined targets in quality or customer service are met.

Total quality management (TQM) Involves an organisation-wide commitment to continuous improvement and satisfying customer needs.

Merit pay Any pay increase awarded to an employee based on their individual performance.

The role of performance measurement and incentives (particularly individual performance appraisal and individual incentives) is a controversial issue in **total quality management (TQM)**. W. Edwards Deming, the founder of TQM, has always opposed performance appraisal and **merit pay** being linked to improvements in quality.[35] A basic tenet of the TQM movement is that the work system or process is the primary determinant of performance and thus is the main source of any off-standard variance. According to Deming, attempts to measure or reward individual performance based on the output of the system detract from the need for a total group effort. TQM recognises the dependence on colleagues, equipment, operating policies and procedures and a range of other factors that can positively or adversely affect performance. Deming describes individual performance evaluations and individual merit pay plans as '... one of the deadly diseases of management'.[36]

Others argue that TQM and an organisation's financial performance are related, so there should be a clear link between pay and quality.[37] Consequently, with the widespread focus on quality and customer service, many companies have used small-group incentives to meet Deming's requirement for a group (rather than individual) focus on quality performance and reward. The approach is to link pay and quality through specifically designed work-team incentive systems. This has two significant advantages. First, the TQM emphasis on team or group performance provides a simple and logical basis for an incentive pay system. Second, incentive payments can be linked to key quality performance indicators — such as a reduction in defects and scrap — and key customer service performance indicators — such as a reduction in customer complaints.

Incentive pay for project teams

Workplace redesign has shifted the emphasis away from individual performance and more towards teams and work groups.[38] Consequently, project teams are now used extensively in many organisations. Generally, the key performance measures for project work are completion on time and within budget. This usually allows the overall task to be divided into 'milestones' that define specific time frames and budgets for each stage of the project. In this respect, project work is often ideally suited to small-group incentives.

This can be illustrated by using the example of an organisation planning the release of a new computer product. First, the milestone events required to meet the timing schedule are identified. Next, management must determine when the group bonuses will be paid (usually when the various groups in the project team meet their schedules). A possible incentive plan that could be applied in this situation is shown in table 13.2. The advantages and disadvantages of such a plan are set out in figure 13.5.[39]

Table 13.2	An example of a project-team incentive plan		
PROJECT MILESTONES	**TIME SCHEDULE**	**PERFORMANCE CRITERIA**	**ELIGIBLE GROUP**
Feasibility study to management	8 weeks from commencement	On time	Project manager
Completion of systems design	12 weeks	On time and within specifications	Systems group
Completion of applications programming	20 weeks	On time and within specifications	Applications group
Completion of hardware selection and planning	24 weeks	On time and within specifications and budget	Operations group
Completion of software programming	20 weeks	On time and within specifications	Software group
Completion of hardware/software installation	12 weeks	On time and within specifications	Operations and software groups
Systems test	8 weeks	On time and within specifications	Project team
Product release	6 weeks	On time and within specifications	Project team
Handover to Marketing Department	2 weeks	On time	Project manager

Large-group (organisation-wide) incentive plans

Many organisations choose to introduce variable pay systems that cover all employees. These organisation-wide plans often work in addition to individual or small-group incentives. Such plans are typically based on one or two broad performance indicators such as achievement of a budget or profit. The principles of designing large-group incentives generally follow those applicable to individual and small-group incentives.

Figure 13.5 The advantages and disadvantages of small-group incentive plans

Large-group incentives
Designed to cover large groups of employees. Typically use broad achievement measures such as profit or sales.

Large-group incentives usually take the form of a bonus plan, an incentive plan or an 'at-risk' incentive. As previously described, a bonus is simply a discretionary amount that is determined and paid at the end of an operating period. If the organisation has had a successful year, for example, it may decide to award a lump-sum bonus of 5 per cent of base pay in recognition of the efforts of all employees. Most bonus plans make little or no distinction between individual contributions, with all employees receiving the same percentage bonus.

Bonus plans allow employees to share in the success of the organisation and they promote a favourable organisational image, but there are some consistent criticisms. First, given their discretionary nature, they do little to influence individual performance. Second, if bonuses are paid regularly, they are often seen as a 'right' and as a form of deferred pay. Third, because they do not differentiate on the basis of performance, high-performing employees often feel that their contributions are not sufficiently recognised. These concerns are highlighted in the comments made by executives in an Australian metal manufacturing organisation:[40]

> 'Sure I got a bonus. Last year I got $7500. Don't ask me how they arrived at that figure, for all I know it could have been $1000 or $10 000.'

> 'Our bonus system doesn't recognise the top people. I got the same as everybody else and yet last year was a really tough year for production. I worked 60-hour weeks including most weekends and I end up getting the same as the finance people who work regular office hours.'

> 'Our bonus system isn't really a bonus, it's a top-up to our salaries. We're paid just on market rates and the bonus lifts our pay a little above market. Without the annual bonus we wouldn't be able to attract people in.'

The design principles and administration of large-group incentives are identical to those for individual and small-group incentive plans. Performance criteria and payout schedules should be predetermined. Then, when the organisation achieves its objectives, the incentive amounts can be distributed. Some percentage of annual profit over the budgeted figure is usually put aside to fund the organisation's incentive plan. The proportion of additional profit that goes to the incentive pool will increase as the above-target profit increases. At the end of the operating period, the incentive fund is expressed as a percentage of total payroll and each employee receives that percentage of their annual pay.

The significant difference between incentive plans designed as an 'add-on' to normal pay and those designed as an 'at-risk' component of the pay structure is in the base salary. 'At-risk' plans set the base salary at a level below that aimed for by an employee, the difference being made up from the incentive plan. The objective is to encourage employees to achieve or better the performance targets. Once the targets are reached, the employees receive the incentive amount and this lifts their total pay to the planned or market value. If the objectives are exceeded, employees receive more than their 'target' salary. Figure 13.6 sets out the advantages and disadvantages of large-group incentive plans.

LARGE-GROUP INCENTIVE PLANS

Advantages
- Encourage employee identification with organisation-wide objectives.
- Control part of remuneration costs if reward is contingent on meeting objectives.
- Promote a positive organisational image.

Disadvantages
- Have a long line of sight because only a few employees can directly influence the end result.
- May leave high performers feeling that their contribution is overlooked.
- Allow poor performers to be 'carried' by the overall effort.

Figure 13.6 The advantages and disadvantages of large-group incentive plans

Recognition programs

Recognition programs are a form of individual or work-group incentive that is usually outside the normal remuneration system.[41] Recognition programs use various forms of reward, including cash, merchandise, travel, time off with pay, badges, plaques and certificates. The performance measures vary depending on the purpose of the program. Awards can relate to reaching specific targets — for example, achieving shift production quotas or exceeding sales budget. Each employee or work-group member who has met the criteria receives the award. The measures may be competitive — for example, the work group with the best safety record or the sales representative with the greatest increase over target. Often, recognition programs are discretionary and permit managers (and sometimes colleagues) to nominate an employee for an award (see table 13.3). The advantages and disadvantages of recognition programs are shown in figure 13.7.

Recognition programs Make use of various rewards such as cash, merchandise, travel, certificates and the like.

Table 13.3	An example of a recognition program		
CASH VALUE	**PERCENTAGE OF EMPLOYEES**	**CRITERIA**	**AUTHORITY LEVEL**
2500	0.5	Significant personal contribution and identifiable impact across whole business	Managing Director
1250	1.0	Significant personal contribution and identifiable impact within a defined area of the business	Managing Director
625	2.5	Important personal contribution and defined impact	Function manager
300	5.0	Personal effort and contribution significantly above job requirements	Immediate manager or supervisor
150	7.5	Personal effort and contribution above job requirements	Immediate manager or supervisor
75	10.0	Commendable personal effort	Peers

Figure 13.7 The advantages and disadvantages of recognition programs

Recognition programs are ideally suited to the situations where:
- a reward process is required for a short-term goal or activity such as 'to introduce the new payroll system by 15 December', 'to increase customer satisfaction ratings by 15 per cent by the end of the first quarter' or 'to clear superseded stock by the end of the month'
- the organisation decides to introduce a process for recognising any outstanding contribution by an individual employee or work group (there are no defined performance measures, simply a desire to reward employees for their contribution)
- the organisation has a strong team orientation and wishes to keep the focus on work-group performance and team incentives while still recognising the specific contribution of individual employees — the recognition program provides a reward while maintaining the team incentive as the primary pay vehicle.

The design and implementation of incentive pay

A range of issues needs to be considered when designing and implementing an incentive pay system. The following discussion is a basic checklist for designing a program that effectively focuses employee attention on the organisation's objectives.[42]

Focus on strategic business objectives

The first step in designing an effective incentive pay system is to define the required performance criteria. If the overall organisational business objectives can be phrased in terms of one or two key indicators (for example, share price and profit after tax), these may be the performance criteria for the CEO and the executive team. However, it is rarely appropriate to use such broad performance criteria for middle managers, supervisors and employees. The aim is to provide as direct a line of sight as possible for all employees included in the incentive system. The question to ask at each level of the organisation is how the department or work group can have the most impact on share price and profit.

A manufacturing department will affect profit, and therefore share price, by increasing the productivity of its operations. Thus, its key performance indicators are likely to be drawn from those issues that affect cost and efficiency. Similarly, a sales department will affect profit by increasing the volume of sales and gross profit margins. Performance indicators for sales employees should reflect this.

Graham Hubbard is *professor of strategic management at Mount Eliza Business School.*

Why pay for no results?

Finally we are beginning to get some good evidence of what we have known from anecdotal sources for some time: chief executive pay rates are not related to performance. These rates are also increasing at a much faster rate than general pay levels, and they are too high. A recent newspaper survey of the top 50 listed companies found that the average chief executive is receiving base pay of $1.5 million and a total of $3.9 million. Another survey showed that performance seems to account for less than 20% of what chief executives receive.

In reality, the picture is different. Excluding three people from the sample (two are based in the United States and the other gains most of his pay from a performance-based bonus), the averages drop to $1.1 million in base pay and $2.9 million in total — a 25% difference. And of this, $1.2 million is in bonuses (which should be good, if pay is related to performance).

Let's compare this with what the chief executives of the First XI long-term winning organisations are getting. They get $1.3 million base pay, $800 000 bonus and $2.5 million on average. In other words, chief executives of long-term winning organisations are paid less than the average top-50 chief executive. This confirms the lack of relationship between general performance and pay.

Is $1.1 million too much as a base payment for a chief executive of a top-50 company in Australia? Is a bonus of 100% too much for good performance? The requirements demanded by seven days a week in these jobs, the enormous responsibility involved and the increasing risk of being sacked for under-performance suggest the amounts are not really excessive.

So what is the real problem? It is the lack of a logical relationship between pay and performance, something made worse by the large termination payments that are given to sacked underperformers. Surveys so far have focused on current pay and current performance — and so does the media. Unfortunately, what we really need for chief executive assessment is long-term pay related to long-term performance, which is much harder to assess and to calculate.

But termination is a very clear decision by a company, and why should underperformers be paid bonuses to leave? The payment of these bonuses is what really sticks in people's throats. Who started putting these clauses in the contracts?

And what about the directors who approve these ridiculous contracts? If indeed they are acting on behalf of their shareholders, why not let the shareholders know all about the essential terms and conditions of the contracts? The bare minimum required by the law, now gradually being made irrelevant by excessively complicated and expensive legislation and regulation, is no longer sufficient. Perhaps in time it will become possible to strike a relationship between pay and performance among those who sit at the boardroom tables. Now there's a thought for some lively research.

Graham Hubbard

Source BRW, 13–19 November 2003, p. 67.

Develop a comprehensive reward framework

The incentive system needs to be integrated into a total reward framework. It is necessary at the design stage to address the issue of base pay and how it fits with the incentive system. What should be the total target pay — that is, base pay plus incentives — for each employee? Should there be just one incentive system? Or are there multiple objectives to be met through different incentive programs?

It is often useful to plan out a reward matrix as shown in table 13.4, to ensure that each performance objective has an associated reward component.

Table 13.4	Integrating the total reward structure

REWARD OBJECTIVES

Reward component	Attract employees	Retain key employees	Productivity	Individual contribution	Employee security	Company performance
Base pay	######	######				
Gainsharing plan			######			
Performance incentive				######		
Corporate profit sharing						######
Superannuation					######	
Other benefits					######	
Career planning						

Key ###### Of prime importance   ▨ Of secondary importance   ☐ Not relevant

Ensure reinforcement of desired behaviours

The aim of an incentive system is to reinforce the organisation's strategic business objectives and priorities for employees. Yet, according to O'Neill and Berry, 'Few companies have a clear statement of the philosophy and rationale underlying their executive remuneration program and what they aim to achieve through their reward structure'.[43] ANZ and Westpac, for example, found that their sales incentives schemes produced fake sales reports and other unethical and fraudulent behaviour on the part of some employees because of ambiguities and lack of monitoring.[44] A recent study shows that less than one-quarter of Australia's companies have any formal process for evaluating plan effectiveness.[45] Three things are necessary for the process to be clear and unambiguous: first, the performance objectives need to be clearly specified; second, the nature of the contribution — whether individual or group — must be defined; and third, the frequency of payment must be such that it continually reinforces the organisation's message.

The general rule for frequency of payment is that lower-paid workers should receive their payment at least monthly, preferably in their normal pay packet. Managers and professional employees should receive their incentive half-yearly or quarterly, and senior executives should receive incentive payments annually.

Is it right for CEOs to have multimillion-dollar packages while some of their employees are earning only minimum wages?

Funding

There are two ways to fund incentive payments. First, the amounts can be provided from the increased profits or decreased costs arising from the achievement of the objectives. Alternatively, the payments can be an additional expense to the organisation. Few incentive plans survive as an additional cost unless there is a commensurate reduction in other costs such as base salaries. This is the approach that organisations sometimes take when introducing an 'at-risk' incentive system.

Generally, incentive plans are funded from increased profits or reduced expenses. It is important to trial the planned system against historic data before implementing it. This allows for the plan to be tested against a series of different scenarios to ensure that the objectives are appropriate and the costs are accurate.

'Fit' with organisational culture

Performance-based remuneration will be most effective when it reinforces the existing organisational culture and management style. Such reinforcement requires giving consideration to issues such as centralisation/decentralisation, the degree of employees' control or autonomy over their work and other characteristics of the organisation.

Summary

The act of relating pay to performance is increasing as organisations seek to become more productive. Incentive plans, moreover, are an effective vehicle for management to communicate to employees what is important and what is not. Organisations typically introduce incentive compensation plans to promote employee identification with the organisation's strategic business objectives, to encourage individual, team or business unit performance, to control fixed compensation costs and to increase remuneration competitiveness.

Incentive compensation plans can be classified in a variety of ways — individual programs, small-group programs, large-group programs and recognition programs. The choice of plan ultimately depends on the objectives to be achieved. Gainsharing, for example, is a small-group incentive system that shares the benefits of productivity improvements with the employees responsible. Types of gainsharing plans include the Scanlon plan, the Rucker plan and Improshare™. Recognition programs are a form of individual or work-group incentive that is usually outside the standard remuneration system. These programs may include cash, merchandise, travel, time off with pay, plaques and certificates.

When designing and implementing an incentive plan, an organisation needs to consider performance criteria, development of an integrated reward framework, reinforcement of desired behaviours, funding and fit with the organisation's culture.

Thirty interactive Wiley Web Questions are available to test your understanding of this chapter at **www.johnwiley.com.au/ highered/hrm5e** *in the student resources area*

terms to know

'at-risk' compensation (p. 488)
base pay (p. 488)
bonus (p. 492)
commission (p. 491)
contribution-based pay (p. 489)
gainsharing (p. 498)
incentive (p. 492)
incentive compensation (p. 491)
individual incentives (p. 493)
large-group incentives (p. 502)
line of sight (p. 493)

merit pay (p. 500)
options (p. 488)
piece-rates (p. 491)
profit sharing (p. 491)
recognition programs (p. 503)
Rucker plans (p. 500)
Scanlon plan (p. 499)
small-group incentives (p. 498)
total quality management (TQM) (p. 500)
variable pay component (p. 493)

review questions

1. What are the advantages and disadvantages of individual incentive plans?
2. What changes to an organisation's culture can be brought about by incentive compensation?
3. How can an incentive plan simultaneously increase individual motivation and group performance?
4. What are the advantages and disadvantages of linking rewards to performance for:
    (a) university academics?
    (b) public servants?
    (c) blue-collar workers?
    (d) sales representatives?
5. Explain in which circumstances you would employ individual, group and organisation-wide incentives.
6. What are the major features of the Scanlon, Rucker and Improshare™ plans?
7. Do you believe it is fair or unfair to reward employees by using incentive plans?
8. 'Financial incentive schemes are based on the false assumption that money has the power to motivate.' Critically discuss.
9. Incentive compensation is gaining in popularity? Why?
10. What are some of the reasons why employees may resist the introduction of incentive plans?

environmental influences on incentive compensation

Describe the key environmental influences from the model (figure 13.8 shown opposite) that have significance for incentive compensation.

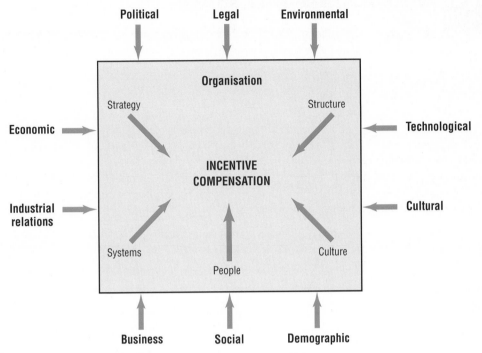

Figure 13.8 Environmental influences on incentive compensation

class debate

Senior executives should be paid like movie stars and sports stars.

or

Incentive compensation is divisive and unAustralian.

what's your view?

Write a 500-word response to the Letter to the Editor on page 499, agreeing or disagreeing with the writer's point of view.

practitioner speaks

As a class, critically discuss the views expressed by Graham Hubbard on page 505.

newsbreak exercise

Read the Newsbreak, 'The pay puzzle' on pages 495–7. What do you think of the author's argument that incentives for senior executives should go a lot deeper than mere money?

soapbox

What do you think? Conduct a mini survey of class members, using the questionnaire below. Critically discuss the findings.

1.	Incentive plans destroy an organisation's collective culture.	YES	NO
2.	All university lecturers should be on an incentive pay system.	YES	NO
3.	Incentive pay is just a ploy to increase management control.	YES	NO
4.	Australia's high income tax rates destroy the positive impact of incentive compensation.	YES	NO
5.	Incentive plans work only with employees who are motivated by money.	YES	NO
6.	Incentive plans are a good way to select out those employees management wants to lose.	YES	NO

online exercise

1. Conduct an online search to investigate employee, trade union and management attitudes towards incentive or 'at-risk' compensation programs. As a class, discuss your findings.
2. Conduct an online search to investigate employee share option programs and the controversy surrounding them. As a class, discuss your findings.

ethical dilemmas

Bonus points

Gerry Compton, Managing Director of Hi Tel Ltd, smiled as he spoke to Julie Chong, the company's newly appointed HR Manager. 'This is one of our best executive incentives.'

'A credit card?' questioned Julie.

'Not just a credit card Julie, a company credit card.'

'I'm sorry, I don't understand', said Julie.

'You will. It's a great scheme. You charge every HR Department expense you can to your credit card and you get the bonus points. Hire a temp — pay by credit card. Purchase a new computer — pay by credit card. Last month, I clocked up over 500 000 bonus points. I've got almost everything in the reward catalogue. Believe me, it's fantastic. Best of all, its tax-free. You'll love it.'

Julie wondered.

Discussion questions

1. What ethical and legal issues are involved with Hi Tel's credit card incentive?
2. What do you think Julie should do? Why?

Partly paid shares

The Managing Director of ABC Industries, Edith Schlosser, enthused 'The aim of the board is to make every one of the top management group rich. It's only fair that you who have made this company so successful should reap the rewards of your efforts.' The executives seated around the gleaming mahogany table murmured their agreement.

'I will ask Lily da Silva, our HR expert who put this scheme together, to outline the details.'

'Thanks Edith', Lily responded. 'From 1 July, we will introduce a new share plan. Each of you will be entitled to purchase a minimum of one million shares. Additional purchases will be allowed up to a maximum of five million shares depending on your length of service, your position and your performance.'

'Lily, that's sounds terrific, but the shares hit $4.50 this morning. Where do I get $4 500 000?' Andy Vargas, Group Marketing Manager, questioned.

Lily smiled. 'You don't. The shares will be issued at one cent, partly paid. All you have to come up with is a minimum of $10 000 and the company will give you an interest-free loan to cover this.'

'I still don't get it', said Andy. 'What's the benefit?'

'The benefit, Andy, is that your partly paid shares will participate in all new bonus share issues. For example, if the board approves a one-for-two bonus issue, your one million shares will become one-and-a-half million. Your new half a million shares will receive all dividends and you can sell them on the market.'

'You mean', said Andy, 'that with a $10 000 interest-free loan, I can get the equivalent of half a million fully paid shares worth at least $2 million?'

'Precisely', replied Lily.

'I love it, Lily', beamed Andy. 'You're the best HR Manager ever.' The delighted faces around the boardroom table grinned in agreement.

Discussion questions

1. What do you think of the new share scheme?
2. What ethical issues are involved in this case?

case studies

The top sales representative

Ian Prentice was angry. 'It's not fair!' he screamed. 'As the boss I should be paid more, not less, than my salespeople.'

'Take it easy, Ian', pleaded Donna Keller, HR Manager for Super Products Ltd. 'We all knew that the new incentive scheme made it possible for the top sales reps to earn heaps if they exceeded their targets. And Sophie Baglioni has done that. She is our top sales representative. We can't afford to lose her. If she can't earn big money, she will quit. You know that as well as I do.'

'Yeah, but it still isn't fair that she earns more than me!' fumed Ian.

Discussion questions

1. What faults may exist in the design of the incentive program at Super Products?
2. What would you do if you were Donna? Explain your answer.
3. Should subordinates be able to earn more than their superiors? Explain your answer.
4. What do you think would happen if the incentive plan were redesigned and a cap placed on incentive earnings?

Improving teaching effectiveness

Abbie Frey, HR Manager for Western University, looked at her notes. She had just come from a university council meeting where the university's strategic objectives for the next five years had been finalised. The council had asked Abbie to develop a set of recommendations to promote teaching effectiveness. In particular, the council wanted Abbie to design a new incentive program for the university's academic staff that would motivate them to improve their teaching. Abbie decided to use the strategic reward systems grid, shown below, to devise a flexible reward program to achieve the objective of teaching excellence.

STRATEGIC REWARD SYSTEM GRID		
Financial incentives		
	Short term	**Long term**
Individual		
Group/team		
Organisational		
Non-financial incentives		
	Short term	**Long term**
Individual		
Group/team		
Organisational		

Exercise

Assume that you are Abbie. In small groups, or individually, devise a program of financial and non-financial rewards that will encourage and reinforce excellent teaching among the university's academic staff.

practical exercises

1. **Employee incentives**

   Break into small groups of four to six. Imagine that you are members of a special compensation committee that has been given the job of developing a list of innovative employee incentives. The incentives may be simple and inexpensive or sophisticated and costly. Brainstorm for 10 to 15 minutes. Write down every suggestion, regardless of how silly it may sound. After you have developed your list, rank all the incentives in order of attractiveness. Identify the motives (using one of the theories of motivation discussed in chapter 11) to which each incentive appeals. Regroup and, as a class, evaluate the best incentives for their originality, practicality (in terms of cost and ease of implementation) and likely effectiveness.

2. **Employee options**

   Break into groups of four to six. Identify a major publicly listed company that has a share option program. Ask the HR Manager the following questions:
   - Why do you have a share option program?
   - How do you decide which employees are eligible for the program?
   - What performance hurdles do employees have to satisfy?
   - Do you regard the program as successful? Why or why not?
   - What measures do you employ to gauge the effectiveness of the program?

   Write a 500-word report on your findings. As a class, review your individual reports.

suggested readings

Beardwell, I. and Holden, L., *Human Resource Management*, Prentice Hall, London, 2001, ch. 12.

CCH, *Australian Master Human Resources Guide*, CCH, Sydney, 2003, ch. 12.

De Cieri, H. and Kramar, R., *Human Resource Management in Australia*, McGraw-Hill, Sydney, 2003, ch. 13.

Dessler, G., Griffiths, J., Lloyd-Walker, B. and Williams, A., *Human Resource Management*, Prentice Hall, Sydney, 1999, ch. 13.

Fisher, C. D., Schoenfeldt, L. F. and Shaw, J. B., *Human Resource Management*, 5th edn, Houghton Mifflin, Boston, 2003, ch. 13.

Henderson, R. I., *Compensation Management in a Knowledge Based World*, 9th edn, Prentice Hall, Upper Saddle River, NJ, 2003.

Ivancevich, J. M. and Lee, S. H., *Human Resource Management in Asia*, 8th edn, McGraw-Hill, Singapore, 2002, ch. 11.

Milkovich, G. T. and Newman, J. M., *Compensation*, 7th edn, McGraw-Hill, New York, 2002.

Mondy, R. W., Noe, R. M. and Premeaux, S. R., *Human Resource Management*, 8th edn, Prentice Hall, Upper Saddle River, NJ, 2002, ch. 11.

Nankervis, A. R., Compton, R. L. and McCarthy, T. E., *Strategic Human Resource Management*, 4th edn, Thomas Nelson, Melbourne, 2002, ch. 12.

online references

www.ahrm.org/aca.htm
www.shrm.org.hrmagazine
www.workforceonline.com

end notes

1. The original text for this chapter was prepared by Graham O'Neill, BA (Hons) (Tasmania), Dip. App. Psych. (Adelaide), FAHRI, MAPS, MACA, Director of Operations, Melbourne, The Hay Group. He is Editor-in-Chief of the John Libby and Co. bi-monthly *Reward Management Bulletin*, has edited several books on compensation and human resources and is a frequent commentator and contributor to professional journals on remuneration and HR issues.

2. G. Morgenson, 'Pay for performance? Companies lower the bar', *International Herald Tribune*, 26 May 2003, p. 9.

3. G. Smith, Chief Investment Strategist for Prudential Securities (USA), reported in 'Editorial: capitalise on US capitalism', *Australian Financial Review*, 8 August 1997.

4. D. Bank, 'As Microsoft is maturing, executives go off line', *Asian Wall Street Journal*, 17 June 1999, p. 1.

5. A. Cornell, 'Wage case', *Boss*, March 2002, pp. 56–9; and G. O'Neill and A. Berry 'Remuneration of Australian executives: a practitioner review', *Asia Pacific Journal of Human Resources*, vol. 40, no. 2, 2002, pp. 238–41.

6. N. Chenoweth, 'Plotting to avoid a hard landing for soft options', *Australian Financial Review*, 11–12 May 2002, pp. 24–5; and 'Executive hand wringing', *Intelligent Investor*, 6 September 2002, p. 3.

7. A. Kohler, 'Moss's pep talk to the troops more a MacBank meaculpa', *Australian Financial Review*, 27–28 July 2002, p. 72.

8. P. McGeehan, 'Bucks still shop at chief's offices', *International Herald Tribune*, 7 April 2003, p. 11.

9. M. Lawson, 'Australian options schemes hit by competitiveness: survey', *Australian Financial Review*, 3 October 1997, p. 20.

10. G. O'Neill and A. Berry, op. cit., p. 229.

11. F. Cameron, 'Fair share', *HR Monthly*, November 2002, p. 19; and G. Weaven. 'The tide of excess', *BRW*, 28 August–3 September 2003, p. 66.

12. M. Hovy, 'Executive pays go to market', *HR Monthly*, May 2003, p. 36.

13. P. Roberts, 'Work appraisal is good, but skip the bonus pay', *Australian Financial Review*, 3 October 1997, p. 46.

14. L. Allen, 'Top pay deals under the gun', *Australian Financial Review*, 31 August 2000, p. 3.

15. T. J. Stanley and W. D. Danko, *The Millionaire Next Door*, Longstreet Press, Atlanta, 1997, p. 171.

16. G. O'Neill, I. Hartnell and R. Clark, 'Managing salaried remuneration: an overview of trends and issues', *Human Resource Management Australia*, vol. 26, no. 1, February 1988, p. 16.

17. *Short Term Incentive Report, 1996–1997* published by Hay Group, Level 11, 1 Spring Street, Melbourne 3000.

18. Hills Industries, *Annual Report*, 2000, p. 3; and Westpac, *Annual Financial Report*, 2000, p. 36.

19. Quoted in A. Ferguson and T. Watts, 'CEOs tack into stormy waters', *Business Review Weekly*, vol. 20, no. 45, 23 November 1998, p. 51.

20. A. Hepworth, 'Incentive plans are being taken on board', *Australian Financial Review*, 5 September 2000, p. 5.

21. Quoted in S. Long, 'Ordinary workers moving to performance related pay', *Australian Financial Review*, 24 March 2000, p. 23. Also see D. Knight, 'The loyalty lure', *HR Monthly*, October 2000, pp. 18–24.

22. See, for example, E. Lawler, *Strategic Pay: Aligning Organization Strategies and Pay Systems*, Jossey-Bass, San Francisco, 1990; and J. Schuster and P. Zingheim, *The New Pay: Linking Employee and Organization Performance*, Lexington Books, New York, 1992.

23. G. O'Neill and P. Payne, 'Performance based pay — is it appropriate for Australia?', *Personnel Today*, February 1989, pp. 12–16; and S. P. Robbins, *Organizational Behavior*, 9th edn, Prentice Hall, Upper Saddle River, NJ, 2001, pp. 198–201.

24. R. P. Gandossy and E. J. Scheffel, 'Variable compensation: maxims for successful design and implementation', *Journal of Compensation and Benefits*, vol. 11, no. 3, 1995, p. 33.

25. G. O'Neill and A. Berry, op. cit., pp. 233–4.

26. R. L. Heneman, *Merit Pay*, Addison Wesley, Reading, Mass., 1992, pp. 44–8; and R. I. Henderson, *Compensation Management*, 7th edn, Prentice Hall, Upper Saddle River, NJ, 1997, pp. 412–14.

27. This is borne out by any of the compensation surveys published in various countries. There is a great deal of interest in group incentives, but individual incentives remain the most common form of variable pay.

28. For further discussion, see C. D. Fisher, L. F. Schoenfeldt and J. B. Shaw, *Human Resource Management*, 5th edn, Houghton Mifflin, Boston, 2003, ch. 13.

29. T. R. Stenhouse, 'The long and the short of gainsharing', *Academy of Management Executive*, vol. 9, no. 1, 1995, p. 77.

30. L. A. Berger and D. R. Berger (eds), *The Compensation Handbook*, 4th edn, McGraw-Hill, New York, 1999, ch. 18.

31. D. Mitchell, D. Lewin and E. Lawler, 'Alternative pay systems, firm performance and productivity', in S. Blinder (ed.), *Paying for Productivity*, Brookings Institution, Washington, 1990, pp. 15–94.

32. R. I. Henderson, op. cit., pp. 362–3.

33. R. I. Henderson, op. cit., pp. 363–4.

34. Research by Watson Wyatt indicates that about 20 per cent of gainsharing plans in the United States are Scanlon plans, 5 per cent are Rucker plans, 10 per cent are based on Improshare™ and about 65 per cent are customised plans.

35. R. Risher, 'Paying employees for quality', *Perspectives, Total Compensation*, vol. 3, no. 6, 1992, pp. 1–4.

36. R. Risher, op. cit., p. 1.

37. G. O'Neill, 'Linking TQM, performance and pay', *Corporate Review*, October 1993, pp. 32–4.

38. R. L. Heneman and C. Von Hippel, 'Balancing group and individual rewards: rewarding individual contributions to the team', *Compensation and Benefits Review*, vol. 27, no. 4, 1995, p. 63.

39. S. Caudron, 'The individual pay to team success', *Personnel Journal*, vol. 73, no. 10, October 1994, pp. 40–6; and C. J. Novak, 'Proceed with caution when playing with teams', *HR Magazine*, vol. 42, no. 4, April 1997, pp. 73–8.

40. These comments are taken from Graham O'Neill's discussions with a number of the organisation's senior executives.

41. S. S. Brooks, 'Non-cash ways to compensate employees', *HR Magazine*, vol. 39, no. 4, April 1994, pp. 38–43.

42. K. Wilkinson, 'Why incentives fail', *HR Monthly*, October 2000, pp. 26–7; and M. A. Stiffler, 'Eliminating the hidden costs buried in your incentive compensation plan', *Compensation and Benefits Review*, vol. 32, no. 1, 2000, pp. 46–54.

43. G. O'Neill and A. Berry, op. cit., p. 243.

44. G. Lekakis, 'Sacked ANZ staff faked sales for bonus', *Australian Financial Review*, 16 October 2000, p. 17.

45. Hay Group, *Short-Term Incentives Report 2000: Trends and Issues*, Hay Group, Melbourne, 2000.

employee benefits

Learning objectives

When you have finished studying this chapter, you should be able to:

- Explain why organisations provide benefits to employees
- Understand the link between strategic business objectives and employee benefits
- List the major types of employee benefits
- Understand the requirements for a sound employee benefits program
- Describe the fundamentals of superannuation
- Appreciate some of the current issues in superannuation.

'The notion of meeting the superannuation costs of staff as part of their employment — which has long been taken for granted — is now disappearing'.[1]

Alison Kahler, financial journalist

Benefits Include financial rewards that are not paid directly in cash to the employee (for example, childcare, healthcare, gym membership, life insurance) and all non-financial rewards (for example, an office with a window, a key to the executive toilet).

The right combination of **benefits** can assist an organisation in reaching its strategic business objectives and provide HR managers with an improved focus and sense of perspective on their organisation's benefit programs.[2] Unfortunately, many conventional benefit programs bear little relationship to the strategic business objectives of the organisation. 'Specifically', Bowen and Wadley argue, 'the distribution of benefits is often inconsistent with the overall philosophy of compensation.'[3] This is because no identifiable benefit philosophy or objectives exist. Reactive decisions are made about benefits in response to specific demands and pressures — rising costs, union demands, taxation changes and competitive pressures producing a piecemeal benefit program that does not help to achieve or reinforce the organisation's strategic business objectives and culture. As a consequence, an opportunity for the HR manager to forge a strategic business partnership with management is lost.

Equal pay for equal work and pay-for-performance philosophies are promoted by many organisations. The reality, however, is that many benefit programs are in direct conflict with these principles. For example, employees with families are frequently provided with extra coverage under medical and health benefit programs; retirement benefits are extended to all irrespective of performance; and the allocation of company cars, club memberships, the payment of union dues and so on are linked to status, not performance.

In fact, most employee benefits are determined by membership of the organisation and have nothing to do with the individual's contribution towards the organisation's strategic business objectives. Consequently, although expensive to organisations, the provision of a benefit is not a motivating reward. Company cars, for example, are given to all employees at a given job level, irrespective of their individual performance.

Benefits are also discriminatory. The receipt of benefits is often determined by age, marital status, gender, seniority, state of health and the like, and not by merit or the value of the individual's contribution to the organisation. Consequently, the type, number and proportion of benefits to direct or cash compensation have an impact on the employee mix.

Unless benefit programs are in harmony with the organisation's strategic business objectives and culture, their design may compromise the organisation's ability to attract and retain the very employees needed to achieve the organisation's strategic business objectives. Poor design can mean that benefit programs may neither improve employee motivation nor be cost-effective. This inhibits the organisation's long-term competitiveness and ability to attract and retain staff.[4] Budget funds allocated for improvement of the superannuation plan at the expense of a childcare benefit program may, for example, make the organisation's benefits package more appealing to older male employees and less appealing to younger female employees.[5]

Farcus

by David Waisglass
Gordon Coulthart

© 1995 Farcus Cartoons   WAISGLASS/COULTHART

'After 25 years of loyal service, all I have is a crummy gold watch and $3 million in office supplies.'

Benefit plan objectives

To ensure that benefit program design fits with the organisation's strategic business objectives and culture, the HR manager needs to ask the following questions:
- How much does the organisation want to spend on total cash and non-cash compensation?
- What proportion of total compensation should be given as pay or benefits?
- What is the total cost the organisation is prepared to pay for a benefit program?
- What benefit costs (if any) will be shared with employees? Is the benefit subject to abuse?
- What benefits are to be included in the organisation's benefit program? What is the need for such benefits? Are they benefits that employees want?
- What is the purpose of the benefits? Do they satisfy the organisation's strategic business objectives? Will they help attract, motivate and retain the right mix of employees? Will they reinforce the desired organisation culture?
- Which employees should receive or be offered benefits? Will employees be able to select the benefits they prefer? How are benefits to be granted — via seniority, performance or other criteria? Will same-sex partners be offered benefits (see figure 14.1)?[6]

The answers to these questions help the HR manager in designing a benefit program by focusing attention on plan objectives, cost containment and relevance. 'Failure to set and meet targets for total benefits costs tends to result in benefits driving costs', claim Bowen and Wadley.[7]

To avoid this dilemma, the organisation must state benefit plan objectives in terms of total benefit costs rather than in terms of the benefits provided.

To remain competitive, Company X must reduce costs, so it moves its operations to a state with lower workers compensation costs.

WHAT IS A DEPENDANT?[8]

A trend that reflects changing social values is the definition of a dependant. Traditionally, a dependant was a legally wed husband or wife and dependent children. Today, the definition of a dependant can include any person with whom the employee has a relationship of mutual support and dependence (financial, emotional or physical). Criteria that can be used to recognise a domestic partnership include sharing a relationship that involves:

(a) a shared commitment
(b) joint responsibility for basic living expenses or each other's common welfare — for example:

(i) sharing a residence
(ii) financial interdependence (being mutually responsible for basic living expenses)
(iii) not being married to anyone else and having no other domestic partner
(iv) both partners being of the age of legal adulthood or the age of consent
(v) partners not being so closely related that legal marriage would be prohibited
(vi) registration as domestic partners in the relevant jurisdiction
(vii) legal competence.

Figure 14.1 Criteria concerning dependants

The growth of employee benefits

Traditionally, employee compensation consisted primarily of direct or cash compensation. A limited range of **fringe benefits** that were of minor value supplemented this. Today, all this has changed. Benefits now cost at least 30 per cent of the payroll and form a similar, significant component of total compensation. Despite this escalating expenditure, few Australian organisations have proactively managed their benefit programs. Instead, many have simply reacted to current trends, taxation changes, union pressures and statutory requirements. That this is so becomes evident when the factors contributing to the growth of benefits in Australian organisations are examined.

Fringe benefits Indirect or non-cash compensation items such as life insurance, medical benefits, additional sick leave and the like.

Taxpayers contribute 69 per cent towards the superannuation of federal MPs. The guaranteed minimum paid by most Australian employers is 9 per cent.

Taxation

Compensation in Australian organisations has been driven by the need for tax minimisation. The punitive tax rates on wages and salaries have placed ever-increasing pressure on employers to allow employees to sacrifice their wages and salaries for a non-cash benefit. Employers have felt pressure to introduce more and more 'tax-free' benefits such as family holidays, improved sick leave, private school fees, home mortgage repayments, fully maintained cars and non-contributory superannuation and to package these in the most tax-effective way for the employee.[9] Recent legislative changes, however, have created so many restrictions that some experts believe that it is no longer worthwhile packaging salaries for employees. Non-luxury cars, motorbikes, superannuation, mobile telephones and laptops appear to be all that can now be packaged tax-effectively.[10]

Union pressure

Unions are in the vanguard of seeking new and improved benefits for their members. Annual leave, sick leave, maternity leave, long service leave, annual leave loading, payment of union dues, provision of uniforms and safety clothing, and retirement benefits are all examples of improved or additional benefits sought by unions.

Status

Some fringe benefits are highly prized as status symbols and can act as powerful motivators. However, in response to competitive pressures, some companies are beginning to ask: Does this add value? Does it support our strategic business objectives? As a consequence, companies are tending to favour linking rewards to the achievement of performance objectives through incentive-based pay and cutting back on costly benefits. Furthermore, the increasing paternalism and involvement in employees' private lives associated with some benefits such as elder-care and adoption assistance are being questioned. Associated with rising benefit costs, this has seen companies increasingly shift benefit responsibilities back to employees.

A federal politician's pension of about $50 000 per year is guaranteed for life after serving eight years or three terms in office. The pension is indexed not to inflation but to the salary of the highest position held by the MP.

Fringe benefits tax (FBT) Australian federal government tax designed to tax organisations on most benefits provided by them to their employees.

Fringe benefits tax

On 1 July 1986, the former Labor government introduced a **fringe benefits tax (FBT)**. This was specifically designed to tax benefits that in the past had escaped the income tax net. Although employees receive the benefit, the FBT is levied on the organisation and is not a deductible expense. All in all, FBT imposes considerable costs and administrative responsibilities upon employers.[11]

Fringe benefits tax is payable on the following benefits:
- airline transport
- car parking
- childcare expenses
- club memberships
- debt waivers
- education expenses
- entertainment benefits
- expense payments
- goods and services
- housing and board
- leisure facilities
- living-away-from-home allowances
- low-interest loans
- motor vehicles
- other benefits
- relocation expenses
- travel expenses of an accompanying spouse.[12]

Fringe benefits tax now generates billions of dollars per year and is regarded by the federal government as a significant source of tax revenue.

Major employee benefits still exempt from FBT include employee amenities, employee share acquisition schemes, superannuation contributions, **workers compensation, accident make-up pay** and medical treatment, occupational health and counselling and safety awards.

While the FBT forced organisations to review their benefit programs, most of the key traditional benefits, such as the company car, remain. This is due to the conservatism of Australian organisations and because it is still more tax-effective in some cases to offer remuneration via fringe benefits than via salary.

Examples of some of the fringe benefits provided by Australian employers include **non-contributory superannuation**, health insurance, maternity leave, paternity leave, telephone payments, mobile phones, professional subscriptions, entertainment expenses, low-interest personal and housing loans, prestige motor vehicles, a second company car, laptops, home computers, flexible working hours, sabbaticals and financial counselling.

Flexible benefit plans

Most organisations have a varied employee population. Differences in age, sex, marital status, number of dependants, financial position and personality make for different benefit needs. To address this, some organisations offer a system of flexible or **cafeteria benefits**. Such programs allow employees to select the particular benefits that match their individual needs. Each employee is allocated a sum of money that can be used to purchase specific benefits from among those provided by the organisation. This enables employees to develop benefit plans that suit their lifestyle.

For example, in a family where both partners work and receive supplementary health benefits, adequate coverage may be provided by just one plan. A flexible benefit plan permits one spouse to select another benefit more appropriate to the family's needs.

While having this obvious advantage, cafeteria benefit plans can be administratively complex as constant monitoring and updating is required. Moreover, employees may fail to choose those benefits that are truly in their best interest and then blame the organisation. Finally, trade unions often do not like cafeteria plans, seeing them as a management effort to restrict benefits and shift the cost to employees.[13] For example, employees in US employer-sponsored health plans are paying almost 50 per cent more for health care than they did just a few years ago.[14]

Types of employee benefits

Organisations provide many non-monetary benefits to their employees. These enhance the attractiveness of the organisation as a place to work and are generally administered by the HR department. Some benefits, such as annual leave, sick leave and workers compensation, are **mandatory benefits** required by law, while others, such as mentoring, are **voluntary benefits** — the product of the organisation's HRM philosophy and competitive practice. Effective communication of employee benefits is necessary if employees are to understand their entitlements and the costs involved. Many organisations now use computerised personal benefit statements to achieve this (see figure 14.2).

Group life insurance

The purpose of group life insurance is to provide financial protection for an employee's dependants upon their death. The benefit may be determined as a fixed lump sum (such as $50 000) or as a multiple of the employee's annual salary (for example, twice the annual salary of $50 000; that is, $100 000).

Healthcare insurance

Although Medicare provides basic health protection, some organisations offer supplementary health benefits. Generally, this takes the form of added medical and hospital benefits, plus assistance with dental, optical and paramedical costs. Because of escalating medical and hospital costs, some organisations are beginning to focus more on managing healthcare by

Workers compensation A legally required benefit that provides medical care, income continuation and rehabilitation expenses for people who sustain job-related injuries or sicknesses.

Accident make-up pay The difference between the workers compensation payment and the employee's actual pay.

Non-contributory superannuation A scheme where all contributions to the retirement plan are made by the employer.

Cafeteria benefits Employees choose their own benefits up to a certain cost per employee.

Mandatory benefits Benefits that must be provided by law (for example, annual leave, workers compensation insurance).

Voluntary benefits Benefits provided voluntarily by an employer (for example, additional annual leave, gym membership, tuition refund).

introducing wellness or preventive health programs to educate and motivate employees to adopt healthier lifestyles.[15] Some employer initiatives in health promotion include on-site exercise facilities, health-risk appraisals (questionnaires about health hazards) and health-risk assessments (physical or biomedical tests that screen for specific health conditions). A significant number of men and women in Australia are either overweight or obese, so the potential value of such programs is obvious.[16]

OZ International
BENEFIT STATEMENT

John J. Irwin

Your benefits have been calculated using your annual base salary as at 1 January 2004, which is $50 000.

Insurance protection

A   *Life*

If you die while in the company's employ, the company will pay your beneficiaries $100 000

B   *Personal accident*

If you die in an accident while in the company's employ, the company will pay your beneficiaries an additional benefit of $100 000

C   *Business travel*

If you die in an accident while travelling on company business (excluding normal daily commuting to and from work), the company will pay your beneficiaries (in additionto A and B) a benefit of $100 000

D   *Long-term disability*

If you become disabled because of illness or injury for a period exceeding six months, the company will pay you a monthly pension for as long as you are disabled or up to age 65, whichever occurs first, of $2 000

Retirement benefits

On your normal retirement age of 65, the company's plan will pay you a monthly pension of $2 000

If you desire, you may convert your pension into a lump sum payment of $240 000

For more information

This statement is only a brief summary of your benefit entitlements. If you have any questions or would like more information, please call S. Ando, Benefits Specialist, on extension 9999.

Figure 14.2 Example of a computerised personal benefit statement

Payment for time not worked

This category includes annual leave, annual leave loading, long service leave, paternity leave, sick leave, maternity leave, jury duty, military service, bereavement leave, compassionate leave, public holidays, education leave sabbaticals and leave for trade union training. Although taken for granted by most employees because many are mandatory benefits, payments for time not worked constitute a significant proportion of the total cost of employee benefits. For example, it is estimated that sick leave alone costs Australian employers $15 billion per year.[17]

Workers compensation insurance

All organisations in Australia are legally obliged to have their employees covered by workers compensation insurance to give them protection against the costs of medical care and loss of income caused by a workplace injury or illness.

The cost of workers compensation is a major concern to government and employers because it accounts for about 3 per cent of total labour costs. Competitive pressures have led to a review of workers compensation systems, a tightening of loopholes, improved worker rehabilitation and increased government and union pressure for the provision of safer workplaces.

Total and permanent disability insurance

Some organisations provide benefits in the event of the employee's total and permanent disability. **Disability insurance** may form part of the employer's retirement plan or may be completely separate. Benefits provided may be a specified sum, a designated percentage of annual income or an amount equal to the employee's accrued or projected retirement benefit.

Disability insurance Insurance designed to protect employees during long-term disablement (and loss of income) through illness or injury.

Childcare

The demographics of the Australian work force suggest that as more and more women enter employment, demands for employer-provided childcare will increase. However, childcare benefits are not only for women. In Australian organisations, children of male staff fill as many places as do children of female staff.[18] Some major benefits claimed for providing childcare services are that they:

- aid recruitment
- reduce absenteeism
- increase employee loyalty
- improve productivity
- reduce labour turnover
- improve the organisation's image
- enhance employee morale.[19]

Two companies that provide childcare are Esso and Lend Lease, and they have established a joint childcare centre in Sydney. The companies say that the program 'has both real and potential impacts on career aspirations, particularly for women' and makes it much easier for women to enter and remain in the work force.[20] High initial costs, loss of government subsidies, taxation burdens and unfamiliarity with childcare options are seen as the major obstacles to more employers introducing childcare programs.[21]

HR managers should note that the mere provision of childcare facilities is not sufficient in itself. The facilities must be of a high standard and operated by qualified staff. The HR department has a very serious responsibility to employees in this respect and must ensure that it clearly identifies what employees really want in childcare if expensive mistakes are to be avoided.

Elder-care

Because the population is ageing, caring for older relatives is becoming more common. For example, in the United States it is estimated that almost one in two people will have to provide some form of care for an elderly relative.[22] Similarly, an Australian study found that for every employee with elder-care responsibilities, an average of three days per year were lost and another four days disrupted. In addition, more than one-third of workers who were adult carers resigned to help an aged or disabled relative.[23] Coupled with a career, caring for an older person can affect an employee's productivity, attendance and morale.[24] Some companies such as Lend Lease, Sydney Water Corporation and Colgate Palmolive have elder-care programs, while many awards provide for carer's leave, which includes elder-care.[25]

Employee assistance programs

Employee assistance programs (EAPs) have become more widespread as more organisations recognise that their success depends on the health and wellbeing of their employees.

Traditional services offered by EAPs include counselling on drug and alcohol abuse, marital and family problems, financial problems and time management. Newer services include counselling on mental health problems, dependant care, bereavement, stress management, community services referral, weight control, health education, smoking cessation and adoption assistance programs.

Such programs reflect both compassion and concern for costs. Alcoholism, for example, is a major problem in Australia, affecting up to one in 10 adult males and costing business and government billions of dollars per year.[26] As with smoking, employers who do not take reasonable steps to prevent alcohol or drug-related harm to employees may be exposing themselves to legal liability.

Employee assistance programs (EAPs) Company-sponsored programs that help employees to cope with personal problems that are interfering with their job performance.

NEWSBREAK

Boomers face tough retirements

By Alison Kahler

Ageing Australians face an imminent financial crisis unless the Federal Government acts quickly to resolve issues identified in the Intergenerational Report released in last week's Budget and introduces reforms to boost retirement savings.

New research by the National Centre for Economic and Social Modelling and AMP has found that most baby boomers will struggle to survive in retirement, let alone sustain the standard of living enjoyed during their working life.

The report found that the average 50 to 64-year old Australian had an average personal wealth of only $240 000 in January 2002. More than half, or $127 000, of their wealth was home equity and would not provide retirement income unless family homes were sold and retirees moved to cheaper properties.

'This is a major policy issue for government and the community. As a nation, we have a real problem', managing director of AMP Financial Services Andrew Mohl said.

Mr Mohl said that 2.7 million Australians faced a bleak future unless spending and tax concessions were revised to create a more equitable savings environment and prevent wealthy individuals from qualifying for pensions.

The average 50 to 64-year old had only $115 000 in assets, including an average $56 000 superannuation investment, outside his or her family home.

This was insufficient to finance a comfortable 20 to 30-year retirement, according to NATSEM director Ann Harding.

'The $115 000 of non-home wealth held by 50 to 64-year olds will generate an annual retirement income of less than $10 000', Professor Harding said.

The aged pension will not provide a reliable safety net because, at its current levels, it will boost income to just under $20 000.

The results of the survey are likely to increase calls for significant reforms of the superannuation system.

'The low superannuation savings highlighted in the survey reflect an immature superannuation system. These people have only had superannuation guarantee contributions since 1992', spokesman for the Association of Superannuation Funds of Australia Ross Clare said.

'It will take 30 to 40 years for the system to mature. Reducing superannuation contributions tax and increasing contributions will help people meet their expectations for retirement', he said.

Source *The Australian Financial Review*, 22 May 2002, p. 5.

Australian organisations that have established EAPs include AGL, BHP Billiton, Lend Lease and Qantas. It must be emphasised that an EAP cannot operate in a vacuum. The EAP must be related to the organisation's strategic HR objectives and be consistent with its culture. Where this is the case, EAPs allow employee problems to be dealt with in a proactive way. This, in turn, provides benefits to both the employee and the organisation.

Preventive health programs

Many organisations now realise that health and fitness are not just a fad and that healthy employees are more productive. Other benefits claimed for health promotion programs include:

- decreased absenteeism
- improved morale
- decreased workers compensation claims
- improved image of the organisation as a concerned and caring employer.

Preventive health programs focus on physical fitness, stress reduction, weight loss and smoking cessation.

Preventive health programs
Programs designed to promote employee health and fitness. Examples include physical fitness, stress reduction, weight loss and smoking cessation.

There has been some criticism in Australia and the United States that such programs remain a perquisite for middle-class, well-educated, productive and healthy employees.[27] In contrast, blue-collar workers are conspicuous by their absence. One US company found that its most motivated and successful employees used the facilities the most. This is despite the fact that in Australia and the United States blue-collar workers have worse health habits than white-collar workers and consequently are at greater risk of heart disease and other illnesses.[28] Tradesmen in Australia smoke twice as much as professional men and exercise half as much. Women in the retail industry smoke 25 per cent more than professional women and exercise half as much.[29] This suggests that the benefits of many corporate health programs are not understood or accepted by the groups that need them the most. Some suggested reasons for this are:

- there is mistrust between blue-collar and white-collar workers
- blue-collar workers feel intimidated
- workers in unhealthy work environments perceive health programs as a sign of management hypocrisy
- physical work makes blue-collar workers too tired to exercise
- lunchbreaks are often too short, which makes exercise impractical
- employees fear that medical screening results may jeopardise job security.[30]

HR managers need to be sensitive to these problems and ensure that blue-collar workers are involved in the planning of health programs. One expert says that for a program to be effective, the following conditions should be met:

- The program should include a range of physical activities, such as aerobics, and be available at least three times per week.
- There should be an accompanying education program that encourages health and fitness.
- There should be an emphasis on participation rather than excellence and an allowance for individual choices.
- Facilities should be conveniently located so exercise can be part of the organisation's normal working day.
- Programs and facilities should be available to all employees.
- There should be a strong commitment from senior management.
- The promotional campaign should target both active and inactive employees.
- The program should be sustained, rather than short term and isolated.[31]

Australian organisations with corporate health programs include AMP, ANZ, Coles Myer, IBM, Lend Lease and Westpac.

Flexible work schedules

Flexible work schedules are designed to provide employees with a choice in the hours that they work. They also permit the organisation to respond quickly to changes in the work force and to satisfy customer demands for increasing information and 24-hour-a-day savings.[32] For example, if women are to be able to balance their dual work roles — at home and on the job — then flexible work schedules are essential. Changing lifestyles, pressure for further education and the advent of the dual-career couple make the 'flexible workplace' an attractive recruiting tool.

The major types of flexible working schedules are listed below.

- *Variable day:* employees may vary the number of hours worked in a day, so long as they work the required 40 hours (or whatever the award states) in a full week. In most cases, employees are required to be at work for a 'core' period such as 10.00 am to 3.00 pm, but can start at 7.00 am one day or finish at 6.00 pm another.
- **Flexitime:** the employee selects a starting time within a band and sticks to it. One employee may opt to start at 6.00 am every day and another employee at 10.30 am.
- *Variable week:* an offspring of the variable day where the employee must complete the award set hours in a fortnight and be in the office every day from Monday to Friday each week. However, the employee chooses the hours worked.
- *Maxiflex:* employees can work the hours required for the week in less than five days and take a three-day weekend. A variation of this flexible work schedule is when the hours to be worked are spread over a fortnight, so that a five- or six-day break may be taken.

Flexitime A system that allows employees to choose their own starting and finishing times within a broad range of available hours.

- *Job sharing:* one job is split between two workers. The employees work on alternate weeks, split days (three days for one employee and two for the other) or some other variation. The employees are not actually sharing a job, but are working independently part-time.
- *Permanent part-time:* workers choose to work less than full-time (for example, three or four hours a day) and receive partial benefits afforded full-time workers.[33]

Flexible work schedules remain the subject of some controversy. For example, a report by the Human Rights and Equal Opportunity Commission claims women workers are often disadvantaged by the introduction of flexible working hours because of the erosion of the predictability and regularity of hours of work for employees.[34] Nevertheless, employers using such arrangements appear to be generally pleased and an increasing number of employees seem set to welcome the availability of flexible work schedules.

This Letter to the Editor provides a provocative viewpoint. Do you agree? See 'What's your view?' on page 533.

Letter to the Editor

Unmarried people shouldn't be entitled to dependent benefits

Dear Editor,

Organisational ethics are being given increasing consideration and greater attention is being paid throughout our community to issues of social responsibility. Given this, I believe that there is a range of less popular ethical issues to which organisations should be turning their minds. One of these is the issue of providing similar benefits to employees who are not married and those who are.

In decades past, organisations would often tailor reward and benefit systems with the employee's family responsibilities in mind. Now, however, organisations don't seem to care whether someone is in a stable relationship or whether their employees are changing partners every week.

Readers might argue that this is as it should be. They would argue that organisations have no place in the bedroom, and that rights to privacy should be respected.

The hypocrisy of this position is easily revealed. For instance, readers should consider that there are multinational corporations around the world who give money to all sorts of bizarre community movements and lobby groups. Whether these groups are trying to protect the endangered giant snails of Western Sydney (and there are some!) or subsidise family planning (read abortion) in the developing world, these decisions represent moral and ethical judgements of significant consequence to others.

In my view, the most endangered species in our society is the traditional family. Not only does the nuclear family provide stability for employees as they enter the workplace, but research continues to show that children living in traditional family structures are likely to do better at school and are less likely to fall into lives of crime and drug abuse. Given these realities, why shouldn't organisations make a moral judgement about the moral choices of their employees, particularly when the provision of benefits also directly affects the organisational bottom line?

I cannot understand why entrepreneurs like Anita Roddick of The Body Shop are viewed as ethical martyrs for their concern for the physical environment (and some aspects of the human environment), while those who express concern about the social survival of our species from a more conservative perspective are satirised for their allegedly politically incorrect views.

Let's not kid ourselves any longer. Both intuition and empirical research support the notion that the traditional nuclear family is the most stable and potentially most prosperous relationship structure for both adults and children. Corporations, like governments, should recognise and reward this reality via their policies and reward systems.

A family man

Source David Poole, University of Western Sydney.

Miscellaneous benefits

Miscellaneous benefits include service awards, share purchase plans, profit sharing, income protection, savings and thrift plans, employee loans, travel insurance, frequent flyer points, tuition refunds, study leave, sabbatical leave, employee discounts, payment of union dues, annual medical exams, free clothing, subsidised canteens, company cars and free parking. In recent times, leading companies (especially high-tech companies) have produced an explosion of non-traditional benefits, including: rock climbing walls; massage services; weight reduction programs, laptops and Internet connections; take-home meals; restaurant vouchers, grocery deliveries at work; in-house florists, hair salons; company boats; acupuncture and health clinics; lap pools, basketball courts, meditation rooms; outdoor walking trails; free fruit baskets; bonus pay at Christmas or Chinese New Year; guesthouses in holiday locations; sabbaticals; free maid services; entertainment and product discounts; nanny services; coffee rooms stocked with free soft drinks, fresh fruit, sweets and pastries; concierge and travel services; and on-site legal offices.[35] Like other benefits, these too must be included in the company's labour costs.

Practitioner speaks

Paula DeLisle is Vice-President, Asia–Pacific Business Development for Watson Wyatt Worldwide, an international consulting firm specialising in human capital and financial management. Based in Hong Kong since 1982, Paula has helped leading local and multinational companies throughout Asia implement their business strategies by providing the best people and financial solutions.

Salary and benefit trends in the Asia–Pacific

Remuneration in the Asia–Pacific region continues to evolve as organisations maintain their focus on cost management and the pursuit of efficiencies. Salary increases have mirrored economic activity in each country, particularly inflation rates. Hence, we see the highest level of salary increases in Indonesia where inflation has been running in double digits for several years. Hong Kong, on the other hand, has suffered with deflation for the past five years, with an aligned flat rate of salary growth and even in some cases a corresponding decrease in the salary package overall.

One exception to this alignment between inflation and salary increase is China, which has experienced strong economic growth and comparatively high salary increases, yet very low inflation. For businesses operating in China, this means profits may suffer as the cost of labour rises disproportionately to price rises.

The most significant compensation trend continues to be the shift away from guaranteed pay, with its fixed cost, towards a far greater emphasis on performance-related pay. Over the past several years, we have seen variable plan design features becoming more sophisticated as plans that are discretionary in nature are replaced by very target-driven performance plans, with multiple performance measures, not just profit. At the same time, companies are vigorously revamping their sales-incentive programs. Restructuring aimed at eliminating costs can only go so far. To gain top-line growth, companies realise that their salespeople are the ultimate agents of increased revenue. Long-term incentives are also becoming increasingly popular and, if designed properly, are viewed as a low-cost incentive to encourage hard work and to focus on shareholder value.

There continues to be a freeze on any improvement of benefits plus a strong interest in cost sharing and greater attention to the cost/value proposition of each benefit plan. An example of this is the shift away from defined benefit retirement plans where the cost and risk belong to the employer, towards a defined contribution plan, which typically requires a contribution from both the employer and the employee and where the investment risk is with the employee.

These changes to the construction of remuneration packages were very much forced because of the difficult economic environment and concerns about the cost of doing business. As global, regional and local economic activity strengthens, we are likely to see a renewed strong demand for talent, which in turn may result in compensation again shifting.

Looking into the crystal ball, the trend towards performance-related pay is likely to continue, with perhaps greater opportunities for increasing the actual bonus payout. In addition, benefit provisions are likely to come back into focus to suit the changing demographic needs of the worker.

Paula DeLisle

Retirement benefits

Superannuation Benefit paid as a pension and/or lump sum to help employees to meet their financial needs in retirement.

Retirees from the Australian work force have usually depended on the federal government's age pension for their financial security. However, the cost burdens associated with this, and the ageing of the Australian population, have seen an ever-increasing push by Labor and Coalition governments towards private **superannuation** funded by compulsory and voluntary contributions. The result is that today less than 30 per cent of employees expect the age pension to be the prime means of funding their retirement.[36]

Although it is estimated that over 90 per cent of Australian workers are eligible to receive some form of superannuation, the adequacy of the actual benefit payable is too low to provide an adequate retirement income (this is especially true for blue-collar workers and women).[37] One study indicates that at least 40 per cent of retirees are living between poverty and parsimony.[38] The reality is that many retired Australians will have a meagre existence. To live comfortably in retirement, it is estimated that retirees should have an income equal to 50–70 per cent of their pre-retirement income.[39] Few achieve this. In Australia, only 17 per cent of people over the aged pension age do not draw any pension at all.[40] Furthermore, the burden on the government's age pension system caused by the ageing population is intensifying pressures to increase the retirement age, place greater restrictions on eligibility and freeze some benefits.

Superannuation in Australia is complex because many of the changes introduced by Labor and Coalition governments have been ill-conceived and, in some cases, unworkable. In the past 20 years there have been more than 1000 changes in superannuation regulations.[41] Consequently, considerable confusion and controversy surrounds superannuation in Australia.[42] Nevertheless, further changes have been proposed, such as linking health cover with superannuation, increasing the compulsory superannuation contribution from a maximum of 9 per cent to 15 per cent, providing portability, and abolishing contributions and investment taxes.[43]

Federal government objectives about superannuation, however, are clear:

- first, to encourage employees to provide for their own retirement rather than to rely on the age pension (yet Australia is the only country that taxes superannuation contributions, annual earnings and pensions/lump sums on retirement)[44]
- second, to minimise the losses of tax revenue brought about by the concessional treatment of superannuation.[45] According to one critic, the government uses superannuation primarily as a means of raising taxes rather than as a way for Australians to save for retirement.[46] For example, it has been estimated that if the government were to levy taxes at the benefits stage and not the contributions stage, individual retirement savings would be boosted by about 30 per cent.[47]

The inherent conflict between these two objectives provides some explanation as to why the situation is so complicated. In an attempt to overcome the confusion and instability surrounding superannuation and to extend superannuation coverage, in 1992 the former federal Labor government implemented the Superannuation Guarantee Levy (SGL). According to the Treasurer at the time, the SGL represented a major step forward in the development of retirement income policy and would bring about income security and higher standards of living for future generations of retirees. Basically, the SGL aims to provide employees with 40 per cent of their working income when they retire.[48] The SGL mandated employer contribution is 9 per cent. However, it is claimed that contributions closer to 16 per cent are needed if reliance on the age pension is to be reduced.[49] The scheme has also been criticised for being overly complex, in need of change, costing jobs, for failing to meet its fundamental objectives with a reasonable level of secure retirement income and lacking compliance.[50] However, the introduction of the SGL has meant that today virtually all working Australians have at least some form of superannuation coverage.

In 1996, the Coalition government introduced further changes that also generated considerable controversy, anger, confusion and accusations of inequity and excessive meddling.[51] Three of the key changes included a 15 per cent surcharge on deductible contributions by employees and the self-employed with taxable income in excess of $70 000 p.a. ($90 527 for the 2002/2003 financial year), increasing the age for superannuation contributions to 70 years, and the introduction of retirement savings accounts to be offered by banks, building societies and credit unions.[52] The superannuation surcharge has been criticised for being a major disincentive to save for retirement.[53]

A change proposed by the Coalition government is to give employees a choice of superannuation funds. Superannuation choice will directly impact all existing industry and company-sponsored funds and may pose some risk for employees.[54] For example, US experience shows that employees make excessively conservative choices, which means a much lower retirement benefit. This indicates that education in investment will be important if employees are to make the decisions best suited to their retirement needs.[55] The Association of Superannuation Funds and some large employers have criticised the proposed change because of the additional administrative costs involved.[56] Even so, the trend is clearly towards giving employees greater choice.

Other proposals for changing superannuation include making it compulsory for employees to take part of their superannuation as a pension instead of taking it all as a lump sum, ensuring the equal treatment of same-sex couples, allowing employees to split their superannuation contribution with their spouse, and increasing the preservation age.

The payment of benefits

Superannuation benefits in Australia traditionally have been in the form of a lump-sum payment in the private sector and a pension in the public sector. Changes in the taxing of lump-sum benefits have initiated moves towards all superannuation benefits being paid in the form of pensions. Nevertheless, most superannuation payouts remain in the form of a lump sum. In conjunction with early retirement, this has led to 'double dipping', with the employee receiving a lump-sum retirement benefit, spending it and then claiming the age pension. In fact, the National Commission of Audit claims that the present arrangements for superannuation and pensions 'actually rewards private dissipation of savings to preserve eligibility for the age pension and related benefits'.[57] As a consequence, the concept of superannuation providing financial independence in retirement has been greatly undermined.

This has resulted in the federal government increasing taxes on lump-sum payments and increasing age, income and asset-testing requirements for the age pension. As most Australian retirees overwhelmingly prefer a lump-sum benefit to a pension, the introduction of such changes has posed some difficulties for the government. In turn, HR managers are experiencing increasing pressure to restructure compensation and benefits packages to try to accommodate these conflicting demands. Executives, in particular, feel frustrated because they have regarded a lump-sum payment at retirement as a form of compensation for the years of long hours, stress and dislocation of family life. Finally, the superannuation problem is further complicated by the number of extremely generous public sector superannuation schemes that have created a highly inequitable situation for private sector employees.[58]

The rationale for superannuation

Superannuation was once regarded as a gratuity from a grateful employer in recognition of an employee's long and faithful service. Payments were provided at management's discretion, with none or few employee rights. This reward philosophy viewed superannuation as a means of retaining key personnel. Personnel who were not valued by management, who quit or who were discharged were regarded as undeserving of superannuation benefits.

Over the years, competitive, social, government and union pressures brought about increasing acceptance of the view that superannuation is a form of deferred income. This earnings philosophy of superannuation is gaining increasing acceptance.

Still another view is that superannuation reflects a moral obligation of employers to provide for their employees' financial wellbeing in old age. This moral philosophy regards employers as being obligated to provide realistic retirement benefits. Advocates of this approach see it as a means of keeping age pension costs contained.

Under present legislation, a couple can retire early and receive almost $17 000 per year in welfare benefits while having $1 million in superannuation assets.

Types of retirement plans

Defined benefit and defined contribution superannuation plans are the two major approaches used by employers to provide retirement benefits for their employees. Recently, defined benefit plans have undergone a decline in popularity.[59]

Defined benefit plans

Defined benefit plans pay out a predetermined amount either as a lump sum or as a monthly pension on the employee's retirement. These plans give employees certainty as to their precise entitlement on retirement. Contributions are determined actuarially and plan formulae are geared to retirement benefits rather than contributions.

A variety of formulae can be used to calculate retirement benefits. The benefits may be calculated as an annual pension or as a once-only lump sum on retirement. The most widely used formula in the private sector (but not the public sector) involves calculating the retiree's average earnings (usually over a three- to five-year period immediately preceding retirement). This is multiplied by the retiree's number of years of credited service with the employer, and then multiplied by an actuarially determined factor typically ranging between 1.25 per cent and 1.5 per cent. This calculation gives an annual pension.

Public servants and politicians have access to government-guaranteed life pensions, while the general community faces uncertain benefits and the risk of outliving their capital.

If the retirement benefit is to be paid in a once-only lump sum, then the annual pension figure will be multiplied by the assumed number of years the retiree will live after retirement. As a rule of thumb, the post-retirement life span used on retirement at 65 years of age is 10 years. Under this assumption, the once-only lump sum retirement benefit will be 10 times the annual pension calculated in accordance with the procedures just set out. If we assume that the average pay rate over the retiree's last three years of employment was $60 000 and that the retiree had worked for the employer for 20 years, and if the factor to be applied is 1.5 per cent, then the retirement benefit would be calculated in the following way:

$60 000 × 20 years × 1.5 per cent = $18 000.

In this instance, the annual pension is $18 000.

A once-only lump sum can be calculated as:

annual pension × 10 years = $18 000 × 10 = $180 000.

There is a global trend for defined benefit plans to be replaced by defined contribution or accumulation plans. This change has been brought about by increased life expectancy (and the associated increase in costs), increased compliance requirements, potential financial liabilities and a desire to transfer risk from the organisation to the employee.[60]

Defined contribution plans

Defined contribution plans, sometimes called accumulation plans, calculate the employee's retirement benefit on the basis of the accumulated contributions and superannuation fund earnings at the time of retirement (that is, the final benefit is the sum of all contributions plus interest earned). The benefit may be paid in the form of a lump sum or a pension (via the purchase of an **annuity**). Defined contribution plans are fully funded, while defined benefit plans require actuarial calculations to determine the amount required to meet promised benefit levels.

Contributions are determined by a formula, usually 5 per cent of the employee's annual salary and an equivalent or greater amount contributed by the employer. It is estimated that over 80 per cent of Australian companies offer defined contribution plans.[61]

Employer and employee contributions

The issue of employee contributions to superannuation is somewhat controversial. In the case of contributory plans, the employee and the employer jointly contribute to the superannuation fund. In the case of non-contributory plans, contributions are made solely by the employer. Most superannuation plans in Australia are of the contributory type. Unions traditionally prefer non-contributory plans.

Issues in superannuation

Retirement age

In Australia, the traditional retirement ages were 65 years for men and 60 years for women. This difference is discriminatory and the pension age for women is being increased gradually from 60 to 65 to bring it into line with the pension age for men. An added dilemma is the question of compulsory retirement — in Australia, it is regarded as discriminatory and therefore illegal.[62]

Unfunded Commonwealth government superannuation liabilities for public servants amount to almost $90 billion, placing an obligation of more than $4000 on each Australian. An additional $40 billion also exists in state government liabilities.

The size of benefits

The size of superannuation benefits in Australia has been steadily increasing. The public sector has accelerated the increase by linking its pension benefits to the cost of living. Private employers simply cannot afford to provide commensurate benefits and are legally prohibited from operating unfunded plans, so the disparity between public and private sector superannuation benefits appears set to continue. (Unfunded Commonwealth government superannuation liabilities amount to almost $90 billion.)[63]

Early retirement

Retirement before the age of 65 years is generally viewed as **early retirement**. Some superannuation plans allow employees to retire with reduced benefits as early as 10 to 15 years before the standard retirement age. The average age of retirement is 58 for an Australian male and 41 for an Australian female.[64]

Early retirement Occurs when an employee retires from an organisation before the standard retirement age.

Major reasons for early retirement are to allow for lifestyle and to permit organisations to open up jobs for younger employees. Another reason is that early retirees in receipt of a lump-sum payment have been able to manipulate their financial circumstances so they can later qualify for the age pension. This 'double dipping' adds greatly to the costs of providing age pensions and reduces the effectiveness of superannuation as a means of providing for employee retirement. For example, an employee could retire at age 55, take a lump-sum superannuation benefit, spend it over 10 years and then apply for an age pension. In an effort to overcome this drain on resources, the government introduced tax incentives to motivate employees to keep their entitlements invested in an approved superannuation fund until they are 65 years of age. According to one Australian expert, if work force participation by 55–70 year olds rose by just 10 per cent, average per capita incomes would increase 4 per cent.[65] A further problem is that serious skill shortages can result because employees are given an incentive to retire early. This has led to calls to stop early retirement and to encourage special training programs and flexible pay arrangements for older workers.[66]

Vesting

Vesting refers to an employee's earned benefit rights. This means that the employee has the right to superannuation benefits even if they leave the organisation before the normal retirement date. Vesting usually applies after a specified number of years of service. If employees leave before vesting occurs, they have a right only to their own contributions to the superannuation plan.

Vesting Provision in a retirement plan that gives employees a right to specific benefits after a stated number of years of service.

Union-sponsored superannuation schemes governed by an award are all fully vested. Many public and private sector schemes remain unvested or only partially vested. Some superannuation schemes also have a **portability** provision, which permits an employee's entitlement to be transferred to another superannuation plan on change of employment.

Portability The ability of an employee to transfer without penalty their accrued retirement benefits from one superannuation plan to another.

Industry funds

Promoted by the trade union movement, industry superannuation funds have experienced spectacular growth. Industry funds now cover more than one-third of the work force.[67]

Considerable controversy arose with the introduction of industry funds. This was partly because of employer fears of the enormous financial power that union-controlled superannuation schemes would possess. Some unions contributed to employer concerns by strong-arm tactics and moves to channel superannuation funds into investments that they designated as politically and socially desirable.[68] Other ongoing criticisms of industry super-annuation funds relate to their appropriateness, lack of flexibility, restricted choice, emphasis on accumulation plans, exclusion of private occupational schemes and politicisation.[69]

In practice, leading industry funds such as the Australian Retirement Fund (ARF), Cbus and REST have pursued traditional investment policies, have been efficiently run, have had low-cost structures and have consistently outperformed their retail competitors.[70] Further-more, industry funds appear to be more member-focused and less driven by shareholder demands and the payment of sales commissions.[71] Union involvement in superannuation, overall, has had a positive and dramatic impact on generating improved retirement benefits for employees.

Industry funds have always provided the lowest fees and very good performance but are seldom recommended by financial planners and accountants because they do not pay commissions.

Superannuation portability

Another controversial issue relates to employee freedom of choice in selecting the fund into which compulsory employer contributions are to be invested. Proponents claim that this is a basic right of all employees. Critics argue that most employees lack knowledge and will be easily exploited by unscrupulous investment advisers resulting in the payment of more exit and entry fees and other fees.[72] A recent study, for example, found that half the population knows nothing about the cost of superannuation and that less than half can understand a superannuation statement.[73]

AIDS, drug-related death and superannuation

The cost of death and disability cover for group superannuation schemes is expected to increase because of claims related to AIDS and drug-related death. As most superannuation schemes demand little or no medical screening, they risk being exposed to increasing costs and financial liabilities.

HR managers acting as fund trustees need to address this problem and develop appro-priate policies. Questions that should be asked include the following:

- Does the organisation wish to cover all employees in the superannuation scheme for ben-efits on death from AIDS and drug-related conditions?
- Is comprehensive cover available from insurers and what will it cost?
- If the insurer rejects an AIDS or drug-related claim, what is the benefit liability under the fund?
- What action, if any, needs to be taken to ascertain the fund's liabilities?
- Do the existing membership conditions apply to future employees or does the organ-isation wish to protect the fund against claims arising from employees who join the fund when they know they are infected with AIDS or are drug dependent?[74]

Women and superannuation

Compared with men, women live longer, earn less and are often out of the paid work force for a substantial part of their adult life. In addition, a high proportion of women in employ-ment are employed in part-time or casual work.

All these factors have imposed severe barriers on women gaining adequate access to superannuation and securing adequate benefits. It is estimated that half of all Australian women retiring in the next 10 years will have superannuation savings of less than $20 000.[75] A study by Rosenman and Winocur found that the major reasons for the low participation rate of women in superannuation schemes were:

- ineligibility on the grounds of age or work status
- the perceived unattractiveness of superannuation for women because of its cost, lack of portability and unsuitability for leaving and returning to the work force
- a belief that their financial future was secured by their husband's or partner's super-annuation scheme.[76]

Rosenman and Winocur concluded that 'by choosing not to join superannuation schemes whatever the circumstances, women are also choosing financial dependence in retirement, be it on a spouse or on the age pension'.[77] Similarly, a survey by Onyx and Watkins found that women were failing to plan for their own futures with the result that an increasing number of women were falling into 'genteel poverty' when their husband either left them or died unexpectedly.[78] A US survey found that 80 per cent of widows living in poverty were not poor before their husband died.[79]

Since one in three marriages now ends in divorce, the need for women to have their own personal superannuation is obvious.

The major recommendations made by Rosenman and Winocur to advance the position of women in superannuation included the following:

- Superannuation schemes should allow part-time and casual workers to join or retain membership.
- Preservation of superannuation benefits should be facilitated and encouraged when women leave the work force to have families.
- Superannuation tax benefits should be extended to women either temporarily or permanently outside the work force who continue to contribute to their own superannuation.
- Portability of superannuation schemes for women across employers should be encouraged.
- In the event of a divorce, a woman's right to a share of the anticipated superannuation benefit accrued during the marriage must be enforced.[80]

Changes are occurring. Women are beginning to plan earlier for their retirement, insurance companies are targeting women as a huge untapped market, superannuation schemes that blatantly discriminate against women have all but disappeared, union pressure for improvement is increasing, and legislation has been introduced requiring superannuation plans to make provision for part-time employees.[81]

Summary

Employee benefits are a rapidly growing part of an employee's total compensation. Social trends, government legislation, union pressure, taxation and competitive forces all make benefits an increasingly attractive but expensive form of compensation. Most employers offer a wide range of benefits. Some benefits, such as annual leave, are required by law, while other benefits, such as childcare, are provided voluntarily by some employers.

To be of value, benefits must be related to the organisation's strategic business objectives and to employee needs. Cost-effective benefits that are preferred by employees are in the organisation's long-term competitive interest as they can be a positive recruiting aid and motivational force. The strategic use of benefits can thus help give an organisation a competitive edge by enabling it to better attract and retain people with the skills it needs to achieve its key business objectives.

Thirty interactive Wiley Web Questions are available to test your understanding of this chapter at **www.johnwiley.com.au/ highered/hrm5e** *in the student resources area*

terms to know

accident make-up pay (p. 519)

annuity (p. 528)

benefits (p. 516)

cafeteria benefits (p. 519)

defined benefit plans (p. 528)

defined contribution plans (p. 528)

disability insurance (p. 521)

early retirement (p. 529)

employee assistance programs (EAPs) (p. 521)

flexitime (p. 523)

fringe benefits (p. 517)

fringe benefits tax (FBT) (p. 518)

mandatory benefits (p. 519)

non-contributory superannuation (p. 519)

portability (p. 529)

preventive health programs (p. 522)

superannuation (p. 526)

vesting (p. 529)

voluntary benefits (p. 519)

workers compensation (p. 519)

review questions

1. Why do employers provide benefits?
2. Which employee benefits do you most desire? Why?
3. Should retirement be compulsory at age 65? Explain the arguments for and against.
4. Why should young employees be concerned about superannuation?
5. Why is it important for a company to effectively communicate benefit costs and other information to its employees?
6. 'Instead of providing benefits, companies should pay cash.' Do you agree or disagree with this statement? Explain your reasoning.
7. How might increasing work force diversity affect benefit design and administration?
8. Why should benefit programs be integrated with corporate and HRM objectives?
9. What role do benefits play in a person's decision to join or leave a company?
10. Which benefits do you think will appeal most to the following employees?
    (a) A 22-year-old single BBA graduate
    (b) A 48-year-old married electrician with four dependent teenage children
    (c) A 25-year-old single parent of a two-year-old child who works part-time as a supermarket cashier
    (d) A 35-year-old university lecturer with a working partner and two children aged seven and nine
    (e) A 55-year-old divorced sales representative with no dependants

environmental influences on employee benefits

Discuss the key environmental influences from the model (figure 14.3 shown opposite) that have significance for employee benefits.

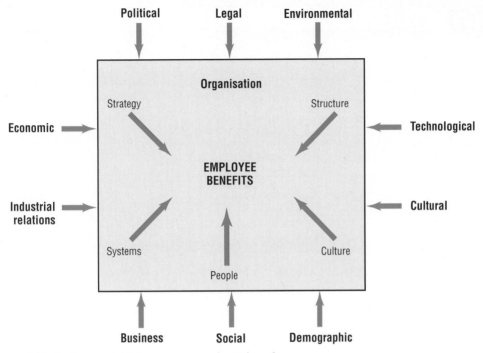

Figure 14.3 Environmental influences on employee benefits

class debate

Superannuation benefits for politicians and public servants should be switched from guaranteed defined benefit plans to defined contribution or accumulation plans as used by most Australians.
Or
Retirement at a specified age (for example, 60 years) should be compulsory for everyone.

what's your view?

Write a 500-word response to the Letter to the Editor on page 524, agreeing or disagreeing with the writer's point of view.

practitioner speaks

Read the article on page 525. Critically discuss the author's claim that the most significant trend is the move away from guaranteed compensation to performance-related compensation. In particular, discuss the impact that this may have on benefits.

newsbreak exercise

Read the Newsbreak 'Boomers face tough retirements' on page 522. As a class, critically review the article and discuss its implications for organisations, HRM and you personally.

What do you think? Conduct a mini survey of class members, using the questionnaire below. Critically discuss the findings.

1.	Taxing employee fringe benefits is unfair.	YES	NO
2.	Dependent children should not be entitled to benefits after the age of 18.	YES	NO
3.	Flexible work schedules are not a benefit; they are simply a means to further exploit workers.	YES	NO
4.	Employees under age 30 should not have to contribute to superannuation.	YES	NO
5.	Companies should pay their employees' union dues.	YES	NO
6.	Unmarried partners should not be entitled to dependent benefits.	YES	NO

online exercise

1. Conduct an online search for information on employee benefits in one of the following locations: Australia, China, Hong Kong, India, Indonesia, Japan, Malaysia, New Zealand, Singapore, Taiwan, Thailand, the United Kingdom or the United States. Write a 500-word executive summary on your findings. Include the web sites that you found useful.
2. Conduct an online search for information on one of the following retirement programs: Mandatory Provident Fund (Hong Kong), Central Provident Fund (Malaysia), Central Provident Fund (Singapore) or Labor Retirement Fund (Taiwan). Prepare a 300-word executive summary highlighting the key features of the selected program.

ethical dilemma

Super at XYZ Ltd

'Look, it's obvious that we have to do something. Funding superannuation is becoming a black hole for this company', barked Keith Barnes, Financial Controller for XYZ Ltd.

'I agree', retorted John Kolikias, XYZ's Managing Director. 'Keeping our defined benefit plan based on final salary may give our employees certainty regarding their super benefits, but with the downturn in the market it is killing us. We have to come up with an additional $30 million this year to keep the plan in the black. Unlike the government, we cannot pass on our underfunding problems to future generations of Australians. We have to be financially responsible.'

Jo Santini, HR Manager, interrupted. 'But if we move to a defined contribution or accumulation plan, that transfers all the risk to employees. The present plan commits us to paying employees a percentage of their final pay regardless of market conditions. Under your proposal, employees will be vulnerable to fluctuations in the stock market. Is that fair?'

'Is it fair that the financial viability of this company is threatened by this employee benefit?' snapped Keith.

'Keith, I hear what you're saying, but think about it for a minute. Our defined benefit plan not only gives our employees a sense of certainty, but it also rewards loyalty by permitting employees to grow their benefits in the years just before they retire. The changes you propose will discriminate against our older and longest-serving employees.'

Keith sighed. 'Jo, converting from a defined benefit plan to a defined contribution plan is a global trend. Continuing with a defined benefit plan is a burden that this company can no longer afford.'

Discussion questions

1. Who do you agree with? Why?
2. What ethical issues are raised in this case?

case studies

Super rip-off at Jet Red

Stan Vines, Marketing Manager for Jet Red, pushed his superannuation statement across Linda Church's desk. 'I tell you Linda, this is a rip-off. How HR ever got us involved with such a plan is beyond me. My fund is down and yet I'm still being charged like a wounded bull. Do you realise that in the past two years the fund manager has lost me more than $80 000? I'm 57 — how am I expected to make that up? I'm due to retire in less than three years.'

Linda studied the statement. 'Well, I must say, it doesn't look good, but the markets have been down across the board.'

'Linda, I understand that. What outrages me is not just the lousy performance but the fees I'm being charged. The fund manager takes out 4 per cent of everything I contribute, then charges me 2 per cent to further lose my money. My super is worth about $400 000. That means I'm paying $8000 a year in management fees alone.'

'But those charges are fairly standard Stan.'

'Maybe so for a retail fund, but not for an industry fund. Look at this article. It says that over five years the average industry fund has outperformed the average retail master trust by 17 per cent.'[82]

'Mmm, that's a big difference', replied Linda.

'You bet it is. Industry funds have outperformed Jet Red's fund manager by a country mile and are much cheaper. I want to change to the Australian Retirement Fund — it has low administration fees and good performance.'

'How much are the fees Stan?'

'Only $1 per week, plus its investment costs are much lower than what I'm paying now. What's more, the performance of its balanced fund has consistently beaten the average for the typical commercial balanced fund.'[83]

Linda sighed. 'I'm afraid it's not quite that simple.'

'What do you mean?' asked Stan.

'Well, our present arrangement is for all company contributions to be paid into Oz Super Managed Funds. You can select an income, balanced or growth fund offered by them, but that is your only choice. You can't change the fund manager.'

'You're telling me that I have to put up with substandard performance and continue to pay outrageous fees? This means I'm losing out twice.'

'I'm afraid so, Stan. You don't have a choice.'

Discussion questions

1. What ethical issues are raised in this case?
2. If you were Linda, what would you do now?

Exercises

1. Form into groups of four to six. Imagine you are members of a task force charged with reviewing Jet Red's superannuation scheme.
   (a) Select a superannuation plan offered by a retail fund manager to compare with the Australian Retirement Fund (ARF).
   (b) Compare the two plans on the basis of cost (entry and exit fees, management fees and other fees) and performance over one, three and five years. (To compare ARF with another superannuation fund, click on the Super Fund Comparator tool at ARF's web site at www.arf.com.au.)[84]
   (c) Write a 500–750 word executive report listing your findings and recommendations.
2. Find out the difference between an income fund, a balanced fund and a growth fund. Which is likely to be most suitable for (a) a 25-year-old employee, (b) a 45-year-old employee and (c) a 55-year-old employee? Explain your answer.

Benefit review at Jet Red

Alan Balkin, Jet Red's Managing Director, shifted in his black leather chair. 'Linda, I want to be sure we're getting value for our money. We spend about 40 per cent of payroll on benefits. I don't have to tell you that's big bucks. I need hard data, not opinions, before I consider any requests for changes to our benefit program.'

Linda Church, HR Manager, and Lal Krishna, Benefits Specialist, looked at each other. 'Okay, Alan', said Linda, 'we'll be back once we get the necessary information.'

Exercises

1. Assume you are part of the HR team assigned by Linda and Lal to survey the present range of benefits offered by Jet Red.
    (a) Design a questionnaire to survey:
        - employee understanding of Jet Red's present benefits program
        - the ranking employees give to existing or alternative benefits
        - changes to the benefit program employees would like to see introduced (for example, improvements in administration, the type of benefits offered, and so on).
    (b) Using your questionnaire, conduct a survey of class members or employees in a local organisation.
    (c) Using Maslow's hierarchy of needs (see pages 415–6) analyse the employees' rankings of benefits.
    (d) Prepare a report for Alan Balkin on your findings.
2. Break into groups of four to six. Compile a list of typical benefits available to the following employees:
    (a) a university lecturer
    (b) a nurse
    (c) an HR manager
    (d) an unskilled casual worker
    (e) a state school teacher
    (f) a private school teacher.
    As a class, review and discuss your findings.

suggested readings

Armstrong, M. and Munis, H., *Reward Management: A Handbook of Remuneration Strategy and Practice*, 4th edn, Kogan Page, London, 2003.

CCH, *Australian Master Human Resource Guide*, CCH, Sydney, 2003, chs 12, 31, 32, 33, 34.

De Cieri, H. and Kramar, R., *Human Resource Management in Australia*, McGraw-Hill, Sydney, 2003, pp. 173, 467, 548–9.

Fisher, C. D., Schoenfeldt, L. F. and Shaw, J. B., *Human Resource Management*, 5th edn, Houghton Mifflin, Boston, 2003, pp. 627–46.

Ivancevich, J. M., *Human Resource Management*, 8th edn, McGraw-Hill, Boston, 2001, ch. 12.

Ivancevich, J. M. and Lee, S. H., *Human Resource Management in Asia*, McGraw-Hill, Singapore, 2002, ch. 12.

Mondy, R. W., Noe, R. M. and Premeaux, S. R., *Human Resource Management*, 8th edn, Prentice Hall, Upper Saddle River, NJ, 2002, ch. 12.

Nankervis, A. R., Compton, R. L. and Baird, M., *Strategic Human Resource Management*, 4th edn, Nelson, Sydney, 2002, pp. 470–1.

Smith, B. and Koken, E., *Retirement Income Streams*, 2nd edn, Wrightbooks, Melbourne, 2002, chs 1, 2, 3, 6.

online references

www.abr.com
www.acaonline.org
www.aetnafinancial.com
www.ahrm.orglaca.htm
www.allbenefits.com
www.amanet.org/periodicals/cbr
www.amp.com.au
www.arf.com.au
www.asx.com.au
www.ato.gov.au
www.benamerica.com
www.benefitslink.com
www.btonline.com.au
www.centrelink.gov.au
www.colonialfirststate.com.au

www.ebri.org
www.fpa.asn.au
www.ing.com.au
www.mic.com.au
www.mlim.com.au
www.moneyweb.com.au
www.perpetualinvestments.com.au
www.quicken.com/retirement
www.SelectingSuper.com.au
www.shrm.org.hrmagazine
www.superannuation.asn.au
www.taxpayer.com.au
www.workforceonline.com
www.zurich.com.au

end notes

1. A. Kahler, 'Super feeding frenzy', *Australian Financial Review*, 22 May 2002, p. 60.
2. K. Mathes, 'Strategic planning: define your mission', *HR Focus*, February 1993, p. 11.
3. D. E. Bowen and C. A. Wadley, 'Designing a strategic benefits program', *Compensation and Benefits Review*, vol. 21, no. 5, 1989, p. 44.
4. R. Anderson, 'Beyond the colour of money', *HR Monthly*, November 1999, p. 32.
5. D. E. Bowen and C. A. Wadley, op. cit., pp. 45–6.
6. Adapted by the author from D. E. Bowen and C. A. Wadley, op. cit., p. 47.
7. D. E. Bowen and C. A. Wadley, op. cit., p. 48.
8. G. Glynn, 'Criteria for identifying domestic partners', *Personnel Journal*, March 1994, p. 12; 'Varied definitions of family', *HR Magazine*, June 1993, p. 20; and M. Fastenau, 'Prejudices that hide behind "values" hamper HR professionalism', *HR Monthly*, November 1996, pp. 26–7.
9. H. Grennan, 'Take your pick', *Bulletin*, 17 December 1996, pp. 48–50.
10. M. Innis, 'Equity: the new salary package', *Australian Financial Review — Special Report*, 22 November 2000, p. 3; M. Lawson, 'The gloss goes off packaging', *Australian Financial Review — Special Report*, 18 May 2000, p. 1; and M. Laurence, 'Beware of package pitfalls', *Personal Investor*, March 2001, p. 83.
11. H. van Leeuwen and F. Buffini, 'Why the system needs fixing', *Australian Financial Review*, 2 July 1997, p. 16

12. M. Laurence, 'FBT's nasty new bite', *Business Review Weekly*, 13 March 1995, pp. 40–5; and S. Bagwell, 'Threat to child-care under fire', *Australian Financial Review*, 15 November 1996, p. 26.
13. J. Main, 'The battle over benefits', *Fortune*, 16 December 1991, p. 59.
14. M. Freudenheim, 'US workers' share of health costs grows', *International Herald Tribune*, 11 September 2003, p. 12.
15. B. E. Wachsman and K. J. Swanson, 'Managed health versus managed care: one part of cost management', *HR Focus*, May 1992, p. 11.
16. Australian Bureau of Statistics, quoted in 'Snapshot', *Bulletin*, 29 December 1992 – 5 January 1993, p. 38.
17. S. Hoyle, 'Sickies cost $15 billion a year: study', *Australian Financial Review*, 5 March 1997, p. 4.
18. S. Neales, 'Tackling the equity issue of company child care', *Australian Financial Review*, 10 April 1990, p. 4.
19. M. N. Martinez, 'Work-life programs reap business benefits', *HR Magazine*, June 1997, pp. 110–14.
20. S. Jackson and L. Briggs, 'Esso, Lend Lease tackle the problem', *Weekend Australian*, 3–4 March 1990, p. 39.
21. S. Bagwell, 'Bean counters set child care agenda', *Australian Financial Review*, 21 May 1997, p. 21; and C. Kenkes, 'Childcare keeps staff, if mix right', *Weekend Australian — Careers*, 22–23 April 2000, p. 1.
22. SHRR, 'The ageing of America will create elder care needs', *Workplace Visions*, May–June 1997, p. 2.
23. New South Wales Department of Women report, *Aged Care Facts for Australian Employers*, reported in A. Moodie, 'Aged care costs in

absenteeism and staff losses', *Australian Financial Review*, 6 June 1997, p. 59.

24. K. Walter, 'Elder care obligations', *HR Magazine*, July 1996, pp. 98–103.

25. A. Moodie, 6 June 1997, op. cit., p. 59.

26. D. Knuckey, 'Drinking on job an $8bn problem', *Weekend Australian*, 2–3 June 1990, p. 35.

27. K. Pechter, 'Corporate fitness and blue collar fears', *Compensation and Benefits Review*, vol. 19, no. 2, 1987, p. 71.

28. K. Pechter, op. cit., pp. 72–3.

29. M. Ragg, 'Companies working on getting fit', *Weekend Australian*, 19 March 1990, p. 13.

30. K. Pechter, op. cit., pp. 73–5.

31. D. James and M. Dobbie, 'Are company health programs really worth their salt?', *Business Review Weekly*, 11 May 1990, p. 94.

32. L. Thornburg, 'Change comes slowly', *HR Magazine*, February 1994, p. 46.

33. D. Plowman, 'Flexible working hours — some labour relations implications', *The Journal of Industrial Relations*, vol. 19, no. 3, 1977, pp. 307–13.

34. Reported in M. Davis, 'Flexible hours can work against women', *Australian Financial Review*, 20 November 1996, p. 5.

35. N. Ravo, 'New perk: the workplace sabbatical', *Australian Financial Review*, 26 September 1997, p. 13; and D. Townshend, 'Points of departure', *Australian Financial Review — Weekend Review*, 22 August 1997, p. 3.

36. BT Funds Management, 'Australians and their savings', *BT Investors Circle*, Autumn 1996, p. 4.

37. 'Personal superannuation', The Rothschild Report No. 18, *Australian Financial Review*, 5 June 1996, p. 11; and H. Van Leeuwen, 'Super savings inadequate, AMP claims', *Australian Financial Review*, 15 July 1997, p. 7.

38. Study by the Association of Superannuation Funds of Australia, the University of New South Wales and the Australian Council of Aging, reported in P. Coombes, 'Retirement budgeting needs rigour', *Australian Financial Review — Special Report*, 22 November 2000, p. 9; and R. Kelly, 'Life's not much fun if you're running on empty', *Australian Financial Review — Special Report*, 25 July 2002, p. 11.

39. J. Collett, 'Don't run out of super fuel', *My Money*, July 2000, p. 21.

40. T. Blue, 'The battle for your super money', *Weekend Australian*, 9–10 October 1999, p. 38.

41. T. Blue, 'Our easy steps on road to riches', *Weekend Australian*, 8–9 January 2000, p. 35.

42. A. Kohler, 'Billion$ badly spent — the super mess', *Australian Financial Review*, 12–16 April 2001, pp. 19, 24, 25.

43. M. Bachelard and G. Price, 'It's not the money — it's the perks', *Weekend Australian*, 8–9 April 2000, p. 38; B. Dunstan, 'Labor promises to renew super policy', *Australian Financial Review*, 28 March 2001, p. 7; and C. Murphy, 'Superannuation choice rules face defeat', *Australian Financial Review*, 10 September 2003, p. 3.

44. N. Shoebridge, 'The one-two-three hit to savings', *Business Review Weekly*, 11 August 2000, p. 10.

45. M. Rice, 'Shaping super for the long term', *Personal Investment*, June 1997, pp. 80–1.

46. M. Laurence, 'The super tax grab', *Business Review Weekly*, 11 August 2000, p. 44.

47. R. Kelly, 'Plugging the looming retirement income gap', *Australian Financial Review — Special Report*, 5 June 2002, p. 27.

48. N. Chenoweth, 'Work your way to poverty', *Bulletin*, 27 July 1993, pp. 63–7.

49. C. Marriott, 'Model behaviour', *Asian Investor*, August–September 2003, p. 14.

50. N. Chenoweth, op. cit., pp. 63–7.

51. C. Butler, 'Meddling spawns super cynics', *Australian Financial Review*, 31 January 1997, p. 38; and B. Dunstan, 'Supertax plans ill conceived', *Australian Financial Review*, 10 February 1997, p. 4.

52. D. & D. Tolhurst, '1996 Federal Budget summary — changes to superannuation', *Directions*, Spring 1996, p. 1.

53. M. Laurence, 'Howard's super failure', *Business Review Weekly*, 9–15 May 2002, p. 10.

54. R. Bowerman, 'Winners and losers in super choice', *Personal Investment*, vol. 15, no. 8, September 1997, p. 6.

55. G. Haramis, 'Choice initiatives give greater control to members', *HR Monthly*, July 1997, p. 34.

56. M. Laurence, 'Benefits and pitfalls in choice of fund', *Business Review Weekly*, vol. 19, 30 June 1997, p. 83.

57. Reported in I. Henderson, 'Warning on super double dipping', *Australian*, 3 July 1996, p. 26.

58. B. Dunstan, 'Federal pollies' retirement plan a super deal', *Australian Financial Review*, 19 August 1996, p. 3.

59. B. G. Landstrom and T. B. Bainbridge, 'Defined lump sum plans', *Compensation and Benefits Review*, vol. 28, no. 1, 1996, pp. 40–50.

60. N. Cicutti, 'Everything you ever wanted to know about pensions but were afraid to ask', *Bloomberg Money*, July 2002, pp. 16–23; and L. Gibbs, 'The changing face of pensions', *Money*, April 2003, p. 91.

61. J. H. Christy and J. Doeble, 'Investor power', *Forbes Global*, 7 February 2000, pp. 76–7.

62. M. Fastenau, 'Retirement age concerns require both options and strategies', *HR Monthly*, February 1997, pp. 40–1.

63. D. Elsum, 'Rethink super for MPs, public servants', *Australian Financial Review*, 29 July 2003, p. 51; and Editorial, 'Super deserves seniors debate', *Australian Financial Review*, 25 July 2003, p. 82.

64. N. Field, 'Trend to early retirement gone too far', *Australian Financial Review*, 13 October 1999, p. 7.

65. C. Richards, reported in C. Murphy, 'Retirees threat to welfare', *Australian Financial Review*, 3–4 May 2003, p. 7.

66. C. Murphy, 'OECD wants a stop to early retirement', *Australian Financial Review*, 7 February 2003, p. 23; and M. McLachlan, 'Older workers must stay on', *Australian Financial Review*, 24–27 April 2003, p. 6.

67. M. Laurence, 'Industry super gets aggressive', *Business Review Weekly*, 5 February 1996, p. 34.

68. N. Way, 'Kelly's crusade gets personal', *Business Review Weekly*, 17 November 2000, p. 41; and Editorial, 'Super vehicle needs tune up', *Australian Financial Review*, 9 July 2002, p. 62.

69. M. Laurence, 5 February 1996, op. cit., pp. 34–8; and M. Russell, 'Let the workers choose super: bosses', *Sydney Morning Herald*, 5 July 1995, p. 6.

70. M. Laurence, 5 February 1996, op. cit., p. 38; N. Way, op. cit., p. 41; and S. Hely, 'Super star fund', *Personal Investor*, September 2003, pp. 68–70.

71. M. Dunlevy, 'Superfund builds on members' labour', *Australian Primespace Supplement*, 20 March 2003, p. 14; and S. Hely, 'The rise and rise of industry super funds,' *Personal Investor*, August–September 2003, p. 14.

72. C. Murphy, 'Superannuation choice rules face defeat', *Australian Financial Review*, 10 September 2003, p. 3.

73. ANZ survey, reported in A. Kahler, 'Super still a mystery to most: survey', *Australian Financial Review*, 3–4 May 2003, p. 3.

74. Adapted from A. Sampson, 'AIDS dangers for super funds', *Australian Business*, 15 March 1989, p. 56.

75. B. Collins, 'Wake up call for women', *Connections*, January–February 2003, p. 18.

76. R. Rosenman and S. Winocur, reported in S. Neales, 'Most women not opting for super, study finds', *Australian Financial Review*, 16 May 1989, p. 12; and A. Lane, 'Women and retirement', *Personal Investment*, May 1997, p. 32.

77. Quoted in S. Neales, 16 May 1989, op. cit., p. 12.

78. J. Onyx and A. Watkins, reported in M. Lawson, 'Women fail to plan for future', *Australian Financial Review*, 15 November 1996, p. 23.

79. R. A. Ogilvie, 'Forget the glass slipper, just go for gold', *My Money*, July 2000, p. 28.

80. S. Neales, 16 May 1989, op. cit., p. 12; and P. Moodie, 'Tax system discriminates against women', *Australian Financial Review*, 14 August 1996, p. 11.

81. B. Quinlivan, 'Women and money: a special report', *Personal Investment*, July 1997, pp. 40–6.

82. S. Hely, September 2003, op. cit., p. 68.

83. Australian Retirement Fund, *Annual Report 2002/2003*, p. 2.

84. Australian Retirement Fund, *Annual Report 2002/2003*, p. 7.

SOLICITING EXCELLENCE: STRATEGIC REWARD MANAGEMENT AT WINTON WYNNE MOORE

John Shields, University of Sydney

You could have cut the air in the conference room with a knife. Charles Wynne, Chief National Partner of Sydney commercial law firm Winton Wynne Moore and Associates, had just delivered his address to the firm's 600 Sydney-based solicitors informing them that the previous financial year had been one of the firm's best profit-making years ever. For all of his up-beat assessment, however, Charles showed remarkably poor judgement and timing in his announcement. Just two weeks earlier, the firm had completed its annual pay reviews, which had resulted in increases lower than in any of the previous five years.

As the caterers rolled out the post-address refreshments, many of the solicitors present muttered darkly to each other that the time and effort they had put into achieving this outstanding financial result had not been adequately recognised or rewarded. Several 20-something high achievers who had put in long hours on very difficult legal cases grumbled about leaving the firm (and possibly the legal profession altogether) to work for organisations where their contributions would be far better rewarded. One of the firm's most successful female corporate tax lawyers spoke of going off to work for a merchant bank renowned for the six-figure bonuses it paid to its commercial litigation team.

Such utterances did not bode well for Felicity Fairchild, the firm's new Director of Human Resources. Charles had invited Felicity along to his address to introduce her to the firm's core work force. However, the conversations that she overheard left her feeling quite unnerved — and she had every reason to suspect that unless she did something to address this undercurrent of reward dissatisfaction, her recent career move would end in disaster. With five years experience as a senior HR administrator in a large not-for-profit organisation — a job that she greatly enjoyed — Felicity had taken a gamble by making a career move into a 'mainstream' corporate HR position. Whatever her initial expectations of her new job, though, she was now under no illusions as to the magnitude of the challenge that awaited her.

The firm's strategy and structure

Winton Wynne Moore and Associates is one of the country's largest national commercial law firms, employing over 800 people in its Sydney office alone. It also has offices in most other Australian capital cities. Its mission is to be 'the provider of choice of commercial legal services to Australian corporations' and its chief goals are to double its business in the highly profitable fields of corporate mergers and acquisitions, insurance litigation and tax law over the next triennium.

Like most other large legal firms, Winton Wynne Moore has a hierarchical structure based on seniority. Being a partnership, the firm is not listed on the stock exchange and responsibility for its governance resides with its 25 partners, all highly experienced and respected members of the legal profession. The firm's 1200 solicitors nationwide are categorised into the following four position grades:

- graduates at law, currently numbering 200
- junior solicitors (with 1–3 years experience), currently numbering 400
- senior solicitors, currently numbering 500
- senior associates, currently numbering 100.

This legal pecking order is also heavily gendered. Although women comprise 50 per cent of the firm's first-year graduates and junior solicitors, they make up only 35 per cent of the senior solicitors and just 25 per cent of the senior associates, while only 5 of the firm's 25 partners are women. In addition to qualified solicitors, the firm employs a large number of legal support staff, including administrative and secretarial staff, librarians and human resource practitioners, of whom over 80 per cent are female. While these workers make a major contribution to the firm's success, they are left in no doubt as to their lowly status in the firm's internal hierarchy. As a woman, Felicity too has quickly come to realise that she faces an uphill battle to invest HR with 'voice' and influence in such a male-dominated authority structure.

Pay for position; promotion for performance

At present, remuneration for Winton Wynne Moore's solicitors consists solely of base pay, which is subject to annual review. To date, these reviews have been overseen by the 'staff partner', Simon Moneypenny QC, with only limited input from the HR Department, which has hitherto mainly handled routine recruitment and payroll administration matters. No one else in the firm apart from Simon and his fellow partners seems to know just how these annual base pay decisions are arrived at. Employees are simply informed that 'a variety of factors will be taken into account' in determining their annual pay rise. Similarly, while pay levels for each of the four grades of solicitors are obviously geared to some combination of seniority, experience and competence, just how pay relativities between grades are fixed remains something of a mystery, with the partners evidently assuming that solicitors learn as they go, adapting and improving their legal knowledge and skills over time.

Solicitors in any given grade receive 'more or less' the same base pay, irrespective of whether their performance is exceptional or just acceptable, with promotion to a higher grade being the firm's preferred way of rewarding consistently high performance. In the absence of any formal system of performance appraisal and review, solicitors' performance is defined and measured in terms of 'billable hours' worked. As is the norm in the legal profession, to ensure that the firm obtains value for money from these base payouts, each solicitor is expected to meet a minimum budgetary requirement for the number of hours billed to clients each day. The minimum requirement is set at an average of 7.5 hours per day, with charge-out rates ranging from $150 per hour for a new graduate to $500 for a senior associate. No additional rewards are in place for those solicitors who exceed their annual billable hours budget. Budget underperformers are simply 'managed out'.

What Simon says

Wishing to discover more about the firm's remuneration practices, Felicity arranged an interview with Simon Moneypenny, who informed her that the solicitors' base pay is determined 'by a variety of things such as the market rate in other major law firms, level of seniority and certain extraordinary qualities a solicitor may possess'. When pressed, Simon volunteered that the 'market' information used to set pay levels for each grade was actually limited to one Melbourne-based law firm with a similar grade structure but also with a reputation for doing insurance litigation 'on the cheap'.

Somewhat sheepishly, Simon also revealed to Felicity that until last year he had shared information on pay ranges with his counterparts in two Sydney-based commercial law firms, but that cooperation had now come to an acrimonious end. To Simon's dismay, despite having reached a gentleman's agreement to set the same pay levels for the ensuing financial year, the two other firms held off announcing their annual pay reviews until after Winton Wynne Moore had done so, then they introduced base pay levels 30 per cent above those offered by Winton Wynne Moore. As a result, the two competitor firms were able to poach some of Winton Wynne Moore's best high-flyers in the highly lucrative areas of mergers and acquisitions and taxation law, and the company had also encountered increasing difficulty in attracting any of the latest batch of top-notch law graduates.

Simon also confided to Felicity that while the existing pay system does incorporate grade-specific pay ranges for the purpose of recognising solicitors with 'extraordinary skills and talent', the range is never more than 10 per cent. Simon explained that this was because the firm wished to avoid internal conflict over pay inequality and because having a uniform rate of pay encouraged teamwork, a common feature of much of the firm's litigation work. Ironically, the fact that the firm encourages secrecy in pay administration actually serves to amplify the negative effect of the small pay disparity within each grade. The outcomes of the annual pay reviews are communicated to solicitors in sealed envelopes marked 'private and confidential' and, as a consequence, there is a great deal of rumour (much of it ill-founded) about disparity in pay for solicitors in the same grade.

Finally, Simon admitted to Felicity that the absence of systematic performance appraisal made it all the more difficult to justify pay differences between individuals in any given grade. He remained convinced, though, that individual performance appraisal is 'more trouble than it is worth and a totally unproductive exercise, especially when it comes to billable hours'.

Felicity's challenge: a new approach to soliciting excellence

The more she heard, the more Felicity wondered whether she had made the right career move; but she is not faint-hearted and also knows that she has much to do and little time to lose. It is clear that there are serious shortcomings with the firm's existing approach to performance, remuneration and reward management. The firm is failing to attract top talent and is losing some of its star performers to competitors and other industries. There is growing dissatisfaction in its core work force with existing base pay levels and the absence of adequate rewards for high performance. No one really understands or can justify the annual pay review outcomes, and pay secrecy simply exacerbates the distrust. Promotion alone cannot motivate solicitors adequately. The limited number of senior associate and partner positions means that the firm cannot reward all high performers with promotion to the top — unless, that is, it wishes to become a 'top-heavy' organisation, which, in any case, would simply devalue the prestige of senior positions.

Felicity's meeting with Simon had one important positive outcome: he agreed to give her a free hand to implement changes to the firm's performance and reward management systems and to guarantee support for her change program at partner level. So what exactly should she propose? Should she recommend a 'scorched earth' approach involving radical change to both base pay and rewards for performance? Should she propose the introduction of performance-related cash incentives? If so, of what type and using what performance measures? Alternatively, should she experiment with performance rewards of a non-cash nature? Should she concentrate on changing the firm's position-based approach to base pay? If so, should change simply involve adjusting pay levels for each grade or should it be more thorough, entailing, say, a move to broadbanding and base pay progression based not on seniority but on personal contribution? And how could she ensure that whatever changes she opts for constitute a cohesive reward package capable of assisting Winton Wynne Moore to achieve its mission and strategic goals?

Questions

1. What additional HR information does Felicity need in order to properly evaluate the nature and extent of the firm's problems in the management of solicitors' performance and rewards? How should she go about obtaining this information?

2. What are the advantages of retaining the existing system of stand-alone position and seniority-based base pay, and what changes would need to be made to make it more viable and effective?

3. If Felicity were to recommend the introduction of a new base pay system configured according to personal contribution rather than position/seniority, how should the new system be structured and implemented?

4. Should Felicity recommend the introduction of an individual performance-related cash incentive plan for the firm's solicitors? If so, what type of incentive? If not, why not?

5. Would it be preferable to opt for a group-based cash incentive scheme?

6. How might rewards of a non-financial nature be of use to the firm in attracting, retaining and motivating high-performing solicitors, particularly women?

7. Would it be appropriate to introduce regular performance appraisals for the firm's solicitors and, if performance appraisals were to be introduced, what form should they take and should they be linked to pay?

8. How could Felicity ensure that her reward initiatives are properly integrated and strategically aligned?

managing human resources

Part 5 is concerned with industrial relations, the management of change and workplace relations, negotiating in the workplace, employee health and safety, and managing diversity. The case study at the end of the part incorporates many of the issues under discussion by using the example of Merino Wool Combing Company.

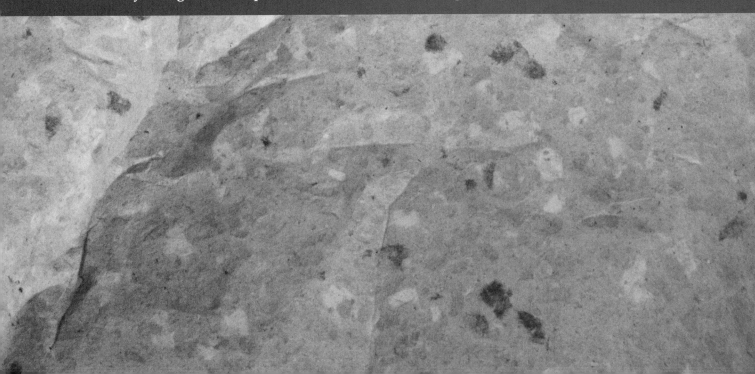

chapter

15

industrial relations

Learning objectives

After studying this chapter, you should be able to:

- Understand the key strategic issues in industrial relations
- Explain the unitarist, pluralist and radical approaches to industrial relations
- Appreciate the role of employers, trade unions and governments in industrial relations
- Discuss individual and collective bargaining, and conciliation and arbitration
- Describe the key elements of the *Workplace Relations Act 1996*.

'The unions are still failing to convince workers that they have an agenda that suits the 21st century.'[1]

Editorial, *The Australian Financial Review*

Australian organisations increasingly are finding themselves in cutthroat competition with the rest of the world. The internationalisation of business means that organisations are now less restricted in their use of workers resident outside of Australia. More and more, employment-related costs and issues are being taken into account when companies make investment decisions. In the cost-sensitive and import-sensitive manufacturing industry, in particular, workplace arrangements that ignore the economic circumstances of individual firms 'will almost certainly result in closures, business failures and job losses'.[2] Trade unions in this environment are also experiencing the scrutiny of the global business community. BHP Billiton's relationship with its unions, for example, is now contingent on the unions 'adding value' and delivering workplace reforms.[3] BHP Billiton's old industrial relations culture, in contrast, was the product of a comfortable protectionist environment where management could appease the unions whenever they raised demands.[4] Militant unions such as the Construction, Forestry, Mining and Energy Union (CFMEU), the Australian Manufacturing Workers Union (AMWU) and the Electrical Trades Union (ETU) nevertheless contain hard line factions, which continue to ignore commercial realities and employ industrial thuggery.[5]

Because of 'closed shops', featherbedding, protectionism, subsidies and the like, some of Australia's industries have been described as sheltered workshops.[6] In fact, in one abattoir, the workers were found to be less productive than those actually working in a sheltered workshop.[7] Australia's food-processing firms lag behind the best international companies because of low labour productivity, poor industrial relations and innovation-shy managers with low performance expectations (motivating overseas companies to invest elsewhere).[8] Similar criticisms are made of the building and construction industry where compulsory unionism (although illegal) is enforced by powerful unions.[9]

Although it is illegal, powerful, militant trade unions are still able to enforce compulsory unionism.

According to former Minister for Industrial Relations, Peter Cook, 'At the heart of the problems underlying Australian industry is the culture that grew up over 90 years of protectionism, which bred complacency, inefficient management, confrontationist industrial relations and a weak international performance in terms of innovation, training and research and development'.[10] The car industry is protected by tariffs of approximately $1 billion per year (which adds about $3000 to the cost of a car for the consumer) and has been described as fat, inefficient and lacking incentive to negotiate competitive agreements with its employees.[11] Patrick Stevedores implemented radical (and controversial) workplace reforms and is planning to bypass Maritime Union labour and further boost productivity by replacing dock workers

with robots.[12] (A trade union researcher similarly claims that future automation will eliminate most mining jobs.[13])

Left-wing critics, however, argue that the demon of globalisation is just a convenient management excuse for cost-cutting and anti-union behaviour designed to decollectivise the workplace and promote market forces. The real problems for Australia's competitiveness, according to such critics, are not in unproductive workplaces, 'but in the boardrooms of banks, large corporations and other centres of financial power'.[14]

International competition nevertheless means that many workers are priced out of the market (especially those with low skills and with only their time to sell). A criticism of Australia's regulated labour market is that it makes it difficult for unskilled workers to get work, protects incompetent employees, increases employers' costs and builds rigidity into the workplace.[15] According to Clark, social security support and Australia's punitive tax rates mean that unemployed members of low-income families have little incentive to seek work.[16] Furthermore, an OECD study shows that the proportion of long-term unemployed rises when the number of regulations enforcing redundancy payments and periods of notice for dismissal increases (because higher dismissal costs make employers reluctant to hire workers).[17] Setting high minimum wages also prices junior and unskilled workers out of jobs and promotes long-term unemployment.[18]

Employment laws and regulations, in addition, place a high cost on business and management time. A study by the Melbourne Institute of Applied Economic and Social Research, for example, found that unfair dismissal laws are discriminatory, inefficient and cost the economy at least 70 000 jobs and $1.3 billion per year.[19] Excessive regulations, high costs and lack of labour flexibility mean that people are no longer viewed as an organisation's greatest asset but rather its greatest liability. Management, as a result, is forced to outsource employees or to utilise professional employee organisations (which manage the client's employees as well as all major HRM activities such as hiring, training, compensation, and so on) to reduce costs, gain flexibility and avoid bureaucratic red tape.[20] Because professional employee organisations free up managers to focus on their core business rather than on employee-related rules, regulations and paperwork, they are now the fastest-growing business service in the United States.[21] In Australia, listed investment company Pacific Strategic Investments has no employees having outsourced all its administration and investment activities.[22]

While there has been improvement in industrial relations, the improvement has been from a very poor base. Continuing concerns over unemployment, massive foreign debt, declining relative standards of living and ever-increasing competition are creating pressures for more industrial relations reform. There is growing union, management and government recognition that economic protectionism breeds stagnation and that global competition breeds high productivity. Higher productivity, in turn, translates into higher pay, better jobs and improved job security.[23] All parties concede that further change is inevitable. The problem is obtaining consensus about the type and degree of change necessary. For example, some advocate a freeing up of the award system and allowing wages to fall to meet the market and for the introduction of more individualistic workplace arrangements. Others, in turn, see this as being anti-union, anti-collectivist and dividing the nation into 'haves' and 'have-nots' through the destruction of comparative wage justice.[24] The way people view the challenges of reform is in a large part influenced by their perspective on industrial relations.

Management cuts costs by reducing the number of employees. As a reward, top managers receive large cash bonuses.

Approaches to industrial relations

Industrial relations (IR), or employee relations (see page 12), involves employees and their unions, employers and their associations and governments and the industrial tribunals that make regulations governing the employment relationship.

Industrial relations is also intimately entwined with political, economic and social forces.[25] Consequently, people differ in their approaches to industrial relations. Some perceive industrial relations in terms of class conflict, others in terms of mutual cooperation and others still in terms of groups with competing interests. HR managers need to understand these varying approaches because they provide the ideological underpinnings for much of the debate about IR reform and the role of HRM.

The unitarist approach

Under the **unitarist approach**, industrial relations is grounded in mutual cooperation, individual treatment, teamwork and the sharing of common objectives.[26] Workplace conflict is seen as a temporary aberration, resulting from poor management, employees who do not fit

Industrial relations Involves employees and their unions, employers and their associations and governments and the industrial tribunals that make regulations governing the employment relationship.

Unitarist approach Industrial relations is grounded in mutual cooperation, individual treatment, teamwork and the sharing of common objectives. Trade unions are regarded as competitors for the employee's commitment and cooperation.

with the organisation's culture or trade union activity. Trade unions are regarded as competitors for the employee's commitment and cooperation. Management's right to manage is accepted because there is no 'them and us'.

The underlying assumption is that it is to the benefit of all to focus on common interests and promote harmony. Conflict in the form of strikes, therefore, is regarded as not only unnecessary, but destructive.

The unitarist approach that underlies much HRM thinking is not without its critics. For example, Osborn says an 'over-emphasis' on value consensus and commonality of interests within organisations means that any diversity of interests within the workplace, the nature of work and the work environment, and the complexity of the underlying historical, economic, social, political, industrial and technological influences that generate tension, dissension, contradictions and conflict in the workplace tend to be ignored. Conflicting interests are disregarded or eschewed as pathological, as trade unions inevitably are. The nature of conflict, the sources and distribution of power (other than that associated with managerial prerogative) and political processes in organisations are either absent or summarily dismissed.[27] In essence, the unitarist approach is seen as a management ideology that legitimises management authority and control, blames conflict on employees rather than management, threatens the existence of unions and is manipulative and exploitative.[28] In this view, HRM is seen as a management tool for seducing employees away from unionism and socialism.[29]

Advocates of the unitarist approach seek a radical overhaul of the industrial relations system. Emphasis is on enterprise industrial relations and direct negotiations with employees. Participation of government, industrial tribunals and unions is not sought or seen as being necessary to achieve good industrial relations.

The pluralist approach

Pluralist approach Regards conflict as inevitable because employers and employees have conflicting interests. Trade unions are seen as a legitimate counter to management authority.

In contrast to the unitarist approach, the **pluralist approach** sees:
* organisations as coalitions of competing interests, where management's role is to mediate among the different interest groups
* trade unions as legitimate representatives of employee interests
* stability in industrial relations as the product of concessions and compromises between management and unions.[30]

Advocates of the pluralist approach argue that in democratic and pluralist societies like Australia, conflict is inevitable. In short, conflict is inherent in all organisations. The legitimacy of management authority is not automatically accepted. Employees join unions to promote their interests and influence management decision making. Unions thus balance the power between management and employees. A strong union movement in the pluralist approach, therefore, is not only desirable, but a necessity. Similarly, society's interests are protected by state intervention through legislation and industrial tribunals, which provide orderly processes for the regulation and resolution of conflict (see figure 15.1).

Proponents of the pluralist approach include many IR academics, labour lawyers, unionists and IR practitioners. The approach is seen as pragmatic and underpins much Australian academic work in industrial relations.[31] Nevertheless, a number of its assumptions have been criticised.[32] Marxists, for example, see power heavily balanced in the favour of management, while many managers believe unions have too much power.[33] Industrial relations consultant (and former union official) Paul Houlihan (reflecting a unitarist approach) argues that IR is about the relationship between employer and employee and not the relationship between the organisations that represent them. 'Employer organisations and unions', says Houlihan, 'have a status they are not entitled to. They impinge on that fundamental relationship in a way that stifles real industrial relations.'[34]

To pressure employers to agree to its demands, a teacher's union places a ban on the processing of exam results.

Australian Industrial Relations Commission (AIRC) Federal industrial tribunal charged with preventing and settling industrial disputes.

Pluralists are likely to seek refinements of the traditional system rather than the introduction of drastic change. The **Australian Industrial Relations Commission (AIRC)**, government, unions and employer associations consequently will be guaranteed continuing roles. Certainly, any attempts to marginalise unions through enterprise bargaining have been strongly resisted. 'The ACTU's position is clear', says a union official, 'it is firmly against the spread of agreements that exclude unions.'[35]

UNION	MANAGEMENT
Strike Employees refuse to work.	*Lockout* Employees are not allowed to enter the workplace.
Bans Employees refuse to undertake particular jobs, to use specified machines or equipment, or to work with certain people.	*Injunction* The company obtains a civil court order to stop a union taking some form of industrial action that it feels is infringing on its legal rights.
Boycott Employees and their union prevent others from doing business with the company.	*Strike breakers* The company uses non-union members or dissident union members (called scabs) to fill the jobs of striking union members.
Picket Employees prevent other employees, customers and suppliers from entering the work site.	*Employer associations* The company uses an employer association (such as the Australian Industry Group) to exert its influence on the union.
Industrial tribunal The union seeks the assistance of an industrial tribunal such as the Australian Industrial Relations Commission to resolve a dispute.	*Industrial tribunal* The company seeks the assistance of an industrial tribunal such as the Australian Industrial Relations Commission to resolve a dispute.

Figure 15.1 The key weapons in adversarial industrial relations

The radical or Marxist approach

Marxists, like pluralists, regard conflict between management and employees as inevitable. However, where pluralists see conflict as inherent in all organisations, Marxists see it as a product of a capitalist society. Adversarial relations in the workplace are simply one aspect of class conflict. The **radical approach** thus focuses on the type of society in which an organisation exists.

Conflict arises not just because of competing interests within the organisation, but because of 'the division within society between those who own or manage the means of production and those who have only their labour to sell'.[36] Industrial conflict is seen as being synonymous with political and social conflict. The solution to employee alienation and exploitation, therefore, is the overthrow of 'the capitalist economic and social system and its replacement by a system in which workers own and control the means of production'.[37] Trade unions are seen as both a logical employee reaction to capitalist exploitation and as part of the overall political process for achieving fundamental changes in society. Unions thus act as 'instruments for challenging the capitalist system of class domination and as schools of solidarity generating consciousness for the class struggle', and their main concerns are issues of control, power and ownership.[38] Concerns with pay rates and conditions of work are secondary, as they focus on improving the workers' position within the capitalist system and not its overthrow.[39] For the Marxists, therefore, all strikes are political.

One Australian radical states: 'Political strikes are a higher form of struggle than economic strikes. Such strikes challenge the government, the state, the rule of the capitalist class. One of our chief tasks is the politicalisation of strikes.'[40] This presents a major challenge for Marxists as research indicates that Australian union members are more interested in 'bread and butter' issues of pay and working conditions than political issues.[41]

Radical approach Sees industrial conflict as an aspect of class conflict. The solution to worker alienation and exploitation is the overthrow of the capitalist system.

Finally, unlike pluralists, Marxists see state intervention via legislation and the creation of industrial tribunals as being supportive of management's interests rather than ensuring a balance of power between competing interests. For Marxists, says Salaman, 'industrial relations is, at best, concerned only with marginal issues and power (relative distribution of pay between employees and the exercise of management's operational authority) rather than fundamental issues (the distribution of wealth and control within society)'.[42] To Marxists, the pluralist approach is supportive of capitalism; the unitarist approach anathema. Comments the leftist 'Australasian Spartacist': '... the trade union bureaucracy is fundamentally loyal to the capitalist system, expressed most directly in its organic links to the ALP social democrats ... to take on and defeat this government orchestrated union busting requires a serious politically organised class struggle fight. A revolutionary workers party ... to do away with the profit system once and for all ...'[43]

IR reforms centred on enterprise bargaining, individual contracts, employee participation, cooperative work cultures and the like consequently face a hostile reception from Marxists. Such initiatives are regarded as nothing more than sophisticated management techniques designed to challenge collective labour and worker militancy and reinforce management control and the continuance of the capitalist system. HR management, in turn, with its underlying unitarist philosophy, emphasis on individualism and questioning of the collective regulation of industrial relations, is viewed as ideologically repugnant, manipulative and exploitive (see figure 15.2).[44] Marxist and radical academics and trade unionists argue that HRM is a threat to employees, does not work and in reality is not practised. The problem, as Grant and Shields point out, is that, if this is all true, how can HRM be a major threat to employees?[45] Furthermore, irrespective of whether HRM is manipulative, the fact is that high-performance HR policies and practices are consistently preferred by workers to situations where they are absent.[46] Finally, high-performance HR policies and practices are employed by the most admired and top performing companies.[47]

THE UNION VIEW: HRM — A WOLF IN SHEEP'S CLOTHING?

Human resource management has become nothing more than an apologist for unreasonable employer demands on working people.

It has become 'consultant speak' to justify a harsher face of modern business — a wolf in sheep's clothing.

HRM is trotted out to justify changes to working conditions and to call for more 'reform'. It has been accompanied by reductions in the award safety net, increased working hours and the eruption of insecure forms of employment.

Research by the Australian Centre for Industrial Relations Research and Training (ACIRRT) shows the rise and rise of human resource management has been matched by:

• The unfair distribution of working hours. Unemployment remains too high while increasing numbers of workers are working longer and longer hours.

• Problems associated with hours worked: over 30 per cent of full-time workers now work more than 50 hours a week and increasing numbers of part-time workers say they need to work more hours. Even 50 per cent of managers want to work fewer hours.

• Unpredictable, irregular and insecure hours: 25 per cent of workers are now casual — with women workers suffering even higher rates of casualisation.

• Mounting intensity of work: people are working harder as well as longer — problems with fatigue, stress and quality of working life mount up.

• A break down in the link between the hours and earnings has occurred. Annualisation of salaries and unpaid overtime have weakened the connection.

Workers' experience does not correspond with the propositions HRM put forward. Workers want to believe what they are hearing, but it does not match the reality of their lives. They are looking for alternative forms to give voice to their scepticism.

Marx and Engels could have been describing HRM in the late 20th century when they wrote in *The Manifesto of the Communist Party*:

'Constant revolutionizing of production, uninterrupted disturbance of all social conditions, everlasting uncertainty and agitation distinguish the bourgeois epoch from all earlier ones. All fixed, fast-frozen relations, with their train of ancient and venerable prejudices and

Figure 15.2 The union view: HRM — a wolf in sheep's clothing?

opinions, are swept away, all new-formed ones become antiquated before they can ossify. All that is solid melts into air, all that is holy is profaned . . .'

Now we have the triumph of transnational business revolutionising its way across all social and workplace relations. Deregulation, market forces and the reduction of collective and social brakes on business are removed. Australian workers, companies, communities and society all struggle in unprecedented times of insecurity, uncertainty and agitation. Fixed positions relent before the unstoppable logic of the market and its own reference point of the 'TINA (There Is No Alternative) Market'.

HRM has become little more than an agent of these triumphal forces. It has become the gate-keeper for management change strategies, ushering out what is socially useful and making way for the socially profane. But in doing so it creates the seeds of its own problems. The contradiction between what HRM promises and the reality of the workplace is too much for workers and the community to reconcile.

This is where the platform for a new type of trade unionism might emerge.

But trade unions have to face up to a few hard realities like making sure they are collective organisations of workers speaking from the realities of working people's lives. Our own constituency has lost faith in our core message:

'Together working people are better and stronger than on their own.' The message has gone unheard by an entire generation of workers and those in many 'sunrise' industries.

Trade unions in the 1980s decided to take the smart decision and consider that capital and deregulation were unbeatable. Most retreated behind barricades of bureaucracy of 'super unions' and we removed ourselves from the people we were meant to represent. Talking more to CEOs we sounded more like the company than the company did. A few took the alternative route to irrelevancy through a retreat to a world of militancy based on false notions of a nation state hidden behind tariff protection. The trouble was each arrived at the same end point — lack of engagement with working people's reality. Both models remain as equally irrelevant to a workforce now highly casualised, fixed term and living in fear of the next 'restructure'.

As the promise of HRM melts into air, the opportunity for unions to influence workplace outcomes again emerges. It remains to be seen if unions are able to put in place the programs to engage workers successfully. HRM has failed to act as the agent brokering the compromise between labour and business. In so doing it provides the trade union movement the platform for our own renewal. The issue for unions is are we up to it?

Figure 15.2 The union view: HRM — a wolf in sheep's clothing?
Source Martin Foley, 'HRM — a wolf in sheep's clothing', *HR Monthly*, June 1999, p. 57.

HRM and industrial relations

The changing role and increasing acceptance of HRM has implications for industrial relations academics and practitioners as well as for HR managers.[48] The emphasis on strategic integration of high-performance HR policies and practices, underpinned by a philosophy of employees as assets, has promoted HRM as business oriented, optimistic and liberating. In contrast, traditional industrial relations seems narrow, pessimistic and static.[49] Moreover, with its focus on cooperation based on the mutuality of employee and organisational objectives, HRM presents a direct challenge to traditional industrial relations centred on conflict inevitability, government intervention and employee representation through trade unions (see figure 15.3).[50] Cherished ideologies and academic theories (and job security) are all under threat. Thus, it is not surprising that HRM has become a topic of considerable controversy.[51]

Plowman says: 'A little bit of ingenuity would enable us to pre-empt the human resource management thrust, and to subsume much of its content into our own paradigm. We also need to counter HRM at the theoretical, educational and administrative levels. The unitarist paradigm underlying HRM should be openly challenged. We need to emphasise that degree courses are about education, not merely training. Many HRM courses are merely training courses in gimmicks. We need to alert administrators that the adoption of courses with inbuilt management biases does long-term harm to academic integrity. Importantly, we must refuse to allow business "benefactors" to call the tune. The HRM thrust should be resisted and repulsed. Not to do so, in my view, would be to put at risk the wellbeing of industrial relations as a field of study.'[52] Boxhall and Dowling likewise note that some academics find the notion of HRM not only distasteful but downright Machiavellian.[53] HRM is seen as a new management tool to secure the levels of compliance and cooperation it requires.[54] Thus, HRM represents nothing more than human resource manipulation and HR managers, in turn, have no claim to being the guardians of humane HRM.[55]

The past — industrial relations	The future — HRM
• Belief that employees are an unavoidable cost of doing business	• Belief that employees are an organisation's most valuable asset
• Belief that conflict is inevitable	• Emphasis on mutual interests and common goals
• Emphasis on 'them and us'	• Emphasis on teamwork
• Little trust between managers and workers	• Increased trust between managers and workers
• Poor communications	• Open communications
• Centralised control by head office staff specialists and by union officials	• Decentralised control with the emphasis on workplace negotiations
• Reliance on external bodies such as the Australian Industrial Relations Commission and employer associations	• Decreased role for the Australian Industrial Relations Commission and employer associations
• Line managers not responsible for industrial relations	• Line managers responsible for industrial relations
• Rigid work practices	• Flexible work practices
• Emphasis on uniformity in pay and conditions	• Emphasis on flexibility in pay and conditions
• Belief that training is a waste	• Belief that training is an investment
• Emphasis on seniority	• Emphasis on ability
• Legalistic and high involvement of industrial lawyers	• Reduced legalism and involvement of industrial lawyers
• Poorly trained managers	• Highly trained managers
• Low employee involvement in decision making	• High employee involvement in decision making
• Employee allegiance to the union	• Employee allegiance to the company

Figure 15.3 HRM and industrial relations

Those who hold such views will only find HRM appealing 'following a much more radical shift of ownership and control in industry'.[56] Given the strong collectivist ethos existing among many Australian and UK academics and trade unionists, it is not surprising that there is considerable opposition to HRM. How strong feelings run on this is shown by the lyrics from an IR academic conference song, 'And all and sundry come and put the boot into HRM'.[57]

Theory, HRM and IR

If HRM is to be a respected area of academic study, it must develop theory. The past decade or so has seen considerable growth in the practice of HRM and its theoretical development. This has brought about the creation of new academic positions in HRM, the change in department names from industrial relations to HRM, and the expansion of courses in HRM. Tensions have arisen from claims that the old industrial relations' emphasis on trade unions and conflict is passé and that its continuing relevance as an area of study is questionable.[58] IR academics transferred into business schools to implant HRM have been faced with the dilemma of what to teach. Serious questions of content exist if HRM is perceived as gimmicky, vocational, lacking in theory, anti-union and legitimising management action and control. IR academic responses range from calls to study political economy, industrial sociology and an understanding of the class structure, to integrating industrial relations and HRM and presenting it as the 'emperor in new clothes' in the form of employment relations or employee relations.[59]

Industrial relations academics may criticise HRM for being theoretically weak, but they cannot dismiss it because it constitutes a teaching threat.[60] Moreover, with a theoretical base in organisational behaviour, personnel psychology and strategic management, HRM offers a broader approach than the narrow 'preoccupation of industrial relations theory and practice in Australia with the institutionalised resolution of conflicting interest'.[61] Boxhall and Dowling note that HRM contributes in three areas where Australian industrial relations has been traditionally weak:

- theory and research on management as an initiator of change in the industrial relations system (rather than unions, tribunals and governments)
- frameworks for understanding enterprise-level relations (rather than centralised award making)
- frameworks for understanding direct and informal management (rather than indirect, formal ones) — that is, employee relations.[62]

Nevertheless, until more rigorous research in HRM (particularly as it relates to the Australian situation) is undertaken, the criticism by some traditional industrial relations academics that HRM is little more than a map providing organisations with principles for managing employees cannot be dismissed as academic paranoia or ideological sour grapes.[63]

Finally, if HRM is to be recognised as pivotal to business, it needs theory because theory explains why events happen. It provides explanations based on logic that are plausible and empirically defensible. Theory enables the HR manager to provide line managers with compelling explanations, interpretations and insights into the organisation's external and internal environments. It explains how and why specific HR policies and practices lead to a particular outcome. Theory thus is essential to explanations of how and why HRM contributes to the organisation's strategic business objectives and employee wellbeing.[64] (It should be noted that IR as an academic discipline is also criticised for being excessively descriptive and lacking in theory, suggesting that IR too is searching to isolate its key characteristics.[65])

Parties in industrial relations

Australian industrial relations has traditionally been dominated by three major parties — government, employers and their associations, and employees and trade unions.[66] The unique system of compulsory **arbitration** that requires the grouping of employers and employees into registered organisations has fostered the growth of trade unions and affected employer approaches to industrial relations.[67] The system is highly institutionalised. The federal government and the Australian Industrial Relations Commission, for example, regulate pay rates and working conditions through legislation and industrial **awards**.[68] Employers and trade unions are clearly bound by a network of rules and regulations that define their rights and obligations. Changes of government, competitive pressures, legislative changes, the continuing decline in union membership, increasing demands for deregulation (and re-regulation) of the labour market and a less centralised industrial relations system have seen the established system of compulsory arbitration revised and revised.[69] One of Australia's leading employer associations the Business Council of Australia (BCA), for example, seeks:

- an enterprise-based employee relations approach, where most matters relating to the terms and conditions of work are settled directly by employers and employees in enterprises
- major changes in the structure of unions to enable only one union to be represented in each workplace and enterprise
- changes to allow employers and employees greater freedom to contract with respect to terms and conditions of work.[70]

Arbitration The submission of a dispute to a third party for a binding decision.

Awards Written determinations setting out the legally enforceable terms and conditions of employment in a firm or industry.

The BCA has been especially critical of:

- the compulsory nature of the arbitration system
- the guarantees enjoyed by unions to represent defined classes of workers
- the absence of a legal framework to ensure compliance with awards and agreements.[71]

The introduction of the *Workplace Relations Act 1996* (see below), with its emphasis on reaching agreements at the enterprise and workplace level, the downplaying of the importance of industrial awards, the erosion of the special role of unions previously guaranteed in the award system, the devolution of IR decision making and the growth of enterprise bargaining, has emphasised the changing roles of the major parties — government industrial tribunals, employer associations and trade unions.[72] The major parties in the new industrial relations are individual employers and employees. Individualism rather than collectivism is emphasised, with the consequence that 'the line between contract based employment law and the collective based industrial law of the award system is blurring'.[73]

The *Workplace Relations Act*, while introducing some major changes, has had its goals of radical reform blunted.[74] Critics, however, argue that the softening of the changes prevented the federal Coalition government from removing protections applying to employee living standards and believe that the Act poses a direct threat to the capacity and structure of unions.[75] Not surprisingly, the **Australian Council of Trade Unions (ACTU)** is agitating for increased regulation and a return to a more centralised system. Items aimed at reversing the Coalition government's reforms include abolishing individual contracts and entrenching in legislation the rights to union bargaining and to strike.[76]

Australian Council of Trade Unions (ACTU) National trade union organisation that represents the Australian trade union movement.

Government and industrial tribunals

Governments have always played a significant part in Australian industrial relations through legislation, **industrial tribunals** and as employers in their own right. Moreover, the approach of government to industrial relations is influenced by the political philosophy of the party in power.[77] The Whitlam Labor government, for example, set pace-setting conditions for federal government employees and encouraged union membership. The Fraser Coalition government introduced legislation that cancelled government collection of union dues and facilitated dismissal of public servants.[78] The Hawke-Keating Labor governments saw significant increases in labour market flexibility and an extension of enterprise bargaining.

Industrial tribunals Refers to government tribunals charged with preventing and settling industrial disputes. The AIRC is Australia's most important industrial tribunal.

The Howard Coalition government has pursued policies promoting decentralised bargaining, non-union agreements and a diminishing role for the Australian Industrial Relations Commission[79] (its interventionist approach to IR is highlighted by its collusion with Patrick Stevedores and the National Farmers Union to de-unionise the waterfront).[80] Labor and Coalition governments, in an effort to secure decisions consistent with their policies, also have sought to influence the AIRC.[81]

Political pressures also strained the relations of the AIRC with the former Labor government and the ACTU.[82] Perceived Labor government damage to the AIRC's integrity and independence and the stacking of senior AIRC positions with ACTU officials caused anger within the Commission and the resignation of Commissioner Turbet (a former union official).[83] The charge of stacking positions was rejected by the ACTU, which argued that at various times the AIRC has been biased in its employer representation.[84] According to Polites, 'industrial relations is seen as a political winner or loser . . . for that reason . . . it has been the plaything of party politics and continues to be so today'.[85]

Should trade unions and companies make financial contributions to political parties irrespective of their members' or shareholders' wishes?

Apart from struggling to maintain its independence, the AIRC is also seeking to redefine its role in the new era of enterprise bargaining and diminution of the importance of awards. The ACTU, although highly critical of the AIRC, still needs it for the continuance of the award system. Furthermore, by restricting access to the AIRC by non-affiliated ACTU organisations, union survival is guaranteed.[86] Other criticisms of the AIRC include its role as a follower of trends rather than a setter and its inability to enforce its decisions.[87]

Recently, the AIRC has been criticised for undermining non-union enterprise agreements and bringing about re-regulation of the federal system by sidestepping the Coalition government's reforms.[88] Interestingly, the AIRC's traditional role was originally challenged not by employer action, but by the break between the ACTU and the federal Labor government with the AIRC.[89] According to one commentator using a football analogy, the AIRC has ceased to be the referee and instead has become a part of the medical staff.[90]

The pivotal role historically played by the AIRC in shaping industrial relations has been subjected to further attack by the *Workplace Relations Act 1996*.[91] A diminished role for the AIRC now appears to be clearly established. For example, the AIRC's focus is restricted to the setting of minimum (safety net) wages and conditions; it has a reduced arbitral role (access by the parties to the AIRC for an arbitrated decision in a dispute has been closely circumscribed to ensure that access to arbitration is a last resort); and it has limited powers to make awards to settle disputes.[92] Some critics are demanding that its powers be reduced further or that it be abolished altogether.[93] However, the AIRC still possesses a powerful, supportive lobby (for example, the federal Labor party, unions, employer associations, industrial advocates and academic specialists all have varying degrees of vested interest in its continuance). The federal Labor Party has already announced plans to restore the AIRC's power when elected.[94]

Employer associations

Employer associations represent employer interests before industrial tribunals and provide a range of services covering training, award interpretation, legislation updates, HRM issues, dispute handling and how to counter union activity. Employer associations, like trade unions, are not monolithic. They differ in size, purpose, power, influence, ideology and IR expertise.[95] Moreover, they have their own institutional interests, which are not necessarily related to those of their members.[96] Employer associations have played an essentially reactive role in Australian IR. Recently, however, a more proactive stance has been taken by the Business Council of Australia. This, in turn, has highlighted the general conservatism and divisions existing in employer ranks. For example, the BCA has adopted a unitarist approach to IR, arguing that Australia needs an IR environment where:

- people can work together most effectively and with the greatest satisfaction
- the highest possible productivity becomes the common goal for all
- healthy enterprise performance provides the best outcomes for employers and employees alike.[97]

The BCA sees the development of enterprise-based employee relations as the key to more harmonious and productive IR. In particular, the BCA seeks to:

1. develop among Australian employers, employees and unions a much higher acceptance of the need for fixed-term commitments; that is,
   (a) awards and agreements should have a specific duration
   (b) the provisions of an award or agreement should be largely unalterable for that specified period
   (c) at the end of the period, the award or agreement should be renewed, extended or renegotiated or otherwise expire
2. prohibit industrial action completely in relation to the content of awards and agreements during their specified terms
3. specify clearly how the industrial and common law and other legislation would apply to industrial action taken during the specified terms of awards and agreements and when they are being renegotiated
4. require over-award bargaining to take place within the same rules as apply to negotiating and complying with awards and agreements
5. provide well-understood procedures for resolving disputes without industrial action during the term of and when awards and agreements are being renewed or renegotiated
6. provide appropriate penalties for
   (a) industrial action during a fixed-term commitment
   (b) failure to follow the procedures for renegotiation.[98]

Critics of the BCA approach see it as aiming to destroy the Australian trade union movement. Dabscheck, for example, says: 'the rationale of the BCA's so-called concern with the individual is an ideological device to undermine the collectives that workers have traditionally used to define and advance their rights and interests at the workplace — namely trade unions. Through the creation of enterprise unions the BCA hopes to wrest workers

Employer associations
Represent employer interests at industrial tribunals and provide a range of IR advisory services, including award interpretation, dispute handling and how to counter union activity.

away from what, for a better term, might be called 'fair dinkum' unions, and via the registration of enterprise agreements break down the coverage of industrial awards. By isolating workers and reducing the relevance and coverage of awards the BCA will be able to substantially redistribute bargaining power in favour of employers.'[99]

In contrast to the BCA, the Australian Chamber of Commerce and Industry (ACCI) and the Australian Industry Group (AiGroup) have tended to pursue a more pluralist approach, showing less enthusiasm than the BCA for decentralising IR or introducing major changes into the existing IR system. Recently, however, the ACCI announced an agenda for further IR reform that includes:

- replacing state systems with a unitary federal system
- reducing award coverage to wages, annual leave, sick leave, maternity/parental leave and equal pay
- introducing a national minimum wage
- restricting the right to strike
- stopping the AIRC from prescribing how work conditions are to be implemented
- requiring the AIRC to calculate the effect its decisions have on jobs.[100]

All employer associations agree that the days of a highly centralised IR system are gone. Employer associations (like the AIRC and trade unions) also face the challenge of defining their role in an IR world increasingly dominated by enterprise bargaining. Professional accounting, consulting and legal firms already have encroached on the traditional territory of employer associations to give advice on 'structuring, negotiating, implementing and monitoring enterprise agreements'.[101] Nevertheless, while the system protects trade unions and unions continue to influence parliamentarians and governments, the ongoing involvement of employer associations in IR is inevitable.

Trade unions

The old system of compulsory arbitration encouraged trade unionism. As registered organisations, **trade unions** had legal protection and a monopoly over representing employee interests before industrial tribunals.

Union concerns have traditionally focused on pay rates, conditions of work and job security. Increasingly, however, unions are moving away from these bread and butter issues and adopting an approach of strategic unionism that includes industrial democracy, social welfare, training, industrial policy and taxation. Moreover, because most awards and industrial agreements set only minimum rates and conditions, unions also seek to negotiate above-award concessions from employers. Some unions, in fact, see enterprise bargaining as being limited to just that.

Trade unions, as with employer associations, are not monolithic organisations. Differences exist in union policies and practices, degree of industry penetration, ideology, power and influence. The Australian Council of Trade Unions is the national peak trade union organisation. Minor central trade union organisations include state and provincial trades and labour councils. The ACTU's functions include:

- advocacy before the AIRC in national wage cases and other major national hearings[102]
- consultation with state and federal governments
- representing the Australian trade union movement internationally on such bodies as the International Labour Organisation (ILO)
- coordinating national industrial campaigns
- intervening in industrial interstate disputes
- encouraging closer cooperation between unions.[103]

The current ACTU agenda centres on promoting fairness in the workplace and society. In particular, the ACTU seeks to:

- win guaranteed worker rights to collective bargaining
- improve job security for casual workers
- improve work and family rights (for example, paid maternity leave)
- impose restrictions on working hours
- restore capital gains tax
- introduce a wealth tax.[104]

Trade unions Formal organisations that represent individuals employed in an organisation, throughout an industry or in an occupation.

Practitioner speaks

Plundered treasure

John Halfpenny became an organiser for the Amalgamated Engineering Union in 1969 and was appointed Victorian state secretary of the Amalgamated Metal Workers Union in 1972. He was secretary of the Victorian Trades Hall Council from 1987 to 1995.

A lot of people think there is a big difference between human resources management and industrial relations but they are both basically about the relationship between workers and employers. I don't think the relationship has changed but the circumstances surrounding that relationship have.

The Australian economy has made two great shifts over time — from agricultural to industrial, with an emphasis on manufacturing, and from industrial to the increasing domination of service industries. Few other countries have dismantled their manufacturing industry as much as Australia. It is hard to find things that are made here. Lots of good things are invented here and then have to be taken overseas to be put into production. It is worse than disappointing — it's outrageous.

Of course, it is cheaper to get things made in places like Vietnam, but people need to make up their minds about what sort of future they want for this country and whether we want to maintain our standard of living and opportunities for worthwhile employment. Maybe if we do, we have to be prepared to have things made here and pay a premium for them.

My recollections of industrial relations go back to the 1950s. For most of my time in the union movement the economy was characterised by long periods of prosperity and short periods of recession. In recent years it has been characterised by shorter periods of prosperity and longer periods of recession. Overall, levels of prosperity have declined and, while some service industries provide good jobs, I think a nation that relies on them tends to become a nation of servants. The Satanic mills of today are the fast-food outlets and call centres.

The view of the unions used to be that they accepted awards as a safety net. Collective bargaining for over-award payments was used to top-up awards and maintain a living wage. At that time, employers were big fans of the arbitration commission and always talking about the need to accept the umpire's decision. Now the roles have been reversed, with the unions forced to rely more heavily on the arbitration system to protect wages and the employers finding it a burden that inhibits their desire to apply an open market philosophy on wage rates and conditions.

In the sixties, seventies and eighties the wages system in Australia was unique by international standards and it was very egalitarian. Wages and conditions like the extra week of annual leave, additional sick leave, additional long service leave, jury service pay and compassionate leave were won on a factory-by-factory basis and then converted into the awards so the whole workforce benefited. The true spirit of trade unionism prevailed — the strong helped the weak.

One of the big things that has happened is that the workforce has become increasingly casualised and people fear not having a job or losing a job. IR is based on economic activity — it is really about who has power.

In periods of prosperity, workers and their unions have power. In recent years, the pendulum has swung and the economic power is with the employers, and their main weapon in dismantling entitlements is fear. Union membership has declined due to unemployment, casualisation, the growth of new industries with no tradition of union membership and the legacy of the Hawke/Keating years when unions lost touch with rank-and-file membership. Labor and Liberal governments have supported labour market deregulation and people feel they must toe the line if they are to keep their jobs. Workers compete with each other rather than uniting but there's a lot of discontent.

When people say 'an organisation's greatest treasure is its people' they are speaking the truth, but it is how they deal with them that counts. The level of effort by unions to work with employers on restructuring to make companies more productive is, I think, quite high and the number of industrial disputes is quite low, but it is nonsense to say Australia must compete on a level playing field — there isn't one.

John Halfpenny

Source *HR Monthly*, May 2003, p. 33.

The ACTU is the dominant public face of the union movement, with the state trades and labour councils being increasingly marginalised. The following have all contributed to the decline of the state bodies: the unique personal relationship between former ACTU Secretary Bill Kelty and former Prime Minister Paul Keating; the Accord; ACTU leadership in superannuation, award restructuring and union amalgamation; the continuing move to the federal award coverage; the advent of enterprise bargaining; and the increasing influence of powerful individual unions. This has led some unions to stop paying their affiliation fees to the state labour councils.[105] Iain Ross, former ACTU Assistant Secretary, however, sees the amalgamation of Australia's 142 trade unions into 20 mega unions, along with enterprise bargaining, leading to a diminished role for the federal body. The ACTU, says Ross, will become a political catalyst for unions, a facilitator of ideas and an information exchange communication centre.[106] In contrast, Cooper argues that a major priority for the ACTU is to rebuild the union movement by strengthening unions in the workplace and increasing membership.[107] In the words of one commentator, '[unions, along with employer associations and the AIRC] are searching for survival techniques in a world that no longer wants much of what they offer'.[108]

Union membership

In 1954, 59 per cent of the Australian work force was unionised.[109] In 1996, the figure was 31 per cent. Today, only about one-quarter of the work force is unionised. (In the private sector, trade union membership is less than 18 per cent.[110]) According to Davis, 'this fall in membership represents a massive challenge for unions'.[111] More open and competitive economies, the need for more flexible labour markets, the decrease in manufacturing and the public sector, the growth of service industries, the increase in women and part-timers in the work force, the loss of union 'closed shops' and changing social attitudes towards unions have all contributed to this decline. In addition, Peetz argues that a conscious effort by employers (with federal Coalition government support) to decollectivise industrial relations has been especially significant.[112] This has created concern among some unionists that:

- the ACTU will represent only a minority of the work force
- the centralised wage system will collapse
- the Coalition government's policies on enterprise bargaining will succeed.[113]

According to Anna Booth, the former Federal Secretary of the Clothing and Allied Trades Union, 'A worst case scenario would see the commission abolished, labour laws deregulated, competition between unions encouraged and the use of voluntary employment agreements … it would be devastating for us'.[114] As a result, many unions have vigorously opposed the introduction of enterprise bargaining and individual contracts. The ACTU, for example, has launched a drive to reunionise BHP Billiton's iron ore operations. Says ACTU Assistant Secretary Richard Marles, 'This really is an ideological battle; they are fundamentally opposed to collective organization'.[115] A similar struggle is occurring within the banking industry where the Finance Sector Union is desperately fighting against individual contracts in an attempt to maintain its presence in the workplace.[116] Although a Federal Court decision concluded that **individual agreements** do not discriminate against unions, it remains Labor Party policy to abolish individual agreements.[117]

The advent of knowledge workers, ructions associated with amalgamations, a focus on political activism at the expense of servicing members, financial insolvency, pressures for more flexible and varied working time arrangements, casualisation of the work force (one in four Australian workers is now a casual employee), privatisation, changes in penalty payments, removal of job demarcations and other workplace rigidities have created additional difficult (and controversial) challenges for trade unions.[118] It is argued, for example, that what appeals to manufacturing and building workers (where unions remain strong) — collectivism, militancy and class conflict — has little appeal for young workers (see figure 15.4).[119] Many knowledge workers, for example, see trade unions 'as irrelevant and politically tainted'.[120] Rejecting such views, the ACTU's Greg Combet claims: '… our polling tells us it is the 18 to 30 years olds who are the most supportive of unions and collective bargaining … these are the people working in pubs, restaurants, shops — many as casuals with

Individual agreements
Include common law contracts and Australian Workplace Agreements.

few skills — who realise their only hope of a fair deal is collective organization.'[121] Other research suggests that it is not the trade union agenda that fails to appeal to younger workers but rather the union movement's male, middle-aged, out-of-touch officials.[122] Unions have also come under increasing scrutiny regarding restrictions on civil liberties, the treatment of women, corruption, political influence and their contribution to economic performance.[123]

Finally, the economic, industrial and political climate has motivated employer-led and Coalition government-supported assaults on unions that have weakened the power of the trade union movement.[124] The transfer from a Labor to a Coalition government has seen a dramatic change in the relationship (and influence) of trade unions with government. A Labor government, in turn, will likely roll back many of the Coalition's reforms and give unions a much bigger influence in the workplace by promoting collective bargaining and union representation and by eliminating or restricting individual agreements. Unions, politically isolated under the Coalition government, have been forced to undergo a critical self-evaluation. Pocock and Wright, for example, claim that the radical change in the political climate has obligated unions to rely less on parliamentary political unionism and to place greater reliance on traditional industrial unionism.[125]

WHY EMPLOYEES JOIN UNIONS

Compulsion
To get a job in a 'closed shop', the employee must join the union.

Protection
Arbitrary and unfair management pushes the employee to join a union as a form of protection.

Social pressure
Pressure from fellow workers may force the employee to become a union member.

Political beliefs
Employees may join because of their political and social beliefs in the desirability of unionism.

Solidarity
A belief in 'strength in unity' may foster union membership.

Tradition
Membership of a union is traditional in the employee's family and social group.

Pay and conditions
Dissatisfaction with low wage rates, poor conditions of work and lack of job security motivate employees to join a union.

Communication
The union can provide a communication link to management, which allows employees to express their dissatisfaction without the fear of punishment by management.

Health and safety
A safe and healthy workplace is important to employees. Where the union is seen to be active in improving the health and safety conditions at work, union membership becomes attractive.

Figure 15.4 The reasons why employees join unions

To survive in the long run, unions must change and become more innovative.[126] Costa, for example, argues 'The trade union movement, if it is to regain relevance, needs to experiment with new products, services and different structural forms'.[127] Suggestions on how to do this include the provision of increased services to members, reduced membership fees and lower costs for services via increased economies of scale, improved delegate training (especially in recruitment, bargaining and dispute resolution), the development of alliances with other community groups, greater use of technology, improved public relations, aggressive recruitment of new members (especially non-unionists in so-called heartland industries), the elimination of craft unionism, the resolution of union coverage to avoid demarcation disputes, single union sites, the introduction of European-style work councils, maintenance of the centralised wage system, the promotion of enterprise bargaining, better training for union officials, the return of a federal Labor government (and the rollback of the federal Coalition government's industrial relations reforms) and the development of a unified ACTU corporate strategy.[128]

The CFMEU, for example, has joined a global coalition of trade unions to target Rio Tinto via a campaign of shareholder activism (individual contracts for all employees is an integral part of Rio Tinto's HR strategy), while other unions have set up their own labour hire firms.[129] The Association of Professional Engineers, Scientists, Managers and Architects (APESMA) provides advice on negotiating individual contracts and the Finance Sector Union (FSU) is seeking to have one of its members elected to the board of the ANZ Banking Group. Finally, the ACTU is targeting high school and university students via school and campus visits, door knocking and using its international network of trade unions to counter declining membership and the economic power of global corporations.[130]

Some of these recommendations (and practices) touch on very sensitive matters that highlight personality, ideological and strategic differences existing within the union movement.[131] Economist Michael Costa, a former officer with the Labor Council of NSW, for example, describes the ACTU's amalgamation strategy as 'fatally flawed', arguing that rather than being expanded, unions need to find new ways to deliver the services their members want.[132] The determination of individual unions to protect their membership base, interlaced with personality clashes, adds to the difficulties of reaching agreement as to what should be done.[133] As a result, there is a fear that sectionalism, narrow militancy, a preoccupation with legalism and a temptation to resort to 'cannibalism' are real dangers that unions face as they seek to adjust to the changing industrial relations environment.[134] Union bureaucracy, in addition, creates an inbuilt resistance to change.[135]

Regardless, there is an increasing realisation among some union leaders that Australia must be internationally competitive and that 'the key issue is how to make the cake bigger, rather than how to divide it'.[136] Says Bill Kelty, 'Trade unions don't die from right wing political pressure, they die if they are not relevant in the work force'.[137] According to Drucker, the best hope for survival is that unions will redirect their role to optimising human resources.[138] Unions should aim to protect their members' jobs and incomes by working with management to improve productivity, quality and competitiveness.[139] 'In the workplace today', says an ACTU research officer, 'pursuit of shared objectives is steadily replacing the confrontation and trenchant divisiveness of yesterday . . . these common workplace aims translate into greater productivity, which in turn enhances Australia's international competitiveness. That in turn provides a sound basis for sustainable recovery and employment growth.'[140]

Industrial relations processes

Collective bargaining The process through which representatives of management and the union meet to negotiate a labour agreement.

Arbitrated awards Outline minimum pay rates and conditions as determined by an industrial tribunal decision.

Consent awards These occur when the parties to an industrial dispute reach agreement without third-party involvement, and the agreement is then ratified by an industrial tribunal. A consent award is binding on the parties in the same way as an arbitrated award.

The processes of industrial relations deal with the mechanisms for handling industrial disputes. They include **collective bargaining** (the process of negotiating between management and groups of employees and/or their unions), conciliation (the process of a third party such as the AIRC assisting management and unions to reach an agreed settlement) and arbitration (the process of a third party such as the AIRC making a judgement).

In Australia, many disputes have been settled by collective bargaining. In particular, direct negotiations are often entered into when dealing with over-award payments and conditions. Moreover, the AIRC traditionally encouraged the parties to first try to resolve a dispute by direct negotiation before getting itself actively involved in the conciliation process. If union–management negotiations broke down and the AIRC as conciliator could not reconcile the differences between the parties, then the AIRC would hear evidence and make a judgement in order to settle the dispute. Decisions of the AIRC relating to wages and conditions are called **arbitrated awards**. Negotiated agreements ratified by the AIRC at the request of both management and the union are called **consent awards**. Consent awards have the same legal status as arbitrated awards and can be seen as 'the outcome of the marriage of collective bargaining to arbitration'.[141]

Union membership slips again

By Cherelle Murphy

Union membership fell drastically last year, figures released yesterday show, dashing trade union organisers' hopes of rebuilding their power base.

The figures, which reveal a decline both in the total number of union members and in the share of the workforce they represent, came after two years of small rises in membership numbers. That had given hope to trade unions that the decades-long membership decline might be reversing.

But according to the Australian Bureau of Statistics, 69 000 fewer people were members of unions in the year to August 2002, pulling down national membership to 1.83 million.

And only 23.1 per cent of the labour force were unionised in 2002, down from 24.5 per cent in 2001. The figure was 51 per cent as recently as 1976.

'These figures concern us', said ACTU secretary Greg Combet.

He said the trend contrasted with community attitudes to union membership, which were positive and improving.

'We have been working away at strategies to focus on our grassroots organisations — to rebuild unionism from the ground up', Mr Combet said.

But he said unions were also having to reinvent themselves and sell to new industries.

'We are trying North American-style organisational tactics in the services industry — in casinos and hotels, in call centres and telecommunications — and we are getting some good results there', he said.

The president of the Queensland Teachers Union, Julie-Ann McCullough, said the organisation put a lot of time into expanding its 37 000-strong membership base.

'You have to deliver services that people are paying for. We are very careful to move with the times.'

Mr Combet said falling union membership had dire consequences for workers. 'There are a record number of workers who don't have paid holiday or sick leave', he said.

Just over 27 per cent of employees were not entitled to paid sick or holiday leave in August last year.

The union movement is not giving up the fight — the ACTU will be releasing a paper called 'Strategies for Growth' next month in an attempt to reverse the negative trend.

Structural changes in the economy and the labour market are the main forces behind the fall in trade union membership. There are now more part-time and casual jobs in service industries than in past decades, and these types of jobs are traditionally not unionised.

Mr Combet also blamed the government, saying it would 'help a lot if you didn't have a government hell-bent on destroying unionism'.

'We can't ignore the fact that the Howard government legislative attacks have an effect — they do.'

Private sector unions have suffered more than their public sector counterparts, where membership has held close to 50 per cent over the last few years. In the private sector, only 17.7 per cent of the workforce are unionised, down from 19.6 per cent in 1999.

Recent large job losses at Ansett and in the banking sector have had a large impact. The data shows that over the year to August, transport union membership fell by 11 200 to 122 500. A net 18 200 deserted the finance and insurance sector over the same period.

Source *The Australian Financial Review*, 1 April 2003, p. 3.

Choice of processes

The way industrial disputes are settled depends on many factors. Generally, it is recognised that the earlier and the lower the level at which conflict is resolved, the better it is for employees, unions and management (see figure 15.5). Inevitably, the longer a dispute continues, the greater the probability that positions will become more entrenched and the atmosphere more emotionally volatile. In such situations, it is not uncommon for the original cause of the dispute to become submerged by a range of other agenda items as other parties with their own vested interests become involved.

Unfortunately, the old conciliation and arbitration system downgraded the role of workplace dispute settlement. As a consequence, the responsibility for industrial relations at the enterprise level of HR managers, line managers and shop stewards was reduced. However, this often suited unions, employer associations, IR lawyers and the AIRC as it promoted their involvement, prestige, control and existence. Furthermore, it encouraged HR managers and union officials to concentrate on developing the advocacy skills and legal knowledge required for success in appearances before the AIRC. Negotiation and conflict resolution skills needed for dispute settlement at the enterprise level were largely neglected.

In addition, the old system fostered reactive and remedial HRM instead of high-performance HRM and saw many managers develop a preference for arbitration to avoid accountability. Finally, the failure of management and unions to develop skill in enterprise dispute resolution was in itself the cause of many grievances or protest strikes.[142]

RESOLVING DISPUTES

1. The employee approaches their immediate supervisor to discuss the grievance.
2. If the grievance remains unresolved, the employee next approaches the shop steward or an employee representative who then approaches the supervisor.
3. If the matter still remains unresolved, the shop steward contacts a union organiser who negotiates with the HR manager and/or a line manager and/or an employer association representative.
4. If the matter is still unresolved, it may be referred to the AIRC for conciliation. If requested by the parties, the AIRC may make a recommendation to resolve the dispute if it is satisfied that all parties will abide by its recommendation.

Figure 15.5 Grievances, disputes and industrial relations processes

Workplace-level grievances

Grievances are the product of employee dissatisfaction or feelings of injustice. As mentioned earlier, IR problems can quickly escalate when not dealt with by management at the enterprise level. As a consequence, the role of the first-line supervisor is critical. Supervisors who have good relationships with their subordinates are a major impediment to union activity.[143] When confronted with an employee grievance, supervisors and HR managers should do the following:

- Listen carefully to what the employee says and try to distinguish between facts and feelings. The key question is, 'Why does the employee feel this way?' To the employee, an imagined wrong and an actual wrong are of equal significance. To resolve a grievance effectively it is necessary to understand the nature of the employee's complaint. 'What is the problem?' rather than 'Is this a valid grievance?' should be focused on. The actual sources of dissatisfaction — real or imaginary — need to be identified. If appropriate, notes should be made to record what has been discussed. Employees should feel that they have had a good hearing. All grievances should be treated seriously and discussed privately. Managers should remain calm and avoid losing their temper or swearing.
- Ensure that they have all the relevant facts. It is unsatisfactory (even dangerous) to act alone on the basis of assumptions or opinions. The work area should be visited and any witnesses identified and interviewed. Management action must be based on fact, not emotion. This may mean extensive checking with other managers and employees, reviewing organisational policies and the award, examining HR or other records, identifying any precedents or accepted workplace practices, and seeking legal, IR or technical advice.
- Avoid lengthy delays. When all the relevant information has been collected, a decision should be made and communicated to the employee and the union representative (if

appropriate). The reason for the decision should be given. Vague justifications such as 'it's organisational policy' or 'my hands are tied by top management' will do little to settle the issue and may exacerbate the dispute. The doctrine of natural justice requires that employees be given the opportunity for a fair hearing and that management's decisions are made without bias and on their merits. Any management decision dealing with employee grievances that is inconsistent with this doctrine is subject to union challenge and rejection by an independent third party such as the AIRC.

- Recognise that sometimes a union is placed in the awkward position of having to argue a case it does not genuinely support. The reality is that some employees are chronic complainers who create just as many headaches for union representatives as they do for management.

In the final analysis, the successful handling of grievances is related to the attitudes of the parties involved. The nature of the IR climate is critical. Bad or ineffective HR policies and practices will have a negative impact. In contrast, high-performance HR policies and practices that encourage managers to know their subordinates as individuals and promote trust and mutual understanding can facilitate the handling of grievances without the need for union or tribunal involvement.[144]

This Letter to the Editor provides a provocative viewpoint. Do you agree? See 'What's your view?' on page 574.

Letter to the Editor

High minimum wages price junior and unskilled workers out of jobs

Dear Editor,

I am writing to add my views to the current debate about minimum wages. While minimum wages have their purpose, their extension across virtually every industry sector is a recipe for disaster.

In particular, I am concerned that the push to create high minimum wages prices many people out of a job, especially the young and the unskilled. The 'bleeding hearts' who demand higher minimum wages for these groups create new pools of unemployment, an outcome precisely opposite to that which they seek.

Simple economics predicts that employers will substitute capital in the form of technology for labour when the price of labour rises too high. We can see this occurring every day in the automation of industries from fast food to petrol retailing. Commonsense and anecdotal evidence indicate that employers hire fewer apprentices and low-skilled workers when their price becomes prohibitive. Moving from local production to importing goods and services is one common response.

Sure, the young and the unskilled need enough money to live on. But it is the question of how much is 'enough' that is the current focus of debate. As a small business owner, it is obvious to me that 'enough' should be defined as the equivalent level of unemployment benefit that the person would draw if they did not have a job, plus a small (10–15 per cent) premium for work force participation. In the majority of jobs, the young and the unskilled do not add sufficient value to justify any more than this. While this may sound callous, to pay more would be to ensure that few in these groups have a job at all. In addition, both groups should be participating in formal and informal training programs and seeking to lift their skill levels in order to move on quickly from the lower-paying positions.

The bleeding hearts should reassess their position. Their push for higher minimum wages does nothing but hurt those groups they are seeking to assist. The tough reality is that governments and employers do need to be 'cruel to be kind' if the unacceptably large pools of unemployed youth and unskilled adults are to be significantly reduced.

The CEO of a locally produced manufacturing company

Source David Poole, University of Western Sydney.

Tribunal-level grievances

When a grievance cannot be resolved at the workplace level, the HR manager may need to present their organisation's case before an industrial tribunal such as the AIRC. Unfortunately, some HR managers are 'tribunal shy' and prefer to delegate this responsibility to the representative of an employer association or a member of the legal profession. Even worse is the situation where top management lacks confidence in the ability of the HR manager to handle the case and directs that they assist an external advocate.

To avoid becoming clerical assistants in settling industrial disputes, HR managers must develop the skills and confidence to take (and be given) the responsibility for advocacy. Who else has (or should have) as much knowledge about past disputes, custom and practice, personalities, pay rates and conditions as an organisation's HR manager? As an industrial advocate, this gives the HR manager a fundamental advantage over employer association or legal advocates. In addition, presiding members of industrial tribunals tend to respond positively when HR managers act as advocates. As most commissioners are not lawyers (and are extremely busy), they generally welcome the opportunity to get to the 'nitty gritty' of the dispute rather than being caught up in legal technicalities or 'broad issues of principle'. In-house advocacy also avoids the personal animosities that sometimes exist between union officials and employer association representatives.

Finally, as Cohen points out, as soon as an employer association representative addresses a group of shop stewards or union members, the perceived ability, knowledge and status of the HR manager is diminished in the eyes of employees, the union and other managers.[145]

Advocacy

Advocates Employer or union representatives who argue a case before an industrial tribunal or court.

Industrial advocacy, although often shrouded in mystique, is really quite straightforward. It essentially involves presenting a case in a logical and understandable way. Nothing more, nothing less. As with good negotiators, good **advocates** do a lot of preparation. They understand that their role is to advance their organisation's (or members') interests and assist the tribunal in the resolution of a dispute. They do not become involved in personal vendettas, emotional outbursts, abuse or unethical behaviour. Successful advocates can be extrovert or quiet in temperament. Their style of advocacy, however, should always be in harmony with their natural personality (see figure 15.6).

CHARACTERISTICS OF SUCCESSFUL ADVOCATES

- *Orderly presentation.* The advocate's arguments should be developed in a logical and clearly understandable way. Thorough preparation is critical.
- *Objectivity.* Loss of objectivity diminishes the advocate's ability to persuade others of the 'correctness' of his/her arguments.
- *Appearance.* Presenting a case before an industrial tribunal is a formal situation. Appropriate business dress is required to convey respect and professionalism.
- *Politeness.* Advocates gain nothing by rude or ill-tempered behaviour and may damage their case, as well as their own reputation.
- *Knowledge of industrial law and industrial relations.* Ignorance in these areas is nothing more than an indication of professional incompetence.
- *Ethical.* Unethical acts cost the advocate the respect and trust of all parties concerned and do untold damage to the organisation's case.
- *Good communicator.* Speaking clearly, avoiding the use of jargon, using visual aids, and so on make for an effective transfer of understanding.

Figure 15.6 Characteristics of successful advocates

HR managers taking up the role of advocate need to be aware that while an industrial tribunal may have many of the formal trappings of a court, it is in fact quite different. Courts are concerned with justice. Industrial tribunals are pragmatic institutions concerned with finding workable solutions to industrial disputes. So pragmatic, in fact, that according to Howard and Fox '... there is reason to suspect that most of the work the tribunals do is to give bureaucratic acknowledgement to something that has already happened, or to something that will inevitably happen'.[146] Because of this, tribunals are not bound by the rules of evidence and can try to get information by any means they see appropriate. Legal qualifications and professional competence are not required to appear before a tribunal. Advocates may be (and sometimes are) illogical, emotional, incoherent, ill-prepared and incompetent. Tribunals are also used for 'political' purposes or personal promotion.

Lastly, because commissioners are allocated an 'industry', an ongoing relationship between advocates and commissioners is common. Consequently, commissioners are well aware of who is competent and who can be trusted.

The *Workplace Relations Act*[147]

Passed in November 1996, the *Workplace Relations Act* reflected the federal Coalition government's aim of encouraging 'a more direct relationship between employers and employees; a much reduced role for third party intervention and greater labour market flexibility'[148] (see figures 15.7 and 15.8). Although subject to much criticism, the changes were moderate and are a continuation of the former Labor government's policy of 'non-union collective bargaining and of enterprise agreements as an alternative to awards for regulating wages and connections'.[149] According to some critics, however, the Act (in conjunction with global market changes) has fundamentally shifted the balance of power away from unions and made it increasingly difficult for them to protect their members. [150]

The objectives of the *Workplace Relations Act* are to:

- give primary responsibility for industrial relations and agreement making to employers and employees at the enterprise and workplace levels
- focus the role of the award system on providing a safety net of fair and enforceable minimum wages and conditions
- ensure freedom of association
- avoid discrimination
- assist employees to balance their work and family responsibilities
- assist in giving effect to Australia's international obligations in respect of labour standards.

Figure 15.7 Objectives of the *Workplace Relations Act*
Source Adapted by the author from *Changes in Federal Workplace Relations Law — Legislation Guide*, Commonwealth Department of Industrial Relations, Canberra, 1996, p. 1.

Australian Workplace Agreements (AWAs) Agreements made directly between an employer and an employee.

Certified Agreements (CAs) Agreements that are the product of negotiations between a corporation and groups of employees or a union(s) and that are subsequently registered by an industrial tribunal.

Pattern bargaining Occurs when the same (or essentially the same) pay and conditions are negotiated for several firms (often in the same industry). Such negotiations are coordinated by union headquarters with clear parameters being set for the local union negotiators. Pattern bargaining is favoured by militant unions and is commonly found in industries that are protected from global competition by tariffs or government subsidies.

One of the primary objectives of the *Workplace Relations Act* was to give employers and employees the primary responsibility for industrial relations and negotiating workplace agreements. A choice is given to the parties between **Australian Workplace Agreements (AWAs)** and **Certified Agreements (CAs)**. AWAs are individual agreements between an employer and their employees. These can be negotiated individually or collectively. (At the professional and managerial level, the trend now appears to favour individual contracts.) The final agreement, however, must be signed by each individual employee. Employees can employ a bargaining agent (for example, a union representative or a private consultant) to negotiate on their behalf. Unions, however, can participate in the negotiation process only by invitation. Not surprisingly, unions and some IR academics do not like AWAs, denouncing them as heavily biased against workers and a means to isolate workers, deunionise the work force, eliminate **pattern bargaining**, increase workloads, and reduce wages and conditions.[151]

KEY FEATURES OF THE *WORKPLACE RELATIONS ACT*

AGREEMENT-MAKING CHOICES

- Formalised and informal. Union and non-union. Individual and collective. Federal/state
- No agreement stream favoured over another

Australian Workplace Agreements (AWAs) — a new option

- Between employee and employer
- Can be negotiated collectively or individually
- Limited right to strike/lockout during bargaining
- Bargaining agents can be appointed
- Signed individually
- Global 'no-disadvantage' test — benchmark against relevant award and any relevant law
- User-friendly EA (Employment Advocate) approval process
- Period to be specified/upper limit of three years
- Can terminate at any time by written agreement

Certified Agreements (CAs) — modified

- Between employer and union(s) or directly with employees
- Collectively negotiated
- Limited right to strike/lockout during bargaining
- No need for underpinning award
- Emphasis on single business CAs — obtaining multi-employer CAs tightly controlled
- Majority approval of employees required
- Global 'no-disadvantage' test — benchmark against relevant award and any relevant law
- AIRC to certify
- New employees automatically covered — unless otherwise agreed
- Apply for an upper limit of three years
- Can be terminated at any time, with majority approval
- AWAs and CAs continue in force after expiry date, unless
  - agreement provides for an alternative *or*
  - replaced by a new agreement, terminated by agreement between the parties or on application of one party, terminated by AIRC if not against the public interest

INDUSTRIAL ACTION

- Protected action — right to strike/lockout during bargaining
- Industrial action prohibited during the term of an agreement
- Strike pay unlawful

- AIRC enhanced powers to stop/prevent unprotected industrial action
- Secondary boycotts provisions restored to Trade Practices Act
- Compliance — higher maximum penalties for breaches of awards/agreements

OPERATING AN EFFECTIVE SYSTEM

Federal/state harmonisation

- Complementary legislation, where needed
- Administrative improvements through collaboration
- Cooperation on service delivery

Flexibility for changing work patterns

- Regular part-time work
- Balancing work and family responsibilities

Striking a fair balance

- Anti-discrimination provisions
- Equal remuneration provisions
- Special arrangements for apprentices and young people in training
- Continuation of junior rates plus access to new wage arrangements for new apprenticeships and traineeships
- Safeguards for vulnerable workers involved in bargaining
- EA's role in relation to women, young people, apprentices, trainees, outworkers and people from a non-English-speaking background

SAFETY NET

- Fair and enforceable minimum wages and conditions
- AIRC to arbitrate safety net adjustments — needs of the low paid
- Awards confined in scope to 20 subject areas ('allowable matters') — AIRC can settle exceptional cases about non-allowable matters
- Awards to be simplified — through AIRC fair and transparent process
- Paid rates → minimum rates, with overall pay safeguarded
- Special case arbitration by AIRC above safety net strictly limited, only in circumstances where bargaining exhausted — disputes threatening serious harm to community/economy, or where employees have been customarily covered by paid rates awards

'FAIR GO ALL ROUND' UNFAIR DISMISSAL

- Balances interests of employees and employers
- Limited to employees covered by federal awards and agreements

Figure 15.8 Key features of the *Workplace Relations Act*

- Simple test applied — harsh, unjust or unreasonable
- Dismissal on discriminatory grounds not allowed*
- Notice still to be given or pay in lieu*
- AIRC to deal with cases. Conciliation stressed. If arbitrated, reinstatement or compensation (with limits). Frivolous or malicious applications discouraged plus possible costs

FREEDOM OF ASSOCIATION
- Voluntary unionism
- Compulsory unionism and preference outlawed
- Protection against coercion and discrimination
- 'Conveniently belong' replaced — greater employee choice of representation
- Enterprise unions
- Limited union right of entry — Industrial Registry Permit needed
- Registered organisations — minimum registration requirement of 50. Disamalgamation of unions
- Twelve-month limit on liability for union dues

ACCESS TO ADVICE, SERVICES AND REMEDIES
The Employment Advocate
- Guarantees the integrity of AWA arrangements
- Readily accessible, user friendly
- Advice and information on AWAs, freedom of association and related matters

*For all employees

- Vetting of AWAs (not via formal hearings)
- Freedom of association and AWA breaches
- Powers to enforce
- Special attention to needs of worker disadvantaged in bargaining
- Publishes aggregated statistics on AWAs

Department of Industrial Relations
- Power to investigate award and CA breaches — voluntary compliance/can prosecute
- Advice and information on workplace relations issues

The AIRC
- Unfair dismissal jurisdiction
- Maintenance of the award safety net
- Award simplification
- Conciliation role in assisting CA making
- Dispute resolution
- Arbitration role within specified limits
- Matters relating to registered organisations

The Federal Court
- Takes over the jurisdiction of the Industrial Relations Court, including injunctions relating to industrial action
- Can impose penalties for discrimination or victimisation under freedom of association
- Approval of union disamalgamation

Figure 15.8 Key features of the *Workplace Relations Act*
Source Based on *Key Features of the New Federal Workplace Relations Law*, Department of Industrial Relations, Canberra, 1996, pp. 4–5.

AWAs are subject to approval by the Employment Advocate (EA), a new statutory office established under the Act. To approve an AWA, the EA will need to be satisfied that:
- it meets the no-disadvantage test — that is, when considered as a whole, the agreement is no less favourable to the employee concerned than the relevant award and any relevant laws
- the employer explained the effect of the AWA to the employee and that the employee genuinely consented to the making of the AWA.

In addition to approving AWAs, the EA's responsibilities include:
- providing advice to employees and employers
- handling alleged breaches of AWAs
- investigating freedom-of-association complaints
- assisting employees in prosecuting breaches
- providing statistics on AWAs.[152]

Uncompetitive companies and trade unions collude to oppose cuts in tariffs that would benefit the community.

Under the Act, CAs can be negotiated directly by corporations with employees, but relevant unions can participate in the negotiations and become parties to an agreement when requested to by a union member. CAs must be ratified by the AIRC. CAs must also meet the same no-disadvantage test as AWAs.

Finally, the AIRC must be satisfied that employees have had the agreement explained to them and that the majority of employees support it.[153] By focusing on the workplace, the Workplace Relations Act promotes decision making by employees. Defining the role of unions as service providers is likely, says Callus, 'to move the industrial system still further away from one based on collective bargaining with unions to one in which agreements negotiated between individuals or non-union collectives have equal legal standing and legitimacy . . . the most likely long-term legacy of the new law is that it will marginalise unions in bargaining to a degree not seen in Australia this century'.[154]

Managers now have an unparalleled opportunity to manage their human resources free from third-party interference. Success depends on their quality and vision.[155] Winley, for example, claims that the pressures of international competition will provide a strong incentive for employers to explore new options rather than relying on past practices.[156] The evidence, however, suggests that high-performance HR policies and practices (which are associated with higher employee work and life satisfaction, greater workplace trust and superior organisational performance) have not been widely implemented, even though research indicates that high-performance HR policies and practices that substitute for some of the traditional functions of trade unions may reduce employee desire to join a union or to perceive trade unions as necessary.[157]

According to the University of Melbourne's Centre for Employment and Labour Relations Law, the focus has been on cost cutting and union busting and not on productivity improvement.[158] In contrast, companies that have introduced AWAs as part of a cultural change program (and not as a cost-cutting exercise) have experienced dramatic increases in productivity, flexibility and competitiveness.[159] The majority of changes in large workplaces, such as downsizing, restructuring, the introduction of new technology and the like, have taken place independently of enterprise bargaining.[160] Thus, despite their cries for more freedom, managers (particularly in large workplaces) have been slow to exploit the opportunities for greater workplace flexibility offered by AWAs.[161]

According to former Workplace Relations Minister, Tony Abbott, managers are reluctant to negotiate non-union agreements because they see them as unusual, risking employee disenchantment and fostering union opposition.[162] Gollan and Davis similarly point out that there has been a lack of management commitment, time and resources to improved HRM in the workplace.[163]

In contrast, the trend to individual agreements and away from unions and the award-based system is clearly more evident in small business. Employees in small business, for example, are six times more likely than those in large companies to have individual agreements. Despite management recalcitrance, more than 40 per cent of employees are now covered by individual agreements and the growth in agreements that do not involve trade union participation appears likely to continue.[164]

Lansbury and Westcott argue that more individualised forms of wage setting and the decline of trade union coverage have not achieved any increased economic competitiveness.[165] Even more scathing are the claims that individualisation of the employment relationship has created material inequality, promoted greed and divided the nation.[166] Finally, some critics remain sceptical that the negotiation of AWAs is anything more than 'take it or leave it' bargaining on employers' terms for a significant percentage of the work force (and a potent excuse for increasing work intensification). Other commentators see them as Australia's 'greatest economic blunder of the 20th century'.[167]

Figure 15.9 outlines the 20 **allowable matters** in the *Workplace Relations Act*.

Allowable matters These are provisions allowed to remain in awards by the *Workplace Relations Act*. No other items can be covered by an award.

Workplace Relations Legislation Amendment (More Jobs, Better Pay) Bill 1999[168]

In 1999, the Howard Coalition government proposed a 'second wave' of changes to workplace relations including:
• the accreditation of private mediators
• the introduction of compulsory secret ballots before strike action
• restrictions on unions' right of entry to workplaces
• additional exclusions from unfair dismissal laws
• further award simplification
• deregistration of unions for breaching court injunctions against industrial action and for breaching freedom of association laws.

The following are the allowable matters in the *Workplace Relations Act*

- classifications of employees and skill-based career paths
- ordinary time hours of work and the times within which they are performed, rest breaks, notice periods and variations to working hours
- rates of pay generally (such as hourly rates and annual salaries), rates of pay for juniors, trainees or apprentices and rates of pay for employees under the supported wage system
- piece rates, tallies and bonuses
- annual leave and leave loadings
- long service leave
- personal/carer's leave, including sick leave, family leave, bereavement leave, compassionate leave, cultural leave and other like forms of leave
- parental leave, including maternity and adoption leave
- public holidays
- allowances
- loadings for working overtime or for casual or shift work
- penalty rates
- redundancy pay
- notice of termination
- stand-down provisions
- dispute settling procedures
- jury service
- type of employment, such as full-time employment, casual employment, regular part-time employment and shift work
- superannuation
- pay and conditions for outworkers, but only to the extent necessary to ensure that their overall pay and conditions of employment are fair and reasonable in comparison with the pay and conditions of employment specified in a relevant award or awards for employees who perform the same kind of work at an employer's business or commercial premises.

Figure 15.9 Allowable matters in the *Workplace Relations Act*
Source Australian Government, Attorney-General's Department, Australian Law Online, http://scaleplus.law.gov.au.

Employer groups, although in favour of the proposals, argued that they did not go far enough. In contrast, trade unions, church and welfare groups and others argued that the changes were unfair and unnecessary. The proposed amendments were defeated, but they remain on the legislative agenda of the Coalition parties.

A single IR system

Another proposal by the Coalition government is to unify Australia's state and federal systems to produce a unitary system of industrial relations. The proposal has generated mixed reactions and has not won widespread acceptance. It has been criticised by employers for lacking clear objectives and overstating the problems of the present system. State governments of all political persuasions, in turn, are mainly also negative, fearing that a dominant federal system of industrial relations would sideline them (although the Victorian Labor government has promised to lobby other states to move to a unitary system).[169]

Future reforms

The Coalition government has unsuccessfully attempted to introduce several other IR reforms, mainly relating to unfair dismissals and the use of secret ballots. It nevertheless continues to push for further changes to liberalise and decentralise wage and employment conditions (and to overcome what it perceives as restrictive AIRC and Federal Court decisions).[170] Critics argue that such Coalition government actions are primarily aimed at trade union and industrial tribunal exclusion.[171] If re-elected, the Coalition government seems certain to aggressively pursue further liberalisation of the workplace. Alternatively, a future Labor government will introduce a raft of changes aimed at guaranteeing the place of trade unions, restoring the powers of the AIRC and undoing many of the Coalition's initiatives.

Summary

The changing nature of global markets and the need to become more customer-driven have forced a critical re-examination of the way industrial relations is handled in Australia. Radical, pluralist and unitarist approaches (in one form or another) all have their supporters. The arguments of their advocates comprise the most extensive (and emotionally charged) industrial relations debate that Australia has witnessed in recent years. The traditional roles and dominance of government, employer associations and unions are being challenged and their place in the industrial relations sun is no longer guaranteed. Aggravating these tensions is the continued politicisation of industrial relations by both major political parties. The IR agenda in the years ahead seems certain to be dominated by further change and controversy.

terms to know

advocates (p. 566)
allowable matters (p. 570)
arbitrated awards (p. 562)
arbitration (p. 555)
Australian Council of Trade Unions (ACTU) (p. 556)
Australian Industrial Relations Commission (AIRC) (p. 550)
Australian Workplace Agreements (AWAs) (p. 567)
awards (p. 555)
Certified Agreements (CAs) (p. 567)
collective bargaining (p. 562)

consent awards (p. 562)
employer associations (p. 557)
individual agreements (p. 560)
industrial relations (p. 549)
industrial tribunals (p. 556)
pattern bargaining (p. 567)
pluralist approach (p. 550)
radical approach (p. 551)
trade unions (p. 558)
unitarist approach (p. 549)

review questions

1. What is an AWA? Are you in favour of AWAs? Explain your reasoning.
2. What significance does the decline in union membership have for Australian industrial relations?
3. Explain the purpose of a trade union. Are you in favour of trade unions? Explain your reasoning.
4. What are the differences between the Marxist, pluralist and unitarist approaches to industrial relations? Which approach do you favour? Why?
5. Describe the key steps in handling employee grievances.
6. Explain the differences between AWAs, CAs and awards.
7. To survive in the long run, unions must change.' Do you agree or disagree with this statement? Why? What changes (if any) would you propose?
8. Explain why some employees join unions and some do not.
9. Explain the meaning of (a) conciliation, (b) arbitration and (c) collective bargaining.
10. What is the role of the Australian Industrial Relations Commission? Is its importance increasing or decreasing? Why?

environmental influences on industrial relations

Identify and discuss the key environmental influences from the diagnostic model (figure 15.10 shown on the next page) that have significance for industrial relations.

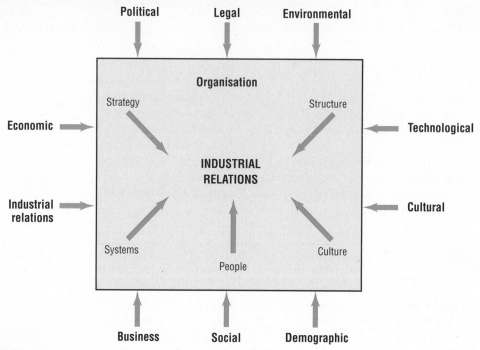

Figure 15.10 Environmental influences on industrial relations

---

class debate

The *Workplace Relations Act 1996*, under the guise of improving productivity and workplace relations, has diminished employee wages and working conditions.
or
HRM is the future and IR is the past.

---

what's your view?

Write a 500-word response to the Letter to the Editor on page 565, agreeing or disagreeing with the writer's point of view.

---

practitioner speaks

Read the article 'Plundered treasure' on page 559. Do you agree or disagree with the author's views? As a class, critically discuss the article.

---

newsbreak exercise

Read the Newsbreak 'Union membership slips again' on page 563. Break into groups of four to six and critically discuss the reasons for the decline in union membership. Identify ways in which the trade union movement could overcome these challenges. Regroup as a class and discuss your findings.

What do you think? Conduct a mini survey of class members, using the questionnaire below. Critically discuss the findings.

1. Workers need trade unions to protect them from management exploitation.	YES	NO
2. Employers and workers should negotiate workplace agreements without union involvement.	YES	NO
3. High minimum wages price unskilled workers out of jobs.	YES	NO
4. HRM stands for human resource manipulation.	YES	NO
5. Industrial conflict is synonymous with class conflict.	YES	NO
6. Tough dismissal laws make employers reluctant to hire workers.	YES	NO

online exercise

Conduct an online search for information about trade unions in two of the following locations: Australia, China, Hong Kong, India, Indonesia, Japan, Malaysia, New Zealand, Singapore, Taiwan, Thailand, Britain or the United States. Write a 500-word report, highlighting your key findings in point form. Include the web addresses that you found useful.

ethical dilemma

A matter of management and union cooperation

The Managing Director of Oz Timber Industries Ltd, Scott Kirwan, pushed his chair away from the gleaming oak table. 'Well, I guess that's it. We're agreed that we stand united against the environmentalists and their opposition to logging the region's old-growth forests?'

'Absolutely, Scott. The union is 100 per cent with you on this. If that mob of protesters is successful, it's going to cost the jobs of hundreds of my members. Unemployment is already a major problem and I don't want to see it get worse', grumbled Eric Martin, Secretary of the United Timberworkers Union.

'I agree Eric, these longhaired hippies and radicals from the big cities just don't understand. The logging industry in this area generates more than $2 billion of business and supports more than 10 000 jobs. But what do the protesters care? All they worry about is that the habitat of some bug that no one has ever heard of might be threatened.'

'Yeah!', snapped Eric. 'That mob never thinks about the workers and their families and what's going to happen to them.'

'The one problem as I see it', interrupted Sarah Menon, HR Manager, 'is that more than 70 per cent of the community is against us.'

'So what?' snapped Eric. 'The public are fools. They've been misled by all the environmentalist propaganda.'

'You can say that again, Eric. Their news releases are straight-out lies. It's a disgrace', added Scott angrily.

'Look, if we don't fight this together', barked Eric, 'there will be no Oz Timber Industries, no timber workers and no bloody union.'

Discussion questions
1. If you were Sarah, what would you do?
2. What ethical issues are raised in this case?

case studies

Sacked on the spot at Jet Red

Bill Armstrong, Operations Manager for Jet Red, is talking to Julie Segal, flight crew supervisor.

Bill   'Now Julie, are you certain that Monica Mehta had the stolen liquor?'

Julie   'Absolutely. The security guards were doing a spot check on crew leaving the plane. Monica's handbag was full of whisky miniatures.'

Bill   'What happened then?'

Julie   'Well, the security guard called me and I went to talk to Monica.'

Bill   'And ...?'

Julie   'Monica denied having stolen anything. She says the liquor must have been planted in her bag by one of the crew members who doesn't like her because she is Indian. Monica also argued that she was being victimised because many other flight crew were stealing. She claims that one of the head office HR staff openly took some bottles on her last flight and the security guards ignored it.'

Bill   'What did you do?'

Julie   'I sacked her on the spot. She knows you can't steal company property.'

Discussion questions

1. What do you think of Julie's actions? How would you have handled the situation?
2. If you were Bill, what would you do? Why?
3. If you were the flight crew union representative, what action would you take? Why?

Exercise

Form into groups of four to six. Break into union and management negotiating teams. Appoint one or two class members as observers. Try to negotiate an agreement over the summary dismissal of Monica Mehta. Complete the negotiator perception sheet below and then review the negotiations using the key points.

NEGOTIATOR PERCEPTIONS

You may have developed some impressions about your counterparts. Circle the adjectives listed below that you feel apply to your counterparts. You may list additional adjectives in the blank spaces.

argumentative	objective	_____	_____
arrogant	patronising	_____	_____
biased	reasonable	_____	_____
confident	scheming	_____	_____
domineering	sincere	_____	_____
emotional	trustworthy	_____	_____
flexible	uncertain	_____	_____
helpful	understanding	_____	_____

NEGOTIATION KEY POINTS

- Did the parties reach agreement?
- Were both parties satisfied with the outcome?
- Do the parties feel their self-respect has been maintained?
- Would the parties negotiate with each other again?
- Will the parties comply with the agreement?
- What constructive/destructive behaviour was observed?
- What would the team members do differently next time around?

Bad times at Jet Red

'Look, we're sick and tired of hearing how Jet Red has to cut costs. Where has it got us? Your restructuring has cut our members' jobs by more than 10 per cent. And now you want more. I don't see you people taking any cuts!' Joe Murphy, Assistant Secretary of the Airline Workers Union, snarled as he glared at the management representatives seated opposite.

'Joe, be reasonable. This airline is on the verge of bankruptcy. We have to reduce our headcount, shut down unprofitable operations and reduce debt. Surely you can see that?' replied Linda Church, Jet Red's HR Manager.

'What I see is my members getting kicked in the guts by a bunch of no-hopers who wouldn't know a good idea if it hit them between the eyes like a meat axe. You people just don't care. Some of my members have been with Jet Red since they left school. And now you want to give them the boot!' Joe snapped angrily.

Linda sighed. 'Come on Joe, that's not fair. I admit the old management was not up to it. But we have a new team now. Alan Balkin is really the only hope this company has. If his initiatives fail, there will be no Jet Red and no jobs. We need to work together on this.'

'How can I work with you lot when all you want to do is take my members' jobs, cut their pay and benefits, and increase their workloads?' Joe growled.

'Joe, you know as well as I do that your members have been overpaid and underworked for years. That was okay when there was no competition. The world has changed. Our cost structure is no longer competitive. What with the impact of SARS, terrorism and increased competition, we're struggling. You know that as well as I do. The good old days are gone; we are no longer protected by the government. We now have to compete.'

'Yeah, at my members' expense', muttered Joe.

'Joe, I'm going to spell it out one more time', Linda answered sharply. 'If your members do not agree to the introduction of competitive pay rates, greater flexibility and expanded job responsibilities, we will be forced to explore other options.'

'Linda, I don't know how many times I have to tell you — the cabin crew will not clean the planes, and especially not the toilets. That is cleaners' work. Have you talked to Bill Ferguson at the Airline Cleaners Union? He won't have a bar of it. If we agreed to your requests, we would have an almighty demarcation dispute on our hands. Where would you be then?' countered Joe.

'With one union, Joe. Yours.'

Joe looked at Linda. 'Let me get this straight. If we agree to play ball with you, Jet Red will give us coverage of all employees?' Joe asked.

'That's right. If we can cut a deal, you will have total coverage of all Jet Red's union members. Except for the pilots, of course', smiled Linda.

Joe leant forward. 'Well, those blokes belong to an association, not a union. If I go for this, I need to give the members something. What can you offer me?'

'Well', said Linda, 'how about career paths, performance bonuses, shares in the company, promotion on ability and increased training and development?'

'Yeah, but where's the sweetener?' asked Joe.

'Higher pay rates. If we get increased flexibility and higher productivity, we can pay more. Sure your members will have to work harder and smarter, but they will be paid for it. They will have higher level jobs than they have now, they will be more skilled and they will have greater job security because the airline will be profitable.'

(continued)

'What about the poor sods who are going to lose their jobs?' asked Joe.

Linda paused. 'Of course, there will be cutbacks. We plan to offer the standard package plus an extra week's pay for every year of service, and outplacement counselling. We can't be fairer than that.'

'And what happens if I can't sell this package to my members?' asked Joe.

'The company will be left with no alternative Joe. We will outsource. We will terminate your members and replace them with casuals, part-timers and overseas hires. We can get equally qualified or better people in New Zealand and the Philippines at much lower cost. There is nothing that requires us to hire people in Australia', answered Linda.

Joe leant back in his chair and glared at Linda. 'What's this country coming to?'

'It's all about survival, Joe. Globalisation has brought the competition into our backyard. We have to slash costs. There is no other way', replied Linda.

Discussion questions

1. If you were Joe, what would you do? Why?
2. Do you agree or disagree with Linda's proposals? Why?
3. If you were a union member, how would you react? What concerns would you have?

practical exercises

1. Break into small groups.
   (a) Arrange to interview two or three union members and find out why they are union members, what they see as the purpose of their trade union and how satisfied they are with their union.
   (b) Arrange to interview one or two HR managers in organisations that have unions. Find out why the HR managers believe their employees join a union, what they see as the purpose of trade unions and how they view the union's role in their organisation.
   (c) As a class, compare and discuss the results of your interviews. What are the major highlights of your findings? What differences (if any) in attitude towards unions were found? Explain these differences.

2. (a) Break into three groups of two to three members. The groups will represent:
   (i) a union
   (ii) management
   (iii) an industrial tribunal.
   (b) Read the case material below, then prepare your arguments, questions, and so on for a meeting before the industrial tribunal to try to resolve the dispute.
   (c) Meet before the industrial tribunal to try to resolve the dispute.
   (d) Review the tribunal appearance.
   (i) Was an agreement reached through conciliation or did the tribunal members have to make a decision? Why, do you think, was this method used to reach agreement?
   (ii) Were both parties satisfied with the outcome? Why? Why not?
   (iii) What constructive/destructive behaviour was observed?
   (iv) What would team members do differently next time?

The General Workers Union (GWU) is in dispute with Allstate Industries Ltd over the following incident.

The GWU Allstate Industries Ltd award contains a clause that states, 'Employees will be allowed 10 minutes paid time to wash up at the end of each shift'. Three days ago, Angela Costa, supervisor of the packing section, found Bill Maloney cleaning up 30 minutes before finishing time. Angela asked: 'Bill, what are you doing quitting so early? If you don't get back to work, you'll have your pay docked.' Bill replied, 'I just finished filling the Acme order, which was a big job, and the next one is Apex which is even bloody bigger! What's the point of working on it now for a few minutes when I'll spend that time tomorrow just checking where I was? Anyway, our award says we get wash up time so I don't see why you're getting your knickers in such a knot!'

'Bill, you're being paid to work, so work! Now get on with it', Angela snapped. Bill glared at Angela, but said nothing. He then turned and picked up a carton to commence work. Angela walked away. As she did so, Bill cursed, 'Stupid dago bitch.'

Infuriated, Angela screamed, 'I heard that, you ignorant pig! You're fired! Get out!'

Additional information

Bill Maloney   Employed as a packer for seven years. Regarded as an average worker. Reprimanded three years ago for insubordination.

Angela Costa   Employed by the company for two years. Regarded as an excellent employee and an above-average supervisor. Promoted to her present position two months ago. Has had no supervisory training.

3. Break into small groups.
    (a) Arrange to interview an employee, a shop steward and a member of management in an organisation that has negotiated an Australian Workplace Agreement.
    (b) Find out how they felt about negotiating the workplace agreements. Were they happy with the process and the results? What were the advantages and disadvantages each saw regarding the negotiation of the workplace agreements?
    (c) On the basis of your interviews, prepare a brief report for management on how negotiating workplace agreements in the organisation can be improved.
4. Break into groups of three to four. Imagine you are part of a management task team designated to investigate industrial relations in one of the following locations: China, Hong Kong, India, Indonesia, Japan, Malaysia, New Zealand, Philippines, Singapore, Thailand, Britain or the United States. You are charged with preparing a two- to three-page summary report for the board of directors highlighting the main features of the location's system and any industrial relations advantages or challenges your organisation may face if it decides to establish operations there.

suggested readings

ACIRRT, *Australia at Work*, Prentice Hall, Sydney, 1999.

Alexander, R. and Lewer, R., *Understanding Australian Industrial Relations*, 6th edn, Thomson, Melbourne, 2004.

Beardwell, I. and Holden, L., *Human Resource Management*, 3rd edn, Financial Times/Prentice Hall, London, 2001, chs 1, 10, 11.

CCH, *Australian Master Human Resources Guide*, CCH, Sydney, 2003, chs 17, 18, 22, 24, 27, 28.

De Cieri, H. and Kramar, R., *Human Resource Management in Australia*, McGraw-Hill, Sydney, 2003, ch. 7.

Deery, S., Plowman, D., Walsh, J. and Brown, M., *Industrial Relations: A Contemporary Analysis*, 3rd edn, McGraw-Hill, Sydney, 2001.

Fisher, C. D., Schoenfeldt, L. F. and Shaw, J. B., *Human Resource Management*, 5th edn, Houghton Mifflin, Boston, 2003, ch. 15.

Gennard, J. and Judge, G., *Employee Relations*, 3rd edn, CIPD, London, 2003, chs 5, 6, 7, 8, 10, 11.

Ivancevich, J. M., *Human Resource Management*, 8th edn, McGraw-Hill, Boston, 2001, ch. 16.

Ivancevich, J. M. and Lee, S. H., *Human Resource Management in Asia*, McGraw-Hill, Singapore, 2002, ch. 14.

Mondy, R. W., Noe, R. M. and Premeaux, S. R., *Human Resource Management*, 8th edn, Prentice Hall, Upper Saddle River, NJ, 2002, chs 14, 15, 16.

Nankervis, A. R., Compton, R. L. and Baird, M., *Strategic Human Resource Management*, 4th edn, Thomas Nelson, South Melbourne, 2002, chs 14, 15.

online references

aflcio.org
mua.tcp.net.au
nimrod.mit.edu/depts/dewey/indrel/html
www.abs.gov.au
www.actu.asn.au
www.aigroup.asn.au
www.AIRC.gov.au
www.amwu.asu.au
www.anf.org.au
www.anu.edu.au/polsci/unions/unions.html
www.australianbusiness.com.au
www.cepv.asn.au
www.cfmeu.asn.au
www.cpsv.org/psv/index.htm

www.deet.gov.au
www.dewrsb.gov.au
www.dir.nsw.gov.au
www.econ.usyd.edu.au/acirrt
www.forbes.com/labourmethod
www.fsunion.org.au
www.hrq.com
www.ilo.org/public.english/index.htm
www.labor.net.au
www.lib.msu.edu/call/main/lir
www.oea.gov.au
www.shrm.org.hrmagazine
www.workplaceinfo.com.au
www.workplaceonline.com

end notes

1. Editorial, 'Unions on a slippery slope', *Australian Financial Review*, 8 April 2003, p. 70.

2. T. Skotnicki, 'Employees feel the worst from Campaign 2000', *Business Review Weekly*, 16 June 2000, p. 35; and E. Lee, 'For love or money?', *South China Morning Post*, 31 March 2001, p. 17.

3. S. Long, 'Different sorts of mettle in the steel and iron division', *Australian Financial Review*, 23 December 1999, p. 5; and S. Long, 'Win for BHP union sting', *Australian Financial Review*, 11 January 2001, p. 8.

4. W. Kasper, 'History is on BHP's side', *Australian Financial Review*, 27 January 2000, p. 17.

5. N. Way, 'Dis-unionity', *Business Review Weekly*, 9 March 2001, pp. 72–4; M. Skulley, 'Union boss pleads guilty', *Australian Financial Review*, 5 November 2003, p. 8; P. Klinger, 'CFMEU control under scrutiny', *Australian Financial Review*, 2 October 2002, p. 7; and Editorial, '... and union bullies must be vanquished', *Australian Financial Review*, 2 October 2002, p. 62.

6. P. K. Ruthven, 'Industry leaders and laggards', *Australian Financial Review*, 26 July 1996, p. 24.

7. N. Way, 'Slow workers', *Business Review Weekly*, 28 May 1993, p. 66.
8. K. Phillips, 'ALP hassle bares union struggle for future', *Australian Financial Review*, 22 May 2002, p. 63.
9. K. Phillips, 'Building a case against unions', *Australian Financial Review*, 5 June 2002, p. 63; S. Strutt, 'Multiplex reaped profits from subbies funds', *Australian Financial Review*, 19 April 2002, p. 7; and J. Murray, 'Industry should adopt freedom of choice', *Australian Financial Review*, 17 April 2002, p. 55.
10. Quoted in R. Gottliebsen, 'Comment', *Business Review Weekly*, 11 December 1992, p. 6; and N. Way, 'Across the tracks', *BRW*, 4 December 2003, p. 29.
11. A. Mitchell, 'Path of reform winds on', *Australian Financial Review*, 13 August 2003, p. 54.
12. S. Long, 'Corrigan plans to replace wharfies with robots', *Australian Financial Review*, 14 August 2000, pp. 1, 5; K. Murphy, 'Waterfront reform fails to impress', *Australian Financial Review*, 5 May 2000, p. 55. For an analysis of the dispute, see R. Morris, 'From productivity crisis to industrial dispute: the 1998 waterfront troubles', *International Employment Relations Review*, vol. 6, no. 1, 2000, pp. 89–106.
13. S. Long, 'Mining jobs gone soon, says researcher', *Australian Financial Review*, 10 January 2001, p. 6.
14. ACIRRT, *Australia at Work*, Prentice Hall, Sydney, 1999, p. 10.
15. A. Mitchell, 'Treasury has fertile argument', *Australian Financial Review*, 25 May 2003, p. 53; P. Saunders, 'How to kill jobs the Australian way', *Australian Financial Review*, 28 July 2003, p. 59; K. Tsumori, 'Unfair dismissal laws deter hiring too', *Australian Financial Review*, 26 August 2002, p. 55; and S. Long, 'A pain for Patrick', *Australian Financial Review*, 24 April 2002, p. 67.
16. D. Clark, 'Fuss and feathers over tax reform', *Personal Investment*, August 1996, pp. 28–32.
17. Reported in E. Shann, 'Adding costs won't work for outsiders', *Business Review Weekly*, 12 November 1993, p. 56.
18. K. Tsumori, 'Low-skilled jobless still out in the cold', *Australian Financial Review*, 18 December 2003, p. 47.
19. Reported in J. Koutsoukis, 'Unfair dismissal laws cost $1.3 bn and are inefficient', *Australian Financial Review*, 30 October 2002, p. 10; and P. Saunders, op. cit., p. 59.
20. P. F. Drucker, 'They're not employees, they're people', *Harvard Business Review*, February 2002, pp. 70–7; and D. Welch, 'How Nissan laps Detroit', *Business Week*, 22 December 2003, pp. 72–4.
21. P. F. Drucker, 2002, op. cit., p. 73.
22. Pacific Strategic Investments, *Annual Report*, Sydney, 2003, p. 7.
23. W. Lewis, 'The secret to competitiveness', *Asian Wall Street Journal*, 1 November 1993, p. 10.
24. B. Pocock and p. Wright, 'Trade unionism in 1996', *Journal of Industrial Relations*, vol. 39, no. 1, 1997, pp. 120–36; D. Moore, 'Better than the Australian Industrial Relations Commission', *Policy*, vol. 15, no. 4, 1999–2000, pp. 11–18; and T. Abbott, 'It's always unfinished business', *Australian Financial Review*, 27 March 2001, p. 43.
25. M. Salaman, *Industrial Relations Theory and Practice*, 2nd edn, Prentice Hall, London, 1992, pp. 5–16.
26. T. A. Kochan and T. A. Barocci, *Human Resource Management and Industrial Relations*, Scott Foresman, Glenview, Ill., 1985, p. 10.
27. J. Osborn, 'Book Review', *Journal of Industrial Relations*, vol. 34, no. 1, 1992, p. 172; and K. N. Kamoche, *Understanding Human Resource Management*, Open University Press, Buckingham, 2001, pp. 24–5.
28. M. Salaman, op. cit., p. 33; H. Guile, D. Sappey and M. Winter, 'Can industrial relations survive without unions?', in M. Bray and D. Kelly (eds), *Issues and Proceedings of the 4th Biennial AIRAANZ Conference*, University of Wollongong, 1–4 February 1989, p. 36; and F. M. Horwitz, 'HRM: An ideological perspective', *Personnel Review*, vol. 19, no. 2, 1990, pp. 10–15.
29. F. M. Horwitz, op. cit., p. 11.
30. D. Farnham, *Employee Relations*, IPM, London, 1993, p. 35.
31. S. J. Deery and D. H. Plowman, *Australian Industrial Relations*, 3rd edn, McGraw-Hill, Sydney, 1991, p. 10.
32. S. J. Deery and D. H. Plowman, op. cit., pp. 11–12.
33. S. J. Deery and D. H. Plowman, op. cit., pp. 9–12; and M. Salaman, op. cit., pp. 33–6.
34. Quoted in J. Karanagh, 'Paul Houlihan', *Business Review Weekly*, 24 November 2000, p. 117.
35. Quoted in 'Badinage', *Business Review Weekly*, June 1993, p. 59.
36. M. Salaman, op. cit., p. 37.
37. T. A. Kochan and T. A. Barocci, op. cit., p. 8.
38. T. Bilton, K. Bonnett, p. Jones, M. Stanworth, K. Sheard and A. Webster, *Introductory Sociology*, Macmillan, London, 1981, p. 237.
39. T. Bilton et al., op. cit., p. 238.
40. L. L. Sharkey, quoted in R. M. Martin, 'The problem of political strikes', in W. A. Howard (ed.), *Perspectives on Australian Industrial Relations*, Longman Cheshire, Melbourne, 1984, p. 69.
41. For example, see D. W. Rawson, *Unions and Unionists in Australia*, Allen & Unwin, Sydney, 1980, p. 98; and N. F. Duffy, 'Conscripts and volunteers', *Australian Bulletin of Labour*, vol. 17, no. 2, 1991, pp. 96–7.
42. M. Salaman, op. cit., p. 38.
43. Reported in 'They say', *Australian Financial Review*, 15 April 1998, p. 10.
44. I. Beardwell and L. Holden, *Human Resource Management*, 3rd edn, Financial Times/Prentice Hall, London, 2001, pp. 24–7; K. Kamoche, op. cit., pp. 1–26; and T. Keenoy, 'HRM: a case of the wolf in sleep's clothing?', *Personnel Review*, vol. 19, no. 2, 1990, pp. 3–9.
45. D. Grant and J. Shields, 'In search of the subject: researching employee reactions to human resource management', *Journal of Industrial Relations*, vol. 44, no. 3, 2002, p. 321.
46. D. Guest, 'Human resource management, corporate performance and employee well being: building the worker into HRM', *Journal of Industrial Relations*, vol. 44, no. 3, 2002, p. 344; and S. Albrecht and A. Travaglione, 'Trust in public sector senior management', *International Journal of Human Resource Management*, vol. 14, no. 1, 2003, p. 79.
47. S. Spreier and S. Sherman, 'Staying ahead of the curve', *Fortune*, 3 March 2003, pp. 41–3; and J. Gould-Williams, 'The importance of

HR practices and workplace trust in achieving superior performance: a study of public sector organizations', *International Journal of Human Resource Management*, vol. 14, no. 1, 2003, pp. 28–54.

48. See J. Purcell, 'Ideology and the end of institutional industrial relations: evidence from the UK', *Labour and Industry*, vol. 5, no. 3, 1993, pp. 37–74.

49. S. Dunn, 'The roots of metaphor in the old and new industrial relations', *British Journal of Industrial Relations*, vol. 28, no. 1, 1990, pp. 1–31.

50. Marxists, for example, see an inherent conflict of interest between the working class and capitalists who own and control the means of production. Similarly, pluralists, while not seeking the overthrow of capitalism, see conflicting interests operating in the workplace that necessitate government regulation and the existence of unions. See T. A. Kochan and T. A. Barocci, op. cit., pp. 8–9; and S. J. Deery and D. H. Plowman, op. cit., pp. 5–17.

51. For example, see V. Taylor, 'Industrial relations and management education', in G. Griffin (ed.), *Current Research in Industrial Relations*, Proceedings of the 5th AIRAANZ Conference, University of Melbourne, 4–7 July 1990, pp. 526–48; T. Keenoy, 'The roots of metaphor in the old and the new industrial relations', *British Journal of Industrial Relations*, vol. 29, no. 2, 1991, pp. 313–28; and K. N. Kamoche, op. cit., pp. 11–26.

52. D. Plowman, 'Industrial relations' teaching and research: trends, pressures, strategies', in G. Griffin (ed.), op. cit., p. 10. Also see H. Guille, D. Sappey and M. Winter, 'Can industrial relations survive without unions?', in G. Griffin (ed.), op. cit., pp. 31–47; and N. Howarth, 'The unitarist renaissance', in M. Bray and D. Kelly (eds), *Issues and Trends in Australian Industrial Relations*, Proceedings of the 4th Biennial AIRAANZ Conference, University of Wollongong, 1–4 February 1989, pp. 407–23.

53. P. F. Boxhall and P. J. Dowling, 'Human resource management and the industrial relations tradition', *Labour and Industry*, vol. 3, no. 2–3, 1990, p. 203.

54. P. Blyton and P. Turnbull (eds), *Reassessing Human Resource Management*, Sage, London, 1992, p. 13; and F. M. Horwitz, op. cit., pp. 10–15.

55. T. Keenoy, 1990, op. cit., pp. 8–9.

56. D. E. Guest, 'Human resource management and industrial relations', *Journal of Management Studies*, vol. 24, no. 5, 1987, p. 520.

57. A. D. Peetz, 'Welcome to AIRAANZ', *AIRAANZ Review*, vol. 1, no. 2, 2000, p. 52.

58. S. Dunn, op. cit., p. 3; P. F. Boxhall, 'The significance of human resource management: a reconsideration of the evidence', *International Journal of Human Resource Management*, vol. 4, no. 3, September 1993, p. 646; and J. Bailey, 'IR? You must be joking', *HR Monthly*, August 2003, pp. 44–5.

59. For example, Gardner and Palmer describe employment relations as bringing HRM and industrial relations together as a field of study. See M. Gardner and G. Palmer, *Employment Relations*, Macmillan, South Melbourne, 1997. Also see M. Fastenau and L. Pullin, 'Employment relations, a framework for regional research', in L. Pullin, M. Fastenau and D. Mortimer, *Regional Employment Relations*: *Contemporary Research*, University of Western Sydney, Nepean, 1996, pp. 1–6; D. Kelly, 'A shock to the system? The impact of HRM on academic IR in Australia in comparison with USA and UK, 1980–1995', *Asia Pacific Journal of Human Resources*, vol. 41, no. 2, 2003, pp. 159–64; and M. Westcott, N. Wailes, T. Todd, and J. Bailey, 'The HRM challenge and the teaching of IR at Australian universities', *Asia Pacific Journal of Human Resources*, vol. 41, no. 2, 2003, pp. 172–89.

60. P. F. Boxhall, op. cit., p. 646; and D. Kelly, op. cit., p. 150.

61. P. F. Boxhall and P. J. Dowling, op. cit., p. 208.

62. P. F. Boxhall and P. J. Dowling, op. cit., p. 209.

63. P. Blyton and P. Turnbull, 'Afterword', in P. Blyton and P. Turnbull (eds), *Reassessing Human Resource Management*, Sage, London, 1992, p. 256; D. E. Guest, 1987, op. cit., pp. 516–17; J. Hallier, 'HRM as a pluralistic forum: assumptions and prospects for developing a distinctive research capability', *International Journal of Human Resource Management*, vol. 4, no. 4, 1993, pp. 945–73; and D. E. Guest, 'Human resource management and performance: a review and a research agenda', *International Journal of Human Resource Management*, vol. 8, no. 3, 1997, pp. 263–76.

64. Based on D. Ulrich, *Human Resource Champions*, Harvard Business School Press, Boston, 1997, pp. 237–8.

65. M. Bray, 'What is distinctive about Industrial Relations', *AIRAANZ Review*, vol. 1, no. 2, 2000, pp. 4–16.

66. In fact, there are six major parties in industrial relations: state and federal government, industrial tribunals, state and federal employers, employer associations, trade unions and employees. S. J. Deery and D. H. Plowman, op. cit., p. 71.

67. S. J. Deery and D. H. Plowman, op. cit., p. 71.

68. Awards are legal decisions made by state or federal industrial tribunals that govern pay rates and conditions of employment. The awards may reflect agreements reached between employers and unions or they may be the product of arbitrated decisions arising from an industrial dispute.

69. M. L. MacIntosh, 'Australian industrial relations in 1992: another turning point', *Asia Pacific Journal of Human Resources*, vol. 31, no. 2, 1993, pp. 52–64.

70. F. G. Hilmer, P. A. McLaughlin, D. K. Macfarlane and J. Rose, 'Enterprise based bargaining units — a better way of working', *Business Council of Australia*, Melbourne, 1989, p. vii.

71. Cited in M. L. MacIntosh, op. cit., p. 61.

72. J. Buchanan, K. Van Barneveld, T. O'Loughlin and B. Pragnell, 'Wages policy and wage determination in 1996', *Journal of Industrial Relations*, vol. 39, no. 1, 1997, p. 119.

73. G. D. John, 'Employer matters in 1996', *Journal of Industrial Relations*, vol. 39, no. 1, 1997, p. 156.

74. T. MacDermott, 'Industrial legislation in 1996: the reform agenda', *Journal of Industrial Relations*, vol. 39, no. 1, 1997, p. 52; and P. Dawkins, 'The tortoise makes a forward move: the economic effects of the Workplace Relations Act', *Australian Bulletin of Labour*, vol. 23, no. 1, 1997, pp. 66–7.

75. R. Gough, 'Australian employee relations in 1996: change and continuity', *International Employment Relations Review*, vol. 2, no. 2, 1996, p. 112; and B. Pocock and P. Wright, op. cit., p. 124.

76. N. Field, 'ACTU bid to undo workplace reform', *Australian Financial Review*, 6 March 2001, p. 7; and K. Murphy, 'Bosses fear Labor's plans for IR change', *Australian Financial Review*, 6 April 2001, p. 17.

77. S. J. Deery and D. H. Plowman, op. cit., p. 92; and E. Davis, 'Industrial relations in Australia', in CCH, *Australian Master Human Resources Guide*, CCH, Sydney, 2003, p. 354.

78. R. Lansbury and E. Davis, 'Australian industrial relations', in G. J. Bamber and R. D. Lansbury (eds), *International and Comparative Industrial Relations*, Allen & Unwin, Sydney, 1987, pp. 102–3.

79. R. D. Lansbury and M. Westcott, 'Collective bargaining employment and competitiveness: the case of Australia', *International Journal of Employment Studies*, vol. 8, no. 1, 2000, p. 123.

80. S. Long, 'Maritime Union captain John Coombes steps down', *Australian Financial Review*, 14 November 2000, p. 11.

81. R. Lansbury and E. Davis, op. cit., p. 102; J. Hewett, 'Fractures in the fragile IR club', *Australian Financial Review*, 19 September 1993, p. 17; and S. J. Deery and D. H. Plowman, op. cit., pp. 334–5.

82. See J. Hewett, op. cit., p. 12; and C. Bolt, 'The AIRC is not a true believer', *Australian Financial Review*, 4 August 1993, p. 15.

83. Reported in C. Bolt, 4 August 1993, op. cit., p. 15.

84. See B. Kelty, 'Bias or balance — autonomy of the AIRC', *Workplace*, no. 7, 1992, pp. 6–10.

85. G. Polites, 'Change and the Industrial Relations Commission', *Industrial Relations Society of Victoria*, Kirby Monograph Series, No. 3, 1991, p. 5.

86. J. Hewett, op. cit., p. 17.

87. N. Field, 'Unions on notice after court issues $200 000 fine', *Australian Financial Review*, 31 March–1 April 2001, p. 7.

88. G. Smith, 'AIRC goes back to its old tricks', *Australian Financial Review*, 2 September 2003, p. 71; D. Williams, 'Bargaining at the limit', *HR Monthly*, March 2003, p. 26–7; and S. Long, 'Back to arbitration', *Australian Financial Review*, 8 May 2002, p. 60.

89. Former ACTU secretary, Bill Kelty, once a close friend of the late Justice Barry Maddern, President of the AIRC, 'accused him of modelling himself on Fidel Castro and likened the Full Bench's decision to vomit'. The federal Labor government dumped similar scorn on the AIRC. See C. Bolt, 4 August 1993, op. cit., p. 15.

90. G. F. Smith, 'Startling breadth of changes has yet to be appreciated', *Australian*, 30 March 1994, p. 4.

91. T. MacDermott, op. cit., p. 53.

92. Commonwealth Department of Industrial Relations, *Changes in Federal Workplace Relations Law — Legislation Guide*, Canberra, 1996, p. 12.

93. D. Barnett, 'IR storm, but Howard is safe', *Australian Financial Review*, 22 August 1997, p. 34.

94. E. Davis, 2003, op. cit., p. 374.

95. R. Lansbury and E. Davis, op. cit., p. 113.

96. J. D. Hill, W. A. Howard and R. D. Lansbury, *Industrial Relations: An Australian Introduction*, Longman Cheshire, Melbourne, 1982, p. 21.

97. F. G. Hilmer et al., op. cit., p. 1.

98. F. G. Hilmer et al., op. cit., p. 10.

99. B. Dabscheck, 'Industrial relations and the irresistible magic wand: the BCA's plan to Americanise Australian industrial relations', in M. Easson and J. Shaw (eds), *Transforming Industrial Relations*, Pluto Press, Sydney, 1990, p. 120, pp. 127–8.

100. T. O'Loughlin, 'IR reforms big on bosses' wish list', *Australian Financial Review*, 15 November 2002, p. 19.

101. C. Bolt, 'A new force in industrial relations', *Australian Financial Review*, 19 August 1993, p. 3; and M. Skulley, 'Reform, but slowly does it', *Australian Financial Review*, 14 November 2003, p. 80.

102. The National Wage Case is a major wage case for a general wage increase. The Equal Pay Case is an example of a major national hearing.

103. TUTA, *An ABC of Trade Unionism*, 3rd edn, TUTA, Wodonga, 1985, p. 3.

104. M. Priest and M. Skulley, 'Judgment day for Combet', *Australian Financial Review*, 18 August 2003, p. 7; M. Skulley, 'ACTU at odds with ALP policy', *Australian Financial Review*, 22 August 2003, p. 5; M. Skulley, 'After the deals, now for the hard part', *Australian Financial Review*, 22 August 2003, p. 5; S. Balogh, 'Unions agree on hours cap', *Australian*, 20 August 2003, p. 4; and G. Combet, 'Unions celebrate their past amid questions over the future', *Australian Financial Review*, 30 November – 1 December 2002, p. 50.

105. N. Way, 'State Labor bodies past their peak', *Business Review Weekly*, 1 June 1993, p. 66.

106. Reported in D. Murphy, 'Man for all factions', *Bulletin*, 3 August 1993, p. 29.

107. R. Cooper, 'Trade unionism in 2002', *Journal of Industrial Relations*, vol. 45, no. 2, 2003, p. 205.

108. J. Hewett, op. cit., p. 17.

109. Reported in P. Berry and G. Kitchener, *Can Unions Survive?*, BWIU, Canberra, 1989, p. 1.

110. N. Way, 'Workers of the world uniting', *BRW*, 13–19 November 2003, p. 64; and K. Phillips, 'Union war is reaching climax', *Australian Financial Review*, 8 August 2002, p. 63.

111. E. Davis, 2003, op. cit., p. 359.

112. D. Peetz, cited in M. Costa, 'Union strategy post the Workplace Relations Act', *Australian Bulletin of Labour*, vol. 23, no. 1, 1997, p. 53.

113. P. Berry and G. Kitchener, op. cit., p. 1.

114. Quoted in N. Way, 'Bargaining: tough lessons', *Business Review Weekly*, 7 February 1992, p. 23.

115. Quoted in S. Long, 'ACTU launches drives to reunionise BHP iron ore', *Australian Financial Review*, 6–7 January 2001, p. 6. Also see N. Way, 'BHP and unions dig in for a stoush', *Business Review Weekly*, 6 April 2001, pp. 46–7.

116. N. Way, 'Collision course', *Business Review Weekly*, 20 October 2000, pp. 36–9.

117. See Editorial, 'Union lessons in BHP ruling', *Australian Financial Review*, 12 January 2001, p. 46.

118. M. Costa, op. cit., p. 57; M. Davis, 'New broom at AWU can see a way out of the red', *Australian Financial Review*, 25 July 1997, p. 19; and

N. Way, 'Abbott dons the workers mantle', *Business Review Weekly*, 20 April 2001, pp. 64–6.

119. N. Way, 'ACTU revival challenge', *Business Review Weekly*, 17 December 1999, p. 20.

120. N. Field, 'Women pull rank and file', *Australian Financial Review*, 21 December 1999, p. 15.

121. Quoted in N. Way, 'Reith: a pattern emerges', *Business Review Weekly*, 30 June 2000, p. 77.

122. J. Waddington and A. Kerr, 'Unions fit for young workers?', *Industrial Relations Journal*, vol. 33, no. 4, 2002, p. 314.

123. S. Kniott, 'Improved resources', *HR Monthly*, April 2003, pp. 42–3; Editorial, 'Unions in war of attrition', *Australian Financial Review*, 19 August 2003, p. 62; and T. O'Loughlin, M. Skulley and M. Priest, 'Secret Cole report lifts lid on rorts', *Australian Financial Review*, 18 September 2003, pp. 1, 4.

124. B. Pocock and P. Wright, op. cit., p. 120; K. Murphy, 'Government denies it has secret plan to break waterfront union', *Australian Financial Review*, 21 August 1997, p. 3; G. Griffin, 'Trade unions in crisis: introduction', *Labour and Industry*, vol. 9, no. 3, 1999, pp. 1–3; and E. Anderson, G. Griffin and J. Teicher, 'The changing roles of public sector unionism', *International Journal of Employment Studies*, vol. 10, no. 2, 2002, p. 71.

125. B. Pocock and P. Wright, op. cit., p. 120.

126. A. Charlwood, 'Why do non union employees want to unionize? Evidence from Britain', *British Journal of Industrial Relations*, vol. 40, no. 3, 2002, p. 488.

127. M. Costa, op. cit., p. 57; and N. Way, 'Unions face the new reality', *Business Review Weekly*, 20 April 2001, p. 12.

128. E. Davis, op. cit., pp. 360–1; P. Berry and G. Kitchener, op. cit., pp. 40–51; B. Pocock and P. Wright, op. cit., pp. 120–36; B. Van Gramberg, J. Teicher and G. Griffin, 'Industrial relations in 1999: workplace relations, legalism and individualization', *Asia Pacific Journal of Human Resources*, vol. 38, no. 2, 2000, pp. 12–14; C. Briggs, M. Cole and J. Buchanan, 'Where are the non-members? Challenges and opportunities in the heartlands for union organizing', *International Journal of Employment Studies*, vol. 10, no. 2, 2002, pp. 1–22; W. J. Diamond and R. B. Freeman, 'Will unionism prosper in cyberspace? The promise of the Internet for employee organization', *British Journal of Industrial Relations*, vol. 40, no. 3, 2002, pp. 569–96; and J. Visser, 'Why fewer workers join unions in Europe: a social custom explanation', *British Journal of Industrial Relations*, vol. 40, no. 3, 2002, p. 425.

129. S. Long, 'Going for Rio', *Australian Financial Review*, 6–7 May 2000, p. 30; N. Way, 'BHP mettle on test in the Pilbara', *BRW*, 14 January 2000, pp. 24–6; and N. Field, 'Women pull rank and file', *Australian Financial Review*, 21 December 1999, p. 15.

130. D. Knight, 'A hard act to follow', *HR Monthly*, December 2000, p. 21; N. Way, 'Boardroom raiding party', *BRW*, 4 December 2003, pp. 66–7; M. Skulley, 'ACTU flags global push', *Australian Financial Review*, 19 September 2002, p. 4; and M. Priest, 'ACTU in doorstep recruitment drive', *Australian Financial Review*, 9 May 2003, p. 5.

131. S. Long, 'Union leaders turn on Kelty', *Australian Financial Review*, 20 February 1997, p. 2; S. Long, 'CFMEU bosses' battle hits court',

Australian Financial Review, 22 March 2001, p. 26; N. Field, 'Unionists to target ASX in May 1 protest', *Australian Financial Review*, 6 April 2001, p. 20; and S. Long, 'Sutton blames the good fight', *Australian Financial Review*, 20 March 2001, p. 9.

132. Reported in D. O'Reilly, 'Crunch time for Kelty', *Bulletin*, 16 February 1993, p. 19.

133. N. Way, 'ACTU sets sights on coverage wars', *Business Review Weekly*, 20 August 1993, p. 32; and N. Way, 'How workers first came last', *Business Review Weekly*, 1 December 2000, pp. 64–7.

134. B. Pocock and P. Wright, op. cit., p. 136.

135. W. J. Diamond and R. B. Freeman, 2002, p. 592.

136. N. Way, 'Unionism's new challenge: survival', *Business Review Weekly*, 19 April 1991, p. 85.

137. Quoted in P. Wilson, 'Power in the balance', *Weekend Australian*, 17–18 July 1993, p. 19.

138. Taken from P. Hamburger, 'A review of P. Drucker, *The New Realities* in "Books"', *Australian Business*, 4 July 1990, p. 93.

139. Unions should retain an ombudsman role against management stupidity and arbitrary abuse of power, according to Drucker. Hamburger, op. cit., p. 93. See also P. Drucker, *The New Realities*, Mandarin, London, 1989, pp. 185–9.

140. M. Gaynor, '10 decent proposals', *Workplace*, Winter 1993, p. 17.

141. J. D. Hill, W. A. Howard and R. D. Lansbury, *Industrial Relations: An Australian Introduction*, Longman Cheshire, Melbourne, 1982, p. 144.

142. B. Dabscheck and J. Niland, *Industrial Relations in Australia*, Allen & Unwin, Sydney, 1982, p. 74.

143. R. W. Mondy and R. M. Noe, *Human Resource Management*, 6th edn, Allyn & Bacon, Boston, 1996, pp. 556–7.

144. This section is based on material taken from G. Dessler, *Human Resource Management*, 7th edn, Prentice Hall, Englewood Cliffs, NJ, 1997, pp. 575–6; D. J. Cherrington, *The Management of Human Resources*, 4th edn, Prentice Hall, Englewood Cliffs, NJ, 1995, pp. 584–9; and M. Samuels, *Supervision and Management*, John Wiley & Sons, Brisbane, 1990, pp. 294–5.

145. P. Cohen, 'Industrial negotiation — why not do it yourself?', unpublished paper, 1981, p. 9.

146. W. A. Howard and C. Fox, *Industrial Relations Reform*, Longman Cheshire, Melbourne, 1988, p. 19.

147. This section is largely derived from Commonwealth Department of Industrial Relations, *Changes in Federal Workplace Relations Law — Legislation Guide*, Canberra, 1996, pp. 1–48; G. Watson and J. Cooper, *Workplace Relations Bill 1996*, Senior Business Leaders Forum, Australian Human Resources Institute and Freehill Hollingdale and Page, 1996, unnumbered; P. Reith, *Workplace Relations and Other Legislation Amendment Bill 1996*, Summary Sheets, Address to Freehill/Australian Human Resources Institute Forum, 11 July 1996, unnumbered; and R. Callus, 'Enterprise bargaining and the transformation of Australian industrial relations', *Asia Pacific Journal of Human Resources*, vol. 35, no. 2, 1997, pp. 23–4.

148. Commonwealth Department of Industrial Relations, 1996, p. 1. For a detailed discussion of the *Workplace Relations Act*, see R. Gough,

op. cit., pp. 91–116; G. D. John, 'Employer matters in 1996', *Journal of Industrial Relations*, vol. 39, no. 1, 1997, pp. 137–56; P. Reith, 'Real reform — the government's industrial relations agenda', *The Sydney Papers*, vol. 8, no. 3, 1996, pp. 1–13; and A. Birmingham, 'A guide to the Workplace Relations Act', *Australian Bulletin of Labour*, vol. 23, no. 1, 1997, pp. 33–47.

149. R. Callus, op. cit., p. 24; R. Gough, op. cit., p. 92; and R. Skeffington, 'The Workplace Relations Act, plus ça change', *Review*, vol. 49, no. 3, March 1997, pp. 10–11.

150. M. J. Watts, 'Wages and wages determination in 2002', *Journal of Industrial Relations*, vol. 45, no. 2, 2003, p. 202.

151. S. Marris, 'Experts split on workplace deals', *Australian*, 10 March 1997, p. 2; S. Balogh, 'Public service faces hardline laws: unions', *Australian*, 24 September 2003, p. 4; K. McAlpine, 'Employees get squashed again', *Australian Financial Review*, 3 September 2003, p. 59; and R. Mitchell, 'Individual contracts not wanted because they are not needed', *Australian*, 8 October 2003, p. 12.

152. Commonwealth Department of Industrial Relations, 1996, pp. 2–3; and P. Reith, 1996, p. 3.

153. Commonwealth Department of Industrial Relations, 1996, p. 3.

154. R. Callus, op. cit., p. 24.

155. A. Birmingham, 'A guide to the Workplace Relations Act 1996', *Australian Bulletin of Labour*, vol. 23, no. 1, 1997, p. 47; V. Winley, 'Workplace Relations Act 1996: implications for business', *Australian Bulletin of Labour*, vol. 23, no. 1, 1997, p. 86; and J. McDonald, 'Risks apparent for both sides under Workplace Relations Act', *HR Monthly*, July 1997, p. 40.

156. V. Winley, op. cit., p. 86.

157. S. Deery, D. Plowman and J. Walsh, *Industrial Relations: A Contemporary Analysis*, McGraw-Hill, Sydney, 1997, p. 2.15; D. Guest, 'Human resource management, corporate performance and employee well being: building the worker into HRM', *Journal of Industrial Relations*, vol. 44, no. 3, 2002, p. 335; B. Blunsden and K. Reed, 'The effects of technical and social conditions on workplace trust', *International Journal of Human Resource Management*, vol. 14, no. 1, 2003, p. 12; G. A. Gelade and M. Ivery, 'The impact of HRM and work climate on organizational performance', *Personnel Psychology*, vol. 56, no. 2, 2003, pp. 383–404; R. Callus, op. cit., p. 20; and P. McGraw and B. Hartley, 'Industrial relations and human resource management practices in Australia and overseas owned workplaces: global or local?', *Journal of Industrial Relations*, vol. 45, no. 1, 2003, pp. 1–22.

158. Study by R. Mitchell and J. Fetter, reported in 'Report slams workplace agreements', *Australian Financial Review*, 25 March 2003, p. 6.

159. C. Fox, 'Survey talks up AWAs' value', *Australian Financial Review*, 21 November 2000, p. 46; and H. Vines, 'Workplace relations: the new focus', *HR Monthly*, November 1999, p. 19.

160. R. Callus, op. cit., p. 22.

161. L. G. Nelson, 'Managers and enterprise bargaining: some preliminary findings', *Asia Pacific Journal of Human Resources*, vol. 35, no. 1, 1997, p. 54.

162. T. O'Loughlin, 'Abbott renews push for AWAs', *Australian Financial Review*, 21 May 2003, p. 4.

163. J. Gollan and E. M. Davis, 'High involvement management and organizational change: beyond rhetoric', *Asia Pacific Journal of Human Resources*, vol. 37, no. 3, 1999, pp. 69–91.

164. Australian Bureau of Statistics figure, reported in A. Urquhart, 'Strong take-up of individual agreements', *Australian Financial Review*, 13 December 2002, p. 8; and J. Burgess, W. Mitchell and A. Preston, 'The Australian labour market in 2002', *Journal of Industrial Relations*, vol. 45, no. 2, 2003, p. 125.

165. R. D. Lansbury and M. Westcott, op. cit., pp. 95–127.

166. ACIRRT, op. cit., p. 8.

167. T. MacDermott, op. cit., p. 55; H. McBride, quoted in D. James, 'Workplace deals may go against co-operation', *Business Review Weekly*, 31 March 1997, p. 79; ACIRRT, op. cit., p. 7; M. Priest, 'Unions draw line on collective power', *Australian Financial Review*, 27 May 2003, p. 3; and P. Sheldon and L. Thornwaite, 'Employer matters in 2002', *Journal of Industrial Relations*, vol. 45, no. 2, 2003, p. 248.

168. This section is based on B. Van Gramberg, J. Teicher and G. Griffin, op. cit., pp. 14–18.

169. N. Field and K. Murphy, 'No gains in single IR system, forum told', *Australian Financial Review*, 18–19 November 2000, p. 5; J. Shaw, 'Single IR system would bring problems', *Australian Financial Review*, 24 November 2000, p. 41; C. Merritt, 'States erupt over Reith plan', *Australian Financial Review*, 20 November 2000, pp. 1, 4; and M. Skulley, 'Vic, feds sign new IR deal', *Australian Financial Review*, 13 November 2003, p. 9.

170. M. Skulley and M. Priest, 'New bills accelerate industrial reform', *Australian Financial Review*, 7 November 2003, p. 3.

171. J. Riley, 'Industrial legislation in 2002', *Journal of Industrial Relations*, vol. 45, no. 2, 2003, p. 151.

chapter 16

managing change and workplace relations

Learning objectives

When you have finished studying this chapter, you should be able to:

- Understand the link between strategic business objectives and organisational change
- Identify the key elements in the management of change
- Describe change and total quality management (TQM)
- Understand change and acquisitions, mergers and divestitures
- Explain the process of change and downsizing
- Discuss change and the establishment of good workplace relations
- Discuss change and the establishment of salaried operations.

'The implicit lifetime employment contract between the corporation and its employees no longer exists. Employer and employee loyalty, as traditionally understood, is a relic of the past.'[1]

B. Rajagopalan, R. Peterson and S. B. Watson

Managing change

Exposure to the global economy has initiated revolutionary change in many organisations. Competition for capital, markets, technology and skilled labour is fierce. Ever-increasing performance standards are demanded. Service industries are replacing manufacturing as the major employer of people. Trade unions face a crisis of legitimacy as their membership declines.[2] Cherished social and workplace values are under threat. Change is everywhere — the work force casualised; lifetime employment gone; unemployment high; job security eroded; traditional skills redundant; career ladders destroyed; stress; work–family conflicts; downsizing; workplace bargaining; new technology; 'virtual' offices; TQM; safety net awards — the list goes on. The workplace is dominated by change (see figure 16.1).

Companies are demanding more, but where are the rewards? Griffith University's David Peetz complains 'Companies are demanding greater commitment from staff but offering none in return'.[3] Predictable work, predictable pay, predictable career, trust and loyalty are disappearing. Now, it is job flexibility, multitasking, marketable skills, at-risk pay and portable careers. Instead of stability and certainty, the workplace offers change, uncertainty and anxiety. ACTU research shows heavy workloads, massive organisational change and increasing job insecurity are major causes of stress in the workplace.[4] More than one in four Australians believe that they are at risk of becoming unemployed. In Hong Kong, workers bemoan their long hours and unpaid overtime.[5] Today, organisations, managers and employees must continually adapt to rapid change to survive and prosper. Rigid hierarchy is being replaced by temporary and ever-changing networks, bureaucratic systems are giving way to flexible processes, and management roles are evolving into relationships focusing on empowerment and coaching.[6] For employees and managers, the choices are stark — be flexible, embrace change and develop marketable skills, or settle for low pay, limited career opportunities or no job.

Change or be changed is the message. Rapid and constant change has altered the traditional employment relationship. The **psychological contract** that organisations have with their employees has undergone a paradigm shift (see also page 371). Loyalty no longer is a guarantee of job security, academic qualifications no longer guarantee a good job, superior performance no longer guarantees job continuity — conventional expectations and assumptions about employment relationships have been swept away.

Psychological contract The unwritten expectations of an employee or employer about what each is entitled to receive and obliged to give.

FORCES FOR CHANGE

External

- Globalisation (for example, increasing competitive pressures)
- Demographic change (for example, an ageing population)
- Technological change (for example, the introduction of robots)
- Economic conditions (for example, exchange rate fluctuations, economic downturns)
- Changing consumer behaviour (for example, new fashions, purchasing via the Internet)
- Changes in government regulations (for example, changes in retail trading hours)
- Shifts in community values (for example, attitudes towards smoking, lifestyle)

Internal

- Crisis (for example, raw materials shortage, financial collapse, death of CEO)
- New information (for example, new ways of working, recognition of need for change)
- Reduced performance (for example, poor quality which leads to the loss of a major customer)
- Lack of talent (for example, increasing demand for people with new skills, knowledge and abilities)
- New organisational structure (for example, flatter, leaner, more flexible structure)

Figure 16.1 Forces for change
Source Asia Pacific Management Co. Ltd, 2004.

The erosion of trust

Downsizing, restructuring and re-engineering in particular have threatened employee perceptions of job security and led to a decline in trust. One recent study, for example, revealed that only about one-third of employees trust management.[7] The absence of open communications, a reluctance by management to involve employees in decisions that affect them, a failure to keep 'surprising changes' to a minimum and a lack of HR leadership have eroded trust and increased employee cynicism.[8] HR managers can promote trust by ensuring that HR policies and practices are fair and equitable (especially during periods of turbulence and change).[9] Performance appraisal systems, for example, if perceived as having unfair procedures or unfair outcomes, produce emotional stress, increased scepticism and reduced commitment.[10] HR managers should keep in mind (and ensure that managers understand) that HR policies and practices not only impact on workplace trust, but are used by employees as markers of the organisation's commitment to them (and reciprocate accordingly).[11] When employees trust management, the likelihood that they will perceive the psychological contract as broken is reduced.[12] The provision of **employee voice** likewise is critical to performance improvement, innovation and the acceptance of change.[13]

When employee expectations are met this leads to increased employee commitment and intention to remain with the organisation. When expectations are not met, this leads to reduced job satisfaction, poor performance and high labour turnover.[14] Employees in low-trust organisations have low energy — they remain sceptical and unenthusiastic about change, performance improvement or other management initiatives.[15]

Employee voice The ability of employees to express their ideas, views and complaints to management.

HRM and change

A primary difference between organisations that succeed and those that fail, says Ulrich, is 'the ability to respond to the pace of change'.[16] HR managers increasingly are taking on the role of **change agent** — to make things happen, to introduce new policies and practices, to alter the way work is performed, to change the culture of the workplace, to make the organisation more responsive, flexible and competitive — and therefore need to monitor the organisation's environment continuously for:

Change agent A person who acts as a catalyst for change.

- uncertainty (what information is available for accurate decision making?)
- volatility (how often is the environment changing?)
- magnitude of change (how drastic are the changes?)
- complexity (how many external and internal influences in the environment are at play?).[17]

According to Denton, an HR manager's success depends on recognising the need for change and implementing it successfully.[18] Consequently, HR managers today must be alert to people and situations requiring change, be receptive to new ideas and ways of doing things and be able to lead and support initiatives for change. Stace and Dunphy, for example, found that high-performing organisations exhibited:

- a move from centralised to decentralised HR
- a trend to adopt a more strategic approach to HR
- the development of performance management systems (integrating MBO, appraisal, development and rewards).[19]

New or changed business and HR strategies, however, require careful introduction. Changing employee behaviour requires a change in the organisation's culture.[20] This is because the whole organisation tends to be affected by change in any part of it (see figure 16.3 on page 595).[21] Consequently, an integrated approach in which culture and employee behaviour are taken into account is required. For example, if changing business conditions call for a changed organisational structure, management should not ignore the impact on culture and the reactions of people who have to work within the new structure. Management thus must examine any change through the eyes of both the organisation and employees. In short, the way change is managed may be more important than the change itself.

What ethical responsibilities does management have when introducing changes that may result in job loss, job insecurity or stress for employees?

Types of change

Radical change

Change may be radical or incremental. **Radical change** (or *transformational change*) produces revolutionary shifts in organisational strategies, culture, systems, structures and human resources (see figure 16.1 above). Decisions to downsize, exit existing industries, merge with a foreign partner, change the corporate culture, appoint a new CEO and the like may see an organisation undergo a dramatic transformation. Qantas, for example, is experiencing radical change in its shift from a government-owned organisation to a publicly listed company facing cutthroat global competition. Radical change is usually the product of a crisis (for example, SARS, terrorism) or some other critical event (such as the appointment of a new CEO or financial distress).

Radical change Produces fundamental changes in the nature of the organisation.

Incremental change

Incremental change is generally perceived as less threatening than radical change because it is evolutionary. Dramatic and sudden shifts are avoided. Examples of incremental change include the introduction of new products, new technologies or new systems that are developments of existing products, technologies or systems (for example, a tobacco company introduces menthol-flavoured cigarettes).

Incremental change Involves gradual or small-step modifications to the organisation's existing strategies, structure, systems, culture and people.

Planned versus unplanned change

Planned change is introduced and systematically implemented by a change agent. It is a systematic response to an identified gap between desired and actual performance. **Unplanned change** is caused by some spontaneous or ad hoc event. Terrorist bombings, the sudden death of the CEO, financial collapse, wildcat strikes or natural disasters (for example, earthquakes) are all examples of events that could initiate unexpected change. The outcomes of unplanned change can be positive or negative.

Planned change Change that is introduced and systematically implemented by a change agent.

Unplanned change Change that is the product of some spontaneous or ad hoc event.

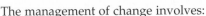

Steps in the change process

The management of change involves:
- determining the need for change
- determining the obstacles to change
- introducing change
- implementing change
- evaluating change.

Determining the need for change

Typically, the need for change becomes apparent when there is a gap between organisation, division, function or individual performance objectives and actual performance. Indicators such as total net profit, sales per employee, labour costs, accident rates and the like can identify performance deficiencies. Alternatively, if a strategic decision is made to enter new businesses (for example, the move into wine making by brewing company Foster's) or to exit existing businesses (for example, Mayne's divestiture of its hospitals division) change will be required (see figure 16.2).

'Successful strategic repositioning', argue Stace and Dunphy, 'often requires radical organisational change and powerful confrontation of entrenched interest groups.'[22] Managers must therefore analyse situations and determine what it is that is preventing the organisation, division, department or individual from achieving a desired performance level or desired future state. Rio Tinto, for example, determined that if its Australian mining operations were to be globally competitive, its rigid labour practices had to change. However, there was powerful union resistance to Rio Tinto's demands for greater labour flexibility through the elimination of demarcation barriers, the hiring and promoting of employees on merit and the rewarding of employees on their performance because of union fears regarding loss of power, reduced working conditions and demands for higher performance. What appears to be a logical and necessary change to management may be perceived by employees as threatening, unnecessary and something to be resisted. According to Strebel: 'top level managers see change as an opportunity to strengthen the business by aligning operations with strategy, to take on new professional challenges and risks, and to advance their careers. For many employees, however, including middle managers, change is neither sought after nor welcomed. It is disruptive and intrusive. It upsets the balance.'[23]

CHANGE TARGETS	CHANGE
Purpose or mission	The fundamental purpose or mission of the organisation is changed (for example, Foster's change from being a domestic beer company to a global lifestyle beverage company producing and marketing beer, wine and spirits).
Objectives	Key business objectives and performance targets are changed (for example, the Commonwealth Bank of Australia's plan to reduce its headcount by 10 per cent).
Strategies	New strategies are introduced (for example, Pacific Strategic Investment Ltd's decision to outsource the management of its investment portfolio and office administration and thus have no employees).
Structure	The organisational structure is changed (for example, from a hierarchical structure to a flat structure).
Systems	New operating, marketing, finance or HR systems are introduced (for example, 360-degree performance appraisals).
Technology	New technology is introduced (for example, the replacement of assembly line workers with robots).
Culture	New core values and beliefs are introduced (for example, to become a learning organisation).
People	People with different skills, abilities and knowledge are hired or promoted (for example, graduates, women, minorities, MBAs, German speakers, people with disabilities, high-tech whizkids).

Figure 16.2 Change targets
Source Asia Pacific Management Co. Ltd, 2004.

Change is thus a *human* as well as a *technical* problem. Managers must therefore be alert to the cultural barriers and supports for change and the modifications to the organisational culture required to promote the strategic change. Westpac, as part of its strategy to transform itself from a large Australian bank into a diversified international financial services group, hired outsiders to introduce new ideas and vitality. Unfortunately, existing employees did not welcome the newcomers and much of the hoped-for energy was dissipated in rivalries and resentment.[24] Research similarly shows that there is an emerging gap between the rhetoric of cultural transformation towards a high-achievement Australian public service (APS) and the reality experienced by employees, with scepticism and resistance being demonstrated.[25] A senior bureaucrat says, 'It is ill informed and wrong to suggest that the APS works well only to the extent that it conforms to the culture of the corporate world'.[26]

Determining obstacles to change

Managers need to identify all the potential barriers to change and determine what it is that is actually generating resistance. Opposition to change may exist throughout the organisation (for example, in the case of a hostile takeover), at divisional level, functional level (for example, the HR department may resist the transfer of HR activities to line managers) and individual levels (for example, employees do not trust their managers). Unions likewise may support change (especially where it advances or protects their members' interests) or oppose it. Iverson found that employee acceptance of change was increased by harmonious industrial relations, but decreased by union membership.[27]

Typically, where changes in power or status are involved, politicking and conflict will surface as individuals, functions or divisions fight to retain or overthrow the status quo. An organisation's existing culture, strategies, structures and systems are powerful barriers to change. Decentralised matrix structures, for example, are more flexible (and therefore easier to change) than highly centralised functional structures.[28] Similarly, some corporate cultures are easier to change than others. Highly authoritarian and bureaucratic cultures such as those found in the large banks and the military demonstrate considerable inertia. Bob Joss, former Managing Director of Westpac, says of its culture: 'It's still in our judgment, far too much of a bureaucratic culture of waiting to be told what to do, of running it by the book and trying to refer to the manual as opposed to people taking responsibility and ownership for the problem, the customers, and delivering the better solution ... I'd say that, in order of magnitude, it's more difficult to change the culture than dealing with financial issues or strategic issues. There's no comparison.'[29] The bureaucratic culture of Telstra is similarly an inhibitor of change.[30] In contrast, more freewheeling cultures (such as Hewlett-Packard's, which promotes flexibility and acceptance of change) are easier to change.[31] Because change challenges the accepted beliefs of managers and workers, its introduction is never likely to be easy.[32]

Introducing change

Managers versus consultants

The introduction of change can be done by internal managers or external consultants. An organisation's own managers, while more knowledgeable about people and business operations, often are too narrow in outlook, too imbued with the existing culture and carry too much political baggage to introduce change successfully. In the case of Westpac, Joss says: 'If you've grown up in middle management one way for 15 or 25 years, you develop a lot of habits and attitudes and values in the way you do things ... to turn that is hard.'[33] Consultants, on the other hand, while politically neutral and possessing broader and more knowledgeable viewpoints, generally do not know the organisation and its people. Consequently, consultants can face considerable obstacles in trying to introduce change. As a result, organisations often combine teams of consultants and managers in an attempt to benefit from both insider know-how and external independence and expertise.

Top-down versus bottom-up

Organisations can introduce change using top-down or bottom-up approaches. Top-down involves management deciding on the change and then implementing it. The emphasis is on speed and action. The top-down approach, while seemingly faster, often faces problems in implementation because of resistance from managers and employees resentful of change being forced on them by their superiors. In contrast, the bottom-up approach involves considerable discussion and consultation with managers and employees. Thus, bottom-up change emphasises participation and communication and the minimisation of uncertainty.

Its major disadvantage is that it is time consuming. The bottom-up approach, however, provides considerable opportunity for management to identify and deal with areas of resistance and other problems before they become serious.

It is important to note that either approach may be successful. The critical point is that the change strategy must be integrated with the organisation's strategic business objectives.[34] According to Stace and Dunphy, 'change agents (internal or external) should therefore select the most effective strategy and style of change, rather than reflexively relying on a change strategy and style compatible with their own personal values'.[35] This has important implications for HR managers who tend to favour less directive and less coercive approaches. In contrast, it appears that line managers lack appreciation of the value of participative approaches to change.[36]

Implementing change[37]

Change progresses through three phases: unfreezing, moving and refreezing. **Unfreezing** involves management preparing the organisation for change (in other words, people see the need for change and are motivated to accept its introduction). Change means that old attitudes, values and behaviours are challenged. The less satisfied people are with the present situation, the more positive they will be to any proposed change.

Moving involves management initiating action to change one or more key organisational variables (such as its structure, systems or culture). During this phase employees need to see clearly why change is necessary, be given any training that is required, and understand what is expected of them and how they will be affected.

Refreezing involves reinforcing the desired outcomes so that the 'new' becomes permanent (in other words, the change is institutionalised and becomes an everyday part of the workplace). Reinforcement may take the form of pay increases, special bonuses, promotion and management recognition. If reinforcement is not undertaken, the desired changes may be prematurely rejected or only partly implemented.

Evaluating change

To measure the effectiveness of change, organisations must compare the before and after situations. Indicators such as employee productivity, job satisfaction, sales and the like can be used to evaluate the effects of the change. If the change proves ineffective, however, a need for even further change is created.

NEWSBREAK

Work in progress

By Jan McCallum

The young Turks singled out to set up the greenfields aluminium site back in the 1980s could have done it by the book — the one that highlighted distrust, demarcation and dictatorial management. But this group had other ideas about how to run Alcoa's new smelter in the southern Victorian town of Portland.

'It was a new frontier', says Wayne Osborn, who was administration manager at the plant back then. 'We all went there with the view that this could be different from the industrial organisation we had worked with before [where] you could see management was often a barrier to people getting their jobs done.'

Osborn and others saw themselves as a new generation of managers, influenced by the radical ideas that had revolutionised Japanese industry. In Australia, despite some attempts to redesign work based on postwar British models, union/employer animosity was high and an adversarial culture was endemic. Employees were given little responsibility for, or ownership of, their jobs. Managers who wanted a new way were often frustrated by old attitudes. After all, who needed change when so much of Australian industry was protected by high tariffs?

By 1986 when Portland was commissioned global pressures on Australian companies were intense and companies faced a more competitive and deregulated environment. The joint venture managed by Alcoa was a chance to break the mould. Here, the young managers figured, was the opportunity to build a more productive culture by getting rid of hierarchies, introducing multiskilling, and experimenting with some dramatic ideas — such as consulting with the workers.

Almost 20 years on, Osborn is managing director of Alcoa Australia and Portland is one of the company's top plants, and one of the three most competitive smelters worldwide. The innovations it spurred have spread throughout Alcoa worldwide, and are credited with enabling the company to increase profits through major workforce changes and improved productivity. And the ideas that seemed so new at Portland are now commonly applied, or at least tried, in many areas of work.

Portland had a difficult birth. The smelter had been built against a volatile industrial backdrop in Victoria, a period during which the militant Builders Laborers' Federation had been deregistered. BLF members had been among those employed on the site. There was also cynicism about whether the smelter would go ahead. Portland is on the other side of Victoria from the electricity generation on which it depends and the small rural community was handed the project on political grounds. The town was first turned upside down by an influx of construction workers, who arrived in 1981, and then the joint venture shut the project for two years in 1983 because of a dispute with the state government over the supply of cheap electricity. It was 1986 before it was completed and opened.

Enter the young Turks. They had no particular role models to guide their approach, but many had attended seminars sponsored by the Federal Government to introduce manufacturers to Japanese production systems. Just-in time production — the idea introduced into Japanese companies such as Toyota in the 1970s — was one of the more radical concepts. JIT meant that you supplied parts for the process only when you needed them. There was also a focus on quality and on treating the next person in the production line as a customer to be served. The worker was the core of the production process, and everything else had to be directed at supporting the core. Managers had to think about how they could facilitate rather than direct work — an approach that led to more autonomy for employees.

'The ethos was that as a manager group we were there to support the people getting the work done to run the smelter', says Osborn.

Managers had to be able to cope with a loss of status. The Portland managers lost some of the trappings: there were no special car spaces and they dropped collars and ties for the same workwear as employees — something that is now standard around the resources industry but which was remarkable at the time. They also lost something less definable: the right to rule, because if employees were expected to take more responsibility and do a wider range of tasks, it meant they had to be given more of a say in the process, and that meant that sometimes they would question the boss.

Union agreement to the new approach was essential, so Portland opened with just three unions, compared with 18 at the smaller Point Henry smelter, also run by Alcoa in Victoria — an important simplification for the time. It was a challenging time for unions, who were generally willing to negotiate as long as they saw members getting benefits. And because of the scale of Portland, it made sense to have large unions because there were fewer jobs for members of smaller, craft-based unions. Portland's scale means the largest union, the Australian Workers' Union, has a full-time organiser on site, which tends to defuse disputes by bringing the parties together early.

A strategy was mapped out before hiring and the emphasis was on recruiting younger people, many of whom had never been to a smelter. The idea was that they would be open to change — and perhaps less likely to have an adversarial approach or a strong allegiance to unions. Anaconda Nickel managing director Peter Johnston, who was a manager at Portland during construction, says Alcoa gave the Portland team a lot of leeway: 'We became the yardstick. Alcoa used these principles right through the organisation over time.'

Central to the experiment were work teams, which were designed to be self-managing — although that task sometimes proved beyond the crews who struggled with the newfound freedom, particularly in a new plant that had not built up maintenance routines and practices. Osborn says the managers had to work hard to build these into the organisation and, in retrospect, that they focused too heavily in the early days on the people side and less on the technical, and had to restore the balance in later years.

(continued)

The company set up a newsroom, with airport-style monitors in lunchrooms, to get communications out to employees. The newsroom ran internal news and came into its own on controversial issues, when people could air their views and put up opposing sides. Osborn recalls that people could be brutally candid, and it was very painful as the smelter moved towards full production and things went wrong. 'But having the message delivered publicly forced you to listen', he says.

The influx of young families into Portland caused a shortage of childcare, so the smelter built a creche. It also built a gym, set up links with community organisations, and began working on ways to recycle waste rather than dump it in landfill. The smelter is surrounded by bushland but was filling 13 000 cubic metres of it a year in 1989 when it began evaluating all its processes. These days, it creates just two cubic metres of waste a month through improved processes and cleaner production.

Six years into its operation, Portland management started negotiations for employees to move from eight- to 12-hour shifts, and to a salary rather than wage-based structure. Osborn says trust was the key to the changes: 'They had seen the organisation had really taken risks and been innovative in making them and their families important to the organisation. It was a huge shift to flexibility in work requirements.'

What's changed, and what remains two decades on from that idealistic start?

Work teams still form the core of Portland and the crews arrange their tasks as they see fit in order to get the job done, with all members able to perform a range of tasks. Because they have some control over the way they organise work, team members can take time out of a shift for family matters, such as a school presentation. Teams have changed work practices and equipment to make their job more productive, and reduced waste through recycling. Employees today say it can take time to make changes because everyone involved is consulted, but it means that changes work and last.

Good communications are still regarded as essential. The newsroom has disappeared under the weight of new technology such as email, but meetings and publications remain key channels for information to be distributed and ideas to be ventilated.

The early years when the company built a culture around people — and acknowledged their needs for a private life — has meant continued focus on work and family policies. In 1993 an Alcoa taskforce was set up to look at this area, and the company contracted an organisational specialist, Dr Graeme Russell, of Macquarie University, to survey 4000 of its 6000 employees in Victoria and Eastern Australia on attitudes to work and family.

The result was more flexible work arrangements, with each location tailoring the policy to its needs. A follow-up survey in 1999 documented improvements in morale, less absenteeism and improved job satisfaction. But it also showed the company needed to change the workplace culture to attract and retain employees. Alcoa has since established contact officers at every site — including Portland — to provide advice on equal opportunity and harassment, and has implemented a program to encourage women into non-traditional roles. It has begun work on retirement planning for older employees, encouraging them to pass on knowledge and allowing them reduced physical work and fewer hours.

The 12-hour shifts that have been a part of Portland for a decade are now being questioned. The Australian Workers' Union, which is the major union onsite and covers 70 to 80 per cent of the 700-strong workforce, is campaigning for a return to eight-hour shifts. The union's organiser for the south-west district of Victoria, Ken Gadsden, says Alcoa would have to employ more people but the health and quality of life of workers would improve. Alcoa, however, argues that the move to 12-hour shifts was universally popular because shift times were less changeable. Wayne Osborn argues that employees have had more certainty over when they work and therefore suffer less from the tiredness caused by irregular hours.

From Alcoa's perspective, Portland has delivered. Osborn says the benefits include a more highly skilled workforce, retained expertise, a safer workplace, and a culture of continuous improvements. He says concepts such as just-in-time manufacture and treating the next person in the production chain as the customer remain valid. He believes executives today won't survive if they cannot operate within a flat management structure. Looking back, he concedes he and his colleagues were sometimes too idealistic, 'but without the idealism you could not move far enough away from the traditional manner in which you could do something'.

Social policy consultant Dr Don Edgar, who advised Alcoa on work and family issues through the 1990s, believes the policy has lasted and developed because top management was committed to it, and because responsibility was pushed down into the workplace so that employees had to identify issues and work on solutions. He said Alcoa also made work and family part of its financial and strategic planning, rather than hiving issues off to human resources staff without enough clout to make serious changes.

Source Boss, June 2003, pp. 42–6.

Workplace change

Change in the workplace does not occur in isolation. This is because a complex set of relationships exists in any work environment (see figure 16.3). Changing the way work is performed in response to changes in technology (for example, the introduction of new equipment) sets off a chain of events. The job to be performed may now require less skill, involve a loss of status, carry a lower pay rate, involve less autonomy for the employee and an unwanted shift in reporting relationships and membership of a different union. Unfortunately, managers often forget this and consequently are often surprised when what appears to be a logical decision for improvement produces employee (and union) anger and resistance.

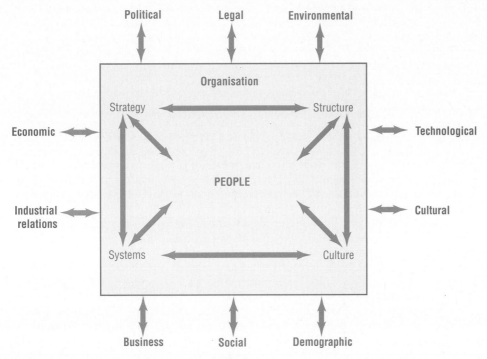

Figure 16.3 Environmental influences and change[38]
Source Asia Pacific Management Co. Ltd, 2004.

High technology is one of the most important causes of organisational change. The introduction of word processors to the workplace clearly changed the way typing and secretarial work was performed. The need for a typing pool and the position of typing pool supervisor were eliminated and the number of typists required was reduced. Because of the distribution of typists throughout the organisation (including the breaking up of the formal work group and informal social groups), the culture of the workplace was changed drastically. A change in technology thus triggered off changes in the structure of the organisation (flatter, less hierarchical), the culture of the workplace (emphasis on the individual rather than the group), the number of people needed (fewer), the nature of the skills required (higher) and in the way work was performed (use of word processors instead of typewriters), and created a need for new policies and procedures (new job descriptions, job classifications, pay rates and reporting relationships).

When implementing change, it is thus critical that managers do not focus exclusively on the factor being changed. The impact of the change on other factors must always be considered, if the real barriers to change are to be identified.

Resistance to change[39]

When managers and employees resist change, it is for a reason. The change is perceived by them as a threat. Some of the common reasons why people resist change include:

- *lack of trust* — not trusting those proposing the change
- *fear of the unknown* — not understanding what is happening or why
- *disrupted habits* — feeling upset when old ways of doing things cannot be followed
- *belief that change is unnecessary* — seeing no need for the proposed change
- *loss of confidence* — feeling incapable of performing well under the new way of doing things
- *loss of control* — feeling that things are being done 'to' them rather than 'by' them or 'with' them
- *poor timing* — feeling overwhelmed or that things are moving too fast
- *work overload* — not having the physical or mental stamina to handle the change
- *loss of face* — feeling inadequate or humiliated because the 'old' ways are no longer perceived as 'good' ways
- *lack of purpose* — not seeing a reason for the change or not understanding its benefits[40]
- *economic loss* — feeling that their pay and benefits may be reduced or that they may lose their job
- *group pressure* — team norms may need to be altered if they conflict with the desired changes.[41]

Reducing resistance to change

Management and employee resistance to change is both common and natural. HR managers ideally should treat any resistance as an opportunity to re-evaluate a proposed change and to identify and deal with the real barriers to the change. Some of the ways managers can overcome employee resistance to change are:

- *Communication:* management should give advance information regarding the reasons for the change, the nature of the change, the planned timing of the change and its possible impact on the organisation and employees. According to McShane and Von Glinow, 'Communication is the highest priority and first strategy required for any organizational change'.[42] Research shows that communication can reduce fear of the unknown and change team behaviours that are in conflict with the proposed changes. Yet, in the majority of workplaces undergoing change, the Australian Centre for Industrial Relations Research and Training found workers effectively had no role in the decision-making process and were simply told that change was to occur. At some workplaces, there was no communication at all — change just happened.[43]
- *Participation:* wherever possible, management and employee participation should be encouraged to give everyone a sense of ownership and involvement regarding the decision to introduce the change. Employees who participate in developing and implementing change are more likely to be supportive than those who have it imposed on them from above. Research clearly shows that participation reduces fear of the unknown and leads to commitment.[44]
- *Guarantee:* if possible, it is desirable that management guarantees that employees will not be disadvantaged. For example, an organisation may guarantee employees the same pay and benefits while they undergo any required training.
- *Certainty:* fear of the unknown is a major cause of employee resistance. Even if unpalatable (for example, if job losses are involved), it is better to let people know exactly where they stand and to detail what is going to happen and when.
- *Counselling:* non-directive counselling has proved a useful management tool in change situations.[45] Non-threatening discussions and counselling can help defuse rebellious and angry feelings and facilitate voluntary employee acceptance of the change.
- *Negotiation:* organisational change is very much a political activity. People have vested interests and will naturally seek to ensure that any change is consistent with their own values and needs. As a result, negotiation may be required to offset some of the costs of

change for those who stand to lose.[46] Unions often use negotiation as a means of modifying changes proposed by management. For example, in exchange for greater workplace flexibility, management may give a guarantee of job security or an increase in pay.
- *Reward:* managers and employees who contribute to the successful introduction of change should be rewarded. Those who accept new work assignments, put in extra effort and help others to adjust to change deserve recognition.
- *Coercion:* this may be necessary when speed is essential and other approaches prove ineffective. Coercion involves the use of threats or punishment against those resisting change, such as transfers, loss of promotion, poor performance ratings, pay cuts and termination.[47]

Change is accelerating and impacting on organisations, the workplace and individuals as never before. In the following sections, changes relating to total quality management, acquisitions, mergers and divestitures, downsizing and workplace industrial relations are discussed. The pressures of these changes threaten many traditional and long-held ways of managing and working. Grappling with these changes are among the greatest challenges facing managers and workers.

Total quality management

The ongoing theme for organisations is change. Worldwide competition sets international standards of performance. Global organisations adopt international best practices to secure a competitive advantage. Organisations that do not change and adapt to the new competitive environment will be defeated in the marketplace and will disappear or be taken over by those that do. The consistent demands for improved performance caused by intense competition, demanding customers, cost pressures and rapid change have made continuous productivity improvement a necessity for survival. Non-stop improvement in quality, productivity and cost containment have become integrated into the strategic business objectives of organisations seeking to match international competition. Reflecting this, **total quality management (TQM)** involves an organisation-wide commitment to **continuous improvement** (which constantly asks (a) is this necessary? and (b) can it be done better?) and meeting customer needs.[48] It means building quality into everything — design, production, purchasing, marketing and human resource management.

The results organisations seek from TQM are:
- an ability to anticipate, meet and exceed customers' expectations
- to gain a competitive advantage via better products and services and improved work processes
- to gain management and employee commitment
- to stay in business.[49]

Total quality management (TQM) Involves an organisation-wide commitment to continuous improvement and satisfying customer needs.

Continuous improvement Focuses on the non-stop improvement of everything and everybody.

Managing quality[50]

Leading organisations manage TQM by implementing and recognising the following:
- *Creating a quality culture.* Quality is reflected in the organisation's strategic business objectives and is communicated throughout the organisation. For example, Maersk Hong Kong uses slogans such as 'No detail too small, no effort too large' and 'Quality second to none' to reinforce its commitment to quality.[51]
- *Venerating the customer.* Organisations strive to ensure that their product or service consistently meets or exceeds their customers' expectations. Yet one survey shows that just four in 10 customers are satisfied with the overall service of Australian banks.[52] Not surprisingly, focusing the banks' bureaucratic cultures on customers is rated as one of the major challenges facing their managements.[53]
- *The championing of TQM by top management.* Senior management commitment is critical to the success of any TQM program.[54] Australian senior managers in publicly listed companies, however, have not shown much genuine enthusiasm for TQM, preferring to focus more on costs and short-term profits.[55]

- *Measuring quality.* Performance monitoring of product and service quality is emphasised so that problems can be easily pinpointed and rectified. Measurement, however, is not done for measurement's sake but for its practical value.
- *Securing union support.* Australian companies with poor industrial relations have struggled to successfully implement TQM.[56]
- *Starting with quality.* Quality assurance is built into every product or service, policy or practice. Quality is part of the corporate culture. Says one expert: 'TQM is not for everyone. If the values implicit in TQM do not fit your company's, it is better to leave the concept alone; you will fall flat on your face if you try to implement it.'[57] However, few companies appreciate the degree of cultural change required and, as a result, TQM programs quickly lose momentum.[58]
- *Striving for high standards.* Motorola, for example, seeks perfect quality, which in turn drives change within the organisation.
- *Rewarding employees for teamwork and quality.* TQM requires management to encourage employees to share ideas and to act on them. This necessitates high levels of communication, interaction and cooperation among team members. Reward systems must recognise and reinforce such behaviour.
- *Recognising that TQM is a strategy that depends for success on the effective management of human resources.* Attracting and selecting people who are motivated by the idea of teamwork, quality and customer service necessitates the introduction of new recruitment and selection processes. Qantas, for example, uses the Hogan Personality Inventory to assess the customer service orientation of prospective cabin crew.[59]
- *Involving people.* The assumption is made that people involved in the process have the best knowledge of how the process works. Using employee know-how is seen as a valuable resource. This requires ongoing training and a corporate culture of continuous learning. Employees must continually acquire new know-how and apply it to improving product and service quality.
- *Training management and employees in leadership and team building.* Exercises and workshops focused on practical skills for working in teams, such as problem solving, communication, negotiation, conflict management and coaching, are common ways of doing this.
- *Recognising that there is no one best way of introducing TQM.* Successful companies tailor TQM to meet their own organisational requirements.

Rigid work practices, poor industrial relations, traditional hierarchical organisational structures and authoritarian management styles are clearly not compatible with TQM. Similarly, TQM does not automatically enhance an employee's job satisfaction and may be perceived as making work more demanding and involving too much responsibility.[60]

Too many organisations also see TQM as a fad or quick fix.[61] The result is half-hearted management commitment, disenchanted employees, failure to improve product quality, customer service and organisational performance, and lost momentum. Similarly, organisations fail to realise that implementing TQM involves considerable changes to the existing corporate culture — they focus almost exclusively on TQM system technology and ignore the people aspect.[62] Says one expert: 'you often find the policies within the organisation don't reflect the values of TQM. Employees are told the company is aiming for quality and the customer comes first, but reviews and management policies reflect the old paradigm rather than the new.'[63]

Australian culture, moreover, has some characteristics (such as individualism, short-term orientation, greater tolerance for uncertainty, and a willingness to take risks and break rules for pragmatic reasons) that are contrary to key TQM values (such as minimisation of variation, adherence to rules, focus on teams, and continuous improvement), which make its ready acceptance unlikely.[64] In fact, there is even some opinion that the quality movement in Australia and elsewhere is in danger of collapsing. For example, the CEO of the Australian Quality Council states: 'The bubble has burst. The movement has gone off.'[65] TQM appears to have promised more than it could deliver and spawned mini bureaucracies, rather than eliminated errors, decreased costs and improved customer satisfaction.[66]

Consequently, the adoption of TQM, says Dawson, 'is a large task which will take a number of years, require considerable planning, involve numerous revisions and modifications to planned changes and is unlikely to be marked by a line of continual improvement from beginning to end'.[67] TQM is thus best regarded as 'a journey, not a destination'.[68]

Acquisitions, mergers and divestitures

In virtually every major industry, the number of companies is shrinking. **Merger** and **acquisition** activity is especially high in technology, telecommunications, media, resources, utilities and financial services.[69] Unions, too, are faced with the need to amalgamate to ensure their survival. The Construction, Forestry, Mining and Energy Union (CFMEU) and the Maritime Union of Australia (MUA), faced with declining memberships in stagnant or low-growth industries, are exploring mergers. Says an MUA official, 'It's time to put a little meat on the bones'.[70]

The goals of such mergers are market dominance to get the size and resources to better compete domestically and internationally; to invest in new technologies and new products; to control distribution channels; and to guarantee access to markets.[71] According to one expert, 'we are moving toward a period of the mega-corporate state in which there will be a few global firms within particular economic sectors'.[72] This presents large companies in Australia with a dilemma — although they may dominate the domestic market, they are too small to compete successfully with mega global corporations (for example, Wal-Mart, with sales approaching US$250 billion and 1.4 million employees, is more than ten times the size of Woolworths) and suffer extreme pressures from unions (fearful of job losses), consumer groups (worried about reduced competition) and government (concerned with public opinion). Finally, many mergers and acquisitions founder because of a clash of corporate cultures (Telstra's merger with OTC failed because Telstra's bureaucratic public service culture stifled the entrepreneurial OTC culture), top management failure to consider people factors, poor planning and 'gamesmanship' resulting from executive egos.[73]

Merger Combination of two or more firms to form one new company, which often has a new corporate identity.

Acquisition Purchase of a firm or company by another firm or company.

Restructuring and human resources

Managing the survivors of organisational restructuring is one of the major challenges facing today's HR manager. As Kohler states, 'the risks and dangers of putting together different organisations and two different cultures will not go away because of a chief executive's global vision'.[74] Problems are particularly likely to arise when conservative, bureaucratic companies team up with entrepreneurial, high-tech companies.[75] HR managers therefore need to play an active role in decisions relating to acquisitions, mergers and **divestitures**. Unfortunately, they are often excluded until a problem arises (even though the evidence shows that the HR aspects of major takeovers and mergers often cause more problems than the legal, financial and administrative aspects).[76] Most companies undertake due diligence when they take over another company; however, most do not carry out due diligence on their target's culture, structure and HR policies and practices.[77] This ignores the fact that although most restructurings start out as financial propositions, they are in fact human transactions.[78]

The clash between **corporate cultures** is a major cause of merger failure. For example, it is estimated that more than half of all merged companies in the United States fail to create value for shareholders because management underestimates 'the complexity of corporate marriage'.[79] Furthermore, these complexities are intensified when organisations from different countries combine.[80] Says one consultant, 'most companies manage their cultures accidentally'.[81] By neglecting the human dimension, managers can destroy the value of the acquired or merged organisation.[82] HR managers therefore need to take a proactive role in educating line managers about the people problems involved in mergers and acquisitions. To do this, HR managers must be credible, possess good facilitating skills and have the ability to build rapport and to partner senior managers in developing transition teams, feedback, goal clarification and culture reinforcement mechanisms. In these ways, HR managers can help their organisations to avoid the HR pitfalls common to many business mergers.[83]

Amazingly, the evidence suggests that takeovers that dramatically change a company are routinely managed part-time by executives with little merger or acquisition experience (and

Divestitures Selling selected operating units for either strategic or financial reasons.

Corporate cultures The values, beliefs, assumptions and symbols that define the way in which the organisation conducts its business.

the less skilled the deal makers are, the greater the HR burden is on the managers in the restructured organisation).[84] According to McKinsey & Co, companies that are most successful at making mergers work 'tend to blend cultural sensitivity with a clear idea from the onset of how they will integrate the two companies'.[85]

Problems associated with ineffective HR management during restructuring include:
- the cost of lost talent — one US study found that more than half the acquired company executives leave within three years of the takeover[86]
- lost productivity
- loss of competitive position
- the expense of union problems — according to one union official, employees unsure of their future because of takeover or merger speculation are less likely to work productively and are more likely to strike[87]
- the cost of miscasting people — the decisions regarding who will go, who will stay and who will go where are made on the basis of expediency, favouritism, hunches, first impressions, highly questionable second-hand information and negotiated trade-offs, according to Pritchett;[88] the result is that important management and executive slots are filled by misfits.

To overcome such problems during a restructuring, the HR manager should focus on:
- ensuring a compelling strategic rationale exists for the acquisition or merger
- moving quickly to meld the two companies
- overcoming conflicting corporate cultures
- creating retention incentives for key employees
- auditing the policies and practices of the acquired company
- ensuring the orientation of new employees
- redesigning the compensation programs
- integrating management styles
- communicating restructuring decisions.

An HR merger specialist stresses 'it's human resources' role to foster and massage the merger and acquisition process to make it an ongoing part of the surviving firm's fabric'.[89]

Downsizing

Downsizing A reduction in a company's work force to improve its bottom line.

Restructuring Involves a major change to an organisation via downsizing, flattening, elimination of departments, and so on.

Downsizing, or **restructuring**, aims to achieve greater organisational efficiency by job elimination. It involves reducing a company's work force in an attempt to improve its financial performance. Downsizing may also be called right sizing, delayering, resource reallocation, decombination, job separation and work force imbalance correction.[90] A 'lean and hungry' organisation rather than a 'fat and comfortable' one is the goal. Increased domestic and international competition, deregulation, mergers and acquisitions, and pressures for increased profitability and performances have all played a part in forcing organisations to cut jobs. Even companies such as IBM, Kodak, Qantas and Xerox, long renowned for their 'no lay-off' policies, now use downsizing as a standard business practice.[91] In Japan, a new generation of CEOs is doing away with lifelong employment in favour of downsizing, cost cutting and spinning off superfluous business units.[92] Stronger, leaner companies, it is argued, are better able to compete.[93]

Likewise, governments and trade unions are not immune. The Finance Sector Union (FSU) faced a major restructuring to avoid insolvency and to arrest a declining membership. Says FSU joint National Secretary, Tony Beck: 'We have to make the transition otherwise we will die.'[94] Similarly, the Australian Manufacturing Workers Union considered tough cost-cutting measures, including job cuts and pay increase rejections.[95]

ANZ CEO John McFarlane says, 'I have an instinct which says you are always better off with as few people as you need to run the business, and pay those people more'.[96] Some experts, however, claim that downsizing is destructive because it eliminates an organisation's memory and sense of values and destroys trust. An American Management Association survey, for example, found that only 30 per cent of companies implementing job cuts since 1990 reported an increase in worker productivity over the next year and only 40 per cent reported an increase in subsequent years.[97] Similarly, a survey of Australian and New Zealand companies showed labour productivity improvements in only one-third of firms that had embarked on downsizing.[98]

Critics further argue that downsizing can lead to each manager trying to look after too many people, with the result that they become overloaded.[99] According to Markels and Murray, 'Despite warnings about downsizing becoming dumbsizing, many US companies continue to make flawed decisions — hasty across-the-board cuts — that come back to haunt them, on the bottom line, in public relations, in strained relationships with customers and suppliers and in demoralized employees'.[100] Similarly, sweeping early retirement and buyout programs may remove not only the deadwood, but also the talented (many of whom may join competitors).[101] Telstra, for example, found that because of union opposition to reductions based on merit, its best people left to join its competition, thus jeopardising its long-term performance.[102] The elimination of middle management jobs, moreover, has produced increased spans of control, time pressures and complexity in those supervisory jobs remaining. Downsizing may also create hardships because of ruthless retrenchment practices, increased stress, longer spells of unemployment and reduced job opportunities (especially for older workers and for those without marketable skills). One Internet retailer, for example, sacked one-third of its staff just days before Christmas — scape (a Village Roadshow/Ten Network joint venture) sacked all but a skeleton staff and then reportedly searched employees' bags on the way out. Others have been sacked by email.[103] Even worse are companies that transfer employees into shelf companies (which have no assets) to avoid paying them their entitlements on termination.[104]

Figure 16.4 lists 10 restructuring mistakes.

TEN RESTRUCTURING MISTAKES

1. Failure to be clear about long- and short-term goals.
2. Use of downsizing as a first resort, rather than as a last resort.
3. Use of non-selective downsizing.
4. Failure to change the ways work is done.
5. Failure to involve workers in the restructuring process.
6. Failure to communicate openly and honestly.
7. Inept handling of those who lose their jobs.
8. Failure to manage survivors effectively.
9. Ignoring the effects on other stakeholders.
10. Failure to evaluate results and learn from mistakes.

Figure 16.4 Ten restructuring mistakes
Source W. Cascio, 'Cutbacks threaten innovation', *HR Monthly*, February 2003, p. 14.

Finally, stress caused by anxiety, guilt and fear of job loss in employees remaining in downsizing organisations ('survivor syndrome') has created a need for HR programs designed to overcome the aftershock associated with large-scale retrenchments.[105] For example, in the United States, one HR vice-president responsible for carrying out downsizing activities reported receiving numerous death threats and being physically attacked, as well as employee fighting and suicides.[106] According to O'Neill and Lenn, 'The real pains of downsizing cannot be minimized. Careers change, families struggle and downsized victims suffer loss of prestige, income and security.'[107] Furthermore, survivors may feel guilty, suffer insecurity, perceive their workload as being higher and their career opportunities as being reduced, and remain unclear about their responsibilities and what managers expect of them.[108] The result is a group of unhappy, overworked employees, who may have to do tasks for which they have not been trained and who still feel they are potential termination targets.[109]

Because downsizing involves change, it requires a strategic, proactive approach to HR management. Unfortunately, too many organisations equate downsizing with across-the-board cost cutting and headcount reduction. In reality, downsizing involves a re-invention of the organisation. The organisation's structure, culture and work processes are all affected. Downsizing is thus a strategic transformation that can be used to change the organisation's culture and the way it does business. In this sense, downsizing becomes part of an organisation's continuous improvement scheme and assumes a long-term perspective instead of short-term cost cutting.[110] Traditional hierarchical organisational structures, for example, can be replaced by flatter, more flexible structures that require greater delegation of responsibility and autonomy for employees, but also involve fewer opportunities for promotion, changed career paths and an emphasis on generalist rather than specialist skills.

As a result, the psychological contract between organisations and employees has changed.[111] Experts predict that the average employee during their working career will change jobs seven or eight times, be unemployed for up to a year and be fired at least once.[112] Employees therefore perceive the employment relationship as temporary, with their prime loyalty being to themselves and not to the organisation. To motivate and retain good people made cynical by downsizing, employers now offer incentives such as continuous learning, career development opportunities and coaching, share options, bonuses, performance-based compensation, flexible benefits, and portable health and retirement plans.[113] The impact on corporate culture of such changes can be dramatic. Furthermore, a 'slash and burn' approach to downsizing (especially if it is repeated) can lead to a collapse of morale and loss of competitive advantage.

According to Littler's research, it is not the *depth* of cutting that matters but the *frequency*.[114] Employers in organisations that continue to downsize find their employees quickly become demoralised because they do not know when it will end.[115] Dunlap states: 'you either get the pain and suffering accomplished in the first 12 months, or you don't do it at all. If a restructuring is done over three years, moods and corporate decisions change. The longer it takes, the greater the opportunity for the old corporate culture to corrupt it.'[116]

Suggestions for making downsizing effective include:
- promoting open and frequent communication to encourage employees to become part of the change process
- retaining employees who have the competencies needed to achieve the organisation's strategic business objectives — across-the-board headcount reductions should be avoided
- targeting specific inefficiencies, redundancies and low-value activities for elimination
- treating employees who lose their jobs with compassion and dignity (see figure 16.5)
- generating excitement about the future by painting a vivid picture of what the organisation plans to become[117]
- planning the restructuring effort and linking it to the organisation's strategic business objectives to ensure that it positions the organisation for the future by having the right people in place after the downsizing is completed.[118]

Change and how managers and employees deal with it are the focus of downsizing. Downsizing should be a product of the organisation aligning its strategic business objectives and shaping its corporate culture to better fit its changing environment. According to De Vries and Balazs, downsizing involves 'the creation of an organisational mindset that concentrates unwaveringly on finding new learning opportunities'.[119] In this sense, they argue 'downsizing' is too narrow and restrictive a term and should be abandoned and replaced with the term 'corporate transformation'.[120] Support for this view comes from research, which shows that those organisations that are the most successful downsizers are ones that use the process strategically.

In short, downsizing has benefits when it is tailored to meet the strategic challenges thrown up by the organisation's environment (irrespective of whether the company is financially healthy or in decline). Without a strategic approach, downsizing easily becomes dumbsizing.[121] Not surprisingly, downsizing has attracted considerable criticism for being a representation of greed, short-sightedness and social irresponsibility.[122]

HOW HR CAN HELP MANAGERS

Now that downsizings and reorganisations have become a necessary part of business for most companies, there are many workers who wouldn't be surprised if they received a layoff notice at some time in their careers. This doesn't mean, however, that employees relish the idea of being laid off. What they want most is to be treated with dignity during the process. Here are 10 basic principles that HR professionals can use to help managers to lay off or eliminate employees in a respectful way. These principles include:

1. *Conduct the meeting in private.* A terminated employee has the right to a private severance meeting conducted by the employee's supervisor, not someone from the HR department. Because termination is a personal issue, employees want to hear the news from their supervisors, not from someone they don't know.

2. *Keep the meeting short and to the point.* The meeting should last no more than 10 to 15 minutes. Employees want to know the facts. They don't want nuances and indirect language. As soon as the employee is seated, explain why you called them in: 'Jo, I'm sorry, but your position has been eliminated.' Repeat the statement if necessary, and ask if they understand it.

3. *Offer support and compassion, but don't give hope of reversing the decision.* For example, tell the employee that this decision has been reviewed at the highest levels, and there's no possibility for appeal. Tell them that efforts have already been made, without success, to find them another assignment.

4. *Explain why the company made the decision.* Tell the employee why they are being laid off: a change in the company's strategic direction, or whatever is the reason for the decision. Don't argue about issues that should

have been resolved long ago. Be firm in telling the employee that the decision is made, and it's final.

5. *Don't make discriminatory statements.* Be aware of the many laws on discrimination and wrongful termination. The HR department should be involved in giving managers advice on what they can and can't say to employees.

6. *Control your emotions.* Don't try to keep the employee from leaving the room (you could be accused of false imprisonment); don't touch (you could be prosecuted for assault and battery); and don't yell (you could be accused of intentional infliction of emotional abuse).

7. *Give the severance package in writing.* When doing this, explain that the company wishes to make the employee's transition as painless as possible. Express confidence in the employee and their prospects. Remind that person that this termination was a business decision, and that you'll do all you can to help them.

8. *Encourage the employee to take positive, rather than destructive, actions.* Tell that person to follow the advice of the outplacement consultant who will help them to move in a positive career direction.

9. *Plan a graceful exit.* Walk the employee to the door or bring the outplacement consultant to them.

10. *Inform other employees, customers and suppliers of the decision.* Don't criticise the employee. Make the statement simple and non-blaming, such as, 'Jo left the company to pursue other interests'.

There should be no winners and losers in a termination. All parties should come out as whole as possible with a promise for a better future.

Joe Meissner is President and founder of Power Marketing, a San Francisco-based outplacement firm.

Figure 16.5 How HR can help managers
Source Joe Meissner, 'How HR can help managers', *Personnel Journal*, November 1993, p. 66.

Workplace relations

> **Workplace relations** Refers to employer–employee relations in a specific workplace (for example, at a factory site or branch office) as distinct from the total organisation or industry.

A company's strategic human resource objectives affect all aspects of **workplace relations**. They impact on rates of pay, recruitment, selection, job security, health and safety, employee motivation and employee attitudes towards the company and union membership. For example, Tabcorp seeks to be recognised as a great place to work by offering employees challenges and opportunities to grow and develop. Leighton Holdings encourages and empowers its people to reach their full potential by making them accountable for the project or business they are managing and by rewarding performance. And Foster's aims to attract, develop and retain the best people by focusing on training and development, offering a challenging and rewarding work environment, and encouraging employees to become shareholders.[123]

Strategic HR objectives also determine how industrial relations are managed. The former BHP's industrial relations strategy was built around pragmatic cooperation with trade unions (masterminded by non-performing, authoritarian managers who never talked to their workers and who had a long history of caving in to unions).[124] In contrast, Rio Tinto favoured direct management of industrial relations via performance-based individual contracts.[125] In terms of saleable coal produced per employee per annum, Rio Tinto workers are among the most productive in the world.[126] Overall in the resources sector, it is claimed that bypassing unions has improved productivity and reduced the number of industrial disputes.[127]

Work climate

The nature of the **work climate** thus has a direct impact on the viability of many HRM activities. For example, where the climate is negative and the union(s) strong, a company may not be able to:

- employ non-union members (the CFMEU, for example, applies 'pressure' on employers' to ensure that all workers on a site are financial members of the union[128])
- terminate an employee's employment without union consent
- allocate rewards according to performance (Telstra unions, for example, are opposed to moves to link all pay rises to performance[129])
- introduce a performance appraisal program
- offer employees membership in a non-union-sponsored superannuation fund
- assign employees to a job without the union's permission
- deal directly with its employees[130]
- introduce an employee participation scheme
- promote employees on merit
- treat employees equally
- introduce change[131]
- do business with non-union organisations or organisations employing members of a different union[132]
- reorganise its business operations without union consent.[133]

Compulsory unionism infringes on individual freedoms, but without it non-union members benefit from union gains without making any sacrifice (via payment of union dues, and so on).

Such situations can foster a feeling in some managers that workplace relations is 'too hard'.[134] This, in turn, produces managers who fail to give priority to HRM, who are reliant on outside bodies, who hand the initiative to the unions and who adopt a reactive and remedial rather than a proactive and preventive approach to industrial relations. For example, the Australian Industrial Relations Commission was long recognised as Telstra's de facto industrial relations department.[135] The consequences are low productivity, labour rigidities, high costs, poor quality products and services, and low employee commitment and motivation. Inefficient work practices in Australia's resource, food processing, waterfront and shipping industries are barriers to competitiveness. Similarly, poor union–management relationships in the coal industry have produced higher labour costs and strike action and developed the perception that Australia is an unreliable supplier.[136] One survey found that the main reasons for the poor performance of Australian coalmines compared with comparable US mines were inefficient work practices and relatively high labour costs.[137]

Another product of adversarial workplace relations is the **closed shop** where employees must join a union regardless of whether they want to or not (**compulsory unionism**).

HR managers have an important role to play in persuading line managers of the strategic benefits of innovative HR policies and practices, especially as the evidence indicates that line managers are critical in influencing employee attitudes and in achieving harmonious workplace relations (see figure 16.6).[138] Finally, union members who work for supervisors who are not union members show less loyalty to, less willingness to work for and less belief in unions.[139]

HUMAN RESOURCE MANAGER	LINE MANAGER
• Provides specialist knowledge on awards, legislation and industrial tribunal procedures. • Represents the company before industrial tribunals. • Helps negotiate disputes and award agreements. • Liaises directly with employer organisations and trade union officials. • Monitors the employee relations climate. • Acts as an advocate to ensure fair and equitable treatment for all employees.	• Via supervisory practices, determines the quality of the relationship with employees. • Ensures award and legal requirements are adhered to. • Resolves employee grievances. • Helps negotiate disputes and award agreements.

Figure 16.6 Roles in industrial relations

Management's role in creating the need for unions

A union is primarily an instrument of protest. Its power base is built on anger and frustration. 'No ... union', argues one expert, 'has ever captured a group of employees without the full cooperation and encouragement of managers who create the need for unionism.'[140] 'Unionism's best recruiter', claims Tas Bull, former National Secretary of the Waterside Workers Federation, 'is the grasping, uncaring nature of most employers'.[141]

HR managers and line managers have a responsibility to identify and treat the causes of employee dissatisfaction and not merely accept the status quo. Managers who do not, foster the growth of unionism. Major unions, for example, are now targeting the IT industry where white-collar employees are expressing anger and frustration with their grim working conditions and decreasing job security.[142] The evidence also indicates that when an employer collects union dues, this results in an increase in union membership (yet many managers enthusiastically continue to act as collecting agencies for unions).[143] 'This is the clearest possible example', says Rawson, 'of collaboration between employers and unions for the expansion and strengthening, at least in the numerical sense, of unionism itself.'[144] Trade unions are fully aware that any move to stop deductions could devastate the union movement and actively seek to include 'deduction clauses' in workplace agreements.[145]

The reactive and defeatist attitudes of some Australian managers is evidenced by a former senior industrial relations figure who comments 'Employers never win; all they can hope to do is slow down the rate at which they lose'.[146] It is difficult to imagine such a view being expressed by any other management function (particularly when Australian and US research indicates that if a thriving, profitable company is the goal, unionisation should be opposed).[147] Unfortunately, with some notable exceptions, few Australian organisations appear to have developed any proactive HR strategies to encourage managers to take responsibility for managing their human resources.[148] In fact, monopolistic, tariff-protected and other industries sheltered from global competition are cocooned, allowing union abuses and incompetent management to flourish.[149]

Practitioner speaks

Maura Fallon is President of Fallon International Limited, Hong Kong, a group that enables senior executives and executive teams in Asia to clarify corporate goals and execute complex decisions using intercultural insight.

Downsizing in Asia

A friend who was laid off was later re-offered his job by his ex-boss, but declined because he was embittered by the way his dismissal was handled. Many executives in Asia have had to dismiss people because of downsizing and poor economic conditions and, unfortunately, feelings of betrayal on the part of the dismissed employees often result. But there can be a happier outcome if management applies more effective human resource techniques during trying times.

The first question is: Are lay-offs necessary? There are alternatives — for example, across-the-board salary cuts, converting some jobs into part-time or moving excess support staff into customer relations roles. There also may be opportunities to place qualified staff with suppliers and customers.

However, if management has determined that staff cutbacks are the only answer, the task involves saving the face of those departing and maintaining the loyalty of both those departing and those remaining on staff. This is especially critical in an Asian cultural context.

Here are some key points to remember:

1. Management at all levels must build trust and confidence in good times and bad. The Chinese character for trust, *zhong* 忠, shows that trust centres on the heart.
2. Give face by recognising contributions and hard work in challenging and stressful times. Thank people for their loyalty. Employees appreciate positive acknowledgement of their accomplishments.
3. Acknowledge the losses personally. Allow people to vent their feelings. It's okay to let the tears flow.
4. Spell out the reasons for the lay-offs. The financial picture should be clear by the time lay-offs occur.
5. Build strong relationships between bosses and their direct reports. Asian employees respect managers who value teamwork.
6. Motivate staff through one-on-one relationships. Critical issues can be addressed during tête-à-tête lunches because the informal atmosphere fosters frank discussion of company developments.
7. Relationship building should take precedence over the use of email. Emphasise face-to-face meetings. Personal connections (*guanxi* 关係) are particularly important during crisis periods.
8. Build group bonds through informal activities such as staff dinners, hiking and boat trips, and include family members at times to build family bonds to the group.
9. Employees and their families need to feel proud of the company. Celebrate successes and bestow awards to individuals.
10. Staff remaining after a lay-off should be told what will change and what will not as people, particularly in Asian cultures, need continuity during unsettled periods. This also enables them to focus on their work between the announcements of new developments.
11. Managers earn loyalty by being seen to 'take care' of staff just as a respected elder would ensure the wellbeing of family members. The remaining staff members should be told how departing 'family' members are being assisted.

An open, proactive, culturally sensitive approach in lay-off situations can go a long way towards maintaining credibility with current employees and avoiding the hard feelings of departing staff whose store of knowledge can be of value when times permit rehiring.

Maura Fallon

Stereotyping in industrial relations

Negative stereotyping is deeply entrenched in the minds of many managers and union officials. This is because the culture and history of workplace relationships has influenced their perceptions of each other's motivations and competence (which in turn influences the level of trust existing between the two).[150] A study by Spillane on the difference between managers and union leaders in their perception of industrial conflict found that: 'Managers were inclined to attribute conflict to employee and union greed, lack of cooperation and poor team spirit. For their part, union leaders blamed the autocratic and selfish attitudes of management as well as the unwillingness of employers to cooperate with labour as the major sources of industrial conflict.'[151] 'The kind of image a worker has of the boss, and the image the boss has of himself and of his workers', argue Stagner and Rosen, 'will determine what each does in a given industrial situation. The image may be erroneous … but the person behaving is guided by his image, to him it is reality. Such images often provide the key to an understanding of an industrial dispute.'[152] The responsibility for eliminating such barriers via improved communication, employee empowerment, the development of personalised relationships and the utilisation of other high-performance HR policies and practices rests with management.[153]

How managers encourage unionism

In practice, however, it is often managers who teach employees to be anti-company and pro-union. Management abuse and neglect ensure that the only way for employees to secure dignity and protection at work is by joining a union. For example, a former union official describes a company where the female secretarial and clerical staff were constantly tearing their stockings on the dilapidated wooden furniture. Management ignored all complaints until one of the clerks caught a splinter under her kneecap. The frustrated staff walked out and sought union help. Management, confronted with a strike and the union, immediately purchased new furniture.[154] Another case involved a casual receptionist who was sacked by her employer for taking time off to see her doctor five months into the term of her pregnancy (despite the fact she had given her employer two weeks notice of the appointment!).[155]

Deloitte Consulting's tough cost cutting and impersonal management were described by a union official as an advertisement for the union, enabling it to sign up 200 members in a few weeks.[156] Qantas ignored numerous complaints from the Australian Services Union about cold wind blasts at its Melbourne check-in counters, leading to a walkout by employees.[157] An Australia Post employee suffered a pay cut for having four personal items on her desk instead of three. The Community and Public Sector Union challenged management over the issue.[158] Manufacturing firm Ferro Corporation had a redundancy package dispute that saw all its management and salaried staff (with the exception of the Managing Director and HR Manager) go on strike.[159] Australian Workers Union Secretary Bill Shorten commented, 'we have strong support for the salaried staff who are being shafted'.[160]

Management by such actions teaches its employees that to get satisfaction, they must go to the union. Bad management is the best recruiting agent available to unions. 'Most union organising campaigns', says Fossum, 'do not arise as the result of a carefully constructed strategy by a national union's organising department. They tend instead to generate from within or around issues of mutual concern that employees see as unfair and/or threatening.'[161]

Union protection

The United Steel Workers of America lists 10 key factors motivating workers to seek union protection. In reality, they constitute a checklist of 'management don'ts'. If management wants to make unionisation attractive to workers, all it needs to do is:
1. ensure that there is a lack of communication between employees and management
2. remain ignorant of workers' problems
3. pay lower wages or salaries than most others in the same geographical area
4. have people doing identical work receiving different rates of pay
5. permit inequities in promotions with regard to seniority
6. have few or no employee benefits
7. offer poor working conditions
8. allow overtime work without compensation
9. constantly pressure and harass employees to complete their work
10. treat employees as if they are unintelligent.[162]

Research shows that employees who are dissatisfied with wages and benefits, job security, information sharing and consultation, promotion opportunities and supervisory treatment favour union representation and do not trust management.[163] Deery, Erwin and Iverson argue that support for trade unions is greater where there is a high degree of industrial conflict and distrust and where employees are unhappy with their employment arrangements.[164] Recent research suggests that about 40 per cent of employees who join a union do so for a 'safety net' in case something goes wrong.[165] In contrast, employees who enjoy higher levels of job satisfaction, an egalitarian culture, training and development, performance-related pay, employment security, good communications and opportunities to participate show greater commitment to the organisation.[166]

This Letter to the Editor provides a provocative viewpoint. Do you agree? See 'What's your view?' on page 617.

Letter to the Editor

Trade unions in Australia have outlived their usefulness

Dear Editor,

Once upon a time, Australian trade unions performed a range of useful functions. These functions primarily involved the need to moderate the excesses of Australia's historically underperforming managers, who often lacked the people skills demanded by organisational change initiatives.

In areas like workplace safety and the pursuit of reasonable wage demands, most unions served Australian workers fairly well. During the mid- to late 1980s, the Hawke government's Accord between unions, business and government provided the unions with an influential role in wage-setting and award-restructuring processes, and probably represented the zenith of union power in this country.

The early years of the new millennium are markedly different to the sleepy years of the 1970s and 1980s, however. As Australian industry struggles to find its niche in the new era of globalisation and hyper-competition, it can no longer afford the luxury of a change-averse trade union movement. While some companies may continue to operate via the old ways of industrial adversarialism, most Australian businesses realise that rapid change is inevitable, and that successful change efforts demand the participation and support of all employees. Multiskilling, flexibility and a preparedness to avoid the old 'work by the book' practices of the past characterise this new environment.

While some unions embrace these processes, most trade unions view them with fear, loathing and resistance. In the higher education sector, for instance, militant unions hinder university leaders' efforts to match resources and academic staffing levels to student demand. As with the hospital in the TV show *Yes, Minister* that won an award for efficiency precisely because it had no patients, higher education unions are forcing universities to maintain departments that have virtually no student demand for their courses. Despite the threats created by the rise of corporate universities and the growth of new methods of delivery, such as Internet-based courses, unions insist on their right to hamper change efforts at every turn. It is not surprising then that the general public begins to view universities as 'sheltered workshops' undeserving of greater public funding. As a consequence, the unions achieve precisely the opposite result to that intended by their change-obstructing actions.

Australian managers of this generation are arguably significantly better people managers than their predecessors. Training in the softer skills in BBA and MBA programs at business schools and in internal company training programs has assisted with this transition. The new managers no longer need unions to tell them what to do or how to do it. They are also well aware that their own performance will be judged on how well they can bring their employees with them in designing and implementing change initiatives.

Unions in Australia are an endangered species, and it is regrettable that they have not gone the way of the dinosaurs before now.

A senior manager from a non-union workplace

Source David Poole, University of Western Sydney.

The self-fulfilling prophecy in industrial relations

Peters and Waterman argue that 'most organisations are governed by rules that assume the average worker is an incompetent, never-do-well, just itching to screw up'.[167] Recent research also suggests that many managers hold assumptions that employees cannot be trusted to make important decisions about their work.[168] Unfortunately, employees treated as irresponsible behave that way. A **self-fulfilling prophecy** takes effect.

In contrast, organisations with proactive HRM have an ingrained philosophy that says, 'respect the individual, make people winners, let them stand out, treat people as adults'.[169] There is an overwhelming emphasis on providing employees with a workplace environment that reflects a shared common purpose.[170] It has been shown, for example, that companies that promote selective hiring, employee participation, information sharing, egalitarianism, training and development, career development, pay for performance, flexible work schedules, teamworking and gainsharing financially outperform those companies that do not.[171]

Self-fulfilling prophecy Occurs when expectations about someone cause them to behave in a way consistent with the expectations.

What employees want

Albrecht and Travaglione found that open communication, procedural justice, organisational support and employee satisfaction with job security led to trust of management, which in turn positively influenced employee commitment, attitudes towards change and turnover intentions.[172] Regrettably, many managers do not know or understand the needs of their employees. For example, research suggests that less than half of Australian workers are satisfied with the way they are treated by their managers.[173] Another survey similarly shows that an overwhelming majority of Australian workers do not trust their managers and regard them as uncommunicative, poor listeners and demonstrating little confidence in workers' abilities.[174] A consistent theme generated by research is that Australian managers need much better 'people' skills if they are to motivate teams of skilled workers and professionals to work effectively towards a common goal.[175]

The job of the union

Trade unions are collective organisations that aim to protect and advance the rights and interests of their members. As such they seek to expose inefficient management, low wages and bad working conditions, improve health and safety, increase worker involvement in decision making, and provide ongoing protection in the workplace.[176] A former Victorian Trades Hall Council secretary says, 'employers would be wise to give careful consideration to increasing the security of their employees ... I guarantee that if we asked people to list in order of priority what most concerned them for the future they would first list job security'.[177] A survey shows 'that workers want unions to concentrate on traditional industrial issues of wages, conditions and job security, and that they are less enthusiastic about issues such as training and career development and balancing work and family responsibilities'.[178] Managers who ignore such basic issues risk alienating their employees and subjecting their companies to unionisation (see figure 16.7).[179]

Trade unions Formal organisations that represent individuals employed in one organisation, throughout an industry or main occupation.

Featherbedding A type of restrictive work practice that involves the use of too many employees for the actual work to be performed.

Demarcation An exclusive right that restricts a specific type of work to members of a particular union. In practice, it operates as a form of job protection.

Strikes Refusal by employees to work until their demands are met by the employer.

Go-slows Occur when workers refuse to work at their normal pace in order to pressure management into making a concession. Often implemented by working strictly according to the rules.

Bad management equals bad workplace relations

Companies pay a heavy penalty for bad human resource management — **featherbedding**, **demarcation**, **strikes**, **go-slows**, reduced productivity and the loss of the right to manage. Remote, faceless managers who tolerate unpleasant, threatening, dangerous, inequitable or discriminatory workplaces foster negative solidarity — 'us against the company' — and stimulate the growth of unions.

Good workplace relations spring from managers who genuinely believe that 'people are the company's most important asset'. An Australian Workplace Industrial Relations Survey shows that the majority of managers want to deal directly with their employees, which suggests that HR managers now have the opportunity to partner line managers in the introduction of more sophisticated HR policies and practices.[180] 'The generals that get the support of their troops', says Paterson, 'are those that pay attention to whether they've got boots, whether they've got rations or whether they're camping on a well drained site. They care about the loss of every individual member and people will risk their lives for those who care and be cynical about those who don't.'[181] Simply put, good industrial relations centres on management that is competent, has integrity, is benevolent, promotes open (and frequent) communication, provides organisational support, demonstrates fairness and equity in organisational HR policies and practices, and stresses mutual commitment to shared objectives.[182]

SUCCESSFUL MANAGEMENT ACTION IN THE WORKPLACE

Success in making unions unnecessary depends on the ability of management to deal effectively with its employees by:

- developing HR values and strategies that delineate management's approach to people management. For example, one mining company established a set of corporate values that included health and safety, openness and integrity, innovation and excellence, cooperation and teamwork, and empowerment and personal fulfilment.[183] Leading innovative companies similarly enhance their competitiveness by investing in their people and having a culture that values HR management.[184]
- placing responsibility for industrial relations with line management. This will require the training of line managers in strategic HRM, as they are the leading edge of HRM implementation.[185]
- encouraging open communication and being prepared to listen.[186] Says an ANZ senior HRM executive, '... what we have done quite consciously is to build better communications with our staff — direct relationships face to face with our staff for matters that affect them in the workplace. And there is no substitute for that'.[187] Yet research indicates that in the majority of workplaces, communications are inadequate.[188] For example, according to one union official, the only time top executives were seen at one steel works was once a year when they drove around in a fleet of white cars.[189]

- ensuring that managers are out of their offices and give employees personal attention. One London-based AMP employee reportedly had his employment terminated via a mobile phone text message.[190]
- ensuring that front-line supervisors are trained and have the necessary authority and rewards to make them feel part of management
- promoting company-sponsored social and sporting events
- recognising loyalty and seniority
- objectively identifying and rewarding performance[191]
- promoting from within
- stressing quality and pride in the company and its products
- eliminating artificial status distinctions such as reserved car parking and executive dining rooms. Flight Centre promotes a strong egalitarian culture where all interpersonal communications (irrespective of rank) are on a first name basis and dress is smart casual.[192]
- introducing profit sharing and employee share purchase schemes
- creating a pleasant and safe physical work environment
- encouraging the development of employee skills by ongoing training and development[193]
- ensuring fair and competitive compensation and benefits
- communicating to employees that management is committed to treating employees fairly and with respect.

Figure 16.7 Successful management action in the workplace

Salaried operations

The introduction of Australian Workplace Agreements, the decline of union coverage, management preference for voluntary unionism and the increasing influence of strategic HRM have stimulated a change from a collectivist and legalistic approach to industrial relations to one emphasising individualism and non-third-party involvement (for example, in organisations such as Rio Tinto).[194] **Salaried operations**, which promote the mutual interests of employees and the organisation, are the natural outcome. In such organisations, all employees are treated as staff rather than as staff and wages (or union) personnel. This aims to remove artificial barriers to cooperative effort and to ensure that all employees are given equal respect and treatment. Salaried operations reflect a strong unitarist influence by emphasising the creation of a more productive, efficient and competitive organisation by enhancing employee commitment and competence. This is done by:

- equal treatment and the elimination of artificial barriers such as status symbols (for example, reserved parking, separate canteens) and different policies for union and staff personnel, which treat employees as first- and second-class citizens
- rewards based on individual effort and achievement rather than on collective negotiation and seniority (research shows that unionised companies are less likely to use performance appraisal and profit-sharing schemes and more likely to favour across-the-board increases.)[195]
- broad job structuring with an emphasis on multiskilling and the elimination of narrow job descriptions (and thus demarcation issues)
- individual performance being used to make promotion decisions as opposed to seniority
- higher pay and fringe benefits (resulting from increased employee productivity)
- mutual interest, cooperation and communication instead of 'them and us' with the subsequent union–management friction
- well-trained supervisors with the confidence and know-how to manage human resources successfully
- decision making being pushed down to the lowest level possible in the organisation to promote individual responsibility and reduce the need for supervision.

Robe River, one of the most efficient and profitable iron ore projects in Australia, has everyone employed on staff conditions and uses a profit-sharing arrangement based on productivity. As a union operation, productivity was 22.5 tonnes per employee compared with 171.5 tonnes as a salaried operation.[196] Similarly, in the United States, leading companies such as IBM, Hewlett-Packard, Kodak, Gillette and Microsoft have avoided unionisation but simultaneously developed reputations as excellent employers.[197] The traditional view of industrial relations inherently involving conflict has been rejected.

It should be noted that not all industrial relations experts agree with this approach. For example, Deery argues that there is little evidence to indicate that trade unions have a negative effect on productivity, that the presence of a 'union voice' can augment rather than hinder productivity, that union membership need not be at the expense of organisational loyalty and that unions ensure fairness and procedural equity in the workplace.[198] Vaughn also argues that the idea of management and employees working closely together in a spirit of shared loyalty, commitment and trust is a romantic vision with little credibility.[199] Research that suggests that unionisation goes hand in hand with higher productivity, however, has been subjected to considerable criticism. Alternative explanations include monopoly effects and inadequate definitions of productivity. Moreover, even if unions do not reduce productivity, the evidence indicates that they do reduce profits and in the longer term the competitive advantage of the organisation.[200] Finally, the overriding hypothesis that high-performance HR policies and practices (which emphasise open and frequent communication, performance-related pay, training and development, and an egalitarian culture) lead to superior organisational performance is clearly supported by current research.[201]

It should be noted that because a company is union-free there is no guarantee that it will employ high-performance HR policies and practices. Research in Britain, for example, shows that, with few exceptions (such as companies that had adopted a strategic HRM approach in greenfield sites), non-union workplaces were characterised by poor communications, little employee involvement, high labour turnover, and high rates of accidents and terminations. Unionised workplaces, in contrast, showed greater innovation in their HR policies and practices (see figure 16.8).[202] A study by Deery and Walsh similarly found non-union workplaces in Australia were marked by inadequate policies relating to equity, fair treatment and safety at work. Labour turnover, as a consequence, was almost double that of unionised workplaces.[203] Another Australian survey also confirms the trade union view of union-free workplaces as having exploited employees suffering high levels of job insecurity, stress and work-related illnesses.[204]

Salaried operations Involves all employees being treated equally as staff rather than salaried (staff) and wages (or union) personnel.

	Union-free workplace	**Unionised workplace**
Strategic HRM (sophisticated)	Harmonious relations	Cooperative relations or industrial warfare*
Non-strategic HRM (unsophisticated)	Covert industrial conflict (absenteeism, high labour turnover)	Overt industrial conflict (strikes)

HRM policies

Low — Union activity — High

* Depends on union's perception of strategic HRM as an opportunity or a threat

Figure 16.8 Strategic HRM and union activity
Source Asia Pacific Management Co. Ltd, 2004.

Such companies are merely preparing the ground for a union upsurge. In Australia and the United States, disenchantment among dot.com workers concerning job security, benefits, forced overtime and low pay is reigniting interest in union membership.[205] Getting employees to be more productive involves more than the absence of unions. It involves management time, commitment and expertise. The quality of management is the critical element in the successful introduction of high-performance HR policies and practices designed to improve productivity and worker satisfaction.

Finally, the presence of a union does not rule out cooperative partnerships between management and employees. For example, in the 1990s Toyota Australia was crippled by strikes that cost the company up to $10 million per day, but the appointment of a new CEO brought about a dramatic improvement in industrial relations. Ken Asano, Toyota's new CEO, emphasises communication (he regularly addresses workers, visits the shop floor and is open about the company's production, export and sales goals), is actively involved in union–management negotiations and is open and approachable. Asano's management style has been acknowledged by union leadership as a major factor in the improved relationship.[206]

Union–management cooperation

The introduction of high-performance HR policies and practices is achieved in only a few organisations and at management's initiative.[207] Moreover, resistance to such change by managers, trade unionists and employees can be great.[208] Guest argues that unions may 'be wiser to see HRM as an opportunity rather than a threat ... rather than oppose HRM, unions should champion it, becoming more enthusiastic than management'.[209] Similarly, Bacon and Storey suggest that trade unions should restructure themselves and align themselves with the organisation's strategy. This they justify on the grounds that many aspects of HRM, such as skill development, career enhancement, employee involvement and open communication, have been advocated by the unions themselves.[210] Furthermore, if unions can discover a 'common cause' or 'shared objective' with management, it makes it possible for employees to demonstrate a dual commitment to the company and the union.[211] Such views, however, are far from universal. Kelly, for example, argues that union cooperation and partnership with management provides only meagre benefits, threatens union survival and recovery, and ignores the antagonistic interests of workers and employers.[212] Nevertheless, the evidence suggests that it is possible for trade unions to be accommodated within the HRM model if a cooperative rather than an adversarial approach is employed.[213]

It would also seem that strategic HRM poses the greatest threat to those unions that have ineffectual leadership, are neglectful of their members, are inactive, do not provide the services that workers require and are unconcerned with the competitive pressures that employers face.[214] Peetz, for example, found that if a union is active and well represented, management efforts to enhance employee involvement have no effect on unionisation. However, if unions are not active in the workplace, such management strategies produce substantial reductions in unionisation.[215] Similarly, research by Kelly and Kelly shows the persistence of 'them and us' attitudes depends on how HRM initiatives are implemented and managed. For example, failure to consult workers, inequality of status, discriminatory benefits and lack of commitment by top management lead to a lack of trust and a failure of the HRM initiatives to change employee attitudes.[216] In turn, those union-free and unionised companies that fail to introduce innovative HR policies and practices will create a hostile workplace and inevitably suffer the re-emergence of militant union power.[217]

The benefits of salaried operations

Organisational benefits claimed for salaried operations include the following:

- *Better utilisation of employee talent via:*
  - elimination of demarcation restrictions and disputes (with the result that fewer people are required). Rio Tinto, for example, suffered from overstaffing (as illustrated by the practice of 'shadowing', where union members are assigned to work alongside outside contractors even though there is no work for them to perform) and inflexibility (as illustrated by the union's control over the allocation of overtime, using seniority instead of assigning the best person for the job).[218] Grocon workers went on strike after a non-union worker picked up a broom to help clean up after a freak rainstorm.[219]
  - flexibility to move people from job to job. Virgin Blue's multiskilled baggage handlers check in passengers, terminal employees also work as flight attendants and flight attendants also clean the planes, giving the company a competitive edge over Qantas, where rigid job demarcations are enforced by its unions.[220]
  - increased emphasis on merit in hiring, pay and promotion decisions. In the coal industry, the former common practice was for companies to recruit employees from the union's list of retrenched mine workers. Selection on merit was not allowed.[221]
- *Increased employee commitment via:*
  - improved pay and benefits
  - improved supervision
  - individual treatment
  - elimination of second-class citizen status (the abolition of reserved parking, time clocks, different holiday benefit plans and share purchase/award programs)
  - recognition of individual performance and personal circumstances (unions are opposed to this — pay linked to individual performance, for example, is seen as reducing the sense of collective action among employees and enhancing management control)[222]
  - increased opportunities for training and skill development
  - increased job satisfaction through job rotation, job enlargement and job enrichment (research shows that job satisfaction is decreased when employees are both attitudinally and behaviourally committed to the union)[223]
  - elimination of friction caused by union–management adversarial relations
  - increased career opportunities and job security
  - increased social and welfare activities such as family picnics and sports days.
- *Elimination of union costs via:*
  - elimination of strikes and other disruptions. According to one study, unions increase employment costs, make change more difficult, encourage trivial grievances, protect unsatisfactory workers, impede communication, promote an adversarial industrial relations climate, inhibit individual rewards, provide a platform for 'trouble' workers, impose restrictions on production, inhibit flexibility and impose unnecessarily high staffing levels. Strikes and inefficiencies at Rio Tinto's Hunter Valley No. 1 Mine, for example, caused production to plummet and profits to drop to about $1 per tonne compared with $20 per tonne at mines with salaried operations.[224] Similarly, it is estimated that poor industrial relations in the Victorian construction industry adds as much as 30 per cent to building costs.[225]
  - elimination of **restrictive work practices**. Research shows that union members are less flexible than non-union members.[226] Telstra, for example, has a very detailed, complex, highly codified and highly regulated system of agreements and employment conditions expressed in 12 awards, 46 registered agreements and numerous unregistered and local agreements. One consequence is that the average time for a disciplinary action is

Restrictive work practices Any practice designed to restrict the efficient and effective operation of an organisation. Examples include featherbedding, demarcations and limits placed on output.

315 days.[227] Optus Communications, in contrast, has a single 15-page agreement covering the same things.[228]

– promotion of loyalty to the company instead of the union
– ability to hire, promote and terminate personnel on the basis of ability and perform–ance instead of on the basis of seniority and union membership. Unions are opposed to such ideas, preferring, for example, to retrench workers on the basis of the 'last on, first off' principle. Although this has been shown to be discriminatory (particularly in the case of female employees who tend to have less seniority because of earlier sex discrimination in hiring), unions claim it is not discriminatory. Tony Maher, Senior Vice-President of the CFMEU's Mining Division, argues that abandoning the 'last on, first off principle' would allow employers to 'pick and choose and play favourites'. Agreements between the Communications, Electrical and Plumbing Union (CEPU) and electrical contractors require employers to give absolute preference in employ-ment to financial union members. Freedom of association has not ended compulsory unionism in Australia.[229]
– ability to manage without union interference. The FSU, for example, is opposed to the Commonwealth Bank's attempts to increase flexibility and improve customer ser-vice.[230] Similarly, the CFMEU fiercely resisted mining company attempts to regain con-trol over recruitment, retrenchment and overtime allocation. For example, it took the former BHP six months to negotiate staggered 'smoko' breaks for its Pilbara iron workers.[231]

Seniority is said to be an objective way of determining who is to be terminated. However, because it ignores performance, an organisation's best workers may be fired and its worst workers retained.

While having considerable advantages, many organisations remain uninterested in salaried operations because of:

• a lack of any identifiable HR strategy linked to the organisation's strategic business objec-tives. The former BHP, in contrast to Rio Tinto, for example, had no philosophical or ideological preference for dealing with unions.[232]
• a lack of managers who are comfortable with and have the know-how to manage a salaried operation successfully. For many managers, managing according to an award or through a union (and as a consequence not having to make a decision and be held accountable) is very attractive. Such managers often make 'sweetheart deals' with unions, which, in turn, are happy to trade off guaranteed membership dues for industrial peace and stability and 'reasonable' pay claims.[233] Questions were raised, for example, over the former BHP's management ability to extract the full benefits of individual contracts. Even the unions had little regard for the former BHP management. ACTU Secretary, Greg Combet, for example, complained: 'The correct procedure for a driver whose truck breaks down is to notify his supervisor, who then advises maintenance. In one instance, the driver used his initiative to directly notify maintenance. He was taken aside and coun-selled for failing to follow the right procedure. That's the sort of management we're dealing with.'[234] Likewise, management weakness and tolerance of bad work practices has seen inefficiencies, high costs and illegal activities entrenched in the construction industry.[235]
• a corporate culture that emphasises formal hierarchy, status differences and an authori-tarian management style. According to one survey, half of Australian managers said they did not consult employees about major organisational changes, including those affecting the way work was done.[236] Telstra's corporate culture remains imbued with a public sector mentality, which restricts its flexibility.[237]
• a management that feels threatened by the emphasis given to employee involvement and participation in decision making
• a management that is frightened of the union. According to the National Farmer's Feder-ation, employers are reluctant to exercise their legal rights for fear of being targeted by the union movement.[238] The building and construction industry, for example, has been described as lawless. The dominant union, the CFMEU, 'has used intimidation, extortion and economic blackmail to enforce its monopoly'.[239] A self-confessed 'enforcer' for the union said it was his job to 'crack heads'.[240]
• a management faced with a labour force controlled by a union monopoly; for example, Australian stevedoring companies and the MUA — this has resulted in the stevedoring companies paying about three times the going commercial rate for waterfront labour.[241]

A company falsifies its books to pay the membership fees of an employee forced to join the union.

Comments one former Labor government minister, 'The maritime union manages to ensure it's very well paid troops get paid more and more for doing less'.[242]

- a management sheltered from vigorous competition. Australian transport and construction companies, for example, treat labour as a cost.[243] In contrast, organisations that are exposed to international competition are more likely to be concerned with productivity improvements and see employees as providing a competitive edge.[244]
- a management that has a short-term orientation and is not prepared to devote the resources and effort needed to make salaried operations work. National Australia Bank says it prefers collective rather than individual agreements because they are easier to negotiate and administer.[245] Comments Peter Sams, Secretary of the NSW Labor Council, 'Compulsory unionism will continue to operate whether it's illegal or not because a lot of employers like to have everyone in the union for ease of negotiation'.[246] This has led to accusations of 'spoon-fed' managers dependent on a centralised system to make their industrial relations decisions for them.[247]

In summary, the concept of salaried operations demands a change in organisational culture, top management commitment, a clearly defined HR strategy, increased emphasis on human relations, a change in the manager's role from boss to coach, counsellor and motivator, and considerable management determination to make it succeed. Not surprisingly, many organisations shy away, preferring the comfort of a more traditional approach to the management of human resources. For those that do accept the challenge, however, the opportunity exists to gain a competitive advantage by maximising profits and growth through flexibility, productivity and employee commitment.

Only union-approved vending machines (for which the union gets a commission on every item sold) are permitted on a company's construction site.

Summary

Australia's integration into the global economy has brought with it dramatic change. Long-standing social and workplace values are now subject to constant challenge. As a result, the workplace is at the forefront of change. Today, managers are expected to act as change agents and workers are expected to be more flexible. All live with job insecurity and uncertainty. Downsizing, for example, has generated stress among employees and calls for the development of new HR policies and practices to help employees to adjust.

Managers now need to determine the need for change, identify obstacles to change, implement change and evaluate its success or failure. Managers also must be alert to the fact that change does not occur in isolation, but involves a complex set of relationships. A change in technology, for example, may trigger a change in employees' status, skill requirements and job security. Similarly, an organisation's decision to buy, sell or merge with another organisation has major HR repercussions.

The ongoing need for improved performance has seen many organisations focus on TQM as a means to gain a competitive advantage. Similarly, competitive pressures have forced changes in the way people are managed in the workplace. Greater emphasis is now being placed on the manager's role in managing workplace relations. A trend towards individual treatment and a decreased role for trade unions is evident. This, in turn, has created an interest in salaried operations where all employees are treated as staff and the commonality of organisation and employee interests is stressed.

Thirty interactive Wiley Web Questions are available to test your understanding of this chapter at **www.johnwiley.com.au/ highered/hrm5e** *in the student resources area*

review questions

1. What are the key steps in the management of change?
2. Why do people resist change? How can resistance to change be overcome?
3. How does change affect people at work? What are some of the current forces for change in the workplace? What are the implications for HR managers?
4. What workplace conditions are most likely to promote the unionisation of an organisation's work force?
5. Are you in favour of or opposed to unions? Explain your position.
6. What is a change agent? How can HR managers act as change agents?
7. What is compulsory unionism? What are the advantages and disadvantages of compulsory unionism?
8. What is TQM? What are the major advantages and disadvantages of TQM?
9. Explain what is meant by seniority. What are the advantages and disadvantages of using seniority to determine pay increases, promotions and terminations?
10. Define salaried operations. Explain why you favour or oppose the concept.

environmental influences on workplace relations

Identify and discuss the key influences from the model (figure 16.9 shown opposite) that have significance for workplace relations.

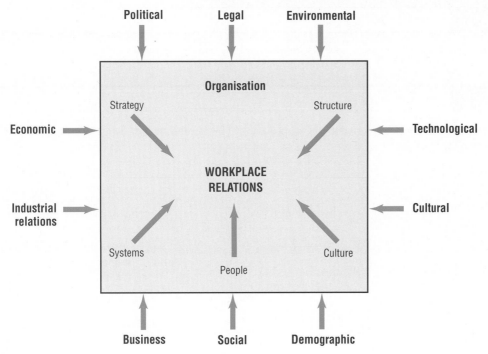

Figure 16.9 Environmental influences on workplace relations

Downsizing destroys morale and reduces the organisation's competitiveness.
Or
Bad workplace relations are the product of bad management.
Or
Professional employees should not join unions.
Or
Powerful unions, not just companies, must obey the law.
Or
Tariff protection fosters union abuse and incompetent management.

practitioner speaks

Read the article on page 606. Explain what is meant by downsizing. What are the arguments for and against downsizing? What is the most significant point made by the author? Why?

what's your view?

Write a 500-word response to the Letter to the Editor on page 608, agreeing or disagreeing with the writer's point of view.

newsbreak exercise

Read the Newsbreak 'Work in progress' on pages 592–4. Identify the major changes introduced. Which were successful/unsuccessful? What lessons did you learn from reading this article?

soapbox

What do you think? Conduct a mini survey of class members, using the questionnaire below. Critically discuss the findings.

1. Union membership should be compulsory.	YES	NO
2. Unions are bad for a firm's competitiveness.	YES	NO
3. Workplace change destroys trust.	YES	NO
4. Unions are essential to protect employee interests.	YES	NO
5. People who refuse to change should be fired.	YES	NO
6. Downsizing sees employees treated as numbers rather than as people.	YES	NO

online exercise

Conduct an online search for information on one of the following: workplace change, corruption in industrial relations, total quality management or downsizing. Prepare a 300–500 word executive summary. Include the web addresses you found useful. As a class, discuss your findings.

ethical dilemma

'Last on, first off' at Jet Red

The decision has been made to outsource all training and development activities at Jet Red. As a result, the HR Department has to reduce its headcount. Someone has to go.

Linda Church, HR Manager, thinks that Con Spanos, Senior Training Officer, should be retrenched. Aged 48, Con's performance history is poor. In contrast, Libby Wu, Training Officer, is an outstanding performer. Aged 31, she has been with Jet Red for just two years. Con, with 29 years of service, is a member of the Airline Workers Union. Libby is not a union member. The union has traditionally enforced a 'last on, first off'

policy when retrenchments have occurred. Linda feels that this is discriminatory because it ignores merit and tends to disadvantage female employees. However, given the power of the union and the need to avoid an industrial dispute, Linda wonders whether she should fire Libby instead.

Discussion questions

1. If you were Linda, what would you do? Why?
2. If you were the union representative, how would you justify the use of the 'last on, first off' principle?
3. What ethical issues are raised in this case?

Change at Global Mining

The atmosphere in the room was tense. Ted Kimoski, Financial Director for Global Mining, had just finished his presentation. John Campbell, Managing Director, sat quietly making notes. After a pause, he broke the silence. 'From what you have shown us Ted, it seems that we face the following problems in Australia. Our mines are not competitive. Benchmarked against international best practice or our own mines in Canada, Indonesia, South Africa and the United States, our production costs are the highest in the world. Our low productivity and high labour costs are killing us. In short, we must cut our Australian losses and expand elsewhere or make our Australian operations more competitive.'

Ted looked directly at John. 'John, that's it in a nutshell. Our Australian operations are bleeding badly. Worse, our financial performance is now affecting the group's overall profitability and ability to grow. If we don't do something about Australia soon, we risk being taken over by Mega Mining. And it certainly will sell off the Australian mines. You are all aware that our share price has dropped 20 per cent in the past six months and that it is now rumoured in the market that we are a potential takeover target.'

John nodded in acknowledgement then turned to face Paul Jaworski, Production Director. 'Paul, what do you think?'

Exercise

Form into groups of three to four. Identify the key factors you will need to consider in formulating an HR strategy for Global Mining. Develop strategic objectives in the areas of industrial relations, recruitment and selection, training and development, and compensation and benefits. Identify potential problems that may hinder the implementation of your new strategy. Suggest possible ways to overcome these challenges.

practical exercises

1. Form into groups of four to six. Identify which external influences shown in figure 16.9 on page 617 affect the industry in which you work, the company for which you work and the job in which you work. What changes are these influences bringing about? Identify and discuss the implications for your organisation's HR management and for you personally.

2. Form into groups of four to six. Assume that you are the senior HR staff member for an organisation that aims to be the fastest-growing, most profitable bank/manufacturer/retailer (select one industry) in the Asia–Pacific region. Identify and discuss the implications of this mission statement for the following HR activities:
   - recruitment and selection
   - training and development
   - compensation and benefits.

3. Form into groups of two to three. Research the stated 'core purpose' of three or four organisations with which you are familiar. You may gather the information from interviews, company web sites or published material such as annual reports. Regroup as a class. Discuss what each stated core purpose tells you about the organisation and its culture. Is it credible? Is it reflected in the organisation's strategies, policies and practices? Identify which core purpose appeals to you most and explain why.

4. In groups of four to six, discuss what you would do in the following situations if you were the HR manager.

(a) Two of your new graduate trainees, Gloria Hamilton and Michael Caplan, are found to have lied about their academic qualifications. Both in fact failed their final year and did not graduate from Western University as stated on their application form. The performance of Michael, who is not a union member, is excellent, while the performance of Gloria, who is a union member, is unsatisfactory.

(b) Your training manager has been accused of copyright infringement by a management consultant. The consultant's customer service training program has been reproduced without permission and illegal photocopies distributed to all managers. It appears that illegal photocopying of training material has been widespread for some time in the training department. Until now, the manager has been highly regarded and was rated superior at the last performance appraisal. He is an active member of the union.

(c) You have been asked to advise the board on a proposed list of senior managers to be retrenched. On meeting with the Managing Director, you comment that there are several top performers who are listed for termination, while some other managers with poor performance records are listed to be retained. The Managing Director simply looks at you and says: 'The ones who are being chopped are the ones who have run out of friends in high places. Performance really doesn't have much to do with it. Surely you realise this?'

(d) By accident, you become aware that your boss, the Managing Director of Oz Enterprises Ltd, has lied on his application form about his academic and professional qualifications. Recently, a union member was dismissed without notice because he had made false statements on his application form.

(e) You are surprised to receive a late-night telephone call from the Secretary of the Industrial Workers Union, Bernie O'Shea, telling you that his union has decided to accept your company's offer and, as a consequence, he has recommended an immediate return to work. You are delighted and immediately ring your boss to inform him. He thanks you, but makes no further comment. Later, by chance, you discover that Bernie was secretly paid $100 000 by your boss to end the strike.

(f) As the new HR Manager for Oz Enterprises Ltd, you are aware that employees in the manufacturing division have suffered from bad management in the past. However, as part of the new management team, you are confident of improving workplace relations in the division. On a plant visit, several workers approach you to inform you that they plan to join the militant Manufacturing Workers Union.

(g) You have just come from a highly confidential meeting with the Managing Director regarding cuts in the senior management staff. One of the managers listed for retrenchment is your friend Ted Palmer. At lunch, Ted tells you in the strictest confidence that he is planning to turn down a job offer that he has received from a competitor because he feels in the long term that he has much better prospects by staying in his present job.

(h) The board has decided to cut employee numbers by 15 per cent. The Manufacturing Manager wants to cut numbers on the basis of seniority, believing this is the fairest means as it rewards loyalty. In contrast, the Marketing Manager wants to cut numbers on the basis of performance, believing that this is the fairest as it rewards merit. The Managing Director has asked you for your recommendation.

5. Form into groups of four to six. Your task is to plan the introduction of salaried operations to a publicly listed company you are familiar with. List the steps you would take to identify the need for change, the potential obstacles to change, how the change will be implemented and how it will be evaluated. Prepare an executive summary (maximum three pages) outlining your recommendations for the consideration of the board of directors.

suggested readings

ACIRRT, *Australia at Work*, Prentice Hall, Sydney, 1999.

Beardwell, I. and Holden, L., *Human Resource Management*, 3rd edn, Financial Times/Prentice Hall, London, 2001, ch. 4.

CCH, *Australian Master Human Resource Guide*, CCH, Sydney, 2003, chs 2, 27, 28.

De Cieri, H. and Kramar, R., *Human Resource Management in Australia*, McGraw-Hill, Sydney, 2003, chs 1, 7.

Fisher, C. D., Schoenfeldt, L. F. and Shaw, J. B., *Human Resource Management*, 5th edn, Houghton Mifflin, Boston, 2003, ch. 10.

Gennard, J. and Judge, G., *Employee Relations*, 3rd edn, CIPD, London, 2003, chs 2, 6, 12.

Ivancevich, J. M. and Lee, S. H., *Human Resource Management in Asia*, McGraw-Hill, Singapore, 2002, ch. 4.

Nankervis, A., Compton, R. and Baird, M., *Strategic Human Resource Management*, 4th edn, Thompson, Sydney, 2002, pp. 108–26.

Robbins, S. P., *Organizational Behavior*, 9th edn, Prentice Hall, Upper Saddle River, NJ, 2000, chs 13, 18.

Schermerhorn, J. R., Hunt, J. G. and Osborn, R. N., *Organizational Behavior*, 8th edn, John Wiley & Sons, New York, 2003, chs 2, 13, 19.

Ulrich, D., *Human Resource Champions*, Harvard Business School Press, Boston, 1997, chs 1, 6.

online references

aflcio.org
hri.eckerd.edu
mua.tcp.net.au
www.actu.asn.au
www.amwu.asn.au
www.cfmeu.asn.au
www.econ.usyd.edu.au/acirrt

www.fortune.com
www.fsunion.org.au
www.hbsp.harvard.edu
www.shrm.org.hrmagazine
www.wfs.org
www.workforceonline.com
www.workplaceinfo.com.au

end notes

1. B. Rajagopalan, R. Peterson and S. B. Watson, 'The rise of free agency: is it inevitable?', *Organizational Dynamics*, vol. 32, no. 1, 2003, p. 93.

2. R. Lansbury, 'Managing change in a challenging environment', in A. R. Nankervis and R. L. Compton, *Readings in Strategic Human Resources*, Nelson, South Melbourne, 1994, p. 135.

3. D. Peetz, quoted in M. Cave, 'Are we working too hard?', *Australian Financial Review*, 20–21 December 2003, p. 23.

4. Reported in K. Murphy, 'Workplace stress costs spiralling', *Australian Financial Review*, 20 October 1997, p. 7.

5. Bulletin Morgan poll, reported in 'Public pulse', *Bulletin*, 2 September 1997, p. 10; B. Rajagopalan, R. Peterson and S. B. Watson, op. cit., p. 93; and L. Yan, 'Employees working longer hours for no additional pay', *South China Morning Post*, 9 April 2004, p. 4.

6. B. Rajagopalan, R. Peterson and S. B. Watson, op. cit., p. 98.

7. R. Fralicx and D. McCauley, 'US workers feel pride in jobs, organizations, but don't trust managers', *Journal of Compensation and Benefits*, vol. 19, no. 3, 2003, p. 42.

8. D. E. Morgan and R. Zeffane, 'Employee involvement, organization change and trust in management', *International Journal of Human Resource Management*, vol. 14, no. 3, 2003, pp 55–75; E. M. Whitener, S. E. Brodt, M. A. Koorsgaard and J. M. Werner, 'Managers as initiators of trust: an exchange relationship framework for understanding managerial trustworthy behaviour', *Academy of Management Review*, vol. 23, 1998, pp. 513–30; and S. Albrecht and A. Travaglione, 'Trust in public sector management', *International Journal of Human Resource Management*, vol. 14, no. 1, 2003, p. 76.

9. S. Albrecht and A. Travaglione, op. cit., p. 88.

10. M. Brown and J. Benson, 'Related to exhaustion? Reactions to performance appraisal processes', *Industrial Relations Journal*, vol. 34, no. 1, 2003, pp. 67–81; and R. Zeffane and J. Connell, 'Trust and HRM in the new millennium', *International Journal of Human Resource Management*, vol. 14, no. 1, 2003, p. 4.

11. E. M. Whitener, 'Do "high commitment" human resource practices affect employee commitment? A cross-level analysis using hierarchical linear modelling', *Journal of Management*, vol. 27, no. 5, 2001, p. 515; and B. Blunsden and K. Reed, 'The effects of technical and social conditions on workplace trust', *International Journal of Human Resource Management*, vol. 14, no. 1, 2003, p. 12.

12. R. Zeffane and J. Connell, op. cit., p. 5.
13. R. C. O'Brien, *Trust*, John Wiley & Sons, Chichester, 2001, pp. 52–53; and J. Schermerhorn, J. G. Hunt and R. J. Osborn, *Organizational Behavior*, 8th edn, John Wiley & Sons, New York, 2003, p. 404.
14. R. Zeffane and J. Connell, op. cit., p. 5.
15. R. C. O'Brien, op. cit., p. xv.
16. D. Ulrich, *Human Resource Champions*, Harvard Business School Press, Boston, Mass., 1997, p. 151.
17. L. R. Gomez-Mejia, D. B. Balkin and R. L. Cardy, *Managing Human Resources*, Prentice Hall, Englewood Cliffs, NJ, 1995, pp. 59–60.
18. D. K. Denton, 'Nine ways to create an atmosphere for change', *HR Magazine*, October 1996, p. 76.
19. D. Stace and D. Dunphy, 'Beyond traditional paternalistic and developmental approaches in organisational change and human resource strategies', in A. R. Nankervis and R. L. Compton, op. cit., p. 95.
20. O. Lundy and A. Cowling, *Strategic Human Resource Management*, Routledge, London, 1996, p. 161; and B. Schneider, A. P. Brief and R. A. Guzzo, 'Creating a climate and culture for sustainable organizational change', *Organizational Dynamics*, vol. 24, no. 4, 1996, pp. 7–19.
21. C. R. Milton, *Human Behaviour in Organizations*, Prentice Hall, Englewood Cliffs, NJ, 1981, p. 372.
22. D. Stace and D. Dunphy, op. cit., p. 87; and R. A. Noe, *Employee Training and Development*, McGraw-Hill, Boston, 2000, pp. 345–9.
23. P. Strebel, 'Why do employees resist change?', *Harvard Business Review*, May–June 1996, p. 86; and S. L. McShane and M. A. Von Glinow, *Organizational Behavior*, McGraw-Hill, Boston, 2000, pp. 474–9.
24. E. Carew, 'Westpac's great escape', *Business Review Weekly*, 8 September 1997, p. 62.
25. J. O'Brien and M. O'Donnell, 'Creating a new moral order? Cultural change in the Australian Public Service', *Labour & Industry*, vol. 10, no. 3, 2000, pp. 56–76.
26. Quoted in G. Barker, 'Yes, Minister', *Australian Financial Review*, 10 October 2000, p. 49.
27. R. D. Iverson, 'Employee acceptance of organizational change: the rate of organizational commitment', *International Journal of Human Resource Management*, vol. 7, no. 1, 1996, pp. 122–49.
28. C. W. L. Hill and G. R. Jones, *Strategic Management Theory*, 2nd edn, Houghton Mifflin, Boston, 1992, p. 417.
29. B. Joss, quoted in J. Gray, 'Westpac needs cultural rebirth', *Australian Financial Review*, 26 September 1997, p. 46.
30. A. Ferguson, 'Ziggy's big call', *Business Review Weekly*, 8 September 2000, pp. 45–51.
31. C. W. L. Hill and G. R. Jones, op. cit., p. 417.
32. R. Zeffane, 'Dynamics of strategic change: critical issues in fostering positive organizational change', *Leadership and Organizational Development Journal*, vol. 17, no. 7, 1996, p. 40.
33. B. Joss, op. cit., p. 46.
34. D. Stace and D. Dunphy, op. cit., p. 91.
35. D. Stace and D. Dunphy, op. cit., p. 93.
36. D. Stace and D. Dunphy, op. cit., p. 93.
37. See K. Lewin, *Field Theory in Social Science*, Harper & Row, New York, 1951, pp. 228–9.
38. Based on and adapted from the Task, Structure, Technology, People change model developed by H. Leavitt. See H. Leavitt, 'Applied organizational change in industry: structural, technological and humanistic approaches', in J. March (ed.), *Handbook of Organizations*, Rand McNally, Chicago, 1965, p. 1145.
39. This section is based on material drawn from J. R. Gordon, R. W. Mondy, A. Sharplin and S. R. Premeaux, *Management and Organizational Behavior*, Allyn & Bacon, Boston, 1990, p. 637; and G. Moorhead and R. W. Griffin, *Organizational Behavior*, 4th edn, Houghton Mifflin, Boston, 1995, pp. 487–8.
40. J. R. Schermerhorn Jr, *Management and Organizational Behavior Essentials*, John Wiley & Sons, New York, 1996, p. 272.
41. S. L. McShane and M. A. Von Glinow, op. cit., p. 473.
42. S. L. McShane and M. A. Von Glinow, op. cit., p. 475.
43. D. Miller and J. R. Johnson, 'Antecedents to willingness to participate in a planned organizational change', *Journal of Applied Communication Research*, vol. 22, 1994, pp. 59–80; and ACIRRT, *Australia at Work*, Prentice Hall, Sydney, 1999, p. 54.
44. D. Hellriegel and J. W. Slocum Jr, *Management*, 6th edn, Addison Wesley, Reading, Mass., 1993, p. 726; and K. T. Dirks, L. L. Cummings and J. J. Pierce, 'Psychological ownership in organizations: conditions under which individuals promote and resist change', *Research in Organizational Change and Development*, vol. 9, 1996, pp. 1–23.
45. J. R. Gordon, R. W. Mondy, A. Sharplin and S. R. Premeaux, op. cit., p. 643.
46. S. L. McShane and M. A. Von Glinow, op. cit., p. 477.
47. S. L. McShane and M. A. Von Glinow, op. cit., p. 479.
48. J. R. Schermerhorn, J. G. Hunt and R. N. Osborn, op. cit., p. 23. See also M. Barad, 'Total Quality Management', in M. Poole and M. Warner (eds), *The Handbook of Human Resource Management*, Thomson, London, 1998, pp. 293–5.
49. S. Bright, 'Total quality management — the implications for personnel professionals', *Consulting Australia*, March 1992, p. 14.
50. Based on The Editors, 'How Asia's outstanding companies manage quality', *World Executive Digest*, June 1992, p. 19; P. Dawson, 'Rejecting magical prescriptions: a process approach to implementing TQM', *Q BIZ*, no. 1, 1995, pp. 4–5; S. Bright, op. cit., pp. 14–15; and R. Blackburn and B. Rosen, 'Does HRM walk the TQM talk?', *HR Magazine*, July 1995, pp. 69–72.
51. The Editors, op. cit., p. 19.
52. Reported in B. O'Riordan, 'Survey says customers unhappy with banks', *Australian Financial Review*, 9 October 1997, p. 27.
53. J. Gray, op. cit., p. 46.
54. A. S. Sohal, 'Success factors in implementing total quality management', *Management*, no. 4, May 1993, p. 6.
55. D. James, 'Keeping up with the norms? Australia has to be in it', *Business Review Weekly*, 8 May 1992, p. 65; and D. James, 'Business lacks commitment to total quality management', *Business Review Weekly*, 5 July 1991, pp. 66–70.

56. D. James, 'Bosses and workers against system', *Business Review Weekly*, 22 September 1997, p. 81.

57. M. Syrett, 'Questions of quality', *Asian Business*, March 1994, p. 38.

58. A. Sampson, 'Quality comes of age', *ABM*, May 1992, p. 126.

59. A. Brown, 'Quality management: issues for human resource management', *Asia Pacific Journal of Human Resources*, vol. 33, no. 3, 1995, pp. 121–2; and D. Cran, 'New program will demand big psychological shifts', *HR Monthly*, February 1997, p. 23.

60. S. S. K. Lam, 'Total quality management and its impact on middle managers and front line workers', *Journal of Management Development*, vol. 15, no. 7, 1996, pp. 37–46; S. P. Robbins, *Organizational Behavior*, 9th edn, Prentice Hall, Upper Saddle River, NJ, 2001, pp. 271–2; and S. L. McShane and M. A. Von Glinow, op. cit., pp. 318–24.

61. D. James, 1992, op. cit., p. 64.

62. D. Cran, op. cit., p. 22.

63. N. Vogel, quoted in A. Sampson, op. cit., p. 126.

64. D. James, 'Rugged individual glory in our culture of resistance', *Business Review Weekly*, 23 October 1995, pp. 142–3; and D. James, 1992, op. cit., p. 64.

65. J. Spouster, quoted in J. Connolly, 'Keys to a world of difference', *Bulletin*, 10 December 1996, p. 52.

66. J. Byrne, 'Management theory — or fad of the month?', *Business Week*, 23 June 1997, p. 37; and A. Gome, 'Quality movement gets a critical report', *Business Review Weekly*, 19 May 1997, pp. 30–1.

67. P. Dawson, op. cit., p. 4.

68. R. Blackburn and B. Rosen, op. cit., p. 72.

69. J. Kavanagh, 'On the prowl . . .', *Business Review Weekly*, 21 July 2000, pp. 76–8.

70. S. Long, 'MUA, CFMEU plan merger', *Australian Financial Review*, 8 November 2000, p. 8.

71. M. J. Mandel, C. Farrell and C. Yang, 'Land of the giants', *Business Week*, 11 September 1995, p. 26; and B. Dunstan, 'Search for critical mass drives merger mania', *Australian Financial Review*, 23 October 1997, p. 16.

72. S. Negaunee, quoted in M. J. Mandel, C. Farrell and C. Yang, op. cit., p. 26.

73. M. Lawson, 'Unwritten rules for mergers', *Australian Financial Review — Special Report*, 3 April 2003, p. 3; J. Shapiro, 'Telstra crunch', *BRW*, 15–21 May 2003, p. 36; and S. Mitchell, 'Roger Corbett's other big W', *Boss*, October 2003, pp. 48–52.

74. A. Kohler, 'Mega-mergers: the race to get big', *Australian Financial Review*, 25–26 October 1997, p. 25; and M. Lawson, 'Culture clashes main blight on M & As', *Australian Financial Review*, 16 November 1998, p. 23.

75. *New York Times*, 'Battle to bridge culture gap', *South China Morning Post — Business*, 31 January 2000, p. 4.

76. J. S. Sturges, 'A method for merger madness', *Personnel Journal*, March 1989, p. 60; O. Lundy and A. Cowling, op. cit., p. 334; and K. Marshall, 'Mergers too often overlook the workforce', *Australian Financial Review*, 1 October 1999, p. 69.

77. *The Economist*, 'The marrying kind', *Australian*, 10 January 1997, p. 30.

78. P. Pritchett, *Making Mergers Work*, Dow Jones/Irwin, Homewood, Ill., 1987, p. 4.

79. *The Economist*, op. cit., p. 30.

80. M. L. Marks, 'Merger management HR's way', *HR Magazine*, May 1991, p. 61.

81. *The Economist*, op. cit., p. 30.

82. L. Empson, 'Extended review: human resource management implications of mergers and acquisitions', *International Journal of Human Resource Management*, vol. 5, no. 3, 1994, p. 781.

83. M. L. Marks, 'Let's make a deal', *HR Magazine*, April 1997, pp. 125–31.

84. *The Economist*, op. cit., p. 30; and P. Pritchett, op. cit., p. 4.

85. *The Economist*, op. cit., p. 30.

86. Study by R. E. Lamalie, cited in P. Pritchett, op. cit., p. 4.

87. Cited in B. Potter, 'Happy staff key to merry mergers', *Australian Financial Review*, 24 September 1986, p. 30.

88. P. Pritchett, op. cit., p. 11.

89. J. S. Sturges, op. cit., p. 69.

90. See V. A. Mabert and R. W. Schmenner, 'Assessing the roller coaster of downsizing', *Business Horizons*, vol. 40, no. 4, 1997, pp. 45–53; and K. Camercon, 'Downsizing', in M. Poole and M. Warner (eds), *The Handbook of Human Resource Management*, Thomson, London, 1998, pp. 55–7.

91. L. R. Gomez-Mejia, D. B. Balkin and R. L. Cardy, op. cit., p. 17; and G. Koretz, 'Big payoffs from layoffs', *Business Week*, 24 February 1997, p. 10.

92. I. M. Kunii, 'Hi tech roars again', *Business Week*, 13 November 2000, pp. 24–5.

93. P. Coy, 'Lean may not be so mean', *Business Week*, 8 September 1997, p. 10.

94. T. Beck, quoted in 'Infighting rocks key bank union', *Australian Financial Review*, 15 October 1997, p. 36.

95. M. Davis, 'AMWU in radical cost cutting plan', *Australian Financial Review*, 8 July 1997, p. 7.

96. J. McFarlane, quoted in J. Kirby, 'Cost controller roaring to go at ANZ Bank', *Business Review Weekly*, 6 October 1997, p. 34; J. M. Ivancevich, *Human Resource Management*, 8th edn, McGraw-Hill, Boston, 2001, p. 451; and S. Dibble, *Keeping Your Valuable Employees*, John Wiley & Sons, New York, 1999, p. 12.

97. Reported in G. Koretz, 'An update on downsizing and how it is paying off', *Business Week*, 25 November 1996, p. 14.

98. Survey by C. Littler and R. Dunford, reported in K. Murphy, 'Downsizing . . . little by Litter', *Australian Financial Review*, 20 September 1996, p. 2.

99. D. James, 'Forget downsizing, now it's participative design', *Business Review Weekly*, 25 November 1996, p. 70.

100. A. Markels and M. Murray, 'Call it downsizing: why firms regret cost cutting', *Asian Wall Street Journal*, 15 May 1996, p. 1.

101. A. Markels and M. Murray, op. cit., p. 1.

102. A. Kohler, 'Telstra: why it may be riskier', *Australian Financial Review*, 6–7 September 1997, p. 28.

103. J. S. Lublin, 'Spin off wave leaves fewer jobs in wake', *Asian Wall Street Journal*, 22 November 1995, p. 7; and M. Bryan, 'The sack dot com style: do it by email', *Australian Financial Review*, 12–16 April 2001, p. 49.

104. M. Priest, 'More companies face payouts', *Australian Financial Review*, 24 September 2003, p. 7.

105. A. Thornhill, M. N. K. Saunders and J. Stead, 'Managing the survivors of change', *Strategic Change*, vol. 5, 1996, pp. 323–30; and ACIRRT, op. cit., pp. 147–55.

106. L. Thornburg, 'Practical ways to cope with suicide', *HR Magazine*, May 1992, p. 62.

107. H. M. O'Neill and D. J. Lenn, 'Voices of survivors: words that downsizing CEOs should hear', *Academy of Management Executive*, vol. 9, no. 4, 1995, p. 23.

108. J. Purcell and S. Hutchinson, 'Lean and mean?', *People Management*, 10 October 1996, p. 29; and G. Ebadan and D. Winstanley, 'Downsizing, delayering and careers — the survivor's perspective', *Human Resource Management Journal*, vol. 7, no. 1, 1997, p. 88.

109. M. K. De Vries and K. Balazs, 'The human side of downsizing', *European Management Journal*, vol. 14, no. 2, 1996, p. 111.

110. M. K. De Vries and K. Balazs, op. cit., p. 112.

111. N. J. Mathys and E. H. Burack, 'Strategic downsizing: human resource planning approaches', *Human Resource Planning*, vol. 16, no. 1, 1993, p. 71; D. Hellriegel and J. W. Slocum Jr, *Management*, 6th edn, Addison Wesley, Reading, Mass., 1993, p. 718; E. McShulskis, 'Job tenures shift for men and women', *HR Magazine*, May 1997, p. 20; C. Hendry and R. Jenkins, 'Psychological contracts and new deals', *Human Resource Management Journal*, vol. 7, no. 1, 1997, pp. 38–44; J. M. Hiltrop, 'Managing the changing psychological contract', *Employee Relations*, vol. 18, no. 1, 1996, pp. 36–49; and E. W. Monson and S. L. Robinson, 'Why employees feel betrayed: a model of how psychological contract violation develops', *Academy of Management Review*, vol. 22, no. 1, 1997, pp. 226–56.

112. D. Hellriegel and J. W. Slocum Jr, op. cit., p. 719.

113. D. Bencivenga, 'Employers and workers come to terms', *HR Magazine*, June 1997, pp. 91–7.

114. C. Littler, 'Cut once to keep morale high', *Australian Financial Review*, 11 June 1996, p. 27.

115. J. Purcell and S. Hutchinson, op. cit., p. 27.

116. A. Dunlap, quoted in T. Sykes, 'The world according to Al', *Australian Financial Review — Weekend Review*, 15 November 1996, p. 3.

117. A. Merryman, 'Managing the pain and the gain', *HR Focus*, December 1995, p. 22.

118. Based on A. Merryman, op. cit., pp. 22–3.

119. M. K. De Vries and K. Balazs, op. cit., p. 120.

120. M. K. De Vries and K. Balazs, op. cit., p. 120.

121. G. D. Bruton, J. K. Keels and C. L. Shook, 'Downsizing the firm: answering the strategic questions', *Academy of Management Executive*, vol. 10, no. 2, 1996, pp. 38–45; and C. R. Littler, R. Dunford, T. Bramble and A. Hede, 'The dynamics of downsizing', *Journal of Human Resources*, vol. 35, no. 1, 1997, pp. 65–79.

122. Knight Ridder, '"Chainsaw" Al Dunlap in Sunbeam work force massacre', *Australian*, 14 November 1996, p. 23; J. Stewart, 'Cutting power to the people at any cost', *Business Review Weekly*, 24 March 1997, p. 70; and L. Lavelle, 'Corporate liposuction can have nasty side effects', *Business Week*, 17 July 2000, pp. 62–3.

123. Foster's Group, *Annual Report*, Melbourne, 2003, p. 26; Leighton Holdings, *Annual Report*, Sydney, 2003, p. 10; and Tabcorp, *Annual Report*, Melbourne, 2003, p. 10.

124. See T. Sykes, 'Killed by its own culture', *Australian Financial Review*, 6 September 2000, p. 34.

125. A. Cornell, 'Rio Tinto versus BHP: and the winner is . . .', *Australian Financial Review*, 25–26 October 1997, pp. 30–1.

126. S. Long, 'All's fair in love and war — the new IR battlefield', *Australian Financial Review*, 16–17 October 1999, p. 30.

127. S. Knitt, 'Improved resources', *HR Monthly*, April 2003, pp. 42–3.

128. P. Klinger, 'Power plays in Perth', *Australian Financial Review*, 9 August 2003, p. 73; and M. Skulley, 'Union chief "threatened managers"', *Australian Financial Review*, 28 October 2003, p. 9.

129. M. Davis and S. Lewis, 'Telstra unions draw their lines', *Australian Financial Review*, 18 July 1997, p. 4.

130. Editorial, 'Time to follow Grocon's lead', *Australian Financial Review*, 5 December 2002, p. 62.

131. A. McCathie, 'Defiant unions are struggling', *Australian Financial Review*, 24 October 2003, p. 28.

132. K. Towers, 'Victorian government pressured by CFMEU', *Australian Financial Review*, 14 May 2003, p. 3; and M. Priest, 'Unions take on NSW', *Australian Financial Review*, 2 October 2003, p. 7.

133. M. Priest, 'Post shops to be franchised', *Australian Financial Review*, 17 November 2003, p. 3.

134. T. E. McCarthy, 'Management's role in improving industrial relations', *Management Review*, vol. 12, no. 7, 1987, p. 2.

135. S. Lewis, 'Unions face hard line stance', *Australian Financial Review*, 12 June 1997, p. 33.

136. J. Earle, 'Producers head for hard yakka at coalface', *Australian*, 7 October 1996, p. 19.

137. Study by Tasman Asia Pacific, reported in M. Davis, 'Open-cut coal mines "below best practice"', *Australian Financial Review*, 23 October 1997, p. 6.

138. D. Davies, 'The role of employment relations in line management', *Management*, July 1994, p. 23; Centre for Corporate Change, 'The supervisor as change agent', *Catalyst*, no. 5, October 1992, p. 1; and P. Saul, 'Managers in the firing line', *Management*, November 1994, pp. 5–8.

139. R. Iverson and D. Buttigieg, 'Union commitment within work groups: the effect of non-union co-workers and supervisors', in

R. Fells and T. Todd (eds), *Current Research in Industrial Relations*, Proceedings of the 10th AIRAANZ Conference, Wollongong, February 1996, p. 226.

140. C. L. Hughes, *Making Unions Unnecessary*, Executive Enterprises, New York, 1976, p. 1.

141. T. Bull, quoted in M. Priest, 'Union elders mourn Bull', *Australian Financial Review*, 17 June 2003, p. 61.

142. D. Crowe and R. Lebihan, 'Unions put the byte on IT sector', *Australian Financial Review*, 19 November 2002, pp. 1, 61.

143. G. Griffin, 'White-collar unionism 1969 to 1981: some determinants of growth', *The Journal of Industrial Relations*, vol. 25, no. 1, March 1983, p. 35.

144. D. W. Rawson, *Unions and Unionists in Australia*, George Allen & Unwin, Sydney, 1978, p. 39.

145. P. Berry and G. Kitchener, *Can Unions Survive?*, BWIU, Canberra, 1989, p. 37; N. Way, 'Bottomline signals tough times ahead for PS unions', *Business Review Weekly*, 24 March 1997, p. 96; and K. Gough, 'Unions win right to take fees from pay', *Australian*, 2 May 2002, p. 2.

146. G. Polites, quoted in P. Stephens, 'Commission decision is a product of the times', *Age*, 7 August 1984, p. 18.

147. R. J. Stone, 'Industrial relations — a case of management failure?', *Human Resource Management Australia*, vol. 25, no. 3, 1987, p. 77.

148. J. Niland and D. Turner, 'Control, consensus or chaos?', in *Managers and Industrial Relations Reform*, Allen & Unwin, Sydney, 1985, p. 174.

149. A. Mitchell, 'Path of reform winds on', *Australian Financial Review*, 13 August 2003, p. 54; M. Skulley and T. O'Loughlin, 'Crackdown on rogue building unions', *Australian Financial Review*, 27 March 2003, pp. 1, 48; G. Lekakis and M. Skulley, 'How unions climbed into the drivers seat', *Australian Financial Review*, 3 July 2003, pp. 60–1; and N. Way, 'Across the tracks', *BRW*, 4–10 December 2003, p. 29.

150. L. Young and K. Daniel, 'Affectual trust in the workplace', *International Journal of Human Resource Management*, vol. 14, no. 1, 2003, p. 147.

151. R. M. Spillane, 'Attitudes of business executives and union leaders to industrial relations', reported in J. D. Hill, W. A. Howard and R. D. Lansbury, *Industrial Relations: An Australian Introduction*, Longman Cheshire, Melbourne, 1982, pp. 120–1.

152. R. Stagner and H. Rosen, *The Psychology for Union–Management Relations*, Tavistock, London, 1968, p. 9.

153. B. Blunsden and K. Reed, 'The effects of technical and social conditions on workplace trust', *International Journal of Human Resource Management*, vol. 14, no. 1, 2003, pp. 12–27; and L. Young and K. Daniel, op. cit., pp. 139–55.

154. J. D. Cameron, 'Aspects of management prerogative — sacred cows?', paper presented at the 18th Convention, Industrial Relations Society of Victoria, 20 October 1984, pp. 6–7.

155. S. Long, 'ACTU fights for casual staff's rights', *Australian Financial Review*, 27 October 2000, p. 17.

156. D. Crowe, 'Dispute sends Deloitte staff scurrying for a union', *Australian Financial Review*, 21 November 2002, p. 24.

157. K. Gough, 'Work freeze puts the heat on Qantas', *Australian*, 3 July 2002, p. 4.

158. AP, '$2900 pay cut for putting photo of friends on office desk', *Straits Times*, 16 July 2002, p. 13.

159. M. Priest, 'Bosses strike a blow for solidarity of the workers', *Australian Financial Review*, 9 September 2003, p. 5.

160. B. Shorten, quoted in M. Priest, September 2003, op. cit., p. 5.

161. J. A. Fossum, 'Strategic issues in labour relations', in C. Fombrun, N. M. Tichy and M. A. Devanna, *Strategic Human Resource Management*, John Wiley & Sons, New York, 1984, p. 353.

162. Reported in R. L. Mathis and J. M. Jackson, *Personnel*, 3rd edn, West, St Paul, 1982, pp. 485–7.

163. W. C. Hamer and F. Smith, 'Work attitudes as predictors of unionisation activity', *Journal of Applied Psychology*, vol. 63, no. 4, 1978, pp. 415–521; J. Cooper and J. Hartley, 'Reconsidering the case for organisational commitment', *Human Resource Management Journal*, vol. 1, no. 3, 1991, pp. 18–23; and D. E. Morgan and R. Zeffane, 'Employee involvement, organizational change and trust in management', vol. 14, no. 1, 2003, pp. 55–75.

164. S. Deery, P. Erwin and R. Iverson, 'Predicting organisational and union commitment: the effect of industrial relations climate', *British Journal of Industrial Relations*, vol. 32, no. 4, 1994, pp. 581–97.

165. S. Bearfield, 'Australian employees' attitudes towards unions', Working Paper 82, ACIRRT, University of Sydney, March 2003, pp. 1, 11.

166. J. Coopey and J. Hartley, 'Reconsidering the case for organisational commitment', *Human Resource Management Journal*, vol. 1, no. 3, 1991, pp. 18–33; and P. Pfeffer, 'Putting people first for organizational success', *Academy of Management Executive*, vol. 13, no. 2, 1999, pp. 37–48.

167. T. J. Peters and R. H. Waterman, *In Search of Excellence*, Harper & Row, New York, 1982, p. 236.

168. D. E. Morgan and R. Zeffane, 'Employee involvement, organizational change and trust in management', *International Journal of Human Resource Management*, vol. 14, no. 1, 2003, p. 69.

169. T. J. Peters and R. H. Waterman, op. cit., p. 277.

170. C. Bongarzoni and R. Compton, 'The impact of the macro industrial relations system on relations at the enterprise level', in R. Blandy and J. Niland (eds), *Alternatives to Arbitration*, Allen & Unwin, Sydney, 1986, p. 128.

171. R. Lansbury, in A. R. Nankervis and R. L. Compton, op. cit., pp. 139–40; J. Pfeffer, op. cit., pp. 37–48; and J. Gould-Williams, 'The importance of HR practices and workplace trust in achieving superior performance: a study of public sector organizations', *International Journal of Human Resource Management*, vol. 14, no. 1, 2003, pp. 28–54.

172. S. A. Albrecht and A. Travaglione, op. cit., pp. 76–92.

173. Survey conducted by Kelly Services, reported in AAP, 'Workers distrust bosses', *Australian Financial Review*, 24 September 2003, p. 6.

174. DDI Asia Pacific survey, reported in M. Lawson, 'Most workers don't trust leaders: survey', *Australian Financial Review*, 4 July 1997, p. 20.

175. Enterprising Nation, *Report of the Industry Task Force on Leadership and Management Skills*, AGPS, Canberra, 1995, p. 25.

176. B. Brookes, *Why Unions?*, CCH, Sydney, 1980, p. 60.

177. K. Stone, quoted in P. Coombes and F. Lucato, 'It's fingers out time folks', *Rydges*, May 1985, p. 19.

178. Research commissioned by the NSW Labor Council, reported in M. Davis, 'Unions losing ground in their heartland, poll finds', *Australian Financial Review*, 1 September 1997, p. 4.

179. J. P. Swann, 'Formal grievance procedures in non-union plants', *Personnel Administrator*, vol. 26, no. 8, 1981, p. 67.

180. Reported in M. Davis, S. Long and K. Murphy, 'Survey uncovers major changes', *Australian Financial Review*, 29 August 1997, p. 8.

181. J. Paterson, 'The management of change and its implications for the personnel function', *IPMA Bulletin*, February 1985, p. 7.

182. R. C. Mayer and J. H. Davis, 'The effects of the performance appraisal system on trust for management: a field quasi experiment', *Journal of Applied Psychology*, vol. 84, 1999, pp. 123–36; and S. Albrecht and A. Travaglione, op. cit., pp. 76–92.

183. North Limited, *1997 Annual Report*, Melbourne, 1997, p. 2.

184. P. H. Mirvis, 'Human resource management: leaders, laggards and followers', *Academy of Management Executive*, vol. 11, no. 2, 1997, pp. 54–5.

185. R. Singh, 'Human resource management: a sceptical look', in B. Towers (ed.), *The Handbook of Human Resource Management*, Blackwell, Oxford, 1992, p. 140.

186. S. Albrecht and A. Travaglione, op. cit., p. 79.

187. P. Wilson, quoted in A. Kohler, 'Reith's Rambos of industrial reform', *Business Review Weekly*, 10 March 1997, p. 22.

188. R. Callus, A. Morehead, M. Cully and J. Buchanan, *Industrial Relations at Work*, Commonwealth Department of Industrial Relations, AGPS, Canberra, 1991, p. 136.

189. A. Wood, 'Brave bid for a better future', *Australian*, 6 May 1997, p. 5.

190. L. Murray, 'AMP's unsentimental bloke', *Australian Financial Review*, 23–24 November 2002, p. 12.

191. A. R. Dunford and I. Palmer, 'Managing for high performance? People management practices in Flight Centre', *Journal of Industrial Relations*, vol. 44, no. 3, 2002, p. 391.

192. J. Pfeffer, op. cit., pp. 37–48.

193. J. Pfeffer, op. cit., pp. 32–48.

194. For a detailed account of how Rio Tinto introduced salaried operations, see J. T. Ludeke, *The Line in the Sand: The Long Road to Staff Employment in Comalco*, Wilkinson Books, Melbourne, 1996.

195. I. Ng and D. Maki, 'Trade union influence on human resource practices', *Industrial Relations*, vol. 33, no. 1, 1994, pp. 121–35.

196. T. Treadgold, 'Robe River echoes in Rio Tinto dispute', *Business Review Weekly*, 29 September 1997, p. 32.

197. L. R. Gomez-Mejia, P. B. Balkin and R. L. Cardy, op. cit., p. 541.

198. S. Deery, 'Industrial relations', in G. L. O'Neill and R. Kramar, *Australian Human Resources Management*, Pitman, Melbourne, 1995, pp. 73–4; and ACIRRT, op. cit., p. 7.

199. E. Vaughn, 'The romance and theatre of managing together', in E. M. Davis and R. D. Lansbury, *Managing Together*, Longman, Melbourne, 1996, p. 25.

200. S. Deery, 'The demise of the trade union as a representative body?', *British Journal of Industrial Relations*, 1995, pp. 537–43; M. Wooden, 'Are Australian trade unions good for productivity?', *Asia Pacific Human Resource Management*, vol. 28, no. 2, 1990, pp. 81–6; and M. Quinlan, 'The reform of Australian industrial relations: contemporary trends and issues', *Asia Pacific Journal of Human Resources*, vol. 34, no. 2, 1996, pp. 3–21.

201. J. Gould-Williams, op. cit., pp. 28–54; G. A. Gelade and M. Ivery, 'The impact of human resource management on organizational performance', *Personnel Psychology*, vol. 56, no. 2, 2003, pp. 383–404; I. Bjorkman and X. Fan, 'Human resource management and the performance of western firms in China', *International Journal of Human Resource Management*, vol. 13, no. 6, 2002, pp. 853–64; and A. K. Paul and R. N. Anantharaman, 'Business strategy, HRM practices and organizational performance: a study of the Indian software industry', *Journal of Transnational Management Development*, vol. 7, no. 3, 2002, pp. 27–51.

202. K. Legge, *Human Resource Management*, Macmillan, London, 1995, p. 331; and S. Deery, D. Plowman and J. Walsh, *Industrial Relations: A Contemporary Analysis*, McGraw-Hill, Sydney, 1997, p. 2.14.

203. Reported in S. Long, 'Staff turnover high in non-union workplaces', *Australian Financial Review*, 14 January 1999, p. 6.

204. N. Way, 'Labor pains', *Business Review Weekly*, 17 March 2000, pp. 74–80.

205. N. Wingfield and Y. J. Reazen, 'Unions find mixed blessings at troubled online business', *Asian Wall Street Journal — Networking*, 3 January 2001, p. N8; and D. Crowe and R. Lebihan, op. cit., pp. 1, 61.

206. Based on J. Thomson, 'Konichiwa mate', *Business Review Weekly*, 21–27 August 2003, pp 26–8.

207. D. E. Guest, 'Human resource management, trade unions and industrial relations', in J. Storey, *Human Resource Management: A Critical Text*, Routledge, London, 1995, p. 134.

208. P. Stuart, 'Labor unions become business partners', *Personnel Journal*, vol. 72, no. 8, 1993, p. 56.

209. D. E. Guest, op. cit., p. 134.

210. N. Bacon and J. Storey, 'Individualism and collectivism and the changing role of trade unions', in P. Ackers, C. Smith and P. Smith (eds), *The New Workplace and Trade Unionism*, Routledge, London, 1996, pp. 54–5.

211. N. Bacon and J. Storey, op. cit., pp. 63–4.

212. J. Kelly, 'Union militancy and social partnership', in P. Ackers, C. Smith and P. Smith (eds), op. cit., pp. 77–109.

213. I. MacLoughlin, 'Inside the non-union firm', in P. Ackers, C. Smith and P. Smith (eds), op. cit., p. 303.

214. S. Aryee and Y. Debra, 'Members' participation in the union: an investigation of some determinants in Singapore', *Human Relations*, vol. 50, no. 2, 1997, pp. 129–47.

215. D. Peetz, 'Deunionisation and union establishment: the impact of workplace change, HRM strategies and workplace unionism', *Labour and Industry*, vol. 8, no. 1, 1997, pp. 21–36.

216. J. Kelly and C. Kelly, '"Them and us": social psychology and "the new industrial relations"', *British Journal of Industrial Relations*, vol. 29, no. 1, 1991, pp. 25–48.

217. S. Kerr and M. A. Von Glinow, 'The future of human resources: plus ça change, plus c'est la meme chose', in D. Ulrich, M. R. Lasey and G. Lake (eds), *Tomorrow's HR Management*, John Wiley & Sons, New York, 1997, p. 179.

218. T. Treadgold, op. cit., pp. 32–3. Also see M. Skulley, 'Victorian liberals attack unions over disruptions', *Australian Financial Review*, 18 April 2002, p. 9.

219. AAP, 'Grocon worker walk out', *Australian Financial Review*, 5 December 2003, p. 4.

220. B. Sandilands, 'Qantas baby flies into cloud', *Australian Financial Review*, 6–7 December 2003, p. 12; and T. Harcourt and M. Priest, 'Jetstar puts Qantas on collision course with unions', *Australian Financial Review*, 5 December 2003, p. 56.

221. S. Long, 'Union offer to CRA to end Vikery Strike', *Australian Financial Review*, 26 July 1996, p. 5.

222. C. Lockyer, 'Pay, performance and reward', in B. Towers (ed.), *The Handbook of Human Resource Management*, Blackwell, Oxford, 1992, p. 248.

223. R. Iverson and D. Buttigieg, 'Union commitment within workgroups: the effect of non union coworkers and supervisors', in R. Fells and T. Todd (eds), *Current Research in Industrial Relations*, Proceedings of the 10th AIRAANZ Conference, Wellington, February 1996, p. 235.

224. T. Treadgold, op. cit., p. 33.

225. J. Stensholt, 'Grocon's redeveloper', *BRW*, 2–8 October 2003, p. 28.

226. S. Deery, D. Plowman, J. Walsh, p. 2.13.

227. A. Kohler, March 1997, op. cit., p. 22.

228. M. Davis, 'Telstra seeks union consent to break with heavy award legacy', *Australian Financial Review*, 21 July 1997, p. 5.

229. M. Davis, March 1997, op. cit., p. 9; M. Davis, 'Government fights union preferences in enterprise deals', *Australian Financial Review*, 3 June 1997, p. 5; and S. Wood, 'A wreath for Reith: we'll miss you', *Australian Financial Review*, 26 March 2001, p. 31.

230. S. Long and M. Davis, 'CBA plans to offer individual contracts', *Australian Financial Review*, 22 July 1997, p. 35; and N. Way,

'Collision course', *Business Review Weekly*, 20 October 2000, pp. 36–9.

231. S. Long, 'Coal and Allied offers $170 weekly pay rise', *Australian Financial Review*, 18 July 1997, p. 5; and S. Bagwell, 'Flexibility is the issue: BHP boss', *Australian Financial Review*, 31 January 2000, p. 3.

232. N. Way, 'BHP mettle on test at the Pilbara', *Business Review Weekly*, 14 January 2000, pp. 24–6.

233. T. Cook, 'IR blueprint recreates the way we work', *Australian*, 24 May 1996, p. 15.

234. N. Way, 14 January 2000, op. cit., p. 26; G. Combet, quoted in N. Way, 'BHP's new challenge, a divided work force', *Business Review Weekly*, 18 February 2000, p. 35; and N. Way, 'BHP and unions dig in for a stoush', *Business Review Weekly*, 6 April 2001, p. 47.

235. K. Barrymore and B. Foley, 'Grollo hits out at union tactics', *Australian Financial Review*, 13 November 2003, p. 57.

236. Survey conducted by Kelly Services, reported in AAP, 24 September 2003, op. cit., p. 6.

237. N. Way, 'Call still waiting', *Shares*, May 2003, p. 37.

238. See K. Murphy, 'Sharp says bosses gone to water', *Australian Financial Review*, 22 September 1997, p. 4; and T. Boreham, 'Industry guarded about anti-union action', *Australian*, 17 November 1995, p. 23.

239. Editorial, 'Lawless industry needs tough bill', *Australian Financial Review*, 19 September 2003, p. 74; M. McLachlan, 'Stop harassment, court warns', *Australian Financial Review*, 29 October 2003, p. 9; and M. Skulley, 'Union official found guilty', *Australian Financial Review*, 4 November 2003, p. 5.

240. G. Carter quoted in K. Towers, 'Union "enforcer" tells of threats', *Australian Financial Review*, 22 February 2002, p. 5.

241. R. Gottliebsen, 'How to counter the wages push', *Business Review Weekly*, 18 November 1997, p. 6.

242. G. Richardson, 'No winners in the final battle of the class war', *Bulletin*, 30 September 1997, p. 37.

243. M. Westfield, 'Corrigan rails against old ways', *Australian*, 22 October 2003, pp. 39–40; and J. Steinsholt, 'Grocon's redeveloper', *BRW*, 2–8 October 2003, pp. 28–30.

244. G. J. Bamber, 'Industrial relations and organisational change: is human resource management strategic in Australia?', in B. Towers (ed.), *The Handbook of Human Resource Management*, Blackwell, Oxford, 1992, p. 89; and N. Way, 'Across the tracks', *BRW*, 4–10 December 2003, p. 29.

245. J. Gray and K. Murphy, 'NAB bowed to FSO demands, says unhappy Reith', *Australian Financial Review*, 7 October 1997, p. 3.

246. P. Sams, quoted in S. Long, 'Unions invoke constitution', *Australian Financial Review*, 5 June 1996, p. 3.

247. R. Gottliebsen, 'A defining moment in our history', *Business Review Weekly*, 27 May 1996, p. 6.

chapter 17

negotiating in the workplace

Learning objectives

When you have finished studying this chapter, you should be able to:

- Understand the importance of trust and ethics in negotiation
- Identify the components of the negotiation planning hierarchy
- Explain the range of negotiation strategies and tactics
- Understand the significance of power, time and information in negotiation
- Describe the key stages in the negotiation process
- Appreciate the importance of thorough preparation to success in negotiation.

'Today's collective bargaining sessions have no place for the uninformed, the inept, or the unskilled.'[1]

A. A. Sloane and F. Witney

Negotiation in industrial relations involves of management (or its representatives) and workers **bargaining** over items such as wages, penalty rates, hours of work and conditions of employment (see figure 17.1). It is fundamental to union–management relations and a key activity for many HR managers.[2]

Negotiation The process by which one party (for example, a union) seeks to get something it wants (for example, a pay increase) from another party (for example, an employer) through persuasion.

Bargaining Another term for negotiation.

Casual work	Part-time work	Sick leave
Disciplinary procedures	Penalty rates:	Special allowances such as:
First aid	• overtime	• dirt
Grievance procedure	• shift work	• noise
Holidays	• holiday work	• height
Hours of work	Piece rates	• wet weather
Job classifications	Probationary period	• cold
Job posting procedures	Profit sharing	Superannuation
Junior rates	Provision of protective	Suspension
Jury duty	clothing and footwear	Termination
Management rights	Rest periods	Time off
Maternity leave	Retirement age	Union bulletin board
Medical examination	Right of entry	Union deductions
Mixed functions	Safety	Union preference
National wage increases	Seniority	Wage rates
No-strike clause	Severance pay	

Figure 17.1 Examples of items bargained over by unions and management

An important characteristic of **collective bargaining** is that the employer–employee relationship is ongoing. The industrial relations system and conservative management moreover 'guarantees' a union presence in most large Australian organisations. HR managers, as a result, must deal with union officials on a range of employee relations issues (see figure 17.1).

Unfortunately, such a prospect can create considerable anxiety and motivate HR managers to delegate their negotiation responsibilities to industrial relations lawyers or employer association representatives.[3] Such external troubleshooters, however, may not have the necessary familiarity with the company and its industrial relations history, and may be more intent on pushing the goals of the employer association than the interests of the individual employer.

Furthermore, the use of such outside consultants reduces the status of the HR manager in the eyes of employees, union officials and company management. Because the HR manager does not accept direct responsibility for the conduct of negotiation, the HR function is perceived as weak and the HR manager as not having the ability, authority or confidence of top management.[4]

Competitive pressures have forced negotiators to seek greater productivity and more labour flexibility through workplace reform. Consequently, the Australian industrial relations system is becoming increasingly decentralised as the focus shifts from centralised tribunals to the local workplace. Decisions imposed on the parties to a dispute by a centralised industrial tribunal are less likely to gain acceptance or to overcome resistance to change in the workplace. In contrast, 'negotiated settlements', claim Hudson and Hawkins, 'can achieve outcomes that result not only in the parties becoming committed to change but also in all parties actively wanting to work together and be involved in implementing the agreed change'.[5] 'This joint ownership', say Hudson and Hawkins, 'may well create synergistic outcomes beyond the expectations of either party.' Finally, **enterprise bargaining** appears to

Collective bargaining The process through which representatives of management and the union meet to negotiate a labour agreement.

Enterprise bargaining Direct negotiation that takes place between an employer or enterprise and its employees and/or their nominated representatives.

achieve a better fit between subject topics and employee concerns. For example, in workplaces with large proportions of female workers, negotiated agreements are more likely to include matters such as childcare, family leave, and health and safety.[6] In an era of increasing employee participation, enterprise bargaining and corporate restructuring, negotiating competence has become an even more critical skill for the HR manager and the individual employee (see figures 17.2 and 17.3).

TYPES OF EMPLOYEE–EMPLOYER NEGOTIATIONS

Consent awards

Union(s) and the employer negotiate directly to reach agreement *within parameters* (20 allowable matters) established by the Australian Industrial Relations Commission (AIRC). The AIRC is notified and, if the negotiated agreement satisfies its requirements, it is registered. Such consent awards possess the same legal and industrial standing as an award arbitrated by the Commission.

Certified Agreements

Union(s) and the employer negotiate directly about *all matters* involved in the employment relationship. Certified Agreements encompass over-award pay and conditions, which are incorporated into the award rate (that is, over-award pay and conditions become the new legal minimum). Such arrangements are also called paid rates awards. Certified Agreements must be approved by the AIRC to be legally enforceable.

Collective bargaining

In the purest form of collective bargaining, all aspects of the employer–employee relationship are subject to negotiation between the employer and the unions.

Enterprise bargaining

Decentralised bargaining conducted at the workplace. All aspects of the employer–employee relationship are subject to negotiation. Negotiations may be between the employer and all employees or groups of employees. Third parties such as unions and independent facilitators may or may not be involved.

Individual bargaining

Individual employment contracts negotiated by an employee and their employer (and approved by the Employment Advocate and/or the AIRC). Called Australian Workplace Agreements, they take the place of awards.

Figure 17.2 Types of employee–employer negotiations

Trust in negotiation

Key questions for HR managers (and union officials) are: How much should I trust the other side? When should I trust them? Are they going to provide misleading information or misrepresent their position? Will they tell the truth? How do I make them trust me? Will they honour the agreement?

Trust is central to the negotiating relationship because it is the basis for effective cooperation. Trust is a measure of the extent to which negotiators believe the other party will honour their promises, respect limits, obey norms and protect their interests.[7] Research suggests that trust in the context of negotiation is based on a cooperative orientation, predictable behaviour and a negotiator holding a problem-solving perspective.[8]

In reality, incentives and pressures force management and union negotiators to mislead, lie and cheat.[9] As a result, without an element of trust, a successful negotiation is unlikely. Trust makes it easier (and safer) for negotiators to cooperate, share information and engage in joint problem solving.[10] The higher the level of trust among negotiators, the more positive the emotional feelings they experience during the negotiations and the higher the likelihood that communications will be truthful, undistorted and candid.[11] Moreover, a reputation for being trustworthy increases a negotiator's ability to influence the other party. The presence of trust in a negotiation thus has an economic pay-off because it promotes cooperative behaviour, reduces harmful conflict and decreases transaction costs. While many negotiators understand the importance of trust, most are also aware that it is not easy to establish and maintain trust in negotiations. In fact, it is easier to destroy trust than to create it because trust-destroying events are more visible and carry more weight.[12] As Spring points out, trust among negotiators, 'is a very fragile element in relationships, taking years to establish and only moments to destroy'.[13] For example, when negotiators are deceived it arouses feelings of hostility, outrage, anger and resentment.[14] This is particularly so in the case of industrial relations negotiations where people from different backgrounds and political persuasions interact.

NEGOTIATING PAY AND CONDITIONS WITH YOUR BOSS

Prepare

- Prepare a checklist of all issues to be negotiated. Make sure everything is covered.
- Justify what you are asking for. Know what you want and why. Back up your requests with hard data.
- Prioritise your requests. Separate the 'musts' from the 'likes'. Identify your 'tradables'.
- List all your strengths, achievements, and so on. Create value. Build up the perceived worth of your qualifications, experience and contributions.
- Know your boss. Review their past negotiating behaviour. Talk to others who have negotiated with your boss. Look for patterns — past behaviour tends to be repeated.
- Sharpen your negotiating skills. Practise. Take the role of your boss. The better you understand the situation from their viewpoint, the better you can predict their concerns and needs (and their likely arguments and how to counter them).

- Know your bottom line. What is the minimum you will settle for? Figure out what your options are if your requests are not met.

Listen

- Plan the key questions you need to ask. Anticipate the key questions that your boss might ask (and your answers).
- To gain influence and power, you must understand what is important to your boss. Listen to what they say.
- Show empathy. Look at the issues through the eyes of your boss. Show how getting what you want can satisfy their needs or concerns.

Adapt

- Be flexible. Explore all options. Consider the package as a whole. Don't focus on money alone.
- Be cooperative.
- Be willing to exchange information.
- Aim to build trust. Employ a problem-solving, win–win approach.

Figure 17.3 Negotiating pay and conditions with your boss
Source Asia Pacific Management Co. Ltd, 2004.

Ethics in negotiation

There are ethical questions regarding how honest, frank and open a negotiator should be. For example, what does 'telling the truth' mean? What constitutes a deviation from the truth? Should the negotiator tell the truth all the time? Is the telling of a 'white' lie in order not to cause hurt or embarrassment 'dishonest', or does it reveal concern for the vulnerability of the other party and their welfare?

Some experienced negotiators claim that negotiating (like poker) is essentially a game, and that concealing or manipulating information, exaggerating, misrepresenting and bluffing are legitimate ways to maximise self-interest in a business context. Lewicki and Stark found that gaining information about the other side's negotiating position and strategy by seeking information from friends, associates and business contacts, concealing one's bottom line, making a high opening demand and conveying the impression that one was not subject to time pressures were viewed as acceptable and likely tactics to be used in a negotiation.[15]

These pragmatic views, however, have been criticised as unethical by others, and controversy over openness and honesty in negotiations continues. Provis, for example, argues that withholding information when it does not involve distortion, deception or conscious misstatement may be acceptable. However, deliberately trying to deceive the other party to gain an advantage makes the negotiator's behaviour unethical.[16]

Negotiators on the management team feign friendship in order to win a concession. Are they being unethical?

Negotiate or trail

Those who ask for more, get more. And men ask for more, more often than women. American research suggests that a woman's approach to negotiating can cost her more than US$500 000 during the course of a career. The experience in Australia is similar. Female university graduates in Australia received only 94.6% of their male counterparts' starting salaries last year, according to the Graduate Careers Council of Australia. It says the reason is that men complete degrees in higher-paying fields, but research by two adademics, in their book *Women Don't Ask: Negotiation and the Gender Divide*, suggest a different explanation.

The implication is that career success depends heavily on being willing to negotiate. Linda Babcock is the James M. Walton professor of economics at Carnegie Mellon University in Pittsburgh. With a fellow academic, Sara Laschever, she observed that female graduates with master's degrees received an average US$4000 less a year than their male counterparts. Fifty-seven per cent of men had negotiated a higher starting salary, compared with 7% of women. Those who had negotiated were able to increase their starting salaries by 7.4% on average, or $US4053, which explains a substantial proportion of the difference between men's and women's average starting pay. The cumulative effect of accepting what is initially offered is believed to amount to a loss of US$568 834 over a 38-year career.

It seems that some women are afraid of appearing aggressive, pushy and self-centred. They are uncomfortable about expressing their worth in dollar terms, and fear that assertiveness will damage relationships.

Lisa Barron, assistant professor of organisation and strategy at the University of California's Graduate School of Management and author of a recent study on women and negotiation, says that men see salary negotiation as an opportunity to advance their interests, whereas none of the women [studied] mentioned positive benefits from negotiating.

Men liken the process to the excitement of a baseball game, while women express anxiety similar to what they feel before visiting the dentist.

How true is this in Australia? *BRW* presented Babcock and Laschever's theories to four young Australians in comparable stages of their careers. The results suggest that generalisations are dangerous.

Lisa Piefke, 32, and Andrew Hills, 32, both employees of the stockbroking firm Wilson HTM, express similar attitudes towards the negotiating process. They both feel it was their right to negotiate a higher starting salary, and both stress the importance of understanding one's worth before beginning the negotiating process.

Piefke rebuts the theory that women do not negotiate. She says she did not accept the first salary figure that was offered by her employer.

Hills comments that in the stockbroking industry, compensation 'reflects whether you're a revenue writer or not'. Piefke agrees, saying the problem tends to be that women are not regarded as revenue writers. 'Female roles are support roles.' These roles are rarely rewarded in line with their worth.

Two others provide support for the gender-difference theory. Fleur Knowles, 26, events co-ordinator for Willow Creek Vineyard on Victoria's Mornington Peninsula, and her partner, Jonathon Hallinan, 28, a property developer, reveal attitudes in line with Babcock and Laschever's work. Hallinan negotiated up by 25% the salary for his first position. Knowles felt her first position was not negotiable, but thought she was entitled to negotiate a more lucrative package when she went to Willow Creek Vineyard. 'I felt I had achieved more.'

Hallinan says he negotiates 'daily'. Knowles named her salary requirements as negotiations commenced. Babcock reports that 'the men we talked to saw negotiation as a bigger part of their lives and a more common event than the women did'.

Hallinan says he negotiates 'daily'. Knowles named her salary requirements as negotiations commenced. Babcock reports that 'the men we talked to saw negotiation as a bigger part of their lives and a more common event than the women did'.

Babcock and Laschever suggest that Western culture has formulated rigid gender-based standards for behaviour; standards that require women to behave modestly and unselfishly and to avoid promoting their own self interest.

Babcock contends that women are taught early on that pushing on their own behalf is unfeminine, unattractive, unwelcome — and ineffective. Children, she argues, are taught to abide by and internalise these standards and, when faced with the need to assert their self-worth as adults, anxiety deters them or interferes with their ability to ask effectively.

What seems unarguable is that passivity is punished. Pay rises and promotions are rarely awarded to those who, while quietly working, believe their effort and talent will be recognised and fairly rewarded. What is not clear is whether this occurs along gender lines; that women in the main are passive and men mostly aggressive.

Certainly Babcock believes so. In one experiment, she and two colleagues, Deborah Small and Michele Gelfaund, observed students playing the Milton Bradley game Boggle. Participants were promised compensation in the range of $3–10. After playing the game each subject was handed $3 and was told: 'Here's three dollars. Is three dollars OK?' The number of women and men who complained about being offered $3 was about the same, but nine times more men asked for more money.

The implication is that women are nine times more likely to accept initial offers of compensation, despite every indication that the figure is negotiable.

Dr Anne Junor, a lecturer at the School of Industrial Relations and Organisational Behavior at the University of New South Wales, expresses concern at the level of anxiety experienced by her students when being interviewed for their first non-casual job. As the graduate job market has reached unprecedented levels of competition, some women (and men) are so grateful to receive any offer that they are 'self-effacing in their demands for remuneration because they don't want to ask for too much'.

Junor supports Babcock and Laschever's theory of societal conditioning. Junor says her students feel that 'the battle has been won'. They feel passe if they perceive that there is an issue. 'This is supposed to be the post-feminist era', they say. 'Don't complain, just get on with it.'

The highly competitive job market has led scholars to examine the effect of competitive pressures on gender behavior. The US academics Uri Gneezy, Muriel Niederle, and Aldo Rustichini suggest that men and women differ in their ability or propensity to perform in competitive environments. Their paper, *Performance in Competitive Environments: Gender Differences* in August's *Quarterly Journal of Economics*, puts forward an alternative view on the gender divide.

They report that, in the workplace, the average performance of men increases while that of women remains the same. 'Men outperform women on average, and more so in the competitive environment', the paper concludes. Whether or not this is true, some women are giving their male counterparts a head start by taking a more passive approach to negotiation.

Kristen Le Mesurier

Source BRW, 16–22 October 2003, pp. 66–7.

The negotiation planning hierarchy

Objectives

No HR manager should enter a negotiation without a clear sense of purpose as to what is to be achieved. Failure to develop clear, strategic industrial relations **objectives** undermines the whole negotiation process. Organisational and HR objectives are the foundations on which the objectives of industrial relations negotiations are developed. However, Nelson found that managers often have no goals or agenda to follow and have no appreciation of the need to have a structure when commencing negotiations.[17]

Without a sense of mission, the objectives of industrial relations negotiations lack common purpose. The HR manager must continually ask: Does the objective of this negotiation

Objectives Measurable targets to be achieved within a certain time frame.

support the organisation's and HR strategic business objectives? If not, problems will be created. HR managers must ensure that overall corporate HR objectives are understood and accepted by the whole management group and not just the HR department. Indeed, when negotiations with unions are viewed as a strategic activity within the organisation and not merely a defensive response to union demands, line managers and top executives become much more active in the negotiation process.[18] Such objectives must reflect and reinforce the corporate culture espoused in the organisation's mission statement.

Clear HR objectives provide the basis for negotiation planning. Without a sense of purpose, industrial relations negotiations become ad hoc and ineffective. The formulation of clear objectives is thus critical to successful negotiations. HR managers who fail to observe such planning basics face frustration, disappointment and a victorious union (see figure 17.4).[19]

THE NEGOTIATION PLANNING HIERARCHY

- **Objectives**

Bargaining objectives give a sense of purpose or direction to the negotiation. Bargaining objectives provide the basis for planning.
Why are we sitting at the negotiating table? What do we want to achieve? What is the purpose of this negotiation?

- **Strategy**

A negotiation strategy is an overall game plan designed to achieve the bargaining objective(s).
What is our strategy? Will it help achieve our objective?

- **Tactics**

A negotiating tactic is a ploy or move used by negotiators to achieve the strategy or game plan.
What tactics will we use? Are they consistent with our selected strategy?

Figure 17.4 The negotiation planning hierarchy

Strategy

Strategy The overall game plan designed to achieve the negotiating objectives.

The **strategy** is the general game plan designed to achieve the objectives of the negotiation. It provides the HR manager with a positioning approach and a guideline for action.

In negotiations, the four strategic options are win–win, win–lose, lose–lose and lose–win (see figure 17.5). All are valid. The HR manager's choice depends on the negotiation objectives established.

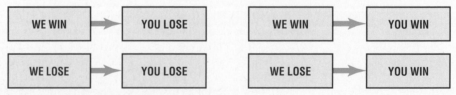

Figure 17.5 The negotiation quadrants

Win–win

Win–win bargaining Sees the negotiation as a cooperative problem-solving exercise that will benefit both parties.

Win–win bargaining is sometimes called *integrative bargaining* because it refers to a cooperative, problem-solving form of negotiation.[20] Both unions and management examine the areas of conflict and try to reach mutually acceptable solutions. Negotiations are conducted in an atmosphere of trust highlighted by open, honest and accurate communication and devoid of power plays and threats. The parties maintain flexibility in their position and regard the outcomes not as fixed but as variables that can be increased and shared.

Examples of this approach occur when a union that is seeking a wage increase is prepared to explore ways to finance the increase via improved productivity, changed work practices and the like. For its part, management does not reject the claim out of hand; it demonstrates a willingness to see the wage demand as evidence of a conflict requiring creative mutual problem solving that will bring benefits to both parties. The 'them and us' attitude evident in Australian employee relations remains a major barrier to the employment of this strategy.

Win–lose

Win–lose bargaining has been the dominant industrial relations strategy used in Australia. Nelson reports that many managers have a superior, patronising approach in negotiations. 'It is', he says, 'as though managers are completely unaware of the opportunities of doing things differently under enterprise bargaining.'[21] As a consequence, negotiations involve ongoing power struggles between unions and management. Each party sees the conflict as a fight to maximise its share. Rewards or outcomes are seen as fixed, so a competitive win–lose relationship exists. This is sometimes called *distributive bargaining*. Getting more becomes a 'them and us' battle in which suspicion, threats, rigidity, power plays, deceit, misinformation and an unwillingness to share information are evident. Given the nature of such negotiations and the high emotional volatility present, they can quickly deteriorate into a state of industrial warfare.

> **Win–lose bargaining** Sees the negotiation as a competitive conflict with one party winning and the other party losing.

Lose–lose

Lose–lose bargaining occurs when neither party achieves an outcome that is beneficial to their true interests. This approach is frequently the unintentional product of other failed strategies. Its presence in Australian industrial relations is evident where the sheer bloody-mindedness of one or both parties fosters the destruction of both. In such cases, threats, sabotage, misrepresentation, industrial thuggery, rigidity, emotional outbursts and chicanery are all present.

Examples arise where an extravagant **log of claims** is pursued, the organisation capitulates and then goes out of business because it is not competitive. Both parties are worse off: the workers have lost their jobs and the organisation is bankrupt.

> **Log of claims** A list of demands covering pay and conditions of work typically made by a union on an employer.

Lose–win

Lose–win bargaining occurs where one party sees benefits in being defeated. In other words, they deliberately sacrifice an immediate gain in the hope of winning a greater benefit in the longer term. This strategy of accommodation is also used when the negotiator's primary objective is to develop or strengthen the relationship with the other party. In this case, the relationship outcome is more important than the substantive outcome. In a long-term relationship it is likely that both sides will at some stage accept a suboptimal outcome in a negotiation in anticipation of a reciprocal accommodation in the future.[22] Management, for example, may give way on an issue to maintain harmonious employee relations or secure a future concession.

Tactics

Tactics are employed in negotiations to alter perceptions about power and reduce the need to make concessions. They are used to help the union or management negotiator to achieve their objectives. As such, they are an essential part of any successful negotiator's armoury. Gambits, ploys or tactics are used to create anger, shock and fear in opponents. Alternatively, they can promote warm, cooperative, friendly behaviour. Tactics are a dynamic part of the process of industrial relations negotiations and cannot be ignored.

> **Tactics** Moves or ploys used to facilitate the successful negotiating strategy.

HR managers must ensure that the tactics selected are consistent with their strategy or general game plan. For example, to have a cooperative win–win strategy but employ an aggressive, unfair or misleading tactic means the tactic is counterproductive and forms a barrier to the achievement of the negotiation objectives. HR managers need to learn to use, recognise and deal with tactics if they seek success in their negotiations.

Common tactics

No authority
When faced with a union request for a concession the HR manager does not want to give, the HR manager can plead lack of authority by saying, 'I'm sorry, but it is beyond my authority' or 'I would like to be able to help but my predecessor got fired for doing that'.

Change the dollars, change the deal
When considering making a wage concession, the HR manager must identify what can be taken out or rearranged in the deal to compensate. A wage concession may mean a change in work practices, penalty payments and the like. The HR manager needs to be creative and explore all options.

Make each concession count
The HR manager must let the union know that the organisation is hurting when asked for a concession. The idea is to flinch, look pained and never admit that it is an easy request. HR managers who make light of a concession find that it loses its trading value.

'Let me think about it'
When the HR manager does not want to make an immediate concession or commitment, they can delay by saying, 'I need some time to think about that', 'Let me make a note of that' or 'I'll get back to you on that'. These responses buy the negotiator time and allow them to think through the response and avoid making mistakes.

'After all I have done for you'
In this case, the union negotiator impresses on the HR manager how much they have done for the HR manager: kept the members from going on strike, persuaded them to reduce their wage demands, and so on. All these things have been done personally for the HR manager — not out of need but out of liking for the HR manager. Next comes the demand: the union representative would like a small favour in return. How can the HR manager refuse? When confronted with this tactic, negotiators need to exercise caution, as a false sense of obligation can prove very expensive.

Conditionalise everything
If forced to make a concession, the HR manager should conditionalise the basis on which it is made. For example, in conceding to a wage demand, the HR manager could say, 'Okay, I'll agree to your request for an increase of $20 per week if we can reduce the staffing on the widget machine'. The 'if' defends the wage concession against further increase. The HR manager has offered not just a wage increase of $20, but a wage increase of $20 plus conditions.

Save it for later
The union representative indicates that they don't want anything in exchange for a concession now but will let the company know later. This is very dangerous. If the HR manager agrees, this will expose the company to an open-ended request.

Ask for more
A deal always looks better to the union representative (and the members) when they 'win' by getting a concession from the company. The HR manager therefore must always ask for more than they expect to get. If not, the HR manager will have insufficient room to manoeuvre.

Fait accompli
The union sends the organisation a draft agreement containing an item not agreed to. The fait accompli tactic is used in the hope that the organisation will agree to the additional item because further negotiations are too time consuming and troublesome. The best defence for the HR manager is to use the tactic too, by deleting the unacceptable item and sending the document back. Tactics that are recognised are not effective.

Shopping list
The HR manager must always get the union's complete 'shopping list' or log of claims before discussing wages. This enables the HR manager to cost concessions accurately,

repackage the deal and avoid an overemphasis on wage concessions. However, as Fells illustrates, the union may hesitate to agree to a final list of demands because its members might raise new issues that the union negotiators as representatives of the membership feel obligated to introduce to the negotiation.[23]

One reason at a time

A negotiator should not spell out all the organisation's arguments immediately. Only one reason, point or argument at a time should be given in support of the organisation's position. Failure to do this allows the union to pick on the weakest argument and destroy it, together with all the negotiator's other points. The negotiator now has nothing left for the next round. The HR manager can maximise the strength of their position by presenting each argument simply and only after the previous point has been neutralised by the union. The HR manager should never lump all the reasons together — to do so is argument dilution.

Make concessions slowly

Concessions should be made slowly and in decreasing amounts. If the maximum wage offer the company is prepared to make is $14 and the initial offer is $7, the first concession should be small. This indicates to the union that the organisation does not have much room to manoeuvre. Making large concessions tells the union that the organisation's original offer was low, and encourages them to expect further large concessions in all aspects of the negotiation.

'Why do you want this?'

After the union makes a demand, the HR manager should ask: 'Why do you want this?' If there is no rationale behind the demand, the union's bluff has been called. The organisation cannot be expected to agree to a concession when the union does not really understand why it is being requested.

Last-minute concessions

This can be a very expensive trap. Management believes the negotiations have ended when suddenly the union makes a few small requests. The organisation should not be tricked into making a concession. The HR manager should indicate that the organisation will be glad to consider the new requests but that of course the union must realise that a change in the amount of wage increase or whatever will now be necessary. A concession should never be given away — it should be traded.

Set aside

This tactic prevents negotiating deadlocks and keeps the negotiations moving. When an impasse has been reached, the negotiators set aside the item in contention and focus their attention on other matters where agreement can be reached. This creates a positive climate and gives momentum to the resolving of the set-aside point of disagreement.

'Take it or leave it'

This expression or more subtle versions of it are 'famous last words', which often are not that at all. The aim is to create pressure. If using this tactic, the negotiator should be serious, firm and polite. It should never be used early in the negotiations unless the intention is to alienate the union. The HR manager should ensure that the union understands that the organisation is quite happy to continue talking but that it is not prepared to make any further concessions.

Even so, a minor concession should be kept in reserve to clinch the deal if required. If the union uses this tactic, the HR manager should ascertain whether it is genuine or just a bluff. A face-saving way out should be kept available if the organisation wishes the union to remain at the negotiating table.

Time to think

Often, a few minutes to gather thoughts can be invaluable to a negotiator. To get time to think, the HR manager can arrange to be interrupted by a telephone call, an urgent message or the like.

Unrealistic demands

Unrealistic demands must not be given legitimacy. If the union makes an outrageous offer or demand, it must be rejected. Failure to do so gives legitimacy to the proposal and sets the parameters of the bargaining zone way outside the organisation's expectations.

Split the difference

When linked with an unrealistic demand, this tactic can position the organisation (or the union) for an overwhelming win or loss at the negotiating table. For example, a fair wage increase may be $30. After some preliminary discussions, the union rejects the company's first offer of $20 and demands $80. The organisation, although disappointed, does not reject it out of hand. After much deliberation, the union representative then says: 'Look, we are all reasonable people on this side of the table. Why don't we split the difference? We will meet you half way — $50. How about it?' The bargaining zone has been set at $20 to $80. To achieve a settlement near $30, let alone below it, will prove an exhausting if not impossible task.

Useful questions that the negotiator can ask to counter this ploy include: 'Why should I accept such a demand?', 'What evidence do you have to support such a claim?' and 'If I agreed to this, how could I justify it to my managing director?' Such questions create pressure on the union as it is not easy to justify an unrealistic demand. Typically, the demand is withdrawn and a more realistic proposal substituted.

Apples and oranges

If the union demands a higher wage increase because the organisation's wages are not competitive, the HR manager must make certain that 'apples and oranges' are not being compared. For example, are the rates detailed by the union for similar work in similar industries in the same geographic location? Are employment conditions and fringe benefits comparable?

The squeeze

This common (and effective) tactic is designed to get the other party to make a concession by placing them under pressure. The union representative says: 'I'm sorry but you will have to do better than that!' The usual reaction of inexperienced management negotiators is to make a concession immediately. Naturally, the union representative then says 'I'm sorry but you will ...', and so on. In contrast, experienced negotiators counter with: 'How much better than that?' No concession has been made and the union representative is now tied into making a commitment without any guarantee of acceptance by the company negotiator.

False demands

When the union makes a demand that is not questioned by the HR manager, it gains validity. The union then generously offers to withdraw the request providing the company agrees to make a concession. By using this technique, a concession can be gained without giving anything in return.

Good guy and bad guy

This is one of the oldest negotiating ploys known. One person on the union negotiating team takes an aggressive, hard-nosed approach (the 'bad guy'), while another is friendly, reasonable and easy to get along with (the 'good guy'). At some stage the bad guy exits (usually in a fit of anger at management's unreasonableness). Next, the good guy makes an offer which, given the circumstances, seems too good to refuse. As the good guy is fair and reasonable, so must be the proposal. HR managers should keep in mind that while a walkout may look spontaneous, many are pure theatre.[24] The best way to handle the good guy/bad guy ploy is to recognise it, let the other side know you recognise it and refuse to go along with it.[25]

Tradition

'It can't be done. It's not standard practice.' The HR manager should be wary of such a statement; it is a ploy to persuade them to do or not do something because of tradition or convention. An example is the almost universal practice of unions serving logs of claims on employers and not vice versa. The negotiator should always question tradition or convention. It is surprising how 'untraditional' the other party can become when pressed to justify a particular convention.

Psychological blackmail

When the union side loses its temper, shows outrage, is insulting or threatening, it is using manipulative tactics designed to win concessions by placing the organisation's representatives under emotional pressure. The HR manager must recognise these tactics for what they are and deal with them accordingly. Some counter-tactics include:

- The HR manager should listen silently. Even the best actors on the union side find it hard to maintain an emotional outburst for any length of time (and, if it is genuine, silence and attentive listening are therapeutic — listening helps defuse anger). Unless it is decided to end the negotiations, management should not respond with similar behaviour — all that will happen is that the situation will become emotional, mistakes will be made and the relationship destroyed.
- The HR manager can ask for a recess.
- The HR manager can indicate that such behaviour is unproductive and unacceptable.
- The HR manager can focus attention on a specific, non-emotional issue.
- The HR manager can use questions such as 'Can you elaborate on why you feel the way you do?' to reduce the other person's anger.

This is not a complete list of tactics that will be faced by the HR manager in negotiating with unions, but it does highlight some of the most common ploys. To be a successful negotiator, the HR manager must be able to recognise and deal with both fair and unfair tactics. It is essential for the HR manager to plan and practise tactics and counter-moves before sitting down at the negotiating table. Anticipating and coping with tactics are basic to success in the negotiation game.

The negotiation process

The negotiation process contains five major stages that vary in significance in each negotiation situation (see figure 17.6).

Preparation

Before meeting with the union, groups of employees or an individual employee, the HR manager needs to prepare carefully and should have:

- factual information such as wage and condition surveys and cost of living data to support the arguments
- a clear understanding of the objectives of the negotiations, and assurance that these are understood and agreed to by other members of the negotiating team and line management
- a costing on all union or employee demands and an awareness of the impact of each concession on organisation profitability and/or costs.

Employers see red in patterns

By Marcus Priest

Employers have threatened to use new anti-pattern-bargaining legislation to head off union attempts to achieve standard industry pay and conditions in the latest wave of enterprise bargaining.

The tactic will stretch union resources to the limit by forcing them to negotiate 1200 separate enterprise agreements over the next five months.

Pattern bargaining occurs when a party attempts to negotiate terms and conditions on an industry-wide basis rather than on an enterprise or workplace basis.

If employers can show that the unions are not genuinely negotiating each and every agreement, the Australian Industrial Relations Commission can suspend or terminate negotiations.

One union, the Australian Manufacturing Workers Union, will be forced to renegotiate at least 450 separate agreements in Victoria due to expire on March 31 or April 1.

The Australian Industry Group's national industrial relations director, Stephen Smith, warned unions not to be surprised 'if employers use the full force of the law to protect their businesses if unlawful action is taken'.

The anti-pattern-bargaining provision was inserted into the Workplace Relations Act late last year. It incorporates the decision of AIRC deputy president Paul Munro in relation to pattern bargaining by unions during 2000.

In that case, Justice Munro suspended negotiations after unions served identical bargaining notices as well as notices of a state-wide stoppage on about 1500 employers.

In introducing the amendment, Workplace Relations Minister Tony Abbott said: 'Pattern bargaining . . . represents an outdated, one-size-fits-all approach to workplace relations where union officials utilised the centralised system to dictate their agenda to both employers and employees.'

AMWU national secretary Doug Cameron said he believed his union could cope with the large number of negotiations. 'Most employers have taken a much more practical approach to issues that we are raising', he said.

'We are confident we can set some decent standards for our members across the industry.'

The national secretary of the Australian Workers Union, Bill Shorten, said opposition to pattern bargaining was motivated by a desire to keep wages down.

'Given that inflation is running at least at 2 to 3 per cent and productivity growth is at 2 per cent, every worker should be getting at least 4 per cent wage increase. It just makes sense', Mr Shorten said.

'But if we demand that, they will say that is pattern bargaining.'

Source *Australian Financial Review*, 23 January 2003, p. 4.

Preparation for negotiation is a complex process and involves both organisation and external specialists. Determining who will be on the negotiation team, the costs of concessions, the public relations aspects, the potential for and the costs of industrial action, the legal implications, and so on take time and effort. The temptation thus exists for the HR manager to ignore this critical part of the negotiation process.

Negotiating with employees and unions is hard work. The amount of preparation done by the HR manager will be revealed at the negotiating table. If the HR manager does not have the time to prepare properly, they should not negotiate. Nothing is more important to success in negotiation than thorough, painstaking preparation. Depressingly, Nelson found that 'when working arrangements are put on the table for discussion and employees make suggestions for improving efficiency, managers have very little, if any, comprehension of what actually goes on in the workplace (see figure 17.7).[26]

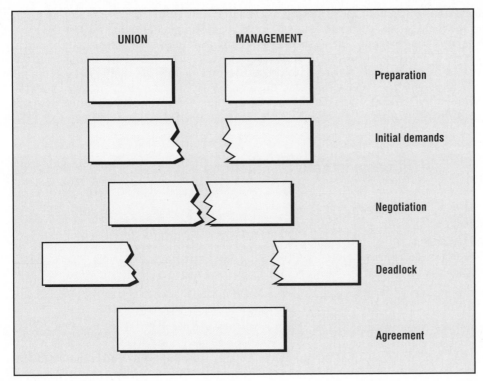

Figure 17.6 The negotiation process

Figure 17.7 Checklist for preparing for union–management negotiations

Initial demands

The first meeting centres on clarifying the demands of each party. The amount of rancour or cooperation demonstrated by the union and management representatives establishes the climate for the negotiations. Successful negotiators focus on the easy issues first as this facilitates the building of a pattern of cooperation and agreement. Resolving the less controversial issues also clearly defines the areas of major conflict. It should be noted that 'research into enterprise bargaining shows that equity issues tend to slip off the bargaining agenda as the attention of negotiators increasingly focuses on other industrial matters'.[27] HR managers, union representatives and employees therefore need to ensure that matters such as sex discrimination, childcare and flexible working hours are not marginalised or ignored (see figure 17.8).

CHECKLIST OF EQUITY PRINCIPLES

Wages

1. Equal remuneration for work of equal value is upheld and advanced by the agreement.
2. In order to eliminate indirect discrimination, negotiations over the agreement recognise that:
   - the elimination of penalty rates may have a disproportionate effect on women due to their lower levels of income
   - the absorption of allowances may not benefit women, since they may not be eligible for many allowances, and
   - any pay packaging arrangements (where a lower pay rate is supplemented by other measures like cars, childcare and/or school fees), will not result in reduced benefits such as losing leave loading and superannuation. Superannuation can be paid by employers on the value of the total remuneration package (rather than just the wage or salary component).

Training

1. All workers have access to training of an equal standard and training is scheduled so that all workers can attend.

2. Entry requirements to training are based on genuine grounds.

Hours and working-time arrangements

1. No changes are made to existing working-time arrangements that currently facilitate the participation of women in work. These arrangements include predictable days and hours of work, working hours that coincide with childcare services and the use of flexitime or rostered days off.
2. Hours specified for a job match job requirements.
3. Conditions attached to part-time work are calculated as the pro rata entitlements of those applying to full-time workers.

Classification structures

1. Classification structures developed via the agreement provide all workers with access to a career path.
2. Job evaluation techniques measure all skills, not individual tasks, particularly skills held by women that previously went unrecognised.
3. Entry point qualifications genuinely match job requirements.
4. Job requirements linked to physical capacity (height, weight, etc.) are reviewed.

Figure 17.8 Checklist of equity principles
Source Human Rights and Equal Opportunity Commission, *Enterprise Bargaining: A Manual for Women in the Workplace*, Sydney (undated), p. 52.

Negotiation

Once the opening positions have been announced, each party must determine what the other wants most and what it will give up to get it. The areas in which the union and management are prepared to negotiate comprise the **bargaining zone** (see figure 17.9). Each party has a tolerance limit beyond which it will not negotiate, but within these parameters a compromise must be made if agreement is to be reached and a deadlock avoided.

Deadlock

Where agreement is not reached, a **deadlock** results. In such cases, the parties will bring pressure on each other and attempt to force a concession and break the impasse (see figure 17.10).

Bargaining zone The parameters between which the union and management are prepared to negotiate comprises the bargaining zone.

Deadlock Occurs when neither side in a negotiation will make a concession.

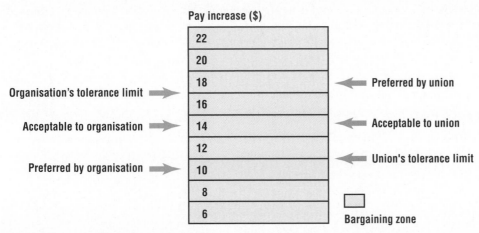

Figure 17.9 An example of a bargaining zone

A union can increase its negotiating power by:	

A union can increase its negotiating power by:
- achieving increased member solidarity via a 'closed shop' (although current legislation does not permit 'closed shops', the reality is that militant unions such as the CFMEU are able to pressure employers into accepting 'no ticket, no work' practices)[28]
- building up strike funds
- arranging support from other unions and vested interest groups
- conducting aggressive publicity and public relations campaigns
- applying pressure on employers and governments via international organisations such as the International Labour Organisation (ILO)

- employing shareholder activism.

Management can increase its negotiating power by:
- utilising alternative labour sources
- threatening to outsource or move offshore
- carrying large inventories
- having ample financial resources to withstand a prolonged stoppage
- conducting aggressive publicity and public relations campaigns
- employing high-performance HR policies and practices.

Figure 17.10 Union and management negotiating power
Source Asia Pacific Management Co. Ltd, 2004.

Unions may strike, impose work bans, go slow, work to rule, and so on to pressure the organisation. The organisation, in turn, may shut down its operations, lock out the union or seek a civil court injunction to prevent the union from taking industrial action.

Alternatively, the assistance of a state or federal industrial tribunal may be sought. The tribunal representative acts as an independent conciliator and helps the deadlocked parties to continue the negotiations and arrive at a solution. If this fails, the tribunal representative may then assume the role of arbitrator. The arbitrator determines the relative merits of the parties' arguments and makes a decision, called an award, which becomes legally binding on both parties.

Agreement

A summary of the stages of negotiation is shown in figure 17.11. This model identifies the sequence of events (preparation, problem solving and resolution) that make for a successful negotiation. In real life, however, union–management negotiations may not proceed in such a systematic way. There may be deadlocks, walkouts and breakdowns without any agreement being reached.

Where an agreement has been reached without recourse to **arbitration**, it must be ratified. For the union, this involves presenting the agreement to its members for approval;

Arbitration The submission of a dispute to a third party for a binding decision.

management in turn may submit it to the company's board of directors. Once approved by both parties, the agreement is then submitted to the appropriate industrial relations tribunal for registration. By this process, the negotiated agreement becomes a consent award.

• Gather information	– Sources of information – Information needs
• Analyse the situation	– Strengths, weaknesses, threats, opportunities
• Assess bargaining power	– Sources of power – Information deficiencies – Time constraints
• Set objectives	– What is the purpose of this negotiation? – What is our objective? – What is their objective?
• Develop strategies	– Which strategy will best achieve our objective? – What is their likely strategy? – How will we deal with it?
• Identify tactics	– Which tactics best support our strategy? – Which tactics are they likely to use? – How will we handle them?
• Explore their needs	– What do they really hunger for?
• Identify areas of agreement and disagreement	– Which are the 'common ground' items? – Which are the stumbling blocks?
• Obtain movement	– How can we repackage the deal? – Which concessions are we prepared to make? – What do we want in exchange?
• Review objectives and strategies	– Are our objectives and strategy still appropriate?
• Apply tactics	– Are they helping our strategy and achieving our objectives?
• Reach settlement	– Check all items have been covered
• Document the agreement	– Confirm what has been agreed

Figure 17.11 A negotiating model

Practical aspects of union negotiation

Management–union relationships in Australia are long term. Divorce is difficult if not impossible (especially in companies insulated from international competition). Confrontationist negotiation strategies therefore are of value only in the short term. If the employer–employee relationship is to be enhanced, a problem-solving approach to negotiation is essential. The organisation that always pushes to get most of the pie, leaving the minimum for the union, is not going to achieve much in terms of employee satisfaction or commitment. The HR manager should bear in mind that at some stage the union will be in a position of power and will be able to even the score. The proactive HR manager thus aims for a bigger pie.

Militant unions only understand one thing in negotiations: power

Dear Editor,

There are some lovely little psychological games that can be played by both sides of the industrial negotiating table. While they might work for some employers, I've learned that there is only one effective tactic in negotiations with unions: go in hard, don't take a backward step and only compromise or give concessions as a last resort.

It is a matter of great regret to me that my staff are represented by one of those old-style, militant trade unions run by blokes who sound like they've recently surfaced from a coalmine in working-class England or Wales. They don't give a damn for the economic viability of my business or for my ideas about how our work should be organised and rewarded. All they care about is screwing me for every last dollar and every last union 'picnic day' they can get. After they've finished with me, they do the same thing with their next target.

I mean, think about this. They turn up with no warning and serve me with a log of claims that has no basis in reality.

I did the sums on the last one and their list of claims added up to a salary equivalent of nearly $20 000 per employee per week! Now, I recognise that my staff may not be the highest paid in the world, but I do my best to share the profits of my business as widely as I can. I seek to accommodate employee needs for extra time off for family or personal reasons, and I try to ensure that their shifts suit their lifestyles and responsibilities. You can imagine how I react when Glynn from the union turns up and nails his union's demands to the door!

I've tried convincing the union of the need for a more harmonious approach to negotiations, but they seem intent on pursuing their own goals to the exclusion of mine. It's really a win–lose approach. They want to win at all costs, and to hell with me. As you can guess, we often end up in the industrial relations court after it reaches the point where I simply refuse to listen to their 'Trotskyist' rubbish any longer.

Consensus and cooperation be damned. The union is driving me out of business, and frankly I'm tempted to sell up and buy a caravan down the coast. How could anybody defend this archaic and irresponsible approach to negotiation?

The angry owner of a metal fabrication business

Source David Poole, University of Western Sydney.

This Letter to the Editor provides a provocative viewpoint. Do you agree? See 'What's your view?' on page 650.

Quid pro quo bargaining

HR managers must always insist on **quid pro quo** bargaining. To do this, what is wanted from the negotiation must be clearly defined:

- *Musts* are issues that, if not won, will cause the organisation to walk away from the negotiating table. Such items are so critical to the organisation that it cannot reach agreement without the union conceding them.
- *Wants* are items that the organisation will go to great lengths to win because they are seen as desirable (but not critical).
- *Gives* are the 'throwaways' — ideally issues or points of high value to the union but of little importance to the organisation.

The HR manager must push for a trade-off for every concession made, even if the issue is a minor one. The HR manager should not fall into the trap of making concessions in the interests of harmonious relations or to get the negotiations moving. The unions will not be grateful. All such behaviour does is to condition the union to ask for more and to designate the organisation's management as weak. Skilled negotiators never give something for nothing.

Quid pro quo Involves a negotiator requesting a trade-off for every concession asked for.

Negotiators are representatives

HR managers must keep in mind that union officials have an electorate (the union members) and that unions are political organisations. Consequently, some demands made by the union representative may be for public consumption only and are not a true indicator of what the substantive issues are.

The HR manager should not accept money claims especially at face value. Wage demands are an easy way for an inarticulate, lazy or out-of-touch union official to try to satisfy the members' needs. In such cases, the solution of more money is temporary. Because the real needs have not been satisfied, worker frustration will very quickly build up and express itself in the form of yet another wage claim. The more the HR manager knows about the organisation's employees, its management, the union representative and the union, the better the HR manager will negotiate.

Management's log of claims

HR managers for too long have assumed a strictly defensive posture in the face of union demands. HR managers must be proactive, not reactive. The organisation must develop its own log of claims. The HR manager should never accept the union argument that tabling a management log of claims is unheard of and will have a negative impact on its relations with the unions.

Leave money until last

The discussion of money should be left until last because it allows the total package to be costed, enables give-and-take to continue with other items in exchange for money, and ensures union interest is maintained in negotiating all the items on the organisation's log of claims.

Keep the package in mind

Each negotiating issue should not be seen as separate and independent. At all times the organisation's representatives must keep in mind the components of the total package and their cost. To underestimate or ignore the cost of non-cash items such as free uniforms, free laundry, subsidised canteen meals and extra wash-up time may prove very expensive. It is important that the union understands the true cost of such items — failure to do so reduces their negotiating value.

Computer simulations can be very useful in answering 'what if' questions regarding the costs of claims and counterclaims. Computer programs that calculate the dollar cost benefits (both direct and indirect) offer considerable time savings and allow negotiators to be better prepared and better informed.

Long-term objectives

A long-term objective should never be sacrificed for a short-term gain. A common example of this in Australia is the agreement by management to collect union dues in the interest of good industrial relations. What is forgone is the long-term opportunity to operate in a union-free environment. The collection of union dues by the organisation and the numerical strength of financial members of the union are directly related.[29]

Time pressures

Negotiations with unions should not be conducted against the clock. To do so involves the risk of having to make more concessions than planned. In negotiations, time is power. Trying to negotiate with the union when pressed for time because of having to catch an aeroplane or attend another meeting puts the HR manager at a distinct disadvantage.

Time pressures make for concessions. Demands are watered down, quid pro quo bargaining is dropped, concessions are given and the power balance is tipped in favour of the union. Sufficient time must always be allowed.

When faced with an approaching **deadline**, the HR manager should not assume that it is non-negotiable. Deadlines come and go. Just as management has a deadline, so does the union. The time pressures on the union should not be underestimated. They exist. The good negotiator always tries to establish what the union's deadline is. Obviously, the organisation's real deadline remains secret.

Deadline The time limit set for the completion of the negotiation.

Listening for success

Active listening is a powerful negotiating tool. Too many HR managers weaken their negotiating position because they talk and do not listen. Information is a source of power in negotiations. To influence the union representatives, the HR manager should ask lots of questions and listen carefully to the answers (see figure 17.12). In this way, the HR manager can learn what it is that the union really wants. The effective negotiator is thus able to look at the issues through the union's eyes.

Active listening Asking lots of questions and carefully listening to the answers.

DEVELOPING YOUR LISTENING SKILLS

Listening is a valuable tool for establishing good rapport and for giving recognition. Simply, it lets other people know how important they are to you, and that their contributions are valuable. The following guidelines may help you develop your listening skills:

Concentrate. Clear your mind of other thoughts. While you are listening use as much of your brain as possible to analyse and organise what the speaker is saying. Key words or short phrases will help you to remember the essence of the conversation.

Don't interrupt. This is not as easy as it sounds, especially if you have an outgoing, expressive personality. Be patient — let the other person finish before you leap in with your response.

Non-verbal messages. Often the non-verbal part of the conversation is as important as the words. Watch that the verbal and non-verbal messages agree.

Give feedback. Expressions such as a smile, a nod, a hand gesture and feedback words such as 'yes', 'I see', 'sure' all indicate an interest from you.

Verify. You can verify the information by rephrasing or repeating what was said to you.

Figure 17.12 Developing your listening skills

Source Extract from 'Better Listening', *Drake Business Review*, vol. 3, no. 2, undated, p. 33.

Check authority to deal

The agreements of industrial relations negotiations are normally subject to the approval of the union members. The HR manager must establish what authority the union representative has. Union officials are not averse to understating their authority. This makes it easier for them to take a hard line and to seek further concessions. The union official who says, 'My members have voted to ratify the agreement subject to a few minor changes' is trying such a ploy.

To avoid being subjected to this tactic, the HR manager should always try to avoid negotiating with more authority than the union counterpart.

Unfortunately, management ego too often gets involved, making it easy for the union to exploit this tactic to the full. The HR manager must remember that the negotiation is not finalised until the agreement has been ratified. Consequently, it is always politic to need the approval of the managing director or the board of directors — even if this may be a total fiction.

The negotiating game

Most negotiations with unions involve some measure of play-acting, exaggeration, manipulation and even outright misrepresentation. To be an effective negotiator, the HR manager must be aware that it is a game, a serious game admittedly, but still a game (see figure 17.13).

UNION NEGOTIATING GAMES

1. Union policy is normally to demand shorter working hours, but 'management has created a major problem for our members by cutting the overtime they can work'.
2. Equal pay is absolutely correct as long as the men always get more money than the women.
3. You must improve the wages of the lower paid and you must also restore the differential after you have done so.
4. If management cannot make an agreement here and now with us, we prefer to deal with the organ grinder rather than the monkey. However, 'we will now report back to our members to see whether they accept what you have proposed'.
5. The effect of legislation intervening in free collective bargaining is a basic assault on trade union rights. 'We demand legislation on industrial democracy, trade union immunities, compulsory time off', and so on.
6. 'Our ban on overtime, together with the work-to-rule and go-slow, is a moderate protest reaction to management's unreasonable stance. Your action in suspending our members is an outrageous provocation and can only serve to worsen the prospects of a settlement.'

Figure 17.13 Union negotiating games
Source Adapted from G. Kennedy, J. Benson and J. McMillan, *Managing Negotiations*, 3rd edn, Hutchinson Business, London, 1987, pp. 158–9.

Tactics need to be recognised for what they are and then dealt with. The good negotiator does not get trapped into losing their temper or allowing the negotiation to degenerate into a verbal fight. Point scoring is most dangerous in industrial relations. If this happens, the argument may be won but not the hearts and minds of the union representatives. The basic aim of industrial relations negotiations is to satisfy the organisation's strategic business objectives, not to demonstrate how smart the management representatives are.

Thirty interactive Wiley Web Questions are available to test your understanding of this chapter at
www.johnwiley.com.au/ highered/hrm5e
in the student resources area

Summary

HR managers more than ever need good negotiating skills if they are to be successful. The increasing importance of enterprise-based employee relations is clear. Consequently, conflicts relating to wages, fringe benefits and conditions of work will increasingly be settled by direct negotiation between employers and employees or their union representatives.

Traditionally, the initiative has been left to the unions. HR managers can no longer be reactive if they wish to be change agents and active contributors to the achievement of the organisation's strategic business objectives. They must develop clear negotiation objectives, linked to the organisation's business and HR strategies, develop their negotiating skills, undertake thorough preparation and pursue a more creative and collaborative approach to employee–management relations.

student study guide

terms to know

active listening (p. 647)
arbitration (p. 643)
bargaining (p. 629)
bargaining zone (p. 642)
collective bargaining (p. 629)
deadline (p. 647)
deadlock (p. 642)
enterprise bargaining (p. 629)

log of claims (p. 635)
negotiation (p. 629)
objectives (p. 633)
quid pro quo (p. 645)
strategy (p. 634)
tactics (p. 635)
win–lose bargaining (p. 635)
win–win bargaining (p. 634)

review questions

1. In preparing to negotiate a new agreement with an organisation or union, what information would you collect before commencing negotiations?
2. How is management and trade union negotiator power influenced by tariff reductions, outsourcing and foreign competition? Who is most affected by these changes — management or unions?
3. Identify any 'management rights' that you believe should not be subject to collective bargaining.
4. What specific personal qualities should a negotiator possess? Which is the most important? Why?
5. What tactics would you use if your choice of negotiating strategy were (a) win–win and (b) win–lose?
6. How would you overcome a situation where the other side has a strong commitment to a particular issue?
7. What should management do when a negotiated settlement is rejected by the union's members?
8. How would you go about building trust in negotiations if you were (a) the HR manager and (b) the union representative?
9. How is integrative bargaining different from distributive bargaining?
10. Give arguments for and against the involvement of lawyers and/or employer association representatives in union–management negotiations.

environmental influences on management–employee negotiations

Discuss the environmental influences from the model (figure 17.14 shown on the following page) that have significance for management–employee negotiations.

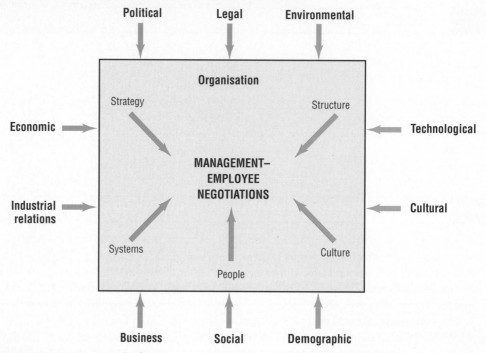

Figure 17.14 Environmental influences on management–employee negotiations

class debate

Deceptive tactics are part and parcel of union–management negotiations and should not be considered unethical.
or
Power rather than trust is what counts in union–management negotiations.

what's your view?

Write a 500-word response to the Letter to the Editor on page 645, agreeing or disagreeing with the writer's point of view.

practitioner speaks

Read the article 'Negotiate or trail' on pages 632–3. As a class, discuss the author's viewpoints, especially the argument that women's natural lack of competitiveness leaves them behind aggressive men in achieving higher pay. Do you agree or disagree? Why?

newsbreak exercise

Read the Newsbreak 'Employers see red in patterns' on page 640. In your own words, explain (a) what pattern bargaining is, (b) why employers are opposed to pattern bargaining, (c) why trade unions favour pattern bargaining and (d) your personal view about pattern bargaining.

soapbox

What do you think? Conduct a mini survey of class members, using the questionnaire below. Critically discuss the findings.

1. The only way to win a negotiation with a difficult opponent is to be tough and demanding.	YES	NO
2. It is okay to misrepresent information and mislead the other party to gain an advantage.	YES	NO
3. You should always make an opening demand that far exceeds what you really want.	YES	NO
4. Being open and cooperative means the other side will perceive you as weak and naive.	YES	NO
5. Making a promise you cannot deliver on is okay if it helps you to get what you want.	YES	NO
6. If you are in a powerful negotiating position, you should exploit your advantage to the maximum.	YES	NO

online exercise

Conduct an online search on one of the following: (a) the importance and role of trust in collective bargaining, (b) what is meant by ethics and how ethics applies to union–management negotiations or (c) three different Australian Workplace Agreements and the manner in which they were negotiated. As a class, discuss your findings.

ethical dilemma

A subtle persuader

Len Goodman, HR Manager for Glorious Development Ltd, sighed and sipped his beer. 'What's up mate? You look like the bloody sky has fallen in.' Len turned. It was Greg Katzenbach, Secretary of the United Industrial Workers of Australia. 'Hi Greg. I'm afraid your mates are giving me a hard time.'

'You mean the blokes in the Federated Construction Workers Union?'

'Yeah, that's them', Len replied.

'What's the problem? Your company is generally pretty reasonable.'

'Yeah', muttered Len, 'but being reasonable has nothing to do with it. We're up against a tight deadline on the Wallis Street project but we're getting hit with wildcat strikes. The Fed officials are okay, but they can't control their members.'

'Whose doing the stirring?' asked Greg.

'Two blokes — Bluey Rodgers and Tony Compton. You know them?'

'Yeah. They're with the Workers Reform Group. They're trying to kick out Bill Dylan and his mates from the Federal leadership. That group have been creating trouble all over town. Bill's tearing his hair out even though he's safe. Those two are a pain in the backside.'

'You're telling me', sighed Len. 'You can't negotiate with them. They just yell and scream. It's an absolute nightmare.'

'Maybe I can help. It'll cost you a couple of thousand.'

'Are you serious Greg?'

'Of course I am.'

'Look, if you can stop those two making trouble I can spring a couple of grand off the record. If we don't complete this project on time we will go under — the penalty clauses will wipe us out.'

'Jeez, I didn't realise it was that bad.'

'Well it is'.

'Leave it to me mate. Consider your problem solved.'

The following week, Len was telephoned by the site manager. 'You'll never guess what. Those two mongrels Rodgers and Compton have quit.'

Len gasped. 'You're kidding!'

'No Len, it's true. They're already off the site.'

Len leant back in his chair, sighed with relief and picked up the phone.

'Greg, is that you? It's Len.'

'Yeah mate, how are things?'

'I owe you. Compton and Rodgers quit this morning. What did you do?'

'You really want to know?'

'Of course I do.'

'Well, both of those blokes are newly married. So I had a couple of our young studs pay their better halves a visit. All they said was that they would be back if hubby didn't find new employment. Your boys must have got the message.'

Discussion questions

1. If you were Len, how would you have handled the situation?
2. What ethical issues are raised in this case?

case study

The absent employee

Allstar Ltd had had a tough year. Sales had plummeted and staff numbers had been reduced by 30 per cent. Each department was now very lean, with every employee assuming a very heavy workload. Allstar's Sales Department in particular was under considerable pressure to improve its performance. A key member of the sales team was Iris Chow. As Internal Sales Coordinator, Iris passed on leads to the outside sales force, answered customer queries, processed all orders and followed up with the shipping department to ensure that all deliveries were made on time. Iris was regarded as competent and hardworking.

However, over the past few months Iris had been taking more and more days off. At first, other members of the department took little notice, but as they had to do her work as well as their own, her persistent absences soon became a sore point. Derek Jacoby, the Sales Manager, was becoming increasingly frustrated with Iris. Under considerable pressure from management, he was stretched to the limit. Now he had the added hassles of declining morale and what to do about Iris. His subordinates started asking 'Why is she always absent?' When approached, Iris became evasive, simply stating that she had some personal problems.

Resentment continued to increase. One afternoon, the company's top sales representative, Susie Andreas, heatedly told Derek that she and several others were going to quit if something wasn't done about Iris. At breaking point, Derek called Iris at home and told her that as she could no longer perform her job, she was fired. Shortly after, Derek received a call from Tony Keating, organiser with the United Office Workers Union, requesting a meeting to discuss the matter of Iris' termination.

Role-play

Form negotiating teams to represent management and the union in the above dispute and try to negotiate a resolution to the dispute.

practical exercises

1. ETHICAL NEGOTIATOR BEHAVIOUR

Listed opposite are a number of common negotiating tactics. Circle the response that best reflects your attitude regarding the appropriateness of their use in negotiations. Break into small groups of four to six and discuss the results. Regroup as a class and review your findings.

1. Give misleading information to trick the other party.

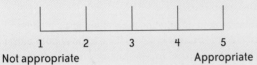

2. Make an extremely high opening demand.

3. Gain information by feigning friendship.

4. Use threats to gain a concession.

5. Offer a bribe to win agreement.

6. Make a promise you know you cannot keep.

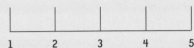

7. Exaggerate the loss you will suffer if the other side does not agree to your demand.

8. Lie about your deadline to put pressure on the other party.

9. Say you do not have the authority to make a decision when in fact you do.

10. Exaggerate the sacrifice you have made when you make a concession.

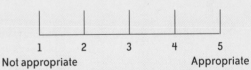

2. **NEGOTIATOR REACTIONS**

Complete the following statements individually, then discuss your responses as a class.

If the other negotiator:	My reaction would be:	If the other negotiator:	My reaction would be:
• Makes a large concession • Loses their temper • Remains silent • Becomes aggressive and demanding • Uses flattery • Offers a bribe • Is insulting • Is friendly		• Is competitive • Is arrogant • Doesn't do what they promise • Is cooperative • Makes an outrageous opening demand • Uses threats • Misrepresents the facts • Walks out	

3. **NEGOTIATING CURRENT ISSUES**

Scan industrial relations news items in newspapers and magazines and draw up a list of negotiating issues and claims, then complete the following tasks:

(a) Break into a number of union and management negotiating teams (two to six members per team) and prepare your negotiating objectives, strategies and tactics. One team should adopt a cooperative win–win approach, the other a competitive win–lose approach.

(b) Appoint one or two class members as observers for each negotiating group.

(c) Negotiate an agreement on the issues and claims.

(d) Review the negotiations using these key points:
- Did the parties reach agreement?
- Were both parties satisfied with the outcome?
- Do the parties feel their self-respect has been maintained?
- Would the parties negotiate with each other again?
- Will the parties comply with the agreement?
- What constructive/destructive behaviour was observed?
- What would the team members do differently next time around?

4. **NEGOTIATION AT WESTERN UNIVERSITY**

Western University is suffering from severe budgetary problems. As a consequence, the university management has been forced to critically examine all its operations. One of the areas identified as having the potential for great savings is the better utilisation of staff. Management has decided to try increasing individual accountability and eliminating staff committees, which are said to be inefficient and costly and to blur accountabilities. In addition, it is proposed to increase the ratio of part-time casual staff to permanent tenured employees. Staff with poor performance are to be dismissed and ways are to be sought to reward staff members who perform.

It is also envisaged that a radical approach to timetabling will be needed, with the university being open during weekends and semester breaks. This will make it necessary for teaching staff to assume extra teaching loads of up to two hours per week, and to teach during traditional holiday periods.

Activity

(a) Form negotiating teams of two to six members representing union and management. Appoint one or two class members as observers for each negotiating group.

(b) Do not read the other team's confidential information brief (see below).

(c) Develop your team's objectives, strategy, tactics and bottom-line position.

(d) With the other party, commence the negotiation.

(e) Time required is approximately one hour.

(f) Complete the negotiator perception sheet below and then discuss.

(g) Review the negotiations using the key points listed in 3(d) above.

Confidential union information

Western University Staff Association represents academic employees only. The union is vehemently opposed to any management initiative that will threaten existing working conditions. In particular, the ideas of extended working hours and appraising the performance of lecturing staff are seen as unacceptable. Moreover, tenure is regarded as sacrosanct and not open to negotiation.

Philosophically, you regard this latest management concern for excellence as smacking of elitism and not in the best interests of either staff or students. You feel management has not paid sufficient attention to the stress faced by staff, the ever-increasing demands on staff time outside of lectures and the increasing pressure to publish and obtain higher qualifications in order to be eligible for promotion.

You believe that management must push for more money from the government and that militant action is required by the university staff to create community awareness of the problems.

Confidential management information

Management is aware that the university must cut costs and become more performance-oriented and that this will involve considerable pain. However, there is a strong feeling that management has been overly sensitive to staff feelings in the past and that now is the time for management to assert itself. In particular, management wishes to give greater power to heads of department to hire and fire, and to reward performance. An outside consultant has been approached to ascertain the feasibility of introducing a performance management program and the linking of pay increases and promotions to individual performance. Management already has a list of recognised poor performers it wishes to terminate or demote.

Management is most anxious to create a climate of academic excellence so that it can attract talented researchers, teachers and administrators. The administration is also aware of a scheme by a privately funded institution to establish a university near the Western University campus. It is rumoured that this venture is being supported financially by local industries because of their dissatisfaction with the quality and relevance of Western University courses.

Negotiator perceptions

You may have developed some impressions about your counterparts. Circle any of the adjectives listed below that you feel apply to your counterparts. You may list additional adjectives in the blank spaces.

argumentative	objective
arrogant	open
biased	patronising
compromising	pleasant
confident	reasonable
cooperative	reliable
devious	rigid
domineering	scheming
easy	sincere
emotional	tough
flexible	trustworthy
helpful	uncertain
honest	understanding

---

5. **CONFLICT AT PACIFIC MANUFACTURING**

Pacific Manufacturing Ltd is a specialist manufacturer of high-quality engineering products. Over the past five years, it has made a successful effort to develop export markets in the Asia–Pacific region. While its products are highly regarded for their technical precision and quality, the company is in danger of losing its hard-won markets because of unreliable deliveries resulting from industrial disputes.

Recently, an order for $500 000 to Japan was cancelled because of the company's inability to meet a shipping deadline. Worse, labour costs have been creeping up, and if the company is to remain competitive, these will have to be reduced. The company originally started as a small high-tech engineering company but has grown rapidly in its 10-year existence. Employees now total 400.

All 320 factory and trades personnel are in the National Metal Workers Union. The remaining personnel are professional managerial and clerical staff and are not unionised.

The company is financially stretched because of its rapid growth and is experiencing severe cash flow problems, which have been aggravated by cancelled orders. In the last financial year, the company made a loss of $8 000 000 because of its failure to satisfy customers' orders. Unless productivity and deliveries can be improved, the company's operations will have to be cut back.

The National Metal Workers Union is currently pressing for an immediate across the board 10 per cent pay increase. The union is represented by a politically ambitious organiser who has taken an extremely hard line. The organiser refuses to even discuss productivity improvement trade-offs until the company grants the 10 per cent across-the-board pay increase and has publicly stated that it is 'just not on for employers to allow workers' standards of living to decline and to seek the elimination of widely accepted and long-standing award conditions'.

Activity

(a) Form negotiating teams of two to six members representing union and management. Appoint one or two class members as observers for each negotiating group.

(b) Do not read the other team's confidential information brief (see below).

(c) Develop your team objectives, strategy, tactics and bottom-line position.

(d) Meet with the other party and commence negotiations.

(e) Time required is approximately one hour.

(f) Review the negotiations using the negotiator perception sheet on page 655 and the negotiation key points listed in 3(d) on page 654.

Management's trade-off requests

1. Eliminate the practice of paying two hours overtime as 'climbing time' for crane drivers.

2. Allow the company to use a mental aptitude test to select personnel to operate the newly purchased, computerised Ajax machining equipment.

3. Cease political strikes such as the recent one-day stoppage to protest the overthrow of the People's Democratic Party government in Tinselville.

4. Stop the practice of employees clocking on then changing into their work clothes before proceeding to work.

5. Cease the practice of 'one man, one job, one machine' with the Delta machine, which has been specially designed as a bank of four machines to be operated by one operator.

6. Eliminate the payment of the disturbance allowance of one hour's pay. Currently, this is paid to all employees contacted at home after hours to do overtime, even if they refuse to work.

7. Introduce a performance appraisal scheme, with performance ratings linked to individual pay increases. Abolish across-the-board pay increases.

8. Cease the practice of annual payouts to employees for unused sick leave.

9. All future wage increases are to take into account the company's profitability and capacity to pay.

Confidential management information

You regard these negotiations as critical to the future financial viability of the business. If concessions are not achieved, it is anticipated that the factory staff will have to be reduced immediately by 30, and possibly up to 60 within six months. In addition, it is planned to terminate 10 office and technical personnel immediately and not to replace others as they leave. Management salaries are to be frozen for the next 12 months.

If the requested changes can be achieved, the Finance Department estimates that the company can achieve a turnaround in less than 18 months and once again enter an expansionary phase. The

company has secretly commenced a feasibility study on transferring all its manufacturing operations to China.

Confidential union information

Your position is quite firm. You want a 10 per cent across-the-board pay increase now. Once this is given, you will be prepared to consider reasonable trade-off requests made by the company. However, you will not consider requests that you regard as impinging on hard-won working conditions or reflecting an individualist rather than a collectivist philosophy.

You want the company to provide incentives to workers to train and retrain, and you want the company to increase its investment in Australia. You regard the company's financial problems as the result of bad management and overstaffing in non-unionised areas. You do not believe that your members should suffer to protect non-union employees.

suggested readings

Alexander, R. and Lewer, J., *Understanding Australian Industrial Relations*, 6th edn, Thomson, Melbourne, 2004, ch. 8.

Clark, R. and Seward J., *Australian Human Resource Management: Framework and Practice*, 3rd edn, McGraw-Hill, Sydney, 2000, pp. 90–5.

Fisher, C. D., Schoenfeldt, L. F. and Shaw, J. B., *Human Resource Management*, 5th edn, Houghton Mifflin, Boston, 2003, pp. 720–31.

Grennard, J. and Judge, G., *Employee Relations*, 3rd edn, CIPD, London, 2003, ch. 9.

Ivancevich, J. M. and Lee, S. H., *Human Resource Management in Asia*, McGraw-Hill, Singapore, 2002, pp. 350–9.

Lewicki, R. J., Saunders, D. M., Barry, M. and Minton, J. W., *Essentials of Negotiation*, 3rd edn, McGraw-Hill, New York, 2003.

Mondy, R. W., Noe, R. M. and Premeaux, S. R., *Human Resource Management*, 8th edn, Prentice Hall, Upper Saddle River, NJ, 2002, ch. 15.

Nankervis, A. R., Compton, R. L. and Baird, M., *Strategic Human Resource Management*, 4th edn, Nelson, Melbourne, 2002, pp. 571–3.

Schermerhorn, J. R., Hunt, J. G. and Osborn, R. N., *Organizational Behavior*, 8th edn, John Wiley & Sons, New York, 2003, pp. 388–93.

Shell, G. R., *Bargaining for Advantage*, Penguin, New York, 2000.

online references

www.adr.org
www.aflcio.org/
www.ilr.cornell.edu

www.shrm.org.hrmagazine
www.workforceonline.com

end notes

1. A. A. Sloane and F. Witney, *Labor Relations*, 10th edn, Prentice Hall, Upper Saddle River, NJ, 2001, p. 217.

2. R. Fells, 'A critical examination of the process of workplace negotiation', *Labour & Industry*, vol. 9, no. 1, 1998, pp. 37–52; and L. Hawkins and M. Hudson, 'Leaders as negotiations', *HR Monthly*, August 1998, pp. 6–8.

3. L. G. Nelson, 'Managers and enterprise bargaining: some preliminary findings', *Asia Pacific Journal of Human Resources*, vol. 35, no. 1, 1997, p. 58.

4. P. Cohen, 'Industrial negotiation — why not do it yourself?', unpublished paper, May 1981, pp. 9–10.

5. M. Hudson and L. Hawkins, *Negotiating Employee Relations*, Pitman, Melbourne, 1995, p. 4.

6. J. Sloan, 'Enterprise bargaining's quest for maturity', *Australian*, 8 November 1996, p. 15.

7. T. J. Griffin and W. R. Daggott, *The Global Negotiator*, Harper Business, New York, 1990, p. 32.

8. R. Ross and J. La Croix, 'Multiple meanings of trust in negotiation theory and research: a literature review and integrative model', *International Journal of Conflict Management*, vol. 7, no. 3, 1996, pp. 314–60.

9. J. B. Barney and W. Hesterly, 'Organizational economics: understanding the relationship between organizations and economic analysis', in S. R. Clegg, C. Hardy and W. R. Nord (eds), *Handbook of Organization Studies*, Sage, London, 1996, pp. 115–47.

10. J. Child and D. Faulkner, *Strategies of Cooperation*, Oxford University Press, Oxford, 1998, p. 46.

11. A. K. Mishra, 'Organizational responses to crises: the centrality of trust', in R. H. Kramer and T. R. Tyler (eds), *Trust in Organizations*, Sage, Thousand Oaks, CA, 1996, pp. 261–87.

12. R. Kramer, 'Trust and distrust in organizations: emerging perspectives, enduring questions', *Annual Review of Psychology*, vol. 59, 1999, pp. 569–98.

13. H. C. Spring, 'Discussion: building new organizational alliances and the role of trust', *Proceedings of the Forty Sixth Annual Meeting of the Industrial Research Association*, Boston, Mass., 1994, p. 35.

14. R. J. Bies and T. M. Tripp, 'Beyond distrust: "Getting even" and the need for revenge', in R. M. Kramer and T. R. Tyler (eds), op. cit., pp. 246–60.

15. R. J. Lewicki and N. Stark, 'What is ethically appropriate in negotiations: an empirical examination of bargaining tactics', *Social Justice Research*, vol. 9, no. 1, 1996, pp. 69–95.

16. C. Provis, 'Ethics, deception and labour negotiation', *Journal of Business Ethics*, vol. 28, 2000, pp. 145–58.

17. L. G. Nelson, op. cit., p. 58.

18. A. Kochan and T. A. Barocci, *Human Resource Management and Industrial Relations*, Scott Foresman, Glenview, Ill., 1985, p. 292.

19. J. M. Ivancevich, *Human Resource Management*, 8th edn, McGraw-Hill, Boston, 2001, pp. 505–6.

20. S. P. Robbins, *Organizational Behavior*, 9th edn, Prentice Hall, Upper Saddle River, NJ, 2001, pp. 397–8.

21. L. G. Nelson, op. cit., pp. 58–9; and S. P. Robbins, op. cit., pp. 396–7.

22. R. J. Lewicki, D. M. Saunders and J. W. Minton, *Negotiation*, 3rd edn, McGraw-Hill, New York, 1999, p. 274.

23. R. Fells, op. cit., p. 42.

24. G. R. Shell, *Bargaining for Advantage*, Penguin, New York, 2000, pp. 183–4.

25. G. R. Shell, op. cit., p. 232.

26. L. G. Nelson, op. cit., p. 59.

27. Human Rights and Equal Opportunity Commission, *Enterprise Bargaining: A Manual for Women in the Workplace*, Sydney (undated), p. 44.

28. For example, see P. Klinger, 'Power plays in Perth', *Australian Financial Review*, 9 August 2003, p. 73; M. Skulley, 'Union chief threatened managers', *Australian Financial Review*, 28 October 2003, p. 9; T. Abbott, 'One law for the unions, another law for the wimps', *Australian Financial Review*, 29–30 March 2003, p. 48; and J. Murray, 'Industry should adopt freedom of choice', *Australian Financial Review*, 17 April 2002, p. 55.

29. P. Berry and G. Kitchener, 'Can unions survive?', *BWIU*, ACT, 1989, pp. 37–8.

chapter

18

employee health and safety

Learning objectives

When you have finished studying this chapter, you should be able to:

- Appreciate the importance of a safe and healthy work environment
- Describe what management and employees must do to create a safe and healthy work environment
- Understand the contribution of TQM to improved occupational health and safety performance
- Discuss some major current health and safety issues
- Identify the major sources of job stress and the possible remedies.

'Only when regulators and industry take strategic responsibility for occupational health and safety can workplaces be free from injury and illness.'[1]

Carolyn Rance, HR writer

Introduction

Occupational health and safety (OHS) Concerned with the provision of a safe and healthy work environment.

Health and safety programs reflect an organisation's strategic concern for employee productivity and quality of work life. As such, they should be linked with the organisation's strategic business objectives to seek competitive advantage by promoting employee commitment, the company's image as a preferred employer, reduced costs and increased productivity. Poor **occupational health and safety (OHS)** performance equates with poor human resource management, and poor ethical, legal and social responsibility. It represents a management failure to realise that safe organisations are more effective organisations.[2] The provision of a safe and healthy working environment is important to all employees. Accidents and illness result in physical and mental suffering and are a major cost for employers and the community because of the loss of experienced workers, increased premiums for workers compensation insurance and decreased morale.

There are about 2900 work-related deaths and 650 000 work-related injuries in Australia each year, and annual economic losses are estimated at more than $27 billion.[3] According to a recent report issued by the Construction, Forestry, Mining and Energy Union, Australian construction sites experience an average of 50 deaths per year. In addition, accidents and deaths cost the construction industry $100 million per year and almost 50 000 weeks of lost working time.[4] Australia's coalmining industry also has an appalling safety record. In China, however, where government regulations are ignored, the death rate from accidents is 500 to 1000 times that experienced in Australian mines.[5] China also has more deaths from work-related illnesses than all of Europe and the United States combined. According to International Labour Organisation data, almost 400 000 Chinese workers died of occupational illnesses in 2002.[6]

Major causes of work injury include mechanical failure, being hit by a moving object, being harmed by chemicals, falls, trips and slips, heat, radiation and electricity, and hitting objects.[7] Major health issues include infectious diseases, hazardous substances, noise, age-related disorders, physical disorders caused by lack of fitness, reproductive disorders, shiftwork and stress-related problems associated with downsizing and restructuring (see figure 18.1).[8]

Occupational health and safety problems account for more lost production time in Australia than industrial disputes. In performance-oriented organisations, considerable attention is given to employee health and safety and the promotion of a corporate culture that puts safety first.[9] Wesfarmers, for example, states that the provision of a safe working environment for employees is a non-negotiable priority and reinforces this by tying executive remuneration to safety performance.[10] At Coles Myer, 20 per cent of executive bonuses are linked to safety and succession issues. [11]

The union proposes that its members performing hazardous work be paid an allowance or 'danger money'. Management agrees.

Making safety part of the organisational culture is an integral part of good HR management. 'The health and safety of our workforce is more than a compliance issue', says Wal King, CEO of Leighton Holdings, 'for us it is about developing and maintaining a safety-conscious culture throughout each operating company.'[12] Delivering a healthy and safe workplace is also part of Boral's culture of respect for employees, contractors and customers. Boral claims that effective management of health and safety contributes to its bottom line through minimising losses, reducing workers compensation costs and, most importantly, protecting its employees.[13]

Responsibility for employee wellbeing is shared by line managers, HR managers, unions and the employees themselves. Ultimate responsibility, however, rests with the employer. This is because it is the employer who has the greatest control over the employee's working environment. Common law and government legislation reinforce this locus of responsibility. It is therefore essential that top management take the lead in establishing the corporate philosophy and objectives for health and safety. At Boral, all divisional safety targets are signed off by the Managing Director. SimsMetal's commitment to health and safety requires monthly board presentations by key operational personnel.[14]

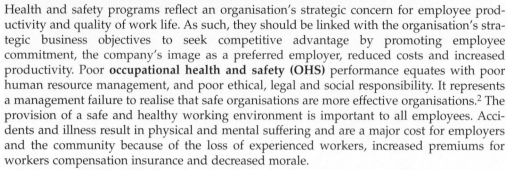

OCCUPATION	POTENTIAL HAZARD	POSSIBLE OUTCOME

Textile workers	Cotton dust
	Noise
	Chemical exposures
	   Aniline-based dyes
	   Formaldehyde
	   Furfuraldehyde
	
	Moving machine parts without barriers
		• Brown lung or byssinosis (a debilitating lung disease)
		• Temporary or permanent hearing loss
		
		• Bladder cancer and liver damage
		• Dermatitis, allergic lung disease, possibly cancer
		• Dermatitis, respiratory irritation, fatigue, headache, tremors, numbness of the tongue
		• Loss of fingers or hands

Hospital workers	Infectious diseases
	   Hepatitis
	   Herpes simplex virus
	Chemical exposure
	   Anaesthetic gases
	   Metallic mercury
	   Inorganic acids and alkalis
	Physical hazards
	   Ionising radiation
	   Microwave radiation
	
	   UV light
	Safety hazards
	   Lifting or carrying
	   Puncture wounds from syringes
		• Liver damage
		• Painful skin lesions
		
		• Spontaneous abortions
		• Poisoning of nervous system and kidneys
		• Irritation to respiratory tract and skin
		
		• Burns, birth defects, cancer
		• Sterility, harm to eyes, possible increased risk of cataracts
		• Burning or sensitisation of skin, skin cancer, cataracts
		
		• Back pain or permanent back injury
		• Infections

Welders	Infrared and visible light radiation
	UV radiation
	Chemical exposure
	   Carbon monoxide
	   Acetylene
	   Metallic oxides
	
	   Phosphine
		• Burns, headaches, fatigue, eye damage
		• Burns, skin tumours, eye damage
		
		• Cardiovascular disease
		• Asphyxiation, fire, explosion
		• Contact dermatitis, eye irritation, respiratory irritation, metal fume fever (symptoms similar to flu), possible kidney damage
		• Lethal at even low doses: irritating to eyes, nose, skin, acts as anaesthetic

Clerical workers	Improperly designed chairs and workstations; lack of movement
	Noise
	Exposure to chemicals
	   Ozone from copy machines
	   Benzene and toluene in rubber cement and 'cleaners'
	
	   Methanol and ammonia in duplicating machine solvents
		• Backache, aggravation of haemorrhoids, varicose veins, and other blood-circulation conditions; eyestrain
		• Hearing impairment, stress reaction
		
		• Irritation of eyes, nose, throat; respiratory damage
		• Benzene is associated with several blood diseases (including leukaemia) and toluene may cause intoxication
		• Irritation to eyes, nose and throat

Figure 18.1 Examples of job safety hazards
Source J. M. Ivancevich, *Human Resource Management*, 8th edn, McGraw-Hill, New York, 2001, p. 533

According to National Safety Council of Australia consultant, Lidia Ferraro, 'Culture is one of the most critical determinants of safety performance'[15]. Ted Kunkel, former President and CEO of Foster's, stresses his company's commitment to an objective of zero harm or injury to its employees because the company sees this as critical to the creation of an inspiring workplace.[16] At Leighton Holdings, the board reviews quarterly safety performance on all construction projects and regards its commitment to the health and safety of its work force as a core value (see figure 18.2).[17] Paperlinx similarly claims that the safety and health of its employees are the cornerstones of its culture and work practices.[18] OneSteel's occupational health and safety policy is outlined in figure 18.3.

LEIGHTON HOLDINGS SAFETY POLICY

The Group's core values guide our actions and include, among other things, a commitment to creating a safe, challenging and fun workplace and ensuring employees return home each day in the same health and condition as when they arrived at work.

The health and safety of our workforce is more than a compliance issue. For us it is about developing and maintaining a safety-conscious culture throughout each operating company. It is with this in mind that Safety Management Committees, consisting of senior managers, have been formed to help establish safety policies in all operating companies. An emphasis on training and awareness programs, including regular safety workshops and reviews, helps improve performance and supports the development of safer working environments. It is an ongoing requirement that each employee undergoes a safety induction course before beginning work on any Group project.

Monthly safety audits occur on all Leighton Group projects, both in Australia and offshore. These audits ensure compliance with our rigorous health and safety policies.

The Board oversees the Group's safety performance, reviewing quarterly performance reports. These reports contain detailed statistics and management analysis of work-related incidents, all based on reporting criteria and targets that are standardised across the Group. The reports also include any remedial action taken or planned, as well as the specific outcomes of such action.

Figure 18.2 Leighton Holdings safety policy
Source Leighton Holdings Ltd, *Concise Annual Report*, 2003, p. 18.

If an employee health and safety program does not have a clear sense of purpose, top management commitment and financial support (see figure 18.2), then it will fail. Depressingly, a recent study shows that 65 per cent of Australia's top 200 companies do not disclose any information about how they manage workplace safety risks. Other research shows that apart from legally required reporting, 90 per cent of companies do not report any details of their safety record, 96 per cent do not publish safety objectives and 80 per cent do not report a system to manage safety risks.[19] Furthermore, many management reporting systems encourage data manipulation rather than effective prevention.[20] Some organisations also complain that accidents are caused by careless workers, and that it is too expensive to spend money on employee health and safety.[21] Even worse are the companies that treat fines for safety violations as a business expense or establish undercapitalised shell subsidiaries so that they can avoid any penalties.

Foreign manual workers (especially illegals) are often exploited. In Japan, a 38-year-old Bangladeshi worker who severed his thumb in a workplace accident dumbfounded doctors after a successful operation to reattach the thumb by his request to amputate his thumb because his furious boss argued that it would save the company money and, if he did not amputate it, he would be fired.[22] In Hong Kong, month after month the same companies appear in court: Gammon, Paul Y-ITC, China State Construction Engineering Corporation and other large contractors are some of the worst repeat offenders.[23] Aoki, a Japanese construction company, was fined only HK$171 000 (approximately A$34 000) after 13 people died when a hoist plunged 17 floors (approximately HK$13 153 or A$2600 per dead worker). Mr Justice Duffy said of Aoki management: 'The knowledge of safety regulations shown … would not fill a postage stamp.'[24] At least one worker is killed on a building site in Hong Kong every week. Hong Kong's accident rate in the construction industry is 25 times worse than in Japan and Singapore.[25] Negligent employers are seldom arrested and fined only lightly if convicted.[26]

OneSteel

OneSteel's Occupational Health and Safety Policy sets the foundation for our approach and commitment to Occupational Health and Safety (OHS).

To put the policy into action OneSteel's approach to safety focuses on three key areas:
- demonstrated management commitment
- systems and standards
- involvement of people.

Demonstrated Management Commitment

A cascading structure for managing OHS throughout the company from Board level to the operations is in place. Key features of this structure include:
- OneSteel Board OHS&E Committee
- OneSteel Lead Team Central Safety Committee
- OneSteel Safety Network — across all OneSteel businesses
- individual business safety committee structures.

Safety has been a key focus with the integration of the Email Metals businesses recently acquired by OneSteel. DuPont Safety and Environmental Management Services has provided evaluation of these businesses and safety leadership training to key personnel.

Systems and Standards

OneSteel's OHS management system is designed to cater for business units of varying size, from an integrated steelworks to a small distribution centre.

The OneSteel Safety Network, in consultation with the Lead Team, developed a framework based on Australian Standard 4801. This allows each business unit to have systems and procedures in place that take into account the complexity of their operation.

An important ingredient to maintain the integrity of OneSteel's OHS management system is undertaking external assessment of progress against defined goals.

Occupational Health and Safety Policy

OneSteel is committed to achieving the highest performance in occupational health and safety with the aim of creating and maintaining a safe and healthy working environment throughout its businesses. Consistent with this, the company will:
- Seek continuous improvement in its occupational health and safety performance taking into account evolving community expectations, management practices, scientific knowledge and technology;
- Comply with all applicable laws, regulations and standards and where adequate laws do not exist, adopt and apply standards that reflect the company's commitment to occupational health and safety;
- Involve employees and contractors in the improvement of occupational health and safety performance;

- Train and hold individual employees accountable for their area of responsibility;
- Manage risk by implementing management systems to identify, assess, monitor and control hazards and by reviewing performance;
- Ensure that OneSteel employees, contractors and visitors are informed of and understand their obligations in respect of this policy;
- Communicate openly with employees, government and the community on occupational health and safety issues; and contribute to the development of relevant occupational health and safety policy, legislation and regulations; and
- Support relevant occupational health and safety research.

Figure 18.3 OneSteel's occupational health and safety policy
Source OneSteel, *Annual Report*, 2002, p. 23.

In Shenzen in southern China, every week one or two workers die in industrial accidents and more than 200 lose arms or legs. Local government officials (illegally) restrict compensation payouts so as not to deter investors.[27] Because the law in China is negotiable, most companies pay their employees nominal compensation and give them bus fare home.[28] Not one of the nine Hong Kong-owned toy factories in the Pearl River Delta strictly complies with Chinese labour regulations, let alone Hong Kong or international standards.[29] According to the Secretary General of the Hong Kong Toy Council, Warren Kwok, Western safety standards are not appropriate for a developing country such as China.[30]

The inability to economically dispose of toxic waste in Australia is threatening the survival of your company. Your finance manager says he can arrange to export the toxic waste to China at a third of the cost via his brother's company in Hong Kong.

Finally, some companies have transferred their OHS risks and hazards by relocating industrial wastes and noxious industries to other countries. For example, Australia has exported used lead-acid batteries to India for recycling, while Hong Kong traders export hazardous electronic scrap from North America to mainland China, where labourers receive about $2.55 per day to pick apart the toxic material.[31]

Australian industries with appallingly low OHS standards include clothing, farming, fishing and forestry. Occupations with high fatalities include plant and machine operators, labourers and tradespeople.[32] Long-haul truck drivers have one of the most dangerous occupations because of ineffective regulation, excessive hours, overloading, speeding and poor vehicle maintenance (one study found that more than 10 per cent of trucks were unroadworthy).[33]

In China, the chemicals, steel, paper and energy industries are notorious emitters of toxins and heavy metals. Environmental pollution in Jiangsu province is estimated to kill 120 000 people every year.[34]

Such employer attitudes and behaviour, which treat occupational health and safety as an expense rather than a strategic investment, are morally bankrupt. They reflect total ignorance of the real significance of accident and illness prevention and explain the greater focus on prosecuting managers and directors under OHS legislation.[35] 'What most impresses managers', says Hopkins, 'is the threat that they might be personally prosecuted in the event of some serious health and safety failure.'[36] ACTU Assistant Secretary, Bill Mansfield, similarly argues for criminal penalties against employers whose reckless behaviour causes workplace deaths.[37] Such an approach, however, has been fiercely resisted by employers, who see it as a shift away from prevention to punishment and the work of left-wing unions.[38]

Badly constructed and managed health and safety programs totally disregard the evidence, which demonstrates that healthy employees are more productive and are less likely to be absent, quit, have accidents or die. Organisations with healthy and safe work environments also have lower insurance and benefits costs and reduced downtime, and experience less damage to plant and equipment (see figure 18.4).

BENEFITS OF A SAFE WORKING ENVIRONMENT

- Improved personal safety
- Reduced overheads
- Reduced claims
- Insurance premium control
- Reduced uninsured losses
- Reduced retraining and relocation
- Improved production
- Reduced spoilage and wastage
- Reduced machine shut-down
- Reduced re-work
- Compliance with *Occupational Health and Safety Act* requirements

Figure 18.4 The benefits of a safe working environment, safe work practices and informed management

Organisations striving to achieve competitive advantage through increased employee commitment, motivation and productivity, reduced operating costs and enhanced public image must align health and safety objectives with their strategic business objectives. Health and safety performance cannot be divorced from employee trust, organisational culture and performance. Du Pont's HR Director for Australia and New Zealand, Graeme Longe, says: 'People are keen to work for a company with a good safety record. These workplaces quickly become recognized as good places to work. They also enjoy good morale — people go home happy when they know they have a safe workplace.'[39]

Sophisticated employers are increasingly aware of the bottom-line costs associated with accidents and ill health. Top-performing companies have workers compensation costs per employee that are less than 10 per cent of the workers compensation costs for the worst-performing companies. A retailer with more than 100 000 employees could thus save millions of dollars by achieving high safety standards.[40]

Organisations such as Boral, Du Pont, Leighton Holdings and Orica see the value of workplace health and safety. It not only provides a safer and healthier workplace, but also leads to improved productivity, quality and more harmonious employee relations. Total quality management (TQM), with its emphasis on improvement and the involvement of the worker, is having a spill-over effect on safety. As in TQM programs, occupational health and safety must be an inherent component of job design and employee training and development. Add-on safety programs are ineffective in reducing occupational injuries — safety and health must be considered when:
• jobs are designed
• employees are selected
• employees are trained and developed.[41]

By applying TQM principles to occupational health and safety, one Victorian company reduced work injuries by 55 per cent and the cost of workcover claims by 65 per cent within three years.[42]

Figure 18.5 outlines 'old' and 'new' management approaches to occupational health and safety.

Government regulation of occupational health and safety

Employers are under growing pressure from professional, community and union groups to accept a greater responsibility for employee health and safety. These pressures have motivated federal and state governments to introduce legislation covering occupational health and safety. Because of constitutional limitations, most legislation is generated by the states, which produces complexity and inconsistencies.[43] Adding to this problem is the half-hearted efforts (or in some cases outright resistance to change) of some governments, companies and unions.[44]

The **National Occupational Health and Safety Commission** is the national consultative body on occupational health and safety in Australia. This organisation has led much of the push to improve Australia's health and safety record, even though it lacks effective legislative or enforcement powers. Under its auspices, all Australian states have now adopted similar health and safety legislation that emphasises a duty of care on employers and workers through education and information rather than detailed regulation. The National Occupational Health and Safety Commission sets national standards, develops strategies, provides statistics, research and consultation services, and produces training packages for employers and employees.[45]

The underlying principles of the Australian system are **self-regulation** and active involvement of employers, the unions and all Australian governments. This **tripartite approach** has been subject to criticism by safety experts and appears to have basically failed.[46] Reasons for this include: confusion over OHS responsibilities; OHS is not seen as a core business activity; economic incentives to improve OHS have decreased; the increased bureaucratisation of OHS; resistance to change; and the overriding of employee health and safety concerns by demands for increased productivity and increased profits. Overall, the evidence also indicates that the legislative approach on its own has been ineffective in bringing improvements to poor-performing and small workplaces.[47]

National Occupational Health and Safety Commission The national consultative organisation on occupational health and safety in Australia.

Self-regulation Applies where employers are held responsible for providing a safe and healthy work environment. Emphasis is placed on education and information rather than detailed government regulation.

Tripartite approach Approach to OHS involving the active participation of employers, unions and government.

MANAGEMENT STYLE

Old — Formal and directive

- command and control
- OHS low priority

New — Committed and open

- participative and consultative
- visible commitment from leadership/senior management
- OHS ongoing demonstrable priority
- accountable for OHS performance
- role of work force and union valued

EMPLOYEES

Old — Directed

- performance measured only by costs
- no ownership of OHS objectives

New — Empowered

- pride in OHS achievements
- people valued and trusted
- OHS part of performance appraisal
- control over OHS/working environment
- people development focus

MANAGEMENT SYSTEMS

Old — OHS marginalised

- OHS system is 'tacked on' (parallel system)
- outcomes-only focus

New — OHS inclusive

- comprehensive management plan
- responsive mechanism for participation and consultation
- OHS included in operational management plans
- technology assessed for OHS implications
- OHS included in work procedures
- process focused

SKILLS

Old — Functional (narrow)

- production focus only
- OHS skills reside in specialists only

New — Problem solving

- problem-solving skills valued and developed
- OHS skills integral to all skills
- workers are multiskilled

ORGANISATIONAL STRUCTURE

Old — Rigid

- steeply hierarchical
- weak links between OHS and production
- control of OHS by experts

New — Flexible

- practices link OHS and design, production, planning, research and development
- OHS responsibility devolved
- team-based work structures
- OHS expertise available as a resource

STRATEGY

Old — Reactive

- meet regulations
- internal focus
- blame the victim
- reliance on only personal protective equipment

New — Preventive

- link between OHS excellence and competitiveness
- continuous improvement
- open to OHS developments
- benchmarking OHS practices
- quality focus
- auditable OHS systems
- OHS integrated with workplace reform

Figure 18.5 'Old' and 'new' approaches to occupational health and safety
Source OHS Best Practice: An Overview, Worksafe Australia, Sydney, November 1992.

Managing workplace health and safety

Health and safety has traditionally been regarded as something of a marginal issue by many managers. Some have assumed that it is a specialist function completely separate from their normal management responsibilities. Frequently, managers believe that appointing a health and safety officer (or nominating someone within their organisation to be responsible for health and safety) is sufficient and absolves them from any further responsibility. As a result, lack of training, and inadequate resources provided by employers to comply with safety and health regulations, are serious problems in Australia.[48]

It appears that employer attitudes remain largely unaltered and most improvements have occurred because of external pressure.[49] This has caused the South Australian OHS Commission to press for employers to be required by law to provide health and safety training for supervisors who are grossly lacking in knowledge when compared with worker and union representatives.[50]

The reality is that effective safety programs do work. Like most human resource management activities, however, they require serious commitment from all the parties involved.

Work-related injuries and illnesses represent a waste of the organisation's human resources. Losses through accidents at work come straight off an organisation's bottom line. Minimising these losses means increased profit. For the financial success of the organisation, health and safety must be regarded as an integral part of human resource management.

Occupational health and safety is not an altruism; it is a necessary and fundamental aspect of any productive organisation. Fewer accidents, diseases and symptoms of stress and improved quality of working life result in less absenteeism, higher productivity, lower health benefit costs, reduced workers compensation charges, lower labour turnover and increased attraction as an employer of choice.

The provision of a safe workplace is thus not only a moral issue, but also one with a positive economic pay-off. Management realisation of this is the starting point in the development of an effective health and safety program.

The importance of top management commitment cannot be overstated. 'The outstanding feature of the approach taken by safety leaders', says Hopkins 'is the fact that the commitment to safety comes from the top.'[51] The Managing Director of Du Pont Australia reads reports of every lost-time accident. He must inform the US head office within 24 hours and detail what is being done to prevent a recurrence. Occupational health and safety is part of Du Pont's core values and is regarded as a strategic advantage because it creates operational discipline — a key success indicator in large organisations.[52] Shell Australia likewise devotes one-third of every board meeting to safety and, in the case of a fatality, the CEO must fly to Shell's Dutch headquarters to explain and report the action taken to prevent a recurrence.[53]

Contrast this with organisations with a culture that says 'accidents and illness are natural in our industry', which only reinforces the acceptance of high rates of injury and disease.[54]

The Du Pont and Shell approaches demonstrate that management is serious about safety and, when employees observe this, they adopt the same attitude. In such organisations, it is obvious that employees are not treated as an expendable resource but as valuable human capital.

Elements of success

Du Pont, honoured more times than any other company by the American National Safety Council, uses visible initiatives from the top and employs powerful induction programs in which would-be employees are encouraged either to accept Du Pont's high occupational health and safety standards or seek employment elsewhere. Du Pont has a well-thought-out OHS philosophy and clearly defined OHS objectives. The Vice-President of Du Pont's Asia–Pacific Safety Resources Business says: 'Safety is only a symptom of how effective you are as a manager. If you can't manage safety, then you can't really manage.'[55] The development of such a culture of safety is a key characteristic of OHS best-practice companies (see figure 18.6).[56] A safety culture helps keep management and workers focused on and committed to OHS. Figures 18.7 and 18.8 show the key elements of successful OHS programs.

Evaluation of health and safety performance[57]

Auditing health and safety enables the HR manager to obtain feedback on the efficiency and effectiveness of the organisation's OHS program and to take the appropriate corrective action. The OHS audit permits performance to be compared over time, risks to be systematically reviewed and checks to be made to ensure that legal and company OHS policy requirements are being met. To do this, the organisation must develop an integrated combination of measures (see figure 18.9) that will provide managers with the necessary data to improve health and safety performance and to build a positive safety culture.

WHAT IS BEST PRACTICE?

'Best practice' refers to those practices that lead to superior performance in a company or enterprise relative to industry or international leaders.

Best practice is a process of continuous improvement achieved by 'benchmarking' practices and performance. This requires companies to:

- analyse their processes and activities to identify those that most impact on performance, and measure how well they are carried out
- compare these practices with those of organisations recognised as having superior performance
- adapt and implement practices based on what has been learned from the other organisations studied and set realistic targets for improved performance.

Figure 18.6 What is best practice?

Source *OHS Best Practice: An Overview*, Worksafe Australia, Sydney, November 1992.

THREE KEY ELEMENTS OF WORKPLACE OHS IMPROVEMENT

Culture

Without a culture which values the wellbeing of everyone in the workplace and which believes all injuries and illnesses can be prevented, people will continue to become ill, be injured and killed.

Adherence to development procedures, proper conduct of training, attention to detail, acceptance of personal responsibility, all workers thinking about every job and caring for others — these are essential values seen in the successful organisation. Visible commitment to them — not just compliance with their application — is required, starting with the most senior management. A positive workplace culture goes beyond workplace consultation. There must be genuine involvement and participation by all employees in OHS.

The task of achieving this culture would be much easier if the workplace existed in isolation. However, the OHS culture of the community in which the workplace exists is also important. That community tends to accept a certain level of workplace illness and injury. While it is possible to achieve excellent performance in spite of this, our challenge is to create a community culture that is increasingly intolerant of poor OHS performance.

Systems

Within organisations, solid systems underpinning OHS must be present. They include induction, training, policies, standards, procedures, audits, safe work practices, safe work organisation, performance measurement, improvement plans and action follow-up. Ensuring that elements such as these are in place will immunise the organisation against OHS performance decay due to staff changes or external pressures. These systems must include formal and durable mechanisms for involving all employees in the OHS programs. It is essential that a supportive culture be in place, otherwise systems can become an end in themselves and bury everything and everyone in bureaucratic procedures — forgetting that the objective is to stop people being hurt.

Hardware

Hardware includes plant, equipment and materials. Important issues are design, purchase, installation, operations, shutdown and maintenance requirements. Hardware must include OHS considerations and it is generally an effective OHS system which ensures that hardware is appropriate and safe.

Figure 18.7 Three key elements of workplace OHS improvement

Source R. Russell, 'The future: a management view', in C. Mayhew and C. L. Peterson (eds), *Occupational Health and Safety in Australia*, Allen & Unwin, Sydney, 1999, pp. 88–9.

SAFETY PROGRAM ELEMENTS

- Develop the organisation's human resource management philosophy and strategic objectives.
- Establish organisational health and safety objectives.
- Demonstrate top management commitment and support.
- Constantly reinforce that employee health and safety is a management responsibility.
- Encourage active participation by all employees.
- Create an all-inclusive health and safety program.
- Introduce ongoing inspections and checks.
- Promptly eliminate identified health and safety hazards.
- Establish appropriate health and safety records.
- Systematically evaluate the program.

Figure 18.8 Safety program elements

HEALTH AND SAFETY PERFORMANCE MEASURES

- Workplace inspections: concerned essentially with what can be observed or inferred from observations on a site.
- Safety tours: systematic or ad hoc reviews of a plant, for example, on a 'walk through' basis.
- Safety sampling: involves reviewing specific aspects of health and safety on a random basis.
- Behaviour sampling: assesses workers' behaviour on a systematic sampling basis to establish the proportion of unsafe work behaviours that might require correction, for example, by training or design improvements.
- Probabilistic risk assessments: such as fault tree analysis, failure modes and effects analysis and event tree analysis, which assign probabilities to foreseen occurrences as a prelude to risk reduction programs.
- HAZOP/HAZAN techniques: represent experts' contingency-based assessments of plant, particularly process plant, as part of a risk assessment program.
- Analysis of accident/ill-health/damage data: evaluates specified past events with a view to prevent recurrences.
- Analysis of near miss data: a more proactive version of the above in which events that might have led to accidents or unwanted incidents are evaluated with a view to prevent more serious outcomes.
- Management Oversight and Risk Tree (MORT): uses a logic tree to analyse organisational functions required in the safe management of high-risk technologies; also used to gain insights during accident investigations, near miss reviews and safety audits.
- Job Safety Analysis (JSA): a semi-formal hazard analysis that evolved from work study techniques and that uses task analysis to identify accident potential within a job.

Figure 18.9 Illustrative management health and safety performance measures

Source I. Glendon and R. Booth, 'Measuring management performance in occupational health and safety', *Journal of Occupational Health and Safety, Australia and New Zealand*, vol. 11, no. 6, 1995, p. 560.

Letter to the Editor

Management shouldn't be held responsible for accident-prone employees

Dear Editor,

Like all good managers, I aim to provide a safe workplace for my staff. Yet I am concerned that the OHS demands now being placed on employers are excessive and unjustified.

While managers should take every precaution to create a safe work environment, they cannot wrap every staff member in cotton wool to make the risks of accidents negligible. Each employee has to bear their share of the responsibility for workplace safety. Unfortunately, our legal system seems to ignore this necessity as it makes huge payouts to injured or disabled workers without seeming to consider the worker's own responsibility for accidents. The result is that all employers are slugged with huge workers compensation insurance premiums, which significantly raise the cost of doing business, often through no fault of their own.

Some employees increase their risk of accidents by coming into work tired from late-night clubbing. Others come to work under the influence of soft and hard drugs or the various medications that cause fatigue and impair reaction times. Still others bring the kinds of emotional and relationship problems to the workplace that make them lose focus on their work. All these problems serve to make workplace accidents a greater possibility.

In my view, OHS laws and compensation courts should take these sorts of issues into account. In doing so, the burden of OHS responsibility should be adjusted so that it bears more evenly and fairly on the reciprocal responsibilities of employers and employees.

As has been the case with legislation in other areas, the movement towards 'no-fault' workers compensation legislation has created as many problems as it has solved. While understandably aimed at simplifying a complex and costly legal minefield, the process remains complex and incomprehensible to most employers and employees. In addition, just as Australia's no-fault divorce laws arguably added elements of unfairness and inequity to the evaluation of marriage break-ups, the no-fault workers compensation system fails to fairly evaluate the contributions of both employers and employees to individual workplace accidents.

While these reforms have made for a faster resolution to OHS claims, they fly in the face of any notion of mutual responsibility for workplace safety.

A concerned OHS officer

Source David Poole, University of Western Sydney.

This Letter to the Editor provides a provocative viewpoint. Do you agree? See 'What's your view?' on page 690.

Current health and safety issues

The provision of a safe and healthy work environment requires more than reducing the number of job-related accidents and injuries. Managers have to 'deal with a variety of practical, legal and ethical issues, many of which involve a careful balancing of individual rights (particularly the right of privacy) with the needs of the organisation'.[58]

Some of the major issues for which HR managers must develop policies include AIDS, economy class syndrome, air rage, terrorism, sexual harassment, smoking, substance abuse, obesity, violence and work–family conflict.

HIV/AIDS Human immunodeficiency virus that causes a breakdown in the body's immune system and can lead to the development of AIDS.

AIDS

It is estimated that more than 40 million people worldwide now live with **HIV/AIDS**, with 25–30 million in Africa alone. The incidence of AIDS in the Australian work force is as high as 1 in 160.[59] The centre of gravity of the global AIDS epidemic is moving rapidly towards

Asia with Indonesia, Cambodia and Papua New Guinea especially at risk. India has around 4 million people living with HIV/AIDS and UN experts predict that by 2010 China could have more than 10 million cases.[60] In Hong Kong, trips to China for prostitution and drug use are dominant factors in the spread of the disease.[61] Mainland Chinese women, in turn, face a significant risk of catching HIV from their bisexual husbands.[62]

Such statistics and trends make it clear that every major organisation will have to deal with AIDS. A survey of Singaporean HR managers found that allowing HIV-infected people to work in a company would cause some employees to quit or refuse a job assignment and would produce increased grievances and complaints.[63] In China, HIV-infected people are prevented from marrying or using public swimming pools. Police are prone to seize their businesses, while medical practitioners inform their employers and refuse to operate on them. Not surprisingly, Chinese are terrified of having, or being associated with, AIDS. Stigma persists despite China having strict laws prohibiting discrimination against those with AIDS or HIV.[64]

Similar discrimination exists in many other Asian countries. In India, parents at one school withdrew their children because two orphaned students were identified as HIV positive.[65] Australia too continues to battle the HIV stigma as the rate of infection increases. One survey found that nearly 40 per cent of HIV/AIDS sufferers experienced less favourable treatment in the provision of health services, while 20 per cent had been discriminated against by insurance companies.[66] Former Chairman of the Federal AIDS Research Review Committee, Russell Scott, cautions: 'Because of public focus and media interest, a single adverse finding against an employer or a hospital under Australian anti-discrimination laws, or a serious industrial dispute arising from employees refusing to work with an AIDS sufferer or HIV-positive individual, could create a crisis in an industry or in the practice of medicine or blacken the industrial landscape. Employers, particularly those with large numbers on the payroll, should carefully develop acceptable, justifiable policies in relation to employees with HIV or AIDS.'[67] See figure 18.10.

You are having a late-night drink with your friend to celebrate her award as top salesperson of the year. You are shocked when she tells you in confidence that she is HIV positive and is having unprotected sex with the purchasing officers of some of the company's largest customers.

AIDS POLICY CHECKLIST

Does a formal written policy exist? If yes, does it:

- guarantee confidentiality to protect the employee's privacy?
- state that the company is against discrimination and is supportive of employment continuance and keeping the employee in productive employment as long as possible?
- clearly identify the employee's entitlements to health, disability and life insurance and other benefits?

- explain to managers and employees what is expected of them?
- provide for management and employee training on what AIDS is and how to deal with AIDS-related issues?
- provide for employee counselling and support?
- indicate consistency with the company's policy on equal employment opportunity?
- have the support of AIDS groups in the community?
- comply with all the company's legal obligations?
- create a sensitive and understanding corporate culture?

Figure 18.10 Things to consider when dealing with a person who has AIDS or who has a family member with AIDS

Source Adapted by the author from J. Monroe Smith, 'How to develop and implement an AIDS workplace policy', *HR Focus*, March 1993, p. 15; and R. Stodghill II, R. Mitchell, K. Thurston and C. Delvale, 'Why AIDS policy must be a special policy', *Business Week*, 1 February 1993, pp. 41–2.

The purpose for such policies is to inform employees about AIDS and how the organisation intends to respond to all the health and HR issues raised by the presence of AIDS in the workplace.

Australian companies that have developed formal or informal AIDS policies include ANZ, BHP Billiton, Coles Myer, Exxon and Qantas. Exxon's policy states that the company will not test for AIDS at the pre-employment examination, and will regard people with AIDS or the HIV antibody as being fit for work while they have continued health and fitness and can perform their job safely. Exxon employees incapacitated for work will be eligible for all benefits relating to illness and any other health benefits, and employees dying from AIDS are eligible for death benefits.

Some organisations, however, are opposed to issuing a special AIDS policy statement because they treat AIDS in the same way as any other disease or condition.

Economy class syndrome

Economy class syndrome
Blood clots caused by cramped airline seating and lack of movement.

Blood clots caused by inactivity and cramped airline seating are now recognised as a risk associated with flying. Twenty-five people have died in recent years at Tokyo's Narita airport because of '**economy class syndrome**'. Problems arise when long hours in cramped conditions cause blood clots to form, which can be fatal if they circulate into the heart and lungs. Experts estimate that between 15 and 20 per cent of passengers on long-haul flights are affected with varying degrees of severity.[68] Airlines have been accused of failing to adequately warn passengers of the potential dangers of tight seat pitches and inactivity during long-distance flights (Qantas and British Airways have some of the tightest seat pitches). According to Skytrax Research, tight seat pitches do not offer enough leg room for the average-size passenger to be able to relax in comfort.[69]

Although it has been alleged that airlines received warnings regarding economy class syndrome more than 30 years ago, Qantas claims there is no proven link between the syndrome and air travel.[70] Nevertheless, a group of Australian air travellers who have suffered the effects of economy class syndrome has launched a class action against Qantas and British Airways.[71]

The health and safety implications of economy class syndrome for business travellers and their organisations are obvious. Drinking water and doing stretching exercises can help maintain normal blood circulation.[72] (However, tests by Britain's Public Health Laboratories show that the airline drinking water is contaminated by *E. Coli* and human waste in 15 per cent of the water fountains on jets using major British airports.[73])

Air rage

Air rage Offensive and violent behaviour by commercial airline passengers. Examples include food throwing, sexual harassment, indecent behaviour, insulting language, abusive conduct and physical assault.

Desk rage Offensive and/or violent employee behaviour occurring in an office environment.

Airlines face a growing problem with '**air rage**'. Cabin crew find themselves involved as targets or because of their attempts to deal with passenger disturbances. Qantas has put its air crew through specialised training in the evaluation, prevention and management of disruptive passenger behaviour. Incidents of air rage include food throwing, sexual harassment, lewd behaviour, insulting language, offensive conduct and physical assault.[74] Cathay Pacific has banned the rock group Oasis from its flights because of rowdy, loutish, drunken behaviour.[75]

Some experts link air rage with other forms of aggressive behaviour such as road rage, bank queue rage, school rage, supermarket rage, **desk rage** and workplace rage. Factors contributing to such violent behaviour include feelings of loss of control and being endangered, and righteous indignation that someone else has broken the rules or is stealing part of one's space or privileges.[76] A clinical psychologist from the University of Western Australia says most air rage incidents are fuelled by growing stress and anger in the community, compounded by alcohol.[77] One recent study showed alcohol was present in 73 per cent of assaults and 84 per cent of offensive behaviour cases. Graham Burrows, Professor of Psychiatry at Melbourne University, says violence accompanied by alcohol abuse is now a major community health issue.[78]

A new form of air rage centres on obese passengers. Says one passenger, 'I have been pinned against an armrest by an overweight passenger twice in the past year; I doubt I can take much more'.[79] Recent research shows that invasion of personal space is the major annoyance of business travellers.[80]

Terrorism

According to a former Director of the US National Security Agency, industry is now a primary target for terrorist groups seeking to impose global political and economic change.[81] Starbucks, for example, has suffered boycotts by anti-war demonstrators and criticism by advocates of higher coffee prices for farmers. McDonald's also has been targeted by anti-war protesters, suicide bombers and French farmers.[82] Two Qantas flight attendants were stabbed by a passenger wielding two 15 cm stakes (which were not detected by airport security).[83]

Australian companies, in response, have increased security measures. These include more visible security personnel, more thorough security checking and increased staff training.[84] Technology also plays a part with the use of video screening, personal tracking devices and armoured cars on the increase. Bodyguards are also becoming more commonplace for senior business executives. Criminal and terrorist kidnappings, physical violence from extremist animal rights and environmental groups, and fear of terrorist attacks have made Australian business executives more alert to the need for personal security.[85]

Companies also need to ensure that employees are trained in security and evacuation procedures. This is especially important for expatriate personnel working in dangerous locations (such as Papua New Guinea and the Philippines) where they are prime kidnap targets. Companies have a duty of care to ensure that employees who are sent overseas are aware of the risks and are given appropriate training. An employee of Yellow Pages (Pacific Access) was awarded $570 000 after she was attacked while working in Papua New Guinea because the company did not give her adequate advice about working in a dangerous environment.

Unfortunately, too many companies still regard security as a cost rather than an investment in safeguarding their human and physical assets.[86] One study indicated that only about half of the companies surveyed had any sort of plan to deal with terrorism.[87]

The NSW Chamber of Commerce recommends that companies:
- provide staff with visible security passes
- develop an action plan in case of crisis
- ensure staff are alert to the presence of unauthorised personnel
- establish contact with local police
- screen mail
- audit all security equipment
- check the credentials of hired security staff.[88]

Sexual harassment

Sexual harassment is a significant issue in the workplace. It includes unwelcome sexual advances, unwanted and persistent physical contact, indecent sexual language and offensive comments, open discussion of a person's sexual behaviour and the unnecessary display of sexual material. Victims often suffer low esteem, anger, stress, humiliation, disinterest in the job and a feeling of powerlessness.[89]

HR managers need to introduce appropriate policies, training and supervision to guarantee every employee's right to work in an environment free from sexual harassment. Failure to do so can impose high costs on the organisation. The Catholic diocese on New York's Long Island, for example, is currently facing sexual abuse lawsuits amounting to US$1.85 billion.[90] Regardless, for some organisations the prime focus remains on protecting financial assets and public image.[91]

Sexual harassment Behaviour involving sexually suggestive remarks, unwanted touching and sexual advances, requests for sexual favours, or other verbal or physical conduct of a sexual nature that is unwanted and that adversely affects a person's employment and/or creates a hostile work environment.

Smoking

More and more companies are enacting workplace smoking policies. They are reacting to the reduced social acceptance of smoking, demands by employees and customers for a smoke-free environment, rising healthcare costs, increased government regulation and concerns over potential sizeable legal liabilities if sued by employees who develop illnesses from passive smoking. HR managers need to be proactive in assessing the risks within their organisation. Enlightened self-interest and ethical considerations suggest that companies provide a smoke-free work environment and promote 'quit smoking' programs, particularly as evidence suggests that the poorest Australians die from lung cancer at nearly twice the rate of the richest (even though cigarettes are expensive).[92, 93]

Companies involved in leisure and entertainment nevertheless fear adverse economic consequences of smoking bans. The Chief Executive of the Australian Hotels Association says: 'We believe staff are adequately protected under occupational health and safety laws. We want to get rid of the smoke, not the smokers.'[94]

NEWSBREAK

Taking workers' welfare into its own hands

By Robin Robertson

In 1994–95, staff at the City of Sydney lost 2179 days to injury. Fast forward to 2002–03, and days lost to injury have plummeted to 124 days.

When the City of Sydney placed a stronger emphasis on safety by putting it in the hands of management instead of leaving it to chance, it was able to run a healthier and safer workforce.

It was able to reduce the number of incidents which led to those lost days: there were 107 incidents in 1993–94 compared with 11 incidents in the past 12 months.

Human resources manager for the City of Sydney Council, Chris Saunders, says the most powerful change it made was to become a self-insurer. 'In June 1997, our workers compensation liability was about $6.5 million. By September 2003, our liability sat at just over $2 million.'

Workers' compensation claims have a tail, as a claim can take some years to be fully realised. Until then, the liability must be anticipated by the insurer.

'We've reduced our workers' compensation liability essentially by being better managers and developing a strategy', Saunders says. 'As a self-insurer, we have total control over prevention, injury management and compensation. We don't rely on an insurance company which puts up the premiums.

'We also have a passionate interest in the ongoing welfare of workers and their return to work.'

The council employs about 1000 people, in tasks ranging from compacting garbage to library management.

'We have innumerable safety plans based on the daily tasks of employees', he says. 'Risks associated with those tasks are all documented. We're not leaving anything to chance.'

And nor is the management of an injured employee left to chance. The employee is tracked from the time of the injury until they return to work. 'Management must understand the system', Saunders says. 'If an employee trips and sprains an ankle, they have an obligation to inform the supervisor immediately. The supervisor decides whether they need first aid or a trip to hospital. Then, we rely on the medical direction of the doctor. We encourage an injured employee to return to work on selected duties.'

He says that the City of Sydney has developed relationships with doctors, who know of the diversity of work on offer when staff are injured and cannot return to their designated job. They can return to alternative, possibly lighter, duties which brings them back to the workforce and under the eye of management.

'The injured employee is assigned a case manager under medical direction until they are fit to return to their usual work', he says.

By identifying the claim early — that is, taking immediate control of any workplace injury — the City of Sydney has a greater chance of controlling the cost.

In terms of prevention, Saunders says that the best way for employees to care about their own health is to give them information about it. 'So we have manual handling programs, first aid, plant safety, noise reduction, a hazardous substances program and drug and alcohol management awareness.

'We also run sun cancer tests and blood pressure tests, and they can assess their own health if they want.

'We spend a lot of money on safety training. For instance, the cleansing department has a 10-minute toolbox meeting every morning, where they will ensure everyone has their safety gear.'

Finally, the culture of safety must be so embedded into management systems that it is maintained by the next generation of managers. 'New people come in all the time', Saunders says. 'And that is the test of your system: if you do not have an OHS system that can be picked up by new managers, then it is lost.'

Source *The Australian Financial Review — Occupational Health and Safety Special Report*, 6 November 2003, p. 15.

In Asia, with the exception of a few locations such as Hong Kong, Singapore and Thailand, tobacco control laws are weak or nonexistent.[95] China has more than 350 million smokers who consume nearly one in every four cigarettes smoked in the world.[96] A recent study suggests that 100 million young Chinese men will die from smoking-related diseases unless habits change.[97] In both China and Hong Kong any moves to tighten control are strongly resisted despite data showing a dramatic increase in teenage smoking, a heavy cost to the government of treating smoking-related illnesses, and 70 per cent of people wanting smoke-free restaurants.[98]

Japanese politicians similarly have stymied plans to introduce anti-smoking policies arguing that it would be unconstitutional and negatively affect the tobacco industry (the dominant tobacco company, Japan Tobacco, has the Japanese government as its major shareholder). It is estimated that 100 000 Japanese die every year from smoking-related diseases.[99]

Substance abuse

There is increasing evidence that more and more employees are turning to alcohol and drugs to overcome stress. The Victorian Occupational Health and Safety Commission enquiry into alcohol and drugs in the workplace found that 20 per cent of women employed as managers and sales representatives are drinking unhealthy amounts of alcohol. According to a British medical expert, sales representatives are more likely than other employees to be heavy smokers, to be addicted to alcohol, to have heart disease and to suffer from stress.[100] In contrast, the largest groups of males consuming hazardous amounts of alcohol are tradesmen and blue-collar workers.[101] Heavy drinkers are also more likely to be single.

In Korea, middle-aged men are turning to drugs because of their declining economic and social status brought about by new technologies and the increasing presence of women in the work force.[102] After-hours drinking is also an established part of Korean corporate culture, and illnesses caused by widespread work-related drinking are now viewed as industrial accidents.[103] A government survey further reports that much Korean worker alcohol consumption is because of job-related stress.[104] In the United States, excessive alcohol consumption kills more than 100 000 people each year.[105]

According to one addiction specialist, many Wall Street employees use cocaine to feel more 'energetic, powerful, sexy and on top of the world'.[106] Some Australian legal advocates similarly use cocaine to enhance their performance and gain an unfair advantage.[107]

Australians smoke more than US$3 billion worth of cannabis per year (equivalent to about 1 per cent of Australia's gross domestic product).[108] Marijuana is the largest (and fastest-growing) cash crop in the United States — it is estimated that more than one-third of Americans over the age of 12 have smoked the drug.[109]

The cost of alcohol and drug problems in Australia is calculated at more than $19 billion per year (see figure 18.11).[110] Drug abuse also costs Hong Kong billions of dollars per year.[111]

If organisations are to deal effectively with workplace **substance abuse**, a clear, unequivocal policy statement defining the rights and responsibilities of the employer and the employee is essential.

Management argues that random drug tests are essential to guarantee workplace safety. The union claims that random drug tests are an invasion of its members' privacy.

Substance abuse Concerned with alcohol, tobacco and other drug addiction.

Obesity

Obesity has become a major health concern and has caused leading companies such as Ford, Honeywell, General Mills and PepsiCo to introduce 'slim down' campaigns to improve employee health and their corporate bottom lines.[112] The University of Chicago describes the obesity problem as a by-product of technological changes that have generated lower food prices coupled with higher-paying but sedentary jobs.[113] In the United States about 300 000 deaths per year are associated with people being overweight.[114] A recent US study found that excess weight accounted for 20 per cent of all female cancer deaths and 14 per cent of all male cancer deaths.[115] Moreover, problems related to obesity are further aggravated by smoking.[116] According to the US Center for Disease Control and Prevention, the number of obese Americans increased by 74 per cent between 1991 and 2001.[117] In Britain, it is predicted that more than half the population will be obese by 2006.[118] Obesity in Australia has more

DRUG	EFFECTS OF ABUSE
Amphetamines (speed)	Depression, insomnia, heart failure, kidney failure, loss of appetite, toxic psychosis
Cannabis (marijuana)	Bronchitis, conjunctivitis, disoriented behaviour, endocrine disorders, impaired judgement
Cocaine	Heart failure
Ecstasy	Collapse, convulsion, dehydration, exhaustion, muscle breakdown, overheating
Heroin	Dependence, drowsiness, nausea, respiratory depression, withdrawal syndrome (watery eyes, runny nose, yawning, loss of appetite, irritability, tremors, panic, chills, sweating, cramps)
Ketamine	Delirium, heart problems, impaired memory, impaired motor function, respiratory problems, tolerance/dependency

Figure 18.11 Substances of abuse

than doubled over the past 20 years as people give up exercise to eat more junk food and watch more television.[119] In Hong Kong, about one in 20 adults are double their ideal body weight.[120] This has been associated with a more than 200 per cent rise in the number of deaths from diabetes.[121]

Obesity can rob years from the lives of employees. Research shows that obesity can shorten the life expectancy of people who are grossly overweight at 40 by 7.1 years for females and by 5.8 years for males.[122] It increases the threat of chronic diseases such as diabetes, heart attacks, hypertension, stroke, gall bladder disease and some forms of cancer. People who are seriously overweight are seven times more likely to develop diabetes, six times more likely to develop high blood pressure and almost twice as likely to have high cholesterol levels as people of average weight.[123]

Experts also warn that obesity is spreading rapidly among children. *Xiao pangzi* or 'little fatties' are increasingly common in China. In Singapore, about 10 per cent of schoolchildren are obese and 5 per cent grossly obese.[124] The number of overweight children in the United States has almost doubled over the past two decades.[125] The prime causes of obesity are processed foods and fast foods rich with sugar and saturated fats and little or no exercise. This has led to bans on the sale of soft drinks and junk food in schools in some US states.

The President's Council on Physical Fitness and Sport claims that about 70 per cent of US adults are overweight and that 40 per cent of children aged 5 to 8 show at least one heart disease risk factor. In another finding, 50 per cent of girls aged 6 to 17 and 25 per cent of boys aged 6 to 12 could not do a single push-up.[126] According to fitness authority Dr Garry Eggar, more than half the Australian population is obese or overweight, with about one in three Australians being a sedentary slob. Recent research by the International Diabetes Institute also confirms the myth of Australians as suntanned athletes. Australians are now in the same fat league as Germany and Britain.[127] Nearly 90 per cent of Australians admitted to hospital with cardiovascular problems do little or no exercise.[128] A Beijing University survey shows that more than half of China's university students take no exercise.[129] In Hong Kong, more than half the people play no sport or do not exercise.[130] The dominant diseases in Singapore

A hospital is in serious financial trouble. If its situation does not improve, it will be forced to cut essential health services. To reduce costs it eliminates its loss-making cafeteria. It profitably leases the space to a fast-food chain renowned for a menu that is high in saturated fats, salt and sugar.

— cancer, heart disease, stroke, hypertension and diabetes — are related to unhealthy life-styles including smoking, physical inactivity, obesity and poor diet.[131]

In the United States, obesity is increasingly being viewed as being 'similar to alcoholism' and therefore to be regarded as a 'disability'.[132] Critics of this approach argue that it encourages people to avoid responsibility for their actions, sees everyone as a victim and encourages legal scams.[133] Rotund burger munchers and other fast-food addicts, for example, have launched legal cases arguing that they were misled into believing that fast food was nutritious and that companies did not warn them of the possible health hazards of eating fast food.[134]

Airlines also face difficulties. Normal-sized passengers complain of being squeezed and pinned against armrests by overweight passengers. Overweight passengers, in turn, complain of discrimination and undersized seats. Cabin crew increasingly are being forced to arbitrate between feuding passengers. The demands of anti-discrimination laws and the frustrations of furious passengers squeezed into a seat against an obese passenger (especially one who has raised the armrest because they could not fit into one seat) have aggravated the work stress of cabin crew. Some airlines, such as Southwest Airlines, have attempted to introduce policies to charge obese passengers for an extra seat.[135]

Finally, there is evidence to suggest that discrimination against obese employees appears to be greater than discrimination based on other characteristics.[136]

Workplace violence

According to the Director of the Australian Institute of Criminology, the use of violence as a means of resolving disputes is deeply rooted in Australian society.[137] Overwhelmingly, violent offenders are working-class males aged 18–30 who have often committed crimes while intoxicated.[138]

All types of employees can encounter anger and aggression in the workplace — police, parking officers, nurses, receptionists, teachers, domestic helpers — virtually anyone in a regulatory, social or service role.[139] Teachers in Hong Kong increasingly face classroom violence. One Australian English language teacher reportedly was regularly abused, spat upon, pushed down stairs, physically assaulted and sexually groped. Such student violence is rarely reported, however, because of fears of adverse publicity by school administrators.[140] Similarly, domestic helpers in Hong Kong, Malaysia and Singapore suffer abuse. Indonesian maids in Malaysia have been scalded with irons, forced to eat cockroaches, kept in cages or handcuffed, physically and sexually assaulted, and had food, water and wages withheld.[141] An Indonesian maid employed by Singaporean Ng Hua Chye was found battered and bruised. Post-mortem reports indicated more than 200 injuries on her body as a result of whipping, kicks, punches, burns and scalding. At death her weight was just 36 kg.[142] Ng was subsequently jailed for $18\frac{1}{2}$ years and caned 12 times for abusing and causing the death of his maid.[143]

Research shows the industries most at risk of **workplace violence** in Australia include health, welfare and community services, restaurants, education, retail, and road and rail transport.[144] Australia's image as a 'safe' country has meant that many companies have no or only poorly developed employee protection programs.[145] Banks have been accused by unions and employees of being slow to respond to security concerns regarding armed robberies because of cost considerations. ANZ is now being sued under the *Occupational Health and Safety Act* by the Finance Sector Union because it reportedly ignored union advice about inadequate security.[146]

A new type of violent behaviour is being expressed by workers who have been dismissed, retrenched or demoted. In the United States, homicide is the most frequent cause of job-related deaths after traffic accidents.[147] Homicides committed by disgruntled current and former employees are now so common that a standardised profile of this type of killer has emerged.[148]

Workplace violence Violent behaviour occurring in the workplace.

Domestic violence

Domestic violence, traditionally thought of as a private, family matter, also needs to be addressed. One in four Australian women, for example, have been subjected to domestic violence, making it a major health problem.[149] In Hong Kong, the economic downturn has been blamed for a 25 per cent surge in family violence.[150] Interestingly, the most dramatic increase has been in the number of Hong Kong men reported as victims of physical abuse. According to one expert, most assaults occur when a woman suspects her husband of having an affair.[151]

Research shows that domestic violence directly affects an employee's psychological well-being, productivity, attendance, physical safety, medical insurance costs and turnover rates, making it a workplace issue.[152] The challenge exists for HR managers not only to find ways of protecting employees from violence, but also to address the pervasive fear, sense of shame and anxiety that these incidents induce.

Workplace bullying

Bullying in the workplace is a health and safety hazard. It is also illegal. Bullying includes persecuting or ganging up on an individual, making unreasonable demands or setting impossible work targets, making restrictive and petty work rules, constant intrusive surveillance, shouting, abusive language, physical assault, and open or implied threats of dismissal or demotion. One survey, for example, shows that lazy workers place pressure on colleagues not to work too hard. If ignored, verbal and physical abuse are suffered.[153] An ACTU survey found that more than half of all employees reported experiencing shouting, ordering, belittling and other intimidating behaviour.[154] Bullying can be present anywhere in the organisation, but most bullies are managers. The incidence of bullying is higher in workplaces with autocratic and arbitrary management.[155] 'Bullying', says Phillips, 'affects all parties — employer, alleged harasser and victim. It can result in reduced efficiency, productivity and profitability, adverse publicity, an unsafe work environment, increased absenteeism, sick leave and staff turnover. In addition there are costs associated with counselling, compensation claims and if necessary legal action.'[156] Research by Griffith University estimates the cost of workplace bullying to Australian employers at $6–13 billion per year.[157]

Work–family conflict

Increasing interest is being shown by HR managers in understanding and managing the work–family interface. This is because employee surveys consistently show that **work–family conflict** affects productivity. People do not go to work in isolation. Everyday events affect them, such as:
- the birth of babies
- coping with infertility
- women re-entering the work force and the impact of this on the good running of the household and on changed household roles
- parents growing old and infirm and needing to have new, viable living arrangements
- adolescent troubles, within the normal to crisis range
- mid-life stresses, including marriage breakdown, living alone and re-marriage.

These all have an enormous impact on the people experiencing those events, wherever they are, including at work.[158] US studies, for example, show that 20 per cent of employees lose time because of appointments involving their children, childcare problems or sick children, and 38 per cent have taken time off work to care for older relatives.[159]

More and more organisations are reorganising the traditional way work has been structured because it is no longer compatible with the needs of today's working families. Recently, it was found that the work–life balance was rated by US professional women as the number one factor in their decision to quit working.[160] Research also shows that working women with caring responsibilities are under more pressure than those who have no caring responsibilities and that married women reported greater pressure than single women.[161]

In response, progressive organisations are introducing flexible work schedules, childcare and elder-care assistance, personal services (such as banking, dry cleaning and hairdressers) and work–family seminars to allow employees to better integrate their work–family responsibilities. Westpac, for example, aims to be an employer of choice by promoting work–life balance. Specific programs include: paid maternity, paternity and adoption leave; mutual negotiation of work hours for part-time employees; and innovative home-based work, job-sharing and childcare arrangements.[162]

Practitioner speaks

Time to pause, reflect and educate

When I started working in this field more than 20 years ago there was relatively little awareness of occupational health and safety in Australia. We had very prescriptive legislation and a view that it was largely a medical rather than workplace issue. Businesses couldn't conceive that they would have to understand work procedures and take action to make workplaces safer.

New legislation, people's changing views on how they want to live their lives in the work environment and the introduction of OHS courses at university and other levels were catalysts for change.

Now we are very aware of what is happening internationally and have a lot of very good professionals working in the area and interacting with overseas agencies. In what I call the early days of working in OHS we would go to conferences and cling to every word the foreign professionals were saying. Now the tables have turned. Australians are sought-after speakers at international conferences and active participants in committees and working parties where the outcomes will guide the future of health and safety for the working community. It's very exciting.

Everything about work has changed — the way we work, the pace of work, business ethics, regulatory requirements, the effect of global markets and attitudes to workplace safety — but we shouldn't think that change has led to perfect workplaces. It has only caused us to think more about health and safety.

Now we are striving to encourage managers and employees to work together to change work practices. Years ago communication wasn't seen as important. If you wanted to change the status of your occupational health and safety you would call in a professional to deliver a report. Management would look at the report and make a decision on whether or not to implement the recommendations. Frequently only the easy and inexpensive things were done. Now employees and unions are better educated on OHS and they are able to put pressure on government to regulate and employers to make improvements.

The establishment of the National Occupational Health and Safety Commission in the mid-1980s provided the first forum for the states, employers and unions to come together and discuss OHS. The development of the recently endorsed National OHS Strategy is a significant step creating a social partnership to work together in improving Australian health and safety standards.

'Safer communities' programs are also boosting awareness. People are becoming more aware of safety in everything they do, from working in the home garage and reading product safety labels to taking more care of themselves at work. People need to grow up thinking about safety if we are to develop a real safety culture in the workplace. Already we can see that younger people will not put up with some of the unsafe and unhealthy work conditions their parents endured and that's a very good outcome.

It is time to pause, reflect and educate rather than pass more legislation. If we keep adding new requirements, we are going to have people throwing up their hands and saying they can't deal with it. It is critical now to have a period when employers and employees are helped to understand and comply fully with current legislation. We already have very good legislation throughout the states. What we need is a lot more thinking about how we can assist workplaces to understand and assess risk and make real changes.

Sylvia Kidziak

Sylvia Kidziak is managing director of SL Engineering, a health, safety and environmental engineering consultancy in Sydney. Her background is in the nuclear and power-generation industries, construction and manufacturing. A commissioner of the National Occupational Health and Safety Commission and adviser to Commonwealth and state governments and industry, she became a Member of the Order of Australia in 2001 for her work on OHS.

Source *HR Monthly*, June 2003, p. 33

What is stress?

Stress has been described as the rate of wear and tear on the body caused by living. It is a general term for the pressures and problems people experience as they go through life. In itself, stress is neither good nor bad. In fact, some degree of stress is normal and necessary for day-to-day survival. Even when people are relaxed there is a minimal amount of stress present. Without stress, energy and motivation would be absent. Stress is unavoidable in human existence.

Stressors

Stressors are the things that cause stress. They are the stimuli or circumstances that bring about a change in people's psychological and/or physiological equilibrium. Surprisingly, whether the stressors are positive or negative, the initial physiological reactions are much the same. Rapid heartbeat, increased blood pressure, dryness in the mouth and quickened breathing are just some of the dominant reactions. Getting fired (negative) and having a romantic encounter (positive) bring about the same physiological reactions. Stress levels increase irrespective of whether the experience is unpleasant or pleasant.

It is only when stress becomes excessive that it threatens people in a harmful way. Too much stress over a prolonged period can make people susceptible to physical and/or mental breakdown. In fact, some experts argue that stress-related illnesses represent up to 75 per cent of all health problems.[163] It is small wonder that stress is often seen as the cause of ulcers, heart attacks, strokes and other degenerative diseases among employees.

Sources of stress

All employees face stress. It is part and parcel of being an employee. How each individual employee handles stress will determine whether they can happily live with it or whether it will destroy both health and career. Much depends on whether the individual employee perceives the stressor as a threat or a challenge.

The sources of employee stress are virtually endless. However, three general groupings can be made — those relating to work, those relating to the personal characteristics of the employee and those relating to the employee's external environment (see figure 18.12).

Although a single stressor may affect a person, stressors usually act in combination to bring about a state of tension. For example, the demands of a new job associated with a transfer interstate, the purchase of a new house, finding new schools for the children and generally settling into a strange environment can together cause major stress to develop in an employee. In fact, research evidence suggests that stressors outside of work, such as those related to personal and family life, are major causes of employee stress.[164]

Work causes of stress

Workplace stress places a heavy burden on organisations through stress-related absenteeism, lateness and decreased ability of employees to perform their work.[165] A survey of mental health and wellbeing found that just under 20 per cent of adult Australians stay away from work more than one day in a month because of depression, substance abuse or anxiety. The most affected groups include women, people in their early 20s, singles and those living alone.[166] A UN study found that high unemployment, job insecurity, short-term contracts and intense time pressures on employees were associated with stress.[167] In Australia longer hours, continuous change, employment uncertainty and bullying are prominent stress causes.[168] Research indicates that almost one-third of Australians are worried about losing their job and feel that they have lost control of their economic future.[169] Says the Director of

Labor Education Research at Cornell University: 'Workers are feeling the ground is constantly shifting under their feet. They don't know who owns them, when they will be outsourced, or what future they have with the company.'[170] In Britain, stress-related issues are now the biggest cause of workplace absence.[171]

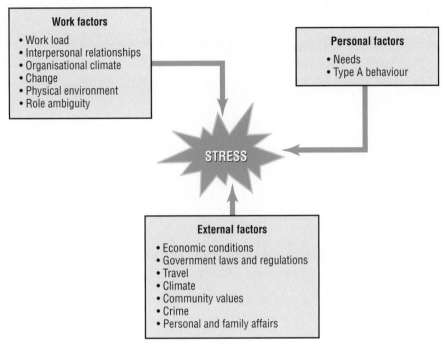

Figure 18.12 Sources of stress

Almost any aspect of work can cause stress. In some professions (such as law, medicine, finance, consulting and technology) a 55-hour week is considered 'part-time', with long hours a prerequisite for tenure and promotion.[172] Software engineers and venture capitalists involved in the Internet revolution were renowned for their 24/7 schedules.[173] Among the most stressful jobs are firefighter/emergency services worker, senior executive, surgeon, police officer and air traffic controller.[174] A recent study found staff at Australian universities suffering from higher stress and ill health than the general community because of increased teaching loads, funding pressures, lack of recognition, poor management and job insecurity.[175]

Some of the major stress factors are outlined below.

Work overload

Having too much to do, information overload, working long hours and having to meet tight deadlines are frequent causes of stress. If experienced over prolonged periods of time, they can lead to **burnout**. Because of economic recession and the struggle to maintain living standards, increasing numbers of employees are finding themselves overworked, stressed out and heavily taxed by the joint demands of work and family life.

A survey of almost 7000 Australian union members found that overwork was leading to serious health and safety concerns, with less than half being happy with their work–family balance.[176] Australians are developing into a nation of 'time poor', 'stress rich' individuals. It is estimated that 40 per cent of Australian workers do not take annual holidays, only 18 per cent take their full entitlements and about 20 per cent have not had a holiday in the past two years.[177] It is also estimated that one in five work more than 50 hours per week. Research indicates that many people now want to work less hours for less money to have a better quality of life.[178] A recent study shows fatigue-related accidents cost the Australian economy almost $2 billion per year.[179] However, other research indicates that nearly half the men and one-third of the women are happy to work long hours because of job satisfaction, career advancement and financial security. Experts argue, however, that long hours are unhealthy,

Burnout A state of mental, emotional and physical exhaustion that results from substantial and prolonged stress.

unsustainable and ultimately unproductive. Nevertheless, the evidence suggests that employees who gain reputations as clock-watchers experience career stagnation.[180]

In Japan, *karoshi*, or death from overwork, is also a serious problem. *Karoshi* occurs most commonly in workplaces where jobs require extremely strenuous effort and where employees work without assistance.[181] In a suicide note one employee wrote: 'I chose this way because I couldn't achieve results even though I worked until becoming completely exhausted.'[182] At least 600 Japanese kill themselves each week. Suicide rates are highest among men in their 40s and 50s — the group most affected by Japan's economic malaise.[183] In many Japanese companies, stress is not considered a problem but a badge of honour for hardworking employees.[184]

Work underload

Rust-out Stress produced from having too little to do.

Perhaps surprisingly, having too little to do can cause stress. Frustration, boredom, dissatisfaction and fatigue give rise to **rust-out**, with a corresponding decline in health. In fact, boredom carries a greater health risk than the stress of working in a demanding job.[185]

Shift work

Shift workers are more likely than day workers to have chronic health problems.[186] Divorce rates are 20–60 per cent higher than for day workers. In addition, they experience less job satisfaction, more accidents, and increased alcohol and drug use and abuse.[187] Overall, shift workers are more likely than other workers to experience problems that affect their job performance.[188] A study by the University of Adelaide found that shift workers who have had one sleepless night can perform as poorly on the job and pose as great a hazard to themselves and their colleagues as those who have been drinking alcohol.[189] Similarly, research by the National Aeronautics and Space Administration indicates that long-haul airline pilots are often fatigued, sleep deprived and probably suffer from sleep disorders.[190] Female shift workers are prone to disrupted menstrual cycles, lower fertility rates and a higher incidence of miscarriage, premature births and babies with low birth weights.[191]

Interpersonal relationships

Unsatisfactory relationships with the boss, subordinates and colleagues are major sources of stress in the workplace. A recent UK study found that unfair and unreasonable bosses are potent workplace stressors who cause increased blood pressure and increased risk of heart attack or stroke in their subordinates.[192] Poor interpersonal relationships are aggravated further in highly political organisations where no objective performance standards exist and personal connections are critical for promotion and survival. Moreover, when managers conduct performance appraisals using subjective measures or 'gut feel', or are subject to such appraisals themselves, stress is produced. This is particularly so where performance ratings have a direct impact on advancement or pay.[193]

Change

Change is an accepted cause of stress. Takeovers, mergers, downsizings and the introduction of new technology can all act as stressors because they require employees to adapt to new and unfamiliar situations. Change can be particularly stressful when it is associated with an organisation's rationalisation involving transfers, terminations and retrenchments because employees face increased job insecurity and uncertain work demands. Job insecurity especially is a great stress producer in most employees.[194]

Organisational climate

Work environments characterised by extreme competition, poor communication and an authoritarian and threatening management style create stress. Such work climates create a vicious circle as managers under stress in turn produce stress in their subordinates and other managers. A US study found the leading cause of workplace stress to be incompetent management.[195]

Employees with heavy workloads, constant deadlines and little say in how they do their work exhibit more heart and cardiovascular problems, greater anxiety and depression, increased use of alcohol and prescription/over-the-counter drugs, and greater susceptibility to infectious diseases.[196] Studies by the University of Pittsburgh show that job dissatisfaction can cause high blood pressure in males. Men who see little chance of promotion, feel uncertain about their careers, have poor relationships with colleagues and/or superiors, and have no opportunities to contribute to decision making are most likely to develop hypertension.[197] An Australian study by Savery indicates that high job dissatisfaction leads to frustration and, if the employee cannot leave, this frustration causes ill health.[198] Gilbertson similarly found that people in HR positions reported significant role stress and lack of power.[199]

Finally, researchers from Boston University discovered that strokes are likely to occur most often on Mondays, suggesting that 'Blue Monday' does exist.[200]

Physical environment

Excessive noise, inappropriate lighting, high or low temperatures, crowding, lack of privacy and an inability to 'personalise' the workplace can all produce stress.[201] Workspace ratios, for example, dropped on average from 30 m² per person in 1997 to 23 m² in 2001, and a further fall of 7 m² is predicted.[202] Living and working in high-rise buildings have both psychological and physical effects on people and have been associated with asthma, allergy proneness, fatigue, headaches, miscarriages, nausea and increased stress.[203] Similarly, workers in airconditioned buildings with poor air quality are more than twice as likely to suffer respiratory problems than workers in naturally ventilated environments.[204] According to recent research, Hong Kong's permanent ambient noise causes large numbers of its residents to suffer from sleep disorders, mood swings and other psychological problems.[205]

Role ambiguity

In organisations where employees do not know what is expected of them, the resulting uncertainty creates stress.[206] In such situations, managers are pressured to anticipate what their duties and responsibilities are, creating an internal fear that their actions are not appropriate and that they will be punished.

Personal factors

A variety of personal factors are also potential sources of stress for the employee at work. For example, a study in Hong Kong suggests that balding men face severe psychological stress.[207] Another Hong Kong survey found that 60 per cent of women and 40 per cent of men are at risk of psychological breakdown during a divorce.[208] Similarly, 80 per cent of Australian managers in one survey changed jobs within a year of a marriage breakdown.[209] US cardiologists Friedman and Rosenman showed that people who were hard driving and competitive, with a strong sense of time urgency and who were chronically impatient with delays (Type A), had more than six times the incidence of heart disease compared with those with opposite characteristics (Type B). The need to achieve, impatience and perfectionism in Type A employees create stress not only in the employees but also in others. Furthermore, Type A employees tend to seek out stressful jobs with long working hours and tight deadlines. In this sense, Type A employees bring stress to themselves. Consequently, it is not surprising to find that Type A employees are more susceptible to heart disease than others.[210]

External factors

Many external or environmental factors can cause stress. For example, a recent survey found that stress levels among Australian CEOs had increased because of increased competition, declining profitability, the state of the economy, labour relations and industry restructure.[211] The main external factors are outlined below.

Economic conditions

Recession can create fears of retrenchment and prolonged unemployment.[212] One research study has shown that anxiety and uncertainty about job security can give rise to as many health problems as unemployment itself.[213] For example, 46 per cent of employees in the United States say they feel more pressure to prove their value to their employers.[214] Family members also experience stress when a loved one becomes unemployed.[215] The stress of unemployment, according to the Australian Society of Sex Educators, Researchers and Therapists, is a major factor in male impotence.[216] A Chinese University of Hong Kong survey similarly found economic worries triggered sexual problems among 50 per cent of its Hong Kong respondents. These in turn lowered quality of life, undermined marital relationships and harmed psychological health.[217]

Another survey found that money is the principal contributing factor to stress in Australian homes.[218] Likewise, a study by the Family Planning Association of Hong Kong indicates that financial pressures are a key factor having a negative effect on the sex lives of Hong Kong couples.[219] Finally, in the United States recessions and the increasing number of lay-offs are blamed for the dramatic increase in workplace murders.[220]

Government laws and regulations

Fringe benefits tax, workers compensation, regulations regarding termination, equal opportunity, occupational health and safety, and so on can all add to the tension experienced by employers and employees. Complying with state, federal and organisational rules and policies was ranked as the number one stressor in a survey of US managers.[221] Similarly, complex and wide-ranging Australian government compliance regimes are creating high levels of stress and ill health among many family and small business managers.[222]

Travel

International travel, or even commuting to work, can induce stress. One US study found that employees who spend more time and effort in commuting have high blood pressure and report being more 'uptight' on arrival at work than their counterparts. The commuter who every day has to fight through peak-hour traffic can generate considerable anger and anxiety.[223]

Similarly, jet lag affects over 70 per cent of travellers who cross time zones (up to 30 per cent of them severely).[224] Travel over long distances through several time zones in a short period of time is a stress producer. Because of the geographic size and isolation of Australia, travel over long distances is the norm rather than the exception.

Classic symptoms of jet lag are fatigue, disorientation, insomnia, headache, reduced mental and physical capacity, and disruption of normal body rhythms. The long-term physical impact of constant travel can be serious. US studies suggest that frequent travellers are more prone to heart attacks because of the stress induced.[225] Finally, cancelled flights, lost baggage, sickness, robberies, missed family functions and family confrontations regarding infidelity are other causes of stress cited by frequent business travellers and their families.[226]

Community values

Where community values differ from those of the individual, stress may result. This is one of the causes of 'culture shock' experienced by international travellers and expatriates. Similarly, where managers hold different values from those of the organisation employing them, stress can be induced. The managers may, in fact, psychologically 'tear themselves apart' as they try to satisfy both sets of values. A competitive lifestyle and its associated stress, according to a study by the University of Hong Kong, is an important factor contributing to Hong Kong having the highest number of stomach ulcer sufferers per capita in the world.[227] Not surprisingly, Hong Kong rates as the most stressful city in the world.[228] Similarly, surveys reveal that Sydney is the most stressful city in Australia.[229] Singaporeans, in turn, cite high costs and a lifestyle that places constant pressure on them to improve themselves or risk falling behind socially and economically as major causes of stress.[230]

Lower socioeconomic groups in Australia have failed to participate fully in lifestyle education programs and, as a consequence, have not enjoyed a reduction in diseases such as heart disease. The Australian Institute of Health has shown that levels of cigarette smoking, physical inactivity and overweight or obesity significantly increase as education levels decrease for both men and women.[231] According to a report by the UN Children's Fund,

Australia has the highest rate of teenage suicides in the industrialised world. Reasons suggested for this include higher aspirations generated by the media, lack of confidence in the future and family disruptions.[232]

Crime

Fear of being robbed, stalked or assaulted provides a background of tension that individuals may only fully recognise when, with some relief, they leave the 'danger zone'.[233] The NSW Bureau of Crime Statistics and Research, for example, found that in Australia there is a burglary every four minutes of every day.[234] A recent poll likewise found almost four in five Australian women believe it is not safe to go out in public places at night.[235] In China, the Philippines and Taiwan businesspeople fear kidnapping.[236] Stress caused by fear of crime also can be severe when visiting places with a reputation of being dangerous, such as Cambodia, Papua New Guinea, the Philippines and Southern China.[237]

Personal and family affairs

Divorce, death of a family member or other crises have been linked to the development of stress-related illnesses. For example, US studies show that ten times as many widows and widowers die in the first year after the death of their spouse as do non-widowed individuals in similar age groups. Likewise, the incidence of illness among divorcees during the first year after divorce is over ten times higher than that for married people over the same period.[238] Unhappy marriages, financial problems and domestic violence are driving many young Mainland Chinese women to suicide according to University of Hong Kong research.[239] A Canadian study into heart disorders shows that men having extra-marital affairs are more likely to die from a heart attack while having sex with their adulterous partner.[240] In Hong Kong, men having extra-marital affairs experience increasing stress after their affairs are discovered by their wives or if lovers keep demanding they get a divorce.[241]

In another study, the cancer rate was shown to be sixteen times higher than normal among people who were anxious, easily upset and prone to depression.[242] Finally, according to Sydney psychologist Dawn Cohen, women in management positions have particular problems because they feel they have to be twice as good as their male counterparts.[243] In addition, women who assume multiple roles — both at work and home — have a higher potential for stress.[244]

Stress and job performance

The level of stress may either help or hinder job performance. Figure 18.13 shows the relationship between stress and job performance. When there is no stress, job challenges are nonexistent. Boredom and frustration develop and impact negatively on performance. As stress increases, performance tends to improve as the employee calls up physical and mental resources to meet the challenges of the job.

Such stimulation is healthy and enables employees to feel a sense of achievement and to get satisfaction from the job. However, if the amount of stress exceeds the optimum and starts to place excessive demands on the employee, the result will be lower performance. At this point, the employee loses the ability to cope, finds difficulty in making decisions and demonstrates erratic behaviour.

If no relief from the stressors is available, stress may build up to a level where the employee reaches breaking point. Should this happen, performance will deteriorate rapidly and the employee may face a total mental and physical breakdown.

Unfortunately, such situations tend to compound, with the employee getting fired for non-performance and then facing added financial and domestic pressures. It is easy to understand why job loss and marriage breakdown often go hand in hand.

Decision making and stress

Perhaps one of the commonest causes of stress in managers is the inability to make decisions and take action. Decision making is paramount in preventing stress. As stress inhibits decision making, a vicious cycle can quickly be established. The manager puts off decisions and then becomes overwhelmed with a backlog of problems requiring action. Stress builds up as the manager now worries about all the decisions still to be made, with the consequence that their ability to deal with new situations decreases. This leads to more worry, more problems and more pressure.

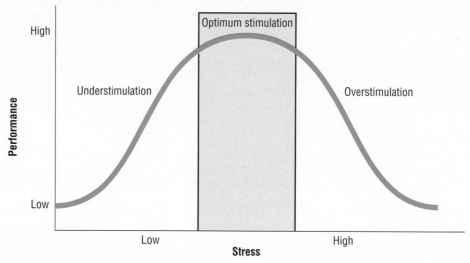

Figure 18.13 Stress and performance curve

Procrastination in decision making may totally immobilise a manager and reduce ability to cope with even the most trivial of problems. To avoid this happening, the manager must ask a key question: 'Whose decision is it?' If it is someone else's responsibility, the manager should immediately direct it to the appropriate person and get on with their own work. If the responsibility for the decision is the manager's, they should take action. A bad decision is better than no decision and the right decision made too late is useless. It is a myth that delay improves the quality of a decision. It is not a myth, however, that delay in decision making is a sure way to increase stress.

Symptoms of stress

The early signs of stress can be recognised easily and it is essential that managers are alert to such warnings in themselves and in the people they work with. Signs to watch for include: a general washed-out feeling; feeling 'nervy', tense or 'uptight'; indigestion; high blood pressure; insomnia; restlessness and a general inability to concentrate; an increase in use of drugs (including alcohol); an increase in smoking; a change in eating habits; an inability to relax; aches and pains; and sexual difficulties.

The more an employee experiences such symptoms, the more likely they are to be the result of too much stress. If ignored, the unrelieved stress will attack the susceptible parts of the employee's body and personality. The end result could be alcoholism, drug taking and degenerative diseases of the stomach, heart, kidney and other parts of the body.

The management of stress

The challenge for every employee is to find the level of stress that stimulates productivity without damaging health. This is achieved through effective stress management. Some basic stress management skills necessary for controlling stress are outlined below.

Relaxation

To avoid the adverse effects of stress, the employee must learn to 'switch off'. The ability to really relax can be learned. Basic tension-relieving exercises such as deep breathing, progressive relaxation techniques and yoga can all be used to beat stress. Other simple ways to relax are listening to music, having sex and having a good laugh.[245] Even patting the dog or cat can help the stress sufferer. In fact, one study suggests that pet birds may have an even greater therapeutic effect than dogs because people make a greater effort to interact with them.[246]

'This position also features a built-in fitness program ... your office is on the 74th floor and the building has no elevators.'

Exercise

Regular physical activity such as ballroom dancing, walking, jogging, swimming, rowing, cycling or tennis will not only improve fitness but also help to counter stress. Before employees commence an exercise program, a medical check-up is advisable. Most aerobic exercises also substantially aid weight loss, thus reducing undue stress on the body. US studies have shown that regular exercise reduces body fat ratios regardless of age. People over 60, for example, gain muscle tone from regular weight training.[247] In fact, people age partly because they do not exercise. It is never too late for employees to improve their physical fitness. Research indicates that organisations that introduce work-site health programs have reduced levels of absenteeism, labour turnover and workers compensation claims.[248]

Diet

Prolonged stress can deplete the body's vitamin supply, making it more susceptible to disease. In addition, when people are under stress their eating habits change: they miss meals and increase the consumption of short-term stimulants such as coffee, alcohol and cigarettes. During stressful periods, maintaining a balanced diet is essential to bodily well-being. Recent research by the National Heart Foundation of Australia shows that senior executives often skip breakfast and lunch and then eat a huge meal at night to compensate, which leads to excessive cholesterol.[249] Another study by the National Institute of Business Management found that workers who overeat are as much as 30 to 50 per cent less productive than those without eating problems.[250]

Talk

Talking about worries or problems can be a very effective way of reducing stress and helping employees to cope with excessive pressure. People typically get an emotional release from their frustrations when they have an opportunity to talk about them. Allowing pressures to build up by 'bottling them up inside' is not an appropriate way to deal with stress.

Planning and time management

Much employee stress is the result of poor planning. Employees must take time out to review their personal and career goals. On the job, time must be set aside for planning future activities. Lack of planning leads to confusion over objectives, wasted activity and considerable frustration. Bottlenecks result when a manager fails to take action, and stress builds up in the manager and those around them. Typically, bottlenecks caused by indecision are the product of mistaken priorities. Being disorganised and 'snowed under' with work demands that fresh priorities be established. Concentrating on low-priority items is a sure way to create tension; there is no substitute for doing the critical jobs first.

Delegation

Poor delegation is a primary cause of managerial failure and stress. Managers need to realise that they cannot make all the decisions — especially all the small day-to-day ones. Alas, many managers are reluctant to delegate. They fear that they will lose status or that others will not be able to do the job as well as they can. Delegation is an essential tool in time management and stress control. Without it, managers risk their sanity.

Living with stress

All employees need to recognise that stress need not be destructive. Awareness of the symptoms and causes of stress permits appropriate interventions. Too much stress is a cause of employee inefficiency and physical and mental breakdown. Relief from excess pressure enhances performance. Employees can live with stress quite happily if they plan, keep a balance between work and leisure, and practise stress-reducing exercise and habits regularly. Employee burnout is avoidable.

Thirty interactive Wiley Web Questions are available to test your understanding of this chapter at **www.johnwiley.com.au/ highered/hrm5e** *in the student resources area*

Summary

Organisations have ethical, legal and business obligations to provide their employees with a safe and healthy working environment. Failure to do so is simply bad management. First, it means human resources are treated as an expense and not as human capital to be valued. Second, it exposes the organisation to excessive risk and legal liability. Third, because the occupational health and safety program has an impact on employee relations, productivity, costs and profits, it affects the organisation's overall economic wellbeing.

Occupational health and safety is part of every manager's job and not just the responsibility of the HR manager or safety specialist. Unfortunately, Australian managers have been slow to accept this and safety is still too often viewed as too difficult and too marginal to the business to be of real concern.[251]

Because occupational health and safety is so important and the benefits so significant, HR managers must be at the forefront in promoting safe and healthy work environments and in stimulating awareness and acceptance by managers of their responsibilities.

student study guide

review questions

1. What is the strategic importance of occupational health and safety?
2. What is HR's role in occupational health and safety?
3. What are some of the major causes of work-related accidents and illnesses?
4. How can managers use the organisation's reward system to promote health and safety?
5. Why should management be concerned about job stress? What can management do to reduce job stress?
6. Is 'overwork' a problem or are people just 'work shy'?
7. 'Some employees are accident-prone.' Do you agree with this statement? Explain your reasoning.
8. Why should management be concerned about employee substance abuse?
9. What are the major stressors in your life? How do you react to them? What stress avoidance measures are you taking?
10. Describe any dangers to your health and safety that you have experienced in a work situation. What did you do about it?

environmental influences on occupational health and safety

Discuss the key environmental influences from the model (figure 18.14 shown on the following page) that have significance for occupational health and safety.

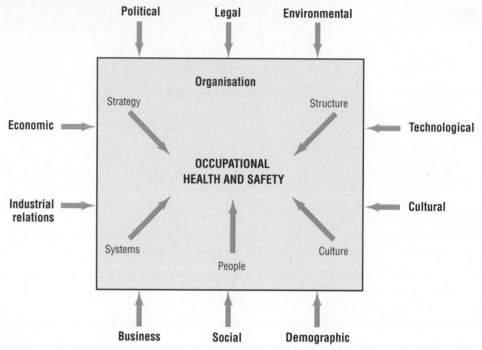

Figure 18.14 Environmental influences on occupational health and safety

class debate

Accidents are caused by accident-prone employees not management.
or
Managers whose irresponsible behaviour results in workplace accidents should be jailed.

what's your view?

Write a 500-word response to the Letter to the Editor on page 670, agreeing or disagreeing with the writer's point of view.

practitioner speaks

Read the article on page 679. As a class, critically discuss the author's view that 'It is time to pause, reflect and educate rather than pass more legislation'.

newsbreak exercise

Read the Newsbreak 'Taking workers' welfare into its own hands' on page 674. What makes for a 'culture of safety'? Describe how management can improve workplace health and safety.

What do you think? Conduct a mini survey of class members, using the questionnaire below. Critically discuss the findings.

1.	It is none of management's business if an employee is HIV positive.	YES	NO
2.	Accident-prone employees should be fired.	YES	NO
3.	Regular drug testing of employees should be compulsory.	YES	NO
4.	People with unhealthy lifestyles should not be considered for employment.	YES	NO
5.	Using cocaine is a personal and not a company matter.	YES	NO
6.	Prosecuting managers is the best way to get companies to take health and safety seriously.	YES	NO

online exercise

Conduct an online search for information on one of the following topics: AIDS, air rage, economy class syndrome, foetus protection, obesity, shiftwork, substance abuse, terrorism or violence in the workplace. Report your findings in 500–750 words. Include the web addresses that you found useful.

ethical dilemma

Jet Red's Operations Manager

Jet Red's HR Manager, Linda Church, sighed as she replaced the phone. Janet Armstrong's anguished pleas echoed in her ears. The pressure of Jet Red's restructuring was telling. She knew all the senior management team was stressed. The demands of Alan Balkin, the Managing Director, were ever-increasing. Bill Armstrong, the Operations Manager, was obviously feeling the pressure. First the Bali bombings, then SARS. Jet Red's sales had plummeted. The never-ending crises and demands for cost reductions were taxing Bill's abilities to the limit. Unable to delegate, Bill had been taking on more and more work. Recently, Bill had started to miss deadlines, make mistakes and become increasingly short-tempered. Linda could see that Bill was caught up in a vicious cycle. She had heard office rumours that he was drinking but had ignored them. Now in desperation Janet had called. She said Bill was depressed and having increasingly

explosive temper tantrums. Janet felt her husband was having a nervous breakdown. She said she was worried that Bill was going to be fired. At 53, she knew he would never get another job. Linda asked whether Bill had spoken to Alan. Mortified, Janet said no. She said Bill was terrified of Alan and begged Linda not to mention to anyone that she had called.

The knock at the door interrupted Linda's musings. It was Alan. 'Sorry to interrupt, but I need you to do something for me.'

'Yes, Alan, what is it?'

'I want you to prepare a separation package for Bill. He's out of his depth. The operations job is too big for him.'

Linda gasped. 'But he's been with Jet Red for over 20 years!'

'I know, but he's yesterday's man. Bill just isn't up to it.'

Discussion questions

1. If you were Linda, what would you do?
2. What ethical issues are raised in this case?

case studies

Jet Red's weighty problem[252]

'We have a problem' declared Linda Church, HR Manager for Jet Red.

'What's up?' asked Alan Balkin, the Managing Director.

'A passenger checking in was refused a seat on our Sydney flight because of her weight.'

'What do you mean?' questioned Alan.

'Apparently, the woman weighs 180 kg and the flight crew refused to allow her to fly because the seat belts wouldn't fit. She's so big that the seat belt couldn't be done up. As a result, the crew refused to let her board because of the safety risk.'

'That seems to be commonsense to me', replied Alan. 'Our prime consideration is the safety of our passengers. If anything happened to her during the flight, we would be in serious trouble. How could we justify letting a passenger fly without a seat belt? Think of the potential legal liabilities and the public relations nightmare we would face. Our image as a safe airline to fly would be destroyed. We would be seen as totally irresponsible.'

'Well', said Linda, 'the woman is claiming that we discriminated against her. She says Jet Red breached her human rights. She is arguing that our refusal to let her fly hurt her dignity and emotions.'

'Surely it's not our problem that she's so fat? Why doesn't she lose weight?'

'I'm afraid that's not the point, Alan. Her lawyers are claiming that we are at fault because our seat belts are not long enough.'

'What do you mean? All our cabin seats and belts are standard. How can it be our fault?'

Linda sighed. 'We told her that it was a safety issue and not deliberate discrimination because of her weight. However, because we didn't clearly specify any restrictions we have on accepting large passengers, we could be at fault.'

'You're kidding me?'

'I'm afraid not, Alan.'

Discussion questions

1. Who do you agree with, the passenger or Jet Red? Why?
2. Should airlines have the right to refuse a seat to an overweight passenger? Explain your reasons.
3. If you were Jet Red's Managing Director, what would you do to prevent such a situation arising in the future?

Toxic foetus

Tina Sexton fumed. 'It's blatant discrimination! The company should never ask such a question. What business is it of theirs whether I'm pregnant or not? I'm qualified to do the job. That's what counts!'

Leslie Crossland, HR Manager for OZ Chemicals, leaned forward. 'Tina, calm down. You know that in the new plant you'll be exposed to toxic substances that may harm a foetus. It's simply not a chance we want to take. How would you feel if you became pregnant and your baby was harmed?'

'That's not the point!' snapped Tina. 'The company has a responsibility to provide a safe working environment.

Refusing to consider women my age for a job in the new plant because we might become pregnant is not fair. It's outright discrimination against women of childbearing age. The company is using this toxic hazard as an excuse to discriminate.'

'Tina, be reasonable. The company can't give you or any other pregnant woman a 100 per cent guarantee that your foetus will not be harmed. We employ the latest and safest technology. What more can we do?'

'As far as I'm concerned, Leslie, the company is not interested in protecting me. It just wants to protect itself and to keep the best-paying jobs for the boys. It should be my decision, not the company's. It's my baby, not yours.'

Discussion questions

1. Do you agree or disagree with (a) Tina or (b) Leslie? Why?
2. Do you think it is appropriate for a company to prohibit pregnant women or women in their childbearing years from working in dangerous or hazardous jobs?

practical exercises

1. HEADPHONES

Jimmy Costello and Danny Thong, packers for Oz Toys, overcome the dull routine of placing toys in boxes all day by listening to music while they work. Both are regarded as good workers. So as not to annoy other workers, Jimmy and Danny both wear headsets. All was well until a new supervisor, Linda De Vries, was appointed to the packing and dispatch section. Linda was horrified to see Jimmy and Danny wearing headsets and told them to remove them immediately. When Jimmy and Danny protested, Linda said it was for their own safety. How could she be sure, Linda said, that both men would hear any alarms or verbal warnings of danger? Moreover, Linda argued that because both Danny and Jimmy listened to their music at high volumes, they could suffer damage to their ears, putting the company legally at risk for not providing a safe and healthy workplace.[253] Danny and Jimmy both disagreed and angrily responded that the wearing of headsets was a personal matter and that they were going to talk to their union representative.

Activities

(a) Break into groups of four to six. Develop an action play to deal with this situation. Regroup and discuss your recommendations

(b) Break into two groups — one to consist of Danny, Jimmy and the union representative; the other to consist of Linda, the factory manager and the HR manager. Your task is to resolve the problem. At the conclusion of the discussion, regroup and review the various points raised and the proposed solutions.

2. TERRORISM

You are the HR Manager for Wonderworld Entertainment Parks. The company currently operates fun parks in Sydney, Surfers Paradise and Singapore. You have just received a telephone call from a person claiming to be a member of World Peace, an extremist terrorist group. The caller has threatened a bomb attack on your Australian fun parks unless your company denounces the Australian government and its environmental policies. The caller says your company is a moral polluter and deserves to be destroyed.

Activity

Break into groups of four to six. Develop an action plan to deal with the threat. Then regroup and discuss your recommendations.

3. KIDNAPPED

Benny Lopez, Marketing Manager, Philippines, is on the telephone. He tells you that Mike Gollan, President, Tony Cortez, Finance Manager, and Teresa Ng, Manager IT, have been kidnapped by terrorists. The terrorists want US$5 million for their release. They have threatened to kill Teresa if they do not receive a reply from Benny within the hour. If the police are contacted, all three will be beheaded. Benny asks you what he should do. Mike's wife is in Australia visiting her parents. She is six months pregnant.

Activity

Break into groups of four to six. Discuss what you would do. Then regroup as a class and review your action plans.

4. **HAZARDS**

Identify a job you are familiar with and list any potential hazards (such as exposure to toxic chemicals, noise, stress, and so on) and their possible effects on the job holder (such as burns, hearing loss, back injury, fatigue, and so on). As a class, discuss your findings.

suggested readings

Bohle, P. and Quinlan, M., *Managing Occupational Health and Safety*, 2nd edn, Macmillan, South Melbourne, 2000.

CCH, *Australian Master Human Resources Guide*, CCH, Sydney, 2003, chs 21, 25.

Clark, R. and Seward, J., *Australian Human Resources: Framework and Practice*, 3rd edn, McGraw-Hill, Sydney, 2000, pp. 130–8.

De Cieri, H and Kramar, R., *Human Resource Management in Australia*, McGraw-Hill, Sydney, 2003, pp. 99–110.

Fisher, C. D., Schoenfeldt, L. F. and Shaw, J. B., *Human Resource Management*, 5th edn, Houghton Mifflin, New York, 2003, ch. 14.

Gennard, J. and Judge, G., *Managing Employee Relations*, CIPD, London, 2003, ch. 13.

Geroy, G. D., Wright, P. C. and Berrell, M. M., *Counting the Costs: Corporate Workaholism and Organisational Performance*, Saint Louis Press, Melbourne, 2000.

Gomez-Majia, L. R., Balkin, D. B. and Cardy, R. L., *Managing Human Resources*, 3rd edn, Prentice Hall, Upper Saddle River, NJ, 2001, ch. 16.

Ivancevich, J. M., *Human Resource Management*, 8th edn, McGraw-Hill, Boston, 2001, ch. 17.

Mayhew, C. and Peterson, C. L. (eds), *Occupational Health and Safety in Australia*, Allen & Unwin, Sydney, 1999.

Mondy, R. W., Noe, R. M. and Premeaux, S. R., *Human Resource Management*, 8th edn, Prentice Hall, Upper Saddle River, NJ, 2002, ch. 13.

Nankervis, A. R., Compton, R. L. and Baird, M., *Strategic Human Resource Management*, 4th edn, Thomson, Melbourne, 2002, ch. 13.

online references

www.acci.asn.au
www.adgih.org
www.britishairways.com/health
www.cdc.gov/niosh/homepage.html
www.dewrsb.gov.au/workplacerelations/legislation/
www.econ.usyd.edu.au/acirrt
www.nationalsecurity.gov.au
www.nla.gov.au/02/law/html

www.nohsc.gov.au/
www.nsc.org
www.osh.net/safeprog.htm
www.osha.gov
www.shrm.org.hrmagazine
www.stopjetlag.com
www.workforceonline.com
www.worksafe.gov.au

end notes

1. C. Rance, 'A long road to the top', *HR Monthly*, June 2003, p. 32.
2. L. Nelson, 'Managing managers in occupational health and safety', *Asia Pacific Journal of Human Resources*, vol. 32, no. 1, 1994, pp. 13–28.
3. F. Buffini, 'Funds expand disclosure push', *Australian Financial Review*, 8 April 2003, p. 4.
4. Reported in N. Lindsay, 'Union steps up worker safety push', *Australian Financial Review*, 10 February 2003, p. 7.
5. S. Long, 'Study outlines flaws in mine safety', *Australian Financial Review*, 6 June 1997, p. 15; and M. Davis, 'Unsafe at any depth?', *Business Review Weekly*, 6 April 1998, pp. 52–6.
6. J. Kahn, 'Ailing Chinese workers pay high price for export boom', *International Herald Tribune*, 19 June 2003, p. 2.

7. Worksafe Australia, 'The top 10 of everything', *Business Review Weekly*, 25 January 1999, p. 14.

8. N. Ellis, 'Old world model has passed its use-by date', *Australian Financial Review — Special Report*, 15 August 2001, p. 10.

9. A. Shaw and V. Blewett, 'Telling tales: OHS and organisational culture', *Journal of Occupational Health and Safety — Australia and New Zealand*, vol. 12, no. 2, 1996, p. 186.

10. Wesfarmers, *Annual Report*, 2002, p. 30.

11. J. Durie, 'It counts, being a numbers man', *Australian Financial Review*, 9 October 2001, p. 60.

12. W. King in Leighton Holdings Ltd, *Annual Report*, 2002, p. 18.

13. Boral, *Annual Review*, 2002, p. 31.

14. Boral, op. cit., p. 31; and SimsMetal, *Annual Report*, 2002, p. 14.

15. L. Ferraro, 'The culture of safety', *HR Monthly*, April 2003, p. 38.

16. Foster's Brewing Group Ltd, *Concise Annual Report*, 2002, p. 27.

17. Leighton Holdings Ltd, *Annual Report*, 2002, p 18.

18. Paperlinx Ltd, *Annual Report*, 2002, p. 27.

19. F. Buffini, op. cit., p. 4.

20. M. Brown, 'Knowing versus doing', *HR Monthly*, June 2002, p. 24.

21. P. Bohle and M. Quinlan, *Managing Occupational Health and Safety*, 2nd edn, Macmillan, South Melbourne, 2000, pp. 90–1.

22. P. Hadfield, 'Illegal worker sacrifices thumb to keep in with boss', *South China Morning Post*, 31 January 2001, p. 12.

23. L. Hopkinson, 'Pollution', *Post Magazine*, 12 March 2000, p. 33; J. Flint, 'Firm's fine condemned as "peanuts"', *Sunday Morning Post*, 22 February 1998, p. 2; and V. Chiu, 'Getting to grips with building site safety', *South China Morning Post*, 8 June 1996, p. 17.

24. Quoted in S. Fluendy, 'To be on the safe side, Aoki leads with its chin', *South China Morning Post — Business*, 12 October 1995, p. 22; and G. Manuel, 'Courts ensure anti-inflationary costs of human life', *South China Morning Post — Business*, 10 September 1994, p. 16.

25. C. S. Wong, 'Safety record slammed', *Eastern Express*, 8 March 1996, p. 2; and J. K. W. Chan and H. C. Chan, 'Construction site safety in Hong Kong', *International Journal of Management*, vol. 14, no. 3, 1997, pp. 334–8.

26. S. Mok, 'Safety onus on workers', *Eastern Express*, 24 June 1996, p. 5.

27. M. O'Neill, 'Injured workers pay high price for industry', *Sunday Morning Post*, 28 November 1999, p. 4.

28. *New York Times*, 'Lives sacrificed to progress', *South China Morning Post*, 8 April 2003, p. A9.

29. P. Bohle and M. Quinlan, op. cit., pp. 2–3.

30. R. Knowles, 'Toying with the lives of workers', *Eastern Express*, 16 January 1996, p. 11.

31. A. M. Chugani, 'HK dealers active in toxic waste dumping', *Sunday Morning Post*, 3 March 2002, p. 2.

32. R. Robertson, 'Manual workers caught in the danger zone', *Australian Financial Review — Special Report*, 22 August 2002, p. 15.

33. Based on P. Bohle and M. Quinlan, op. cit., pp. 4–5.

34. M. Chan, 'Industry blamed for cancer deaths', *South China Morning Post*, 19 April 2003, p. A4.

35. C. McLean, 'Prosecutions emphasise personal liability of managers', *HR Monthly*, November 1996, p. 20.

36. A. Hopkins, *Making Safety Work*, Allen & Unwin, Sydney, 1995, p. x.

37. R. Robertson, 'Keeping the workforce off the sick list', *Australian Financial Review — Special Report*, 22 August 2002, p. 14.

38. K. Gough, 'Work's bill of wrongs', *Australian*, 30 April 2002, p. 9.

39. B. Bennett, 'Safety is a strategic advantage: Du Pont', *Australian Financial Review — Special Report*, 15 August 2001, p. 9.

40. M. Brown, 'Protecting profits means protecting staff', *Australian Financial Review*, 12 December 2001, p. 55.

41. R. F. Scherer, J. D. Brodzinski and E. A. Crable, 'The human factor', *HR Magazine*, April 1993, p. 95.

42. Example cited in 'No other investment can offer such excellent returns', Occupational Health and Safety Authority, Melbourne, undated, p. 12.

43. P. Somerville, 'Balancing risk', *HR Monthly*, April 2001, p. 20.

44. G. Robotham, 'OHS makes slow progress', *HR Monthly*, August 1999, pp. 30–1; and T. O'Loughlin, 'Abbott seizes the chance to turn up the heat again', *Australian Financial Review*, 14 April 2003, p. 6.

45. M. Dobbie, 'Tougher laws force greater awareness', *Business Review Weekly*, 11 May 1990, p. 109; and R. Robertson, 'Action plan spells out life saving priorities', *Australian Financial Review — Special Report*, 22 August 2002, p. 19.

46. M. Saunders, 'Our safety record questioned', *Australian*, 12 March 1997, p. 29; G. Robotham, op. cit., pp. 30–1.

47. C. Mayhew and C. L. Peterson (eds), *Occupational Health and Safety in Australia*, Allen & Unwin, Sydney, 1999, p. 90.

48. P. Ruzek, 'A stern test for tripartism', *Personnel Today*, June 1990, p. 10; M. Saunders, 'Our safety record questioned', *Australian*, 12 March 1997, p. 29; T. Harris, 'Bribes and rorts culture ignores safety of miners', *Australian*, 10 April 1997, p. 2; and C. Sobieralski, 'Effective health and safety committees', *HR Monthly*, May 2000, pp. 42–3.

49. P. Bohle and M. Quinlan, op. cit., pp. 1–7; and C. Mayhew and C. L. Peterson, op. cit., pp. 1–10.

50. Reported in P. Ruzek, op. cit., p. 12.

51. A. Hopkins, op. cit., p. 187.

52. B. Bennett, op. cit., p. 9.

53. A. Hopkins, op. cit., p. 187.

54. A. Shaw and V. Blewett, 'Telling tales: OHS and organisational culture', *Journal of Occupational Health and Safety — Australia and New Zealand*, vol. 12, no. 2, 1996, p. 185.

55. B. Bennett, op. cit., p. 9.

56. A. Hopkins, op. cit., p. 187.

57. This section is based on I. Glendon, 'Safety auditing', *Journal of Occupational Health and Safety — Australia and New Zealand*, vol. 11, no. 6, 1995, pp. 569–75; and I. Glendon and R. Booth, 'Measuring management performance in occupational health and safety', *Journal of Occupational Health and Safety — Australia and New Zealand*, vol. 11, no. 6, 1995, pp. 559–65.

58. L. R. Gomez-Meijia, D. B. Balkin and R. Cardy, *Managing Human Resources*, 3rd edn, Prentice-Hall, Englewood Cliffs, NJ, 2001, p. 33.

59. E. Leopold, 'UN steps up fight against AIDS', *Courier-Mail*, 26 June 2001, p. 14; Reuters, 'The worst year yet for HIV cases and AIDS deaths: UN', *South China Morning Post*, 26 November 2003, p. A10; and M. Richardson, 'AIDS: the shadow over Asia's growth', *South China Morning Post*, 28 November 2003, p. A23.

60. Agencies, 'UN warns Asia to keep AIDS in check', *South China Morning Post*, 27 November 2002, p. 10.

61. E. Lee, 'SAR sitting on AIDS time bomb', *Sunday Morning Post*, 25 June 2000, p. 3.

62. Agence France-Presse, 'Women face AIDS risk from bisexual husbands, says study', *South China Morning Post*, 21 June 2003, p. A4.

63. V. Lim and G. L. Loo, 'Facing AIDS in the workplace', *Human Resources*, vol. 2, no. 11, 1999, pp. 22–3.

64. E. Rosenthal, 'In China lives as outcasts force AIDS patients together', *International Herald Tribune*, 15 January 2003, p. 6.

65. Agence France-Presse, 'Pupils flee HIV-positive children', *South China Morning Post*, 8 March 2003, p. E2.

66. N. Squires, 'Australia battles HIV stigma as infection rate rises', *South China Morning Post*, 2 December 2002, p. 12.

67. R. Scott, 'Negotiating the minefield of AIDS in the workplace', *Australian Financial Review*, 1 June 1989, p. 12; and J. Catanzariti, 'Commission puts bar on HIV discrimination', *Weekend Australian*, 5–6 April 1997, p. 38.

68. H. Phillips, 'Fatal fliers less likely to be Asian', *South China Morning Post*, 30 October 2000, p.3; and M. Tessier, 'Tragedy in economy class', *Hong Kong iMail*, 12 March 2001, pp. A22–A23.

69. 'Airlines' pitch puts travellers in comfort zone', *Australian Financial Review — Special Report*, 28 November 2003, p. 5.

70. *The Observer*, 'Air death warnings ignored for 30 years', *South China Morning Post*, 15 January 2001, p. 9; and L. Creffield, 'Australia launches probe into dangers', *South China Morning Post*, 15 January 2001, p. 9.

71. Agence France-Presse, 'Deep vein thrombosis claim allowed', *South China Morning Post*, 21 December 2002, p. 11.

72. Based on E. Lee, '40 pc of lung blood clots linked to flying', *South China Morning Post*, 16 January 2001, p. 1; 'Twenty five die at Narita after cramped flights', *South China Morning Post*, 29 December 2000, p. 1; R. Maynard, 'Airlines face suit over economy class syndrome', *South China Morning Post*, 12 December 2000, p. 11; and E. Lee 'A hidden killer that preys on travellers', *South China Morning Post*, 16 January 2001, p. 15.

73. *The Observer*, op. cit., p. 9.

74. A. Keenan, 'Violence going over our heads', *Weekend Australian*, 8–9 April 2000, p. 9; G. Peters, 'Battered airline crews demand law on air rage', *South China Morning Post*, 6 July 2000, p. 9; and B. Porter 'Airline battles in-flight crime', *South China Morning Post*, 29 April 2000, p. 10.

75. J. Pegg, 'Tougher air rage laws urged', *Sunday Morning Post*, 8 August 1999, p. 3.

76. B. Sandilands, 'Travel tantrums are all the rage', *Australian Financial Review — Special Report*, 8 November 2000, p. 6; N. Briger, 'The big thing', *Post Magazine*, 7 June 1998, p. 4; and D. Costello, 'Desk rage incidents erupt in more offices', *Asian Wall Street Journal*, 18 January 2001, p. N1.

77. A. Keenan, op. cit., p. 9.

78. Quoted in M. Safe, 'All the rage', *Australian Magazine*, 29–30 January 2000, pp. 18–23.

79. I. Driscoll, 'The broader issue', *South China Morning Post — Features*, 13 May 2002, p. 1.

80. 'Air-borne business preferences', *Australian Financial Review Magazine*, May 2003, p. 10.

81. G. Barker, 'Business top terror targets', *Australian Financial Review*, 8 April 2003, p. 9.

82. H. Jung, 'Starbuck's growth makes it a target', *International Herald Tribune*, 16 April 2003, p. 14.

83. J. Koutsoukis and A. Day, 'Security review after Qantas stabbings', *Australian Financial Review*, 30 May 2003, p. 5.

84. T. Perinotto, 'Higher vigilance here to stay', *Australian Financial Review*, 8 April 2003, p. 62.

85. T. Elliott, 'Playing it safe', *Australian Financial Review*, 4 January 2002, p. 44; and R. Heller, 'Roadside warrior', *Forbes Global*, 17 March 2003, p. 10.

86. This section is based on M. Cave and A. Shand, 'The serious business of terror proofing companies', *Australian Financial Review*, 19–20 October 2002, p. 26.

87. M. Priest, 'Few plan for terrorist attack', *Australian Financial Review*, 21 February 2003, p. 24.

88. M. Priest, op. cit., p. 24.

89. S. Halliday, 'Many employers still reluctant to tackle workplace harassment', *HR Monthly*, November 1992, pp. 19–20.

90. Reuters, 'Catholic diocese in New York faces HK$14 billion sexual abuse suit from 34 men', *South China Morning Post*, 16 April 2003, p. A1.

91. J. Margo, 'Healing the psychological scars of sexual assault', *Australian Financial Review*, 8 May 2003, p. 67.

92. G. Thompson, 'Where there's smoke…', *HR Monthly*, March 2000, p. 31.

93. S. Stock, 'Smoking takes toll in poor', *Weekend Australian*, 15–16 April 2000, p. 5.

94. I. Haberfield and D. Wilson, 'Pubs safe in smoke ban push', *Sunday Herald Sun*, 23 December 2001, p. 17.

95. Associated Press, 'Thailand curbs indoor smoking', *South China Morning Post*, 9 November 2002, p. 13.

96. E. Tang, J. G. Juang and J. Luo, 'China opens to foreign smokes', *International Herald Tribune*, 12 February 2003, p. 31.

97. P. Moy and V. Button, 'China's smoking time bomb', *South China Morning Post*, 17 August 2001, p. 1.

98. L. Yeung, 'Schoolboy smokers soar 40 pc in five years: poll', *South China Morning Post — Education*, 7 September 2002, p. 1; J. Moir, 'SAR weighs action over public cost of smoking', *South China Morning Post — Business*, 9 December 1999, p. 1; L. Ho, 'Majority want smoke free restaurants', *South China Morning Post*, 18 March 2000; p. 7; and C. Y. Chow, 'Teenage smoking surges', *South China Morning Post*, 22 November 2000, p. 1.

99. A. Cornell, 'What a drag: Japanese politicians reduce anti-smoking laws to ashes', *Australian Financial Review*, 28 January 2000, p. 34.

100. M. Donnell, 'The really great salesmen don't quite sell themselves', *International Management*, vol. 43, no. 5, 1988, p. 84.

101. C. Murphy, 'It pays to drink a little', *Australian Financial Review*, 10 May 2002, p. 16.

102. R. D. Du Mars, 'Lost generation of men turns to drugs as internet age passes them by', *South China Morning Post*, 23 March 2000, p. 12.

103. 'Accident insurance to cover illness from drinking on the job', *South China Morning Post*, 22 January 2002, p. 11.

104. Agence France-Presse, 'Seoul sobers up to work induced drinking', *South China Morning Post*, 22 January 2002, p. 1.

105. D. H. Hensrud, 'To your health?', *Fortune*, 8 January 2001, p. 94; and R. Sharpe, 'The ban on drugs is what gives pushers their oomph', *Business Week*, 11 December 2000, pp. 5–6.

106. D. A. Washton, quoted in *The Guardian*, 'Wall Street gets its kicks from cocaine', *South China Morning Post — Business*, 4 December 2000, p. 6.

107. Y. Ross, 'Lawyers, drugs and money: addressing substance abuse', *Australian Financial Review*, 6 December 2002, p. 53.

108. Reuters, 'Cannabis spend nearly the same as beer study', *Australian Financial Review*, 1 October 1999, p. 24; and 'We are a nation that likes its pot', *Far Eastern Economic Review*, 11 November 1999, p. 29.

109. *The Guardian*, 'Drugs, sex and sweat fuel US black market', *South China Morning Post*, 3 May 2003, p. A11.

110. A. Peart, 'What's your poison?', *HR Monthly*, October 2000, pp. 44–5.

111. A. So, 'Abuse costs $4.2 billion, study finds', *South China Morning Post*, 19 January 2001, p. 4; and Staff reporters, 'Abuse of Ecstasy and "ice" soars', *Sunday Morning Post*, 11 February 2001, p. 6.

112. A. M. Freudenheim, 'Firms aim to trim fat, literally', *International Herald Tribune*, 19 June 2003, p. 12.

113. Agence France-Presse, 'Obesity, diabetes levels jump in America', *South China Morning Post*, 2 January 2003, p. 9.

114. P. Bowring, 'Burgers — deadlier than al-Qaeda?', *South China Morning Post*, 24 February 2003, p. 15.

115. R. Mishra, 'Obesity and disease risk', *International Herald Tribune*, 25 April 2003, p. 7.

116. S. Mydans, 'A hungry Asia grows fat', *International Herald Tribune*, 15–16 March 2003, pp. 1, 4.

117. Agence France-Presse, 'Obesity diabetes levels jump in America', *South China Morning Post*, 2 January 2003, p. 9.

118. *The Guardian*, 'Spread of obesity fattens diet food market's profits', *South China Morning Post*, 1 June 2002, p. 11.

119. Agence France-Presse, 'Australians swap surf and sun for TV, chips — and fat', *South China Morning Post*, 6 May 2003, p. A8.

120. S. Schwartz, 'Obesity crisis lurks behind closed doors', *South China Morning Post*, 7 November 2002, p. 5.

121. F. Chan, 'Death rate from cardiovascular diseases soars as HK men get fatter', *South China Morning Post*, 30 December, 2002, p. 3.

122. Reuters, 'Carrying that extra weight can take years off your life, say researchers', *South China Morning Post*, 8 January 2003, p. 13.

123. Agence France-Presse, 'Obesity, diabetes levels jump in America', *South China Morning Post*, 2 January 2003, p. 9.

124. Deutshe Presse-Agentur, 'So big, so cute and so at risk', *South China Morning Post*, 25 September 2002, p. 12.

125. A. Starr, 'Why US kids don't eat right', *Business Week*, 3 March 2003, p. 39.

126. Reported in P. Hay, 'Fit for life', *BBC Worldwide Asia Pacific*, no. 33, July 1995, p. 16.

127. Agence France-Presse, 'Australians swap surf and sun for TV, chips — and fat', *South China Morning Post*, 6 May 2003, p. A8.

128. Reported in R. Harrison, 'Who are you gonna call? Gut busters?', *BBC Worldwide Asia Pacific*, no. 33, July 1995, pp. 21–2.

129. Reported in 'Pampered slobs', *Hong Kong Standard*, 25 April 1996, p. 6.

130. V. Button, 'More than half shun sport and exercise', *South China Morning Post*, 18 September 2002, p. 8.

131. Survey cited in I. Stewart, 'Unhealthy lifestyles cause alarm', *South China Morning Post*, 2 February 1993, p. 9.

132. C. O. Fisher, L. F. Schoenfeldt and J. B. Shaw, *Human Resource Management*, 5th edn, Houghton Mifflin, New York, 2003, p. 197.

133. K. Sinclair, 'Fat chance of justice for the real victims of scandals', *South China Morning Post*, 31 July 2002, p. 15.

134. K. Sinclair, op. cit., p. 15; and Reuters, 'McFries make you McFat …, McObviously says Maccas', *Australian Financial Review*, 22 November 2002, p. 55.

135. I. Driscoll, 'The broader issue', *South China Morning Post — Features*, 13 May 2002, p. 1; and M. Freudenheim, 'Firms aim to trim fat, literally', *International Herald Tribune*, 19 June 2003, p. 12.

136. M. V. Roehling, 'Weight based discrimination in employment: psychological and legal aspects', *Personnel Psychology*, vol. 32, 1999, pp. 969–1016.

137. Reported in 'Violence deeply set in Australia', *South China Morning Post*, 16 June 1993, p. 14.

138. 'Violence deeply set in Australia', op. cit., p. 14.

139. K. Kaur, 'Woman punched her maid for grousing over pay', *The Straits Times*, 4 April 1997, p. 40; M. B. Benitez, 'One in four foreign helpers abused', *South China Morning Post*, 15 February 2001, p. 2; and E. Lee, 'Medics in the firing line', *Sunday Morning Post — Review*, 11 February 2001, p. 1.

140. 'Teacher was routinely groped, spat upon and pushed down stairs', *South China Morning Post*, 7 February 2003, p. 14; and P. Bunce, 'Violence in schools rarely reported', *South China Morning Post*, 11 February 2003, p. 14.

141. S. H. Yong, 'Slave labour', *South China Morning Post*, 15 March 2003, p. A15.

142. K. Ho and E. Chong, 'Starved, battered, dead…', *Straits Times*, 20 July 2002, p. H1.

143. E. Chong, '18½ years, caning for man who abused maid', *Straits Times*, 20 July 2002, p. 4.

144. G. Safe, 'Australian workers in danger', *Weekend Australian*, 7–8 August 1999, p. 23.

145. R. Shrapnel, 'Protecting your people', *HR Monthly*, December 1998, pp. 6–8.

146. M. Priest, 'Lawyers add to cost of keeping banks safe', *Australian Financial Review*, 14 March 2003, p. 17.

147. E. McShulskis, 'Protecting against workplace violence', *HR Magazine*, February 1997, p. 20.

148. B. Hale, 'Beware the killer who works beside you', *Australian Financial Review*, 15 September 1997, p. 12.

149. A. Larriera, 'One in four women bashed: study', *Sydney Morning Herald*, 4 July 1995, p. 3; C. W. Li, 'Facing up to domestic abuse', *Sunday Morning Post*, 14 January 2001, p. 5; and Editorial, 'Aboriginal women deserve better deal', *Australian*, 16 April 2001, p. 8.

150. P. Moy, 'Alarm at drastic rise in number of battered spouses', *South China Morning Post*, 11 February 2003, p. 6.

151. P. Moy, 'Husbands take a beating as wives lash out', *South China Morning Post*, 20 November 2002, p. 4.

152. Reported in 'Addressing domestic violence research capsules', *Training and Development*, vol. 49, no. 7, 1995, p. 60. See also J. A. Kinney, 'When domestic violence strikes the workplace', *HR Magazine*, August 1995, pp. 74–8.

153. 'Employees terrorised by peer pressure at work', *Human Resources*, November 2000, p. 10.

154. Based on R. Robertson, 'Firms count the cost of bullying', *Australian Financial Review*, 31 October 2000, p. 26.

155. S. Long, 'Bullying: a new illness', *Australian Financial Review*, 15 March 2000, p. 19.

156. L. Phillips, 'Behaving badly', *HR Monthly*, September 2000, pp. 36–7; and A. Burrell, 'Broker bastardisation no laughing matter for juniors and "Jew boys"', *Australian Financial Review*, 7 February 2001, p. MW16.

157. M. Sheehan, P. McCarthy, M. Barker and M. Henderson, 'Mean testing', *HR Monthly*, February 2002, pp. 34–6.

158. R. Galbally, 'The impact of family on work', *Management*, August 1993, p. 16.

159. S. Long, 'Children pay for our long working day', *Australian Financial Review*, 4 April 2001, p. 55.

160. Reported in E. McShulskis, 'Work/life programs increase employee retention', *HR Magazine*, June 1997, p. 31.

161. S. Field and R. Bramwell, 'An investigation into the relationship between caring responsibilities and the levels of perceived pressure reported by female employees', *Journal of Occupational and Organizational Psychology*, vol. 71, no. 2, 1998, pp. 165–70; S. Clark and K. Whitehead, 'The struggle to juggle it all', *South China Morning Post — Education*, 7 April 2001, p. 8; and C. Arnst, 'Being a mother doesn't pay', *Business Week*, 12 March 2001, p. 8.

162. Westpac, *Concise Annual Report*, 2002, p. 26.

163. P. Bohle and M. Quinlan, op. cit., pp. 87–8, 195–204.

164. J. Arbose, 'Home truths about stress', *Management Review*, June 1980, p. ix.

165. C. Peterson, 'Dealing with stress related disorders in the public sector', in C. Mayhew and C. L. Peterson (eds), *Occupational Health and Safety in Australia*, Allen & Unwin, Sydney, 1999, ch. 13; and A. E. Schwartz, 'Why do managers burn out?', *Human Resources*, January 2003, pp. 28–30.

166. K. Cummins, 'Mental health study shows lots to worry about', *Australian Financial Review*, 11 October 1999, p. 4.

167. S. Long, 'Work-related mental health problems on the rise', *Australian Financial Review*, 10 January 2001, p. 31.

168. C. Fox, 'Stressed employees are bad for business', *Australian Financial Review*, 21 May 2002, p. 67.

169. J. Este, 'The failure of happiness inc.', *Weekend Australian — Review*, 23–24 October 1999, p. 6.

170. P. Fong, 'Why blue collar workers still have the jitters', *Business Week*, 11 December 2000, pp. 4, A10.

171. 'Workplace stress on the rise', *Human Resources*, November 2002, p. 2.

172. K. J. Dunham, 'Workers yearn for the luxury of a nine-to-five work day', *Asian Wall Street Journal*, 18 January 2001, p. N4; and *The Guardian*, 'Putting in the hours at work leads to success', *South China Morning Post — Business*, 19 March 2001, p. 7.

173. C. Hymowitz and R. E. Silverman, 'Softer economy, greater stress', *Asian Wall Street Journal*, 18 January 2001, pp. N1, N4.

174. C. Saltau, 'Pressure packs hefty punch', *Sunday Age*, 23 July 2000, p. 8.

175. J. Madden, 'Uni staff score top marks on stress test', *Australian*, 4 July 2002, p. 3.

176. C. N. Field, 'Workers' balancing act fails', *Australian Financial Review*, 3 September 1999, p. 14; and N. Tabakoff, 'Why you are a candidate for burnout', *Business Review Weekly*, 3 December 1999, pp. 84–9.

177. D. Macken, 'Desperately seeking holiday', *Australian Financial Review*, 2–3 December 2000, p. 2.

178. J. Jones, 'Time out', *South China Morning Post*, 14 January 1997, p. 17.

179. N. Field, 'Wake up call for workers, fatigue kills', *Australian Financial Review*, 26 October 1999, p. 3.

180. M. Priest, 'An addiction to overtime', *Australian Financial Review*, 21 March 2003, p. 69.

181. R. Burbury, 'Stress rich will test goodwill', *Australian Financial Review*, 18 April 2000, p. 46.

182. Quoted in I. Foyuno, 'A silent epidemic', *Far Eastern Economic Review*, 28 September 2000, p. 78.

183. W. Pesek, 'Hard times breed despair in Japan', *International Herald Tribune*, 12 March 2003, p. B2.

184. P. Hadfield, 'Bosses bite the bullet on suicidal staff', *South China Morning Post*, 22 November 2000, p. 16.

185. R. Leider and S. Bucholz, 'The rust out syndrome', *Training and Development*, vol. 49, no. 3, 1995, pp. 7–9.

186. S. Mardon, 'Screen applicants for shift compatibility', *HR Magazine*, January 1997, pp. 53–5.

187. D. Filipowski, 'Problems are common among shift workers', *Personnel Journal*, August 1993, p. 34.

188. E. McShulskis, 'Support your shift workers', *HR Magazine*, June 1997, p. 20.

189. Reported in J. Kevin, 'Sleepy workers bad as drinkers', *Australian*, 21 January 1995, p. 3.

190. D. Phillips, 'Pilots may soon fight sleep with sleep', *International Herald Tribune*, 28 December 1992, p. 1.

191. Research by Dr Meredith Wallace, health and work behaviour consultant, cited in G. Stickels, 'When the body clock and the time clock are out of sync', *Business Review Weekly*, 28 August 1995, pp. 65–6.

192. Reuters, 'Bad bosses raise the risk of heart attacks', *South China Morning Post*, 25 June 2003, p. A8.

193. S. P. Robbins, *Organizational Behavior*, 9th edn, Prentice-Hall, Upper Saddle River, NJ, 2001, p. 566.

194. J. S. Lublin, 'Takeovers can take toll on workers', *Asian Wall Street Journal*, 18 January 2001, p. N7; and S. L. McShane and M. A. Von Glinow, *Organizational Behavior*, McGraw-Hill, Boston, 2000, p. 141.

195. Reported in *Boardroom Reports*, November 1991, p. 11.

196. J. Santa-Barbara, 'When workplace stress stifles productivity', *Drake Business Review*, November 2002, p. 28.

197. Research at the University of Pittsburgh, reported in *Boardroom Reports*, March 1988, p. 5.

198. L. K. Savery, 'The influence of job factors on employee satisfaction', *Journal of Managerial Psychology*, vol. 4, no. 1, 1989, p. 29; and J. M. Ivancevich, *Human Resource Management*, 8th edn, McGraw-Hill, Boston, 2001, p. 545.

199. D. Gilbertson, 'Personnel and industrial relations staff in New Zealand: a role stress perspective', paper presented at the 1992 ANZAM Conference, Auckland, 1992, pp. 1–17.

200. Study cited in 'They're not kidding when they say Blue Monday', *Business Week*, 18 May 1992, p. 85.

201. C. Ng, 'Driven to action over advert din', *South China Morning Post*, 23 April 2001, p. 16.

202. A. F. Tyndall, 'Office staff face squeeze', *Australian Financial Review*, 29 April 2003, p. 64.

203. A. Takeshita, 'High rise stress increases ailments of residents, workers', *Nikkei Weekly*, 4 October 1993, p. 24; G. Overell, 'Indoor air becomes an issue', *Australian Property News*, 10 October 1996, p. 6; and P. Somerville, 'Basic building blocks', *HR Monthly*, November 2001, p. 43.

204. A. Smith, 'Cooled air linked with workers' ills', *South China Morning Post*, 22 September 1997, p. 5; and F. Chan, 'Poor air quality in many offices harms workforce', *South China Morning Post*, 9 December 2002, p. 5.

205. H. Philips, 'Noise levels linked to health problems', *South China Morning Post*, 2 June 2003, p. C3.

206. J. Quah and K. M. Campbell, 'Role conflict and role ambiguity as factors in work stress among managers in Singapore: some moderator variables', *Research and Practice in Human Resource Management*, vol. 2, no. 1, 1994, pp. 21–33.

207. Reported in C. Jasper, 'This week', *Window*, 2 July 1993, p. 3.

208. S. Kwok, 'Survey reveals high mental cost of divorce', *South China Morning Post*, 21 April 1999, p. 5.

209. Survey by Profile Management Consultants, cited in 'Splitting headache', *ABM*, May 1992, p. 20.

210. G. Sadri and G. A. Marcoulides, 'The dynamics of occupational stress: proposing and testing a model', *Research and Practice in Human Resource Management*, vol. 2, no. 1, 1994, pp. 1–19.

211. Reported in 'CEO stress rising', *HR Monthly*, September 1997, p. 53.

212. M. Gordon, 'Australia: not relaxed, not comfortable', *Weekend Australian*, 9–10 August 1997, p. 3.

213. S. Long, 'Work-related mental health problems on the rise', *Australian Financial Review*, 10 January 2001, p. 31.

214. Reported in D. Filipowski, 'Perspectives', *Personnel Journal*, June 1993, p. 34.

215. 'How job loss affects children', *HR Focus — Supplement*, December 1993, p. 4.

216. S. Green, 'Tough times keep sex therapists busy', *South China Morning Post — Review*, 16 January 1993, p. 5.

217. P. Moy, 'Economic worries spoil joy of sex', *South China Morning Post*, 5 March 2002, p. 5.

218. Australian Social Monitor Survey, cited in HSBC Asset Management advertisement, *Business Review Weekly*, 10 April 1995, p. 17.

219. Reported in C. Y. Chow, 'For most married women, sex is a bore', *South China Morning Post*, 13 May 2003, p. C3.

220. P. Stuart, 'Murder on the job', *Personnel Journal*, February 1992, pp. 72–84.

221. W. H. Gmelch, *Beyond Stress to Effective Management*, John Wiley & Sons, New York, 1982, p. 76.

222. T. Jonas and I. Stewart, 'Red tape making family business a gloomy affair', *Australian Financial Review*, 9 December 1999, p. 21.

223. C. Spielberger, *Understanding Stress/Anxiety*, Harper & Row, New York, 1979, pp. 29–30; W. H. Gmelch, op. cit., pp. 21–2; and A. Hepworth, 'The new commuter families', *Australian Financial Review*, 6 April 2001, p. 13.

224. Reported in *Boardroom Reports*, July 1988, p. 16.

225. D. Adams, 'No easy cure for groggy feeling', *Australian — Supplement*, 15 May 1986, p. 2; and W. H. Gmelch, op. cit., pp. 21–2.

226. S. Krueger, 'Sex and the business traveller', *Age*, 5 August 1997, p. B1; and C. Tolhurst, 'Tough times for the ones left behind', *Australian Financial Review*, 8 August 1997, p. 50.

227. Study cited in K. Daswani, 'Hong Kong lifestyle hard to stomach', *South China Morning Post*, 19 July 1992, p. 3.

228. S. Mulley, 'How to survive stress capital of the world', *South China Morning Post — Review*, 19 November 1994, p. 4.

229. A. Sampson, 'Stressed out in Sydney', *Australian Business Management*, May 1993, p. 23.

230. Reported in Associated Press, 'Stressed citizens eager to emigrate', *South China Morning Post*, 16 August 1997, p. 10.

231. B. Gilbert, 'The myths and realities of executive health', *Management*, August 1993, pp. 8–10.

232. G. Chan, 'Teenage suicide rate highest in the world', *Weekend Australian*, 18–19 September 1993, p. 2; D. Bagnall, 'Suicide generation', *Bulletin*, 23 May 1995, pp. 16–79; J. Salmon, 'Youth suicide: why us?', *Weekend Australian*, 4–5 January 1997, p. 19; and M. de La Harpe, 'Suicide a crucial men's health issue', *Campus Review*, 9–15 October 1996, p. 11.

233. B. Martin, 'Fear stalks the land', *Bulletin*, 24 June 1997, p. 12.

234. NSW Bureau of Crime Statistics and Research 1997, quoted in Securities advertisement, *Australian Financial Review*, 15 April 1997, p. 9.

235. Bulletin–Morgan Poll reported in 'National', *Bulletin*, 24 June 1997, p. 10.

236. B. Cheesman, 'Taipei's top tycoons fear new kidnap outbreak', *Australian Financial Review*, 29 April 1997, p. 12.

237. T. Harris, 'Armed robbery, extortion lead jump in crime', *Australian*, 25 July 1997, p. 5; and N. Fraser, 'Crime wave brings cloud of depression', *Sunday Morning Post*, 27 April 1997, p. 3.

238. R. Galbally, 'The impact of family on work', *Management*, August 1993, pp. 16–17; and 'Research reveals men's divorce woes', *Campus Review*, 23–29 October 1996, p. 13.

239. V. Yu, 'Family conflict is pushing Chinese women to the brink', *South China Morning Post*, 18 April 2003, p. A4.

240. Reported in 'Warning: extra-marital sex can kill', *Australian*, 9 February 1996, p. 3.

241. N. Lee, 'Cheating husbands get a shoulder to cry on', *Sunday Morning Post*, 1 September 1996, p. 3.

242. Reported in *Boardroom Reports*, June 1988, p. 6.

243. Reported in S. Bagwell, 'The untranquil business women — a new target', *Times on Sunday*, 13 December 1987, p. 18.

244. 'Study pinpoints the causes of stress for working women', *HR Focus*, September 1993, p. 24.

245. S. L. McShane and M. A. Von Glinow, op. cit., pp. 147–54; and S. P. Robbins, op. cit., pp. 570–1.

246. Study by A. Katcher, University of Pennsylvania, School of Veterinary Medicine, reported in *Boardroom Reports*, June 1987, p. 5; and Reuter, 'Seal of praise for men's best friend', *Eastern Express*, 8 March 1996, p. 7.

247. Research by W. J. Evans, US Department of Agriculture's Human Research Center on Aging, reported in *Boardroom Reports*, 13 July 1988, p. 5.

248. J. Stone, 'Drug and alcohol abuse: barriers to effective Australian workplace strategies', *Management*, August 1993, pp. 11–14.

249. M. Lawson, 'Executives' eating patterns a concern for health carers', *Australian Financial Review*, 2 May 2003, p. 25.

250. Reported in *Boardroom Reports*, 1 October 1987, p. 15.

251. G. Robotham, 'OHS making slow progress', *HR Monthly*, August 1999, pp. 30–1.

252. Based partly on S. Lee, '180 kg passenger grounded by airline demands apology', *South China Morning Post*, 18 January 2003, p. 4.

253. Wearing noisy headphones can cause the same sort of ear damage as industrial noise trauma. See R. Maynard, 'Personal stereos causing deafness', *South China Morning Post*, 8 December 1998, p. 11.

chapter 19

managing diversity[1]

This chapter was written by Dr Maureen Fastenau, Senior Lecturer in Management at RMIT University

Learning objectives

When you have finished studying this chapter, you should be able to:

- Define and distinguish the three different approaches to managing diversity in the workplace
- Compare and contrast how each approach to managing diversity enhances equal opportunities in employment
- Explain how managing diversity contributes to the strategic objective of HRM
- Define and distinguish the three different types of discrimination
- Identify harassment as a particular form of discrimination and recommend appropriate management responses
- Define the concept of merit.

'. . . this study [the AMA's 'Senior Management Teams: Profiles and Performance' study] confirms what many who work . . . in diverse settings have long suspected. Diverse groups provide valuable opportunities for learning and for productivity in a variety of settings.'[2]

American Management Association

Competitive advantage
A special edge that allows organisations to better deal with business challenges.

Diversity The variety of people who make up an organisation's work force, in terms of age, gender, ethnicity, occupation, length of service, and so on.

Organisations operating in increasingly competitive domestic and global marketplaces cannot afford to ignore any source of possible **competitive advantage**. Many managers and management texts assert that employees are a primary asset of any organisation. However, many organisations' HRM policies and practices give little consideration to the **diversity** of the work force and the implications of that diversity for the effective management and use of employees, individually and in groups. In other words, many organisations practise 'one size fits all' HRM, ignoring significant differences among their workers. Managing diversity means recognising that there is no such thing as the 'average worker' and that competitive advantage can be gained by those organisations that value and accommodate difference.

Many places, including Australia, Japan, Hong Kong and New Zealand, have equal opportunity or anti-discrimination legislation.[3] This legislation was enacted for two reasons: (1) for social justice (that is, to give legal support to the notion that all people in a society should have equal opportunities to enjoy the benefits of that society, including employment); and (2) for economic considerations (that is, to encourage businesses to use the human resources of society most effectively, thus benefiting not only businesses and individuals but also society as a whole). The strength of anti-discrimination legislation — its effectiveness in ensuring that all people regardless of specified characteristics, such as disability, sex and race or ethnicity, have equal employment opportunities — varies considerably from country to country.

Organisations that ignore or merely undertake basic compliance with anti-discrimination legislation fail to recognise and capitalise on the benefits of a diverse work force. Organisations that hire, value, accommodate and reward **non-traditional employees** as well as traditional or 'usual' employees can gain a competitive advantage whereby employee differences present opportunities to (1) improve staff management practices, (2) alter the workplace and work practices in ways that increase efficiency and safety, (3) make products and facilities more accessible to and appropriate for clients and customers, and (4) identify new products, services and markets. Furthermore, such organisations offer their employees an environment that values and supports them because they are different, not despite their difference.

Non-traditional employees
Employees who differ from those usually employed in a particular occupation, organisation or industry because of sex, race/ethnicity, disability or some other characteristic.

Managing diversity: a strategic approach to HRM

The HR manager's responsibilities

It is the responsibility of HR practitioners to facilitate the organisation's ability to use staff efficiently and effectively to achieve strategic business objectives. They are also responsible for ensuring that all employees are rewarded fairly and equitably for their contributions to the organisation. Fair and equitable rewards include not only wages/salaries, but also opportunities for training and career development and the provision of a work environment in which all workers are treated with respect. Ensuring that all employees are treated fairly and equitably is not only a matter of legal and ethical responsibility, but also recognises that employees who perceive unfair or inequitable treatment may be less likely to be committed to the organisation and thus may be less productive (see chapter 11 on employee motivation).

The HR manager can achieve these outcomes by:

- identifying significant differences in the work force of their organisation and in the labour market(s) from which they draw employees
- exploring the potential advantages to be gained from hiring persons from particular groups

- identifying relevant diversity factors existing in the present work force
- developing, implementing, monitoring and evaluating staff management practices that facilitate the ability of each employee to contribute effectively to the organisation and to be rewarded appropriately.

It is also the professional and business responsibility of the HR manager to establish audit measures that identify and quantify the advantages gained from diversity employment practices and that minimise the costs of diversity employment.

Taking the strategic approach

The difference between companies that do and do not develop a strategic approach to managing diversity can be demonstrated by the experiences of two Australian companies: a bank and a newspaper publisher.[4]

A major bank with over 30 000 employees has linked its **diversity strategies** with its business objectives. Two of the bank's business objectives are: (1) to be the employer of choice for persons seeking to work in the finance industry; and (2) to be responsive to a diverse customer base.

Diversity strategies Encompass equal employment opportunity, affirmative action or diversity management strategies.

The bank's managers recognised that to achieve these objectives, the bank needed to address the terms and conditions of employment and the promotional opportunities of its female staff. The managers recognised this because the HR and equal opportunity staff were able to demonstrate that the failure to provide the bank's female staff with flexible working conditions and ensure access to promotional opportunities were costly to the bank in terms of turnover and lost skills and knowledge. Furthermore, they were able to demonstrate what these losses meant in terms of the bank's strategic objectives.

The bank's affirmative action strategies were linked to its business objectives, and monitoring processes were established to ensure the affirmative action strategies achieved the desired results, both in terms of affirmative action objectives and in terms of the bank's business objectives. Auditing measures were set up to enable the managers and the HR staff to determine the effectiveness of the affirmative action strategies.

As a result of its strategic approach to diversity management, the bank was able to achieve real advances in ensuring equitable employment opportunities: there was a 13 per cent increase in the number of women in management, and flexible working conditions were included in the bank's new enterprise agreement. The bank's affirmative action strategies also contributed to its business objective to be the 'employer of choice' in the banking industry: the quality of male and female applicants rose, and turnover costs were substantially reduced.

The newspaper publishing company, on the other hand, has not taken a strategic approach to affirmative action and thus has achieved little. There apparently has been no effort to link affirmative action strategies to business objectives, so there would be little encouragement or direction to managers to achieve affirmative action goals. The lack of a strategic approach is suggested by the fact that the company cannot even determine whether it has communicated its affirmative action policy to its staff. While there has been some discussion of the need to broaden women's employment and increase women's promotional opportunities, no strategies have been formulated nor have any auditing and evaluation measures been established.

The business case for managing diversity

Does managing diversity provide organisations with business benefits? There are three main arguments put forward for creating and managing work force diversity: (1) the shrinking labour pool of traditional workers requires employers more than ever before to access, utilise and reward the talents and contributions of non-traditional employees; (2) it helps to make the organisation and its products/services more attractive and responsive to diverse customer markets, domestic and global; and (3) diverse work groups have improved performance outcomes. A fourth reason is that staff management practices that address the different needs of employees from different groups will result in lower HR costs. As with many areas of HR practice, the data that show the effects of diversity management practices on business outcomes are neither readily available nor conclusive.

A recent US research project studied four companies to determine whether diversity strategies and practices improved business performance.[5] The four companies are all major US organisations with well-established and highly lauded diversity programs. The study considered the effects of race and gender on financial performance. The researchers found little evidence to support an argument that diverse work groups performed better than more homogenous work groups.

However, the researchers noted (as has other research) that more diverse work groups were more productive and effective when innovation and creativity were required — especially in organisational environments supportive of diversity, with appropriate HR practices and managers and employees trained in communication and interpersonal skills. Organisational cultures (people- or competition-orientation) and strategies (customer- or growth-orientation) also influenced whether diversity was more likely to result in positive, neutral or negative business performance outcomes.

This study was limited in its research sample as well as in its criteria for measuring the business benefits of diversity practices and work force diversity. Other research has indicated that diversity practices do have business benefits.[6] For example, a study in the mid-1990s found that companies with excellent diversity practices had higher share prices compared with companies sued for discrimination.[7] Another study revealed that having women in top management positions when a company is making its initial public offering has a positive effect on share price and short- and long-term financial performance.[8] This effect was seen recently when Gail Kelly was appointed CEO of St George Bank: when her appointment was announced, $97 million was added to the value of Australia's nineteenth largest company (or 20 cents per share).[9]

Business benefits may also be achieved by reducing HR costs through the retention and improved utilisation of non-traditional employees. For example, the international professional services firm Deloitte Touche Tohmatsu initiated diversity management strategies that reduced the voluntary turnover of senior female accounting staff to a rate closer to that of their male counterparts.[10] Xerox reported that its EEO measures contributed to staff retention, thereby saving the company over A$2 million in recruitment and selection costs over a five-year period.[11] NRMA found that it was expending over $6 million per year in direct, quantifiable recruitment and selection costs to replace the 35 per cent of its staff, mostly women, resigning each year. The implementation of various EEO and AA strategies dramatically reduced these costs.[12]

Australia is one of the few developed countries without a national paid maternity leave program.[13] A number of Australian organisations have, however, found that paid maternity leave results in business benefits. Westpac Bank, the first Australian bank to offer paid maternity leave to its staff, saved $6 million over five years by increasing the return rate of female staff from maternity leave. Similarly, over a five-year period NRMA increased its return rate from maternity leave from 32 per cent to 85 per cent with the introduction of paid maternity leave. A senior National Australia Bank executive observed that 'while [paid maternity leave] is a substantial investment in our people, we have done sufficient cost-analysis to know that we reap the dividends in terms of employee productivity, job satisfaction, and retention'.[14]

Approaches to managing diversity

Equal employment opportunity (EEO) Giving people a fair chance to succeed by avoiding discrimination based on unrelated job factors such as age, race, sex or nationality.

There are three approaches to managing diversity in employment: (1) anti-discrimination (often referred to as equal opportunity (EO) or **equal employment opportunity (EEO)**); (2) affirmative action; and (3) diversity management. The goal of all these approaches to managing diversity is to facilitate equitable employment opportunities for all employees and for applicants for employment. The principal argument for anti-discrimination is often social justice; affirmative action and diversity management, while not ignoring social justice arguments, often build their case on arguments of business advantage or benefit.

Organisations that take either an anti-discrimination or affirmative action approach are usually responding to state and federal legislation. Increasingly, organisations in countries with a decade or more of experience with legislative approaches to managing diversity are considering the implementation of a diversity management approach. This approach is a management initiative, rather than merely compliance with a legal requirement. It is based not only on social justice rationales and legislative requirements of anti-discrimination and affirmative action, but also on arguments (and growing evidence) that it makes good business sense.

Legal obligations

Anti-discrimination and **affirmative action (AA)** are legal requirements, thus imposing legal obligations and liabilities on employers. (Note: 'Employer' is used in this chapter to refer to an organisation/company, a person who owns a company, or a manager of a business/organisation.) You should be aware that laws are applicable only in the political unit (for example, nation, state, city, and so on) where they have been enacted. Also, even though many laws concerned with discrimination have the same or similar titles, they are not exactly the same.[15] For example, both the South Australian and Victoria state anti-discrimination laws are entitled 'Equal Opportunity Act', but only the Victorian legislation prohibits discrimination on the basis of physical appearance.

HR professionals need to determine which laws are applicable for their organisation. They then want to ensure the adoption of organisational policies and practices both to minimise legal liabilities and gain the benefits of equitable employment practices. It can also be good practice for HR professionals to consider generally laws regarding anti-discrimination and equitable employment even if they are not applicable because their organisation does not operate in that state or country.

So, for example, HR professionals working for a company operating only in South Australia or in Hong Kong may wish to ensure, even though there is no legal prohibition against it in either that state or country, that physical appearance does not influence employment decisions. If physical appearance is not relevant to a person's ability to perform the job, regardless of whether it is illegal, using it to make employment decisions may mean that the most suitable person in terms of actual job requirements might be overlooked.[16]

Anti-discrimination
Elimination of any practice that makes distinctions between different groups based on age, sex, and other characteristics identified in EO legislation and that results in one group being advantaged and the other group disadvantaged.

Affirmative action (AA)
Programs that require firms to make special efforts to recruit, hire and promote women and/ or members of minority groups.

Anti-discrimination legislation: Australia

The first anti-discrimination Act in Australia was South Australia's *Prohibition of Discrimination Act 1966*, which addressed racial discrimination. It was not until the Australian Parliament ratified the International Labour Organisation's Convention 111 — Discrimination (Employment and Occupation) that the Australian states, notably South Australia, Victoria and New South Wales, enacted sex discrimination legislation.

The federal government at the time considered enacting legislation to prohibit discrimination against women, but strong public resistance dissuaded the then Liberal government from taking this step. The first national anti-discrimination Act in Australia was the *Racial Discrimination Act 1975*, which was enacted after Australia ratified the International Convention on the Elimination of All Forms of Racial Discrimination. The federal *Sex Discrimination Act* was not enacted until 1984. Queensland, Tasmania, the Australian Capital Territory and the Northern Territory did not enact anti-discrimination legislation until the 1990s.

Federal anti-discrimination legislation

The federal anti-discrimination and AA legislation in Australia includes: the *Racial Discrimination Act 1975*, the *Sex Discrimination Act 1984*, the *Disability Discrimination Act 1992*, the *Human Rights and Equal Opportunity Commission Act 1986*, the *Equal Opportunity for Women in the Workplace Act 1999* (EOWW Act) (formerly the Affirmative Action (Equal Employment Opportunity for Women) Act 1986) and the *Equal Employment Opportunity (Commonwealth Authorities) Act 1987*.

Other federal legislation also contains anti-discrimination provisions with implications for various aspects of the employment relationship and of which HR practitioners should be aware. These include the *Workplace Relations Act 1996* and the *Privacy Amendment (Private Sector) Act 2000*.[17] In the winter 2003 session of Parliament, the government introduced the Age Discrimination Bill, which is designed to prohibit employment on the basis of age.[18] This legislation is a response not only to increasing evidence of age discrimination, but also to the demographic trend of an ageing work force with its implications for the work force, taxation and welfare.

State anti-discrimination legislation

In addition to the federal legislation, all Australian states and territories have anti-discrimination or equal opportunity legislation.[19] There is also public service legislation at both state and federal levels that contains provisions to promote EEO and to establish AA-style programs to improve the employment opportunities of not only women but also Aboriginal Australians and Torres Strait Islanders, people with disabilities and people from non-English-speaking backgrounds. The public service legislation covers government departments and public authorities (such as hospitals, the Roads and Traffic Authority and TAFE colleges).

Anti-discrimination legislation in other Asia–Pacific countries

New Zealand's first anti-discrimination legislation was the *Race Relations Act 1971*. This Act was later repealed and replaced with the *Human Rights Act 1993*, which prohibits discrimination based on sex, pregnancy, marital status, religious and ethical beliefs, colour, race, ethnicity/national origin, disability, age, political opinion, employment status, family status and sex orientation. Sexual harassment is covered under Pt III (Personal Grievances) of the *Employment Contracts Act 1991*. The *New Zealand Bill of Rights Act 1990* and the *Employment Relations Act 2000* (see Part 9 — Personal Grievances, Disputes, and Enforcement) also contain anti-discrimination provisions.

Other countries in the Asia–Pacific region, including Japan in 1985 and Hong Kong in 1996, have enacted EEO laws. Taiwan's Women's Employment Promotion Measure took effect in 1994, but it is only an administrative directive rather than a law.

Indonesia and Singapore do not have any anti-discrimination laws. While Indonesia's constitution includes provisions that could be seen to encourage equal opportunities in employment, the failure to implement anti-discrimination legislation to support the constitutional provisions has meant in reality that women often endure inequitable treatment in the work force. Indonesian women are left with no legal recourse against discriminatory employment practices, and employers in Indonesia have no legal incentive to adopt and implement equitable employment practices. Additionally, the enactment of protective legislation (for example, prohibiting women's employment in certain 'dangerous' occupations and limiting their access to night employment) and requirements for employers to provide certain paid leave entitlements to women has worked to disadvantage them further in the workplace.[20]

The Singaporean government has implemented various policies that facilitate women's participation in the work force. These include various tax relief schemes, such as the 'relief of foreign maid levy', which provides a tax rebate for employed women hiring a foreign maid to assist with childcare and domestic responsibilities, and subsidies for childcare centres.[21] Women now make up 50 per cent of graduates from Singaporean universities.

Singaporean women do, however, experience government-sanctioned discrimination, both active and passive.[22] The government, for example, has permitted the setting of a maximum quota for the number of women admitted to medical schools and has failed to address working conditions (for example, childcare arrangements and flexible work hours) that would allow female doctors to continue to practice. The failure of the Singaporean government to extend the Employment Act to cover domestic workers, the majority of whom are women, has left these female employees without adequate coverage. The absence of anti-discrimination laws has also allowed pay discrimination to occur between men's and women's work in both public and private sectors.

Characteristics identified in anti-discrimination legislation

Equal opportunity or anti-discrimination legislation prohibits discrimination in employment. This means that employers may not discriminate against people based on the characteristics identified in the legislation. Characteristics often found in Australian anti-discrimination legislation (and also in the anti-discrimination legislation of many other countries) include:

- sex (often incorrectly thought to be limited to women)
- race/ethnicity/nationality
- disability (physical, sensory, intellectual, psychological, presumed)
- marital status (single, married, divorced, widowed, de facto)
- parental status
- pregnancy
- religious beliefs and activities
- political beliefs and activities
- trade union membership (or non-membership)
- age
- transgender/transsexuality.

It is important to remember that not every characteristic listed above is included in every piece of anti-discrimination legislation.

There are also a number of other characteristics that have been included more recently in some anti-discrimination legislation in Australia, including:

- physical appearance
- industrial activity
- sexual preference/orientation
- gender identity
- breastfeeding
- carer status.

Every person is covered by this legislation. Many characteristics apply to everyone: we all have a sex, an age and a marital status, for example. Some may not apply to any one person at a given time, but may apply at a later time. People who do not have a disability, for example, could become disabled at any time as a result of accident or illness.

An airline demands that obese passengers pay for two seats if they cannot fit comfortably into a standard sized seat.

Who experiences discrimination in the workplace?

The legislation clearly recognises that every person faces the possibility of being discriminated against and of discriminating against someone else, although perhaps unintentionally. A range of historical sociocultural factors, however, mean that some groups are more likely to be discriminated against in employment. Women, for example, are generally disadvantaged in the work force, regardless of the country in which they live; thus they are more likely to face discrimination in employment than are men.

Some of the employment disadvantage that women suffer is a result of direct, conscious discrimination: for example, an employer refusing to employ a qualified woman in a specific job or occupation because she is a woman. Some of it is the product of more subtle indirect or structural discriminations. This does not mean, however, that men never experience discrimination in employment because of their sex, just that it is less likely. There have been cases of men alleging that they have been discriminated against because of their sex (see figure 19.1).[23]

Similarly, racial discrimination is more likely to happen to men and women who do not belong to the dominant racial or ethnic group in their country.[24] Australia's dominant racial/ethnic group is white and of an Anglo-Celtic ancestry. It is rare for white men and women in Australia to allege that they have been racially discriminated against, but it has happened.[25] The dominant racial/ethnic group is not necessarily the numerically largest racial/ethnic group in a society.

The following Letter to the Editor provides a provocative viewpoint. Do you agree? See 'What's your view?' on page 734.

The office manager argues against employing an otherwise well-qualified applicant for a bookkeeping position saying she is too fat.

Fear of accusations of sexual abuse is causing men to reject primary teaching as a career.

If people want to discriminate, they will, regardless of any EEO legislation

Dear Editor,

Governmental efforts to socially engineer the workplace through programs like EEO are doomed to failure, since people cannot simply be bent, shaped and moulded in this way.

Both commonsense and empirical research tell us that the support of senior managers is the key ingredient in any successful organisational change program. This is particularly true for programs of cultural change. The modelling of key behaviours by senior managers provides a powerful indicator that the organisation is serious about change, and such changes are also more likely to succeed if they are reinforced in company policies and reward systems.

The keys to the effective creation and management of a diverse work force are no different. The acceptance of cultural differences within the workplace depends on appropriate policies and systems being implemented, from diversity training programs through to the need to link performance appraisal processes and the effective management of diversity.

Changing the culture from within represents the best possible chance of successfully managing diversity and minimising discrimination in the workplace. In contrast, government-mandated programs are doomed to failure, for a number of reasons. In the first place, citizens of countries across the developed world are cynical and wary of government efforts to socially engineer their lives. This cynicism extends to EEO programs and their enthusiasm for 'outing' and publicly embarrassing non-complying organisations. These efforts only result in greater cynicism about the programs rather than motivating greater compliance.

In addition, EEO programs reek of the 'political correctness' that has become linked to well-meaning but politically and culturally insensitive social reform programs around the globe. In the eyes of most managers, such programs bring significant compliance costs and endless paperwork, but few direct benefits. These managers understand that organisational change is more likely to be successful when it is viewed as arising from within the organisation rather than being imposed by external forces.

While legislating EEO did indeed serve the valuable purpose of drawing the attention of organisations to the benefits of effectively managing diversity and the need to develop policies to combat workplace discrimination and harassment, it is time for governmental EEO programs to be abolished. Unfortunately, people will discriminate against each other regardless of the presence of EEO programs. The best response of managers is to model more appropriate behaviour in their own working lives, and to reinforce this approach through strong company policies.

A Vice-President of Human Resources

Source David Poole, University of Western Sydney.

Can a characteristic be a legitimate employment criterion?

It should be noted that if an employer can clearly demonstrate that any of the characteristics specified in the legislation is an actual job requirement — that is, necessary for the performance of the functions of the position — then the employer may make employment decisions based on that characteristic. A church seeking a minister, for example, may specify particular religious beliefs because they are critical to the function of the position, or a director casting a play may specify the sex of actors for specific roles.

However, a shop owner with customers principally from the Chinese community could not advertise for a Chinese shop assistant. The functions of a shop assistant could be done by anyone with the required skills — being Chinese is not an essential characteristic of a shop assistant. But if the shop assistant needs to be able to speak Chinese because most of the shop's customers speak or prefer to speak only Chinese, then this would be a legitimate job requirement that the shop owner could specify. While it is more likely that someone of

Chinese ancestry will be able to speak Chinese than will someone of another ethnic background, any shop assistant with the required language skills could apply and should be considered for the position. The employer, by clearly stating what is required to do the job to a satisfactory standard, both complies with the equal opportunity law and is more likely to attract suitable applicants and choose the best applicant based on actual job requirements.

Ensure the classroom windows remain clear of artwork, have a female chaperone in attendance when administering first aid and, when swimming, hands should be kept above the water at all times. These are a few of the precautions that men working in the early childhood sector must take each day as a first layer of protection against suspicious minds.

They are faced daily by colleagues and parents who are distrustful of their motivation for working with the young. And it is in this environment that worthy candidates are gradually eliminated and early childhood education loses its capacity to equip children for the real world.

Dealing with misconceptions and apprehension, men in early childhood education comprise a rare and battle-scarred few.

According to lecturer Lyn Briers, of Moreton Institute of TAFE in Brisbane, initial enrolment in early childhood courses for men runs from zero in some intakes to a boom year of six (out of 60) students, many of whom will drop out.

'Men can be discouraged both by the minimal pay packet and community attitudes', she says. 'Traditionally we've seen the care and education of children as a woman's role, but there's really no reason for this to continue, as both [sexes] have something to offer.'

Although the reasons for the lack of men in early childhood education appear obvious, the solutions are not, according to Jennifer Sumsion of Macquarie University's Institute of Early Childhood.

'Only a small proportion of men, maybe 2.5 to 3 per cent, are currently in the field, yet the number continues to fall', Sumsion says. 'Although there are no tangible barriers to their involvement, plenty of sociocultural ones exist, from suspicion of paedophile tendencies to wondering why these men would choose to follow such an untraditional male career path.'

Only those men who build support networks and remain positive under pressure will survive what Sumsion refers to as the 'ticking bomb' environment in which they work.

Figure 19.1 Public ignorance is discouraging men from teaching
Source L. Bettison, 'Goodbye, sir', *The Australian*, 23 May 2001, p. 27.

Anti-discrimination in employment and employment-related areas

Anti-discrimination legislation prohibits discrimination in all aspects of employment, including:
- recruitment and selection
- terms and conditions of employment
- training and development
- promotion and transfer
- termination.

Anti-discrimination legislation not only prohibits discrimination in employment, it also prohibits discrimination in the provision of goods and services. This is important for HR practitioners, managers and employees to note because employees who discriminate against customers or clients of the organisation may expose the organisation, as well as themselves, to legal liabilities. This requirement has implications for HR functions, including the selection of staff, training programs, performance appraisal, criteria for dismissal of employees, and so on.

Anti-discrimination legislation is passive legislation

Anti-discrimination legislation is often described as 'passive legislation'. This means that a person alleging violation of the legislation must make a complaint — for example, while an employer is prohibited from refusing to hire a woman for a particular job because she is a woman, the employer will be liable for discrimination only if the person discriminated against makes a complaint to an equal opportunity commission or tribunal. The employer must determine whether to be socially responsible by complying with the law or to risk being caught and penalised for discrimination.

The costs of discrimination

The costs of failing to ensure equal opportunity in employment and in the provision of goods and services are high, whether or not any complaints are filed against the organisation. Organisations that fail to ensure equal opportunity for all employees can experience low staff morale, high turnover rates, lower productivity and high absenteeism. Discrimination by employees against customers or clients can result in lost business as well as damage to the organisation's reputation, which can affect the share price and the willingness of potential employees to apply for positions, and can lead to further loss of customers, and so on.

Workplace discrimination or harassment that causes an employee earning $30 000 per year to take 10 days stress leave will cost the organisation over $1600 just in sick leave pay, and much more when the costs of things such as lost productivity and the wages of a replacement worker are included. Replacing a junior or middle manager who resigns as a result of discrimination or harassment will cost an organisation over $50 000 in costs associated with the recruitment, selection and training of a new employee, as well as the performance difference between an experienced and a new employee.[26]

Additionally, an organisation that gains a reputation for discriminatory practices may find itself regarded as a less attractive employer not only by persons from the groups discriminated against but also by traditional employees, and thus it may find it has a more limited applicant pool from which to select suitable employees. Organisations that discriminate in the provision of goods and services may find that they lose customers or clients: people from the discriminated groups may take their business elsewhere.

If a person who is discriminated against brings a legal action, then the organisation will find itself facing substantial costs to defend the action. These costs can amount to tens of thousands of dollars — even hundreds of thousands of dollars. Costs include not only legal fees and the amount of any financial award made to the complainant, but also the time of employees (spent consulting legal representatives, compiling evidence, and so on) and the disruptions in the workplace, which can result in lower productivity, increased absenteeism, and so on. Even if the matter is handled within the organisation, the costs are not inconsequential. The Anti-Discrimination Board of New South Wales estimates that an organisation will spend an average $35 000 to resolve a discrimination complaint in-house.[27] The costs of discrimination were recently highlighted when it was revealed that the Victoria Police has spent over $1 million resolving discrimination complaints (see figure 19.2).

Victoria Police has spent more than $1 million settling complaints of discrimination, harassment and bullying within the force over the past 3 years.

... The figure also indicates a continuing pattern of payouts following the landmark 1998 $125 000 Anti-Discrimination Tribunal payout to [a woman police officer found to have been sexually harassed].

... [A] former senior sergeant who worked as an independent conciliator between 2000 and 2002 ... broker[ing] settlement of complaints of discrimination and harassment ... [said]: 'This is public money coming out of a very tight police budget ... Every time they pay out $30 000 on settling a complaint, that's another police car. When they pay out $100 000, that's another trained police officer'

.... [T]he head of the [Victoria Police] Equity and Diversity Unit ... said about $500 000 had been paid in settlements in 17 cases. The other $500 000-plus had gone on costs of legal fees, investigations, counselling and courses to assist complainants with career development.

Figure 19.2 The costs of discrimination
Source L. Porter, 'Police pay out $1 m for bullies, *Sunday Age*, 3 August 2003, p. 1.

Affirmative action legislation

Anti-discrimination is a process-based approach to managing difference and mainly focuses on addressing direct discrimination (see the section on direct discrimination below). It is based on the premise that treating everyone in the same way will lead to equal outcomes. However, equal treatment can result in indirect discrimination and result in unequal outcomes, even when not intended. Indirect discrimination (see the section on indirect discrimination below) is frequently the outcome of treating everyone the same.

Given that indirect discrimination is often not obviously discriminatory and that the passive nature of anti-discrimination legislation was not producing the desired result of increasing women's employment opportunities, the Australian government enacted the *Affirmative Action (Equal Employment Opportunity for Women) Act 1986*. In 1999, this act was amended and re-titled as the *Equal Opportunity for Women in the Workplace Act 1999* (EOWW Act).

AA legislation is outcome focused. It requires organisations to consider how affirmative action programs can achieve equitable outcomes. It recognises that treating everyone the same will benefit some individuals and groups, while disadvantaging others. Because people are different, the mere fact of treating everyone as if they were the same will result in some people being advantaged, and others disadvantaged.

The EOWW Act

The EOWW Act applies to all organisations (excluding those in the public sector, which are covered by public service legislation) employing 100 or more workers. It covers private sector companies, unions, group training schemes, non-government schools, community organisations and all higher education institutions.

The EOWW Act is 'active' legislation. It requires employers to develop policies and practices to redress the results of historic and structural discrimination in the workplace. Employers must file a report annually with the Equal Opportunity for Women in the Workplace Agency (formerly the Affirmative Action Agency).

Employers who fail to comply with the reporting requirements can be named in Parliament. They may also be barred from tendering for government contracts or be unable to benefit from various government programs designed to support employment and develop businesses. In 2002, 28 companies (or less than 1 per cent of organisations covered by the legislation) did not submit a report.[28] On the other hand, after 15 years of AA legislation, the Agency's annual report noted that 14 per cent of reporting organisations either were just commencing their AA programs or had made slow progress, and that another 69 per cent had only moderate achievements.[29]

In 1996, the Agency adopted its Policy for Waiving Affirmative Action Report Requirements to reward those companies that have achieved 'the development and implementation of successful affirmative action programs'. In 1996, less than 5 per cent of the more than 2000 reporting organisations were deemed best-practice organisations. In 1997, a further 45 organisations were granted the waiver from reporting. By 1998, 291 organisations had been granted reporting waivers (12.5 per cent of the 2334 companies reporting to the Agency). In 2001, 206 had been granted reporting waivers (approximately 8 per cent of reporting organisations).[30]

The EEOW Act requires that employers not only eliminate direct discrimination, but also address indirect and structural or systemic discrimination (see below) which prevents women from having equal access to employment opportunities. It should be noted that the reasons for the differences in women's and men's work force participation patterns are the result of complex historical and sociocultural factors that are not always within the scope of individual organisations to resolve.[31] Individual organisations can, however, implement numerous HR strategies to address the inequities encountered by women in employment as a result of indirect and systemic discrimination.

The EEOW Act specifically applies to women, but the principles of affirmative action could be applied to enhance the employment opportunities of any group that has been disadvantaged in employment. Federal and Victorian public service legislation, for example, require government departments and public authorities to develop AA-style programs to address the employment disadvantage experienced not only by women, but also by

Aboriginal Australians and Torres Strait Islanders, people with disabilities and people from non-English-speaking backgrounds.

Affirmative action: not 'reverse' or 'positive' discrimination

Reverse discrimination
Discrimination against persons who are not designated as members of a minority or disadvantaged class.

Affirmative action in Australia and many other countries generally does not involve **'reverse' discrimination** (or 'positive' discrimination). Setting targets or forward estimates, as recommended by AA legislation, is not about setting quotas; rather, it is about setting benchmarks by which an organisation can measure the success of particular strategies. In other words, targets or forward estimates are audit measures to determine the effectiveness of a particular strategy to achieve a desired outcome.

Neither the EEOW Act nor its predecessor legislation requires organisations to employ or promote persons (that is, women in the case of the Australian legislation) unqualified or less qualified for positions merely to comply with the legislation. But the legislation does require organisations to consider whether their policies and practices may indirectly discriminate against women. It also permits organisations to establish programs specifically directed at members of the disadvantaged group to redress previous discrimination.

An organisation seeking to employ a chef, for example, could use the completion of a relevant apprenticeship as a selection criterion for all applicants. This would prevent many otherwise qualified women from applying for the job — or being selected if they did apply — because women are much less likely than men to have completed an apprenticeship. This is a form of indirect discrimination. An affirmative action approach encourages organisations to consider why fewer women apply for the position or why fewer women are as likely as men to meet the selection criteria. HR practitioners could then consider whether there are alternative selection criteria by which applicants could demonstrate their competency.

Broadening the selection criteria to allow applicants to demonstrate their knowledge and skills in a number of ways allows non-traditional applicants to be considered for positions that would previously have been closed to them. Sometimes, especially to persons who were previously advantaged by the limitation (for example, completion of an apprenticeship), an applicant who presents different qualifications can seem to be less qualified and thus their appointment is viewed as 'reverse' or 'positive' discrimination.[32]

AA strategies can be adopted to make employment opportunities more accessible to groups underrepresented in an organisation's work force or in particular parts of the work force. For example, in 1994, women made up less than 25 per cent of managers in Australian organisations. And the higher the level of management, the fewer women were to be found: women made up 35 per cent of junior managers in Australian private sector organisations, 24 per cent of middle management, 15 per cent of senior management and only 8 per cent of executive management. Such proportions are even found in those industries dominated by women: for example, in 1994 women made up 78 per cent of employees in the health and community services sector but held only 34 per cent of executive management positions; similarly, women made up 65 per cent of employees in the education industry but held only 17 per cent of executive management positions. The hospitality industry is a more gender-mixed sector but still shows a similar pattern: women hold 48 per cent of junior and middle management positions but only 29 per cent and 20 per cent of senior management and executive management positions, respectively.[33]

In 1998, women represented 27.3 per cent of managers in *companies reporting to the Equal Opportunity for Women in the Workplace Agency*. While this is only a marginal improvement since 1994, it is significant that Australian Bureau of Statistics data for *all Australian companies* reveal that the percentage of women managers decreased from 23.9 per cent to 23.6 per cent between 1990 and 1998.[34] In other words, the implementation of affirmative action programs can make a difference in women's employment and career development opportunities.

However, it was recently estimated that at this pace of change it will take 177 years (or approximately seven generations) for women to achieve equality in the Australian work force. The Equal Opportunity for Women in the Workplace Agency's 2002 Census of Women Executive Managers and Census of Women Board Directors reveal how far organisations need to go to achieve equitable employment for women. These reports highlighted that 54 per cent of Australia's top 200 companies did not have any women at the highest levels of management. They also revealed that only 5 per cent of executive positions in core business areas (the areas from which most senior executive and board positions are filled) are held by women.[35]

Women are less likely than men to enter the ranks of management for a number of reasons.[36] An AA program is designed to identify the reasons for women's lesser participation and then to develop appropriate practices to address the causes of inequitable outcomes.

For example, one factor that limits women's ability to achieve managerial status is that they often lack access to the informal mentoring and networking offered to male colleagues.[37] Of course, not all men who aspire to be managers have mentors, but men are much more likely than women to be mentored or to have access to managerial networks (which have predominantly male membership). As an alternative to these informal mentoring and networking arrangements from which women are largely excluded (often without conscious intent), some organisations have established formal mentoring programs for women or management training or information networks specifically for women.

The offering of programs specifically targeted at or designed for women may appear to be discriminatory, especially to those who are process-oriented rather than outcome-oriented. Such programs can appear discriminatory to men from minority ethnic groups, for example, and to other men who have been unable to access and benefit from the informal networking and mentoring provided by male colleagues and superiors. They can also appear discriminatory to men who do benefit from the informal networking and mentoring but are unaware of the benefits or believe that the benefits are merit based rather than a result of such processes as homosocial reproduction or 'comfort cloning' (see below).

In other words, beliefs about how fairness is achieved — through procedures equally applied or through alternatives enabling equal access to the possibility of achieving the desired outcome — can shape employees' perceptions of whether a particular approach or program is fair. Also, experience of other forms of discrimination or unfairness may make it difficult for some people to support AA strategies from which they do not benefit; AA strategies may seem just another benefit from which they are excluded. Ignorance about organisational processes and interpersonal relationships can limit people's understanding of processes and structures that advantage some and disadvantage others.[38]

While affirmative action is not synonymous with 'reverse' or 'positive' discrimination in Australia, there are countries in which AA does take this form. Malaysia, for example, has had 'reverse' or 'positive' discrimination requirements designed to redress certain imbalances in society that are associated with race/ethnicity. Malays are given preference over other ethnic groups (primarily Chinese and Indian) in new housing developments, public sector jobs and state university admissions.[39] They are also allocated 30 per cent of the equity in new companies.[40] However, in 2003 the racial affirmative action policy was ended, at least with regard to the allocation of places in Malaysian universities, and this is seen to have implications for university employment.[41]

Other countries, such as the United States, occasionally set court-allocated quotas when a company has failed, usually repeatedly, to properly implement EEO and AA programs. The presence of mandated 'reverse' or 'positive' discrimination or quotas usually reflects either structural discrimination that is deeply entrenched and/or persistent direct discrimination.

Establishing and implementing an AA program

An easy assumption to make is that AA programs are required only by those organisations with a male-dominated work force. But, as Santa Sabina College's experience (see figure 19.3) indicates, even organisations with predominantly female work forces can benefit from analysing their employment practices in terms of work force diversity factors.

The EOWW Act outlines the following steps to ensure compliance with the legislation's requirement that employers develop and implement workplace programs designed to achieve equal employment opportunities for women (see Pt II(8) of the Act):

1. Appoint staff with sufficient authority and status to develop, implement and review the workplace program.
2. Consult with employees, particularly women employees, or their nominated representatives. (A step in the AA Act, but omitted from the EOWW Act, is consulting with relevant unions.)

3. Prepare a work force profile.
4. Analyse the organisation's work force profile to determine issues that need to be addressed in order to achieve equal employment opportunities for women.
5. Identify specific actions to be taken to address identified EEO issues and devise effectiveness measures that permit monitoring and evaluation.
6. Submit a report annually to the EOWW Agency, unless a waiver has been obtained from the Agency.

These steps are similar to those recommended in the Act's predecessor (the *Affirmative Action (Equal Employment Opportunity for Women) Act 1986* — the AA Act). The EOWW Act presumes the issuance of an affirmative action or equal employment opportunity policy, a step clearly specified by the AA Act.

Step 1. Set the policy and appoint staff

By issuing a policy statement, the organisation commits to taking active measures to eliminate discrimination against women in its work force. Implementation of any policy requires the appointment of staff with responsibility to ensure the development and implementation of appropriate strategies and practices and to monitor and evaluate those strategies and practices to ensure they achieve the desired outcomes.

Step 2. Consult with staff

Consultation with employees is necessary for several reasons, including: (1) ascertaining the needs and interests of employees, particularly women; and (2) facilitating discussion of local organisational matters with employees directly (see figure 19.3).

STEPPING THROUGH THE PROCESS WITH SANTA SABINA COLLEGE

Sydney-based Santa Sabina College, an independent Catholic school for girls and primary school boys, is committed to retaining its highly valued staff and providing them with an environment that enables them to perform at their best. *Action News* spoke to Santa Sabina's HR Director, Elizabeth Bennett, to find out how they do it.

- **Assess your workplace**

  A statistical assessment of the female-dominated College showed that 67% of women employees were full time and 28% part time, and the majority were of child-bearing age. 'We identified there was a need for more part-time work and job sharing, as well as the provision of a childcare centre.'

- **Prioritise the issue**

  Acutely aware of the workplace disruption and high cost of staff and turnover, the College believes that 'enabling women to balance work and family commitments is a necessity'. Aligning business goals and EO goals, the College prioritised the development and implementation of a Job-Sharing Policy and the provision of a childcare centre.

- **Take action**

  After establishing a childcare centre for the use of College staff, the College then focused on the development of the Job-Sharing Policy. 'The involvement of the wider staff in the formulation of this policy has meant that staff see Equal Opportunity as encompassing more than just the provision of childcare', observed Ms Bennett.

- **Evaluate the effectiveness**

  Currently, the 40-place childcare centre caters for 14 children belonging to members of staff, which 'led to a rate of return to work after maternity leave of 87% — a significant improvement on the figures of three years ago'. In addition, the number of part-time and job-sharing roles has increased to 36% in 2000.

- **Plan future actions**

  The College recognises that 'people are our resources' and actively promotes commitment to advancing women through on-going consultation with staff. So what's in the pipeline for Santa Sabina's future? We also provide a Stay in Touch program for those on maternity leave, the flexibility to combine breastfeeding breaks in the workday and a private room where mothers can express and store their breastmilk.'

Figure 19.3 Stepping through the process with Santa Sabina College
Source *Action News* (EOWW Agency), Issue 44, Summer 2001, p. 7.

It is particularly important to consult female workers directly, and often separately from male workers, so that women's interests and concerns may be adequately raised. Women may feel constrained from speaking freely in the presence of men. An organisation undertaking AA strategies should determine what women see to be the problems and solutions for inequities in employment.

Step 3. Prepare a work force profile
The HR staff need to collect data about the work force profile by sex. Information may include: the number and percentage of women and men employed in particular occupations and classification levels, the salaries and benefits of men and women employed in the same or equivalent jobs, the promotion rates of men and women, and so on.

Step 4. Analyse the work force profile
By analysing the organisation's employment profile by sex, the HR manager can determine patterns of discrimination. A pattern of discrimination could be found, for example, if women are more likely to be employed in certain occupations (employment as secretaries, nurses, and so on) and not in others (employment as plumbers, dentists, and so on). Other patterns of discrimination may be found in the classification levels at which women are employed (more or less likely than their male counterparts to be managers or managers at particular levels — junior, middle, senior, executive) or in salaries (paid similar or different salaries from those of their male counterparts for positions requiring equivalent experience and qualifications). Or, are women less likely to undertake training or to be promoted than are their male counterparts? Do women have higher turnover rates or absenteeism?

Once the patterns of discrimination are determined, the HR manager can consider whether particular policies and practices of the organisation may have caused the inequality. The HR manager may wish to consult with employees, particularly female employees, to discuss the patterns and seek observations and suggestions from employees about how to address the situation.

Step 5. Develop, monitor and evaluate AA strategies, practices and programs
The organisation can then take steps to minimise or eliminate discrimination. If the organisation finds that women are less likely to be promoted into supervisory positions, for example, it may consider factors that contributed to this situation. It could be that employees wishing to be considered for supervisory positions need to complete an in-house training program that is offered only on weekends, and because women are less likely than men to be able to attend training outside business hours, fewer women are able to meet the training requirement. Offering the training during business hours or providing/reimbursing childcare for weekend sessions would enable more women to access the training and thus more women would be eligible for promotion.

There are likely to be other reasons why women find it difficult to access the training or why they are less interested in accessing the training. Is the training offered in a location where women feel uncomfortable or unwelcome? Or, given that women are more reliant on public transportation than are men, is the training in a location that is difficult to get to? Is the problem not the training itself, but the fact that supervisors are expected to act and interact with their subordinates in ways that make promotion seem less attractive to women, thus discouraging them from undertaking management training?

Consultation with female employees enables the HR manager to discover how to best provide appropriate training in an appropriate manner that encourages female employees to access the training required for promotion. It also allows the HR manager to understand why women may be less likely to undertake the training program.

Having developed a strategy to address the inequity, the HR manager should monitor the implementation of the strategy and evaluate its effectiveness. Monitoring the implementation will allow the strategy to be modified, if necessary, to ensure that it accomplishes the outcome desired.

In the above example of encouraging women to access management training, the strategy of offering training during business hours could be considered successful if more women undertake the program. If women still do not access the training, the HR manager's monitoring of the implementation will help determine why the strategy is unsuccessful and the intervention required. It could be that women are not allowed to take the time off from their work to attend the training sessions, so the HR manager would need to speak with supervisors to get their cooperation. It could be that women are not attending the training sessions because they regard the atmosphere as hostile, so the HR manager would need to determine the source of hostility and take appropriate steps to create a more welcoming atmosphere at training sessions. It could be that the trainer tells sexist jokes or uses lots of sports imagery, so the HR manager would need to instruct the trainer to be more inclusive or consider hiring other trainers.

Monitoring the AA strategy is not sufficient in itself. The HR manager needs to evaluate the effectiveness of the strategy to address discrimination; this involves setting up objectives and forward estimates. Generally, objectives and forward estimates should be quantifiable results: for example, a 20 per cent increase in the number of women attending the training program over 12 months, or a 20 per cent increase in the number of women completing the program, or enrolment of 44 women in the program. The objectives and forward estimates should be reasonable — that is, achievable, but requiring 'stretch' to achieve.

Imagine that the organisation meets its objective of increasing the number of women completing the training program by 20 per cent over 12 months, but only 1 per cent of the newly appointed supervisors are women. A study of promotion patterns for the company over a number of years shows that women make up only 1 per cent of supervisors appointed each year. The HR manager would now want to consider why the number of female appointments in supervisory positions did not change despite the increased number of women completing the training. Again, there are a number of possible explanations: women may work in narrow occupational areas (occupational segregation), so there are fewer opportunities for promotion regardless of the number of women qualified for promotion. Or perhaps the people making the promotion decisions may directly, whether consciously or unconsciously, discriminate against women. Or women may be less likely to apply for supervisory positions despite having completed the training. Another reason may be that women may lack other qualifications or experience required for promotion.

The answer is likely to be a combination of several reasons, and the HR manager would need to develop strategies to address each of the factors that contribute to inequitable promotion outcomes. Again, the HR manager should consult with female employees as well as supervisors and managers to determine further strategies for achieving an increased number of women in supervisory positions in the organisation.

Linking AA strategies to organisational objectives

If AA strategies are to achieve real and permanent changes to organisational employment practices with corresponding benefits of equitable employment opportunities for members of the targeted group(s), these strategies need to be linked to organisational objectives. In other words, affirmative action strategies must be seen to benefit the organisation as well as members of the targeted group(s). A strategic HR manager therefore not only seeks to demonstrate the success of AA strategies in terms of achieving equitable employment opportunities for the targeted group, but also wants to be able to demonstrate how AA strategies help the organisation achieve its strategic objectives.

If, for example, the organisation has as one of its organisational objectives to be the employer of choice for people seeking employment in that industry or particular occupation, the HR manager would want to demonstrate that AA strategies helped achieve that objective. This was the case for Westpac Bank when it initiated its *paid* maternity leave program. (Note: By law, female employees in Australia are entitled to six weeks *unpaid* confinement leave, and many industrial awards and enterprise agreements also contain provisions for up to 12 months *unpaid* maternity leave.) Westpac was the first Australian bank to offer its female employees paid (six weeks) maternity leave. This AA strategy not only increased retention of women staff; it also resulted in an increase in the number and quality of female — and male — applicants for Westpac positions. By monitoring resignations and returns from maternity leave and the quality of applicants pre- and post-introduction of the paid maternity leave program, the HR manager was able to demonstrate how an AA (and an HR) strategy facilitated achievement of organisational objectives.[42]

Diversity management

Diversity management is management initiated, rather than required by law. It was initially associated with cultural diversity based on ethnicity or race. It now also encompasses diversity based on the characteristics specified in anti-discrimination laws as well as those that are never likely to be included in such legislation. These latter characteristics can include levels of literacy and numeracy skills, career and life stages, occupational or professional identifications, decision-making or problem-solving styles, approaches to risk-taking, and so on. An organisation will want to identify and manage those characteristics that are likely to have a significant impact on the organisation's ability to achieve its strategic objectives.

While it is important that the wide range of characteristics that distinguish individuals and groups within an organisation are identified and determination is made about their significance in order to enable effective management of a diverse work force, HR practitioners should ensure that the major characteristics (for example, sex, race, disability) that have resulted in discrimination and disadvantage are not minimised or ignored in implementing diversity management strategies. A diversity management approach should not be allowed to trivialise the significant employment disadvantages suffered by women, people from a non-English-speaking background, Aboriginal Australians and Torres Strait Islanders and people with disabilities, nor redirect resources from addressing the causes of disadvantage for persons from these groups.

Differences between diversity management and anti-discrimination and AA approaches

Diversity management differs from anti-discrimination and AA not only in addressing more characteristics but also in being management initiated.

- *Differences between anti-discrimination and diversity management*
  Unlike anti-discrimination, diversity management respects and accommodates difference and requires significant changes to the organisation's culture. Anti-discrimination is essentially an assimilation approach: those who are different from the traditional work force are expected to conform to the values and behaviours of the **dominant or traditional employees/group**. Non-traditional workers are required to assimilate into the organisational culture while few, if any, accommodations are made to recognise that the non-traditional worker may find the 'accepted way of doing things' inappropriate or unproductive.

  Anti-discrimination approaches often ignore and devalue non-traditional employees' experiences or approaches. As a result, non-traditional workers may experience stress and expend considerable energy just trying to fit in. Numerous studies of female managers find that the failure of their employers to manage diversity creates stress and feelings of being devalued, which ultimately lead a number of women to decide to resign their positions. Evidence of the failure to manage diversity includes making the women feel like outsiders on the management team, maintaining a 'macho' organisational culture, offering women lower remuneration and benefits than those offered to male counterparts, requiring women to outperform male peers to secure equal advancement, often making women wait longer for promotion, and denying women access to information networks, mentors and role models.[43]

- *Differences between affirmative action and diversity management*
  Diversity management is also different from AA, although it is similar in its consideration of how current staff management practices may indirectly and structurally disadvantage non-traditional workers. AA seeks to identify and address factors that hamper non-traditional employees from contributing to the achievement of the organisation's objectives. Diversity management seeks not only to accommodate difference, but also to recreate the organisational culture to value and respect difference.

The difference between the three approaches to managing difference are best explained by example. An organisation taking an anti-discrimination approach to managing difference would generally expect non-traditional employees to comply with the employment practices already in place. Thus, the organisation would be unlikely to address women's childbearing

Diversity management Activities involved in integrating non-traditional employees (such as women and minorities) into the work force and using their diversity to the organisation's competitive advantage as well as considering other work force diversity characteristics that need to be addressed to ensure fair and effective utilisation of employees.

Dominant or traditional employees/group Employees who come from the majority group. In Australia, the dominant racial/ethnic group are people, particularly men, of Anglo-Celtic ancestry.

and childrearing functions by creating maternity leave or family-friendly policies, such as family leave, working from home or job sharing. Female employees would be expected to make their own individual and private arrangements to balance their work and family responsibilities.

An organisation taking an AA approach would identify the policies and practices that hamper the effective participation of non-traditional groups. It would determine difference so as to develop HRM practices that allow non-traditional employees to work more effectively within the existing structures and value system of the organisation. Having determined that women require support to manage their work and family responsibilities, the organisation might adopt a maternity leave policy. Many Australian organisations, for example, allow women to take up to 12 months unpaid maternity leave, allowing them to return to their previous position or an equivalent position, and thereby protecting a woman's employment while she cares for her baby. Other practices introduced to help women combine their work and family obligations include part-time work, job sharing, working from home and work-based childcare.

It should be noted that these practices, while valuable to working women with families, often do not alter the culture of the organisation. Thus, women continue to experience disadvantage in their career development and in accessing other employment opportunities.[44] This has also been referred to as the 'mommy track'.

An organisation taking a diversity management approach, like those taking an AA approach, would consider whether and how current staff management practices indirectly or systemically disadvantage non-traditional workers. However, unlike an AA-driven organisation, this organisation would consider not merely how to accommodate difference, but how the culture of the organisation needs to be altered to respect and value that difference.

An AA approach would seek to develop policies and practices that would help women to meet their family and work commitments without altering the organisational culture and values, but diversity management is about considering whether the organisation's values, and thus its policies and practices, respect employees' family commitments and encourage those employees that use family-friendly policies and practices (see the Deloitte Touche Tohmatsu example below).

A recent case demonstrates how affirmative action policies without organisational commitment and cultural change can result in continuing disadvantage.[45] A female employee who had been with an organisation for 11 years applied for maternity leave. Her manager expressed anger and hostility when she advised him of this application. Reportedly, he indicated his annoyance with having three female staff away on maternity leave and stated that he would employ only men in the future.

Near the conclusion of her maternity leave, the woman advised her manager of her anticipated return date and sought clarification of the arrangements that would be made regarding her return to her position. Given the provisions in both anti-discrimination law and the company's family leave policy, she expected to return to the position she held prior to taking the maternity leave — or to a comparable position. She found, however, that while she would retain her job classification (job title, pay level, classification grade and benefits), she would be assigned a different job. The evidence indicated that the new job was inferior in status, responsibility, strategic significance to the organisation and reporting relationships.

While there is some indication that there was a 'personality clash' between the manager and the female employee, the court found that the reason for her effective demotion was discrimination. The court determined that if she had not taken maternity leave, she would not have been reassigned to an inferior position but, rather, would have retained her more prestigious position.

The organisation has a family leave policy (this policy is provided in the court decision) and its Code of Ethics contains a provision stating that 'recruitment and selection for specific jobs and career progression will be determined by personal merit, competency, and the individual's potential to effectively perform the job'. A similar statement on the company's web site advises potential applicants of the working conditions at the company.[46] The evidence presented suggests, however, that while both the HR staff and the manager were aware of the law and the company's policy, they had little commitment to supporting the intent behind them. As a result, not only did the employee suffer constructive dismissal, but the organisation faced a damages claim of almost a quarter of a million dollars, as well as having to meet both its own and the plaintiff's legal costs.

An example of diversity management: Deloitte Touche Tohmatsu[47]

International professional services firm Deloitte Touche Tohmatsu offers a case study in the creation of a culture that recognises and accommodates diversity as a strategy to achieve sustained competitive advantage. Deloitte began to foster a diversity culture after senior management became worried by the high level of resignations of female accounting staff.

Consultation with both male and female staff revealed that the culture was 'heavy on ... testosterone', which was particularly alienating and discouraging for women. It also revealed that many male staff were dissatisfied with the family-unfriendly work practices and organisational culture. However, the introduction of family-friendly and work–life balance programs did not produce significant results until organisational cultural change was also achieved.

The success of the firm's diversity culture is measured by not only the reduction in the attrition rate of female staff, but also the increased number of women advancing to partner status, including several employed on a part-time basis. It is also measured by the importance of the firm's diversity culture on applicants' decisions to accept offers of employment: 98 per cent of female applicants and 88 per cent of male applicants recently indicated that Deloitte's diversity culture positively influenced their decision to accept a job offer. Additionally, new clients increasingly cite the firm's commitment to its people as a factor in the decision to employ Deloitte as their professional services firm.

Ensuring diversity management benefits employees as well as the organisation

There is a concern with diversity management that organisations will capitalise on certain employee differences while 'ghettoising' non-traditional employees within the organisation. Australian organisations, for example, are showing increasing interest in capitalising on the multicultural nature of the work force. Qantas, Australia's international airline, and Prestige, a manufacturing company, offer two examples of Australian businesses that have used their ethnically diverse work force to achieve organisational objectives. The Qantas catering service, for example, secured millions of dollars in catering contracts from other airlines by using its multicultural staff to develop menus and food preparation to meet the culinary requirements of different cultural groups. Prestige was on the verge of closing down as a result of business losses when it turned to its multicultural staff for advice on how to market its products appropriately in various countries. Implementing marketing strategies that were culturally sensitive, this company increased its export sales from 0 per cent to 15 per cent in two years.[48]

The question is whether the multicultural employees have gained greater access to employment opportunities within the organisation commensurate with their contribution to their employers' successes. Furthermore, have they gained access to employment opportunities that are not specifically tied to their ethnicity? Do multicultural employees gain access to positions in the marketing department, for example, or is their knowledge of a non-Australian culture plundered to benefit the organisation without any improvement to their own employment opportunities? Are people from a particular culture locked into jobs associated with that culture and excluded from other positions? Are 'national' market directors selected from individuals from the relevant national background (for example, a person of Japanese ancestry chosen as Marketing Director in Japan, an Indonesian chosen for the position in Indonesia, and so on) but not considered for the position of Asia–Pacific Regional Marketing Director (for example, an Anglo-Australian is chosen instead)?

Do you feel some concern that perhaps the organisation may be discriminating in seeking a person of Japanese ancestry to work as the director of marketing in Japan? How could the organisation avoid a complaint of discrimination? (See the discussion regarding the Chinese shop assistant on pages 708–9.)

Practitioner speaks

Developing an AA/EOWW program

Cyndi Stow is the Human Resources Manager for John Wiley & Sons Australia, Ltd. She became responsible for the company's EEO program in the 1995/1996 reporting year.

Turning theory into practice

Developing and implementing an affirmative action/equal opportunity for women in the workplace (AA/EOWW) program requires creativity and a commitment to establishing an organisational culture with equitable and transparent HR practices that maximise available talent. This sounds good in theory, but how does an HR practitioner turn it into a reality?

It's about your organisation

The program needs to be about *your* organisation. Like peeling through the layers of an onion, you can reveal a wealth of meaningful information about the way human resources are managed in your organisation through the use of staff surveys.

Staff surveys at Wiley Australia

I first surveyed our staff in 1995 on a broad range of issues to establish a comprehensive employment profile of the organisation. This survey was the first step in developing a new organisational culture — one in which attitudes and perceptions of individuals in the business were aggregated into statistics, giving staff a 'voice' in matters relating to human resource practices and policies that were important to them. Developing this change in organisational culture was consistent with the company's goal to make Wiley 'the place to be'.

How we went about it

The success of our initial staff survey, and subsequent surveys, has relied to a great extent upon a consultative approach:

- The CEO was consulted during the development of staff surveys, providing management with a stake in the process.
- A committee comprising management and non-management staff was established to act as a focus group. It was also consulted during the development and implementation of the survey.
- Staff were offered a voluntary opportunity to participate in the surveys and were assured of the confidentiality of their responses. Only aggregated statistics were included in the reports evaluating survey results.
- All staff were provided with an evaluation of survey responses and the company's recommended action plan.

    Don't bulldoze your way through the process and alienate HR along the way. Consider the importance of consultation and of giving stakeholders a 'buy-in' to the process.

What the surveys revealed

The initial survey provided us with statistics on the numbers of men and women in the organisation in management and non-management positions, their age ranges, and the numbers and age ranges of their children. We compared the length of time they expected to stay with the company with the time they expected to remain in the work force. We also gathered information on training and career development opportunities that they had received and their desired expectations for development opportunities. Perceptions on whether promotions and compensation were fair and equitable and whether they had experienced any form of discrimination or sex-based harassment during their employment with the company were also identified.

Developing an HR strategy

From survey responses, we identified a broad range of issues that were important to our staff. This profile highlighted information that had not previously been examined by senior management. HR strategies were subsequently developed and included establishing family-friendly policies, career development programs and transparent compensation policies. Over the years we have continued to survey staff on a wide range of HR practices including the annual performance appraisal process and quality of work–life issues. This process provides us with an ongoing HR strategic agenda.

Gaining the necessary political influence

Examining sensitive issues can be potentially threatening for an organisation as it may reveal facts or perceptions other than those traditionally accepted by the management hierarchy. However, without such close examination, organisations are limited to establishing an HR strategy based solely on management perceptions and anecdotal comment. Therefore, HR practitioners need support from the highest levels in the organisation to effectively examine such sensitive issues. Successful programs will commonly have the CEO as a champion for equitable HR practices, as is the case at Wiley Australia.

The benefits

In particular, HR practitioners need to identify and eliminate barriers to women in the workplace — this is only commonsense. They need to consider how to develop *all* the people in the organisation to their fullest potential, so that the organisation can utilise *all* the talent and creativity available. We cannot afford to have lesser expectations from, or rewards for, women in the workplace. Until HR practitioners can deliver an inclusive organisational approach across all levels of human resource practice, it will limit the potential return on investment for the organisation's highest cost — its people.

Cyndi Stow

Discrimination

Discrimination is any practice that distinguishes different groups based on characteristics defined in the anti-discrimination legislation (for example, sex, race, disability, marital or parental status) and results in one group being advantaged and the other group being disadvantaged. Discrimination does not have to be conscious or intended to be illegal.

Distinguishing between discrimination and unfairness

HR practitioners need to distinguish between discrimination and **unfairness**. Discrimination is behaviour that is prohibited by the anti-discrimination legislation. Thus, it is discriminatory to refuse to hire a person on the basis of race, or to pay a woman less than her male counterparts because she is a woman, or to refuse to hire a person with a disability if reasonable accommodation could be made to allow that person to undertake the functions of the position. It would be unfair, but not discriminatory, to deny an otherwise qualified person a training or promotional opportunity merely because they had not completed high school.

Both discrimination and unfairness are examples of poor HR practices, but discrimination can result in legal action as well as adverse staff management outcomes. HR practitioners will want to ensure that HR policies and practices are both non-discriminatory and fair. The problem is that practices that are designed to eliminate discrimination can appear to some people to be unfair.

A person's perception of whether an HR practice is fair or unfair depends, at least in part, on whether that person determines fairness based on a sense of 'distributive justice' (a focus on the allocation of outcomes: equity in outcomes) or 'procedural justice' (a focus on the process by which allocation of outcomes is determined: treating everyone the same). Those societies and individuals who determine fairness through procedural means (treating everyone the same) will often look on AA and diversity management approaches as unfair and as a form of 'reverse' discrimination.[49]

Discrimination can occur when a person receives less favourable treatment than received by others because:

- they have a characteristic identified in the legislation

Discrimination Any practice that makes distinctions between different groups based on characteristics identified in anti-discrimination legislation such as sex, race, age, religion, and so on, which results in particular individuals or groups being advantaged and others disadvantaged.

Unfairness Unfairness involves treating a person differently and adversely based on irrelevant criteria or characteristics. This adverse treatment cannot be addressed under anti-discrimination legislation — in other words, such adverse distinctions are unfair but not illegal.

- assumptions are made about the person based on certain characteristics (for example, the assumption that a female employee will be unavailable to work overtime because she has children, or that a person with a mobility impairment will be unable to drive a car)
- unreasonable conditions or requirements are set.

Employers' responsibility to prevent discrimination

An employer can be held vicariously liable for the discriminatory acts of employees (that is, the employer can be held liable for the acts of employees). Thus, it is important that employees are well informed of desired behaviour in anti-discrimination and AA matters and that proper steps are taken to respond to any complaints of discrimination.

Employers need to ensure that their employment practices do not discriminate against employees and applicants for employment. They also need to ensure that their employees do not discriminate against other employees or against applicants. Furthermore, they need to ensure that employees do not discriminate against customers and clients.

The mere creation and dissemination of policies regarding anti-discrimination and AA are not sufficient steps to meet the employer's legal responsibilities. Employers must demonstrate that employees have been adequately informed of the policies and advised and assisted to behave in a non-discriminatory manner. Advising employees of their responsibilities is not a one-off exercise. As new employees are hired, they need to be advised of the policies and expected behaviour. And existing employees should be regularly advised of the organisation's anti-discrimination and AA policies, the expectations of appropriate behaviour and possible penalties for failing to comply with the policies.

The employer must also ensure that employees are properly supervised to minimise the possibility of discriminatory behaviour occurring. This, in turn, means that supervisors and managers need to be advised of their responsibilities, trained to meet those responsibilities and held accountable for upholding those responsibilities (possibly through performance evaluations). Additionally, appropriate complaint and grievance processes must be in place, and complaints must be investigated properly. Organisations will want to ensure that managers, supervisors and employees are well aware that they may be held legally liable for their own discriminatory behaviour in the workplace and that it is in their own interests as well as the interests of the organisation to ensure that they behave in a non-discriminatory manner towards all staff and anyone else they encounter in the exercise of their employment.

An employer's obligations under the anti-discrimination legislation are not restricted to equitable employment practices. Employers are also obliged to ensure that discrimination does not occur in the provision of goods and services; employers are legally liable for the discriminatory actions of their employees while providing goods and services.

An example is when KPMG, a major accounting firm, was forced to defend itself in a sex discrimination case because one of its staff allocated shares in a float of the fruit-processing company SPC on the basis of sex. The float was oversubscribed, so the staff member, following instructions from the underwriter, issued shares only to the man when 'there was more than one application from a mixed-sex household or from people who shared the same name and address'.[50] Thus, the woman in such a household was discriminated against on the grounds of sex and possibly also on the grounds of marital status. The case was ultimately resolved after several days of hearings before the Human Rights and Equal Opportunity Tribunal when KPMG agreed to make a public apology, but not before the firm had incurred sizable legal costs and adverse publicity.

The HR manager and other managers and supervisors also need to realise that behaviour apparently considered acceptable by employees in that organisation may still have an adverse effect on the organisation. Employees may not find racist or sexist jokes or pornographic posters discriminatory, for example, but clients who hear or see them may be offended and decide not to do business with the organisation. This is an example of the value of a diversity management approach. This approach values difference and, as a result, fosters an organisational culture respectful of individuals, so the organisation's employees, customers and visitors are less likely to find an environment or practice that denigrates, devalues or disrespects them.

Types of discrimination

There are three types of discrimination: (1) direct, (2) indirect and (3) structural or systemic. Direct discrimination occurs when irrelevant criteria exclude a person from an employment opportunity — for example, when a woman applying for a job is told 'We don't hire women'. Indirect discrimination occurs when a seemingly neutral policy or practice or a criterion irrelevant to the job advantages one group of people and disadvantages others — for example, requiring security guards to be at least 1.8 metres tall excludes almost all women as well as most men from certain ethnic or racial groups. Occupational segregation is an example of structural or systemic discrimination, where discrimination has become embedded in an organisation as a product of longstanding direct and indirect discrimination — for example, social and cultural expectations discourage many women from becoming engineers and organisational practices often deny women engineers job opportunities, while a hostile work environment may force them to leave their jobs and the profession.

Direct discrimination

Direct discrimination occurs when a decision or action of one person or group excludes another person or group from a benefit or opportunity or significantly reduces their chances of obtaining a benefit or opportunity because a personal characteristic irrelevant to the situation is applied as a barrier. Direct discrimination is often the product of stereotypes about particular groups:

> ... direct discrimination is where you make assumptions about a person just because they happen to belong to a particular group of people, as opposed to checking out their particular individual skills, abilities, and talents. It happens when you put a person into a box labelled 'women', 'men', 'Lebanese', and so on, rather than treating the person as an individual.[51]

Direct discrimination is often, but not always, blatant and easy to identify. It can include remarks such as 'No Vietnamese need apply', 'We don't hire Catholics', 'A person in a wheelchair can't do this job' and 'It isn't worth training female staff — they just get married and quit'. It can also include behaviour such as hostile or intimidating questioning of non-traditional applicants during selection interviews.[52]

Stereotyping may be another example of direct discrimination, although sometimes the discriminator is unaware of making decisions based on stereotypes because the stereotypes have become unconscious beliefs or assumptions. A manager may refuse to hire a woman as a forklift driver, for example, believing it is inappropriate for a woman to do such work. Similarly, a man could be refused a job as a secretary, childcare worker or nurse because these occupations are not deemed as being 'men's work'.

Another example of direct discrimination would be if race were the sole reason why two employees from different ethnic or racial groups (for example, an Anglo-Australian and a Turk, or a Hong Kong Chinese and a mainland Chinese) were paid different salaries for doing the same job. Direct discrimination may even occur in a downsizing situation if management decides to first terminate the employment of people with disabilities 'because they can always collect social welfare'. In all these situations, an employment decision has been made to disadvantage a person based on a characteristic that is irrelevant to the employment issue.

Direct discrimination can also be presumed from outcomes. Assume a company has hired only men as management trainees yet half the applicants for these positions were women, all with relevant tertiary qualifications and work experience. This suggests that the company is directly discriminating against women, even if there have been no overt discriminatory statements or behaviours. It may be that the selectors are unaware of their discriminatory practice; they may honestly believe they have chosen the best-qualified applicants.

Direct discrimination Refers to any bias towards a person based on characteristics such as age, sex, race, etc. Direct discrimination is often the product of stereotypes about a particular group. It can be expressed through a refusal to hire, dismissal, providing unfavourable working conditions or limited opportunities.

Homosocial reproduction
Sometimes called 'comfort cloning'. Occurs when existing groups of people replicate themselves through selecting people like themselves to join their group or by selecting applicants most similar to those already employed in the position.

This could be an example of a process called '**homosocial reproduction**' or 'comfort cloning'. This is the process, often unconscious, whereby a group of selectors replicate themselves if selecting for a position similar to their own — for example, male managers selecting other men for managerial positions or a group of midwives hiring only women for midwifery positions.[53] Selectors will replicate as closely as possible, particularly with regard to sex and race/ethnicity, to themselves. Homosocial reproduction may also occur when selectors select for other positions: choosing applicants most like those already in similar positions within the organisation. For example, a selection panel may prefer women applicants for secretarial positions.

Antoinette Bishop coined the term 'comfort cloning', which captures the essence of homosocial reproduction — that is, an often unconscious need or desire to be comfortable with the people with whom one associates, in this instance, with the people with whom one works. This captures both the replication of oneself in selecting peers (for example, a manager selecting another manager) as well as in selecting people for subordinate positions (for example, hiring women to be secretaries).

Indirect discrimination

Indirect discrimination
Occurs when policies, procedures and practices that appear to be neutral (that is, non-discriminatory) produce adverse outcomes for people with specific characteristics.

Indirect discrimination occurs when policies, procedures and/or practices that appear neutral (that is, non-discriminatory) have an adverse outcome for persons with a particular characteristic, thus reducing the employment opportunities for those persons.[54] The criteria for determining indirect discrimination are enunciated in anti-discrimination legislation, including the *Victorian Equal Opportunity Act 1995* and the federal *Sex Discrimination Act*:

> A person discriminates against a [woman] if that person requires [her] to comply with a requirement or condition:
> – with which a substantially higher proportion of [men] comply or are able to comply,
> – with which [she] does not or is not able to comply, and
> – which is not reasonable in the circumstances of the situation.

Other groups besides women can be the subjects of indirect discrimination: for example, in the above definition substitute persons with a visual impairment for women and persons without a visual impairment for men. It is important to note that indirect discrimination can be found only if the person alleging discrimination is required to meet an unreasonable criterion or condition.

Most anti-discrimination legislation sets out the standards to determine reasonableness. Section 9(2) of the *Victorian Equal Opportunity Act 1995*, for example, specifies:

1. What are the consequences of failing to meet the requirement or condition?
2. What are the costs of alternative requirements, conditions or practices?
3. What are the financial circumstances of the person on whom the alternative requirement might be imposed?

Thus, it is not unreasonable, for example, to require an airline pilot to be sighted and to have specified levels of visual acuity — these are necessary job requirements.[55] It would not therefore be indirect discrimination for a blind person to be denied employment as an airline pilot. While the consequences of the blind applicant not meeting the vision requirements mean that they will be excluded from an opportunity to be employed as a pilot, the employer has no reasonable alternatives that would allow a blind person to be employed as a pilot. Further, employment of a blind person as a pilot could subject the employer to costly legal obligations if an accident occurred. It should be noted, however, that technological advances mean that many tasks that previously could not be handled by people with disabilities can now be undertaken by them. Research suggests that the accommodations required to allow people with disabilities to work competently and effectively are often low cost, with many costing less than $50.[56]

The case of *Australian Iron and Steel Pty Ltd v. Banovic* clearly established the concept of indirect discrimination in Australian law.[57] This case involved a group of women who applied for employment in a steel mill in the late 1970s. The women failed to secure employment and brought an equal opportunity case. It was found that they had been discriminated against, and the company was compelled to employ them.

Several years later, the company experienced a business downturn and was forced to terminate the employment of a number of workers. The company used a common practice for determining whose employment would be terminated: 'last hired, first fired'.

The group of women who had been employed as a result of their equal opportunity suit filed a second suit alleging indirect discrimination. They argued that if they had been hired at the time of their original application, they would not be among those to be fired; the males who had applied at the same time as the women's original application were not in danger of termination.

The court found that the policy indirectly discriminated against the women. The policy of 'last hired, first fired' seemed to be non-discriminatory — both men and women who had been hired after a certain date (last hired) were to be fired — but the previous discrimination meant the women were being treated differently from the men in the original applicant cohort who had been employed in the late 1970s.

The height requirement of a number of police forces several years ago is another example of indirect discrimination. All applicants had to be at least a minimum height. This was a seemingly neutral policy: every applicant who met this criterion could go on for further consideration. However, this criterion worked to eliminate from selection most women, regardless of ethnic group, and many men from certain ethnic groups. Thus, it was a form of indirect discrimination. The height requirement had not been intended to be discriminatory. It was thought that height would give police officers greater ability to control unruly individuals and crowd situations. As it turns out, height is not a good criterion on which to judge a person's interpersonal skills and abilities to control violent or potentially violent situations.

Structural or systemic discrimination

Structural or systemic discrimination is the product of longstanding direct and indirect discrimination. It is the result of the interaction of decisions, actions, regulations, policies, practices, social attitudes and so on that allow discrimination to become embedded within the system. The 'system' may be both society as a whole and/or individual organisations and their cultures.

The occupational segregation of the work force is an example of systemic discrimination. Occupational segregation occurs both in the work force at large and in the microcosm of individual organisations. Secretaries are more likely to be women and engineers are more likely to be men, for example — both across the national work force and in any individual organisation.

How deeply embedded beliefs about men's and women's proper social and employment roles are in society and in organisations is revealed even in newer industries such as information technology.[58]

Table 19.1 shows the occupational distribution of the male and female work forces in Australia over the period 1986 (the year in which the AA legislation was first introduced) to 2001. For example, in 2001, 5.7 per cent of the female work force and 12.1 per cent of the male work force were employed as managers and administrators. Until the mid-1990s, the percentage of women and men employed as managers and administrators remained stable, but in 1998 there was a dramatic decline for both men and women. This might have been a result of factors such as downsizing and the flattening of organisational hierarchies that characterised the 1990s. It might also in part have been a result of a change to the coding system used by the Australian Bureau of Statistics. The dramatic increase in the percentage of women in the 'Professionals' category may be attributed, in part, to the inclusion of Nursing and Teaching, two female-dominated occupations, in the 'Professional' category; previously these two occupations were categorised as 'Para-professional'.

The patterns in employment identified in table 19.1 suggest how deeply entrenched discrimination is within societies. Note that women are 'crowded' into a narrow range of occupational categories, particularly clerical and sales/service occupations, while men are much more evenly distributed across the categories.

Table 19.2 considers the occupational distribution of the Australian work force by sex. For example, in 1986, 77.5 per cent of managers and administrators were men, whereas only 22.5 per cent were women. The most recent data (2001) indicate a small increase in the

Structural or systemic discrimination A form of hidden discrimination that is the product of social conditioning and that has become embedded within the system; for example, the view that it is 'natural' for women to be secretaries and men to be engineers.

Women are prohibited from combat roles in the military. Men are not. Is this sexual discrimination?

percentage of female managers but, as noted earlier, this increase is at the lower levels of management, and few women have achieved senior and board-level management positions.

Table 19.1   Occupation of employed persons aged 15 years or more, Australia (percentage)

	WOMEN					MEN				
	1986	1992	1995	1998	2001	1986	1992	1995	1998	2001
Managers and administrators	6.3	6.7	6.1	3.5	5.7	14.0	14.7	14.2	9.6	12.1
Professionals	11.9	13.9	14.2	20.0	21.2	12.1	13.8	13.7	16.2	15.8
Para-professionals	6.4	6.7	6.3	8.8	11.4	5.5	5.6	5.2	11.5	12.0
Tradespersons	4.3	3.7	3.6	3.1	3.0	24.8	23.3	22.8	21.8	19.9
Clerks	32.6	30.6	29.9			7.4	6.5	6.1		
Salespersons and personal service workers	22.0	23.7	26.3	53.2*	47.3	8.4	9.1	10.75	15.2*	15.3
Plant and machine operators, drivers	3.3	2.4	2.3	2.7	2.5	10.8	10.6	10.7	14.3	12.7
Labourers and related workers	13.1	12.4	12.3	8.6	7.0	16.9	16.4	16.8	11.3	10.0

* Categories of clerks and salespersons and personal service workers combined in 1998 data.

Source Data derived from Australian Bureau of Statistics, *Women in Australia*, ABS, Canberra, 1993; 'Women at work — facts and figures', *Women & Work*, vol. 16, no. 2, July–October 1995; and Commonwealth Office of the Status of Women, *Women in Australia 1999*, Department of Prime Minister and Cabinet, Canberra, 1999, Table 4.11: Occupation in main job: August 1998, 2001 Census data provided by Office of the Status of Women from ABS data; and private communication, 5 August 2003.

Table 19.2   Distribution by sex in occupation of employed persons aged 15 years or more, Australia (percentage)

	1986		1995		1998		2001	
	WOMEN	MEN	WOMEN	MEN	WOMEN	MEN	WOMEN	MEN
Managers and administrators	22.5	77.5	24.6	75.4	22.3	77.7	28.0	72.0
Professionals	38.9	61.1	44.1	55.1	49.0	51.0	52.5	47.5
Para-professionals	42.9	57.1	47.8	52.2	37.5	62.5	44.0	56.0
Tradespersons	10.1	89.9	10.8	89.2	9.9	90.1	11.0	89.0
Clerks	74.0	26.0	78.9	21.1				
Salespersons and personal service workers	62.9	37.1	64.7	35.3	73.1*	26.9*	71.8	28.2
Plant and machine operators, drivers	16.5	83.5	14.0	86.0	13.0	87.0	13.8	86.2
Labourers and related workers	33.4	66.6	35.9	64.1	37.2	62.8	36.8	63.2

* Categories of clerks and salespersons and personal service workers combined in 1998 data.

Source Data derived from Australian Bureau of Statistics, *Women in Australia*, ABS, Canberra, 1993; 'Women at work — facts and figures', *Women & Work*, vol. 16, no. 2, July–October 1995; and Commonwealth Office of the Status of Women, *Women in Australia 1999*, Department of Prime Minister and Cabinet, Canberra, 1999, Table 4.11: Occupation in main job: August 1998. 2001 Census data provided by Office of the Status of Women from ABS data; and private communication, 5 August 2003.

NEWSBREAK

Equity is still a long way off

By Fiona Buffini

So girls, your teacher said you could do anything. He — or more likely she — was wrong.

'Our educators have given young women the impression that they can do anything — and that is demonstrably not true', Saatchi & Saatchi Australia chairwoman Sandra Yates said yesterday.

'There is a real disconnect between what your education leads you to believe will happen when you get into the workforce and what the reality is.'

Australia's second annual census of women in leadership shows women hold only 8.8 per cent of senior executive positions and 8.4 per cent of board seats in the top 200 listed companies.

That is up 0.4 and 0.2 percentage points respectively on last year, but almost half of the top 200 have no women in executive positions. Only four of the top 200 have a female chief executive.

'I have to say, looking back, that this report finally puts the nail in that old shibboleth that time will deliver equity for women', Ms Yates said at the launch of the census yesterday.

'Whoever bought that particular pup should abandon it right now — it's clearly not true.'

Even when women make it to the top management team, 62 per cent hold 'staff' or supporting roles in human resources or legal departments while 74 per cent of male managers hold 'line' positions with direct responsibility for profit or clients.

The Equal Opportunity for Women in the Workplace Agency conducted the study.

Federal director Fiona Krautil said a major barrier for women was their lack of experience in jobs 'where the money is made'.

'We have this huge gap, with women clustered in staff roles with limited career opportunities — and to some degree languishing in these roles', she said.

The results also showed that Australia was falling further behind countries such as the United States where women held nearly 16 per cent of top management roles.

'I feel disappointed and frustrated … with the leaders of Australian businesses that they still don't recognise the contribution that women have to make to Australian business success', Ms Krautil said.

Women comprise half the Australian workforce and 43 per cent of middle managers and professionals.

Ms Krautil said women often did not recognise the importance of operational roles, maybe opting to 'work with people', so missed out on key experience.

'And many Australian men can't imagine women in these roles because they've never worked with them', she said.

As a manager at Esso in the 1980s, Ms Krautil recalled one of the oil company's brightest young female engineers having a career development discussion with her boss.

'"Well, what do you want to be?" he said. She said, "I want to be the production manager". To which he replied, "You're aiming a bit high aren't you?"

'That is an unconscious thing', she said. 'Most of our managers in Australia are unconsciously incompetent in

managing diversity and yet they think they know it all.'

The census was based on methods developed by US organisation Catalyst in partnership with Macquarie University and sponsors ANZ and Edith Cowan University.

It shows software, telecommunications, retailing and health care among the best industries in promoting women into executive jobs. Consumer durables, pharmaceuticals, real estate, hotels, restaurants, food and beverage are among the worst.

'I think there's been a failure somewhere along the line and I wouldn't like to make an accusation on the basis of gender but we all know who's really in charge', Ms Yates said.

She said men just did not see diversity as a bottom-line issue.

'It is a missed opportunity', she said. 'We're not globally competitive and we're not going to be because we don't seem to attach any urgency to this.'

While today's business leaders did not usually disregard things that would make them more money, many CEOs were 'surrounded by a bunch of blokes with the same attitudes and beliefs as them — there's no one to kickstart the debate', she said.

Their daughters may turn out to be 'our best secret weapon', she predicted.

'The majority of male business leaders now have probably got daughters in their 20s and 30s and they are now having to focus on what happens to women generically is now happening to their own little princess all of a sudden. That tends to focus their attention.'

Source *Australian Financial Review*, 2 October 2003, p. 6.

Structural or systemic discrimination often appears to be the natural order because it has become so embedded in the system. Systemic discrimination is also difficult to address because even those who are disadvantaged often accept the outcomes of the discrimination as 'natural'. There is no reason why women are particularly suited to being secretaries, for example, but women are more likely to seek out this occupation than plumbing or engineering work. In fact, until the early twentieth century, secretaries were much more likely to be men than women.[59] The fact that systemic discrimination is a product of wider social factors and seemingly often the 'choice' of those who are disadvantaged makes it difficult for organisations to address it. But this difficulty does not mean that organisations are not obliged to try.

Organisational efforts to address systemic discrimination require long-range strategies as well as cooperation with other organisations, including educational and training institutions and professional bodies. For example, engineering is one of the most male-dominated occupations. Organisations that employ engineers and seek to hire more female engineers will need to address the structural factors that discourage women from studying in this area (see figure 19.4).

The male domination of a number of professions can discourage women from entering those professions. Recognising this, the University of Melbourne recently sought and was granted an exemption from the Victorian *Equal Opportunity Act* allowing it to reserve three of its Engineering postdoctoral fellowships specifically for women.

This exemption allows the university to address gender imbalance in both the Engineering faculty's academic staffing and its student body: Currently, only 32 of the 206 academic staff are women, and only 17 of the 91 postdoctoral positions are held by women.

Associate Professor Doreen Thomas, head of Electrical and Electronic Engineering and the only female associate professor in the Engineering faculty, commented that increasing the number of women in Engineering would mean that women would not have to walk the 'lonely road' she experienced. She noted further that, as a result, female students and staff would be offered professional and academic role models that would encourage other women to enter the Engineering profession and provide support for career development and advancement.

Associate Professor Thomas also suggested that since Engineering links science and society, a more gender-inclusive profession would benefit the whole community as well as women.

Figure 19.4 Addressing some of the structural factors that discourage women from studying engineering
Source Based on S. Milovanic, 'Uni wins PhD places for female engineers,' *Age*, 2 August 2003, p. 8.

A number of organisations have implemented strategies such as providing scholarships for female engineering students and supporting campaigns to encourage young women to consider engineering studies. Other strategies are focused on the organisation: recruitment campaigns that particularly target female applicants for engineering positions; the financing of the engineering studies of women already employed by the organisation; the use of policies and practices that encourage female engineers to remain on staff by ensuring that the work environment is not hostile or unwelcoming to women (for example, maternity leave policies, job descriptions and expectations that accommodate family responsibilities, and the enforcement of sexual harassment policies), and so on.

Harassment

Harassment Behaviour designed to make a person feel unwelcome, offended, humiliated and/or intimidated.

Racial vilification A particular form of discrimination sometimes called racial harassment.

Harassment is a particular form of discrimination, and sexual harassment and racial harassment (sometimes referred to as **racial vilification**) are prohibited under anti-discrimination legislation.[60] This discussion focuses on sexual harassment, but HR managers will want to ensure that no employee is harassed for any reason.[61]

To harass someone is:
- to exhaust or wear out with trouble
- to harry

- to trouble or vex by repeated attacks
- to worry or distress with annoying importunity.

Harassment is behaviour designed to make a person feel unwelcome, offended, humiliated and/or intimidated. It is illegal if it adversely affects a person's employment. However, it has been argued that harassment that creates a hostile work environment is discrimination, even if the employee cannot show any specific employment detriment as a result of the harassment.

Sexual harassment is not about sexual attraction; it is about the abuse of power. Both men and women can be the victims of sexual harassment, and both men and women can be harassers. However, because sexual harassment is about the abuse of power, and men are more often the holders of power in most organisations, women are much more likely to be sexually harassed than are men.

Sexual harassment may take the following forms:
- quid pro quo harassment in which a person is required to accept or perform sexual behaviour to gain an employment benefit (for example, to be hired or promoted, or to be awarded a salary increase) or to avoid some employment detriment (for example, to avoid being fired or transferred)
- harassment that creates a sexually permeated or hostile work environment (for example, displays of sexually explicit material, constant discussion of sexual matters)
- criminal behaviour (for example, sexual assault or obscene communications).

Sexual harassment is defined as physical, visual, verbal or non-verbal behaviour of a sexual nature that is *uninvited* and *unwelcome* and that adversely affects or could adversely affect a person's employment. Sexually harassing behaviour can include:
- uninvited and unwelcome touching
- sexual comments and jokes
- displays of sexually explicit materials, including posters, pin-ups, graffiti and magazines
- speculations about or intrusive questions into a person's private life
- sex-based insults or taunts.

The anti-discrimination legislation makes it illegal for an employer to sexually harass employees. The employer is also vicariously liable for the behaviour of employees, so the employer will be held legally responsible if an employee harasses another employee (unless the employer has taken reasonable steps to prevent harassing behaviour from occurring in the workplace). In Victoria, employers are also liable for the behaviour of their employees in other workplaces.

The mere development and dissemination of a sexual harassment policy is usually not regarded as satisfying the employer's responsibility to prevent sexual harassment. Employers need to ensure that employees are properly advised of expected behaviour, ensure that employees are properly supervised to minimise the likelihood of sexually harassing behaviour occurring, and respond seriously, appropriately and speedily to any complaints of harassment within the framework of the organisation's grievance procedures.

The costs of sexual harassment are not inexpensive. Sydney University law lecturer Therese MacDermott advises employers that the average compensation award in Australian sexual harassment cases is $35 000. This does not include an organisation's legal costs in defending a sexual harassment case, so these costs could easily rise to $150 000 or $200 000, or more. In addition, an organisation will accrue further costs — including the time of staff involved in preparing the case and attending hearings as well as disruptions to work and the workplace — which could easily add tens of thousands of dollars to the costs. Even if the person harassed decides not to bring a legal action, it is likely that they will seek another employer. As a result, an employer will incur replacement costs. Replacing a middle manager, for example, could easily cost $50 000 in recruitment, selection and training expenses.[62]

Perhaps the seriousness of the costs of sexual harassment to organisations, along with the telling failure of many organisations to appropriately deal with sexual harassment in the workplace, is highlighted by American International Group's (a major international insurance company) announcement of policies to cover directors, officers and their employing companies against losses arising from sexual harassment claims both in Australia and internationally. American International Group already offers similar policies to companies operating in the United States, Britain, Europe and Japan.[63]

Sexual harassment Behaviour involving sexually suggestive remarks, unwanted touching and sexual advances, requests for sexual favours, or other verbal or physical conduct of a sexual nature that is unwanted and that adversely affects a person's employment and/or creates a hostile work environment.

Merit

Merit Concerned with excellence, superiority and/or being the best qualified.

Merit is a key concept in employment. There are often fears that programs designed to address difference in the workplace will undermine this concept — in other words, that anti-discrimination, AA and diversity management will require organisations to hire, promote, reward and retain unqualified or less qualified people.

There are few organisations that would acknowledge making employment decisions on any other basis than merit. Yet there are numerous examples of employment decisions made on other criteria. The *Australian Iron and Steel Pty Ltd v. Banovic* decision discussed earlier, for example, revealed a termination decision based on seniority rather than merit. It may be argued that more experienced workers are more valuable than less experienced workers, and thus that seniority is a shorthand measure of value. But this assumption is dangerous given that length of service does not necessarily mean quality of work performance or breadth of experience or relevant experience or work commitment. Seniority is at best an imprecise measure of relative merit; it is merely a measure of relative time served. NRMA introduced a merit-based promotion system to replace the 'old boys' network', that previously determined promotion decisions.[64] Rio Tinto, as part of its industrial dispute with the Construction, Forestry, Mining and Energy Union, challenged the traditional practice of hiring only from the union-maintained list of retrenched members.[65] It may be suggested that merit is championed when a privileged group fears the loss of its advantage.

Actually, the major difficulty with the concept of merit is that it usually is presented as an objective concept, free of biases and assumptions — that is, free of prejudice and discrimination. But merit is often a subjective concept. Furthermore, the criteria for and measures of merit may actually be forms of indirect discrimination.

Merit is most clearly and frequently incorporated into selection, whether for initial appointment or for promotion. Many managers would claim that a number of other HR decisions are made on the basis of merit: for example, choosing the recipient of a training opportunity or workers for a particular project, setting performance measures, determining amounts of performance bonuses or salary increases for individual employees, and so on. There may be a seeming objectivity to these processes, but likely hidden assumptions and prejudices may actually result in subjective outcomes.[66]

There are two competencies tested in selection processes: functional competency and organisational competency.[67] **Functional competency** is the most obviously tested in selection processes and the most familiar. It focuses on the criteria required to undertake the position's functions, to benefit from the training opportunity, and so on. Functional competency asks the questions: 'Does the applicant/employee meet the level of skills, knowledge and experience needed to perform to a satisfactory level?' and 'Does the applicant have suitable qualifications?' Such questions would suggest that selection decisions are made on an objective basis. However, as we have already seen with the requirement for a completed apprenticeship for a chef's position, the determination of what are considered acceptable qualifications may be indirectly discriminatory. Similarly, determinations of what qualifies as an acceptable level of skill, knowledge and experience may also be based on criteria that are appropriate to one group and that are not an appropriate measure for another group.

Functional competency Concerned with job-specific competencies. For example, can the person satisfy the skills, knowledge and experience requirements of the job to perform at a satisfactory level?

Having determined functional competency, however flawed that decision may be, selectors usually make their final determination on the basis of their perception of each applicant's presumed organisational competency. Selectors' decisions about organisational competency are often based on homosocial reproduction. **Organisational competency** (or 'fit') is concerned with what and how a person can contribute to the achievement of organisational objectives in *addition* to their functional (or job-specific) competencies. It is often a judgement about how well the applicant will fit into the organisational culture, and selectors often presume that applicants similar to the existing employees in that type of job are more suitable. Decisions about organisational competency based on homosocial reproduction result in such structural discriminations as occupational segregation (for example, women, but rarely men, employed as secretaries and primary school teachers; men, but rarely

Organisational competency Often a judgement concerning the similarity of an applicant or employee to the existing work force, with that similarity viewed as being an advantage or desirable. Should involve a consideration of the balance of 'fit' (similarity) and 'flexibility' (difference) required by the organisation, as well as a determination on which criteria fit or flexibility should be sought.

women, employed as senior managers and engineers). AA and diversity management approaches bring into the open the organisational competency component of selection decisions and compel organisations to consider whether and when homogeneity and diversity are desirable.[68]

A brief critique of diversity management

Diversity management offers both employers and employees a valuable and respectful approach to developing and maintaining the employment relationship, but it also has the potential to perpetuate and intensify discriminatory practices and outcomes. As with much of management, including HRM, values play a significant part in determining whether diversity management offers meaningful benefits to the parties to the employment relationship or simply becomes a mechanism for exploitation. The relative power of the parties to the relationship also affects the benefit/exploitation outcomes of diversity management strategies. In addition, the forces of globalisation affect an organisation's ability and commitment to managing work force diversity in a manner that respects and values difference.[69]

A convicted paedophile is employed as a school bus driver.

The parties to the employment relationship include not only the most obvious ones of employer/managers and employees, but also the community (both the immediate community in which the organisation operates and the larger community, which is often represented by government). Shareholders in the organisation, unions (both those representing workers in the relevant workplace and industry and those representing workers in other industries), special interest groups, and families of employees and managers are also participants in shaping and reinforcing the employment relationship. The values of these various parties, as well as their power to affect the relationship and their willingness to do so, will determine whether diversity management, like any other approach to the employment relationship, will be mutually beneficial or exploitative.

The need to manage diversity arises out of the changing demographics of the work force as well as changing social values and the globalisation of economies and markets. It is not surprising, therefore, that diversity management is a concept of particular interest to immigrant societies, such as Australia, the United States, Canada and Britain, which have multicultural work forces. It is also of interest in those societies where women are increasingly becoming long-term participants in the work force as a result of increasing investment (both societal and individual) in their education and training as well as other factors (for example, rising divorce rates and financial necessity) that encourage or necessitate women's continued work force participation. Furthermore, multinational companies are discovering the benefits of recognising cultural diversity in managing work forces in host countries as well as in developing and marketing products in those countries.

The attractiveness of the diversity management approach is that it appears to offer mutual benefits. Employers can facilitate, through the development and implementation of diversity management strategies, increases in productivity and profitability by removing barriers to employee effectiveness. Employees, particularly those who have been disadvantaged in the past, can gain more equitable access to the benefits of employment as well as work in more hospitable employment environments.

One of the dangers of diversity management is that it may encourage and legitimise stereotyping. One area where this can be seen is the development of 'family-friendly' policies. These policies include flexitime, part-time work, parental leave to care for sick children, and childcare facilities or arrangements. These policies are labelled 'family-friendly' but they are often perceived as 'for women only'. As a result, they perpetuate the stereotype of women as mothers and wives first and employees second, with consequent judgements made about women's commitment to work (thereby affecting their opportunities for promotion, overtime, particular job assignments, and training and development programs). While many women benefit from these policies, the policies work to perpetuate discriminatory employment outcomes and reinforce stereotypes about women.

Without a change in organisational culture, men are unlikely to access these policies because such access is perceived to be a measure of work commitment (or rather, lack of commitment), with consequent adverse effects on a person's career. Also, there is evidence that the introduction of a number of flexible-time arrangements have benefited employers, yet have not only failed to accommodate female employees' actual time flexibility requirements but have also reduced their income as a result of lost penalty rates and overtime allowances.[70]

Another danger with diversity management is that it may increase the costs of employment in a country such that organisations transfer their operations to offshore locations where they can gain greater profit through lower employment costs. The global economy, without a comparable global regulatory agency with regard to employment, can result in not only loss of jobs in one country but also maintenance of exploitative employment practices in another.

Thirty interactive Wiley Web Questions are available to test your understanding of this chapter at
www.johnwiley.com.au/ highered/hrm5e
in the student resources area

Summary

There are few, if any, organisations today that can rely on their environments staying the same. A work force that reflects the diversity of the community — the market — it serves is likely to be better placed to achieve its organisational objectives if it uses the strengths and flexibilities offered by that diversity. Managing the diversity of the work force can enable organisations to benefit from the range of experiences, perceptions, ways of doing things and knowledge of various cultures that employees from different backgrounds bring to the organisation and to their work. Managing the work environment in a way that is harassment-free and non-discriminatory creates a respectful workplace in which all employees are valued and encouraged to contribute for the benefit of the organisation as well as themselves. Recognising that merit involves not only functional competency but also organisational competency, and that organisational competency benefits from diversity as well as similarities, will enable managers to select, reward, develop and retain staff in ways that enhance the organisation's flexibility and creative opportunities yet provide stability.

student study guide

terms to know

affirmative action (AA) (p. 705)
anti-discrimination (p. 705)
competitive advantage (p. 702)
direct discrimination (p. 723)
discrimination (p. 721)
diversity (p. 702)
diversity management (p. 717)
diversity strategies (p. 703)

dominant or traditional employees/group (p. 717)
equal employment opportunity (EEO) (p. 704)
functional competency (p. 730)
harassment (p. 728)
homosocial reproduction (p. 724)
indirect discrimination (p. 724)

merit (p. 730)
non-traditional employees (p. 702)
organisational competency (p. 730)
racial vilification (p. 728)
reverse discrimination (p. 712)
sexual harassment (p. 729)
structural or systemic discrimination (p. 725)
unfairness (p. 721)

review questions

1. Describe the three different types of discrimination. Give an example of how each type of discrimination could occur in the selection process and suggest an HR practice that could minimise this type of discrimination occurring during selection.

2. Draw up a table identifying the key aspects of each of three approaches to managing diversity. How do these approaches differ?

3. Some people argue that managing diversity just adds costly programs and practices to managing staff without providing any organisational benefits. Do you agree or disagree? Why?

4. You must choose between two well-qualified applicants, one male and one female. The successful applicant will be assigned to head a work group that is 80 per cent female. Which applicant would you choose? Explain your answer. If the successful applicant is to be assigned to a work group that is 80 per cent male, would you make a different decision? Why or why not?

5. Consider tables 19.1 and 19.2 on page 726. What do they suggest about work force discrimination in Australia? How might an organisation's HR department address the situations indicated in the tables?

6. You are an HR adviser and an employee has complained to you that her manager has repeatedly asked her out on a date, and she has repeatedly refused. She says she regards this behaviour as sexual harassment and she wants it stopped. Is this an example of harassment? Explain your answer. How could the HR department deal with this situation? If the person repeatedly asking for dates were a fellow employee, rather than a manager, would you view this situation as harassment? Why or why not? If a female employee were repeatedly asking a male employee for a date, would you regard it as harassment? Why or why not?

7. Discuss how misunderstandings about functional and organisational competencies can result in discriminatory employment decisions.

8. An employee has been accused of sexual harassment of a colleague. The company has a sexual harassment policy, implemented four years ago. Since the introduction of the policy, no staff training has occurred, but the policy is posted on staff noticeboards. Is the employer vicariously liable for the harassing and discriminatory behaviour of its employee? Why or why not?

9. 'Equal employment opportunity and affirmative action are just legal ways of discriminating.' Do you agree or disagree with this statement? Explain your reasoning.

10. It has been argued that AA stigmatises the group that it was designed to benefit. Do you agree? What steps could HR managers take to minimise the perception that employees from AA-targeted groups are lacking in merit?

environmental influences on diversity management

Describe the key environmental influences from the model (figure 19.5 shown below) that have significance for diversity management.

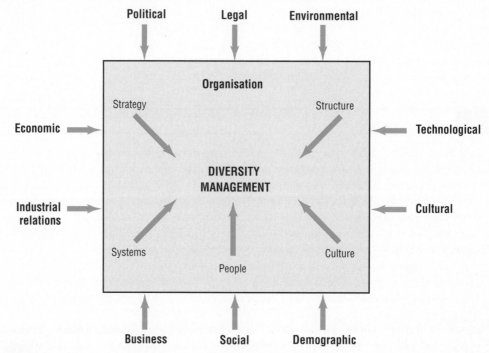

Figure 19.5 Environmental influences on diversity management

class debate

The prime beneficiaries of equal employment opportunity legislation are white, middle-class women.
or
To reduce potential sexual harassment claims, organisations should have a policy that prohibits employees from dating each other.

what's your view?

Write a 500-word response to the Letter to the Editor on page 708, agreeing or disagreeing with the writer's point of view.

practitioner speaks

Read the article on pages 720–1. Design a survey questionnaire to audit the status of a company's EEO program. Regroup as a class and discuss your proposals.

newsbreak exercise

Read the Newsbreak 'Equity is still a long way off' on page 727. Critically review the article and discuss your individual views in class.

soapbox

What do you think? Conduct a mini survey of class members, using the questionnaire below. Critically discuss the findings.

1. Employers should not be expected to employ workers with disabilities if they have to pay for special equipment or make other accommodations.	YES	NO
2. Men and women have inherently different skills and capabilities.	YES	NO
3. Women who are sexually harassed usually do something to provoke the behaviour.	YES	NO
4. Employees who complain of racial discrimination when ethnic jokes are told in the workplace lack a sense of humour.	YES	NO
5. Employers should not be held responsible for the harassing and discriminatory behaviour of their employees.	YES	NO
6. EEO often results in less qualified, non-traditional applicants being selected over better qualified, traditional applicants.	YES	NO

online exercise

Conduct an online search for information on one of the following topics: work–life balance, family-friendly policies, paid maternity leave, workplace accommodation of disabled employees or employment of non-traditional employees (for example, men in female-dominated occupations, women in male-dominated occupations). Compare the situation in Australia with a country of your choice. Summarise your findings in a report of 500–750 words. Include the web addresses that you found useful.

ethical dilemma

Capable women

Capability Products is a major national company. It employs 2492 employees and its work force demographics are as follows:

- 35 per cent of employees are women. Most female employees are from a non-English-speaking background (NESB) and are employed in production, clerical and secretarial positions.
- 2 per cent of managers are women, all of whom are from an Anglo-Australian background as are all the male managers at senior level and 86 per cent of the male managers at middle level.

- 34 per cent of the supervisors and entry-level managers are men from a NESB.
- 65 per cent of employees are first or second generation Australians from a NESB.
- 21 per cent of professional and senior technical staff are women, the majority from an Anglo-Australian background.

The HR Manager has just announced that the organisation is going to develop an affirmative action program, 'Capable Women', to encourage and support female staff in advancing into management positions. Among the programs that will be

established are a mentoring program for women seeking a management career; an on-the-job training program to ensure female professional and technical staff are included in management project teams; and an education support program for female staff enrolled in MBA programs, which will include a childcare subsidy, five days study leave each semester and an allowance to defray costs associated with study (books, and so on).

There has been much grumbling among the male employees about the new program. They complain that it is favouritism and reverse discrimination. Particularly angry about the 'Capable Women' program are male employees from a NESB who believe that they have few opportunities themselves to advance into management and are being further disadvantaged by the

assistance provided to female employees, particularly Anglo-Australian women.

Discussion questions

1. Is affirmative action reverse discrimination? Explain your answer.
2. Why might men see this affirmative action program as discriminatory? Is it actually discriminatory? Why or why not?
3. How might the HR Manager respond to the concerns and complaints of the male employees, particularly the male employees from a NESB?
4. What ethical issues are raised in this case?

case studies

Mount Massey Hospital

Grace Hardy is a nurse who works in the orthopaedic ward of the Mount Massey Hospital. She has complained that she is being sexually harassed by doctors and also by patients and their relatives. She provides the following examples of incidents she believes are sexual harassment. One doctor repeatedly brushes against her at patients' bedsides and is always touching her shoulder. Another doctor refers to her in

front of patients and other staff as 'Sexy Gracie'. A long-term male patient often tells her sex-based jokes, even though she has indicated to him that she is uncomfortable with such humour and has asked him to stop; other staff have told her that she is being too sensitive and should just put up with it. Male friends of a long-term female patient have on several occasions made sexually suggestive remarks to her and said they would be waiting for her when her shift finishes.

Discussion questions

1. Are any of the situations experienced by Grace sexual harassment? What criteria have you used to determine which are sexual harassment?
2. Does an employer have any responsibility for the behaviour of customers (patients, in this case) and their friends? Why or why not?
3. Does the hospital have any responsibility to address the situations experienced by Grace? Why or why not?
4. What steps could the hospital take to address the problems raised by Grace?

Too old for new training?

Tony Garcia has worked for his employer, Jet Red, for almost 25 years, starting as a clerical officer and being promoted through the ranks to supervise a work team of 12. He has always received above-average annual performance ratings. Soon after celebrating his 60th birthday, Tony overhears his supervisor, Tom Stackpole, criticising his work in front of other staff members. Tom also gripes that older employees are just too set in their ways to adapt to the changes sweeping the company. Tony later complains that he is not scheduled for

training in the new software being introduced to facilitate the efficient processing of sales orders. After he has expressed his dissatisfaction, he and several other long-serving employees are assigned to the last training session (even though places are available in the earlier training sessions). When Tony again complains, Tom says that older workers like Tony are harder to train and suggests that with all the turmoil at Jet Red it is perhaps time to consider retirement and to give the younger employees a chance. Tony threatens to take the matter to the Equal Opportunity Tribunal.

1. Do you think this is an example of discrimination? Explain your answer.
2. What is the basis for Tom's behaviour towards Tony?
3. How could the HR Department manage this situation?

Not wanted at Jet Red: fatties, uglies or wrinklies

'Look, let's get one thing straight!' The sharp-toned voice of Stan Vines, Marketing Manager at Jet Red, cut off Linda Church, HR Manager, in mid-sentence. 'We're in the business of promoting an image of a young, vital, "with it" airline. We sell our passengers a portrait of style and status. Customers come to us because they want to fly with an airline that has flair. If our flight crew are not young, slim and attractive, what does that say to our customers? Linda, we are marketing to a group with big dollars to spend. A young market where image is everything. Our flight crew have to be attractive. I don't care how well qualified an applicant is. I don't want fatties, wrinklies or uglies attending to our passengers. They don't fit with our new public image.'

Linda shrugged. 'Okay, Stan, have it your way, but we are setting ourselves up to be charged with using unfair or discriminatory hiring practices.'

'Linda, I don't know if you realise it, but this is a business and we give the customers what they want. If we don't discriminate in hiring, our customers will go elsewhere. We can use an employment agency to filter out anyone who doesn't meet our age and physical requirements, so I don't see what the problem is. Our target market wants to be surrounded by beautiful people. It's part of the attraction of flying the new Jet Red. Who would you sooner be served by Linda? Some ageing, overweight doughnut-head or a young, athletic hunk?'

'Don't be ridiculous Stan!' Linda snapped.

'It's not me who's being ridiculous. You live in some HR dream world, Linda. It's about time you put your energies into helping this company implement its strategies and making a profit. Face reality. If there is no profit, there will be no jobs for anyone — attractive or not.'

Discussion questions

1. Do you agree or disagree with Stan's comments? Explain your reasoning.
2. If you were Linda, how would you explain to candidates classified as 'fatties, uglies or wrinklies' why their application was unsuccessful?
3. What is the difference between discrimination and unfairness?
4. Is this a case of (a) discrimination, (b) unfairness or (c) neither (a) nor (b)? Explain your answer.
5. What are the possible adverse outcomes of Jet Red's failure to employ older and less physically attractive staff?
6. Is the use of an employment agency to filter out undesired applicants a discriminatory practice? Explain your reasoning.

practical exercises

If you were the HR Manager, what would you do in the following situations?

(a) The senior management team asks you to justify the benefits to the organisation of managing diversity.
(b) An external applicant for a senior professional position has recently won a highly publicised racial discrimination lawsuit.

(c) An independent consultant hired to review customer satisfaction levels advises that customers from particular ethnic/national groups have reported that they believe they have been ignored by sales staff, offered less attractive packages and been subjected to unnecessary credit checks.

(d) A requirement for promotion to assistant manager is that all in-house applicants have completed the organisation's management training workshop. The workshop is offered only after work hours in the evenings. No female staff have ever enrolled in this workshop.

(e) A review of supervisory positions reveals that both women and men are supervisors of women-only work groups, no women supervise any men-only work groups and most mixed work groups are supervised by men.

(f) A group of male staff have complained that allowing applicants to demonstrate suitable knowledge and experience in ways other than completion of an apprenticeship will result in the hiring of incompetent personnel.

(g) A manager states that he recently had two applications from people with Down's syndrome (who have mild intellectual impairment and minor speech problems), but he refused to hire them, although they were quite capable of doing the work involved both at the counter and in the food preparation area. The manager argues that customers will object to being waited on by someone 'who looks and sounds funny', and he has a right not to hire someone who will adversely affect his business.

(h) Staff are sending sexist and racist jokes to each other via the company's intranet.

(i) A staff member keeps religious material on her desk in plain view and always ends conversations with staff and clients saying 'God bless you'.

suggested readings

Anti-Discrimination Board of New South Wales, *Anti-Discrimination and Equal Employment Opportunity (EEO) Guidelines*, Sydney, 1997.

Bacchi, C. L., *The Politics of Affirmative Action: Women, Equality and Category Politics*, Sage Publications, London, 1996.

CCH, *Australian Master Human Resources Guide*, CCH, Sydney, 2003, chs 19, 20, 44.

De Cieri, H. and Kramar, R., *Human Resource Management in Australia*, McGraw-Hill, Sydney, 2003, chs. 3, 8.

Fisher, C. D., Schoenfeldt, L. F. and Shaw, J. B., *Human Resource Management*, 5th edn, Houghton Mifflin, Boston, 2003, ch. 5.

Hunter, R., *Indirect Discrimination in the Workplace*, The Federation Press, Sydney, 1992.

Ivancevich, J. M. and Lee, S. H., *Human Resource Management in Asia*, McGraw-Hill, Singapore, 2002, ch. 13.

Mondy, R. W., Noe, R. M. and Premeaux, S. R., *Human Resource Management*, 8th edn, Prentice Hall, Upper Saddle River, NJ, 2002, ch. 3.

Nankervis, A. R., Compton, R. L. and Baird, M., *Strategic Human Resource Management*, 4th edn, Nelson, Melbourne, 2002, ch. 5.

Osborne, M., *Sexual Harassment: A Code of Practice*, Human Rights and Equal Opportunity Commission, Sydney, 1996.

Smith, C. R. and Hutchinson, J., *Gender: A Strategic Management Issue*, Business and Professional Publishing, Sydney, 1995.

online references

www.abs.gov.au

www.austlii.edu.au

www.business-humanrights.org

www.dewrsb.gov.au

www.eeo.gov.au

www.eeoc.gov

www.eeotrust.org.nz

www.eoc.og.hk

www.eoc.sa.gov.au

www.equalopportunity.on.ca

www.hereoc.gov.au

www.icdi.wvu.edu

www.ilo.org/public/english/employment/gems/eeo
www.info.gov.hk/justice
www.jil.go.jp/bulletin
www.justice.tas.gov.au/adc/adcfrontpage.htm
www.lawlink.nsw.gov.au/adb

www.lawlink.nsw.gov.au/caselaw/caselaw.nsf/pages/adt
www.mwa.govt.nz
www.shrm.org
www.un.org/womenwatch
www.workforce.com

end notes

1. This chapter was written by Dr Maureen Fastenau, Senior Lecturer in Management at RMIT University, Australia. Maureen practised for a number of years as a manager of EEO and AA programs, and continues to consult to private and public sector organisations in EEO, AA, diversity management, and sexual and racial harassment, as well as to research in these areas. Maureen was until recently the EEO columnist for *HR Monthly*, the professional journal of the AHRI, and is the founding editor of the *International Employment Relations Review*.

2. American Management Association, 'Senior management teams: profiles and performance: summary of key findings', p. 7 (www.amanet.org/research/pdfs/senior.pdf, accessed 7 November 2003).

3. Countries in the Asia–Pacific and Pacific Rim regions with anti-discrimination legislation include: New Zealand (see *Equal Pay Act 1972*, *Parental Leave and Employment Protection Act 1987*, *Human Rights Act 1993*, *Human Rights Amendment Act 1994*, Pt III (Personal Grievances) of the *Employment Contracts Act 1991*, *New Zealand Bill of Rights Act 1990* and the *Employment Relations Act 2000*, particularly Part 9 (Personal Grievances, Disputes, and Enforcements)), Hong Kong (see *Sex Discrimination Ordinance* and *Disability Discrimination Ordinance*, both enacted in 1996, and the *Family Status Discrimination Ordinance 1997*), Japan (see *The Basic Law for a Gender-Equal Society (Law No. 78 of 1999)* replacing 1985 legislation) and Taiwan (see Women's Employment Promotion Measure, although this is an administrative directive rather than legislation). Indonesia has not enacted any anti-discrimination laws, but its constitution contains provisions that are a foundation for EEO (see article 27(1): 'All citizens have equal status before the law and in the government and shall abide by the law and the government without exception'; article 27(2): 'Every citizen has the right to work and to live in human dignity'; and article 31(1): 'Every citizen has the right to education'). Singapore also has no specific anti-discrimination laws, but the government has implemented a number of policies to facilitate women's employment opportunities. See note 19 for anti-discrimination legislation for the Australian states.

4. See 'A finance sector organisation' and 'A media sector organisation', case studies in Affirmative Action Agency, *Annual Report 1994–1995*, AGPS, Canberra, 1995, pp. 6, 10.

5. T. Kochan, K. Bezrukova, R. Ely, S. Jackson, A. Joshi, K. Jehn, J. Leonard, D. Levine and D. Thomas, 'The effects of diversity on business performance', Report of the Diversity Network, October 2002 (www.shrm.org/foundation/kochan_keyfindings.asp, accessed 23 July 2003). This study has been published in *Human Resource Management*, vol. 42, no. 1, 2003, pp. 3–21. See also F. Hansen, 'Diversity's business case doesn't add up', *Workforce*, April 2003, pp. 28–32 and related articles (available also from the *Workforce* web site at www.workforce.com).

6. A. Rajan and S. Harris, 'The measure of success', *Personnel Today*, 16 September 2003, p. 22; R. Orland, A. McMillan, K. Chadwick and S. Dwyer, 'Employing an innovation strategy in racially diverse workforces', *Group & Organization Management*, vol. 28, no. 1, 2003, pp. 107–27; R. Orland, 'Racial diversity, business strategy, and firm performance: a resource-based view', *Academy of Management Journal*, vol. 43, no. 2, 2000, pp. 164–77; and E. S. W. Ng and R. L. Tung, 'Ethno-cultural diversity and organizational effectiveness: a field study', *International Journal of Human Resource Management*, vol. 9, no. 6, 1998, pp. 980–95.

7. P. Wright, S. P. Ferris, J. S. Hiller and M. Kroll, 'Competitiveness through management of diversity: effects on stock price valuation', *Academy of Management Journal*, vol. 38, no. 1, 1995, pp. 272–87. See also, C. B. Shrader, V. B. Blackburn and P. Iles, 'Women in management and firm financial performance: an exploratory study', *Journal of Managerial Issues*, vol. 9, no. 3, 1997, pp. 355–72; R. Erhardt, J. Werbel and C. Shrader, 'Executive board diversity: its effects on organizational performance', paper presented at the 2002 Academy of Management Conference; R. Litz and C. Foler, 'When he and she sell seashells: exploring the relationship between gender balance and firm performance', paper presented at the 2002 Academy of Management Conference, Denver, Colorado, 9–14 August 2002.

8. Theresa M. Welbourne, 'Wall Street likes its women: an examination of women in the top management teams of initial public offerings', Working Paper 99-07, Center for Advanced Human Resource Studies, School of Industrial and Labor Relations, Cornell University, New York, 1999.

9. 'Women = profits', *EOWA Action News*, March 2002 (www.eeo.gov.au, accessed 7 November 2003).

10. G. Flynn, 'Deloitte & Touche change women's minds', *Personnel Journal*, vol. 75, no. 4, April 1996, pp. 56+; and L. Trimberger, 'Deloitte & Touche: retaining women means success', *HR Focus*, November 1998, pp. 7+. For current information, see the company's web site at

www.dc.com. See also L. P. Wooten, 'What makes women-friendly public accounting firms tick? The diffusion of human resource management knowledge through institutional and resource pressures', *Sex Roles*, vol. 45, no. 5–6, 2001, pp. 277–97.

11. Anti-Discrimination Board of New South Wales, *Affirmative Action and Equal Employment Opportunity (EEO) Guidelines*, Sydney, 1997, pp. 19–20.

12. P. Roberts, 'NRMA finds lowering staff turnover pays off', *Australian Financial Review*, 1 May 1996, p. 29.

13. The most recent Australian discussion about paid maternity leave was launched in 2002 with the publication of a discussion paper *Valuing Parenthood* (Sex Discrimination Unit, Human Rights and Equal Opportunity Commission, *Valuing Parenthood: Options for Paid Maternity Leave: Interim Paper 2002*, Human Rights and Equal Opportunity Commission, Sydney, 2002). However, no provisions for paid maternity leave were included in the federal budget for 2003, and the Prime Minister, John Howard, signalled that the issue was not currently under consideration. See Phillip Hudson, 'Family benefits revamp dumped', *Age*, 4 August 2003, p. 1; and John Howard, 'How we support families', *Age*, 4 August 2003, p. 13.

14. Equal Opportunity for Women in the Workplace Agency, 'Benefits of providing paid maternity leave' (www.eeo.gov.au, accessed 30 July 2003).

15. The CCH publication *Australian and New Zealand Equal Opportunity Law and Practice* includes a section that discusses the particular components of and differences between the various Australian anti-discrimination laws. This provides a handy overview for the HR manager but is not a substitute for legal advice. As with any HR policies and practices that can give rise to legal liabilities, the HR manager will need to determine whether specific legal advice is required.

16. M. Hosoda, E. F. Stone-Romero and G. Coats, 'The effectiveness of physical attractiveness on job-related outcomes: a meta-analysis of experimental studies', *Personnel Psychology*, vol. 56, no. 1, 2003, pp. 431+; and J. Fowler-Hermes, 'The beauty and the best in the workplace: appearance-based discrimination claims under EEO laws', *Florida Bar Journal*, vol. 75, no. 4, 2001, pp. 32–8. See also T. Dusevic, M. Gunn and M. Coorey, 'Good lookers do well while plain pay the penalty', *Weekend Australian*, 20–21 May 1995, pp. 1, 2; D. Hamermesh and J. Biddle, 'Beauty and the labour market', *American Economic Review*, vol. 84, no. 5, 1994, pp. 1174–94; and C. M. Marlowe, S. L. Schneider and C. E. Nelson, 'Gender and attractiveness biases in hiring decisions: are more experienced managers less biased?', *Journal of Applied Psychology*, vol. 81, no. 1, 1996, pp. 11–21.

17. It should be noted that the Workplace Relations Act encourages the decentralisation of industrial negotiation, which results in declining union membership. Research suggests that female workers are more advantaged in industrial systems characterised by high union density. See G. Whitehouse, 'Legislation and labour market gender

inequality: an analysis of OECD countries', *Work, Employment and Society*, vol. 6, no. 1, 1996, pp. 65–86; and K. Heiler, B. Arovaska and R. Hall, 'Good and bad bargaining for women: do unions make a difference?', *Labour and Industry*, vol. 10, no. 2, 1999, pp. 101–27. See also P. V. Wunnava and N. O. Peled, 'Union wage premiums by gender and race: evidence from PSID 1980–1991', *Journal of Labor Research*, vol. 20, no. 3, 1999, pp. 415+; and J. Burgess, W. Mitchell and A. Preston, 'The Australian labour market 2002', *Journal of Industrial Relations*, vol. 45, no. 2, 2003, pp. 125–50.

18. The Age Discrimination Bill can be accessed at the web site scaleplus.law.gov.au/html/bills/0/2003/rtf/03108b.rtf, and further information about the Bill is available at the Attorney General's web site at www.ag.gov.au.

19. The Australian state and territory anti-discrimination legislation includes: South Australia's *Equal Opportunity Act 1984*, which replaces earlier sex, racial and handicapped persons anti-discrimination legislation, and the *Racial Vilification Act 1996*; New South Wales' *Anti-Discrimination Act 1977* and *Disability Services Act 1993*; Queensland's *Anti-Discrimination Act 1991*; Western Australia's *Equal Opportunity Act 1984*; Tasmania's *Anti-Discrimination Act 1998*; Victoria's *Equal Opportunity Act 1995*, which replaces earlier legislation, and Section 17 of the *Racial and Religious Tolerance Act 2001*; the Australian Capital Territory's *Discrimination Act 1991*; and the Northern Territory's *Anti-Discrimination Act 1996*.

20. International Labour Organisation (ILO Office Jakarta), '5 medium-term employment promotion', p. 7 (www.un.or.id/ilo/english/chap5.htm, accessed 25 September 2000).

21. For information on tax relief schemes, see the Singapore government's web site at www.gov.sg.

22. United Nations General Assembly, *Report of the Committee on the Elimination of Discrimination Against Women (2001)*, Official Records, 56th Session, Supplement No. 38 (A/56/38), paragraphs 54–96 (www.hri.ca/fortherecord2001/documentation/genassembly/a-56-38.htm, accessed 29 October 2003).

23. For example, *Askey-Doran v. Fremantle Women's Health Centre* (2001) EOC93–116 and *Brennan v. NSW Brigades* (1996) EOC 92–825.

24. See, for example, B. Birnbauer and C. Miller, 'Race in the marketplace', *Age*, 5 July 1997, p. A27; and *Oyekanmi v. National Forge Operations Pty Ltd* (1996) EOC 92–797.

25. Jody Scott, 'Token damages for manager abused by blacks', *Australian*, 2 May 1995, p. 7; *Wilson v. Budsoar Pty Ltd* (1996) EOC 92–871; and B. Lane, 'ATSIC makes deal with white accuser', *Australian*, 16 May 1995, p. 6.

26. Anti-Discrimination Board of New South Wales, *Anti-Discrimination and Equal Employment Opportunity (EEO) Guidelines*, Sydney, 1997, p. 19.

27. Anti-Discrimination Board of New South Wales, op. cit., p. 19.

28. Equal Opportunity for Women in the Workplace Agency, 'List of non-compliant organizations (1-6-01 to 31-5-02)' (www.eeo.gov.au, accessed 29 July 2003).

29. Equal Opportunity for Women in the Workplace Agency, *Annual Report 2001–2002*, Canberra, 2002, p. 19.

30. A. J. Sheridan, 'Affirmative action in Australia — employment statistics can't tell the whole story', *Women in Management Review*, vol. 10, no. 2, 1995, pp. 26–34; Affirmative Action Agency, *Annual Report 1998/99*, AGPS, Canberra, 1999, p. 20; and Equal Opportunity for Women in the Workplace Agency, *Annual Report 2001–2002*, p. 29 and Appendix B.

31. See the following reviews in *International Employment Relations Review*, vol. 3, no. 1, 1997: M. Fastenau, 'Australian women's employment, 1986–1996: a period of glacial change', pp. 61–89; P. Debroux, 'Women at work in a changing environment: the Japanese experience', pp. 37–59; R. I. Westwood and S. M. Leung, 'Between patriarchy and opportunity: women and employment in Hong Kong 1960s–1990s', pp. 109–27; and E. Hall, 'The status of women's employment in New Zealand: issues and directions', pp. 91–107.

32. For a discussion of how members of a previously advantaged group (men) perceive AA strategies in selection, see M. E. Heilman, W. F. McCullough and D. Gilbert, 'The other side of affirmative action: reactions of nonbeneficiaries to a sex-based preferential selection', *Journal of Applied Psychology*, vol. 81, no. 4, 1996, pp. 346–57.

33. Affirmative Action Agency, *Annual Report 1994–1995*, AGPS, Canberra, 1995, pp. 19–20.

34. Equal Opportunity for Women in the Workplace Agency, 'Women in management', *Action News*, Issue 40, December 1999, pp. 14–15 (www.eeo.gov.au/resources_pub/newsletter/issue40.html, accessed 26 September 2000).

35. Equal Opportunity for Women in the Workplace Agency, 'Business blind to women's talent', media release, 28 February 2003 (www.eeo.gov.au, accessed on 29 July 2003).

36. While women have increased their participation in lower level (for example, supervisory) and middle management roles, they continue to experience the 'glass ceiling' at the highest levels of management. The 2003 Women and Leadership Census revealed that women hold only 8.8 per cent of executive management positions and 8.4 per cent of board positions. These data should be considered in the light of the fact that women make up 47 per cent of the Australian work force and hold 43 per cent of managerial and professional positions. However, women hold only 4.2 per cent of the line management positions from which senior managers and board directors are drawn. Equal Opportunity for Women in the Workplace Agency, 'Lack of profit centre experience thwarts women's careers: 2003 Census', media release, 1 October 2003 (www.eeo.gov.au, accessed 29 October 2003).

37. K. Stephenson and V. Krebs, 'A more accurate way to measure diversity', *Personnel Journal*, vol. 72, no. 10, 1993, pp. 66–72, 74.

38. See M. E. Heilman, W. F. McCullough and D. Gilbert, op. cit., pp. 346–57.

39. B. Gilley, 'Affirmative action', *Far Eastern Economic Review*, 10 August 2000, p. 26.

40. I. Stewart, 'PM attacks Chinese, Malay extremists', *South China Morning Post*, 1 September 2000, p. 12.

41. D. Cohen, 'Malaysians drop racial quota rules', *Australian*, 2 April 2003, p. 37.

42. F. Krautil (Director, Affirmative Action Agency), 'Competition and best practice in diversity management', speech given at Griffith University, Queensland, 4 November 1999, p. 14 (www.eeo.gov.au).

43. See, for example, P. A. Bellamy and K. Ramsay, *Barriers to Women Working in Corporate Management*, Report to the Women's Employment, Education and Training Advisory Group, AGPS, Canberra, 1994. See also J. Marshall, *Women Managers Moving On: Exploring Career and Life Choices*, Routledge, London, 1995.

44. See C. Kermond, 'Career hurdle for mothers', *Age*, 30 June 1997, p. A7. This article reports research presented by Professor Saroj Parasuraman, Drexel University, Philadelphia, at the International Industrial and Organisational Psychology Conference held in Melbourne. Professor Parasuraman reported that organisations 'withhold career opportunities from employees believed to be highly committed to their families'. Those employees who access family-friendly policies and practices are likely to be perceived as being more committed to their families than to their careers and to the organisation. Professor Parasuraman concluded that 'While the organisation eulogises the family and extols it as a desirable virtue, it doesn't really want to know about it'. See also D. K. Jacobs, 'Back from the mommy track', *New York Times*, 9 October 1994, pp. F1, F6.

45. *Thomson v. Orica Australia Pty Ltd* [2002] FCA 939 (30 July 2002).

46. See Orica's web site at www.orica.com.au.

47. D. M. McCracken, 'Winning the talent war for women: sometimes it takes a revolution', *Harvard Business Review*, November–December 2000, pp. 159–67; L. Trimberger, op. cit., pp. 7+; G. Flynn, op. cit., pp. 56+. See also the 'Women's initiative' section of the firm's web site at www.deloitte.com.

48. Anti-Discrimination Board of New South Wales, op. cit., p. 20.

49. M. E. Heilman, W. F. McCullough and D. Gilbert, op. cit., pp. 346–7.

50. S. Das, 'Woman sues over share allocation', *Age*, 26 March 1996, p. A4.

51. Anti-Discrimination Board of New South Wales, op. cit., p. 6.

52. See, for example, *C & Ors v. Australian Telecommunications Corporation* (1992) EOC 92–437. In this case, several female RMIT engineering students faced hostile questioning from a male selection panel when interviewing for work placements. The types of questions and the style of questioning differed dramatically from the interview situation experienced by their male counterparts. Although the organisation had an equal opportunity policy as well as a policy that selection panel members had to have been trained in selection procedures, including equal opportunity matters, the selectors neither complied with the policy nor met the requirement for selection training.

53. The term 'homosocial reproduction' was coined by J. Lipman-Blumen, 'Toward a homosocial theory of sex roles: an explanation of sex segregation of social institutions', in M. Blaxall and B. Reagan (eds), *Women and the Workplace*, University of Chicago Press, Chicago, 1976.

54. An excellent study of the concept of indirect discrimination is presented by R. Hunter, *Indirect Discrimination in the Workplace*, The Federation Press, Sydney, 1992.

55. The use of medical, skills, intelligence and psychological tests needs to be carefully monitored to ensure that they do not lead to indirect discrimination. For a discussion of a discriminatory use of a medical test in a selection process, see M. Fastenau, 'Discrimination claimed — and won — over medical test', *HR Monthly*, September 1993, pp. 6–7.

56. The Job Accommodation Network web site (www.jan.wvu.edu/media) offers valuable information about equipment, technologies and work redesign that can enable persons with particular disabilities to successfully undertake a variety of different types of jobs.

57. (1989) EOC 92–271.

58. R. Woolnough, 'Vanishing IT women', *Computer Weekly*, 27 February 2003, p. 33; and 'Glass ceiling for women in high-tech industry revealed', *Women in Business*, vol. 53, no. 4, 2001, p. 15.

59. M. Wolfe, 'But how fast can you type, sir?', *New York Times*, 22 May 1994, p. F11.

60. The Human Rights and Equal Opportunity Commission's booklet *Sexual Harassment: A Code of Practice* (Sydney, 1996) is an excellent guide for employers about their obligations in the area of sexual harassment and steps to take to minimise possibilities for sexual harassment in the workplace. Copies can be obtained from the Commission, GPO Box 5218, Sydney, New South Wales 2001.

61. A more detailed discussion of sexual harassment can be found in M. Fastenau, 'Sexual harassment: the creation and perpetuation of hostile and discriminatory workplaces', in R. Stone (ed.), *Readings in Human Resource Management*, vol. 3, John Wiley & Sons, Brisbane, 1998, pp. 393–401.

62. F. Carruthers, 'Sexual harassment costs soar, employers suffer', *Australian*, 21 March 1997, p. 3.

63. T. Blue, 'Insurer covers bosses for sexual harassment', *Australian*, 19 March 1997, p. 3.

64. P. Roberts, op. cit., p. 29.

65. A. Kohler, 'Gender: CRA's latest battle line', *Age*, 24 November 1995, p. 3.

66. See D. Lander and G. O'Neill, 'Pay equity: apples, oranges and a can of worms', *Asia Pacific Human Resource Management*, vol. 29, no. 1, 1991, pp. 16–28. This article reports how gender bias is built into job evaluation tools, which are supposedly objective measures for determining the relative worth of jobs.

67. For a fuller discussion of the concept of functional and organisational competencies, see M. Fastenau, 'Selection on merit is not an objective measure', *HR Monthly*, November 1994, pp. 20–1.

68. Gary N. Powell, 'Reinforcing and extending today's organizations: the simultaneous pursuit of person–organization fit and diversity', *Organizational Dynamics*, vol. 26, no. 3, 1998, pp. 50–61.

69. For a critique of the diversity management approach, see M. Humphries and S. Grice, 'Equal employment opportunity and the management of diversity: a global discourse of assimilation?', *Journal of Organizational Change Management*, vol. 8, no. 5, 1996, pp. 17–32; and D. A. Thomas and R. J. Ely, 'Making differences matter: a new paradigm for managing diversity', *Harvard Business Review*, September–October 1996, pp. 79–90.

70. See, for example, S. Charlesworth, *Stretching Flexibility: Enterprise Bargaining, Women Workers and Changes to Working Hours*, Report of the Flexible Working Hours and Women Project, Human Rights and Equal Opportunity Commission, Sydney, 1996.

MERINO WOOL COMBING COMPANY: SEARCHING FOR INNOVATION AND PRODUCTIVITY IN A GLOBAL ECONOMY

Erica French and Glenda Maconachie, Queensland University of Technology

Merino Wool Combing Company (MWC) was established in Bendigo in the 1930s as a family-operated business. Its main activity was to take greasy wool straight from the sheep's back after shearing and process it in readiness for spinning. From there, MWC grew into a small public company with 100 employees. Between the 1930s and the 1980s MWC was successful in the market, and up to 95 per cent of its product was exported to overseas markets for spinning. The globalisation of markets in the 1970s and 1980s had a significant impact on MWC's profitability. Increased competition from low-waged countries, particularly South America, began to affect MWC's viability to such an extent that it seemed that the company might close. Increased tariffs in the European Union in the 1990s also resulted in restrictions on Australian exports, which affected MWC.

In the mid-1990s, a large Italian wool-spinning company offered to take over MWC's operations and the company accepted the offer. The Italian company was seeking to control its value chain through this acquisition and was keen to introduce a high-technology basis to the Australian subsidiary. As MWC was largely technologically obsolete in the eyes of the parent company, the strategic plan was to construct a new technologically advanced plant on the outskirts of Geelong (150 km away) as a greenfield site and close the Bendigo plant. The new plant would also introduce innovative ways of working to facilitate the technology and international competition.

The old processing plant at Bendigo had a fully unionised work force. Workers were advised that jobs would be available at the new plant in Geelong, but that the number of workers required was only half that working at Bendigo. The company also advised that it would be introducing Australian Workplace Agreements (AWAs) to set terms and conditions of employment individually with workers at the new plant, rather than having a Certified Agreement with union consultation. All workers at the new plant would be hired by a newly formed company and there would be no carry over of seniority, long service leave, and so on. Workers interested in relocating were asked to submit an application and interviews were conducted by members of the parent company in conjunction with MWC's own HR Manager. Most workers (90 per cent) applied for positions in the Geelong plant, while a few decided to retire. However, only 20 employees from the Bendigo plant were selected for transfer — the other positions were filled by new recruits in Geelong.

Workers not chosen for employment in Geelong contacted the textile union complaining about the manner in which the selection process had been conducted. It was argued that selection was biased against more mature workers with considerable work experience in the old processing plant. Workers suggested that the questions about technology and education levels were used to discriminate unfairly against older workers without really considering their potential for training or retraining. In addition, it was alleged that workers who were active in the union and females with family responsibilities were excluded from selection.

While the new plant was being constructed, the Bendigo plant continued to operate. The union undertook extensive discussions with management at the Bendigo plant regarding the discrimination allegations raised above. After a group of workers threatened to take their case to the Anti-Discrimination Tribunal and industrial action was threatened by the majority of workers, management agreed to negotiate redundancy packages for workers not transferring to the new plant.

Once the Geelong plant was ready for operation, AWAs were negotiated with the new recruits before the Bendigo workers ceased work. The Bendigo workers who relocated discovered that while their pay and most conditions of employment were little different from those at the old plant, their wages were now annualised and they were required to work flexible hours. This meant that overtime usually performed in busy periods was not paid when it was conducted but was calculated as a certain number of hours worked over a yearly period, with the additional overtime pay included in the weekly pay. Workers found that they were required to work longer hours in peak production periods and would have reduced work hours in the off-season. In practice, this meant that workers would be required to work a roster of 12-hour days for 10 consecutive days and then have four days off for a period of 12 weeks in the peak season. This was a rotating roster to ensure that the factory was continuously operational. During the off-peak season workers would undertake a nine-day fortnight working five hours each day.

Workers at the Geelong plant were to become multiskilled to assist with productivity and efficiency in the plant and to facilitate the flexible roster system. A modular training package was developed with an external training institution allowing workers to undertake training both on and off the job. Modules were available in the classroom in the off-peak season and workers were encouraged to continue their training and development. The company rewarded training with extra pay levels and opportunities for advancement in the organisation. In the first two years of operation, management was surprised with the enthusiasm of workers for the training modules. While management had initially guaranteed that all training would be rewarded, the costs of upgrading pay levels and the lack of opportunities for advancement resulted in a change of policy. Training remained available to workers, but rewards were limited to specific quotas in pay levels and to available positions.

After three years of operation it was time to renegotiate the AWAs. Management was advised that the workers no longer wanted AWAs and wanted a union-negotiated enterprise agreement. Workers' reasons for wanting a union-negotiated agreement included health and safety issues associated with the flexible roster system as well as its impact on work and family balance. In addition, the workers were unhappy with the training/rewards balance. Since the opening of the Geelong plant management had steadfastly ignored worker suggestions and complaints about working conditions and work processes. Now, during this bargaining period, the workers desired union support throughout the negotiations. Management refused to negotiate with the union and workers began industrial action in support of their claim for a Certified Agreement and changed working conditions.

This action ultimately resulted in the plant being non-operational for five months. This fact, combined with a global downturn in the industry, where wool prices dropped by 34 per cent, led the Italian parent company to close the Geelong plant in November 2003.

Questions

1. Had the workers gone on strike over the selection process for employment at the Geelong plant, what might have been the consequences for workers and the union?
2. How might management have prevented accusations of discrimination on the grounds of age, union activity and family responsibility in the selection process?
3. Discuss the benefits and limitations of flexible working arrangements in industries with pronounced seasonal operations.
4. How might management have changed its training policy and still encouraged and motivated workers to undertake training?

5. How might management have better handled conflict within the organisation?
6. Using theoretical approaches, how would you characterise the different views held by management and workers? Is there any way these views could be reconciled?
7. What health and safety obligations does management have in respect of its flexible roster system? How might it meet these obligations?
8. What benefits were there for MWC in relocating to Geelong?
9. How did training create a more flexible work force?
10. How did multiskilling assist MWC to improve productivity and efficiency to compete in a global market?

human resources in a changing world

Part 6 deals with international human resource management and the challenge of managing international assignments. The case study at the end of the part incorporates these topics using the example of outsourcing IT services to India.

chapter 20

international human resource management

Learning objectives

When you have finished studying this chapter, you should be able to:

- Describe the major differences between domestic and international HRM
- Understand some of the key cross-cultural issues dealing with communication, ethics, trust, management style and EEO
- Describe the major challenges faced in international HRM relating to performance appraisal, training and development, compensation and benefits, and industrial relations
- Explain the major characteristics of HRM in China and Japan.

'Australian companies are undermining their chances of success overseas by not paying enough attention to cultural issues'.[1]

A. Nankervis and R. Grainger

Introduction

International operations are strategically important for Australian companies such as Amcor, BHP Billiton, Brambles, Foster's, Lend Lease, Paperlinx, QBE and Westfield Holdings. These companies are now affected more by global influences than by Australian domestic influences and must develop global business objectives and strategies to succeed. They must consider the influences of differing national cultures, political systems and economic situations on their strategic business objectives, corporate culture and the way in which they operate. In turn, these companies must decide how and to what degree they will be sensitive to national cultures without diluting their core values and strategic objectives.

In short, internationalisation means increased complexity. The external environment now includes not just local but also foreign influences (see figure 20.1). Companies have to be alert to changes in foreign labour markets, government regulations, inflation rates, union pressures, and so on. Strategic business objectives are now the product of an analysis of numerous competing and different environments. Thus, organisational performance depends on a good fit between the organisation's key business objectives and strategies and domestic and foreign environmental demands. However, research suggests that companies are often ill prepared for internationalisation and that strategic HRM issues are regarded as peripheral.[2]

FACTORS CREATING THE GLOBAL MARKETPLACE AND GLOBAL ORGANISATIONS

- Global technology and telecommunications (enhanced by fibre-optics)
- Satellites and computer technology
- Competitiveness of global corporations
- Convergence of global lifestyles and values, accelerated by global languages
- Emergence of global market drivers
- Lowering of costs of doing business globally

- Globalisation of financial markets, resources and services
- Emergence of the knowledge economy and era
- Work force mobility
- Privatisation and globalisation of government services
- Emergence of open and unrestricted (free) trade

Figure 20.1 Factors creating the global marketplace

Source M. J. Marquardt, 'How to go global: creating the global organization', *Monash Mt Eliza Business Review*, vol. 1, no. 3, 1998, p. 30.

It is not surprising, therefore, that while the internationalisation of business has increased opportunities for organisations and their employees, it has also created a myriad of HRM challenges related to a multicultural work force that is geographically dispersed.[3] Lend Lease, for example, has 80 per cent of its employees offshore.[4]

Local employee Someone who lives and works in their home country.

Expatriate Someone who lives and works in a foreign country.

Who should manage a new overseas venture — a **local employee** or an **expatriate**? How will people be selected? How should locals and expatriates be compensated? What should be done about industrial relations? How will employees' performance be measured? What HRM policies and practices will apply? These and similar HR questions can make international people management complex, costly and administratively chaotic. Fisher, Schoenfeldt and Shaw comment: 'Human resource managers in multinational corporations must achieve two somewhat conflicting strategic objectives. First, they must integrate human resource policies across a number of subsidiaries in different countries so that overall corporate objectives can be achieved. At the same time, the approach to HRM must be sufficiently flexible to allow for sufficient differences in the types of HR policies and practices that are most effective in different business and cultural settings.'[5]

Major differences between **domestic HRM** and **international HRM**, for example, include:

- additional activities such as taxation, international relocation, expatriate remuneration, cross-cultural training and repatriation
- increased complexities such as currency fluctuations, foreign HR policies and practices, and differing labour laws
- increased involvement in the employee's personal life — for example, assistance with personal taxation, voter registration, housing, children's education, health, recreation and spouse employment
- a more complex employee mix, such as a mix of people from different cultures and ethnic backgrounds as a more significant part of the work force
- more complex external influences, such as different cultures, political systems, ethics and laws
- increased risks, such as emergency exits for illness, personal security, kidnapping and terrorism (see figure 20.2).

Domestic HRM HRM as practised within the geographical boundaries of one country. Its focus is the management of people in a single-country context.

International HRM HRM as practised by multinational organisations. Its focus is the management of people in a multi-country context.

HRM ACTIVITY	EXAMPLES OF ADDED ACTIVITIES AND COMPLEXITIES FOR INTERNATIONAL HRM	
HR planning	• Multiple information sources • Nonexistent or unreliable data	• Diverse employee mix • Multiple labour sources
HRIS	• Multiple legal requirements	• Cross-border data flows
Recruitment	• Multiple recruitment locations	• Multiple recruitment sources
Selection	• Multiple selection criteria • Expatriate selection • Employee privacy	• EEO complications • Relocations (visas, customs, transport, passports)
Performance appraisal	• Multi-location appraisals (format, language, criteria)	• Expatriate appraisals
HRD	• Expatriate orientation • Cross-cultural training	• Development of global managers
Career development	• International exposure • Monitoring expatriate careers	• Re-entry
Compensation	• Multiple pay structures • Multiple currencies • Multiple tax systems	• Cultural differences (motivation, importance of money) • Expatriate compensation
Benefits	• Multiple benefit programs • Multiple currencies • Multiple legal requirements	• Expatriate benefits (home leave, housing, education)
Industrial relations	• Multiple labour laws • Different attitudes towards unions	• Government controls
Health and safety	• Multiple legal requirements • Security • Terrorism	• Disease • Expatriate medical issues

Figure 20.2 International HRM activities
Source Asia Pacific Management Co. Ltd, 2004.

HR managers and organisations that fail to comprehend this new international orientation and its complexities are unlikely to ever realise the full potential of their overseas ventures. The challenge of instilling a global orientation among employees is particularly critical.[6]

International HRM policy

The key questions to ask when developing an international HRM policy are: What type of organisation is desired (an Australian organisation with overseas operations, an Australian multinational or a truly global organisation with its headquarters based in Australia)? What are the organisation's key values? What makes this organisation successful? What is the organisation's purpose? What type of corporate culture is desired? Possible orientations are outlined in table 20.1.

Table 20.1	Orientation to international operations		
	AUSTRALIAN ORGANISATION WITH INTERNATIONAL OPERATIONS	**AUSTRALIAN MULTINATIONAL ORGANISATION**	**AUSTRALIAN GLOBAL ORGANISATION**
Personnel	All senior and many middle management positions held by Australians	Localisation of some management positions but all top corporate positions held by Australians	All management positions open to the best people regardless of nationality
Decision making	Highly centralised in Australia; large head office	Some decentralisation to regional or area headquarters; head office in Australia	Decentralised, with small global headquarters in Australia (or elsewhere)
Communication	Instruction and advice from Australian head office to subsidiaries	Regional headquarters are the main source of communication, but with instructions and advice coming from Australian head office	Two-way communication between overseas operations and head office and among the various overseas operations
HRM policies and practices	Predominantly Australian with some modification to satisfy foreign legal requirements	Australian for expatriates, with separate localised policies and practices for foreign employees in each location	Benchmarked on best international practice
Corporate culture	Australian	Mix of Australian and local	International

Clarifying these points establishes the basic flavour of the organisation. It determines to what degree home country values and management practices will be imposed on the overseas operations. It also permits an organisation to identify those core values that are critical to its success and that make it unique. Whirlpool, for example, imposes its performance management system worldwide because it feels the system encompasses the company's vision and values. The company argues that it is not trying to overcome national culture, but rather is trying to build a united global enterprise.[7] This critical examination facilitates the modification (or elimination) of peripheral home-country HRM policies and practices that inhibit the acquisition, development, reward and motivation, maintenance and departure of the organisation's international human resources. Specific examples of HRM policy that may need to be addressed are outlined below:

- Should pay-for-performance programs be transplanted without alteration to seniority-oriented societies such as South Korea and Japan?
- Should the Australian organisation's posture on EEO be applied irrespective of the social, legal and/or political situation in foreign locations such as Indonesia, South Korea, Japan, Malaysia and Saudi Arabia?
- Should Australian, US or local job titles be used (for example, President instead of Managing Director)?
- What is the organisation's attitude towards industrial relations and trade unions?
- Should the Australian mix of cash compensation and benefits be applied in overseas locations?
- What degree of autonomy on HRM matters should be given to the offshore operations?
- What is the organisation's attitude towards the localisation of management in the foreign operation?

Global view

To be effective, HRM policies must reflect an international view rather than a narrow, Australian head-office perspective. David Moffat, CEO of GE Capital in Australia, says: 'The idea is that companies are driven by a common culture, driven globally by an incessant commitment to sharing ideas, challenging what we do every day. Then they are closely linked in global networks. The factors that drive GE are transnational. Who can argue with excellence; who can argue with a loathing of bureaucracy?'[8] Managers must have global vision. The task of transforming domestic managers into international managers is a strategic HRM challenge facing many multinationals. Unfortunately, inadequacies in this area are a virtual guarantee of failure.

A study of multinational disasters concludes that 'the primary causes of failure in multinational ventures stem from a lack of understanding of the essential differences in managing human resources, at all levels, in foreign environments'.[9] One writer puts it very bluntly: 'the choice facing the multinational firm is clear: either increase its global character in order to compete worldwide or give up and disappear.'[10] Japan's Ministry of International Trade and Industry found that overseas operations of Japanese corporations were far less profitable than US and European companies. A major reason for this was the reluctance of Japanese firms to hire local managers.[11] Thus, the development and promotion of global rather than merely domestic HRM policies is critical for international business success.

HR technology implications[12]

Companies are leveraging technology to manage the complexities of global HRM and to deliver high-quality service. Companies use either a common system universal to all locations (for example, SAP, PeopleSoft, Lawson and Oracle) or a set of non-standard systems unique to each location to handle their HR programs and information needs. The problem with the latter is that data are often late, incomplete and/or inaccurate. However, because of time and cost factors they are the most commonly used. To reduce the negative impact of such problems some companies are developing service centres utilising self-service technology and HRIS databases to eliminate routine work and to push the delivery point back to the employee or line manager (see chapter 3).

 ## Key cross-cultural issues

Communication

Cross-cultural communication can be a minefield for the international manager. Gestures, facial expressions, behaviour and words can have different meanings and connotations. For example, 'Yes' to an Australian means yes, but to a Japanese it may mean yes, I agree with you, or yes, I have heard you (but I don't agree with you).

Cross-cultural communication Occurs when a person from one culture (for example, an Australian) communicates with a person from another culture (for example, a Chinese). Misunderstandings may occur because of differences in language, values, attitudes and beliefs.

Cultures also differ in the importance they place on *what* is actually said or written (low context) versus *how* it is said or written (high context). Hong Kong Chinese regard the number 4 as unlucky because in Cantonese it sounds the same as the word for death. As a result, many buildings in Hong Kong do not have a 'fourth' floor. The number 9, in contrast, is considered lucky because it sounds the same as 'longevity'. (In 1994, a Hong Kong businessman paid HK$13 million — almost A$2.5 million — for the car numberplate 9.[13])

China, Korea and Japan have **high-context cultures** where considerable importance is given to non-verbal or situational cues. For effective communication, it is essential that people accurately interpret the intentions of others. Good personal relations help. Family relationships, school and regional ties also can enhance understanding and trust.[14] In contrast, Australia, Canada, the United States and Britain have **low-context cultures** where what is said is what is meant. For example, when a Japanese manager sighs this may mean 'That is difficult', 'I'll have to think about it' or 'I'll try'. The Australian manager asks 'How can the problem be overcome?' or 'When can you give me an answer?' and the Japanese manager is perplexed. Why does the foreigner persist with all these requests when they have already been told that the answer is 'No'? The Australian manager, in turn, wonders why the Japanese manager is so vague and evasive. Can they be trusted? Why won't they say what they mean?

Because of the importance of context, Japanese prefer to communicate face to face or by telephone rather than by impersonal means such as fax, mail and email. Getting to know the other party via recreational activities such as dining out, nightclubbing and golf are extremely important in high-context cultures. While such activities are also employed in low-context cultures, their significance is not as critical. Relationship-building is so important that Japanese companies spend US$35 billion per year on business entertainment (which is more than the government spends on defence).[15]

Silence is another cultural difference. Chinese and Japanese negotiators use, and are used to, silence in their business meetings and negotiations. Australians, in contrast, find periods of silence (especially if prolonged) unsettling or even threatening. Silence may be used as 'thinking time' or to avoid having to say no. Not answering a letter, for example, is a pragmatic way out of an uncomfortable situation for a Japanese executive.[16]

In meetings, Chinese, Koreans and Japanese are often reluctant to express their views for fear of making a mistake, saying something foolish or expressing an opinion that conflicts with their colleagues (or worse, their superior).[17] Face is a critical factor in doing business in Asia, and concerns a person's reputation and the respect they are held in by others. Face emphasises behaviour that promotes harmony, tolerance and solidarity.[18]

Australians tend to be direct in speaking their minds. Independence and freedom of expression are valued. Many Asians, in contrast, are much more cautious. Value is given to comments that bolster other people's reputation, prestige and status.[19] As a result, much importance is given to respecting hierarchy, rank and seniority. Comments Blackman: 'In China, the age, status, position, style and manner of a foreign negotiator will all have a bearing on the negotiation. Because these things count.'[20] Any slight causing loss of face will be deeply felt and not forgotten.[21] Stephen Vines, the founding editor of the now defunct Hong Kong English language newspaper *Eastern Express*, was allegedly fired in a humiliating way by the former group Chairman Ma Ching-Kwan. Reportedly, Ma lost face when he was refused

'I think we made a big impression. They love Aussie informality.'

entry to a dinner party for Deng Xiao Ping's younger brother. (Deng was apparently upset by a series of satirical articles that had appeared in the paper and that Vines had refused to stop publishing.[22]) In Asia, direct confrontation is generally considered both rude and undesirable. In Australia, the United States and other individualistic cultures, saying what one thinks is viewed much more positively. From the clash of ideas it is felt a better solution can be found; time is not wasted 'beating around the bush', and everyone knows exactly where they stand. In group-oriented cultures, such as China, Korea and Japan, the emphasis is on saving one's face and that of other group members (and especially that of a superior).

Finally, it should be remembered that appearance is important in cross-cultural communication. Dress in Hong Kong, Japan and Korea is conservative and conventional. Australians venturing forth in shorts and long white socks (irrespective of temperature) are seen as disrespectful country bumpkins who do not deserve to be taken seriously.

Ethics

Ethics has to do with morality and standards of behaviour. What is considered ethical (and legal) in one culture may be viewed as unethical (and illegal) in another. Australian HR managers cannot assume that their standards will be shared by others or will be seen as right. Deciding what is 'right' and 'wrong', moreover, is not easy when different ethical standards are in conflict. There is a common saying in China, for example, that government officials only speak the truth when they are drunk or careless. To speak the truth could upset a superior and destroy a bureaucrat's career.[23] In Japan, the *Yakuza* (gangsters) have been employed by legitimate companies (and the government) to break up demonstrations, protect politicians and businessmen, and intimidate people.[24]

Ethics Deals with what is good and bad or right and wrong, or with moral duty and obligation. Ethical behaviour may require higher standards than that established by law.

NEWSBREAK

Uni largesse included new suits for visiting Chinese

By Lisa Allen

Staff at an offshoot of the University of Technology, Sydney, bought business suits for Chinese officials and provided free travel, accommodation and sightseeing for a Chinese family.

The NSW Auditor-General's report also found an Insearch staff member had received $5400 for tax advice, while a Shanghai University employee had received a $953 gift.

The audit report, which also raises concerns about the commercial activities of other NSW universities, found Insearch staff frequently had free lunches to welcome and farewell colleagues. They also used its credit cards for private purchases.

Auditor-General Bob Sendt has referred the Insearch matter to the Independent Commission Against Corruption, which has yet to release its findings.

Mr Sendt said yesterday the decision to pay $2326 for three business suits for foreign delegates was 'presumably to gain business for the company from Chinese officials'.

'The occasional business lunch is understandable, but agencies need to ensure public funds are not spent for private benefit.'

Insearch said it had since 'counselled' the manager involved and set down new controls.

Source *The Australian Financial Review*, 30 May 2003, p. 8.

Bribery and **corruption** are also rampart in many parts of Asia.[25] Thailand's national Police Chief recently declared that he was sure that 'more than half' of the police force was honest.[26] According to World Bank estimates, corrupt Filipino tax and customs officials skim off half of every peso collected in tax.[27] Indonesia's corrupt legal system is a major hazard of doing business there and has been described as the law of the jungle.[28] Singapore firms, for example, are withdrawing from Indonesia because of graft and corruption.[29] In Japan, bribery and corruption are synonyms for government. The legal system is largely ignored for

Corruption Includes fraud, bribery, graft and the payment of secret commissions and kickbacks.

backroom deals with gangsters and bureaucrats. Corruption is especially evident in agriculture, distribution and construction.[30] Similarly, there are almost daily reports of Indian and Chinese government officials being arrested for graft and corruption.[31]

The dilemma for the international manager is, if certain behaviour is acceptable in the host country, should their home country standards be imposed? Difficult questions can arise. What is the difference between a business gift and a bribe? At what point does business entertainment become immoral? Is the payment of $20 'speed money' to an underpaid civil servant to process a visa application acceptable, whereas $20 000 to secure a contract is unacceptable? Is it ethical to hire an employee from a competitor in order to obtain trade secrets or other confidential information? Should a company do business in countries with corrupt and/or totalitarian regimes where human rights are suppressed and the right to form independent trade unions is nonexistent? Is it ethical to export Australia's dirty and dangerous manufacturing processes to a third world country? These and other questions can pose serious ethical, moral and professional dilemmas for HR managers.

BHP Billiton and Telstra are two multinationals that have issued guidelines to help their managers to deal with the corruption quagmire. International lawyer Bill O'Shea says, 'My advice to clients is just don't do it . . . if you do it once they have you over a barrel and they will keep demanding it of you'.[32] A related problem is the unforeseen consequence of a manager doing what is 'right'. A US manager in China who (in accordance with company policy) fired a subordinate for theft (and notified the police) was horrified to later learn that the sacked employee had been summarily executed.[33]

It is recommended that companies take the following steps to ensure that their responses to different cultural environments are both appropriate and ethical:[34]

- Develop a clearly articulated set of core values as the basis for global policies and decision making. An organisation's culture will influence the ethical behaviour of its employees. A culture that supports ethical standards of behaviour gives employees a clear guide as to what is acceptable and what is not acceptable. Likewise, one that tolerates or encourages corrupt behaviour will cause ethical standards to decline.
- Train employees to ask questions that will help them to make business decisions that are both culturally sensitive and flexible within the context of those core values. Lo suggests that to find the minimum standards acceptable for practical businesspeople, four basic questions need to be asked:
  1. *Is it legal?* Any business act must be legal before it can be considered ethical.
  2. *Does it respect human life?* Any business act that endangers or harms life is unethical (even if it is legal). The failure to provide a healthy and safe work environment is unethical because it ignores the importance of human life. The payment of below-subsistence wages is also unethical because it deprives workers of the right to survive.
  3. *Does it conform with the ethics of established trade practice?* Ethical business behaviour should be consistent with the codes of conduct of trade associations, professional bodies and the business community at large.
  4. *Does it trouble my conscience?* A person's conscience is the product of religious faith, moral belief and philosophical conviction. Although subjective, ethical behaviour is what a person's feelings say is right.[35]
- Balance the need for policy with the need for flexibility or imagination (for example, a cash payment may not be acceptable, but a business trip to Sydney head office could be).

A company refuses to engage in unethical practices but, as a result, puts itself at a competitive disadvantage.

Trust

A hot issue in organisations and international business is **trust**. This is because employment and business relationships depend on trust. Colleague, subordinate, superior, client, customer and supplier relationships are all influenced by the degree of trust that exists. In the multinational organisation trust is necessary for quick and coordinated global action, the development of employee commitment and social harmony.[36] In joint ventures, trust and commitment are the essential elements for a long-term business relationship.[37] Commercial negotiations, negotiations with trade unions, superior and subordinate negotiations — all require trust for success.

The following Letter to the Editor provides a provocative viewpoint. Do you agree? See 'What's your view?' on page 769.

Letter to the Editor

Western managers who resort to bribery and corruption in any location in which they do business should be prosecuted

Dear Editor,

I am sick and tired of hearing the drivel of managers attempting to excuse unethical behaviour when operating overseas. There are few reasons, if any, why corporations should bend their ethical yardstick in order to achieve international business success.

My argument is simple. Profits do not outrank morality. As Richard De George argues: 'some firms that operate in corrupt environments claim explicitly or implicitly that it is ethically justifiable for them to do whatever they must to stay in business. But their claim is too broad to be defensible. Ethics does not permit a company to capitulate to corruption.'

How can anyone seriously claim that values like honesty and integrity are culturally relative? Ethical values transcend cultures and are relevant for all environments at all times. It is naive in the extreme to argue that the accommodation of corrupt behaviour is a reasonable response to cross-cultural ethical conflict, as is argued by some management theorists.

Australian companies have been able to avoid this issue for far too long. What is needed is an equivalent of the *US Foreign Corrupt Practices Act*, which ensures that North American corporations behave with ethical consistency no matter where they are doing business. While Australia has recently legislated to prohibit corruption between Australian companies and overseas government officials and bureaucrats, this does not go far enough.

Progressive corporations should also consider accepting the ethical principles formulated by international executives in groups such as the Caux Round Table, an association of US executives committed to ethical values, which seems to have other corporations agreeing to the same highly ethical values. Alongside principles such as respect for domestic and international laws and the environment, the group advocates the 'avoidance of illicit operations' including bribery and money laundering.

Australia's current attitude is that ethical problems do not exist because they are not easily visible. This head-in-the-sand approach denies the many negative consequences arising from corrupt conduct in international environments. One ethical consequence is that staff returning to Australia bring their newly acquired ethical relativism with them, thus potentially lowering ethical standards in their home office. Similarly, staff thrown into the ethical wilderness in overseas locations are commonly beset by considerable anxiety and stress as they tear themselves apart in the battle between conscience and company.

At the end of the day, organisations must recognise that international profits are sometimes not worth the pain of whoring corporate morality to the fickleness of ethical relativism. Managers should have the courage to resist corruption in all its manifestations, particularly in the international context where organisational reputations are constantly on the line.

An HR manager with a multinational corporation

Source David Poole, University of Western Sydney.

Culture has an impact on trust. Fukuyama divides societies into low trust (for example, China) and high trust (for example, Australia and the United States). Trust arises when a society 'shares a set of moral values in such a way as to create expectations of regular and honest behaviour'.[38] In Chinese society, a sharp distinction is made between family members and non-family members. Family ties provide the basis for trust. In Chinese enterprises, family members fill key management positions. These are the people the *taipan* (big boss) can trust to meet their family obligations. Loyalty, rather than technical ability or job performance, is what counts. Chinese management style, as a consequence, is often described as personalistic — HRM decisions are made on the basis of the manager's personal relations with subordinates.[39] Non-family members rarely are given equity. They frequently complain of a lack of openness when dealing with the boss and of the 'glass ceiling' that prevents them from gaining senior positions.[40] Consequently, skilled and ambitious workers favour starting their own business as soon as they acquire sufficient capital and experience rather than pursuing a career in someone else's family business.[41]

The pervasive distrust of strangers and the reluctance to appoint non-family members to positions of importance place limits on the efficiency and size of the typical Chinese family company.[42] The vast majority of small businesses in Hong Kong, Taiwan and Singapore are owned by single families. Even large companies such as Cheung Kong, Wharf Holdings and Bank of East Asia remain family managed. In high-trust cultures, in contrast, there is a greater trust of strangers (because of established legal systems), which permits unrelated people to work together. Professional managers can be employed for their technical competence and not their family ties.

Management style

Management style Reflects the particular approach used by a manager to achieve goals through other people.

Culture affects **management style**. Effective managers do not use one style of leadership but adjust their style to each situation. Subordinates in a national culture, however, will expect an overriding style from their managers. A manipulative or autocratic style, for example, is compatible with cultures that emphasise hierarchy and status. In contrast, in cultures where differences in power and status are de-emphasised a participatory, more egalitarian approach will be sought. Thus, in **high power distance cultures** (such as Hong Kong, China, India, Korea and Singapore) subordinates will expect their managers to make the decisions and tell them what to do, and managers will expect their instructions to be implemented without question. For example, when Singapore's Senior Minister Lee Kuan Yew says something, 'traditionally, he is not offering an opinion'.[43] Bangladesh managers are mainly autocratic and resistant to the idea of employee empowerment. [44] Japanese managers, in contrast, while paternalistic, allow their subordinates much greater involvement in decision making.[45] As a consequence, Australian managers may complain that their Chinese or Korean subordinates lack initiative, and never voice an opinion or idea. Zhu and Dowling, for example, claim that because of their education and experience, mainland Chinese managers 'lack decision making skills and are wary of taking personal initiatives'.[46]

High power distance cultures Cultures where employees obey orders and treat superiors with respect, and where hierarchy and status are emphasised.

Low power distance cultures Cultures where employees expect to be involved in decisions that affect them and to be treated as an equal, and where hierarchy and status are de-emphasised.

In **low power distance cultures** (such as Australia and the United States) employees will expect to have a much greater say in decision making and more autonomy in their work. These expectations, however, may not be reflective of the underlying cultural values elsewhere. Chinese and Koreans, for example, emphasise the importance of hierarchy in interpersonal relations. This produces a greater acceptance of unequal, authoritarian relationships.[47] In some Asian airlines, the hierarchical culture in the cockpit means no one will question the pilot (even if the pilot is making a mistake) and that discipline is sometimes enforced physically. A leaked Korean Air report, for example, cites an incident in which a captain hit his co-pilot for making a mistake.[48]

Equal employment opportunity (EEO)

Equal opportunity laws are the product of society's social values. In some cultures, the status of men and women, young and old, gays and lesbians, and various ethnic and religious groups may not be the same. For example, the most commonplace descriptions of Mainland Chinese by Hong Kong Chinese university students include dirty, unlawful, corrupt, backward, uneducated and poor.[49] In Saudi Arabia, women are not permitted to drive and do not hold senior managerial positions.[50] In India, where people are divided by a caste system, the *Harijans* (the lowest caste) are predominantly found in low-level jobs.[51] In Indonesia and Malaysia, preferential treatment is given to *bumiputras* (sons of the soil). Malaysia has legislation favouring Malays over other ethnic groups in government employment and university access. In Indonesia, children of communists and former political prisoners experience difficulties in getting employment with the military or public service.[52] Migrant workers (from rural areas) are China's untouchables. They are subject to economic and political exploitation by both employers and government officials.[53] One factory (owned by Hong Kong and Taiwanese businessmen) refused to provide workers with drinking water, forcing them to drink from a fishpond. When the workers protested, they were fired.[54] Another Hong Kong-funded factory strip-searched its workers (mainly women) after four diamonds went missing.[55]

The international HR manager must be alert to such differences. Foreign EEO laws may be quite different from those applying in Australia (for example, China and Japan have no specific laws against sexual harassment and in Thailand trading sex for good grades by university undergraduates is commonplace).[56] In addition, although anti-discrimination laws exist, companies and governments may ignore or try to avoid them. No leading Japanese company, for example, will knowingly employ a *burakumin* or *eta* (outcast) even though they are Japanese and are not descended from Koreans. Similarly, other ethnic minorities such as Ainu and Koreans born in Japan are excluded from employment. Japanese people consider such issues sensitive and they remain unmentioned. Nevertheless, discrimination is entrenched and members of such groups are not accepted as 'true' Japanese.[57] Top companies use lawyers and private detectives to check the 'blood line' of prospective employees, and use unofficial copies of the *Koseki*, or Family Register, which gives a complete history of every Japanese family. Families involved in marriage negotiations take similar action.[58] Japanese firms operating in the United States also tend to locate where minorities (especially African-Americans) are not present.[59]

A company practices EEO but puts itself in conflict with the local culture.

Performance appraisal

For companies that operate internationally, performance measurement is a complex issue. In Korean companies, evaluation is based not only on performance but also on the employee's disposition. Performance evaluation in Thai firms is based on the employee's attitude towards the company rather than on actual job performance.[60] Performance appraisal in mainland Chinese firms depends on the quality of personal relations, political attitudes and output.[61] Fundamental questions to be asked include: What do we mean by performance? What performance criteria will be used? Will the same criteria be used for head office employees, expatriates and local employees? Will performance be assessed on an individual or a group basis? Are programs such as management by objectives (MBO) culturally appropriate? (The evidence suggests the answer is yes for Germany, no for France.) How will feedback be given, directly or indirectly? (In China and Japan, indirect feedback, or feedback via a mutually respected third party or by withdrawing a favour, may be more appropriate.)

Simply exporting the head office program may end in disaster if it is not culturally sensitive. In Japan, the dominant work unit is the group and not the individual. Job descriptions give only a generalised understanding of the work to be performed. To single out one person as being superior or more productive than other group members may be considered not only wrong but also personally humiliating to the highly rated employee. In Japan, the adage is 'the nail that sticks up gets hammered down'.[62] Local Hong Kong companies appear to overcome this problem by allowing their managers and employees to collude to produce a harmonious result.[63]

Similarly, different criteria may be required for the evaluation of expatriate performance. Some experts suggest that consideration be given not only to the expatriate's technical skills and the work performed, but also to personality variables (such as cultural empathy, communication skills, flexibility and stress tolerance) and the work environment (for example, lack of workable telephones, potable water, constant blackouts, and so on).[64] Comments Shanghai-based Xerox China General Manager Howard Holley: 'I find the biggest gap has been between what I can actually accomplish here versus what I was used to accomplishing in the United States with the same or fewer resources.'[65] Finally, it is important that the performance criteria be valid. In an overseas location, performance criteria may be polluted by exchange rate fluctuations, government controls, bribery and corruption, and other hidden barriers.

Training and development

Organisations that operate internationally face a number of unique challenges in training and developing their employees. Matters relating to the diversity of the work force, language and cultural differences impinge on all aspects of the training and development activity. Should programs be conducted in English or the host-country language? Are there cultural attitudes that conflict with company philosophies and practices? (For example: How will employees in the host country relate to female managers? Is a participative learning style the most effective? Are some topics taboo? Should programs be formal or informal? How should training be evaluated?)

Spencer and Chiu, for example, found differences between Hong Kong Chinese managers and Western managers in their preferred approaches to giving and securing feedback, learning, handling conflict and contributing in teams.[66] Similarly, Saner and Yiu claim that many non-US students experience difficulties with the traditional case study method, which, in turn, reduces its effectiveness as a teaching medium.[67] Finally, there may be significant cultural differences that need to be acknowledged when defining the training needs of managers. Byham claims that, compared with US companies, Japanese firms stress technical knowledge and skills but attach relatively little importance to leadership, communication and interpersonal skills.[68]

Consequently, when an organisation enters the international training and development area, the HR manager needs to be sensitive to local customs and expectations. The HR manager must deal with questions regarding local, national and corporate culture, the ethnocentricity of particular approaches and interventions, ethics and the value placed on training and development.[69]

Compensation

A foreign company pays in excess of the local minimum wage and offers superior working conditions. It is criticised for attracting scarce professionals away from universities and hospitals to perform semi-skilled work.

National culture is an important consideration in strategic compensation. Cultures that value hierarchy and status differentials (for example, China, Indonesia and the Philippines) will employ compensation strategies that promote and reinforce differences in status. In contrast, more egalitarian reward systems are used in cultures where status differentials are minimised (for example, Australia and Sweden). Individualistic cultures (such as Australia and the United States) likewise will adopt compensation strategies that reward individual performance and the acquisition of individual skills and know-how. In collectivist or group-oriented cultures (such as China, Korea and Japan), organisations will base their rewards more on group performance and individual seniority (in recognition of the employee's time as a group member).[70] In Japanese and Korean companies, for example, base pay is primarily tied to educational qualifications and length of service.

Risk-averse cultures will prefer bureaucratic reward systems that emphasise fixed (guaranteed) and not variable (at-risk) pay. Profit-sharing and incentive pay programs may prove less effective where risk-taking is discouraged or where employees may be punished for showing initiative instead of respect. In Thai companies, for example, pay increases linked to inflation are given to all employees regardless of their performance. While most Australian and US companies reward individual performance (via merit pay and incentive pay), Japanese companies, in contrast, prefer to recognise group membership, loyalty and employee needs (for example, additional allowances relate to family size, travel and housing needs). US company Lincoln Electric found that its incentive program based on the belief that all employees would be willing to work harder to increase their income was highly successful in the United States, Canada and Australia, but a failure in Germany.[71]

Industrial relations

Industrial relations philosophies and practices vary around the globe. About one-quarter of the Australian work force is unionised. Membership is even lower in Hong Kong and the

United States. In China, employees can join only state-sponsored unions. Any attempt to establish independent unions is quickly squashed and the organisers jailed.[72] **Craft unions** traditionally have dominated in Australia and Britain; in contrast, **enterprise-based unions** are the norm in Japan. Employees in the United States can vote whether to have a union, but Australian workers in some industries (in practice) have no choice. Collective bargaining is more likely to be at the local or enterprise level in Japan and the United States, whereas until recently Australians primarily resolved conflict within a legal framework involving peak employer associations and the trade union hierarchy. Despite declining memberships, unions have considerable economic and political clout in Australia but not in Hong Kong and Taiwan. Industrial relations in Australia has traditionally been characterised by a 'them and us' attitude, while in Japan and Singapore it is characterised by cooperation and employee identification with the company and its objectives. Cultural, economic and political differences clearly express themselves in industrial relations.

HR managers should ensure that:

- practices adhere to and reinforce strategic HRM objectives and policies and are in harmony with the desired corporate culture
- concessions granted in one location do not create damaging precedents for the rest of the organisation
- ethical and legal obligations are met. For example, in response to criticism that its contract suppliers in Indonesia, Thailand and Vietnam run poorly managed sweatshops, Nike funded monitoring studies by the non-profit organisation Global Alliance.[73] 'Monitoring isn't a philanthropic gesture', claims Slater, 'but a way of reducing risk. Revelations by the media or independent organizations of dangerous or abusive conditions are a CEO's nightmare, and can poison years of brandbuilding.'[74]

It is obvious that the special problems and considerations involved in global industrial relations require managers to demonstrate considerable cultural sensitivity. Flexibility and an understanding of the unique conditions of the host country's work force are essential, as is the imagination to translate organisational HRM objectives and policies into appropriate industrial relations practices on a worldwide scale. To undertake these measures successfully, Australian multinationals must be well versed in international industrial relations and be aware that each industrial relations system is unique.

HRM in China

The labour market

The Chinese labour market is characterised by a vast pool of poorly qualified personnel (more than 15 per cent of the population are illiterate). The shortage of top-class professionals and managers is acute (especially in areas such as accounting, HRM and marketing). Aggravating such shortages is the concentration of professionals in the major coastal cities of Beijing, Shanghai and Guangzhou. Consequently, foreign companies have had to pay a premium and develop their HR programs (especially those relating to mentoring, overseas experience, career planning, and training and development) to make themselves employers of choice and to stem labour turnover. Achieving employee commitment, not surprisingly, is a key HR strategy of foreign firms in China.[75]

State-owned enterprises

In state-owned enterprises (SOEs), an 'iron rice bowl' philosophy still exists. The guarantee of lifelong employment, while threatened, is dominant in many state-owned enterprises because of the enormous social pressures to keep surplus workers. Performance appraisals traditionally have been subjective, with an overriding emphasis given to whether the worker is politically correct. In addition to assessment by superiors appraisals still include self-assessment and peer group discussion.[76]

Compensation in SOEs has three components: a *monetary wage* (base pay, group bonus and various allowances such as for shift work, cost of living, hazards, and so on); a *social wage* (which includes insurance for sickness, accidents, disability, funeral costs, medical costs and pension); and *non-material incentives* (which are moral encouragements, such as loyalty to the Communist Party and honorary titles like 'model worker' and 'labour hero').

SOE employees are attracted to foreign firms because of improved pay and working conditions, more opportunities for personal development; the chance to live and work overseas, and less political pressure (representatives of the Communist Party of China are partly responsible for managing SOEs and HR managers until recently were required by law to be party members).[77]

HR challenges for foreign enterprises

Specific challenges facing the international HR manager in China include: the absence of reliable market data; expenditure on training and development is often wasted, because people quit as soon as the training is completed; labour laws are complicated (for example, different provinces have different legislation) and often vague (leaving their interpretation open to local officials, which breeds corruption); termination of surplus staff is difficult, if not impossible; talented professionals and managers are hard to locate and recruit; remuneration often involves complex legal arrangements and an array of benefits unique to China; and finally, Chinese managers traditionally have not been subject to pressures to perform or operate efficiently.[78]

HR managers in China also face a number of overriding problems. First, nothing is ever black and white — everything is negotiable (there is a popular saying 'Nothing is illegal in China, but at the same time, nothing is legal either').[79] Second, politics impacts on all HRM activities (independent trade unions, for example, are not permitted). Third, the change from a command to a market economy has created legal and regulatory ambiguities that foster corruption, deception and unscrupulous management practices.[80]

Personal files

Personal files are a major hindrance to labour mobility. Everyone in China has a personal file (normally started when a person reaches the age of 12). It covers the individual's personal history; evaluations by superiors and officials; an outline of the person's political background; records of rewards, punishments, promotions and demotions; and references and the names of referees. Before an applicant can transfer to a new job or work for a foreign enterprise it is necessary for the person's work unit to release their personal file.

Performance appraisals

Correct political attitudes, loyalty to the boss and seniority traditionally have been the main criteria determining performance ratings in Chinese organisations. With the advent of joint ventures and wholly foreign-owned subsidiaries, and increasing pressures for performance improvement, more objective measures are slowly being introduced (especially in SOEs where there is a desperate need to break the 'iron rice bowl'). Cultural values impact on performance appraisal. Zhao says: 'The manager who criticizes a subordinate ... causes that subordinate to lose face ... This means that criticism of performance on the job must be handled in a very delicate way, with criticisms disguised as suggestions for improvement.'[81] Straight-speaking Australian managers must be sensitive to the Chinese concern for face if they are to be effective.[82]

Finally, research suggests that development-oriented performance appraisal systems that promote career development aspirations and long-term development opportunities facilitate localisation, develop technical expertise and foster employee commitment.[83]

Recruitment and selection

Although labour reforms and market pressures have created greater flexibilities, the Chinese system is still overly bureaucratic and rigid. Often, joint ventures with SOEs are grossly overstaffed, making it difficult to hire new and better-qualified employees. Sophisticated selection techniques such as psychological testing are used only in joint ventures and wholly foreign-owned companies. In Chinese enterprises, reliance on the interview (or multiple interviews) is most common. Recruiting methods include newspaper advertisements, job fairs, and private and government employment agencies. The use of personal connections or networks is a popular method used by both employers and employees. (This approach can create problems, however, if the person recommended is not hired or proves to be unsatisfactory and has to be fired.[84])

Major concerns for employers in China are:
- Does the applicant have the technical skills required? (Fake qualifications are common.)
- Does the applicant have sufficient relevant experience?
- Will the applicant be able to adjust to the corporate culture of a foreign enterprise?
- Does the candidate have sufficient English language skills (especially for professional and managerial appointments)?
- Is the candidate honest? (Multiple background checks are essential in newly developing countries such as China.)
- Is the résumé free from misinformation (for example, title inflation, bogus qualifications and inflated salary)?

Compensation and benefits

Compensation and benefits practices tend to be chaotic. Marked differences exist between companies, industries and geographic locations.[85] Added to this is the problem of obtaining accurate information on compensation and benefits. A company's remuneration package may include base salary, bonuses, allowances (for education, family, meals, transport, living, clothing, showers, haircuts and laundry), housing (or housing assistance), insurance, medical benefits, superannuation and various types of paid leave (such as annual leave, sick leave, marriage leave, compassionate leave, leave for child-feeding and domestic leave for couples living in different provinces).

Training and development

For many Chinese employees, the opportunity to learn a new skill is a powerful motivator (especially if it involves attending training and development programs overseas). Having a professionally developed training and development program is key to building employee commitment and being seen as an employer of choice. Lack of skilled workers (especially managers) has been identified by the government as a major barrier to modernisation and the introduction of new technology and industrial reform, and is a major source of complaint from foreign companies.[86]

HRM in Japan

The traditional features of HRM in Japan are lifelong employment, a seniority-based wage and promotional system, and enterprise-based unions. However, the onslaught of international competition, the transition to a service economy, an ageing work force (which burdens companies with increasing numbers of highly paid, elderly, less productive employees) and the emergence of a mobile, technically literate young work force less committed to the 'one company, one career' ideal are forcing change.[87]

Lifelong employment

Under **lifelong employment**, the individual enters the company from school or university and is given assured employment until the age of 55 or 57. As a concept, it is practised only by major and medium-sized companies and is now under threat. When a Japanese male joins a company, he expects to remain with that one company for the rest of his entire working life. He does not anticipate that he will be laid off, dismissed or retrenched. Moreover, he personally does not seek to job hunt or switch companies. He is there for life. In contrast, female employees are expected to resign on getting married.

Lifelong employment A situation where an employee is 'guaranteed' a job for their entire working life.

Practitioner speaks

The Japanese way of management

Tatsuo Tanaka *(BA Law, Keio University) is Director, Chief Executive for China of The Bank of Tokyo-Mitsubishi, Ltd. He has more than 30 years' banking experience. From 2001 to 2003, during his assignment in Hong Kong, he also held various directorships inside and outside of the banking industry. Tatsuo Tanaka is now based in Tokyo, travelling frequently to China and Hong Kong.*

During the 1980s, it emerged that many Japanese companies were sharing a host of similar problems: they were highly rigid and bureaucratic; their decision-making processes were slow; their management systems made it unclear where responsibilities lay; they had failed to respond to the need of specialisation; and their seniority-based promotion systems nurtured managers who had not paid enough attention to front-line operations and whose mottoes included inaction, avoidance of responsibility and being risk-averse.

Many people have suggested that these problems were a result of the unique Japanese way of management, which allegedly is also responsible for the prolonged sluggishness of the Japanese economy. But I do not fully agree with this view.

Indeed, many Japanese companies are still successful under the present economic downturn. These companies can be divided into two groups. In the first group are companies that have concentrated on reducing costs and lowering prices under deflationary pressures. In the second group are companies that have continued to create their own unique new values. In the latter group, the managers usually have the following characteristics: first, they maintain their own refined ways of thinking; second, they have a keen sense of risk; third, they are experienced at crises and failures; and fourth, they have a strong sense of duty and ethics.

It should be noted that many of the companies that have continued to be successful since the 1980s are neither the large companies that have given up the much-condemned Japanese way of management nor the small- and medium-sized companies that have refused to accept the Japanese management practice.

The fundamental problem of many failing Japanese companies seems to lie with their managers. Those successful companies that experienced a slowdown due to bureaucratisation showed a recovery after having installed charismatic, high-calibre managers, who usually have experience in front-line operations. It should be emphasised that incapable managers are not unique to companies that implement Japanese-style management practices — they are a universal phenomenon.

In this regard, what Japanese companies need to do is construct a personnel training system, within the Japanese style of management (which has solid strengths such as long-term vision, humanism, fast communication flows and a strong sense of unity), which can cultivate and promote expertise in diverse areas and which also places more emphasis on front-line operations. However, such changes may lead to the loss of superficial equality that is the main characteristic of the seniority-based system, and there will be a new task of how to maintain the unity of the corporate culture.

Tatsuo Tanaka

A protective and hierarchical management style pervades all areas of large Japanese organisations. Companies will spend money on training and development because they know that their employees will not quit to go to a job that offers more money. Training, in addition, is seen as a very effective means of demonstrating management's interest in the employee and directing his attention away from union influences.

A further advantage gained from lifelong employment is flexibility in job allocation. Even among blue-collar workers, there are no problems over demarcation issues. Likewise, because of the strong sense of job security, employees favour the introduction of highly mechanised or automated processes (a situation not normally found with labour in Australia or the United States).

Another striking characteristic of Japanese-style HRM is the emphasis placed on maintaining harmonious relations within the organisation. Given lifelong employment, employees know that they are going to have to work (and play) together for the rest of their working lives. Consequently, the creation of a cooperative, supportive and happy working group is essential.

Lifelong employment means that mid-career hires are the exception in Japanese companies. Employment at any time except immediately after graduation from high school or university was until recently extremely rare. Workers over 40 who lost their jobs were held to have received a form of 'death' sentence (for example, it is estimated that 'salary men' in their forties and fifties now account for 40 per cent of Japan's suicides).[88] Job security is thus an extremely important consideration in gaining a motivated and satisfied work force in Japan. The termination of personnel (even poor performers) is a sensitive and emotional issue. Generally, only when the very existence of the company is threatened will Japanese management move to cut the work force (and then only with the consent of the union). The union, for its part, will willingly accept a lower rate of wage increase (or no increase) or even a reduction in wages in an effort to try to keep the company 'family' together.

A seniority-based wage and promotion system

A better name for the **seniority system** is the system of merit by years. The Japanese feel that an individual who has been in a job longer can obviously perform it better. Thus, 'seniority' is the only 'true and fair' merit system. It is understood by all and is not influenced by the personal whims of a supervisor. This gives the Japanese a strong sense of security and certainty. Employees 'know' what their minimum salary and their minimum 'position' in the company will be at a particular age. For example, a university graduate expects to be a *Kacho* (section chief) by his mid-thirties. It should be noted, however, that at about this point there is a subtle change of emphasis, and ability rather than seniority tends to be stressed. Thus, promotion to *Bucho* (manager) and higher classifications is more selective. Even so, seniority remains important and 'equivalent' face-saving job titles will be found for those who have been passed over. This is because, from a social as well as a business point of view, the recognition of seniority by some form of title change is seen as being necessary to maintain the status or 'face' of the employee (in the office, at home and outside).

Seniority system Where the length of time that an employee has worked with an organisation is given recognition and priority for promotions and salary increases.

Enterprise-based unions

Enterprise-based unions in Japan are company unions. The word 'union' in Japan has a different meaning from that which it is given in Australia or the United States. The union in Japan is perhaps best thought of as being an organised group within the company family that ensures that its voice is heard. Its basic aims are not all that different from those of management. Given lifelong employment, the union has a vested interest in ensuring the continued profitability and existence of the company. Japanese-style unions are generally seen as being an excellent communication channel by both managers and employees.

Almost every manager in a Japanese company will, in fact, have been a member of the union, as membership of the union normally includes all people up to professional and sub-managerial levels. This exposure gives Japanese managers an excellent understanding of how the union works and allows them to maintain close relationships with union leaders and members. It must be stressed that union membership is restricted to full-time permanent employees hired directly from school or university. The company union has no interest in the working conditions of casual or part-time workers, as these groups are not regarded as being members of the corporate family.

Pay for performance

For the average Japanese employee, pay for performance may create insecurity and uncertainty. The Japanese generally know after the annual 'Spring Offensive' held in April each year what the increase to their base salary will be. Amounts for individual companies and industries are publicised widely in the press and are closely linked to company and industry profitability. Merit is recognised primarily through special monthly merit allowances or by additions to annual bonus payments.

Unlike the US or Australian approach, a 'typical' compensation package in Japan consists of monthly base salary, a bonus normally paid twice a year in June and December, and a number of monthly allowances for position, merit, housing, commutation, special skills and meals. It is via this allowance system that differences in compensation come about. The base monthly salary for personnel of the same age and qualifications is identical in amount. In other words, the Japanese system has the flexibility of treating every one the same, but differently.

Promotion based on ability

US and Australian companies generally emphasise promotion based on ability. This is in contrast to the Japanese approach, where seniority receives greater recognition. In Australia and the United States, it is generally felt that the individual who has contributed the most to the achievement of the company's goals should advance and take on additional responsibilities. In contrast, in Japan the group is regarded as being more important than the individual.

US and Australian companies talk about the top performer's 'right' to be promoted, whereas in Japan companies talk about 'duty'. One of the key duties for a Japanese employee is to help maintain harmonious relations within the group. Superior performers, if young or female, may, as a result, hesitate to accept a position that would upset the established order. If a younger person is placed in a position of seniority over an older person from the same university, a sense of uneasiness may arise, because in the company social structure the older person is the patron of his college junior. To disturb this key internal social relationship can be uncomfortable and embarrassing for all concerned.[89] As a result, younger employees may prefer to 'wait their turn' rather than upset group harmony and face the possibility of being isolated by their fellow workers.

The fundamental differences

US and Australian companies emphasise profitability. Simply stated, without profits there will be no jobs. With profits there are increased opportunities for growth and advancement. Individual opportunity is stressed. Those making the greatest contribution to profit achievement are rewarded the most (at least in theory). A large element of contract typically exists in US and Australian employment relationships. Employees may be required to sign secrecy agreements, 'no compete' agreements and a formal employment contract. Similarly, jobs are evaluated by methods that do not take into account the employee's personal situation (such as age, marital status and number of dependants).

To the Japanese, this is a 'cold' approach. Japanese companies emphasise their obligations to employees (not to shareholders). This does not mean that Japanese companies are uninterested in profits. However, there is an overriding sense of obligation because of the family nature of the organisation.

Unlike in Australia and the United States, the interests of women, minorities and individuals are secondary to the maintenance of group harmony (which at all times is placed above individual interests).

Finally, Japanese companies have a very strong spiritual relationship with their employees. The individual employee in the Japanese language refers to his company as his home. He does not introduce himself as an engineer or a chemist but as a Mitsui man or a Mitsubishi man, for example. His economic relationship with the company is personalised. A cynic who accepts Maslow's theories (see page 415) could well argue that a Japanese company, by providing for all the employee's basic needs, permits the employee to devote his total energies to achieving the company's goals.

The future

The 'traditional' Japanese approach to HRM is now under threat. Questions are being asked about the continuing validity of such concepts as lifelong employment and the seniority-based pay and promotion systems.[90] The prolonged economic downturn, the need to become more competitive, the 'cultural challenges' posed by high-tech industries and the increasing demands for reform by foreign investors are all adding to the pressures for change. As is the case in Australia, Japanese firms subjected to international competition are the leaders in introducing more innovative and flexible HR policies and practices.

Summary

International HRM is complex, difficult and critical to global business success. The organisation that has not thought through its domestic HRM policies and practices will find that its transition to international activities will be both painful and expensive. Without a solid base on which to build, the development of an international HRM policy risks being ad hoc, wasteful and alienating to domestic, expatriate and foreign employees. A successful policy requires clearly developed HRM objectives that are intimately tied to the organisation's global strategic business objectives.

In international business, the underlying impact of culture is evident in the way people interact with and manage others. Not surprisingly, the approaches to HRM in cultures such as China and Japan are very different from those employed in Australia.

Thirty interactive Wiley Web Questions are available to test your understanding of this chapter at **www.johnwiley.com.au/ highered/hrm5e** *in the student resources area*

terms to know

corruption (p. 755)
craft unions (p. 761)
cross-cultural communication (p. 753)
domestic HRM (p. 751)
enterprise-based unions (p. 761)
ethics (p. 755)
expatriate (p. 750)
high-context cultures (p. 754)
high power distance cultures (p. 758)

international HRM (p. 751)
lifelong employment (p. 763)
local employee (p. 750)
low-context cultures (p. 754)
low power distance cultures (p. 758)
management style (p. 758)
seniority system (p. 765)
trust (p. 756)

review questions

1. What are the main differences between domestic HRM and international HRM?
2. What are the major HRM issues that a company should consider before going international?
3. What role does EEO play in international HRM?
4. To what extent should a company export its domestic HRM policies and practices to its international operations?
5. What are some of the barriers that may hinder cross-cultural communication? How might these be overcome?
6. How would you describe Australian and Japanese management styles?
7. What is trust? Why is it especially important in international HRM?
8. Outline the similarities and differences in HRM policies and practices between Australia and China.
9. What is ethics? What are some ethical problems that may be encountered when doing business internationally?
10. What advice would you give to a sales manager who is about to commence a three-year assignment in Japan? How would your advice differ if the person were being transferred to Indonesia?

environmental influences on international HRM

Describe the key environmental influences from the model (figure 20.3 shown opposite) that have significance for international HRM.

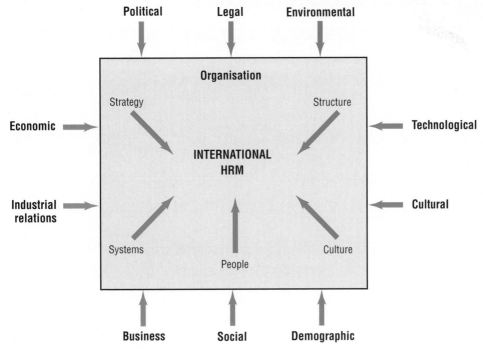

Figure 20.3 Environmental influences on international HRM

soapbox

What do you think? Conduct a mini survey of class members, using the questionnaire below. Critically discuss the findings.

1.	Managers should not resort to bribery, even when it is an accepted local practice.	YES	NO
2.	Companies operating in a foreign location should implement local and not home country HR policies and practices.	YES	NO
3.	The use of child labour is acceptable in developing countries.	YES	NO
4.	A foreign company operating in Australia should be allowed to implement HRM policies and practices consistent with its home country culture.	YES	NO
5.	What is considered ethical varies from one culture to another.	YES	NO
6.	Australian companies operating overseas should be managed by Australians.	YES	NO

online exercise

Conduct an online search for information on (a) child labour, (b) 'sweatshops' in the Asia–Pacific region or (c) trade unions in either China or Indonesia. As a class, discuss your findings.

ethical dilemmas

Between a rock and a hard place at Jet Red[91]

'This garbage collection business. How serious is it?' questioned Alan Balkin, Managing Director of Jet Red.

'Very serious. Our present contractor is Mafia linked. We are being charged an exorbitant amount. It's like an extra "tax" on doing business in New York. We are being ripped off', replied Stella Chow, General Manager, USA.

'Well, why don't we change contractors? How on earth did we get mixed up with these people in the first place?' demanded Alan.

'No choice. The Mafia had a virtual monopoly over garbage collection until recently. You dealt with them or no one. You wanted your garbage collected, then the Mob collected it. Very simple!' Chow said with a resigned shrug.

'The point is', interrupted Linda Church, HR Manager, 'we now have a choice. We have received a proposal from a new company that is not linked to the Mob. They charge 40 per cent less — money that will go straight onto our bottom line!'

'Well, why don't we change? I'm appalled to think a reputable company like Jet Red is doing business with criminals', gasped Alan.

Stella looked at Linda, then said, 'You see, Alan, the problem is, if we change collectors, the Mob might retaliate. We are a people business. The safety and welfare of our customers and employees are paramount. We can't afford to have any of our planes or facilities damaged. If we change contractors, there is a risk. A big risk. The consequences could be terrible. You can imagine the publicity if anything happened. It would be a public relations nightmare'.

'The question, I take it then, is can we take the chance?' grimaced Alan.

Discussion questions

1. What would you do in this situation? Why?
2. What ethical questions are raised in this case?

Free drinks

You are conducting a training program in Hong Kong with members of the executive team from the China Agricultural Import and Export Company of Guangdong Province, your joint venture partner. Your company is paying their expenses during their Hong Kong stay. All has been going well. The training program has been extremely well received. At the end of today's training session, the hotel manager, who appears somewhat embarrassed, speaks to you. He tells you that for the last two days, all the ashtrays, bathrobes and towels along with all the liquor and confectionery from the refrigerators in your guests' rooms have 'disappeared'. He says the hotel has no option but to charge for all the 'consumed' items. He wonders, however, if you are aware about what is happening and the costs involved.

Discussion question

What would you do in this situation? Why?

---

case studies

Crisis at Western University

Abbie Frey, HR Manager for Western University, knocked sharply then entered the book-lined office of Professor Poon, the Dean of the School of Business. 'Sorry to disturb you, but I need to speak to you urgently.'

Poon angrily swivelled his chair away from the computer screen to face Abbie. 'Abbie, what is it?' Poon snapped, annoyed at the interruption.

'We have a crisis on our hands. It's our MBA class in Jakarta. The Golden Paradise Hotel has been attacked by terrorists. Apparently, there was an enormous explosion near the seminar rooms. At least 13 people have been killed. We don't know if any of our staff or students have been hurt.'

'Oh no, that's terrible! How many of our people are likely to be involved?'

'Five', replied Abbie. 'Stella Chatzky, Steve Plovnick, Percy Samuels, Mary Lee and Ron Mazzolis. Mary Lee is five months pregnant.'

'Oh, no! What about the students?'

'Seventy-three were enrolled. How many were actually in class is anyone's guess, as we don't mark attendance.'

Poon, his face grey with shock, gasped 'What do you suggest we do?'

Discussion questions

1. What short-term and long-term HR issues may arise because of this incident?
2. Are there any special ethical issues that need to be considered in this case?

Exercise

Form into groups of four to six. Imagine that you are members of the university task force charged with dealing with the situation. Develop a plan of action. Regroup as a class and review your recommendations.

HR promotion at International Industries

You are the Vice-President of Human Resources at General Industries Asia (GIA) Ltd. Five years ago, GIA became a wholly owned subsidiary of International Industries Ltd. Prior to its takeover, GIA was controlled by the Tse family and was listed on the Hong Kong Stock Exchange.

GIA was a traditional Chinese family-owned organisation but has undergone major change since the takeover. The company management is now less paternalistic and more performance-oriented. Performance appraisal and pay-for-performance systems have been introduced and several senior personnel are now non-Chinese. However, the present Managing Director, Robert Tse, continues to manage in a traditional Chinese way and pays only lip service to many of the changes that have been introduced. It is rumoured that next year Tse will be appointed as Chairman of GIA and that his replacement as Managing Director will come from one of International's overseas subsidiaries.

Yesterday, you were informed by Robert Tse, your administrative boss, that Head Office in Sydney has confirmed your appointment as Vice-President of Human Resources, Europe. You have been asked by your functional boss in Sydney, Patrick O'Malley, to nominate your successor from one of your three direct reports (John Chow, Training and Development Manager, Anita Law, Compensation and Benefits Manager, and Henry Cheung, Employment and Planning Manager) for the consideration of Robert, Patrick and International's newly appointed President, Lisa Glazewski.

You decide to write a brief summary about each employee and then make your decision.

John Chow

John Chow is a BBA graduate from a Hong Kong university. His Cantonese and English are excellent. He is 41 years old and married with three school-age children. John has worked for you for four years. He is very dependable, and can always be relied upon to do things the way you want. He is always polite and never loses his temper or disagrees with you. In fact, John seems to have developed the ability to anticipate your wishes. He is extremely hardworking, and is always first in the office in the morning and last to leave at night. John is well liked by senior management, who regard him as a loyal, competent and very diligent employee who can be trusted to do the right thing. John's office is always immaculate. His subordinates are all reliable, competent and hardworking. John emphasises harmony in his dealings with others, even if this sometimes means that unfairness is the result. John's training and development programs are well organised and consistently receive good ratings. Your only concern is that John, while competent, never initiates any major changes or innovations, preferring to implement your ideas in accordance with your wishes. You know that Robert and many of the Chinese senior managers would be very comfortable with the appointment of John. You worry, however, that some senior managers in head office may see John as too conservative and 'too Chinese' for the job.

Anita Law

Anita is 31 and unmarried and she has worked for you for three years. Educated in the United States, she has excellent Cantonese and English language skills. Anita is highly motivated but, unlike John, works in fits and starts. She is very goal-oriented and consistently outperforms. The problem is that Anita does not follow procedures and is very outspoken.

She openly challenges others and does not tolerate fools easily. Whenever there is a difficult job to be done, Anita is the person you turn to. She is liked by her subordinates and respected for her ability by her colleagues. Anita, however, has some critics. Robert, for example, regards Anita as too direct, too aggressive and too Americanised and in the past he has attempted to lower her performance ratings and reduce her bonus payments. However, he never objects when you recommend Anita for a demanding assignment (especially if it involves head office). Head office managers (including Patrick) frequently make direct contact with Anita seeking her advice and assistance (even in areas outside her direct responsibility). Robert says that Anita's high standing with head office is because of her good looks, Western attitudes and fluent English. He claims that Anita's interpersonal skills are not appropriate for a Chinese woman and that she upsets the harmony of the office.

Henry Cheung

Henry Cheung is 33 and unmarried. He has worked for you for just over two years. Henry is always immaculately and expensively dressed. He is completely at ease with both Chinese and foreigners. Educated in Hong Kong and London, Henry regards himself as a citizen of the world. Henry is smooth, sophisticated and persuasive. He has no hesitation assuming responsibility and impresses others as being extremely optimistic, self-confident and competent. Henry participates in all company social functions and has a wide range of contacts both within and outside the company. Everyone knows Henry and most enjoy his company, although some Hong Kong employees complain that he is a 'shoe polisher' who spends too much time ingratiating himself with senior management. You too feel that while Henry strives to impress others as being warm and friendly, he is really a very skilled manipulator. Head office visitors love Henry and actively socialise with him. Patrick, for example, always plays tennis with Henry when in Hong Kong. While Henry's performance is extremely good, you sense that he is the most cunning and calculating of your subordinates. He always tests the water and will not commit to a position if he perceives that someone powerful is opposed. You have the uneasy feeling that Henry always acts in the way that best serves his own interests. Nevertheless, you have to admit that Henry is extremely intelligent, very hardworking and politically very well connected.

Discussion questions

1. Which candidate would you select? Why?
2. How would you explain to the other two candidates why they did not get the job?

---

practical exercises

What would you do in the following situations if you were the HR Manager?

(a) A senior executive of your company has been arrested by the Public Security Bureau in Guangzhou. He is charged with having 'a romantic liaison' with a local woman in his hotel.

(b) Your manufacturing plant in Malaysia is on strike because several of the female assembly-line workers insist on wearing traditional Islamic clothing, including the Jilbab veil. The production manager says that not only is it unsafe, but company policy requires employees to wear company-provided uniforms when in the factory.

(c) The Managing Director of your Indonesian manufacturing plant is an extremely competent and well-connected manager. You are made aware that he takes a 'payment' from every new employee joining your company.

(d) You have just informed an employee that he is to be the new President of your South Korean subsidiary. He tells you that he is HIV positive and that he suspects that the South Korean government prohibits the entry of all HIV-infected people.

(e) The 17-year-old daughter of your Pacific Area Marketing Director has been arrested by the Thai police for attempted drug smuggling.

(f) The wife of your Hong Kong based Asia–Pacific Marketing Director rings you in Sydney and tells you that her husband is having an affair with his secretary. She demands that the secretary be fired.

(g) The President of your Singapore operations informs you that her husband has been diagnosed as HIV positive. She says he has been requested to leave by the Singapore government.

(h) Your largest contract manufacturer in Indonesia has been charged by an internationally renowned human rights activist with condoning sexual harassment, physical beatings, forced overtime and underpayment in his factories.

(i) Your plant in Shanghai is undergoing restructuring. The families of the fired workers have staged a sit-in and are holding all the senior managers (including two expatriates) as hostages.

(j) The son of your local manager in the Philippines has been kidnapped. The manager is a Chinese Filipino and comes from a wealthy family.

(k) The distributor of your premier brand of beer in Cambodia employs 'beer girls' to promote sales. You read in a newspaper report that the girls supplement their US$50 per month salary by sometimes going home with customers.

(l) Your sales manager in Indonesia is involved in a fatal 'hit and run' accident. The identity of the driver and the car remain undetected by police.

(m) The expatriate manager in charge of sales and marketing in your Manila office is having an affair with one of her subordinates.

(n) Your Vice-President of Business Development has been charged with assaulting a Hong Kong taxi driver who he claimed had cheated him.

(o) After a company-sponsored party celebrating the company's record sales performance, the Sales and Marketing Manager is arrested by the Hong Kong Police for being drunk and disorderly.

(p) Your Mine Manager at a remote site in Indonesia has received a 'request' from the local army commander that his soldiers provide 'security services' for the mine. You are aware that other foreign companies have experienced 'incidents' after refusing such requests.

(q) Tom Smith, your Vice-President of Marketing located in Seoul, announces that he is going to marry his maid.

(r) The wife of your most senior expatriate in Thailand has committed suicide. It is rumoured that the manager was having an affair with his Thai secretary.

(s) Your joint venture partner in a new hotel development in Shanghai demands that his mistress be appointed General Manager.

suggested readings

Beardwell, I. and Holden, L., *Human Resource Management*, 3rd edn, Financial Times/Prentice Hall, London, 2001, chs 15, 16, 17.

Bennett, M. and Bell, A., *Leadership and Talent in Asia*, John Wiley & Sons, Singapore, 2004.

CCH, *Australian Master Human Resources Guide*, CCH, Sydney, 2003, chs 7, 41, 42.

De Cieri, H. and Kramar, R., *Human Resource Management in Australia*, McGraw-Hill, Sydney, ch. 14.

Dowling, P. J., Welch, D. E. and Schuler, R. S., *International Human Resource Management*, 3rd edn, Southwestern, Cincinnati, 1999, chs 1, 2, 4, 5, 8, 9.

Fisher, C. D., Schoenfeldt, L. F. and Shaw, J. B., *Human Resource Management*, 5th edn, Houghton Mifflin, Boston, 2003, ch. 17.

Ivancevich, J. M. *Human Resource Management*, 8th edn, McGraw-Hill, Boston, 2001, ch. 4.

Ivancevich, J. M., and Lee, S. H., *Human Resource Management in Asia*, McGraw-Hill, Singapore, 2002, ch. 15.

Mondy, R. W., Noe, R. M. and Premeaux, S. R., *Human Resource Management*, 8th edn, Prentice Hall, Upper Saddle River, NJ, 2002, ch. 17.

Nankervis, A. R., Compton, R. L. and Baird, M., *Strategic Human Resource Management*, 4th edn, Nelson, Melbourne, 2002, ch. 17.

online references

members.ozemail.com.au/~gbs001/
www.chinasafety.gov.cn
www.chrm.gov.cn
www.globalinterface.com.au
www.ihrm.org
www.ilo.org
www.mcb.co.uk/hr
www.mop.gov.cn

www.shrm.org.hrmagazine
www.shrm.org/international
www.shrmglobal.org
www.stats.gov.cn
www.t-bird.edu
www.webofculture.com
www.workforceonline.com
www.worldbiz.com/australia.html

end notes

1. A. Nankervis and R. Grainger, 'Foreign affairs', *HR Monthly*, June 2001, p. 42.

2. D. E. Welch and L. S. Welch, 'Pre-expatriation, the role of HR factors in the early stages of internationalization', *International Journal of Human Resource Management*, vol. 8, no. 4, 1997, pp. 402–13.

3. B. W. Stening and E. V. Ngan, 'The cultural context of human resource management in East Asia', *Asia Pacific Journal of Human Resources*, vol. 35, no. 2, 1997, pp. 3–15.

4. J. Walker, 'Sitting ducks', *Shares*, November 2000, p. 32.

5. C. D. Fisher, L. F. Schoenfeldt and J. B. Shaw, *Human Resource Management*, 4th edn, Houghton Mifflin, Boston, 1999, p. 806.

6. W. F. Cascio, 'International human resource management issues for the 1990s', *Asia Pacific Journal of Human Resources*, vol. 30, no. 4, 1992, p. 2.

7. 'Whirlpool Corporation includes global employees in global vision', *CCH Ideas and Trends — Human Resource Management*, no. 330, 29 March 1995, p. 58.

8. Quoted in D. James, 'Globalisation', *Business Review Weekly*, 24 September 1999, p. 75.

9. P. V. Morgan, 'International HRM: fact or fiction?', *Personnel Administrator*, September, 1986, p. 45.

10. V. Pucik, 'The international management of human resources', in C. Fombrun, N. M. Tichy and M. A. Deranna (eds), *Strategic Human Resources Management*, John Wiley & Sons, New York, 1984, pp. 403, 404.

11. B. Fulford, 'Dependence on foreign units rises', *South China Morning Post — Business*, 10 July 1998, p. 8; and J. Legewie, 'Too Japanese to succeed in China', *Far Eastern Economic Review*, 7 December 2000, p. 37.

12. This section is based on A. J. Walker, 'The global HR model', *HR Focus*, April 1998, pp. S9–S10.

13. A. So, 'Driver buys his boss a $1.8 m number plate', *Sunday Morning Post*, 11 February 2001, p. 2.

14. M. Chen, *Asian Management Systems*, Routledge, London, 1995, p. 219.

15. P. C. S. Chan, 'A $35 billion expense account', *Asia Inc.*, July 1999, p. 56.

16. A. M. Whitehill, *Japanese Management*, Routledge, London, 1992, p. 223.

17. M. Chen, op. cit., p. 219.

18. C. Blackman, *Negotiating China*, Allen & Unwin, Sydney, 1997, p. 17; and R. Mead, *International Management*, Blackwell, Oxford, 1995, p. 291.

19. C. Blackman, op. cit., p. 18.

20. C. Blackman, op. cit., p. 19.

21. C. Blackman, op. cit., p. 19.

22. See S. Bradford, 'Press group acted against its foes: editor', *South China Morning Post*, 27 February 2001, p. 7; and P. Y. Mo, 'Editor fired over boss's loss of face, court told', *South China Morning Post*, 21 February 2001, p. 2.

23. D. Fang, 'For mainland cadres, truth remains elusive', *South China Morning Post*, 3 July 2003, p. A7. Also see D. Ahlstrom, M. N. Young and A. Nair, 'Deceptive managerial practices in China: strategies for foreign firms', *Business Horizons*, vol. 45, no. 6, 2002, pp. 49–59.

24. D. McNeill, 'The untouchables', *South China Morning Post*, 27 August 2003, p. C5, and J. Ryall, 'Japanese gangsters cash in on taxpayers', *South China Morning Post*, 26 July 2003, p. A8.

25. Y. Luo, 'Corruption and organization in Asian management systems', *Asia Pacific Journal of Management*, vol. 19, no. 2/3, 2002, p. 405.

26. Sant Sarutanond, quoted in S. Mydans, 'Thai sex king sees staid new world', *International Herald Tribune*, 31 July 2003, p. 5.

27. R. Robles, 'Officials face graft change in Philippines', *South China Morning Post*, 22 July 2003, p. A8.

28. T. Dodd, 'Mystery creditors, law of the jungle claims ANZ', *Australian Financial Review*, 21 February 2001, p. 9; and V. England, 'Rotten to the core', *Sunday Morning Post*, 1 August 1999, p. 9.

29. K. Loveard, 'A love affair sours', *Asia Inc.*, June 2002, pp. 33–6.

30. A. Cornell, 'Graft: synonym for government in Japan', *Australian Financial Review*, 29 January 2001, p. 8; and B. Fulford, 'Japan's dirty secrets', *Forbes Global*, 30 October 2000, pp. 24–9.

31. C. M. Dwyer, 'China tops the world as the worst place to do business', *Australian Financial Review*, 14 February 2001, p. 11; and Asia News Network, 'Vajpayee calls graft India's biggest enemy', *The Straits Times*, 18 April 2001, p. 14.

32. Quoted in K. Towers, 'Paying bribes is a dangerous game', *Australian Financial Review — Special Report*, 8 June 2000, p. 53.

33. Cited in P. Digh, 'Shades of gray', *Human Resources*, vol. 2, no. 4, 1997, p. 8.

34. P. Digh, op. cit., p. 8.

35. This section is based on C. Lo, 'An ethical framework for business behaviour', *Ethics and Society Newsletter*, May 1997, pp. 11–14.

36. C. A. Bartlett and S. Ghoshal, *Transnational Management*, 3rd edn, McGraw-Hill, Boston, 2000, p. 602.

37. H. W. Lane and J. J. DiStefano, *International Management Behavior*, 2nd edn, PWS-Kent, Boston, 1992, pp. 215–16.

38. F. Fukuyama, *Trust*, The Free Press, New York, 1995, p. 153.

39. F. Fukuyama, op. cit., p. 77.

40. F. Fukuyama, op. cit., p. 76.

41. R. Whittey, *Business Systems in East Asia*, Sage, London, 1992, p. 60.

42. F. Fukuyama, op. cit., chs 8, 9.

43. Political analyst Seoh Chiang Nee, quoted in Reuters, 'Media companies weigh options as losses continue', *South China Morning Post*, 6 December 2003, p. B14.

44. M. K. Miah, M. Wakabayashi and N. Takahashi, 'Cross cultural comparisons of HRM styles: based on Japanese companies, Japanese subsidiaries in Bangladesh and Bangladesh companies', *Global Business Review*, vol. 4, no. 1, 2003, pp. 77–98.

45. R. M. Hodgetts and F. Luthans, *International Management*, 4th edn, McGraw-Hill, Boston, 2000, p. 410.

46. C. J. Zhu and P. J. Dowling, 'Managing people during economic transition: the development of HR practices in China', *Asia Pacific Journal of Human Resources*, vol. 38, no. 2, 2000, p. 101.

47. R. I. Westwood (ed.), *Organizational Behavior: Southeast Asian Perspectives*, Longman, Hong Kong, 1992, p. 126.

48. W. Arnold, 'Internal Korean Air study details safety challenges', *Asian Wall Street Journal*, 8 April 1999, pp. 1–2.

49. N. K. Lau, 'Hong Kong's worst enemy? Its superiority complex', *South China Morning Post*, 23 January 2003, p. 15.

50. M. Tayeb, 'Conducting research across cultures: overcoming drawbacks and obstacles', *International Journal of Cross Cultural Management*, vol. 1, no. 1, 2001, p. 104.

51. M. H. Tayeb, *The Management of a Multicultural Workforce*, John Wiley & Sons, Chichester, 1996, p. 181.

52. J. Grant, 'Communist parents plague job seekers', *South China Morning Post*, 29 September 1997, p. 14.

53. J. Kahn, 'A migrant worker seeking salvation, finds only hardship', *International Herald Tribune*, 27 August 2003, p. 2.

54. Associated Press, 'Migrant workers fired over protest', *South China Morning Post*, 25 June 2003, p. A9.

55. T. Mitchell, '$91 000 payout to humiliated factory workers', *South China Morning Post*, 24 August 2002, p. 7.

56. R. M. Hodgetts and F. Luthans, op. cit., p. 76.

57. H. W. French, 'Outsiders waiting to be insiders', *International Herald Tribune*, 24 July 2003, pp. 1, 6; and B. Pearson, 'Corporate Japan's dirty little secret', *Australian Financial Review*, 28 June 2004, p. 11.

58. See W. Horsley and R. Buckley, *Nippon New Superpower*, BBC Books, London, 1990, pp. 234–5; and P. Tasker, *Inside Japan*, Sidgwick & Jackson, London, 1987, pp. 24–5.

59. R. M. Hodgetts and F. Luthans, op. cit., pp. 76–7.

60. C. H. Tan and D. Torrington, *Human Resource Management for Southeast Asia and Hong Kong*, 2nd edn, Prentice Hall, Singapore, 1998, p. 282.

61. Y. Lu and I. Bjorkman, 'Human resource management in international joint ventures in China', *Journal of General Management*, vol. 23, no. 4, 1998, p. 69.

62. This section is largely based on A. M. Whitehill, op. cit., pp. 201–11; R. Whitley, *Business Systems in East Asia*, Sage, London, 1992, pp. 39–40; T. Jackson (ed.), *Cross Cultural Management*, Butterworth-Heinemann, Oxford, 1995, p. 157; and A. W. Harzing and J. Van Ruysseveldt (eds), *International Human Resource Management*, Sage, London, 1995, pp. 151–2.

63. P. S. Kirkbride and S. F. Y. Tang, 'Personnel management in Hong Kong: a review of current issues', *Asia Pacific Human Resource Management*, vol. 27, no. 2, 1989, pp. 45–57.

64. T. Jackson, 1995, op. cit., pp. 358–61; and P. J. Dowling, R. S. Schuler and D. E. Welch, *International Dimensions of Human Resource Management*, 2nd edn, Wordsworth, Belmont, CA, 1994, ch. 4.

65. H. Holley, 'Shanghai surprise — it's no western city', *South China Morning Post — Business*, 25 September 2000, p. 6.

66. N. Spencer and B. Chiu, 'Management and learning styles in a Hong Kong organization', *Asia Pacific Journal of Human Resources*, vol. 34, no. 2, 1996, pp. 115–16.

67. R. Saner and L. Yiu, 'European and Asian resistance to the use of the American case method in management training: possible cultural and systemic incongruences', *International Journal of Human Resource Management*, vol. 5, no. 4, 1994, pp. 953–76.

68. W. C. Byham, *Shogun Management*, Harper Business, New York, 1993, pp. 191–3.

69. See L. A. Peterson, 'International HRD: what we know and don't know', *Human Resource Development Quarterly*, vol. 8, no. 1, 1997, pp. 63–79.

70. J. J. Martocchio, *Strategic Compensation*, Prentice Hall, Upper Saddle River, NJ, 1998, pp. 30–3.

71. R. Hodgetts, 'A conversation with Donald F. Hastings of the Lincoln Electric Company', *Organizational Dynamics*, vol. 25, no. 3, 1997, p. 69; and T. Jackson, 'The management of people across cultures: valuing people differently', *Human Resource Management*, vol. 41, no. 4, 2002, p. 472.

72. C. Y. Chow, 'Workers arrested for setting up illegal union', *South China Morning Post*, 8 December 2003, p. A9.

73. S. Shu, 'Nike factory report cites violations', *Asian Wall Street Journal*, 22 February 2001, pp. 1, 4.

74. J. Slater, 'The inspector calls', *Far Eastern Economic Review*, 6 July 2000, p. 32.

75. R. Verburg, 'Developing HRM in foreign–Chinese joint ventures', *European Management Journal*, vol. 14, no. 5, 1996, p. 519.

76. C. J. Zhu and P. J. Dowling, op. cit., pp. 90–3.

77. C. K. S. Au, 'Cultural aspects of HRM in China', *HK Staff*, 5 March 1992, p. 6; and R. Verburg, op. cit., p. 520.

78. S. Sze, 'Mainland in need of business leadership', *South China Morning Post — Classified*, 6 December 2003, p. 14.

79. P. M. Wright, H. Mitsuhashi and R. S. K. Chua, 'HRM in multinationals' operations in China: building human capital and organizational capability', *Asia Pacific Journal of Human Resources*, vol. 36, no. 2, 1998, pp. 10–11.

80. D. Ahlstrom, M. N. Young and A. Nair, op. cit., p. 52.

81. S. Zhao, 'Human resource management in China', *Asia Pacific Journal of Human Resources*, vol. 32, no. 2, 1994, p. 6.

82. S. Zhao, op. cit., p. 6.

83. N. Lindholm, 'Performance management in MNC subsidiaries in China: a study of host country managers and professionals', *Asia Pacific Journal of Human Resources*, vol. 37, no. 3, 1999, pp. 18–35.

84. M. Born, 'Shortening the odds in the China recruitment lottery', *China Staff*, June 1996, pp. 6–7.

85. R. A. Swaak, 'The role of human resources in China', *Compensation and Benefits Review*, vol. 27, no. 5, 1995, p. 46.

86. C. J. Zhu and P. J. Dowling, op. cit., pp. 95–7.

87. J. Selmer, 'Human resource management in Asia Pacific', in M. Warner (ed.), *Management in Asia*, Thomson Learning, Padstow, Cornwall, 2000, pp. 104–8.

88. S. Curtain, 'Why the "salaryman" generation has lost the will to live', *South China Morning Post*, 20 February 2003, p. 16.

89. N. Onishi, 'In Japanese workplaces, titles take a cut', *International Herald Tribune*, 31 October 2003, pp. 1, 10.

90. N. Dalton and J. Benson, 'Innovation and changes in Japanese human resource management', *Asia Pacific Journal of Human Resources*, vol. 40, no. 3, 2002, pp. 345–62.

91. This case is partly based on material appearing in R. Behar, 'Talk about tough competition', *Fortune*, 15 January 1996, pp. 62–71.

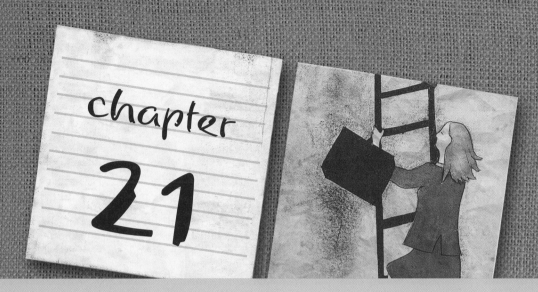

chapter 21

managing international assignments

Learning objectives

When you have finished studying this chapter, you should be able to:

- Understand the key factors in selecting a person for an international assignment
- Explain the major adjustment difficulties encountered by expatriate managers and their families
- Understand the importance of expatriate orientation and the meaning of culture shock
- Appreciate the importance of career planning and repatriation
- Explain the basic components of an expatriate compensation and benefits program.

'There is a commonly held, but erroneous view, that expatriation to a foreign culture is more difficult than repatriation to the home culture.'[1]

L. Elphinstone, psychologist

Introduction

This is the decade of the global enterprise. Increasingly, organisations that traditionally focused on domestic markets are looking internationally. Executives also are becoming more international. The list of Australian Chairmen and CEOs of US companies includes Charlie Bell (McDonald's) Geoff Bible (Philip Morris), Douglas Daft (Coca-Cola), Rod Eddington (British Airways) and James Wolfensohn (The World Bank).[2] An organisation with a head office in Australia and its major operations overseas is no longer unique. Such firms cannot claim to be distinctively Australian and it is not easy to define what is an Australian product or service. Brambles and Burns Philp, for example, both generate more than half their earnings outside of Australia.[3] The conventional bonds between local multinational organisations and Australia are fast disappearing. Corporate decisions are increasingly being driven by the dictates of global competition, not national allegiance. 'The logic of the global manager is clear: to undertake activities anywhere around the world that will maximize the performance of the company, enlarge its market share and boost the price of its stock.'[4] Says the CEO of one consulting firm: 'Our clients demand people who are mobile and internationally literate. So do we.'[5]

ABB (Asea Brown Bovery), the product of a merger between Sweden's Asea, Switzerland's Brown Bovery and the US Combustion Engineering Inc., is an example of this new global organisation. Generating more than US$35 billion in annual revenue with 220 000 employees in more than 140 countries, ABB has its head office in Zurich, has an executive committee of Swedes, Swiss, Germans and Americans, conducts business in English and keeps account books in US dollars. Says its former President and CEO: 'ABB is a company with no geographical center, no national axe to grind. We are a federation of national companies with a global coordination center.'[6]

Recruitment

Local nationals Citizens of the host country in which the business is located; for example, a Singaporean working for an Australian company in Singapore.

Expatriate Someone who lives and works in a foreign country.

Third-country national A citizen of a country differing from the home or host country; for example, a Singaporean working for an Australian company in Hong Kong.

Home-country national An expatriate who is a citizen of the country where a multinational company is headquartered; for example, an American working in Singapore for a company with its headquarters in the United States.

Host-country national A local employee of the foreign location working for a multinational; for example, a Singaporean working in Singapore for a US multinational.

This trend requires recruitment of people who can manage global organisations. It cannot be overemphasised how crucial qualified managers are to international business success.[7] Aryee, for example, argues that 'international experience should be considered a prerequisite for advancement into the top management ranks of globalizing firms'.[8] Consequently, staffing foreign operations has become a key HRM responsibility. Typically, most positions are filled by **local nationals** because:

- It is usually cheaper to hire nationals of the host country than to send in expatriate staff from the home country. (An **expatriate** is someone who lives and works away from their own country — for example, an Australian working in Singapore for a US multinational. The Australian in this case is called a **third-country national**. A **home-country national** is an expatriate who is a citizen of the country where the multinational company is headquartered — for example, an American working in Singapore for a US multinational. A **host-country national** is a local employee of the foreign location working for the multinational — for example, a Singaporean working in Singapore for a US multinational.)
- There are often restrictions or even total prohibitions on the hiring of home-country personnel in the host location.
- Local personnel are more familiar with the local business environment.

Nevertheless, the use of expatriate managers in key management roles is still common. Expatriates are usually employed when:

- a new venture is being established in a foreign location
- the company sees an international assignment as essential to the development of high-flying executives
- local personnel do not have the required managerial or technological expertise, or both
- the parent company in the home country wants to exercise a high degree of centralised control

- the business project or investment is short term
- the company is concerned with legally protecting highly specialised technical know-how
- local nationals resist transfer outside their home country and are perceived as lacking mobility
- the appointment of local nationals may create racial, religious, social and/or political problems
- the parent company has a strategic need to be seen as a foreign enterprise
- local employees are extremely nationalistic and easily subject to government control and influence
- head office management is more confident and relaxed with someone they know well.

Expatriate selection

Expatriate selection is much more difficult than domestic selection. Expatriates confront many new challenges both in the workplace and the community — 'culture shock differences in work-related norms, isolation, homesickness, differences in health care, housing, schooling, cuisine, language, customs, sex roles and cost of living, to name but a few'.[9] Organisations involved in international HR selection often do not recognise these issues. In fact, many firms use selection procedures that vary little from those employed in domestic selection.[10] Organisations still predominantly use employee technical competence and past job performance as the key selection criteria.[11] Such an approach assumes that a successful manager in Sydney will also be successful in Jakarta.[12] Managers ignore or marginalise human relations skills, understanding of the host-country culture, ability to adapt, family issues and language fluency.[13] Failure of assignment in many cases, however, is the result of a lack of personal adjustment rather than a lack of technical skills.[14] Furthermore, research shows that in many companies expatriate selection is often haphazard and irrational.[15]

'A set of competencies and skills which lead to success in a home country', says Richard Phelps, former Director, Compensation and Human Resource Practice, Towers Perrin Hong Kong, 'does not always equate to success in a foreign setting. Organizations need to understand that in choosing expatriates, they should take into account differences in the business, social and cultural environment in the specific country and the impact on the potential expatriate, spouse and dependants. High performers at home can easily become poor performers abroad and the negative consequences are highly geared for both employer and employee.'[16] In short, the cost of transferring the wrong person overseas is enormous.[17] *China Daily*, for example, experienced the following HR problems in an 18-month period:
- a British copy editor quit after his wife committed suicide
- a US editor had to be repatriated for refusing to sign China's standard work contract
- a New Zealand copy editor had to be shipped home after repeatedly showing up for work drunk, ranting at the staff and smashing unopened beer bottles against the walls of the company-provided apartment.[18]

'It's a dirty secret among the human resources community as to the number of times executives fail to fulfil the terms of their contracts', says a vice-president of an international executive search firm based in Hong Kong. 'The cost it implies in terms of dispensing cash and losing clients is enormous.'[19] According to Lipper, 'The stress an overseas move places on spouses and children will ultimately affect the worker, no matter how dedicated he or she is to the company'.[20]

Stone's study found that both local managers and expatriate managers perceive the essential selection criteria as the expatriate's ability to adapt and the adaptability of the partner and family.[21] Respondents in the survey were also unanimous in their rankings of the least important criteria: academic qualifications, knowledge of the language of the host country and understanding of the home-country culture. Baruch also argues that a genuine appreciation of the host-country culture and customs is more important than knowing the local language.[22] Brewster's study of European multinationals, in contrast, found that respondents gave high ratings to education and language skills, with Dutch and French multinationals being particularly concerned with language.[23] Filipino, Indonesian and Thai managers in Stone's survey rated 'human factors' higher than did Hong Kong and Singaporean Chinese managers, who emphasised technical skills. Franke and Nicholson similarly found that North Americans placed a higher value on selection criteria related to partner support, gender equality and dual career issues than did their Asian counterparts.[24] This suggests that the perception of the importance of various selection criteria may be affected by cultural values.

Stone's findings also indicate that Australian women managers rate education as a more important selection criterion than do their male counterparts, suggesting that gender as well as culture may affect expatriate selection decisions. Overall, the research into expatriate selection shows that certain personal attributes, behaviours, skills and experiences are desirable if an expatriate manager is to be successful. These include technical skills, effective communication and listening skills, host-country language skills, stress tolerance, empathy and flexibility in dealing with foreign cultures, political skills, extensive foreign travel and previous international experience.[25] Finally, definite danger signs include alcohol or drug dependency, marital discord, racist attitudes, ethnocentrism and serious health problems. Countries such as Brunei, China, South Korea and Singapore require that all expatriates be AIDS-free and HIV-free, and in Singapore, any foreigner who tests HIV positive is asked to leave.[26]

Selection of female expatriates

Expatriate experience is becoming increasingly important for advancement as organisations expand internationally.[27] Women who aspire to higher management must pursue international assignments.[28] Unfortunately, women are seldom given the chance to secure an expatriate posting and still suffer from unsystematic selection procedures and negative assumptions regarding their suitability.[29] A recent UK survey, for example, found that international HR managers believe that female candidates are not qualified, lack experience, have family obligations and dual career obstacles, and would not be acceptable to host-country employees and customers.[30] Although women account for some 30 per cent of students in MBA programs in the United States, they make up only 14 per cent of those chosen by corporate America for an overseas assignment. A major reason for this appears to be that male bosses overestimate the problems the female executive will face and consequently believe that they will be less effective.[31] Furthermore, expatriate women tend to be young, working in junior positions and found in non-line functions such as finance, HRM and legal.[32] Research by Forster suggests that women who are single or in 'traditional' marriages have a better chance of being selected for an international assignment.[33] Successful female expatriates recommend that women make sure that their managers know they are interested in working overseas, demonstrate their ability to be culturally flexible and ensure that they have family support. The same advice applies to men, but because women are assumed to be less mobile than men, they need to be particularly vocal in expressing their interest.[34]

The problems faced by female expatriates in Asia are similar to those faced by men, particularly the culture shock and adjustments to new ways of doing business. What makes it more difficult for women is their lack of acceptance in international management by certain expatriates and locals. Expatriate Mary Chiew, for example, claims that on Asian airlines everything is geared to the male and that there is poor security in many Asian hotels.[35] However, Westwood and Leung argue that gender is something of a non-issue for expatriate women managers in pragmatic Hong Kong. Many surveyed foreign women felt the situation for women managers was better in Hong Kong than in their home country and that 'the worst forms of sexism they encountered came from expatriate, not local males'.[36]

Practitioner speaks

Cross-cultural diversity

Critical to doing business in China is attending a banquet with local Chinese dignitaries held in your honour. Food is a large part of the daily routine for Chinese and they go to a great deal of trouble to present an impressive culinary delight. Attending a banquet of scrumptious local delicacies is a great indulgence for me. However, local Chinese closely note all the peripheral aspects of my behaviour as a consultant. Do I drink alcohol or smoke? What type of conversation do I pursue? Do I behave 'properly' as an imperative of doing business in China? When the senior official insisted that I smoke after a banquet, I did, as it was culturally a sign of friendship. I had abstained from smoking during the banquet, as this would have set a precedent because I was the guest of honour.

Doing business in China 'as an Australian woman' has made me realise that gender differences do not always affect making management decisions and creating mutually beneficial long-term business relationships. My experience of business in China has been a combination of elated success in gaining business and despondency realising that my failures were a lack of understanding of Chinese cultural norms and behaviours. As an Australian woman doing business in China I became aware of the gender difference of being a female, like acceptance and social status. Through research and discussions I modified my behaviour and accepted this as only a difference, not a barrier between cultures. I found this through asking questions to fulfil my curiosity. The answers drew me closer to the processes and introductions to people in China who could help me.

To understand the cross-cultural differences I read widely. I specifically read books like *China for Women* (Spinifex Press), about the history and contemporary life of women in China, *Wild Swans* (by Juan Chang, Flamingo Press) and *The Good Women of China* (by Xinran, Chatto & Windus, 2002). On the Web I found sites that explained cultural idiosyncratic traits like introduction protocols, preferred colours and gifts, and protocols for banquets.

The strengths of being a foreigner/expatriate/woman from Australia doing business in China far outweigh the weaknesses. Avoiding conversations about ethics, religion and gender is wise in many cultures, but don't be surprised if you are asked about your preferences on these matters in China. Chinese listen carefully to responses that Australians would find personal and offensive, but this is part of the relationship-building process in Chinese culture.

Business in China does not always go as expected. Being watched, mimicked, pursued and inspected has led to compromised, hurried, inaccurate or incorrect business decisions.

Understanding the cultural differences is the catalyst to a successful business deal. The best way to bridge the cross-cultural gap is to research the region and, when immersed, apply your research. The process may appear long and sometimes arduous but asking questions and doing research about cultural differences can ease the frustration associated with cross-cultural misunderstanding.

Pamela Jackson

Pamela Jackson was originally employed in a range of senior marketing positions and now acts as a consultant to enterprises in Australia, Singapore and China, providing a portfolio of management services such as leadership and cross-cultural development.

But differences in sex roles can be an added obstacle in some cultures where the Western concept of women in management is virtually nonexistent.[37] One study found that men and women in Japan and China associate success in management with characteristics commonly ascribed to men.[38] This means that women can find it extremely difficult to establish the network of business contacts and relationships so necessary to doing business in Asia. In short, if the assignment is tough for a man, it will be even tougher for a woman.[39] Eddy Ng, Jardine Fleming's Head of HR, comments: 'Someone will ask me, "Eddy should I hire a black, female senior manager to manage the business in Japan?" If they've been exposed, perhaps done a lot of travelling, the answer is "possibly". But if it's a traditional male-dominated Japanese company, you had better think twice.'[40] 'The bottom line is that the culture to which a woman is posted must be accepting of women in the particular business role concerned.'[41]

In contrast, Black and others argue that even in traditionally male-dominated societies such as Japan and South Korea, women perform just as well as men do.[42] There is also evidence to suggest that expatriate women have an advantage over men because of their greater visibility, easier access to top management and more open communications.[43] Nevertheless, it is extremely important that organisations pay sufficient attention to selecting and orienting women expatriates entering the Asian arena.[44] A realistic job preview is therefore essential.

Ability to adapt is the critical factor in the selection of female expatriates, as it is with male expatriates. Adler reports that marital status concerns companies when selecting female expatriates, but this does not rate highly as a selection factor in the results obtained by Stone.[45] Again, the surveyed managers did not perceive adaptability of the partner and family as important in the selection of female expatriates. Possibly this is because female expatriates tend to be single, so the problem is ignored.

An Australian female expatriate claims she is being discriminated against because her male colleagues (Australian and Japanese) exclude her when they go nightclubbing in Tokyo.

NEWSBREAK

It's no expat on the back when overseas

By Catherine Fox

The expat senior executive who spent a night in custody at Heathrow airport because he was still using a tourist visa wasn't happy about the incarceration.

In a significant oversight, he and his employer had failed to have immigration details sorted out before he moved to a job in London, says Bob Gillen, a partner at accountancy firm PricewaterhouseCoopers. And that's not good enough these days as the level of global mobility in the workforce steadily increases.

Even before the outbreak of severe acute respiratory syndrome and the spate of terrorist attacks, there were risks involved in moving employees internationally. Now the risks are even higher and the companies ignoring them are likely to find significant corporate governance dimensions.

'There's a huge debate about corporate governance, but I'm finding it's been focused on remuneration, board performance and independence.

'In the area I work, global mobility — poor management policy is creating risks for companies. A lot of things are done to save money or for expediency, which was common practice five to 10 years ago, but there's a new environment.'

SARS and terrorism are obviously having an effect on the movement of employees overseas and the risks involved. The rising cost of the process is hitting as well, and there are fewer traditional expat assignments these days, partly because of the expense.

'Expatriate assignments are no longer the norm. Now companies say the next stage of your career is in the UK, then maybe France or Germany, but there's no guarantee you'll come back, so then you are on your own. This is the future — global mobility is increasing but in a different manner.'

This change has been driven by cost of expatriate moves, usually calculated to be three to five times the base salary of the employee. On the other hand, simply offering an employee a job overseas does not involve the usual expat package of allowances, trips home and housing costs.

Regardless of the conditions for the move overseas, companies need to look at tax compliance in the countries involved, employment laws, immigration details, the selection, retention and repatriation of candidates, and the duty of care they have to the employee, Gillen says.

'Where does the duty of care start and stop for an employer in a global mobility environment? It's more than just an HR issue, it's a tax issue. Most jurisdictions are not set up for taxing people who are globally mobile . . . most companies don't know the risk they are running each time a return is lodged.'

Some Australian multinationals are reacting to the rising costs and risks of expatriate moves by keeping some executives in Australia but requiring more business travel.

'I'm talking to lots of international organisations about key risk assessments and many have not thought these issues through. They are really shocked. This is the next layer of corporate governance and there's no point having all that debate unless the operational practices support it.'

Companies typically continue to look at the global mobility of workers in cost-related terms, although that should not be the main framework.

'It's always cost, never value or risk. Cost is no longer the critical element, it's risk and value management', he says.

Candidate selection is another critical component of the process, which in the past involved a familiarisation trip and cultural briefings.

Both are now unusual steps because of the cost, yet failures are far more costly.

'We just had a company's expat fail in Singapore. The employee had some real cultural issues, but there was no cultural briefing. They brought him back and sent someone else, but the exercise cost them $315 000 instead of the $2000 to $3000 for a cultural briefing.'

The resignation rate among employees returning home at the end of an assignment can be high within the first two years of their return, Gillen says. Mostly this is due to little planning for the homecoming.

'Poor management when they are away contributes. But when these people are overseas they are in small offices and are quite senior.

'They are away for three years or so and come back and there's no plan for them, sometimes not a job or a desk. Career progression is a big thing. Of course, expat benefits are so good and you come back to a local salary and different lifestyle.'

In the future, according to Gillen, expat assignments are likely to be limited to technical people such as engineers with specific skills.

Globe-hopping will continue within companies, but as a part of career progression rather than a specific term in another country.

That wider spread of employees across the world creates other risks.

'Companies haven't focused on what that means. I asked a company to tell me where all their people were in Asia if there's a terrorist attack and they didn't know', says Gillen. 'But that information should be accessible and the norm.'

Source *Australian Financial Review*, 23 September 2003, p. 59.

Stone's results suggest that physical appearance is unimportant, but Adler indicates that her female respondents 'by Western standards were very good looking'.[46] Consistent with Adler's comment, a US study found that 'beautyism' is a powerful influence on personnel decisions.[47] Similarly, one writer claims that discrimination in employment against unattractive women is persistent, persuasive and most insidious because no one will admit that it exists.[48]

Willingness to accept an expatriate assignment

HR managers are experiencing difficulty finding qualified candidates for international assignments with candidates increasingly reluctant to accept an overseas posting.[49] An

A newly appointed expatriate to the Philippines is mugged and robbed. He requests an immediate transfer back to Australia.

international executive search firm, for example, reported that 40 US executives rejected approaches to become the senior HR manager of a major company based in Singapore.[50] A survey of 70 international organisations similarly found that people sent overseas were often the sole candidate for the position and were not necessarily the most suitable.[51] Surveys consistently suggest that many international assignments are rejected as a result of partner career concerns (most companies still do not provide compensation for partner loss of income).[52] In addition, since 9/11 and SARS companies are facing a tougher time persuading managers to accept international assignments to perceived high-risk locations such as Indonesia, Papua New Guinea and the Philippines.[53]

Other factors challenging a candidate's decision to accept an expatriate assignment include the similarity or dissimilarity of the culture of the host location, healthcare, housing, pollution, schooling, sporting and recreational facilities, family ties, company relocation policies, remoteness from corporate power centres, financial cost, repatriation problems, career goals, partner support and the personality of the candidate.[54] Aryee, Chay and Chen, for example, claim that an extrovert personality is a significant positive predictor of a candidate's willingness to accept an expatriate assignment regardless of the cultural similarity or dissimilarity of the host country.[55] As a result of the reluctance of employees to move internationally, companies are exploring alternatives to long-term assignments such as shorter assignments, greater reliance on local hires, increased business travel and telecommuting, and more use of videoconferencing.[56]

Expatriate failure

Research indicates that the manager's inability to adapt and the partner's inability to adapt are the major cause of expatriate failure.[57] Other major reasons for early departure include poor performance, failure of the family to adjust to the new culture, missing family and friends at home, concerns over safety and healthcare, education problems, the partner's career and inadequate compensation.[58] Organisations may be aware of the importance of such factors but give them little weight in the selection process.[59] Studies consistently show that technical expertise is the prime selection criterion.[60] One seasoned expatriate in the Philippines cynically argues that the typical corporate conversation goes: 'Of course ability to adapt is the most important factor in an overseas posting, but I am sure Bill and his family will be okay. Now let's consider the really important things.'[61] Tung comments that 'given the increasing demand for personnel who can function effectively abroad and the relatively high incidence of failure, there certainly appears to be room for improvement in this area'.[62] Indicators of a failed international assignment include premature ending of the assignment, an employee quitting the organisation soon after repatriation, underperformance, eroding business relationships, lost business opportunities and low morale.[63]

The expatriate

The expatriate with an aggressive or rigid personality or with family problems will probably fail (especially if located in a developing country).[64] The person most likely to succeed will be one who is flexible and open minded, has empathy for the local people, experiences no role conflict and has colleague and family support.[65] A lack of family and organisational support and an inability to adapt to the local culture were among the main reasons for expatriate failure found in a Hong Kong survey of 16 multinational companies.[66]

According to one expert, 'Australians, accustomed to the more direct and pragmatic style of business at home, completely underestimate the degree to which personal qualities are taken into account by Asians in deciding whether to do business.'[67] The acuteness of the problem is demonstrated by a joint Australian–Indonesian government survey, which found that cultural ignorance was the main stumbling block in doing business between the two countries.[68] A proposed Australian–Malaysian joint venture to manufacture light aircraft collapsed because of lack of trust, clashes of business cultures and poor communication.[69]

An Australian expatriate experienced in Asia blames such communication problems on senior managers who make decisions without the necessary cultural knowledge and experience.[70] Finally, a perceived similarity between cultures can lead managers to underestimate the actual differences. Selmer and Shiu, for example, found that a common Chinese cultural heritage aggravated the adjustment problems of Hong Kong managers in mainland China instead of facilitating acclimatisation.[71] Likewise, research on Australian and UK expatriates suggests that the perceived cultural closeness between the two does not eliminate culture risk. As a result, cross-cultural training is critical for all expatriates regardless of the cultural distance between the home and host cultures.[72]

The following Letter to the Editor provides a provocative viewpoint. Do you agree? See 'What's your view?' on page 797.

Letter to the Editor

EEO principles should not apply in expatriate selection

Dear Editor,

Like most managers, I support the application of EEO principles to Australian workplaces. I am concerned, however, that the extension of EEO principles to the selection of managers for overseas locations could place organisations at great risk.

Let's be honest. Some ethnic cultures are hostile at best to the idea of women undertaking particular jobs. Males dominate the senior positions in corporations across the world, and this is especially the case in the Asia–Pacific region. Given that most men are more comfortable dealing and negotiating with other men, it strikes me as foolish that Australian organisations would even consider placing women in critical positions within these cultures — this is only setting them up for the inevitable failure that will follow.

Many organisations also worry, with some justification, that placing women managers in international posts raises ethical and legal concerns. If organisations have a duty of care to their employees, the possibility of women being sexually harassed or assaulted in other countries places this duty in question. The danger of personal harm and the possibility of litigation in the event of harassment or assault may make the selection of women managers a risky proposition for Australian organisations operating offshore.

In any event, most of the female managers that I know appear to be less than enthusiastic about undertaking international assignments. Many older females are immobilised by family commitments, while younger female managers are often loathe to give up their social commitments and relationships.

I also note from the research literature that physical appearance is often a key factor in expatriate selection, and that good looks can 'open doors' for female expatriate employees in the Asian business environment. If we are to move down the EEO path, this 'unspoken' preference for attractive women will have to be removed in some way. Yet the reality of business in the region is that an attractive physical appearance may improve an expatriate's chances of corporate success.

Taken together, these arguments indicate that expatriate selection is a far too culturally complex issue for the use of blunt government legislative instruments such as EEO. Australian corporations should be free to make their own selection decisions on the basis of the specific context and cultural environment in which they operate.

An HR manager with international responsibilities

Source David Poole, University of Western Sydney.

The female partner

Perhaps the greatest weakness in the expatriate selection process is organisations' failure to realise that an overseas assignment is a family venture.[73] Most organisations do not include the family in the selection process, even though research indicates that partner involvement has a positive impact on adjustment.[74] One expatriate wife explained: 'The company treated me as if I were just so much excess baggage, I wasn't asked if I wanted to move overseas, I wasn't given adequate information about life over here. I wasn't screened or counselled about how I might mix in with the local people and even my language training was arranged as a sort of afterthought.'[75] It appears that the family situation in Japanese companies is similarly neglected.[76]

De Cieri, Dowling and Taylor found that the most important predictor of psychological adjustment for Australian expatriate wives was assistance from the organisation.[77] Taylor and Napier similarly found that both men and women adjust better to their environment when their firms help them with cross-cultural training.[78] Research by Aycan showed that 'successful adjustment was a function of not only the expatriate manager's personal characteristics but also of the organizational (both parent and local) support and preparation for expatriation'.[79] A study in Hong Kong, however, showed that expatriate wives were most dissatisfied with the lack of orientation training (over 50 per cent had received none) and inadequate assistance.[80] Davidson and Kinzel similarly found the support offered by Australian firms to the families of expatriates to be inadequate.[81] Anderson also showed that organisational support was primarily related to work matters and did not adequately address the personal aspects of relocation or the personal needs of partners and family.[82]

Research clearly indicates that 'a spouse or family member who is undergoing severe culture shock and/or selecting inappropriate behaviours to deal with the stress of relocating affects the morale and performance of the expatriate manager'.[83] Similarly, it has been shown that a significant and positive relationship exists between partner and expatriate adjustment.[84] An estimated 20–30 per cent of expatriates fail in their assignment, mostly because their wives fail to adjust.[85] Some locations are extremely difficult for wives. Professional women may also be dealing with the fact that their career has come to a halt. Furthermore, 'in most expatriate communities, the prevailing attitude towards women who want to work is negative'.[86] This is aggravated by 'the condescension exhibited by organisations which hire women "as a favour" or "to help them out"'.[87] As a result, wives 'are very cynical of companies regarding the lip service paid to their predicament. They indicate there is little or no recognition or appreciation for their situation'.[88] Comments one expatriate: 'They said they would provide assistance to my wife for a similar job that she had. We got there and they said, "Well, maybe she can teach English".'[89] Consistent with this, in a recent study Anderson reported that organisations give minimal support for partners and little assistance finding work overseas.[90] Employment assistance that companies can give to a partner includes paying fees for job counselling, paying the costs of printing a résumé, providing referrals to other companies, covering the costs of job-hunting trips, placing the partner within the company and providing introductions to executive search firms or job placement agencies.[91]

A wife may also find that she is frequently left alone while her husband travels. In a survey of IBM employees, 25 per cent felt that family problems resulted from business travel.[92] Hong Kong and Singaporean businessmen who travel regularly or relocate to China, for example, have a reputation for acquiring mistresses and new families.[93] In Hong Kong, the second family is a major cause of family break-ups and is an ongoing social problem.[94] Even when the husband is 'in town', he may be out entertaining clients several times a week. Loneliness and culture shock can make life a 'living hell' for many partners. Consequently, some end up feeling totally isolated and useless; withdrawal, extra-marital affairs, alcohol and drug abuse become the way out. One seasoned HR manager commented that 'the wife is the "Achilles heel" of the appointment'.[95]

The male partner

The increasing number of female expatriates has seen the emergence of a new figure — the trailing male partner. The issues associated with dual career relocations are likely to be exacerbated even further in this scenario.[96] Husbands and wives face some formidable challenges living and working overseas.[97] But the trailing male partner often has a more difficult time adjusting to an overseas assignment than does his female counterpart.[98] First, the host location (for example, Singapore) may not recognise a husband as a dependant and therefore refuse to let him stay unless he obtains employment. Second, there is typically no social network or infrastructure established to support a dependent male partner. Third, social interaction with female expatriate partners may be difficult as a result of fear of gossip and lack of common interests. Fourth, the trailing male partner upsets traditional stereotypes and can generate persistent ribbing from other expatriates and locals about being 'a kept man', 'the lady of the house', and so on.[99]

However, before a couple's departure, few organisations provide counselling for men (or for women) on personal adjustment and career and educational opportunities in the host location, despite research showing that career concerns of expatriate partners limit the selection of the best candidate for a position and are the most commonly stated reason for candidates declining an international assignment.[100] 'Consideration must be given not only to the careers of both spouses', say Reynolds and Bennett, 'but also to their life goals, the overseas cultural, economic and cultural environment and the sponsoring organization's resources.'[101] For example, organisations could arrange career and life planning counselling, intercompany networking, job-hunting/fact-finding trips, continuing education tuition assistance, commuter marriage support, short-term assignments and miscellaneous support services. Such services could include special allowances for the trailing partner's professional development, trips to seminars and conferences, childcare expenses and marriage counselling by expatriate family therapists.[102] HR managers who take a proactive approach to female expatriates and their partners will create a competitive edge for their organisation in attracting and retaining superior employees.[103]

Implications for HR managers

HR managers can improve an organisation's international selection processes by:
- helping selection managers to become aware of the core cultural values existing in the host society
- assessing the adaptability of the expatriate and their family
- using orientation programs to facilitate adjustment
- ensuring that technical qualifications are not overemphasised.

A company rejects a qualified applicant for an assignment in Hong Kong because they have six dependent children, which the company says makes the appointment uneconomical. The candidate claims discrimination.

Cross-cultural orientation

Managers selected for an overseas tour of duty typically get little or no preparation. Research shows that organisations commit relatively few resources to **orientation**.[104] One recent survey, for example, found that almost two out of three expatriates were dissatisfied with HR's ability to explain procedures for medical and security emergencies and to help them locate local healthcare services. A similar number also rated coordination between host and home country HR negatively.[105] It is critical for expatriates and their families to understand the culture, history, geography, politics and economics of their destination because proper orientation eases entry into the new society. Black's study of expatriate Japanese managers in the United States found that pre-departure knowledge was significantly and positively related to work success, interaction and general adjustments.[106] Selmer similarly found that expatriates who had received orientation training adjusted more quickly and were more satisfied than those who had not.[107]

Given that most organisations present an international assignment as a significant career opportunity, Derr and Oddou suggest that it is reasonable to assume that organisations provide appropriate support systems. Alas, US research indicates that over 65 per cent of organisations have no orientation training at all and it is estimated that less than half of US families receive any preparation before they leave on an overseas assignment.[108] Australian

Orientation The introduction of the expatriate and their family to the culture, living conditions, etc. of the host country.

survey results appear much better, with 90 per cent of organisations reporting that they provide some form of orientation training for their expatriates.[109]

However, closer examination reveals that much of what qualifies as orientation training among Australian organisations simply consists of 'information packs', which are often outdated, incomplete and irrelevant.[110] Consistent with this, Anderson found that respondents rated organisation-sponsored orientation programs as being less effective than other sources of information accessed by expatriates in preparing for their new assignment.[111] Worse, 50 per cent of the organisations in one survey reported having no orientation at all for the partner.[112] Says one expert: 'There are still a lot of companies that are "hairy chested" macho companies that say "look, we're giving you an airline ticket and a cabcharge docket, what more do you want?".'[113]

To prepare for an international assignment, Copeland and Griggs suggest that the expatriate and their family study the following:

- social and business etiquette
- history and folklore
- current affairs, including relations with the home country
- the culture's values and priorities
- geography, especially the cities
- sources of pride such as artists, musicians, novelists, sports, great achievements of the culture, and including things to see and do
- religion and the role of religion in daily life
- political structure and current players
- practical matters such as transportation, currency, time zones, hours of business, medical facilities, housing and schooling
- the language.[114]

Without this kind of study, people may commit social sins that will make their acceptance difficult or even impossible (a high risk given that Australian managers rate poorly on cross-cultural skills).[115] Thompson points out that 'There are potential disasters in body language and many subtleties in non-verbal communication, such as never showing anger or disdain'.[116] Managers generally understand that language differences can cause major barriers to communication, but they often do not understand that non-verbal barriers can cause even greater problems.[117]

Extreme situations can result in tragedy. *The Economist* cites a case in the Pacific where an oil company's expatriate employees placed young local workers in supervisory positions.[118] Within a week, all the young supervisors had had their throats cut. No one had told the expatriates that age was equated with superior status.

An effective orientation program can give the expatriate and their family an empathy for the host country and its people, promoting understanding. Selmer, for example, recommends some kind of pre-assignment involvement with the foreign operation to clarify expatriate expectations of the work environment.[119] According to a US survey, cultural orientation programs are credited with raising expatriate productivity and increasing the expatriate's satisfaction with the foreign assignment.[120]

Unfortunately, too many organisations do not offer orientation training because:

- top management sees it as unnecessary
- such training is perceived to be ineffective and/or too expensive
- there is insufficient time before the expatriate departs.[121]

Both the expatriate and their partner should also receive a clear explanation of relevant HRM policies. This should cover how compensation and benefits will be paid, what allowances are involved and how they are calculated, when home leave is due and how it should be taken, and who is the returning sponsor. People must understand their entitlements and their obligations. Much anxiety, frustration and antagonism can be avoided by sharing such information.[122]

Figure 21.1 outlines the different stages that expatriates should go through to prepare themselves for an international assignment.

PREPARING FOR AN INTERNATIONAL ASSIGNMENT

Stage I: self-evaluation and general awareness

- Ask yourself: 'Is an international assignment really for me?'
- Find out if your spouse and family are supportive of your decision.
- Collect general information on international job opportunities that are available to you.

Stage II: activities to complete before you are selected for an international assignment

- Choose a general geographic region where you would like to be assigned. Be sure your company has job opportunities in this region.
- Do your technical skills match those required for most of your firm's international assignments? If not, begin refining your technical skills.
- Begin learning the language, customs and etiquette of your chosen region.
- Develop an awareness of the culture and value systems of your chosen region.
- Develop stress management techniques.
- Make your superior aware of your interest in an international assignment.

Stage III: activities to complete after you are selected for the assignment

- Attend any training sessions provided by your company.
- Attend programs at local universities and develop skills not covered by your company's training program.
- Confer with colleagues who have experience in your assigned country.
- Speak with expatriates and foreign nationals of your assigned country.
- Include your spouse in your training program.
- If possible, visit your assigned host country with your spouse before your scheduled departure.

Figure 21.1 Different stages of preparing yourself for an international assignment
Source H. Tu and S. E. Sullivan, 'Preparing yourself for an international assignment', *Business Horizons*, vol. 37, no. 1, 1994, p. 68.

Culture shock

Culture shock The stress produced by the inability to adjust to a different cultural environment.

Most expatriates living overseas experience **culture shock** as the result of stress overload.[123] Culture shock is induced by the removal of familiar cues. Reading street signs or newspapers, catching a bus or making a telephone call can suddenly become nightmarish experiences. People feel lost and threatened.[124] Locals are seen as irrational or stupid, and their institutions are seen as incompetent, backward and corrupt.

Proper orientation can alleviate the negative impact of culture shock. The expatriate family can take positive steps to deal with culture shock problems, rather than suffering. Selmer, for example, found that expatriates in China who interact with the locals are less surprised and frustrated by cultural differences compared to expatriates who are isolated from the host culture by living in compounds. This is because interaction teaches the expatriates how to behave.[125]

Common symptoms of culture shock include requests for a transfer or return home, and indifference or dissatisfaction with every aspect of the host location, the company, the housing, and so on. The home country becomes an ideal, a paradise against which the local situation is compared. The comparison is always negative and the locals are subjected to endless denigration. Given such stress, some expatriates withdraw from all social activities; alcoholism, drug abuse, extra-marital affairs, family break-up and suicide are often the result.[126] The quality of the expatriate's work deteriorates, personal relationships break down and the expatriate becomes a source of frustration and embarrassment to the company.[127]

Career planning and repatriation

It is desirable for every expatriate to have a mentor or sponsor. Such a person can encourage employees to accept overseas assignments, improve the coordination of the transfer and facilitate **repatriation**. It is easy for expatriates to become divorced from the home-country operation, so they need to know that they have a senior manager in the home office looking after their interests and ensuring that they are considered for promotions (and are not forgotten and put into a holding position on repatriation!). The mentor provides a contact point, ensuring that the expatriate is kept up to date with news from home. Corporate isolation is a major concern of most expatriates, along with lack of feedback on performance and inadequate career planning.[128] Selmer, Ebrahimmi and Li found that mainland Chinese expatriates assigned to Hong Kong were given very limited access to corporate development activities, indicating little interest on the part of the Chinese parent organisations in the development of their expatriates' careers.[129] These career-related problems are worsened by the fact that multinational companies rarely have a credible expatriate performance appraisal system.[130]

Returning home can be another major frustration for expatriates. The overseas assignment meant that they were the person on the spot who made the decisions, but back at head office they are part of a large bureaucracy and their decision-making responsibilities are limited.[131] 'Time and again', says Nancy Carter, Director of International Human Resources for KMPG, 'we see people who have thrived on the independence that typically accompanies international assignments return to a more traditional job where they are not challenged to utilize the skills they've developed.'[132] Worse, the expatriate is often placed in a project assignment, waiting for a position to be found or terminated. One study found that almost 80 per cent of expatriates felt that their new job was a demotion.[133] As a result, it is not surprising that an estimated 40 per cent of returning expatriates quit within one year.[134] Given the economic climate, these are valid concerns for expatriates. Expatriates must take responsibility for their own careers because they no longer can assume their employer will take care of them.[135] Expatriates are particularly vulnerable if their organisation has undergone a merger or acquisition during their absence.[136]

Poor career management produces labour turnover and reduced morale in other expatriates. Employees in the home office, for example, quickly conclude that an overseas assignment is the 'kiss of death' and refuse to entertain the idea.[137] Feldman and Thomas found that expatriates' perceptions of international assignments as helping their long-term career plans are significantly and positively related to their overall performance, relationship with host nationals, skill acquisition, intent to remain, job satisfaction and mutual influence. In contrast, expatriates who see less of a relationship between their international assignment and their long-term career plans experience greater psychological stress.[138] As a result, it is critical that expatriate assignments are integrated into career planning, have top management support and are valued within the organisation.[139]

In short, many multinationals need to reassess their policies and improve their treatment of returning expatriates. Expatriates struggle to accept being told that they are out of touch and must be prepared to accept a junior position until they learn the ropes again. One study found that over 90 per cent of returning expatriates believed that their international experience was not valued.[140]

Re-entry stress also affects expatriates and their families, with more than 60 per cent experiencing significant 'reverse culture shock'.[141] Says one consultant, 'If people don't realise what it is going to be like, you are bringing back a time bomb'.[142] Importantly, one study found that more than 60 per cent of expatriates and over 80 per cent of families receive no re-entry orientation.[143] Repatriation problems include financial difficulties, organisational problems, family upsets and work issues.[144] A partner can experience special problems. Having the primary responsibility of helping family members adjust to living back in the home country, the wife often bears the brunt. Furthermore, partners may 'feel intimidated by the thought of re-entry into the world of work' because they have lost touch with their profession and suffered in career terms.[145] The organisation can help by providing counselling and assistance to partners in their efforts to re-enter the job market. Unfortunately, few companies offer such help.[146]

Performance appraisal

Performance appraisal is a matter of serious concern for many expatriates. This is because performance appraisal is often handled badly by their organisations.[147] Companies fail to take into account the added complexities that come with international appraisals. Key issues involving performance expectations, performance measures and who will be responsible for the conduct of the appraisals are left vague or undecided. Worse, some head office managers ignore the international appraisal and do not incorporate it into the career development process. The end result is that expatriates perceive the appraisal process as unfair and a source of never-ending frustration.

To overcome such problems, the HR manager needs to ensure that the following key issues are clarified before the expatriate commences their overseas assignment:
- What are the organisation's performance expectations?
- What criteria and standards will be used to measure performance?
- Who will conduct the evaluation — a local manager, a head office manager, or both?
- What will be the frequency of the appraisals?
- What consideration will be given to local environmental influences? (For example, volatility of foreign exchange rate fluctuations, availability of skilled labour, political instability, corruption, and so on.)
- Is the appraisal positively incorporated into the career development process?
- Are head office managers cognisant of the local business environment?
- Are there any cultural influences that may distort the measurement of the expatriate's performance? (For example, will a local manager have the same understanding of what constitutes good performance as a head office manager? Will a local manager be comfortable giving meaningful feedback to an expatriate?)[148]

Expatriate compensation and benefits

HR managers must be familiar with the fundamentals of international compensation and the special needs and requirements of expatriates. Blindly cloning expatriate policies and practices developed elsewhere is both inappropriate and unprofessional. It can create dissatisfaction and ill will among expatriates and saddle the organisation with 'an exorbitant and unnecessary financial burden'.[149] Research suggests that some organisations, instead of treating international assignments as an important part of corporate strategy and employee development, simply throw money at the problem.[150]

Competitive pressures have caused many firms to shift their focus to cost containment and the promotion of international assignments as a business and career opportunity. However, this emphasis is again being evaluated as managers become increasingly unwilling to accept international assignments that are perceived as dangerous, unhealthy or disruptive. According to one expert, people would rather quit than take an assignment in places such as Colombia, Indonesia, Iraq, Nigeria and Saudi Arabia. Even Singapore is being treated with apprehension by US executives.

As a result, some companies are now dramatically increasing their foreign service, hardship and danger allowances.[151]

Program development

To be effective, an expatriate compensation program must:
- provide an incentive to leave the home country
- maintain a home-country standard of living
- facilitate re-entry into the home country
- provide for the education of children
- help the expatriate family maintain its relationships with family, friends and business associates
- be cost-effective.

Thus, designing and managing the compensation of employees working in a foreign location creates an entirely new set of issues for the HR manager. Many organisations fail to develop clearly defined policies and procedures in this area, resulting in frustration, confusion and unnecessary expense. The extent of the cost is indicated by one survey which found 'that the added cost of filling overseas posts with expatriates can reduce pre-tax profit from international operations by as much as 20 per cent'.[152] Increased competition and the shift to performance pay mean that companies increasingly are being forced to critically examine the expenses associated with expatriate compensation and to ensure that the maximum amount is channelled into performance-linked rather than guaranteed compensation.

Expatriate packages

The additional compensation expatriates require means that they are expensive — as a general rule, they cost two to four times their annual **base pay**. A study of 35 UK-based multinationals revealed that the most common reasons for paying additional premiums were 'climatic conditions, separation from friends and relatives, cultural shock, political instability and economic risks in conditions of unstable currencies'.[153] Such premiums and allowances — especially if they are inflated by cost-of-living adjustments and housing prices — can undermine an organisation's competitiveness.[154] As a result, the need for some of these components in **expatriate packages** has been questioned (leading to reduction, elimination or repackaging in a more cost-effective format).[155] However, terrorism, kidnappings and candidate fears regarding personal and family health and safety are causing companies to reconsider this emphasis on cost reduction and it appears that firms are again becoming more willing to increase expatriate packages (especially for perceived dangerous locations).[156]

Foreign service premium

Foreign service premium is paid as compensation for being located outside of the home country. Regardless of what people in Australia believe about places such as New York, Paris and Singapore, they are not home; compensation for living outside of Australia and away from family and friends is justified. This allowance is usually paid tax-free to the expatriate and is calculated as a percentage (usually 10–15 per cent) of base pay. Some companies have now replaced the foreign service premium with a mobility allowance, which is paid as a two-part lump sum at the beginning and end of the assignment.[157]

Hardship or site allowance

Hardship allowance is either determined as a percentage of base pay (0–35 per cent) or paid as a flat amount. The most common practice is to use the percentage approach. The allowance is paid to compensate for hardship resulting from physical isolation, cultural and language differences, extremes of climate, political instability, health and security fears, inadequate housing, education, medical assistance and shopping, and other inconveniences.

Base pay Standard pay that an employee receives for doing a job. It is used as the basis for calculating other allowances and benefits.

Expatriate packages Total compensation and benefits given to personnel on a foreign assignment. Includes base pay, foreign service premium, hardship allowance, housing assistance, education allowance, relocation allowance and other special allowances and benefits associated with a foreign assignment.

Foreign service premium Paid to the expatriate as compensation for being located outside of their home country.

Hardship allowance Paid to compensate the expatriate for hardship resulting from physical isolation, cultural and language differences, extremes of climate, political instability, health concerns, security worries and other inconveniences.

Cost-of-living allowance

'This is the most debatable item in the make-up of expatriate pay. It is also the one that costs employers the most money, in administration as well as in direct payment to the expatriates.'[158] The **cost-of-living allowance (COLA)** has two prime aims:
- to protect the expatriate's standard of living against cost-of-living differences between the host country and the home country
- to offer some protection against exchange rate fluctuations.

The COLA, like other premiums, is being subjected to close management scrutiny. As a result, changes have appeared in the way that companies calculate the COLA. For example, some companies now use an international basket of goods for all expatriates, regardless of their country of origin (instead of a special COLA based on the assignee's home country). Other modifications include the reduced weighting or elimination of certain items in the basket of goods used to calculate the COLA indexes (for example, luxury items such as alcohol and cigarettes). Such changes reduce the COLA, freeing up funds for increased incentive rewards.[159]

Taxation

Expatriates may not be subject to Australian tax when working overseas, so they can experience a tax break in locations such as Hong Kong. However, if they are assigned to high-tax countries such as India, the resulting tax burden can be disastrous. One solution is for expatriates to be taxed at the standard Australian rate as if they were still living in Australia and for the organisation to pay all local taxes. This has some advantages. It means that the tax liability is known and understood. It also maintains equity between personnel in the home office and expatriates. This approach is called **tax equalisation**.

Another approach is to let expatriates pay local taxes and to 'tax protect' them: the expatriate is not reimbursed unless the foreign taxes exceed those theoretically payable in Australia. **Tax protection** has advantages for expatriates assigned to low-tax countries because they experience a tax windfall, but it can produce ill feeling among Australian-based personnel and expatriates located in high-tax countries. Furthermore, labour mobility can be negatively affected when employees seek to be assigned to low-tax countries and refuse assignments in high-tax countries.

Cost-of-living allowance (COLA) Designed to protect the expatriate's standard of living from cost-of-living differences between the host country and the home country and to offer some protection against exchange rate fluctuations.

Tax equalisation Ensures that the expatriate does not suffer a loss or windfall gain because of differences between home-country tax and the host-country tax obligations. This is achieved by the expatriate being taxed at the home-country tax rate irrespective of the host-country tax rate.

Tax protection Ensures that the expatriate does not suffer a loss in spendable income because of higher host-country taxes (by reimbursing the expatriate if the actual host-country taxes exceed the hypothetical home-country tax obligation).

Minimisation of potential problems

The above discussion shows the major components likely to be present in any sophisticated expatriate compensation program. However, a program must also deal with matters such as education, housing, health insurance, home leave, cars, house selection trips, sale of the Australian home, temporary living, language instruction, shipment of furniture and club membership. Expatriate compensation is complex, but most potential problems can be minimised if HR managers:
- establish a clear expatriate policy that reflects organisational and HRM objectives, is consistent with the corporate culture and has the support of top management
- communicate the policy to both the employee and their partner
- ensure that the expatriate package is competitive
- give the same care and attention to the international compensation and benefits program as is given to the home-country program
- ensure that the international compensation and benefits program is cost-effective.

A company bases its expatriate compensation package on the home country salary. An Indian expatriate in Sydney complains that it is unfair that his Chinese colleague from Singapore receives more than he does. He says the company is discriminating against people from low-wage countries.

Compensation of third-country nationals (TCNs)

A recent development for Australian and Asian multinationals has been the use of third-country nationals (TCNs) to staff their offshore operations. (A TCN is a citizen of a country different from the home or host country — for example, a Malaysian working for an Australian subsidiary in Hong Kong.) Apart from all the standard questions that are raised in developing a policy for parent-company expatriates, the use of third-country nationals raises a particular set of problems. A New Zealander may be quite happy to be placed on an Australian pay scale and be treated as an Australian, but expatriates from Hong Kong, Japan, Singapore and the United States are unlikely to be satisfied. Moreover, the significant negative differences in pay structures are further aggravated by high Australian income taxes.

Problems of internal equity can also arise. An Australian manager based in Hong Kong, for example, will be paid less than a US, Japanese or Singaporean expatriate or a local counterpart. There is a logical explanation for this from the organisation's point of view, but it generally does not sit well with expatriates who find themselves in this position. Furthermore, dissatisfaction is virtually guaranteed if an organisation has a mix of third-country nationals working alongside each other in similar (or identical) positions but receiving markedly different levels of remuneration.

Some organisations, attempting to overcome such difficulties, elect to pay an international-base pay and benefits (often based on a US pay structure), ignoring nationality or place of hire. The creation of such an international cadre has advantages because it maintains equity among expatriates and it is seen as being internationally competitive.

Unfortunately, problems can arise if home-country personnel become jealous of the high pay received by their counterparts or subordinates. Labour mobility may also suffer, with Australian, New Zealand and Filipino expatriates reluctant to return home because of the dramatic decline in their material standard of living.

In developing an international compensation program for third-country nationals, HR managers should consider the following questions.

- Is the third-country national seen as part of the organisation's international talent bank available for assignment anywhere, any time?
- Is the third-country national tied to the home country in terms of retirement benefits?
- Are the differences between the third-country national's home-base pay and the international-base pay such that they constitute a major problem in equity?
- Does the company have a small or large number of third-country nationals in expatriate positions?
- Is the company likely to increase or decrease its use of third-country nationals in expatriate positions?
- Does the company wish to establish an elite cadre of international executives who see their careers as being in international management?

Summary

The internationalisation of business has created ever-expanding opportunities for more and more people to work overseas. Along with this has come a range of new HR challenges. How will expatriates be selected? What determines failure or success in an international assignment? How should expatriates be compensated?

Many criteria are used in selecting expatriate managers, but some of the most important include family adaptability, technical skills, effective communication and listening skills, host-country language skills, stress tolerance, and empathy and flexibility in dealing with foreign cultures. The evidence suggests that female expatriates are just as effective as male expatriates, even in male-dominated cultures such as Japan and South Korea.

The most common reasons for expatriate failure are the inability of the expatriate and/or family members (especially the partner) to adapt to living and working in the foreign culture. Failure by companies to adequately prepare the expatriate and their family through

Thirty interactive Wiley Web Questions are available to test your understanding of this chapter at **www.johnwiley.com.au/ highered/hrm5e** *in the student resources area*

systematic orientation appears to be a significant barrier to easing expatriate adjustment to the new location.

Finally, compensating expatriates can be both complex and expensive. Although there is no one perfect way of compensating expatriates, the package should be cost-effective, fair and consistent with the organisation's overall business objectives and culture.

student study guide

review questions

1. What are the most important criteria in expatriate selection? Explain your answer.
2. What are the major advantages and disadvantages of employing expatriates? How can the disadvantages be managed?
3. How can a company assist a dual career couple when one partner is offered an expatriate assignment?
4. What is a trailing partner? Why should companies be concerned about trailing partners?
5. Many expatriates fail because they cannot cope with a different culture. What would you do to reduce the risk of expatriate failure?
6. What is re-entry shock? What factors contribute to re-entry shock? How can these be overcome?
7. What special challenges do expatriates and their families face when transferred to a foreign location?
8. Discuss the major factors involved in expatriate performance appraisal.
9. What are the major issues involved in the design of expatriate orientation programs?
10. What are the major issues a company must consider when developing an expatriate compensation program?

environmental influences on expatriate management

Describe the key influences from the model (figure 21.2 shown opposite) that have significance for expatriate management.

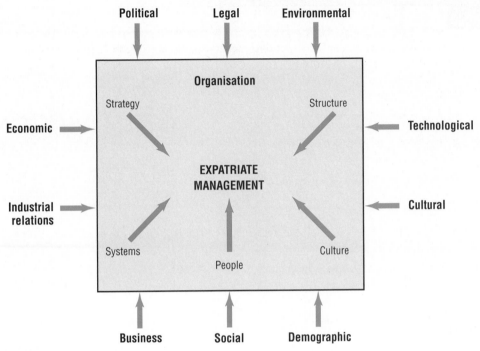

Figure 21.2 Environmental influences on expatriate management

---

Women should not be considered for expatriate assignments in dangerous locations.

what's your view?

Write a 500-word response to the Letter to the Editor on page 785, agreeing or disagreeing with the writer's point of view.

practitioner speaks

Read the article 'Cross-cultural diversity' on page 781. As a class, critically discuss the major points raised by Pamela Jackson.

newsbreak exercise

Read the Newsbreak 'It's no expat on the back when overseas' on pages 782–3. Critically discuss the author's view that managing expatriates involves more than just controlling costs.

case studies

A friendly drink

You are enjoying your first Kaesing party in a Seoul restaurant. The food and entertainment have been lavish. Your Korean hosts have been very hospitable and everything seems to be progressing smoothly. Mr Park, the senior Korean, fills his glass with whisky and passes it to you to drink. You suddenly became concerned. You are worried about the health risks (especially AIDS and hepatitis) and about having to drink so much liquor in one hit. In fact, the whole idea of exchanging drinking glasses with others strikes you as repugnant.

Discussion question

What would you do? Why?

The noisy eater

Ken Shimada was happy. His interviews with the Executive Search Consultant, Michio Ishii, had gone extremely well and now he had been invited to dinner by Winston Eldridge III. Ken knew that if this meeting went well he would be certain to be offered the position of President for American Heritage Inc.'s Asian operations. As the Chairman and largest stockholder, Eldridge was the decision maker. A man in his early sixties, he was a Bostonian of conservative and aristocratic manner. All seemed to be progressing smoothly until the soup was served. Ken slurped the soup Japanese-style, making considerable noise. Eldridge was horrified. Suddenly, Ken sensed that he had lost the job.

Discussion questions

1. How could this situation have been avoided?
2. What would you do now assuming you were (a) Ken Shimada, (b) Michio Ishii and (c) Winston Eldridge?

The angry professor

Professor Harry Barbarian faced his Kowloon University class of year one business administration students. 'Okay', said Harry, 'let's see what you have learned from the case study.'

Harry noticed that suddenly all the students were staring intently at the floor. Willie Wong, in particular, seemed to be fascinated by the floor tiles.

'Mr Wong, you look like an intelligent fellow. Tell me, what do you think? How would you solve the problem?' Willie said nothing, and became even more absorbed in the floor tiles.

'Come on, man, you haven't lost your tongue, have you? Tell me, what would you do?' Willie muttered a desperate 'I'm not sure.'

Harry exploded 'What do you mean, you're not sure? Haven't you got a brain? Answer me, man, what do you think?'

Willie's face reddened. He continued staring at the floor.

Discussion questions

1. Why was Willie reluctant to answer the question?
2. Why did the professor behave the way he did?

Not original

Professor Harry Barbarian looked at Tina Wong's assignment in amazement. He read the pages again. There before his very eyes, copied word for word, were several pages from a well-known textbook. Harry wondered what Tina was attempting to achieve. The differences in the standard of English expression were so great that it would be obvious to anyone that the work was written by two different people. Harry marked Tina's assignment with a failing grade. When Tina received her paper, she was very disappointed. As she thought of the long hours she had spent completing the assignment, she became angry and thought the professor to be very hard and unfair.

Discussion questions

1. Was the professor hard and unfair?
2. Was Tina justified in feeling angry?

The adventures of Pete and Eva Expat — culture clash!

Pete Expat had just received notice that his shipment of 13 boxes had arrived. Aware that he could not manage on his own, Pete sought assistance.

The HR Manager at Pete's place of employment said that a van and some helpers were available. Pete met the van in front of his office. In the van were the driver, Tony Tsang, a young man of 22 or so and two women, Ah Lo and Ah Wu, who were old enough to be Pete's mother.

Pete was shocked and embarrassed when it became apparent that the two women with their trolleys were to pick up the boxes. Pete protested that the boxes were too heavy and asked Tony to help. Tony replied sharply that his job was to drive and mind the van while the others picked up the boxes. The women looked on in wonderment as Pete proceeded to pick up all the big boxes and carry them by himself.

Discussion questions

1. Why did Pete behave the way he did?
2. Why did Tony behave the way he did?
3. If you were Pete, what would you have done?
4. What cultural differences are demonstrated in this case?

Pete and Eva Expat knocked on the door of Local and Lilly Wu's flat. This is the first time that the Expats have visited the Wu family at home.

As they enter, Local and Lilly introduce them to their two children, Winnie and Willie. 'This is Uncle and Auntie', says Local. 'Hello, Uncle Pete and Auntie Eva', respond Winnie and Willie.

'Oh, don't call us Uncle and Auntie', says Eva, 'it makes us sound so old — just call us Pete and Eva.' The children look at their parents, who seem somewhat uncomfortable. The Expats wonder why their friendly gesture seems to be a cause of concern. After all, being called Uncle and Auntie seems so stuffy and formal.

Discussion questions

1. Why was the reaction of Local and Lilly Wu different from what the Expats expected?
2. If you were Local and Lilly Wu, how would you handle the situation?

Local and Lily Wu have just celebrated their 15th wedding anniversary. Pete and Eva Expat present them with an expensive clock. They are nonplussed when Local and Lily appear upset with the gift.

Discussion questions

1. Why was the reaction of Local and Lilly Wu different from what the Expats expected?
2. If you were Local and Lilly Wu, how would you handle the situation?

practical exercises

1. Form into small groups of three to four. Choose an overseas location for an expatriate assignment and discuss the following questions, then regroup as a class and review your findings.
   - How much do you know about _____ ? Where can you find out more information about _____ ?
   - What do you think life will be like in _____ ?
   - What difficulties, if any, do you anticipate you will have to deal with in _____ ?
   - How might your family feel about your assignment to _____ ?
   - What do you believe it takes to adjust to the culture in _____ ?
   - What do you expect will be the personal benefits/costs of living and working in _____ ?
   - List three adjectives to describe the people of _____ .
   - List three adjectives you think the people of _____ would use to describe Australians.
2. Break into small groups of three to four. Review the interview checklist below. What questions would you add/change/delete? (Give particular consideration to employee privacy, EEO and legal concerns.) Prepare a revised form for a location of your choice, then regroup as a class and discuss your findings.

INTERVIEW CHECKLIST

1. (a) Is the candidate keen to go to China?

   Very ☐   Fairly ☐   Not very ☐

   (b) If affirmative, which location is the candidate most interested in?

Beijing	Very ☐	Fairly ☐	Not very ☐	Definitely not ☐
Shanghai	Very ☐	Fairly ☐	Not very ☐	Definitely not ☐
Guangzhou	Very ☐	Fairly ☐	Not very ☐	Definitely not ☐

2. Is the candidate's partner keen to go to China?

   Very ☐   Fairly ☐   Not very ☐

3. Are the candidate's children keen to go to China?

   Very ☐   Fairly ☐   Not very ☐

4. Have the candidate and their family had a medical check-up?

   Yes ☐   No ☐

5. Are the candidate and their family physically fit?

   Medical problems   Yes ☐   No ☐

   HIV positive   Yes ☐   No ☐

   Emotional problems Yes ☐   No ☐

   If yes, give details:

   _____

   (continued)

6. Does the candidate or any family member have drug or alcohol problems?

   Yes ☐ No ☐

   If yes, give details:

   _____

7. Does the candidate or their family have a 'social adjustment problem' that may make the adjustment to China difficult?

   Yes ☐ No ☐

   If yes, give details:

   _____

8. How do the candidate and their family feel about living in an apartment?

9. How do the candidate and their partner feel about driving in China?

10. How does the candidate feel about the *possibility* of having to spend 1 to 1½ hours travelling to work?

11. How do the candidate and their family feel about not having easy access to a wide range of Australian recreational and sporting facilities?

12. Do the candidate and their partner understand the type of educational facilities available?

    Yes ☐ No ☐ Don't know ☐

    If yes, how do they feel about it? ————————————————————————

13. Does the partner want to work in China? Will this be a problem?

14. What are the family's hobbies? Does the partner have any special skills or hobbies?

15. Does the family understand the type of religious facilities available?

    Yes ☐ No ☐ Don't know ☐

    If yes, how do they feel about it? ————————————————————————

16. Does the family (particularly the partner) have strong ties to any aged/sick relative in Australia?

    Yes ☐ No ☐ Don't know ☐

    If yes, is this going to be a problem?

    Yes ☐ No ☐

17. Has the family ever been outside of Australia?

    Yes ☐ No ☐

    If yes, where ————————————————————————————————

18. Is the family very status conscious?

    Yes ☐ No ☐ Don't know ☐

19. Is the family regarded as a happy, stable unit?

    Yes ☐ No ☐ Don't know ☐

20. How does the family feel about China? (Are there signs of excessive concern over food, language, hygiene, pollution, security, etc.?)

21. What further information do the candidate and their family need to give them a satisfactory picture of what it will be like living and working in China?

suggested readings

Beardwell, I. and Holden, L., *Human Resource Management*, 3rd edn, Financial Times/Prentice Hall, London, 2001, ch. 15.

CCH, *Australian Master Human Resources Guide*, CCH, Sydney, 2003, chs 7, 41, 42.

De Cieri, H. and Kramar, R., *Human Resource Management in Australia*, McGraw-Hill, Sydney, 2003, ch. 14.

Dowling, P. J., Welch, D. E. and Schuler, R. S., International Human Resource Management, 3rd edn, South-Western, Cincinnati, Ohio, 1999, Chs 3, 4, 5, 6, 7.

Fisher, C. D., Schoenfeldt, L. F. and Shaw, J. B., *Human Resource Management*, 5th edn, Houghton Mifflin, Boston, 2003, ch. 17.

Ivancevich, J. M., *Human Resource Management*, 8th edn, McGraw-Hill, Boston, 2001, ch. 4.

Ivancevich, J. M. and Lee, S. N., *Human Resource Management in Asia*, McGraw-Hill, Singapore, 2002, ch. 15.

Mondy, R. W., Noe, R. M. and Premeaux, S. R., *Human Resource Management*, 8th edn, Prentice Hall, Upper Saddle River, NJ, 2002, ch. 17.

Nankervis, A. R., Compton, R. L. and Baird, M., *Strategic Human Resource Management*, 4th edn, Nelson, Melbourne, 2002, ch. 17.

online references

expatexpert.com
www.asiaxpat.com
www.crownrelo.com
www.djr.com
www.ds-osac.org
www.expatforum.com
www.fco.gov.uk/travel

www.iht.com/athome.html
www.internationalsos.com
www.intl-risk.com
www.rebglobal.com
www.shrm.org.hrmagazine
www.travel.state.gov/travel_warnings.html
www.workforceonline.com

end notes

1. L. Elphinstone, 'Returning valve', *HR Monthly*, December 2002, p. 14.
2. A. Shand, 'Smedley loose: CEOs are feeling the heat', *Australian Financial Review*, 17–18 June 2000, p. 14.
3. D. Kitney and S. Mitchell, 'Big Australians on the move', *Australian Financial Review*, 16 August 1999, p. 14.
4. R. B. Reich, 'Who is them?', *Harvard Business Review*, February 1991, pp. 77–88.
5. Quoted in C. Matlack and K. Capell, 'Managers without borders', *Business Week*, 20 November 2000, p. 59.
6. W. Taylor, 'The logic of global business: an interview with ABB's Percey Barnevik', *Harvard Business Review*, February 1991, p. 92; and G. Lindahl, 'Globalising leadership: tapping the creative potential of cultural diversity', *Monash/Mt Eliza Business Review*, vol. 1, no. 13, 1998, p. 24.
7. G. Beeth, 'Multicultural managers wanted', *Management Review*, vol. 86, no. 5, 1997, pp. 17–21.
8. S. Aryee, 'Selection and training of expatriate employees', in N. Anderson and P. Herriot, *International Handbook of Selection and Assessment*, John Wiley & Sons, Chichester, 1997, p. 158.
9. M. E. Mendenhall, E. Dunbar and G. R. Oddou, 'Expatriate selection training and career pathing: a review and critique', *Human Resource Management*, vol. 26, no. 3, 1987, p. 331; and Y. Stedham and M. Nechita, 'The expatriate assignment: research and management practice', *Asia Pacific Journal of Human Resources*, vol. 35, no. 1, 1997, pp. 80–1.
10. J. E. Heller, 'Criteria for selecting an international manager', *Personnel*, vol. 57, no. 3, 1980, p. 53; R. M. Hodgetts and F. Luthans, *International Management*, 4th edn, McGraw-Hill, Boston, 2000, pp. 432–4; and S. Aryee, op. cit., p. 147.
11. M. E. Mendenhall, E. Dunbar and G. R. Oddou, op. cit., p. 332; P. Enderwick and D. Hodgson, 'Expatriate management practices of New Zealand business', *International Journal of Human Resource Management*, vol. 4, no. 2, 1994, p. 420; R. M. Hodgetts and F. Luthans, op. cit., pp. 433–4; and J. Franke and N. Nicholson, 'Who shall we send? Cultural and other influences on the rating of selection criteria for expatriate assignments', *International Journal of Cross Cultural Management*, vol. 2, no. 1, 2002, p. 23.
12. M. E. Mendenhall, E. Dunbar and G. R. Oddou, op. cit., p. 333. See also J. Black and M. Mendenhall, 'Cross cultural training effectiveness: a review and a theoretical framework for future research', *Academy of Management Review*, vol. 15, no. 1, 1990, p. 114.

13. R. J. Stone, 'Expatriate selection and orientation', *Human Resource Management Australia*, vol. 24, no. 3, 1986, p. 24; R. L. Tung, 'Human resource management, international', in M. Poole and M. Werner (eds), *The Handbook of Human Resource Management*, Thomson, London, 1998, p. 375; and J. Franke and N. Nicholson, op. cit., p. 23.

14. M. Harvey, 'The selection of managers for foreign assignments: a planning perspective', *Columbia Journal of World Business*, vol. 32, 1997, p. 112.

15. H. Harris and C. Brewster, 'The coffee machine system: how international selection really works', *International Journal of Human Resource Management*, vol. 10, no. 3, 1999, pp. 488–500.

16. R. Phelps, personal correspondence with the author, 28 June 1992. See also M. Harvey, op. cit., p. 116.

17. M. E. Mendenhall, E. Dunbar and G. R. Oddou, op. cit., p. 331; and G. M. Wederspahn, 'Costing failures in expatriate human resource management', *Human Resource Planning*, vol. 15, no. 3, 1992, pp. 27–35.

18. H. Lipper, 'Employers manoeuver to help expats survive China', *Asian Wall Street Journal*, 16 September 1997, p. 13.

19. R. V. Sears, quoted in H. Lipper, op. cit., p. 13.

20. H. Lipper, op. cit., p. 13.

21. R. J. Stone, 'Expatriate selection and failure', *Human Resource Planning*, vol. 14, no. 1, 1991, pp. 9–18.

22. Y. Baruch, 'No such thing as a global manager', *Business Horizons*, vol. 45, no. 1, 2002, p. 41.

23. C. Brewster, *The Management of Expatriates*, Cranfield School of Management, Human Resources Center, No. 2, 1988, p. 35.

24. J. Franke and N. Nicholson, op. cit., p. 30.

25. N. Forster, 'International managers and mobile families: the professional and personal dynamics of trans-national career pathing and job mobility in the 1990s', *International Journal of Human Resource Management*, vol. 3, no. 3, 1992, pp. 605–23; J. S. Black and M. Mendenhall, 'Cross training effectiveness: a review and theoretical framework for future research', *Academy of Management Review*, vol. 15, no. 1, 1990, pp. 113–36; M. Harvey, op. cit., pp. 102–18; S. Aryee, op. cit., pp. 147–60; A. Fish and J. Wood, 'Cross cultural management competence in Australian business enterprise', *Asia Pacific Journal of Human Resources*, vol. 35, no. 1, 1997, pp. 37–52; J. S. Black, H. B. Gregersen, M. E. Mendenhall and L. K. Stroh, *Globalizing People Through International Assignments*, Addison Wesley, Reading, Mass., 1999, pp. 59–63. J. Selmer, 'Practice makes perfect? International experience and expatriate adjustment', *Management International Review*, vol. 42, no. 1, 2002, p. 71; M. Harvey and M. Novicevic, 'The role of political competence in global assignments of expatriate managers', *Journal of International Management*, vol. 8, no. 4, 2002, p. 402; and M. Harvey and M. Novicevic, 'The hyper competitive global marketplace: the importance of intuition and creativity in expatriate managers', *Journal of World Business*, vol. 37, no. 2, 2002, p. 131.

26. C. M. Solomon and B. Porter, 'Expatriates with AIDS to be ejected', *South China Morning Post*, 19 February 2000, p. 11.

27. A. Fish and J. Wood, 'A review of expatriate staffing practices in Australian business enterprises', *International Journal of Human Resource Management*, vol. 7, no. 4, 1996, p. 849.

28. M. Domsch and B. Lichtenberger, 'Foreign assignments for female German managers', *International Executive*, vol. 34, no. 4, 1992, pp. 345–55.

29. M. Domsch and B. Lichtenberger, op. cit., pp. 345–6; N. J. Adler, 'Pacific Basin managers: a gaijin, not a woman', *Human Resource Management*, vol. 26, no. 2, 1987, p. 169; and N. K. Napier and S. Taylor, *Western Women Working in Japan*, Quorum, Westport, Conn., 1995, pp. 192–3.

30. H. Harris, 'Think international manager think male: why are women not selected for international assignments?', *Thunderbird International Business Review*, vol. 44, no. 2, 2002, pp. 175–203.

31. G. Kovetz, 'A woman's place is …', *Business Week*, 13 September 1999, p. 12; and J. S. Black, H. B. Gregersen, M. E. Mendenhall and L. K. Stroh, op. cit., p. 64.

32. N. J. Adler, op. cit., pp. 178–9; and M. Domsch and B. Lichtenberger, op. cit., p. 350.

33. N. Forster, 'The persistent myth of high expatriate failure rates: a reappraisal', *International Journal of Human Resource Management*, vol. 8, no. 4, 1997, p. 429.

34. Reported in Dow Jones Newswires, 'Why more women stay home to work', *Australian Financial Review*, 30 June 1999, p. 16.

35. Reported in C. Tolhurst, 'Service slipping through the gender gap', *Australian Financial Review — Special Report*, 12 July 2000, p. 8; and P. R. Olsen, 'Safety for traveling women', *International Herald Tribune*, 28 November, 2003, p. 8.

36. R. I. Westwood and S. M. Leung, 'The female expatriate manager experience', *International Studies of Management and Organization*, vol. 24, no. 3, 1994, p. 81.

37. M. Downes, 'SIHRM: overseas staffing considerations at the environmental level', *Journal of International Management*, vol. 2, no. 1, 1996, p. 34.

38. V. E. Schein, R. Mueller, T. Lituchy and J. Liu, 'Think manager — think male: a global phenomenon?', *Journal of Organizational Behaviour*, vol. 17, no. 1, 1996, pp. 33–41.

39. Taylor and Napier found that while female expatriates in Japan can be successful and bring some advantages to the assignment, they face special challenges — for example, resistance by Japanese female subordinates to working for a foreign woman. S. Taylor and N. Napier, 'Working in Japan: lessons from women expatriates', *Sloan Management Review*, vol. 37, no. 3, 1996, pp. 76–84.

40. Quoted in C. Parson, 'Tactics put people first', *South China Morning Post — Business*, 15 January 2001, p. 10.

41. Anonymous reviewer comment, April 2001.

42. J. S. Black, H. B. Gregersen, M. E. Mendenhall and L. K. Stroh, op. cit., p. 64.

43. N. K. Napier and S. Taylor, 1995, op. cit., p. 192.

44. Some of the problems faced by women working internationally include being mistaken for a prostitute, receiving less than adequate service compared with the service given to their male counterparts, being treated as the 'tea lady', experiencing jealousy

from expatriate wives, not being taken seriously, being sexually harassed and experiencing problems with personal safety. See L. Bernier, 'Fear of flying', *International Management*, vol. 43, no. 7/8, 1988, pp. 55–9; D. Couture, 'Western women in Japanese business', *The Journal*, American Chamber of Commerce in Japan, January 1992, pp. 30–5; R. Robertson, 'Product not gender holds key to foreign markets', *Australian Financial Review*, 4 March 1997, p. 39; and E. D. Davison and B. J. Punnett, 'International assignments: is there a role for gender and race in decisions?', *International Journal of Human Resource Management*, vol. 6, no. 2, 1995, p. 431.

45. N. J. Adler, op. cit., p. 177; and R. J. Stone, 1991, op. cit., pp. 9–18.

46. N. J. Adler, op. cit., p. 179.

47. T. F. Cash, B. Gillen and D. S. Burns, 'Sexism and "beautyism" in personnel consultant decision making', *Journal of Applied Psychology*, vol. 62, no. 3, 1977, pp. 301–10.

48. Quoted in 'Equality for uglies', *Time*, 21 February 1972, p. 8.

49. R. A. Swaak, 'Today's expatriate family: dual careers and other obstacles', *Compensation and Benefits Review*, vol. 27, no. 3, 1995, pp. 21–6; J. S. Lublin, 'US managers demur to stints abroad now', *Asian Wall Street Journal*, 29 September 2003, p. A10; and B. Rosen, 'Fewer but more senior employees are being sent overseas', *International Herald Tribune*, 21–22 June 2003, p. 16.

50. J. S. Lublin, 2003, op. cit., p. A10.

51. Arthur Andersen survey of 21 000 employees, reported in J. Nicol, 'Inside the mind of the expat', *South China Morning Post*, 9 November 2002, p. 14.

52. 'Family issues main reasons for turning down overseas assignments', *International HR Update*, September 1996, p. 2.

53. J. S. Lublin, 2003, op. cit., p. A10.

54. S. Aryee, Y. W. Chay and J. Chen, 'An investigation of the willingness of managerial employees to accept an expatriate assignment', *Journal of Organizational Behavior*, vol. 17, 1996, pp. 267–83; D. Welch, 'HRM implications of globalization', *Journal of General Management*, vol. 19, no. 4, 1994, pp. 57–8; Political and Economic Risk Consultancy survey, reported in 'Which way to the beach?', *Far Eastern Economic Review*, 13 April 2000, p. 70; H. Phillips, 'Firms push for cleaner air as HK loses appeal as posting', *South China Morning Post*, 20 January 2003, p. 6, and P. K. Jagersma and D. M. Van Gorp, 'International HRM: the Dutch experience', *Journal of General Management*, vol. 28, no. 2, 2002, p. 83.

55. S. Aryee, Y. W. Chay and J. Chen, op. cit., p. 279.

56. B. Rosen, op. cit., p. 16.

57. R. J. Stone, 1991, op. cit., p. 384; R. L. Tung, 1998, op. cit., pp. 375–6; and R. L. Tung, 'Selection and training procedures of US, European and Japanese multinationals', *California Management Review*, vol. 25, no. 1, 1982, pp. 63–7.

58. G. S. Insch and J. D. Daniels, 'Causes and consequences of declining early departures from foreign assignments', *Business Horizons*, vol. 45, no. 6, 2002, p. 41.

59. M. E. Mendenhall, E. Dunbar and G. R. Oddou, op. cit., p. 333.

60. C. Brewster, op. cit., p. 13; and R. A. Swaak, 'Expatriate failures: too many, too much cost, too little planning', *Compensation and Benefits Review*, vol. 27, no. 6, 1995, p. 50.

61. Quoted in R. J. Stone, 1991, op. cit., p. 11.

62. R. Tung, 1982, op. cit., p. 64.

63. P. Novelli, *1996–1997 International Assignee Research Project*, HFS Mobility Services Inc. and Berlitz Languages Inc., Princeton, NJ, 1997, p. 1; and C. M. Solomon, 'Danger below! Spot failing global assignments', *Personnel Journal*, vol. 75, no. 11, 1996, pp. 278–85.

64. National Foreign Trade Council, 'Study of global sourcing and selection finds troubling rate of assignment failures', *International HR Update*, March 1996, p. 6.

65. S. Aryee and R. J. Stone, 'Work experiences, work adjustment and psychological well being of expatriate employees in Hong Kong', *International Journal of Human Resource Management*, vol. 7, no. 1, 1996, pp. 150–64.

66. SHL Hong Kong Ltd survey, reported in S. Fenton, 'The price of instability', *Asian Wall Street Journal*, 3–4 December 1999, p. 3.

67. T. Maher, 'Manners maketh the deal', *Business Review Weekly*, 14–20 January 1984, p. 61.

68. M. Chipperfield, 'Getting to know Asians, and then trading with them', *Australian*, 15 May 1986, p. 11.

69. I. Jarrett, 'Oz starts north', *Asian Business*, May 1993, p. 64.

70. M. Chipperfield, op. cit., p. 11. See also R. Callick, 'Meeting challenge of Vietnam', *Australian Financial Review*, 29 November 1996, p. 19.

71. J. Selmer and L. S. C. Shiu, 'Coming home? Adjustment of Hong Kong Chinese expatriate business managers assigned to the People's Republic of China', *International Journal of Intercultural Relations*, vol. 23, no. 3, 1999, pp. 447–65.

72. M. Fenwick, R. Edwards and P. J. Buckley, 'Is cultural similarity misleading? The experience of Australian manufacturers in Britain', *International Business Review*, vol. 12, no. 3, 2003, pp. 297–309.

73. A complicating factor is that an increasing number of international selections now involve blended or split families. See W. Coyle, 'Family dynamics at heart of relocation success', *HR Monthly*, November 1996, p. 10.

74. J. S. Black and H. B. Gregersen, 'The other half of the picture: antecedents of spouse cross cultural adjustment', *Journal of International Business Studies*, vol. 22, no. 3, 1991, pp. 461–77; C. M. Solomon, 'CEO mom: the tie that binds a global family', *Personnel Journal*, March 1996, pp. 80–93; M. Ridney, 'Global families: surviving an overseas move', *Management Review*, vol. 85, no. 6, 1996, pp. 57–61; and R. Hodgetts and F. Luthans, op. cit., pp. 436–7.

75. G. Wederspahn, 'Cultural awareness for managers', *The Corporate Expatriate*, May 1986, p. 5.

76. K. J. Fukuda and P. Chu, 'Wrestling with expatriate family problems', *International Studies of Management and Organization*, vol. 24, no. 3, 1994, pp. 36–47.

77. H. De Cieri, P. J. Dowling and K. F. Taylor, 'The psychological impact of expatriate relocation on partners', *International Journal of Human Resource Management*, vol. 2, no. 3, 1991, pp. 377–414.

78. S. Taylor and N. K. Napier, 'Successful women expatriates: the case of Japan', *Journal of International Management*, vol. 2, no. 1, 1996, pp. 51–78.

79. Z. Aycan, 'Expatriate adjustment as a multifaceted phenomenon: individual and organizational predictors', *International Journal of Human Resource Management*, vol. 8, no. 4, 1997, pp. 451–2.

80. E. Lee and W. B. Hudgens, 'The perceptions of expatriate spouses on organisational assistance in international transfers', *Business Research Centre Working Paper*, Hong Kong Baptist College, June 1991, pp. 1–22; and J. S. Lublin, 'Overseas stint can overwhelm family', *Asian Wall Street Journal*, 2 February 1999, p. 6.

81. P. Davidson and E. Kinzel, 'Supporting the expatriate: a survey of Australian management practice', *Asia Pacific Journal of Human Resources*, vol. 33, no. 3, 1995, pp. 105–6.

82. B. Anderson, 'The preparation of Australian expatriates for relocation to South East Asia', *Asia Pacific Journal of Human Resources*, vol. 36, no. 3, 1998, pp. 50–65.

83. M. E. Mendenhall, E. Dunbar and G. R. Oddou, op. cit., p. 333.

84. J. S. Black, 'Work role transitions: a study of American expatriate managers in Japan', *Journal of International Business Studies*, vol. 19, 1998, pp. 277–94; and J. S. Black and G. K. Stephens, 'The influence of the spouse on American expatriate adjustment in overseas assignments', *Journal of Management*, vol. 15, 1989, pp. 529–44.

85. R. Tung, 'US multinationals: a study of their selection and training procedures for overseas assignments', *Academy of Management Proceedings*, 1979, pp. 298–301.

86. N. J. Piet-Pelon and B. Hornby, *Women Overseas*, Institute of Personnel Management, Wimbledon, 1986, p. 86.

87. N. J. Piet-Pelon and B. Hornby, op. cit., p. 87.

88. B. Fitzgerald-Turner, 'Myths of expatriate life', *HR Magazine*, June 1997, p. 70.

89. Quoted in P. Novelli, op. cit., p. 19.

90. B. A. Anderson, 'When expatriation means follow that woman', *Asia Pacific Journal of Human Resources*, vol. 39, no. 3, 2001, p. 109.

91. H. C. Collie, 'The changing face of corporate relocation', *HRM Magazine*, March 1998, p. 102.

92. Reported in B. Phillips, 'On the road to a wrecked marriage', *Business Review Weekly*, 21 May 1999, p. 89.

93. M. O'Neill 'Thriving business of being a mistress', *South China Morning Post*, 2 January 1999, p. 10; C. Sui, 'Shenzen women wary of "unfaithful" SAR husbands', *South China Morning Post*, 4 January 1999, p. 3; and S. M. M. on, '24-hour Lowu bad for economy and marriage', *South China Morning Post*, 2 May 2000, p. 4.

94. N. Lee, 'Duplicitous liaisons', *Far Eastern Economic Review*, 20 April 1995, pp. 64–5.

95. R. Feil, 'Smoothing the path for expatriate wives', *Australian*, 18 November 1986, p. 12.

96. M. G. Harvey, 'The impact of dual career families on international relocations', *Human Resource Management Review*, vol. 5, no. 3, 1995, p. 237; and N. Foster, 'The persistent myth of high expatriate failure rates: a re-appraisal', *International Journal of Human Resource Management*, vol. 8, no. 4, 1997, p. 423.

97. L. Greenbury, 'Follow that expatriate woman!', *People Management*, vol. 2, no. 24, 1996, pp. 6–7.

98. M. Lacheze, 'And husband came too', *Expatriate*, vol. 12, no. 3, 1989, p. 2.

99. See also B. J. Punnett, O. Crocker and M. A. Stevens, 'The challenge for women expatriates and spouses: some empirical evidence', *International Journal of Human Resource Management*, vol. 3, no. 3, 1992, pp. 585–92.

100. P. R. Harris and D. L. Harris, 'Women managers and professionals abroad', *Journal of Managerial Psychology*, vol. 3, no. 4, 1988, p. 2; and research by Windham International and the National Foreign Trade Council, reported in 'HRM update', *HR Magazine*, December 1992, pp. 21–2. See also survey by Pricewaterhouse covering over 200 companies in 13 European countries, reported in 'Managing expatriates', *Multinational Employer*, vol. 10, no. 3, 1993, p. 13.

101. C. Reynolds and R. Bennett, 'The career couple challenge', *Personnel Journal*, vol. 70, no. 3, 1991, p. 48.

102. C. Reynolds and R. Bennett, op. cit., p. 48. See also R. Bennett, 'Solving the dual international career dilemma', *HR News*, January 1993, p. C5.

103. B. J. Punnett, O. Crocker and M. A. Stevens, op. cit., pp. 585, 590.

104. P. Davidson and E. Kinzel, 'Supporting an expatriate: a survey of Australian management practice', *Asia Pacific Journal of Human Resources*, vol. 33, no. 3, 1995, p. 110; and K. Hutchings, 'Cross cultural preparation of Australian expatriates in China: the need for greater attention to training', *Asia Pacific Journal of Management*, vol. 20, no. 3, 2003, p. 375.

105. Reported in 'Expats want more support from HR', *Human Resources*, July–August 2002, p. 4.

106. J. S. Black, 'Factors related to the adjustment of Japanese expatriate managers in America', *Proceedings of the International Conference on Personnel and Human Resource Management*, Hong Kong, 12–15 December 1989, pp. 390–8.

107. J. Selmer, 'To train or not to train? European expatriate managers in China', *International Journal of Cross Cultural Management*, vol. 2, no. 1, 2002, p. 37.

108. C. B. Derr and G. R. Oddou, 'Are US multinationals adequately preparing future American leaders for global competition?', *International Journal of Human Resource Management*, vol. 2, no. 2, 1991, p. 230; and E. Olson, 'Training firms offer help in bridging cultural divides', *International Herald Tribune*, 21–22 June 2003, p. 17.

109. R. J. Stone, 1991, op. cit., p. 13.

110. D. Hisco, 'The Australian banker overseas', *Australian Institute of Bankers Centenary Scholarship Report*, Melbourne, 1987, p. 7.

111. B. Anderson, op. cit., pp. 60–2.

112. R. J. Stone, 1991, op. cit., p. 13.

113. M. Sims, quoted in 'Smart moves', *Australian Financial Review Magazine*, August 1997, p. 21.

114. Adapted by the author from L. Copeland and L. Griggs, *Going International*, Random House, New York, 1985, p. 216.

115. K. Hutchings, op. cit., p. 376.

116. Quoted in 'Blunting culture shock', *University of Melbourne Gazette*, 1985, p. 7.

117. M. Munter, 'Cross cultural communication for managers', *Business Horizons*, vol. 36, no. 3, May–June 1993, pp. 76–7.

118. 'Mad dogs and expatriates', *Economist*, 3 March 1984, p. 67.

119. J. Selmer, 'What do expatriate managers know about their HCN subordinates' work values? Swedish executives in Hong Kong', *Transnational Management Development*, vol. 2, no. 3, 1996, p. 17.

120. Survey by Organization Resources Counsellors Inc., reported in 'Companies praise the benefits of cultural orientation training', *HR Focus*, August 1993, p. 18.

121. J. McEnery and G. Des Harnais, 'Culture shock', *Training and Development Journal*, vol. 44, no. 4, 1990, p. 44.

122. M. Shilling, 'Avoid expatriate culture shock', *HR Magazine*, July 1993, p. 62.

123. L. Copeland and L. Griggs, op. cit., p. 195; and R. M. Hodgetts and F. Luthans, op. cit., pp. 440–1.

124. Fear regarding personal security may be justified in some locations. Kidnapping, for example, is a major concern in the Philippines. Other 'hot' spots include Indonesia, Papua New Guinea and southern China. G. Maslen, 'Jakarta international schools on alert', *South China Morning Post*, 29 November 2003, p. E3; and C. H. Conde, 'Abductions in Philippines spark death penalty debate', *International Herald Tribune*, 25 November 2003, pp. 1, 4.

125. J. Selmer, 'Effects of coping strategies on sociocultural and psychological adjustment of western expatriate managers in the PRC', *Journal of World Business*, vol. 34, no. 1, 1999, p. 47.

126. Australian troops sent to Cambodia on peacekeeping duty suffered a 60 per cent divorce rate, for example. Reported in 'The enemy within', *Bulletin*, 12 October 1993, p. 31.

127. For example, see S. T. Davies, 'The price of privilege', *Magazine*, 3 January 1993, pp. 7–9.

128. 1992 SHRM/CCH survey, reported in *Human Resources Management*, Commerce Clearing House, 8 July 1992, pp. 1–12; C. G. Howard, 'Out of sight, not out of mind', *Personnel Administrator*, vol. 33, no. 6, 1987, pp. 82–90; and R. L. Tung, 1998, op. cit., pp. 386–7.

129. J. Selmer, B. P. Ebrahimmi and M. T. Li, 'Corporate career support: Chinese mainland expatriates in Hong Kong', *Career Development International*, vol. 5, no. 1, 2000, pp. 5–12.

130. M. Harvey, 'Focusing the international personnel performance appraisal process', *Human Resource Development Quarterly*, vol. 8, no. 1, 1997, p. 42.

131. K. Welds, 'The return trip', *HR Magazine*, June 1991, p. 113.

132. N. Carter, quoted in E. McShulskis, 'How effective are your expatriates?', *HRM Magazine*, December 1996, p. 14.

133. J. S. Black and H. B. Gregersen, 'When Yankee comes home: factors related to expatriate and spouse repatriation adjustment', *Journal of International Business Studies*, vol. 22, no. 3, 1991, pp. 671–95.

134. Survey reported in J. Nicol, 'Inside the mind of an expat', *South China Morning Post*, 9 November 2002, p. 14.

135. J. S. Lublin, 'Warning to expats: maybe you can't go home again', *Asian Wall Street Journal*, 27–28 August 1993, pp. 1, 20; and D. C. Feldman and H. B. Tompson, 'Entry shock, culture shock: socialising the new breed of global managers', *Human Resource Management*, vol. 31, no. 4, 1992, pp. 352–3.

136. D. C. Feldman and D. C. Thomas, 'Career management issues facing expatriates', *Journal of International Business Studies*, vol. 23, no. 2, 1992, pp. 285–6.

137. J. S. Black, 'Returning expatriates feel foreign in their native land', *Personnel*, vol. 68, no. 8, 1991, p. 17; and J. S. Black, H. B. Gregersen, M. E. Mendenhall and L. K. Stroh, op. cit., pp. 69–70.

138. D. C. Feldman and D. C. Thomas, op. cit., p. 283.

139. G. K. Stahl, E. L. Miller and R. L. Tung, 'Toward the boundaryless career: a closer look at the expatriate career concept and the perceived implications of an international assignment', *Journal of World Business*, vol. 37, no. 3, 2002, pp. 216–27.

140. J. S. Black, 1991, op. cit., p. 17.

141. J. S. Black, 1991, op. cit., p. 17.

142. S. Green, 'How a rude awakening can lead to good life', *Sunday Morning Post, Agenda*, 6 April 1997, p. 2.

143. J. S. Black, 1991, op. cit., p. 17; and J. S. Black, B. Gregersen, M. E. Mendenhall and L. K. Stroh, op. cit., pp. 204–8.

144. M. Shilling, 'How to win at repatriation', *Personnel Journal*, September 1993, p. 40; and J. S. Black, B. Gregersen, M. E. Mendenhall and L. K. Stroh, op. cit., pp. 202–8.

145. J. Wallach and G. Metcalf, 'The hidden problem of re-entry', *Bridge*, vol. 5, no. 4, 1980, p. 18.

146. See C. M. Solomon, 'Repatriation: up, down or out?', *Personnel Journal*, January 1995, pp. 28–37; and J. S. Black, B. Gregersen, M. E. Mendenhall and L. K. Stroh, op. cit., pp. 202–33.

147. D. R. Briscoe, *International Human Resource Management*, Prentice Hall, Englewood Cliffs, NJ, 1995, p. 103.

148. P. Evans, V. Pucik and J. L. Barsoux, *The Global Challenge*, McGraw-Hill/Irwin, Boston, 2002, pp. 128–30; and D. C. Martin and K. M. Bartol, 'Factors influencing expatriate performance appraisal system success: an organizational perspective', *Journal of International Management*, vol. 9, no. 2, 2003, pp. 115–32.

149. R. Payne, 'Rewarding the expatriate executive', in G. O'Neill (ed.), *Corporate Remuneration in the 1990s*, Longman Cheshire, Melbourne, 1990, p. 65; and R. M. Hodgetts and F. Luthans, op. cit., pp. 442–6.

150. N. Forster and M. Jackson, 'Expatriate management policies in UK companies new to the international scene', *International Journal of Human Resource Management*, vol. 7, no. 1, 1996, p. 192.

151. J. S. Lublin, 2003, op. cit., p. A10.

152. M. R. Foote, 'Controlling the cost of international compensation', *Harvard Business Review*, June 1977, p. 123; and M. S. Schell and C. M. Solomon, *Capitalizing on the Global Workforce*, McGraw-Hill, New York, 1997, pp. 113–16.

153. D. Young, 'Fair compensation for expatriates', *Harvard Business Review*, April 1973, p. 93.

154. W. R. Sheridan and P. T. Hansen, 'Linking international business and expatriate compensation strategies', *ACA Journal*, Spring 1996, pp. 66–79.

155. W. R. Sheridan and P. T. Hansen, op. cit., pp. 66–70; C. D. Fisher, L. F. Schoenfeldt and J. B. Shaw, *Human Resource Management*, 5th edn, Houghton Mifflin, Boston, 2003, pp. 840–3; T. Phillis, 'Moving out', *HR Monthly*, August 2003, pp. 38–9; and C. Rance, 'Managing a global workforce', *HR Monthly*, August 2003, pp. 34–6.

156. J. S. Lublin, 2003, op. cit., p. A10.

157. C. M. Solomon, 1995, op. cit., p. 73; and J. S. Black, B. Gregersen, M. E. Mendenhall and L. K. Stroh, op. cit., p. 183.

158. D. Young, op. cit., p. 95.

159. K. A. Freeman and J. S. Kane, 'An alternative approach to expatriate allowances: an "international citizen"', *International Executive*, vol. 37, no. 3, 1994, p. 254; and G. W. Latta, 'Expatriate compensation practices', in L. A. Berger and D. R. Berger (eds), *The Compensation Handbook*, 4th edn, McGraw-Hill, New York, 2000, pp. 612–13.

OUTSOURCING IT-ENABLED SERVICES TO INDIA: SOUND STRATEGY OR SOCIAL SUICIDE?

Mohan Thite, Griffith University

Robert Perry, the HR Director of Tel Alliance, a major telecommunications company in Australasia, had just come back to his office after addressing the annual meeting of HR professionals in the company. He had a smile on his face because the company had just posted handsome profits after many years of sluggish growth and declining revenue, and the board of directors had openly acknowledged the strategic contribution made by the HR Division in this remarkable turnaround.

With the smile still on his face, Robert turned his attention to the new email from his CEO, Jack Clinton, marked 'Urgent and confidential'. The email, addressed to all functional directors, said: 'I have called an urgent meeting of all directors on Monday morning to review our policy of outsourcing IT-enabled services (ITES) to strategic business partners in India.'

The message came as a surprise to Robert. He started wondering what could have prompted the CEO to call an urgent meeting on this issue, particularly as it was well known in the company that outsourcing ITES to India had had a very healthy impact on the company's bottom line. While walking to the coffee room, Robert recalled how Tel Alliance had come to rely more and more on Indian IT companies in IT services, including call centre operations.

It all started three years ago when Tel Alliance undertook a major review of its IT strategy. At that time, the IT Division was notorious for cost overruns, missing deadlines, a critical shortage of IT personnel with the latest skills and misreading technology trends affecting the business. Being a telecommunications company, Tel Alliance operated in an extremely volatile market characterised by hyper global competition, rapid technological obsolescence and heavy investment in technology with uncertain returns.

Robert recalled how the IT Director and the Finance Director had made an exciting presentation to management about the strategic benefits of outsourcing IT services to India. They pointed out that more than 50 per cent of Fortune 500 companies outsourced their IT-related operations overseas to countries like India, where labour costs offered dramatic savings — upwards of 70 per cent.[1] In fact, what was said at the meeting was open knowledge.

It was already being recognised worldwide that India, the world's largest democracy and home to one billion people, had surprisingly emerged as a software powerhouse in the global IT arena. From 1995 to 2000, exports of IT services by the Indian software industry grew at a staggering annual rate of 62.3 per cent.[2] At the time when the IT industry was experiencing an unprecedented boom period, due to a variety of factors such as the emergence of e-commerce, dot.coms and the Y2K scare, there was a worldwide shortage of IT personnel and India, with the world's second-largest pool of English-speaking scientific and technical professionals, offered high-quality and cost-effective IT services. What started with the outsourcing of low-level IT maintenance to Indian companies rapidly grew to include the development of critical IT projects. This IT outsourcing revolution was led by the United States, which issued more than 50 per cent of the work permits for foreign IT workers to Indian IT professionals.[3] This trend slowly picked up in other developed countries, such as Britain, Japan, Germany, Singapore and Italy.

Against this background, management did not need much convincing to follow the trend. In fact, many Indian IT professionals had already worked for Tel Alliance as subcontractors and provided excellent on-site services. Now the proposal was to use offshore IT services from Indian IT

companies. Once an IT project was given the financial go-ahead, it would be outsourced to an Indian company whose IT analysts would come to Australia to meet with potential users of the new system and draw up a detailed needs analysis. They would then return to India to get the coding done by Indian IT programmers under remote supervision from Australian managers, and come back to Australia to implement the system. They would maintain and modify the system, as required, from India on a long-term basis.

Despite teething problems, IT outsourcing had worked remarkably well and delivered promised benefits. In fact, it worked so well that the company decided to outsource its growing call centre operations to India, again in line with global trends. Once the dot.com bubble had burst and Y2K fears proved unfounded, the IT industry worldwide went into recession. But not so in India as the country had just discovered another niche market: back-office outsourcing. Again, it all started as a trickle with the outsourcing of global ticketing systems by major airlines and medical records transcriptions and bills processing by insurance companies.

This also coincided with another trend — the replacement of face-to-face customer service with call centres to exploit revolutionary developments in communications technology. As customer service reached new heights with round-the-clock attention to customers, countries like India proved to be cost-effective — the differences in time zones between India and North America/Europe enabled Indian companies to provide night-time customer service to overseas customers via the phone while it was still daytime in India. Also, when call centres in Western countries experienced high labour turnover due to a work environment characterised by routine, high pressure and long hours of work, unemployed graduates in India queued up to take the jobs, which to them were relatively highly paid, even though their pay was 50–70 per cent less than their Western counterparts.

Tel Alliance initially started back-office outsourcing with technical call centre assistance, whereby its customers could email or call a technical help desk in Australia and the messages/calls were automatically diverted to an Indian call centre for reply. As this system worked relatively well, the company went one step further and outsourced its general business-related call centre activities to India. This meant that customers who wanted to transact day-to-day business, such as account balances, bill payments, fault reporting and product enquiries, were also diverted, without their knowledge, to Indian call centres.

In fact, when Robert had recently visited Tel Alliance's call centre partners in India, based in Bangalore, Hyderabad and Gurgaon (near Delhi), he was surprised to learn that Indian call centre staff were regularly trained in Australian language and culture. They even called themselves by Australian-sounding names and were actively encouraged to develop an Aussie accent! By 2003, the top five Indian IT companies had set up offices in Australia and were actively sourcing business with companies in the finance, telecommunications, aviation, manufacturing and retail industries.

Thus, it was no wonder that the CEO's email came as a surprise to Robert. Since it was a Friday afternoon, Robert was in a weekend mood and brushed aside further thoughts. On Monday morning, Jack Clinton, the CEO of Tel Alliance, briskly walked into the boardroom and was pleased to see all the functional directors in attendance. Jack wasted no time to come to the topic.

'Good morning, ladies and gentlemen. The main purpose of today's meeting is to review our entire ITES outsourcing model. As you know, the model has worked pretty well from the point of view of cost savings and productivity improvement. However, some recent developments have led me to believe that we need to revisit this model and retune it. While there is no need for alarm at this stage, I feel that, if left unattended, these developments have the potential to cause major damage to our community image as a corporate citizen and therefore I want to be proactive and address this issue while it is still manageable.

'Let me highlight some of the present and potential problems with our current ITES outsourcing model.

'You might have read about recent media reports highlighting how tech jobs are heading overseas at the cost of local employment.[4] It is a fact that at Tel Alliance, over the years, we have significantly reduced the number of IT personnel and call centre staff. There is a growing political row over the loss of domestic jobs due to outsourcing. In fact, some politicians in the United States and Britain, as well as in Australia, have proposed bans on awarding contracts to firms that use foreign workers.

'It is unfortunate that politicians play with the concept of globalisation as it suits them. However, we need to be sensitive to public opinion and we need to reassure them that we will not ignore local community concerns in pursuit of corporate objectives. It is sometimes hard to argue against a political stand that favours a vendor providing local jobs and local investment even though from a purely business point of view that vendor may be more expensive and less productive compared to global standards. The economic and business reasons for IT outsourcing may be compelling, but jobs disappearing to India is an emotive issue.[5]

'As the politicians and trade unions step up their pressure against the loss of local jobs, many Australian companies, including Tel Alliance, are being accused of 'breathtaking hypocrisy' in outsourcing.[6] Even the Australian Computer Society has suggested that outsourcing tech jobs is a potential disaster for the economy, because it threatens 70 000 local IT jobs. The pressure even landed one local IT company in the Industrial Relations Commission because it was accused of forcing its employees to accept a 50 per cent pay cut to remain as competitive as foreign outsourcing firms.[7]

'There are problems on the quality front too. In terms of the help desk, few firms now believe that Indian IT companies can provide the level of quality and services they need and many have started bringing the help-desk function back in-house.[8] Even though at present the quality of service by Indian firms is not a major issue at Tel Alliance, we need to keep a close watch because there is obviously the potential for failure when administering back-office operations from another country, in another time zone, where the law, communications technologies and industrial relations are of a very different standard from those in Australia.[9]

'The software industry in India has its own problems too. They include poor infrastructure, lack of cultural and business familiarity with Western countries, increasing labour turnover and ballooning wage bills.[10] In the long run, this might erode the cost and quality advantage that India enjoys in the ITES market, and companies like Tel Alliance could be forced to look elsewhere to derive similar advantages.

'Thus, our ITES model is not as rosy as it appears and we may need to rethink our strategy on outsourcing. Some of you may argue that the business case of IT outsourcing to India remains strong and that in a hyper competitive market with fast-eroding profit margins, it is a strategic business compulsion to stick to core competencies and outsource everything else. I agree and also believe that as the effects of economic recession wear off and employment levels in the IT industry come back to healthy levels, the current protests will slowly fade away from public notice.[11] However, in the meantime, we need to be sensitive to current debate on IT outsourcing and proactively monitor the pros and cons of a fast-changing business scenario. I now invite your comments and suggestions.'

Questions

1. If you were the HR Director of Tel Alliance, what comments and suggestions would you give to the CEO from an international HR perspective?

2. Assume that you have just received the results of an employee morale survey, which indicates that the employees in your IT division and call centre feel very demoralised and stressed due to the potential threats to their jobs from outsourcing. How would you deal with this situation?

3. The employees of an Indian outsourcing firm working on-site in Australia have lodged a complaint that they are not receiving proper cooperation from local Tel Alliance employees in performing their work and that they have been the target of racial abuse in the workplace. How would you respond to these complaints?

4. The External Relations Department has reported to management that many customers have called to complain that they could not understand the accent of Indian call centre staff and that, in many instances, the call centre representative did not seem to know or understand the local business environment to be able to resolve the issue. (*Note:* Credit card transactions are still a rarity in India.) The matter has been referred to HR to help enhance customer service quality. What do you recommend?

5. Some Indian call centre staff have complained that they have received abusive treatment from Australian customers who demand to know where they are from and why they are snatching Australian jobs. The staff have been prohibited by the Indian management from revealing their true name and location. Would you recommend that customers be told upfront as to where their calls are being transferred?

End notes

1. 'Outsourcing customer service: 50% to 67% of leading companies continue outsourcing operations', PRNewswire, 17 December 2003 (biz.yahoo.com/prnews/031217/clw017_1.html).
2. National Association of Software & Services Companies, *The Indian Software Industry in India: A Strategic Review*, NASSCOM, New Delhi, 2001.
3. P. Engardia, 'Corporate America's silent partner: India', *Business Week*, 15 December 2003.
4. E. Connors and R. Lebihan, 'More Telstra jobs head overseas', *Australian Financial Review*, 9 September 2003; and J. O'Rourke, 'IT jobs go overseas for lower pay rates', *Sun-Herald*, 29 December 2002.
5. J. Kirby, 'Australian jobs go west', *BRW*, 6 March 2003.
6. E. Connors, '"Breathtaking hypocrisy" in outsourcing, says union', *Australian Financial Review*, 9 September 2003.
7. J. Kirby, op. cit.
8. Computerwire/Datamonitor 'Lehman moves helpdesk out of India', posted 18 December 2003 (www.theregister.co.uk/content/53/34582.html).
9. J. Kirby, op. cit.
10. J. Fox, 'Call centres hang-ups in India', *Fortune*, 22 December 2003; and N. M. Agrawal and M. Thite, 'HR issues, challenges and strategies in Indian software services industry', *International Journal of Human Resources Development and Management*, vol. 3, no. 3, 2003, pp. 249–64.
11. P. Engardia, op. cit.

part

7

assessing human resource management

Part 7 deals with how to effectively evaluate HRM. The case study at the end of the part incorporates this topic using the example of Acme Financial Services.

chapter 22

assessing HRM effectiveness

Learning objectives

When you have finished studying this chapter, you should be able to:

- Understand the importance of assessing HRM effectiveness
- Describe the approaches used in assessing HRM effectiveness
- Identify the information and common measures used in assessing HRM effectiveness
- Understand the importance of measuring and communicating the contribution of HRM to the achievement of the organisation's strategic business objectives
- Describe the HR scorecard and its application.

'Not only is it possible to measure the effect of human performance; it is necessary for maintaining a viable position in the market'.[1]

Jac Fitz-Enz

Introduction

'In forward looking organisations', says Kenney, 'the HR manager's major goal is to create a new kind of employment relationship, in which employees believe their greatest success and satisfaction will come from actively seeking ways to contribute to the organisation's success.'[2] Consequently, many HR managers now 'report directly to the CEO and spend much of their time aligning human resources with business strategy'[3] They are being held accountable for contributing to measurable strategic business objectives. 'To support the articulation of strategic HR priorities', says Howes, 'it is important to determine performance indicators to measure the impact of HR strategy.'[4]

HR managers have a desperate need to demonstrate the costs and benefits of the HR function. Alas, too few HR managers make the effort to analyse the return on the organisation's HR expenditure. A recent survey, for example, found that few companies undertake cost–benefit analyses of their work–family policies.[5] Similarly, some HR managers feel that quantifying HR runs counter to their basic values.[6] Such feelings are justified by the belief that HR contributions are intangible and cannot be measured.[7] In the United States, it is estimated that fewer than 50 per cent of HR departments measure anything quantitatively.[8]

Odiorne says that such a view invites two immediate questions:
- How can the HR function insist that other functions do something that it itself evades?
- If the output of the HR function is so vague that it cannot be described or measured, what would the organisation be missing if it were eliminated?[9]

As a result, line managers perceive many HR activities as luxuries that can be eliminated when economic times are tough. This emphasis also explains in large part why HR managers have traditionally not been accorded much status and influence in their organisations.[10] 'Profits aren't measured in terms of goodness, righteousness or other aesthetics indexes', says Fitz-Enz. 'They are expressed in hard dollars. Therefore, if the human resource department wants to join the profit team along with marketing, manufacturing and the rest of the high status departments, it will have to start looking for and pointing out its contribution to profits.'[11] Interestingly, some forward-looking companies such as Scandia AFS, a Scandinavian insurance firm, now use important non-financial measures such as intellectual knowledge and corporate culture characteristics that contribute to their success.[12]

The HR function, however, is not different and should not be treated differently. Its outcomes must be measured in economic terms.[13] HR must prove its worth by quantifying the value of its policies and programs so that investments will be made in areas such as training and development and childcare programs.[14] Organisations live and die by the bottom line. A function that adds to the bottom line is important. A function that does not do so invariably deserves and gets less status, influence, security and money.[15] 'It is essential', stresses Howes, 'that the HR function be able to articulate how HR initiatives are linked to, and driven by, the strategic priorities of the organisation. An effective audit of the HR function must assess this level of alignment because of its importance in leveraging the best return from the investment in HR and in people-related initiatives.'[16]

Failure to do so means that the HR function:
- views line managers as the enemy who frustrate the 'professional' approach to HRM
- depends on top management support to overcome line management resistance
- gives up or introduces HR programs without line management support
- measures success in superficial terms such as number of training programs conducted.[17]

According to Cascio, the challenge is to:
- demonstrate the costs associated with the mismanagement of human resources (for example, controllable turnover and absenteeism costs)
- demonstrate the benefits and the return on investment associated with the wise management of people (for example, the benefits associated with valid employee selection programs and employee assistance programs).[18]

HR managers must make a choice, says Mercer. 'They can continue to provide a service that is valued to a degree. Or, human resource managers can fully enter the real business arena of their organisations by becoming part of the profit-generating team that runs the show.'[19]

The HR audit

An **HR audit** involves a systematic analysis and evaluation of the HRM function. It provides feedback to both management and HR specialists on the value of the contribution of the HR function to the organisation's strategic objectives (see figure 22.1).

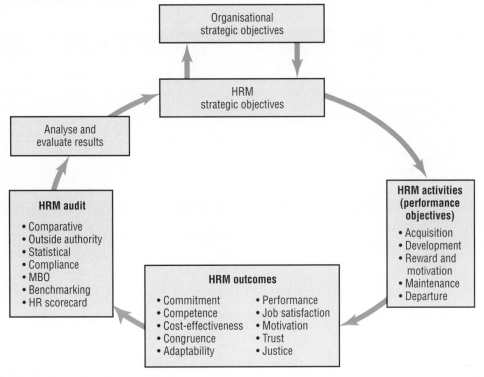

Figure 22.1 The HRM audit process
Source Asia Pacific Management Co. Ltd, 2004.

An HR audit shows that employees are using the company's tuition refund program to advance their careers outside.

Furthermore, generating a meaningful set of measures that can be tracked over time indicates objectively how well the HR function is performing in terms of relative productivity and cost-effectiveness. In summary, the HRM audit facilitates:

- evaluation of the performance of the HR function
- compliance with laws, policies, regulations and procedures
- contribution by the HR function to the organisation's strategic objectives
- development of the professionalism of HR personnel by subjecting their function to management scrutiny
- improvement in the HR function's image with management by demonstrating its impact on profits.[20]

Approaches to the HR audit

Five key approaches to conducting an HR audit can be identified:

1. *Comparative approach.* The audit compares the firm (or division) with another firm (or division) to uncover areas of poor performance. This approach commonly is used to compare the results of specific activities or programs. It helps to detect areas of needed improvement.[21] A development of this is *benchmarking*, where HR performance indicators are compared with available data from 'best practice' firms (or divisions).

HR audit Involves a systematic analysis and evaluation of the efficiency and effectiveness of the HRM function and its contribution to the achievement of the organisation's strategic objectives.

2. *Outside authority approach.* The audit relies on the expertise of a consultant or published research findings as a standard against which activities or programs are evaluated. The consultant or research findings may help diagnose the cause of problems.
3. *Statistical approach.* From existing records, the audit generates statistical standards against which activities and programs are evaluated. With these numerical standards, the audit may uncover errors while they are still minor.
4. *Compliance approach.* By sampling elements of the HR information system, the audit looks for deviations from laws and company policies or procedures. Through fact-finding efforts, the audit can determine whether there is compliance with company policies and legal regulations.
5. *Management by objectives (MBO) approach.* When an MBO approach is applied to the HR area, the audit can compare actual results with stated objectives. Areas of poor performance can be detected and reported and corrective action taken.[22]

As would be expected, no one approach is universally appropriate to every situation and every organisation. Because each HR function is unique, the HR manager must select the approach (or approaches) that best fits the organisation's culture and generates the performance indicators that can be best translated into cold, hard cash. As Cascio points out, the language of management is dollars, not correlation coefficients.[23] A list of typical items that can be costed out is shown in figure 22.2.

Auditing HR activities reduces employees to numbers on a page or dollars in a budget.

HR ACTIVITIES THAT CAN BE DOLLAR COSTED

Recruitment and selection
- Advertising expenses
- Administration costs (for example, the cost of processing job applications)
- Costs of interviewers' time
- Employment test expenses
- Consultants' fees
- Legal expenses (for example, for contract preparation)
- Time to fill a vacancy
- Cost per hire

Compensation and benefits
- Payroll costs
- Benefit costs (for example, costs of sick leave, maternity leave, superannuation, etc.)
- Insurance premiums

HRD
- Training program expenses
- Training consultants' fees
- Training material expenses (for example, books, videos, etc.)

Health and safety
- Costs of accidents
- Workers compensation insurance
- Lost time because of accidents

Industrial relations
- Lost time because of industrial disputes
- Absenteeism
- Labour turnover

Figure 22.2 Examples of HR activities that can be dollar costed
Source Asia Pacific Management Co. Ltd, 2004.

Audit information

Information that can be used as a database for measurement of HR activities is available both from within the organisation (for example, HR budgets, employment interview records, grievance complaints, production records, performance appraisal records, and so on) and outside the organisation (for example, pay surveys, benchmarking data, industry surveys, and so on). Data may be hard or quantitative (for example, financial) or soft or qualitative (for example, observation, interview and focus group data). Much of what HR deals with is intangible, so soft data are often used. Although data may vary in type, their purpose is to enable the HR manager to establish performance measures, evaluate performance, identify cause and effect relationships, and integrate HR activities with the organisation's strategic business objectives.

This Letter to the Editor provides a provocative viewpoint. Do you agree? See 'What's your view?' on page 837.

Letter to the Editor

Assessing HR effectiveness places the emphasis on money, not people

Dear Editor,

In an effort to prove the value of HR, HR managers appear to be increasingly engaged in futile attempts to quantify the costs and benefits of HR activities. In doing so, they hope to show that HR has 'strategic' relevance to organisations and should be given the same intra-company status as functions such as production, marketing and finance.

Unfortunately, apart from the obvious measures of HR effectiveness, such as measuring absenteeism and monitoring work stoppages and other industrial relations issues, most human behaviour in organisations is unquantifiable.

For instance, the proponents of HR evaluation argue that one way in which the effectiveness of HR can be measured is by considering the morale of employees. This can be done by asking staff whether they agree or disagree with statements such as 'This is a good place to work'. Questions like this are, unfortunately, 'motherhood statements' of the worst kind. Who knows what 'a good place to work' is? Is it one where salary levels are above the industry average, or it is one where the airconditioning system keeps people comfortable? Furthermore, is the statement asking respondents to compare their current workplace to previous workplaces, or is it asking them to compare life at work this week with

life at work last week? There is no objective reference point, and the question is fraught with ambiguity.

In addition, it is arguable whether 'a good place to work' in the eyes of employees has any correlation whatsoever with productivity or organisational success. Corporate life is littered with the carcasses of companies that were great places to work but that nevertheless failed for any of a variety of reasons.

Some have noted that the evaluation of HR activities is a complex process wrapped up in issues of power, politics, value judgements and human interests. If this is true, then HR managers may be better off avoiding the interdepartmental 'turf wars' associated with proving the worth of their particular function. They would be better served by taking the high moral ground and continuously asserting the self-evident value of instituting and resourcing appropriate HR practices across the entire organisation.

Thus, rather than attempting to gain the perception of equivalence with key organisational functions, HRM should stress its historically valuable support role in working with other functional areas and with senior management to improve the execution and operationalisation of organisational strategies and change management processes. This would allay much of the cynicism of senior managers as they continue to observe HRM's seemingly futile attempts to recast itself as the equal or better of the other business disciplines.

The CEO of a diversified multinational corporation

Source David Poole, University of Western Sydney.

Evaluating the HR climate

The climate in an organisation has an impact on employee motivation, performance, job satisfaction and morale.[24] The quality of the **HR climate** can be measured by examining employee turnover, absenteeism, health and safety records, and employee attitude surveys. These criteria may also be used in assessing the performance of the HR function.

HR climate Covers employee perceptions about the work environment that affect motivation and behaviour (such as the physical environment, the culture of the organisation, its management style, the openness of communications, and HR policies and practices).

Employee turnover

Employee turnover refers to the process of employees leaving an organisation and having to be replaced.[25] Employee turnover in Australia and Hong Kong traditionally has been high and is a major factor inhibiting improved labour productivity.

Employee turnover The loss of employees by the organisation. It represents those employees who depart for a variety of reasons.

High labour turnover involves increased costs in recruitment, selection, orientation and training.[26] Furthermore, labour turnover may lead to disruption of production, problems in quality control, poorer communications and an inability to develop teamwork and morale. In fact, Knowles identifies labour turnover as one of the most sensitive variables in depicting deterioration in Australian organisations.[27] Reinforcing this view, a recent study shows serious deficiencies in the selection, induction and socialisation practices of many Australian organisations.[28]

Computing employee turnover

Standard methods of computing employee turnover are:

$$\text{Separation rate} = \frac{\text{Number of separations during the month}}{\text{Total number of employees at mid-month}} \times 100$$

$$\text{Resignation rate} = \frac{\text{Total resignations}}{\text{Total number of employees}} \times 100$$

$$\text{Avoidable turnover} = \frac{\text{Total separations} - \text{unavoidable separations}}{\text{Total number of employees at mid-month}} \times 100$$

Unavoidable separations include terminations of temporary employment, promotions, failure to return after maternity leave, transfers and separations due to illness, death, marriage or retirement. Avoidable turnover gives an excellent measure of the HR climate as it directs attention to that part of employee turnover that can be reduced. It also represents the portion of labour turnover that management has the most capacity to influence by better HR management (via improved recruitment, selection, orientation, training, working conditions, compensation and benefits, and opportunities for advancement).[29] Ironically, low turnover (associated with good management and organisational health) may be worse than high turnover if top performers are not being retained.[30] Turnover quality as opposed to turnover quantity must also be considered.

Exit interviews

Exit interviews are conducted with employees who are separating from the organisation to ascertain what they think and feel about the organisation (see figure 22.3). Exit interviews are the most popular means of monitoring labour turnover in Asia.[31] Exit interviews have two goals: to maintain good public relations with the departing employee and to discover the employee's reasons for leaving. Properly handled, the exit interview can yield much revealing information about the HR climate. One survey, for example, found that exit interviews produced useful data on how management and company policies could be improved.[32] A good exit interview process can thus help the HR manager to diagnose an organisation's weaknesses and confirm its strengths.[33]

Separation rate A standard method of computing employee turnover. Includes both avoidable and unavoidable separations.

Resignation rate A standard method of computing employee turnover that focuses on that part of employee turnover due to resignations.

Avoidable turnover A standard method of computing employee turnover that focuses on that part of employee turnover that can be reduced by managerial action.

Exit interviews An employee's final interview following separation. The purpose of the interview is to find out the reasons why the employee is leaving (if the separation is voluntary) or to provide counselling and/or assistance in finding a new job (if the separation is involuntary).

EXIT INTERVIEW QUESTIONS

- Why are you leaving?
- Where are you going?
  - geographic location
  - name of organisation
  - position title
  - compensation details
- What do you think of your:
  - compensation and benefits?
  - job?
  - supervision?
  - colleagues?
  - working conditions?
  - promotional opportunities?
  - training?
- What did you like/dislike about the company?
- Would you consider returning to the company?
- Would you recommend the company to others as a good place to work?
- What could have been done to prevent your departure?
- Do you have any suggestions or comments on how to improve things?

Figure 22.3 Exit interview questions

Post-exit interviews

Other methods of obtaining information about why an employee has left an organisation include the post-exit interview (often by telephone) and the **post-exit questionnaire**. The latter is mailed to separating employees shortly after they leave the organisation. This approach may get a more honest explanation, especially if confidentiality is guaranteed (see figure 22.4).

Post-exit questionnaire
Survey questionnaire used with departed employees to find out why they left the organisation, their feelings about the company, their supervision, and so on.

POST-EXIT QUESTIONNAIRE

	Yes	In part	No
My job lived up to my expectations	☐	☐	☐

	Good	Fair	Poor
My working conditions were	☐	☐	☐
My job orientation was	☐	☐	☐
My training was	☐	☐	☐
My pay was	☐	☐	☐
My benefits were	☐	☐	☐
My treatment by my supervisor was	☐	☐	☐

My major reason/s for leaving were dissatisfaction with

Pay	☐
Benefits	☐
Conditions	☐
Supervision	☐
Training	☐
Opportunities	☐
Other	☐

What could we have done to prevent you from leaving?

_____
_____
_____

What suggestions do you have to make our organisation a better place to work?

_____
_____
_____

Figure 22.4 Post-exit questionnaire

Costs of turnover

The costs of labour turnover are surprisingly high. For example, the US Department of Labor estimates that it costs a company one-third of a new employee's annual salary to replace an employee.[34] The cost of replacing executives is approximately 150 per cent of annual salary, making it a significant cost to companies 'in terms of knowledge capital and resources to find a replacement'.[35] These costs include the direct costs of recruiting, interviewing, testing, reference checking and so on, plus the administrative costs associated with placing a new employee on the payroll. Indirect costs such as underutilised facilities until the new employee is hired and reduced productivity while the new employee is learning the job must also be considered. A study by Hewitt Associates found that labour turnover at one US$30 billion service division of a US high-tech company cost US$150 million per year.[36]

Causes of turnover

The two variables most related to labour turnover are job dissatisfaction and economic conditions (see figure 22.5).[37] In the former case, organisations with poor working conditions, undesirable jobs, pay inequities and restricted opportunities for advancement can predict a high level of labour turnover. In the latter case, an inverse relationship is revealed between the state of the economy and the rate of employee turnover. When the economy is depressed, for example, turnover in most organisations goes down.[38] Research findings indicate that Australian male and female managers resign for basically the same reasons.[39]

The Gallup Organisation drew on interviews and questionnaires completed by more than one million employees over 25 years. Using sophisticated statistical techniques such as factor analysis, regression analysis and concurrent validity studies, Gallup researchers identified the questions that would measure whether employees were likely to stay with their employer.

Ultimately, the full range of factors was reduced to aspects that seem to measure the 'core elements' that attract and retain productive employees. Gallup summarises these as 12 questions:

1. Do I know what is expected of me?
2. Do I have the materials and equipment I need to do my work right?
3. At work, do I have the opportunity to do what I do best every day?
4. In the past seven days, have I received recognition or praise for good work?
5. Does my supervisor, or someone at work, seem to care about me as a person?
6. Is there someone at work who encourages my development?
7. At work, do my opinions seem to count?
8. Does the mission of my company make me feel like my work is important?
9. Are my colleagues committed to doing quality work?
10. Do I have a best friend at work?
11. In the past six months, have I talked with someone about my progress?
12. At work, have I had the opportunity to learn and grow?

The answers to these questions seem particularly important to the most productive and talented employees. They reveal aspects of the workplace that will retain key staff; however, they seem less important to underperforming staff. Therefore, they have the potential to encourage the best to stay without encouraging those that an employer is less interested in retaining.

The research focused on more than just job satisfaction. Many employees apparently have great jobs in lousy workplaces. Some have lousy jobs in great workplaces, and they stay because the workplace is great. Gallup defined 'great workplaces' as those that performed well on four measurable outcomes: employee retention, customer satisfaction, productivity and profitability.

Figure 22.5 The 12-step program for keeping employees
Source H. Onsman, 'The secret of a happy office', *Business Review Weekly*, 11 June 1999, p. 46.

Absenteeism

Absenteeism The failure of employees to report to work when they are scheduled to do so.

Absenteeism is any failure to report to work, as scheduled, regardless of reason.[40] It does not include planned absences such as annual leave, public holidays or rostered days off. Unauthorised or unscheduled absenteeism is a major social problem with costs for the individual worker, the economy and the general community.[41] Unfortunately, there is a misconception among some employees that absences (such as taking a 'sickie' after a late night) are excusable. From a business standpoint, all unscheduled absences cost money.[42] Experience shows that better attendance equates with better quality, lower costs and greater productivity.[43] Australia Post, for example, developed a new sick leave policy after discovering that 80 per cent of all sick leave at the organisation was taken by 20 per cent of the work force.[44]

The costs of absenteeism

The costs of employee absenteeism, according to Cascio, stem from three main sources:
- costs associated with absentees themselves (for example, pay and benefits)
- costs associated with managing problems of absenteeism (for example, pay and benefits to supervisors for counselling absentees, completing necessary reports, recruiting and training substitute employees)
- costs not associated either with absentees or with managing absenteeism problems (for example, machine down-time, extra scrap and wasted materials, overtime costs for replacement workers).[45]

One US study estimates that a 2.5 per cent reduction in productivity occurs for each 1 per cent increase in absenteeism.[46] Yet some HR managers do not see the need to keep records or take action to reduce absenteeism.

According to Allen and Iggins 'we live in an absenteeism culture. Taking a day off and calling in sick is supported and encouraged by our society. Many people's attitude is "The time is coming to us"'.[47]

Employers are also guilty of supporting absenteeism as a cultural phenomenon. They expect people to take sick days when they aren't sick, and accept it as one of the costs of doing business. Absenteeism is so routine that employers budget around it, make overtime allowances for it and hire more workers than they need to take up the slack it causes. It is estimated that 'sickies' cost Australian industry more than $2 billion per year.[48]

Computing absenteeism rates

Methods of computing absenteeism rates recommended by the Productivity Council of Australia are as follows.

The *frequency rate* gives a measure of the number of absences that occur. It does not take into account the length of the absences.

$$\text{Frequency rate} = \frac{\text{Total number of separate absences}}{\text{Average strength of work force}}$$

Consider, for example, that a firm has an average work strength of 60 people and that there were 180 separate absences (of more than one hour's duration) over a period of one month. Then, the frequency rate for the month is:

$$\frac{180}{60} = 3$$

The *absence rate* gives a measure of how much working time was lost through absence during a particular period.

$$\text{Absence rate} = \frac{\text{Total labour hours lost through absences}}{\text{Total labour hours rostered}} \times 100$$

For example, consider that a firm with 100 employees had a total of 16 000 labour hours rostered in a particular month, and that there were absences totalling 800 hours in that period. Then, the absence rate for the month would be:

$$\frac{800}{1600} = 5 \text{ per cent}^{49}$$

Calculating absenteeism cost/savings

Cascio has suggested using the cost of absenteeism at Time 1 as a baseline from which to measure the financial gains associated with some strategy (such as discipline or positive incentives to come to work) to reduce absenteeism. Then, at some later time (Time 2), the total cost of absenteeism is calculated again. The difference between the Time 2 figure and the Time 1 figure, minus the cost of implementing the strategy to reduce absenteeism, represents net gain.[50]

An approach developed in Australia by Isherwood calculates the organisation's net extra profit for the year if there had been no absenteeism. There are three steps:

- An estimate is made of the increase in dollar value of production if no employees were absent.
- An estimate is made of the costs of production of this extra output.
- The difference between the two estimates is equal to the cost of absenteeism.[51]

Causes of absenteeism

A model for analysing the causes of absenteeism developed by Steers and Rhodes suggests that both ability to attend and motivation to attend are key factors. Variables such as transportation that affect the employee's ability to attend work are generally beyond the organisation's control. However, the employee's motivation to attend work is affected by variables such as job satisfaction and attendance incentives, which are very much subject to the organisation's control. Australian studies have identified a relationship between absence and such factors as job boredom, poor interpersonal communication and poor management–employee relations.[52]

NEWSBREAK

Time for a check-up

By Steve Van Emmerick

Given Australia's multicultural and diverse society, it's not surprising that many Australian organisations have diversity strategies. However, these strategies, which involve managing a workforce in an inclusive way to better serve an increasingly diverse client base, are not always uniformly successful.

Diversity audits are a new tool that can help to improve diversity management. A diversity audit involves taking a quantitative and qualitative reading of employee attitudes, perceptions and characteristics, and analysing the results to determine which actions will help achieve strategic goals.

The signs that an organisation's diversity management is failing is when HR managers and CEOs have different perspectives.

HR managers point to symptoms such as high staff turnover, absenteeism and grievance actions.

These symptoms can have strong bottom-line effects that organisations in today's competitive marketplace can ill afford. For example, estimates of the costs of staff turnover range from 95 per cent to 290 per cent of an employee's annual salary. Serious-grievance procedures are estimated to cost on average $35 000 for each case, and have significant effects on the people involved and negative effects on workplace harmony.

HR managers who conduct a diversity audit give themselves the tools to prevent such problems, rather than just reacting to them.

Surveys indicate that CEOs believe good diversity management can help address vital issues such as difficulties in penetrating export markets and problematic alliances with joint-venture partners.

In this regard, a diversity audit helps by identifying the right people and strategies to deal with customers and joint-venture partners who are culturally different.

A productive continuous improvement strategy involves four stages: symptom, diagnosis, prescription and action. However, when it comes to diversity management in Australia, companies generally jump from symptom to action — often with disappointing results. A diversity audit provides the diagnosis and prescription, completing the continuous improvement cycle.

In the first stage, the organisation identifies the symptoms it wants to audit to address. The audit usually uncovers additional symptoms. Next, the audit measures the attitudes, perceptions and characteristics of the workforce. This diagnosis results in a prescription — recommended actions based on audit measures, key performance indicators, policies and goals.

In the action stage, the organisation uses the diagnosis and prescription to improve company policies, their communication and implementation; to make marketing more appropriate to customers; and to train managers to manage diversity in the workforce more effectively.

The continuous improvement cycle can then be repeated to tackle issues such as reducing staff turnover, increasing productivity and targeting new markets.

The prescriptions that flow from diversity audits vary according to the purpose of the audit and the specific issues that exist within an organisation. However, several themes emerge.

Firstly, workers who feel a strong sense of inclusion in an organisation will be more productive and satisfied with their work. This helps to reduce symptoms such as staff turnover, absenteeism, low productivity and grievance procedures. Simply conducting the diversity audit can help, by making workers aware that managers do care about workers' job satisfaction.

Secondly, audits often highlight the widely differing perceptions of managers and workers. Managers are frequently surprised to find that workers feel uninvolved in decision-making, unappreciated, and cynical about the fairness and transparency of promotion decisions. Prescriptions from the audit can deal with the issues workers care most strongly about.

Thirdly, audits can uncover hidden skills in employees that managers were unaware of. These skills may help in targeting new markets.

Even though Australian business and political leaders have recognised the benefits of engaging in an increasingly diverse global marketplace, vital data that would provide a prescription for effective diversity management is not being captured.

According to the University of Melbourne's Centre for International Business, most Australian companies do not keep even the most basic diversity records, such as data relating to ethnic background, language skills or age. Even fewer companies analyse such data to determine how it can help them achieve their goals. This means that companies that do effectively collect and manage this information have a real competitive and sustainable advantage.

An audit can shed light on underlying perceptions and attitudes that may need to be addressed in order for the organisation's workforce to function smoothly. This often indicates an organisation's strengths and weaknesses, which may otherwise go undetected by management for years.

In the past, diversity management was mainly about legal compliance. However, developments in the United States suggest that the new focus is linking diversity to real bottom-line results.

US diversity management specialist Edward Hubbard has found that the concrete data obtained from a diversity audit provides powerful feedback to CEOs on the value of HR programs and useful information on the type of programs that deliver value.

Australians live in an increasingly diverse world. If managers ignore this reality then the health of a company's corporate culture and the bottom line can suffer. Many companies have diversity strategies, but implementing a diversity strategy without undertaking a diversity audit is equivalent to taking a cure without the proper diagnosis and prescription.

Source *HR Monthly*, April 2003, pp. 46–7.

Absenteeism data

A national survey into absence rates shows that the overall absence rate attributed to sickness and accidents is 4 per cent. This means that 40 out of every 1000 employees are absent at any one time. On average, nine-and-a-half days each year are lost as a result of unscheduled absence, which is much greater than time lost through strikes. Interestingly, one recent study shows that on Fridays there are between two to three times more workers absent than on any other day of the week.[53] The overall loss of working time through unscheduled absence obviously represents a heavy cost to the Australian economy.

Occupational injuries and illnesses

Statistical records of occupational injuries and illnesses in Australia are not complete. The Australian Bureau of Statistics stopped collating information on workplace accidents several years ago and the responsibility now rests with the states.[54] Nevertheless, most major organisations do maintain records on occupational injuries and illnesses that can be used to measure health and safety performance and costs. Expenses associated with workplace accidents include administrative expenses, medical costs, workers compensation insurance payments and loss of productivity. Cascio's approach to measuring the costs of absenteeism is just as valid for injuries and illnesses.

Statistical records of occupational injuries and illnesses also can be used to compute a **lost-time injury** incidence rate for a particular organisation. The standard formula for computing the incidence rate is:

Lost-time injury A severe job-related injury that causes an employee to be absent from the job.

$$\text{Lost-time injury incidence rate} = \frac{\text{Number of lost-time injuries}}{\text{Number of employees}}$$

Incidence rates of this type enable comparisons of safety records to be made both among different employers and across different industries. These rates are also useful for comparing the safety records of particular work groups and departments within the one organisation.[55]

Employee attitude surveys

One of the most objective and economical methods of obtaining information on HRM performance is the **attitude survey**.[56] Because attitudes are a major factor in determining employee behaviour, they reveal much about how an individual feels towards the organisation, towards particular departments and activities, and towards management and other employees. For example, survey results at Qantas show a strong relationship between employee satisfaction and customer satisfaction. In dollar terms, according to one expert, a 1 per cent change on a scoreboard survey was worth $17 million on the Qantas bottom line.[57] Surveys can be carried out by interview or by self-administered questionnaires, using in-house HR specialists or external consultants.

Nankervis claims that substantial benefits can accrue to an organisation from a well-conducted employee attitude survey. These include:
- the generation of a large number of development suggestions
- evidence for changes in policy and practice
- the communication of management concern and willingness to involve employees in the organisation's decision making
- an opportunity for employees to release pent-up feelings about the organisation
- discovery of unknown grievances.[58]

If well planned and administered, employee attitude surveys can thus give the HR manager an invaluable insight into what employees are thinking. They can also be used to act as a driver for change and to specifically address business problems associated with productivity, turnover, absenteeism, tardiness, work group effectiveness, mergers, acquisitions or reorganisations, and industrial relations (see figure 22.6).[59]

An employee attitude survey should be conducted only if top management is thoroughly committed to:
- informing employees of the results of the survey
- implementing changes indicated by the survey results.[60]

If these two actions do not occur, then employees will see the survey as a waste of time. Even worse, warns Mercer, is when no improvements are implemented. This makes employees feel betrayed and less trusting of the organisation than they were before the survey.[61] Reinforcing this view, Nankervis says that it is important to remember that employee expectations are raised by the holding of an employee attitude survey. If the expectations are unsatisfied, then increased cynicism and deteriorating morale are likely.[62]

Guidelines for conducting a survey

Some guidelines for conducting a survey are as follows.
- A single, one-time survey is much less valuable than repeated surveys. It is important to measure trends and changes in direction.
- As a means of cutting costs, and thereby making more frequent surveys, use of sampling should be considered.
- Develop company, plant and department norms or yardsticks. In time, these can have more meaning than most outside comparisons.
- To make comparisons over time, 'freeze' the scale; that is, standardise it. Questions of special momentary interest can be added, but keep the basic checklist constant.
- Attempt to relate attitude scores to specific HRM policies and practices.
- Watch replies to individual questions for their diagnostic values.
- Do not attempt to conduct a survey without expert help and advice.
- Never violate an employee's confidence.
- Show employees and management how attitude scale results have been used to effect improvements.
- Bring employees and line managers in on the planning.[63]

The major steps involved in conducting an employee attitude survey from inception to reporting the findings are shown in figure 22.7.

EMPLOYEE SURVEY

Does your superior understand what your job is? ☐ Yes ☐ No ☐ Uncertain

Do you understand what your superior expects
from you in your job? ☐ Yes ☐ No ☐ Uncertain

Do you understand how your job contributes to
the organisation's objectives? ☐ Yes ☐ No ☐ Uncertain

Do you know what your superior thinks of your
performance? ☐ Yes ☐ No ☐ Uncertain

How do you believe your performance is measured?

☐ Results ☐ Personal relationship with superior

☐ Don't know ☐ Other (please specify)

When did you last sit down with your superior and discuss:

	Within last 12 months	Over 12 months ago	Never
(a) Your performance?	☐	☐	☐
(b) Your training and development?	☐	☐	☐
(c) Your career aspirations?	☐	☐	☐

Do you feel you are well paid for the job you do? ☐ Yes ☐ No ☐ Uncertain

Do you feel your pay increases reflect your
performance of your job? ☐ Yes ☐ No ☐ Uncertain

Do you feel you get sufficient warning of changes
that affect your work? ☐ Yes ☐ No ☐ Uncertain

Does your superior share information with you
and keep you fully informed of what is going on? ☐ Yes ☐ No ☐ Uncertain

Do you feel your superior is interested in you and
your career? ☐ Yes ☐ No ☐ Uncertain

My superior is aware of the problems existing at
my level in the organisation. ☐ Yes ☐ No ☐ Uncertain

Does your superior do a good job of motivating you? ☐ Yes ☐ No ☐ Uncertain

My earnings are better than I would receive for
similar work elsewhere. ☐ Yes ☐ No ☐ Uncertain

I receive sufficient recognition and credit for the
work I do. ☐ Yes ☐ No ☐ Uncertain

I feel secure in my job. ☐ Yes ☐ No ☐ Uncertain

There are ample opportunities for promotion
and advancement within this organisation. ☐ Yes ☐ No ☐ Uncertain

I feel really involved as part of the organisation team. ☐ Yes ☐ No ☐ Uncertain

Working conditions in this organisation are:

☐ Excellent ☐ Good ☐ About average ☐ Below average

Social activities in this organisation are:

☐ Excellent ☐ Good ☐ About average ☐ Below average

Benefits such as superannuation, sick leave, etc. are:

☐ Excellent ☐ Good ☐ About average ☐ Below average

My superior is really interested in knowing how I feel. ☐ Yes ☐ No ☐ Uncertain

Creative thinking and innovation by employees
is encouraged by this organisation. ☐ Yes ☐ No ☐ Uncertain

This organisation is concerned with improving
conditions and benefits for its employees. ☐ Yes ☐ No ☐ Uncertain

Figure 22.6 Employee attitude survey used to explore the HR climate (selected sample questions)
Source Asia Pacific Management Co. Ltd, 2004.

PHASE	KEY QUESTIONS/ISSUES	ACTIVITIES
Validation	Commitment to survey process and corrective action	Interviews with key managers
	Need for survey: – problem indicators – survey objectives.	Employee focus groups
	Survey effectiveness in achieving objectives	Problem analysis
Administration plan	Survey population/appropriate survey units	Development of project plan outlining tasks, time frames and responsibilities
	Sampling strategy, participant anonymity, processing alternatives	Communications, orientation for managers
	Administration method and logistics	
	Pre-/post-survey communication	
	Feedback method and logistics	
	Resource procurement and allocation	
Questionnaire development	Appropriate survey structure and content	Prototype instrument development
Pilot test	Is the meaning of each question clear?	Pre-testing design with employees
	Do response categories facilitate valid responses?	Final modifications to instrument
	Does the instrument elicit the information sought?	
Administration	Effective internal management and follow-up	Questionnaire distribution and administration
Data analysis	Return rate	Data input, computer processing
	Preliminary results	
Report to management	Broad-based trends	Analyses and interpretation
	'Hot spots'	Presentation development
	General conclusions	Management review
	Recommendation for follow-up activities	
Management/ employee feedback	Verification/clarification of findings	Communication development, feedback meetings
	Recommendations for change	
	Employee involvement	
Action planning	Commitment to action plans based on findings	Short- and long-term planning and implementation

Figure 22.7 Major components of an employee attitude survey process

Source P. Sheibor, 'The seven deadly sins of employee attitude surveys', *Personnel*, vol. 66, no. 6, June 1989, p. 68. Reprinted by permission of the publisher. © 1989 American Management Association, New York (www.amanet.org). All rights reserved.

Transformational research[64]

Transformational research
An information-gathering approach designed to help organisations to create an improved employment relationship.

A recent information-gathering approach (**transformational research**) is designed to help organisations to create a new kind of employment relationship. It attempts to do this by:

- involving employees in developing the terms of their new employment relationship

- acknowledging that a complex set of work and non-work factors affects employee attitudes and behaviour
- changing the focus of employee research, so that it centres on ways to encourage employees to deliver the performance necessary to achieve the organisation's business objectives rather than on ways to improve employee satisfaction. For example, a company could ask employees why they thought the company was planning to introduce flexitime, a new medical program or a new incentive plan. Based on the information obtained, the company could better design, communicate and implement the change and increase the probability that it will have the desired impact on employee behaviour (see figure 22.8).

1. Reaching our profitability and market-share goals depends on our ability to sustain a company culture that fosters employees' involvement, individual development and job satisfaction. It is important that you feel a sense of ownership in our strategy for change. Please answer these questions to tell us how well we are meeting this objective:

	Strongly disagree			Strongly agree
A. I have a clear understanding of what I can do to help the company become more profitable.	1	2	3	4
B. I believe that what I do will make an important difference in how profitable the company will be.	1	2	3	4
C. I am confident that I will be well rewarded for helping the company become more profitable.	1	2	3	4
D. I believe it is each employee's responsibility to stay 'employable' by continuously learning and building job skills.	1	2	3	4
E. My job is changing in ways that will:				
• benefit me	1	2	3	4
• benefit the company.	1	2	3	4

2. 'Alignment' is an important part of changing our company and environment. Alignment means that our policies, practices and programs are 'in line with' and support the changes we want to make. How close do you feel we are in making these changes to reach these goals?
The company is moving

• from several management levels to flatter, 'just enough' levels of management.	1	2	3	4
• from people trained for specific jobs with limited flexibility to broad job definitions and people broadly trained for flexibility.	1	2	3	4
• from strict policies, practices and rules to collaboration leading to creative and innovative approaches to resolving problems.	1	2	3	4
• from a focus on individual contribution to an emphasis on team contribution as well as individual contribution.	1	2	3	4
• from divisions that operate independently to cross-divisional cooperation.	1	2	3	4

Figure 22.8 Sample questions from transformational research studies

Source S. M. Kenney, 'Transformational research: a tool for creating the new employer–employee relationship', *Compensation and Benefits Review*, vol. 27, no. 1, 1995, p. 26.

According to Kenney, companies increasingly are realising that 'by understanding more about their employees' needs, focus and goals, they can develop an HR strategy that will help them produce the employee work efforts necessary for business success'.[65]

Practitioner speaks

Achieving employer-of-choice status

Mick Bennett is a psychologist whose career has included working both as an academic and a consultant. He is currently the Asia–Pacific Regional Manager for Hewitt Associates based in Hong Kong.

Many organisations aspire to being an employer of choice. With this aspiration comes an increased expectation on the HR function to develop best-in-class or benchmarked policies and processes that will achieve employer-of-choice status. Hewitt Associates, in conjunction with various media and academic partners, has over the past three years conducted Best Employer studies covering more than 1000 companies in 10 countries. The studies have also directly measured the attitudes and beliefs of hundreds of thousands of employees.

Best Employers are chosen based on three measures: a CEO questionnaire, a People Practices Inventory and an Engagement Survey. On the basis of this quantitative data and qualitative comments, Best Employers are chosen by panels of independent judges operating 'blind' — that is, with no name or links to the identity of the company. Once Best Employers have been chosen by the panels, it is possible to compare the 'Best' with the 'Rest'.

We can now state with absolute confidence that the defining characteristics of Best Employers are not their HR policies and processes. The key differentiators are leadership and culture — it is these factors that create an environment with which HR can be effective. Our research in the Asia–Pacific identifies one particular trait among great leaders: they have an unrelenting and passionate focus on their people as a source of competitive advantage.

Employees in Best Employers believe their senior leadership provides a clear direction for the future (90 per cent of the Best, 54 per cent of the Rest). They are also seen as being open and honest in communications (91 per cent versus 59 per cent). Similarly, employees in Best Employers consistently rate their organisations extremely high in terms of cultural factors such as agility, decisiveness and being results-oriented. Best Employers do not define different values, but they do live the values much more effectively than others.

Given the importance of leadership and culture, are there any HR practices that seem to be characteristic of Best Employers? Yes, there are two. The first is differentiation based on talent. Best Employers have aggressive talent management programs. They identify high potentials, they reward their best people significantly better than other companies and they expose their best people in a variety of roles that will challenge and grow them.

The second is execution. HR Best Employers are less concerned with elegance, although many do have sophisticated HR practices. What is more important is whether the practices are applied. Best Employers recruit for 'fit' with culture and values more than they do for skill. They put much more emphasis on orientation and on-boarding. In Best Employers, managers have honest and direct conversations about performance, they see a core part of their role as being that of coach, and Best Employers clearly define expectations about how people are accountable for outcomes.

These characteristics pay off because employees are engaged — they say good things, do not intend to leave and will work hard to help the company prosper. Engaged employees then work harder for customers, look for ways of improving the business and are focused on creating great business results. It's a double win — satisfied employees working hard for the company. All the data suggest HR cannot do this on their own.

Mick Bennett

Focus groups[66]

Originally designed for use in market research, **focus groups** can be useful in uncovering information and suggestions that employees may be reluctant to disclose. The focus group interview is loosely structured and is designed to promote free-flowing discussion. Unlike traditional focus groups, employee focus groups are confidential and management is not involved. Each focus group is made up of 8–12 participants and led by a trained external consultant. Sessions last between one and two hours.

The consultant introduces a topic or questions, such as: How would employees improve the way the company is managed? Do employees understand the rationale for restructuring? What do employees think of the company's pay-for-performance program? Individuals are asked to give their views and reactions. Group dynamics tend to generate considerable comment and elicit responses that employees may not express independently. Consequently, a good leader can obtain a thorough understanding of the problem or situation. The consultant prepares a summary of the group's comments and suggestions for management.

For focus groups to be successful, it is essential that employees know that their identity will be protected. Consequently, the consultant should instruct participants that the proceedings are confidential and are not to be discussed outside the focus group.

The Hong Kong Housing Authority, KCRC and Cathay Pacific Airways are examples of large organisations that use employee focus groups.

> **Focus groups** Groups of employees who are brought together to confidentially discuss specific HR topics such as a company's pay-for-performance program, restructuring, quality of management, and so on.

Benchmarking

Benchmarking is a relatively new approach to evaluating HR performance and is a key quality improvement technique. It permits an organisation to study and adapt the 'best' business practices by comparing its performance on specific activities with those in 'best-practice' organisations. According to Marshall, benchmarking involves an organisation learning about its own practices, searching for the best practice that will lead to superior performance and making the necessary changes.[67]

Increasingly, benchmarking is being seen as necessary for survival. Competitive pressures to improve customer service, time to market and financial performance are driving managers to study recognised industry leaders, learn their secrets and adapt these ideas to their own organisations.[68] Benchmarking, however, is more than just copying.[69] Because no two organisations are exactly alike, practices may not be directly transferable. Deming cautions 'Adapt, don't adopt'.[70]

Moreover, it is necessary to understand the theory behind the practice. According to Glanz and Dailey, benchmarking HR practices serves a number of purposes:
- It enables the manager to audit how effectively HR meets the needs of the organisation.
- It enables an organisation to learn from those who excel in an HR practice.
- It identifies HR areas where performance can be improved.
- It can be used to create a need for change.
- It can be used to help set direction and priorities for an HR department.[71]

Although there are a number of approaches to benchmarking, there is general agreement on the key ingredients:
- *Don't go on a fishing expedition.* The manager should pick a specific area to be improved and then do the necessary homework. This includes a thorough study of their own organisation's practices and a careful selection of organisations that excel in the practice.
- *Send out people who will have to make the changes.* Practitioners need to see for themselves. It will not help if senior managers or consultants do the benchmarking, then come back and tell the 'owner' of the practice what to do. Visits should be kept short and teams small.
- *Be prepared to exchange information.* The manager should be prepared to answer any questions asked by another organisation.
- *Avoid legal problems.* Discussions that might imply illegal activities lead to trouble and should be avoided.

> **Benchmarking** The identification of best practices among competitors and non-competitors that make them superior performers.

- *Respect the confidentiality of the data given.* Organisations that are relaxed about sharing information with the manager's organisation may not want that information going to a competitor.[72]

Benchmarking is not for the half-hearted manager. It involves a major transformation in attitudes and practices.[73] The shift to workplace bargaining, where wage increases are linked to the reform of the work practices and their adoption, is a major challenge. Moreover, common elements in the 'best-practice' revolution include increased work force participation and more flexible organisational structures, both of which are often resisted by craft unions and middle managers.[74] But as James and Gottliebsen point out, 'they face Hobson's choice: either change their ways or watch their employer and their jobs self-destruct'.[75] In benchmarking, the HR manager has a powerful management change tool.

Measuring HR outcomes

The diagnostic model used in this book gives a framework for evaluating HR's performance (see figure 1.9 on page 23). It should be noted that because organisations differ in their circumstances, individual measures will vary in their significance. The model provides the HR manager with a combination of quantitative and qualitative measures that can be employed to show HR's strategic contribution to the organisation's objectives and employee wellbeing (see figure 22.9).

HRM OUTCOMES	INDICATORS	HOW MEASURED
• Commitment	• Attachment to job • Identification with company	• Questionnaire • Interviews • Focus groups • Observation • Performance ratings • Customer feedback
• Competence	• Abilities • Knowledge • Skills	• Pencil and paper test • Oral examination • Work sample • Observation • Number of promotable employees • Performance ratings • Customer feedback
• Cost-effectiveness	• Dollar value	• Cost–benefit analysis
• Congruence	• Acceptance of core values • Consistency between employee and company objectives	• Questionnaire • Interviews • Focus groups
• Adaptability	• Flexibility • Acceptance of change • Innovation • Creativity	• Questionnaire • Interviews • Focus groups • Performance ratings • Observation

HRM OUTCOMES	INDICATORS	HOW MEASURED
• Performance	• Sales • Profit • Accidents • Quality • Productivity • Customer satisfaction	• Customer feedback • Sales statistics • Profit and loss statement • OH&S statistics • Manufacturing statistics • Performance ratings
• Job satisfaction	• Attitudes • Labour turnover • Absenteeism	• Questionnaire • Interviews • Focus groups • Absenteeism statistics • Turnover statistics • Grievances frequency • Strike figures
• Motivation	• Attitudes • Job performance • Absenteeism	• Questionnaire • Interviews • Focus groups • Observation • Performance ratings
• Trust	• Satisfaction with management • Free exchange of information • Cooperation • Openness • Honesty	• Questionnaire • Interviews • Focus groups • Observation • Performance ratings
• Justice	• Perceptions of fairness • Treatment by supervisors • Ethical behaviour • Grievances • Industrial disputes • Turnover • Satisfaction with HR systems • Satisfaction with management	• Questionnaire • Interviews • Focus groups • Observation • Performance ratings • Audit of HR systems • Demographic analyses • Turnover statistics • Grievances frequency • Strike figures • Third-party audit

Figure 22.9 Measures of HR outcomes
Source Asia Pacific Management Co. Ltd, 2004.

The HR scorecard[76]

Created by Becker, Huselid and Ulrich to measure HR's contribution to the bottom line, the **HR scorecard** (a development of the balanced scorecard, see page 300) promotes the achievement of an organisation's strategic objectives. The HR scorecard allows HR managers to

HR scorecard A measurement system designed to show HR's impact on the achievement of the organisation's strategic objectives and financial performance.

strategically plan and measure the results of HR's contributions. It is based on the assumptions that people are the basis of value creation and that if something cannot be measured, it cannot be managed.

Strategic HRM demands that HR managers deliver technical HRM services such as recruitment and selection in a way that supports the achievement of the organisation's strategic objectives. However, because HR's contributions to organisational performance are difficult to measure, they are often ignored. The HR scorecard attempts to overcome this problem by focusing on the role of HR as an implementer of corporate strategy.[77] The HR manager must answer questions such as:

- Which strategic objectives/outcomes are critical (as opposed to desirable)?
- What are the drivers of performance?
- How will performance be measured?
- What are the barriers to the achievement of each strategic objective/outcome?
- Is HR providing the organisation with the right people in the right place at the right time?
- Do employees have the abilities, skills, knowledge and motivation to achieve the organisation's strategic objectives?
- If not, what needs to change?

High-performance work system An arrangement whereby HR systems are aligned with the organisation's strategic business objectives and HR activities are efficiently performed.

Becker, Huselid and Ulrich argue the need for a **high-performance work system** (HPWS), which is embedded in the organisation's strategy. This will help the organisation to gain a competitive edge by:

- building and maintaining a cadre of talented people, through linking selection and promotion decisions to validated competency models
- developing strategies that provide timely and effective support for the skills required by the organisation's strategic business objectives
- enacting compensation and performance management policies that attract, retain and motivate high-potential people.[78]

To demonstrate HR's strategic contribution, the HR scorecard highlights the following:

- *Cost control* (reducing costs and enhancing operational efficiency). Traditional measures such as accident costs, cost per hire, the number of training courses taught, the percentage of payroll spent on training and turnover costs are employed.
- *Value creation* (ensuring that HR activities are aligned with the organisation's strategic objectives). Strategic measures such as changes in employees' mindsets, customer satisfaction with the company's hiring process, the extent of organisational learning, survey results on becoming the employer of choice and the extent to which information is communicated effectively to employees are employed.

The HR scorecard emphasises the measurement of performance from the perspective of strategic implementation and not just financial results. Examples of high-performance work measures include: How many *exceptional* candidates did we recruit for each *strategic* job opening? What proportion of new hires have been selected using *validated* selection methods? What percentage of employees is regularly assessed via a *formal* performance appraisal? What percentage of total compensation is represented by *variable* pay? What is the number and quality of *cross-functional* teams?[79]

The benefits of the HR scorecard

- It reinforces the distinction between *technical HR* (HR outcomes that focus on HR efficiency) and *strategic HR* (HR outcomes that serve to execute the organisation's strategic business objectives).
- It focuses attention on *leading indicators* that drive the implementation of the organisation's strategic business objectives and emphasise the future. In contrast, traditional evaluation approaches focus on *lagging indicators* such as financial measures, which reflect what has happened in the past.
- It assesses HR's contribution to strategic implementation and the 'bottom line'.
- It allows HR managers to manage their strategic responsibilities effectively.
- It promotes flexibility and change.[80]

Becker, Huselid and Ulrich caution that the HR scorecard is not a panacea for all the problems of a badly managed HR function. It can, however, provide HR managers with a more rigorous method of assessment of HR performance, help deliver improved HR performance and integrate HR activities with organisational strategy.[81]

Criticisms of the HR scorecard

The HR scorecard, like its predecessor the balanced scorecard, forces HR managers to go beyond conventional financial measures and take a strategic approach. The problem (as with the balanced scorecard) is that this is not always an easy or economical thing to do.

The HR scorecard (like the balanced scorecard) needs to be subjected to further study before any definite conclusions can be made about its usefulness.[82] HR managers also need to do a cost–benefit analysis of the HR scorecard process to ensure that it is economically justifiable (particularly as the measurement of HR intangibles often requires the introduction of new measures whose validity and reliability may be uncertain).[83]

Finally, HR managers must measure the costs/benefits not only to the organisation but also to employees. There is little value in creating higher performance if the long-term costs include increased stress and reduced employee motivation.[84]

Measuring performance places employees under stress.

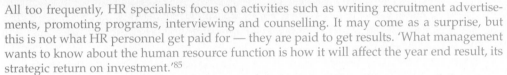

Summary

All too frequently, HR specialists focus on activities such as writing recruitment advertisements, promoting programs, interviewing and counselling. It may come as a surprise, but this is not what HR personnel get paid for — they are paid to get results. 'What management wants to know about the human resource function is how it will affect the year end result, its strategic return on investment.'[85]

HR managers must ensure that their function facilitates the achievement of the organisation's strategic business objectives and that performance is expressed in quantifiable terms using facts, figures and dollars. Only then can the HRM function be seen as not belonging among the expense items and the HR manager can be recognised as a strategic business partner. The hard reality is that until HRM can show a substantial and quantifiable positive effect on the bottom line, it will not be given a place at the strategic decision-making table.[86] A recent development in the measurement of HR performance is the HR scorecard, which attempts to show how HR adds value by linking HR activities to measures (for example, profitability) that line managers understand.

Thirty interactive Wiley Web Questions are available to test your understanding of this chapter at **www.johnwiley.com.au/ highered/hrm5e** *in the student resources area*

terms to know

absenteeism (p. 822)

attitude survey (p. 826)

avoidable turnover (p. 820)

benchmarking (p. 831)

employee turnover (p. 819)

exit interviews (p. 820)

focus groups (p. 831)

HR audit (p. 817)

HR climate (p. 819)

HR scorecard (p. 833)

high-performance work system (p. 834)

lost-time injury (p. 825)

post-exit questionnaire (p. 821)

resignation rate (p. 820)

separation rate (p. 820)

transformational research (p. 828)

review questions

1. Why should HRM activities be assessed?
2. Can the HR function be efficient but not effective? Explain your answer.
3. 'You cannot measure the quality of HR services.' Do you agree or disagree with this statement? Give reasons for your answer.
4. 'HRM lacks status and influence because it does not speak the language of line management?' Do you agree or disagree with this statement? Give reasons for your answer.
5. What is the HR scorecard? Explain how it can be used for measuring HR performance.
6. How would you evaluate an organisation's performance appraisal program?
7. How would you conduct an employee attitude survey?
8. What is the HR climate? How would you measure it?
9. How can exit interviews help to identify HR problems?
10. What is labour turnover? How is it measured? Is there an optimal turnover level?

environmental influences on the assesment of HRM

Describe the key influences from the model (figure 22.10 shown opposite) that have significance for the assessment of HRM.

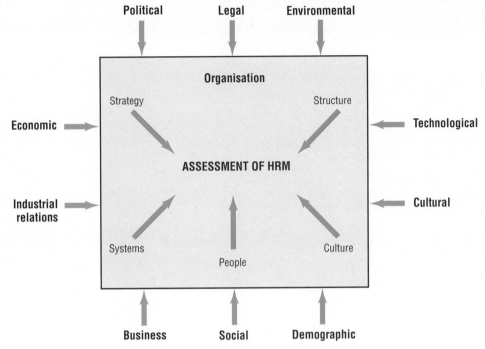

Figure 22.10 Environmental influences on the assessment of HRM

class debate

The HR scorecard is just another management fad that will pass with time.
or
Assessing HRM emphasises money, not people.

what's your view?

Write a 500-word response to the Letter to the Editor on page 819, agreeing or disagreeing with the writer's point of view.

practitioner speaks

Read the article on page 830. Write a 300-word report explaining why you agree or disagree with the author's views.

newsbreak exercise

Read the Newsbreak 'Time for a check-up' on pages 824–5. Critically review the article. Prepare a one-page executive summary explaining why you would recommend/not recommend a diversity audit be conducted in your organisation.

soapbox

What do you think? Conduct a mini survey of class members, using the questionnaire below. Critically discuss the findings.

1.	Organisations live and die by the bottom line.	YES	NO
2.	HR contributions are intangible and cannot be measured.	YES	NO
3.	Measuring the performance of HR insults its professional status.	YES	NO
4.	HRM deals with people; not profits.	YES	NO
5.	Attitude surveys are an invasion of employee privacy.	YES	NO
6.	HR managers lack power and status because they are not bottom-line oriented.	YES	NO

online exercise

Conduct an online search for information on one of the following: absenteeism, labour turnover, benchmarking or the balanced scorecard. Summarise your conclusions in a 300-word report and include the web addresses that you found useful. As a class, discuss your findings.

ethical dilemma

A matter of standards at Western University

Mary Lee, a lecturer in the Department of Management at Western University, was annoyed. She had just presented her HRM class exam results and 23 of her 71 students had failed.

Dr John Smith, the Head of Department, openly expressed his concerns about the high failure rate. Mary stated that the failed students had very poor English language skills and had great difficulty answering the analytical questions. Discussion among the staff members regarding the failed students indicated that most had failed or barely passed their other subjects.

Mary expressed concern that the university's graduates risked becoming unemployable because of their lack of knowledge and marketable skills. She questioned whether some of the students should even be at university and wondered how they could have passed Year 1. Percy Samuels, Senior Lecturer in OB, laughed and said that standards were now so low that even the 'brain dead' could pass.

John flushed and replied angrily that competition was severe and that Western University could not afford to fail so many students, especially fee-paying students. The Dean, he stressed, would never accept such a high number of failures given the university's precarious financial situation.

Percy sarcastically recommended that all student marks be increased by 25 per cent, which would mean that only two students would fail. John said he thought this was a workable situation. Mary reluctantly agreed.

Discussion questions

1. What do you think of this situation?
2. Was John being unethical or just realistic?
3. If you were Mary, what would you have done?

case studies

What's wrong at XYZ Ltd?

Jo Santini sighed. She looked at Bob Cohen, Employment Manager for XYZ Ltd. 'Are you sure, Bob?' she asked.

'Of course I am. There's nothing wrong with our recruitment and selection procedures. I keep on telling you it's our training programs — they're just not doing the job.'

'Jo, that just isn't so!' shouted Elspeth Kim, XYZ's Training and Development Manager. 'Our programs are relevant, up to date and highly regarded.'

'Well, it seems to me', said Jo, 'as manager of this department, we have got a problem. The figures are clear. We have high turnover and the skills of some of our trainees are definitely below average. Why? Is it that we are selecting the wrong people? Is it that our training programs are not appropriate? Or is it something else? We have to find out.'

Discussion questions

1. Explain how you would conduct an audit of the selection and training functions at XYZ Ltd.
2. What possible explanations could there be for the unsatisfactory situation at XYZ Ltd? How would you go about testing them?

Jet Red's fat smokers

Linda Church, Jet Red's HR Manager, clicked forward the next slide of her PowerPoint presentation. The black figures were stark against the yellow background. 'As you can see, our audit of the medical plan shows some startling figures. Employees who are overweight and smoke cost considerably more than those who are of average weight and do not smoke. You can also see that obese smokers lose more days from illness and have a higher rate of general absenteeism.'

'So, what are you suggesting we do about it, Linda?' asked Alan Balkin, Jet Red's Managing Director.

Before Linda could answer, Stan Vines, Marketing Manager, bellowed 'It's simple. Don't hire any more fatties or smokers and fire the ones we have!'

'Are you serious?' questioned Linda.

'You bet I am. Look at the job time wasted with people going outside for a smoke. To say nothing of the mess they make. It really gives visitors a terrible impression. And one other thing — let's get rid of the chocolate biscuits and sweets we provide free of charge. It's an unnecessary cost and just encourages people to eat junk food.'

'I agree with Stan' stated Bill Armstrong, Operations Manager. 'Why should the company encourage such behaviour? We're going broke. We want to employ people who are going to make us money, not cost us money.'

'For heaven's sake, you just can't make decisions like that!' snapped Linda. 'Just because someone is obese or smokes doesn't mean they aren't a productive employee.'

'Sure, there will be individual exceptions, but your own figures show that the average fat smoker costs this company a lot of money', retorted Bill.

'Linda, get real!' Stan barked. 'We're trying to run a business, not a rest home for overweight smokers.'

Jeff Davis, Manager, Finance and Accounting, interrupted the exchange. 'Look, it's obvious that there's a problem. But we need more information. For example, is there a relationship between these factors and performance? For all we know, some of our best people may be overweight smokers. And there is one more thing. What about employee privacy — will that be an issue?'

'Not to mention the matter of discrimination', sighed Linda.

Discussion questions

1. Who do you agree with? Why?
2. Should audits of HR activities cover the physical attributes and personal habits of employees?

Exercise

Break into groups of four to six. Interview an HR manager or a union representative to ascertain their views regarding the potential liability of employers that provide free snacks (such as biscuits and candies, or cigarettes and alcoholic beverages) for their employees to consume. Write a 500-word report summarising your findings.

A matter of turnover at Jet Red

Alan Balkin, Managing Director of Jet Red, turned to Linda Church, the HR Manager. 'Well, Linda', asked Alan, 'What have you got for us?'

Linda moved to the head of the boardroom table and turned to face the airline's senior management. 'As you are well aware, our focus has been on improving customer service. Overall, the feedback we are getting is extremely positive. However, we are starting to experience some difficulties.'

'Why is that, Linda?' asked Alan.

Linda displayed a PowerPoint slide showing the labour turnover figures for the airline. 'Although these are only year-to-date figures', said Linda, 'it's quite clear that we are experiencing a dramatic increase in labour turnover in some departments. If the current trend continues, theoretically we will have lost every one of our existing head office employees by the end of the year.'

Alan turned to Stan Vines, Marketing Manager, and said 'Stan, any comments?'

Stan paused then replied, 'Yes, I think the problem lies in the quality of people the HR Department is sending us. With the current rate of unemployment, I would think we should be able to attract better-qualified applicants. Frankly, some of the people we attract are just not up to scratch. What's more, a lot our turnover is involuntary. We've been house cleaning and getting rid of the poor performers.'

Before Linda could respond, Alan turned to the Finance and Accounting Manager, Jeff Davis, and said, 'Jeff, what about your department?'

'Well, I agree with Linda that turnover in some departments is too high but in others there is virtually none at all. The problem as I see it is that we are losing too many good people and keeping too much of the deadwood.'

'I support Jeff's comments. It's the quality, not the quantity, of people leaving that's the problem' interjected Bill Armstrong, Operations Manager. 'Our flight crew personnel all moan and groan but they never quit. Yet that is where we have some our worst performers.'

The Engineering Manager, Peter Wiley, said 'You're all wrong. We're losing people because of all the changes at Jet Red. The place is becoming a madhouse. The best people are leaving because of all the pressure and uncertainty.'

Alan looked around the table and then said, 'It seems clear to me that we have some problems. It's also evident that we don't have any agreement as to what the causes are. Lots of speculation but no facts! Linda, I suggest you get your act together and have a report ready for our meeting next Friday detailing the precise nature of our turnover problem and what we should do about it.'

Discussion questions

1. What other possible causes of labour turnover could be present?
2. If you were Linda, how would you go about preparing the labour turnover report for the meeting? What information would you need? How would you collect it?
3. What impact could ongoing labour turnover (or lack of turnover) have on customer service?

practical exercises

Using the survey questionnaire in figure 22.6 on page 827, conduct an attitude survey of your workmates (or classmates). Examine (a) what the survey results reveal about the HR climate and (b) what action steps should be recommended. Review your experience in doing the survey and discuss the strengths and weaknesses of attitude surveys as a means of identifying human resource problems.

suggested readings

Becker, B. E., Huselid, M. A. and Ulrich, D., *The HR Scorecard*, Harvard Business School Press, Boston, Mass., 2001.

Boxhall, P. and Purcell, J., *Strategy and Human Resource Management*, Palgrave/Macmillan, Basingstoke, 2003, ch. 1.

Cascio, W. F., *Costing Human Resources*, 4th edn, Southwestern, Cincinnati, Ohio, 2000.

CCH, *Australian Master Human Resources Guide*, CCH, Sydney, 2003, ch. 6.

Clark, R and Seward, J., *Australian Human Resources Management: Framework and Practice*, 3rd edn, McGraw-Hill, Sydney, 2000, pp. 183–6, 502–16.

De Cieri, H. and Kramar, R., *Human Resource Management in Australia*, McGraw-Hill, Sydney, 2003, ch. 16.

Fitz-Enz, J., *The ROI of Human Capital*, AMACOM, New York, 2000.

Fitz-Enz, J. and Davison, B., *How to Measure Human Resources Management*, 3rd edn, McGraw-Hill, New York, 2002.

Ivancevich, J. M., *Human Resource Management*, 8th edn, McGraw-Hill, Boston, 2001, pp. 559–63.

Ivancevich, J. M. and Lee, S. H., *Human Resource Management in Asia*, McGraw-Hill, Singapore, 2002, ch. 16.

Nankervis, A. R., Compton, R. L. and Baird, M., *Strategic Human Resource Management*, 4th edn, Nelson, South Melbourne, 2002, ch. 16

online references

www.ahri.com.au
www.cica.ca
www.ifac.org
www.isrsurveys.com
www.jrmc.com.au

www.montague.com
www.owlbusiness.com.au
www.shrm.org.hrmagazine
www.workforceonline.com

end notes

1. J. Fitz-Enz, *The ROI of Human Capital*, AMACOM, New York, 2000, pp. 22–3.
2. S. M. Kenney, 'Transformational research: a tool for creating the new employer–employee relationship', *Compensation and Benefits Review*, vol. 27, no. 1, 1995, p. 23.
3. R. J. Anthony, 'Human resources in the forefront', *HR Focus*, October 1995, p. 6.
4. P. Howes, 'Does HR benchmarking have a real role to play in organisational success?', *HR Monthly*, September 1997, p. 44.
5. Business Council of Australia survey, reported in F. Buffini, 'Glass ceiling proves a shattering turnoff', *Australian Financial Review*, 3 October 2003, p. 11.
6. R. J. Grossman, 'Measuring up', *HR Magazine*, January 2000, pp. 28–35.
7. L. Pickett, 'Conversations about measurement and human resource effectiveness', *Corporate Management*, vol. 46, no. 6, 1994, p. 255.
8. R. J. Grossman, op. cit., p. 28.
9. G. S. Odiorne, 'Evaluating the human resource program', in J. J. Famularo (ed.), *Handbook of Human Resources Administration*, 2nd edn, McGraw-Hill, New York, 1986, p. 9.5.
10. W. Cascio, 'The dollar impact of staff behaviour', *Personnel Today*, April 1990, p. 8.
11. J. Fitz-Enz, 'Quantifying the human resources function', *Personnel*, vol. 57, no. 2, 1980, pp. 41–52, reprinted in K. Perlman, F. L. Schmidt and W. C. Hammer, *Contemporary Problems in Personnel*, 3rd edn, John Wiley & Sons, New York, 1983, p. 273; N. M. Sorensen, 'Measuring HR for success', *Training and Development*, vol. 49, no. 9, 1995, pp. 49–51; and D. M. Burrows, 'Increase HR's contributions to profits', *HR Magazine*, September 1996, pp. 103–10.
12. L. Thornburg, 'Accounting for knowledge', *HR Magazine*, October 1994, pp. 50–6; and P. Howes, 'Measuring human capital', *HR Monthly*, April 2000, pp. 48–9.
13. W. Cascio, op. cit., p. 8.
14. S. Spodman, 'Human resource management', *Credit Union Magazine*, March 1998, pp. 70–6.
15. M. W. Mercer, *Turning Your Human Resource Department into a Profit Center*, AMACOM, New York, 1989, p. 6.
16. P. Howes, 'Measurement is prerequisite for auditing the HR function', *HR Monthly*, April 1997, p. 46.
17. G. S. Odiorne, op. cit., pp. 9.7, 9.8.

18. W. Cascio, op. cit., p. 8.

19. M. W. Mercer, op. cit., p. 3.

20. V. P. Kraitis, 'The personnel audit', *Personnel Administrator*, November 1981, pp. 29–34; and W. B. Werther Jnr and K. Davis, *Human Resources and Personnel Management*, 5th edn, McGraw-Hill, New York, 1996, p. 560.

21. The Australian Human Resources Institute and HRM Consulting together promote and develop the HR Benchmarking Program, which is Australia's biggest source of benchmarking data. Members of the program receive data specifically tailored to their organisation's needs. Further information on the HR Benchmarking Program can be obtained from Peter Howes, Principal of HRMConsulting, Tel: (07) 3236 1300.

22. Adapted from W. B. Werther and K. Davis, op. cit., p. 565. For a more detailed discussion see G. S. Odiorne, op. cit., pp. 9.1, 9.7.

23. W. Cascio, op. cit., p. 8.

24. A. W. Sherman and G. W. Bohlander, *Managing Human Resources*, 9th edn, Southwestern, Cincinnati, Ohio, 1992, p. 678; and W. French, *Human Resources Management*, 3rd edn, Houghton Mifflin, Boston, 1994, p. 90.

25. R. L. Mathis and J. H. Jackson, *Human Resource Management*, 8th edn, West, St Paul, Minn., 1997, p. 75.

26. J. Abbott, H. De Cieri and R. Iverson, 'Costing turnover: implications of work/family conflict at management level', *Asia Pacific Journal of Human Resources*, vol. 36, no. 1, 1998, pp. 25–43.

27. M. C. Knowles, 'Labour turnover: aspects of its significance', *Journal of Industrial Relations*, vol. 18, no. 1, 1976, pp. 67–75.

28. A. Ellerby and K. Barrett, 'Increased costs eat into profits', *HR Monthly*, June 1999, p. 23.

29. A. W. Sherman and G. W. Bohlander, op. cit., p. 679.

30. P. J. Harkins and L. Kurtz, 'The real cost of employee turnover', *World Executive's Digest*, October 1991, p. 87.

31. Drake Beam Morin survey, reported in K. Leo, 'Employers in renewed efforts to stem staff turnover', *Sunday Morning Post*, 17 September 2000, p. 4.

32. R. Half, 'Managers learn from exit interviews', *Personnel Journal*, May 1994, p. 16.

33. P. Brotherton, 'Exit interviews can provide a reality check', *HR Magazine*, August 1996, p. 45; and S. Moran, 'Just a word before you go', *Boss*, February 2004, pp. 40–2.

34. G. L. White, 'Employee turnover: the hidden drain on profits', *HR Focus*, January 1995, p. 15. Also see P. Howes, 'Labor turnover escalating into a huge cost structure', *HR Monthly*, May 1998.

35. P. Ray, 'Hire executives who'll stay', *HR Magazine*, June 1996, p. 19.

36. A. S. Harrison, 'War for talented staff set to heat up', *South China Morning Post*, 21 October 2000, p. 3.

37. D. J. Cherrington, *The Management of Human Resources*, 4th edn, Prentice Hall, Englewood Cliffs, NJ, 1995, p. 73.

38. D. J. Cherrington, op. cit., p. 73.

39. S. Trudgett, 'Resignation of women managers: dispelling the myths', *Asia Pacific Journal of Human Resources*, vol. 38, no. 1, 2000, pp. 67–83.

40. W. Cascio, op. cit., p. 9.

41. M. Buschak, C. Craven and R. Ledman, 'Managing absenteeism for greater productivity', *SAM Advanced Management Journal*, vol. 66, no. 1, 1996, p. 26; and A. Ellerby and K. Barrett, 'Increased costs eat into profits', *HR Monthly*, June 1999, pp. 22–6.

42. W. Cascio, op. cit., p. 9.

43. L. E. Hazzard, 'A union says yes to attendance', *Personnel Journal*, November 1990, pp. 47–9.

44. M. Priest, 'Health checks in the mail for postal sickies', *Australian Financial Review*, 31 July 2003, p. 3.

45. W. Cascio, op. cit., p. 9.

46. 'Auditing absenteeism', *Special Bulletin, No. 12-A*, Division of Labor Standards, US Dept of Labor, 1943, p. 1.

47. R. F. Allen and M. Iggins, 'The absenteeism culture: becoming attendance oriented', *Personnel*, vol. 56, no. 1, 1979, p. 30; and J. Moullakis, 'Sickies go untouched', *Australian Financial Review*, 8 April 2003, p. 6.

48. J. Moullakis, op. cit., p. 6; and A. Hepworth, 'In search of a cure for the sickie', *Australian Financial Review*, 10–11 July 2004, p. 6.

49. See *Guide for Supervisors — Minimizing Absence*, Productivity Promotion Council of Australia brochure, undated, pages unnumbered.

50. W. Cascio, op. cit., p. 9.

51. R. Isherwood, 'The financial effects of absence from work', *Bulletin of Industrial Psychology and Personnel Practice*, vol. 8, no. 2, 1952, p. 22–6.

52. R. M. Steers and S. R. Rhodes, 'Major influences on employee attendance: a process model', *Journal of Applied Psychology*, vol. 63, no. 4, 1978, pp. 390–6; D. Dunphy, H. Andreatta and L. Timms, 'Redesigning the work organisation at Philips', *Work and People*, vol. 2, no. 1, 1976, pp. 3–11; R. Harkness and B. Krupinski, 'A survey of absence rates', *Work and People*, vol. 3, no. 2, 1977, pp. 3–9; and P. M. Muchinsky, *Psychology Applied to Work*, 5th edn, Brooks/Cole, Pacific Grove, CA, 1997, pp. 83–4.

53. Australian Bureau of Statistics survey, reported in D. Macken, 'Dress down Friday is now goof off day', *Australian Financial Review*, 7 July 2000, p. 9.

54. P. Ruzek, 'A stern test for tripartism', *Personnel Today*, June 1990, p. 8.

55. Standards Association of Australia, *Recording and Measuring Work Injury Experience*, Australian Standard 1885, June 1976, p. 21.

56. R. A. Fleck, 'The employee attitude survey as a management tool', *Personnel Management*, vol. 10, no. 3, 1972, pp. 34–8.

57. M. Story, 'Employee surveys reveal trends in corporate behaviour', *Human Resources*, vol. 1, no. 2, 1996, p. 3.

58. A. Nankervis, 'Employee attitude surveys can help morale', *Weekend Australian*, 24–25 March 1990, p. 39.

59. M. W. Mercer, op. cit., p. 150; and M. Allix, 'Surveys plumb corporate depths', *Asian Business*, November 1996, pp. 62–4.

60. M. W. Mercer, op. cit., p. 151.

61. M. W. Mercer, op. cit., p. 151.

62. A. Nankervis, op. cit., p. 39. See also P. Sheibor, 'The seven deadly sins of employee attitude surveys', *Personnel*, vol. 66, no. 6, 1989, pp. 66–71.

63. This list is based on D. Yoder, H. G. Heneman, J. G. Turnbull and C. H. Stone, *Handbook of Personnel Management and Labor Relations*, McGraw-Hill, New York, 1958, pp. 14–23.

64. This section is based on S. M. Kenney, op. cit., pp. 23–8.

65. S. M. Kenney, op. cit., p. 28.

66. This section is largely based on M. M. Kennedy, 'How do employees really feel about your company?', *Boardroom Reports*, August 1994, pp. 11–12.

67. B. Marshall, 'Benchmarking: buzzword or business advantage?', *Human Resources*, vol. 2, no. 3, 1997, p. 11; and D. Stauffer, 'Measure for measure', *Boss*, November 2003, pp. 18–19.

68. D. J. Ford, 'Benchmarking HRD', *Training and Development*, vol. 47, no. 6, 1993, p. 37.

69. G. H. Watson, *Strategic Benchmarking*, John Wiley & Sons, New York, 1993, p. 2.

70. Quoted in G. H. Watson, op. cit., p. 3.

71. E. F. Glanz and L. K. Dailey, 'Benchmarking', *Human Resource Management*, vol. 31, no. 1–2, 1992, p. 9; and R. L. Mathis and J. H. Jackson, *Human Resource Management*, 8th edn, West, Minneapolis/St Paul, 1997, p. 588.

72. Based on 'Benchmarker's guide', *Fortune*, 19 October 1992, p. 82.

73. A. C. Deutsch, 'Working wide of the mark', *Business Review Weekly*, 30 July 1999, p. 48.

74. Best practice', *Workplace*, Spring 1992, p. 2; and D. James and R. Gottliebsen, 'World best practice: a matter of survival', *Business Review Weekly*, 17 January 1992, p. 40.

75. D. James and R. Gottliebsen, op. cit., p. 34.

76. This section is largely drawn from B. E. Becker, M. A. Huselid and D. Ulrich, *The HR Scorecard*, Harvard Business School Press, Boston, Mass., 2001.

77. B. E. Becker, M. A. Huselid and D. Ulrich, op. cit., p. 4.

78. B. E. Becker, M. A. Huselid and D. Ulrich, op. cit., p. 13.

79. B. E. Becker, M. A. Huselid and D. Ulrich, op. cit., p. 63.

80. B. E. Becker, M. A. Huselid and D. Ulrich, op. cit., pp. 75–7.

81. B. E. Becker, M. A. Huselid and D. Ulrich, op. cit., pp. 204–5.

82. E. M. Olsin and S. F. Slater, 'The balanced scorecard: competitive strategy and performance', *Business Horizons*, vol. 45, no. 3, 2002, p. 12.

83. N. B. Olve and A. Sjostrand, *The Balanced Scorecard*, Capstone, Oxford, 2002, pp. 25–6.

84. P. Boxhall and J. Purcell, *Strategy and Human Resource Management*, Palgrave/Macmillan, Basingstoke, 2003, pp. 19–20.

85. C. Rance, 'Investing in people', *Age — Employment Section*, 5 August 1989, p. 3.

86. Based on an anonymous reviewer comment, 7 July 1997.

ASSESSING MANAGERIAL BENCH STRENGTH
HRM Consulting

Acme Financial Services (AFS) is a financial services company that operates in all Australian states. As at 30 June 2003, the company employed just under 4300 employees. The bank's four business units are:

- institutional banking
- financial services
- personal banking
- corporate shared services.

The bank's major challenge is to continue to automate existing services, increase efficiency and improve integration with the lifestyles and needs of its customers. The bank sees that developing new products and services, particularly financial services, will be essential to customer retention. The provision of these new services will require the development of new skills within the existing work force.

The bank's portfolios are in growth mode, but it is forecast that these growth opportunities should be achieved within current staffing levels. AFS currently has a number of branches in regional centres. The organisation is planning to transfer these business operations to centrally located call centres (requiring considerably fewer staff) and at the same time to boost the range and quality of its financial service options, particularly for personal bankers.

AFS is an established bank. Its market share in relation to home-lending services has recently been eroded by mortgage lenders.

The challenge

A number of general factors have raised the importance of strong leadership/management in any business:

- more complex and global business challenges — significant decisions need to be made faster and with less information, so executives need to be more skilled and globally savvy
- dynamic organisational structures with evolving position descriptions
- the increasing importance of human capital as a competitive advantage.

These and other reasons (summarised below) have also raised the importance of having a strong managerial 'bench' — that is, candidates capable of appointment to a senior management position. The other reasons are:

- the elimination of middle management — each promotion is a larger jump in required skills
- labour market changes
  - an ageing work force and a shortage of labour
  - decreased organisational loyalty
  - technology facilitating increased job movement
- diversity as an important part of an organisation's work force strategy
- research shows that effective succession management can prevent more than 20 per cent of the root causes of growth stalls in large companies (Corporate Strategy Board, *Stall Points*, 2000).

There are several dimensions to managerial succession that need to be considered:

1. depth — the number of successors for each position
2. quality — successor performance levels
3. readiness — the time frame for succession.

Considering this range of dimensions, Acme's approach is to evaluate its managerial bench strength (MBS) using a suite of measures, rather than one single measure. The suite of measures encompasses both contextual and performance HR indicators, as follows:

CONTEXTUAL MEASURES	PERFORMANCE INDICATORS
➢ Managerial staffing rate ➢ Managerial turnover rate (various) ➢ Tenure profile of managers ➢ Sub-manager turnover rate — total ➢ Employee growth rate ➢ Age profile of managers	➢ Sub-manager promotion/transfer ratio ➢ Successor pool depth ➢ Managerial hiring source ratio ➢ Gender profile (manager) ➢ Ethnicity profile (manager) ➢ Successor pool coverage ➢ Successor quality rating ➢ Managerial position occupancy rate

Interpretive notes for these measures are shown below.

Contextual measures

MEASURE	FORMULA	DESCRIPTION OF MEASURE	INTERPRETIVE NOTES
Managerial staffing rate	*Managerial FTE/total FTE100*	This measure indicates the relative number of managers to other organisational staff, and assists in the interpretation of input, process and output MBS measures.	A high result (a 'top-heavy' managerial profile — 75th percentile and above) may place greater strain on the organisation's capacity to develop a strong managerial bench, because a larger pool of successor candidates may need to be identified and developed.
Managerial turnover rate — total	*Total managerial terminations /total managerial headcount*	This measure indicates the percentage of managers who leave the organisation for whatever reason during the reporting period. It assists interpretation of input, process and output MBS measures.	A high result (75th percentile and above) will place greater strain on the organisation's capacity to develop a strong managerial bench, because a larger pool of successor candidates may need to be identified and developed — within a shorter space of time. A high result may also be due to an organisational downsizing/M&A initiative, which could reduce the number of management positions and place less strain on capacity to identify a strong managerial bench. Therefore, this measure needs to be interpreted in conjunction with the managerial staffing rate.
Managerial turnover rate — voluntary	*Total managerial voluntary terminations/total managerial headcount*	This measure indicates the percentage of managers who leave the organisation of their own accord during the reporting period. It assists interpretation of input, process and output MBS measures.	A high result (75th percentile and above) will place greater strain on the organisation's capacity to develop a strong managerial bench, because a larger pool of successor candidates may need to be identified and developed — within a shorter space of time.

(continued)

MEASURE	FORMULA	DESCRIPTION OF MEASURE	INTERPRETIVE NOTES
Managerial turnover rate — involuntary	*Total managerial involuntary terminations /total managerial headcount*	This measure indicates the percentage of managers who were terminated at the organisation's discretion during the reporting period. It assists interpretation of input, process and output MBS measures.	A high result (75th percentile and above) may be due to an organisational downsizing/M&A initiative, which could reduce the number of management positions and place less strain on capacity to identify a strong managerial bench. Therefore, this measure needs to be interpreted in conjunction with the managerial staffing rate.
Managerial turnover rate by tenure profile	*Number of terminating managers with x yrs service/total number of managers*	This measure indicates the proportion of managers within a particular tenure group who effect voluntary separation.	A high turnover among managers with less than three years service will place greater strain on the organisation's capacity to develop a strong managerial bench, because a larger pool of successor candidates may need to be identified and developed — within a shorter space of time.
Tenure profile of managers	*Percentage of managers in each defined tenure range*	This measure shows the number of managers in various tenure groups as a proportion of the total number of managers in the organisation.	A high proportion of managers with low tenure (less than three years) may be reflective of rapid growth or high turnover at managerial level (see notes above concerning turnover levels in interpreting MBS). On the other hand, a high proportion of managers with long tenure may be reflective of approaching retirement, and future high managerial turnover. A high proportion of managers with 'mid-term' tenure may be reflective of stability within the organisation — possibly restricting opportunities for potential successors and stimulating turnover within the successor pool.
Sub-manager turnover rate — total	*Total terminations at the level of staff from whom the successor pool is drawn/total headcount of staff from whom the successor pool is drawn*	This measure indicates the percentage of sub-managers who leave the organisation for whatever reason during the reporting period. It assists interpretation of input, process and output MBS measures.	A high result (75th percentile and above) means there is constant change in the composition of the successor pool, which will place greater strain on the organisation's capacity to develop a strong managerial bench.
Employee growth rate	*Percentage increase in work force size*	This measure indicates the rate of growth in the organisation's work force.	A high result (75th percentile and above) will place greater strain on the organisation's capacity to develop a strong managerial bench, because a larger pool of successor candidates may need to be identified and developed — within a shorter space of time. This measure needs to be interpreted in conjunction with the managerial staffing rate. High growth in the sub-manager rate and stable numbers at the managerial level will result in a larger successor pool (though the increased responsibility of managing a larger work force may increase turnover at managerial level).
Age profile of managerial group	*Percentage of managers in each defined age range*	This measure shows the number of managers in various age groups as a proportion of the total number of managers in the organisation.	A high proportion of younger managers could restrict opportunities for the successor level and increase turnover at this level, placing greater strain on MBS. A high proportion of older managers could suggest imminent retirement and the need for a strong managerial bench. *Note:* The age profile of the potential successor pool also needs to be monitored.

part 7 case study

Performance indicators

MEASURE	FORMULA	DESCRIPTION OF MEASURE	TARGET RANGE	INTERPRETIVE NOTES
Sub-manager promotion/ transfer ratio	*Number of promotions of sub-manager/ number of transfers at sub-manager level*	The number of sub-managers internally promoted for every sub-manager internally transferred to a new position. This will be an increasingly important measure as organisations endeavour to provide satisfying careers for staff in increasingly flat organisational structures.	Emphasis on lateral movement can assist to recognise and develop employees, ensure job satisfaction, and avoid retirement on the job. For these reasons the target range is the 25th percentile.	A high result (high in relation to the target range) indicates more promotions than transfers. A low result will suggest that sub-managers are acquiring a range of developmental experiences through job transfers.
Successor pool depth	*Number of people identified as capable of promotion to manager/ number managerial positions*	This measure indicates the average number of potential successors available to fill each managerial position.	Because of the benefit of having a wide choice from which to choose managerial successors, the target range for this measure is the 75th percentile.	A high result indicates that a relatively large number of successors are capable of promotion to managerial level. However, it does not indicate the quality of the successor pool, nor whether the successor pool includes successors for each managerial position.
Managerial hiring source ratio	*Number of managerial internal hires for each managerial external hire*	This measure indicates the number of internal recruits at managerial level for every external recruit at managerial level.	Because of the benefits to be gained from developing and promoting/transferring employees, the desired result for the recruitment source ratio is around the 75th percentile. However, if the organisation were actively recruiting externally to bring new skills and ideas to the organisation, a lower result would be expected.	A high result suggests strong managerial bench strength. However, a high result could be due to organisational restructuring rather than an effective management development strategy. A low result could suggest a 'shallow and/or narrow' managerial bench, or it could suggest organisational growth/ new direction and an active strategy to bring new skills and ideas to the organisation.
Managerial gender profile	*Number of male managers for every female manager*	This measure enables an organisation to monitor the gender balance of its managerial work force.	As skill levels are generally distributed throughout the population regardless of gender, organisations should aim to have an appropriate mix of male and female managers to ensure that they are developing and recruiting the best people available. The desired range for this measure is often held to be the median (within the industry), but an ideal target for organisations would be 1:1, as this is more representative of the work force participation rates of the population at large.	This would need to be considered within the industry, as some industries are traditionally dominated by one or other gender.

(continued)

part 7 case study

MEASURE	FORMULA	DESCRIPTION OF MEASURE	TARGET RANGE	INTERPRETIVE NOTES
Managerial ethnicity profile	*Number of ethnic group managers for every non-ethnic group manager*	This measure enables an organisation to monitor the ethnic balance of its managerial work force.	As skill levels are generally distributed throughout the population regardless of ethnicity, an organisation should aim for its managers to have an appropriate mix of ethnic backgrounds, to ensure the organisation is developing and recruiting the best people available. The desired range for this measure is often held to be the median, but an ideal target would be to reflect the ethnic profile of the work force at large.	This would need to be considered within the region to account for different ethnic demographics across geography.
Successor pool coverage (% roles with defined successors)	*Number of managerial positions with identified successors/ total number of managerial positions*	This measure indicates the percentage of managerial positions that have at least one defined successor.	As the aim is to maximise the number of positions with identified successors, the target range for this measure is the 75th percentile.	A high result could indicate that all or many managerial positions have an identified successor, but this would not indicate: • the breadth of the successor pool (that is, whether positions have more than one identified successor) • the quality of individuals within the successor pool.
Successor quality rating	*Current managers' assessment of the quality of the successor pool*	This measure would poll (through surveys, interviews, focus groups, and such) the opinions of current managers about the quality of the successor pool.	The aim is to achieve a high quality rating, so the target for this measure is the 75th percentile.	It would need to be determined whether managers were simply rating their own successors, or the quality of the successor pool for all managerial positions. As this measure involves human opinion, it is necessarily subjective, and potentially liable to the bias of individual managers. For example, managers who feel threatened by up-and-coming successors may provide a low rating. Alternatively, if a component of managerial performance pay is dependent on successor development, managers may provide an artificially high poll rating.
Managerial position occupancy rate	*Number of managerial positions filled/ total number of managerial positions*	This measure indicates the percentage of managerial positions with occupants during the period.	As the aim is to have all managerial positions productively filled, the target for this measure is the 75th percentile.	A high result may indicate an effective management development program with strong management bench strength. However, a high result does not necessarily reflect on the quality of the managerial appointments. Also, high turnover and/or employee growth rate and/or organisational change will affect the interpretation of this measure. It would need to be determined whether 'acting' or relieving appointments should be counted as occupied, or not.

Questions

As Director of HR Planning, you are responsible for reporting to Acme's board on the current strength of the managerial bench (MBS) and proposed strategies to ensure continuing bench strength. Specifically, you have to undertake the following in preparation for the next board meeting:

1. Analyse Acme's performance on the MBS contextual indicators as shown below. What does this analysis tell you about the strengths and opportunities facing Acme in ensuring continuing managerial bench strength?

Table 1	Management bench strength — contextual indicators			
	PERCENTILE POSITION			
BENCHMARK	**BELOW 25TH**	**25TH–50TH**	**50TH–75TH**	**ABOVE 75TH**
Managerial staffing rate			X	
Managerial turnover rate — total		X		
Managerial turnover rate — voluntary		X		
Managerial turnover rate — involuntary		X		
Managerial turnover rate < 1 yr			X	
Managerial turnover rate 1–3 yrs		X		
Managerial turnover rate 3–5 yrs		X		
Managerial turnover rate 5–10 yrs		X		
Managerial turnover rate 10+ yrs	X			
Tenure profile of managers			X	
Employee growth rate				X
Age profile of managers				X
Sub-manager turnover rate — total		X		

Desired position   [X]   Acme's result

2. In the light of these contextual indicators, analyse Acme's performance on the MBS performance indicators as shown below. What are the priority improvement areas for Acme in terms of managerial bench strength?

Table 2   Management bench strength — performance indicators

BENCHMARK	PERCENTILE POSITION			
	BELOW 25TH	25TH–50TH	50TH–75TH	ABOVE 75TH
Sub-manager promotion/transfer ratio	▨			X
Successor pool depth		X		▨
Managerial hiring source ratio				X ▨
Gender profile (manager)			▨	X
Ethnicity profile (manager)		X	▨	
Successor pool coverage			X	▨
Successor quality rating	X			▨
Managerial position occupancy rate				X ▨

▨ Desired position | X | Acme's result

3. For the top two or three priority improvement areas, what strategies would you propose to effect the required improvement?
4. In preparing this report to the board, what other information sources (for example, corporate) should you consult?

Institutes and societies relevant to the HR manager

Australian Human Resources Institute (AHRI)
National office
Level 2, 153 Park Street
South Melbourne VIC 3205
Tel: 1300 656 746
Fax: (03) 9696 4532
Email: enquiries@ahri.com.au

Australian Institute of Training and Development (AITD)
National office
PO Box 5452
West Chatswood NSW 1515
Tel: 1300 138 862 or (02) 9419 4966
Fax: (02) 9419 4142
Email: national@aitd.com.au

Australian Institute of Management
National office
PO Box 112
St Kilda VIC 3182
Tel: (03) 9534 8181
Fax: (03) 9534 5050
Email: vic_enquiry@aimvic.com.au

Regional offices
Canberra
Deakin House
50 Geils Court
Deakin ACT 2600
Tel: (02) 6282 1914
Fax: (02) 6285 3961
Email: act@aim.com.au

New South Wales
PO Box 328
North Sydney NSW 2059
Tel: (02) 9956 3030
Fax: (02) 9956 5613
Email: nsw@aim.com.au

Tasmania
PO Box 1069
Hobart TAS 7001
Tel: (03) 6224 3408
Fax: (03) 6225 3441
Email: Sandra@eisa.net.au

South Australia
224 Hindley Street
Adelaide SA 5000
Tel: (08) 8229 3820
Fax: (08) 8231 2414
Email: sa@aim.com.au

Western Australia
PO Box 195
Wembley WA 6913
Tel: (08) 9383 8088 or (08) 9383 8000
Fax: (08) 9387 6171
Email: aimwa@aimwa.asn.au

Queensland/Northern Territory
PO Box 200
Spring Hill QLD 4004
Tel: (07) 3832 0151
Fax: (07) 3832 2497
Email: qld+nt@aim.com.au

Australian Psychological Society
PO Box 126
Carlton South VIC 3053
Tel: (03) 8662 3300
Fax: (03) 9663 6177
Email: natloff@psychsociety.com.au

Australian Industrial Relations Society
PO Box 1557
Sydney NSW 2001
Email: irsa@irsa.asn.au

Company web sites

Australian company web sites

www.amcor.com.au
Amcor Ltd
www.amplimited.com
AMP Ltd
www.anz.com
ANZ Ltd
www.bhpbilliton.com
BHP Billiton
www.boral.com.au
Boral
www.ccamatil.com
Coca-Cola Amatil Ltd
www.commbank.com.au
Commonwealth Bank
www.fostersgroup.com
Foster's Group
www.leighton.com.au
Leighton Holdings Ltd
www.macquarie.com.au
Macquarie Bank
www.national.com.au
National Australia Bank Ltd
www.onesteel.com
One Steel Ltd
www.p-s-i.com.au
Pacific Strategic Investments Ltd
www.qbe.com
QBE Insurance Group Ltd
www.southcorp.au
Southcorp Ltd
www.stgeorge.com.au
St George Bank Ltd
www.stockland.com.au
Stockland Ltd
www.telecom.co.nz
Telecom New Zealand Ltd
www.telstra.com.au

Telstra Corporation Ltd
www.westfield.com.au
Westfield Holdings Ltd
www.westpac.com.au
Westpac Ltd
www.woolworthslimited.com.au
Woolworths Ltd

Hong Kong company web sites

www.cathaypacific.com
Cathay Pacific
www.hayco.com.hk
Hayco
www.hgc.com.hk
Hutchinson Global Communications
www.philips.com.hk
Philips

US company web sites

www.apple.com
Apple
www.bankamerica.com
Bank of America
www.bpamoco.com
BP Amoco
www.campbellsoup.com
Campbells Soup
www.daimlerchrysler.com
Daimlerchrysler
www.dell.com
Dell
www.disney.com
Disney
www.ford.com
Ford
www.prudential.com
Prudential

absenteeism The failure of employees to report to work when they are scheduled to do so.

access Concerned with who will have the right to enter, change or retrieve data via the HRIS. For example, will there be decentralised access capability (line managers and employees) or will access be centralised and tightly controlled (HR only)?

accident make-up pay The difference between the workers compensation payment and the employee's actual pay.

accident-prone The proposition that certain employees have specific characteristics that make them more likely to have accidents, and that these same employees cause or are involved in most accidents.

accreditation The process of certifying the professional competence of HR specialists.

achievement motivation The desire to be successful in competitive situations or to perform in terms of a standard of excellence.

acquisition Purchase of a firm or company by another firm or company.

across-the-board increases General pay increases awarded to all employees irrespective of performance.

action learning Based on learning by experience. Uses real problems from the work situation for trainees to solve.

active listening Asking lots of questions and carefully listening to the answers.

activity phase (training) Concerned with selecting the training methods and learning principles to be employed in a training program.

adaptability Relates to the extent that HRM policies foster employee and organisational readiness for and acceptance of change.

administrative experts Refers to the efficiency of HR managers and the effective management of HR activities (such as selection, etc.) so that they create value.

adventure training Adventure or wilderness training presents managers with physical and mental challenges such as abseiling, canoeing and bushwalking. The aim is to promote self-awareness, confidence and teamwork.

advertised recruitment Communicating to the public an organisation's HR requirements using the media (such as newspaper advertisements).

advocates Employer or union representatives who argue a case before an industrial tribunal or court.

affirmative action (AA) Programs that require firms to make special efforts to recruit, hire and promote women and members of minority groups.

ageing population Occurs when the number of older people increases relative to the number of young people in the population.

AIDS (acquired immune deficiency syndrome) A disease that undermines the body's immune system, leaving the person susceptible to a wide range of fatal diseases.

air rage Offensive and violent behaviour by commercial airline passengers. Examples include food throwing, sexual harassment, indecent behaviour, insulting language, abusive conduct and physical assault.

alcoholism A treatable disease characterised by uncontrolled and compulsive drinking that interferes with normal living patterns.

allowable matters These are provisions allowed to remain in awards by the *Workplace Relations Act*. No other items can be covered by an award.

annuity A type of investment that pays a specific income for life or for a guaranteed period of time (typically 10 years). Annuities are usually purchased from insurance companies, benevolent societies or trade unions.

anti-discrimination Elimination of any practice that makes distinctions between different groups based on age, sex, and other characteristics identified in EO legislation and that results in one group being advantaged and the other group disadvantaged.

application form Basic source of employment information covering qualifications, experience and other job-related data.

apprenticeship training A combination of classroom and on-the-job training.

aptitude tests Measure of special abilities (such as clerical, linguistic, musical and artistic abilities) that are required in specific jobs.

arbitrated awards Outline minimum pay rates and conditions as determined by an industrial tribunal decision.

arbitration The submission of a dispute to a third party for a binding decision.

assessment centres Use interviews, tests, simulations, games and observations to evaluate an individual's potential.

assessment phase (training) Establishes what training is needed, by whom, when and where so that training objectives can be established.

'at-risk' compensation Variable rewards that are payable only when a performance target is met.

attitude survey A systematic method of determining what employees think about their job, supervision and the organisation.

Australian Council of Trade Unions (ACTU) National trade union organisation that represents the Australian trade union movement.

Australian Industrial Relations Commission (AIRC) Federal industrial tribunal charged with preventing and settling industrial disputes.

Australian Workplace Agreements (AWAs) Agreements made directly between an employer and an employee.

automatic progression Sometimes called incremental pay scales. Pay increases occur automatically each year on a specified date, irrespective of performance.

autonomous work teams Represents job enrichment at the group level. This is achieved by creating self-managed work teams responsible for accomplishing defined performance objectives.

autonomy The extent to which the job provides the employee freedom to plan, schedule and decide about work procedures.

avoidable turnover A standard method of computing employee turnover that focuses on that part of employee turnover that can be reduced by managerial action.

awards Written determinations setting out the legally enforceable terms and conditions of employment in a firm or industry.

background investigation Process of checking job applicant information prior to an employment offer being made.

balanced scorecard (BS) A performance management technique that evaluates organisational performance in four key areas: people, internal operations, customer satifaction and financial.

bargaining Another term for negotiation.

bargaining zone The parameters between which the union and management are prepared to negotiate comprises the bargaining zone.

base pay Standard pay that an employee receives for doing a job. It is used as the basis for calculating other allowances and benefits.

behaviour modelling The process of learning from other people's experience by simulating (copying) their behaviour.

behaviour observation scale (BOS) Performance appraisal system that uses critical incidents to develop a list of desired behaviours needed to perform a specific job successfully.

behaviourally anchored rating scale (BARS) A performance appraisal method that combines elements of the traditional rating scale and critical incidents method.

benchmark jobs Jobs that are similar or comparable in content across firms.

benchmarking The identification of best practices among competitors and non-competitors that make them superior performers.

benefits Include financial rewards that are not paid directly in cash to the employee (for example, childcare, healthcare, gym membership, life insurance) and all non-financial rewards (for example, an office with a window, a key to the executive toilet).

biographical information blanks (BIBs) A specially designed application form that is used to obtain comprehensive information about an employee's background, attitudes, hobbies, sports, early life experiences, and so on.

blue circle pay rates Pay rates that are below the range minimum for a job.

body language Non-verbal signals (such as facial expressions) that can indicate what a person is really thinking or feeling.

bonus A discretionary reward provided after the achievement of a goal.

bottom line Refers to a final result, such as the net profit after taxes.

boundaryless careers Careers that involve switching jobs, specialisations, companies, industries and locations. They may involve upwards, downwards and sideways moves.

broadbanding Collapses numerous job grades with narrow pay bands in a pay structure into a few broad job grades with wide pay bands.

bullying Examples of workplace bullying include persecuting or ganging up on an individual; making unreasonable demands or setting impossible work targets; restrictive and petty work rules; constant, intrusive surveillance; abusive language; physical assault; and open or implied threats of dismissal or demotion.

burnout A state of mental, emotional and physical exhaustion that results from substantial and prolonged stress.

business games Simulations that represent actual business situations.

cafeteria benefits Employees choose their own benefits up to a certain cost per employee.

campus recruiting Recruiting activities conducted at a college or university campus.

career All the jobs that an employee has held in their working life.

career counselling Involves the giving of information and advice to employees to facilitate their career planning and development.

career meltdown Occurs when an employee's career commences a downward spiral. Typically characterised by termination, demotion, being bypassed for promotion and being politically marginalised.

career path Flexible line of progression through which an employee moves during their employment with an organisation.

career planning and development Giving employees assistance to develop realistic career goals and the opportunities to realise them.

career plateau Point in an individual's career where the probability of further advancement is negligible.

career transition Involves a significant change in an employee's career via transfer, demotion, promotion, overseas assignment or switch from one occupation to another.

central processing unit (CPU) This is the computer's brain. It controls the interpretation and execution of instructions. It causes data to be read, stored, manipulated and printed.

central tendency A common error that occurs when every employee is incorrectly rated near the average or middle of the scale.

Certified Agreements (CAs) Agreements that are the product of negotiations between a corporation and a group of employees or a union(s) and that are subsequently registered by an industrial tribunal.

change agent A person who acts as a catalyst for change.

charter of professional standards Statement of an organisation's ethical values and standards that guides the professional conduct of its employees.

classification method A job evaluation method by which classes or grades are defined to describe a group of jobs.

closed shop Exists when a job applicant cannot be hired by an employer unless he or she is a member of a designated union.

coaching An on-the-job approach to management development in which the manager is given an opportunity to teach on a one-to-one basis.

collective bargaining The process through which representatives of management and the union meet to negotiate a labour agreement.

collectivism The emphasis given by a culture to group relationships.

commission An individual incentive system whereby an employee is paid either a percentage or flat sum amount on the revenue of sales volume they generate.

commitment Relates to the extent that HRM policies enhance employee identification with and attachment to their job and the organisation.

common law 'Case law' developed in the court system. It is the body of previous judgements that determine the law.

communication The process of transferring meanings from a sender to a receiver.

compa ratio (pay index) The ratio between the average pay for a particular job point or grade and the midpoint of the pay range for that point or grade.

compensation What employees receive in exchange for their work. Includes pay and benefits (total compensation) or just pay (cash compensation).

compensatory approach Involves considering all the selection data (favourable and unfavourable) before a selection decision is made.

competence Relates to the extent that HRM policies attract, retain, motivate and develop employees with the abilities, skills, knowledge and competencies to achieve the organisation's strategic objectives.

competencies (*see* unit of competency) Multiple units of competency.

competency (*also* competence) The ability to perform tasks and duties to the standard expected in employment.

competency-based assessment (CBA) The gathering and judging of evidence in order to decide whether a person has achieved a standard of competence.

competency-based training (CBT) Training that develops the skills, knowledge and attitudes required to achieve competency standards.

competency profiling Job analysis method that focuses on the skills and behaviours needed to perform a job successfully.

competency standard An industry-determined specification of performance that sets out the skills, knowledge and attitudes required to operate effectively in employment. Competency standards are made up of units of competency, which are themselves made up of elements of competency, together with performance criteria, a range of variables, and an evidence guide. Competency standards are an endorsed component of a training package.

competitive advantage A special edge that allows organisations to better deal with business challenges.

competitive analysis Review of the competitive forces in an industry, including the threat of new entrants, bargaining power of buyers and suppliers and the threat of substitute products or services.

compulsory unionism An arrangement whereby union membership is a necessary condition of employment.

computer-based training Uses computers as a learning vehicle to provide interactive drills, problem solving, simulations and gaming. The emphasis is on self-managed learning.

conciliation Occurs when a dispute involves a third party (a conciliator) who tries to facilitate agreement between unions and management.

conduct guide A formal statement of expected professional conduct and ethical rules.

congruence Relates to the extent that HRM policies generate (or sustain) and promote the simultaneous achievement of employee goals and the organisation's strategic business objectives.

conscript mindset Employees are externally motivated (that is, they are coerced by management) to perform.

consent agreement Occurs when the parties to an industrial dispute reach agreement without third party involvement. If ratified by an industrial tribunal, it becomes a consent award and is binding on the parties in the same way as an arbitrated award.

consent awards These occur when the parties to an industrial dispute reach agreement without third party involvement, and the agreement is then ratified by an industrial tribunal. A consent award is binding on the parties in the same way as an arbitrated award.

constructive dismissal Dismissal by the employer where the employer acts in a manner suggesting that they no longer wish to be bound by the terms of the contract.

content theories Attempt to explain motivation in terms of factors that initiate employee behaviour.

contingent workers Temporary or part-time employees.

continuous improvement Focuses on the non-stop improvement of everything and everybody.

continuous reinforcement Occurs when rewards are given after each desired behaviour.

contract Legal agreement, enforceable by law, that sets forth the relationship between parties regarding the performance of a specific action.

contracts of a fixed term Contracts of employment that provide that the employment will end on a specified date or upon the completion of a specific task.

contracts of indefinite duration Continuing employment that ends only after one party gives the other party notice that they wish to terminate the contract.

contribution-based pay A pay plan designed to directly link rewards to the contributions made by an individual employee.

contributory superannuation Scheme where the employee (along with the company) is required to make a regular contribution (typically 5 per cent of monthly base pay) to their retirement plan.

corporate culture The values, beliefs, assumptions and symbols that define the way in which the organisation conducts its business.

correlation coefficient A statistical procedure showing the strength of the relationship between two variables; for example, between an employee's test score and on-the-job performance.

corruption Includes fraud, bribery, graft and the payment of secret commissions and kickbacks.

cost–benefit analysis Involves an evaluation of the tangible and intangible costs and benefits resulting from a decision.

cost centre A unit in which managers are held responsible for all associated costs; for example, administrative and service departments where inputs are measured in financial terms, but outputs are not.

cost-effectiveness Relates to the extent that HRM policies reduce personnel-related costs, help correctly size the organisation, eliminate unnecessary work, reduce compensation and benefit costs, reduce labour turnover, etc.

cost-of-living allowance (COLA) Designed to protect the expatriate's standard of living from cost-of-living differences between the host country and the home country and to offer some protection against exchange rate fluctuations.

craft unions Unions that include workers who have a common skill; for example, carpenters or plumbers.

criterion validity A type of validity based on showing that scores on the test (predictors) are related to job performance (criterion).

critical incident An example of employee behaviour that illustrates effective or ineffective job performance.

critical incident method A performance appraisal technique that requires a written record of highly favourable and highly unfavourable employee work behaviour.

cross-cultural communication Occurs when a person from one culture (for example, an Australian) communicates with a person from another culture (for example, a Chinese). Misunderstandings may occur because of differences in language, values, attitudes and beliefs.

culture shock The stress produced by the inability to adjust to a different cultural environment.

cut-off score The score on a test below which an applicant will not be considered for employment.

data Unprocessed facts and figures (sometimes called raw data). Processed data are organised into information that is ready for analysis.

database management Involves the input, storage, manipulation and output of data.

deadline The time limit set for the completion of the negotiation.

deadlock Occurs when neither side in a negotiation will make a concession.

decision making Choosing from alternatives.

defined benefit plans Retirement plans that specify the actual benefit payable upon retirement.

defined contribution plans Retirement plans that specify employer and employee contributions, but do not specify what the actual benefit at retirement will be.

delegation Giving decision-making responsibilities to subordinates.

Delphi technique Obtains predictions from a panel of experts about some specific future occurrence. The collective estimates are fed back to individual panel members until general agreement is reached.

demarcation An exclusive right that restricts a specific type of work to members of a particular union. In practice, it operates as a form of job protection.

demotion The process of moving a worker to a lower level of duties and responsibilities, which typically involves a pay cut.

desk rage Offensive and/or violent employee behaviour occurring in an office environment.

development Involves those activities that prepare an employee for future responsibilities.

diary/log A written record of the duties performed by an employee.

direct discrimination Refers to any overt bias towards a person based on characteristics such as age, sex, race, etc. Direct discrimination is often the product of stereotypes about a particular group. It can be expressed through a refusal to hire,

dismissal, providing unfavourable working conditions or limited opportunities.

disability insurance Insurance designed to protect employees during long-term disablement (and loss of income) through illness or injury.

disciplinary action Invoking a penalty against an employee who fails to meet organisational standards or comply with organisational rules.

discrimination Any practice that makes distinctions between different groups based on characteristics identified in anti-discrimination legislation such as sex, race, age, religion and so on, which results in particular individuals or groups being advantaged and others disadvantaged.

distribution of learning Relates to the scheduling of training activities. In most cases, spacing out training produces more rapid learning and better retention.

distributive justice The extent to which employees are treated in the same way by the organisation irrespective of their status or personal characteristics.

diversity The variety of people who make up an organisation's work force, in terms of age, gender, ethnicity, occupation, length of service, and so on.

diversity management Activities involved in integrating non-traditional employees (such as women and minorities) into the work force and using their diversity to the firm's competitive advantage, as well as considering other work force characteristics that need to be addressed to ensure fair and effective utilisation of employees.

diversity strategies Encompass equal employment opportunity, affirmative action or diversity management strategies.

divestitures Selling selected operating units for either strategic or financial reasons.

division of labour Process of dividing work and assigning tasks to workers.

domestic HRM HRM as practised within the geographical boundaries of one country. Its focus is the management of people in a single-country context.

dominant or traditional employees/group Employees who come from the majority group. In Australia, the dominant racial/ethnic group are people, particularly men, of Anglo-Celtic ancestry.

downshifters Employees who make a voluntary long-term lifestyle change involving less work, less income and less consumption.

downsizing A reduction in a company's work force to improve its bottom line.

dual career Situation where both spouses or partners have career responsibilities and aspirations.

early retirement Occurs when an employee retires from an organisation before the standard retirement age.

economy class syndrome Blood clots caused by cramped airline seating and lack of movement.

education Activities designed to improve the knowledge, understanding and abilities of an individual.

effectiveness Determining appropriate objectives; 'doing the right things'.

efficiency Minimum use of resources to achieve the organisation's objectives; 'doing things right'.

electronic recruiting Recruiting via the Internet (external) and intranet (internal). Sometimes called cybercruiting.

employability Having marketable skills (skills that are attractive to employers).

employee assistance programs (EAPs) Company-sponsored programs that help employees to cope with personal problems that are interfering with their job performance.

employee champion Requires the HR manager to be the employee's voice in management decisions.

employee motivation *See motivation.*

employee relations (ER) Deals primarily with employee attitudes and behaviour and the relationships between an organisation and its employees. Sometimes regarded as being the same as industrial relations (IR). However, ER focuses more on workplace relations than traditional IR, which emphasises industrial tribunals, trade unions, employer associations and government and their roles in the making of rules governing the employer–employee relationship.

employee turnover *See turnover.*

employee voice The ability of employees to express their ideas, views and complaints to management.

employee's duties Those duties and obligations defined at law that an employee must fulfil.

employer associations Represent employer interests at industrial tribunals and provide a range of IR advisory services, including award interpretation, dispute handling and how to counter union activity.

employer's duties Those duties and obligations defined at law that an employer must fulfil.

employment contract An informal (oral) or formal (written) agreement between an employer and an employee specifying the legal rights and obligations of each party.

employment interview A conversation with a purpose between an interviewer and a job applicant.

employment relations Attempt to integrate HR and IR. Views industrial relations and HRM as its constituent parts.

employment tests Attempt to assess the match between the applicant and the job requirements. Examples include typing, welding and driving tests.

empowerment Giving employees a reasonable amount of authority and the means and decision guidelines for exercising it.

enterprise bargaining Direct negotiation that takes place between an employer or enterprise and its employees and/or their nominated representatives.

enterprise-based unions Unions that restrict membership to employees of a particular company.

environmental influences Existing (and potential) opportunities and threats present in the organisation's external and internal environments.

equal employment opportunity (EEO) Giving people a fair chance to succeed by avoiding discrimination based on unrelated job factors such as age, race, sex or nationality.

equal opportunity Concept that all individuals should have equal consideration and treatment in employment regardless of their sex, race, religion or other non-job-related factors.

equity theory of motivation A theory that assumes that people have a strong need to balance their inputs of labour and their rewards.

essay description A written statement describing an employee's strengths, weaknesses, past performance and future development prepared by the rater.

ethical behaviour Behaviour that is morally accepted as 'good' and 'right'.

ethics Deals with what is good and bad or right and wrong, or with moral duty and obligation. Ethical behaviour may require higher standards than that established by law.

evaluation phase (training) Concerned with measuring how well a training activity met its objectives.

executive leasing Similar to temporary help except that the focus is on supplying management and professional personnel.

executive recruiters Firms specialising in locating qualified candidates for top management jobs.

executive search Sometimes called 'head-hunting'. Executive search firms specialise in identifying top-level executives for key positions and approaching them directly.

exit interviews An employee's final interview following separation. The purpose of the interview is to find out the reasons why the employee is leaving (if the separation is voluntary) or to provide counselling and/or assistance in finding a new job (if the separation is involuntary).

expatriate Someone who lives and works in a foreign country.

expatriate packages Total compensation and benefits given to personnel on a foreign assignment. Includes base pay, foreign service premium, hardship allowance, housing assistance, education allowance, relocation allowance and other special allowances and benefits associated with a foreign assignment.

expectancy The employee's perceived probability that exerting a given amount of effort will lead to performance.

exposure Employee behaviour designed to make management aware of the employee's abilities and achievements.

external equity Payment of employees at rates comparable with those paid for similar jobs elsewhere.

extinction Withdrawal of a positive reinforcer so that the undesired behaviour gets weaker and eventually disappears.

face validity Refers to where a test item or question appears to make sense or to be logical.

factor comparison system A job evaluation technique that involves comparing (ranking) jobs on a range of factors such as know-how, responsibility, etc. Each factor ranking for each job is converted to points. The total number of points for the factors equals the job size.

featherbedding A type of restrictive work practice that involves the use of too many employees for the actual work to be performed.

feedback The extent to which the job permits the employee to obtain clear and direct knowledge about how well they are doing.

fixed interval schedule The frequency of reinforcement is determined by an interval of time (for example, hour, day, week, month, year).

fixed ratio schedule Occurs when an employee is rewarded after producing a fixed number of items or performing an activity a fixed number of times.

flame-out track A situation where employees work to excess, make lots of money, acquire lots of assets and then quit to take an open-ended sabbatical.

flat organisation structure Organisation structure with a wide span of control, few managerial levels and a short chain of command.

flexitime A system that allows employees to choose their own starting and finishing times within a broad range of available hours.

focus groups Groups of employees who are brought together to confidentially discuss specific HR topics such as a company's pay-for-performance program, restructuring, quality of management, and so on.

foreign service premium Paid to the expatriate as compensation for being located outside of their home country.

fringe benefits Indirect or non-cash compensation items such as life insurance, medical benefits, sick leave and the like.

fringe benefits tax (FBT) Australian federal government tax designed to tax organisations on the benefits provided by them to their employees.

functional competency Concerned with job-specific competencies. For example, can the person satisfy the skills, knowledge and experience requirements of the job to perform at a satisfactory level?

Functional Job Analysis Job analysis method that uses standardised statements and terminology to describe the nature of jobs and to prepare job descriptions and job specifications.

gainsharing An incentive system that shares the gains from productivity improvements with the employees who made the improvements.

gender The social construction of males and females. It describes what is seen as appropriate rules and behaviour for men and women.

general union A union that represents workers without regard to their skill, qualifications, occupation or industry (for example, the Australian Workers Union).

genetic screening Biological testing that can determine whether a job applicant is genetically susceptible to certain diseases, such as cancer and heart disease or to specific chemical substances.

glass ceiling Occurs when people can see higher-level positions but are blocked by an unseen barrier, such as discrimination.

glass walls A hypothetical barrier that faces women (and minorities) in moving across functions in an organisation.

goal A specified desired result. Goals are the qualitative or quantitative values set for an indicator.

goal setting The process of defining an objective or target to achieve. Gives a sense of purpose or direction to an action.

go-slows Occur when workers refuse to work at their normal pace in order to pressure management into making a concession. Often implemented by working strictly according to the rules.

government employment agencies Typically specialise in assisting blue-collar clerical and secretarial personnel to find employment.

grading Employees' performance is matched with a specific grade definition such as superior, good, acceptable, marginal and unsatisfactory.

graphic scales Rating scale that numerically evaluates employee performance using specific employee behaviour or characteristics (for example, quality and quantity of output, reliability, etc.).

graphology The study of handwriting for the purpose of measuring personality.

grey ceiling Occurs when people can see higher level positions but are blocked by age discrimination.

grievance Any dispute or difference arising between the employer and an employee or the union.

grievance procedure A formal, systematic process that permits employees to complain about matters affecting them and their work.

group incentives Incentives designed to recognise group as opposed to individual performance.

group interviews Meetings in which several job applicants interact in the presence of one or more company observers.

halo effect A problem that occurs during performance appraisal, when a supervisor's rating of a subordinate on one factor biases the rating of that person on other factors.

harassment Behaviour designed to make a person feel unwelcome, offended, humiliated and/or intimidated.

hardship allowance Paid to compensate the expatriate for hardship resulting from physical isolation, cultural and language differences, extremes of climate, political instability and other inconveniences.

hardware The physical parts of a computer; for example, the hard drive.

health and safety committee Joint employer–employee committee responsible for examining OHS matters in the workplace.

health and safety representative (HSR) Employee charged with representing the OHS interests of a work group.

high-context cultures Cultures where non-verbal communications (such as body language and gestures) and indirect language are used to transfer meaning. China and Japan are examples of high-context cultures.

high-performance work system An arrangement whereby HR systems are aligned with the organisation's strategic business objectives and HR activities are efficiently performed.

high power distance cultures Cultures where employees obey orders and treat superiors with respect, and where hierarchy and status are emphasised.

HIV/AIDS Human immunodeficiency virus that causes a breakdown in the body's immune system and can lead to the development of AIDS.

HIV/AIDS testing Medical tests designed to determine the presence of AIDS in job applicants or existing employees.

home-country national An expatriate who is a citizen of the country where a multinational company is headquartered; for example, an American working for a company with its headquarters in the United States.

homosocial reproduction Sometimes called 'comfort cloning'. Occurs when existing groups of people replicate themselves through selecting people like themselves to join their group or by selecting applicants most similar to those already employed in the position.

honesty tests Tests designed to evaluate a candidate's honesty and integrity.

horizontal loading Job enrichment through the addition of tasks of a similar nature.

host-country national A local employee of the foreign location working for a multinational; for example, a Singaporean working in Singapore for a US multinational.

hostile work environment Occurs when an employee is subjected to unwanted harassment in the workplace.

HR audit Involves a systematic analysis and evaluation of the efficiency and effectiveness of the HRM function and its contribution to the achievement of the organisation's strategic objectives.

HR climate Covers employee perceptions about the work environment that affect motivation and behaviour (such as the culture of the organisation, its management style, the openness of communications, and HR policies and practices).

HRIS security Concerned with the protection of HRIS data from invasion and abuse by unauthorised parties.

HRM activities HR activities such as job analysis, HR planning, recruitment, etc.

HR scorecard A measurement system designed to show HR's impact on the achievement of the organisation's strategic objectives and financial performance.

human capital The knowledge, skills and abilities of an organisation's employees.

human relations movement Recognises that employees seek more than financial rewards from their jobs. Focus is on group norms and behaviour.

human resource development (HRD) Includes training and development, career planning and development, and performance appraisal. Its focus is on the acquisition of the required attitudes, knowledge and skills to facilitate the achievement of employee career goals and organisational strategic objectives.

human resource information system (HRIS) A computerised system used to gather, store, analyse and retrieve data, in order to provide timely and accurate reports on the management of people in organisations.

human resource management (HRM) Involves the productive use of people in achieving the organisation's strategic business objectives and the satisfaction of individual employee needs.

human resource planning The process of systematically reviewing human resource requirements to ensure that the required number of employees, with the required skills, are available when they are needed.

human resource strategy A firm's deliberate use of human resources to help it to gain or maintain an edge against its competitors in the marketplace.

humanistic (soft) HRM Recognises the need for the integration of HR policies and practices with the organisation's strategic business objectives, but places emphasis on employee development, collaboration, participation, trust and informed choice.

hygiene factors Lower-order employee needs that are met by pay, working conditions, interpersonal relations, supervision, company policy and administration.

in-basket exercises *See in-basket training.*

in-basket training A simulation in which the participant is asked to establish priorities for handling a number of business papers, such as memoranda, reports and telephone messages, that would typically cross a manager's desk.

incentive A reward to be given if a specified goal is achieved.

incentive compensation Compensation that is linked to performance by rewarding employees for actual results achieved instead of seniority or hours worked.

incremental change Involves gradual or small-step modifications to the organisation's existing strategies, structure, systems, culture and people.

indicators A means for measuring progress towards meeting a responsibility.

indirect discrimination Occurs when policies, procedures and practices that appear to be neutral (that is, non-discriminatory) produce adverse outcomes for people with specific characteristics.

individual agreements Include common law contracts and Australian Workplace Agreements.

individual incentives Incentives directly linked to individual (as opposed to group or team) performance.

individualism The emphasis given by a culture to individual self-interest.

industrial democracy Type of employee participation that involves a redistribution of decision-making power from management to employees (often via a trade union).

industrial relations Involves employees and their unions, employers and their associations and governments and the industrial tribunals that make regulations governing the employment relationship.

industrial tribunals Refers to government tribunals charged with preventing and settling industrial disputes. The AIRC is Australia's most important industrial tribunal.

industrial unions Sometimes called general unions. Include all types of workers ranging from unskilled to skilled.

information Data that have been analysed and processed.

instrumental (hard) HRM Stresses the rational, quantitative aspects of managing human resources. Performance improvement and improved competitive advantage are highlighted.

instrumentality The degree to which an employee believes that performing at a specific level will bring about a desired result.

intellectual capital The knowledge that exists within an organisation.

intellectual disability Refers to an impairment of a person's mental functioning. A person is determined to have an intellectual disability if they have an IQ score of less than 70–5 and have difficulties with adaptive skills (e.g. following and understanding directions). Intellectual disabilities may result from genetic factors (e.g. Down Syndrome), physical factors (e.g. injuries, accident, infection) or environmental factors (e.g. inadequate nutrition).

intelligence tests Measure an individual's intelligence (IQ) (that is, ability to reason).

interactional justice The extent to which the organisatin treats its employees with dignity and respect.

interest tests Aim to measure how an applicant's interest patterns compare with the interest patterns of successful people in a specific job.

internal equity Payment to employees according to the relative values of their jobs within an organisation.

international HRM HRM as practised by multinational organisations. Its focus is the management of people in a multi-country context.

Internet A global network of electronic information sources. It enables people to send mail, access reference material, share documents electronically and send computer software directly from one computer to another.

interviews The job analyst interviews the job holder about the duties performed.

intranet A network of computers that enables employees within an organisation to communicate with each other.

IT (information technology) department Department responsible for the methods and equipment that provide information about all aspects of the organisation's operations.

job A group of tasks that must be performed if an organisation is to achieve its objectives. One or many persons may be employed in the same job.

job analysis A systematic investigation of the tasks, duties and responsibilities of a job and the necessary knowledge, skills and abilities a person needs to perform the job adequately.

job analysis questionnaire Questionnaire specially designed to collect information about job content, how the job is done and the personal requirements needed to do the job successfully.

job analysts People who collect information about job content, how the job is done and the personal requirements needed to do the job successfully.

Job Characteristics Model An example of comprehensive job enrichment. It combines both horizontal and vertical loading to stimulate employee motivation and satisfaction.

job characteristics theory *See Job Characteristics Model.*

job description A written statement explaining what a job holder does, how the work is performed, where and when it is performed and the performance standards to be met.

job design Specification of the content of a job, the material and equipment required to do the job, and the relation of the job to other jobs.

job dissatisfaction Employee dissatisfaction caused by poor pay, working conditions, supervision and/or company policy and administration.

job enlargement The horizontal expansion of a job by adding similar level responsibilities.

job enrichment The vertical expansion of a job by adding planning and decision-making responsibilities.

job evaluation The systematic determination of the relative worth of jobs within an organisation.

job grading A job evaluation method that sizes jobs using a series of written classifications.

job hierarchy A list of jobs in order of their importance to the organisation, from lowest to highest.

job posting Advertising of job openings to current employees via bulletin boards, newsletters, personal letters or computerised posting programs.

job pricing Placing a dollar value on the worth of a job.

job ranking A job evaluation method that sizes jobs by placing them in rank order.

job rotation Increases task variety by moving employees from one task to another.

job satisfaction The degree to which employees have positive attitudes about their jobs.

job sharing A concept that allows two or more people to share a single full-time job.

job specialisation or simplification Involves employees performing standardised, repetitive and routine tasks.

job specification A written statement of the qualifications, skills and know-how a person needs to perform a given job successfully.

justice Relates to perceptions of fairness.

knowledge management Deals with an organisation's ability to collect, store, share and apply knowledge in order to enhance its survival and success.

knowledge worker A worker who transforms information into a product or service.

labour market The geographical area from which employees are recruited for a particular job.

large-group incentives Designed to cover large groups of employees. Typically use broad achievement measures such as profit or sales.

lateral careers Career path where an employee undertakes a series of lateral moves (often in different functions) instead of moving upward within the organisation.

lay off Separation of the employee from the organisation because of economic or business reasons.

lean organisation Organisation with relatively few managers overall and a low ratio of staff managers to line managers.

learning curve A graphical representation of the rate at which a person learns something over time.

learning organisations Organisations where the focus is on the acquisition, sharing and utilisation of knowledge to survive and prosper.

leniency bias Occurs when employees are rated more highly than their performance warrants.

lifelong employment A situation where an employee is 'guaranteed' a job for their entire working life.

line manager A manager who is authorised to direct the work of subordinates and is responsible for accomplishing the organisation's objectives.

line of sight The relationship between employee control and influence over the end result. The more direct the relationship, the stronger the line of sight.

local area network (LAN) Computer network connecting a group of computers within one work site, allowing them to exchange data and share hardware and software.

local employee Someone who lives and works in their home country.

local nationals Citizens of the host country in which the business is located; for example, a Singaporean working for an Australian company in Singapore.

lockout Refusal by management to let workers enter a plant or building to work.

log of claims A list of demands covering pay and conditions of work typically made by a union on an employer.

lost-time injury A severe job-related injury that causes an employee to be absent from the job.

low-context cultures Cultures where verbal communications are explicit and direct. What is said is what is meant. Australia and the United States are examples of low-context cultures.

low power distance cultures Cultures where employees expect to be involved in decisions that affect them and to be treated as an equal, and where hierarchy and status are de-emphasised.

mainframes The biggest, fastest and most expensive class of computer.

management The art of getting things done through people.

management by objectives (MBO) Involves setting specific measurable goals with each employee and then periodically reviewing the progress made.

management development Any attempt to improve current or future management performance by imparting knowledge, changing attitudes or increasing skills.

Management Position Description Questionnaire Job analysis method that uses a behaviourally oriented, structured questionnaire to describe, compare, classify and evaluate management positions.

management recruitment consultants Concentrate on advertised recruiting for professional and managerial positions.

management style Reflects the particular approach used by a manager to achieve goals through other people.

managerial prerogatives The decision-making rights considered by management as essential for the efficient and effective operation of the organisation.

managing diversity *See diversity management.*

mandatory benefits Benefits that must be provided by law (for example, annual leave, workers compensation insurance).

mandatory retirement Designated age at which all employees must retire from the organisation (usually 65 years).

market postures Determine where an organisation seeks to be in the pay market — above market, market average or below market.

Markov analysis A mathematical technique used to forecast the availability of internal job candidates.

medical examination Examination to determine whether an applicant is physically fit to perform a job.

mentor A person (generally an experienced manager) who helps a younger employee to advance their career by offering advice, giving instruction and opening up career opportunities.

mentoring A developmentally oriented relationship between senior and junior colleagues or peers that involves advising, role modelling, sharing contacts and giving general support.

merger Combination of two or more firms to form one new company, which often has a new corporate identity.

merit Concerned with excellence, superiority and/or being the best qualified.

merit grid A technique used to allocate rewards linked to performance.

merit pay Any pay increase awarded to an employee based on their individual performance.

microcomputer The smallest and least expensive class of computer. Generally called a personal computer (PC).

microprocessor The logic, mathematic and central functions contained in a computer chip.

middle managers Managers who are concerned with implementing the plans and policies of top managers.

minicomputers Computers that are more powerful than microcomputers but less powerful than mainframes.

mission General purpose or reason for an organisation's existence.

mission statements The operational, ethical and financial reasons for an organisation's existence.

motivation That which energises, directs and sustains human behaviour.

motivators Job-centred factors such as achievement and responsibility which, when present in a job, motivate employees.

motivator factors Higher-order employee needs for achievement, recognition, an interesting job, responsibility and advancement.

moving The second phase of change, which involves taking action to alter something so that change occurs.

multimedia training Training that combines audiovisual training methods with computer-based training.

multisource evaluations (360-degree appraisals) Seek performance feedback on employees from their colleagues, superiors, customers and subordinates. Popular in companies with teams, TQM and employee involvement programs.

National Occupational Health and Safety Commission The national consultative organisation on occupational health and safety in Australia.

needs hierarchy Sequence of five human needs, as proposed by Maslow — physiological, safety, social, esteem, and self-actualisation needs.

negative educational equity Occurs when the poor reputation of a university qualification causes the applicant to also be perceived in a negative light.

negative reinforcement Also called avoidance learning. Involves the withdrawal or withholding of punishment when the desired behaviour occurs.

negotiation The process by which one party (for example, a union) seeks to get something it wants (for example, a pay increase) from another party (for example, an employer) through persuasion.

networking Using informed contacts inside and outside an organisation.

non-contributory superannuation A scheme where all contributions to the retirement plan are made by the employer.

non-traditional employees Employees who differ from those usually employed in a particular occupation, organisation or industry because of sex, race/ethnicity, disability or some other characteristic.

norms Rules of standards that establish the behaviour of group members.

notice Notice of termination is required if one party to a contract of employment wishes to bring the contract to an end.

objectives Measurable targets to be achieved within a certain time frame.

observation The job analyst observes an employee working and records the duties performed.

occupational health and safety (OHS) Concerned with the provision of a safe and healthy work environment.

occupational union A union that represents workers from one occupation (for example, nurses or teachers).

off-the-job training Employment training that takes place away from the workplace.

off-the-shelf Commercially available HRIS software.

on-the-job training Employment training that takes place at the job site and tends to be directly related to the job.

operant conditioning Also called learning by reinforcement or behaviour modification. Focuses on rewards and punishments and the effect that they have on employee behaviour.

optimal turnover Employee turnover that sees unwanted (i.e. low performing) employees depart and valued (i.e. high performing) employees stay.

options Give employees the option to buy shares at a favourable price at some future date (usually, but not always, if certain performance targets are met).

organisation chart Shows the relationships between jobs and those given authority to do those jobs.

organisation incentives Cover all employees in an organisation and can take the form of a bonus, standard incentive or 'at-risk' incentive.

organisational competency Often a judgement concerning the similarity of an applicant or employee to the existing work force, with that similarity viewed as being an advantage or desirable. Should involve a consideration of the balance of 'fit' (similarity) and 'flexibility' (difference) required by the organisation, as well as a determination on which criteria fit or flexibility should be sought.

organisational culture *See corporate culture.*

organisational structure Refers to the organisation's framework or design.

orientation (expatriate) The introduction of the expatriate and their family to the culture, living conditions, etc. of the host country.

orientation (new hire) The introduction of new employees to their job, their colleagues and the organisation.

outplacement Special assistance given to terminated employees to help them to find jobs with other organisations.

outsourcing Subcontracting work to an outside company that specialises in and is more efficient at doing that kind of work. International outsourcing is called offshoring.

panel interviews Interviews in which a group of interviewers question the applicant.

partial reinforcement Occurs when rewards are given occasionally after each desired behaviour; that is, the desired behaviour is not rewarded each and every time.

participation rates Refers to the numbers of a particular group in the work force. For example, the increased participation rate of women in the work force is one of the most significant demographic changes to occur in recent times.

pattern bargaining Occurs when the same (or essentially the same) pay and conditions are negotiated for several firms (often in the same industry). Such negotiations are coordinated by union headquarters with clear parameters being set for the local union negotiators. Pattern bargaining is favoured by militant unions and is commonly found in industries that are protected from global competition by tariffs or government subsidies.

patterned interview An interview using a set sequence of questions that every candidate is asked in the same way.

pay compression Occurs when workers perceive that the pay differential between their pay and that of employees in jobs above or below them is too small.

pay for performance A pay system that rewards employees on the basis of their performance.

pay formula The straight line (least squares) formula used to calculate the organisation's pay line.

pay line Graphically depicts the compensation currently being paid for jobs related to job size.

pay policy A firm's decision to pay above, below or at the market rate for its jobs.

pay policy line A graphical representation of the organisation's predicted pay midpoints.

pay range Sets the minimum and maximum scheduled amounts paid for a job at a particular job size.

pay reviews Management reviews of present pay rates to determine whether an increase is to be given and, if so, how much and when.

pay secrecy Occurs where pay rates are kept confidential between the employer and the employee.

pay structure Presents all pay ranges over the whole spectrum of job sizes.

pay survey The vehicle for relating an organisation's pay rates to those for similar jobs in other organisations.

payment in lieu of notice Payment of all wages that would have been receivable if the employee was required to work during the notice period.

peer evaluation Employees at the same level in the organisation rate one another's performance. Sometimes called peer review.

peer review A performance appraisal system in which workers at the same level in the organisation rate one another.

performance Relates to the achievement or non-achievement of specific results designated to be accomplished.

performance appraisal Concerned with determining how well employees are doing their jobs, communicating that information to employees, agreeing on new objectives and establishing a plan for performance improvement.

performance appraisal record Document used to record the performance ratings and supervisor comments on an employee's performance.

performance management Aims to improve organisational, functional, unit and individual performance by linking the objectives of each. Incorporates job design, recruitment and selection, training and development, career planning and compensation and benefits, in addition to performance appraisal.

performance range A pay administration technique used to better align performance with rewards.

performance review discussion Where the manager and subordinate mutually review the employee's job responsibilities, performance improvement and career goals.

performance standards The benchmarks against which performance is measured.

personality tests Measure basic aspects of a person's personality or temperament (such as level of motivation, assertiveness, sociability, etc.).

personnel management (PM) Emphasis is on the administration of activities such as selection, training, welfare and industrial relations. As such, it is regarded as reactive and non-strategic.

physical disability Refers to an impairment of the body (e.g. someone who is missing a limb or who is paralysed). It can also include impairments to physical abilities resulting from diseases or conditions such as arthritis, back injuries and muscular dystrophy. Sometimes, people also refer to sensory disabilities (e.g. visual or hearing impairments) as physical disabilities.

piece-rates Incentive system in which compensation is based on the number of units produced or sold.

placement Assignment of an employee to a new or different job.

plan Action step that shows how an objective or goal is to be achieved.

planned change Change that is introduced and systematically implemented by a change agent.

plateauing A career condition that occurs when job functions and work content remain the same because of a lack of promotional opportunities within the firm.

pluralist approach Regards conflict as inevitable because employers and employees have conflicting interests. Trade unions are seen as a legitimate counter to management authority.

point system An approach to job evaluation in which numerical values are assigned to specific job factors and the sum of those values provides a quantitative assessment of a job's relative worth.

policies General statements that serve to guide decision making.

polygraph Lie detector that records changes in a person's physiology (such as heart rate, blood pressure) in response to a structured set of questions.

portability The ability of an employee to transfer without penalty their accrued retirement benefits from one superannuation plan to another.

Position Analysis Questionnaire Job analysis method that uses a structured questionnaire for quantitatively assessing jobs.

Position Classification Inventory Job analysis questionnaire that can be used to classify occupations and assess person–job fit.

positive reinforcement Encourages a desired behaviour by repeatedly pairing the desired behaviour with rewards.

post-exit questionnaire Survey questionnaire used with departed employees to find out why they left the organisation, their feelings about the company, their supervision, and so on.

power distance The acceptance by a culture of power and status differences.

predictor A selection criterion, such as the level of education or scores on an intelligence test.

prejudice Where a manager demonstrates a positive or negative bias.

preventive health programs Programs designed to promote employee health and fitness. Examples include physical fitness, stress reduction, weight loss and smoking cessation.

proactive When managers anticipate problems and take corrective measures to minimise their effect.

procedural justice The extent to which organisational policies and procedures are fairly administered.

procedures Specific statements that define the action to be taken in a particular situation.

process theories Attempt to explain motivation in terms of the thought processes that employees go through in choosing their behaviour.

productivity The overall output of goods and services produced, divided by the inputs needed to generate that output.

profession An occupation having a common body of knowledge, a code of ethics and a procedure for certifying its practitioners.

professional association Group of specialists who join together to advance their profession and enhance their own personal development.

professional ethics Rules and principles that define right and wrong professional conduct.

professional literature Literature relating to a particular academic discipline or professional occupation.

profit centre A unit where performance is measured by the difference between revenues and expenditures.

profit share Reward program that gives employees additional income based on the profitability of a work unit division or the entire organisation.

profit sharing A plan whereby employees share in the company's profits.

programmed instruction Based on the principles of operant conditioning. It involves presenting questions or facts, getting the trainee to respond and then giving the trainee immediate feedback on the correctness of their answer.

promotion The movement of a person to a higher level position in the company.

promotion from within Policy that gives preference to existing employees when filling a job vacancy.

psychological contract The unwritten expectations of an employee or employer about what each is entitled to receive and obliged to give.

punishment Occurs when negative consequences are experienced after the undesired behaviour is demonstrated.

qualitative HR forecasting The use of the opinions of experts to predict future HR requirements.

quality circles Small groups of employees who meet regularly to identify and solve work-related problems.

quality of work life Involves the implementation of HRM policies and practices designed to promote organisational performance and employee wellbeing (including management style, freedom to make decisions, pay and benefits, working conditions, safety, and meaningful work).

quantitative HR forecasting The use of statistical and mathematical techniques to forecast the demand for and supply of labour.

quid pro quo Involves a negotiator requesting a trade-off for every concession asked for.

racial vilification A particular form of discrimination sometimes called racial harassment.

radical approach Sees industrial conflict as an aspect of class conflict. The solution to worker alienation and exploitation is the overthrow of the capitalist system.

radical change Produces fundamental changes in the nature of the organisation.

ranking The manager compares their subordinates' performance then ranks each in order from 'best' to 'worst'.

rater errors Errors in the evaluation of an employee's performance resulting from leniency, strictness, bias, central tendency, prejudice, recency effect and the like.

reactive When managers wait until a problem occurs before taking action.

realistic job preview A method of conveying job information to an applicant in an unbiased manner, including both positive and negative factors.

reasonable notice The amount of notice to be given in individual circumstances where no period is contemplated in the contract.

recency effect The use of most recent events to evaluate employee performance instead of using a longer, more comprehensive time frame.

recognition programs Make use of various rewards such as cash, merchandise, travel, certificates and the like.

recruitment The process of seeking and attracting a pool of qualified applicants from which candidates for job vacancies can be selected.

recruitment consultancies Privately owned employment agencies.

recruitment methods The specific means by which potential employees are attracted to an organisation.

recruitment sources Where qualified individuals are located.

red circle pay rates Pay rates that are above the range maximum for a job.

redundancy Termination of the employment contract by the employer due to the permanent elimination of the position.

re-entry The repatriation or return of an expatriate to their home country after an international assignment.

re-entry shock The reverse culture shock experienced when the expatriate returns to their home country.

reference check (background investigation) Investigation of the background of job candidates. Includes contacting previous employers, verifying dates of employment, pay and job title, as well as reports from credit agencies, letters of reference, and so on.

refreezing The final phase of change, which involves reinforcing the desired outcomes so that change is institutionalised.

reinforcement The strengthening or weakening of a behaviour through the use of rewards or punishments.

relationship capital The value of an organisation's relationships with its suppliers, customers and competitors.

relationship effect Occurs where the nature of the superior/ subordinate relationship influences a performance rating.

reliability The ability of a test or other selection technique to produce similar results or scores for an individual on separate occasions.

renewal capital The intellectual property (patents, trademarks, copyrights, licences) of an organisation that have marketable value.

repatriation The return of the expatriate to their home country on the completion of an overseas assignment.

replacement chart A visual representation of which employee will replace the existing incumbent in a designated position when it becomes vacant.

reports The presentation of organised information (processed data).

resignation Voluntary departure of an employee from a job.

resignation rate A standard method of computing employee turnover that focuses on that part of employee turnover due to resignations.

responsibilities Major areas in which the employee is accountable for achieving results.

restrictive work practices Any practice designed to restrict the efficient and effective operation of an organisation. Examples include featherbedding, demarcations and limits placed on output.

restructuring Involves a major change to an organisation via downsizing, flattening, elimination of departments, and so on.

retirement Permanent separation of an employee from the company (usually at a specified age; for example, age 60).

retrenchment Employee termination because of changing business, financial, technological or organisational circumstances.

reverse discrimination Discrimination against persons who are not designated as members of a minority or disadvantaged class.

role ambiguity Occurs when employees are uncertain of what they are expected to do in a job.

role conflict A condition that occurs when an individual is expected to achieve opposing goals.

role-playing A training technique where the trainee assumes a role in order to learn how others feel and think.

role-plays Training activities in which participants assume the roles of specific people in situations (such as the roles of interviewer and job applicant), act out the event and then review the implications of their behaviour.

Rucker plans Gainsharing plans that calculate employee gains using a value-added formula.

rust-out Stress produced from having too little to do.

salaried operations Involves all employees being treated equally as staff rather than salaried (staff) and wages (or union) personnel.

salary Compensation that is consistent from period to period and is not directly related to the number of hours worked by the employee.

Scanlon plan A gainsharing plan designed to link employee rewards to the firm's performance.

scientific management Explanation of employee motivation based on the work of Frederick Taylor. Emphasises the division of labour, task specialisation, time measurement and the use of monetary rewards.

secondary boycott The practice of a union attempting to encourage third parties (such as suppliers and customers) to stop doing business with a firm.

selection The process of choosing from a group of applicants the best qualified candidate.

selection criteria Key factors in making a decision to hire or not to hire a person. May include qualifications, experience, special skills, abilities or aptitudes. Selection criteria must be job-related.

self-actualisation Becoming what one is capable of becoming.

self-evaluation Occurs where employees evaluate their own performance.

self-fulfilling prophecy Occurs when expectations about someone cause them to behave in a way consistent with the expectations.

self-regulation (OHS) Applies where employers are held responsible for providing a safe and healthy work environment. Emphasis is placed on education and information rather than detailed government regulation.

seniority The length of an employee's service with the organisation in relation to other employees.

seniority-based pay Occurs where pay levels and increases are determined by length of time on the job and not performance.

seniority system Where the length of time that an employee has worked with an organisation is given recognition and priority for promotions and pay increases.

separation rate A standard method of computing employee turnover. Includes both avoidable and unavoidable separations.

sex Relates to having male or female physical characteristics.

sexual harassment Behaviour involving sexually suggestive remarks, unwanted touching and sexual advances, requests for sexual favours, or other verbal or physical conduct of a sexual nature that is unwanted and that adversely affects a person's employment and/or creates a hostile work environment.

shop stewards Elected union officials who represent union members to management when workers have complaints.

sick leave Provides pay for an employee when they are absent from work because of illness.

simulation A training device designed to reproduce a real-world situation in a risk-controlled learning environment.

skill-based pay A system that compensates employees on the basis of job-related skills and the knowledge they possess.

skills inventory A company-maintained record of employees' abilities, skills, knowledge and education.

skills variety The degree to which a job holder requires a variety of skills and talents to perform the job.

small-group incentives Incentives designed to reward work teams, project groups or departments.

social loafing Occurs when an employee expends less effort and performs at a lower level when working in a group than when working alone.

socio-technical enrichment Focuses on the relationship between technology and groups of workers. The aim is to integrate people with technology.

software The program of instructions that makes computers perform.

specialisation Occurs when a very limited number of tasks are grouped into one job.

split halves method A method of determining the reliability of a test by dividing the results into two parts and then correlating the results of the two parts.

sponsor A sponsor is a person who creates career development opportunities for others.

staff personnel People in an organisation who provide advice and specialised support services to line personnel.

stakeholder Any individual group or organisation that is affected by or has a vested interest in an organisation's policies and decisions.

statutes In the context of employment, statutes legislate the minimum conditions of employment that must apply in any employer–employee relationship.

stock option plan The opportunity for employees to buy a specified amount of stock (shares) in the company in the future at or below the current market price.

strategic choice Refers to managers being proactive (as opposed to reactive) in facilitating the organisation's successful adaptation to changes in its environment.

strategic compensation Involves compensation practices being aligned with the achievement of the organisation's strategic business objectives.

strategic HRM Focuses on the linking of all HR activities with the organisation's strategic business objectives.

strategic intent Sustained obsession to achieve a challenging long-term objective.

strategic partner Refers to HR managers being an essential part of the management team running an organisation and contributing to the achievement of the organisation's objectives by translating business strategy into action.

strategic planning The determination of overall organisational purposes and goals and how they are to be achieved.

strategic recruitment The linking of recruiting activities to the organisation's strategic business objectives and culture.

strategic selection The linking of selection activities to the organisation's strategic business objectives and culture.

strategy Defines the direction in which an organisation intends to move and establishes the framework for action by which it intends to get there.

strategy (negotiating) The overall game plan designed to achieve the negotiating objectives.

strategy formulation Involves selecting an organisation's mission, key objectives and business strategies.

strategy implementation Involves designing an organisation's structure and control systems and evaluating the selected strategies in achieving the organisation's key objectives.

stress A condition of strain that affects one's emotions, thought processes and physical condition.

stressors The conditions that cause stress.

strictness bias Occurs when employees are rated lower than their performance justifies.

strikes Refusal by employees to work until their demands are met by the employer.

strikebreakers Non-union employees hired to replace striking union workers; also called scabs.

structural capital The knowledge that is captured and retained in an organisation's systems and structures.

structural or systemic discrimination A form of hidden discrimination that is the product of social conditioning and that has become embedded within the system; for example, the view that it is 'natural' for women to be secretaries and men to be engineers.

structured interview Uses a predetermined checklist of questions that usually are asked of all applicants.

subordinate evaluations Sometimes called upward appraisals. Involve the subordinate evaluating the performance of their superior.

substance abuse Concerned with alcohol, tobacco and other drug addiction.

succession planning A systematic, long-term career development activity that focuses on preparing high-potential employees to fill key professional and management positions so that the organisation can achieve its strategic objectives.

successive hurdles approach Involves the screening out of candidates at each stage of the selection process.

summary dismissal Dismissal based on an employee's serious ('repudiatory') breach of the employment contract. Effectively, dismissal occurs without giving any notice.

superannuation Benefit paid as a pension and/or lump sum to help employees to meet their financial needs in retirement.

supervisors Lowest level of managers, responsible for managing operating employees.

SWOT analysis Review of an organisation's strengths and weaknesses and the opportunities and threats in its environment.

sympathy strike Strike mounted by workers not directly involved in an industrial dispute to support strikers who are directly involved.

systematic approach to training A three-step approach to training that involves: (a) assessment of training needs; (b) conduct of the training activity; and (c) evaluation of the training activity.

tactics (negotiating) Moves or ploys used to facilitate the successful negotiating strategy.

tall organisation structure Organisation structure with a narrow span of control, many managerial levels and a long chain of command.

task identity Means doing an identifiable piece of work, thus enabling the worker to have a sense of responsibility and pride.

task significance Means knowing that the work one does is important to others in the organisation and outside it.

tax equalisation Ensures that the expatriate does not suffer a loss or windfall gain because of differences between home-country tax and the host-country tax obligations. This is achieved by the expatriate being taxed at the home-country tax rate irrespective of the host-country tax rate.

tax protection Ensures that the expatriate does not suffer a loss in spendable income because of higher host-country taxes (by reimbursing the expatriate if the actual host-country taxes exceed the hypothetical home-country tax obligation).

team appraisals Appraisals that are specially designed to evaluate how well a team has performed.

telecommuting Involves employees working outside the office (often at home) and maintaining contact via the telephone, fax and computer.

test–retest method Determines selection test reliability by giving the test twice to the same group of individuals and correlating the two sets of scores.

Theory X The assumption that employees dislike work, are lazy, seek to avoid responsibility and must be coerced to perform.

Theory Y The assumption that employees are creative, seek responsibility and can exercise self-direction.

third-country national A citizen of a country differing from the home or host country; for example, a Singaporean working for an Australian company in Hong Kong.

360-degree appraisal See multisource evaluations.

total compensation The package of quantifiable rewards an employee receives for their labour; includes three components: base compensation, incentives and indirect compensation/benefits.

total quality management (TQM) Involves an organisation-wide commitment to continuous improvement and satisfying customer needs.

trade unions Formal organisations that represent individuals employed in one organisation, throughout an industry or in an occupation.

traditional career path A vertical line of career progression from one specific job to the next, more senior job.

training Represents activities that teach employees how to better perform their present jobs.

training needs analysis Identifies training needs and translates them into training objectives.

transfer of training Relates to the transfer of training to the work situation. The greater the transfer, the more effective the training.

transfers Occur when an employee is moved from one job to another that is relatively equal in pay, responsibility and organisational level.

transformational research An information-gathering approach designed to help organisations to create an improved employment relationship.

tripartite approach (OHS) Approach to OHS involving the active participation of employers, unions and government.

trust A measure of how willing employees are to share information, cooperate with one another and not take advantage of each other.

turnover The loss of employees by the organisation. It represents those employees who depart for a variety of reasons.

turnover analysis Involves an examination of why employees leave an organisation.

understudy assignment An appointment to gain exposure to some specific knowledge and/or skill.

unfair contract A contract that a relevant industrial tribunal can vary if the contract is unfair, harsh or unconscionable.

unfair dismissal Occurs where a dismissal is harsh, unjust or unreasonable, but need not involve a fundamental breach of the employment relationship.

unfairness Unfairness involves treating a person differently and adversely based on irrelevant criteria or characteristics. This adverse treatment cannot be addressed under anti-discrimination legislation — in other words, such adverse distinctions are unfair but not illegal.

unfreezing The first phase of change, which involves preparing the organisation for change.

union preference Situation where job applicants who are union members have to be given preference in employment over non-union members.

unitarist approach Industrial relations is grounded in mutual cooperation, individual treatment, teamwork and the sharing of common objectives. Trade unions are regarded as competitors for the employee's commitment and cooperation.

unit of competency A component of a competency standard. A unit of competency is a statement of a key function or role in a particular job or occupation.

unplanned change Change that is the product of some spontaneous or ad hoc event.

unstructured interview Uses few, if any, planned questions. It enables the interviewer to pursue, in depth, the applicant's responses.

upward appraisals Appraisals where the subordinate evaluates the performance of a superior.

valence The value or importance that an employee places on a potential result or reward that can be achieved.

validity The ability of a test or other selection technique to measure what it sets out to measure.

value-added Activity that increases worth or utility.

vapourware Software that purports to undertake certain tasks but in reality cannot accomplish them.

variable interval schedule Rewards are administered at varied intervals.

variable pay component That part of pay that is not guaranteed and is at-risk; that is, it is paid only if the performance target is met.

variable ratio schedule Rewards are administered only after an employee has performed the desired behaviour a number of times.

vertical careers Traditional career path where an employee enters the organisation at a junior level and progresses upward to more senior positions over a period of time.

vertical loading Job enrichment through increased opportunities for responsibility, decision making, recognition, personal growth and achievement.

vestibule training Training that takes place away from the production area on equipment that closely resembles the actual equipment used on the job.

vesting Provision in a retirement plan that gives employees a right to specific benefits after a stated number of years of service.

voluntary benefits Benefits provided voluntarily by an employer (for example, additional annual leave, gym membership, tuition refund).

volunteer mindset Employees are internally motivated (that is, they are self-motivated) to perform.

wage Pay directly calculated on the basis of time worked.

web site The web address or location of an organisation; for example, the web site for BHP Billiton is www.bhpbilliton.com.

web-based training Refers to training that is delivered via the Internet.

wellness programs Organisation-sponsored programs designed to prevent illness and promote employee wellbeing.

wildcat strikes Spontaneous work stoppages that take place in violation of the labour contract and are officially against the wishes of the union leaders.

win–lose bargaining Sees the negotiation as a competitive conflict with one party winning and the other party losing.

win–win bargaining Sees the negotiation as a cooperative problem-solving exercise that will benefit both parties.

work climate Refers to the overall 'feeling' of the work environment as conveyed by the physical layout and surroundings, employee social interaction and employee–management relationships.

workers compensation A legally required benefit that provides medical care, income continuation and rehabilitation expenses for people who sustain job-related injuries or sicknesses.

work–family conflict The conflicting demands made on an individual by home and work.

workplace policy A document of general application that is prepared by the employer and is designed to govern (either with or without contractual force) any and all aspects of the conduct, rights and obligations of the parties to a contract of employment.

workplace relations Refers to employer–employee relations in a specific workplace (for example, at a factory site or branch office) as distinct from the total organisation or industry.

workplace violence Violent behaviour occurring in the workplace.

wrongful dismissal Occurs when an employee's employment is terminated by an employer for reasons that are in breach of the employment contract.

name index

A

Abbott, T.   570
Adler, N.   782
Al-Bala'a, C.   342
Albrecht, S. A.   609
Allan, C.   150
Allen, L.   242, 755
Allen, R. F.   823
Anderson, B.   785, 788
Anderson, G.   251
Anderson, P.   151
Andrewartha, G.   328
Andrews, J. R.   389
Anzellotti, P.   203
Argus, D.   27
Arvey, R. O.   241
Aryee, S.   378, 383, 778, 784
Asano, K.   612
Aycan, Z.   785

B

Bacon, N.   612
Balazs, K.   602
Barclay, L. A.   193
Barrett, P.   390
Bartlett, C. A.   5
Burch, Y.   779
Barwick, J.   383
Bass, A. R.   193
Beck, T.   600
Becker, B. E.   833, 834
Becker, G. S.   332
Beckham, D.   382
Bell, A.   8, 201
Bell, C.   778
Bennett, M.   831, 832
Bennett, R.   786
Bennington, L.   208
Benson, J.   78
Berenholtz, R. N.   97, 246
Berger, Y.   250
Berry, A.   506
Bible, G.   778
Bishop, A.   724
Bjorkman, I.   4
Black, J. S.   782, 786
Blackman, C.   754
Blair, J.   75
Boffini, F.   727
Bongazoni, C.   243
Booth, A.   560
Bosch, J.   416
Boudreau J.   75
Bowen, D. E.   516
Boxhall, P.   188, 275, 554, 555
Boyle, C. D.   236

C

Brady, A.   234
Branson, R.   430
Brass, C.   149
Braysich, J.   241
Brewster, C.   779
Brierley, L.   344
Brinkies, J.   405
Buarch, P.   241
Buffett, W.   457
Bull, T.   605
Burrows, G.   673
Byham, W. C.   760

Callus, R.   569
Cardy, R. L.   279
Carmichael, L.   328
Carson, K. P.   279
Carter, N.   790
Cascio, W.   149, 227, 816, 818, 822, 823, 825
Catanzariti, J.   76, 99, 133, 246
Cave, M.   303
Chambers, J.   372
Chang, P. L.   4
Chapman, G.   85
Chay, Y. W.   784
Chen, J.   784
Chen, W. L.   4
Cherrington, D.   142
Chiew, M.   780
Chopard, G.   334
Chown, A.   200
Chuawiwat, C.   77
Cicutto, F.   27, 458
Clark, R.   391
Clarke, L.   4
Cleveland, N.   324
Clough, H.   46
Cohen, D.   685
Collins, J. C.   14
Combet, G.   457, 561, 614
Cook, M.   291
Cook, P.   548
Cooper, R.   559
Copeland, L.   788
Cornelius, E. T.   193
Costa, M.   561, 562
Cox, M.   460
Craft, L.   205
Cuban, M.   248
Curtain, R.   331

D

Dabscheck, B.   557
Daft, D.   778

Dailey, L. K.   830
Danko, W. D.   488
Davidson, P.   31, 785
Davis, E.   560, 570
Dawson, P.   598
Day, A.   202
De Cieri, H.   785
De Fillippi, R. J.   371
De Lisle, P.   525
De Nisi, A. S.   297
De Vries, M. K.   602
Debrah, Y.   17, 207
Decker, P. J.   193
Deery, S.   608, 611
Demming, W. E.   277, 279, 500, 830
Deng, X. P.   754
Denton, D. K.   588
Derr, C. B.   787
Dibble, S.   139
Dobbins, G. H.   279
Dolmat-Connell, J.   300
Dowling, P.   554, 555, 758, 785
Drucker, P.   19, 60, 310, 562
Dunlap, A.   602
Dunn, P. A.   246
Dunphy, D.   588, 589, 592
Dwyer, M.   233, 243

E

Ebrahimmi, B. P.   790
Eddington, R.   778
Eddy, J.   86
Eggar, G.   677
Elphinstone, L.   777
Emery, F.   329
Erwin, P.   608
Eunson, B.   169

F

Fallon, M.   606
Fan, X.   4
Farley, J. A.   193
Fastenau, M.   701, 739
Feldman, D. C.   791
Fenech, T.   83
Ferraro, L.   662
Findlay, P.   280
Fish, A.   65
Fisher, C. D.   236, 750
Fitz-Enz, J.   815, 816
Fletcher, J.   26
Foley, M.   553
Folger, R.   3
Forster, N.   780
Fossum, J. A.   607

Fox, A.   150
Fox, C.   8, 782
Franke, J.   780
Fraser, T.   371
Friedman, M. D.   683
Fukuyama, F.   757

G

Gadiel, M.   77
Galante, S. P.   21
Gardner, M.   294
Geisinger, K. F.   193
Ghoshal, S.   5
Gibbon, T.   202
Gilbert, D.   203
Gilbertson, D.   683
Glanz, E. F.   830
Gloet, M.   10, 364
Goldrick, P.   240
Gollan, J.   570
Gollan, P. J.   171, 172
Goodale, J. G.   75
Goodyear, C.   62
Gottliebsen, R.   831
Gould, R.   241
Grainger, R.   750
Gratton, L.   4
Green, P.   237
Greenspun, P.   385
Grigg, P.   245
Griggs, L.   788
Grover, R.   458
Guest, D.   4, 612

H

Hackman, J. R.   166, 167
Halfpenny, J.   559, 560
Hall, D. T.   75
Hamel, G.   14
Handy, C.   371
Harn, T. J.   240
Harrington, C.   203
Harris, N. J.   197
Hawkins, L.   629
Hay, D.   14
Herzberg, F.   172, 416, 417, 418
Hewson, J.   233
Hofstede, G.   285, 299, 416
Hogan, J.   236
Hogan, R.   236
Holley, H.   759
Hollman, R. W.   290
Hopkins, A.   667
Houghton, C.   150
Houlihan, P.   550
Howes, P.   816

Hubbard, G.   504, 509
Hudson, M.   629
Huselid, M. A.   833, 834

I

Iggins, M.   823
Isherwood, R.   823
Ivancevich, J. M.   143, 661
Iverson, R. D.   591, 608

J

Jackson, P.   781, 797
Jackson, S.   21
James, D.   495, 831
Janz, T.   237
Jawahar, I. M.   291
Johnson, D.   298
Jones, B.   332
Jones, C.   371
Joss, B.   591

K

Kahler, A.   515, 522
Kallenbach, S.   239
Kanter, R. M.   15
Karpin, D.   328
Kealing, B.   488
Kearney, W. J.   306
Keating, P.   559
Kelly, C.   613
Kelly, G.   282, 704
Kelly, J.   612, 613
Kelty, B.   559, 562
Kenney, S. M.   816, 830
Kerr, S.   423
Kidziak, S.   668
Kiechel, W.   289
King, L.   382
King, W.   660
Kinzel, E.   785
Kirkpatrick, D. L.   350
Kirnan, J. P.   193
Kiyosaki, R.   382
Knowles, M.   358, 820
Kohler, A.   599
Kolb, D. A.   357
Kunkel, T.   44, 662
Kwok, W.   664

L

Lahey, K.   370
Lam, M.   301, 302
Lambert, K.   458
Lansbury, R.   207, 283, 570
Latham, C. P.   338
Lawler, E. E.   156, 426

Le Mesurier, K.   632, 633
Lee, K.Y.   758
Leece, P.   276, 287, 293
Lenn, D. J.   601
Leslie, M.   203
Leung, A.   781
Lewicki, R. J.   631
Lewis, L.   62
Li, F. S. (Alan) 378
Li, F. S. (Sean) 378
Li, F. W.   378
Li, K. C.   378
Li, K. P.   378
Li, K. S.   378
Li, M. T.   790
Li, S.   427, 428, 433
Lim, V.   78
Lipper, H.   779
Littler, C.   602
Livingston, E. M.   197
Lles, P.   210
Lloyd, J.   381
Lo, C.   756
Longe, G.   665

M

Ma, C. K.   754
MacDermott, T.   729
Mackay, C. B.   64
Macken, D.   374
Magnusen, K.   253
Maher, T.   614
Markels, A.   601
Marles, R.   150, 560
Marshall, B.   830
Martin, C. L.   252
Maslow, A.   415, 416, 418
Matthews, B. P.   193
Mayer, H.   328
Mayo, E.   413
McAllister, I.   207
McCallum, J.   592
McCarthy, T.   240
McClelland, D.   417, 418
McCoy, S.   80
McDonald, P.   385
McFarlane, J.   62, 600
McGregor, D.   414
McKenna, E. P.   384
McLagen, P. A.   330
McLaughlin, A.   188
McNally, J.   451
McNealy, S.   381
McShane, S. L.   596
Mercer, M. W.   6, 816, 826
Michalandos, M.   99
Miller, H. E.   241

Milton-Smith, J.   355
Miner, J. B.   426
Moffat, D.   753
Mohl, A.   371
Monsfield, B.   664
Moore, F.   329
Moore, R.   207
Morgan, D.   490
Morgenson, G.   487
Morris, B.   385
Murphy, C.   343, 563
Murphy, K. R.   291
Murray, D.   85, 457
Murray, M.   601

N

Nagao, D. H.   252
Nankervis, A. R.   276, 287, 293,
   749, 826
Napier, N. K.   785
Nelson, L. G.   633, 640
Newton, T.   280
Ng, E.   782
Nicholson, N.   780
Niemyer, E. S.   340
Nugent, H.   378

O

O'Connell, S. E.   81
Oddou, G. R.   787
Odiorne, G. S.   816
Ogbonna, E.   225
Ogden, M.   371
Oldham, G. R.   166, 167
O'Neill, G.   442, 463, 464, 506
O'Neill, H. M.   601
Onyx, J.   530
Osborn, J.   550
O'Shea, B.   756

P

Packer, J.   378
Palmer, G.   294
Paterson, J.   610
Patmore, G.   171, 172
Patrick, T.   371
Pearce, J.   291
Peetz, D.   150, 151, 560, 587, 612
Pennington, D.   328
Peters, L. H.   297
Peters, T.   149, 609
Peterson, P.   76
Pfeffer, J.   4, 226, 327
Phelps, R.   779
Philips, J. J.   210
Phillips, L.   679

Plowman, D.   553
Pocock, B.   561
Pontifax, M.   241
Poole, D.   11, 64, 83, 117, 165, 208,
   234, 293, 380, 429, 459, 499,
   524, 565, 608, 644, 670, 708,
   757, 788, 819
Porras, J. I.   14
Porter, L.   291
Power, C.   105
Prahalad, C. K.   14
Pratt, V.   205
Price, D.   19
Priest, M.   76, 150, 639
Pritchett, P.   600
Provis, C.   631
Purcell, J.   188, 275

R

Raelin, J. A.   159
Ramlall, S.   347
Rance, C.   659
Rawson, D. W.   605
Reddin, D.   190
Reddin, W.   451
Redman, T.   193, 207
Regel, R. W.   290
Reingold, J.   458
Reynolds, C.   786
Rhodes, S. R.   823
Rich, J.   488
Roberts, B. W.   236
Robertson, R.   675
Robinson, A. G.   345
Rosen, H.   607
Rosenman, R.   530, 531
Rosenman, R. H.   683
Ross, I.   559
Rowe, B.   239, 246
Rucker, J.   488
Russell, B.   150

S

Sack, H.   378
Salaman, G.   210
Salaman, M.   552
Salmon, P.   75
Sams, P.   615
Samuelson, R.   440
Saner, R.   760
Savery, L.   683
Scanlon, J.   499
Scheoenfeldt, L. F.   750
Schermerhorn, J. R.   425
Schmidt, N.   235
Schneider, B.   235

subject index

A

ABN Amro 62
Aboriginal Australians 209, 210
absenteeism 822f
academic standards 50
action learning 344
adaptability 28
advertisement rating grid 217
Advertiser newspaper 122
Affirmative Action Agency 205, 711
age discrimination 113
ageing population 59
AGL 522
AIDS Research Review Committee 672
AIDS/HIV 226, 249f, 530, 670f, 780
air rage 672
Alcoa 208, 592f
Amcor 387, 750
American International Group 729
American Management Association 328, 600, 701
American National Safety Council 667
American Productivity & Quality Center 282
American Psychological Association 254
AMP 283, 371
Ansell International 62
Ansett 488
Anti-Discrimination Board of NSW 710
ANZ 6, 27, 61, 62, 80, 206, 233, 347, 441, 449, 506, 562, 600, 622, 678
appearance 242f, 382
applicant evaluation form 247f
application forms 241
    and the law 113f
    EEO requirements 231f
    selection 225, 230
aptitude tests 235
arbitration 555, 643
ArsDigita 385
Asea Brown Bovery (ABB) 62, 778
assessment centres 253f, 302
Association of Professional Engineers, Scientists, Managers & Architects (APESMA) 562
AT Kearney 61
AT&T 287
attitude surveys 826f
Australia Post 607
Australia Postal Corporation 118, 822
Australian Bureau of Statistics 207, 209, 327, 712, 725, 726, 825
Australian Centre for Industrial Relations Research & Training 327, 596
Australian Chamber of Commerce & Industry (ACCI) 558
Australian Council for Educational Research (ACER) 236

Australian Council of Trade Unions (ACTU) 371, 457, 556, 558, 559, 560, 561, 562, 587, 614, 664, 679
Australian Graduate School of Management 377
Australian Hotels Association 675
Australian Human Resources Institute (AHRI) 389, 390, 391
Australian Industrial Relations Commission 105, 107, 126, 150, 430, 550, 555, 556, 557, 558, 559, 564, 569, 571, 590, 604
Australian Industry Group (AiGroup) 558
Australian Institute of Criminology 678
Australian Institute of Directors 457
Australian Institute of Management (Western Australia) 282
Australian Law Reform Commission 250
Australian Manufacturing Workers Union (AMWU) 548, 600
Australian National University (ANU) 385
Australian Public Service (APS) 282
Australian Quality Council 598
Australian Retirement Fund (ARF) 530
Australian Services Union (ASU) 607
Australian Society of Sex Educators 684
Australian Standard Classification of Occupations (ASCO) 154, 155
Australian Workers Union (AWU) 250, 607
Australian Workplace Agreements (AWAs) 560, 567f, 610
Australian Workplace Industrial Relations Survey 173, 610
autonomous work teams 165f
autonomy 167
AXA 61, 80

B

Baker & McKenzie 61, 99, 202, 203, 204
balanced scorecard 300f
Bank of East Asia 378, 758
Bank of Tokyo Mitsubishi 764
BBC 331
behaviourally anchored rating scales (BARS) 297
behaviour modelling 343
behaviour observation scales (BOS) 298
Beijing University 677
benchmarking 350, 817, 830f
benefits 516f
    defined 516, 517
    flexible plan 519
    plan objectives 517
    retirement 526f
    statement 520
    statutory 118f
    strategy 516f

taxation 518
    types of 519f
    union pressure and 518
Berkshire Hathaway 457
BHP Billiton 4, 15, 16, 26, 57, 62, 253, 346, 441, 449, 522, 548, 560, 672, 750, 756
biographical information blank 251
body language 241
Booz Allen Hamilton 372
Boral 660, 665
Boston Consulting Group 377
Boston University 683
bottom line 5
boundaryless careers 371
Boyden International (Japan) 188
Brambles 127, 750, 778
British Airways 673, 778
broadbanding 454f
Burns Philp 778
Business Council of Australia (BCA) 555, 556, 557, 558
business games 253

C

Campbell's Soup 27, 298
career planning and development 12, 370f
    boundaryless careers 370
    career counselling 375
    career management defined 371
    career meltdown 383
    career planning defined 371
    career plateau 382f
    career transition 382f
    careers in HRM 386f
    downshifters 385
    dual careers 383
    employability 372f
    employee responsibility 372
    factors in career development 376f
    flame-out track 385
    HR planning 371, 372
    HR responsibility 375f
    lifelong careers 370
    lifelong learning 371
    negative educational equity 378
    outplacement 385f
    uses of 376
    vertical careers 371
casualisation of the work force 60
Cathay Pacific 61, 253, 347, 673, 830
Cbus 530
Center for Disease Control & Prevention (USA) 676
Certified Agreements 567f, 630
change 18, 586f
    acquisitions, mergers and divestitures 599

Hong Kong and Shanghai Bank   253, 449
Hong Kong Housing Authority   830
Hong Kong Toy Council   664
Hong Kong University of Science &
    Technology   377
horizontal loading   163
HR scorecard   833f
HRM activities   5f
HRM and the law   99f
    Australian Workplace Agreements   106
    awards   108
    Certified Agreements   107f
    common law duties   109f
    confidentiality agreements   103
    contracts   100f
    discrimination   110f
    dismissal   119f
    intellectual property   103f
    legal obligations   100f
    moral rights   104f
    recruitment and selection   110f
    statutes   106
    statutory agreements   106
    workplace policy   102
HRM Consulting   844
HRM evaluation   815f
    absenteeism   822f
    attitude surveys   826f
    audit   817
    benchmarking   830f
    climate   819f
    employee turnover   819f
    exit interviews   820f
    focus groups   830
    HR scorecard   833f
    measuring HR outcomes   832f
    occupational injuries and illnesses   825f
    transformational research   828f
HSBC Holdings   61, 62
human relations movement   414
human resource development (HRD)   12, 327f
    action learning   344
    activities   339f
    assessment of training needs   338f
    competency based training   328, 344
    corporate universities   346
    defined   327
    education   327
    evaluation   347f
    knowledge management   334f
    learning organisations   332f
    methods and techniques   335f
    multimedia training   347
    need for   329f
    orientation programs   351f
    performance appraisal   336
    psychological principles of learning   355f

strategic   331f
supervisory and management
    training   354f
training defined   335
training technologies   346f
web-based training   347
human resource information systems
    (HRIS)   75f
    access   88
    confidentiality   80f
    data and report extraction   88
    data items   79
    database management   78
    decision-making process   84
    evaluating   91
    flexibility   80
    hardware   87
    hardware issues   89f
    integrated database   76, 81
    Internet and HRM   90f
    IT department   88f
    key issues   87f
    legal and management concerns   82f
    off-the-shelf systems   84
    outsourcing   87
    payroll   78f
    security   81, 82
    software   87
    uses of   79f
    vapourware   87f
human resource management (HRM)
    change   588f
    defined   4
    diagnostic model   23
    environmental influences   22
    ethics   13
    evaluation   28
    high performance   4, 23
    humanistic   8
    instrumental   8
    international   749f
    Internet   90f
    managing diversity   702f
    myths   6
    objectives   21f
    outsourcing   60f
    plans   21f
    policies and procedures   22
    professional status   390f
    strategic   20f, 22f
    strategies   19f
human resource manager
    administrative expert   9, 10
    careers   386f
    change agent   9, 10
    competencies   157, 389

employee champion   9, 10
experience   390
managing diversity   702f
remuneration   386f
role   9
strategic partner   9
human resource planning (HRP)   11, 45f, 144
    academic standards   50
    approaches to   51f
    defined   45
    environmental influences   48f
    globalisation   48f
    needs   47f
    purpose of   46
    requirements   64f
    short versus long term   47f
    strategic HRM planning   45, 46
    women in the work force   50
Human Rights & Equal Employment
    Opportunity Commission   524
Human Rights & Equal Opportunity
    Tribunal   722
Human Rights and Equal Opportunity
    Commission   116
*Human Rights and Equal Opportunity
    Commission Act 1986*   106, 110
hygiene factors   416

I

IBM   27, 48, 91, 166, 168, 201, 208, 334, 343,
    344, 378, 386, 415, 417,
    600, 611, 785
Improshare ™   500, 507
in-basket exercises   253, 341
incentive compensation   491f
India   48, 49, 61, 62, 207, 309, 671, 672, 713,
    758, 809f
Indonesia   671, 706, 755, 758, 760, 761, 784,
    792
industrial awards   555, 562, 630
industrial democracy   170f
industrial relations   12, 25, 549f
    advocacy   566f
    allowable matters in   570, 571
    approaches to   549f
    arbitrated awards   562
    consent awards   562
    employer associations   557f
    government role   556
    grievances   564f
    and HRM   553f
    individual agreements   560
    international   760f
    parties to   555f
    processes   562f

stress 284, 680f, 789f, 791
strikes 609
substance abuse 250, 675
succession planning 56f
Sun Microsystems 347, 381, 384
superannuation 519, 526f
   portability 529, 530
   vesting 529
Superannuation Guarantee Levy (SGL) 526
Swinburne University 405
SWOT analysis 17
Sydney Water Corporation 521

T

Tabcorp 604
TAFE 331, 336
Taiwan 379, 685, 706, 758, 759, 761
talent scarcity 45f
Tandou 6
task identity 166
task significance 166
Telstra 19, 26, 449, 599, 601, 604, 613, 614, 756
Ten Network 601
termination 119f
Termination, Change & Redundancy
     Case 1984 121
terrorism 673f
Texas Instruments 296, 417
Thailand 676, 755, 759, 761
theory X & theory Y 414f
Thomson DBM 198
TMP e Resourcing 199
Tokyo University 377
total quality management (TQM) 285, 287, 334, 500, 587, 597f, 665
Towers Perrin 442, 779
Toyota 327, 612
Trade Practices Act 1974 112
trade unions 548f, 558f, 609f
   benefits 518
   defined 609
   job of 609
   membership 560f
   need for 605f
   pay for performance 441
   performance appraisal 276f, 282
   psychological testing 188, 225
   recruitment 200
   selection 252, 254

seniority based pay 458
   superannuation 529f
training and development 144, 327f
   activities 339f
   defined 335
   evaluation 347f
   needs analysis 339
   supervisory and management 354f
   systematic approach 337f
   technologies 346f
Training Guarantee Scheme 328
training within industry (TWI) 345f
trend projection 52
trust 30, 588, 596, 609, 630f, 756f, 784
turnover analysis 54

U

UBS 61, 188
Unilever 378
United Steel Workers of America 667
University of Adelaide 682
University of Chicago 377, 676
University of Hong Kong 684, 685
University of Melbourne 377, 570, 673, 728
University of NSW 207, 377
University of Pennsylvania 377
University of Phoenix 347
University of Pittsburgh 683
University of Queensland 377
University of South Australia 327
University of Sydney 458, 489, 540, 729
University of Technology, Sydney 206, 755
University of Western Australia 277, 673

V

value added 18
vertical loading 163
Victoria Police 710
Victorian Occupational Health & Safety
     Commission 676
Victorian Trades Hall Council 609
Vietnam 791
Village Roadshow 601
violence 678f
   bullying 678
   domestic 678f
   workplace 677
Virgin Blue 8, 613
Visa 378
Visy Industries 378

Visy Paper Pty Ltd 107
volunteer mindset 15
Volvo 166

W

Wal-Mart 599
Walt Disney 15
Waseda University 377
Waterside Workers Federation 605
Watson Wyatt 74, 282, 388, 416, 450, 453, 525
WD & HO Wills Holdings Ltd 121
Wesfarmers 660
Western Electric 414
Westfield Holdings 27, 57, 750
Westpac, 18, 20, 27, 77, 187, 208, 387, 441, 488, 489, 490, 506, 590, 591, 704, 716
Wharf Holdings 758
Whirlpool 164, 752
WMC Resources 250
women in the work force 50
   barriers in employment 205
   careers 384
   glass ceiling 205f
   glass walls 206
   recruitment of 204f
   sales 206
   superannuation 530f
   trades 206
Woolworths 18, 450, 599
work climate 604f
work–family conflict 383f, 679
work overload 681f
workers compensation 519, 520
workplace relations 603f
Workplace Relations Act 1996 106, 107, 113, 120, 121, 122, 123, 124, 125, 126, 127, 556, 557, 567f, 706
Workplace Relations Legislation Amendment
   (More Jobs, Better Pay) Bill 1999 570
workplace surveillance 300, 303
World Bank 778

X

Xerox 166, 168, 600, 704, 759

Y

Yamaha 15